BURNETT-HALL

ON

ENVIRONMENTAL LAW

SECOND EDITION

BURNETT-HALL

ON

ENVIRONMENTAL LAW

SECOND EDITION

GENERAL EDITORS

Richard Burnett-Hall, M.A. (Cantab.)
Solicitor and Chartered Patent Agent,
Consultant, Bristows

Brian Jones, LLB, M.A. (Cantab.)
Consultant, Herbert Smith LLP,
Honorary Professor, University of Wales (Aberystwyth)

SWEET & MAXWELL

 THOMSON REUTERS

First edition 1995

Published in 2009 by Thomson Reuters (Legal) Limited
(Registered in England & Wales, Company No 1679046.
Registered Office and address for service: 100 Avenue Road, London, NW3 3PF)
trading as Sweet & Maxwell

For further information on our products and services, visit:
htttp://www.sweetandmaxwell.co.uk

Typeset by YHT Ltd, London
Printed in the UK by CPI William Clowes, Beccles, NR34 7TL

ISBN: 978 0 421 74810 1

No natural forests were destroyed to make this product;
only farmed timber was used and replanted.

British Library Cataloguing in Publication Data
A CIP catalogue record for this book is available
from the British Library.

EDITORS

Valerie Fogleman
Consultant, Stevens & Bolton LLP; Professor of Law, Cardiff University;
Visiting Professor, University of Ghent

David Hart QC
Barrister, 1 Crown Office Row

CONTRIBUTORS

Michael Bedford
Barrister, 2-3 Gray's Inn Square

Caroline Cross
Barrister, 1 Crown Office Row

Peter Davies
Associate Professor of Law, University of Nottingham

Matthew Donmall
Barrister, 1 Crown Office Row

Rosalind English
Academic Consultant, 1 Crown Office Row

Martha Grekos
Barrister, Berwin Leighton Paisner LLP

Richard Ground
Barrister, 2-3 Gray's Inn Square

Jeremy Hyam
Barrister, 1 Crown Office Row

John Jolliffe
Barrister, 1 Crown Office Row

Suzanne Lambert
Barrister, 1 Crown Office Row

Robert Lee
Professor of Law, Cardiff University

Rachel Marcus
Barrister, 1 Crown Office Row

Angus McCullough
Barrister, 1 Crown Office Row

Angela Morris
Barrister, 23 Essex Street, London

Richard Mumford
Barrister, 1 Crown Office Row

Gordon Nardell
Barrister, 39 Essex Street, London

Wendy Outhwaite
Barrister, 1 Crown Office Row

Neil Parpworth
Principal Lecturer in Law, De Montfort University

Owain Thomas
Barrister, 1 Crown Office Row

PREFACE

When the first edition of this work was written in the mid-1990s, environmental law was still a comparatively new concept in the United Kingdom. The Water Act 1989 and the Environmental Protection Act 1990, and the creation of what proved to be an unexpectedly vigorous National Rivers Authority, had transformed the previous lax regime of environmental protection, in which many of the regulatory authorities were themselves among the worst polluters. Although the level of activity that many law firms and environmental consultants had anticipated failed to materialise as rapidly as they had planned for, the new regime had taken root. The transformation was largely completed by the Environment Act 1995, with the creation of the Environment Agency in England and Wales and the Scottish Environment Protection Agency in Scotland, and (eventually) the setting up of the present regime for dealing with contaminated land.[1]

The subsequent developments in environmental law have largely been incremental, rather than radical. In the mid-1990s, the principal environmental concern of most people was the impact of pollutants on humans and other living organisms, whether in the air, water or land. A sound regulatory system was in place; the contentious issues were mostly whether the applicable standards were unduly or insufficiently demanding, and whether the standards were being effectively enforced in practice. Since then there have been several major revisions to the legislation, notably new EU Water and Waste Framework Directives, the REACH regime for chemicals, and the introduction of a comprehensive environmental permitting regime for virtually all major processes requiring regulatory control. Nevertheless, important though these are, they build on previous legislation rather than departing substantially from it. One development that can whole-heartedly be welcomed is the much greater awareness of the judiciary these days of the proper application and interpretation of European law; one can reasonably hope that there will never again be such disastrously wrong decisions as occurred in the "Lappel Bank" litigation[2] in the early 1990s.

---

[1] Discussed in Chapter 16.
[2] Starting with *R. v Swale Borough Council and Medway Ports Authority, ex p. RSPB* [1991] J.P.L. 39, and leading up to the ECJ decision in Case C-44/95 *R v Secretary of State for the Environment, ex p. RSPB* [1996] ECR I-3805.

A more distinct development has been the introduction of the EU Environmental Liability Directive.[3] This is an important harmonising measure; in the United Kingdom its main impact is likely to be in its application to the protected species and natural habitats within the scope of the EU Birds and Habitats Directives. Apart from this, there are perhaps three issues in particular that may come to be seen as especially significant in the evolution of environmental law and practice over recent years: access to justice, regulatory reform, and climate change.

Access to justice is, in many respects, a re-embodiment of the old question: *quis custodiet ipsos custodes?* The day to day activities of the Environment Agency are, quite rightly, not subject to direct Government control, but nor is the Agency directly accountable to the members of the public immediately affected by its decisions. Even where public authorities are democratically elected, their regulatory decisions rarely play a significant part in subsequent elections. Judicial review is generally the only recourse for third parties who wish to contest a regulatory decision, but this procedure has numerous defects from their point of view – it is liable to be prohibitively expensive, especially given that the loser must generally pay the other side's costs, and that the discretionary nature of the remedy makes it very hard to assess in advance the chance of succeeding; an objector who has sufficient resources may be held not to have "standing" to seek a review; the Courts, in a judicial review, allow a regulator far more leeway before quashing its decisions on grounds of unreasonableness than would occur in an appeal on the merits; and even a successful outcome may merely result in the regulator re-deciding the issue in the same way as before, but on grounds that are less susceptible to challenge.

For those adversely affected by decisions of the Environment Agency and other regulatory authorities, the need for affordable access to justice has become an increasingly significant issue over recent years. A series of judicial reviews instigated by NGOs have brought about an appreciably more relaxed attitude to standing, though the other problems with the judicial review procedure remain. The access to justice provisions of Article 9 of the 1998 Åarhus Convention[4] have driven efforts to find a solution, and the constructive recommendations, made in May 2008, of the Working Group on Access to Environmental Justice chaired by Sullivan J. are very encouraging and most welcome. It is to be hoped they will soon be adopted.

One of the most recent developments before this book went to print was the passing of the Regulatory Enforcement and Sanctions Act 2008 (RESA).[5] The use of the criminal law to enforce absolute liability offences may have been acceptable in the days when fines were no more than a slap

---

[3] Discussed in Chapter 5.
[4] Discussed in Chapter 6.
[5] Discussed in Chapter 2.

on the wrist, intended to discourage what, in the words of Lush J. in the 1874 case of *Davies v Harvey*,[6] were seen as "acts ... which are not criminal in any real sense but are acts which in the public interest are prohibited under a penalty". Regulatory enforcement today has to deal with a wide range of situations, from intentional breaches of the law to save money, through inadvertent but avoidable breaches arising from poor management, to strict liability offences unwittingly committed by a company that has done all that could reasonably be expected to ensure compliance. Dealing with this variety of situations requires a much more gradated approach than the blunt instrument of prosecuting strict liability criminal offences, especially as this is liable to lead to fines bearing little relationship with the "moral" culpability of convicted defendants. The use of civil penalties not merely, or even primarily, to punish, but to recoup improperly gained profits and to compensate for damage caused by a breach, was pioneered in the United States. Their use under RESA should prove a most valuable development. The devil is however in the detail, and much of the essential detail of exactly how the new regime will operate in the field of environmental regulation has yet to be seen.

One uncertain aspect of particular concern is whether a tribunal hearing appeals against decisions on the part of the Environment Agency on the ground of unreasonableness will treat these as merits appeals, as is to be hoped, or whether they will tend to uphold the decisions unless they can be shown to be "*Wednesbury* unreasonable" – a hurdle that would (one suspects) prove insurmountable for most appellants. It is worth noting that decisions of Patent Office examiners in the United Kingdom and elsewhere, even on complex matters such as the obviousness of the subject matter of a patent application, have for many years been subject to what are effectively merits appeals, notwithstanding that the examiners' decisions are taken by people applying a high degree of experience, skill and judgment. The appeals tribunals review *de novo* the cases that come before them, and if thought fit substitute their own opinion for that of the examiner. There seems no reason why a suitably qualified and experienced tribunal hearing environmental appeals should not act similarly.

The issue of climate change came to public attention as a result of the conference at Rio de Janeiro in 1992 at which the United Nations Climate Change Convention was adopted. It took another five years for the Kyoto Protocol to be agreed, and a further eight years before the Protocol entered into force in February 2005. This glacial progress was in sharp contrast to the rapid amassing of ever more cogent evidence that climate change was occurring at a much faster pace than had been expected, affecting both developed and undeveloped countries, and making the measures necessary to halt and then reverse it increasingly demanding and urgent. Too many United Kingdom politicians have displayed a degree of complacency,

---

[6] [1874] Law Rep. 9 Q.B. 433

claiming credit for the country meeting its Kyoto targets, despite this being achieved largely through one-off measures, namely moving from coal to gas-fired power stations, and losing its most polluting manufacturing industries to Far Eastern countries with at best rudimentary pollution controls. If an accounting system were in place that properly allocated greenhouse gas emissions to imported goods, the UK's position would look far less favourable. Nevertheless the Stern Review on the Economics of Climate Change, published in October 2006, made a cogent case for action, showing how the costs entailed are entirely manageable, even if the science was eventually found to be wrong and the preventive measures unnecessary, while if the science is right the costs of failing to take appropriate action are likely to be immense. Though the need for positive action is now generally accepted, it is much less clear that the necessary practical measures will also be.

The legislative response to climate change illustrates a broader development that will undoubtedly play an increasing part in the future – the use of economic instruments rather than command and control regimes to influence behaviour. Taxation of polluting activities by the UK's Climate Change Levy, landfill tax, and increasing the vehicle excise duty on the more polluting cars, are examples of one type of instrument. More sophisticated are the trading schemes, such as that under the European Emissions Trading Scheme and the Kyoto Protocol's "flexible mechanisms" to reduce the emission of greenhouse gases, and the ability of English local authorities to trade their landfill allowances[7] so as to encourage the development of alternatives to landfill. As these trading schemes become more widespread, there will be considerable need for lawyers who understand both the legal and economic contexts to assist and advise parties carrying out such trades. This edition contains a new chapter[8] devoted exclusively to climate change – the topic may well need still more space in future editions.

Addressing climate change effectively is of critical importance to us all. Of no less importance is the issue of sustainability, which has tended to become submerged in the concerns over climate. Lip service has been paid to sustainability over the years, but with little practical effect. The dramatic rise in commodity prices for a few months earlier this year briefly focussed attention on resource use and conservation but, following the subsequent almost equally dramatic fall in these prices, that attention has moved elsewhere. As a result of the recent turmoil in the financial markets, it is now generally accepted that growth stimulated by excessive credit is unsustainable and cannot continue indefinitely. Nevertheless, though a period of recession is now forecast, public pronouncements of economists and politicians all envisage that the economy should in due course revert

---

[7] Under the Waste and Emissions Trading Act 2003.
[8] Chapter 7.

once more to continued growth. What has yet to be generally recognised is that sustainable growth can only continue at all if it is derived exclusively from increases in efficiency and productivity, whereby the same resources produce a greater output, coupled with re-use and recycling of the materials employed. The Preface to the first edition addressed this issue; no apologies are made for doing so again. By its very nature it will not go away.

This new edition benefits from the expertise of a significant number of authors. It is very much to their credit that they met the exacting deadlines set by ourselves, and responded so positively to our comments on drafts. We are most grateful to all of them for their contributions to the work, providing a depth of legal and practical knowledge that no one person could hope to possess. We would like to mention David Hart QC, in particular, who helped greatly in getting this project under way, and then provided advice and assistance in the preparation of several chapters for which he was not directly responsible, as well as those for which he was.

The time that has elapsed since the first edition has meant that virtually all the chapters have been written entirely anew; a few, such as those on Radioactive Substances and Genetically Modified Organisms, were able to make use of some of the previous text, but even they have been subject to extensive updating and rewriting. The authorship of the various chapters is as follows.

Chapter 1	Sources of Environmental Law	Neil Parpworth, with Gordon Nardell (section on human rights)
Chapter 2	Environmental Regulators and their Enforcement Powers	Valerie Fogleman
Chapter 3	Criminal Prosecutions and Sentencing	Angela Morris
Chapter 4	Civil Liabilities in the Context of Environmental Harm	Jeremy Hyam and Rosalind English
Chapter 5	Environmental Liability Directive	Valerie Fogleman
Chapter 6	Public Accountability: Public Law, Public Participation and Access to Information	Caroline Cross and Rachel Marcus
Chapter 7	Climate Change Law	Peter Davies
Chapter 8	Environmental Impact Assessments	Richard Ground and Michael Bedford

As in any work on environmental law, one of the most intractable issues is where to draw the boundaries – what to include and what to leave out. In a single volume that must remain portable, it is impossible to be comprehensive on every aspect. We hope we have got the balance right, but recognise that some readers may well wish for more on whatever topic is of particular concern to them. The objective has been to survey the legal framework of each topic, including relevant case law, and to point up and discuss legally uncertain or contentious aspects likely to be of practical concern. In many cases there are specialist works that deal with the topic in question in greater depth, and where appropriate we have been glad to be able to direct readers to additional sources of legal analysis and guidance. In some cases, such as the chapter on Chemicals, the procedural aspects of obtaining authorisations and the controls over transport are felt to be of comparatively slight interest to many readers, while those who do need information on such matters are generally well served by official guidance. That chapter is accordingly appreciably shorter than its equivalent in the first edition.

There has also inevitably been the separate question of what topics should be omitted altogether. Although much environmental law is aimed at protecting human health, health and safety legislation as such is not covered – it is compendiously addressed in works devoted exclusively to it, and little purpose would be achieved in covering it again here. Nevertheless it is touched on where it would be misleading not to mention it at all, for example as in the controls on the handling and use of asbestos. Pharmaceuticals regulation shares many aspects with that of e.g. chemicals, pesticides (more properly, plant protection products) and genetically modified organisms, but it is a highly specialised area that, if addressed adequately, would throw the rest of the book out of balance, and accordingly has not been covered.

European Community law is central to any review of domestic environmental law. For a considerable while following the United Kingdom's accession to the EEC, as it then was, UK legislation transposing directives generally attempted to prescribe what was believed to be their intended effect, sometimes with questionable accuracy, so that attention always had to be given to whether or not the directive had been properly implemented, and to the legal consequences if it had not. With the modern tendency to transpose EU Directives verbatim, these problems are largely avoided. As a result, the main focus can quite properly be on the underlying EU legislation, and that is the approach taken in this book.

Since the last edition, powers over environmental regulation have been devolved to Scotland and, to a considerable extent, Wales also. Northern Ireland has for decades operated substantially independently of the rest of the UK. With the passage of time, environmental legislation increasingly differs between these jurisdictions, even if only in matters of detail – while they must of course all give effect to EU legislation that is binding on the UK, there are often areas of discretion that can be and are exercised differently. It has reluctantly been decided that to attempt to cover at all adequately the environmental law of all four separate jurisdictions of the UK, or even two or three of them, is now simply not possible in a single volume. Consequently, this work only aims to state the law as it applies in England. In many instances this will also be the law in Wales, as much environmental legislation still applies equally to both jurisdictions – indeed, depending on its subject matter, new legislation may still apply to the UK as whole – but it cannot be taken for granted that the law of England is also that of the other jurisdictions, or any of them. Local advice may well be called for.

New legislation, and new and revised proposals for legislation, are issued constantly, both by the EU institutions and by Whitehall. Inevitably, in preparing a work such as this, some important developments emerging in the following months will be left out whenever the final deadline is drawn, but we have tried to indicate likely future changes where these are known. The law stated here is as it applied on October 22, 2008.

Richard Burnett-Hall   Brian Jones
October 31, 2008

FROM THE PREFACE TO THE FIRST EDITION OF "ENVIRONMENTAL LAW"

Public concern for improved protection of the environment has developed since the early 1980s from being the pre-occupation of a small minority to where it is now an almost daily news item. "The environment" is an important element of the policies of all the major political parties, and the government has since 1990 formally set out annual reports on its policies and achievements in this field. Though these may, perhaps inevitably, be less than wholly objective, such a public display of concern and commitment would have been unimaginable ten years ago. The Water Act 1989 and the Environmental Protection Act 1990 have brought about a transformation of the substantive environmental law of Great Britain (most of the changes have yet to reach Northern Ireland), and their practical implementation through secondary legislation is largely complete.

Most of the major industrial firms now have or are developing active environmental policies. While this may have been largely led by those with experience of the dire consequences in the USA of failure to pay sufficient attention to environmental issues there, the culture change in industry is perceptibly taking root in the United Kingdom also, even though there is a considerable way still to go, particularly among smaller businesses. The United Kingdom Environmental Law Association has grown, from its foundation in 1987, when environmental law was considered by only a handful of firms to be a practice area in its own right, to a membership of one thousand, reflecting the spreading need for lawyers in all of industry and private practice, local government and academia, who have a proper understanding of the subject. The practice of environmental law in the United Kingdom can fairly be said to have come of age, and it is therefore an appropriate time to produce this survey of it.

Britain can be rightly proud of the pioneering legislation it introduced in the mid-19th century to protect public health and to control direct pollution of air and water (though rather less merit can be claimed for the much later development and enforcement of the laws on waste disposal). These laws and their immediate successors were operated largely independently of each other, separate regulatory bodies being developed to administer them, and this pattern of uncoordinated regulation persisted right up to the 1980s. However with the introduction of integrated pollution control and the now imminent full amalgamation of the regulatory authorities, both our environmental law and the regime for its practical implementation have been brought towards a coherent whole.

Nevertheless, as has all too often been observed, having effective environmental legislation is of little value unless it is vigorously enforced, and enforcement in the United Kingdom has in the past undoubtedly been inadequate. While the previous legislation was theoretically capable of providing effective control and undoubtedly mitigated the worst excesses, its main defect to modern eyes lay primarily in the virtual absence of mandatory numerical standards, which both left a large degree of discretion in the hands of the regulators and also exacerbated the difficulties in obtaining a conviction except in the most blatant instances of non-compliance. To this was added a strong reluctance to take enforcement action in the Courts, partly through lack of resources, but at least as much from regarding (with the best of motives) a prosecution as a sign of failure by the regulators to induce compliance voluntarily. All this was coupled with a persistent failure by the courts to impose such penalties on those who were convicted as would operate as a serious deterrent both to them and others.

What appears not to have been sufficiently appreciated by those in a position to improve this record is that responsible industry—and much of it is so—has no objection to firm and fair enforcement against itself. A real concern is that, if it invests considerable money and management effort in securing good environmental behaviour on its part, its less responsible competitors who fail to do so may be able to get away with it. A culture of environmental responsibility within industry can only flourish if all those who cut corners are firmly dealt with—and not just those whose mere size gives them prominence. Furthermore the evidence is overwhelming that when organisations become committed to ensuring that their operations stay in compliance, far from this imposing extra costs as is often supposed, the improved management systems they set up almost invariably result in significant savings. The resourcing of the regulators by charging for permits, the declarations of increased willingness to prosecute, the recent reforms of the law, and the generally significantly greater penalties available to the magistrates courts, all create potential for effective change. Increased public access to environmental information will put additional pressure on the authorities to set demanding standards and to enforce them, and will facilitate the bringing of private actions, both criminal and civil.

Strong enforcement can however only be acceptable if the law itself is perceived to be reasonable. There will always be room for dispute in the setting of limits on permissible discharges to the environment. The effects of chronic exposure of man and other living organisms to low levels of chemical substances cannot be predicted with any precision from laboratory tests—and extensive testing on animals is in any event itself undesirable and discouraged by EC legislation. Limits that are always set on the basis of worst case assumptions will inevitably both burden the community with excessive costs and lead to undue fears when they are marginally exceeded; limits set on any other basis may perhaps prove in the long term to have been too lax. Ultimately a decision must be made that balances the publicly perceived risks against the publicly perceived benefits to be derived from the activity in question; unless made solely by reference to the use of best available technology (virtually irrespective of cost) it cannot therefore be a purely scientific assessment by technical experts alone, vital though their contribution is. While the US system arguably gives excessive weight to popular sentiment in determining environmental regulations, the tenuous degree of political accountability that there has been for standard setting in EC legislation—with the notable exception of the standards for small car exhaust emissions, which tends to prove the rule—is surely also hard to justify. Some development in this respect must be expected, as a result of the greater influence of the European Parliament following the Maastricht Treaty, leading to demands for increasingly stringent standards. To keep these standards realistic will require additional effort from industry to inform the public fully on the relevant risks and benefits, but this must be preferable to a paternalistic regime that is liable to result eventually in public cynicism and rejection of the real benefits that industry can give.

These issues are however matters of administrative detail by comparison with the fundamental issue with which virtually every country is faced, whether or not it chooses to make any effective response, namely how sustainable lifestyles—let alone sustainable development—are to be achieved world-wide. It can scarcely be contended that the present pattern of global economic activity is sustainable, but it is axiomatic that what is not sustainable must at some point come to an end. If that end is not planned for, it is likely to be nasty and brutish, though maybe unpleasantly long drawn out. Planning for it requires political, indeed moral, decisions on how limited resources are to be shared between richer and poorer countries and between present and future generations. The development of environmental law over the coming years will be increasingly influenced by how this over-riding issue is handled. The European Community's Fifth Action Programme on the environment is called "Towards Sustainability". Only time will tell whether the Community and its member states have the strength to make effective steps to that goal.

Richard Burnett-Hall
Bristows, Cooke & Carpmael   February 1995

ACKNOWLEDGEMENTS

Grateful acknowledgement is made for permission to reproduce from the undermentioned works:

Principles of European Environmental Law, edited by Richard Macrory with Ian Havercroft and Ray Purdy (Groningen: Europa Law Publishing, 2004)

Alexandre Kiss and Dinah Shelton, *International Environmental Law*, 3rd edition (Ardsley, NY: Transnational Publishers Inc., 2004)

While every care has been taken to establish and acknowledge copyright, and contact copyright owners, the publishers tender their apologies for any accidental infringement. They would be pleased to come to a suitable arrangement with the rightful owners in each case.

SUMMARY OF CONTENTS

FULL TABLE OF CONTENTS

Chapter 9
ENVIRONMENTAL IMPACT ASSESSMENTS   487

Chapter 10
NATURE CONSERVATION   521

Chapter 12
WATER ABSTRACTION   643

Chapter 13
LAND DRAINAGE, FLOOD DEFENCE AND COAST PROTECTION   659

Chapter 17
STATUTORY NUISANCE AND CONTROLS OVER NOISE

Chapter 18
CHEMICALS

Chapter 19

GENETICALLY MODIFIED ORGANISMS   965

Chapter 20

RADIOACTIVE SUBSTANCES AND NUCLEAR INSTALLATIONS   985

TABLES OF CASES

TABLE OF UK CASES

1

li

EUROPEAN COURT OF JUSTICE AND COURT OF FIRST INSTANCE

Alphabetical List of Cases

EUROPEAN COURT OF HUMAN RIGHTS AND EUROPEAN HUMAN RIGHTS COMMISSION

CASES BEFORE THE
INFORMATION COMMISSIONER

TABLES OF LEGISLATION

TABLE OF UK STATUTES

TABLE OF UK STATUTORY INSTRUMENTS

TABLE OF EUROPEAN AND INTERNATIONAL CONVENTIONS

TABLE OF EU REGULATIONS

TABLE OF EU DIRECTIVES

TABLE OF ABBREVIATIONS

Note: Where the term "q.v." is used in this Table, the expression concerned is described more fully in the Glossary

Å	Ångstrom (q.v.)
AAP	Area Action Plan
AATF	Approved Authorised Treatment Facilities
AAUs	Assigned Amount Units (tradable units issued to 'Kyoto' Annex I countries)
ACBE	Advisory Committee on Business and the Environment
ACDP	Advisory Committee on Dangerous Pathogens
ACGM	Advisory Committee on Genetic Manipulation
ACOP	Approved Code of Practice
ACP	Advisory Committee on Pesticides
ACRE	Advisory Committee on Releases to the Environment (of micro-organisms) appointed under section 124 of the E.P.A.
ACTS	Advisory Committee on Toxic Substances
ADAS	Agricultural Development and Advisory Service
ADI	Acceptable Daily Intake (q.v.)
ADR	*Accord Européen relatif au transport international des marchandises Dangéreuses par Route* (European Agreement on the International Carriage of Dangerous Goods by Road)
ALARA	As Low As Reasonably Achievable
ALARP	As Low As Reasonably Practicable
AONB	Area of Outstanding Natural Beauty
AOSIS	Association of Small Island States
AoSP	Area of Special Protection
AOX	Absorbable organic halides
AQMAU	Air Quality Monitoring Assessment Unit
ASCOBANS	Agreement on the Conservation of Small Cetaceans of the Baltic and North Seas
ASTM	American Society for Testing and Materials
ATF	Authorised Treatment Facilities
BAT	Best Available Technology – the standard required under IPPC (q.v.)

BATNEEC	Best Available Techniques Not Entailing Excessive Cost – the standard required under IPC (*q.v.*)
BATRRT	Best Available Treatment, Recovery and Recycling Techniques
BCH	Biosafety Clearing House (set up under the Cartagena Protocol, *q.v.*)
BCME	bis (chlormethyl) ether
BCN	Breach of Condition Notice
BOD	Biochemical (or Biological) Oxygen Demand (*q.v.*)
BPEO	Best Practicable Environmental Option (*q.v.*)
BPM	Best Practicable Means
Bq	Becquerel. A unit of radioactivity in the SI system
BREEAM	Building Research Establishment Environmental Assessment Method
BS	British Standard. BS 7750 is the specification for environmental management systems
BTU	British Thermal Unit (obs.)
C	Centigrade
CA	Competent Authority
CABE	Commission for Architecture and the Built Environment
CAS	Chemical Abstracts Service, a division of the American Chemical Society of Columbus, Ohio, USA. It has set up a classification system and information bank on millions of chemical compounds in which each compound is assigned a unique CAS number as described in the CAS Registry Handbook ISSN 0093-058X.
CCA	(UK) Climate Change Agreement
CCL	(UK) Climate Change Levy
CCPO	(The UK) Climate Change Projects Office
CCW	Countryside Council for Wales
CDDA	Company Directors Disqualification Act 1986
CDM	Clean Development Mechanism (a Kyoto 'flexible mechanism')
CERs	Certified Emission Reductions (tradable units created by 'Kyoto' CDM projects)
CERT	Carbon Emissions Reduction Target
CFCs	chlorofluorocarbons (*q.v.*)
CGL	Comprehensive General Liability (insurance)
CH_4	Methane (a 'Kyoto' greenhouse gas)
CHP	Combined Heat and Power
CHIS	Covert Human Intelligence Sources
CHIP	The Chemicals (Hazard Information and Packaging for Supply) Regulations 2002
CHP	Combined Heat and Power
Ci	Curie. A unit of radioactivity (= 3.7×10^{10} Bq)

CIL	Community Infrastructure Levy
CITES	Convention on International Trade in Endangered Species of Wild Flora and Fauna
CJA	Criminal Justice Act 2003
CMCHA	Corporate Manslaughter and Corporate Homicide Act 2007
CMTs	Carcinogens, Mutagens and Teratogens
CNAEA	Clean Neighbourhood and Environment Act 2005
CNCC	Council for Nature Conservation and the Countryside (Northern Ireland)
CO/CO_2	carbon monoxide/carbon dioxide
CO_2e	Carbon Dioxide Equivalent *(q.v.)*
COD	Chemical Oxygen Demand *(q.v.)*
COMAH	Control of Major Accident Hazards Regulations 1999
COP	Code of Practice
	Conference of the Parties (e.g. under the Kyoto Protocol)
COPA	Control of Pollution Act 1974
CoRWM	Committee on Radioactive Waste Management
COSHH	The Control of Substances Hazardous to Health Regulations 2002
COT	The Committee on Toxicity of Chemicals in Food, Consumer Products and the Environment
COTC	Certificate of Technical Competence (in respect of the handling of waste)
COTIF	The Convention Concerning the Carriage of Goods by Rail (Cmnd. 8535)
CPIA	Criminal Procedure and Investigation Act 1996
CPL	The Classification, Packaging and Labelling of Dangerous Substances Directive 92/32 (and others)
CPR	(1) Criminal Procedure Rules 2005
	(2) Civil Procedure Rules
CRI	Chemical Release Inventory
CRISTAL	Contract Regarding an Interim Supplement to Tanker Liabilities for Oil Pollution
CROWA	Countryside and Rights of Way Act 2000
CSD	The Commission for Sustainable Development; established under the UN ECOSOC to take responsibility for the implementation of Agenda 21
CTC	carbon tetrachloride (CCl_4)
dB	decibel
DBBT	dibromo benzyl toluene; monomethyl dibromo diphenyl methane.
DCLG	Department of Communities and Local Government
DDT	dichloro diphenyl trichloroethane. An insecticide now generally banned due to its ability to bioaccumulate and non-biodegradability

DECC	Department of Energy and Climate Change
DEMOS	[The] DTI's Environmental Management Options Scheme
DNA	deoxyribonucleic acid (a nucleic acid consisting of a long chain of nucleotide units)
DPD	Development Plan Document
DREF	Dose Rate Effectiveness Factor (a term used in toxicology)
DWI	Drinking Water Inspectorate
EA	(1) Environmental Assessment
	(2) Environment Agency
	(3) Environment Act 1995
EAP	Environmental Action Programme
EC	The European Community/Communities (the EEC, the European Coal and Steel Community, and Euratom)
ECCP	European Climate Change Programme
ECHA	European Chemicals Agency, the central body responsible for administering the REACH (*q.v.*) regime. The 'H' indicates Helsinki, where the Agency is based.
ECHR	European Convention on Human Rights
ECJ	European Court of Justice
ECN	The Environmental Change Network
EComHR	European Commission of Human Rights
ECOSOC	(1) The (EC) Economic and Social Committee; one of the Community's institutions established under Article 193 of the Rome Treaty
	(2) The (UN) Economic and Social Council; a United Nations body under which the CSD (*q.v.*) has been established
EctHR	European Court of Human Rights
EDC	ethylene dichloride; 1,2-dichloroethane
EEC	The European Economic Community (now the European Union)
EEE	Electrical and Electronic Equipment
EFSC	European Food Safety Committee
EFW	Energy from Waste
EH	English Heritage
EIA	Environmental Impact Assessment
EIL	Environmental Impairment Liability (insurance)
EINECS	European Inventory of Existing Commercial chemical Substances ([1990] O.J. C146A)
EIR	Environmental Information Regulations 2004 (and 1992)
EIS	Environmental Impact Statement (also ES)
ELINCS	European List of Notified Chemical Substances (6th edition contained in COM 2003 / 642 final, October 29, 2003)

ELV	(1) Emission Limit Value
	(2) End of Life Vehicles Directive 2000/53
EMAS	The EC Eco-Management and Audit Scheme
EMF	Electromagnetic field
EMS	Environmental Management System
EPA	(1) Environmental Protection Act 1990 (UK)
	(2) Environmental Protection Agency (the US Agency is sometimes referred to as the USEPA)
EPC	Energy Performance Certificate
EQO	Environmental Quality Objective (*q.v.*)
EQS	Environmental Quality Standard (*q.v.*)
ERPA	Emissions Reduction Purchase Agreement
ERRA	European Recovery and Recycling Association
ERUs	Emissions Reduction Units (tradable units created by 'Kyoto' JI projects)
ES	Environmental Statement
ESA	Environmentally Sensitive Area
ETS	(The EU) Emissions Trading Scheme
ETSU	Energy Technology Support Unit
EU	European Union
EUCLID	European Chemicals Information Database; the database of all chemical substances notified to the European Commission pursuant to Directive 793/93
EWC	European Waste Catalogue
FA	Finance Act (e.g. 1996 on landfill tax)
FAC	Food Advisory Committee
FEPA	Food and Environment Protection Act 1985
FGD	Flue Gas Desulphurisation
FOG	Fat, Oil and Grease
FOI (A)	Freedom of Information (Act 2000)
G	giga-. Used as prefix before units: 10^9
g, gm	gram
GDL	Generalised Derived Limits
GDPO	The Town and Country Planning (General Development Procedure) Order 1995
GEF	Global Environment Facility
GHG	Greenhouse Gas
GHS	The (United Nations) Globally Harmonised System for classifying chemicals according to their characteristics e.g. corrosive, toxic, etc.
GLA	Greater London Authority
GLP	Good Laboratory Practice
GMO	Genetically Modified Organism (*q.v.*)
GPDO	The Town and Country Planning (General Permitted Development) Order 1995

GPR	Ground Penetrating Radar (used in surveys for underground objects)
GTAC	Gene Therapy Advisory Committee
GWP	Global Warming Potential (*q.v.*)
HASS	High Activity Sealed Sources [Directive 2003/122]
HBFCs	hydrobromofluorocarbons (*q.v.*)
HCB	hexachlorobenzene
HCBD	hexachlorobutadiene
HCFCs	hydrochlorofluorocarbons (*q.v.*)
HCH	hexachlorocyclohexane (also sometimes HCCH); gamma-HCH is Lindane
HDPE	(see PE)
HEDSET	Harmonised Electronic Data Set; the computerised data on a chemical substance held by the European Commission pursuant to Directive 793/93 (see EUCLID)
HFCs	hydrofluorocarbons (a class of 'Kyoto' greenhouse gases)
HMIP	Her Majesty's Inspectorate of Pollution (England & Wales) (now merged into the Environment Agency)
HMIPI	Her Majesty's Industrial Pollution Inspectorate (Scotland) (now merged into the Scottish Environment Protection Agency)
HRA	Human Rights Act 1998
HSA	Hazardous Substances Authority
HSC	(1) Health and Safety Commission (2) Hazardous Substances Consent
HSE	Health and Safety Executive
HSWA	Health and Safety at Work etc. Act 1974
HWD	Hazardous Waste Directive 91/189
IARC	The International Agency for Research on Cancer (part of the WHO)
ICRP	International Commission on Radiological Protection
IDB	Internal Drainage Board
IETA	International Emissions Trading Association
IMO	International Maritime Organisation
INCPEN	Industry Council for Packaging and the Environment
INES	International Nuclear Event Scale
IPC	Integrated Pollution Control (now superseded by IPPC)
IPCC	Intergovernmental Panel on Climate Change
IPPC	Integrated Pollution Prevention and Control
IR	Infra-Red
IRPTC	International Register of Potentially Toxic Chemicals; a register operated by an office of UNEP based in Geneva
ISO	International Standards Organisation
IUCN	International Union for the Conservation of Nature
IUPAC	International Union of Pure and Applied Chemistry. The

	IUPAC nomenclature of organic compounds is generally regarded as definitive
JI	Joint Implementation (a Kyoto 'flexible mechanism')
JNCC	Joint Nature Conservation Committee
JR	Judicial Review
LAAPC	Local Authority Air Pollution Control
LAAs	Local Area Agreements
LAWDC	Local Authority Waste Disposal Company
LC_{50}	Lethal Concentration: a measure of acute toxicity by reference to the concentration that kills 50 percent of the organisms under test
LCA	Life Cycle Analysis
LCP	Large Combustion Plant (*e.g.* the EC LCP Directive 88/609)
LD_{50}	Lethal Dose: a measure of acute toxicity by reference to the dose that kills 50 percent of the organisms under test
LDA	The London Development Agency
LDDs	Local Development Documents
LDF	Local Development Framework
LDO	Local Development Order
LDPE	(see PE)
LDS	Local Development Scheme
LFG	Landfill Gas. The potentially explosive gas, consisting primarily of methane, resulting from the anaerobic decomposition of matter at landfill sites
LIFE	*L'Instrument Financiel pour l'Environment* (the EC Financial Instrument for the Environment established by Regulation 1973/92)
LNG	Liquefied Natural Gas
LNR	Local Nature Reserve
LPG	Liquefied Petroleum Gas (normally a mixture mainly of propane and butane)
LPO	Limestone Pavement Order
LULUCF	Land Use, Land Use Change, and Forestry
M	mega-. Used as prefix before units: 10^{-6}
m	milli-. Used as prefix before units: 10^{-3}
μ	(1) micro-. Used as prefix before units: 10^{-6}
	(2) micron. 10^{-6} metre, one thousandth of a millimetre
MAC	Maximum Allowable/Admissible Concentration
MAPP	Major Accident Prevention Policy
MCA	Magistrates Courts Act 1980
MCZ	Marine Conservation Zone (proposed in Draft Marine Bill published 3 April 2008)
MEL	Maximum Exposure Limit (*e.g.* of hazardous substances at the workplace)

ml	Millilitre
MMG	Marine Minerals Guidance
MMO	Marine Management Organisation (proposed by Draft Marine Bill published 3 April 2008)
MNR	Marine Nature Reserve
MOP	Meeting of the Parties
MP	Melting Point
MPA	(1) Minerals Planning Authority
	(2) Metropolitan Police Authority
MPG	Mineral Planning Guidance
MPS	Minerals Policy Statement
MRF	Materials Recycling Facility
MRL	Maximum Residue Limit (*e.g.* of pesticides in food-stuffs)
MSDS	Material Safety Data Sheet (also simply SDS)
MTBE	methyl tertiary butyl ether
MW	(1) Molecular Weight
	(2) Megawatts
MWth/MW(th)	Megawatts thermal—used to express the rated thermal input of a power generator (see Input Rating)
n	nano-. Used as prefix before units: 10^{-9}
N_2O	Nitrous oxide (a 'Kyoto' greenhouse gas)
NAP	National Allocation Plan (for emissions trading purposes)
NAWDC	National Association of Waste Disposal Contractors
NCC	Nature Conservancy Council (now defunct)
NDA	Nuclear Decommissioning Authority
NE	Natural England
NERC	Natural Environment Research Council
NFFO	Non-Fossil Fuel Obligation
NGO	Non-Governmental Organisation
NHA	Natural Heritage Area—a site designation under the Natural Heritage (Scotland) Act 1991
NIA	The Nuclear Installations Act 1965
NNR	National Nature Reserve
NOEL	No Observed Effect Level. The maximum level of a dose or exposure at which no effect is observed
NONS	The Notification of New Substances Regulations 1993
NO_x	Nitrogen Oxides. A general expression covering all the various oxides of nitrogen, *e.g.* N_2O, N_2O_3, NO_2
NPIS	The UK National Poisons Information Service, based in Birmingham
NRA	(1) Nature Reserve Agreement (under the Countryside Act 1949)
	(2) National Rivers Authority (now merged into the Environment Agency)
NRPB	National Radiological Protection Board

NSA	Nitrate Sensitive Area
NTP	Normal Temperature and Pressure. Now obsolete, see STP
NVZ	Nitrate Vulnerable Zone, designated under the EC Nitrates Directive 91/676
OECD	Organisation for Economic Co-operation and Development
OEL	Occupational Exposure Limit
OES	Occupational Exposure Standard
OFWAT	Office of Water Services
p	(1) pico-. Used as prefix before units: 10^{-12}
	(2) para-. In organic chemistry used to denote substitution at the 1,4 positions in a benzene ring (*i.e.* on opposite carbon atoms)
PAH	polycyclic aromatic hydrocarbon(s)
PAP	Pre-Action Protocol
PBB	Polybrominated Biphenyls
PBDE	Polybrominated Diphenyl Ethers
PCB	polychlorinated biphenyl(s)
PCDD	polychlorinated dibenzo-dioxin(s)
PCDF	polychlorinated dibenzo-difuran(s)
PCH	polychlorinated hydrocarbons
PCMH	Plea and Case Management Hearing
PCO	Protective Costs Order
PCP	Pentachlorophenol
PCPA	Planning and Compulsory Purchase Act 2004
PCT	polychlorinated terphenyl(s)
PD	Practice Direction
PDO	Potentially Damaging Operation
PE	polyethylene. It may be made by polymerising ethylene in either a high pressure or a low pressure process, producing low density polyethylene (LDPE) or high density poly-ethylene (HDPE) respectively
pe	population equivalent (*q.v.*)
PEC	Predicted Environmental Concentration; relevant to risk assessments of potential releases of chemicals to the environment
PER	(1) perchlorethylene ($CCl_2:CCl_2$)
	(2) Polluting Emissions Register (EC)
PERN	Packaging Export Recovery Note
PET	polyethylene terephthalate. A clear plastic, of which beverage bottles are often made.
PFA	Pulverised Fuel Ash
PFCs	Perfluorocarbons (a class of 'Kyoto' greenhouse gases)
PGS	Planning Gain Supplement

pH	(*pouvoir Hydrogène*) A measure of the acidity or alkalinity of an aqueous solution. pH7 is neutral, lower values being increasingly acidic, higher values being increasingly alkaline
PIC	Prior Informed Consent
PM_{10} / $PM_{2.5}$	Particle Measurement (see Glossary) used when expressing the concentration in air of particles with diameters of 10 or 2.5 microns
PMN	Pre-Market Notication (of new chemical substances)
PNEC	Predicted No-Effect Concentration; relevant to, *e.g.* ecotoxicity assessments of chemicals
POCA	Proceeds of Crime Act 2002
POPs	Persistent Organic Pollutants, e.g. DDT, PCBs, the 'Drins (*q.v.*). They are the subject of the EU POPs Regulation 850/2004
POST	Parliamentary Office of Science and Technology
PP	Polypropylene
ppb	parts per billion
PPC	Pollution Prevention Control
PPE	Personal Protective Equipment
PPG	Planning Policy Guidance
ppm	parts per million
PPS	Planning Policy Statement
PRN	Packaging Recovery Note
PSD	The UK Pesticides Safety Directorate, an agency of the HSE
psi	Pounds per Square Inch (a unit of pressure)
PSI	Potential Strategic Importance
PSR	Pre-Sentence Report
PVC	polyvinyl chloride
QA	Quality Assurance
Rad	Radiation Absorbed Dose (*q.v.*)
RCEP	Royal Commission on Environmental Pollution
RDF	Refuse Derived Fuel
REACH	The Registration, Evaluation, Authorisation and restriction of Chemical substances (the name given to EU Regulation 1907/2006)
REPs	Regulation Environmental Principles (Environment Agency)
RID	Regulations concerning the International Carriage of Dangerous Goods by Rail
RIMNET	Radioactive Incident Monitoring Network
RIPA	Regulation of Investigative Powers Act 2000
RMUs	Removal Units (tradable units created by 'Kyoto' LULUCF projects)

ROC	(UK) Renewables Obligation Certificate
RPA	River Purification Authority (Scotland)
RPB	(1) Regional Planning Board
	(2) River Purification Board (Scotland)
RPG	Regional Planning Guidance
RSA	Radioactive Substances Act 1993
RSS	Regional Spatial Strategies
RWMAC	Radioactive Waste Management Advisory Committee
SAC	Special Area for Conservation, designated under the EC Habitats Directive 92/43
SCA	Serious Crime Act 2007
SCI	(1) Site of Community Importance, under the EC Habitats Directive 92/43
	(2) Statement of Community Involvement
SCPO	Serious Crime Prevention Order
SDS	Safety Data Sheet (also MSDS)
SEA	Strategic Environmental Assessment
SEPA	Scottish Environment Protection Agency
SF_6	Sulphur hexafluoride (a very potent 'Kyoto' greenhouse gas)
SGC	Sentencing Guidelines Council
SIDS	Screening Information Data Set. The name given to an OECD chemicals testing programme
SNH	Scottish Natural Heritage
SNIF	Standard Notification Information Format. The format for Information to be sent to the European Commission on new chemical substances and proposed releases of genetically modified organisms
SOAFD	Scottish Office Agriculture and Fisheries Department
SOCA	Serious Organised Crime Agency
SORG	The Stratospheric Ozone Review Group
SO_x	Sulphur Oxides. A general expression covering the various oxides of sulphur *e.g.* SO_2, SO_3
SPA	Special Protection Area, designated under the EC Birds Directive 79/409
SPG	Supplementary Planning Guidance
SPOSH	Significant possibility of significant harm
SPZ	Simplified Planning Zone
SSSI	Site of Special Scientific Interest
STEL	Short Term Exposure Limit (*e.g.* of hazardous substances at the workplace)
STP	(1) Standard Temperature and Pressure. The standard conditions used for comparing volumes of gases, *i.e.* 0°C and standard atmospheric pressure (760 mm mercury). The term is now used in preference to NTP

	(2) Sewage Treatment Plant
Sv	Sievert (*q.v.*)
SVHC	Substances of Very High Concern, a category of substances in, and specifically controlled by, the REACH (*q.v.*) regime
SWQO	Statutory Water Quality Objective
T	tera-. Used as a prefix before units = 10^{12}
TBZ	thiabendazole. A fungicide—E233
TCB	Trichlorobenzene
TCDD	2,3,7,8—tetrachlorodibenzo-p-dioxin. Regarded as the most toxic of the family of dioxins and furans (see also TEQ)
TCE	Trichloroethylene
TCPA	Town and Country Planning Act (1947, 1990)
TEQ	Toxic Equivalent (of TCCD). Used to define the toxicity of a mixture of dioxins and/or furans by ascribing a weighting factor to each relating their toxicity to that of TCCD
THM	trihalomethane (CHX_3 where X = any halogen)
TLV	Threshold Limit Value (a term used in the USA equivalent to MEL or OEL (*q.v.*) in the UK
TOC	Total Organic Carbon (*q.v.*)
TRI	Toxics Release Inventory (US)
TWA	Time Weighted Average
UCO	The Town and Country Planning (Use Classes) Order 1987 (as amended)
UKBAP	United Kingdom Biodiversity Action Plan
UNCED	United Nations Conference on Environment and Development (at Rio de Janeiro in June 1992)
UNCLOS	United Nations Convention on the Law Of the Sea
UN-ECE	United Nations—Economic Commission for Europe
UNED	United Nations Environment and Development
UNEP	United Nations Environment Programme
UNFCCC	United Nations Framework Convention on Climate Change 1992
UST	Underground Storage Tank
UV	Ultra-Violet
VCM	Vinyl Chloride Monomer, a toxic substance which polymerises to PVC
VOCs	Volatile Organic Carbons
WAMITAB	Waste Management Industry Training Advisory Board
WATCH	Working Group on the Assessment of Toxic Chemicals
WCA	(1) Wildlife and Countryside Act 1981
	(2) Waste Collection Authority
WDA	Waste Disposal Authority

WEEE	Waste Electrical and Electronic Equipment
WET	Whole Effluent Toxicity. A WET test considers the toxicity of an effluent stream as a whole as opposed to that of its individual components
WFD	(1) Waste Framework Directive (currently 2006/12)
	(2) Water Framework Directive 2000/60
WHO	World Health Organisation
WIA	Water Industry Act 1991
WID	Waste Incineration Directive 2000/76
WMP	Waste Management Paper
WQO	Water Quality Objective
WQS	Water Quality Standard
WRA	(1) Waste Regulation Authority
	(2) Water Resources Act 1991
YJCEA	Youth Justice and Criminal Evidence 1999

GLOSSARY

The explanations of the expressions in this Glossary are intended to assist the non-technical reader in understanding them in the context of environmental legislation and discussion of environmental issues. Accordingly while it is hoped there are no material inaccuracies, on occasion the precision and comprehensiveness to be found in scientific dictionaries have been eschewed in favour of intelligibility for the layman and relevance to the present subject.

Aarhus Convention
:   The Convention on Access to Information, Public Participation in Decision-Making and Access to Justice in Environmental Matters, signed at Aarhus (Århus), Denmark, on June 25, 1998, and which came into force on October 30, 2001. The European Community has been a party to the Convention since May 2005.

Acid, acidic
:   (Strictly) anything having a pH (*q.v.*) below 7. Strongly acidic substances have a pH of 1–2 or less, and are substantially completely dissociated into hydrogen ions (positive) and anions (negative).

Acid Rain
:   Rain (including cloud, fog and snow) which has been acidified by SO_x and NO_x (*q.v.*) present in the atmosphere, leading in particular to damage to trees and other vegetation, the leaching out of essential nutrients from the soil, and acidifying and raising the concentration of metallic salts in rivers and lakes. The term is used in practice to extend also to the deposit of dry acids from the atmosphere.

Acceptable Daily Intake
:   The amount of a substance, e.g. a food additive, that can be ingested daily over a life-time without incurring an appreciable health risk. It may be calculated by dividing the relevant NOEL (*q.v.*)

in mg per kg body weight per day by a safety factor, which is typically around 100.

Activated carbon   A form of carbon that has a high surface area per gram, used in water treatment and other processes to absorb unwanted substances in fluids passed over it.

Active ingredient/ substance   The component of, e.g. a pharmaceutical or pesticide composition that provides the desired effect; the balance will consist primarily of an inert carrier or excipient, though there may also be e.g. wetting or solubilising agents and adjuvants.

Acute (exposure)   A single short-term (often high level) exposure; *cf.* "chronic (exposure)".

Aerobic   Requiring air, e.g. aerobic bacteria which can only function in the presence of oxygen. In the aerobic digestion of organic (*q.v.*) matter (i.e. composting), aerobic bacteria use oxygen from the air, as they break down the organic molecules, and convert it into carbon dioxide – a reaction that also produces heat.

Agenda 21   The programme of action agreed internationally at the UNCED (*q.v.*) at Rio de Janeiro in 1992, designed to lead towards sustainable development. So called as this issue was item 21 on the conference agenda.

Alkali   See "Base".

Alkane   A straight or branched chain fully saturated hydrocarbon, e.g. methane, propane, butane.

Ambient conditions   The normally existing state of potentially variable conditions at a particular location, e.g. the temperature and pressure, or the concentrations of pollutants or other substances in the air or water.

Anaerobic   Not requiring air, e.g. anaerobic bacteria which function in the absence of air. They produce for example methane in the decomposition of organic (*q.v.*) matter.

Ångstrom — A measure of length used in relation to distances between atoms and the wavelength of high frequency radiation, approximately 10^{-8} cm.

Aromatic compounds — Organic (*q.v.*) compounds containing one or more benzene rings or "condensed" ring structures (e.g. toluene, xylene, naphthalene, PCBs). They are to be contrasted with aliphatic compounds which are compounds containing a straight, branched or cyclic carbon chain but with no benzene or condensed ring structures.

Asbestos — Fibrous impure magnesium silicate. It exists in a variety of forms, all of which are highly toxic by inhalation of dust particles and carcinogenic. Amosite (brown asbestos) and crocidolite (blue asbestos) are particularly hazardous; chrysotile (white asbestos) and the amphibole forms (anthophyllite, tremolite and actinolite) somewhat less so.

Base, basic — Alkali, alkaline. (Strictly) anything having a pH (*q.v.*) above 7. Strong bases have a pH of 13–14 or more, and are substantially completely dissociated into hydroxyl ions (negative) and cations (positive).

Becquerel — A measure of radioactivity, being the number of nuclear transformations or disintegrations per second. Becquerel has replaced curie as the standard unit; 1 curie = 3.7×10^{10} becquerels.

Best Practicable Environmental Option — (For the purposes of IPC) the option which for a given set of objectives provides the most benefit or least damage to the environment as a whole, at acceptable cost in the long term as well as the short term, as a result of releases of substances from a process.

Bioaccumulate — The tendency of compounds, e.g. several types of pesticide and PCBs, to accumulate in animal tissues, and thus to increase in concentration in a series of animals up the food chain, prejudicing the survival of those at the top, either directly or indirectly by interfering with their reproductive cycle. The latter is the more lethal to a species, since toxic effects killing some only of the individuals in a population directly may merely remove weaker members or older ones that have already reproduced.

Biochemical Oxygen Demand

A measure of water quality, specifically its content of organic material, by reference to the amount of oxygen used by micro-organisms to break down the organic molecules in a sample of water. For any given content of organics, the figure is reduced by substances that inhibit the action of micro-organisms, such as heavy metals, chlorine and pesticides, and increased by the presence of ammonia and hydrogen sulphide which are themselves oxidised; *cf.* Chemical Oxygen Demand.

Biodegradable

The propensity of a substance to decompose under the action of biological organisms. Whether it in fact does so depends on the surrounding conditions being at least tolerable by the relevant organisms. In the absence of air (as is often so, deep in a landfill), aerobic (*q.v.*) bacteria will not be effective to degrade anything; nevertheless the anaerobic (*q.v.*) bacteria present will not necessarily decompose substances described as biodegradable. The ratio of COD to BOD (*q.v.*) may be used as measure of the biodegradability of substances in water.

Builder

A component of commercial detergents designed to improve their performance by associating with the deleterious metal ions present in hard water (e.g. calcium, magnesium), maintaining the detergent solution alkaline, keeping soil particles suspended and so preventing their re-deposition on the items being washed, and stabilising the physical properties of a washing powder. The most common builders are phosphates, in particular sodium tripolyphosphate, which can lead to eutrophication (*q.v.*). However their use enables less detergent to be used, and many alternatives available at comparable cost themselves have environmental and/or technical disadvantages.

Carbon Dioxide Equivalent

A means of accounting for the differing global warming potentials (GWPs) of greenhouse gases, in particular those covered by the Kyoto Protocol, whereby all quantities of the various gases are expressed as tonnes of Carbon Dioxide Equivalent. These quantities are calculated by multiplying the actual tonnages of any one gas that are emitted or reduced, as the case may be, by its GWP.

Carcinogenic

Substances and preparations which, if they are inhaled or ingested or if they penetrate the skin, may induce cancer or increase its incidence, *cf.* mutagenic, teratogenic.

Cartagena Protocol

A protocol to the UN Convention on Biological Diversity. It is primarily concerned with the safe handling, international transfer, and use of Genetically Modified Organisms.

Chemical Oxygen Demand

A measure of water quality, specifically its content of organic material, by reference to the amount of potassium dichromate (an oxidising agent) required to oxidise the organic material in a sample of water after inorganic substances (such as ammonia and hydrogen sulphide) have been removed. Unlike the BOD (*q.v.*) test, it does not distinguish between biodegradable and non-bio-degradable organic molecules, and so will not necessarily give closely similar results, but it is a relatively cheap and simple test to operate.

Chlorofluorocarbons

(CFCs). A range of alkanes (*q.v.*) in which all the hydrogen atoms are substituted by both chlorine and fluorine atoms. They are very stable and inert in normal circumstances but decompose in the stratosphere where the chlorine released combines with ozone in the ozone layer, so depleting it.

Chromatography

A general term for a variety of related methods of

separating out the components of complex mixtures, typically by differential adsorption, prior to identifying the relative amounts present. Often of use in analyses of pollutants in samples of soil and groundwater.

Chronic (exposure)

Exposure (generally low level) over a long period; *cf.* "acute (exposure)".

Co-disposal

The mixing of different waste types in a landfill, desirably in order to promote a beneficial interaction between them that reduces or eliminates potentially harmful properties of one or more of the wastes. In practice it often did little more than dilute the more hazardous wastes. It used to be favoured in the UK, but is now prohibited.

Copolymer/ copolymerisation

See Monomer.

Critical load

The maximum load of a defined pollutant or pollutants that a given eco-system is known to be able to tolerate without suffering adverse effects. UK policy on the control of acid emissions to atmosphere is based to a large extent on seeking to avoid acid deposition on any site exceeding the critical load for that site.

Cryptosporidium

A microscopic parasite found in many environments, including animals and water, capable of causing ill-health in some circumstances. Its significance in water supplies was the subject of a report of the National Advisory Group (the Badenoch Report, 1990).

Diffuse source

See "non-point source".

Dioxins

A large family of highly toxic chlorinated organic (*q.v.*) compounds, the most toxic being TCDD. They are readily formed in the combustion products of mixed organic compounds and chlorine containing compounds; their formation in incinerators is generally thought to be minimised by very high temperatures, low residence times, and rapid cooling of emissions.

"Drins"	The chemically related chlorine-containing pesticides aldrin, isodrin, dieldrin and endrin.
Ecotoxic	Harmful to the environment.
Environmental Quality Objective	A classification of receiving waters by reference to their suitability for a specified purpose.
Environmental Quality Standard	An environmental quality specification defined by reference to numerical limit values for prescribed parameters, generally being concentrations of particular substances in water or air.
Epidemiology	The study of rates of disease among different population groups.
Eutrophication	Making a waterbody rich in nutrients. The consequence of excessive amounts of nutrients in water encourages undue growth of algae and aquatic plants. On the death of these, their decay under the action of aerobic bacteria may extract an excessive amount of dissolved oxygen from the water and make it uninhabitable for fish and other aquatic fauna. Following loss of the oxygen, anaerobic bacteria then continue the decay, mostly at the bottom of the water, producing toxins liable to kill any of the remaining fish and other fauna that have survived the loss of oxygen.
Flash point	The temperature at which the vapour formed by a liquid or volatile solid that is exposed to air will be capable of ignition.
Fugitive emissions	Uncontrolled leaks of gases and volatile liquids from, *e.g.* joints and valves of pipes, tanks and process plant.
Genetically Modified Organism	(Broadly) a reproducible organism of which the naturally occurring gene sequence has been modified by genetic engineering techniques. The UK Regulations on the contained use and deliberate release of GMOs (SI 2000/2831 and SI 2002/2443, respectively, both as amended) contain more detailed definitions, which differ somewhat from each other.

GENHAZ — An adaptation of HAZOP (*q.v.*). A procedure designed to identify potential hazards resulting from the release of genetically modified organisms to the environment.

Geomorphological — Pertaining to the study of present-day landscapes and their origins.

Giga- — 10^9.

Global Warming Potential — The relative global warming effect of a greenhouse gas over a period of 100 years, as compared with Carbon Dioxide (which, by definition, has a GWP of 1). GWPs vary very widely; the figures produced by the IPCC in its "2nd Assessment Report 1995" are those used in emissions trading under the Kyoto Protocol. The IPCC figures are: Methane 21; Nitrous oxide 310; Sulphur hexafluoride 23,900; Hydrofluorocarbons 140 – 11,700; Perfluorocarbons 6,500 – 9,200. For further detail see http://www.defra.gov.uk/environment/climatechange/about/g-gas-list.htm.

Gray (Gy) — The amount of radiation energy absorbed per unit weight of human tissue – the absorbed dose – is measured in rads or Grays. 1 Gray, the SI unit, is 100 rads, and equals 1 joule / kilogram.

Groundwater — Water contained in, and so capable of flowing (slowly) through, permeable underground strata (aquifers) lying over, and possibly also under, relatively impermeable strata. Since the planes of underground strata may be at wholly different angles to those of the ground surface above, and the groundwater subject to hydrostatic pressure, there is no necessary relationship between the direction of flow of (e.g. contaminated) groundwater and that of surface water above.

Half-life — A measure of the rate of decay of radioactive substances or of decomposition of relatively persistent substances. In the steady state (however fast or slow the actual rate), the time taken for half of any given quantity to decay or decompose (i.e. the half-life) is constant. The time for all of it to do so is theoretically always infinite; hence of the two only the half-life is a useful measure.

Halogen

Any of the elements forming Group VII of the Periodic Table: fluorine, chlorine, bromine, iodine.

Halons

A range of alkanes (q.v.) in which all the hydrogen atoms are substituted by halogen atoms. In distinction from the very similar chlorofluorocarbons (q.v.), the halogen atoms include both fluorine and bromine—chlorine may, but need not, be present. Bromine is an even more effective ozone-depleter than chlorine.

Hazard

A set of circumstances that may cause harm (from temporary minor harm to catastrophe); cf. "risk".

HAZOP

Hazard and Operability Study. A procedure for identifying the potential hazards of any operation, typically used in the designing of safe chemical manufacturing plant.

Heavy metals

Metals with an atomic number greater than that of sodium which form soaps with fatty acids (e.g. stearic acid). Most metals in fact come within this definition including e.g. copper, cobalt, cadmium, chromium.

Heterocyclic compounds

Organic compounds with a ring structure that includes an atom other than carbon, e.g. nitrogen, oxygen or sulphur, as a member of the ring.

Hydrocarbons

Organic compounds consisting exclusively of carbon and hydrogen, e.g. methane (CH_4), benzene (C_6H_6), polyethylene and the principal constituents of oils and petrol.

Hydrobromofluoro-carbons

(HBFCs). A range of organic compounds analogous to HCFCs, but containing bromine in place of chlorine.

Hydrochlorofluoro-carbons

(HCFCs). Organic compounds related to CFCs, but in which one or more hydrogen atoms remain unsubstituted by chlorine or fluorine.

In vitro

A term applied to experiments carried out on artificial systems such as cell cultures in, e.g. test tubes, rather than in vivo, i.e. on a live animal.

Input Rating

A generator may be rated by reference either to the energy it consumes (the rated input) or to the power it produces (the rated output), the ratio of the rated output to the rated input being its conversion factor. A thermal input rating is calculated from the maximum rate at which the intended fuel can be burned multiplied by the net calorific value of the fuel.

Kyoto Protocol

A protocol to the 1992 United Nations Framework Convention on Climate Change. It was agreed at Kyoto in 1997, and entered into force in February 2005. It establishes a system of "flexible mechanisms", enabling the trading of greenhouse gas allowances, and the achievement of emissions reductions through Joint Implementation and the Clean Development Mechanism.

Latency Period

The lapse of time between exposure to the cause of a disease or other injury and its manifestation.

Leachate

The liquid emanating from underground strata. The term is most commonly applied to liquid derived from waste sites, when it is liable to contain toxic decomposition products and/or toxic materials from the waste, such as heavy metal compounds, pesticides, etc., and so pollute groundwater.

MARPOL

The 1973 International Convention for the Prevention of (Marine) Pollution from Ships, as modified by its 1978 Protocol.

Mean

The arithmetical average of a set of figures obtained by dividing their aggregate by the number of figures in the set cf. "median".

Median

In a set of figures of varying amounts, the median is that amount which divides the set into equal halves, so that the number of figures in the set that are larger than it is the same as the number of those that are smaller. The median is often a more meaningful figure than the mean in a skewed sample where a few figures are markedly greater (or smaller) than the remainder.

Mega- 10^6.

Mesothelioma   Cancer of the lining of the chest, associated exclusively with exposure to asbestos, particularly crocidolite.

Metabolism   Biotransformation. The conversion of a foreign compound that has been absorbed by a biological system (*e.g.* an animal or plant) into other substances. The process operates in most cases to reduce or eliminate any toxic effects of the foreign compound (detoxication), but it may on occasion result in increased toxicity (toxication). The ability to metabolise a toxic substance may vary widely between species, and also between different strains and between the sexes of the same species. This can render it difficult or impossible to extrapolate to man with any certainty, still less precision, test results obtained from animals.

Metabolite   A substance to which a foreign compound is converted through metabolism (*q.v.*).

Methaemoglobinaemia   A rare blood condition (commonly known as "blue baby syndrome") affecting young babies, caused by excessive nitrate intake, *e.g.* from drinking water.

Micro- 10^{-6}

Monomer   A compound, nearly always organic, capable of reacting with itself (and often with other monomers) to form a long chain molecule, called a polymer (or copolymer, as the case may be) made up of numerous units of the monomer(s) in sequence. For the purposes of REACH (*q.v.*) a (co)polymer molecule must be made up of at least 3 such monomer units. In practice, commercial (co)polymer molecules will often have hundreds or even thousands of such units; the actual product being a mixture of (co)polymer molecules of differing lengths. The properties of the product depend, inter alia, on the mean/median molecule length and the extent of variation between long and short molecules, which must therefore be carefully controlled. The chemical reaction that creates a (co)polymer from one or more monomers is called (co)polymerisation.

Montreal Protocol A protocol to the Vienna Convention for the protection of the ozone layer, signed at Montreal, which laid down timetables, subsequently accelerated, for the global phasing out of CFCs, halons and other ozone depleting substances.

Mutagenic Substances and preparations which, if they are inhaled or ingested, or if they penetrate the skin, may induce hereditary genetic defects or increase their incidence (as defined in Directive 91/689/EEC).

Nano- 10^{-9}

Nanotechnology The technology involved in working with materials on the nanoscale – this is generally taken to mean molecular structures with dimensions of from 1 to 100 nanometres approximately, i.e. 10^{-9} to 10^{-7} metres. Materials on this scale tend to exhibit properties very different from those found at conventional, much larger scales.

Natura 2000 A "coherent European ecological network" of special areas of conservation established under Article 3 of the EC Habitats Directive 92/43, which also includes the special protection areas designated under the EC Birds Directive 79/409.

Nitrates A term frequently used to signify the inorganic compounds, such as ammonium nitrate ($NH_4.NO_3$), used as agricultural fertilisers. Their presence in water in substantial quantities can lead to eutrophication (*q.v.*).

Non-point source A diffuse source of pollutants, e.g. a field from which pesticides or fertilisers may seep into a watercourse, or a railway line; to be distinguished from a point source, *e.g.* an outfall from drains or a sewer, or a chimney stack.

Organic compounds   Carbon based compounds; in distinction from inorganic compounds. Organic compounds usually contain a stable chain of carbon atoms combined with at least some hydrogen atoms (as in hydrocarbons) but often also halogens, oxygen, nitrogen, etc.

Organohalogens   Organic compounds containing halogen atoms bound to carbon atoms (e.g. CFCs, HCFCs). Many organochlorine compounds in particular are highly toxic pesticides, e.g. dieldrin, DDT.

OSPAR Convention   The 1992 Convention for the Protection of the marine Environment of the North-East Atlantic, merging the earlier Oslo (1972) and Paris (1974) Conventions.

Ozone   A gas with a molecule consisting of three oxygen atoms, *i.e.* O_3 (oxygen gas consists of two, *i.e.* O_2). Low level ozone, liable to be formed by the action of the sun on mixtures of hydrocarbons and NO_x (typical components of vehicle exhausts) causes respiratory problems.

Ozone layer   The layer of ozone in the stratosphere that absorbs, and so filters out, ultraviolet rays that would otherwise reach the earth's surface. It is attacked by the chlorine and bromine atoms released from CFCs, halons, HCFCs and HBFCs, which compounds are therefore referred to as "ozone depleters".

Percentile   Literally, a one hundredth part. The term is used when setting limits to be met by a series of samples. Thus a 95 percentile limit must be met by 95 per cent of the samples. (In the absence of other conditions, this places no restraint on the amount by which the remaining 5 per cent may breach that limit).

Perch   Perching occurs where an isolated pocket of

liquid, e.g. water, is held in a stratum over an impermeable layer that is itself set in or on a permeable stratum containing the local body of groundwater.

Percutaneous (absorption)	(Absorption) through the skin.
Perfluorocarbons	Organic compounds composed only of carbon and fluorine. They are possible substitutes for CFCs since they have similar properties but (having no chlorine) do not harm the ozone layer; however their global-warming potential (*q.v.*) is very high.
Persistence	The property of a substance that remains chemically unchanged following release into the environment, *i.e.* it does not react with other compounds and is not metabolised on take-up by living organisms.
Pesticide	A generic term used to encompass, e.g. insecticides, herbicides, fumigants, fungicides and rodenticides.
Phosphates	Components of many standard formulations of both detergents, where they are used as builders (*q.v.*), and fertilisers. In water they act as nutrients for algae and plant life and in substantial quantities can thus lead to eutrophication (*q.v.*).
Photochemical reaction	A chemical reaction that is stimulated by the action of light, e.g. in the production of low level ozone from the components of vehicle exhausts.
Physiographical	A term used in some statutory definitions of nature conservation meaning geomorphological (*q.v.*).
Pico-	10^{-12}
PM_{10} / $PM_{2.5}$	An expression used to indicate the concentration in air of particles with either 10 or 2.5 microns maximum diameter. The smaller their diameter,

the further into the lungs particles can go, and the more harmful they are liable to be.

Point source   See "non-point source".

Polymer/polymerisation   See Monomer.

Population equivalent   A term relating the polluting load of an organic discharge to the number of people who would normally cause an equivalent load. For the purposes of such a calculation, one person is assumed to produce daily a domestic effluent with a BOD of 60g of oxygen.

Rad   A unit of measurement of the amount of radiation energy absorbed per unit weight of human tissue. See Gray.

Radon   A radioactive inert gas, a decay product of radioactive substances such as uranium and thorium. It occurs naturally in many parts of Britain and is liable to accumulate at ground level in buildings in the absence of adequate ventilation.

Ringelmann Chart   A chart used for assessing the darkness of smoke, *e.g.* for the purposes of the Clean Air Act 1993. It consists of five squares, of which one is white and the remainder represent various shades of grey. These shades are produced by the effect of 20 equally spaced vertical lines crossing 20 equally spaced horizontal ones. The lines vary in thickness from one square to the next. The four grey shades produced thus define: Ringelmann 1–20% obscured; Ringelmann 2–40% obscured; Ringelmann 3–60% obscured; Ringelmann 4–80% obscured; "Dark smoke" is at least as dark as Ringelmann 2; "black smoke" is at least as dark as Ringelmann 4. The chart is described in BS 2742C and its use in BS 2742.

Risk   The probability of an adverse effect occurring. In relation to a toxic substance, it is a function both of its toxicity to those at risk of exposure to it and of the duration, intensity and frequency of exposure.

Saturated In organic chemistry, carbon atoms linked by a single bond or a molecule where all the carbon atoms in a chain are linked by single bonds only, *i.e.* there are no double or triple bonds; *cf.* "unsaturated".

Scrub The treatment of flue gases to remove polluting components such as SO_x and NO_x.

Sievert A measure of the dose of radiation received over a period of time adjusted to take account of the differing biological effects of different types of radiation. Natural background radiation in the UK provides an annual average dose of around 0.002 Sv, *i.e.* 2 mSv.

Synergy Synergy is displayed when two (or more) substances together produce consequences greater than the aggregate of those produced by each of them separately.

Tera- 10^{12}.

Teratogenic Substances and preparations which, if they are inhaled or ingested or if they penetrate the skin, may induce non-hereditary congenital malformations or increase their incidence (as defined in Directive 91/689/EEC).

Total Organic Carbon A measure of water quality, specifically its content of carbon in organic material, obtained by any of a number of different tests in which the carbon in the organic material is totally oxidised to carbon dioxide. It has greater sensitivity than the COD (*q.v.*) test, and is fast and convenient, but more expensive.

Toxicology The study of harmful interactions between chemical substances and biological systems (including, but not limited to, humans).

Unsaturated In organic chemistry, a pair of carbon atoms linked by a double or a triple bond or a molecule containing at least one such carbon pair. Hydrogenation, for example, may lead to one or two hydrogen atoms, as the case may be, becoming attached to each of these carbons; thus the bond becomes single and the molecule "saturated" (*q.v.*).

Vadose zone   The unsaturated stratum of ground between the surface and the water table.

Water table   The level of the upper surface of the saturated zone containing ground-water.

Chapter 1

Sources of Environmental Law

Introduction

The significance of European Community legislation in determining the   **1–001** content of the substantive environmental law of the United Kingdom can hardly be overstated. Environmental law is of course administered almost entirely by government bodies and other "emanations of the state", who are required to give effect to European Community law, even where applicable United Kingdom law is or may be inconsistent. While there may be relatively few aspects where United Kingdom law is incontrovertibly in conflict with European Community law—most questions of non-compliance arise from matters of omission rather than commission—there are bound to be far more where interpretation of United Kingdom legislation could and should be determined by reference to the relevant European Community law and the policy objectives underlying it, not least the basic principles set out in Article 174 of the Rome Treaty.[1] Accordingly in this chapter, attention will focus on, amongst other things, the legal basis on which European Community environmental law is made and the nature and scope of the principles which it reflects. Given that non-compliance with Community environmental law is liable to be an issue for all 27 Member States from time to time, it will be necessary to consider how the states may be made to comply with their obligations. The emergence of the doctrine of "direct effect" will therefore be explained in this chapter, as will the formal infringement proceedings which the European Commission may initiate pursuant to Articles 226 to 228 of the Rome Treaty. The chapter concludes with a consideration of the extent to which the European Convention for the Protection of Human Rights and Fundamental Freedoms (ECHR) constitutes a source of legally enforceable environmental rights.

The opening section in this chapter provides a brief explanation of several key aspects of international environmental law. Since international environmental law is a subject in its own right, it cannot be dealt with in anything other than a tangential way in this book. Accordingly, in what follows, we shall confine our discussion to the legal status of treaties and conventions signed by the UK government as well as how, with the aid of

---

[1] See para.1–020 below.

an example, international environmental law has influenced UK and European environmental law and policy.

International Environmental Law and its Impact on UK Law

International conventions

1–002 International conventions are often one of the principal motive forces behind new environmental legislation. Many of these have been promoted by the United Nations, through the United Nations Environment Programme (UNEP), the Organisation for Economic Cooperation and Development (the OECD), and the Council of Europe. There has been no uniform practice with regard to the manner of participation of EC Member States in these conventions. Individual states may be signatories to them, as may the European Community as a single body. In the latter case, the convention will then be implemented through Community legislation.

There is no standard geographical coverage for an environmental treaty. Thus whilst some may be limited in their application,[2] others may extend to cover the whole international community.[3] Kiss and Shelton point out that "a broad global framework of international law has been established for the four "traditional" sectors of the environment: water, soil, atmosphere and biological diversity".[4] They also make it clear that although the subject matter and geographical scope of environmental treaties varies, such treaties "have common characteristics, use similar legal techniques, and often are interrelated".[5] They identify the main characteristics which these treaties share as follows:

"(1) an absence of reciprocity of obligations, (2) interrelated or cross-referenced provisions from one instrument to another, (3) framework agreements, (4) frequent interim application, (5) the creation of new institutions or the utilisation of already existing ones to promote continuous cooperation, (6) innovative compliance and non-compliance procedures and (7) simplified means of modification or amendment".[6]

---

[2] See, for example, the Paris Convention for the Protection of the Environment of the North-East Atlantic (1992).
[3] See, for example, the United Nations Convention on the Law of the Sea (UNCLOS) (1982) which entered into force on November 16, 1994.
[4] A.C. Kiss and D. Shelton, *International Environmental Law*, 3rd edition (Transnational Publishers Inc, 2004), p.70.
[5] ibid., p.71.
[6] ibid.

Treaties and the UK: prerogative power of government

The power which the United Kingdom government possesses to sign an **1–003** international convention or treaty[7] derives from the royal prerogative, i.e. those common law powers which are unique to the Crown. Despite the fact that the House of Lords has held that the exercise of certain prerogative powers is susceptible to judicial review,[8] the treaty-making power is in a category of prerogative powers which are regarded by the courts as non-justiciable on account of their nature and subject matter.[9] Accordingly, a decision made by the government to enter into an environmental treaty is beyond legal challenge.

Translating international conventions into United Kingdom law is effected in a variety of ways. By contrast with many other countries,[10] international treaties[11] generally create no legal rights or obligations whatsoever within the United Kingdom, unless and until they are incorporated in UK or binding European legislation.[12] In other words, the act of signing a treaty does not automatically make it part of UK law. Treaties are therefore not self-executing. Accordingly, national obligations under an international convention may be complied with by way of government policies, relating to the environment, including the provision or withholding of financial resources for particular activities or bodies and the

---

[7] In his *Textbook on International Law*, 6th edition, (Oxford Universtiy Press, 2007), Dixon points out that conventions or treaties are "the only way states can create international law consciously": at p.26.

[8] See *Council of Civil Service Unions v Minister for the Civil Service* [1985] A.C. 374 (often referred to as the *GCHQ* case).

[9] Per Lord Roskill at 418. Prior to *GCHQ*, Lord Denning had observed in *Blackburn v Attorney-General* [1971] 2 All E.R. 1380 that: "The Treaty-making power of this country rests not in the courts, but in the Crown; that is, Her Majesty acting on the advice of her Ministers. When her Ministers negotiate and sign a treaty, even a treaty of such paramount importance as this proposed one [the Rome Treaty], they act on behalf of the country as a whole. They exercise the prerogative of the Crown. Their action in so doing cannot be challenged or questioned in these courts" (at 1382). *GCHQ* and several cases decided since, e.g. *Maclaine Watson & Co Ltd v Attorney General* [1990] 2 A.C. 418 and *R. v Secretary of State for Commonwealth and Foreign Affairs, Ex p Rees-Mogg* [1994] Q.B. 552, confirm the continued non-justiciable nature of the treaty-making power.

[10] Under whose constitutions international treaties and conventions may be self-executing, i.e. they form part of domestic law either immediately on ratification or by way of a formal vote of approval in their parliament.

[11] The Vienna Convention on the Law of Treaties (May 23, 1969) defines a "Treaty" as: "an international agreement concluded between States in written form and governed by international law, whether embodied in a single instrument or in two or more related instruments and whatever its particular designation".

[12] Thus, for example, in *A and others v Secretary of State for the Home Department (No.2)* [2006] 2 A.C. 221, Lord Bingham commented that "a treaty, even if ratified by the United Kingdom, has no binding force in the domestic law of this country unless it is given effect by statute or expresses principles of customary international law": at [27]. See further below for a brief discussion of the basis on which customary international law applies in the UK. As regards the status of the European Convention on Human Rights before commencement of the Human Rights Act 1998, see below, para.1–077 fn.315.

issue of guidance or instructions to local authorities and other administrative organisations, often by way of Departmental Circulars.

Customary international law within the UK

1–004   The legal position in relation to conventions or treaties, the principal source of international law, can be contrasted with that in relation to another important source of international law, customary law. As its name implies, this type of international law evolves out of the customs and practices of states rather than being made. As a consequence of its evolutionary nature, it is by no means a straightforward task to determine whether or not a particular customary law exists. In order to do so, it is necessary to establish the existence of a number of elements or factors. These include the existence of a state practice which is reasonably consistent and which is generally applied.[13] Unlike treaties or conventions, customary international law has long been accepted as part of the common law of England and Wales. Thus Shaw identifies several eighteenth century cases in which this acceptance was "vigorously stated".[14] In the years that have followed, several theories have been advanced to explain why customary international law takes effect in English law. One theory, the transformation theory, contends that customary international law only has effect in domestic law where it has been "expressly and specifically 'transformed' into municipal law by the use of the appropriate constitutional machinery, such as an Act of Parliament".[15] In other words, the theory replicates the ratification and incorporation theory which explains how treaties and conventions take effect in UK law.

An alternative theory, the doctrine of incorporation, provides that international customary law automatically takes effect in UK without the need to be formally incorporated via the mechanism of an Act of Parliament or some other legal instrument. As Shaw points out, the incorporation doctrine is evidenced in a number of more recent judicial pronouncements, most notably in the *Pinochet* litigation where, for example, Lord Lloyd referred to the "well-established principles of customary international law, which principles form part of the common law of England".[16]

---

[13] For a fuller discussion of the elements of customary law, see Dixon, *Textbook on International Law*, 6th edition, (OUP, 2007), pp.31–37.

[14] See Malcom N. Shaw, *International Law*, 5th edition (Cambridge University Press, 2003), p.129. The cases to which the author refers are *Buvot v Barbuit* (1737) Cases t Talbot 281 and *Triquet v Bath* (1764) 3 Burr 1478.

[15] Shaw, *International Law*, p.219.

[16] See *R. v Bow Street Metropolitan Stipendiary Magistrate and others, ex parte Pinochet Ugarte* [2000] 1 A.C. 61 at 98, cited in *International Law*, p.135. It will be remembered that the *Pinochet* litigation concerned attempts by the Spanish government to have the former Head of State of Chile extradited on the ground of allegedly having ordered the murder of Spanish nationals in Chile.

Trans-boundary pollution: requirement for action at international level

Some forms of environmental pollution may be localised in their effect. **1–005**
Thus, for example, the fly-tipping of waste on land may well result in
adverse consequences for the land in question but, depending on the
nature of what has been dumped, its impact is less likely to be felt more
widely. Discharging pollutants into the atmosphere or into rivers or seas is,
however, an activity which is far more likely to lead to widespread adverse
affects. The consequences of the emission of chemical substances from
industrial chimneys may be felt hundreds or even thousands of miles away
from the original point of discharge due to the action of the wind and air
currents, and the same is obviously true of marine pollution as well. Given
that these types of pollution are no respecters of national boundaries it
follows that devising effective responses to them may only be achieved at
the international level. Over the years therefore, a number of important
treaties and conventions have been drafted in order to tackle the problems
associated with environmental pollution. They are, however, too numerous
to be identified and considered in a book of this nature. For present purposes, we shall confine our discussion to a relatively brief examination of
one of the more important international environmental treaties to have
influenced the development of law and policy within the UK in relation to
marine pollution caused by ships.

Illustrative environmental treaty: MARPOL

International Convention for the Prevention of Marine Pollution from Ships, 1973 as modified by the 1978 Protocol (MARPOL)

The MARPOL Convention[17] is the principal international convention **1–006**
relating to the prevention of pollution caused by ships to the marine
environment. It is concerned with pollution caused in two distinct ways:
through the operational activities of ships; and as a consequence of maritime accidents.[18] Although the latter cause tends to attract considerable
media attention and publicity due to its spectacular consequences as illustrated by, for example, the running aground of the *Torrey Canyon* in

---

[17] For a fuller discussion of MARPOL, see Howarth and McGillivray's *Water Pollution and Water Quality Law* (Shaw & Sons, 2001) paras 19.5–19.19.5.6 (pp. 1011–1017) and paras 19.10–19.10.6 (pp. 1029–1039).
[18] The fourth preamble to MARPOL states that the Convention aims to "achieve the complete elimination of intentional pollution of the marine environment by oil and other harmful substances and the minimisation of accidental discharge of such substances".

1967,[19] operational pollution presents a very significant yet less visible threat to the marine environment.

Background to MARPOL

1–007 The historical background to MARPOL includes a conference organised by the United Kingdom government in 1954 which resulted in the adoption of the International Convention for the Prevention of Pollution of the Sea by Oil (OILPOL). One of the key features of the convention was the establishment of "prohibited zones"[20] within which the discharge of oil or of mixtures of oil containing more than 100 parts per million was expressly forbidden. Although OILPOL represented a significant development, incidents such as the *Torrey Canyon* disaster and the general growth in oil trade demonstrated that there was a need for a more concerted effort to address marine pollution emanating from ships. Accordingly in 1973 an International Conference was held which resulted in the adoption of the International Convention for the Prevention of Pollution from Ships. The Convention recognised that ships were the cause of other forms of pollution as well as oil pollution. However, three years after its adoption, it had not been ratified by a sufficient number of states to enter into force. In February 1978, following a spate of pollution incidents caused by oil tankers, the International Maritime Organisation[21] organised a conference on tanker safety and pollution prevention. The practical consequence was the signing of a Protocol which breathed new life into the 1973 Convention in that the Protocol and the Convention were combined to become the MARPOL Convention 73/78.

Annexes to MARPOL

1–008 MARPOL is a genuinely international convention which applies throughout the world. Since entering into force on October 2, 1983, it has been the subject of many revisions and amendments.[22] The substance of the Convention is to be found in six Annexes which are concerned with: regulations for the prevention of pollution by oil (Annex I); regulations for

---

[19] The *Torrey Canyon* was a Liberian registered oil tanker which ran aground on rocks between Land's End and the Scilly Isles on March 18, 1967. Its cargo of 120,000 tons of crude oil leaked into the sea and caused considerable pollution along the coastline of southern Britain and the Normandy coast of France.

[20] These extended for a distance of at least 50 miles from the nearest land.

[21] This body was established in 1948 under a convention adopted by the United Nations. Originally known as the Inter-Governmental Maritime Consultative Organisation its name was changed to the International Maritime Organisation (IMO) in 1982.

[22] These are adopted either by IMO's Marine Environment Protection Committee (MEPC) or as a consequence of a Convention attended by the MARPOL Contracting States.

the control of pollution by noxious liquid substances in bulk (Annex II); prevention of pollution by harmful substances carried by sea in packaged form (Annex III); prevention of pollution by sewage from ships (Annex IV); prevention of pollution by garbage from ships (Annex V); and prevention of air pollution from ships (Annex VI). Parties to MARPOL are required to accept Annexes I and II. Annexes III-VI are voluntary. As at June 30, 2008, there were 146 Contracting States in relation to Annexes I and II. Annexes III to VI have entered into force on different dates and have been ratified by varying numbers of Contracting States.[23]

The United Kingdom is a signatory to the MARPOL Convention. The power to give effect in UK law to provisions found in international conventions relating to the prevention of pollution from ships is currently to be found in section 128 of the Merchant Shipping Act 1995.[24] This power, which is exercised by the making of an Order in Council, has been used on various occasions to give effect to the MARPOL Annexes. Thus, for example, the Merchant Shipping (Prevention of Oil Pollution) Regulations 1996,[25] as amended,[26] give effect in UK law to the obligations set out in Annexes I and II of MARPOL. These Regulations apply in respect of UK vessels wherever located and to other ships whilst they are present in UK territorial waters. They do not apply, however, in respect of naval ships.[27]

The detail of the compulsory Annexes (I and II) and the associated implementing legislation is beyond the scope of our discussion. For present purposes it is sufficient to note several key features of the Convention regime. The first of these concerns the fact that the Convention does provide for permissible oil discharges provided that certain conditions are satisfied. These include: that the oil tanker in question is not within a "specified area" at the time of the discharge; that it is more than 50 miles from the nearest land; that the rate of discharge does not exceed 30 litres per mile traveled by the ship; and that the total quantity of oil which may be discharged in any voyage does not exceed 1/30,000 of the total cargo carrying capacity of the vessel. "Specified areas" are those areas which are considered to be especially vulnerable to the harmful effects of oil pollution with the result that discharges to them are either further restricted or prohibited. Originally the "specified areas" included the Mediterranean Sea area, the Baltic Sea area, the Red Sea area, the Gulf of Aden area and

---

[23] The date of entry into force and the number of Contracting States as of June 30, 2008, are as follows: Annex III (July 1, 1992, 128); Annex IV (September 27, 2003, 119); Annex V (December 31, 1988, 134); and Annex VI (May 19, 2005, 51). These figures are taken from IMO's own website—see *http://www.imo.org/Conventions/mainframe.asp?topic_id=247*.

[24] It should be noted that the power is exercisable even where the relevant intended convention or treaty has yet to enter into force: see section 128(2) of the 1995 Act.

[25] SI 1996/2154.

[26] The 1996 Regulations have been amended on various occasions in order to take account of revisions and amendments made to Annexes I and II of the MARPOL Convention: see SI 1997/1910, SI 1999/1957, SI 2000/483, SI 2004/303, SI 2004/2110, and SI 2005/1916.

[27] See MARPOL, Article 3(3) and the 1996 Regulations, reg.2(2).

the Antartic area. Amendments made to Annex I in 1997 added the North Western European waters to this list of "specified areas". These waters cover the North Sea, the Irish Sea, the English Channel, the Celtic Sea and parts of the North East Atlantic to the West of Ireland.

1–009   The Convention regime also provides for the conduct of regular surveys and the certification of oil tankers above a certain specified range. Patently the purpose of this is to ensure that vessels engaged in the potentially hazardous activity of transporting oil across the seas and oceans are fit for purpose. These vessels are also subject to an obligation to keep oil records in a form as prescribed by Annex I of MARPOL. An oil record will contain, amongst other things, statements of all the occasions on which oil or oily mixtures have been discharged into the sea. The records must be readily available for inspection. Failure to keep an oil record constitutes an offence, as does knowingly making a false or misleading statement in an oil record.[28]

Annex I to MARPOL provides for the control of pollution by noxious liquid substances in bulk. For the purposes of the Annex, such substances are divided into four categories (A–D), with category A substances being those which present the greatest danger to marine resources and human health, and category D substances presenting a recognisable hazard to either marine resources or human health. Domestic implementation of these provisions has been achieved through the Merchant Shipping (Dangerous or Noxious Liquid Substances in Bulk) Regulations 1996.[29] The regime set out therein is broadly analogous to that which applies in relation to oil discharges, as outlined above.

MARPOL Annexes IV, V and VI have also been implemented in UK law by delegated legislation made pursuant to section 128 of the Merchant Shipping Act 1995.[30] In the case of Annex VI, section 128(1) was amended by section 2(1) and (2) of the Merchant Shipping (Pollution) Act 2006 in order to enable this to happen.[31]

Golden Fleece Maritime Inc

1–010   The place of the MARPOL Convention in UK law can be illustrated with the aid of a recent case. In *Golden Fleece Maritime Inc v ST Shipping and Transport Inc (The Elli)*,[32] the issue to be determined was whether the owners of vessels were liable to the charterers where as a result of

---

[28] See s.142(6)–(8) of the Merchant Shipping Act 1995.

[29] SI 1996/3010.

[30] In relation to the implementation of Annexes IV and V, see the Merchant Shipping (Prevention of Pollution by Sewage and Garbage) Order 2006, SI 2006/2950. This Order revoked an Order of the same name made in 1988 (SI 1988/2252).

[31] See the Merchant Shipping (Prevention of Air Pollution from Ships) Order 2006, SI 2006/1248.

[32] [2008] EWCA Civ 584; [2008] 2 Lloyd's Rep 119.

amendments made to the MARPOL Convention, the oil tankers in question were no longer fit to be used for the transportation of fuel oil. The MARPOL amendment required that the cargo tanks on oil tankers be double-hulled so as to reduce the risk of oil escape in the event of a collision or running aground. It was, in the words of Longmore LJ, the "final logical step"[33] in a series of amendments and developments which the signatories to the Convention had introduced in order to improve the design of tanker vessels. The tankers, which had been hired under the terms of a standard charterparty, were treated as being double-sided by the parties.[34] One of the clauses in the agreement, clause 52, was headed eligibility and compliance. It provided, amongst other things, that:

"Owners further warrant that the vessel does, and will, fully comply with all applicable conventions, laws, regulations and ordinances of any international, national, state or local government entity having jurisdiction including, but not limited to ... MARPOL 1973/1978 as amended and extended...".

In the Commercial Court, Cooke J had upheld the charterers' contentions that they were entitled to be compensated for loss of profits incurred as a result of the owners' breach of their obligation to provide vessels which were fit to transport fuel oil.[35] In agreeing with that decision, Longmore LJ remarked in the Court of Appeal that:

"the authorities do not, on analysis, yield any principle of law that the terms of a time charter as to fitness to carry the cargo or seaworthiness relate only to the physical condition of the vessel and can never embrace legal fitness to carry the cargo".[36]

In other words, the stricter terms of the amended MARPOL could not be complied with by the vessels[37] and as a consequence, the owners were in breach of the time charters and the charterers were entitled to be compensated for their losses.

---

[33] ibid. at [2].
[34] Longmore LJ pointed out that this was "not strictly accurate" because a small part of each side of the vessels was in fact not double-sided: ibid. at [4].
[35] [2008] 1 Lloyd's Rep 262.
[36] [2008] 2 Lloyd's Rep 119 at [17].
[37] Regulation 13H of MARPOL provided for an exemption from the need to be double-hulled. However, the exemption applied in respect of vessels with "double-sides not used for the carriage of oil and extending to the entire cargo tank length". Given Longmore LJ's earlier observation that neither vessel was in fact double-sided, the exemption could not apply to them: see [8]–[10].

R (on the application of International Association of Independent Tanker Owners) v Secretary of State for Transport

1–011   The legal significance of MARPOL has also recently been at issue in proceedings heard both domestically and at the European level. In *R (on the application of International Association of Independent Tanker Owners v Secretary of State for Transport*,[38] the claimants[39] sought judicial review of Articles 4[40] and 5[41] of EC Directive 2005/35/EC relating to ship source pollution of the marine environment on the basis that they were inconsistent with existing international law on marine pollution, including certain provisions of MARPOL, in that they provided for a stricter liability regime for accidental discharges. Following the sinking of the oil tanker the *Prestige* off the coast of Portugal in November 2002 which resulted in the pollution of substantial parts of the Spanish and French coastlines, the Community decided to take legislative action. Paragraph 7 of the preamble to the Directive identifies the perceived shortcomings in international law which it sought to address as follows:

"Neither the international regime for civil liability and compensation of oil pollution nor that relating to pollution by other hazardous or noxious substances provides sufficient dissuasive effects to discourage the parties involved in the transport of hazardous cargos by sea from engaging in substandard practices; the required dissuasive effects can only be achieved through the introduction of penalties applying to any person who causes or contributes to marine pollution; penalties should be applicable not only to the ship owner or the master of the ship, but also the owner of the cargo, the classification society or any other person involved".

The claimants represented nearly 80 per cent of the world's tanker fleet. They doubted the jurisdiction of the Community under international law to legislate in accordance with Directive 2005/35/EC. In particular, the claimants raised four arguments which, they contended, demonstrated that

---

[38] [2006] EWHC 1577 (Admin); [2007] Env. L.R. 8.

[39] In addition to INTERTANKO, the claimants were the International Association of Dry Cargo Shipowners, the Greek Shipping Co-operation Committee, Lloyd's Register and the International Salvage Union.

[40] This provides that: "Member States shall ensure that ship-source discharges of polluting substances into any of the areas referred to in Article 3(1) are regarded as infringements if committed with intent, recklessly or by serious negligence. These infringements are regarded as criminal offences ...".

[41] This states that: "(1) A discharge of polluting substances into any of the areas referred to in Article 3(1) shall not be regarded as an infringement if it satisfies the conditions set out in Annex I, Regulations 9, 10, 11(a) or 11(c) or in Annex II, Regulations 5, 6(a) or 6(c) of MARPOL 73/78. (2) A discharge of polluting substances into the areas referred to in Article 3(1)(c), (d) and (e) shall not be regarded as an infringement for the owner, the master or the crew when acting under the master's responsibility if he satisfies the conditions set out in Annex I, Regulation 11(b) or in Annex II, Regulation 6(b) of MARPOL 73/78".

their belief that the Directive was invalid was well-founded. The first three arguments[42] were as follows: whether it was lawful for the EU to legislate independently of MARPOL for third country vessels in the high seas or in the Exclusive Economic Zone; whether it was lawful for the EU to legislate for the territorial sea otherwise than in accordance with MARPOL; and whether the standard of liability in the Directive ("serious negligence") breached the right of innocent passage. In the judgment of Hodge J, all three arguments were "well founded". Accordingly, he referred various questions to the European Court of Justice for its opinion pursuant to Article 234 of the Rome Treaty.

In the judgment of the European Court of Justice,[43] as a general principle, the validity of a measure of secondary Community legislation could be affected by the fact that it was incompatible with rules of international law. Such a principle was, however, subject to two conditions: that the Community was bound by the rules in question; and that a review of the validity of Community legislation could only occur where this was not precluded by the nature and broad logic of the international treaty, and that the provisions of the treaty itself were unconditional and sufficiently precise.[44]

In determining whether MARPOL met these conditions, the European Court noted at the outset that the Community is not a signatory to the Convention. Moreover, it observed that:

"it does not appear that the Community has assumed, under the EC Treaty, the powers previously exercised by the Member States in the field to which MARPOL 73/78 applies, nor that, consequently, its provisions have the effect of binding the Community".[45]

MARPOL was therefore capable of being distinguished from the General Agreement on Tariffs and Trade (GATT),[46] in respect of which "the Community progressively assumed powers previously exercised by the Member States, with the consequence that it became bound by the obligations flowing from that agreement".[47] In explaining its reasoning, the Court observed:

"It is true that all Member States of the Community are parties to MARPOL 73/78. Nevertheless, in the absence of a full transfer of the

---

[42] The fourth argument, that the standard of liability adopted by the Directive ("serious negligence") was not consistent with legal certainty and/or with the duty to give legal reasons for the Directive, was rejected by the Administrative Court.
[43] Case C-308/06 R. (on the application of International Association of Independent Tanker Owners v Secretary of State [2008] 3 C.M.L.R. 9.
[44] ibid., at paras 43–45.
[45] ibid., at para.48.
[46] This agreement was originally signed by 23 countries in October 1947. Its purpose was to liberalise trade between its signatories. The agreement now falls under the umbrella of the World Trade Organisation which was established in 1995.
[47] [2008] 3 C.M.L.R. 9, at para.48.

powers previously exercised by the Member States to the Community, the latter cannot, simply because all those States are parties to MARPOL 73/78, be bound by the rules set out therein, which it has not itself approved".[48]

Given that the Community was not bound by MARPOL, it followed in the judgment of the Court that "the mere fact that Directive 2005/35 has the objective of incorporating certain rules set out in the Convention into Community law is ... not sufficient for it to be incumbent upon the Court to review the directive's legality in the light of the Convention".[49] Neither, for that matter, did the Court consider that the general rule that the powers of the Community must be exercised in accordance with international law, including customary international law, applied in the present case because none of the relevant provisions of MARPOL expressed customary international law. Thus in the judgment of the Court, the validity of Directive 2005/35 could not be assessed in the light of MARPOL.[50]

European Environmental Law

The Treaty of Rome

1–012 The original Treaty of Rome contained no mention of the environment whatsoever. The first official mention of environmental protection came in a declaration made in October 1972 by the heads of the then six EC Member States:

> "Economic expansion is not an end in itself: its firm aim should be to enable disparities in living conditions to be reduced. It must take place with the participation of all the social partners. It should result in an improvement in the quality of life as well as in standards of living. As befits the genius of Europe, particular attention will be given to intangible values and to protecting the environment, so that progress may really be put at the service of mankind".[51]

It was only with the adoption of the Single European Act, which came into effect on July 1, 1987, that specific provision was made in the Rome Treaty for environmental concerns. The principal amendments in this respect were the incorporation of a new Article 100a providing:[52]

---

[48] ibid., at para.49.
[49] ibid., at para.50.
[50] The Court reached the same conclusion in relation to UNCLOS on the basis that that Convention "does not establish rules intended to apply directly and immediately to individuals and to confer upon them rights or freedoms capable of being relied upon against States ...": at para.64.
[51] Quoted in the Introduction to the 1st Action Programme; [1975] OJ C112 at p.5.
[52] para.3.

"3. The Commission, in its proposals envisaged in paragraph 1 concerning health, safety, environmental protection and consumer protection, will take as a base a high level of protection"

and three new Articles 130r, 130s and 130t setting out the basic principles of Community action on the environment. These last three were revised by the Maastricht Treaty. They have also been renumbered following the Treaty of Amsterdam. The relevant Articles are thus now Articles 174, 175 and 176.[53]

Environmental Action Programmes

European Community law on the environment is shaped to some degree by international conventions; other pressures for change develop from political interaction within and between the Council of Ministers, the European Commission and the European Parliament. Legislation can only be initiated by the Commission, but it in practice will not develop proposals on its own initiative where it considers there is unlikely to be sufficient consensus within the Council of Ministers for them to be adopted. It may however be requested to do so by the European Parliament. The Commission works within a broad agenda laid down in the current "Action Programme on the Environment". There have been six such programmes since 1973, the first four converging periods of four or five years, as shown in table 1/I.   1–013

Table 1/I

Action Programme	Period	OJ Reference	
1st	1973–1976	[1973] OJ C112	1–014
2nd	1977–1981	[1977] OJ C139	
3rd	1982–1986	[1983] OJ C46	
4th	1987–1992	[1987] OJ C328	
5th	1993–2001	[1993] OJ C138	
6th	2002–2012	[2002] OJ L242/1	

The Programmes, which are approved in general terms by the Council, only set out broad policy objectives, and justifications for these; there is no certainty that proposals will be brought forward to meet all of these objectives in full, and in fact matters are often carried over from one Programme to the next (if not abandoned). Moreover, proposals which   1–015

---

[53] These will be discussed in more detail below.

have not originally been referred to in a Programme may still nevertheless be brought forward.

The 1st Action Programme set out 11 "Principles of a Community Environmental Policy" that continued to be supported in subsequent Programmes. These may be summarised as follows:

(1) Pollution should be prevented at source rather than dealt with after the event;

(2) Environmental issues must be taken into account at the earliest possible stage in planning and other technical decision making processes;

(3) Abusive exploitation of natural resources is to be avoided;

(4) The standard of knowledge in the EC should be improved to promote effective action for environmental conservation and improvement;

(5) The polluter should pay for preventing and eliminating "nuisances", subject to limited exceptions and transitional arrangements;

(6) Activities in one country should not degrade the environment of another;

(7) The EC and the Member States must in their environment policies have regard to the interests of developing countries and should aim to prevent or minimise any adverse effects on their economic development;

(8) There should be a clearly defined long-term European environmental policy that includes participation in international organisations and co-operation at both regional and international levels;

(9) Environmental protection is a matter for everyone in the EC, at all levels; their co-operation, and the harnessing of social forces, is necessary for success. Education should ensure the whole community accepts its responsibilities for future generations;

(10) Appropriate action levels must be established—local, regional, national, Community and international—for each type of pollution and area to be protected;

(11) Major aspects of national environmental protection policies should be harmonised. Economic growth should not be viewed for purely quantitative aspects.

The 5th Action Programme

1–016 The 5th Action Programme, adopted in 1993, was entitled "Towards Sustainability" and it marked a departure from previous programmes in its approach. In particular, it concerned itself not with specific environmental media and how they should be protected, but with five sectors of economic activity: industry, energy, transport, agriculture and tourism. The Programme addressed particular themes and set out targets in several areas including climate change, acidification and air quality, protection of nature and bio-diversity, the management of water resources, the urban environment, coastal zones and waste management. In an important section,[54] the Programme reviewed the range of instruments that are available to achieve environmental control and improvement, and deliberately aimed to move away from the conventional "command and control" approach typical of the previous Action Programmes. It recognised that sustainable economic activity cannot be achieved simply by setting out controls that must be complied with.

Accordingly, it stated that:

"environmental policy will rest on four main sets of instruments: regulatory instruments, market-based instruments (including economic and fiscal instruments and voluntary agreements), horizontal supporting instruments (research, information, education, etc.) and financial support mechanisms".

The Programme stated that the ultimate goal of sustainable development could only be achieved by concerted action on the part of all the relevant "actors" working together in partnership, and it thus sought to implement the concept of "shared responsibility" involving, for example, a division of powers and responsibilities between the Community, the Member States, and regional and local authorities; in other cases the relevant actors may be enterprises, the general public and consumers.

The 6th Action Programme

The 6th Action Environmental Programme (6EAP) was formally adopted   **1–017** on July 22, 2002, by a co-decision of the European Parliament and Council based on Article 175(3) of the Rome Treaty and acting in accordance with the procedure laid down in Article 251 of the Treaty. It has been suggested that:

"the fact that the 6EAP is the result of a formal inter-institutional co-decision process provided for in the Treaty, gives it a particular kind of political importance and legitimacy which its predecessors lacked. It is not merely a Commission programme, but a formal act of the European Parliament and Council based on a Commission proposal, embodying a commitment of all three institutions".[55]

---

[54] Chapter 7.
[55] See the Introduction to "Drowning in Process? The Implementation of the EU's 6th Environmental Action Programme", An Institute for European Environmental Policy Report for the European Environmental Bureau (April 2006).

Continuing the trend begun by its immediate predecessor, it is to run for a loner period than the first four Action Programmes (2002–12).

The 6EAP or 6th Action Programme identifies four "key environmental priorities" which are to be met by the Community in the areas of: climate change; nature and biodiversity; environment and health and quality of life; and natural resources and wastes.[56] The Action Programme then proceeds to stipulate a number of principles and overall aims in respect of the priority areas and with regard to the implementation of the Action Programme as a whole. Thus it is stated, for example, that the Programme aims to ensure a high level of environmental protection and to achieve a "decoupling between environmental pressures and economic growth". It is also stated that the Programme shall be based "particularly on the polluter-pays principle, the precautionary principle and preventive action, and the principle of rectification of pollution at source".[57] Article 3 outlines the "strategic approaches" which are to be taken to meet the aims and objectives set out in the Programme. These include: the development of new Community legislation and the amendment of existing legislation; encouraging the more effective implementation and enforcement of EC environmental law; the integration of environmental protection requirements into the preparation, definition and implementation of Community policies and activities; and the promotion of sustainable production and consumption patterns by the effective implementation of the principles set out in Article 2 of the Programme.

An important feature of the 6th Action Programme is the introduction of "thematic strategies" which represent the framework for action at the European level in order to achieve the aims and objectives of the Programme. Seven thematic strategies are to be drawn up in the fields of: air pollution; soil protection; protection and conservation of the marine environment; the sustainable use of pesticides; improving the quality of the urban environment; sustainable use of natural resources; and waste recycling and prevention. Article 4(1) provides that these thematic strategies should be developed and implemented in close consultation with "relevant parties", e.g. NGOs, industry and public authorities. It also provides that the thematic strategies "should be presented to the European Parliament and the Council within 3 years of the adoption of the Programme at the latest".

Mid-term Review

1–018   Given the ten year life span of the 6th Action Programme, it is not surprising that it provided for a "mid term" review of the progress which has been made towards achieving its aims and objectives and an assessment of

---

[56] art.1(4).
[57] art.2(1). The key environmental principles which are to be found in art.174(2) of the Treaty are discussed further below.

the need to change orientation. That review was finally completed by the Commission almost a year later than scheduled.[58] It purports to address three distinct questions: the extent to which the EU is currently meeting the commitments made in the 6th Action Programme; the extent to which the most recent scientific evidence either confirms or denies that the approach set out in the Programme is sufficient to meet the current environmental challenges; whether the EU's strategic approach to environmental policy should be reassessed in the light of the changed political context since 2002. In truth, however, the mid-term review is rather light on the detailed information which would be required in order to answer these questions. Instead, it favours a more broad-brush approach. It should be noted that the review regards the EU's environment policy as "one of its major achievements" although it also acknowledges that "the EU is not yet on the path of sustainable environmental development". Several observations made in the review are a source of disappointment. Thus it is admitted that there "has only been limited progress with the fundamental issues of integrating environmental concerns into other policy areas and improving the enforcement of EU legislation". In relation to the latter, the conclusion to the review is more positive than the discussion on which it is based where it is stated that "the high number of complaints and infringement procedures are a sign that the implementation of environmental legislation remains far from satisfactory".[59] The review expresses the view that the 6th Action Programme remains "the correct framework for future action at Community level". It also claims that the "EU is generally on-track with adopting the measures outlined in the Action Programme" whilst at the same time recognising that "five years into a ten-year Programme . . . is too early to see the results of most of the measures proposed under the 6th EAP". Arguably, an assertion of this kind undermines the value of the mid-term review itself.

The mid-term review or, more precisely, the level of progress which the mid-term review reports, has elicited criticism in some quarters. The European Parliament, for example, believes that there are good reasons to deplore a number of features of the present situation. Thus it considers it deplorable that "the European Union is not on schedule with the implementation of the measures planned in the Action Programme, contrary to what the Commission claims in its own mid-term review", and that the "objective of halting the decline of biodiversity by 2010 will probably not be attained and that the proposed strategies for protecting the marine environment and soil will not produce concrete environmental results by 2012". It is significant that although the Parliament considers that the introduction of the thematic strategies has "increased the importance of

---

[58] See COM (2007) 225 final, published on April 30, 2007. The review itself makes no mention of the delay in its publication. In a resolution adopted by the European Parliament on April 16, 2008, that body considered the delay to be "regrettable".

[59] See COM (2007) 225 final, at para.5.4.

the pre-legislative processes and created additional opportunities for sta-keholder involvement and a more strategic approach to EU legislative policy", it is also of the view that such strategies have "lengthened the duration of the environmental policy-making process by delaying the for-mulation of concrete policy proposals and the adoption of resulting mea-sures". There is no clear view here as to whether the benefits of the thematic strategy approach are considered to outweigh its detriments. Nevertheless, additional delay in a process which was already known for its tardiness is a source of regret.

The Action programmes do not set out detailed proposals for legislation. Such proposals are usually issued by the Commission in draft form leading to a consultation among the Member States and relevant organisations.[60] The draft legislation is normally then followed by the text of a formal proposal.[61] The subsequent procedure depends on the Rome Treaty article under which the legislation is proceeding.

Enacting European Environmental Law

Articles 100 and 235: the early legislative basis

1–019   Once it is decided that there is a need for a particular Community envir-onmental policy and that legal instruments need to be made in order to give effect to that policy, it becomes necessary to identify a legal basis on which environmental legislation can be made. As was noted previously, the Rome Treaty was originally silent on the environment. Accordingly, early Community environmental law was made under either Article 100 or Article 235 of the Rome Treaty. The former empowered the Council "to issue directives for the approximation of such laws, regulations or admin-istrative provisions of the Member States as directly affect the establish-ment or functioning of the common market". Despite the overtly economic nature of the rationale for legislating under this provision, it was used as the basis for directives which also had an environmental focus. Thus, for example, the Drinking Water Directive[62] was made under the authority of Article 100 for the reason that any disparity between Member States' provisions on the quality of water for human consumption "may create differences in the conditions of competition and, as a result, directly affect the operation of the common market". Article 235 had a remit which was

---

[60] The most effective time for influencing new legislation is before it has been crystallised in formal proposals. For those outside the normal network of consultees, it will often be highly desirable to have contacts in the European Commission, government departments or industry organisations, in order to keep up to date with what consultations are in progress and on how responses may have been reflected in drafts for legislation. A wealth of information on consultations, etc. is now of course accessible via the internet.
[61] Published in the C series of the Official Journal.
[62] Directive 80/778/EEC.

wider than harmonising national laws in order to facilitate the establishment of the common market. It provided:

"If action by the Community should prove necessary to attain, in the course of the operation of the common market, one of the objectives of the Community and this Treaty has not provided the necessary powers, the Community shall, acting unanimously on a proposal from the Commission and after consulting the European Parliament, take the appropriate measures".

It was not uncommon in the early stages of enacting environmental law for measures to be adopted on the basis of both Articles 100 and 235.[63] Although neither legal base for making Community environmental law had been designed with this purpose in mind, their somewhat shaky foundations were strengthened by two important factors: the promotion of a Community environmental policy enjoyed the unanimous support of the Member States;[64] and the European Court of Justice accepted that economic concerns were capable of justifying the enactment of environmental measures. Thus in *Commission v Italy*,[65] the Court explained:

"Provisions which are made necessary by considerations relating to the environment and health may be a burden upon undertakings to which they apply and if there is no harmonisation of national provisions on the matter, competition may be appreciably distorted".[66]

In the later case of *Procureur de la Republique v Association de Défense des Brûleurs d'Huiles Usagées*,[67] where the European Court was asked on a preliminary reference to determine whether Articles 5 and 6 of the Waste Oils Directive[68] conformed with the terms of the Rome Treaty, the Court identified environmental protection as "one of the Community's essential objectives" despite the apparent silence of the Treaty on the matter.

Title XIX: The environment

As was noted previously, the turning point in the present context occurred 1–020 in 1987 when specific provision for environmental concerns was finally made by the Single European Act. The key Treaty Articles relating to the

---

[63] Holder and Lee cite the Environmental Impact Assessment Directive 83/337/EEC as an example of an environmental measure made on this dual legal basis: see *Environmental Protection, Law and Policy: Text and Materials*, 2nd edition (Cambridge: Cambridge University Press, 2007), p.159.

[64] The truth of this assertion is borne out by the fact that both Article 100 and Article 235 required the Council to adopt the relevant acts unanimously.

[65] Case 91/79 [1980] E.C.R. 1099.

[66] At 1106.

[67] Case 240/83 [1985] E.C.R. 531.

[68] Directive 75/439/EEC. Krämer has identified this provision as "the very first environmental Directive": see *EC Environmental Law*, 6th edition (London: Sweet and Maxwell, 2007), para.10–48, p.381.

environment are now Articles 174–176. The most significant parts of Article 174 provide as follows:

"1. Community policy on the environment shall contribute to pursuit of the following objectives:

— preserving, protecting and improving the quality of the environment,
— protecting human health,
— prudent and rationale utilisation of natural resources,
— promoting measures at international level to deal with regional or worldwide environmental problems.

2. Community policy on the environment shall aim at a high level protection taking into account the diversity of situations in the various regions of the Community. It shall be based on the precautionary principle and on the principles that preventive action should be taken, that environmental damage should as priority be rectified at source and that the polluter should pay. In this context, harmonisation measures answering environmental protection requirements shall include, where appropriate, a safeguard clause allowing Member States to take provisional measures, for non-economic environmental reasons, subject to a Community inspection procedure.

3. In preparing its policy on the environment, the Community shall take account of:

— available scientific and technical data,
— environmental conditions in the various regions of the Community,
— the potential benefits and costs of action or lack of action,
— the economic and social development of the Community as a whole and the balanced development of its regions".

Article 175

1–021   Article 175 sets out the current legal basis[69] on which Community environmental law is made. By virtue of Article 175(1):

"The Council, acting in accordance with the procedure referred to in Article 251 and after consulting the Economic and Social Committee and the Committee of the Regions, shall decide what action is to be

---

[69] This is often referred to as the principle of attribution. Determining the legal basis on which Community environmental law is made is more than a mere academic exercise. It is important for a number of reasons. These include that establishing the legal basis will make clear the extent of the Community's competence to legislate in the relevant field. It will also identify which decision-making process has to be followed for enacting the environmental law.

taken by the Community in order to achieve the objectives referred to in Article 174".

It is clear from this provision that the legislative procedure to be followed in relation to the adoption of an act pursuant to Article 175(1) is that which is provided for in Article 251 of the Rome Treaty. It is also clear that there is a mandatory obligation to consult both the Economic and Social Committee[70] and the Committee of the Regions.[71]

The co-decision procedure

Article 251 provides for a co-decision procedure which accords the   **1–022** Council and the European Parliament equal weight in the legislative process. Before that process can take place, however, these two institutions must first be in possession of a proposal from another Community institution, the Commission.[72] In other words, the Commission is the catalyst for Community law on the environment. Once a proposal has been received, the Council must first obtain the opinion of the European Parliament on the matter. Once this has been done, the Council acting by a qualified majority[73] has three potential courses of action available to it. Where the Parliament has not proposed any amendments, the Council may adopt the proposed act. If the Parliament has suggested amendments in its opinion and the Council approves of all of them, it may adopt the proposed act as amended. In all other cases, the Council is required to adopt a common position and communicate that position to the Parliament along with its reasons for adopting it. The Parliament will also be notified by the Commission of its position. The co-decision procedure then places the onus on the Parliament to act within a period of three months[74] from the date of receipt of the Council's common position. If the Parliament approves the common position, the act in question is deemed to have been

---

[70] This is an advisory body which represents the interests of various sectors such as producers, farmers, workers and the professions: see Article 257 of the Rome Treaty. The members of the Committee are appointed by the Council for a renewable four-year term.

[71] This Committee was originally established as a consequence of the Maastricht Treaty. It represents regional and local bodies within the Community and, like the Economic and Social Committee, plays an advisory role in relation to both the Council and the Commission.

[72] art.251(2).

[73] The Treaty often requires the Council to act by a qualified majority. Where this is the case, the votes of each Member State are weighted in accordance with Article 205. The weighting of the votes is such that the more populous Member States have the most votes and the least populous Member States have the least votes. Thus, for example, Germany, France, Italy and the UK all currently have 29 votes, whereas Cyprus, Estonia, Latvia, Slovenia, Luxembourg and Malta have four votes each. Not surprisingly, the weighting of votes within the Council is a highly contentious issue amongst the Member States. In order for a proposal from the Commission to be adopted, it is necessary for at least 255 votes (out of a total of 346) to be cast in its favour by a majority of the Member States.

[74] This period may be extended by a maximum of one month at the initiative of the Parliament or Council: see art.251(7).

adopted in accordance with the common position. The same outcome will arise where the Parliament has failed to take a decision on the common position. If, however, the Parliament rejects the common position by an absolute majority of its members, the proposed act is deemed not to have been adopted.[75] Alternatively, the Parliament may, acting by an absolute majority of its members, propose amendments to the common position. Where this happens, the onus transfers once again, this time back to the Council.

The time frame for the Council to act is also three months.[76] If, within this period and acting by a qualified majority, it approves all the amendments which the Parliament has made to its common position, the act is deemed to have been adopted in the form of the amended common position. Where, however, the Commission has delivered a negative opinion on an amendment proposed by the Parliament, Article 251(3) requires the Council to act unanimously when approving it. In the event that the Council does not approve all the amendments, its President, in agreement with the President of the Parliament, shall within six weeks[77] convene a meeting of the Conciliation Committee.[78] The task of the Committee is to reach an agreement on a joint text[79] by a qualified majority of its Council members and by a majority of its Parliamentary representatives. The Commission takes part in the Committee's proceedings and is required to "take all the necessary initiatives with a view to reconciling the positions of the European Parliament and the Council". If within six weeks[80] of being convened the Committee approves a joint text,[81] the Parliament and the Council each have a further period of six weeks[82] within which to approve the act in accordance with the joint text. Approval from the Parliament must be in the form of an absolute majority of the votes cast. The Council is able to approve the joint text by a qualified majority. A failure by either institution to approve the joint text results in the act being deemed not to have been adopted.

---

[75] Under the co-decision procedure the Parliament therefore has the power to veto legislation.

[76] See fn.74.

[77] This period may be extended by a maximum of two weeks at the initiative of the Parliament or Council: see art.251(7).

[78] The Conciliation Committee is composed of an equal number of Members of the Council (or their representatives) and representatives of the Parliament: see art.251(4).

[79] The starting point for the discussion is to address the Council's common position on the basis of the amendments proposed by the Parliament.

[80] See fn.77.

[81] It is possible that the Conciliation Committee may not be able to reach agreement on a joint text. Where this is the case, the proposed act will be deemed not to have been adopted: see art.251(6).

[82] See fn.77.

An alternative legislative procedure

Article 175(2) provides for the adoption of certain categories of environ- **1–023**
mental measures by a different means to that set out in Article 175(1) (and
Article 251). It entitles the Council acting unanimously on a proposal from
the Commission and after consulting the Parliament, the Economic and
Social Committee and the Committee of the Regions, to adopt: provisions
of a fiscal nature; measures affecting town and country planning, the
quantitative measurement of water resources (or their availability) or land
use (not including waste management); and measures significantly affecting a Member State's choice between different energy sources and the
general structure of its energy supply. The role of the European Parliament
under this provision is limited to that of being a consultee; it does not
therefore have the same influence that it has under the co-decision procedure described above.

General action programmes

Article 175(3) states that: **1–024**

> "In other areas, general action programmes setting out priority objec-
> tives to be attained shall be adopted by the Council, acting in accordance
> with the procedure referred to in Article 251 and after consulting the
> Economic and Social Committee and the Committee of the Regions".

As Krämer has pointed out, the initiative for drafting a general action
programme lies with the Commission.[83] Whether or not it submits a
proposal to the Council is a matter for its own judgment. If it does decide
to do so, the proposal may be limited to a specific facet of environmental
policy, or it may be far more wide reaching as is the case with the Community's Environmental Action Programmes.[84] Once a proposal has been
received, Article 175(3) makes it clear that the Council must act in
accordance with the co-decision procedure as set out in Article 251 (and
described above).

Other bases for legislating

The present discussion has focused on Article 175 as the legal basis for **1–025**
enacting Community environmental law since, as Krämer has observed,
"the Council favours Article 175 in environmental matters".[85] That preference should not hide the fact, however, that there are other legal bases in
the Rome Treaty on which environmental legislation can be made, and that
the Council has a discretion in the matter. That discretion is likely to be

---

[83] See Krämer, *EC Environmental Law*, para.2–74, p.89.
[84] Discussed above.
[85] See Krämer, *EC Environmental Law*, para.2–60, p.79.

exercised in favour of a legal basis other than Article 175 where the provision in question extends into other non-environmental policy areas for which the Community is competent to legislate. Thus, for example, a measure which seeks to achieve the progressive establishment of the internal market may be made pursuant to Article 95 even though it also relates to the fulfillment of an aspect of the Community's environmental policy.[86] The Council's choice of a particular legal basis for making environmental law has important consequences not least of which is that it will thereby determine which decision-making procedure is to be used.[87] A dual legal basis is, as previously mentioned, a plausible choice where an environmental measure has both environmental and non-environmental emphases of equal weight. However, where one emphasis is subordinate to the other, the European Court of Justice has adopted a test which focuses on the centre of gravity of the Directive in question.[88] In other words, the correct legal basis for making the law is determined by having regard to the provisions of the measure and identifying whether or not they principally relate to a particular field of action, with only incidental effects on another policy field, or whether they relate equally to both policy fields. In the case of the former, the relevant Directive clearly has a centre of gravity and should therefore be made under the most appropriate Treaty provision. In the latter case, the provision may legitimately be made on a dual basis.

Legal Instruments of European Environmental Policy

Regulations and Directives distinguished

1–026　EC environmental legislation is mostly in the form of Directives, although there are some environmental measures which have taken the form of Regulations. Regulations have direct effect immediately on their coming into force and, in principle at least, require no domestic legislation to implement them. In practice, however, this is often needed to set up appropriate administrative structures and, for example, to provide for penalties for breach of a Regulation's requirements. A Directive, on the other hand, "shall be binding, as to the result to be achieved, upon each member state to which it is addressed, but shall leave to the national authorities the choice of form and methods".[89] Accordingly Regulations

---

[86] Environmental measures may also be made pursuant to other Treaty provisions such as Articles 37 or 80 because their primary focus relates to the development of the Community's agricultural or transport policy, respectively.

[87] As noted previously, this will be specified in the Treaty provision itself.

[88] See, for example, Cases C-164 and 165/97 *European Parliament v Council* [1999] E.C.R. I-1139.

[89] Rome Treaty, Article 249.

are used where uniformity is required, typically where international conventions are to be given effect.[90] They have also been used where there are strong reasons for ensuring identical implementation in all Member States, e.g. in relation to shipments of waste,[91] to overcome the quite frequent substantial delays and other failures by Member States to implement Directives in time or at all. Regulations have also been utilised in respect of administrative matters, such as the establishment of the European Environment Agency.[92]

Unlike Regulations, a Directive cannot place legal obligations on individuals and most other legal persons unless and until it has been given effect in national law by implementing legislation—every Directive specifies a final date for this.[93] Nevertheless, it is not uncommon for the requisite legislation either not to have been brought into effect by the implementation date, or else for it to have failed to give full effect to the Directive's requirements. In these circumstances, the doctrines of "direct effect" and "indirect effect" are of particular importance before national courts.[94] At the European level, infringement proceedings brought by the Commission against a Member State in the European Court may be an effective means of bringing a recalcitrant state to heel.[95]

Environmental Directives

Although it is the case that Directives are sometimes very detailed provisions running to a great many Articles, in the environmental sphere, it is increasingly common for them to be quite general in nature dealing with matters of policy in a broad non-specific way. The use of "framework" or "mother" Directives as they are sometimes called thus provides a means of outlining in a general sense rules, requirements etc. the detail of which may be more specifically dealt with at a later date by one or more "daughter" directives. While an advantage of legislating in this way is that Member States are more likely to take the necessary steps to transpose the relevant Directive into national law, difficulties may arise where it is necessary to determine whether or not the Member State is actually complying with the terms of the Directive. Moreover, the European Court of Justice has made it clear that it will not accept the argument that a Member State has taken all reasonably practicable steps to implement the requirements of a

1–027

---

[90] For example the phasing out of CFCs, halons and other ozone-depleting compounds under the Montreal Protocol; see para.14–058.
[91] See Regulation 259/93.
[92] See Regulation 1210/90.
[93] Case C-91/92 *Paolo Faccini Dori v Recreb Srl* [1994] E.C.R. I-3325.
[94] These are explained in the next section of this chapter.
[95] See further below at paras 1–042 to 1–057.

Directive; what is required is actual compliance with the obligations laid down in the Directive.[96]

The Doctrine of Direct Effect

1–028   The doctrine of "direct effect" is a creation of the European Court of Justice. It is not expressly provided for in the Rome Treaty although it has been contended by the Court that since the Treaty confers rights on the citizens of the Member States, it is implicit that those rights must be capable of being enforced before national courts.

The decision in Van Gend en Loos

1–029   The doctrine was first articulated by the European Court in a judgment[97] which Hartley has described as "one of the most important judgments ever handed down by the Court".[98] The case itself concerned import duties imposed on a chemical substance imported into the Netherlands by Van Gend from the former West Germany. The Dutch revenue applied an import duty of 8 per cent whereas Van Gend contended that it should have continued to impose the previous duty of 3 per cent. It was argued that by increasing the duty after the entry into force of the Rome Treaty (January 1, 1958), the Dutch government had acted contrary to Article 12 of the Treaty. Two questions were referred to the European Court by the Netherlands Revenue Tribunal. The first of these was "whether Article 12 of the Treaty has direct application in national law in the sense that nationals of Member States may on the basis of this Article lay claim to rights which the national court must protect". In a much cited passage, the European Court opined:

> "... the Community constitutes a new legal order of international law for the benefit of which the States have limited their sovereign rights, albeit within limited fields, and the subjects of which comprise not only

---

[96] See, e.g., Case C-337/89 *Commission v United Kingdom* [1992] E.C.R. 6103, and Case C-56/90 *Commission v United Kingdom* [1993] E.C.R. I-4109. In the first of these cases, the Commission brought proceedings against the UK in respect of its alleged failure to implement the terms of the Drinking Water Directive, 80/778/EEC. The second case related to an alleged failure to ensure that the quality of bathing waters in the bathing areas of Blackpool, Formby and Southport conformed to the limit values set out in Article 3 of the Bathing Waters Directive, 76/160/EEC. In both cases, the relevant Directives did allow a Member State to derogate from its obligations in certain prescribed circumstances. However, by claiming that it had taken all reasonably practicable steps to fulfil its obligations, the UK was seeking to introduce a further ground on which to derogate in addition to those expressly provided for under the Directives themselves.

[97] Case 26/62 *NV Alegemane Transporten Expeditie Onderneming Van Gend en Loos v Nederlandse administratie der belastingen* [1963] E.C.R. 1.

[98] T. C. Hartley, *The Foundations of European Community Law* 6th edition (Oxford: Oxford University Press, 2007), p.192.

Member States but also their nationals. Independently of the legislation of Member States, Community law therefore not only imposes obligations on individuals but is also intended to confer upon them rights which become part of their legal heritage. These rights arise not only where they are expressly granted by the Treaty, but also by reason of obligations which the Treaty imposes in a clearly defined way upon individuals as well as upon the Member States and upon the institutions of the Community".[99]

Extending the doctrine of direct effect

The significance of the decision in *Van Gend en Loos* cannot be overstated. **1–030**
Initially its implications were limited to the recognition that Treaty Articles were capable of conferring legally enforceable rights on individuals. In other words, Treaty Articles were capable of having *direct effect*. It was not long, however, before the implications of *Van Gend en Loos* became more far-reaching as a consequence of a string of decisions in which the European Court extended the doctrine of direct effect to other legal instruments referred to in what is now Article 249 of the Rome Treaty.[100] For present purposes the most significant development occurred when the European Court held in *Van Duyn v Home Office*[101] that Directives were capable of having direct effect. Such a development had originally seemed unlikely following *Van Gend en Loos* given that in that case, the Court laid down a test for direct effect which included that the implementation of the Euopean measure must not be conditional upon a positive legislative measure enacted under national law. Since Directives implicitly require implementation by Member States as a consequence of the wording of Article 249,[102] it might have been thought that they could not be capable of having direct effect. However, in *Van Duyn*, the Court did not allow this obstacle to prevent its further development of the doctrine. It sought to justify its decision on various grounds including the argument that the "useful effect" of Directives would be greatly weakened if individuals were not able to invoke them before national courts. Although this was a policy rather than a legal argument, it "won the day"[103] since it provided a practical solution to the problem of Member States failing to implement Directives. Whereas proceedings under Articles 226 to 228 are often slow

---

[99] [1963] E.C.R. 1, para.11.
[100] See, for example, Case 39/72 *Commission v Italy* [1973] E.C.R. 101, where the direct effect of Regulations was confirmed by the European Court. Previously the Court had held likewise in relation to Decisions: Case 9/70 *Grad v Finanzamt Traunstein* [1970] E.C.R. 825.
[101] Case 41/74 [1974] E.C.R. 1337.
[102] The relevant part of which provides as follows: "A directive shall be binding, as to the result to be achieved, upon each Member State to which it is addressed, but shall leave the national authorities the choice of form and methods".
[103] Hartley, *The Foundations of European Community Law*, p.203.

and cumbersome,[104] enabling individuals to enforce rights before their own national courts transfers the burden of ensuring compliance on to those same courts. It also makes it more likely that instances of non-compliance will be detected and that, where they are, they will be resolved more expeditiously.

Subsequently, the European Court of Justice has expressed the doctrine of "direct effect" in the following terms:

"(W)herever the provisions of a Directive appear, as far as their subject matter is concerned, to be unconditional and sufficiently precise, those provisions may, in the absence of implementing measures adopted within the prescribed period, be relied upon . . . in so far as the provisions define rights which individuals are able to assert against the state".[105]

Directives: the importance of the time limit for implementation

1–031   A Member State that has failed to comply with the requirements imposed on it by a Directive within the prescribed period may not plead, as against individuals, its own failure to perform these obligations. Were the position otherwise, the "useful effect" or *effet utile* of a Directive would be considerably lessened. The time limit for implementing Directives is very important in the context of the doctrine of direct effect. In *Pubblico Ministero v Ratti*,[106] the European Court held that a Directive is only capable of having direct effect once the time limit has expired. Prior to that expiry, a Member State may be entitled to argue that it is exercising the discretion accorded to it under Article 249 as to the form and methods of implementing the "result to be achieved" in the Directive. Inactivity is therefore permissible during the transposition period. Is it the case, however, that a Member State is free to adopt national rules at variance with an environmental Directive during the same period?

Inter-Environnement Wallonie ASBL v Région Wallonne

1–032   This was the argument which was advanced by a number of national governments[107] in *Inter-Environnement Wallonie ASBL v Région Wallonne*,[108] where the European Court was invited to consider several ques-

---

[104] See further below at paras 1–042 to 1–057.
[105] Case 8/81, *Becker v Finanzamt Münster-Innenstadt* [1982] E.C.R. 53; [1982] 1 C.M.L.R. 499; Case 152/84, *Marshall v Southampton and South-West Hampshire Area Health Authority* [1986] E.C.R. 723, [1986] 1 C.M.L.R. 688.
[106] Case 148/78 [1979] E.C.R. 1629.
[107] These were the Belgian, French and UK governments.
[108] Case C-129/96 [1997] E.C.R. I-7411.

tions, including whether Articles 5 and 189 of the Rome Treaty[109] precluded such a course of action by a Member State. In giving judgment, the
Court noted that since the purpose of the time limit in a Directive is to give
a Member State the necessary opportunity to transpose the provision, a
State "cannot be faulted for not having transposed the directive into their
internal legal order before expiry of that period".[110] However, the Court
further noted that during the transposition period it was incumbent on a
Member State to "take the necessary measures to ensure that the result
prescribed by the directive is achieved at the end of that period".[111]
Accordingly, it followed from the obligations laid down in Articles 5 and
189 and from the Directive itself,[112] that during the transposition period
Member States "must refrain from taking any measures liable seriously to
compromise the result prescribed".[113] Whether or not the relevant national
provisions were likely to have that effect was a matter for national courts to
determine taking into account various considerations, including whether
the provisions purport to constitute full transposition of the Directive or a
staged implementation, and their duration. In a case where the provisions
in question are intended to constitute "full and definitive transposition",
the Court was of the view that "their compatibility with the directive might
give rise to the presumption that the result prescribed by the directive will
not be achieved within the period prescribed if it is impossible to amend
them in time".[114]

An emanation of the state?

A significant restriction on the direct effect doctrine as it applies in relation   **1–033**
to Directives is that it only gives individual rights against the "state" and
not against other individuals. In other words, Directives are *vertically* rather
than *horizontally* directly effective.[115] However, for this purpose "the state"
has received a wide interpretation in a series of decisions of the European
Court, and includes independent authorities responsible for the maintenance of public order and safety,[116] public authorities providing public

---

[109] Now Articles 10 and 249, respectively.
[110] [1997] E.C.R. I-7411, para.43.
[111] para.44.
[112] The Directive in question was the Waste Framework Directive, 75/442/EEC, as amended
by Directive 91/156/EEC.
[113] [1997] E.C.R. I-7411, para.45.
[114] para.48.
[115] Treaty Articles and Regulations are capable of being both vertically and directly effective:
see Case 43/75 *Defrenne v Sabena* [1976] E.C.R. 455. In other words, from the standpoint
of the individual, these legal instruments are a potential source of rights *and* obligations.
[116] See Case 222/84, *Johnson v Chief Constable of the Royal Ulster Constabulary* [1986] E.C.R.
1651, [1986] 3 C.M.L.R. 240, [1987] Q.B. 129.

health services,[117] and the governing body of a school.[118] All such bodies are regarded as "emanations of the state" and accordingly capable of being directly subject to the obligations of a Directive. It matters not in what capacity the state is acting, whether as employer or as public authority. What constitutes an "emanation of the state" has been defined in the following terms:

> "It follows, from the foregoing that a body, whatever its legal form,[119] which has been made responsible, pursuant to a measure adopted by the state, for providing a public service under the control of the state, and has for that purpose special powers beyond those which result from the normal rules applicable in relations between individuals, is included in any event among the bodies against which the provisions of a Directive capable of having direct effect may be relied upon".[120]

Foster v British Gas

1–034   In the case in question, the British Gas Corporation (i.e. the publicly owned body before privatisation) was held to be directly subject to a Directive relating to equal treatment of men and women as regards retirement ages. The quotation from *Foster* makes it clear that the mere fact that a body may be in private ownership does not automatically exclude it from being an emanation of the state—the question is whether it has the special powers and responsibilities that the Court referred to. On receiving the judgment of the European Court, the House of Lords gave extensive consideration as to whether the British Gas Corporation had the responsibilities and powers referred to and held that it had.[121] The decision in *Foster* was later applied in *Griffin v South West Water Services*,[122] where Blackburne J held that the defendant, a water and sewerage undertaker, was a "state authority against which a person may rely upon provisions of

---

[117] See Case 152/84, *Marshall v Southampton and South-West Hampshire Area Health Authority* [1986] E.C.R. 723, [1986] 1 C.M.L.R. 688.

[118] See *National Union of Teachers v Governing Body of St Mary's Church of England (Aided) Junior School* [1997] I.R.L.R. 242.

[119] It has been suggested that this form of words is sufficiently broad to ensure that private citizens may in certain circumstances amount to an "emanation of the state" for the purposes of the doctrine of direct effect: see P. Wennerås, *The Enforcement of EC Environmental Law* (Oxford: Oxford University Press, 2007), p. 46. The European Court of Justice confirmed that this was so in Case C-157/02, *Rieser Internationale Transporte GmbH v Autobahnen-und Schnellstraßen-Finanzierungs-AG (Asfinag)* [2004] E.C.R. I-1477, where it was held, amongst other things, that "the provisions of a directive capable of having direct effect may be relied upon against a legal person governed by private law where the state has entrusted to that legal person the task of levying tolls for the use of public road networks and when it has direct or indirect control of the legal person" (para.29).

[120] Case C-188/89 *Foster v British Gas* [1990] 1 E.C.R. 3313, [1990] 2 C.M.L.R. 833, [1990] 3 All E.R. 897, para.[20].

[121] [1991] 2 A.C. 396, [1991] 2 W.L.R. 1075, [1991] 2 All E.R. 705.

[122] [1995] I.R.L.R. 15.

EU directives in domestic courts and tribunals". In view of the number of privatised utilities which currently exist the decision in *Griffin* is clearly important.[123] It had been an arguable point whether the utility companies were capable of being bound by directives. *Griffin* makes it clear that they are.

Doughty v Rolls-Royce

The mere fact that the state may own a majority, or even all, of a company's share capital does not, however, automatically make that company an emanation of the state. As was observed in *Doughty v Rolls-Royce plc*,[124] a case which turned on whether a Directive was binding on Rolls-Royce by virtue solely of all its shares being owned by the government, the House of Lords in *Foster* would not have devoted the time they did to the responsibilities and powers of British Gas had the majority control held by the state been a sufficient criterion on its own. In *Doughty* it was held that, although 100 per cent owned by the state, Rolls-Royce plc behaved at all times as a commercial company and had no special responsibilities and powers such as to make directives directly binding on it.

1–035

The Doctrine of Indirect Effect

National courts must, where possible, give effect to European Community legislation. Thus in *Von Colson and Kamann v Land Nordrhein-Westfalen*,[125] the European Court stated:

1–036

> "It is for the national court to interpret and apply the legislation adopted for the implementation of the directive in conformity with the requirements of Community law, in so far as it is given discretion to do so under national law".[126]

In truth, there is little to object to in this statement. Where national law has been made with the express or implied purpose of implementing a Directive, it would defy reason not to interpret it in conformity with the requirements of the European provision. Indeed to do otherwise would be to act contrary to the intentions of those who made the national law. It would also run the very great risk of producing inconsistency between national and European law. In the later joined cases of *Pfeiffer and others v*

---

[123] See P. Craig, "Directives: Direct Effect, Indirect Effect and the Construction of National Legislation" (1997) 22 EL Rev 519.
[124] [1992] I.R.L.R. 126.
[125] Case 14/83 [1986] 2 C.M.L.R. 430.
[126] para.28.

Deutsches Rotes Kreuz, Kreisverband Waldshut eV,[127] the European Court explained the legal basis of indirect effect as follows:

"The requirement for national law to be interpreted in conformity with Community law is *inherent in the system of the Treaty*, since it permits the national court, for the matters within its jurisdiction, to ensure the full effectiveness of Community law when it determines the dispute before it".[128]

The interpretive obligation which *Von Colson* established is patently qualified by the inclusion of the words "in so far as it is given discretion to do so under national law". Thus where the constitutional arrangements of a Member State confine the courts to the role of interpreter rather than the maker of law, as in the United Kingdom, *Von Colson* does not compel a court to cross the boundary between the two roles. In other words, as one commentator has contended, the interpretive obligation "is not absolute and is not designed to give national courts a legislative function to allow them to re-write national law".[129]

In a later case, the *Von Colson* doctrine was applied so that when interpreting national law, a national court should do so, as far as possible, in the light of the wording and purpose of any relevant European directive, whether the national law originated before or after adoption of the directive.[130] Though this is expressly stated in the European Court's judgment in *Marleasing*, there is a case for arguing that it is not within its powers to lay down rules for the interpretation of national legislation, particularly where that rule achieves by a "back door route"[131] the horizontal direct effect of measures which are not directly effective.

Domestic construction of EU law

1–037   Courts in the United Kingdom will undoubtedly seek to give effect to domestic legislation in a manner that is consistent with a directive that it is intended to implement. Indeed where the domestic legislation is evidently intended to give effect to a directive, the Courts have a duty to give it a purposive construction, implying further words if necessary, to achieve that. Thus in *Litster v Forth Dry Dock & Engineering Co Ltd*,[132] a construction of the United Kingdom Regulations in issue was adopted that it

---

[127] Cases C-397/01 to 401/01 [2004] E.C.R. I-8835.
[128] para.114 (emphasis added).
[129] Drake, "Twenty years after *Von Colson*: the impact of 'indirect effect' on the protection of the individual's Community rights" (2005) 30 EL Rev 329 at 342.
[130] Case C-106/99 *Marleasing S.A. v La Commercial Internacional de Elementacion S.A.* [1992] 1 C.M.L.R. 305.
[131] See Hartley, *The Foundations of European Community Law*, p.217.
[132] [1990] 1 A.C. 546.

was said would be impermissible if they were to be read on their own.[133] A Court should not come to a decision which would result in the United Kingdom being in breach of its Treaty obligations "in the absence of the most compulsive context rendering any other conclusion impossible".[134]

The duty to adopt a purposive construction is, however, limited to interpreting national legislation. It does not require UK courts to construe a contractual agreement in conformity with a European Directive. In *White v White and another*,[135] Lord Nicholls explained:

"The rationale of the *Marleasing* case is that the duty of Member States under Article 5[136] is binding on all the authorities of Member States, including the courts. The courts must apply national law accordingly, whenever the law was enacted or made. But it is one matter to apply this principle to national law. Whatever form it may take, law is made by authorities of the State. It is quite another to apply this principle to contracts made between citizens. The *Marleasing* principle cannot be stretched to the length of requiring contracts to be interpreted in a manner that would impose on one or other of the parties obligations which, the *Marleasing* case apart, the contract did not impose".[137]

Having thus explained in outline the doctrines of direct and indirect effect, it is now necessary to consider the implementation of European environmental law.

Implementing European Environmental Law

Articles 10 and 175(4)

In the years since the Community established an environmental policy, the institutions have exercised their legislative powers to make a great many environmental laws. Member States are under an obligation to implement these measures as a consequence of two Treaty provisions: Articles 10 and 175(4). The former provides that: 1–038

"Member States shall take appropriate measures, whether general or particular, to ensure fulfillment of the obligations arising out of this

---

[133] Per Lord Oliver at 576. In the recent case of *Byrne v Motor Insurer's Bureau* [2007] EWHC 1268 (QB); [2007] 3 All E.R. 499, Flaux J commented that: "The application of this principle in English courts leads to a broad approach to statutory interpretation way beyond what would be permissible under domestic law … The only real limit to this approach to interpretation seems to be that, although the approach may change the meaning of the legislation, it must not conflict with a fundamental feature of the legislation"—at [39].

[134] Per Lord Oliver [1990] 1 A.C. 546, at 563. See also *Webb v EMO Air Cargo Ltd* [1993] 1 W.L.R. 49, at 59.

[135] [2001] UKHL 9; [2001] 2 All E.R. 43.

[136] Now Article 10 of the Rome Treaty.

[137] [2001] 2 All E.R., at 22.

Treaty or resulting from action taken by the institutions of the Community. They shall facilitate the achievement of the Community's tasks. They shall abstain from any measure which would jeopardise the attainment of the objectives of this Treaty".

The obligations arising under Article 10 apply in relation to Community law and policy generally. Article 175(4) imposes more specific obligations in relation to Community environmental policy. It provides that:

"Without prejudice to certain measures of a Community nature, the Member States shall finance and implement the environment policy".

It has been suggested that Article 175(4) is "somewhat superfluous"[138] given the general nature of Article 10. Although this is undoubtedly correct, making specific provision does serve to emphasise the importance of the Member States' obligations and how the onus is very much on them to make Community environmental policy work in practice.

Transposing environmental Directives

1–039   Once an environmental Directive has entered into force,[139] Member States are obliged within a clearly specified period to transpose it into their own domestic law.[140] Thus, for example, the Bathing Water Directive 2006/7/EC, makes provision for its own implementation in Article 18. This states:

"1.   Member States shall bring into force the laws, regulations and administrative provisions necessary to comply with this Directive by 24 March 2008. They shall forthwith inform the Commission thereof.

When Member States adopt these measures, they shall contain a reference to this Directive or shall be accompanied by such a reference on the occasion of their official publication. The methods of making such reference shall be laid down by Member States.

2.   Member States shall communicate to the Commission the texts of the main provisions of national law that they adopt in the field covered by this Directive".

Given that the environment is a devolved matter under the devolution legislation,[141] the responsibility for transposing and implementing the

---

[138] See Krämer, *EC Environmental Law*, para.12–02, p.418.
[139] The Directive will itself specify the number of days following its publication in the *Official Journal* when this will occur.
[140] Such an obligation would not arise, however, where a Directive makes provisions which clearly cannot be applied in a particular Member State. Thus, for example, land-locked Member States would not need to implement Directives which make provisions for coastal waters—see Krämer, *EC Environmental Law*, para.12–04, p.422.
[141] See the Scotland Act 1998, the Northern Ireland Act 1998 and the Government of Wales Act 2006.

Bathing Water Directive falls on the respective national governments. In the case of England and Wales, the Directive is implemented by the Bathing Water Regulations 2008, SI 2008/1097.

The obligation to transpose environmental directives into national law requires that the Member State does so by way of a binding legal instrument. As Krämer has noted, the European Court of Justice has "on numerous occasions, rejected Member States' attempts to transpose the requirements of an environmental directive into national law by means of a multi-annual plan, an administrative circular or similar instrument".[142] Thus in *Commission v Germany*,[143] for example, where the Commission applied for a declaration that the German government had not adopted all the laws, regulations and administrative provisions needed in order to fully transpose Directives 75/440/EEC and 79/869/EEC into national law, the European Court of Justice held, inter alia:

"It follows that Article 3(1) of Directive 75/440 has not been shown to have been implemented with unquestionable binding force, nor in a specific, precise and clear manner as required under the Court's case-law in order to satisfy the requirements of legal certainty and that, in any event, certain measures pleaded have not been proved or were not adopted until after the expiry of the time limit set in the reasoned opinion".[144]

What does transposition entail?

In a further case also involving proceedings brought by the Commission   **1–040** against the German government, the European Court of Justice gave an indication as to what transposition entails in the following terms:

"The transposition of a directive into domestic law does not necessarily require that its provisions be incorporated formally and verbatim in express, specific legislation; a general legal context may, depending on the content of the directive, be adequate for the purpose provided that it does indeed guarantee the full application of the directive in a sufficiently clear and precise manner so that, where the directive is intended to create rights for individuals, the persons concerned can ascertain the full extent of their rights and where appropriate, rely on them before the national courts".[145]

---

[142] See Krämer, *EC Environmental Law*, at para.12–03, p.420. In support of these remarks Krämer cites a number of cases. These include: Case C-96/81, *Commission v Netherlands* [1982] E.C.R. 1791, Case C-13/90, *Commission v France* [1991] E.C.R. I-4327, and Case C-262/95, *Commission v Germany* [1996] E.C.R. I-5729.
[143] Case C-58/89, [1991] E.C.R. 4983.
[144] para.18.
[145] Case C-131/88 *Commission v Germany* [1991] E.C.R. I-825, para.6.

Policing EU environmental law: the role of the Commission

1–041   In addition to being responsible for the elaboration of Community policy, the Commission is under a duty by virtue of Article 211 to ensure that the provisions of the Rome Treaty and the measures taken by the institutions pursuant thereto are applied. In order for it to fulfil its role as guardian of the Treaty and comply with its Article 211 duty, it is necessary for the Commission to monitor Member States' compliance with environmental directives. Where it becomes apparent that a Member State has failed to implement a Community environmental law into its own national legal system, the Commission may decide to institute infringement proceedings against the state.

Infringement proceedings

1–042   Community law can be enforced against Member States in two key ways: by individuals before national courts as a result of the doctrines of direct effect and state liability in damages: and by proceedings brought by the Commission against the state before the European Court of Justice pursuant to Articles 226–228 of the Rome Treaty.[146] In this chapter we shall focus on the enforcement of Community environmental law by the Commission.[147] Although Article 226 of the Treaty specifies a formal infringement procedure which is to be followed, it should not be forgotten that it will be preceded by an informal investigation on the part of the Commission to determine whether there is a prima facie infringement of Community law on the part of the Member State. That investigation may take place due to the Commission acting on its own initiative where, for example, a Member State has failed to submit a report on the measures which it has taken to give effect to a Community environmental law in its own domestic legal system. An alternative catalyst for an informal investigation might be the receipt of a complaint from an EU citizen or nongovernmental organisation (NGO). Whatever the reason why an informal investigation was commenced, its conclusion will place the Commission in a better position to determine whether or not infringement proceedings pursuant to Article 226 ought to be undertaken.

---

[146] Article 227 of the Treaty provides for the possibility of a Member State bringing another Member State before the European Court where it considers that there has been a failure to fulfil an obligation under the Treaty. Since the procedure has never been used in the environmental context it will not be considered further: see Krämer, "Statistics on Environmental Judgments by the EC Court of Justice" (2006) 18 J.Env.L. 407 at 409.

[147] The doctrine of direct effect and the principle of state liability in damages are both creations of the European Court of Justice rather than being expressly provided for in the Rome Treaty itself. The former has been discussed above. The latter will be considered in Chapter 4.

Infringement proceedings: the administrative stage

The first paragraph of Article 226 of the Rome Treaty provides as follows: **1–043**

"If the Commission considers that a Member State has failed to fulfil an obligation under this Treaty,[148] it shall deliver a reasoned opinion on the matter after giving the State concerned the opportunity to submit its observations".

Although not expressly referred to above, the first stage of the formal infringement procedure consists of the Commission issuing a Member State with a letter of formal notice in which it sets out its reasons for believing that the Member State is failing to comply with Community environmental law.[149] It is important that this is communicated in a clear and unequivocal manner. A failure to do so may result in the proceedings later being nullified.[150] The Member State will then have a specified period of time from the date of receipt of the letter within which to submit its observations on the case. What has been described by the European Court of Justice as "an essential procedural requirement"[151] thus affords a Member State the opportunity to defend itself against the allegation of having infringed Community law. It thereby ensures that the infringement procedure is compliant with the *audi alteram partem* doctrine.

A reasoned opinion

If the Member State fails to reply or if the Commission is not satisfied by   **1–044**
the response which it receives, Article 226 requires the Commission to deliver a reasoned opinion.[152] It would thus appear to have no discretion in the matter. The reasoned opinion will set out the nature of the alleged infringement of Community law. It will also indicate what the Member State needs to do in order to bring the infringement to an end. The wording of the reasoned opinion is clearly important.[153] If the case is subsequently heard by the European Court of Justice, the allegation set out in the reasoned opinion will form the subject-matter of the application. An

---

[148] A violation of an obligation set down in Community legislation which has been enacted under a Treaty Article falls within the scope of Article 226 since as Hartley observes, "violation of the legislation would constitute a violation of the Treaty provision empowering its enactment": see Hartley, *The Foundations of European Community Law*, p.299.
[149] It has been stated by the Commission that around 70 per cent of complaints can be closed before a formal notice is sent: see COM (2007) 502 final, p.3.
[150] See Hartley, *The Foundations of European Community Law*, p.302.
[151] Case 31/69 *Commission v Italy* [1970] E.C.R. 25, para.13.
[152] The Commission is on record as saying that approximately 85 per cent of complaints are closed before a reasoned opinion is delivered: see COM (2007) 502 final, p.3.
[153] It ought to be noted that the Commission does not publish either letters of formal notice or reasoned opinions issued pursuant to Article 226. Krämer has contended that this may well be contrary to EC Regulation 1049/2001 on access to documents: see "Access to Letters of Formal Notice and Reasoned Opinions in Environmental Law Matters" (2003) 12 *European Environmental Law Review* 197.

attempt to introduce allegations at the judicial stage of the infringement proceedings which were not raised during the administrative stage will be ruled inadmissible by the European Court.[154]

Commission discretion

1–045   The delivery of a reasoned opinion brings the administrative stage of infringement proceedings to an end.[155] A Member State will have a period of time, specified in the reasoned opinion itself,[156] within which to end its violation of Community law. During that time the Member State is effectively protected against the Commission instituting formal legal proceedings before the European Court. If, however, on the expiry of the relevant time the Commission is of the view that the Member State continues to be in breach of Community law, it has a discretion as to whether or not to bring the matter to the attention of the Court. This is evident from the second paragraph of Article 226 which provides:

> "If the State concerned does not comply with the opinion within the period laid down by the Commission, the latter may bring the matter before the Court of Justice".

The use of the permissive "may" makes it clear that the Commission is not formally obliged to institute Article 226 proceedings; it has a discretion in the matter. Accordingly, even if it was of the view that a Member State was clearly in breach of Community environmental law, it could exercise its discretion not to bring the matter before the European Court. This may occur where, for example, it is evident from the Member State's observations that although it accepts that it is in breach of Community law, it is genuinely taking steps to bring that infringement to an end and that whilst this will not be achieved within the time limit specified in the reasoned opinion, there are good reasons for believing that compliance will occur shortly thereafter. The discretion accorded to the Commission under Article 226 is therefore considerable. It would seem to be beyond the reach of legal challenge. Thus in *Commission v Germany*,[157] for example, the European Court of Justice expressed the view that the Commission "alone

---

[154] Case 298/86 *Commission v Belgium* [1988] E.C.R. 4343.

[155] It has been noted that this stage (Krämer refers to it as the "pre-Court procedure") under Article 226 normally takes longer than the Court stage. In 2007 the Commission observed: "It takes an average of 19 months to close a complaint before a letter of formal notice is sent; 36 months where a case is closed between the letter of formal notice and reasoned opinion, and 50 months where the case is closed after the reasoned opinion and before the case is sent to the Court, producing an average time for all cases of 26 months": see COM (2007) 502 final, p.3. There are a number of reasons which explain the lengthy nature of the process. These include the fact that the administrative stage involves several formal decisions needing to be reached by the Commission which only deals with infringement cases twice a year: see (2006) 18 J.Env.L. 407 at 415.

[156] The period of time specified in either a letter of formal notice or a reasoned opinion is normally two months: see (2006) 18 J.Env.L. 407 at 417.

[157] Case C-422/92 [1995] E.C.R. I-1097.

is ... competent to decide whether it is appropriate to bring proceedings".[158] It has been contended, however, that "in the interests of accountability ... such discretion needs to be exercised within defined and well-understood parameters"[159] given that the Commission has both political and enforcement functions under the Treaty which may make it subject to "political influence at every stage of an investigation or infringement procedure".[160]

Some different kinds of non-implementation

Following the establishment of a Community environmental policy the emphasis in the early years was very much on giving legislative effect to the Commission's proposals as set out in the Action Programmes and other documents. Accordingly, as Hattan has noted, "the Commission did not actively pursue non-implementation cases in the environmental field until the mid-1980s".[161] Non-implementation of Community environmental law can take one of several guises.[162] It may involve a failure on the part of the Member State to transpose into national law the requirements of a Directive so that the rights and duties set down in the provision do not take effect in the domestic legal system. A complete failure to transpose an environmental Directive can be relatively easily identified given that Directives impose a duty on Member States to notify the Commission of the measures which have been taken domestically to implement the provision. Partial or bad transposition may be less easily identifiable. The Commission refers to non-transposition cases as "non-communication cases". In its *Seventh Annual Survey on the Implementation and Enforcement of Community Environmental Law*,[163] it stated that it endeavors to pursue non-communication cases "as rapidly as possible with a view to having relevant national legislation adopted quickly".[164] It also noted that whilst the number of cases of failing to communicate national implementing measures stood at 124 for the environment sector, this was "considerably lower than in other policy areas".[165]

1–046

---

[158] para.22.
[159] Hattan, "The Implementation of EU Environmental Law" (2003) 15 J.Env.L. 273 at 275.
[160] Williams, "Enforcing European Environmental Law: Can the European Commission be held to Account?" (2002) *Yearbook of European Environmental Law* 271.
[161] (2003) 15 J.Env.L. 273 at 276.
[162] The distinctions which follow are made for ease of explanation. In truth, there may often be overlaps between them. Thus, a failure to implement a Community environmental directive may actually entail failings at more than one stage of the implementation process.
[163] The Seventh Annual Survey on the Implementation and Enforcement of Community Environmental Law, SEC (2006) 1143.
[164] ibid. p.6.
[165] ibid.

Non-conformity

1–047 The second category of non-implementation case focuses on the issue of conformity. Community environmental law has not been properly implemented where national laws do not conform with the standards and requirements laid down in the relevant EU legislation. Assessing conformity is by no means a straightforward task for an under-resourced Commission. Accordingly in more recent times, the Commission has "moved to an approach of strategic annual conformity checking by outside legal experts".[166]

Bad application

1–048 The final category of non-implementation case concerns whether or not Community environmental law has actually been applied in practice. This may be rather difficult to determine, especially since the Commission does not possess inspection powers in the environmental field. Thus it is largely dependent upon complaints from EU citizens and NGOs and questions and petitions from the European Parliament as a way of drawing attention to what it terms the "bad application" of Community environmental law. Non-application cases are also those which are most likely to be time consuming and cause political controversy since Member States are unlikely to take kindly to the suggestion that they are failing to give proper effect to Community law.

Commission policy vis-à-vis non-implementation

1–049 Until 1996, the Commission exercised its discretion in relation to ensuring the proper application of Community environmental law in the absence of a clearly defined strategy. In that year, however, it published a Communication[167] setting out how it would address the issue of the "implementation gap"[168] or deficit in respect of Community environmental law. The emphasis in that document is on enforcement action being taken in respect of non-transposition and non-conformity cases rather than non-application cases. The Commission has sought to justify this approach by pointing out that what may appear at first glance to be a non-application case may in fact be a case involving inadequate transposition or con-

---

[166] ibid.

[167] COM (96) 500 final, [1996] C4-0591/96.

[168] Commentators have tended to use this term to describe the phenomenon whereby Member States have not properly complied with their obligations to implement Community environmental law: see, for example, M. Lee, *EU Environmental Law* (Hart Publishing, 2005) where Chapter 3 is entitled "The Implementation Gap".

formity.[169] However, as Hattan points out, a number of implications flow from such an approach. Chief amongst these is that:

> "failure by the Commission to pursue aggressively non-application cases could result in a large hole in the practical implementation of EU environmental legislation, particularly if citizens do not have effective access to national courts for environmental matters".[170]

Importantly, however, the Commission's actual use of enforcement proceedings does not seem to reflect its stated strategy. Hattan's analysis of the data[171] reveals that the Commission has pursued rather more non-application cases than would be expected given the supposed emphasis on non-transposition and non-conformity cases. Accordingly, she contends that the Commission's "unofficial policy" on implementation is in practice "more sophisticated" than the strategy set out in the Communication. That unofficial policy does involve the Commission pursuing non-application cases, especially those where there has been a failure by the Member State to establish the correct infrastructure in order to implement a Directive, e.g. the designation of nitrate vulnerable zones and bathing waters pursuant to the Nitrate and Bathing Waters Directives, respectively, or those "which on their face appear to be non-application matters, but which actually reflect deeper transposition and conformity issues". Hattan contends in relation to the former that:

> "whilst technically such cases relate to the non-application of EU law, in reality there are many similarities with non-conformity cases, in that both aim to ensure that the correct framework is put in place, be that in terms of the proper legal framework (conformity) or the proper structural framework (application)".[172]

In the light of these observations there is a strong case for arguing that the Commission needs to produce a more transparent policy in respect of those non-application cases which it will pursue. There is also a case for arguing that an under-resourced DG Environment needs more staff in order for it to be able to "pursue a consistent and proactive approach towards implementation issues"[173] since as Krämer has commented:

> "The practical application of environmental provisions is the most serious problem that national, Community and international environmental

---

[169] See *16th Annual Report on Monitoring the Application of Community Environmental Law* (1998) COM [1999] C354/1, p.63.

[170] (2003) 15 J.Env.L. 273 at 279. The author also draws attention to how "failure to pursue individual complaints relating to instances of non-application may result in disillusionment with the complaint system" and that there is a danger that by over-looking non-application cases, the Commission is simply "passing the buck" to the Member States: ibid. at 280.

[171] Chiefly the Commission's annual reports.

[172] (2003) 15 J.Env.L. 273 at 283.

[173] ibid. at 287.

law faces. Even a piece of national legislation that copies a Directive word for word will remain a mere piece of paper unless it is applied".[174]

The Judicial Stage

1–050 Where the Commission does decide to bring infringement proceedings before the European Court of Justice pursuant to Article 226, the Court is entitled to consider the issues raised by the infringements specified in the reasoned opinion. In the proceedings it will be no defence for a Member State to argue that there are other states which have also failed to implement the relevant environmental Directive and yet which are not being proceeded against.[175] Where the Court finds that a breach of Community law has been established, it gives judgment against the State to that effect. The judgment itself will not specify what the Member State is required to do in order to bring the violation to an end; that is a matter for the State to determine. The binding effect of the Court's judgment is evident from Article 228(1) which provides:

"If the Court of Justice finds that a Member State has failed to fulfil an obligation under this treaty, the State shall be requested to take the necessary measures to comply with the judgment of the Court of Justice".

Based on statistics gleaned from official publications,[176] Krämer draws attention to the fact that between 1984 and 2004, there was a "slow, but continuous, increase in the number of judgments that had not been complied with by the end of the year".[177] Thus whereas in 1990 the relevant number of judgments stood at 14, by 2004 this had risen to 81.[178]

Further proceedings before the European Court

1–051 As originally enacted the Rome Treaty made no provision for what was to happen in the event that a Member State failed to comply with a ruling of the European Court of Justice. Now, however, the amended Article 228 provides for the possibility of further proceedings to secure compliance with a Court ruling. These proceedings correspond to those provided for in

---

[174] See Krämer, *EC Environmental Law*, para.12–07, p.424.
[175] The general principle was established in Cases 52, 55/65 *Germany v Commission* [1966] E.C.R. 159 at para.170–2.
[176] Krämer's frustration at the poor quality of environmental information is evident when he concludes his discussion by suggesting that the Commission "should take a serious look at its present communication policy in the environmental sector, get away from cheap publicity and commonplaces and supply the European citizens with information that is correct, up to date, usable and useful": see "Statistics on Environmental Judgments by the EC Court of Justice" (2006) 18 J.Env.L. 407 at 421.
[177] ibid. at 410.
[178] ibid. Table 5 at 412.

Article 226. Accordingly, where the Commission considers that a Member State has not taken the necessary measures to comply with a judgment of the Court, Article 228(2) requires it to issue a reasoned opinion to that effect. The issuing of a reasoned opinion will be preceded by giving the State concerned an opportunity to submit its observations. Where the Member State fails to take the necessary steps or measures to comply with the Court judgment within a time limit specified by the Commission, the latter may bring the case before the Court. If the Commission does decide to do this, it is required to "specify the amount of the lump sum or penalty payment[179] to be paid by the Member State concerned which it considers appropriate in the circumstances".[180] Given this obligation it has been necessary for the Commission to publicise the method which it uses to calculate penalties.[181] Essentially this involves a standard sum (€600 per day[182]) which is then multiplied by two coefficients relating to the seriousness and duration of the infringement. The sum of this calculation is then itself multiplied by a factor based on the State's GDP and the number of votes which it has in the Council. The purpose of this is to enable the "Member State's ability to pay to be reflected while keeping the variation between Member States within a reasonable range".[183]

Commission v Greece

It is noteworthy that in the years since provision has been made for the Court to impose fines under Article 228, several of the limited number of cases heard by the Court have involved infringements of Community environmental law and subsequent failures to comply with a Court ruling to that effect. Thus in *Commission v Greece*,[184] the Commission sought to enforce an earlier European Court ruling[185] in which it had been held that the Greek government had failed to comply with various obligations under Directives 75/442/EEC and 78/319 EEC. As a preliminary to addressing the substantive issues, the Greek government argued that the action was inadmissible on the ground that the provisions empowering the European Court to impose a penalty payment or lump sum had entered into force after the initiation of the infringement procedure against it. Although the Greek government acknowledged that a fine related to future rather than past non-compliance, it contended that a fine did have retrospective ele-

1–052

---

[179] In effect a payment of a specified sum of money for each day or other period of time (perhaps even annually) which passes without the violation having been remedied.
[180] art.228(2), subparagraph 2.
[181] See [1997] OJ C63/2 and "Commission Communication on the application of Article 228", SEC (2005) 1658.
[182] The 1997 Communication had set the standard sum at €500 per day.
[183] See Case C-387/97 *Commission v Greece* [2000] E.C.R. I-5047 (discussed below).
[184] Case C-387/97 [2000] E.C.R. I-5047. Hartley has noted that this was the first case which was brought before the European Court of Justice under what is now Article 228 (it was then Article 171): see *The Foundations of European Community Law*, p.318.
[185] Case C-45/91 *Commission v Greece* [1992] E.C.R. I-2509.

ments. The European Court of Justice rejected the plea. In its judgment, the action was admissible because all of the stages of the pre-litigation procedure, including the letter of formal notice sent to the Greek government by the Commission, had occurred after the relevant amendments to what was then Article 171 of the Rome Treaty had entered into force.

With regard to the substance of the case, the Greek government accepted that solid waste, in particular household refuse, was still being tipped into one of its rivers contrary to the obligation imposed by Article 4 of Directive 75/442/EEC to dispose of waste without endangering human health or harming the environment. In its defence, it contended that local opposition had delayed the establishment of a mechanical recycling and composting plant and a landfill site which collectively would have remedied the situation. The European Court of Justice rejected this argument. In its judgment, it was:

"settled case-law that a Member State may not plead internal circumstances, such as difficulties of implementation which emerge at the stage when a Community measure is put into effect, to justify a failure to comply with obligations and time-limits laid down by Community law".[186]

Accordingly, the Greek government was held not to have complied with the judgment in Case C-45/91 in so much as it continued to fail to fulfil its obligation under Article 4 of Directive 75/442/EEC.

The second substantive charge leveled at the Greek government by the Commission was that it continued to allow the tipping of toxic and dangerous wastes into the same river contrary to the obligation imposed by Article 5 of Directive 78/319 EEC. In its defence, the Geek government asserted that such a practice no longer took place. Given that there was a dispute of fact between the parties, the European Court made it clear that the onus was on the Commission to provide the necessary information to allow the Court to determine the extent to which a Member State had failed to comply with a judgment of the Court.[187] Since no such information was available, it had not been proved that the Greek government continued to fail to comply with its obligations under Article 5 of Directive 78/319 EEC.

1–053   The third claim advanced by the Commission was that the Greek government had failed to comply with its obligation under Article 6 of Directive 75/442/EEC to draw up waste disposal plans, and its obligation under Article 12 of Directive 78/319 to draw up, and keep up to date, plans for the disposal of toxic waste and dangerous waste. The European Court of Justice accepted that this claim was made out. In its judgment:

[186] para.70.
[187] para.73.

"contrary to the claims of the Greek government, legislation or specific measures amounting only to a series of ad hoc normative interventions that are incapable of constituting an organised and coordinated system for the disposal of waste and toxic and dangerous waste cannot be regarded as plans which the Member States are required to adopt under Article 6 of Directive 75/442 and Article 12 of Directive 78/319".[188]

Having found against the Greek government on two out of the three substantive issues raised by the case, it was necessary for the European Court to determine an appropriate penalty payment. In doing so, it recognised the importance of the Commission's three criteria, the seriousness of the infringement, its duration and the deterrent effect of a penalty, to that calculation. It was the view of the European Court that these guidelines "help to ensure that [the Commission] acts in a manner which is transparent, foreseeable and consistent with legal certainty".[189] Accordingly, given that the breaches had been serious and their duration "considerable", the Court imposed a penalty payment of €20,000 for each day of delay in implementing the measures necessary to comply with the judgment in Case C-45/91.[190]

Commission v Spain

In *Commission v Spain*,[191] the Commission sought a declaration that by not   **1–054** taking the necessary measures to ensure that the quality of its inshore bathing waters conformed to the limit values set out in Article 3 of the Bathing Waters Directive,[192] Spain had failed to comply with its obligation to do so as required by Article 4 of the Directive, and that in not complying with the ruling of the European Court of Justice to that effect in *Commission v Spain*,[193] it was therefore in breach of Article 228 of the Rome Treaty. The Commission also sought an order that Spain pay the sum of €45,600 per day for each day on which there was further delay in complying with the Court's earlier ruling. It was argued on behalf of Spain that the action ought to be dismissed on the ground that the Commission had not given it sufficient time[194] before concluding that the earlier ruling had not been complied with. In relation to the Commission's determination of the

---

[188] para.76.
[189] para.87.
[190] The penalty payment was to take effect from the date of delivery of judgment in the present case until the date on which it could finally be said that the earlier judgment had been complied with. In other words, the penalty was to act as a punishment for a continuing failure to comply with the earlier judgment rather than as a punishment for past non-compliance.
[191] Case C-278/01 [2003] E.C.R. I-14141.
[192] Directive 76/160/EEC.
[193] Case C-92/96 [1998] E.C.R. I-505.
[194] Spain had actually been given from February 12, 1998 (the date of the judgment in the original case) until September 27, 2000 (the date of expiry of the period laid down in the reasoned opinion issued pursuant to Article 228) to fully comply with the judgment.

penalty payment, Spain argued that a daily penalty payment was an inappropriate mechanism for achieving compliance with the earlier ruling and that an annual payment to be paid when the results for each bathing water season were available was to be preferred.

In giving judgment, the Court noted in relation to the first of these arguments that "Article 228 EC does not specify the period within which the judgment must be complied with". However, in accordance with the "settled case-law",[195] it considered that "the importance of immediate and uniform application of Community law means that the process of compliance must be initiated at once and completed as soon as possible".[196] On the facts,[197] the Court concluded that a sufficient period of time had been given to Spain to comply with the earlier ruling. Accordingly, it held that Spain had not taken all the measures necessary to comply with the judgment in *Commission v Spain* and that it had therefore failed to fulfil its obligations under Article 228. With regard to the penalty proposed by the Commission, the Court pointed out that "the Commission's suggestions cannot bind the Court and merely constitute a useful point of reference".[198] It is clear, therefore, that the fixing of a penalty payment or lump sum pursuant to Article 228 is a matter for the discretion of the European Court of Justice. In exercising that discretion, the Court considered in the present case that any penalty imposed must be "appropriate to the circumstances and proportionate to both the breach that has been found and to the ability to pay of the Member State concerned".[199] Applying that approach, the Court accepted Spain's argument that an annual as opposed to a daily penalty was more appropriate. It did so on the basis that determining whether or not an infringement of the Directive's terms had been brought to an end could only take place annually, following the submission by the Member State of the annual report on the implementation of the Directive as required by Article 13 of the Directive itself. With regard to the calculation of quantum of the annual penalty payment to be imposed on Spain, the Court accepted the Commission's method as set out in its Communication.[200] It did, however, adjust downwards the

---

[195] See Case 131/84 *Commission v Italy* [1985] E.C.R. 3531, Case 169/87 *Commission v France* [1988] E.C.R. 4093, and Case C-334/94 *Commission v France* [1996] E.C.R. I-1307 as referred to by the European Court of Justice in Case C-387/97 *Commission v Greece* [2000] E.C.R. I-5047, at para.82.

[196] [2003] E.C.R. I-14141, at para.27.

[197] It was common ground that inshore bathing water in Spain had not been brought into conformity with the mandatory values set out in the Bathing Waters Directive at the time of the Article 228 proceedings. The Court was of the view that since there had been "three bathing seasons between the delivery of the judgment in *Commission v Spain* and expiry of the time-limit laid down in the reasoned opinion in this case", it followed that Spain had received a reasonable time to comply with the Court's judgment: at para.30. This was the case even if it was accepted that compliance with the judgment called for "complex and long-term operations" as the Spanish government claimed.

[198] para.41.

[199] ibid.

[200] 96/C 242/07 (August 21, 1996).

value ascribed to the coefficient relating to the duration of the infringement on the basis that the Commission's suggestion had been "too harsh". The end result was that the amount of the penalty payment was fixed at €624,150 per year and per 1 per cent of bathing areas which do not in the future conform to the limit values in the Directive.

Commission v France

An even more recent case, *Commission v France*,[201] also merits considera- **1–055** tion in the present context. The proceedings arose out of the French government's failure to comply with various European Regulations relating to fishing conservation measures[202] and a European Court decision to that effect.[203] There is no need to rehearse the details of the case, but several aspects of the proceedings and the outcome are worthy of comment. The first of these concerns the fact that prior to the Court hearing, the Commission had issued not one but two reasoned opinions, in which it was stated that it was of the view that the French government had failed to comply with the earlier ruling. Although the European Court did not itself comment adversely upon the issue of what it termed a "supplementary reasoned opinion",[204] one commentator has pointed out that the practice is "procedurally unnecessary, and should be avoided as it causes further delays".[205] Article 228 merely refers to the need for the Commission to issue a reasoned opinion. However, since it does not preclude the issue of more than one reasoned opinion, the Commission is not acting improperly if it chooses to follow this course. Where it does do so, as in the instant case, it inevitably lengthens the proceedings. Thus there was a gap of more than four years between the issue of the first and the second reasoned opinions.

A second point to note about the case concerns the fact that the Commission was able to use its own inspectors who visited various French ports and obtained evidence that, for example, undersized fish were being offered for sale in breach of European law, in order to prove its case against the French government. As was noted previously, the Commission lacks corresponding inspection powers in the environmental field. It has been suggested that although the Member States are unlikely to agree to direct inspection powers being conferred on the Commission in the environmental context, a compromise solution would be for such powers to become available where a Member State has been found to be in breach of its obligations by a European Court judgment.[206]

---

[201] Case C-304/02 [2005] E.C.R. I-6263.
[202] See, e.g. Council Regulations 2057/82, 2241/87 and 2847/93.
[203] Case C-64/88 *Commission v France* [1991] E.C.R. I-2727.
[204] [2005] E.C.R. I-6263, at para.18.
[205] See Wennarås, *The Enforcement of EC Environmental Law*, p.275.
[206] See a comment on Case C-304/02 *Commission v France* by Macrory in ENDS Report (2005) 367 at pp.50–51.

The third point to emerge from *Commission v France* relates to the question whether Article 228 empowers the European Court to impose a lump sum penalty in addition to or as an alternative to a penalty payment for a failure to comply with a previous judgment. The possibility of imposing both forms of penalty in respect of the same failure divided those who made submissions to the Court. The Commission and a number of national governments[207] took the view that the two forms of penalty measure were complementary in that they were each striving to achieve a deterrent effect. Accordingly it was contended that:

"a combination of those measures should be regarded as one and the same means of achieving the objective laid down by Article 228 EC, that is to say not only to induce the Member State concerned to comply with the initial judgment but also, from a wider viewpoint, to reduce the possibility of similar infringements being committed again".[208]

Various other states which included France, Germany, Spain and Italy took a contrary view. They argued that the use of the word "or" in Article 228(2) bore a disjunctive meaning so that either a lump sum or a penalty payment could be imposed, but not both. It was also contended that the imposition of more than one financial penalty was contrary to the principle of the same conduct not being punished twice, and that it would compromise equal treatment between Member States because it had not been considered in the earlier cases of *Greece v Commission* and *Commission v Spain*.[209]

1–056 In the judgment of the European Court, both forms of penalty payment pursue the objective of inducing a defaulting Member State to comply with a judgment confirming a breach of its European obligations. The complementary nature of the measures was explained as follows:

"While the imposition of a penalty payment seems particularly suited to inducing a Member State to put an end as soon as possible to a breach of obligations which, in the absence of such a measure, would tend to persist, the imposition of a lump sum is based more on assessment of the effects on public and private interests of the failure of the Member State concerned to comply with its obligations, in particular where the breach has persisted for a long period since the judgment which initially established it".[210]

Thus the Court was of the opinion that recourse to both types of penalty payment in respect of the same breach of obligations was not precluded by Article 228(2). Such a conclusion could be supported by according the word "or" in that Article a cumulative meaning. The Court rejected the

---

[207] These included the Danish, Dutch and UK governments.
[208] [2005] E.C.R. I-6263, at para.77.
[209] See above.
[210] [2005] E.C.R. I-6263, at para.81.

argument that imposing both types of penalty would amount to punishing the same conduct twice by pointing out that each penalty has its own function as is evident from the passage quoted above. Moreover, it was of the view that "the fact that both measures were not imposed in the cases decided previously cannot in itself constitute an obstacle to the imposition of both in a subsequent case, if, having regard to the nature, seriousness and persistence of the breach of obligations established, that appears appropriate".[211] Article 228(2) provides for what the Court termed a "special judicial procedure" which unlike civil proceedings is not intended to compensate for damage caused by a Member State, but is instead intended to place the state under "economic pressure" to put an end to its breach of obligations.

The final point to note about the decision in *Commission v France* relates to the quantum of financial penalties imposed by the Court. With regard to the penalty payment, the Court accepted the Commission's suggestion that the sum be calculated by multiplying the basic amount (€500) by a coefficient of 10 (on a scale of 1 to 20) for the seriousness of the infringement, by a coefficient of 3 on a scale of 1 to 30 for the duration of the infringement, and by a coefficient of 21.1 (to reflect France's GDP and its number of votes in the Council). In rejecting French arguments that the coefficient of 10 for the seriousness of the infringement was too high, the Court observed that "failure to comply with the technical measures of conservation prescribed by the common policy, in particular the requirements regarding the minimum size of fish ... jeopardises pursuit of the fundamental objective of common fisheries policy".[212] Thus the Court imposed a penalty payment of €57,761,250[213] on France for each complete period of six months from the delivery of its judgment throughout which the judgment in Case C-64/88 had still not been fully complied with. A lump sum payment was considered to be "essential" given that the breach of France's fishery conservation obligations had persisted for so long. Thus the Court arrived at a figure of €20,000,000 without explaining how it had been calculated.[214]

---

[211] para.86.

[212] para.105.

[213] This was calculated by multiplying the Commission's suggested daily penalty payment of €316,500 by 182.5 to reflect a half-yearly payment.

[214] Since the judgment in the case the Commission has published its "Communication on the Application of Article 228" SEC (2005) 1658, which contains calculation methods relating to lump sums as well as to penalty payments. It should not be forgotten, however, that it is ultimately for the Court to decide the appropriate level of financial penalty to impose under Article 228.

Article 228 in practice

1–057   The principal aim of the penalty payment provided for in Article 228 is to ensure that Member States remedy their breach of obligations as soon as possible.[215] It is perhaps significant that the first case brought under this new procedure, *Commission v Greece*, was an environmental pollution case. It should be noted, however, that "the Commission has been sparing in the use of its power to bring applications before the Court under the Article 228 procedure".[216] Thus between 1992 and 2006, it would appear that the Commission brought only six cases (including those referred to above) under Article 228 and its predecessor, Article 171.[217] Also, it should be noted that the procedure under Article 228 takes a very long time to complete. In the six cases referred to, the time span between the formal opening of the Article 226 procedure (sending the letter of formal notice) and the delivery of the Court's judgment under Article 228 was, as Krämer has noted, 109, 106, 175, 120, 134 and 170 months. Since on average this amounts to "119 months or almost ten years",[218] there is a danger that delay is likely to blunt the deterrent effect of the proceedings. That deterrent effect may be further blunted if, following the Court's ruling, the Member State is not actually obliged to pay the penalty payment imposed.[219]

General Principles of Environmental Law

The integration principle

1–058   Article 6 of the Rome Treaty states as follows:

"Environmental protection requirements must be integrated into the definition and implementation of the Community policies and activities referred to in Article 3, in particular with a view to promoting sustainable development".

---

[215] See Case C-387/97 *Commission v Greece* [2000] E.C.R. I-5047, at para.90.
[216] Hartley, *The Foundations of European Community Law*, p.318.
[217] See Krämer, (2006) 18 J.Env.L. 407 at 413.
[218] ibid.
[219] Krämer draws attention to the fact that following the decision in Case C-278/01 *Commission v Spain* [2003] E.C.R. I-14141 (discussed above), the Spanish government did not pay anything after the Commission had filed the case due to "a gross legal misrepresentation" concerning the requirements of the Bathing Waters Directive 76/160/EEC. In effect, the Commission interpreted the Directive's requirement that 95 per cent of the bathing water measurements sampled comply with the values laid down in the Directive to apply to all Spanish inland bathing waters when in fact, the requirement applied to each individual bathing water. In other words, the Commission conflated individual bathing water compliance with overall compliance which is not in fact the same thing. As Krämer rightly points out, this interpretation reflects neither the wording of the Directive nor the decision of the Court: see (2006) 18 J.Env.L. 407 at 412.

The antecedents of the integration principle are to be found in the Community Environmental Action Programmes and earlier provisions of the Rome Treaty. Thus, for example, the First Action programme recognised that:

"the activities of the Communities in the different sectors in which they operate (agricultural policy, social policy, regional policy, industrial policy, energy policy, etc) must take account of concern for the protection and improvement of the environment. Furthermore, such concerns must be taken into consideration in the elaboration and implementation of these policies".[220]

Eventually the integration principle was reflected in primary legislation as a result of the Single European Act. Thus Article 130r of the Rome Treaty provided that "environmental protection requirements shall be a component of the Community's other policies". Although this was a significant development, it might be argued that the brevity of this statement of fact coupled with its inclusion in that part of the Treaty which specifically related to the environment had the tendency to understate the importance of the principle. The Maastricht Treaty sought to address the first of these shortcomings by further elaborating on the principle,[221] and the Amsterdam Treaty dealt with the other matter by transferring the principle to what is now Article 6.

Importance and logic

The significance of the integration principle cannot be overstated. Its **1–059** emergence represents an important landmark in the development of an environmental policy at Community level. From its initially humble origins, the principle now stands alone as a very clear and prominent reminder to Community policy makers that in making and framing their policies, proper regard must be had to environmental considerations.[222] It calls for, in the words of Krämer, "a continuous 'greening' of all Community policies".[223] However, as Krämer also points out, Article 6 does not go so far as to allow environmental requirements to prevail over other requirements. Rather, "the different objectives of the EC Treaty rank at the same level and the policy must endeavour to achieve all of them".[224]

---

[220] [1973] OJ C112, p.11.
[221] Post-Maastricht the reformulated integration principle was expressed thus: "Environmental protection requirements must be integrated into the definition and implementation of other Community policies".
[222] Jans makes the point that Article 6 "is worded more forcefully" than the principle as originally introduced by the Single European Act: see J.H. Jans, *European Environmental Law*, 2nd edition (Europa Law Publishing: 2000) p.17.
[223] Krämer, *EC Environmental Law*, para.1–25, p.21.
[224] ibid.

The Community "policies and activities" to which the integration principle applies are those referred to in Article 3 of the Treaty. They include: a common commercial policy; common agriculture and fisheries policies; a common transport policy; a system ensuring that competition in the internal market is not distorted; and measures in the spheres of energy, civil protection and tourism.[225]

There seems to be a measure of consensus amongst commentators as to what "environmental protection requirements" are for the purposes of Article 6. Thus both Krämer and Jans argue that this phrase is wide enough to include the environmental policy objectives specified in Article 174(1) and environmental principles such as the precautionary principle and the preventive action principle expressly referred to in Article 174(2).[226]

1–060   The inescapable logic of the integration principle cannot be denied. It is intuitively right for "environmental protection requirements" to be taken into account when formulating other policies such as transport or agriculture which patently have the potential to cause significant damage to the environment if they are allowed to develop unchecked by environmental considerations. Article 6 also serves to overcome what Krämer has referred to as the "artificiality" which arises where Community policies in different sectors are regarded as isolated initiatives rather than as a part of a more coherent whole. Where Community action cuts across several sectors, *e.g.* pollution-abatement measures for cars, Krämer rightly points out that "it seems rather old-fashioned to classify a specific measure as belonging to a specific policy".[227] The integration principle lessens the need to make such distinctions.

The precautionary principle

1–061   Article 174(2) of the Rome Treaty declares that Community policy on the environment shall be "based on the precautionary principle"[228] in addition to various other principles such as the "polluter should pay".[229] Despite the undoubted importance of the principle, its precise origins are not entirely clear.[230] It is also worth noting that the Rome Treaty makes no

---

[225] Article 3 actually consists of 21 paragraphs.

[226] See Krämer, *EC Environmental Law*, para.1–26, p.22, and Jans, *European Environmental Law*, p.18.

[227] Krämer, *EC Environmental Law*, para.1–26, p.22.

[228] Reference to the "precautionary principle" was inserted into the Rome Treaty in 1993 as a consequence of an amendment made by the Maastricht Treaty.

[229] The polluter pays principle is discussed below.

[230] It has been suggested, however, that the principle was first articulated as the *Vorsorgeprinzip* in Germany—see, for example, Wegener "Principles into Practice—The German Case", Chapter 7 in *Principles of European Environmental Law*, (Groningen: Europa Law Publishing, 2004), edited by R. Macrory, p.103.

attempt to define what is meant by the "precautionary principle".[231] In the absence of a Treaty definition it is therefore necessary to have regard to the views of the European Commission, the European Court of Justice and the domestic courts on the meaning and content of the principle. First, however, regard may be had to the *Rio Declaration on Environment and Development* on the basis that Principle 15 of the *Declaration* states:

"[W]here there are threats of serious or irreversible damage, lack of full scientific certainty shall not be used as a reason for postponing cost-effective measures to prevent environmental degradation".[232]

Since these are not the words of a statute, we should perhaps refrain from analyzing them too closely. Nevertheless, the essence of the precautionary principle which emerges from this often quoted definition is that it may be legitimate to take action in order to prevent environmental harm from occurring even where science has yet to establish a direct causal link between the activity in question and the relevant harm. Rather than waiting until that link been conclusively established, the precautionary principle justifies taking action at an earlier stage in the interests of environmental protection. Patently, therefore, the precautionary principle operates in the field of scientific uncertainty where the existence or magnitude of a risk to the environment of carrying out or not carrying out a particular activity is yet to be conclusively determined. The *Rio Declaration* precautionary principle is not without limits. It would only apply in the event of a threat of "serious or irreversible damage". Thus the prospect of less serious or relatively minor environmental damage would not fall within the scope of the principle and hence would not justify a precautionary approach. Also, it is limited to requiring the taking of "cost-effective measures to prevent environmental degradation". In other words, measures whose benefits are outweighed by their costs would not need to be taken under this formulation of the principle. It is because of these limits that the *Rio Declaration* definition tends to be classified as propounding a "weak" version of the precautionary principle. A stronger version of the principle would have little regard for cost-benefit analysis. Instead, those who wished to undertake a particular activity or give effect to a policy would need to be able to demonstrate that it was safe to do so. In short, the burden of proof would be upon them to show that the available scientific evidence supported their intentions. The difficulty with this version is, however, that it places a great deal of emphasis upon innovation only taking place where there is a complete absence of risk to the environment. It is highly unlikely that this will be capable of being proved since in the words of the European Commission's *Communication on the Precautionary Principle*, zero risk is

---

[231] It has been suggested that the lack of a definition arguably reflects the "inherent ambiguity" as to the meaning and application of the principle: see Stokes "Liberalising the Threshold of Precaution" (2005) 7 *Environmental Law Review* 206 at 211.

[232] The *Declaration* may be accessed at *http://www.un.org/esa/sustdev/documents/docs.htm.*

"something which rarely exists".[233] Accordingly, scientific uncertainty would act as a bar on innovation and potentially beneficial activities would not be pursued.[234]

Pfizer Animal Health SA v Council

1–062 There have been a number of judicial decisions on the precautionary principle at the European level.[235] In *Pfizer Animal Health SA v Council*,[236] the Court of First Instance was faced with a challenge to the lawfulness of EC Regulation 2821/98 which placed a ban on the use of a number of antibiotics as additives in animal feedstuffs.[237] The ban had been imposed on the ground that there was a risk that the resistance to these antibiotics which animals might accordingly develop could be transmitted to humans once the animals entered the food chain. Pfizer was the sole manufacturer of one of the banned antibiotics, virginiamycin. It was their contention that the Community institutions had been wrong to take the view that the use of virginiamycin as a growth promoter constituted a risk to human health and that preventive measures should be taken.[238] In the opinion of Pfizer, the available scientific data did not establish a link between the use of virginiamycin as an additive and the development of streptogramin resistance in humans. They argued for an application of the precautionary principle whereby the Community institutions "must show that the risk, although it has not actually become a reality, is nevertheless probable".[239]

In delivering its judgment, the Court of First Instance commented that:

"where there is scientific uncertainty as to the existence or extent of risks to human health, the Community institutions may, by reason of the

---

[233] COM (2000) 1 final, p.17. This Communication informs interested parties of the manner in which the Commission applies or intends to apply the precautionary principle. It is likely to be invoked: "where scientific information is insufficient, inconclusive, or uncertain and where there are indications that the possible effects on the environment, or human, animal or plant health may be potentially dangerous and inconsistent with the chosen level of protection" (at para.1.). It should be noted, however, that in Case T-13/99 *Pfizer Animal Health SA v Council* [2002] E.C.R. II-3305, the Court of First Instance rejected the argument that the contested regulation was unlawful because it was inconsistent with the Communication. In the Court's judgment, since the Communication's publication post-dated that of the regulation by more than a year, it was incapable of operating as a self-imposed limitation on the discretion of the Community institutions: see paras 118–122.

[234] For a more sustained critique of the "strong" version of the precautionary principle, see Sunstein "Beyond the Precautionary Principle" (2003) 151 *University of Pennsylvania Law Review* 1003.

[235] See, for example, Case T70/99 *Alpharma Inc v Council* [2002] E.C.R. II-3495.

[236] Case T-13/99 [2002] E.C.R. II-3305.

[237] The antibiotics in question were growth promoters; they were added to feedstuffs in order to reduce the time that it took animals to reach the desirable weight for slaughter.

[238] It is worth noting in passing that virginiamycin had been in use for some 30 years and that it was used by approximately 50 per cent of farmers in the EU: see [2002] E.C.R. II-3305, at para.466.

[239] para.130.

precautionary principle, take protective measures without having to wait until the reality and seriousness of those risks become fully apparent ...".[240]

Of greater significance, however, were the Court's comments in relation to when the precautionary principle ought to be applied. Its application will, the Court noted, "by definition coincide with a situation in which there is scientific uncertainty".[241] Where this is the case, the Court was of the view that:

"a risk assessment cannot be required to provide the Community institutions with conclusive scientific evidence of the reality of the risk and the seriousness of the potential adverse effects were that risk to become a reality ...".[242]

In other words, the threshold for applying the precautionary principle must not be placed too high. Conversely, the Court expressed the view that "a preventative measure cannot properly be based on a purely hypothetical approach to the risk, founded on mere conjecture which has not been scientifically verified".[243] A middle course between the need for "conclusive scientific evidence" on the one hand and a "purely hypothetical approach" on the other was expressed by the Court as follows:

"... a preventive measure may be taken only if the risk, although the reality and extent thereof have not been fully demonstrated by conclusive scientific evidence, appears nevertheless to be adequately backed up by the scientific data available at the time when the measure was taken".[244]

It has previously been noted that a cost-benefit analysis is a central feature of a weak conception of the precautionary principle. In *Pfizer* it was contended by the company that the Community institutions had failed to carry out a cost/benefit analysis and that had they done so, they would have arrived at a less onerous solution which would have achieved the objective of protecting human health without requiring virginiamycin to be banned. In other words, the ban was a disproportionate response. The Court of First Instance rejected this submission on the facts. It was:

"apparent from the documents before the Court that an assessment of this kind was made in several of the reports by international bodies which had been submitted to the institutions during the procedure culminating in adoption of the contested regulation".[245]

---

[240] para.139.
[241] para.142.
[242] ibid.
[243] para.143.
[244] para.144.
[245] At para.469.

Moreover, in response to Pfizer's claims that the Community institutions made errors when weighing up the various options, the Court observed that "the legality of the contested regulation could be called in question only if the institutions had made a manifest error of assessment in deciding upon their policy".[246] In the judgment of the Court, public health "must take precedence over economic considerations".[247] Although the Court accepted that the existence of alternatives to the use of antibiotics may entail an alteration in farming methods and hence the possibility of higher production costs and higher meat prices, that of itself did not suggest that the policy choice made by the institutions had been unreasonable.

The importance of Pfizer

1–063 The decision in *Pfizer* is important in that it provides some guidance as to what is meant by the precautionary principle as a matter of EU law.[248] It can be argued that the meaning favoured by the Court leans more in the direction of the "strong" rather than the "weak" conception of the principle. However, whilst the Court of First Instance gave some indication as to the limits or boundaries of the precautionary principle, it was less forthcoming as to the circumstances in which the principle may be triggered. In other words, it did not clarify what level of risk above a zero level would entitle EU institutions to adopt a precautionary approach. Accordingly, the institutions would seem to have a wide discretion available to them in matters of risk assessment and management having regard to the particular circumstances of the case.

Waddenzee

1–064 In a more recent case, *Waddenzee*,[249] where two environmental NGOs challenged the issuing of licences by a Dutch Secretary of State to carry out mechanical cockle-fishing at a site protected under the Birds Directive[250] and the Habitats Directive,[251] the national court referred a number of questions to the European Court of Justice for a preliminary ruling pur-

---

[246] At para.470.

[247] ibid.

[248] Douma comments that *Pfizer* was "the first judgment in which the interpretation and correct application of the precautionary principle are extensively discussed by the Luxembourg judiciary": see "Fleshing out the Precautionary Principle by the Court of First Instance" (2003) 15 J.Env.L. 372 at 394. It should not be forgotten, however, that the precautionary principle also applies in national as well as supra-national jurisdictions, e.g. Germany, France and Australia.

[249] Case C-127/02 [2004] E.C.R. I-7405. The full case name is *Landelijke Vereniging tot Behoud van de Waddenzee and Nederlandse Vereniging tot Bescheraning van Vogels v Staatssecretaris van Landbouw, Natuurbeheer en Visserij*. It has been shortened in the text for ease of reference.

[250] Directive 79/409/EEC.

[251] Directive 92/43/EEC.

suant to Article 234 of the Rome Treaty. One such question[252] required the Court to determine when an "appropriate assessment" under Article 6(3) of the Habitats Directive ought to be carried out. Having regard to the wording of the Article,[253] the European Court of Justice noted that the requirement of an "appropriate assessment" was conditional upon the plan or project being *likely* to have a significant effect on the site. Thus the trigger for the environmental protection mechanism provided for in Article 6(3) was not that the plan or project would definitely have significant effects, but rather, it followed from "the mere probability that such an effect attached to that plan or project".[254] In a passage that has been much quoted since, the European Court of Justice stated that pursuant to Article 6(3):

> "... the competent national authorities, taking account of the conclusions of the appropriate assessment of the implications of mechanical cockle fishing for the site concerned, in the light of the site's conservation objectives, are to authorise such activity only if they have made certain that it will not adversely affect the integrity of that site. That is the case where no reasonable scientific doubt remains as to absence of such effects ...".[255]

The decision in *Waddenzee* has been heralded as evidence of a willingness on the part of the European Court of Justice to adopt an increasingly liberal approach to determining the threshold for applying the precautionary principle. By this it is meant that the courts are "increasingly willing to extend its scope of application, broadening the meaning of 'uncertainty' in relation to which the precautionary principle operates".[256]

R v Secretary of State for Trade and Industry, Ex p Duddridge

An opportunity for the English courts to consider the precautionary principle presented itself in *R v Secretary of State for Trade and Industry, Ex p Duddridge*.[257] Section 3(3) of the Electricity Act 1989 imposed a duty on the Secretary of State to exercise his functions under Part I of the Act in a manner which he considered best calculated to, amongst other things, **1–065**

---

[252] The referral also sought the Court's opinion on, inter alia, whether Article 6(3) of the Habitats Directive had direct effect. The Court concluded that it did.

[253] The first sentence in Article 6(3) provided as follows: "Any plan or project not directly connected with or necessary to the management of the site but likely to have a significant effect thereon, either individually or in combination with other plans or projects, shall be subject to appropriate assessment of its implications for the site in view of the site's conservation objectives".

[254] [2004] E.C.R. I-7405, para.41.

[255] para.59.

[256] See Stokes "Liberalising the Threshold of Precaution" (2005) 7 *Environmental Law Review* 206 at 210.

[257] [1995] Env. L.R. 151 (DC), [1996] Env. L.R. 325 (CA).

protect the public from dangers arising from the generation, transmission or supply of electricity. By virtue of section 29(1) of the Act, he had the power to make regulations in order to protect the public from such dangers as well as from dangers arising from the use of electricity supplied or from the installation, maintenance or use of any electric line or electrical plant. The applicants sought judicial review (on behalf of their children) of the Secretary of State's decision not to issue regulations to the National Grid Company so as to restrict the electromagnetic fields (EMFs) from electric cables which were being laid as part of the national grid. They alleged that the non-ionising radiation which would be emitted from the cables and which would enter their homes and schools, would be at such a level as would or might expose them to the risk of developing childhood leukaemia. In short, the applicants urged the Secretary of Sate to take a "precautionary view" of the risk of damage to health. It was their contention that rather than asking himself whether there was any evidence of a possible risk, the Secretary of State had instead asked himself whether there was evidence that exposure to EMFs did give rise to a risk of childhood leukaemia. On behalf of the applicants it was contended that this was contrary to the precautionary principle which the Secretary of State was obliged to apply as a matter of Community law, or under the then Government's policy as expressed in the White Paper, *This Common Inheritance*,[258] or as a matter of commonsense.[259]

In delivering the leading judgment in the Divisional Court, Smith LJ stressed that "it is not the function of this Court to decide whether there is in fact an increased risk of leukaemia from exposure to high levels of EMFs. Still less is it for the Court to decide whether these applicants will be at any such increased risk".[260] The evidence of the expert witnesses

[258] (1990) Cm 1200. In para.1.15 of the White Paper it was stated: "We must act on the facts and the most accurate interpretation of them, using the best scientific and economic information. That does not mean we must sit back and wait until we have 100% evidence about everything. Where the state of the planet is at stake, the risks can be so high and the costs of corrective action so great, that prevention is better and cheaper than cure. We must analyse the possible benefits and costs both of action and inaction. Where there are significant risks of damage to the environment, the government will be prepared to limit the use of potentially dangerous materials or the spread of potentially dangerous pollutants, even where scientific knowledge is not conclusive, if the balance of likely costs and benefits justifies it. This precautionary principle applies particularly where there are good grounds for judging either that action taken promptly at comparatively low cost may avoid more costly damage later, or that irreversible effects may follow if action is delayed".
[259] In an Australian case heard in the New South Wales Land and Environment Court, *Leatch v National Parks and Wildlife Service and Shoalhaven City Council* 81 LGERA 270, Stein J had stated: "In my opinion the precautionary principle is a statement of commonsense and has already been applied by decision makers in appropriate circumstances prior to the principle being spelt out". Stein J went on to observe that the precautionary principle: ". . . is directed towards the prevention of serious or irreversible harm to the environment in situations of scientific uncertainty. Its premise is that where uncertainty or ignorance exists, concerning the nature or scope of environmental harm (whether this follows from policies, decisions or activities), decision makers should be cautious".
[260] [1995] Env. L.R. 151 at 155.

called by both sides revealed that there was no great difference of opinion between them; it was accepted that there was a possibility of a connection between EMFs and childhood leukaemia but that there was a need for further research. Had the Secretary of State been under a legal obligation to apply the precautionary principle, the circumstances were such that he would have been obliged to apply it in considering whether to issue the regulations sought. Crucially, however, the Divisional Court held that he was under no such legal obligation. With regard to the policy statement in the White Paper,[261] Smith LJ observed:

"If the Government announces a policy which it intends to adopt without being under any obligation to do so, it must be entitled to define the limits of that policy in any way it wishes. If the Government says it will apply a precautionary policy when it perceives a significant risk of harm, it must, in my view, be entitled to apply that threshold for action. The Secretary of State says that he has considered the need for regulations in the light of this policy and has concluded that such are neither necessary nor appropriate. In my judgment, on the basis of the advice he has received, his conclusion that there is no significant risk of developing cancer from exposure to EMFs cannot be impugned as wholly unreasonable or perverse".[262]

Turning to the argument that commonsense obliged the Secretary of State to apply a precautionary approach, Smith LJ had little hesitation in rejecting such a "startling proposition". The argument that the Secretary of State was under a duty imposed by Community law to apply the precautionary principle received a fuller consideration. It required the Divisional Court to determine into which category Article 130r of the Rome Treaty fell[263]: those Articles which have direct effect and which confer rights on citizens of the Member States; those Articles which impose an immediate duty of compliance on Member States; or those Articles which impose no obligation in their own right but which may do so after the Community acting through its institutions has promulgated a measure which does impose binding obligations on Member States. Having set out the substance of Articles 130r, 130s and 130t, Smith LJ observed:

---

[261] Reference to the precautionary principle has also appeared in later UK policy documents, most notably in *Better Quality of Life: A Strategy for Sustainable Development* (HMSO 1999). Here it was stated that: "The Precautionary principle means that it is not acceptable just to say we can't be sure that serious damage will happen, so we'll do nothing to prevent it. Precaution is not just relevant to environmental damage—for example, chemicals which may affect wildlife may also affect human health. At the same time, precautionary action must be based on objective assessment of the costs and benefits of action. The principle does not mean that we only permit activities if we are sure that serious harm will not arise, or there is proof that the benefits outweigh all possible risks. That would severely hinder progress towards improvements in the quality of life" (at 4.1).

[262] [1995] Env. L.R. 151 at 164.

[263] The case pre-dates the revisions made to the Rome Treaty by the Maastricht Treaty and the renumbering of the Articles by the Amsterdam Treaty.

"... if the applicant's submission be right that Article 130r imposes an immediate obligation upon Member States, it would follow that since November 1993, Secretaries of State in several government departments and their counterparts in every other country within the Community, have been obliged to apply the precautionary principle to a wide range of legislation. That would entail the need to conduct cost-benefit analyses in respect of every known risk of damage to the environment and every known risk to human health from the environment. They would then be obliged to legislate in every case in which the cost-benefit analysis showed that action would be reasonable. All this would be obligatory as a matter of national initiative, in the absence of any definition of the precautionary principle and before any formulation of a coherent policy on the environment. I find quite remarkable the proposition that each state should be obliged to act alone on the basis of so general a statement of objectives and considerations".[264]

It was thus clear from the wording of the relevant Articles that Article 130r fell into the third category of Article in that it laid down principles upon which future Community environmental policy would be based; it did not impose obligations on Member States to act in a particular way and therefore did not apply in relation to the Secretary of State's refusal to issue the regulations sought. The Divisional Court therefore dismissed the application. In a briefer judgment, the Court of Appeal upheld that ruling.[265] In the words of Sir Iain Glidewell:

"... Article 130r sets out the aims which the Community policy shall be designed to achieve and the principles to which such a policy should adhere. The Article does not of itself place any obligation on any organ of a national government. The repeated use of the future tense makes it clear that the Article itself does not contain or create such a policy".[266]

R (on the application of Amvac Chemical UK Ltd) v Secretary of State for Environment, Food and Rural Affairs

1–066   In the more recent case of *R (on the application of Amvac Chemical UK Ltd) v Secretary of State for Environment, Food and Rural Affairs*,[267] the claimant company challenged a decision to suspend regulatory approvals for dichlorvos, a pesticide with both agricultural and non-agricultural uses,[268] on a number of grounds. The present discussion will, however, be confined to the ground of challenge which related to the precautionary principle. It

[264] [1995] Env. L.R. 151 at 167.
[265] [1996] Env. L.R. 325.
[266] At 333.
[267] [2001] EWHC 1011 (Admin).
[268] The claimant manufactured dichlovos for non-agricultural uses only.

was not the claimant's contention that the defendants were necessarily under a duty to follow the principle. Rather, it was contended that although the defendants purported to follow the principle, they had in fact failed to do so. In order to succeed on this ground, Crane J explained that the claimant needed to establish the following three things:

"First, it must show that mechanisms were in place, as part of the application of the precautionary principle, to carry out an appropriate risk assessment. Secondly, it must show that the Defendants purported to follow the principle and its ancillary mechanisms. Thirdly, it must show that there was a failure to follow such mechanisms".[269]

Having been referred to several UK government policy documents in which the precautionary principle had been discussed, and two English cases in which the principle was considered,[270] Crane J observed:

"I am prepared to accept that on a substantive challenge to a regulatory decision, it may in some fields of regulation be relevant to take into account the precautionary principle and, more important, its limitations. It may be relevant to refer to the principle in a substantive challenge in the field of pesticide approval. However, my very firm conclusion is that there is—at least so far—no settled, specific or identifiable mechanism of risk assessment in the field of pesticide approval that the claimant is entitled to rely on as part of the "precautionary principle", viewed as a separate basis for challenging a decision".[271]

Although Crane J was prepared to accept that in reaching their decision the defendants had not been entitled to ignore either the need to assess any risk or act on a rational basis, he did not consider that they had purported "to apply the precautionary principle as a term of art or any settled, specific or identifiable mechanism or methodology". Since the defendants were not purporting to adopt any particular mechanism, the decision to suspend regulatory approvals for dichlorvos could not be successfully challenged as being contrary to the precautionary principle.

Concluding remarks

The importance of the precautionary principle in relation to environmental 1–067 and public health policy matters is patent. Even if the content of the

---

[269] [2001] EWHC 1011 (Admin) at [68].
[270] The cases were *R v Leicester City Council, Ex p Blackfordby and Boothorpe Action Group Ltd* [2000] JPL 1266, and *R (on the application of Murray) v Derbyshire County Council* (2000), unreported, October 6, 2000. In neither case was the principle accorded a very full consideration. In the former case, this seems to be because in the words of Richards J, the precautionary principle submission had been "briefly advanced and again plucked out of the air in the course of oral argument".
[271] [2001] EWHC 1011 (Admin) at [84].

principle is "nebulous"[272] and its application and impact is case-specific, it does represent an "important foundation of environmental law and risk management".[273] It is not, of course, a panacea. It is, however, "a useful tool for a more systematic response to the problem of scientific uncertainty in environment and health decision-making".[274]

The preventive action principle

1–068   The origins of this principle can be traced to the Community's Environmental Action Programmes. Thus as Krämer has pointed out,[275] the first principle of the First Action Programme[276] stated: "The best environmental policy concerns preventing the creation of pollution or nuisances at source, rather than subsequently trying to counteract their effects". The principle was subsequently referred to in the Second Action Programme, and the Third Action Programme[277] "focused strongly on the prevention principle".[278] Eventually the principle was inserted into the Rome Treaty itself.[279] Accordingly, Article 174(2) provides, inter alia, that Community policy on the environment shall be based on the principle that "preventive action should be taken".

Lack of Treaty definition

1–069   As with the precautionary principle, there is no definition in the Treaty of the preventive principle or what "preventive action" amounts to. Evidently, however, it requires that action is taken at an early stage in respect of the threat of environmental pollution. In other words, the principle requires that action is taken so as to prevent pollution from occurring rather than in order to deal with pollution which has occurred.[280] The preventive principle ought therefore to be a central plank of any meaningful environment policy. Complying with the principle is patently advantageous to the environment. It also makes economic good-sense in that it is likely to be cheaper to spend money on pollution preventing measures at the outset

---

[272] Stallworthy *Understanding Environmental Law*, (London: Sweet & Maxwell, 2008), p.155.
[273] Fisher, "Is the Precautionary Principle Justiciable?" (2001) 13 J.Env.L. 315 at 315.
[274] Segger and Gehring "The WTO and Precaution: Sustainable Development and Implications of the WTO Asbestos Dispute" (2003) 15 J.Env.L. 289 at 292.
[275] See "The Genesis of Environmental Principles", Chapter 3 in *Principles of European Environmental Law*, p.38.
[276] [1973] OJ C112.
[277] In the Third Action Programme it was stated that it was necessary that: "the preventive side of environmental policy be strengthened in the framework of an overall strategy" : see [1983] OJ C46.
[278] See Jans, *European Environmental Law*, p.35.
[279] This was achieved by the Single European Act.
[280] Jans has contended that "put simply", the principle recognises that "prevention is better than cure": see *European Environmental Law*, p.35.

rather than to pay for the costs of remediation once pollution has occurred. Krämer has suggested that the content of the prevention principle lacks independence from that of the precautionary principle. Thus he observes:

"There seems to be no Community action which would be possible under the precautionary principle, but not under the prevention principle—and vice versa. Since both principles are, in practice, almost always used together and there is no definition for either of them in the EC Treaty, the added legal value of one to the other is not visible; therefore, they should be used synonymously".[281]

Practical application

As with other environmental principles, in order to be genuinely effective and meaningful, it is necessary for the preventive principle to be more than a declaratory statement; it needs to be incorporated into the relevant legal frameworks. A number of EC Environmental Directives illustrate the application of the preventive principle.[282] Directive 85/337/EEC,[283] as amended,[284] on the assessment of the effect of certain public and private projects on the environment (the Environmental Impact Assessment Directive) is a good example of a Community law which reflects the preventive principle.[285] Thus in the preamble to the Directive it is stated, inter alia, that: **1-070**

"Whereas the 1973 and 1977 action programmes of the European countries on the environment, as well as the 1983 action programme ... stress that the best environmental policy consists in preventing the creation of pollution or nuisances at source, rather than subsequently trying to counteract their effects; whereas they affirm the need to take effects on the environment into account at the earliest possible stage in all technical planning and decision-making processes".

---

[281] Krämer, *EC Environmental Law*, para.1–31, p.25. This view may be contrasted with that of Jans who argues that: "The prevention principle must not be confused with the precautionary principle, which is in essence more far-reaching ...": see *European Environmental Law*, p.35.

[282] See, for example, Directive 94/62 on packaging and packaging waste.

[283] Moore has identified the Directive as giving rise to "the first direct impact of European Community law on domestic town and country planning law": see V. Moore, *A Practical Approach to Planning Law* 10th edition (Oxford: Oxford University Press, 2007), para.13–01, at p.221.

[284] See Directive 97/11/EC.

[285] Environmental Impact Assessment is discussed in Chapter 9 of this book.

Rectification of environmental damage at source

1–071 The principle that environmental damage ought to be rectified at source was originally set out in the Community's First Environmental Action programme as follows: "The best environmental policy consists in preventing the creation of pollution or nuisances at source, rather than subsequently trying to counteract their effects".[286] It is evident from this that the principle is closely related to the preventive action principle. Despite being articulated, neither the First nor the Second Action Programmes offered much in the way of an explanation of the principle. Krämer considers there "would have been good reason to do so" since the principle was clearly relevant in the context of the debate at the time between the UK and other Member States as to whether emission standards or quality standards was the preferable approach for dealing with discharges to water.[287] In his opinion, the argument in favour of emission standards could have been supported by reference to the need to rectify environmental harm or pollution at source. Subsequent Action Programmes have touched upon the principle without actually referring to it by name.[288]

Aspirational rather than practical

1–072 There has been no definition at the European level as to what "rectification" of environmental damage actually means in practice despite the fact that the principle now appears in Article 174(2) of the Rome Treaty.[289] Krämer has contended that the principle "represents wishful thinking rather than reality".[290] In support of this observation he argues that:

> ". . . to rectify environmental damage from cars—air pollution, land use, noise, traffic congestion, waste generation etc—at source would mean that cars would have to be abolished or at the very least absolute priority be given to public transport, the price of fuel be increased in order to reduce the use of cars, restrictions on the making of cars—maximum fuel consumption, maximum speed and so on—be imposed or other measures taken".[291]

However, as he rightly points out, "this would have implications on production, employment and investment for which no country in the world

---

[286] [1973] OJ C112.
[287] See "The Genesis of Environmental Principles" Chapter 3 in Macrory, *Principles of European Environmental Law*, p.41.
[288] Krämer comments that "the Fourth Action Programme discussed 'source-oriented controls' without mentioning the principle and without making any concrete proposals": ibid.
[289] It was inserted into the Treaty by the Single European Act.
[290] Krämer, *EC Environmental Law*, para.1–32, p.26.
[291] ibid.

seems to be prepared".[292] The rectification of environmental damage at source principle may therefore be regarded as one of the weaker environmental principles in that it articulates an aspiration rather than a firm foundation on which environmental policy can be developed.[293]

The polluter pays principle

On May 26, 1972 the Organisation for Economic Cooperation and Development (OECD) issued a recommendation in which it expressed the polluter pays principle as follows:

> "the polluter should bear the expenses of carrying out the measures decided by public authorities to ensure that the environment is in an acceptable state. In other words, the cost of these measures should be reflected in the cost of goods and services which cause pollution in production and/or consumption. Such measures should not be accompanied by subsidies that would create distortions in international trade and investment".

As with a number of the other environmental principles discussed in this chapter, the genesis of the polluter pays principle at the European level is to be found in the Community Action Programmes. Thus the First Action Programme stated that the "cost of preventing and eliminating nuisances must in principle be borne by the polluter".[294] The enduring nature of the principle is evidenced by the fact that it has been a feature of successive Action Programmes and has also been discussed in Council Recommendations[295] and a Commission Report.[296] Indeed in the current sixth Action Programme, there is a commitment to:

> "... promote the polluter pays principle, through the use of market based instruments, including the use of emissions trading, environmental taxes, charges and subsidies, to internalise the negative as well as the positive impacts on the environment".

1–073

---

[292] ibid.
[293] In an earlier publication Krämer concludes his discussion of the principle with the observation that "overall the rectification principle has not played any significant role in the legislation and practice of EC institutions in the area of environmental policy": see "The Genesis of Environmental Principles", Chapter 3 in Macrory, *Principles of European Environmental Law*, p.43.
[294] See principle 5.
[295] Recommendation of November 7, 1974 [1974] OJ C68, p.1; Recommendation 75/436 of March 3, 1975 [1975] OJ 194, p.1.
[296] Fourth Report on Competition Policy, (1975), No.175.

The polluter pays principle is designed to ensure that the full costs of environmental damage caused by polluting activities are borne exclusively by the polluter.[297] Historically, air, water and (to a degree) land have been treated as free resources that industry has been able to pollute at little or no cost to itself, and thereby pass on to the community, directly or indirectly, costs attributable to its own operations. The polluter pays principle aims to avoid such a misallocation of economic resources by requiring these additional costs of an economic activity to be factored into the accounts of the relevant undertaking. This is sometimes referred to as internalising external costs. If a commercial activity is not viable when required to bear its full costs then, provided that its competitors are subject to the same regime, it should not continue. Additionally, the development of cleaner technologies is encouraged by the application of the principle. Indiscriminate subsidies for waste disposal operations, or even for the installation of pollution abatement equipment, are consequently inconsistent with this. The principle is thus in essence an economic instrument.

Presence in primary and secondary legislation

1–074   The polluter pays principle was inserted into the Rome Treaty by the Single European Act. Thus Article 174(2) provides that Community environmental policy shall be based on a number of principles, including that "the polluter should pay".[298] The principle has also been expressly referred to in a number of secondary laws. Thus, for example, Article 9(1) of the Water Framework Directive[299] provides that:

> "Member States shall take account of the principle of recovery of the costs of water services, including environmental and resource costs, having regard to the economic analysis conducted according to Annex III, and in accordance in particular with the *polluter pays principle*".[300]

A more recent example of the polluter pays principle being given legislative effect is in the Environmental Liability Directive.[301] In addition to being

---

[297] Krämer has commented that the polluter pays principle featured at an early stage in the development of Community environmental policy because the Commission wished to allay any fears that Member States may have had that the development of such a policy at the European level would necessitate an increase in their own individual contributions to the EC budget: see "The Genesis of Environmental Principles", Chapter 3 in Macrory, *Principles of European Environmental Law*, p.43.

[298] Krämer draws attention to the fact that the wording of the principle is expressed differently in the various linguistic versions of the Treaty. Thus, for example, whilst the English text refers to "the polluter should pay", other versions refer to the "polluter pays" and the German version is based on the causation principle. It should be noted that each version of the text is of equal value; no one version enjoys superiority over the others.

[299] Directive 2000/60.

[300] Emphasis added.

[301] Directive 2004/35.

expressly referred to on several occasions in the Directive itself,[302] the pervasive effect of the principle is evidenced by Article 1 which states that: "The purpose of this Directive is to establish a framework of environmental liability based on the 'polluter-pays' principle, to prevent and remedy environmental damage".

Imprecise content

Despite the antiquity and strong ethical foundations of the polluter pays principle, its content is less easy to determine. Proclaiming that "the polluter should pay" is a simple statement which is intuitively fair, but of necessity it requires an investigation into issues such as who is the polluter? For what should they be made to pay? How much should they be made to pay? And so on. This lack of certainty as to the meaning of the principle inevitably leads to misunderstandings. It would be a gross distortion of the principle to regard it as authorising unchecked pollution of the environment provided that the polluter is prepared to pay for the harm caused. Beyond such extremes, however, it is difficult to be more precise.

1–075

R v Secretary of State for the Environment and another, Ex p Standley and Metson

Macrory and Havercroft have contended that "there have been few cases to date before the UK courts where the polluter pays principle has been considered at any length or in any great detail".[303] The most noteworthy case which they identify is *R v Secretary of State for the Environment and another, Ex p Standley and Metson*,[304] where members of two groups of farmers sought to challenge the designation of two Nitrate Vulnerable Zones (NVZs) under the Protection of Water Against Agricultural Pollution (England and Wales) Regulations 1996[305] which had been made in order to give effect to obligations arising under the Nitrates Directive.[306] In designating 68 NVZs under the Regulations, the UK government had

1–076

---

[302] See recitals (2) and (18). In the former it is stated: "The prevention and remedying of environmental damage should be implemented through the furtherance of the *'polluter pays' principle*, as indicated in the Treaty and in line with the principle of sustainable development. The fundamental principle of this Directive should therefore be that an operator whose activity has caused the environmental damage or the imminent threat of such damage is to be held financially liable, in order to induce operators to adopt measures and develop practices to minimise the risks of environmental damage so that their exposure to financial liabilities is reduced" (emphasis added).

[303] See "Environmental Principles in the United Kingdom", Chapter 12 in Macrory, *Principles of European Environmental Law*, p.200.

[304] [1997] Env. L.R. 589.

[305] SI 1996/888.

[306] Directive 91/676/EC.

adopted a three-stage approach which was explained by the Head of the Water Quality Division at the then Department of the Environment as follows:

> "As a first step bodies of water were identified on this basis which were either heavily polluted or showed the clear potential to be heavily polluted by nitrates. Secondly, the known areas of land draining into those waters (and not any areas of land draining into the rivers upstream of those waters) were identified. Thirdly, having regard in particular to the land use and other characteristics of the areas of land and the bodies of water in question, an assessment was made as to whether agricultural sources were making a significant contribution to the levels of pollution detected".[307]

The applicants contended that this approach was flawed. They argued that the correct approach was for the government to first consider the sources of nitrate pollution and then proceed to identify only those waters where it could be said that the maximum levels of nitrate as prescribed by the Directive[308] were exceeded by virtue of agricultural inputs alone. They argued in the alternative that the approach taken by the UK government meant that they were required to bear the costs of nitrate pollution caused by sources other than agriculture and that this was therefore contrary to the polluter pays principle. Since Potts J came to the conclusion that he could not with complete confidence resolve the issue of construction raised by the application, he exercised his discretion under Article 177 of the Rome Treaty (now Article 234) and referred the matter to the European Court of Justice for a preliminary ruling.

As is not infrequently the case, the judgment of the European Court was preceded by an Advocate General's Opinion which was longer than the judgment itself. For present purposes it is sufficient to confine ourselves to what Advocate General Léger had to say specifically about the polluter pays principle. In his opinion, the principle:

> "... must be understood as requiring the person who causes the pollution, and that person alone, to bear not only the costs of remedying pollution ... but also those arising from the implementation of a policy of prevention".[309]

Explained in this way, it is evident that the polluter pays principle may be applied at two different stages: after pollution has occurred where remediation is the primary objective; or in order to prevent pollution from

---

[307] See Case C-293/97 *R v Secretary of State for the Environment & another* [1999] Env. L.R. 801, at para.13 of the judgment of the European Court of Justice.
[308] The limit was 50 mg per litre of water.
[309] Case C-293/97 *R v Secretary of State for the Environment & another* [1999] Env. L.R. 801, at 819.

occurring. Based on this understanding of the principle, the Advocate General concluded that:

"... the Directive must be interpreted as requiring the Member States to impose on farmers only the cost of plant for the reduction or avoidance of the water pollution caused by nitrates for which farmers are responsible, to the exclusion of any other cost. That interpretation therefore complies strictly with the polluter pays principle".[310]

The European Court of Justice was of the opinion that the interpretation argued for by the applicants "would lead to exclusion from the scope of the Directive of numerous cases where agricultural sources make a significant contribution to the pollution, a result which would be contrary to the Directive's spirit and purpose".[311] Accordingly, it accepted that the UK government's approach to giving effect to its obligations under the Nitrates Directive was appropriate in the circumstances.

The European Convention on Human Rights[312]

The European Convention on Human Rights[313] ("the Convention") can   **1–077** be thought of as a special case of international treaty law. In force from 1953, it bound the UK in a strict sense only on the international level. But its distinguishing feature was the creation of an individual right of complaint to the Strasbourg-based supervisory institutions, the European Court of Human Rights (ECtHR) and, down to November 1998, the European Commission of Human Rights (EComHR).[314] Thus the Convention accreted a body of case-law dealing directly with the relationship between citizen and UK State and therefore especially apt to influence UK legal thinking. But it was not until October 2, 2000, the commencement date of the Human Rights Act 1998 (HRA), that the Convention and its surrounding case-law *acquis* became a formal source of UK law.[315]

Like the EU Treaty, the Convention came into being as a text with

---

[310] ibid. at 820.

[311] ibid. at 828.

[312] Articles 2 to 18 of the Convention and Articles 1 to 3 of its First Protocol are appended to this Chapter.

[313] European Convention for the Protection of Human Rights and Fundamental Freedoms, UKTS 70 (1950), Cmd. 8969.

[314] Protocol 11 to the Convention merged the former part-time Court and Commission to form the present full-time Court.

[315] Technically the Convention entered force as part of the legal order in Scotland and Wales a year or so earlier under the provisions of the Scotland Act 1998 and Government of Wales Act 1998 defining the powers of the devolved institutions. For the general judicial approach to the pre-HRA status of the Convention, see (among others) *R. v Secretary of State for the Home Department, ex parte Brind* [1991] 1 A.C. 696; *Middlebrook Mushrooms Ltd v TGWU* [1993] IRLR 232, CA; *Derbyshire County Council v Times Newspapers Ltd* [1993] A.C. 534; *R. v Ministry of Defence, ex parte Smith and others* [1996] 1 Q.B. 517.

apparently nothing to say about environmental issues.[316] But by contrast with the EU regime, the Convention's emergence as a source of environmental law results from judicial rather than legislative intervention. The ECtHR adopts a dynamic approach to interpretation of the Convention, treating it as a "living instrument" moving with the times to reflect contemporary social priorities.[317] Thus the ECtHR has come to accept that "private life" and "home" in Article 8(1) encompass the physical quality of the environment in which one leads one's private life and establishes one's home.[318] "Determination of civil rights and obligations" in Article 6 has gradually been extended beyond traditional judicial proceedings to encompass a wide range of administrative processes including environmental and planning controls, all now required to meet enforceable standards of procedural fairness. Article 2—the right to life—has escaped its confines as a prohibition on use of lethal force by the State, forming the basis of liability for the most serious failures of environmental regulation.[319]

In theory, the idea that the citizen can claim a *right* to a particular standard of environmental protection has far-reaching consequences for UK law. The various legislative frameworks for control of development and environmentally hazardous activities follow a common structure, based on discretionary decision-making by regulatory bodies. Decisions of those bodies impact on a range of stakeholders: the developer/operator; affected third parties; public and non-governmental bodies with an interest in the subject-matter; and the amorphous wider community whose collective interest the system of regulation is meant to serve. The system of discretionary decision-making rarely treats the interests of any particular stakeholder as paramount. Instead, the law dissolves those interests into the melting pot of factors to be assessed and balanced. A traditional public law challenge—even by those most closely affected—cannot succeed unless the claimant clears the high hurdle of showing that the balance has been struck in a wholly irrational way.[320] In contrast, the Convention typically starts from the position that a citizen has a right, and it is for the State to establish that any measure that interferes with the right is not merely a rational but a *justified and proportionate* response to the "legitimate aim" it serves.[321]

1–078   The practical results of the HRA, in the environmental field at least, have been less ground-breaking than many anticipated. A number of early upsets with far-reaching implications were eventually reversed.

---

[316] See above, para.1–012.

[317] *Tyrer v UK* (1978) ser.A no.26.

[318] *Powell and Rayner v UK* (1990) 12 EHRR 355; *López Ostra v Spain* (1994) 20 EHRR 277; *Guerra v Italy* (1998) 26 EHRR 357.

[319] *Öneryildiz v Turkey* (2005) 41 EHRR 325. See para.4–086.

[320] For a striking example, see *R. v Leicestershire County Council, ex parte Blackfordby and Boothorpe Action Group* [2001] Env. L.R. 2.

[321] *Sunday Times v UK* (1979) 2 EHRR 245.

In *Alconbury*[322] the Divisional Court created a minor earthquake by finding that the Secretary of State's power to call in planning and similar applications for his own determination was "structurally incompatible" with the right to an independent and impartial tribunal under Article 6(1). The Secretary of State lacked independence because he was both policy-maker and decision-taker, and statutory review by the High Court on ordinary public law grounds was insufficient to cure the defect. The House of Lords restored the status quo, emphasising the democratic arguments in favour of retaining the decision-taking function in the hands of accountable bodies such as ministers and local authorities. "Strengthening the rule of law", remarked Lord Hoffmann, did not mean "inaugurating the rule of lawyers".[323]

In *Marcic v Thames Water Utilities Ltd* a householder sued a sewerage undertaker under Article 8 of the Convention, Article 1 of the First Protocol,[324] and at common law, for continued failure to take remedial steps necessary to prevent repeated overspills of untreated sewage into his home. He succeeded at first instance and in the Court of Appeal.[325] But the House of Lords once more curbed the enthusiasm of the courts below. The elaborate statutory funding scheme for the water industry left no room for imposing liability in individual cases, and since the scheme enabled aggrieved individuals to challenge the regulator's decisions by judicial review, Parliament had struck a Convention-compatible balance.[326]

Underlying these high-profile reversals are important general features of **1–079** Convention law that tend to militate against judicial interventionism in the ordinary run of environmental cases. In particular, the Strasbourg and domestic judiciary alike recognise that courts are not well placed to second-guess conclusions reached by public bodies in a field where decision-making often reflects specialised technical assessments or complex trade-offs between competing political and economic considerations. The ECtHR typically allows the national authorities a broad "margin of appreciation" to reach judgments of this kind. In *Hatton and others v UK*,[327] the Court expressly declined to adopt a "special approach" based

---

[322] *R. (Alconbury Developments Ltd and others) v SSETR* [2001] 2 All E.R. 929, DC, [2003] 2 A.C. 295, HL.

[323] ibid., para.129. In the wake of *Alconbury* the courts have accepted, on similar grounds, the Convention compatibility of other regulatory schemes in the environmental field: *R (Langton and Allen) v DEFRA* [2002] Env. L.R. 20 (disposal requirements under Animal By-Products Order 1999); *William Sinclair Holdings Ltd v English Nature*, [2001] EWHC Admin 408 (designation of SSSI); *R. (Whitmey) v Commons Commissioners* [2005] QB 282 (registration of village green). See also paras 6–039 and 6–040.

[324] Article 1 of the First Protocol protects against interferences with property.

[325] [2001] 3 All E.R. 698, Technology & Construction Court (HHJ Havery QC); [2002] Q.B. 929, CA. The Court of Appeal imposed liability at common law, a course the judge had not felt open to him, but approved the judge's conclusions on the Convention issues.

[326] [2003] 3 W.L.R. 1603, HL. See further paras 4–019 and 4–093.

[327] (2003) 37 EHRR 28, Grand Chamber judgment, reversing the Chamber (2002) 34 EHRR 1.

on "a special status of environmental human rights". Instead the Court held that despite the impact of the impugned decision (permission for night flights at Heathrow Airport) on individuals, it was to be treated as a "general policy" matter in which the government must be "left a choice".[328]

The domestic courts have accepted that review under the Convention involves a more intense scrutiny of official decisions than the *Wednesbury* test.[329] But they have nevertheless affirmed that their public law role remains one of secondary review, not primary assessment of the merits.[330] The courts afford the administration a context-sensitive "discretionary area of judgment", at its broadest when the subject-matter involves "questions of social or economic policy".[331] The courts have tended to place environmental decision-making firmly in that category.[332] A particularly laissez-faire approach applies where the complaint concerns a regulatory interference with property rights.[333] To put it crudely, in the environmental context the expectation is that only the starkest facts will persuade the courts that a decision-maker has overstepped the bounds of proportionality.

That is not to say that the Convention has been without its effect on domestic environmental law and practice; but its net impact is rather less pronounced than that of Community law and so merits briefer treatment in this book. While the courts have declined to treat the HRA as a prompt for radical re-writing of the environmental statute book or the law of tort, they have been prepared to make adjustments to the parameters of civil liability, regulatory procedures and public law review. It is also right to say that scope remains for human rights arguments in the regulatory decision-making process itself, even if the courts have largely set their face against

---

[328] (2003) 37 EHRR 28 at paras 122–123. See also paras 101–103, and the ECtHR's earlier judgment in *Buckley v UK* (1997) 23 EHRR 101. *Hatton is* discussed further at paras 4-087 to 4-089.

[329] *R. v Secretary of State for the Home Department, ex parte Mahmood* [2001] 1 W.L.R. 840, CA; *R. v Secretary of State for the Home Department, ex parte Daly* [2001] 2 W.L.R. 1622, Lord Steyn at paras 25–27 propounding a three-stage test, culminating in the question whether the "means used to impair the right" are "no more than is necessary" to accomplish the objective.

[330] *ex parte Daly, op. cit.,* para.28.

[331] *R. (SB) v Governors of Denbigh High School* [2007] 1 A.C. 100, Lord Hoffmann at para.63 citing *R v DPP, ex parte Kebilene* [2000] 2 A.C. 326 per Lord Hope.

[332] *Lough v First Secretary of State* [2004] 1 W.L.R. 2557, Pill LJ at paras 42–43, and see the extensive discussion of Strasbourg and domestic case law at 28–41.

[333] In *R. (Clays Lane Housing Co-operative Ltd) v The Housing Corporation* [2005] 1 W.L.R. 2229, the Court of Appeal held that where questions of justification arise in a complaint of infringement of Article 1 of the First Protocol, the *Daly* "no more than necessary" test (above, n.329) is displaced in favour of a generalised "fair balance" test, in practice little more stringent than *Wednesbury*. See also *R. v North Lincs Council, ex parte Horticultural & Garden Products Ltd* [1998] Env. L.R. 295.

interfering in the result.[334] Relevant developments are examined further as part of this book's treatment of the individual areas of law concerned, in particular in Chapters 4 (civil liability), 6 (public accountability) and 8 (the planning system). There are, however, a number of general features of the law—particularly the rules governing the workings of the HRA—that are most conveniently explained in overview here.

Status of Strasbourg case-law

HRA section 2 requires a court or tribunal to take account of the case-law   1–080
of the ECtHR and former EComHR. Where the ECtHR accepts an application as admissible (the vast majority are rejected), judgment is usually given by a Chamber of seven judges. But the Court can also sit as a Grand Chamber of 17. The ECtHR does not operate a doctrine of precedent as such. But it generally follows its previous decisions unless persuaded otherwise, and accords a Grand Chamber judgment greater weight than a Chamber judgment. Reasoned admissibility decisions of the ECtHR and former EComHR also carry some weight. These often deal with issues of importance to the operation of the HRA, such as "victim" status and the scope of State responsibility (see below). The House of Lords has held that "in the absence of special circumstances" domestic courts should "follow any clear and constant jurisprudence" of the ECtHR.[335] In the light of the "living instrument" principle, that duty includes keeping pace with the ECtHR's evolving thinking.[336]

The HRA and legislation

HRA section 3(1) demands that legislation must, "so far as it is possible to   1–081
do so" be read and given effect so as to be compatible with Convention rights. If primary legislation is so clear that it is impossible to give it a Convention-compatible reading, then it remains valid and enforceable;[337]

---

[334] For examples of Convention arguments tipping the scales in planning decisions in favour of granting permission when "ordinary" policy considerations point to refusal, see the following: (i) APP/C0603/V/1068930 (*Hadfield/Macclesfield BC*)—development permitted despite conflict with green belt policy since refusal of permission (and consequent demolition) would be a disproportionate interference with rights under Article 8 and Article 1 of the First Protocol; (ii) APP/Q3305/C/95 et al (*Hannis and others/Mendip DC*, the "King's Hill Collective" case)—siting of "low impact" dwellings permitted, taking into account Articles 8 and 9; (iii) *Basildon DC v SSETR*, January 5, 2001, CO/3311/2000, Ouseley J refusing to interfere with decision permitting retention of residential caravan in the green belt on basis of argument under Article 2 of the First Protocol in relation to stability of children's education.

[335] *Alconbury* [2003] 2 A.C. 295, Lord Slynn at para.26. For a discussion of permissible departures from Strasbourg case-law see *Ofulue v Bossert* [2008] UKHRR 447, CA.

[336] *R. (Ullah) v Special Adjudicator* [2004] 2 A.C. 323.

[337] HRA, s. 3(2)(b), (c). But subordinate legislation that is incompatible with the Convention can be quashed (or disregarded as invalid) in the ordinary way *unless* the parent statute *requires* it to provide as it does.

that is, the court must ultimately apply the incompatible legislation. However, in that event HRA section 4 empowers the court (if it is one of the higher courts listed in section 4(5))[338] to make a declaration of incompatibility. A declaration of incompatibility prompts the legislature to consider changing the offending part of the legislation. It also triggers the ministerial power under section 10 to make fast-track changes through a remedial order.

The section 3(1) duty requires the court to adopt, where necessary, a strongly non-literal or even strained reading of legislative language. Words may be read down, read in or read out. The doctrine of Parliamentary sovereignty imposes limits on the court's interpretative powers: an interpretation is not a "possible" one if it would conflict, expressly or by necessary implication, with an essential feature of the statute.[339] However, since Parliament intended a declaration of incompatibility to be a last resort, the court should be very slow to admit defeat in its effort to give legislation a Convention-compatible meaning.[340]

Whose activities does the HRA catch?

1–082   HRA section 6(1) makes it unlawful for a public authority to act in a way which is incompatible with a Convention right. Section 7 gives courts and tribunals jurisdiction to consider complaints about acts made unlawful by section 6. Section 8 empowers a court or tribunal, if it finds a complaint under section 7 well founded, to grant a "just and appropriate" remedy. These provisions create a new species of claim, analogous to breach of statutory duty. But against whom?

Section 6 defines "public authority" inclusively not exhaustively, forcing the domestic courts to grapple with the question of which bodies, beyond the obvious cases of government departments, local authorities and the like, qualify as "hybrid" public authorities under the "one or more functions of a public nature" test laid down by section 6(3)(b). The statutory language echoes the familiar judicial approach to identifying bodies that are amenable to judicial review in English law. Similar language is used to define "public authority" in the Freedom of Information Act 2000.[341] The intention underlying HRA section 6 is that it should be possible to assert Convention rights against those bodies for whose acts, in the eyes of the ECtHR, the State is responsible under the international law of the Convention: *Y.L. v Birmingham City Council*.[342] As *YL* illustrates (it concerned

---

[338] The High Court, Court of Appeal, House of Lords, Judicial Committee of the Privy Council, Courts Martial Appeal Court.

[339] In re S (care order: implementation of care plan) [2002] 2 A.C. 291; R. (Anderson) v Secretary of State for the Home Department [2003] 1 A.C. 837.

[340] Ghaidan v Godin-Mendoza [2004] 3 W.L.R. 113, Lord Steyn at paras 26–34.

[341] These topics are considered further at paras 6–113 and 6–114.

[342] [2008] 1 A.C. 95, Baroness Hale paras 55, 56.

contracted-out adult care services), this can be difficult to apply to the increasingly commercial and contract-based structure of contemporary administration. However, it would suggest that in principle section 6 embraces a wider range of bodies than are amenable to ordinary judicial review. In the environmental field, the High Court and Court of Appeal in *Marcic*[343] proceeded on the basis that a privatised utility undertaker was caught by section 6.

These limits on the reach of section 6 raise the question how far the HRA imports the Convention into legal relations between parties neither of whom is a "public authority": much the same issue of "horizontal effect" as arises in relation to unimplemented Community directives.[344] This is particularly important in relation to the contribution of the Convention to development of civil liability for environmental harm, a topic explored in Chapter 4. In brief, the HRA offers two main routes to horizontal effect: section 6(3)(a), which makes every court and tribunal a public authority; and the general interpretative requirement under section 3.

The role of courts and tribunals as public authorities has three aspects. **1–083** First, the court or tribunal must itself act compatibly with Convention requirements—chiefly found in Article 6—about the conduct of the proceedings. In the environmental field this is relevant to issues such as admission of evidence obtained under compulsory investigative powers from a person accused of an environmental offence.[345] This is not a species of "horizontal" effect as such; in this situation the court recognisably functions as part of the State, bound to avoid infringing Convention rights by its own behaviour.

Second, where the court is asked to make an order against a person (D) at the suit of another (P), the court must ensure that the order is compatible with D's substantive Convention rights. That generally means that the impact of the order on D's rights must be proportionate to the aim the litigation serves. In this situation P will often be a public authority: for example, a local authority seeking an injunction under planning legislation to defend the countryside against unauthorised development, requiring a balance to be struck between environmental protection on the one hand, and rights of individuals in relation to private life and home under Article 8 on the other.[346] But the courts have occasionally found it necessary to moderate their remedial zeal in proceedings between private parties.[347] Hence section 6(3)(a) may affect the scope of relief available in private law

---

[343] Above, para.1–078.
[344] See paras 4–070 and 4–071 below.
[345] *R. v Hertfordshire County Council, ex parte Green Environmental Industries* [2000] 2 W.L.R. 373, HL.
[346] *South Buckinghamshire DC v Porter* [2003] 2 W.L.R. 1547, HL.
[347] *John v Express Newspapers PLC* [2000] 3 All E.R. 257, CA; *Cream Holdings v Banerjee* [2005] 1 A.C. 253.

environmental cases, e.g. an application for an injunction to restrain an alleged nuisance.

Third comes the function of the courts in giving effect to the State's positive obligations under the Convention. This is perhaps the truest case of "horizontal effect" since it offers the citizen the prospect of deploying Convention rights, not merely as a guarantee of due process or a means of defence (as the two previous paragraphs contemplate), but as new substantive ammunition against the environmental impacts of private or commercial activities. The ECtHR recognises that in some circumstances, not only must the State refrain from interfering with Convention rights, but it is positively bound to ensure that its legal system adequately guards the citizen against the excesses of others' conduct in order to strike the "fair balance" the Convention requires.[348] Post-HRA, the domestic courts have acknowledged that they may have to develop the boundaries of the common law so as to impose liability where the Convention demands it.[349] Several landmark judgments of the ECtHR on positive obligations concern inadequate regulation of environmental impacts.[350] Chapter 4 contains a discussion of the relevant case-law in the context of civil liability for environmental harm.[351]

1-084   Turning to HRA section 3(1), the interpretative duty applies to every piece of legislation, including provisions concerned solely with private law rights and obligations of individuals. A number of leading cases involving section 3 have concerned quintessentially private law issues such as succession to property interests and enforceability of consumer contracts.[352] By legislating in the sphere of individual rights and duties, the State effectively assumes responsibility for the impact of the resulting law on human rights. The operation of section 3(1) is not confined to the judicial system; the section is an instruction to all those who interpret and apply legislation. So the section is of equal interest to practitioners in the advisory and transactional sphere as to those who bring and defend litigation.

Some features of HRA proceedings

1-085   The aim of HRA section 7 is to ensure that human rights claims slot as seamlessly as possible into existing classes of domestic legal proceedings. The detailed rules for advancing Convention arguments in litigation are

---

[348] *X. and Y. v Netherlands* (1985) Ser A 91; *Glaser v UK* [2000] 3 FCR 193.
[349] *Venables and Thompson v News Group Newspapers and others* [2001] 1 All E.R. 908, Fam D; *Mosley v News Group Newspapers Ltd* [2008] EWHC 1777 (Q.B.).
[350] *López Ostra v Spain* (1994) 20 EHRR 277; *Guerra v Italy* (1998) 26 EHRR 357.
[351] See paras 4-083 to 4-092.
[352] *Fitzpatrick v Sterling Housing Association* [1999] 4 All E.R. 705, HL; *Ghaidan v Godin-Mendoza* [2004] 3 W.L.R. 113; *Wilson v First County Trust Ltd (No. 2)* [2003] 3 W.L.R. 568.

generally found in rules of court.[353] But two specific features of section 7 should be noted: the "victim" rule and the special one-year limitation period. A few remarks are also due here about factual issues in Convention cases.

Section 7(1) provides that a person can only bring a Convention complaint about a public authority before a court or tribunal if he or she "is (or would be) a victim of the unlawful act". Section 7(7) cross-refers to the "victim" requirement for applications to the ECtHR under Article 34 of the Convention. In broad terms, the Strasbourg case-law on Article 34 limits "victims" to those who can claim to be "directly affected" by an alleged violation of a Convention right.[354] It is not open to a person to make a Convention complaint on behalf of the general public.[355] That is unlikely to pose a problem in private law proceedings where the object of the claim is generally to compensate or prevent some identifiable harm to the claimant.[356] But it creates a potential difficulty in public law cases. The English courts have adopted a liberal approach to the "sufficient interest" test for standing to bring a judicial review claim, enabling (for example) environmental NGOs to litigate issues of public importance.[357] But section 7(3) makes clear that only a "victim" has sufficient interest[358] to make a Convention complaint on judicial review. Standing in judicial review is considered further in Chapter 6.[359]

Section 7(5) requires proceedings to be commenced within one year beginning with the date on which the act complained of took place, or "such longer period as the court or tribunal considers just having regard to all the circumstances". It is important to note that this provision *only* applies to proceedings brought under section 7(1)(a)—that is where, generally speaking, but for the HRA there would be no available forum in which to raise the Convention argument. In many cases, Convention arguments are likely to come before the court under section 7(1)(b), which entitles the victim to "rely on the Convention ... in any legal proceedings" alongside other causes of action or grounds for review stemming from the same facts. Those cases are governed by the usual limitation period

---

[353] e.g. in England, para.15.1 of the Practice Direction to Civil Procedure Rules Part 16 (contents of statement of case).

[354] *Corigliano v Italy* (1983) 5 EHRR 334, para.31; and see *R. (Hooper) v Secretary of State for Work and Pensions* [2003] 1 W.L.R. 2623, paras 29–37.

[355] An *actio popularis*, in Strasbourg parlance.

[356] Indeed, as explained in Chapter 4, the "victim" test in conjunction with the scope of Article 8 has resulted in a *broadening* of the class of persons entitled to bring certain private law environmental claims: see paras 4–014 and 4–015.

[357] *R. v Inspectorate of Pollution, ex parte Greenpeace (No. 2)* [1994] 4 All E.R. 329; *R. v Secretary of State for Foreign and Commonwealth Affairs, ex parte World Development Movement Ltd* [1995] 1 W.L.R. 386.

[358] In Scotland, "title and interest to sue": s.7(4). See *Adams v Advocate General for Scotland* (2002) UKHRR 1189.

[359] paras 6–051 to 6–056. Note that there is an exception to the "victim" rule to enable the Commission for Equality and Human Rights to raise Convention issues by bringing proceedings, including judicial review, in its own name: Equality Act s. 30(3).

applicable to proceedings of that type.[360] Indeed section 7(5) contains an express saving for "stricter" time limits for any particular procedure—for example, the very short periods within which judicial review claims[361] and many statutory environmental appeals must be commenced.

1–086   The HRA does not create any special rules of evidence, but certain principles of Strasbourg case-law are relevant to the way in which domestic courts handle particular kinds of factual issue in relation to the burden and standard of proof in Convention claims.

In *Fadeyeva v Russia*,[362] the ECtHR "reiterated" that the standard of proof in proceedings before that Court is generally "beyond reasonable doubt".[363] But there is little sign that this apparent routine insistence on the criminal standard of proof has been imported into domestic Convention litigation. *Fadeyeva* concerned an Article 8 complaint in relation to the effects of pollution from a steelworks.[364] The emissions were alleged to have seriously prejudiced the applicant's health, and the government disputed much of the applicant's factual case. In reality, the underlying facts of Convention litigation are often undisputed: the real argument is about where, given those facts, the balance lies. Often the answer turns not on primary fact but on "social facts" that illuminate the legislative or regulatory response to a particular mischief or goal, and to which ordinary concepts of proof cannot readily be applied. Even where there is a dispute of primary fact, the ECtHR readily draws inferences in an applicant's favour, especially as the relevant evidence will often be uniquely in the possession of the respondent government. In practice the ECtHR adopts a flexible approach, with the standard to which the claimant must prove the facts supporting an alleged violation of the Convention varying according the nature and seriousness of what is said to have taken place.[365]

The domestic courts dislike having different standards of proof in different classes of non-criminal proceedings.[366] There is no indication that the UK judiciary are imposing any greater evidential burden on Convention claimants than on those making domestic claims in similar circumstances. Indeed if anything the HRA has resulted in new burdens on defendants, at least in the public law context. Where the court examines

---

[360] In relation to civil claims, see para.4–076.
[361] See paras 6–057 to 6–064.
[362] (2005) 41 EHRR 376.
[363] Judgment, para.79.
[364] The case is considered in para.4–091 below.
[365] para.79 of the *Fadeyeva* judgment continued: "Such proof may follow from the coexistence of sufficiently strong, clear and concordant inferences or of similar unrebutted presumptions of fact. It should also be noted that it has been the Court's practice to allow flexibility in this respect, taking into consideration the nature of the substantive right at stake and any evidentiary difficulties involved. In certain instances, only the respondent Government have access to information capable of corroborating or refuting the applicant's allegations; consequently, a rigorous application of the principle *affirmanti, non neganti, incumbit probatio* is impossible (see *Aktaş v Turkey*, no. 24351/94, § 272, ECHR 2003–V)."
[366] *Re. B. (Children)* [2008] 3 W.L.R. 1, HL.

questions of justification for an interference with a Convention right—in an Article 8 case, for example—once the claimant has made out the interference, the burden shifts to the decision-maker to establish sufficient justification. That contrasts with judicial review on traditional *Wednesbury* grounds,[367] in which the burden throughout rests squarely on the claimant to meet the high threshold of irrationality. The domestic courts have also acknowledged that greater insistence on defendant's disclosure may be necessary in judicial review proceedings to enable the court adequately to resolve questions of justification.[368]

Remedies under the HRA

The court or tribunal has power under section 8(1) to "grant such relief or **1–087** remedy, or make such order, within its powers as it considers just and appropriate". The effect of this provision is that if a court or tribunal has power to grant a particular remedy in cases within its usual jurisdiction—including damages (see the next paragraph)—then it can also grant that remedy to deal with an act of a public authority that is incompatible with a Convention right. That includes apprehended as well as past acts, so the court can grant a pre-emptive remedy such as an interim injunction to prevent an interference with a Convention right.[369] Section 8(1) also enables the court to exercise its procedural powers—for example, to exclude evidence or stay proceedings—in order to remedy or prevent an incompatible act.

Damages may be awarded by a court or tribunal that has power to award damages or compensation in civil proceedings.[370] The power to award damages is discretionary and expressly linked to the practice of the ECtHR in awarding compensation to provide "just satisfaction" under Article 41 of the Convention.[371] In the context of this book, two pertinent points arise about damages: first, the availability of damages in judicial review proceedings, and second, the relationship between the common law and the HRA as regards the basis for awarding and quantifying damages for environmental harm.

---

[367] See below, paras 6–027 to 6–033.
[368] *Tweed v Parades Commission for Northern Ireland* [2007] 1 A.C. 650.
[369] In *William Sinclair Holdings Ltd v English Nature*, [2001] EWHC Admin 408, an interim injunction was granted to a party claiming that the procedure for designation of an SSSI infringed its rights under Article 6(1) where the commercial harm it would have suffered had relief been refused outweighed the brief delay in the designation process caused by the grant of relief. See also the interim proceedings in *R. (M.W.H. and H. Ward Estates Limited) v Monmouthshire County Council* [2001] EWHC Admin 1150: injunction initially granted to restrain entry by Council under s.64 Land Drainage Act 1991, but discharged at permission hearing.
[370] s.8(2). Where a finding of an incompatible act is made by a court or tribunal that lacks power to award damages, the victim may seek to claim damages in a civil court on the basis of the finding. For the procedure in England and Wales see CPR 33.9.
[371] s.8(3), (4).

1–088   As regards judicial review, it is well established that a person is not entitled to damages merely because he or she successfully overturns a decision on public law grounds, even if the decision has caused demonstrable loss. Ordinarily damages are available only if the facts also disclose an independent civil cause of action such as breach of statutory duty or misfeasance in public office. The judicial review procedure is ill-equipped for the kind of factual investigation that such claims typically involve. However, the UK courts which deal with judicial review proceedings—the High Court (in England and Wales and Northern Ireland) and the Court of Session (in Scotland)—are entitled to award damages under section 8(1), with the result that if a claim or petition for judicial review succeeds on the basis that the decision is incompatible with a Convention rights, the court also has jurisdiction to award damages for harm shown to have resulted from the decision.

In England and Wales, Part 54 of the Civil Procedure Rules, which came into force alongside the HRA, expressly permits the inclusion of a claim for damages in proceedings for judicial review.[372] If the claimant succeeds in establishing the unlawfulness of an act or decision on Convention grounds following a substantive hearing, the usual practice is to stand over damages issues to be determined separately.

1–089   The link between HRA damages and the "just satisfaction" principle has created uncertainty because of the lack of transparency in the ECtHR's approach to making awards under Article 41.[373] Even where the State's behaviour has given rise to quantifiable loss, the ECtHR frequently concludes that the finding of a violation itself constitutes "just satisfaction", limiting any monetary award to reimbursement (usually partial) of the successful applicant's legal costs.

Compensation—when it is awarded—falls into two categories: pecuniary damage and non-pecuniary or "moral" damage, akin to "special" and "general" damages in English law. However, the ECtHR's procedures do not lend themselves to detailed investigation of quantum issues, and even where an applicant can show some specific pecuniary loss in consequence of the violation, the ECtHR tends to assess it on a rather unscientific "equitable" basis. Non-pecuniary harm is approached with an even broader brush, often as an award in round figures somewhere between €4,000 and €15,000 depending on the nature and seriousness of the violation (though the relationship is not always easy to discern). In *Hatton and others v UK*,[374] the Chamber (before its findings on liability were overturned by the Grand Chamber) awarded each applicant £4,000 for

---

[372] But judicial review may not be used to claim a monetary remedy alone: CPR 54.3(2).
[373] See generally Law Commission, *Damages under the Human Rights Act 1998* (Law Com no.266); Clayton and Tomlinson, *The Law of Human Rights*, (Oxford University Press, 2000), Chapter 21.
[374] (2002) 34 EHRR 1.

non-pecuniary harm to compensate for sleep disruption from night flights at Heathrow Airport.

The ECtHR has occasionally taken a more analytical approach. In *Smith, Grady, Lustig-Prean and Beckett v UK (No. 2)*,[375] the Court considered evidence of the probability that the applicants, had they not been dismissed in circumstances which violated Article 8, would have progressed in their careers and accrued the relevant financial benefits. It calculated pecuniary loss accordingly. This is much the same as the approach taken in EU employment cases where loss results from a breach of Community equal treatment legislation.[376] In addition to substantial sums for lost pay and pensions, the ECtHR awarded each applicant £19,000 for injured feelings.

In the face of the varied record of the ECtHR, the UK courts have adopted a rather confused approach to HRA damages. In *Anufrijeva v Southwark LBC*,[377] the allegations (breach of positive obligations under Article 8) were in the nature of maladministration by public bodies administering social welfare schemes. The Court of Appeal held that damages were "not an automatic entitlement but ... a remedy of 'last resort'", and "where the breach arises from maladministration, in those cases where an award of damages is appropriate, the scale of such damages should be modest" there being "no ready comparator" except perhaps awards of compensation by the Ombudsman.[378] In *R. (Greenfield) v Secretary of State for the Home Department*,[379] the House of Lords refused to award damages following a breach of Article 6 in disciplinary proceedings against a prisoner that resulted in his serving an additional 21 days' imprisonment. Lord Bingham observed that "the 1998 Act is not a tort statute"; its purpose was "not to give victims better remedies at home than they could recover in Strasbourg but to give them the same remedies without the delay and expense of resort to Strasbourg". The House declined an invitation to adopt tribunal awards in discrimination cases as an appropriate yardstick for quantum. Domestic courts should instead follow the ECtHR's "equitable" approach to compensation in the sense that awards are "not precisely calculated but are judged by the court to be fair in the individual case", and "should not aim to be significantly more or less generous than the [ECtHR] might be expected to be, in a case where it was willing to make an award at all."[380]

Both decisions are of course authoritative statements of principle. But **1–090** they concerned novel forms of liability which could not have arisen under

---

[375] Article 41 judgments (2001) 31 EHRR 23 and 24. This was the final Strasbourg leg of the litigation that began in *R. v Ministry of Defence, ex parte Smith*, above, fn. 315.
[376] e.g. *Cannock v Ministry of Defence* [1994] IRC 918.
[377] [2004] Q.B. 1124.
[378] ibid., paras 56, 74–75.
[379] [2005] 1 W.L.R. 673.
[380] ibid., paras 18, 19.

the previous law. It is submitted that neither decision prevents a more scientific or generous approach where there is a "ready comparator" under pre-existing law, particularly as the ECtHR has taken exactly that approach in such circumstances.

In *Marcic* the first instance judge, having imposed liability under the Convention but not at common law, gave a separate judgment on relief.[381] He refused to order the defendant to undertake remedial work. But he made an award that included damages for future losses, effectively assimilating the approach under the HRA to the equitable practice in nuisance cases of granting damages in lieu of an injunction. He held that nothing in the Strasbourg case-law prevented this approach.[382]

With the Court of Appeal's decision to hold Thames liable at common law, the resulting award of tort damages displaced the requirement for just satisfaction,[383] making the judge's decision academic; and of course neither the common law nor HRA award survives the eventual decision of the House of Lords on liability.[384] However, the judge's approach appears entirely consistent with Article 41 and the language of section 8(1). In a case where a public authority's violation of Convention rights closely resembles an act giving rise to liability in tort, it seems both just and appropriate to harmonise the approach to compensation. As against a public authority defendant a court might, on a given set of facts, equally well reach the same result on liability either by adjusting the common law rules pursuant to the State's positive obligations under the Convention or by directly finding the authority to have acted unlawfully under HRA section 6.[385] It would be entirely arbitrary for there to be a fundamental difference in approach to compensation as between these two legal analyses of the same facts.

---

[381] *Marcic v Thames Water Utilities Ltd (No.2)* [2001] 4 All E.R. 326, TCC.
[382] ibid., paras 18, 19.
[383] See *Dobson v Thames Water Utilities Ltd* [2007] EWHC 2021 (TCC), paras 189–211. This case is considered further below in Chapter 4, para.4–019.
[384] See above, para.1–078.
[385] *Dennis v Ministry of Defence* [2003] EWHC 793 (Q.B.) was just such a case. The court preferred, for reasons given at judgment paras 46 and 47, to impose liability at common law. See further below in Chapter 4, para.4–023.

The European Convention for the Protection of Human Rights and Fundamental Freedoms—Articles 2 to 18 and Articles 1 to 3 of the First Protocol

Note that Articles 13 and 15 are not among the "Convention Rights" as defined by section 1(1) of the Human Rights Act 1998. These two Articles are accordingly here marked with an asterisk and shown in italics.

Article 2. Right to life

1. Everyone's right to life shall be protected by law. No one shall be deprived of his life intentionally save in the execution of a sentence of a court following his conviction of a crime for which this penalty is provided by law.
2. Deprivation of life shall not be regarded as inflicted in contravention of this article when it results from the use of force which is no more than absolutely necessary:

    a. in defence of any person from unlawful violence;
    b. in order to effect a lawful arrest or to prevent the escape of a person lawfully detained;
    c. in action lawfully taken for the purpose of quelling a riot or insurrection.

Article 3. Prohibition of torture

No one shall be subjected to torture or to inhuman or degrading treatment or punishment.

Article 4. Prohibition of slavery and forced labour

1. No one shall be held in slavery or servitude.
2. No one shall be required to perform forced or compulsory labour.
3. For the purpose of this article the term "forced or compulsory labour" shall not include:

    a. any work required to be done in the ordinary course of detention imposed according to the provisions of Article 5 of this Convention or during conditional release from such detention;

b. any service of a military character or, in case of conscientious objectors in countries where they are recognised, service exacted instead of compulsory military service;

c. any service exacted in case of an emergency or calamity threatening the life or well-being of the community;

d. any work or service which forms part of normal civic obligations.

Article 5. Right to liberty and security

1. Everyone has the right to liberty and security of person. No one shall be deprived of his liberty save in the following cases and in accordance with a procedure prescribed by law:

   a. the lawful detention of a person after conviction by a competent court;

   b. the lawful arrest or detention of a person for non-compliance with the lawful order of a court or in order to secure the fulfilment of any obligation prescribed by law;

   c. the lawful arrest or detention of a person effected for the purpose of bringing him before the competent legal authority on reasonable suspicion of having committed an offence or when it is reasonably considered necessary to prevent his committing an offence or fleeing after having done so;

   d. the detention of a minor by lawful order for the purpose of educational supervision or his lawful detention for the purpose of bringing him before the competent legal authority;

   e. the lawful detention of persons for the prevention of the spreading of infectious diseases, of persons of unsound mind, alcoholics or drug addicts or vagrants;

   f. the lawful arrest or detention of a person to prevent his effecting an unauthorised entry into the country or of a person against whom action is being taken with a view to deportation or extradition.

2. Everyone who is arrested shall be informed promptly, in a language which he understands, of the reasons for his arrest and of any charge against him.

3. Everyone arrested or detained in accordance with the provisions of paragraph 1.c of this article shall be brought promptly before a judge or other officer authorised by law to exercise judicial power and shall be entitled to trial within a reasonable time or to release pending trial. Release may be conditioned by guarantees to appear for trial.

4. Everyone who is deprived of his liberty by arrest or detention shall be entitled to take proceedings by which the lawfulness of his detention shall be decided speedily by a court and his release ordered if the detention is not lawful.

5. Everyone who has been the victim of arrest or detention in contravention of the provisions of this article shall have an enforceable right to compensation.

Article 6. Right to a fair trial

1. In the determination of his civil rights and obligations or of any criminal charge against him, everyone is entitled to a fair and public hearing within a reasonable time by an independent and impartial tribunal established by law. Judgment shall be pronounced publicly but the press and public may be excluded from all or part of the trial in the interests of morals, public order or national security in a democratic society, where the interests of juveniles or the protection of the private life of the parties so require, or to the extent strictly necessary in the opinion of the court in special circumstances where publicity would prejudice the interests of justice.
2. Everyone charged with a criminal offence shall be presumed innocent until proved guilty according to law.
3. Everyone charged with a criminal offence has the following minimum rights:

    a. to be informed promptly, in a language which he understands and in detail, of the nature and cause of the accusation against him;
    b. to have adequate time and facilities for the preparation of his defence;
    c. to defend himself in person or through legal assistance of his own choosing or, if he has not sufficient means to pay for legal assistance, to be given it free when the interests of justice so require;
    d. to examine or have examined witnesses against him and to obtain the attendance and examination of witnesses on his behalf under the same conditions as witnesses against him;
    e. to have the free assistance of an interpreter if he cannot understand or speak the language used in court.

Article 7. No punishment without law

1. No one shall be held guilty of any criminal offence on account of any act or omission which did not constitute a criminal offence under national or international law at the time when it was committed. Nor shall a heavier penalty be imposed than the one that was applicable at the time the criminal offence was committed.
2. This article shall not prejudice the trial and punishment of any person for any act or omission which, at the time when it was committed, was criminal according to the general principles of law recognised by civilised nations.

Article 8. Right to respect for private and family life

1. Everyone has the right to respect for his private and family life, his home and his correspondence.
2. There shall be no interference by a public authority with the exercise of this right except such as is in accordance with the law and is necessary in a democratic society in the interests of national security,

public safety or the economic well-being of the country, for the prevention of disorder or crime, for the protection of health or morals, or for the protection of the rights and freedoms of others.

Article 9. Freedom of thought, conscience and religion

1. Everyone has the right to freedom of thought, conscience and religion; this right includes freedom to change his religion or belief and freedom, either alone or in community with others and in public or private, to manifest his religion or belief, in worship, teaching, practice and observance. Freedom to manifest one's religion or beliefs shall be subject only to such limitations as are prescribed by law and are necessary in a democratic society in the interests of public safety, for the protection of public order, health or morals, or for the protection of the rights and freedoms of others.

Article 10. Freedom of expression

1. Everyone has the right to freedom of expression. This right shall include freedom to hold opinions and to receive and impart information and ideas without interference by public authority and regardless of frontiers. This article shall not prevent States from requiring the licensing of broadcasting, television or cinema enterprises.
2. The exercise of these freedoms, since it carries with it duties and responsibilities, may be subject to such formalities, conditions, restrictions or penalties as are prescribed by law and are necessary in a democratic society, in the interests of national security, territorial integrity or public safety, for the prevention of disorder or crime, for the protection of health or morals, for the protection of the reputation or rights of others, for preventing the disclosure of information received in confidence, or for maintaining the authority and impartiality of the judiciary.

Article 11. Freedom of assembly and association

1. Everyone has the right to freedom of peaceful assembly and to freedom of association with others, including the right to form and to join trade unions for the protection of his interests.
2. No restrictions shall be placed on the exercise of these rights other than such as are prescribed by law and are necessary in a democratic society in the interests of national security or public safety, for the prevention of disorder or crime, for the protection of health or morals or for the protection of the rights and freedoms of others. This article shall not prevent the imposition of lawful restrictions on the exercise of these rights by members of the armed forces, of the police or of the administration of the State.

Article 12. Right to marry

Men and women of marriageable age have the right to marry and to found a family, according to the national laws governing the exercise of this right.

*Article 13. Right to an effective remedy

Everyone whose rights and freedoms as set forth in this Convention are violated shall have an effective remedy before a national authority notwithstanding that the violation has been committed by persons acting in an official capacity.

Article 14. Prohibition of discrimination

The enjoyment of the rights and freedoms set forth in this Convention shall be secured without discrimination on any ground such as sex, race, colour, language, religion, political or other opinion, national or social origin, association with a national minority, property, birth or other status.

*Article 15. Derogation in time of emergency

1. *In time of war or other public emergency threatening the life of the nation any High Contracting Party may take measures derogating from its obligations under this Convention to the extent strictly required by the exigencies of the situation, provided that such measures are not inconsistent with its other obligations under international law.*

2. *No derogation from Article 2, except in respect of deaths resulting from lawful acts of war, or from Articles 3, 4 (paragraph 1) and 7 shall be made under this provision.*

3. *Any High Contracting Party availing itself of this right of derogation shall keep the Secretary General of the Council of Europe fully informed of the measures which it has taken and the reasons therefor. It shall also inform the Secretary General of the Council of Europe when such measures have ceased to operate and the provisions of the Convention are again being fully executed.*

Article 16. Restrictions on political activity of aliens

Nothing in Articles 10, 11 and 14 shall be regarded as preventing the High Contracting Parties from imposing restrictions on the political activity of aliens.

Article 17. Prohibition of abuse of rights

Nothing in this Convention may be interpreted as implying for any State, group or person any right to engage in any activity or perform any act aimed at the destruction of any of the rights and freedoms set forth herein or at their limitation to a greater extent than is provided for in the Convention.

Article 18. Limitation on use of restrictions on rights

The restrictions permitted under this Convention to the said rights and freedoms shall not be applied for any purpose other than those for which they have been prescribed.

First Protocol to the Convention

Article 1. Protection of property

Every natural or legal person is entitled to the peaceful enjoyment of his possessions. No one shall be deprived of his possessions except in the public interest and subject to the conditions provided for by law and by the general principles of international law. The preceding provisions shall not, however, in any way impair the right of a State to enforce such laws as it deems necessary to control the use of property in accordance with the general interest or to secure the payment of taxes or other contributions or penalties.

Article 2. Right to education

No person shall be denied the right to education. In the exercise of any functions which it assumes in relation to education and to teaching, the State shall respect the right of parents to ensure such education and teaching in conformity with their own religious and philosophical convictions.

Article 3. Right to free elections

The High Contracting Parties undertake to hold free elections at reasonable intervals by secret ballot, under conditions which will ensure the free expression of the opinion of the people in the choice of the legislature.

Chapter 2

ENVIRONMENTAL REGULATORS AND THEIR ENFORCEMENT POWERS

Introduction

Most environmental legislation in England is enforced by the Environment   **2–001**
Agency and local authorities. The Environment Agency does not, however,
develop the environmental policy or draft the secondary legislation that it
enforces. Rather, the Department for Environment, Food and Rural
Affairs (Defra) is responsible for developing environmental policy and for
drafting most of the regulations and guidance that make up the legislation.
On occasion, other government departments may also be involved.

This chapter describes Defra and its role in the enforcement of environmental legislation followed by a brief discussion of the role of other
government departments. It then examines the structure, duties and
responsibilities of the Environment Agency, and its role in implementing
and enforcing environmental legislation, and also discusses the role played
by local authorities and other regulatory bodies. Finally, it reviews the
enforcement powers granted by the Regulatory Enforcement and Sanctions Act 2008 (RES Act), in particular, the power granted to the Environment Agency and other authorities to use civil penalties in addition to
their traditional enforcement procedures.[1]

Department for Environment, Food and Rural Affairs

Defra has oversight responsibility for environmental policy in England.   **2–002**
The scope of this responsibility is broad: it includes responsibility for
integrated pollution prevention and control, local air pollution control, air
quality, the remediation of contaminated land and water quality. Among
other things, Defra advises Ministers on environmental policy, negotiates
European Union (EU) environmental Directives and other EU environmental legislation on behalf of the UK Government, and prepares secondary environmental legislation, including statutory guidance as well as
regulations. As part of the process of transposing EU legislation into

---

[1] Powers to prosecute criminal environmental offences are discussed in Chapter 3. Powers
related to environmental permitting are discussed in Chapter 14.

English law, Defra prepares consultation papers on draft legislation, holds meetings with stakeholders, reviews comments to its consultation papers and prepares draft legislation.

Defra's role is thus critical to the enforcement of environmental legislation in England. This is because over 80 per cent of environmental legislation in the United Kingdom is secondary legislation to transpose EU Directives or to supplement EU Regulations. Defra may work with the Environment Agency in developing such legislation. For example, Defra developed the environmental permitting programme (which introduced a single permitting regime for waste and pollution prevention and control operations) in conjunction with the Environment Agency. In other environmental legislation, such as the Environmental Liability Directive,[2] Defra negotiated the Directive at EU level and developed the regulations and guidance to transpose it into domestic law, with the Agency submitting comments as part of the consultation process.

Defra is headed by the Secretary of State for Environment, Food and Rural Affairs, who is a member of the Cabinet. The Secretary of State, assisted by ministers, sets objectives for the Environment Agency in respect of its functions and its contribution to sustainable development. The Secretary appoints the chairman and members of the Agency's Board with the exception of the member for Wales, who is appointed by the National Assembly for Wales. In addition, the Secretary approves the Agency's budget and the Government's grant to the Agency for activities in England and also approves its regulatory and charging regimes.

2–003   Defra has eight Departmental Strategic Objectives. The six environment-related objectives are:

- to tackle climate change on an international and domestic basis by reducing greenhouse gas emissions;
- to help ensure a healthy, resilient, productive and diverse natural environment;
- to create sustainable patterns of consumption and production;
- to help ensure that the economy and society is resilient to environmental risk and able to adapt to the impacts of climate change;
- to assist in developing and maintaining a thriving farming and food sector with an improving net impact on the environment; and
- to champion sustainable development on a government-wide basis both in the United Kingdom and internationally.[3]

[2] Directive 2004/35/CE of the European Parliament and of the Council on environmental liability with regard to the prevention and remedying of damage, as amended. [2004] OJ L143/56.

[3] See *http://www.defra.gov.uk/corporate/what-do-we-do/index.htm.*

In addition, Defra is the lead government department on two Public Service Agreements.[4] These Agreements, which are key cross-government priorities, are (i) securing a healthy natural environment both for the present and the future, and (ii) leading the global effort to avoid dangerous climate change.

On October 4, 2008, the Prime Minister established a Department of Climate Change and Energy. Relevant functions formerly carried out by Defra and the Department for Business Enterprise & Regulatory Reform (BERR), including implementation of the EU Emissions Trading Scheme and responsibilities and duties under the forthcoming Climate Change Act, will be carried out by the new department.

Other Policy-Making Government Departments

The other main UK Government departments with policy-making responsibilities for environment-related matters are BERR and the Department for Communities and Local Government (CLG).   2–004

Department for Business Enterprise and Regulatory Reform (BERR)

BERR is the lead UK Government department for producer responsibility legislation. Among other things, it was the UK lead on the negotiation, and is responsible for implementation in the UK, of the restriction of hazardous substances Directive (RoHS Directive),[5] the waste electrical and electronic equipment Directive (WEEE Directive)[6] and the batteries Directive.[7] In addition, BERR has split responsibility, with Defra, for the Packaging Waste Directive.[8] In this latter respect, BERR leads on single market aspects of the Packaging Waste Directive, whilst Defra leads on UK waste policy and all other aspects of the domestic implementation of the Directive including setting targets for recycling and the recovery of waste.   2–005

---

[4] Public Service Agreements were introduced in the 1998 Comprehensive Spending Review. They set out the top cross-government priorities as part of the reviews.

[5] Directive 2002/95/EC of the European Parliament and of the Council on the restriction of the use of certain hazardous substances in electrical and electronic equipment. [2002] OJ L037/19.

[6] Directive 2002/96/EC of the European Parliament and of the Council on waste electrical and electronic equipment. [2002] OJ L037/24.

[7] Directive 2006/66/EC of the European Parliament and of the Council on batteries and accumulators and waste batteries and accumulators, as amended. [2006] OJ L266/1.

[8] Directive 94/62/EC of the European Parliament and of the Council on packaging and packaging waste. [1994] OJ L365/10.

Department for Communities and Local Government (CLG)

2–006   CLG is the UK Government department with responsibility for town and country planning legislation. This responsibility includes implementation of the Mining Wastes Directive,[9] the Natural Habitats Directive,[10] the Wild Birds Directive[11] and the Environmental Impact Assessment Directive.[12] Other environmental-related responsibilities of CLG include publication of planning policy statements (PPSs) on environmental issues. Such PPSs include PPS 23 "Planning and Pollution Control", which has annexes on pollution control, air and water quality and development on land affected by contamination[13] and PPS 9 "Biodiversity and geological conservation".[14] Other guidance published by CLG includes the Sustainable Development Action Plan 2007–08,[15] the policy statement on Building a Greener Future[16] and guidance on the energy performance of buildings.[17] In addition, the CLG publishes the Code for Sustainable Homes.[18]

Like BERR, CLG shares some responsibilities concerning environmental Directives with Defra. For example, Defra was the UK lead at the EU negotiating level on the Mining Wastes Directive,[19] working closely with CLG and BERR.

Environment Agency

2–007   The Environment Agency was created as a public body corporate by the Environment Act 1995. It became fully operational on April 1, 1996 when it took over responsibility for functions formerly carried out by the

---

[9] Directive 2006/21/EC on the management of waste from the extractive industries. [2006] OJ L102/15.

[10] Council Directive 92/43/EEC on the conservation of natural habitats and of wild fauna and flora. [1992] OJ L206/7.

[11] Council Directive 79/409/EEC on the conservation of wild birds. [1979] OJ L103/1.

[12] Council Directive 85/337/EEC on the assessment of the effects of certain public and private projects on the environment. [1985] OJ L175/40.

[13] Department for Communities and Local Government, Planning Policy Statement 23, "Planning and Pollution Control" (November 3, 2004).

[14] Department for Communities and Local Government, Planning Policy Statement 9, "Biodiversity and Geological Conservation" (August 16, 2005).

[15] Department for Communities and Local Government, "Sustainable development action plan" 2007–08 (January 9, 2008).

[16] Department for Communities and Local Government, "Building a greener future: policy statement" (July 23, 2007).

[17] See, e.g., Department for Communities and Local Government, "A guide to generating energy performance certificates for similar buildings owned by the same landlord" (July 30, 2008).

[18] Department for Communities and Local Government, "The Code for Sustainable Homes: Setting the standard for sustainability in new homes" (February 27, 2008).

[19] Directive 2006/21/EC on the management of waste from the extractive industries. [2006] OJ L102/15.

National Rivers Authority, HM Inspectorate of Pollution and the waste regulation authorities.

The Agency is a non-departmental public body of Defra[20] which means, among other things, that the Agency is accountable to the Secretary of State for Environment, Food and Rural Affairs for its day-to-day operations in England. The Agency is, thus, less powerful than other environmental enforcement authorities in some jurisdictions. For example, the United States Congress delegates rule-making power to the Environmental Protection Agency (EPA). This means that the EPA not only enforces federal environmental legislation; it also drafts and issues the regulations that it enforces. In contrast, the Environment Agency implements and enforces secondary legislation drafted by Defra, although it may prepare draft guidance, such as draft guidance for the pollution prevention and control programme, prior to Defra holding consultations on it.

The principal aim of the Environment Agency, set out in section 4(1) of the Environment Act 1995, is to discharge its functions "so to protect or enhance the environment, taken as a whole, as to make the contribution towards attaining the objective of achieving sustainable development" mentioned in section 4(3).[21] Sections 4(3) and 4(4) require the Agency, in determining what this contribution might be, to have regard to ministerial guidance.[22]

The Agency's principal responsibilities are: 2–008

- integrated pollution prevention and control;
- waste management including regulation of the treatment, storage, transportation and disposal of controlled waste, the provision of technical guidance on waste management, and carrying out surveys to identify waste disposal needs and priorities;
- the regulation of radioactive substances, including controls on the disposal of radioactive waste, the storage and use of radioactive substances at non-nuclear sites, and the monitoring of radioactivity levels in the environment;
- water quality, including the preservation and improvement of water quality in rivers, estuaries, coastal waters and groundwater, the control of pollution in such waters, implementation of the discharge consent system, the monitoring of trade effluent discharges and sewage treatment works, and the monitoring of the quality of fresh water, groundwater and tidal waters;
- land quality, including implementation and enforcement of Part 2A of the Environmental Protection Act 1990 in respect of special sites,

---

[20] The Environment Agency also operates in Wales where it is a non-departmental public body of the National Assembly for Wales.

[21] Environment Act 1995, s.4(1).

[22] See Department for Environment, Food and Rural Affairs, The Environment Agency's Objectives and Contributions to Sustainable Development: Statutory Guidance by the Secretary of State for Environment, Food and Rural Affairs (December 2002).

various other duties and responsibilities under Part 2A, and the publication of periodic reports on the state of contaminated land in England and Wales;

- water resources, including the exercise of powers concerning the proper use of such resources, the regulation of licensed water abstractions, various duties and responsibilities imposed by the Water Framework Directive,[23] and the publication of information concerning the demand for water and available resources;

- flood risk management, including all matters related to flood defence, educating the public on flood risk, advising local authorities in relation to development in flood plains, providing flood warnings and responding to incidents of flooding;

- navigation on inland waters, including the maintenance and improvement of navigation on rivers and other navigable waters, and the licensing of boats using such waters;

- conservation and enhancement of the water environment, areas of natural beauty and environmental sensitivity and the encouragement of biodiversity;

- water recreation, including promotion of the recreational use of water and access along rivers and other waters; and

- fisheries, including the maintenance and improvement of salmon, trout, freshwater and eel fisheries, regulation of these fisheries, and notifying Defra and the National Assembly for Wales of outbreaks of notifiable fish disease in England and Wales, respectively.

Other functions carried out by the Environment Agency include assembling and disseminating environmental data that has been gathered from its monitoring activities and other sources and carrying out research in respect of its activities.

The Environment Agency has developed various strategies to assist it in carrying out its functions. For example, its revised Climate Change Adaptation Strategy for 2008–11 includes action plans for water quality, chemicals, air quality, radioactive substances regulation, and marine recreation and navigation.

The Agency is managed by a Board of 14 members who, as indicated above, are appointed by the Secretary for Environment, Food and Rural Affairs and one member who is appointed by the National Assembly for Wales. The Board meets six times a year. Day-to-day management of the Agency is handled by the Chief Executive and the Agency's staff.

2–009   The Environment Agency employs approximately 12,000 people. It is funded mainly through grant-in-aid from government (60 per cent), statutory charging schemes and flood defence levies (29 per cent). Its total

---

[23] Directive 2000/60/EC of the European Parliament and of the Council establishing a framework for Community action in the field of water policy. [2000] OJ L327/1.

expenditure for 2006–07 was £1.065 billion. This expenditure was allocated as follows:

- flood risk management—£581 million (55 per cent);
- preventing and controlling pollution—£311 million (29 per cent); and
- other water management functions—£173 million (16 per cent).

The Agency's head office is split between Bristol and London. The head office is responsible for the Agency's corporate management, which includes the development of policy, setting strategic and operational objectives and managing its performance.

The Environment Agency has eight regions: Southern; Thames; South West; Midlands; Anglian; Wales; North West; and North East. In turn, the regions are divided into areas (23 in total), each of which has an area office.

Local Authorities

Local authorities are responsible for the enforcement of various environ- 2–010 mental laws, in particular, the statutory nuisance regime, noise legislation, air quality legislation under both the local authority pollution prevention and control regime and other air quality legislation. The local authorities are the primary enforcing authorities for Part 2A of the Environmental Protection Act 1990, and have duties and responsibilities under the Environmental Liability Directive.[24] In addition, they implement and enforce planning legislation under the Town and Country Planning Acts.

CLG is the UK Government department with responsibility for national policy for local authorities.

Other Enforcement Authorities

Other regulatory authorities that have duties and responsibilities for 2–011 environmental matters are Natural England and the Health and Safety Executive (HSE).

Natural England

Natural England has duties and responsibilities for sites of special scientific 2–012 interest (SSSIs), nature reserves and other designated sensitive ecological areas under conservation legislation including the Conservation (Natural

---

[24] Directive 2004/35/CE of the European Parliament and of the Council on environmental liability with regard to the prevention and remedying of damage, as amended. [2004] OJ L143/56.

Habitats, Etc.) Regulations 1994, as amended,[25] the Wildlife and Countryside Act 1981, as amended by the Countryside and Rights of Way Act 2000, and the National Parks and Access to the Countryside Act 1949. In addition, Natural England is responsible for the restoration of damage to EU protected species and natural habitats on land as well as the restoration of damage to other flora and fauna on SSSIs.[26]

Health and Safety Executive

2–013   The HSE has environmental-related responsibilities in addition to its general responsibilities for health and safety in the workplace. Its environmental-related responsibilities include implementation and enforcement of the Genetically Modified Organisms (Contained Use) Regulations 2000,[27] and the Control of Major Accident Hazards Regulations 1999, as amended (the COMAH Regulations).[28] The HSE shares responsibility for implementing and enforcing the COMAH Regulations with the Environment Agency, which has joint oversight of the remediation of damage caused by installations that are subject to the regulations.[29]

Regulatory Enforcement and Sanctions Act 2008

2–014   The enforcement powers of the Environment Agency and other regulatory authorities that enforce environmental legislation have traditionally been based on criminal law. Indeed, as discussed in chapter 3, virtually all environmental offences when this book went to print are criminal offences. This situation is changing due to enactment of the Regulatory Enforcement and Sanctions Act 2008 (the RES Act).

The RES Act has greatly expanded the enforcement powers of the Environment Agency, local authorities and a large number of other authorities with—and without—responsibility for environmental legislation. The Act accomplished this, subject to ministerial orders being issued before the authorities may use the powers, by extending their enforcement powers to include four new civil administrative sanctions.

---

[25] SI 1994/2716.
[26] See Chapter 5.
[27] SI 2000/2831. The HSE is responsible for the licensing and oversight of the contained use of genetically modified organisms.
[28] SI 1999/743. CLG has responsibility for land-use planning aspects of the regulations.
[29] The HSE and the Environment Agency have entered into a memorandum of understanding under which the Agency is responsible for environmental damage and the HSE is responsible for harm to human health and health and safety issues.

1. *Hampton Report*

The RES Act received the Royal Assent on July 21, 2008. It originates **2–015** from the Hampton Report which was commissioned by HM Treasury to review regulatory inspection and enforcement.[30] The Hampton Report recommended a risk-based and proportional approach to regulation to ensure that regulatory enforcement concentrated on higher risk businesses rather than those with good compliance records. Among other things, the report recommended that:

- regulators should continue to be independent in making decisions, but should be accountable for the efficiency and effectiveness of their activities;
- businesses should not be inspected without a reason for an inspection;
- businesses should not have to provide unnecessary information to regulators and, in particular, should not have to provide the same information to more than one regulator;
- regulators should be able quickly to identify businesses that persistently breach regulations;
- regulators should provide authoritative and accessible advice easily and cheaply; and
- regulators should recognise their key role in facilitating and encouraging economic progress and should, therefore, intervene in a business only when a clear case to do so exists.

The Hampton Report also recommended a comprehensive review of regulatory penalty regimes, having concluded that the regimes of individual regulators were often cumbersome, ineffective and inflexible. It concluded, in particular, that the regimes tended to rely too heavily on criminal prosecution.

A key outcome of the Hampton Report was an invitation to Professor Richard Macrory to carry out a comprehensive review of regulatory sanctions to examine their consistency with the risk-based approach recommended by it and, when the sanctions were not consistent, to suggest ways in which to apply the risk-based approach to them.

2. *Macrory Report*

Professor Macrory published his report (the Macrory Report), entitled **2–016** *Regulatory Justice: Making Sanctions Effective*, on November 28, 2006. It examined the sanctioning regimes of 56 national regulators. The extensive review analysed the regimes of large national regulators such as the Environment Agency, the Financial Services Authority and the HSE, as

---

[30] Philip Hampton, The Hampton Report, "Reducing Administrative Burdens: effective inspections and enforcement". HMSO, 2005, final report.

well as small regulators such as the 468 local authorities in the United Kingdom. Enforcement activities of local authorities examined in the review included: environmental health; planning; building control; licensing; and trading standards and related services.[31] Professor Macrory concurred in the Hampton Report's conclusion that there was a heavy reliance on criminal sanctions as a formal response to regulatory non-compliance. He further concluded that such reliance had resulted in:

- the enforcement of sanctions that do not sufficiently punish or deter non-compliance with regulations because of their limited scope to punish businesses, for example, the requirement to take a defendant company's financial means into account when setting a fine has resulted in low fines for many serious offences;
- the potential for disproportionate prosecution in cases in which the defendant had not committed an offence intentionally or wilfully;
- decisions not to prosecute by regulatory authorities due to the cost and time involved in doing so; and
- the loss of stigma previously associated with a criminal conviction for non-compliance with regulations due, among other things, to the lack of apparent difference between the prosecution of a strict liability offence committed by a legitimate business, and the prosecution of an offence committed by a rogue who deliberately flouted the law.[32]

Professor Macrory also concluded that the lack of flexibility in enforcement options had restricted the ability of regulatory authorities to respond effectively to incidents of regulatory non-compliance.[33] He stated that if, however, administrative penalties and other forms of sanctions were to be created, the most egregious offences, such as those involving intent or recklessness, could be handled in the criminal courts, whilst regulatory authorities would be able to apply a range of sanctioning tools to other offences by using a risk-based approach.

The Macrory Report set out six penalties principles, known as the Macrory Principles, to which regulatory authorities should have regard in designing their sanctioning regimes. The principles state that a sanction should:

(i) Aim to change the behaviour of the offender;
(ii) Aim to eliminate any financial gain or benefit from non-compliance;
(iii) Be responsive and consider what is appropriate for the particular offender and regulatory issue, which can include punishment and the public stigma that should be associated with a criminal convention;

[31] See Macrory Report: *Regulatory Justice: Making Sanctions Effective*, Cabinet office, 2004, annex C, para.C20.
[32] ibid. pp.15–16, para.1.14.
[33] ibid. p.15, para.1.18.

(iv) Be proportionate to the nature of the offence and the harm caused;
(v) Aim to restore the harm caused by regulatory non-compliance, where appropriate; and
(vi) Aim to deter future non-compliance.[34]

The report also set out the characteristics that should apply to a regulatory authority's sanctioning regime. It stated that regulators should:

(i)   Publish an enforcement policy;
(ii) Measure outcomes not just outputs;
(iii) Justify their choice of enforcement actions year on year to stake-holders, Ministers and Parliament;
(iv) Follow-up enforcement actions where appropriate;
(v)   Enforce in a transparent manner;
(vi) Be transparent in the way in which they apply and determine administrative penalties; and
(vii) Avoid perverse incentives that might influence the choice of sanc-tioning response.[35]

In particular, Professor Macrory recommended that the range of sanc-tioning options available to regulatory authorities should be extended to include civil sanctions.[36] The UK Government accepted all of Professor Macrory's recommendations,[37] and the RES Act implements the recom-mendations concerning civil penalties.

3. Structure of the Regulatory Enforcement and Sanctions Act 2008

The RES Act has four parts. Parts 1, 3 and 4 came into force on October 1, **2–017**
2008. Part 2 will come into force on April 6, 2009. In July 2008, BERR published Guidance to the Act (Guidance).[38] On September 10, 2008, it published a Consultation on the Primary Authority Scheme under Part 2 of the RES Act (Consultation).[39]

Part 1 of the RES Act re-established, as a statutory corporation, the Local Better Regulation Office (LBRO), which had been established in May 2007 as a Government-owned company. The LBRO's objective is to help local authority regulatory services carry out their relevant functions in an effective manner that does not create unnecessary burdens and that

---

[34] ibid. p.10, Box E1.
[35] ibid.
[36] ibid.
[37] See Department for Business Enterprise & Regulatory Reform, Regulatory Enforcement and Sanctions Act 2008; Guidance to the Act, para.31 (July 2008).
[38] Department for Business Enterprise & Regulatory Reform, Regulatory Enforcement and Sanctions Act 2008; Guidance to the Act (July 2008).
[39] Department for Business Enterprise & Regulatory Reform, Regulatory Enforcement and Sanctions Act 2008; Consultation on the Primary Authority Scheme (September 2008).

complies with the five key principles of good regulation, namely, consistency, transparency, proportionality, accountability and targeting.[40] The local authorities' relevant functions include environmental protection and public health and safety.

Part 2 of the RES Act established a primary authority scheme under which the LBRO will nominate a single local authority as the primary authority for a particular business when the business carries on an activity that is subject to regulation by more than one local authority.[41] If another local authority (known as an "enforcing authority") proposes taking "enforcement action" against such a business, it must contact the primary authority before it may do so. If the primary authority considers that the enforcement action is inconsistent with advice or guidance provided by it to the business, it may direct the enforcing authority not to carry out its proposed action.[42]

2–018   The RES Act defines an "enforcement action" to mean:

    (a) any action which relates to securing compliance with any restriction, requirement or condition in the event of breach (or putative breach) of a restriction, requirement or condition;

    (b) any action taken with a view to or in connection with the imposition of any sanction (criminal or otherwise) in respect of an act or omission; [and]

    (c) any action taken with a view to or in connection with the pursuit of any remedy conferred by an enactment in respect of an act or omission.[43]

Emergency actions are exempt from the duty to contact the primary authority before carrying out enforcement actions. There are two categories of emergency actions; those involving a response to serious imminent harm, and other emergency actions. The Consultation provides the examples of prohibition notices under the Health and Safety at Work etc. Act 1974 and emergency prohibition notices under the Food Safety Act 1990 as examples of emergency actions involving a response to serious imminent harm.[44] It provides the example of an emergency action in the second category as an abatement notice to silence an intruder alarm under the statutory nuisance regime set out in the Environmental Protection Act 1990.[45]

The purpose of the primary authority scheme is to bring certainty and

---

[40] The principles are set out in section 21 of the Legislative and Regulatory Reform Act 2006.
[41] RES Act, s.26.
[42] ibid. s.28.
[43] ibid. s.28(5).
[44] Consultation, p.23, para.68; see Health and Safety at Work etc. Act 1974, s.22; Food Safety Act 1990, s.12.
[45] Consultation, p.26, para.78; see Environmental Protection Act 1990, Part 3.

consistency to businesses by providing one authority with the primary responsibility for giving advice and guidance to the business.

4. *Civil sanctions*

The RES Act creates four civil sanctions to supplement the existing enforcement powers of the regulatory authorities. The purpose of the civil sanctions is to provide regulatory authorities with an extended sanctioning toolkit to supplement existing criminal sanctions so as to allow regulatory authorities to select the best approach to respond to an offence in light of its surrounding circumstances.   2–019

The power to use the civil sanctions created by the RES Act is not granted directly to a regulatory authority. Instead, Part 3 of the Act authorises the relevant Minister to issue an order that provides a regulatory authority with access to the sanctions subject to the following process. First, the Minister must be satisfied that the authority will comply with the principles of good regulation, which are, as indicated above, transparency, accountability, proportionality, consistency and targeting, in using them. In making this determination, the Minister must review evidence generated by the Hampton Implementation Reviews if such a review has been carried out.

The Minister must then request the Panel for Regulatory Accountability, as appropriate, for its agreement prior to continuing the process to grant the sanctioning powers to the regulatory authority.[46] The next stage is a public consultation on the proposed grant of the powers. Finally, both Houses of Parliament must vote to grant the powers to the regulatory authority under the affirmative Statutory Instrument procedure.[47]

In respect of local authorities, the Minister must consult with the LBRO and also with the national regulatory authority when the national authority works with local authorities in the relevant area of regulation. Local authorities will be granted the civil sanctioning powers as a whole rather than individually.   2–020

Once a regulatory authority has been granted the power to use the civil sanctions, its use of the powers is to be kept under review. If, for instance, the Minister considers that the regulatory authority is persistently misusing the powers, he may issue a direction suspending them.[48]

Three classes of regulators may be granted the authority to use the civil sanctioning powers. Firstly, the Environment Agency, the HSE and Natural England are specifically designated by the RES Act as authorities that

---

[46] The Panel for Regulatory Accountability, chaired by the Prime Minister, must clear all regulatory proposals that are likely to impose a major new burden on business, excluding proposals for emergency legislation and tax matters.
[47] Guidance, para.33.
[48] ibid., para.34.

may be authorised to do so.[49] Secondly, regulatory authorities that enforce offences under provisions of specified statutes may be authorised to use the powers. Of these statutes, those that include environmental enforcement powers are:

- the Clean Air Act 1993 (emissions of smoke and other specified air pollutants);
- the Clean Neighbourhoods and Environment Act 2005, Part 7 (noise);
- the Control of Pollution Act 1974, Part 3 (noise);
- the Control of Pollution (Amendment) Act 1989, sections 1, 5 and 7 (transportation of controlled waste);
- the Environment Act 1995, section 110 (obstruction of authorised persons in the exercise or performance of their duties);
- the Environmental Protection Act 1990, Part 2 (waste), Part 2A (contaminated land regime), Part 3 (statutory nuisances and clean air controls) and section 118 (genetically modified organisms);
- the Health and Safety at Work etc Act 1974 (health and safety at workplaces); and
- the Water Resources Act 1991 (water pollution and other water related offences).

Thirdly, authorities that have enforcement powers set out in secondary legislation issued under specified statutes may be authorised to use the powers. The secondary legislation issued under the following statutory provisions contains the applicable environmental enforcement powers:

- the Environment Act 1995, sections 87 (air quality) and 95 (producer responsibility);
- the Environmental Protection Act 1990, sections 140 (injurious substances or articles) and 156 (regulations giving effect to EU and international obligations);
- the Pollution Prevention and Control Act 1999, sections 2 and 3 (pollution prevention and control); and
- the Water Resources Act 1991, section 92 (precautions against pollution).

If any of the three classes of regulatory authorities described above wishes to use the sanctions, it must publish Penalty Guidance and an Enforcement Policy detailing how it will use the powers. Prior to publication of the Penalty Guidance and the Enforcement Policy, the authority must hold a public consultation.

2–021   The LBRO will publish the Penalty Guidance and Enforcement Policy in consultation with the relevant government departments in respect of local authorities. If both local authorities and a national authority enforce

---

[49] RES Act, Sch.5.

the same legislation, the national authority will be the lead authority in consultation with the relevant central government department, local authorities and the LBRO.[50]

The Penalty Guidance for each regulatory authority and local authorities, as a whole, must describe:

- the authority's proposed use of civil sanctions;
- the circumstances in which the authority will use the sanctions and the manner in which it will do so;
- the circumstances, such as a successful defence, in which a regulatory authority may not impose a sanction;
- the methods of calculating a civil penalty, including factors such as discounts from the penalty for voluntary reporting;
- the right of a business to make representations or objections in respect of a regulatory authority's notice of intent to use a sanction against it; and
- the business' right to appeal a sanction.[51]

The Enforcement Policy, as its name implies, focuses on the enforcement of the civil sanctions in respect of particular offences. As with the Penalty Guidance, the authority must hold a public consultation prior to issuing it.

The Enforcement Policy for each regulatory authority and local authorities as a whole must describe:

- the sanctions that are applicable to each type of offence;
- the way in which the regulatory authority will usually bring an action to punish an offence, for example, whether the authority will usually commence a criminal prosecution or issue a fixed monetary penalty; and
- the circumstances that will determine the sanction that is likely to be used by the regulatory authority in bringing an enforcement action to respond to the offence, for example, prosecuting a person who has a history of failing to comply with the relevant legislation.[52]

The RES Act did not, of course, introduce the concept of enforcement policies. Many regulatory authorities including the Environment Agency[53] and the HSE[54] have long had enforcement policies, which they publish on their websites.

---

[50] Guidance, para.70.
[51] RES Act s.63; see Guidance, para.69.
[52] RES Act s.63; see Guidance, para.69.
[53] Enforcement and Prosecution Policy, No. EAS/8001/1/1 (August 7, 2008); see *http://www.environment-agency.gov.uk/commondata/acrobat/enforcementpolicy_112935.pdf*. The Environment Agency also publishes Guidance for the Enforcement and Prosecution Policy, Doc No. 354_03 (Version 18) (April 7, 2008); see *http://www.environmentagency.gov.uk/commondata/acrobat/epp_1803748.pdf*.
[54] Enforcement Policy Statement, HSE41 (August 2008); see *http://www.hse.gov.uk/pubns/hse41.pdf*.

The four civil sanctions created by the RES Act are: fixed monetary penalties; discretionary requirements; stop notices; and enforcement undertakings.

Fixed monetary penalties

2–022 A fixed monetary penalty is a relatively low fine which may be used by a regulatory authority for a minor, low level regulatory non-compliance. The amount of the fine must be specified in the ministerial order. The regulatory authority, therefore, has no discretion concerning the amount of the penalty but it does have discretion whether to apply it. The maximum amount of the fine for a fixed monetary penalty may not exceed the maximum fine for an offence that is tried summarily and is punishable on summary conviction by a fine,[55] that is, usually £5,000.[56]

A regulatory authority may set a flat amount of penalty for an offence, or it may set varying amounts based on factors such as the size of the non-complying business. The Guidance to the RES Act gives the example of a potential £50 fine for an offence committed by a sole trader, and a potential £100 fine for the same offence committed by a company. A further example is a £50 fine on a business that carries out an activity without a licence for one week, and a £100 fine on a business that carries out the activity without a licence for two weeks.

Prior to issuing a fixed monetary penalty, the regulatory authority must serve a notice of intent on the business against which the penalty will be imposed. The notice must state that the authority proposes to impose the penalty. It must also set out other specified information such as the effect of making a "discharge payment" (that is, a payment accepting liability), the potential availability of defences, the right to make representations and objections to the imposition of the penalty and the deadlines for making the same.[57] Neither the period allowed for making representations and objections nor that allowed for discharging the penalty may exceed 28 days. The ministerial order may set a discharge payment at a lower level than the level of the penalty. In addition, it may specify additional penalties and interest for late payment.[58]

2–023 The authority must not impose a fixed monetary penalty unless it is satisfied beyond a reasonable doubt (i.e. the criminal standard of proof) that the person on whom it is to be imposed has committed the relevant

---

[55] RES Act, s.39(4). The maximum amount applies regardless of whether the offence is also triable on indictment and is also punishable by a term of imprisonment.
[56] Guidance, para.36.
[57] RES Act., s.40.
[58] ibid., s.40.

offence.[59] A business that receives a fixed penalty notice cannot subsequently be prosecuted for the original offence.[60]

The civil courts may enforce an unpaid notice, together with any interest and late penalty payment, as a civil debt. In addition to pursuing the debt through the civil courts, the ministerial order may provide for an unpaid amount to be recoverable as if it was an order of a county court or the High Court. If a regulatory authority follows this latter process in seeking to collect an unpaid amount, it must apply to the relevant court for an order. The authority may then enforce the order[61] by a warrant of execution, a charging order or a third party debt order.[62]

Pursuant to Professor Macrory's recommendation that a regulatory authority should not be allowed to access money recovered from fines, the RES Act provides that the proceeds of fines should be paid into the Consolidated Fund.[63] Professor Macrory had reasoned that financial penalties should not be capable of being viewed by regulatory authorities as a means of raising revenue from businesses regulated by them. He considered that doing so could create inappropriate incentives to a regulatory authority to use such penalties.[64]

Imposition of discretionary requirements

The second category of civil sanctions established by the RES Act is known as "discretionary requirements". These requirements may be imposed for mid to high level regulatory breaches. A "discretionary requirement" is defined by the RES Act to mean a requirement:

2–024

- to pay a monetary penalty in the amount determined by the authority (known as a "variable monetary penalty");
- to take specified steps within a specified period, both to be determined by the regulatory authority, to ensure that the offence does not continue or recur (known as a "compliance requirement"); and/or
- to take specified steps within a specified period, both to be determined by the regulatory authority, to ensure that the position is restored, as far as possible, to the state it would have been in if the

---

[59] RES Act, s.39(2).
[60] ibid., s.41(b).
[61] Guidance, para.40.
[62] A warrant of execution allows a bailiff to size goods or money up to the value of the amount sought to be recovered. A charging order is placed on the defendant's real or personal property. A third party debt order generally prohibits the defendant withdrawing money from a bank or building society account. Ibid. para.41.
[63] RES Act, s.69. The Consolidated Fund is the general UK Government fund managed by the Treasury at the Bank of England.
[64] Macrory Report, p.49, para.3.45.

offence had not been committed (known as a "restoration requirement").[65]

The regulatory authority may impose a combination of these requirements if it considers that doing so is best suited to the circumstances.[66] As with a fixed monetary penalty, the authority must serve a notice of intent on the business on which it proposes to impose a discretionary requirement. The notice must set out the business' right to make representations and objections. The authority must decide, among other things, whether to impose the discretionary requirement, whether to modify it, or whether to impose any other relevant discretionary requirement. If the authority decides to impose a discretionary requirement, it must serve a final notice setting out specified information including the grounds for the imposition, the deadline for payment, the right to appeal the notice and the consequences of non-compliance.[67] A regulatory authority may impose a discretionary requirement only if it is satisfied beyond a reasonable doubt that an offence has been committed. Here also the criminal standard of proof applies, notwithstanding the proceedings being essentially administrative and the "civil" nature of the available sanctions.

Variable Monetary Penalties

2–025 The reason for the flexibility in the amount of the variable monetary penalty is to allow the regulatory authority to set the penalty at a level that both removes from the business any financial gain it may have obtained from committing the offence, and also takes account of the gravity of the business' failure to comply and its history of compliance. If the regulatory authority wishes to be granted the power to impose variable monetary penalties, it must publish guidance setting out the factors that it proposes to take into account in determining their level as well as other factors that may aggravate or mitigate the level of any penalty. The Guidance provides the following examples of aggravating and mitigating factors, stating that they are intended to be illustrative rather than exhaustive. It further states that the aggravating and mitigating factors to be considered by a regulatory authority will depend on the regulatory area and the circumstances of individual cases.

The illustrative aggravating factors set out in the Guidance are:

- the seriousness of the non-compliance with the legislation, such as harm to human health or the environment or the length of time of the non-compliance;
- the business' history of non-compliance;
- the financial gain to the business as a result of the non-compliance;

[65] RES Act, s.42.
[66] Guidance, para.44.
[67] RES Act, s.43.

- the conduct of the business after its discovery of the non-compliance; and
- previous actions taken by regulatory authorities to help the business bring itself into compliance with the relevant regulatory requirements.

The illustrative mitigating factors set out in the Guidance are:

- a previously good compliance record;
- the actions taken by the business to eliminate or reduce the risk of damage resulting from the non-compliance;
- the voluntary reporting of the non-compliance;
- the actions taken by the business to repair the harm caused by its non-compliance with the legislation; and
- the business' co-operation with the regulatory authority in responding to the non-compliance.

The maximum level of a variable monetary penalty for an offence that is triable summarily (that is, may be heard only in a magistrates court) and is punishable only by a fine, is the same as the maximum level for that offence, usually £5,000.[68]

The maximum level of a variable monetary penalty for other offences may be substantial, especially when—as is generally the case—an offender has benefitted financially by failing to comply with the law. Experience in the United States illustrates the potentially high level of such penalties, and as this experience was clearly taken into account by Professor Macrory when proposing the use of variable monetary penalties, a brief description of the US system is given here.[69]

The level of penalties for federal civil environmental offences in the   2–026
United States is determined as follows. First, Congress enacts legislation which, among other things, establishes the maximum penalty for all civil judicial and administrative environmental offences. Other legislation directs the United States Environmental Protection Agency (EPA) (and other federal agencies) regularly to adjust the maximum amount of the penalties for inflation[70] in order to maintain their deterrent effect and to further the policy goals of the relevant legislation. For example, on March 15, 2004, the EPA published regulations that increased the maximum

---

[68] Guidance, para.47.
[69] See M. Woods & R. Macrory, *Environmental Civil Penalties: A More Proportionate Response to Regulatory Breach* (University College London, 2003).
[70] See Civil Monetary Penalty Inflation Adjustment Rule, 40 Code of Federal Regulations part 19, issued pursuant to section 4 of the Federal Civil Penalties Inflation Adjustment Act of 1990, 28 United States Code s.2461 note, as amended by the Debt Collection Improvement Act of 1996, 31 United States Code s.3701 note. The period for increasing the penalties for inflation is four years although this tends to be extended due, among other things, to take account of comments to the proposed rule adjusting the level of the penalties.

amount of civil penalties imposed by it by 17.23 per cent from January 1997 levels.[71]

Second, the EPA publishes enforcement response policies for the settlement of administrative and judicial civil actions brought under various statutes such as the Clean Water Act, the Clean Air Act and the Resource Conservation and Recovery Act. The policies set out the way in which the EPA and the United States Department of Justice (DOJ)[72] will generally calculate the amount sought by the United States Government in settlement of a civil action.[73] The purpose of the guidance is to ensure a consistent national approach in assessing the settlement amount for such penalties whilst providing the relevant EPA and/or DOJ staff with flexibility to determine the penalty amount in individual cases.

The policies include guidance on the component of the penalty attributable to the economic benefit gained by the offender and a "gravity amount", which may be adjusted in response to individual circumstances, to deter future breaches of the law by the same offender and other members of the regulated community. A computer model developed by the EPA, known as the BEN computer model, is used in calculating the economic benefit.[74] The factors that are taken into account by the EPA and the DOJ in determining the level of a settlement penalty track the factors established by Congress for courts to consider in imposing penalties for the relevant offences. For example, the Clean Water Act provides that:

"In determining the amount of a civil penalty the court shall consider the seriousness of the violation or violations, the economic benefit (if any) resulting from the violation, any history of such violations, any good-faith efforts to comply with the applicable requirements, the economic impact of the penalty on the violator, and such other matters as justice may require".[75]

Examples of the high levels of some civil penalties for federal environmental offences in the United States include the following:

- US$34 million assessed against the Colonial Pipeline Company in 2003 for breaching the Clean Water Act by illegally discharging approximately 1,450,000 gallons of petroleum products including oil

---

[71] Environmental Protection Agency, Civil Monetary Penalty Inflation Adjustment Rule, 69 Federal Register 7121 (February 13, 2004).

[72] Federal agencies, including the EPA, do not institute judicial actions. Instead, the DOJ brings the actions on their behalf.

[73] See, e.g. Environmental Protection Agency, RCRA Civil Penalty Policy (June 2003). See also listed federal civil penalty policy and guidance documents at: *http://www.epa.gov/compliance/resources/policies/civil/index.html.*

[74] The BEN User's Manual is available on: *http://www.uiowa.edu/~c091611a/Chaps123.pdf.* For a discussion of civil penalties for environmental offences in the United States, see V. Fogleman, *Environmental Liabilities and Insurance in England and the United States* (London: Witherbys, 2005) pp. 50–51.

[75] 33 United States Code s.1319(d).

into rivers, streams and wetlands along its 5,300 mile pipeline network as a result of operator error, mechanical damage and corrosion;
the settlement included an additional US$30 million to upgrade the
company's operations and to repair and upgrade its pipeline;

- US$20 million assessed against Massey Energy Company in 2008 for
breaching the Clean Water Act by exceeding emission levels for water
discharges at its coal mines and facilities in West Virginia and Ken-
tucky over 4,500 times between January 2000 and December 2006;
the settlement included an additional US$10 million to improve
pollution controls at the company's mines; and

- US$3.5 million against Chevron USA in 2003 for breaches of the
Clean Air Act; Chevron also agreed to spend about US$275 million
in air pollution controls at its refineries.

Compliance and restoration requirements

The Guidance states that examples of compliance requirements, the sec-   **2–027**
ond category of discretionary requirements, are providing training, making
good unsafe equipment and changing a process. Examples of restoration
requirements set out in the Guidance are the remediation of contamination
that has resulted from the business' offence and the reimbursement of
customers' money.[76]

Undertakings

The ministerial order that provides a regulatory authority with the power to   **2–028**
impose discretionary requirements must state that a business may offer the
authority an undertaking to carry out specified actions to benefit a third
party affected by the offence, including the payment of compensation. For
example, a business that receives a notice of intent to issue a variable
monetary penalty may offer to pay compensation to persons affected by the
offence. If the authority agrees with the offer, which must be offered by the
business to the authority before the authority serves a final notice, it may
reduce the amount of the penalty to take account of the compensation.[77]

A business that receives a variable monetary penalty cannot be prosecuted for the original offence, even if it fails to pay the penalty.[78] This is not
however the case where only non-monetary discretionary requirements
have been imposed and/or undertakings have been given in lieu of a variable monetary penalty, and these have not been complied with. The
Guidance states that because such requirements are less punitive than a
variable monetary penalty, a business that fails to comply with them may
subsequently be criminally prosecuted for the original offence.[79] Alter-

[76] Guidance, para.44.
[77] ibid., para.48.
[78] RES Act, s.44(2).
[79] Guidance, para.50.

natively, the Minister may issue an order that authorises the authority to issue a monetary penalty for failure to comply with the discretionary requirement.[80] If a regulatory authority is authorised to issue non-compliance penalties, the ministerial order must set out:

- the amount of the penalty including the method of calculating it;
- the serving of a notice by the regulatory authority to impose the penalty; and
- the business' right to appeal the notice.[81]

Even if a regulatory authority may not bring a prosecution against a company, this prohibition does not prevent the authority from prosecuting one or more directors and officers of that company in respect of the same offence. Most environmental legislation contains provisions that allow the prosecution of directors and officers who consented to, connived in, or were negligent in respect of the commission of an offence by their company.[82]

Stop notices

2–029　A stop notice is a notice that requires a business to cease carrying out an activity specified in the notice until it has carried out steps, also set out in the notice, to comply with it.[83] The notice thus differs from fixed and variable monetary penalties in that it generally seeks to prevent a business from creating or continuing a risk of future harm rather than sanctioning the business for past harm caused by it.

More precisely, a ministerial order may provide that a regulatory authority may serve a stop notice if:

- the business is carrying out an activity in a manner that the authority reasonably believes:
  - is causing, or is presenting a significant risk of causing, serious harm to human health, the environment (including the health of animals and plants), or the financial health of consumers; and
  - carrying out the activity in such a manner involves or is likely to involve the commission of a relevant offence; or
- the authority reasonably believes that the business is likely to carry out a particular activity, and that:

---

[80] Guidance, para.50.
[81] ibid., para.50.
[82] See, e.g. Water Resources Act 1991, s.217(1); Landfill (England and Wales) Regulations 2002, SI 2002/1559, reg.17(3).
[83] RES Act, s.46(2), (5).

- such activity will cause or present a significant risk of causing serious harm to human health, the environment (including the health of animals and plants), or the financial health of consumers; and
- the business' carrying out of the activity will, or will be likely to, involve the commission of a relevant offence.

The stop notice must set out the grounds on which it is based, the business' right to appeal it and the consequences of non-compliance.[84] Failure to comply with a stop notice is a criminal offence.[85]

Due to the potentially serious harm to a business caused by the issuance of a stop notice, a ministerial order that provides a regulatory authority with the power to serve one must authorise the business to apply for compensation from the regulatory authority if it considers that the stop notice should not have been issued and that issuance of the notice has caused it to suffer loss. The Guidance states that compensation may be appropriate if a business successfully appeals the service of a stop notice and the regulatory authority is considered to have acted unreasonably or in serious default. It further states that compensation may not be appropriate if the reason for the success of the appeal is a technicality.[86] A business may appeal an authority's decision not to award compensation as well as the amount of any compensation that is awarded.[87]

If the person on whom a stop notice is served complies with it to the **2–030** satisfaction of the authority, the authority must issue a completion certificate. Issuance of the completion certificate terminates the effectiveness of the notice. The business has the right to appeal an authority's decision not to issue a completion certificate in addition to a right to appeal against the authority's service of the notice itself.[88]

Enforcement undertakings

An enforcement undertaking is an undertaking by a business to carry out **2–031** an action specified in the undertaking within the period also specified in the undertaking. An enforcement undertaking differs from the other civil penalties set out in the RES Act in that the business makes the decision

---

[84] RES Act, s.47(3).
[85] ibid., s.49(1). A person who breaches a stop notice is subject to a fine not exceeding £20,000, imprisonment for up to 12 months, or both, on summary conviction, that is, conviction in the magistrates court. On conviction on indictment in the Crown Court, the penalty is an unlimited fine, imprisonment for up to two years, or both. (Ibid.) The 12 month maximum prison term on summary conviction is subject to the coming into force of section 154(1) of the Criminal Justice Act 2003. Prior to that time, the maximum prison term on summary conviction is six months. Ibid. s.49(2).
[86] Guidance, para.56.
[87] RES Act, s.57.
[88] ibid., s.47.

whether to offer the undertaking to the authority rather than the regulatory authority initiating an action against the business. The business' decision, which may be made following discussions with the authority, is based on the business having recognised that it is in breach of applicable legislation. If the authority has reasonable grounds to suspect that the business has indeed committed an offence, it may accept the undertaking.

An enforcement undertaking may specify that the business will carry out the following actions:

- an action to ensure that the offence does not continue or recur;
- an action to ensure that the position is restored, as far as possible, to its state as if the offence had not been committed;
- an action, including a monetary payment, to benefit any person who has been affected by the offence; and
- any other action specified in the ministerial order.[89]

The ministerial order may also provide that a business may offer an undertaking to make compensation payments, reimbursement or redress to affected parties and enter into a commitment to provide a service such as funding or implementation of a compliance education programme to the community.[90]

The ministerial order may also set out various specified provisions including:

- the procedures by which a business may enter into an undertaking with the regulatory authority;
- the terms of the undertaking and any variation of it;
- the publication of the undertaking by the regulatory authority;
- circumstances that are considered by the authority to indicate compliance with an undertaking;
- monitoring of an undertaking by the regulatory authority; and
- certification by the authority that the business has complied with the undertaking and the right to appeal against the authority's refusal to provide the certification.

If the regulatory authority accepts an undertaking, the business may not be convicted of the original offence and may not have a fixed monetary penalty or a discretionary requirement imposed on it.[91] The regulatory authority may, however, impose a criminal or other sanction on the business, provided the ministerial order so states, if the business has only partially complied with the undertaking, has provided inaccurate, misleading or incomplete information or has otherwise breached the undertaking.[92]

---

[89] RES Act, s.50(3); see Guidance, para.60.
[90] Guidance, paras 4.27–.28.
[91] RES Act, s.50(4).
[92] ibid., s.50(5).

There is no right to appeal an undertaking with the limited exception   **2–032**
of an appeal against the failure of the regulatory authority to issue a
certificate, if relevant, to the business on completion of the undertaking.[93]

Professor Macrory has described enforceable undertakings, in the
consultation document published before the Macrory Report, as "an
additional sanction that could be used further up the enforcement pyr-
amid."[94] He stated that an enforceable undertaking is similar to an
enforcement notice in that it is an alternative to payment of a fine for a
regulatory non-compliance. He further stated that whereas an enforcement
notice is relevant to serious offences due to its potential to impose a significant financial or reputation cost on a business that fails to comply with
regulatory requirements, an enforceable undertaking may include a
restorative element.

Professor Macrory also discussed the use of a combination of an
enforceable undertaking and a fine, which he called an "undertaking plus".
The imposition of an undertaking plus would be subject to the agreement
of both the regulatory authority and the person who committed the
offence. It could, for example, include an agreement on the deadline for
carrying out the specified actions set out in the enforceable undertaking.[95]

Costs

A ministerial order that provides a regulatory authority with the power to   **2–033**
issue a stop notice or to impose a discretionary requirement (but not a fixed
monetary penalty or an enforceable undertaking) may, subject to the
approval of HM Treasury, authorise the regulatory authority to recover its
costs. Costs that are subject to recovery include investigation and administration costs and the cost of obtaining legal or other expert advice. The
business may be granted a right of appeal against the amount of costs
charged and the requirement to pay them.[96]

Appeals

A person on whom a fixed monetary penalty, a discretionary requirement   **2–034**
or a stop notice is served has the right to appeal it to either the First-tier
Tribunal or the statutory tribunal specified in the ministerial order granting
the regulatory authority the power to enforce the civil sanctions. The First-
tier Tribunal is a new generic tribunal that was established by the Tribu-

---

[93] Guidance, para.61.
[94] Richard Macrory, "Regulatory Justice: Sanctioning in a Post-Hampton World" (consultation document), p.68, para.4.26 (May 2006).
[95] Macrory Report, p.68, para.4.30.
[96] Guidance, para.67.

nals, Courts and Enforcement Act 2007, which consolidated many former tribunals. The First-tier Tribunal is divided into chambers,[97] with a General Regulatory Chamber to hear appeals against the RES Act civil sanctions. Appeals are heard by a tribunal judge who may sit alone or with one or two other members of the Tribunal who have expertise in the relevant regulatory area.[98]

The grounds of appeal for a fixed monetary penalty, a discretionary requirement or a stop notice differ depending on the sanction. As a general rule, however, the business on which a civil sanction is imposed may appeal it on the grounds that the regulatory authority's decision to impose the sanction:

- was based on an error of fact;
- was wrong in law; or
- was unreasonable.[99]

The reasons for an appeal based on the regulatory authority's decision to impose it being unreasonable include, depending on the applicable civil penalty, whether the amount of the penalty was unreasonable or whether the nature of the specified compliance requirement was unreasonable.[100] It is not clear in such cases whether the Tribunal will consider individual cases on their merits and, thus, substitute its judgement for that of the regulatory authority or whether the applicable criterion is "Wednesbury unreasonableness".[101] It seems likely that the Tribunal will review appeals on "unreasonableness" on their merits, and will be less inclined than courts in judicial review cases to defer to the regulatory authority's decision, unless the Tribunal considers either that the authority has specific expertise in the subject matter or, in the case of the reasonableness of a monetary penalty, the amount of the penalty is outside the zone of reasonability. A factor that will be included in the Tribunal's decision on "unreasonableness" will, of course, be the authority's compliance (or not) with its Penalty Guidance.[102]

The ministerial order may grant the First-tier Tribunal the power to

---

[97] Tribunals, Courts and Enforcement Act 2007, s.7.
[98] See Guidance, para.63.
[99] ibid., para.64.
[100] ibid., para.49.
[101] "Wednesbury unreasonableness" occurs when an authority has come to a conclusion so unreasonable that no reasonable authority could ever have come to it; *Associated Provincial Picture Houses v Wednesbury Corporation* [1948] 1 K.B. 223 at 233. A decision that is "Wednesbury unreasonable" or irrational has been said to be one that "is so outrageous in its defiance of logic or accepted moral standards that no sensible person who had applied his mind to the question to be decided could have arrived at it"; *Council of Civil Service Unions v Minister for the Civil Service* (the *GCHQ* case), per Lord Diplock, [1985] AC 374 at 411. For a fuller discussion of this see paras 6–027 to 6–033 below. Accordingly if an appellant has to establish Wednesday unreasonableness, he will be faced with an extremely high hurdle, that will rarely be surmountable.
[102] See text accompanying fn.51.

confirm or withdraw the notice or requirement, to take other steps such as imposing another sanction, or to remit the decision back to the regulatory authority for a further decision. The ministerial order may also provide that the notice or requirement may be suspended during an appeal. The Government intends to make detailed procedural rules to govern the Tribunal's use of its powers. Those rules will include, among other things, the time limits for appeals. The limits may vary for the different types of sanctions.[103]

A defendant who is unsuccessful in an appeal to the First-tier Tribunal   **2–035**
has a right of appeal on application, with permission from the First-tier or Upper Tribunal, to the Upper Tribunal on a point of law except for specified excluded decisions.[104] The defendant has a further right of appeal on application, with permission from the Upper Tribunal or the Court of Appeal, from the Upper Tribunal to the Court of Appeal, again on a point of law except for excluded decisions.[105]

Publicity

Each regulatory authority that uses the civil sanctions granted by the RES   **2–036**
Act must publish details of their enforcement actions. The details include the matter in which the sanction has been imposed, the discharge of a fixed monetary penalty and the acceptance of a discretionary requirement.[106] Exceptions from publication exist for sanctions that have been successfully appealed by a business or for which the ministerial order provides an exception.[107] The publication provisions in the RES Act do not prohibit a regulatory authority from continuing to publish details of its enforcement actions including, for example, press releases regarding individual cases.

Regulatory burden

The RES Act grants the Minister the power to require a regulatory   **2–037**
authority to identify and remove any unnecessary regulatory burdens when it is practicable and proportionate to remove them. In addition, it bars a regulatory authority from imposing unnecessary burdens.[108] The Guidance describes an "unnecessary burden" as a duty or requirement that the

---

[103] RES Act, s.54.
[104] Tribunals, Courts and Enforcement Act 2007, s.11.
[105] ibid., s.13. The term "excluded decisions" is defined by section 13(8) of the 2007 Act. The term includes, for example, a decision of the Upper Tribunal to review, or not to review, an earlier decision of the tribunal.
[106] RES Act, s.65.
[107] Guidance, paras 71–72.
[108] RES Act, s.72.

authority has discretion to exercise and that has been identified by the regulatory authority as:

- disproportionate to the authority's policy objective because it exceeds the measures that are necessary to achieve the objective;
- is targeted at situations in which regulatory action is not necessary to achieve the authority's policy objective; and
- is imposed in circumstances in which the desired objective could have been achieved in a less burdensome way.[109]

The regulatory authorities' duty to review the burden on businesses presented by its enforcement powers is continuous and includes a duty to report annually on actions taken by the authority.[110]

---

[109] Guidance, para.74.
[110] ibid., para.74.

Chapter 3

CRIMINAL PROSECUTIONS AND SENTENCING

Introduction[1]

This chapter is primarily concerned with the procedural aspects of how   **3–001** environmental law offences are enforced in the criminal courts, and the sentences that may be imposed on those found guilty, but it also includes an outline of some of the legal concepts relevant to environmental law enforcement. The Regulatory Enforcement and Sanctions Act 2008 which provides for the use of administrative, rather than criminal, sanctions for regulatory offences, is likely to have a major effect on how environmental law is enforced in the United Kingdom.[2] Nevertheless, it may well be some time before this occurs in practice, and in any event the criminal law must and always will be a last resort for dealing with those responsible for wilful or reckless illegal conduct.

Under English common law, two distinct elements must be present for a person to be guilty of a crime. The first is the deliberate and voluntary performance of or participation in the act which is said to be criminal (i.e. the "actus reus"), and the second is the mental element (or "mens rea"), this being the accused's guilty mind or knowledge of the act, whether that be in the form of intention or recklessness. An often borrowed explanation defines mens rea as "intention, knowledge or recklessness with respect to all the elements of the offence together with any ulterior intent which the definition of crime requires".[3]

Virtually all environmental offences are now statute-based. Nevertheless, apart from inchoate offences such as conspiracy and attempt, the common law offence of public nuisance may still be used to deal with certain "crimes against the environment". Even this has, to a substantial extent, been subject to legislative codification.[4] Moreover, a recent judgment of

---

[1] Many of the acronyms used within this chapter may be unfamiliar to lawyers who are not regularly involved in criminal matters. Any readers needing assistance in this respect are directed to the Table of Abbreviations at the front of the book.

[2] See Chapter 2.

[3] Smith and Hogan, *Criminal Law*, 11th edition, (Oxford University Press, 2005) pp.110–113.

[4] See e.g. the nuisance parking offences created by ss.3–9 of the Clean Neighbourhood and Environment Act 2005.

the House of Lords has confirmed that it should only be used where there is no statutory provision which covers the conduct in question.[5]

Strict liability

3–002 In contrast with common law offences, many, probably most, statutory environmental offences require no proof of knowledge, intent, recklessness, negligence, dishonesty or any other mental element which would normally be an essential ingredient. In these cases "the presumption [of mens rea] can be displaced either by the words of the statute creating the offence or by the subject matter with which it deals and both must be considered".[6] Such offences are said to be of strict liability. Strict liability applies of course to many categories of statutory offences. Where it has been imposed there is one common thread linking them—public policy requires certain sorts of offending behaviour to be readily dealt with if the public interest is to be adequately protected, and having to prove mens rea is judged to be an excessive obstacle. Nevertheless, in some, but far from all, cases the defence may be entitled to avoid liability by showing e.g. that due diligence was exercised to avoid commission of the offence.

The modern law on strict liability has been the subject of several comparatively recent decisions of the House of Lords.[7] There is disquiet in some quarters that the more serious environmental offences, which are potentially subject to lengthy custodial sentences and unlimited financial penalties, bypass the primary rule that to be guilty of a criminal offence one must also have a guilty mind. Nevertheless the courts have not only approved the principle of strict liability, but confirmed that it does not infringe a defendant's right to a fair trial under Article 6 of the European Convention on Human Rights,[8] nor give rise to any incompatibility with the presumption of innocence guaranteed by Article 6(2).[9]

Corporate liability

3–003 Until recently corporate criminal liability was based upon two distinct routes: either that which attaches through vicarious liability, where the company is responsible for the acts or omissions of its employees, or direct liability where the company is held responsible because the offence is

---

[5] *R v Rimmington; R v Goldstein* [2006] 1 Cr.App.R 17.

[6] Per Wright J. in *Sherras v De Rutzen* [1895] 1 Q.B. 918.

[7] See *Lim Chin Aik v The Queen* [1963] AC 160; *Sweet v Parsley* [1970] AC 132; *Gammon (Hong Kong) Ltd v Attorney-General of Hong Kong* [1985] AC 1; and *B (A Minor) v Director of Public Prosecutions* [2000] 2 A.C. 428.

[8] *R v Deyemi and Edwards*, unreported August 13, 2007; *Barnfather v Islington LBC and another*, *The Times* March 20, 2003.

[9] *R v G*, unreported April 12, 2006, but see by contrast the observations of Bingham L.J. in *Sheldrake v DPP; Att Gen Reference* (No.2 of 2006), October 15, 2004.

committed by or with the knowledge of someone who is a "directing or controlling mind of the company".

However the notion that corporate liability can only be established where the employees responsible were of sufficient seniority to act as the "controlling mind of the company"[10] is no longer good law. The courts' approach to corporate responsibility for environmental offences, particularly those of strict liability, was underlined by the House of Lords decision in *Alphacell* and has been endorsed by several later decisions including *National Rivers Authority v Alfred McAlpine Homes East Limited*.[11] The court in *Alfred McAlpine* held that to sustain a prosecution under s.85(1) WRA the question was whether, as a matter of common sense, the company caused the pollution of controlled waters. Accordingly a company would be criminally liable for causing pollution which resulted from the *acts* or *omissions* of its employees *acting within the course and scope of their employment*, regardless of whether they could be said to be exercising the controlling mind and will of the company (save only where some third party acted in such a way as to interrupt the chain of causation). In short, *Alphacell* was an illustration of vicarious liability—clearly in that case those representing the directing mind and will of the company had not themselves, in any meaningful sense, personally caused the polluting matter to escape. In *Tesco v Nattrass* a prosecution was brought against Tesco for an offence under s.24(1) of the Trade Description Act 1968. One of its stores had run out of reduced price soap powder, but had failed to remove advertising for it when they put normally priced soap powder on the shelf. The defence of due diligence was available to the company unless the store manager's failure could be attributed to the company. The House of Lords held that the store manager was not of sufficient stature to be identified as a "directing mind" of the company and, therefore, the defence of due diligence was available. Thus, the distinction between *NRA v Alfred McAlpine* and *Tesco v Nattrass* is not whether the company was liable for committing an offence, but whether it could invoke a statutory defence.

The courts thus require a purposive approach to be used to interpret the scope of a statutory offence in order to determine whose acts will be attributed to the company; and a robust attitude has been adopted with environmental offences of strict liability.[12] In some non-environmental categories of strict liability offence, culpability will only attach to a company if there is proof of knowledge or connivance on the part of the directing mind of the company.[13] There is, for example, a contrast between how the courts have dealt with companies involved in environmental offences and their attitude to the employers of drivers committing tacho-

[10] *Tesco Supermarkets v Nattrass* [1972] A.C. 153.
[11] *National Rivers Authority (Southern Region) v Alfred McAlpine Homes East Limited* [1994] Env. L.R. 198.
[12] *NRA v Alfred McAlpine* as above.
[13] *Seaboard Offshore Ltd v Secretary of State for Transport* [1994] 2 All E.R. 99 HL.

graph offences contrary to EU Regulations and the Transport Act 1968. These latter are strict liability offences as regards the employee, but for a prosecution to succeed against a corporate employer the courts have held that there must be some evidence upon which a court can properly infer that the employer gave a positive mandate or some other sufficient act to "cause" the tachograph offence to occur; mere acquiescence in those circumstances is insufficient.[14]

3–004   Where a statutory "due diligence" defence is provided, such as in s.33(7) of the EPA 1990, a company can still be caught even when its employee is not strictly speaking acting within the scope of his employment. Again a purposive approach to statutory interpretation is taken. A company may be liable for the errant employee who is not acting within the scope of his employment if the purpose of the statute requires the company to be held accountable for what actually happened.[15] Whether liability arises may be a question of fact and degree, but some assistance can be gleaned from case law not specific to environmental offences. In *Meridian Global Funds Management Asia v Securities Commission*[16] two senior investment managers improperly used their authority to provide bridging funds in order to obtain a controlling holding in a cash-rich New Zealand company. One manager continued to buy and sell securities without supervision, and the board only met once a year. In considering whether the company was responsible for the unauthorised acts of its employees, Lord Hoffman considered the rules of attribution, whereby as a necessary part of corporate personality there should be rules by which acts of its employees are attributed to the company. It will not be sufficient to show that the primary rules of attribution (which might be found in a company's articles of association) divest it of responsibility for errant employees, since a company builds on the primary rules of attribution by using general rules of attribution, namely the principles of agency. If a company appoints servants and agents whose acts count as the acts of the company, then the company itself can be held liable for their actions. Where a special rule of attribution may be necessary before a company should be held liable, the court will apply the usual canons of interpretation, taking into account the language of the statute and its contents and policy,[17] since "undertakings by corporations would be worth little if the company could avoid liability for what its employees had done on the grounds that the board did not know about it".[18] Similarly in *Meridian Global* the policy of notification under the particular statute was to compel, in fast-moving markets,

---

[14] See *Redhead Freight Ltd v Shulman* [1989] RTR 1; *Vehicle Inspectorate v Southern Coaches and Others* TLR 23/2/00 and *Vehicle Inspectorate v Nuttall* [1999] CLR 674.
[15] See *Shanks & McEwan v Environment Agency* [1995] 1 W.L.R. 1356.
[16] [1998] 4 All E.R. 286.
[17] See *R v British Steel* [1995] 3 W.L.R. 1356, *Re Supply of Ready Mix Concrete (no 2) Director General of Fair Trading v Pioneer Concrete (UK)* [1995] 1 All E.R. 135.
[18] *Re Supply of Ready Mix Concrete (no 2) Director General of Fair Trading v Pioneer Concrete (UK)* [1995] 1 All E.R. 135.

immediate disclosure of the identity of substantial security holders in public issues. The court concluded that the policy of the Act would be defeated if the board of Meridian could escape liability by only meeting once a year. To put it another way "this would put a premium on the board paying as little attention as possible to what its [employees] were doing". *R v British Steel* involved health and safety issues which the court considered "requires more stringent protection with a section cast in absolute terms creating absolute prohibition". In summary, if the court interprets the necessary purpose behind the statute as policing the acts of the company and its management, then the company may not be able to avoid liability, even if prima facie the employee is acting beyond the strict code of his employment, simply because the company (in the form of the board of directors) did not know what was going on.

All of this now has to be set against the decision of the High Court in *Express Dairies (t/a Express Dairies Distribution) v Environment Agency*.[19] This was an appeal from the Redditch magistrates court by way of case stated. The appellant was prosecuted under section 217(3) of the Water Resources Act 1991 (the WRA). The appellant owned a dairy depot. One of its customers was a private contractor (Ian Purdy) who bought milk from it. The appellant also allowed Mr. Purdy to use its premises to take delivery of cream from an outside supplier. In the course of taking delivery of the cream 10 litres escaped down the surface water drains. Although this incident was an isolated occurrence, and a general risk assessment had been made, it was admitted that no thought had been given to the question of how to reduce the risk of a spillage or how to prevent environmental damage if a spillage should occur. In summarising the connection between section 85(1) and 217(3) of the WRA, Kennedy L.J. said this:

> "if a landowner ... is going to permit an operation on his land which gives rise to a risk of pollution then, ... in order not to fall foul of section 85(1) he must carry out a risk assessment and respond to what that assessment reveals. Otherwise if pollution does occur it might be impossible for him to say that the offence committed by those using his land was not due to one or more of his acts or defaults".

Thus, the court can and will look at the policy of protection behind the statute to determine when corporate liability should arise. Where the offence is one of absolute prohibition—such as polluting a water course—a company that has failed to carry out a comprehensive risk assessment, which may lead to a lack of supervision and errant employees, servants or agents contravening the law, cannot evade responsibility on the grounds that those at the top did not know what was going on. Following this decision it is clear that corporate liability will be affected very considerably by deficiencies in the risk assessment, and still more by the failure of a

---

[19] [2004] EWHC 1710.

company to carry out adequate environmental risk assessment as part of its duties. Furthermore, it is no good having policies and procedures for risk assessments in place if they are not effectively implemented. Hence if a company is going to permit operations (either through its employees or third parties) which carry with it a risk of pollution, it must carry out a proper risk assessment, and act on the results.

Liability of directors and managers

3–005 Quite apart from the criminal liability of corporate bodies, their directors, managers, secretaries or others who are effectively running the business are themselves vulnerable to prosecution in certain situations. It is noteworthy that in health and safety legislation the directors and officers of the company are frequently prosecuted alongside the company in a way that happens rarely in environmental prosecutions, unless there is a serious pollution incident and direct evidence of a specific individual's involvement. Section 217(1) of the WRA and s.157 of the Environmental Protection Act 1991 (the EPA) are two examples of statutes which enable a prosecutor to get behind the corporate façade to officers who are responsible for an offence by their company.[20]

In practice these provisions are almost exclusively used to attack the small or medium sized company where the directors' involvement will be easier to establish. Inevitably the larger the company, the more difficult it is to establish a link between the facts of the company's offence and individual company officers. In determining who may be responsible within the company, the title that an officer has attributed to himself is irrelevant; it is the existence and scope of his authority which matters.[21] In order to establish the liability of an officer of a company under the WRA or the EPA provisions, there must be both an offence committed by the company and also specific evidence of the consent, connivance or neglect by the officer. Though these and similar provisions are applicable to all offences by companies under these statutes, prosecutors are especially liable to invoke them where there is a suspicion that unscrupulous officers of a company are profiting from its unlawful activities, or are moving company funds between one legal entity and another to avoid paying large fines at court. Moreover, the use made of the Proceeds of Crime Act (POCA) 2002[22] and

---

[20] The two sections are in substantially identical terms. WRA s.217(1) reads:
"Where a body corporate is guilty of an offence under this Act and that offence is proved to have been committed with the consent or connivance of, or to be attributable to any neglect on the part of, any director, manager, secretary or other similar officer of the body corporate or any person who was purporting to act in any such capacity, then he, as well as the body corporate, shall be guilty of that offence and shall be liable to be proceeded against and punished accordingly."
[21] *Woodhouse v Walsall MBC* [1994] Env. L.R. 30.
[22] See ENDS reports 392, (August 2007), and 396, (January 2008)—£75,000 seized from the operators of an illegal landfill site.

its descendant the Serious Crime Act 2007[23] are being seen by the Environment Agency and other regulatory bodies as one of the most effective weapons against all perpetrators of environmental crime, and not just corporations. It has the clear benefit of enabling offenders to be reached where numerous companies have been established to obfuscate responsibility.

Defences to environmental offences

There are relatively few real defences to a charge of strict liability. **3–006** Obviously a defence will succeed if the accused can show that he has no sufficient connection with the polluting act. Another defence is the "Act of God", i.e. an act which is so unnatural and/or unexpected as to break the chain of causation.[24] A company, faced with a strict liability offence caused by its servants or agents, may also be able to break the chain of causation between them and it, and so avoid liability, if it can demonstrate that, (i) it implemented a full risk assessment, (ii) the servants or agents acted ultra vires, and (iii) those involved in the management of the company could not reasonably have known what the servants and agents were doing, despite fully implementing the risk assessment.

In certain circumstances statute provides for a defence of due diligence, or taking all reasonable steps, e.g. s.33(7) EPA or s.89 WRA. The prosecution must first prove a contravention to the criminal standard, but then the burden of establishing the statutory defence, on the balance of probabilities, lies on the defendant. A due diligence defence is one of fact and degree, but it will be construed narrowly by the courts in order to protect the "strict" nature of liability in environmental crime. A management system of waste disposal which relied merely upon the provision of a skip into which the producer of the waste deposited material, but failed to require information to be given to the person who was responsible for disposing of the skip's contents, was not sufficient to fulfil the requirement in s.3(4) of the Control of Pollution Act 1974 that the person must take care to inform himself whether the deposit contravened section 3(1) of the Act. The transporter of waste had to take care to inform himself on each occasion in relation to each deposit as to the nature of the consignment in order to avail himself of the defence in s.3(4).[25] An offence was committed by his failing to do so. In determining whether a person took all reasonable precautions and exercised due diligence, the court will have regard to any published guidance on the topic. There is a marked contrast between environmental cases and those in other areas of the law where the due

---

[23] This came into force on April 6, 2008.
[24] See *Impress (Worcester) Ltd v Rees* [1971] 2 AER 357, but this case should now be read alongside *Express Dairies and The Environment Agency v Block PLC* (1998) Env. L.R. 607.
[25] *Durham County Council v Peter Connors Industrial Services Limited* [1993] Env. L.R. 197.

diligence defence applies as to the necessity to make full and proper enquiries.[26] However, in the light of the *Express Dairies*[27] case, the need for both a proper risk assessment by an organisation and also an effective response to what that assessment has revealed must be established by those accused of an environmental offence.

In certain limited situations, acting under instruction from an employer may be a defence. EPA s.33(7)(b) is one of the few statutory examples. Again such a defence will be a question of fact and degree. Where an employee raises such a defence, the employer may assert that the employee was not acting in accordance with any instruction given by the management, but outside the scope of his employment. In this situation both the employer and the employee may find themselves conducting "cut-throat" defences, blaming each other.

3–007   Under some statutes, for example WRA s.89 and EPA s.33(7)(c), acts done in an emergency can also be a defence, depending on the circumstances. Under EPA s.33(7)(c), for example, it must be shown that what the accused did was done to avoid danger to human health, and that all such steps as were reasonably practicable were taken to minimise the pollution and harm to human health. This also may now be subject to the *Express Dairies* considerations of risk assessment and proper risk management. Such statutory defences usually require that regulators be alerted swiftly.

Certain statutes provide that having a reasonable excuse is a defence for an offending act, for example s.5(7) of the Control of Pollution (Amendment) Act 1989. The burden of establishing this lies on the defendant, though what is required of him will depend on the circumstances of the case. What is clear from the authorities, such as they are, is that a tribunal should be slow to rule that facts in a particular case cannot amount to a good reason or a reasonable excuse *as a matter of law*.[28] One example of where such a defence might be defeated is if the defendant does not give evidence to explain or support his "reasonable excuse". In these circumstances the tribunal might, as it did in *R v Bown*,[29] conclude as a matter of law that the evidential burden placed upon the defendant had not been discharged. Acting under a misapprehension might amount to a reasonable excuse,[30] and even forgetfulness can contribute to such a defence.[31]

Finally, many statutes create an explicit defence where there is authority

---

[26] See *Popley v Scott* [2001] Crim LR 416; *Kilhey Court Hotels Ltd v Wigan MBC* 169 JP 1 QBD; R *(on application of Bilon) v WH Smith Trading* [2001] Crim LR 850; *Cambridgeshire CC v Kama* 171 JP 194 DC.

[27] [2004] EWHC 1710 (Admin).

[28] See *R v Bown* [2003] EWCA Crim 1989 considered in *R v Wang* [2003] EWCA Crim 3228 HL.

[29] [2003] EWCA Crim 1989.

[30] *R v Nicholson* [2006] EWCA Crim 1518.

[31] *R v Glidewell (CA)* [1999] 163 JP 557, *R v Jolie (CA)* [2003] EWCA Crim 1543, *R v Bird* [2004] EWCA Crim 64.

to discharge or otherwise operate in accordance with a licence or permit issued by a regulator such as the Environment Agency. An inevitable corollary is that where a licensee fails to comply with his licence conditions, he will be potentially separately liable both for that non-compliance and also for any pollution thereby caused.

When to Prosecute

The regulator's decision as to what sanction or sanctions should be deployed in response to a breach of environmental law will inevitably vary from case to case. Immediate sanction in the form of enforcement notices will invariably be used where the offence is minor and can be rectified easily. There are numerous factors which may affect whether an environmental transgression will be the subject of a prosecution; the Incident Categorisation[32] adopted by the Environment Agency indicates those factors which are likely to affect such a decision. The scale and environmental impact of an alleged offence are among the prime factors affecting the outcome. The more serious the incident, the more likely the prospect of prosecution, even if the offender is of good character. Thus, the environmentally compliant defendant of good character who is responsible for creating a Category 1 pollution incident is as likely to be at risk of prosecution as the repeat offender who ignores a number of enforcement notices resulting in a Category 2 pollution incident.

3–008

Category 1 pollution incidents include offences where there has been: (i) persistent and extensive effects upon the quality of media such as air, water or land, (ii) damage to humans, (iii) serious or long-term damage to the ecosystem or to the amenity, or (iv) substantial damage to agriculture or commerce. For these, prosecution is almost invariably the response.

In the case of Category 2 incidents, the likelihood of prosecution depends upon the extent to which there has been a *significant* effect on the quality of air, land or water or damage to the ecosystem, a reduction in amenity value, significant damage to agriculture and/or commerce and/or impact on human beings. The difference between Categories 1 and 2 depends on the regulator's view of what is "significant" damage. If there is evidence to demonstrate that the incident was intentional (in the sense of being deliberate) or reckless it is likely to warrant a prosecution, but this is not inevitable as with a Category 1 incident. Other factors may play a part in determining whether there is to be a prosecution, for example, whether the accused has committed any offences before, or has ignored enforcement notices. The regulator may also have regard to the risk management procedures in place at the time of the incident, the attitude towards the incident by the accused, such as their response to assisting in any clean-up

---

[32] See Environment Agency Facts and Figures—pollution incident categories.

operation and their approach to co-operation with any investigation of the matter. Public interest factors including the frequency of smaller Category 2 incidents being committed in a locality (such as illegal fly tipping) where a deterrent element is needed *pour encourager les autres*. If the matter is not regarded as sufficiently "significant" to demand a prosecution the matter will probably be dealt with by way of a formal caution, at least provided the defendant's attitude towards the regulator is co-operative.

3–009 Category 3 incidents are those where there is a relatively minor effect on the quality of air, land or water. They will rarely be prosecuted unless the accused has shown himself to be a recidivist offender of such magnitude that a warning would not be considered sufficient in the public interest. In most cases these incidents will be dealt with by way of a warning. Category 4 incidents are those where no impact has occurred and are likely to be dealt with by a warning at most.

Since the offender's attitude is relevant in considering whether to prosecute, wilful obstruction will almost certainly guarantee it. Should he, or a witness, make a false statement or declaration in the course of the investigation they could find themselves charged with attempting to pervert the course of justice, for which, being a common law offence, the sentence is at large. Operating without a required Environment Agency permit will generally attract a prosecution unless the activity is of such low risk that this is considered a disproportionate response, or unless it was inadvertent and is immediately corrected on being alerted to the need for a permit. An offence that is committed deliberately or recklessly will normally result in a prosecution. Where it is committed negligently, the regulator will seek to distinguish culpable negligence from simple incompetence, but ignorance of procedure or best practice will not afford a defence, and is unlikely to persuade a regulator to adopt a sympathetic approach to an accused. Since it is part of the regulator's duty to ensure best business practice through enforcement of proper risk management and compliance, those who chose to ignore published guidance, whether that be for profit motives or other reasons, can expect little sympathy from either the regulator or the court, and this is particularly so where there is an unfair impact upon competing legitimate operators. A noticeable increase of environmental offences in a geographical area will also have a bearing upon whether the regulator takes enforcement action through the criminal courts.[33]

Of course all prosecution authorities must have regard to the guidance given in the Code for Crown Prosecutors as to whether the necessary evidential threshold has been met such as will provide a realistic prospect of securing a conviction.[34] In deciding whether the threshold test has been met the prosecutor will consider the evidence gleaned from witness state-

---

[33] Since 2005 the Northern Ireland Environmental and Heritage Service environmental crime team has overseen 244 successful prosecutions against illegal waste offences generating £568,415 in fines.

[34] The Code for Crown Prosecutors.

ments, any sampling evidence, the chain of continuity over sampling, and information obtained as a result of section 108 EA[35] statements, or information that may be required to be provided under legislation, such as by section 71(2) EPA notices (which require the recipient to furnish any information that the authority reasonably considers it needs within a specified time),[36] together with information from the accused (should he choose to give an account in an interview under caution[37]). Information properly obtained from statutory notices can be used in subsequent prosecutions, and a failure to provide the information on the grounds that it may incriminate the individual is not a reasonable excuse for withholding it.[38] The terms of EA section 108, which require a person to produce "records" are not exhaustive, and will not justify a prosecutor embarking upon a fishing expedition. This provision is limited to records which are required to be kept under the pollution control enactments[39] or those which the investigator considers "necessary" for him to see.[40] Inevitably the decision as to what is "necessary" is subjective and will depend upon the facts of each case, but it should be borne in mind that once the information is in the hands of the prosecutor it could be used to request further information from a defendant, either before or at the time of his attendance for interview under caution. Documents created in contemplation of legal proceedings for example will, prima facie, be privileged. It is also open to question whether this is true also of information contained in draft consultation documents. There is no harm in questioning the basis upon which the records are deemed "necessary"; however if there is justification for a request then a refusal to comply may be viewed as obstruction and an aggravating feature in any subsequent prosecution. Such conduct may find its way into the subsequent case summary prepared by the regulator which is commonly known as a *Friskies* Report.[41]

Interviews under caution

Since the Environment Agency cannot compel a party to attend for interview, how a person responds to a request to attend may be crucial to the decision whether to prosecute or not. If the defendant decides that he is

3–010

---

[35] Arguably the information obtained under s.108 statements can now be adduced in evidence using the hearsay provisions in ss.114–118 of the CJA 2003.

[36] And the failure to provide such information without reasonable excuse is an offence in itself. See s.71(3) EPA 1990.

[37] There is no legal obligation on a person to attend an interview under caution and the Environment Agency or other regulator cannot compel them.

[38] *R v Hertfordshire County Council ex p Green Environmental Industries Ltd and another* 95 LGR 424 DC.

[39] Section 108(4)(k)(i) Environmental Protection Act 1995.

[40] Section 108(4)(c) and (k)(ii) EPA.

[41] *R v Friskies Petcare (UK) Ltd* [2000] 2 Cr.App.R.(S) 401. See para.3–021.

content to answer questions, then it is not unreasonable to establish in advance the topics which the investigator is likely to cover, since there may be documents or information which the defendant wants to disclose. However, asking for a list of the questions to be provided prior to the interview will in practice be greeted by a firm refusal. Of course the defendant is not obliged to attend for interview at all, but this may backfire in the long run because the attitude taken towards the regulator is a factor which a court may take into account in determining the sentence, in particular the level of any fine (which may be greater if the refusal has caused investigative costs to increase). Furthermore, any documents which the defendant does take with him will remain with the investigator and may be admissible in evidence under the business documents provisions of the Criminal Justice Act 2003.[42] It is worth remembering that an interview under caution conducted by a regulator is subject to exactly the same provisions of the Police and Criminal Evidence Act 1984 and the Code of Practice as an interview conducted by a police officer—this means that the defendant is not obliged to answer questions. However, any failure to do so may count against him: firstly, the investigator may decide that he has something to hide and gather evidence another way and, secondly, it is an aggravating feature when it comes to the court sentencing considerations. In the case of the defendant who has attended for interview and answered all of the questions, the prosecutor is obliged, as a matter of fairness to the defendant, to place this before the court in mitigation, and the court is likely to have considerable regard to it.

Of all the factors which determine whether an accused will be prosecuted for a pollution incident, perhaps one of the most compelling is if the accused has gained financially from the offence, especially if there is evidence to show that he has profited at the expense of the environment. The accused's position will be aggravated if he has ignored earlier warnings or enforcement notices whilst generating large profits from unlawful practices.

Where there is an expectation that the accused will receive a substantial financial penalty and has the resources to pay it, this may also have an effect upon the decision to prosecute. In the current climate prosecutors are expected to have regard to the cost/benefit analysis of prosecution in deciding whether to pursue a case. Since public funds are not limitless, and resources have to be apportioned between competing interests, lengthy (and often costly) investigations which are expected to derive little financial benefit are liable to fall at an early stage, on the grounds that it is against the public interest to pursue such a course. Recent prosecutions show that the Environment Agency has been working with the Assets Recovery Agency (now called the Serious Organised Crime Agency (SOCA)) to persuade the courts to denounce flagrant transgressions through financial sanction and then attack the profits of the company by the use of the

---

[42] See ss.114–118, discussed below.

Proceeds of Crime Act 2002.[43] The Environment Agency has pledged to refer all cases to the Asset Recovery Agency where a defendant is suspected of earning more than £5,000 as a result of their crime. SOCA will now undertake this function and they have been given further powers to seek civil recovery of these proceeds under the new Serious Crime Act 2007. What this means is, where profits have been made at the expense of the environment, the Environment Agency, in partnership with SOCA, can attack a defendant on two fronts, namely seeking criminal sanctions for breach of the criminal law, and recouping the profits through asset recovery. It remains to be seen how widespread the use of POCA will be by environmental regulators, but successful seizures will only encourage the use of this as another weapon in the enforcement process.[44]

Bad character

Two of the sharpest tools in the prosecutor's armoury were introduced by the Criminal Justice Act 2003. The prosecution can now introduce into evidence a defendant's previous environmental transgressions as part of their case. These transgressions do not necessarily have to be criminal convictions, since section 98 defines "bad character" as "evidence of, or a disposition towards, misconduct". The latter is further defined in section 112 as criminal convictions or "other reprehensible behaviour". This is sufficiently widely drawn to encompass just about *any* conduct which might be described as being discreditable, provided it has a relevance to the case in hand. If the previous conduct has "to do with the alleged facts of the offence with which the defendant is charged, or is evidence of misconduct in connection with the investigation or prosecution of that offence",[45] then technically it is *not* bad character for the purposes of the Act and its admissibility is automatic.[46] In such circumstances the prosecutor need do no more than demonstrate that the previous conduct falls within the ambit of section 98 to succeed in placing the evidence before the court.[47] If, however, the previous behaviour is "bad character" then it only becomes admissible if it can pass through one of the "gateways" in Section

3–011

---

[43] See ENDS reports, 392 (August 2007) and 396 (January 2008)—£75,000 seized from the operators of an illegal landfill site.
[44] The Regulatory Enforcement and Sanctions Act is likely to lead to administratve sanctions ensuring that substantially all proceeds of unlawful activities are recouped in monetary penalties. See further, Chapter 2, paras 2–025 and 2–026.
[45] Section 98(a) and (b).
[46] Although this may be subject to the court's exclusionary discretion under by Section 78 PACE.
[47] For guidance on what "has to do with the alleged facts of the case" means see *R v Edwards and Others* [2006] EWCA Crim 3244 and *R v McNeill* [2007] EWCA Crim 2927.

101. There are seven "gateways" by which the prosecution can adduce evidence of bad character.[48]

The s.101(1)(d) "gateway" is "that the evidence is relevant to an important matter in issue between the defendant and the prosecution". This is expanded upon in s.103 of the Act which makes it clear that "a matter in issue between the defendant and the prosecution" may "include" (but is not limited to) "whether the defendant has a propensity to commit offences of a kind with which he is charged".[49] In a case where a defendant (individual or company) has previous environmental convictions of the same or similar nature, the prosecutor can seek to adduce those convictions as evidence of propensity.[50] This might succeed even where the defendant has committed similar offences abroad,[51] and will be of particular interest to prosecuting authorities who know that the company has offices abroad. In such circumstances it is not good enough simply to adduce the fact of the conviction or a summary of the previous offences without more. If the prosecution wishes to adduce more than the mere fact of the conviction, then they have to obtain the statements and other evidence upon which the conviction is based, and make an application to the court in accordance with Part 35 of the Criminal Procedure Rules 2005 (the CPR).

Well-researched evidence on the point and a properly drafted application focused on the correct "gateway" of the bad character provisions may make all the difference as to its success or failure. Conversely, the defence should be prepared to question the basis of the application and insist on seeing all of the material upon which it is based long before it reaches the court. Mistakes do happen and prompt action may avoid prejudicial material finding its way to a court which is inaccurate or incomplete. This has a particular bearing on the prosecution of a company (or group of companies). Since each company is a separate legal entity it is important to ensure that any application to adduce bad character relates to the correct company, since the conviction of one company within a group will not necessarily be admissible as bad character in relation to another company within the same group.

Hearsay provisions

3–012   Over and above evidence of a defendant's bad character, the relatively new hearsay provisions in the Criminal Justice Act 2003 may allow the prose-

---

[48] Listed in s.101((1)(a)–(g).
[49] Section 103(1)(a) and (b).
[50] For further guidance on this topic see *R v Hanson, Gilmore and P* [2005]2 Cr.App.R. 21 and Prof Spencer's book—*Evidence of Bad Character.*
[51] *R v Kordasinski* [2007] Cr.App.R. 17.

cutor to adduce evidence which would previously have been inadmissible[52] because a witness is unavailable to attend court. The court must consider a number of factors in deciding whether the hearsay evidence is admissible. These are:

(i) its probative value,
(ii) what other evidence there is about the subject,
(iii) how important the evidence is in the context of the case as a whole,
(iv) the circumstances in which the statement was made,
(v) how reliable the maker of the statement is,
(vi) how reliable the evidence of the making of the statement is,
(vii) whether oral evidence of the matter can be given (from another source),
(viii) how difficult it will be for the defendant to challenge the statement, and
(ix) the degree of prejudice it will cause to a defendant.

The court is under no obligation to reach a conclusion on all nine factors before deciding the admissibility of the evidence, but it must have regard to them and any other relevant factors.[53] What this means in practice is that, provided the prosecution has established good reason for the evidence to be admitted, the judge's decision is unlikely to be the subject of an appeal (by the defendant) since the Court of Appeal will rarely interfere with the exercise of a trial judge's discretion. This may have particular relevance to information disclosed by an individual (such as an employee) to an investigating officer in the course of his enquiries about a defendant's activities which has been obtained by the Environment Agency under its s.108 EA powers. Where a witness has made a statement which the prosecution intends to rely upon, they are now better able to adduce that evidence if, at the time of the trial, that person is unable or unwilling to attend court, [54] unable to be traced,[55] or out of the jurisdiction.[56]

Where documents are created by a number of people during the course of a trade or business, it is not always easy for the prosecution to specifically identify each person who has contributed to the creation of the document. A classic example of this would be the use to be made of accounting or computer records from a business where the information may have come from different people over a period of time. The "business document" provisions in section 117 of the Criminal Justice Act 2003 help the prosecution (and sometimes the defence) to adduce evidence when it might

---

[52] CJA s.114 applies equally to the prosecutor and the defence and is compatible with Article 6 ECHR—see *R v Xhabria* [2006] 1 Cr.App.R. 26 and *R v Taylor* [2006] 2 Cr.App.R. 14.
[53] *R v Taylor* as above.
[54] Section 116(1) and (2)(a), (b) and (e).
[55] Section 116(1) and (2)(d).
[56] Section 116(1) and (2)(c) and see *Grant v The State* [2007] 1 A.C.1 PC as to the interplay between s.116 and Article 6(3)(d) of the ECHR.

otherwise be impossible. The provisions closely follow those of its predecessor,[57] but the applicant should always check that the information sought to be adduced was created *by a person* in the course of a trade, business, profession or other occupation, because section 117 does not apply to automatically generated material where there has been no human input.[58]

Sentencing

3–013   In an ideal world, the starting point for sentencing in environmental crimes should have been the Sentencing Advisory Panel's Advice to the Court of Appeal (October 1999). Unfortunately, the Court of Appeal declined the opportunity to lay down specific guidelines for environmental offences in a Sentencing Guideline. Instead they determined that the guidelines given in *R v Howe (Engineers) Limited*[59] were sufficient.[60] For reasons which will be discussed later, these guidelines have continued to assist the courts as a useful tool in determining the appropriate sentence, but they have limitations. In all cases, the sentencing starting point is section 142 Criminal Justice Act 2003.[61] Imprisonment for environmental offences is a weapon of last resort for both the Magistrates' and Crown Courts. It is used rarely, because in most cases the defendant is a company. Ironically the courts have a wider range of sentencing powers for an individual who, for instance, is convicted of unauthorised depositing or keeping of chemical waste,[62] as opposed to a company prosecuted for the same offences. In 2007 at least seven people were sent to prison all of whom were operating illegal waste activities, the longest of which was for 18 months.[63] Where the offence is sufficiently serious to have crossed the threshold for a custodial sentence, but immediate imprisonment is considered unnecessary, the Crown Court can impose a sentence of between 28 and 51 weeks imprisonment suspended for a period of up to two years (the sentence period is limited to six months in the magistrates court).[64] If the court decides that the custody threshold has not been reached, it can impose a community order on the defendant. The benefit of suspended sentence and

---

[57] Section 24 of the Criminal Justice Act 1988.
[58] *R v McCarthy* [1998] RTR 374. See also *R v Humphris* [2005] 169 JP 441 for the limitations on the use of material adduced under s.117 CJA.
[59] [1999] 2 All E.R. 249.
[60] *R v Milford Haven Port Authority* [2000] Env.L.R. 673 (the "Sea Empress").
[61] This applies to all offences committed after April 5, 2005.
[62] *R v Garrett* [1997] 1 Cr.App.R.(S) 109; *R v Moynihan* [1999] 1 Cr.App.R.(S) 294.
[63] ENDS report 396 (January 2008).
[64] Sections 189–198 CJA 2003 for offences committed on or after April 4, 2005. Offences before this were dealt with by PCCA(S) S.118.

community orders is that the court can attach specific requirements to it:[65] If the defendant fails to perform the specified task, he can be brought back before the court on breach proceedings which may result in an immediate custodial sentence being imposed in substitution. Since the sentence and community-based penalties are only relevant to individual offenders, the director of a company may find himself at risk of greater punishment than the company itself, which can only be fined. Moreover, the company director may also risk being the subject of restrictions on his ability to hold any directorship, either indefinitely or for a period of time. The test for the court is whether the offender had some relevant factual connection with the company[66] and since most environmental offences only allow for the prosecution of the director if the company is guilty, the provisions of sections 1 and 2 of the Company Directors Disqualification Act 1986[67] (the CDDA) will apply. Section 1(1)(a) of the Act gives the court a discretionary power to make a disqualification order against a person, preventing him from acting as a director of a company, or as a receiver of a company's property, or from being concerned or taking part, in any way, whether directly or indirectly, in the promotion, formation or management of a company without the leave of the court. Section 2 of the Act gives the crown court power to disqualify a person for a period of up to 15 years.[68] Since the Act gives the sentencing tribunal a general and unfettered discretion[69] and board level involvement is an essential part of the twenty-first century trading ethic, it is perhaps surprising how infrequently the CDDA is used in cases of environmental offences.

Fines are still the most frequent form of sanction in environmental crimes, both for individuals and companies. There are concerns that levels of fines imposed by Magistrates and Crown Courts are so diverse that prediction is very difficult. In some cases it might be appropriate to comment that the level of fine imposed is such that the "polluter does not pay enough" but many factors will contribute to the level of a financial penalty and some of these may be geographical. In determining the correct level of the fine the court must have regard to the offender's circumstances.[70]

What is difficult to glean from any of the cases which have been subject to consideration by the Court of Appeal, is any guiding principles, over and above those found in the leading case of *R v Howe and Son (Engineers)*

---

[65] Where for example the offender has been convicted of a "nuisance" environmental offence such as fly-posting or fly-tipping they can be directed to perform an activity work requirement (defined by s.201(2) as activities whose purpose is that of reparation e.g. cleaning up areas where the offence occurred. Where the offence is one of stealing, trapping or otherwise damaging wildlife a prohibited activity or exclusion requirement can be attached (ss.203 and 205).

[66] *R v Goodman* 97 Cr.App.R. 210 CA.

[67] As amended by the Insolvency Act 2000.

[68] The magistrates court can disqualify a person for a maximum of five years.

[69] See *R v Young* (S.K.) 12 Cr.App.R.(S) 262.

[70] Section 164 CJA 2003.

Ltd,[71] which might give a defendant some idea as to the level of fine which might be imposed.[72] In summary, the factors which the Court of Appeal considered relevant to the level of fine are: (i) how far short of the appropriate standard the defendant fell; (ii) where death has occurred as a result of the breach, this will be considered to be an aggravating feature, and the penalty should reflect public disquiet; (iii) the size of the company and its financial strength or weakness is irrelevant to the degree of care required to be taken by a company in matters of safety;[73] (iv) the degree of risk and the extent of the danger created by the offence; (v) the extent of the breaches i.e. whether it was an isolated incident, or continued over a period of time; (vi) the defendant's resources. Particularly aggravating features would be the failure to heed warnings, or financial gain at the expense of safety.

3–014   If the sentencing authorities illustrate anything, it is the gulf between the Crown Court's approach and that of the Court of Appeal in determining the correct level of fine to be imposed. In the most noteworthy cases[74] the Crown Court fines were reduced by 75 per cent or more. In trying to extract the aggravating and mitigating features which might affect the level of fine, concerns have been raised about the continued use of *Howe* (which was a Health and Safety prosecution) as the guiding light for environmental cases.[75] There are certain obvious features which health and safety and environmental cases have in common, but there are also significant differences. In health and safety prosecutions, the death of a person is obviously one of, if not the most, significant aggravating feature which will affect sentence. To date there have been no recorded prosecutions by the police or Environment Agency where it is said that the environmental offence has caused death.[76] From practical experience, and also borrowing from the guidance given in the various authorities, including the Sentencing Advisory Panel and other sources, the following is an attempt to enumerate those factors which may be taken into account in assessing the likely level of fine in any particular case:

---

[71] [1999] 2 Cr.App.R.(S) 37.

[72] ENDS reports 396, 397—Portsmouth Water Ltd—£10,000 fine for pollution incident killing 287 fish; Welsh Water Ltd—£6,700 fine for pollution incident killing 168 fish; Adam Khan and Dr. Clean(UK) Ltd—£50,000 fine for pollution incident killing 755 fish and 2.5km river affected. Compare this with the fine of £266,681 imposed on Shell UK in March 2008 after the after the release of toxic gas escaped from a corroded pipe into the atmosphere (NB this was a HSE prosecution where the escape placed many employees and others at risk from the escape and potential explosion).

[73] By contrast see *R v Switchgear Engineering Services Ltd* [2007] L.S.Gazette, 27, CA.

[74] *R v Milford Haven Port Authority* [2000] Env. L.R. 673, *R v Anglian Water Service* [2004] Env. L.R. 10 and *R v Cemex Cement Ltd* [2007] EWCA Crim 1759.

[75] For a full appraisal of the problem see "Environmental Offences: the need for sentencing guidelines in the Crown Court" by Neil Parpworth [2008] JPL Issue 1, and the Sentencing Advisory Panel advice to the Court of Appeal on the need for guidelines in environmental cases.

[76] This may change with the introduction of the Corporate Manslaughter and Corporate Homicide Act 2007.

(i) The gravity of the breach of the law and how far short of the appropriate standard the defendant fell in failing to meet that requisite standard.[77]

(ii) In deciding 1 above, the court should have regard to whether there had been any or any proper risk assessment *conducted*.[78]

(iii) In deciding 1 and 2 above the court should have regard to whether any risk assessment was effectively *implemented* (i.e. acknowledged policy without practical application).

(iv) Egregious disregard to environmental regulation and the likely harm resulting there from.

(v) Deliberately breaching environmental legislation and regulation with a *view* to financial gain.

(vi) Whether the defendant has *actually* profited financially from the failure to take the necessary environmental safety measures or ran risks to save money.

(vii) Where appropriate, if the defendant is a company, the fine should be sufficient to have an impact on the shareholders of a company.

(viii) The resources of the defendant, and the effect a fine will have on its business. In considering this aspect, the size of a company and its financial strength or weakness should not necessarily be the over-riding consideration.

(ix) The degree of risk and the extent of the danger created by the offence.[79]

(x) Whether the offence was an isolated incident or continued over a period of time.

(xi) The failure to heed warnings (whether they come from employees, the public or the regulator).

(xii) That the pollutant was noxious, widespread and/or pervasive or liable to have long-lasting effects.

(xiii) The defendant's attitude towards the regulator at the time of the commission of the offence (e.g. did the defendant notify the regulator as soon as they realised that they had committed an offence or did they try to cover it up).

(xiv) The defendant's attitude towards the regulator in alleviating the worst effects of the pollution (e.g. did the defendant assist in trying the stem the pollution or did they leave the clean-up operation to the regulator).

(xv) The defendant's attitude towards the regulator during the ensuing investigation (e.g. did the defendant offer a full explanation at the

---

[77] To be assessed by reference to the relevant guidance on acceptable business practice.

[78] As per *Express Dairies*.

[79] Note that the new Magistrates Court Sentencing Guidance in relation to environmental offences specifies that the lack of actual damage does not render an offence merely technical; it is still serious if it creates a material risk.

(xvi) The defendant's attitude towards members of the public—in particular local residents affected by a pollution incident.

(xvii) The defendant's bad character, including previous meetings with the regulator, warning letters, enforcement notices and any criminal convictions.

(xviii) Whether the problem has been alleviated by expenditure on equipment or the introduction of new policies and procedures to prevent future transgression.

(xix) The environmental impact that the offence has had upon a local community or amenity, in particular if it has caused public or local outrage.[80]

(xx) A timely plea of guilty.

(xxi) Offers of compensation to affected parties.

Other financial powers that the court can utilise especially where there has been significant financial gain and/or substantial environmental harm are through the use of confiscation orders[81] and compensation orders.[82] The court is limited, however, in the making of a compensation order to "personal injury, loss or damage which results[83] from the offence of which the offender is convicted". Sentences such as Conditional Discharges or Anti-Social Behaviour orders are very rarely used in environmental cases.[84]

The Proceeds of Crime Act 2002 and the Serious Crime Act 2007—POCA and SCA

3–015   In 2002 the Lord Chief Justice described confiscation orders as being one of the most successful weapons which can be used to discourage offending that is committed to enrich the offender.[85] Until relatively recently, the court could not attack realisable property held by a company which was owned or controlled by the defendant, but where the defendant uses the corporate structure as a device to conduct his criminal activities, the court is now able to lift the corporate veil and treat the assets of the company as

---

[80] Such as in cases of the trade in importation of rare animals and birds or the stealing of birds eggs from local wildlife conservancies.

[81] See para.3–015.

[82] Section 130 of the Powers Criminal Courts (Sentencing) Act 2000.

[83] Meaning "whether it can fairly be said to result from the offence": *Rowlston v Kenny* [1982] 4 Cr.App.R(S) 85.

[84] Though they may be used in minor noise abatement cases as a method of future control of the defendant.

[85] *Sekhon* [2002] EWCA Crim 2954.

those of the defendant.[86] If there is prima facie evidence that a defendant is in day to day control of the company, is the ultimate beneficial owner (even if through nominees) or can be shown to have personally benefited from the company's activities, then the company assets can be part of any restraint and confiscation orders which the court may consider making. Part 2 of the Proceeds of Crime Act 2002 extended Crown Court (and to a limited extent the Magistrates Court[87]) powers to make confiscation orders, and made the Crown Court the main venue for confiscation for offences committed on or after March 23, 2003.[88] The Assets Recovery Agency (now abolished and replaced by the Serious Organised Crime Agency[89]) was set up to attack criminal enterprises by removing the assets obtained from their illegal activities. The Environment Agency as the main prosecutor of environmental crime was rather slow to take up the invitation, but recent criminal cases have demonstrated that there is now an impetus to make use of these additional sanctions.[90]

If a defendant has (i) been convicted of an offence at the Crown Court, (ii) pleaded guilty at the Magistrates Court or (iii) been committed to the Crown Court for confiscation proceedings, and the prosecutor requests the court to so proceed, or the court believes it appropriate to do so, then the court *must* proceed to determine whether the defendant has a criminal lifestyle as defined by section 75 POCA and has benefited from his general criminal conduct or, if he does not have a criminal lifestyle, whether he has benefited from his particular criminal conduct as defined by section 76 POCA.[91] If it is a criminal lifestyle case, then the court is entitled to make certain assumptions about his receipt of property and expenditure over a six year period. If the court decides on a balance of probabilities that a defendant has benefited from either his criminal lifestyle or from his particular criminal conduct, then it must determine the recoverable amount and make a confiscation order in that sum.[92] If a court proposes to sentence the defendant at the same time as making a confiscation order, it has

---

[86] See *Re H* [1996] 2 All E.R. 391, *R v Dimsey and Allen* [2000] 1 Cr.App.R(S) 497; *Trustor AB v Smallbone (2)* [2001] 1 W.L.R. 1177; *CPS v Compton* [2002] EWCA Civ 1720; *Omar* [2004] EWCA Crim 2320 and *Re K* [2005] EWCA Crim 619.

[87] By the Serious Organised Crime and Police Act 2006.

[88] There is some question as to whether the prosecution can only use POCA for post March 23, 2003 offences—see *R v Aslam* Crim LR 145 CA but cf *RCPO v Hill* [2005] EWCA 3271.

[89] See para.3–016.

[90] On December 17, 2007, two men were ordered to pay more than £40,000 in fines and costs and £75,000 assets were recovered after they were found guilty of using a site as an illegal landfill in which they dumped hazardous waste. On February 1, 2008, the defendant and his company—John Craxford Plant Hire Ltd—paid £88,937 in fines and costs and handed over £1.2 million in assets.

[91] Section 6(4)(a)–(c) Proceeds of Crime Act 2002.

[92] Section 6(5) POCA 2002.

power to order an individual to serve a sentence in default of payment,[93] or if the defendant is a company the default will be expressed by the accrual of interest.[94] However, if the sentence is dealt with before the confiscation hearing the court must *not* make any orders for fines or compensation.[95] Thus in environmental cases (where long periods of imprisonment are unlikely to be imposed) the prosecutor is likely to ask for the confiscation and sentence hearings to be heard at the same time. What recent cases demonstrate is the extent to which the Environment Agency and the Asset Recovery Agency have successfully worked together to prosecute individuals and companies where the defendant is convicted of an offence or committed to the Crown Court for trial or with a view to a confiscation order being made.[96]

The starting point for all confiscation hearings will be the prosecutor's statement. For environmental offences the "criminal lifestyle" provisions in the Proceeds of Crime Act are only relevant if the offence is conduct which forms "a course of criminal activity", or is committed over at least six months and the defendant has benefited from the conduct. In these circumstances the test is not satisfied unless the defendant has received a "relevant benefit", being a sum of not less than £5,000. If the court decides that there has been no "criminal lifestyle", then it must go on to decide if the defendant has benefited from his particular criminal conduct (which can include not only the offences on an indictment but also offences which the accused has asked to be taken into consideration for the purpose of sentencing).[97] If so, the court will assess the benefit by considering the property obtained *as a result of* or *in connection with* his conduct.[98] In doing this it should be borne in mind that "obtain" for the purposes of assessing property is not synonymous with "retain" and so the defendant who uses profits to buy property which is put into another's name will not escape liability through this device. Once the property is identified, the court will then assess the value of the benefit. The amount of the benefit is calculated as the value of the property obtained and not just the net profit.[99] If the defendant has disposed of the property by the time of the confiscation hearing the court will look to comparable market values to assess a benefit figure. The court will identify all free[100] property in which the defendant

---

[93] £50,000–£100,000 = two years maximum sentence; £100,000–£250,000 = three years maximum; £250,000–£1m = five years maximum, and over £1m equals 10 years maximum sentence.

[94] See *Greenacre* [2007] EWHC 1193 (Admin) and *Hartley* [2007] EWHC 1924 (Admin).

[95] Section 15(3)and (4) POCA.

[96] See s.6 POCA.

[97] Defined by s.76(1) POCA as conduct which amounts to an offence in England and Wales or would if committed in England or Wales.

[98] Section 76(4)(7) and see *Jennings v CPS* [2005] CWCA Civ 746. Possession of property for a short time is enough: *Wilkes* [2003] EWCA Crim 949, *Davy* [2003] EWCA Crim 781.

[99] *Banks* [1997] 2 Cr.App.R. 110.

[100] In the sense of free from charging orders etc.

has an interest, calculate its market value, deduct any priority obligations and add in all "tainted gifts".[101] If a defendant serves upon the prosecution a "Basis of Plea", which sets out the important aspects of his case on a guilty plea, including the extent to which he says he has benefited from his criminal conduct, then the prosecution is at liberty to accept or reject it. However, even if the prosecution accepts a defendant's Basis of Plea, in which he seeks to limit his culpability for the offence and the extent of any benefit received, it is worth bearing in mind that this will not necessarily bind a court, particularly if the court considers the Basis of Plea is inadequate.[102] In practice, where a defendant pleads guilty, it is worthwhile having meaningful discussions with the prosecutor in advance of a confiscation hearing, if there is prospect of agreement as to the benefit and recoverable amount. An effective but little used tool in the Act remains the distinction between confiscation and compensation. Section 13[103] allows a court to make a compensation order as well as a confiscation order, but if there is good reason, the court can order that some or all of that compensation be paid out of funds confiscated under POCA.[104]

On April 1 and 6, 2008, many of the provisions of the Serious Crime Act **3–016** 2007 (SCA 2007) came into force,[105] replacing the Proceeds of Crime Act for offences committed after those dates. The Act abolishes the common law offence of incitement,[106] and replaces it with three offences of encouraging or assisting crime.[107] The Act also abolished the Asset Recovery Agency[108] and replaced it with the Serious Organised Crime Agency (SOCA).[109] The Act creates a new scheme of Serious Crime Prevention Orders (SCPO) which are designed to "frustrate crime in England and Wales". Section 1 allows the High Court to make these serious crime prevention orders, which contain prohibitions, restrictions, requirements and other terms, where it is satisfied that a person has been involved in serious crime, whether in the UK or elsewhere, and it has reasonable grounds to believe that the order would protect the public by preventing, restricting or disrupting involvement by the person in serious crime, subject to the certain safeguards in sections 6 to 15. Section 19 gives

---

[101] Which can include monies or other items paid over to relatives and nominees and made after the date the offence was committed.

[102] *R v Bakewell* [2006] EWCA Crim 2, *R v Lazarus* [2004] EWCA Crim 2297.

[103] PCC(S)A 2000.

[104] Section 13 POCA.

[105] See the SCA 2007(Commencement No.2 and Transitional and Transitory Provisions and Savings) Order 2008 (SI 2008/755).

[106] Section 59.

[107] Sections 44–46. See also "Encouraging or Assisting Crime". L.H. Leigh. Archbold News Issue 1, February 2008, page 6.

[108] There was criticism of ARA because it had failed to meet its 2005–6 target for recovery of criminal assets and yet ARA's annual report for the same year reported that it had met all of its key operational targets and recovered 15.9 million, more than its base budget of £15.5 million.

[109] Section 74 and Schs 8–9.

the Crown Court the same powers as the High Court under section 1, whether the person has been convicted in the Crown Court or committed for sentence. "Serious crime" specifically includes certain environmental offences in Part 1 of Schedule 1,[110] and the authority applying for such an order need only prove the issues on the balance of probabilities.[111] A serious crime prevention order is a new kind of civil injunction, the breach of which is a crime punishable on summary conviction by up to six months imprisonment and a fine up to level five. If convicted on indictment, the Crown Court has unlimited powers to fine and imprison for up to five years.[112] A person is said to be involved in a serious crime if they have, (a) committed a serious crime (i.e. convicted of one), (b) facilitated the commission by another of a serious crime, or (c) conducted themselves in a way that was likely to facilitate the commission of a serious offence.[113] A crime prevention order can be imposed by the Crown Court on an individual or corporation, partnership or unincorporated association. The crime prevention order may include prohibitions or restrictions on, or requirements in relation to, an individual's or corporation's financial, property or business dealings or holdings. Section 5(3) SCA sets out the examples of prohibitions and restrictions which can be imposed upon an individual; section 5(4) deals with corporations, partnerships and unincorporated associations. An example of a requirement that may be imposed upon a person by a serious crime prevention order includes a requirement within a time specified in the order to answer questions, provide information or produce documents to a law enforcement officer.[114]

Corporate Manslaughter

3–017   The Corporate Manslaughter and Corporate Homicide Act 2007 took nearly 10 years to find its way on to the statute book. The Act came into force on April 6, 2008. It has been heralded by some as the first step on the path to making directors subject to criminal sanction for breach of statu-

---

[110] Section 13 of sch.1, Part 1 of SCA defines the four categories of "serious offence" as offences committed contrary to: (i) s.1 Salmon and Fresh Water Fisheries Act 1975 (fishing for salmon, trout or freshwater fish with prohibited implements etc); (ii) s.12 Wildlife and Countryside Act 1981 (releasing or allowing to escape wild animals which are not ordinarily resident in or a regular visitor to Great Britain in a wild state), (iii) s.33 EPA (prohibition on unauthorised or harmful deposit, treatment or disposal etc of waste); (iv) s.8 Control of Trade in Endangered Species (Enforcement Regs) 1997 (purchase and sale etc of endangered species and provision of false statements and certificates).
[111] ss.35–36 SCA.
[112] ss.25–29 SCA.
[113] ss.5(3) SCA.
[114] SCA s.5(a) and (b).

tory duties, but the Act does not go that far. The legislation was drafted to avoid the pitfalls experienced by prosecutors in charging directors and companies with manslaughter by gross negligence.[115] If sufficient evidence could not be adduced to demonstrate that the directing minds of a company were responsible for the act or failure that caused the fatality, then the directors would be acquitted. Where this happened, the company was also entitled to be found not guilty, as a matter of course, for lack of any mens rea. Since the reality of decision and policy making in large companies and other organisations rarely centres on a few key individuals, the Act has displaced the old concept of corporate criminal responsibility in this particular context, with an approach which allows liability to be assessed on a broader basis, and so provides a more effective means of making companies accountable for serious management failings.

An "organisation"[116] is guilty of an offence under the Act if the way in which its activities are managed or organised causes a person's death and amounts to a gross breach of a relevant duty of care owed by the organisation to the deceased.[117] The Act does not create new duties of care, but relies upon those already established in the civil law of negligence. The legislation is radical to the extent that once a judge has decided that there is a duty of care, a jury will now be asked to consider how the fatal activity was managed or organised throughout the organisation, including any systems and processes for managing safety and how these were operated in practice. This means that the management of an organisation by its senior officers will be carefully scrutinised. Juries will be asked to consider the extent to which the organisation was in breach of its obligations, and how serious those failings were. This will include considering any attitudes or practices that have tolerated the breaches. If the failure to manage or organise activities properly was such as to constitute a "gross breach" of the applicable duty of care, and also caused the victim's death, then the "organisation" will be guilty of corporate manslaughter. The Act concerns itself with the way in which an organisation is managed at different levels in order to determine how responsibility was being discharged, and thus underpins the requirement that senior management cannot escape liability by delegation. The fines for these offences are limitless, but the Sentencing Guidelines Council is presently working on guidance to the courts to assist in such cases. It is likely that the advice will be to encourage the courts to

---

[115] See e.g. the problems highlighted by the failure of the prosecutions in connection with the Hatfield railway disaster in which the charges of gross negligence manslaughter against the five directors and Balfour Beatty were dismissed at the end of the prosecution case by Mackay J.

[116] s.2 makes the Act applicable to corporations including those incorporated abroad provided they operate in the UK, government departments or other bodies, police forces partnerships, trade unions and employers associations.

[117] ss.1 and 2 of CMCHA 2007.

impose severe fines where such incidents occur.[118] In the worst cases, the court will be able to make a remedial order requiring a company to take steps to remedy management failures, in addition to any financial penalty. Furthermore, the court may order that the company or organisation publicise the fact that it has been convicted of the offence, together with details and the level of any fine.[119]

Obtaining and adducing evidence

3–018 It is trite to say that without good evidence a prosecution cannot succeed, but evidence can come in many forms and through almost any medium. Surveillance techniques by the use of photographic and video evidence may be enough to avoid many witnesses having to provide statements describing the same activity by the culprit. Surveillance techniques employed by a prosecuting authority may be the subject of the Regulation of Investigative Powers Act 2000 (RIPA),[120] and in these circumstances the prosecutor will need to satisfy the court that the authority for surveillance has been correctly obtained before the evidence obtained from such observations will be admissible as evidence.[121] As with any other source of material the surveillance information, the source material and all other documents which relate to it are subject to the disclosure rules,[122] and Article 6 ECHR. From the defendant's perspective an application to see the authority will usually be dealt with under the Criminal Procedure and Investigation Act 1996 (CPIA).[123] Similarly, "covert human intelligence sources" known as CHIS, i.e. informants, are rarely part of the prosecution's armoury in environmental cases, but where offences are serious or complex, or there is a need for infiltration into areas involving organised crime, it will be interesting to see whether the regulators adopt the proactive approach which has long been common within the Revenue and Customs Prosecution Office for example. Over and above the use of surveillance material, evidence can now be received by video and/or tape

[118] In 2004, Thames Trains was fined £2 million over the Paddington rail crash in which 31 people died after the train passed through a red light at Ladbroke Grove and collided with an on-coming train. In 2005 Transco was fined a record £15 million after being convicted of breaching health and safety laws which caused the death of four people in a house in Lanarkshire. The gas explosion was caused by a leaking gas main which destroyed the house and its occupants. In 2005, Balfour Beatty was fined £10 million (reduced on appeal to £7.5 million) for its part in the Hatfield Rail Disaster, in which four people died and 102 were injured when a King's Cross to Leeds train came off the tracks at 115mph. Network Rail was fined £3.5 million for its failures in respect of the same incident.
[119] The publicity order provisions will not come into force until the Sentencing Guidelines Council has provided advice on the relevant guidelines—this is expected in autumn 2008.
[120] Part II of the Regulation of Investigative Powers Act 2000, the Code of Practice—Covert Surveillance and Covert Human Intelligence Sources issued by the Home Office.
[121] For particular guidance on this topic see *R v Harmes and Crane* [2006] EWCA Crim 928.
[122] See s.1 CPIA, the disclosure rules and the Code of Practice on Covert Surveillance.
[123] This will be a PII application by the prosecutor and a s.8 CPIA request by the defence.

recording of a witnesses account and/or video link either from the court or elsewhere.[124] Moreover, in cases where witnesses have been intimidated, the introduction of their evidence has been made considerably easier by the CJA 2003.[125] Moreover, s.139 CJA allows the prosecutor to provide a witness with a copy of their statement, without leave of the court, thus aiding a witness whose memory has faded.

Magistrates Courts

It is estimated that somewhere in the region of 95 per cent of all criminal cases are dealt with by Magistrates Courts, and the bulk of environmental cases are resolved there. The powers and limits of the Magistrates Court are found within the Magistrates Court Act 1980 as amended by the Criminal Justice Act 2003 and should be read together with the Criminal Procedure Rules 2005 Part 7.[126]

3–019

As indicated above, Magistrates Courts deal with three types of cases in differing capacities—

- Summary offences. These are the minor offences where a party is not entitled to elect trial by jury at the Crown Court.[127]
- Either-way offences. These are offences which, as the name implies, can be tried by the Magistrates Court or the Crown Court. A large proportion of environmental offences fall into this category.
- Indictable only offences. These are the very serious offences such as murder, manslaughter, rape and robbery. These offences can only be dealt with in the Crown Court, and the Magistrates Courts' role in the administration of such cases is limited to their transfer to the Crown Court.[128] Until recently there were no environmental offences which were categorised as indictable only. Arguably this may have changed in that certain organisations including corporations and partnerships may be vulnerable to indictable-only charges under the Corporate Manslaughter and Corporate Homicide Act 2007.[129]

Cases in the Magistrates Courts may be dealt with in one of two ways, either by lay Justices or a District Judge. Lay Justices normally sit as a group of three with a legally qualified clerk to the court to assist them. Lay Benches usually consist of a broad mix of people chosen to reflect the local

---

[124] For further consideration of this matter see s.16–18 and s.24–31 Youth Justice and Criminal Evidence Act 1999 and s.51–56 CJA 2003.

[125] e.g. through the use of screens in court so the witness is shielded from the defendant—s.23 YJCEA 1999 or where the witness has failed to attend court by reading the statement after application under s.116(2)(e) CJA 2003.

[126] In force from April 5, 2005.

[127] MCA 1980 s.2(1).

[128] See s.51.

[129] See para.3–017.

community who are, therefore, alive to local community concerns, such as the organisation of a landfill site, over fishing of local streams and rivers, fly tipping, water or air pollution, or the theft of eggs from a local nature reserve. Magistrates are entitled to take such local knowledge into account.

District Judges (formerly known as stipendiary magistrates) are qualified lawyers. They sit as full time judges in the Magistrates Court and preside over the more complicated trials and committals as well as overseeing the day to day running of a court. The District Judge can, and often does, sit without the need for a legally qualified clerk to the court in attendance. District Judges will be expected to deal with more serious or complex matters where issues of law may arise on guilty pleas, summary trials, either-way offences where the defendant has elected to remain in the Magistrates Court, and the more complex committals for sentence. If either party considers that the case should be dealt with by a District Judge they should advise the court at the earliest opportunity. An application to be tried by a District Judge is usually granted, but if made late, the parties may find themselves waiting for a long time before the matter can be heard.

The starting point for any environmental offence which is summary only, or triable either way, will be for the prosecutor to lay an "information" before the court, giving a brief account of the alleged offence and the legislation alleged to have been transgressed. On the basis of the information laid, the court will then issue a summons against the defendant in the same terms as the information. There are few offences which are likely to attract an immediate application for a warrant to arrest an individual, although changes to section 33 of the EPA[130] regarding the increase in penalties for the illegal deposit, treatment and disposal of controlled waste, may affect this. Similarly the introduction of the Corporate Manslaughter and Corporate Homicide Act 2007 gives enforcement authorities the power to arrest directors of a company who are suspected of causing a person's death. Except in summary only cases, the prosecution has a duty to disclose various relevant materials to the defence prior to the defendant's first appearance at the court. The extent of this obligation depends upon whether the alleged offence is either-way or indictment-only.[131]

Summary offences

3–020   The criminal process for these offences starts with the prosecutor laying what the Act describes as "an information".[132] Almost all environmental offences will start in this way. The information is a document which describes the offence which the prosecutor suspects has been committed

---

[130] Amended by s.41 of the Clean Neighbourhood and Environment Act 2005.
[131] See the Protocol for the Provision of Advance Information, Prosecution Evidence and Disclosure of Unused Material in the Magistrates Court 2006.
[132] s.1(1)(a) MCA 1980.

together with sufficient particulars to provide reasonable details about the nature of the charge. The information must contain sufficient detail about the charge in clear unambiguous language to justify the application for the court to issue a summons. This does not mean that it needs to specify all of the elements of the offence or negate any matters upon which the accused may rely,[133] but there must be enough to satisfy the court that there is good and proper reason to grant the application to issue the summons. In reality, the information is drafted by lawyers for the prosecuting authority. Separate informations must be laid for each offence alleged,[134] and a separate summons will then be issued reflecting each information, otherwise there is a risk of the summons being bad for duplicity because it charges more than one offence. On receipt of the summons, its wording should always be checked because, all too often, it has followed a standard format which may not fit the facts of the case. If so, it should be corrected at the earliest opportunity; the court may even require the ill-drafted summons to be withdrawn and fresh information laid, before it is satisfied that a new summons should be issued. As far as the detail in the information is concerned, in practice these contain only the barest facts of the allegations. Since this document may be the subject of an application for disclosure at a later stage, it is generally acknowledged by prosecutors that it should avoid mentioning anything which might be of a sensitive nature.[135]

Serving the summons

Part 4 of the Criminal Procedure Rules deals with the mechanics of serving   **3–021** the summons. The summons has to be signed either by the justice issuing it or state the justices' name and be authenticated by the clerk of the magistrates' court.[136] Service on a person other than a corporation may be effected either by: (i) delivery to the accused in person, (ii) leaving it with another at the last known abode of the accused or, (iii) sending it by post to the accused's last known address. Service of a summons issued to a corporation for the purposes of the Rules is deemed to be effective upon a corporation if it is delivered to the registered office or posted to the same. If there is no registered office then any place where the corporation trades or conducts its business will be sufficient. If the party has not been notified of the proceedings and is unaware of the hearing date, the subsequent proceedings are invalid.[137] On the other hand, if the prosecutor can demonstrate that the address to which the summons was sent is an operative one

---

[133] CPR 2005, Pt 7, R 7.2.
[134] CPR 2005 Pt 7, R 7.3(1).
[135] e.g. that there has been a surveillance operation which may necessitate a Public Interest Immunity application in due course.
[136] CPR Pt 4, Rule 7.7.
[137] s.14 MCA 1980.

where trade is taking place, then simply ignoring the mail will not be sufficient reason to excuse non-attendance (the summons will specify the time and date for the hearing). The accused could even find the case being heard in his absence with the added expense of trying to have the matter overturned by the Crown Court at a later stage. In that event the Crown Court will be reluctant to overturn any decision without very good reason.

In the case of environmental prosecutions, the return date may typically be between six and eight weeks from the issue date on the summons. At the return date the defendant will be expected to enter a plea of guilty or not guilty. Under the Protocol for the Provision of Advance Information, Prosecution Evidence and Disclosure of Unused Material in the Magistrates Court 2006 ("the Protocol") the prosecution is not obliged to provide advance disclosure to the accused in respect of summary-only offences.[138] However, in practice there is room for a pragmatic approach to be taken (recognised by Rule 1.8 of the Criminal Procedure Rules) that strict adherence to the letter of the Protocol can be counter-productive if a party claims that they are disadvantaged by having no information in order to consider their position properly, with consequential time and costs wasted because adjournments may be needed. A polite written or oral request for *some* information which will assist in the readiness for plea and effective trial management may be sufficient to progress the matter at a very early stage. Moreover, since the court is obliged by its own guidance to deal with cases "fairly and justly", it should be reluctant to push a party into entering a plea where they claim such disadvantage by reason of no disclosure. The court may look unfavourably upon the party adhering to the strict letter of the Protocol (which has particular relevance to costs), and sympathetically upon the party trying to advance the case effectively as well expeditiously.

If the case is going to be dealt with by way of a guilty plea at the first hearing, prosecutors such as the Environment Agency will be obliged to provide some form of written document (i.e. a Friskies Schedule[139]) to the Magistrates Court, setting out the brief facts of the case together with the aggravating and mitigating factors which the court should take into account when considering sentence. If the accused has decided to plead guilty in advance of the date fixed for the hearing, it is advisable, depending upon whom the prosecuting authority is, to write to them and the court indicating the same. Where possible they should request a copy of the Friskies Schedule in advance of the hearing so that they can consider and meet it. Not all prosecuting authorities who deal with environmental offences are obliged to prepare a Friskies Schedule.[140] The Environment Agency and many local authorities will do so as a matter of course, but if

[138] para.1.2.
[139] So named after *R v Friskies Petcare* [2000] 2 Cr.App.R.(S) 401.
[140] The Health and Safety Executive, the Environment Agency and Local Authorities are obliged. The Crown Prosecution Service is not.

the case is brought under the Wildlife and Countryside Act 1981 (for instance trading in or stealing wild birds) the prosecutor could be either the police, English Nature or RCPO.[141] In such circumstances, it would be advisable for the accused to speak to the prosecutor in advance of the hearing to try to iron out any issues between them, and not least whether the basis upon which the defendant intends to plea guilty is acceptable to the prosecution.

On the return date the Magistrates will hear the information, and pro-   **3–022** vided that the accused has received sufficient information, the charge will be put to him in order for him to enter a plea of guilty or not guilty. If the defendant is an individual or a sole trader he will be required to attend the court to enter a plea of guilty. The court has no power to enter a guilty plea on behalf of a person where they have not acknowledged their guilt. In the case of a corporation, a director will not have to attend the hearing provided the company is legally represented and its lawyer is instructed to appear and enter a plea on its behalf. If the first appearance is an effective hearing, the Magistrates will then consider all of the relevant information about the offence (which might be contained within a Friskies Schedule) and the offender (including any previous conviction) before determining whether to proceed to sentence immediately. It should be borne in mind that if the court decides to sentence immediately its sentencing powers are limited to the imposition of a bind-over (i.e. a promise to the court to be of good behaviour or keep the peace), absolute or conditional discharges and, most commonly, fines. Given the current issues surrounding environmental protection, there are very few instances where a bind-over, or absolute or conditional discharge, would even be considered. Examples might include a local authority prosecution of an individual who through ignorance rather than malice has failed to notify in writing that he is aware of a rat infestation on his property, or the first-time offender selling two or three cars on a public highway, who has co-operated with the prosecution authority, and made funds available to pay for the removal and/or prosecution costs but is not able to pay a financial penalty as well. These examples will generally only apply to individuals with limited means; the repeat offender, business (whether large or small) and/or the corporation who comes before a court for any environmental offence and claims liquidity problems *must* provide the court with documentary proof of the same before such assertions will be entertained, let alone accepted.

Whatever the offence, every criminal court is obliged by statute to take account of an early guilty plea[142] and give credit for it.[143] This means that a guilty plea on the first occasion must result in a lesser penalty plus reduced costs. For the guilty plea of a first-time offender of a summary-only

---

[141] Revenue and Customs Prosecutions Office.
[142] s.144 Criminal Justice Act 2003.
[143] s.174(2) Criminal Justice Act 2003. See also Sentencing Guideline Council "Reduction for a Guilty Plea" Guidance, revised 2007.

environmental offence, the court will not impose a sentence of imprisonment without adjourning for a Pre-Sentence Report (PSR). In such circumstances, defendants who are of good character or have few previous convictions (i.e. which are historical and/or minor) should take with them any documents to court, such as bank statements, which might assist the Justices in deciding what they can realistically afford to pay if a financial penalty is to be imposed. If, however, after hearing the facts of the case the Justices consider that they are unable to proceed immediately to sentence they will adjourn the case for up to four weeks[144] for the Probation Service to prepare a Pre-Sentence Report. In these circumstances the court's sentencing options are considerably enhanced and they may be looking at the imposition of community based penalties such as community orders, or in the extreme cases imprisonment or a suspended sentence. Imprisonment and suspended sentences are rightly reserved for the most heinous of environmental offences where the magistrates' sentencing powers are sufficient to allow them to mark the gravity of the case without sending it to the Crown Court, but which cannot be adequately dealt with by a financial penalty alone. Two examples of the sort of case where the defendant may well receive a prison sentence are operating illegally within the waste industry, and the illegal import of protected species.

If a summary-only matter is to be contested, the accused must enter a not guilty plea and the hearing will turn into an administrative exercise for fixing a trial date sufficiently far ahead for the parties to have time to prepare their case. It is important to have some idea of the issues the court will be required to focus on, and an estimated length of time that the case will take, because these factors have an impact upon how quickly the matter will be heard. Furthermore, if the matter is likely to raise issues of law—whether they be issues regarding the charge itself or admissibility of evidence—the more advance notice a court has, the better able it will be to determine whether the matter can be tried by a lay Bench or requires a District Judge's experience. The prosecutor should be alive to any legal issues which pre-hearing discussions can help to narrow down and determine whether the case is suitable to be heard by lay Magistrates or a more experienced district judge. Because lay Magistrates sit part-time, it is as well for the parties to reach agreement on a realistic time estimate for the trial which will avoid the undesirable situation of a case being adjourned part-heard to a future date when the Bench can reconvene. It goes without saying that adjourning summary trials part-heard is time-consuming, costly and repetitious for both sides.

---

[144] s.10(3) MCA 1980.

Disclosure duties

The disclosure duties are governed by a combination of legislation, Pro-   **3–023**
tocol and guidance, but the important consideration in any case will
depend upon the date when the investigation began. There may be a few
cases still proceeding through the courts under the old regime, and,
therefore it is necessary to set it out shortly. If the investigation began after
April 1, 1997 but on or before April 5, 2005 then a two stage process for
the disclosure of unused material applies. In these circumstances only
material which the prosecutor considers "might undermine the case for the
prosecution" fails to be disclosed. The legislation refers to this as "primary
disclosure".[145] After consideration of the material and within a given time
frame, the defence will be obliged to serve a Defence Case Statement
setting out its case and why it takes issue with the prosecution case. It is the
contents of this document which will trigger any further or "secondary"
disclosure. The test the prosecutor must apply at that stage is whether it
has any further material in its possession which might reasonably be
expected to assist the case for the accused. If it does, it must disclose it. If
the defence knows that there is material which would help it, then a well
drafted Defence Case Statement makes the task of the prosecutor easier in
reaching a decision to disclose, and more difficult to justify non-disclosure
of material which can be shown (a) to exist, (b)to be in the possession of or
knowledge of the prosecution, and (c)to assist the defence case. On the
other hand, one should not expect an ill-drafted Defence Case Statement
to trigger the production of more material. The guidance and protocols
issued in the last three years regarding proper adherence to the CPIA
regime and the Criminal Procedure Rules for effective case management
have made courts less sympathetic to what may be perceived as "fishing
expeditions" brought by the defence under section 8 CPIA seeking further
disclosure, and parties are in danger of leaving empty handed, if not
threatened with wasted costs orders, in the pursuit of such applications.

If the investigation began on or after April 5, 2005, and this will apply to
most cases now, there is duty upon the prosecutor to provide "initial"
disclosure,[146] namely material which might reasonably be considered
capable of undermining the case for the prosecution *or* of assisting the case
for the accused. This test is more onerous on the prosecutor than the
previous Criminal Procedure and Investigation Act two stage process, but
this is the trade off for prosecutors being expected to apply the rules of
disclosure rigorously from the outset to avoid unnecessary applications and
hearings. This duty applies up to the time of any guilty verdict under the

---

[145] s.3 CPIA 1996.
[146] CJA 2003, s.32.

provisions of the CPIA.[147] Thereafter there is a residual duty at common law[148] until the appeal procedure is exhausted.

Offences triable either-way

3–024   These offences are commenced in the same way as a summary-only offence by the laying of the information. In this case, however, the prosecution's duty regarding disclosure starts at an early stage with the provision of Advance Information. It is incumbent upon the recipient of the summons to "request" any Advance Disclosure "before" the first hearing. That the words in inverted commas are so emphasised in paragraph 1.2 of the Protocol[149] is perhaps indicative of the attitude now prevailing that disclosure must only take place where necessary and the onus is on the defence to make some of the running from the outset. If further support is needed for that, paragraph V of the introduction to the Protocol should assist. The Criminal Procedure Rules impose an obligation upon the prosecutor to provide the requested information and on the court to ensure that the accused is aware of the prosecutor's obligation.[150] If the request is made promptly the prosecutor must provide the accused with copies of the written statements of evidence upon which they intend to rely and/or a summary of the facts and matters which they propose to adduce at trial. Where there is good reason to fear that the provision of statements might provoke threats to a witness the prosecutor is justified in withholding it;[151] in such circumstances a summary of the facts will probably be provided instead.

Assuming that the prosecutor has complied with the Rules, the return date will be an effective hearing, and the issue of venue and plea will be considered. In the case of a company, a representative of the company need not be present at the initial stage provided there is someone present who is authorised to enter a plea on the company's behalf. If the company representative indicates that there will be a guilty plea, then the charge will formally be put and a verdict of guilty entered. If the defence and prosecution have communicated before the hearing then the prosecutor might have a short Friskies Schedule available for the court setting out the brief facts together with the aggravating and mitigating factors. It is important that the accused or his legal representative considers this document in advance of the hearing because they may wish to add or refute matters contained in it. The document once before the court may affect the Jus-

---

[147] CJA 2003, s.7A.
[148] See *R v Makin* (2004) 148 S.J. 821 CA.
[149] Protocol for the Provision of Advance Information, Prosecution Evidence and Disclosure of Unused Material in the Magistrates Court 2005.
[150] CPR 2005 21.4.
[151] CPR 21.5.

tices' decision as to whether to retain the matter for sentence or send the case to the Crown Court for this purpose. More often the matter will be adjourned for the Friskies Schedule to be prepared. In the unusual situation that the parties are in a position to deal with the matter at the first appearance, the company or its representative must have a set of the most up to date company accounts available for the court. Representations regarding the ability to pay and the state of the finances will not be accepted by a court solely on the word of the company representative without more.

If the matter is contested, a "not guilty" indication will be given to the court. Thereafter the court will hear representations from the prosecutor and the defence regarding the suitability of venue. The parties should seek to agree, if they can, on whether the case could or should be heard in the Magistrates Court. This being an administrative part of the trial process, it is often dealt with in the absence of the accused provided they have legal representation.[152] Ultimately it is the court which decides whether a case is suitable for trial in the Magistrates Court,[153] by taking into account the nature of the case, its complexity, the extent of their sentencing powers and whether they are dealing with one or multiple offences. Schedule 3, Part 1 of the CJA has added to the factors which the Magistrates will consider when deciding which venue is suitable. One consideration will be the category of environmental offence itself, Category 1 offences being the most serious.[154] Another consideration is that in most environmental cases, remaining in the Magistrate's Court places limits on sentence (notably on the financial penalties), and this is particularly important where the defendant is not a first offender.

A number of environmental offences now carry the exceptional summary maxima (or ESM) which has increased the fine which a Magistrates Court can impose. For example, the sentencing powers for waste offences contravening section 33 of the EPA have been extended from £20,000 to £50,000 and/or 6 months imprisonment, and for polluting controlled waters under the WRA 1991 to £20,000 and 3 months imprisonment.[155] In relation to other offences, such as carrying on a prescribed process in breach of authorisation or killing protected birds and their eggs, the magistrates can impose a sentence of imprisonment of up to 6 months and a fine not exceeding level 5 (i.e. £5,000). A defendant would be well advised to know what the qualifications are to put a case into the ESM

3–025

---

[152] s.23 MCA 1980.
[153] MCA 1980 s.19.
[154] See paras 3–008 and 3–009.
[155] This came into force on June 7, 2005—see sections 41 and 105 of the Clean Neighbourhood and Environment Act 2005.

category,[156] but if the Magistrates Court considers that even the ESM is insufficient for their sentencing purposes, that is a good indicator of the seriousness with which the Court views the case, and of the likelihood of a substantial financial penalty to follow. A perusal of the latest advice to magistrates from the Sentencing Guidelines Council (the SGC) effective from August 4, 2008,[157] emphasises the fact that fines for corporate offenders should be substantial enough to have a "real economic impact".[158] Especially in the case of large companies, the appropriate level of fine may be beyond the summary limits, in which case the matter should be committed to the Crown Court for sentence. Magistrates are generally careful not to penalise smaller companies beyond their ability to pay, but profitability, turnover and liquidity should be part of their consideration. If a company fails to produce its accounts, the court can assume that it can pay whatever level of fine is imposed.

If the Justices decide that they will deal with the matter summarily, the accused can now ask for an indication of sentence,[159] i.e. whether he can expect to receive a custodial or non-custodial sentence. The Justices are under no obligation to give any indication but if they do, then the accused may decide whether he wishes to change his plea or proceed to trial. Obviously this procedure does not affect a company charged with an offence, but where an individual or a company director is also facing prosecution, the indication of sentence may have a substantial impact upon the future progress of the case. If such an approach is to be made by the defence, both parties must be in a position to present the court with an agreed set of facts which should be signed by both sides and acknowledged as an agreed basis of plea.[160] This document must set out in clear unambiguous terms the facts of the prosecution's case and what facts are accepted and disputed by the defence. In many respects the document has a similar status to a Friskies Schedule, save that the latter is prepared *after* a guilty plea is entered. The accuracy of the document is very important. If the parties fail to agree a set of facts before the plea is tendered this could potentially undermine any indication which the court might be minded to give. There is little chance that any court (particularly a lay Bench) will give any indication on sentence without a comprehensive set of agreed facts,

---

[156] The categories are (i) that the offence is serious enough to justify a penalty above the normal statutory maximum (ii) the matters involved should be susceptible to fairly easy proof; (iii) the offence should be lucrative either because it will give rise to large profits or because it will result in significant savings (iv) it must also be likely to be committed by companies or those with considerable resources. See SGC—*http://www.sentencing-guidelines.gov.uk.*

[157] See SGC—*http://www.sentencing-guidelines.gov.uk.*

[158] Magistrates Court Sentencing Guideline para.11, page 183.

[159] s.19 MCA 1980 as amended by Sch.3, Part 1 of the CJA 2003.

[160] See *R v Goodyear* [2005] 2 Cr.App.R 20, for the Court of the Appeal guidance on this issue.

and even if they have such a document, they are under no obligation to give one.

Ultimately it is the Court's view of the case which will determine the most suitable venue but in reality they pay considerable attention to the views of the prosecutor. Even if they start off thinking that the matter is suitable for summary trial there is a residual power to correct mistakes so that they can turn a summary trial into a committal hearing and vice versa.[161] Once the decision on venue is complete and assuming the matter remains in the lower court, arraignment will take place. A date will be fixed sufficiently in advance for all parties to gather their evidence and witnesses. The court will want to know whether the matter is suitable to be tried by a lay Magistrates or a District Judge because this will affect its listing. Trial venue and sentence venue can be different. If convicted, the court will take account of their findings of fact, antecedents and any other relevant matters before making a decision on whether it has sufficient sentencing powers or should commit the case to the Crown Court.

If, having heard representations from the prosecutor and the defence, the Justices consider the case more suitable for Crown Court trial, they must inform the accused and then discharge their function as examining magistrates for the purposes of transferring the matter to the Crown Court.[162] In most cases the matter will be adjourned to another date for the prosecutor to prepare the committal bundle which satisfies the statutory criteria.[163] Thereafter the Justices (or one alone) can sit in the capacity of examining magistrates for the purposes of committal and commit the defendant to the Crown Court without consideration of the evidence.[164] If there is insufficient evidence to justify the charge the matter <u>must</u> be raised by the defence at that stage, and the court is obliged to consider the issues as examining magistrates and rule on it. If the submission is successful, the magistrates are obliged to discharge the accused.[165] However, discharging the summons is not always the end of the matter. In the rare circumstances where this happens, it is more likely that the prosecutor will withdraw the charge beforehand and then reconsider the case before proceeding. Discharging or withdrawing the charge does not afford a defendant a verdict of not guilty and therefore, there being no acquittal, a submission of "autrefois acquit" will not be possible if the prosecutor decides to redraft the summons.

---

[161] s.25 MCA 1980.
[162] s.6 MCA 1980.
[163] s.5A-E MCA 1980.
[164] s.6(2) MCA 1980.
[165] s.6(1) MCA 1980. If there is a serious issue of law raised, then the justices are enjoined not to determine it and should leave it to the Crown Court: *R v Chichester Justices and Another, ex parte Chichester District Council* [1990] JPL 820.

Indictable only offences

3–026 The Magistrates have little involvement in this category of offence save to transfer them to the Crown Court and, where applicable, to consider bail. There are no environmental offences created by statute or under the common law which fall into this category; except for, where the facts occur in an environmental pollution context, the offence created by the Corporate Manslaughter and Corporate Homicide Act 2007.

The Crown Court

3–027 Cases either committed to or transferred from the Magistrates Court are classified into three categories:

- Class 1: the most serious of cases including misprision of treason, murder, genocide etc. The only offences to which this would apply in the context of environmental offences are those captured by the new Corporate Manslaughter and Corporate Homicide Act 2007.
- Class 2: numerous sexual offences,
- Class 3: all offences not listed in classes 1 and 2. This is where almost all environmental offences are classified, and although the offence itself can be serious with far-reaching consequences to the environment, there has been little recognition of their seriousness as a "category" of offence.

Class 1 cases may be tried only by: (i) a High Court Judge, or (ii) a Circuit Judge, a Deputy High Court Judge or a Deputy Circuit Judge, provided that they are authorised by the Lord Chief Justice and the Presiding Judge has released the case for trial to such a judge. Class 2 cases may be tried by a Circuit Judge, a Deputy High Court Judge or a Recorder provided that in all such cases such judge is authorised by the LCJ and the case has been assigned to the judge by order under the direction of the Presiding Judge or Resident Judge in accordance with guidance given by Presiding Judges. Class 3 cases may be tried by a High Court Judge or, in accordance with the guidance, by a Circuit Judge or Deputy Circuit Judge.

Cases committed to the Crown Court for trial under section 6 of the MCA 1980

3–028 This includes a substantial number of environmental offences, including the EPA waste offences and Category 1 WRA incidents. When the committal takes place, the Magistrates Court will inform the Defendant which Crown Court it is to be transferred to and when he is expected to attend that Court for a Plea and Case Management Hearing (PCMH)—this normally takes place within six to seven weeks of the committal. The draft indictment will have been served with the committal bundle, but it does not always follow that the draft indictment is the final version. It is always worth checking with a prosecution authority in advance of the PCMH hearing whether there are any changes to the form of the proposed indictment since amendments served on the day may leave the defendant at a disadvantage if the judge insists on the defendant being arraigned. If the changes are substantial, late service will usually justify an adjournment of the PCMH to a future date. This is particularly important because arraignment takes place at the PCMH hearing, and if there has been a change of heart the defendant will want to claim the maximum credit for a guilty plea.

Once the charges on the indictment are in final form, the PCMH will take place, at which stage a defendant will be expected to enter a plea of guilty or not guilty. Again, in the case of corporations, this procedure does not require a director or company representative to attend court provided they have a legal representative present and/or have written to the court to notify them of the plea to be entered on the company's behalf.[166] As for partnerships, since the partners are jointly and severally liable, those charged will be required to attend; they can speak on behalf of themselves as well as the partnership.

In all other situations the defendant must attend and it is worth noting that question five of the PCMH form requires the legal representative to confirm to the court that advice has specifically been given on the issue of maximum credit for a guilty plea. If a not guilty plea is entered, the credit available for a guilty plea will be lost, and the prosecution costs will increase substantially the closer the matter gets to trial. Many of the questions on the PCMH form underline the emphasis on case management by the parties and trial judge; the former should be in a position to advise the court on such matters as the realistic length of a trial, the issues involved and any expert evidence to be called. The information provided in the PCMH form will be an indicator to the court what sort of case it is dealing with and the seniority of trial judge needed.

If the defence wishes to air any legal issues before arraignment it must **3–029** advise the prosecutor, the court and any co-defendant in advance of the hearing. This is particularly important where there is an application to stay the proceedings, for example on the grounds that there has been an abuse of process, such as unacceptable delay. Anyone wishing to do this must comply with the Practice Direction[167] on this point, in particular, the court will expect to see a written skeleton argument in advance of the hearing.

Where the Crown Court acts as the appellate court from a conviction by the magistrate's court, the hearing will be *de novo*. The Circuit Judge will sit

[166] s.33 Criminal Justice Act 1925.
[167] [2002] 1 W.L.R. 2870.

with two magistrates to try the case and hear all of the evidence again. If a defendant opts for an appeal, the prosecutor may present more evidence at the rehearing. If the appeal is dismissed, sentence and costs are at large. Consequently an appeal against sentence can sometimes have the contrary effect of increasing not decreasing the sentence.[168]

Cases committed to the Crown Court under section 51 of the Crime and Disorder Act 1998

3–030   This procedure is for indictment-only offences, and would only apply to "environmental" offences under the Corporate Manslaughter and Corporate Homicide Act 2007. In such circumstances, the Magistrate's role is limited to formally transferring the case to the Crown Court for the preliminary hearing. In such circumstances the prosecuting authority may have served some papers, but they are not obliged to serve the evidence bundle at this stage, and the defence may have received little information by the time of the preliminary hearing. The judge will set a timetable for the service of the prosecution papers on the defence (usually within six weeks but much will depend on the complexity of the case) and, thereafter, a date for the pleas and Case Management Hearing.

Disclosure and the Defence Case Statement

3–031   In the case of all offences transferred to the Crown Court, a stage will be reached after the service of the evidence upon which the prosecutor seeks to rely at trial (i.e. the used material) when "initial disclosure" of unused material will have to be made. This is usually done at the same time as the service of the committal bundle, and is accompanied by a standard form letter stating for the benefit of the defence and the court that the prosecutor is aware of, and has complied with, their obligations under the provisions of the CPIA. Once this has been done, the defence will be obliged to serve a Defence Case Statement upon the prosecution. Section 5 of the CPIA, as amended, outlines what the Defence Case Statement should contain and there are penalties, which courts now invoke more frequently, if the Defence Case Statement is lacking in material particulars. In short, a "says all and means nothing" Defence Case Statement will not suffice. Furthermore, prosecuting authorities have become more robust in their approach to disclosure, and less inclined to hand over volumes of unused

---

[168] As happened at Newtownards Crown Court on January 14, 2008, when Ignatius Geddis appealed against fines totalling £32,500 for five breaches of a waste management licence. The fine was increased to a total of £40,000 although the appeal against the suspended sentence was allowed. *http://www.northernireland.gov.uk/news*.

material on the back of a threadbare Defence Case Statement, let alone a written request for the same.

Nevertheless, the prosecution is obliged to be fair in its assessment of disclosure. The preamble to the guidance given by the Attorney General in 2005 is fundamental: "fairness requires full disclosure should be made of all material held by the prosecution that weakens its case or strengthens that of the defence". This Guidance followed closely on the heels of the considerations of the House of Lords in respect of the prosecution's duty of disclosure when faced with issues of public interest immunity in the case of *R v H and C*.[169] What is clear from all of the guidance that has followed the changes to the CPIA regime and *R v H and C* is that the prosecution is expected to have a good grasp of the material it holds or has access to or knowledge of, that records of such material *must* be properly maintained throughout the trial process, and the duty to review remains at all times with them (and only in limited circumstances with the trial judge). It follows therefore, that a well-drafted Defence Case Statement which succinctly identifies all matters with which the defence takes issue can trigger further disclosure. It may then be the foundation for a subsequent section 8 CPIA application where the prosecution has not undertaken its disclosure function in accordance with the Act. Courts do not look favourably upon prosecuting authorities who fail to adhere to their disclosure duties, since it can have serious costs implications if a later revelation means an aborted trial or, in the worst case scenario, a conviction overturned by the Court of Appeal. The guidance is worthy of consideration before any Case Statement is drafted.[170]

There are few examples of environmental offences which might qualify to be tried in the Crown Court as long, complex or serious. However, disasters such as the one at Buncefield in Hertfordshire[171] may fall into such a category should the matter be prosecuted. The prosecution of companies who fall foul of the Corporate Manslaughter and Corporate Homicide Act 2007 may change the approach to environmental cases in the future.

[169] [2004] 2 AC 134, [2004] UKHL 3.
[170] See the Attorney General's Guidelines on Disclosure 2005. See also CPIA Code of Practice and the Protocol for the Control and Management of Unused Material in the Crown Court 2006.
[171] Buncefield Depot fire December 11, 2005.

Chapter 4

CIVIL LIABILITIES IN THE CONTEXT OF ENVIRONMENTAL HARM

PRIVATE LAW AS A MECHANISM FOR ENVIRONMENTAL REGULATION

The multiplicity of grounds of action in English common law for redress **4–001** for environmental harm is by no means indicative of its comprehensive coverage; quite the contrary. Claimants tend to base their actions, quite understandably, on a number of alternative grounds in hope that they may avoid being defeated by one or other of the preconditions for action in these separate torts. Overall, the protection afforded by the common law may be regarded as somewhat incomplete. Moreover, the variety of possible grounds of action is wont to give rise at times to some confusion.

This chapter will explore these components of the various private law actions which are most commonly relied upon in actions involving environmental harm: private nuisance, the action for damages arising out of public nuisance, the Rule in *Rylands v Fletcher*, trespass, negligence, and the action for breach of statutory duty. It will then consider the extent to which the scope of such liability at common law may in recent times have been supplemented by the possibility of an action for damages under the Human Rights Act 1998 or a claim for compensation against the state under the Francovich principle or through the doctrine of direct effect of EC Directives.

Private Nuisance

Private nuisance is the only tort pre-eminently and exclusively concerned **4–002** with "land use" or "environmental" matters, and is therefore the principal concern of this section of the chapter. The key features to note are that:

(i) Nuisance is a tort in respect of the interference with rights in respect of land. Such interference may affect (a) the land itself; (b) the claimant's use or enjoyment of that land; or (c) servitudes or rights connected with the land. It is the general type of harm (interference with land, the use and enjoyment of land, or rights in connection

159

with land), as distinct from the particular conduct causing it, which gives the tort its unifying feature.[1]

(ii) Nuisance is a tort which centres around the concept of reasonableness between neighbours: "the very essence of a private nuisance is that it is the unreasonable use by a man of his land to the detriment of his neighbour".[2]

(iii) Nuisance is closely associated with the concept of negligence, in particular the utilisation of the concept of reasonableness between neighbours, and the application of the principles of forseeability of harm and remoteness of damage.

(iv) the ready availability of injunctive relief (both interim and final) for claims in nuisance means that in contrast with negligence it can on occasion be used either by individuals or groups as an effective tool to counter environmental harm.[3] A person who wants to obtain an injunction for nuisance must prove his legal right and an actual or threatened infringement by the defendant, and also overcome all equitable defences such as laches, acquiescence or estoppel. However, if he succeeds in doing this he is prima facie entitled to an injunction to prevent the continuation of the nuisance. He may also be entitled to damages for past nuisance.[4]

It will be apparent from the above summary that a nuisance action may arise in many different circumstances; from physical damage to land, interference with enjoyment of land, or the interference with some legal interest over land, such as an easement or a right to light or air. The tort relates both to activities on land and also the condition of the land so that the defendant will not escape liability if the damage flows from the passive state, for example, of a landfill site (as distinct from actual operations on that site).

While in many cases there will be a degree of overlap, Lord Westbury in *St Helens Smelting Co. v Tipping*[5] marked what he considered to be an important distinction between interference with land, and interference with use and enjoyment of that land:

"... it is a very desirable thing to mark the difference between an action brought for a nuisance upon the ground that the alleged nuisance produces a material injury to the property, and an action brought for a nuisance on the ground that the thing alleged to be a nuisance is productive of sensible personal discomfort. With regard to the latter, namely, the personal inconvenience and interference with one's enjoyment, one's quiet, one's personal freedom anything that discomposes or

---

[1] See Fleming, *The Law of Torts*, 9th edition (LBC Information Services, 1998) p.457.
[2] *Miller v Jackson and Others* [1977] A.C. 966, 980D.
[3] ibid.
[4] See *Jaggard v Sawyer* [1995] 1 W.L.R. 269 per Millet L.J. p.287G.
[5] (1865) 11 HL Cas 642, at 650.

injuriously affects the senses or the nerves, whether that may or may not be denominated a nuisance, must undoubtedly depend greatly on the circumstances of the place where the thing complained of actually occurs. ... But when an occupation is carried on by one person in the neighbourhood of another, and the result of that trade, or occupation or business, is a material injury to property, then there unquestionably arises a very different consideration. ... in a case of that description, the submission which is required from persons living in society to that amount of discomfort which may be necessary for the legitimate and free exercise of the trade of their neighbours, would not apply to circumstances the immediate result of which is sensible injury to the value of the property".

The rationale behind this distinction appears to have been based on (i) the high degree of protection historically afforded by the common law to property rights; (ii) the fact that such damage is more readily quantifiable; and (iii) the consideration that to allow the defendant a defence to property damage based on considerations of locality would be too favourable to defendants.[6]

While undoubtedly this distinction remains, it has a potential to cause confusion as to where the margin between nuisance and other torts affecting the senses (e.g. personal injury) lies. As Lord Hoffmann observed in *Hunter v Canary Wharf*[7]:

"There has been some inclination to treat *[St Helens v Tipping]* as having divided nuisance into two torts, one of causing 'material injury to the property' such as flooding or depositing poisonous substances on crops, and the other of causing 'sensible personal discomfort', such as excessive noise or smells ... there has been a tendency to regard cases in the second category as actions in respect of the discomfort or even personal injury which the plaintiff has suffered or is likely to suffer. On this view, the plaintiff's interest in the land becomes no more than a qualifying condition or springboard which entitles him to sue for injury to himself ... but the premise is quite mistaken. In the case of nuisances 'productive of sensible personal discomfort' the action is not for causing discomfort to the person, but, as in the case of the first category, for causing injury to the land. True it is that the land has not suffered sensible injury, but its utility has been diminished by the existence of the nuisance. It is for an unlawful threat to the utility of his land that the possessor or occupier is entitled to an injunction and it is for the diminution in such utility that he is entitled to compensation."

---

[6] Preferring *Bamford v Turnley* ((1860) 3 B & S 62; 122 ER 25) to the conflicting decision of *Hole v Barlow* in the Court of Common Pleas (1858) 4 CBNS 334.

[7] [1997] A.C. 655.

This is not to say that the distinction between interference with the land itself, and interference with enjoyment of the land is not without continuing importance. First because locality, i.e. the character of the neighbourhood, is not relevant to property damage but is relevant to damage to the enjoyment of the land; and second, because the availability of injunctive relief and the calculation of damages may vary according to the nature of the right sought to be protected or compensated for.

Material damage to property

4–003   Damage to property can take many different forms e.g. vapours exhaling from works onto the claimant's property injuring trees and shrubs[8], flooding because of a defective drainage system[9]; a tree struck by lightning which, although felled by the defendant, continued to smoulder resulting in a fire spreading to the claimant's land,[10] a landslip onto the claimant's land.[11] The rule that has developed in this line of cases is that if the defendant is aware or ought to be aware of the risk of damage to his neighbour's property and fails to take reasonable steps to prevent it, he is liable for the consequences of that risk eventuating—the *Leakey* principle. In the more recent case of *Holbeck Hall Hotel v Scarborough Borough Council*,[12] the erosion of a cliff owned by the defendant caused part of the claimant's hotel to collapse. The Court of Appeal confirmed that the *Leakey* principle extended to rights of support and analysed the general, though measured, duty under the *Leakey* principle.

Material interference with the use and enjoyment of land

4–004   As with damage to the land itself, interference with use or enjoyment of land may take many and various forms, for example; smells or vapours,[13] smoke or noxious fumes,[14] vibrations,[15] and using a house for prostitution.[16] Generally speaking however the nuisance will generally arise from something which emanates from the defendant's land and injuriously interferes with a neighbour's use or enjoyment of their land.[17] Since what one is dealing with is "enjoyment of the land" and "anything which dis-

---

[8] *St Helens v Tipping* (1865) 11 HL Cas 642.
[9] *Sedleigh-Denfield v O' Callaghan* [1940] A.C. 880.
[10] *Goldman v Hargrave* [1967] 1 A.C. 645.
[11] *Leakey v National Trust* [1980] Q.B. 485.
[12] [2000] Q.B. 836 (CA).
[13] *Walter v Selfe* (1851) 4 De G. & Sm. 315; *Bamford v Turnley* (1860) 3 B & S 62.
[14] *Crump v Lambert* (1867) L.R. 3 Eq.
[15] *Shelfer v City of London Electric Lighting Co.* [1895] 1 Ch.287.
[16] *Thompson- Schwab v Costaki* [1956] 1 W.L.R. 335.
[17] Although the fact that nuisance emanates from the defendant's land is not a necessary condition. In *Halsey v Esso Petroleum* [1961] 1 W.L.R. 683, part of the nuisance was caused by oil tankers entering and leaving an oil depot, the nuisance being caused to the claimant's property, but emanating from the use of the vehicles on the public highway.

composes or injuriously affects the senses or nerves"[18] it is always a question of degree whether the interference with comfort or convenience is sufficiently serious to constitute a nuisance.

Interference with rights connected with land

Although generally outwith the scope of this book, and more the province of property law, the third category of nuisance is nuisance to rights connected with land, in particular servitudes—e.g. easements, profits à prendre and natural rights such as abstracting water from a stream running through property.[19] Examples of this type of nuisances are obstructions of a right of way,[20] or the blocking of an acquired right to light.[21] In these cases a claimant must show a substantial degree of interference with the servitude. Thus in *Colls v Home and Colonial Stores Ltd*,[22] it was held that to constitute an actionable obstruction of ancient lights it was not enough that the light was less than before. There must be a substantial privation of light, enough to render the occupation of the house uncomfortable according to the ordinary notions of mankind and (in the case of business premises) to prevent the plaintiff from carrying on his business as beneficially as before. Similar principles in relation to substantial interference were applied in respect of the obstruction of a private right of way in *Pettey v Parsons*.[23] Once the claimant has proved such substantial interference then, generally speaking, the conduct of the defendant is irrelevant, as is the "convenience" of the locality, the benefit of the activity to the community, or the care taken by the defendant to avoid the damage in question. Effectively such claims are sui generis, see Lord McNaghten in *Colls v Home and Colonial Stores*.

4–005

Contrast with public nuisance

The history of the tort of private nuisance and of the crime of public nuisance are closely related.[24] Both types of nuisance have a common function as curbs on behaviour which from time to time and place to place may breach the bounds of what is acceptable (whether in relation to land and between individuals, or in relation to "anti-social" behaviour generally). Although as a general working rule it is probably true to say that the more ancient the precedent on nuisance, the less relevance it has to modern conditions, since the tort has evolved to reflect changes in use of land in an

4–006

[18] Per Lord Westbury in *St Helens v Tipping* above.
[19] *Swindon Waterworks Co. v Wilts and Berks Canal Navigation Co.* (1875) L.R. 7 HL 697.
[20] *Pettey v Parsons* [1914] 2 Ch.653.
[21] *Colls v Home and Colonial Stores Ltd* [1904] A.C. 179; *Warren v Brown* [1900] 2 Q.B. 722.
[22] Above.
[23] [1914] 2 Ch.653.
[24] See further below at paras 4–040 to 4–043.

industrialised society, it is nonetheless the case that that which is at the heart of nuisance complaints now, e.g. noise, vibrations, smells, smoke and dust, are no different from that which form the basis of many of the old precedents. The famous dissent of Pollock C.B. in *Bamford v Turnley*[25] (a case of brick-burning) must be borne in mind when considering whether a particular use of land amounts to a nuisance affecting enjoyment of land:

> "Most certainly in my judgment it cannot be laid down as a legal pro-position or doctrine, that anything which, under any circumstances, lessens the comfort or endangers the health or safety of a neighbour, must necessarily be an actionable nuisance. That may be a nuisance in Grosvenor Square which would be none in Smithfield Market, that may be a nuisance at midnight which would not be so at midday, that may be a nuisance which would be no nuisance if temporary or occasional only ..."

The modern conditions referred to above include the wide range of stat-utory controls which are now in place to regulate the use of land and protect the environment. Those statutory controls include proceedings for statutory nuisance under sections 79–82 of the Environmental Protection Act 1990 either by a local authority or by "any person aggrieved" by a statutory nuisance.[26] Such statutory controls are likely to be highly relevant if not determinative of some private nuisance claims. Two points however should be noted: (i) the field of private nuisance is potentially wider than the scope of statutory control (e.g. statutory nuisance) and (ii) a claim in private nuisance may afford a better remedy than does the outcome of the statutory procedure—particularly in the form of compensation.

Pre-requisites to a claim in private nuisance

4-007   The preconditions for an action in private nuisance are:

(a) The claimant must be an occupier of land, the defendant a "neighbour";[27]

(b) There must be unreasonable use of land on the part of the defendant;[28]

---

[25] (1862) 122 ER 27.

[26] Considered further in Chapter 7.

[27] "Neighbour" here connotes being within the sphere of operation of the defendant's nui-sance causing activities.

[28] *Cambridge Water Co Ltd v Eastern Counties Leather plc* [1994] 2 A.C. 264, per Lord Goff at 299E—"The effect [of *Bamford v Turnley*] is that, if the user is reasonable, the defendant will not be liable for consequent harm to his neighbour's enjoyment of his land; but if the user is not reasonable, the defendant will be liable, even though he may have exercised reasonable care and skill to avoid it." For more detail on the *Cambridge Water* case see para.4–046.

(c) It must be shown that the defendant knew or ought to have known that damage to the claimant's land, or his use and occupation of such land, might occur;[29]

(d) It must be shown that there has been a substantial interference with the claimant's land, his enjoyment of his land or an interest or right connected with it.[30]

The principle that the defendant's user must be unreasonable, in that it must unduly interfere with the comfortable and convenient enjoyment by the claimant of his land, requires some expansion. It must be shown that the defendant's conduct in the operation of his plant, in terms of emissions of noise and/or odour, has been unreasonable, taking into account all the circumstances of the case. Thus owner occupiers in a block of flats are not liable to one another simply because the party wall between their flats is not an adequate sound barrier so that ordinary noise from one flat unreasonably interferes with the use and enjoyment of the other.[31] There must be an unreasonable use of the land (e.g. putting a washing machine hard up against the party wall), which makes the use of land neither ordinary, nor "conveniently done". Essentially a complaint of nuisance relates to a state of affairs[32] but this is not to say that the interference need be a continuous or a regular occurrence. It may be of an intermittent nature, or in an extreme case, a one-off event can amount to an actionable nuisance. Thus in *Midwood & Co. Ltd. v Manchester Corporation*[33] an electric main installed by the defendants fused. This caused an explosion and a fire whereby the plaintiffs' goods were damaged. The Court of Appeal held that the defendants were liable, all the Lords Justices being of the opinion that they had caused a nuisance. But clearly the duration of the nuisance complained of, its character and quality, are highly relevant in establishing liability. For example, in *Matania v National Provincial Bank Ltd*,[34] a nuisance was established in relation to dust and noise caused by building operations which were carried out without proper precautions being taken. Indeed the incidence of the noise and/or odour may be unpredictable—"living in expectation of disturbance" may be part of the nuisance, as the first

---

[29] See per Lord Goff in *Cambridge Water* at 300F: "But it by no means follows that the defendant should be held liable for damage of a type which he could not reasonably foresee; and the development of the law of negligence in the past 60 years points strongly towards a requirement that such foreseeability should be a prerequisite of liability in damages for nuisance, as it is of liability in negligence".

[30] Nuisance like negligence is an "action on the case" with the consequence that unless until damage has been caused to the plaintiff the tort is not complete—see per Lord Goff in *Cambridge Water* at 295B.

[31] See for example, *Baxter v Camden London Borough Council* [1999] 1 All E.R. 237 CA.

[32] See *Stone v Bolton* [1950] 1 KB 201 at 208 per Jenkins L.J.: "the causing or permitting of a state of affairs from which damage is likely to result."

[33] [1905] 2 KB 597.

[34] [1936] 2 All E.R. 633.

instance decision of *Blackburn v ARC Limited*[35] suggests. The following sections of this chapter analyse each of these aspects in turn.

Undue or unreasonable interference

4–008   As noted above, the central question in private nuisance cases is whether the interference caused by one person's use of land to the detriment of another's is unreasonable. This has been put variously by the courts, and it is necessary to look at different ways in which they have sought to express this balancing exercise between a claimant's and a defendant's different expectations as to how land may reasonably be used.

Lord Millett observed in *Southwark LBC v Mills*:[36]

> "The use of the word 'reasonable' in this context is apt to be misunderstood. It is no answer to an action for nuisance to say that the defendant is only making reasonable use of his land. As Sir George Jessel insisted in Broder v Saillard (1876) 2 Ch D 692, 701–2 that is not the question. What is reasonable from the point of view of one party may be completely unreasonable from the point of the other. It is not enough for a landowner to act reasonably in his own interest. He must also be considerate of the interest of his neighbour. The governing principle is good neighbourliness, and this involves reciprocity. A landowner must show the same consideration for his neighbour as he would expect his neighbour to show for him."

This point is put another way by Bramwell B in *Bamford v Turnley*[37] who, in considering the defence to nuisance of reasonable user, considered that two conditions must be satisfied, namely the acts complained of must (i) "be necessary for the common and ordinary use and occupation of land" and (ii) must be "conveniently done", which is to say, done with proper consideration for the interests of neighbouring occupiers.

Lord Goff in *Cambridge Water*[38] equated the principle of reasonable user with

> "the principle of give and take between neighbouring occupiers of land, under which "those acts necessary for the common and ordinary use and occupation of land and houses" may be done, if conveniently done, without subjecting those who do them to an action."[39]

---

[35] (1998) Env. L.R. 469 at 529 citing *Kennaway v Thompson* (1981) 1 Q.B. 88 p.91.

[36] [2001] A.C. 1 p.20.

[37] 3 B & S 62, pp.83–4.

[38] [1994] 2 A.C. 264.

[39] Note Lord Goff's description of the "similarity of function" between the principle of reasonable user as applied in the law of nuisance and the principle of natural use of the land in *Rylands v Fletcher*. See *Bamford v Turnley* (1862) 3 B. & S. 62, 83, per Bramwell B.

The point is perhaps most succinctly put by Lawton L.J. in *Kennaway v Thompson*:[40]

> "The question is whether the neighbour is using his property reasonably, having regard to the fact that he has a neighbour. The neighbour who is complaining must remember, too, that the other man can use his property in a reasonable way and there must be a measure of give and take and live and let live."

Two particular factors relevant to the reasonableness or otherwise of a **4–009** defendant's conduct or user were highlighted in the test approved by the Court of Appeal in *Murdoch v Glacier Metal Co. Ltd*,[41] where Pill L.J. said:

> "The test to be applied in considering whether there was a nuisance was, the parties agree, accurately stated by the learned Recorder. He said '. . . the issue is whether according to the standards of the average person and taking into account the character of the neighbourhood the noise and the glare were sufficiently serious to constitute a nuisance.' "

This passage suggests that; (i) it is the standard of the average person, or reasonable man which determines the question of nuisance (e.g. abnormal sensitivity can be ignored[42]); (ii) the interference must be of some seriousness, and (iii) reasonableness is largely determined by the character of the neighbourhood and the history of use of the premises in question.

Character of the neighbourhood

It is often said that it is no defence to a claim in nuisance to say that the **4–010** claimant "came to the nuisance"—*Bliss v Hall*;[43] *Miller v Jackson*,[44] but this proposition is subject to the general principle that regard must be had to the character of the neighbourhood in which the claimant finds himself.

Character of the neighbourhood is clearly relevant for determining whether or not a nuisance is occurring: in the well-known dictum, "what would be a nuisance in Belgrave Square would not necessarily be so in Bermondsey"—*Sturges v Bridgman*[45], as uttered by Thesiger LJ. In order to determine the character, the nature and history of the locality must be taken into account together with any special use or uses to which it has been put. This is not of course to say that in a heavily industrialised area there is a freedom to behave at will regardless of the interests of neigh-

---

[40] [1981] 1 Q.B. 88 at 94D.
[41] [1998] Env. L.R. 732.
[42] See e.g. *Robinson v Kilvert* (1889) 41 Ch.D88 as interpreted by *National Rail Infrastructure Ltd v CJ Morris* [2004] EWCA Civ 172.
[43] (1838) 4 Bing N.C. 183.
[44] [1977] Q.B. 966.
[45] (1879) 11 Ch D 852, 865.

bours. This is well demonstrated by *Rushmer v Polsue and Alfieri Ltd*[46] where Cozens Hardy L.J. said:

"It does not follow that because I live, say, in the manufacturing part of Sheffield I cannot complain if a steam hammer is introduced next door, and so worked as to render sleep at night almost impossible, although previously to its introduction my house was a reasonably comfortable abode, having regard to the local standard; and it would be no answer to say that the steam-hammer is of the most modern approved pattern and is reasonably well worked. In short, if a substantial addition is found as a fact in any particular case, it is no answer to say that the neighbourhood is noisy, and that the defendant's machinery is of first class character."

Rather, the point about character of the neighbourhood is that it conditions what the reasonable man might expect to find, and, more importantly, should expect to have to put up with—e.g. ordinary traffic noise in an urban area and rural smells in the countryside. It is obvious therefore that what is reasonable or unreasonable interference is always highly fact sensitive and necessarily must take into account the particular circumstances (and locality) of the case in question. It is doubtful that the Human Rights Act 1998, and the Articles of the European Convention on Human Rights make any substantial difference to this approach although it has been suggested[47] that the rule about the character of the neighbourhood rule is incompatible with human rights law. The argument goes that if Article 14 of the European Convention requires that Convention rights are to be enjoyed without discrimination, why should it matter whether the locality is "run down" or "high class". But the argument is slightly unrealistic since every inquiry into a potential nuisance, whether under Article 8, Article 1 Protocol 1, or at common law, is essentially fact sensitive and looks at the particular effect on the complainant and objectively at the conduct of the alleged wrongdoer. Such objective consideration must necessarily take into account the character of the neighbourhood.

4–011   A potential tortfeasor cannot rely on his own tortious actions as having themselves changed the character of the locality in question. The point is well illustrated by *Dennis v Ministry of Defence*,[48] in which the submission of the defendant was that "the character of the neighbourhood should include RAF Wittering as an established feature."[49] The use was long-established, since the Royal Flying Corps commenced flying there in 1916, with noisier Harrier jump jets arriving in 1969. The claimants responded that the character of the area did not include an operational RAF Wittering, but even if it did, it did not include the Harriers as a fresh source of noise. In response to these submissions, Buckley J commented:

[46] [1906] 1 Ch 234.
[47] Bell and McGillivray *Environmental Law*, 7th ed. (Oxford University Press, 2008) p.334.
[48] [2003] EWHC 793 (Q.B.).
[49] ibid. para.31.

"Nor do I think that a consideration of the character of the neighbourhood tips the balance against finding the Harriers a nuisance. The area remains essentially rural, with villages and individual residences. As [counsel for the claimants] submitted, it would be odd if a potential tortfeasor could itself so alter the character of the neighbourhood over the years as to create a nuisance with impunity."

The judge added:

"However, with the introduction of the V-bombers and more particularly the Harriers, matters changed dramatically. To an extent a court can only take a neighbourhood as it finds it, but that cannot permit an undertaking in an area such as the one in question here to generate an ever increasing level of noise."

Another example which illustrates that the character of the area (and hence the standard applicable to nuisance) does not change because an existing use intensifies is *Crump v Lambert*.[50] In that case the Court held that the claimant could sue in respect of increased smoke and noise in Walsall, even though he lived in an area in which there was "a great deal of smoke and some noise." The defendant had introduced "a completely new state of things as regards the Plaintiff's house and grounds, and ... the smoke and noise materially interfere with the comfort of human existence in the house and grounds".

A stark further example is *Wheeler v Saunders*,[51] In that case the claimants sued for nuisance in respect of smells emanating from a pig farm operated by the defendant. The defendant had obtained planning permission, despite the claimant's objection, to build two Trowbridge houses to accommodate pigs for breeding, one of which was only 11 metres from the claimant's house. The Court of Appeal concluded that the character of the neighbourhood had not changed by reason of the grant of planning permission. Thus although the nuisance of which the claimant's claimed was the inevitable result of implementation of the planning permission, that permission could not be said to allow a change in the character of the neighbourhood.

Additionally, even if a change in the character of the neighbourhood can be identified, for example, a rural area becoming residential, or residential/industrial, such a change will not of itself provide a defence to nuisance, it will only alter the standard to be applied to the defendant's undertaking. This point is well made in *Allen v Gulf Oil*,[52] per Lord Wilberforce, where he contrasts the difference between the effect of statutory authority—to authorise *any* nuisance (subject to the defendants satisfying the inevitability

---

[50] (1867) 3 L.R. Eq 409.
[51] [1996] Ch 19, 35H.
[52] [1981] A.C. 1001, at 1014.

test, as explained below)—and "merely authorising a change in the environment and an alteration of standard."

4–012 This contrast can be seen in Buckley J's decision in *Gillingham Borough Council v Medway (Chatham) Dock Co. Ltd*[53] (a major port development in Chatham), as compared with (and disapproved by) the Court of Appeal decisions in *Wheeler v J.J. Saunders Ltd*,[54] (a new pig unit) and *Hunter v Canary Wharf*[55] (a major new tower development in London's Docklands).

In *Gillingham*, Buckley J sought to equate the effect of statutory authority and planning permission[56] ("I believe that principle [of statutory authority] should be utilised in respect of planning permission"). However this was rejected in both *Wheeler*,[57] and in *Hunter*.[58] The Court of Appeal explained the distinction between the defence of statutory authority (discussed in the section on defences below) which is a discrete and limited basis for immunity, and planning permission which does not give immunity against suit in nuisance for an activity authorised by that permission. The policy reason for this conclusion is explained by Peter Gibson L.J. in *Wheeler*, who said:

"... I am not prepared to accept that the principle applied in the Gillingham case must be taken to apply to every planning decision. The court should be slow to acquiesce in the extinction of private rights without compensation as a result of administrative decisions which cannot be appealed and are difficult to challenge."[59]

The administrative decisions referred to here are those of planning authorities. There is no appeal by objectors against the grant of planning permission by such authorities, and hence challenges are limited to judicial review, which is not generally merits-based.[60] The reference to private rights being extinguished is important. These are essentially property or property related (i.e. use of property) rights.

It is not the case, however, that the existence of a planning permission is irrelevant to a private nuisance claim. A planning permission *may* affect the character of a neighbourhood but this depends on whether and to what extent there has been implementation of the relevant permission, and the nature of the implementation; namely whether it does in fact amount to a change in character.

4–013 The decisions in *Wheeler* and *Hunter* support the following three propositions:

[53] [1993] Q.B. 343.
[54] [1996] Ch 19.
[55] [1997] A.C. 655.
[56] At 359E.
[57] At 30C, 34H–35G, and 37C.
[58] At 669B.
[59] At 35G.
[60] See Ch 6.

(i) At highest, the *Gillingham* case only decided that "strategic" planning decisions, affected by considerations of public interest, may legalise certain nuisances by changing the nature of the locality;[61]

(ii) The *Gillingham* decision is restricted to those cases where the effects of the development make a specific and substantial change in the nature of the locality.

(iii) As noted above, it is the *actual* development as opposed to development *plans* which may be relevant.

It may be said that the first of these propositions does not help to answer a more basic question, namely "when will this be the case?" In other words, when will the character of a neighbourhood be substantially changed such that the standard of comfort and convenience of its inhabitants to which its inhabitants are entitled, is likewise substantially altered?

The above decisions were recently considered in *Watson v Croft Promosport*,[62] a case concerning noise from a motor racing circuit which was within the scope of a planning permission and supporting section 106 TCPA 1990 agreement. While in general terms accepting the propositions above to the effect that a change in the character of the neighbourhood is more likely to be identified where there has been a "strategic" planning decision affected by considerations of public interest, Simon J observed the following passage from Lord Hoffmann's speech in *Hunter*, which tends to support the view that the character of the neighbourhood may, in some cases, be changed by a non-strategic planning decision:[63]

"The power of the planning authority to grant or refuse permission, subject to such conditions as it thinks fit, provides a mechanism for control of the unrestricted right to build which can be used for the protection of people living in the vicinity of a development. In such a case as this, where development is likely to have an impact upon many people over a large area, the planning system is, I think, a far more appropriate form of control, from the point of view of both the developer and the public, than enlarging the right to bring actions in nuisance at common law. It enables the issues to be debated before an expert forum at a planning inquiry and gives the developer the advantage of certainty as to what he is entitled to build."

To this it should be added that *Wheeler* suggests that even if a nuisance were to be authorised by a planning permission, this would only be in circumstances where the nuisance was an inevitable consequence of the planning permission.[64] This is an important limitation, as most permissions

---

[61] *Wheeler* at 30D per Staughton LJ, 35E-F per Peter Gibson LJ, and *Hunter v Canary Wharf* per Lord Cooke at 722: "the tower falls fairly within the scope of a 'strategic planning decision affected by considerations of public interest'".

[62] [2008] EWHC 759 (Q.B.), and subject to an appeal to be heard in early 2009.

[63] At 710 B-D.

[64] At 27H, 29H, 33D, 36D, 38D, of *Wheeler* and see *Gillingham* at 360D and *Hunter* at 669F.

do not require or indeed explicitly envisage a particular minimum level of activity on the defendant's land, so the land *could* be used for the permitted purpose without causing a nuisance.

Proprietary interest

4–014 It is fundamental to an action in private nuisance that the claimant should have a legal right connected with the occupation of land which has in some way been interfered with or damaged. In practice this means that only those with an exclusive possession of land can bring an action in nuisance, e.g. freehold owners, tenants in occupation, licensees with exclusive possession. In the extreme case of *Foster v Warblington UDC*,[65] the claimant "occupied" some oyster ponds for the purposes of farming oysters, something which had gone on for generations at that site. The Court of Appeal held that irrespective of the question of title to the soil or to a several fishery, the plaintiff, as occupier of the oyster ponds, was entitled to maintain his action for trespass/nuisance against those responsible for polluting the oyster ponds.

The proprietary interest requirement was confirmed by the House of Lords in *Hunter v Canary Wharf Ltd*,[66] where an additional claim by the non-proprietary partners and children of the claimants in respect of harm to their enjoyment of their homes, caused by the defendants, was rejected as inconsistent with the basis of nuisance as a tort protecting rights in property, rather than personal rights. Essentially, and as recognised by Lord Cooke in his dissent in *Hunter* (at 717F), the proprietary interest requirement is one of policy:

> "Logically it is possible to say that the right to sue for interference with the amenities of a home should be confined to those with proprietary interests ... No less logically the right can be accorded to all who live in the home. Which test should be adopted, that is to say which should be the governing principle, is a question of the policy of the law. It is a question not capable of being answered by analysis alone."

Perhaps significantly in *Khatun v 180 others v United Kingdom*[67] (the European Commission of Human Rights (ECHR) follow-up to *Hunter*) the ECHR considered all the *Hunter* applicants were protected by Article 8 and not just those with a proprietary right to the land in question.

Although the traditional principle is that nuisance is a wrong to the owner or occupier, the question arises whether a present occupier can sue for damage caused to property owned by his predecessor in title, but which

---

[65] [1906] 1 KB 648.

[66] [1997] A.C. 655.

[67] Unreported July 1, 1998. The claim was in event unsuccessful, as the interference was justified under art.8(2) of the Convention.

is continuing. In *Delaware Mansions Ltd v Westminster City Council*,[68] the House of Lords held the defendants liable in nuisance in respect of tree root damage to a block of flats notwithstanding that the claimants were not the owners or occupiers at the time the damage occurred.

While undoubtedly the tort of nuisance requires a proprietary interest as **4–015** a pre-condition to sue, in many cases there may be an allied claim for a breach of a Convention right. A victim of nuisance may be able to prove breach of Article 8 which may give rise to a separate claim for damages under the Human Rights Act 1998. Such a claim is not limited to those persons who have a proprietary interest. In such circumstances, the question arises as to what, if any, extent the children are entitled to claims for damages over and above that which their parents (the owners of the proprietary interest) are entitled to recover by way of tortious damages for nuisance. It is notable that in other areas of the law certain judges have recognised the importance of developing the common law in harmony with human rights jurisprudence, particularly where different approaches to the same question appear to yield different results.[69] For example in the Court of Appeal in *Van Colle*, a claim against the police for negligence in failing to protect a member of the public from being murdered by a person known to harbour an intention to kill that person, Pill L.J. held it was unacceptable that a court, bound by section 6 of the 1998 Act, should judge such a case by different standards depending on whether or not the claim is specifically brought under the Convention. The decision whether a duty of care exists in a particular situation should in a common law claim require a consideration of Article 2 rights. In the same case, Rimer L.J. considered that "where a common law duty covers the same ground as a Convention right, it should, so far as practicable, develop in harmony with it".[70] These statements were approved by Lord Bingham on appeal,[71] though other members of the House of Lords were not so sure about their applicability. As Lord Brown put it:[72]

"Convention claims have very different objectives from civil actions. Where civil actions are designed essentially to compensate claimants for their losses, Convention claims are intended rather to uphold minimum human rights standards and to vindicate those rights."

---

[68] [2002] 1 A.C. 321.
[69] See in particular, *Smith v Chief Constable of Sussex* [2008] EWCA 39; *Van Colle v Chief Constable of Hertfordshire* [2007] EWCA Civ 325, [2008] UKHL 50.
[70] para.45.
[71] para.58.
[72] para.138.

Foreseeability

4–016   Foreseeability of damage is a pre-requisite for a claim in nuisance. The celebrated Privy Council decision in the public nuisance case of *Overseas Tankship (UK) Ltd v Miller Steamship Co. Pty (The Wagon Mound) (No. 2)*[73] is still widely accepted as establishing that foreseeability of harm is a prerequisite to the recovery of damages in private nuisance and must be read alongside Lord Goff's speech in *Cambridge Water*. In the latter case the defendant escaped liability for pollution of groundwater caused by accidental seepage of chemicals accidentally spilt in its tanning process because the damage in question was not of a kind which was foreseeable. Lord Goff pointed out[74] that in cases of nuisance which have arisen through natural causes, or by the act of an independent third party, "the applicable principles in nuisance have become closely associated with those applicable in negligence", referring to *Sedleigh-Denfield* and *Goldman v Hargrave*.[75] He continued:

> "... it by no means follows that the defendant should be held liable for damage of a type which he could not reasonably foresee; and the development of the law of negligence in the last sixty years strongly points towards a requirement that such foreseeability should be a pre-requisite of liability in damages for nuisance, as it is of liability in negligence."[76]

In *Cambridge Water*,[77] the standard of foreseeability adopted was that of the relevant supervisor. On the facts it was held that no reasonable supervisor would have forseen groundwater pollution from repeated spillages of small amount of solvent. A similar approach was followed in *Savage and Another v Fairclough* where a farmer was held not to be liable for damage caused by contamination of a water supply by nitrates from animal wastes on the basis that at the relevant time this consequence was not reasonably foreseeable by the standard of "the hypothetical good farmer" running a farm such as that in question.[78]

Where the damage is caused by a natural occurrence such as a landslide, failure to prevent the nuisance may result in liability;[79] the same principle extends to nuisance created by trespassers provided that that the defendant knew or ought to have known of it, and essentially allowed the nuisance to

---

[73] [1967] 1 A.C. 617.
[74] At 75D.
[75] [1967] 1 A.C. 645.
[76] [1994] 2 A.C. 264 at 300. per Lord Goff.
[77] See fn.26 above and para.4–046.
[78] *Savage v Fairclough* [2000] Env. L.R. 183.
[79] *Leakey v National Trust* [1980] Q.B. 485.

continue.[80] What has now become known as the *Leakey* principle[81] establishes that occupation of land carries with it a duty to one's neighbour. An occupier must do whatever is reasonable in all the circumstances to prevent hazards on his land, however they may arise, from causing damage to a neighbour.[82] Liability for these natural occurrences is discussed further in Chapter 13 on flooding liabilities.

Defences to a nuisance claim

Prescription

Twenty years continuance of a nuisance will legalise a private nuisance by prescription. To acquire such a right by prescription to commit nuisance requires the right to be capable of forming an easement—in other words a right to do or enjoy something in relation to the the dominant tenement affecting the unfettered use of the servient tenement. It must be a benefit not enjoyed by the owner of the dominant tenement as an essential incident of his ownership of his land, that is to say without the need for any grant by the owner of the servient tenement. e.g. a right to discharge rainwater onto a neighbour's land from the eaves of one's roof.[83]   4–017

The defence is of rare application, because whether a right to commit a nuisance by means of smoke, smells, noise or vibration can ever be acquired by prescription is highly doubtful since it is unclear how such rights are capable of existing as easements. However, there are dicta that a right may be acquired by prescription to annoy a neighbour by smoke, smells and noise.[84] That said, there is no reported case where such a right has in fact arisen. An additional requirement is that the easement or right created must be of sufficient clarity and certainty so that there can be "measurement and determination of the user by which the extent of the prescriptive rights is acquired".[85] A good example of the difficulty in having a right to commit a nuisance can be seen in *Dennis*, above, where the fact that Harriers had flown in proximity to the claimants' house since 1969 did not give rise to a prescriptive right. This is because a prescriptive right needs to be capable of forming the subject matter of an easement, and the judge noted that it was impossible to see how the right to overfly and create a certain level of noise could form a sufficiently precise grant. The other principal test for a prescriptive right was also not satisfied in the

---

[80] *Lippiatt v South Gloucestershire County Council* [2000] Q.B. 51.
[81] See Ramsey J in *Dobson v Thames Water Utilities and others* [2007] EWHC 2021 (TCC) para.23.
[82] See discussion on riparian owners at para.12–002.
[83] *Thomas v Thomas* (1835) 2 CM & R. 34; *Fay v Prentice* (1845) 1 CB 828; *Harvey v Walters* (1873) L.R. 8 CP 162.
[84] *Waterfield v Goodwin* (1957) 105 L.J. 332; *Khyatt v Morgan* [1961] NZLR 1020 at 1024.
[85] *Hully v Silversprings Bleaching Co.* [1922] 2 Ch. 281.

Dennis case; any sustained protests by the claimant would enable him to contend that the continued flying was not "as of right."

Statutory authority

4–018   The leading case on statutory authority is *Allen v Gulf Oil.*[86] In that case, inhabitants of a neighbouring village brought proceedings in relation to the construction and operation of an oil refinery which had been built by Gulf Oil under the Gulf Oil Refining Act 1965. The proceedings were for nuisance in the operation of the refinery, alternatively for negligence in the construction and operation of that refinery. Lord Wilberforce, with whom the majority agreed, set out the relevant principles which apply to a case where there is a defence raised of statutory authority. He said:

> "We are here in the well charted field of statutory authority. It is now well settled that where Parliament by express direction or by necessary implication has authorised the construction and use of an undertaking or works, that carries with it an authority to do what is authorised with immunity from any action based on nuisance. The right of action is taken away: *Hammersmith and City Railway Co. v Brand* (1869) L.R. 4 H.L. 171, 215 per Lord Cairns. To this there is made the qualification, or condition, that the statutory powers are exercised without "negligence"—that word here being used in a special sense so as to require the undertaker, as a condition of obtaining immunity from action, to carry out the work and conduct the operation with all reasonable regard and care for the interests of other persons: *Geddis v Proprietors of Bann Reservoir* (1878) 3 App.Cas. 430, 455 per Lord Blackburn. It is within the same principle that immunity from action is withheld where the terms of the statute are permissive only, in which case the powers conferred must be exercised in strict conformity with private rights: *Metropolitan Asylum District v Hill* (1881) 6 App.Cas. 193".

A further example which demonstrates the need for all reasonable care to be taken, is *Tate & Lyle v Greater London Council,*[87] a claim in public nuisance where the defendant, acting under statutory authority constructed ferry terminals in the Thames. The construction of the ferry terminals was negligent in that it prevented proper access to the claimant's jetty. The defence of statutory authority was rejected because reasonable care had not been taken in the construction under statutory authority. The quantum of damage was calculated by reference to the difference between the costs incurred to the claimants had the works been carried out under statutory authority without negligence, and the actual costs.

---

[86] *Allen v Gulf Oil Refining* [1981] A.C. 1001.
[87] [1983] 2 A.C. 509.

Statutory Authority: Marcic

A slightly different form of the defence of statutory authority arises where   **4–019**
the defendant acts under a statutory scheme which is inconsistent with
there being *any* common law liability in nuisance. The *Leakey* principle
exemplifies the standard of conduct expected today of an occupier of land
towards his neighbour. But certain statutory undertakers, such as water
utilities, are not an ordinary occupier of land and operate within a scheme
imposed and enforced by statute. The complexities which this may give rise
to are demonstrated by *Marcic v Thames Water Utilities Ltd.*[88]

The Water Industry Act 1991 (WIA) creates a regime of duties,
requiring sewerage utilities to provide adequate sewerage systems, and
which were enforceable by Ofwat (the Water Services Regulation
Authority). Ofwat, as the economic regulator of the industry, had to
determine what works of improvement to those systems could properly be
charged by the utilities to their customers A claim was made by Mr Marcic
against Thames Water in respect of flooding to his property from one of
Thames Water's external sewers. He sought a mandatory order compelling
Thames Water to improve its sewerage system. In addition he sought
damages, relying on the common law cause of action in nuisance and on
Article 8(1) and Article 1 Protocol 1 of the European Convention of
Human Rights 1950, as set out in Schedule 1 to the Human Rights Act
1998.[89]

The Court of Appeal[90] held that Thames Water was under a common
law duty to Mr Marcic to take such steps as, in all the circumstances, were
reasonable to prevent the discharge of surface and foul water onto Mr
Marcic's property. However, that decision was reversed by the House of
Lords which held that the existence of a cause of action in nuisance for
flooding in these circumstances would be inconsistent with the complex
statutory scheme under which Thames Water operated and which was
enforceable by Ofwat. Lord Nicholls said that:[91]

> "The existence of a ... common law right [parallel to the statutory
> scheme], whereby individual householders who suffer sewer flooding
> may themselves bring court proceedings when no enforcement order has
> been made, would set at nought the statutory scheme. It would effec-
> tively supplant the regulatory role the director[92] was intended to dis-
> charge when questions of sewer flooding arise."

The Lords took the view that the nature of the defendant, and the existence
and contents of the relevant statute in *Marcic*, distinguished it from the

---

[88] [2003] UKHL 66.
[89] This aspect of his claim is also discussed in paras 1–078 and 1–090.
[90] [2002] Q.B. 929.
[91] para.35.
[92] i.e. Ofwat.

Leakey line of cases, and thus exempted it from the principle of nuisance liability upheld in those cases. As Lord Nicholls put it: "Thames Water is no ordinary occupier of land" and its "obligations regarding these sewers cannot sensibly be considered without regard to the ... statutory scheme".

Dobson v Thames Water[93] applied the *Marcic* principle to another element of the exercise of Thames's sewerage functions, namely its duty to deal with the contents of sewers at sewerage works. Ramsey J held that the *Marcic* principle did apply to such works, but only to circumstances where the steps which the claimants said should have been carried out were of a capital, rather than a maintenance, nature. The former claims were barred by *Marcic*, whereas all other claims were to be judged under the *Allen* principles set out above.

Statutory authority—planning permission?

4-020 At paragraphs 4–012 and 4–013 above, we have looked at the debate as to whether planning permission may ever be said to amount to statutory authority to carry out an activity, as distinct from amounting to a change in the character of the area when implemented.

Act of a trespasser

4-021 This defence simply means that an occupier is not usually liable for nuisance caused by a trespasser on his land. It is applicable where the occupier can show that he neither knew nor ought to have known of the nuisance in time to correct or avoid it.

Ignorance of material facts

4-022 In *Ilford Urban District Council v Beal*[94] the defendant built a wall on her land some eight or nine feet under which ran the claimant's sewer which cracked as a result of the building of the wall. She was held not liable in nuisance or negligence because she could not reasonably have been expected to have known of the fact that the sewer was there.

Act in public interest no defence

4-023 Short of having statutory authority to commit a nuisance, the public interest served by the carrying on of a particular activity (e.g. a landfill or composting site) does not confer on the defendant a licence to commit what would otherwise be a nuisance. While public interest therefore may

[93] [2007] EWHC 2021 (TCC).
[94] [1925] 1 KB 671.

not be a defence as such, it is a relevant consideration as regards determination of the question of reasonableness of user. It may also be relevant
to the question of remedy, as considered below. The point was considered
in the case of *Dennis v MOD* [2003] EWHC 793, where the claimant
claimed damages in nuisance for noise caused by low flying aircraft.
Buckley J. considered what the effect of a public interest in an activity
continuing should be where that activity would otherwise constitute a
nuisance. Allowing the claim in nuisance but refusing any injunctive relief
to prevent the continuation of training pilots at RAF Wittering Buckley J.
held:

"Where there is a real public interest in a particular use of land, I can see
no objection in principle to taking that public interest into account, in
one way or another, in deciding what is best to be done ... The problem
with putting the public interest into the scales when deciding whether a
nuisance exists, is simply that if the answer is no, not because the claimant is being over sensitive, but because his private rights must be
subjugated to the public interest, it might well be unjust that he should
suffer the damage for the benefit of all. If it is to be held that there is no
nuisance, there can be no remedy at common law. As this case illustrates, the greater the public interest, the greater may be the interference.
If public interest is considered at the remedy stage and since the court
has a discretion, the nuisance may continue but the public, in one way or
another, pays for its own benefit ... The principles or policy underlying
these considerations are that public interest should be considered and
that selected individuals should not bear the cost of the public benefit. I
am in favour of giving effect to those principles. I believe it is necessary to
do so if the common law in this area is to be consistent with the
developing jurisprudence on human rights."

Remedies

The primary remedy in nuisance is the grant of an injunction to stop the   **4–024**
activity complained of. Damages are awardable in respect of the period
before the injunction is granted, and may also be awarded in lieu of
injunction. A highly qualified and circumscribed right of abatement, may
in appropriate circumstances be available as remedies for private nuisance.
These remedies are now considered further:

Injunction

As noted above, the primary remedy for an action in nuisance is an   **4–025**
injunction. Indeed the injunction is often seen as the touchstone of what

distinguishes an action of nuisance from one of negligence, as explained by Lord Denning in *Miller v Jackson*:[95]

> "The tort of nuisance in many cases overlaps the tort of negligence. The boundary lines were discussed in two adjoining cases in the Privy Council Overseas Tankship (UK) Ltd v Miller Steamship Co. Pty. (The Wagon Mound No.2) [1967] 1 A.C. 617, 639, and Goldman v Hargrave [1967] 1 A.C. 645, 657. But there is at any rate one important distinction between them. It lies in the remedy sought. Is it damages? Or an injunction? If the plaintiff seeks a remedy in damages for injury done to him or his property he can lay his claim in either negligence or nuisance. But if he seeks an injunction to stop the playing of cricket altogether I think he must make his claim in nuisance".

General

4–026 An injunction is an order by the Court requiring a party either to do a specific act (a mandatory injunction) or to refrain from doing a particular act (prohibitory injunction). Injunctions may be perpetual (following final judgment) or interim (issued at an interolocutory stage before the final hearing). Further, an injunction may be made even before there has been any infringement of the claimant's rights, but there is a real reason to fear that unless restrained by injunction such infringement is likely to occur—a *quia timet* injunction. Generally speaking mandatory injunctions are far rarer than prohibitory injuctions, and are seldom made at the interim stage. A failure to comply with the terms of an injunction results will be a contempt of court for which the punishment may be imprisonment up to two years. It is for this reason that the terms of any injunction must be expressed in clear terms such that the person injuncted knows precisely what he can and cannot do in the light of the order made.

In order to bring an injunction the claimant must have a cause of action. Any interim injunction is made ancillary to a substantive claim in the action but need not necessarily be in a form which can be granted after a final hearing. The most common types of injunction it the environmental sphere are injunctions to restrain nuisance by noise, smells, vibration, dust or pollution; to restrain breaches of planning control (Town and Country Planning Act 1990 s.187B); damage to protected trees (s.214 T CPA 1990) or damage to listed buildings (s.44A of the Planning (Listed Buildings and Conservation Areas) Act 1990).

The first principle of an injunction whether interim or final, is that damages are not an adequate remedy.[96] Damages are likely to be an adequate remedy where the wrongdoing has ceased and there is no likelihood of recurrence.

---

[95] [1977] Q.B. 966.
[96] Per Lindley L.J. in *London and Blackwall Railway Co. v Cross* (1886) 31 Ch D 354 at 369.

Interim injunctions

To succeed in an application for an interim injunction requires the appli-   4–027
cant to demonstrate: (i) a serious question to be tried; (ii) the inadequacy
of damages as a remedy; and (iii) that the balance of convenience lies in
favour of the grant of an injunction.[97] If the claimant obtains an interim
injunction but subsequently fails at trial, the defendant may have unjustly
been restrained from lawfully carrying on his business and the claimant will
be liable for any loss or damage sustained. There is therefore a routine
practice of requiring the claimant for an injunction to provide an undertaking in damages if his claim ultimately fails. In the environmental sphere
this practice may mean that the private citizen, if not of substantial means,
is unable to provide a suitable undertaking (say against a large petrochemical company) as the price of the injunction. The requirement that an
interim injunction should contain an undertaking by the applicant to
compensate the respondent is expressly stated in the CPR[98] and the failure
to provide an undertaking will usually result in the refusal of the injunction.
Ultimately however it is a matter of impression, and the Court retains a
discretion not to require an undertaking in exceptional cases. Thus in *Allen
v Jambo Holdings*[99] a widow sought a Mareva injunction to restrain the
removal of an aircraft belonging to a company in Nigeria, after her husband
had been decapitated and killed by the aircraft's propeller at Leavesden
aerodrome. Lord Denning MR said:

> "It is said that whenever a Mareva injunction is granted the plaintiff has
> to give the cross-undertaking in damages. Suppose the widow should
> lose this case altogether. She is legally aided. Her undertaking is worth
> nothing. I would not assent to that argument. As Shaw L.J. said in the
> course of the argument, a legally aided plaintiff is by our statutes not to
> be in any worse position by reason of being legally aided than any other
> plaintiff would be. I do not see why a poor plaintiff should be denied a
> Mareva injunction just because he is poor, whereas a rich plaintiff would
> get it. One has to look at these matters broadly. As a matter of con-
> venience, balancing one side against the other, it seems to me that an
> injunction should go to restrain the removal of this aircraft".

The routine practice referred to above, of requiring a claimant's undertaking in damages in nuisance cases may have to be reconsidered in the
light of the Report of the Working Group on Access to Environmental
Justice.[100] This group was set up to examine how the UK's obligations
under the Aarhus convention might properly be respected under the

---

[97] See *American Cyanamid v Ethicon* [1975] A.C. 396.
[98] Practice Direction (Interim Injunctions) para.5.1(1).
[99] [1980] 1 W.L.R. 1252.
[100] "The Sullivan Report"—May 2008.

existing administrative law system. At paragraph 82 the working party concluded (in relation to public law cases):

"Aarhus[101] provides a robust justification for the removal of the need to provide a cross-undertaking in damages in environmental cases ... We recommend that the requirement to provide a cross-undertaking in damages should not apply in environmental cases falling within Aarhus where the court is satisfied that an injunction is required to prevent significant environmental damage and to preserve the factual basis of proceedings. In such cases it will be incumbent on the court and its administration to ensure that the full case is heard promptly".

It might be suggested that a similar approach could equally apply to private law environmental cases. Under Article 9(2) of the Aarhus Convention members of the public, where they meet the criteria, if any, laid down in national law, must;

"have access to administrative or judicial procedures to challenge acts or omissions by private parties and public authorities which contravene provisions of its national laws relating to the environment".

"National laws" in this context, must include the common law on private nuisance. If that is correct, then in order to have effective access to justice the requirement for a cross-undertaking in damages should be removed, particularly in cases where there is a strong prima facie case of infringement, and no other adequate timely[102] remedy. Against this suggestion is the consideration that relief from the requirement for an undertaking in damages should only apply where the private party is seeking to protect the public interest generally, or at least, the case has a significant public law/public interest component beyond that of the mere private interest of the individual.

Final injunction

4–028   If the claimant does establish infringement of his legal right and overcomes any equitable defences which may have been raised such as laches, acquiescence or estoppel, he is on the face of it entitled to an injunction against continuing infringement, although the court may in its discretion withhold injunctive relief and award damages instead.[103] The defences of laches acquiescence and estoppel so far as they relate to nuisance are discussed below.

---

[101] The Aarhus Convention, discussed in Chapter 6.
[102] art.9(4) of the Aarhus Convention expressly requires that procedures are "timely".
[103] *Jaggard v Sawyer* [1995] 1 W.L.R. 269; *Nelson v Nicholson* September 1, 2000 (CA) unreported.

Damages in lieu of an injunction

As noted above, if equitable defences are overcome, then an injunction   4–029
should follow. In *Shelfer v City of London Electric Lighting Co.* [1895] 1 Ch.
287, the opening paragraph of the headnote, which correctly summarises
the judgment, reads:

> "Lord Cairns Act 1858, in conferring on the courts of equity a jur-
> isdiction to award damages instead of an injunction, has not altered the
> settled principles upon which those courts interfered by way of injunc-
> tion; and in cases of continuing actionable nuisance the jurisdiction so
> conferred ought only to be exercised under very exceptional
> circumstances".

The Shelfer principles

AL Smith L.J. in his judgment sets out what he called a good working rule   4–030
for the award of damages in substitution for an injunction. The key factors
to consider are (i) whether the injury to the claimant's legal rights is small;
(ii) whether the injury can be estimated in money; (iii) whether it could be
adequately compensated by a small money payment; (iv) whether it would
be oppressive to the defendant to grant an injunction; (v) whether the
claimant had shown that he only wanted money; (vi) whether the conduct
of the claimant rendered it unjust to give him more than pecuniary relief;
and (vii) whether there were any other circumstances which justified the
refusal of an injunction.

In *Jaggard v Sawyer*, the defendants built a house at the end of a private
road. Although the claimant threatened an injunction to enforce a
restrictive covenant in the course of the building works, he did not in fact
make an application with the result that by the time the matter came on for
trial the building was fully erected and the Court held it would be
oppressive to grant an injunction and awarded £700 in lieu of an injunction. In the course of their judgment the Court of Appeal reviewed the
Shelfer line of authority and were careful to observe that although a good
working rule, it was just that, and should not be regarded as a judicial
straightjacket.

In the more recent case of *Regan v Paul Properties*,[104] the *Shelfer* principles and the observations of the Court in *Jaggard* were again reconsidered.
The claimant owned a maisonette on the first and second floors of a
building some 12.8 metres away and almost directly opposite two buildings
where the defendants a development partnership were in the course of
building a mixed commercial and residential development. The claimant
was concerned of the effect of the development on his right to light. The

[104] [2006] EWCA Civ 1319.

defendant denied that there was an actionable nuisance or interference with the claimant's right to light. The claimant brought proceedings for an injunction. The judge at first instance found that the defendant had committed an actionable nuisance, but that the claimant should be awarded damages only since he had not persuaded the Court that damages were inadequate. The Court of Appeal, allowing the claimant's appeal held that the claimant was prima facie entitled to an injunction against a person committing a wrongful act, such as continuing nuisance, and that the court's discretion to award damages instead of an injunction should not be exercised to deprive a claimant of his prima facie right save under very exceptional circumstances.

4–031   The Court in *Regan* emphasised certain comments of Lord Bingham MR and Millet L.J. in *Jaggard v Sawyer:*[105]

> "Laid down just one hundred years ago, AL Smith LJ's checklist has stood the test of time; but it needs to be remembered that it is only a working rule and does not purport to be an exhaustive statement of the circumstances in which damages may be awarded instead of an injunction."

These observations in *Jaggard*, led Simon J. in *Watson v Croft Promosport*[106] to conclude that an injunction should not be granted against a motor racing circuit which operated noisy activities up to 140 days a year because of two primary factors: (i) a culpable delay of approximately two years and (ii) the willingness of the claimant to accept compensation in respect of part of the damage claimed. Both limbs of this reasoning are open to question. The power to award damages in lieu of an injunction under s.50 of the Supreme Court Act 1981 includes a power to grant a limited injunction and to award damages to compensate for the limitation.[107] On the face of it, there is nothing wrong in principle with a claimant seeking a remedy partly by way of injunction and partly by way of damages. As to culpable delay, this really goes to the question of discretion and whether in all the circumstances to grant the injunction after such delay was "oppressive" to the defendant.[108] Mere delay should not suffice, or at least does not suffice for the equitable defences of acquiescence or laches (see below).

---

[105] (CA) [1995] 1 W.L.R. 262 at 278B.
[106] [2008] EWHC 759 (Q.B.), subject to appeal.
[107] *Chiron Corp v Organon Teknika Ltd* (No.10) [1995] FSR 325.
[108] The crucial test as applied by the Court in *Jaggard*, and on which each case will turn is the question of whether in all the circumstances it would be oppressive to grant the injunction sought: per Sir Thomas Bingham MR at 283B: "It is important to bear in mind that the test is one of oppression, and the court should not slide into application of a general balance of convenience test".

Assessment of damages for damages in lieu

A further difficult question that arises is the proper assessment of damages   **4–032**
in lieu of an injunction. As we have seen, in *Jaggard v Sawyer*, the Court
awarded just £700 as damages in lieu. This valuation was based on the
Wrotham Park[109] approach. In that case a developer build a number of
houses in breach of a covenant restraining him from building save in
accordance with a lay-out plan submitted and approved by the claimants.
No interlocutory relief was sought, but subsequently, after the buildings
had been completed a mandatory injunction was sought to demolish the
houses built in breach of the covenant. Brightman J. refused the injunction.
He concluded that a just substitute for a mandatory injunction would be
"such a sum of money as might reasonably have been demanded by the
plaintiffs from the developer as a quid pro quo for relaxing the covenant."
The proper legal basis for the calculation of such sum (it was 5 per cent of
the defendant's expected profit from the venture) is explained by Sir
Robert Megarry V-C in *Tito v Wadell (No. 2)*[110]:

"If the plaintiff has the right to present some act being done without his
consent, and the defendant does the act without seeking that consent,
the plaintiff has suffered a loss in that the defendant has taken without
paying for it something for which the plaintiff could have required
payment, namely, the right to do the act. The court therefore makes the
defendant pay what he ought to have paid the plaintiff, for that is what
the plaintiff has lost. The basis of computation is not, it will be observed
in any way directly related to wasted expenditure or other loss that the
defendant is escaping by reason of an injunction being refused: it is the
loss that the plaintiff has suffered by the defendant not having observed
the obligation to obtain the plaintiff's consent."

The proper approach is therefore to value the loss of the right as that
which a reasonable seller would sell it for. As Sir Thomas Bingham MR
makes clear in *Jaggard* at 282H, in situations of this kind a plaintiff should
not be treated as eager to sell, which he very probably is not, but equally
the court will not value the right at the ransom price which a very reluctant
plaintiff might put on it.

In *Tamares v Fairpoint (No.2)*,[111] Gabriel Moss Q.C. summarised the
relevant principles, when assessing on a *Wrotham Park* basis:

(i) the overall principle is that the Court must attempt to find what
would be a fair result of a hypothetical negotiation between the
parties;

---

[109] *Wrotham Park Estate Co. Ltd v Parkside Homes Ltd* [1974] 1 W.L.R. 798.
[110] [1977] Ch 106 335
[111] [2007] 1 W.L.R. 2167.

(ii)   the context, including the nature and seriousness of the breach must be kept in mind;

(iii) the right to prevent development gives the owner of the right a significant bargaining position;

(iv)   the owner of the right with such a bargaining position will normally be expected to receive some part of the likely profit from the development;

(v)   if there is no evidence of the likely size of that profit, the court can do its best by awarding a suitable multiple of the damages for loss of amenity;

(vi)   if there is such evidence, the court should normally award a sum which takes into account a fair percentage of the profit;

(vii) the size of the award should not in any event be so large that the development would not have taken place had such a sum been payable;

(viii) after arriving at such a figure which takes into consideration all the above and any other relevant factors, the court needs to consider whether "the deal feels right".

In the recent case of *Forsyth-Grant v Allen*[112] the Appellant claimed that the construction of two houses infringed a right of light enjoyed by her hotel. She sought not just damages but an account of profits from the respondents. The Court of Appeal, reviewing the authorities, confirmed that whatever the jurisprudential basis of the award of damages (i.e. whether it was restitutionary or not) it remained distinct from the remedy of account of profits. That remedy was to be kept within the narrow bounds set by *Attorney-General v Blake*.[113] On the facts, damages were assessed by reference to the capitalised diminution in letting value, rather than by a *Wrotham Park* calculation, because it produced a higher figure. A similar approach to calculation was adopted in *Watson v Croft Promosport*,[114] where the Court finding a nuisance, but refusing an injunction, awarded damages in lieu by reference to the diminution of the capital value of the property with the nuisance continuing.

Awards for damages in lieu are made under what was formerly the Lord Cairns Act, but what is now s.50 of the Supreme Court Act 1981.

---

[112] [2008] EWCA Civ 505.
[113] [2000] UKHL 45; [2001] A.C. 268.
[114] Above.

Defences to equitable remedies

Laches

Laches is a defence or bar to a claim for equitable remedies, in this context   **4–033**
for example if an injunction is sought.[115] If the claimant has been tardy in
bringing the claim, and the circumstances of the delay were such that the
claimant should be treated as both having acquiesced in the defendant's
activities and having waived his claim in circumstances in which it would
be inequitable and practically unjust to give him any remedy, the doctrine
of laches applies. The doctrine is described by Sir Barnes Peacock in
Lindsay Petroleum v Hurd[116] as follows:

> "Where it would be practically unjust to give a remedy, either because a
> party has, by his conduct, done that which might fairly be regarded as
> equivalent to a waiver of it, or where by his conduct and neglect he has,
> though perhaps not waiving that remedy, yet put the other party in a
> situation in which it would not be reasonable to place him if the remedy
> were afterwards to be asserted, in either of these cases lapse of time and
> delay are most material. But in every case, if an argument against relief,
> which otherwise would be just, is founded upon mere delay, that delay of
> course not amounting to a bar by any statute of limitations, the validity
> of that defence must be tried upon principles substantially equitable.
> Two circumstances, always important in such cases, are the length of the
> delay and the nature of the acts done during the interval, which might
> affect either party and cause a balance of justice or injustice in taking the
> one course or the other, so far as relates to the remedy."

Laches in other words looks to undue delay, to any change of position by
the defendants resulting from that delay, and to the unreasonableness and
injustice of stopping the defendants from carrying on doing what they have
been doing for a considerable time. Mere delay is not sufficient to form the
defence of laches, rather, the defence of laches is underpinned by the
concept of unconscionability.

Acquiescence

Acquiescence is also an equitable doctrine under which equitable relief   **4–034**
(whether injunction or damages in lieu) will be barred on the ground that
there has been delay coupled with some other factor(s) which, in all the

---

[115] See Snell's *Equity*, 31st edition (Sweet & Maxwell, 2007) paras 5–16 and 5–19 and *Chitty
on Contracts*, 20th edition (Sweet & Maxwell, 2002) Vol 1 paras 28–134 to 28–138 (both
citing, amongst other authorities, *Lindsay Petroleum Co v Hurd* (1874) L.R. PC 221 noted
below).
[116] (1874) L.R. 5 PC 221 at 239–240.

circumstances, makes it unconscionable for a party to continue to seek to enforce rights which he undoubtedly had at the date when the nuisance commenced.

The circumstances in which acquiescence may be established are illustrated in two recent decisions of the Court of Appeal: *Gafford v Graham*[117] and *Harris v Williams Wynne*.[118] In *Gafford* the claimant was not able to sue for the conversion of a neighbouring bungalow and the extension to a barn (both in clear breach of restrictive covenant) because he had not complained about them until three years after the works had been completed and "before that he had effectively treated the conversion of the bungalow and the extension to the barn as incidents which were closed" per Nourse L.J. at 81.

The test is whether it is unconscionable for the claimant to enforce his rights. The second case, *Harris*, upheld the lower court's decision that detriment to the defendant is usually required to establish unconscionability, but not always. If detriment is present it will usually lead the court to conclude that it would be unconscionable for the party whose decision it was not to enforce his rights, at the time when he first became aware of them, subsequently to reverse that decision and seek to enforce those rights. "But absent detriment the court needs to find some other factor which makes it unconscionable for the party having the benefit of the rights to change his mind"[119]—probably some sort of dishonesty or sharp practice.

4–035 It will be noted that in *Gafford* the Court concluded that acquiescence was a bar to all relief in respect of the bungalow and the barn. But the specific facts of the case are important. The plaintiff was suing for breach of restrictive covenant. As *Harris* makes clear, damages for such breaches at common law are likely to be nominal, and therefore any claim must be made under Lord Cairns' Act (enabling damages to be awarded in lieu of an injunction), if at all. *Harris* also explains that the Court's ruling in *Gafford* was on the basis that acquiescence as found in that case deprived the Court of jurisdiction to grant an injunction, and so damages under Lord Cairns' Act (as explained above) were not available.

Delay and oppression

4–036 Being a discretionary remedy, delay may well be a relevant factor, but the circumstances in which delay falling short of acquiescence is a good reason for not granting an injunction should be limited having regard to the guidance in *Shelfer v City of London Electric Lighting Co.*[120] and subsequent cases to that effect: see the discussion of *Watson* in paragraph 4–031 above.

---

[117] (1998) 77 P&CR 73.
[118] [2006] EWCA Civ 104.
[119] ibid., para.39.
[120] [1895] 1 Ch.287.

Damages in nuisance

The purpose of damages in nuisance, as with other torts is to put the **4–037** innocent party in the position he would have been had the wrong not been committed. Where monetary redress is sought, the measure of damages will depend on the type of nuisance under consideration but is usually calculated on the basis of diminution in the loss of the amenity value of the land, or the diminution of the actual value of the land, or, if different, the cost of reinstatement of damaged land.

In the case of nuisance causing material damage to property[121] the remedy, whether by way of injunction or damages is for causing damage to the land. In the case of nuisance which do not cause physical damage to the land, but are "productive of sensible personal discomfort"[122] it is important to appreciate that the damage is not for causing discomfort to the person but, as in the case of physical damage, damage to the land. As Lord Hoffman puts it in *Hunter*, while the land has not itself suffered injury, the utility of the land has been diminished by the existence of the nuisance. It is for an unlawful threat to that utility that the possessor or occupier is entitled to an injunction, and it is for the diminution in such utility that he is entitled to compensation.

So in a case where, for example, noxious odours have affected the claimant's property, the proper measure of damages should be the diminution of the value of the land whether sale or rental. But this is not the only way of measuring loss. In the case of a transitory nuisance, the capital value of the property will seldom be reduced. In such cases the owner or occupier is entitled to compensation by reference to the diminution in the amenity value of the property during the period for which the nuisance persisted. It is true that amenity value for the land may be difficult to calculate, because it involves placing a value on intangibles, but this should not result in a decision which relieves the wrong-doer of the necessity of paying damages and the law is sufficiently flexible to allow this to happen.[123] Assessment by reference to the physical inconvenience and stress and even illness to the claimant however is not an appropriate measure of damages.[124] This is because the damage is to the amenity of the land and not the person. The injury to the "amenity of the land" consists in the fact that the persons upon it are liable to suffer inconvenience, annoyance or illness. Again as explained by Lord Hoffman in *Hunter*:

"It follows that damages for nuisance recoverable by the possessor or occupier may be affected by the size, commodiousness and value of his

---

[121] e.g. the damage to hedges trees and shrubs in *St Helens Smelting Co. v Tipping* (1865) 11 HL Cas. 642.

[122] The phrase used by Lord Westbury in *St Helens Smelting Co. v Tipping* ibid.

[123] Per Lord Hoffman in *Hunter v Canary Wharf* [1997] A.C. 655 citing *Ruxley Electronics v Forsyth* [1996] A.C. 344.

[124] See Lord Hoffman in *Hunter v Canary Wharf* [1997] A.C. 655 at 706.

property but cannot be increased merely because more people are in occupation and therefore suffer greater collective discomfort. If more than one person has an interest in the property, the damages will have to be divided among them".[125]

4–038   Quantification of such damage is often difficult and may result in a relatively modest award. For example, in *Milka v Chetwynd Animal By-Products (1995) Ltd*,[126] HHJ Diehl Q.C. rejected the argument that there should be any analogy with personal injury damages and held that three years of intermittent emission of offensive and noxious odours invading the claimant's two properties, and said that the sum "cannot be assessed mathematically but should be moderate in amount". He awarded £1,000 per year for each year of the nuisance.

By way of counter-example, and in what must probably be regarded as an exceptional case, Buckley J. in *Dennis v Ministry of Defence*[127] awarded £50,000 as an assessment of loss of amenity in the absence of proper evidential grounds a claim for diminution in letting value. The size of this award reflects the size of the estate in question, with a value worth some £12 million if unaffected by the nuisance.

Where conduct which is a nuisance also gives rise to personal injury, a separate personal injury negligence action will lie, and the damages in that personal injury claim will be calculated along ordinary personal injury lines: the mesothelioma cases arising out of culpable escape of asbestos are a good example of this.[128]

As mentioned later in this chapter, exemplary damages are rarely, if ever, available for environmental harm. In the *Camelford* litigation,[129] where a number of people took action in respect of harm they alleged they had suffered from drinking water that was polluted by the defendant water company, the court observed that exemplary damages would be entirely inappropriate in a case where the water company had been convicted and fined for causing a public nuisance, and because of the large number of claimants affected. Such damages, said the court, would simply amount to an undeserved "windfall" based solely on the defendant's conduct. In 2002 the House of Lords effectively put an end to the debate in the environmental context by ruling that if exemplary damages were to be retained at all, they should not be available for causes of action for negligence, nuisance and strict liability.[130]

---

[125] At 706H-707A.
[126] January 19, 2000 (unreported).
[127] [2003] EWHC 793.
[128] *Margereson v J.W. Roberts Ltd* [1996] Env. L.R. 304 CA.
[129] *A.B. v South West Water Services Ltd* [1993] Q.B. 507.
[130] *Kuddus v Chief Constable of Leicestershire* [2002] 2 A.C. 122.

Limitation

The limitation period which applies to claims founded on private or public   **4–039**
nuisance is generally six years from the date on which the cause of action
accrued, which is when damage was caused to the claimant.[131] However, in
the case of a continuing nuisance a claimant will be able to recover losses
resulting from the effects of the nuisance in question over the last six years;
for example a claimant affected by odours for the past 10 years will be able
to recover damages for those odours in respect of the last six years. If the
claim also includes a claim in personal injury is involved, the basic limitation period is three years. These limitation periods primarily apply to
claims for damages for past nuisances. They do not apply to equitable
remedies such as injunctions for continuing nuisances, although, as we
have seen, a claimant seeking such relief must act with reasonable
diligence.

Public Nuisance

Public nuisance is a criminal offence, but requires treatment in this chapter   **4–040**
because of the remedies which may be pursued by individuals who can
prove special damage arising out of the harm caused to the community at
large. Its origins and development alongside the tort of private nuisance are
traced in *R v Rimmington*.[132] As Lord Bingham explained:

> "It became clear over time that there were some acts and omissions
> which were socially objectionable but could not found an action in pri-
> vate nuisance because the injury was suffered by the local community as
> a whole rather than by individual victims and because members of the
> public suffered injury to their rights as such rather than as private owners
> or occupiers of land.... Conduct of this kind came to be treated and
> punishable as such. In an unpoliced and unregulated society, in which
> local government was rudimentary or non-existent, common nuisance,
> as the offence was known, came to be (in the words of J R Spencer,
> 'Public Nuisance—A Critical Examination' [1989] CLJ 55, 59) "a rag-
> bag of odds and ends which we should nowadays call 'public welfare
> offences'. But central to the content of the crime was the suffering of
> common injury by members of the public by interference with rights
> enjoyed by them as such. I shall, to avoid wearisome repetition, refer to
> this feature in this opinion as "the requirement of common injury".

Moreover as Lord Rodger observes, a private individual can sue only if he
can show that the public nuisance has caused him special injury over and
above that suffered by the public in general.

---

[131] s.2 of the Limitation Act 1980.
[132] [2006] 1 A.C. 467.

The definition in *Archbold, Criminal Pleading, Evidence and Practice* describes the offence as follows:

"A person is guilty of a public nuisance (also known as a common nuisance), who (a) does an act not warranted by law, or (b) omits to discharge a legal duty, if the effect of the act or omission is to endanger the life, health, property, morals, or comfort of the public, or to obstruct the public in the exercise or enjoyment of rights common to all Her Majesty's subjects."

A core element of the crime of public nuisance is that the defendant's act should affect the community, a section of the public, rather than simply individuals. Obvious examples would be the release of smoke or fumes which affect a village or neighbourhood or the emission of loud noises which disturb the neighbourhood. In such cases the release or emission or each release or emission affects the public in the area. Of course if one were to break it down, the general effect on the community might well be seen to be made up of a collection of private nuisances occurring more or less simultaneously. As Romer L.J. said in *Attorney General v PYA Quarries Ltd*:[133]

"Some public nuisances (for example, the pollution of rivers) can often be established without the necessity of calling a number of individual complainants as witnesses. In general, however, a public nuisance is proved by the cumulative effect which it is shown to have had on the people living within its sphere of influence. In other words, a normal and legitimate way of proving a public nuisance is to prove a sufficiently large collection of private nuisances."

This insight is relevant from the point of view of proof. As Lord Rodger observes in *R v Rimmington*:

"Although the number of houses affected by the flying splinters of stone: the dust and vibration presumably varied a bit from blast to blast, each blast tended to affect homes in the vicinity of the quarry and a picture of the overall effect of the blasting on the community could be built up from the evidence of individual residents about its effects on them".

The significance of public nuisance to environmental lawyers is that, in addition to its role as a criminal offence of some seriousness, courts are empowered to grant relief, both by way of an injunction at the relation of the Attorney General, and also through the remedies in tort that are available to a claimant who has suffered special or particular damage as a result of a public nuisance. To show special damage, an individual must show that "he has sustained a particular damage or injury other than and

---

[133] [1957] 2 Q.B. 169.

beyond, the general injury to the public and that such damage is substantial".[134] Though most kinds of harm will be relevant damage in such circumstances, such as physical damage to property and economic loss,[135] it is not clear whether inconvenience that is not directly translatable into financial loss will suffice. Typically, a claim in public nuisance may assist the owner of a property specifically affected by a public nuisance affecting the highway in the immediate vicinity.[136] In addition, claims in public nuisance have the advantage that they are not defeated by a claim for prescriptive rights; one cannot in law "prescribe" against the Crown who is nominally the ultimate guardian of the public benefits at issue in this tort.

There was some doubt as to whether the decisions of *Hunter v Canary Wharf Ltd*[137] and *Transco Plc v Stockport MBC*[138] were authority for the proposition that damages for personal injury should no longer be recoverable in public nuisance, based on the principle that such claims are not recoverable in private nuisance. This point was recently considered in *Claimants appearing on the register of the Corby Group Litigation v Corby Borough Council*.[139] The Court of Appeal held that there was no implied reversal of the long-established principle that damages for personal injury could be recovered in public nuisance. The local authority (Corby) argued that Professor Newark's article "the Boundaries of Nuisance",[140] which was considered by the House of Lords in *Hunter*, provided powerful support for an argument that personal injury damages should only be recoverable in negligence. However the Court of Appeal considered that since the essence of the right protected by public nuisance was the right not to be adversely affected by an unlawful act or omission whose effect was to endanger the life and health of the public, it was difficult to see why a person who had been exposed to such unlawful act or omission should not be able to recover damages for the personal injury thereby caused in the tort of public nuisance. 4–041

Bowden: damage to community as a whole

An interesting claim (although ultimately unsuccessful) in public nuisance was made in the case of *Bowden v South West Water*.[141] In a claim considered also below in the context of an action under the *Francovich* principle, a mussel fisherman complained that the sea had become threatened, and his livelihood had been damaged, by the discharge of sewage into the 4–042

---

[134] *Benjamin v Storr* [1874–86] All E.R. Rep. Ext. 2000.
[135] *Tate & Lyle v GLC* [1983] 1 A.C. 509: siltation of the River Thames affecting the plaintiff's rights of navigation.
[136] Obstruction of the highway affecting the claimant's business is the typical example.
[137] [1997] A.C. 655 HL.
[138] [2003] UKHL 61, [2004] A.C. 1. See para.4–048 below.
[139] [2008] EWCA Civ 463.
[140] (1949) 65 LQR 480.
[141] *Bowden v South West Water and Another* [1999] 3 CMLR.

sea by South West Water. Mr Bowden claimed to enjoy private, enforceable rights under one or more of the Bathing Waters Directive,[142] the Shellfish Waters Directive[143] and the Urban Waste Water Directive.[144]

One of the appellant's arguments in support of his claim in public nuisance was that the defendants were in breach of these three directives and in breach of Section 7 of the Sea Fisheries (Shellfish) Act 1967. He submitted that the United Kingdom's breach of the directives in question amounted to a criminal offence; by what is now Article 249 of the EC Treaty, he contended, one or all of the directives was binding upon the UK as to the results to be achieved (clean water) and that a failure to comply and to achieve the results required by the directives amounted to an unlawful act and a breach of duty which stemmed from the directive and was sufficient to establish the unlawfulness of the actions for the purpose of public nuisance. The interference to his right to harvest mussels was the indirect consequence of the defendants' acts, which, though originally done pursuant to their statutory authorisation as sewerage undertakers, became unlawful because the water failed to comply with the quality required by the various directives. The Court of Appeal, dismissed his claim, because the interference was too "remote" to give rise to an action in public nuisance, by which they meant that there must be common injury to the community as a whole, not just injury to an individual or small group of individuals.

Conditions for liability in public nuisance

4–043 Liability in public nuisance is strict. Once the nuisance is proven and the defendant is shown to have caused it, then the legal burden is on the defendant to justify his actions.[145] As such it is a potentially very useful ground of action for environmental protection, particularly since the historical case law[146] has frequently involved environmental catastrophes of one sort or another.

Rylands v Fletcher

4–044 The classic formulation for this separate tort was laid down by Blackburn J in the original nineteenth century case of *Rylands v Fletcher*[147] where he stated that where a person who brings on to his land an inherently

---

[142] 76/160/EEC OJ L31.1.
[143] 79/923/EEC OJ L281/47.
[144] 91/271/EC OJ L135/40. See also para.11-032 on the Court of Appeal ruling in respect to his Francovich action.
[145] *Southport Corporation v Esso Petroleum Co. Ltd.* [1954] 2 Q.B. 182.
[146] The oil spills in *Southport*, the water contamination in (*Camelford*) *A.B. v South West Water*, and the blasting from the quarries in *PYA Quarries* are three examples from leading cases.
[147] [1861–73] All E.R. Rep.1.

hazardous thing (whether an animal, a noxious substance or large quantities of water, for example) if it then escapes he is strictly liable for all the damage that results. Subsequent cases tended to restrict the rule and it was only in *Cambridge Water*[148] that the House of Lords undertook a root and branch review of the rule, and reaffirmed its existence as an aspect, or subspecies,[149] of the law of nuisance applicable to escapes from land.

The essential requirements for liability drawn from *Rylands* are that:

(i) The defendant must bring and keep something on his land for his own purposes.

(ii) That thing must be not naturally there—namely the concept of "non-natural" user of land.

(iii) There must be an escape of that thing which affects the claimant's use of his land.

(iv) The harm complained of must be a foreseeable consequence of that escape[150]—expressed in *Rylands* as the "natural and anticipated consequence".

Foreseeability under the rule in Rylands v Fletcher

Cambridge Water did not alter these preconditions but simply emphasised **4–045**
the condition of foreseeability, which had always been implicit in the tort, as (iv) above makes clear. As the House of Lords noted, the two torts, of escape under *Rylands v Fletcher*, and of nuisance, are closely related. The emphasis their Lordships placed on foreseeability brings them into even closer proximity; not only must the thing which escapes be of such a nature as to be likely to cause harm if it does escape, but also the kind of harm which occurs must be reasonably foreseeable if damages are to be awarded, otherwise the damage will in law be regarded too remote. But it is important to note that, as *Rylands* itself confirms, the defendant is liable even if he could not reasonably have foreseen that there would have been an escape;[151] the foreseeability test only applies to limit recovery to the foreseeable consequences of the escape which did occur. In this one regard, liability is stricter than in a claim for private nuisance.

"Natural" or "reasonable" or "ordinary user"

This is conceptually the trickiest element of the tort, though *Cambridge* **4–046**
Water and *Transco* have eased some of these problems. In modern society it is difficult, if not entirely artificial, to describe the existence of most sub-

---

[148] [1994] 2 W.L.R. 53, as discussed in para.4–046 below.
[149] Lord Bingham's phrase in *Transco plc v Stockport MBC* [2004] 2 A.C. 1.
[150] *Cambridge Water Co Ltd v Eastern Counties Leather plc* [1993] UKHL 12, [1994] 2 A.C. 264.
[151] Well summarised by Lord Hoffman at para.33 of *Transco*.

stances or materials on land as "non-natural". The case law preceding *Cambridge Water* demonstrates this difficulty; indeed that case itself points up how impossible it is to locate an activity on a scale from "natural" to "non-natural". In 1983 Cambridge Water, a statutory drinking water supplier, was testing the water it was abstracting from a borehole to check, inter alia, that it met the requirements of the then current EC Drinking Water Directive, as these had to be complied with by September 1985. It found that two chlorinated organic solvents were present in significant concentrations, well in excess of the maximum limits prescribed in the Directive. The borehole was therefore shut down in October 1983. Eventually a tannery, Eastern Counties Leather, was found to be a source of these solvents. For many years Eastern Counties had used them for degreasing leather, and up until 1976 had brought them on to its site in drums (after which a bulk handling system was used). Transferring solvents from the drums was not carefully controlled, and over the years substantial quantities had been spilt. These had percolated through the soil into the chalk aquifer that fed Cambridge Water's borehole. Cambridge Water sued Eastern Counties in nuisance, negligence and under the rule in *Rylands v Fletcher*. The evidence in the case was that at the material time, i.e. up to 1976, Eastern Counties was not aware that the solvents were harmful or that, if spilt, they might enter an aquifer (it was supposed that they simply evaporated), and still less that they might reach any drinking water borehole. At first instance the claims under all three heads were dismissed; the only one maintained on appeal was liability under the rule in *Rylands v Fletcher*.

The use of organochlorine solvents in a tannery was held at first instance to be a natural use of land in an industrial estate, providing employment to the local community. But in the House of Lords Lord Goff commented that

"the storage of substantial quantities of chemicals on industrial premises should be regarded as an almost classic case of non-natural use; and I find it very difficult to think that it should be thought objectionable to impose strict liability for damage caused in the event of their escape."

Lord Goff continued:

"It may well be that, now that it is recognised that foreseeability of harm of the relevant type is a prerequisite of liability in damages under the rule, the courts may feel less pressure to extend the concept of natural use to circumstances such as those in the present case; and in due course it may become easier to control this exception, and to ensure that it has a more recognisable basis of principle".[152]

---

[152] paras 157 et seq.

So the "non-natural" user criterion is easier to satisfy in the light of this ruling than the pre-*Cambridge Water* cases suggested. Storage of ordinarily-encountered chemicals or substances will undoubtedly fall within the scope of the rule.

The result in *Transco* confirmed this principle. Some of their Lordships, especially Lord Bingham,[153] thought the rule could be better expressed as applying only to extraordinary and unusual user (as opposed to non-natural user). Hence a domestic water supply, including to an 11-storey block of flats, was "an entirely normal and routine" use of land not amounting to non-natural user. It would therefore be wrong to assume that the relaxation of the criterion effected by *Cambridge Water* brings all potentially dangerous activities within the scope of the rule.

Escape from C's land to D's land

The "escape" requirement relates back to the nature of the control of the   4–047
land from which the offending substance emanates. There is no need to establish legal title of the defendant to the land, nor does the "escape" have to be accidental. Occupation or control of the land at the time of the escape is enough.

The escape must also affect land in which the claimant has a legal interest; in *Transco* Lord Scott doubted whether this requirement was satisfied where the claimant's only interest in land was an easement of support over the defendant's land from which the substance escaped.

Conclusion

It is unlikely that the rule in *Rylands v Fletcher* will develop as a major tool   4–048
for environmental regulation, largely because their Lordships in *Cambridge Water* placed a bar against any trend towards strict liability for damages caused by ultra-hazardous operations; the imposition of strict liability in such circumstances, in their view, was a matter for Parliament rather than the courts. Hence foreseeability will play a continuing part in limiting liability under the rule.

The most recent analysis of the role played by the rule in modern society may be found in the case of *Transco Plc v Stockport MBC*[154] where water leaked from a substantial pipe serving a block of flats owned by the council, which caused the collapse of a nearby disused embankment resulting in the exposure of a high pressure gas main requiring work to prevent it from causing serious damage to a neighbouring golf club. The claimant sued the council for the escape of the water. The claim was dismissed in the Court of Appeal and in the House of Lords, principally on the ground that the

---

[153] [2003] UKHL 61, [2004] 2 A.C. 1, para.11, para.13.
[154] [2003] UKHL 61, [2004] 2 A.C. 1.

user was not "non-natural". However, the defendants unsuccessfully sought to uphold the decision of the Court of Appeal on an additional ground, namely that the principles in *Rylands v Fletcher* should be absorbed into the law of negligence. The general conclusion of the House of Lords was that *Rylands v Fletcher* remains a separate tort applicable to environmental damage, because there will always be a class of cases, however small, where liability should be imposed regardless of fault.

Trespass to Land

4–049   In the environmental context we are concerned with trespass to land. This consists in any unjustifiable intrusion by one person upon the land in the possession of another.[155] The tort of trespass is distinguishable from nuisance because it is actionable per se (i.e. without proof of damage) The essential features of the tort are that:

(i)   it is actionable per se;
(ii)   it is in respect of a proprietary interest only;
(iii) direct harm is required;
(iv)   trespass must be intentional or negligent.

The first requirement stems from the historical development of the tort, which differentiated it from an action for trespass on the case, which dealt with harm which was consequential on the defendant's action. In pure trespass, the damage must be forcible and direct, in other words the injury inflicted on person or property must be so closely associated with the act as to be considered a direct part of it. (Actions for trespass on the case formed the basis for the development of the separate torts of nuisance and negligence).

Despite this somewhat archaic precondition, it is of potentially useful application to environmental harm simply because it is quite easy for noxious substances to manifest themselves immediately on a potential claimant's property; trespass may be committed to the air above and the underlying strata of land.[156] As Tromans and Turrall-Clarke have pointed out in their comprehensive survey on the law relating to contaminated land:

"...if the difficulties of direct injury and title to sue can be surmounted, trespass is a powerful remedy since it is actionable irrespective of fault and without proof of actual damage".[157]

---

[155] Blackstone's Commentaries, Vol. 3 p.209.
[156] The first arose in a Canadian case, *McDonald v Associated Fuels* (1954) 3 DLR 775; the second was exemplified in *Corbett v Hill* (1870) L.R. 9 Eq. 671.
[157] Stephen Tromans and Robert Turrall-Clarke, *Contaminated Land*, 2nd Edition, (Sweet and Maxwell, 2008), p. 385.

The concept of direct injury is the key to distinguishing between when an action in trespass will be appropriate and when one in nuisance: the causes of action are mutually exclusive. The direct injury or harm in question need not involve damage: mere interference with proprietary rights will suffice. Thus a person who walks over another's land without permission renders himself liable to an action for trespass and an injunction even though no damage to the property has been caused.

An important example in the environmental context is depositing waste **4–050** on another person's land. This is a trespass even though the underlying land may not be contaminated.[158] This should be contrasted with the position where the defendant causes such material to pass on to or over the claimant's land merely as a result of the exercise of his own rights of property, for example, allowing tree roots to grow onto his neighbour's land.[159] The reason the former is a trespass and the latter a nuisance is because the interference with the proprietary right of the claimant is direct rather than indirect.

This concept is well demonstrated in *Esso Petroleum v Southport Corporation*.[160] Oil which had been jettisoned from the defendant's oil tanker polluted the claimant's foreshore. Neither Lord Radcliffe nor Lord Tucker considered an action in trespass (which had been pleaded in the alternative although not argued at trial) could succeed because the oil was jettisoned in the estuary and there was no certainty or inevitability that it would have ended up on the claimant's foreshore.[161]

Defences

Amongst the defences to trespass, and relevant in the environmental **4–051** context, is the defence of justification by necessity, namely the plea that it was necessary to enter upon the land to preserve life or property. Any danger which would justify such action must be immediate and obvious and no reasonable person would conclude that there was no alternative to the act of trespass.[162] This defence was unsuccessfully relied upon by the defendants in *Monsanto v Tilly*,[163] who carried out a trespass for the purpose of uprooting genetically modified plants and crops which they believed represented a threat to public safety. Similar defences have been invoked (albeit equally unsuccessfully on the law) in the environmental

---

[158] It also gives rise to a specific statutory claim for any losses under section 73(6) of the EPA 1990.
[159] *Butler v Standard Telephones and Cables Ltd* [1940] 1 KB 399.
[160] [1956] A.C. 218.
[161] They also dismissed such a claim on an additional ground, namely that it was well established that a person whose land adjoins a highway or navigable waters and who has suffered damage cannot recover in trespass in the absence of negligence on the part of the person who has caused the damage: ibid. at 244–245.
[162] *Workman v Cooper* [1961] 2 Q.B. 143.
[163] [2000] Env. L.R. 313.

protestor cases of *Secretary of State for Transport v Haughian*[164] and *Mayor and Burgesses of the London Borough of Bromley v Susanna*.[165]

Remedies

4–052   A successful claimant in a trespass action does not have to show that he has suffered actual loss and so may always recover at least nominal damages. If he shows actual damage to have been suffered as a result of direct injury, he is entitled to receive damages to compensate him for his loss, even though the losses may have flowed indirectly from that injury. These damages will be calculated on the basis of the consequent loss to the claimant, depending on whether the circumstances indicate that this should be diminution in the value of the land or the cost of reinstatement. Though there is a considerable body of case law on this, it ultimately comes down to whether any proposed reinstatement is reasonable.[166] If the reinstatement is out of all proportion to the diminution in value of the land this will not be allowed. An injunction may be granted to prevent a continuing trespass or a repetition of a trespass or where a trespass is threatened.

Limitation

4–053   The general rule is that an action for trespass must be brought within six years from the date on which the cause of action accrued (as in private nuisance).[167] In environmental cases it is worth noting that where the defendant's offending substance remains on the claimant's land, this may constitute a new trespass each day—it is thus a continuing tort and a new limitation period likewise starts afresh each day in relation to the damage caused by that day's trespass, though time continues to run in relation to that caused on previous days.

Negligence

4–054   The cardinal principles of negligence are as follows:

(i)   There must be a duty of care owed by the defendant to the claimant.
(ii)   The defendant must be shown to have breached his duty of care.
(iii)   The claimant must have suffered damage which was a foreseeable consequence of the claimant's breach of duty.

---

[164] [1997] Env. L.R. 59 (CA): trespassers on the Newbury bypass site alleging breach of the EIA Directive.
[165] [1998] Env. L.R. D13 (CA); trespassers on a development site alleging breaches of environmental and conservation legislation if the development were to proceed.
[166] *Scutt v Lomax*, CA, January 25, 2000 (destruction of chattels and trees), and *Bryant v Macklin* [2005] EWCA Civ 762 (damage to trees through livestock).
[167] s.2 of the Limitation Act 1980.

A full discussion of the tort of negligence is beyond the scope of this chapter, but so far as it is relevant to environmental matters the following features are important.

First, unlike nuisance or trespass there is no requirement that the claimant have an interest in property. Second, and perhaps most disadvantageously to those who seek to rely on negligence in the environmental context, it requires proof of fault or carelessness. In environmental matters where professional skill and expertise is often in play, the relevant standard of care is that set out in *Bolam v Friern Hospital Management Committee*[168] per McNair J. Although relating to doctors specifically, it is of widespread application to all areas of professional skill:

> "[A doctor] is not guilty of negligence if he has acted in accordance with a practice accepted as proper by a responsible body of [medical] men skilled in that particular art. . . . Putting it the other way around, a man is not negligent, if he is acting in accordance with such a practice merely because there is a body of opinion which takes a contrary view."

As Bingham L.J. put it in *Eckersley v Binnie and Partners*,[169] concerning engineer's liabilities for a methane gas explanation: "the law does not require of a professional man that he be a paragon combining the qualities of polymath and prophet."

This test is subject to the qualification that it is open, in an exceptional case, to the Court to hold an accepted professional practice to be negligent. Lord Browne-Wilkinson explained in the later case of *Bolitho v City & Hackney HA*[170] that the *Bolam* test required the court to be satisfied "that exponents of the body of medical opinion relied upon can demonstrate that such opinion has a logical basis." An example of this in the environmental context might be a claim in negligence for personal injury caused by agricultural water pollution where the escape occurred despite the farmer complying with all relevant codes of good agricultural practice.[171]

Where no professional skill or expertise is involved the relevant duty is   **4–055** one of taking "reasonable care" in the course of the activity in question, and if that is established, an action in negligence fails. Compare an action for nuisance where the carrying out of an operation with all reasonable care is no defence, if its impact upon the claimant's use of his own land is unreasonable.[172]

In the field of environmental liability all the relevant statutory provisions and particular requirement of licences or permits will be relevant to whether there is a breach of duty of care. The Compensation Act of 2006

---

[168] [1957] 1 W.L.R. 582.
[169] [1998] 18 Con. L.R. 1 at 80, dissenting as to the result.
[170] [1988] A.C. 232.
[171] No claim for personal injury lies in either private nuisance or *Rylands v Fletcher*, so the point is far from academic.
[172] *Rapier v London Tramways* [1893] 2 Ch. 588.

enjoins the courts, when considering a claim in negligence or breach of statutory duty,[173] and determining what steps a defendant should have taken, to have regard to whether these steps might prevent a desirable activity being undertaken at all, or whether such requirements might discourage persons from undertaking functions in connection with a desirable activity.[174] This provision must tend to reinforce the position of a defendant relying on permit compliance or compliance with codes of practice in response to a claim in negligence. Its corollary is that claims in nuisance and under the rule in *Rylands v Fletcher* are more attractive to claimants because the 2006 Act does not apply to these causes of action.

As for foreseeability, there must be a close relationship between the type of harm that could have been foreseen and that which actually occurred. In *Cambridge Water*, spillages of solvent did occur but the harmfulness of the substances and their propensity to migrate through aquifers meant that the kind of damage suffered by the water company was not then foreseeable. The case may have been differently decided had the facts occurred rather more recently, when awareness of the effect of certain substances on groundwater has massively increased and the standards expected by regulatory authorities, as reinforced by water pollution directives, are considerably higher.

4-056 There are a number of cases where harm by pollution has been held to be foreseeable; the Canadian case of *Gertson v Municipality of Metropolitan Toronto*[175] held the defendant liable for the escape of landfill gas in 1963 from a pit that had been filled between 1958–59; and in *Eckersley* a methane gas explosion case pleaded in negligence, the Court of Appeal considered that there were a number of factors relevant to the liability of operators to foresee the possible presence of methane as a natural phenomenon. The majority of the Court of Appeal held the engineers liable, by references to the speech of Lord Reid in the *Wagon Mound* concerning remote risks:[176]

"It does not follow that, no matter what the circumstances may be, it is justifiable to neglect a risk of such a small magnitude. A reasonable man would only neglect such a risk if he had a valid reason for doing so; e.g. it would involve considerable expense to eliminate the risk. He would weigh the risk against the difficulty of eliminating it."

Negligence actions are possible against public authorities who are or become involved in operations where problems subsequently occur. For

[173] The not entirely straightforward question of whether claims under the Human Rights Act and under the *Francovich* question are claims for breach of statutory duty is considered below.
[174] s.1.
[175] (1973) 41 D.L.R. (3rd) 646. The claim was pleaded in negligence, nuisance and *Rylands v Fletcher*, though in English law a personal injury claim can only lie in negligence.
[176] (1988) 18 Con. L.R. 1, at 52, per Russell LJ, citing Lord Reid at [1967] A.C. 617 at 642.

example, a local authority owes a duty of care in negligence in respect of the inspection functions of its officers; see *Welton v North Cornwall DC*.[177] In that case an environmental health officer from the Council inspected premises and made a series of negligent misstatements as to the need for substantial building works to comply with Regulations issued under the Food Safety Act. Relying on such misstatements the claimants carried out substantial building works, 90 per cent of which proved to be unnecessary in order to comply with the Regulations. The Court held that the officer had assumed a responsibility to take care in relation to the statements he made and that the officer had been acting outside his statutory powers hence it was unnecessary to consider whether the imposition of a duty of care superimposed on a statutory duty was fair, just and reasonable. Interestingly however, the Court went on to hold that in any event the officer's conduct had been such that it was fair, just and reasonable, and that in accordance with public policy a duty of care should be imposed.

Importantly, the circumstances in which a duty of care in negligence will be superimposed upon an existing statutory duty, is an area of the law which is in a state of constant development. A helpful distillation of the relevant principles is to be found in *Rice v Secretary of State for Trade and Industry; Thompson v Secretary of State for Trade and Industry*,[178] where the Court of Appeal considered their Lordships' speeches in both *Stovin v Wise* and *Gorringe v Calderdale Metropolitan Borough Council*. May L.J. said at paragraph 42:

"Drawing together and synthesising the threads of these authorities, a statute containing broad target duties owed to the public at large, and which does not itself confer on individuals a right of action for breach of statutory duty, is unlikely to give rise to a common law duty of care, breach of which will support a claim by an individual for damages. Such a public law duty is enforceable, if it is justiciable at all, only by judicial review. There may, however, be relationships, arising out of the existence and exercise of statutory powers or duties, between a public authority and one or more individuals from which the public authority is to be taken to have assumed responsibility to guard against foreseeable injury or loss to the individuals caused by breach of the duty. There is then a sufficient relationship of proximity and it is fair, just and reasonable that a duty of care should be imposed. In order to determine whether the law should impose such a duty, an intense focus on the particular facts and the particular statutory background is necessary."

---

[177] *Welton v North Cornwall DC* [1997] 1 W.L.R. 570: but compare cases such as *Lam v Torbay BC* [1997] PIQR P488, where a claim involving the allegedly incompetent regulation of a polluting process via the planning and statutory nuisance processes was dismissed by the CA.

[178] [2007] EWCA Civ 289.

Breach of Statutory Duty

4–057　In addition to, and sometimes in parallel with the common law, are specific statutory duties with respect to the protection of the environment. We have noted section 73(6) of EPA 1990, where a claim for damages is specifically provided for. Similarly, there are provisions considered in Chapter 20 concerning damage arising from nuclear installations. However, the circumstances, in environmental disputes, where an action for breach of statutory duty will lie where this is not set out specifically in the statute will be rare. This is because environmental statutes are generally classic examples of public welfare statutes where the courts are reluctant to construe Parliament as having had an intention to confer such a private law benefit on individual claimants. Unsuccessful claims under various water statutes, dismissed at first instance in *Bowden v South West Water*,[179] are good examples of this in the environmental context, though the underlying principles are drawn from the general law in cases such as *X v Bedfordshire CC*.[180]

Other Mechanisms for Controlling/Preventing Environmental Damage:

4–058　Clearly there are other private law legal mechanisms which can on occasion assist to control environmental damage, and can give rise to civil claims. Among them, are the use of property law, including freehold covenants and easements. Equally, it might be said that on occasion an easement may allow an interference with land which would otherwise be a nuisance. Likewise planning conditions or obligations such as section 106 agreements may address or mitigate environmental damage, It is frequently the case that planning authorities will require mitigation measures (such as noise attenuation bunds around noisy activities) or will set limits to noise and working times on construction or demolition projects. While such limits of themselves are not (for reasons given in the foregoing sections) likely to be determinative of the question of nuisance, and may not confer a civil remedy they may provide effective restraints on the causing of environmental harm.

---

[179] [1998] Env. L.R. 445.
[180] [1995] 2 A.C. 633.

COMMUNITY LAW

As other chapters in this book make amply clear, the protection provided   **4–059** for the environment by Community law seems, on the face of it, the most generous and far-reaching of any of the existing common law regimes. Article 2 EC states that the Community has as its task to promote "a high level of protection and improvement of the quality of the environment", whilst Article 6 EC provides that "environmental protection requirements must be integrated into the definition and implementation of the Community policies and activities".

Enforcement of these protective norms however is a different matter altogether. The following section of this chapter explores the development under EU law of state civil liability in the context of environmental harm, and considers whether in fact the current state of play is sufficient to fill in the gaps left by the somewhat piecemeal imposition of common law civil liability in this country.

Despite the early efflorescence of environmental regulation at a community level, little was achieved by the Commission's efforts to enforce this legislation by infringement proceedings against member states when they failed to transpose or correctly implement directives. The glacial speed of infringement proceedings did little, for example, to clean up rivers or aquifers that had been illegally poisoned by waste. But at least the assumption by the EC institutions of their authority over such matters brought environmental protection within their competence—a somewhat prescient move, considering the resistance Member States now show to new moves by the Community to impose their authority over other areas of public life.

Competence is important because the ability to take action under   **4–060** Community law—for EU institutions as well as individuals—depends on the extent of the Community's jurisdiction. The Community has no inherent powers, and must keep to the powers conferred on it by the treaties. This means that the Community institutions may only legislate within the limits of its existing powers, and the European Court of Justice (ECJ) may only rule on questions concerning those powers. But in the *ERT*[181] case the European Court affirmed that it would review the compatibility of EC law with general principles of law. In that case the ECJ referred to the European Convention on Human Rights as having "special significance" as a key source of inspiration for the general principles of EC law, even though there is no formal incorporation of the ECHR in EC law. By drawing on a non-binding international instrument the Court asserted its freedom to go beyond the remit of EC Treaty principles. In the meantime subsequent treaties have considerably enhanced the community's

---

[181] Case 260/89, [1991] E.C.R. I -2925.

sphere of competence. In the environmental context, water and air pollution, waste, nuclear safety and nature conservation are now governed by community legislation, bringing state action within the jurisdiction of the ECJ, either as an implementation or derogation question. That Court, in other words, is competent to consider the adequacy of the measures taken by the Member State in implementing the relevant Community directive in domestic law, and it can also consider the legality of any claim a member state may make to be entitled to restrict its implementation.

In principle, the European Commission has always had powers to enforce EC precepts on disposal of waste and other matters but there has been a marked failure of enforcement proceedings to deter member states from ignoring these rules. Part of the problem is the fact that the ECJ may only hand down a declaratory decision in the initial stages of infringement proceedings, and therefore the effective use of community law came to depend on the willingness of individual claimants or pressure groups to request preliminary references to the ECJ[182] or to seek redress directly before the court. The former avenue is not usually open to environmental litigants since individuals or groups may only request a reference if an EC decision or community act is directly addressed to them, which is rarely the case with environmental legislation. The latter option is potentially more useful and it is therefore worth looking briefly at the evolution of state liability for breach of EC law in non-environmental cases in order to understand how the proper enforcement of environmental legislation at an EC level is now possible.

It must however be stressed at the outset that for reasons relating to financial incentives, differences in national notions of individual rights and lack of harmonisation of the community's own environmental laws themselves, it is still a relatively unexplored field of litigation, when compared, for example, to actions arising out of alleged gender discrimination or restrictions on the free movement of services or goods. The main problem is that in environmental law it is as difficult to discern the nature of the rights behind various environmental directives (is a person a proper "subject" of a water cleanliness measure?) as it is to understand what kind of remedies might be appropriate (the eventual cleaning up of the water may be of no direct benefit to the individual which has gone to the expense of taking the claim; on the other hand, damages to individuals do nothing to clean up rivers).

4–061   The focus of this chapter is on private actions via the *Francovich* principle or under the doctrine of "direct effect". It is not proposed to repeat the

---

[182] Article 234 EC allows individuals to assert in national courts that their Member States have broken a Community provision, which then triggers a reference by the national court to the ECJ for a ruling on the matter. This procedure has effectively enlisted the national courts as enforcers and appliers of EC law.

wealth of academic and case commentary on either of these avenues[183], but to consider the development of the case law that has developed in the light of the community's competence to legislate on environmental matters, and its usefulness to individual claimants and groups now and in the future.

Francovich and the Doctrine of Direct Effect

EC law consists of Treaty provisions, Regulations and directives. Provided they are sufficiently precise and unconditional, Treaty Articles and Regulations take effect from the moment they enter into force, and they generally have horizontal effect, meaning that they can be enforced against private parties, not just against the state. Treaty provisions and Regulations are directly applicable[184] because they are not dependent until further action of a legislative or executive nature by the Member States.[185] There are not however many candidates in the environmental context for legislation by Regulation or Treaty Article; directives are therefore the focus of this section, and since they are addressed to governments of Member States they are not in principle enforceable by individuals against states until implemented by those Member States.[186] Moreover, there is nothing in the wording of the Treaty to suggest that other kinds of Community legislation—apart from Regulations—should be directly applicable, so it would appear that directives would always have to be implemented before they can be invoked and relied upon by individuals before national courts. Indeed Article 249 EC states that a directive is binding "only as to the result to be achieved" but leaves "the choice of form and methods" to the national authorities.

4–062

Nevertheless, the doctrine of direct effect was applied to directives, most notably in the *Van Duyn* case in 1974,[187] which removed any doubt about the eligibility of certain directives for grounding claims before national courts. But even those directives whose provisions are considered to have direct effect only operate vertically; in other words individuals may only rely on them in order to obtain relief against the state, not other individuals or private parties. To succeed in such an action a claimant must prove that

---

[183] De Burca (1992) "Giving Effect to European Community" MLR 215; Craig (1997) "Directives: Direct Effect, Indirect Effect, and the Construction of National Legislation" ELR 519; *European Community Law in the English Courts*, Andenas and Jacobs (eds) (Oxford: Clarendon Press, 1998); *State Liability in Damages for Breach of Community Law in the National Courts*, Heukel and McDonnell (eds), *The Action for Damages in Community Law* (The Hague: Kluwer, 1997); *Non Contractual Liability of the European Communities*, Schermers, Heukel, Mead (eds) (Dordrecht: Nijhoff, 1988); *Direct Effect of European Law*, *Prinssen and Schrauwen* (eds) (Goningen: European Law Publishing, 2004).
[184] Article 249 EC states that a regulation is "directly applicable in all Member States".
[185] *Van Gend en Loos*, Case 26/62, [1963] E.C.R. 1.
[186] Article [249] EC.
[187] *Van Duyn v Home Office*, Case 41/74 [1974] E.C.R. 1337.

the state has failed properly to implement the directive in question and has therefore caused quantifiable injury.

Most EC legislation concerning the environment comes in the form of directives and therefore these will be the focus of the following discussion.

Direct Effect of Directives

4–063 The abundance of case law and comment on this concept has tended to obscure rather than clarify the principle of direct effect and its relationship with a *Francovich* action, particularly in the context of environmental protection. Only the bare bones of this jurisprudence will be laid out here, before we go on to consider the prospects for success of an action for compensation for environmental harm.

The doctrine of direct effect derives from the principle of "effectiveness" of Community law, the foremost authority for which is the *Van Duyn* judgment, which laid down the principle of the "useful effect" of Community law, otherwise known as *effet utile*. In other words, where the Community authorities have, by directive, imposed on Member States the obligation to pursue a particular course of conduct, the useful effect of such an act would be weakened if the individuals were prevented from relying on it before their national courts.

With time, the precise underpinnings for the doctrine of direct effect became less important than the question of what circumstances should obtain in order that individuals could rely on this doctrine to enforce directives in national courts. This in turn led to the formulation underlying the so-called *Francovich* action.

Francovich

4–064 The *Francovich*[188] case concerned an EC Directive intended to ensure that full payment of salary arrears was received by employees on the event of insolvency of the employer. Italy failed to implement this Directive and a group of employees who had been unable to obtain these arrears of pay sued the Italian government, claiming damages for non-implementation. The Court ruled that there is a general principle inherent in the Treaty that a Member State is liable to compensate individuals for loss caused to them as a result of the violation of Community law for which the Member State is responsible. However for this liability to arise, three requirements must be satisfied;

    (i) the rule of law infringed must be intended to confer rights on individuals,

---

[188] Joined cases C-6 and 9/90 *Francovich and Others* [1991] E.C.R. I-5357.

(ii) the infringement must be sufficiently serious,

(iii) there must be a direct causal link between the breach of obligation and damage sustained.

It is important to remember that before this ruling was laid down the position was that for direct effect to apply, not only the beneficiaries, but the subject matter and the content of the right had to be ascertainable with sufficient precision. *Van Duyn* itself concerned Directive 64/221, which allowed Member States to restrict the movement of non-national on grounds such as public policy. The claimant had been denied entry to the UK because of her association with the Church of Scientology. She relied on the (non implemented) directive, arguing that such refusal could only be lawful under Community law if it was based on personal conduct. She was successful; the obligation imposed was clear, precise and legally complete and the Court ruled that she was therefore able to rely on it before the national court. In another early case on direct effect, *Ratti*,[189] the claimant's firm had packaged its products in conformity with two non-implemented directives. He was prosecuted when it transpired that this packaging did not comply with the relevant Italian legislation and he argued that his compliance with the directives was sufficient. The ECJ ruled that the directive whose deadline for implementation had expired was directly effective and therefore *Ratti* was afforded a defence to the charges under Community law. The rationale for this judgment laid the way for *Francovich* and clearly articulated the estoppel argument for direct effect: a Member State should have implemented a directive by its deadline date, and if it had not done so it could not rely on that wrongdoing so as to deny the binding effect of the directive itself after the date for the implementation itself had passed.[190]

Unfortunately for the *Francovich* claimants, the direct effect doctrine was of no avail to them since the relevant directive in their case failed to meet the requirement of ascertainability. However, the ECJ took the opportunity of laying down a different rule: that the subject of a directive could claim damages for the state's failure to pass the legislation required by the directive, that failure having deprived him of rights that could have been asserted in the national court simply as part of the national legal order.

So even though the claimants in *Francovich* were themselves unsuccessful, that case established that even if the directive itself is not sufficiently precise and unconditional to give rise to an individual claim in damages, there should be a remedy for certain breaches of EC law.

---

[189] Case 148/78 *Pubblico Ministerio v Tullio Ratti* [1979[E.C.R. 1629.
[190] para.23 of the judgment.

Rights for Individuals: Environmental Directives

4–065 *Francovich* has given rise to a great deal of controversy as to what the ECJ actually meant when it said that the directive in issue must be intended to confer rights on individuals. In a number of challenges to Member States in this field[191] it has been argued that all that the ECJ meant by this first condition[192] was that the directive must be capable of giving rise to claims by individuals, and that it is not necessary to show specifically that the implementation of the directive was intended to confer on this claimant or class of claimants the right that they assert against the state, and for the absence of which they seek damages.

This argument invariably fails because the failure of the state to transpose into domestic law the right granted to individuals by the directive must (under the third of the three conditions for liability set out above) cause the loss and damage of which the subject complains. The only way the court can know whether the subject has suffered a relevant loss is by ascertaining the content of the right that should have been created in domestic law. In other words, the failure of the Member State only causes the subject loss if that failure deprives them of the right that they would wish to assert in domestic proceedings. It is that right that must be found in the terms of the directive. If it is not there, the failure of the member state to transpose that directive has not caused the subject any relevant loss. In *Poole*,[193] the appellants complained that they had suffered losses in the course of underwriting at Lloyd's because the UK government had wrongly failed to transpose Directive 73/239 and as a result the market had been inadequately regulated, thus leading to the acceptance of risks that under a proper system of regulation would not have arisen.

The Court of Appeal rejected this argument. The first condition of *Francovich*, when read in the light of the second and third condition, meant that it was necessary for the right in the directive to be the very right that had caused the particular loss in the claimant's case. If one group of persons was accorded the right to sue in the national court in order to support the objectives of a directive, it was very unlikely that a different group of persons needed to be given such a right as well.

So what does this mean for environmental claimants? In the past, the protective scope of environmental directives in Community law has been seen to extend to the public interest only, and not held to create concrete enforceable individual rights. It is certainly a necessary condition for the application of the *Francovich* doctrine that the directive should not merely

---

[191] This argument was advanced, unsuccessfully, in relation to harmonizing Directives in the banking field in Case-C22/02 *Peter Paul*; it also formed the basis for the appeal in *Poole and Others v HM Treasury* [2007] EWCA Civ 1021, again unsuccessful.

[192] Identified in para.40 of *Francovich*.

[193] See fn.131.

make provision for general welfare issues such as the protection of the environment.

However, this precondition seems to have become less of an obstacle with time.[194] It has been noted in discussions on environmental protection under EC law[195] that in a number of infringement actions the ECJ has found individual rights in directives relating to air and water quality, at least where human health is concerned.[196] In the first of these cases[197] the Commission sought a ruling in relation to the proper implementation of the Air Quality Directive[198]. The ECJ held that mandatory rules were necessary to require administrative authorities to ensure that the concentration of sulphur in the air does not exceed certain limit values. Putting values into legislation was not sufficient. The general conclusion was that, by setting environmental quality standards the directives aimed at protecting, inter alia, human health, and so created rights and obligations for individuals.[199] This should be contrasted with the restrictive domestic approach to claims for breach of statutory duty which was noted above.[200]

4–066

But these ECJ cases were infringement proceedings. The ECJ—and national courts, following its lead—seem to take a different approach to the existence of individual rights in directives in state liability proceedings under the direct effect doctrine or in *Francovich* actions. The cases of *BCCI*[201] and *Peter Paul*[202] make this amply clear. In *BCCI* the House of Lords said that the directive in question was only intended as a measure to harmonize the regulation of banking, and did not confer a right of damages for depositors who suffered loss by reason of the failure of the supervisory bodies. There was, in other words, no provision in that directive which entailed the granting of rights to individuals. In *Peter Paul*, banking clients sought compensation for infringements of supervisory obligations of banking regulators based on *Francovich* liability. The ECJ rejected their claim, despite the fact that the interests of the depositors were mentioned in the recitals of the directives concerned.

In the light of this, commentators have suggested that "rights" as referred to in infringement proceedings may not be sufficient for *Francovich* liability. Prechal suggests for example that the ECJ's case law in infringement proceedings should not be interpreted as meaning that the directives give rise to concrete individual (environmental) rights. Indeed she regards

---

[194] See Plender J.'s discussion of the German concept of Schutzgesetz in this context in *Cooper v Attorney General* [2008] EWHC 2178 (Q.B.) para.55(i).
[195] See Wennerås, *The Enforcement of EC Environmental Law* (OUP, 2007) and Prechal, *Directives in EC Law*, 2nd Edition (OUP, 2005).
[196] C-361/88; C-58/89; C-59/89; C-298/95.
[197] C-361/88, *Commission v Germany* [1991] E.C.R. I-2597.
[198] Directive 80/779 [1980] OJ L29/30.
[199] See esp C-131/88 *Commission v Germany* [1991] ECJ I-825.
[200] See para.4–055.
[201] [2000] 3 CMLR 2005.
[202] C-222/02 [2004] E.C.R. I-9425.

the transplant of a "right", labelled as such in infringement proceedings, to the area of state liability as nothing less than a "perilous undertaking". Such an approach would in her view wrongly conflate the question whether a directive confers on a consumer a direct and enforceable right to receive a particular benefit on the one hand, and the question, on the other, whether a Member State has appropriately implemented a directive by providing sufficient legal remedies.[203]

4–067   Another commentator has pointed out that the scope for actions under environmental directives may be reduced by the increased reliance in that context on framework directives, driven by the trend towards subsidiarity and flexibility. Wennerås cites as an example this "paradigm shift" in the adoption of the IPPC Directive.[204] The notion of best available techniques (or BAT) for prescribing emissions standards militates against the characterisation of the directive as sufficiently "unconditional"—because further action is required to make the obligations intelligible—and thus makes compliance with EC environmental law increasingly difficult to monitor and "undermines effective enforcement".[205]

But the proceedings taken to enforce various environmental directives have been helpful in establishing the idea that individual rights are in the frame; take for example the ECJ's encouraging assertion in the enforcement of the Groundwater Directive against Germany that: "The purpose of these provisions of this directive is thus to create rights and obligations for individuals".[206] And in a series of judicial review cases concerning the Environmental Impact Directive,[207] the ECJ held that individuals could rely on its provisions before national courts.[208] In these reference proceedings the ECJ considerably narrowed down the discretion of Member States to decide whether or not a project would have a sufficiently significant impact to warrant an environmental impact assessment (EIA). The Court ruled that for any project that is likely to have a significant impact on the environment, an EIA is necessary, and whilst this is a procedural right only, it considerably enhances the ability of individuals to object to or at least delay the commencement of a project or development. It is also worth noting that even though the EIA Directive contains a reference in its preamble to public health, in the jurisprudence the public health dimension was not in issue; individuals could simply rely on the provisions of the directive because of the doctrine of *effet utile*.

---

[203] Prechal, op.cit., p.110, referring in particular to AG Mischo in Case C-340-96, *Commission v UK*.

[204] Directive 96/61 EC.

[205] Pål Wennerås, *The Enforcement of EC Environmental Law* (OUP, 2007) p. 44.

[206] para.7.

[207] Directive 85/337/EEC, see Chapter 9.

[208] C-72/95 Kraaijeveld [1996] E.C.R. I-5403,; Case C-201/02 Wells [2004] E.C.R. I-723;and C-127/02 Waddenzee [2004] ECR-I 7405. In this last case the ECJ ruled that provisions pertaining to pure environmental protection under Directive 92/43/EC are also capable of producing direct effect from which individuals can derive rights.

It may be that closer attention should be paid to the German system of conceptualising these "rights" as "interests" in a way that is more transparent and principled than the notion of rights as legal claims in common law jurisdictions. As Prechal says, the distinction (in German law) between general and individual interest is not black and white but a matter of degree. The general interest is protected by legal rules; these benefit the community or large groups of people. But whether, over and above that, the legal rule in question protects the special interest which some individuals might have is a problem of interpretation of the provision at issue.[209] See the interesting application of this German notion of Schutzgesetz in a recent EIA case, *Cooper v Attorney General*.[210]

Assuming that the ECJ will continue to assert itself and the need to ensure the effectiveness of Community law as the primary basis for direct effect, it may be that the case law under the *Francovich* "grant of rights for individuals" regime will develop in the direction of environmental protection even though the relevant directives, on their face, aim at benefits for the public as a whole.

It may therefore be instructive at this stage to look again at *Bowden*,[211] as a demonstration of how a *Francovich* claim may become interlinked with a number of claims at common law for damage for environmental harm. **4–068**

It will be remembered from the discussion of *Bowden* earlier in this chapter that a number of claims were considered as preliminary points, under private and public nuisance, negligence, as well as a *Francovich* claim for state liability under three EC Directives. The Court of Appeal accepted that state liability was arguable in the light of the Commission infringement proceedings under the Groundwater Directive infringement Case C-131/88. However the claimant was only able to make out a case on one of the directives. The Court of Appeal concluded that he could rely on the Directive on Shellfish Waters for the purposes of a state liability claim under *Francovich*, because this directive was for the direct benefit of a limited class of shellfishermen. The Court drew a distinction between this limited directive and the public welfare aims of the Urban Waste Water Treatment Directive and the Bathing Water Directive, but it is significant that the reasoning behind their decision to uphold the Shellfish Waters argument was underpinned by the need for *effet utile*. Beldam L.J. acknowledged the significant part played "in securing compliance with, and enforcement of, European directives by the granting of rights to individuals".

For this reason even the somewhat restricted success of the *Francovich* action in *Bowden* may be cause for optimism for similar environmental claims.[212]

---

[209] Prechal, op cit p.119.
[210] [2008] EWHC 2178 (Q.B.), para.51.
[211] *Bowden v South West Water and Another* [1999] 3 CMLR, discussed earlier at para.4–042.
[212] The matter never came to a full trial; the decision was on a preliminary point only.

Environmental Impact Assessment Directive: Enforcement by Individuals

4-069   In a way the "granting of rights" requirement may be seen not so much as imposing a severe restriction on state liability, but a necessary vehicle for *effet utile*, and as such should be generously interpreted. As noted above, the ECJ in *Kraaijeveld*[213] concluded that individuals could rely on the EIA Directive in spite of the fact that none of its provisions specifically protected the claimants' interest in the context of this particular case. In this case the claimants contested a zoning plan adopted by the local council according to which the waterway to which they had access would no longer be linked to navigable waterways. It was argued that the removal of access to navigable waterways would be ruinous to Kraaijeveld's business, whose economic activity was related to waterways. The ECJ held that an assessment should have been carried out under the directive even though it did not specifically protect the claimant's rights or interests of access to the waterway.

Although, on the face of it, *Kraaijeveld* was simply a review on the legality of the government's action under Community law, not a case asserting direct effect of an environmental directive[214] the trend has continued. In *Wells*[215], the claimant relied on the EIA Directive (a piece of legislation which cannot be interpreted as conferring rights on individuals in the traditional sense) in her complaint that an EIA had not been undertaken of mining operations by the quarry operators concerned. She contended that the authorities had failed to comply with their obligations under the directive to carry out an assessment and therefore she sought revocation or modification of the planning permission. On a reference to the ECJ that Court ruled that the state was required to nullify the consequences of a breach of Community law and to make good any harm caused to individuals by the failure to carry out an environmental impact assessment.

Again, there was some surprise at this judgment since the obligation concerned was essentially procedural and therefore did not have the necessary precision or content to give rise to individual rights. And it is true that the ECJ was at pains to stress that the principle of legal certainty prevented this—or any other directive—from creating *obligations* for individuals.[216] But by asserting the right of individuals to rely on a directive such as the one in question, the ECJ has opened the way for environmental interest groups to rely on the provisions of a directive even if the provisions do not specifically endow them with standing—if for example some pro-

---

[213] C-72/95 [1996] E.C.R. I-5403.
[214] See Prechal, op.cit. pp.235–237.
[215] Case C-201/02 *Wells v Secretary of State for Transport, Local Government and the Regions* [2004] E.C.R. I-723.
[216] See para.56.

cedural obligation has not been observed, resulting in a project or development with a significant adverse impact on the surrounding area.

Horizontality: "Forbidden Territory"

This in turn brings with it the probable, if not inevitable, result of negative 4–070
consequences for third parties, such as withdrawal of a permit given to an undertaking in accordance with national rules but in violation of the rules laid down in the directive at issue. This is problematic, since it is a fundamental tenet of Community law that no obligations between private parties should arise from the doctrine of direct effect of directives— otherwise known as "horizontality". Nevertheless "mere adverse repercussions on the rights of third parties"[217] may well ensue, and these should not prevent an individual from invoking the provisions of a directive against the Member State concerned.

As we have said, private parties may not bring suits for breach of directives against other private parties. Most claims alleging breach of EU law will be taken against public authorities as straightforward public authorities or "emanations of the state" in the *Foster* sense.[218] In the field of environmental litigation most potential defendants will meet these criteria—former public utilities, for example, which, though now privatised, are still responsible for vast areas of economic activity, such as energy and water supply, and sewerage. New forms of energy supply however will not necessarily come from bodies exercising quasi public functions.[219]

The effect of the cases on the EIA Directive is to create a possible avenue of horizontal action in environmental protection: failure to notify the authorities, for example, of reasons for exemption from an EIA for a particular developer may be invoked by private parties in proceedings against the public authority that allowed the developer to go ahead—perhaps resulting in proceedings against the developer. This is what is called "exclusionary horizontal direct effect", and along with the principle laid down in *Marleasing*,[220] that national courts must interpret national law "as far as possible" in the light of the wording and the purpose of EC Directives, these may open the field for individual claimants and even NGOs to

---

[217] ECJ in *Wells*, para.56.
[218] C-188/89 [1990] I-3313. To be an emanation of the state, a body;
  1) must fulfil a public service,
  2) must have been made responsible for that service pursuant to a measure adopted by the state,
  3) must be under the control of the state, and
  4) it must have special powers beyond those which result from the normal rules applicable in relations between individuals.
[219] See the discussion on public authorities in relation to the Human Rights Act in Chapter 1.
[220] C-106/89 [1990] E.C.R. I-1799, para.8.

rely on EC environmental protection law in actions against public authorities, whose outcome affects the rights of private parties.[221]

A good example of this is the case of *Huddleston*,[222] concerning, as in *Wells*, the granting of planning permission to quarry works without an EIA under the directive. This case raised the question whether a court can do anything about a deeming provision in the statutory planning regime which, in clear breach of a directive which the United Kingdom was required to implement, enabled a company to revive a mining permission by registering it with the local mineral planning authority without providing an environmental impact assessment. It was therefore an interesting example of direct effect in action because it was the claimant's case that whilst the public authority, Durham County Council, had its hands tied by the legislation, it was nevertheless open to him as an affected individual to insist that the state (of which Durham County Council is a part) should not be able to rely upon its own admitted wrong in failing properly to implement the directive to ignore its duty to enforce proper assessments by developers. And it followed from this argument that the court, either by reading the deeming provision down so that it complied with the directive, or by simply disapplying it, should give effect to the United Kingdom's community obligations. The respondent mining company, Sherburn Stone Company Ltd, contended that this constituted the forbidden act of giving direct effect to an unimplemented directive as between individuals—here Mr Huddleston (the claimant) and Sherburn (the third party "beneficiary" of the state's failure to have properly implemented the directive). In particular, to give it direct effect would be to expose Sherburn both to the uncovenanted obligation to carry out an EIA and to criminal sanctions if they did not.

4–071   The dilemma boiled down to this: because the state may not lawfully take advantage of its own failure to implement a directive, state bodies are to be treated in domestic law as if an unimplemented directive had been implemented. On the other hand, because Community directives are addressed to states, they cannot by themselves alter the legal relations between individuals. It is sometimes inevitable, however, that treating the state as having implemented a directive will operate directly to the benefit of one individual and the detriment of another.

Sedley L.J. in *Huddleston* sought to square this circle by articulating the problem thus: there was a "fundamental difference" between imposing legal obligations on an individual which limit his freedom of action vis-à-vis other individuals, and placing conditions upon that individual's entitlement to secure a benefit from the state. The latter, which is what the

---

[221] Another example is *Wildlife Fund v Autonome Provinz Bozen*, Case C435/97 (decided September 16, 1999) where it held that an individual could call the state to account for the non-implementation of the EIA directive, an intervention which directly and adversely affected the developer.

[222] [1999] EWHC Admin 757.

mining company were facing, came into the category of permitted trans-position from community to domestic law as surely as the former did not.

The respondents raised another objection to Mr Huddleston's case, which was that the County Council, as an emanation of the state, could not hide behind an individual applicant in order to take advantage of direct effect. But the solution to this problem was quite clear, in Sedley LJ's view, and lay at the heart of the rationale for direct effect:

"the failure of the state to transpose a Directive inevitably renders the state itself impotent to implement it; but for an individual with a recognised interest in proper implementation, it is precisely the state's failure which disables it from taking refuge in its own wrongdoing; and it is this which in turn entitles the citizen ... to assert rights conferred by the Directive either as a sword or as a shield against the state, though not directly against another individual."

It is quite a different matter if the effect of interpreting national law in accordance with a non-implemented directive is to impose criminal liability for an act which does not otherwise offend against national law. The principle of legal certainty forbids this: see *Kolpinghuis*[223] and, in the environmental context, *Arcaro*.[224]

Remedies

In most cases redress for breach of EU law in the environmental context is   4–072 an indirect and distant affair. An individual with a successful claim in tort or breach of statutory duty has in his sights a particular result, whether it be monetary compensation, an injunction or an order for specific perfor-mance. A claimant for judicial review on the other hand does not have such a certain outcome as a reward for his efforts. Mr Huddleston at least was awarded a favourable judgment and his costs. But the consequences of such a ruling are uncertain since the only outcome is an order that the relevant council should carry out an environmental impact assessment, which may in the end be favourable to the developer. The party taking a claim for redress for environmental harm under a rule of EC law has to rely on judicial review of the legality of the act giving rise to the alleged harm; essentially they will be challenging individual licences or planning per-missions, or failure to make such decisions. And where the directive is open-ended and generous in allocation of discretion to national authorities, the prospects for success of such an action are limited. It is generally not possible to obtain an injunction or specific performance in respect of a

---

[223] *Officier van Justitie v Kolpinghuis Nijmegen BV* [1989] CMLR 18.
[224] [1997] 1 CMLR 179.

provision which is not binding on the member state, or which confers policy discretion with which the judiciary may not meddle.

Of course where environmental directives are addressed substantively to individuals, and have been implemented in national law, private claimants may seek redress against other private parties. And it will be remembered from paragraph 4–062 above that Treaty Articles and Regulations are directly applicable in national law, provided they are sufficiently precise and unconditional. This means that they have horizontal effect, in other words claimants may seek compensation from private parties for harm suffered.[225]

Remedies for infringements of EC law are left to national courts, but any remedy granted must be no less favourable than those that apply to litigants with claims under national law.[226] The test is for equivalence, not identity, and the national court must consider "the purpose and the essential characteristics of allegedly similar domestic actions".[227]

4–073 Remedies must be "effective", which means that conditions should not be framed in such a way as to render virtually impossible the exercise of rights conferred by Community law.[228] The principle of effective judicial protection[229] means that in a Community based on the rule of law everybody must have the opportunity to assert, on his own initiative, his rights before the courts. This entails a number of obligations on member states.

Standing

4–074 The national rules on standing are a case in point, particularly with environmental directives where it may be difficult to establish which persons are protected and should accordingly be able to bring an action or challenge a decision, since these directives aim at protecting the environment as such, rather than being concerned with securing advantages to individual members of given classes separately. Unfortunately there is not yet a body of case law that clarifies the position in relation to environmental pressure groups; in theory at least it should be possible that group actions intended to uphold environmental protection measures set out in directives should be enforced against any local rule restricting locus standi; this was after all the line of reasoning in a case concerning unfair terms detrimental to consumers' interests.[230]

The UK has relatively liberal standing requirements in relation to

---

[225] Case-C-453/99 *Courage* [2001] ECR-I6297 and Joined Cases C-295 to 298/04 *Manfredi* [2006] ECR-I-6619.
[226] *Rewe-Zentralfinanz*, C-33/76 [1976] E.C.R. 1989; Comet, C-45/76 [1976] E.C.R. 2043.
[227] Case C-326/96, *Levez*, [1999] IRLR 36 at para.43.
[228] C-261/95 *Palmisani* (1997) E.C.R. I—4025.
[229] Case 45/76 *Comet* [1976] E.C.R. 2043 and *Rewe*, Case 33/76 [1976] E.C.R. 1989, reinforced by *Johnston* C-222/84 [1986] E.C.R. 1651.
[230] Joined Cases C-240 to 244/98 *Oceano* [2000] E.C.R. I-4941.

NGOs, and therefore the principle of equivalence would suggest that where the underlying basis for a challenge to an act or failure to act is a rule of EC law, then locus standi should be granted to the litigants.[231] Furthermore, the ECJ has held that it is necessary under the judicial protection doctrine that individuals and environmental groups are able to assert their interests in nature conservation before national courts.[232] In *Huddleston* the issue of compliance with the EIA Directive would not have arisen at all had not Mr Huddleston, a retired quarry engineer who lived nearby, not stepped into the breach and commenced judicial review proceedings, joining cause with Durham Council. He claimed that he had a right to the valuable benefits accorded to him by the 1985 Directive, which were denied to him when Durham was deemed to have granted "development consent" to Sherburn without first according him his right to take an informed part in the consultation process.

Courts

The doctrine of supremacy of EC law creates certain obligations for the national courts themselves. Article 10 EC obliges national courts to raise issues pertaining to Community law of their own motion in so far as they have such powers under domestic law. This is because in so far as community law, including directives, forms part of the legal norms valid within the member state, the courts must apply it accordingly and where necessary of their own motion. In *Kraaijeveld* the ECJ suggested that whilst EC law does not confer a general power on national courts to consider points of EC law of their own motion, if they have a discretion or duty to raise points of national law of their own motion then they must apply such discretion or obligation to points of Community law.[233] An example from domestic law is the case of *Berkeley*,[234] where the House of Lords used its discretion to prioritise EC law over the principle of legal certainty. Here planning permission that had been granted for the construction of a football stadium without an EIA under Directive 85/337/EEC was quashed, since their Lordships viewed it as the duty of the court under Article 10 EC to ensure fulfilment of the UK's obligations under the Treaty. Moreover, as emanations of the state, courts have a direct responsibility to perform obligations of the state under community law.

4–075

---

[231] The question of locus standi in judicial review proceedings is discussed in detail in Chapter 6.

[232] Case C-374/98 *Commission v France* [2000] E.C.R. I-10799, para.54.

[233] Case 72/95 [1996] E.C.R. I-5403, para.60.

[234] *Berkeley v Secretary of State for the Environment* [2001] 13 JEL 89.

Limitation

4–076 Time limits are also a component of the right of access to court. Again, these are left to the discretion of the member state, but they must not be less favourable for claimants taking EC points than other litigants. Of course in the environmental context time limits may severely compromise claimants' chances of success since the damage may only manifest itself some time after the technical requirements of a particular directive have been breached. As Wennerås has pointed out: "although environmental pollution or damage may often be easily detected, it can be very difficult and time-consuming to gather data showing the exact extent of damage, the operator responsible, and a causal link."[235]

Some guidance may be found in the ECJ ruling in the field of competition law, in which it was held that a national rule under which the limitation period begins to run from the day on which an anti-competitive agreement or concerted practice was adopted could make it practically impossible to exercise the right to seek compensation for the harm caused, particularly if the limitation period is a short one and not capable of being suspended.[236] But the ECJ generally allows considerable latitude in the determination of limitation periods, given the considerable diversity or practice in different Member States. The limitation period of six years for nuisance for example[237] would not probably not offend the principle of effective judicial protection if the action were to involve a breach of EU law.

Judicial review remedies

4–077 The minimum remedy required by Community law is the setting aside of incompatible national measures. Having done that it is up to the national legal system to decide what order—unlawfulness, compensation etc—to grant. Community law stops at the point of setting aside, then national law takes over—e.g. in the withdrawal of an environmental permit, etc.

In order to qualify for redress in judicial review proceedings the claim must meet the requirement for a *Francovich* action—the second *Francovich* condition—that the breach should be "sufficiently serious". The court must be satisfied that the respondent state "has manifestly and gravely disregarded the limits on its discretion".[238] So the degree of discretion left to the Member State is an important consideration; the more discretion, the less likely that the individual will be able to prove damage. As noted

---

[235] op.cit. p.98.
[236] C-295-298/04 *Manfredi v Loyd Adriatico Assicurazion SpA* [2006] E.C.R. I-6619.
[237] See para.4–039 above.
[238] Applying the words used by the ECJ in *Brasserie du Pêcheur* [1999] Q.B. 404, 499F.

before in this section, directives framed to protect the environment tend to be open ended and generous in their margin of discretion.

The "successful" environmental cases considered above[239] were all essentially judicial review proceedings concerning the UK's EIA obligations. Since most proceedings challenging administrative action or legislation in breach of EC law takes place in the administrative courts, remedies are limited,[240] as the basic rule in English public law is that there is no automatic claim for damages for unlawful action. There is no general right to recover damages for loss caused by ultra vires acts of public authorities. Some recognised tort claim is necessary—in this context, it would have to be a claim that satisfied the stringent conditions of *Francovich* together with *Factortame* (i.e. sufficiently serious breach, of a provision of Community law which was intended to confer rights on individuals and such an individual has suffered loss).

A finding of illegality in the UK courts does not, in cases not falling   4–078 within *Francovich* or within a recognised common law tort, result in the award of any specific remedy, let alone a right to monetary compensation, but it may be the case, particularly in environmental litigation, that other forms of remedy are of more interest to the claimant than money—such as the suspension or revocation of a permit in the environmental impact assessment cases.

The question central to this chapter is what remedies in private law are available and most useful to claimants in environmental litigation. It is clear that where the *Francovich* conditions are met and causation is established, national courts are under an obligation to provide remedies for actions in breach of EC law. There is the concomitant duty to redress failure to act, particularly if that failure involves the non-implementation of a directive giving rights to individuals. Cases on injunctions are governed by *Factortame*. In that particular case the restriction on the power of courts to grant interim relief was imposed by national law. The ECJ removed that restriction in order to remedy a breach of Community law.[241] Following *Factortame*, it is now established that where a restriction on their remedial powers exists, national courts should depart, by disapplication, from the relevant rules—even though there is no explicit Community law provision serving as the basis of the power for doing this.

On occasion this may conflict with the principle of legal certainty. The doctrine of supremacy of EC law means that national law which conflicts with it must be set aside.[242] However, in 1998[243] the ECJ held that this principle of supremacy did not require that national measures adopted in

[239] See discussion on *Huddleston*, and fn.148 above.
[240] Subject to section 31(4) of the Supreme Court Act 1981, which provides that limitation periods should be extended if it is equitable to do so.
[241] See Prechal, op.cit., p.170.
[242] Case 6/64 Costa-Enel [1964] E.C.R. 585.
[243] Joined Cases C-10 to 22–97 INCOGE [1998] E.C.R. I-6307.

breach of Community law should be presumed to be non-existent, with the relevant Community provision consequently endowed with retroactive effect. So where contracts are entered into under national law which is subsequently found to be in breach, they are not automatically rendered invalid.

4–079   The fact of the matter is that the availability of remedies is inextricably tied up with the question of whether there are rights in the first place—in English law, in any case—which brings us back to the convoluted debate around the requirement for "individual rights". Common law practitioners have had relatively little difficulty in absorbing the concept of these "rights" under EC law because our focus is on remedies—the cause of action, or a particular set of facts, gives rise to a remedy, which we call a right with no further ado. It amounts to no more than saying, in the EC law sense, that you have a right not to be subjected to an ultra vires act.[244]

It may be that, in time, the debate over whether state liability for environmental harm may be established via a *Francovich* action will become largely academic, because the adoption of Directive 2004/35/EC on the Prevention and Remedying of Environmental Damage[245] has essentially broadened the obligation on national authorities to ensure that preventative and remedial measures are taken by operators that have infringed those of the environmental directives that are listed in the annex to the directive. This is not the place to discuss the Environmental Liability Directive (the subject of Chapter 5), but it is useful to note it as part of the background scheme, particularly since Articles 12 and 13 of the Directive confers rights on individuals and NGOs to request authorities to take action against offending operators.

Quantum

4–080   As mentioned above damage for environmental loss is calculated on diminution of value or cost of reinstatement. In *Wells*, the ECJ ruled that national authorities were required to "make good any harm caused by the failure to carry out an environmental impact assessment, and in *Factortame* the Court made the more general stipulation that reparation must be "commensurate with the loss or damage sustained".[246] In any event monetary compensation will not be the most appropriate form of relief in most environmental actions, and where it is, *Francovich* provides the avenue whereby it might be obtained. The availability of exemplary damages is

---

[244] See Prechal, op.cit., p.104.
[245] The "Environmental Liability Directive", [2004] OJ L143/56, discussed fully in Chapter 5.
[246] Joined Cases C-46 and 48/93 *Brasserie du Pêcheur and ex parte Factortame* [1996] E.C.R. I-1029, para.82.

debatable, to say the least. Although the ECJ held in *Factortame* that the principle of equivalence meant that:

"an award of exemplary damages pursuant to a claim or an action founded on Community law cannot be ruled out if such damages could be awarded pursuant to a similar claim or action founded on domestic law",

the trend in the UK at least is firmly against the characterisation of compensation as punitive[247] except in extremely restricted circumstances.[248]

HUMAN RIGHTS

The following section deals with the impact on domestic environmental   4–081
law of the Human Rights Act (HRA) and the European Convention on Human Rights 1950 as incorporated by Schedule 1 of the Act which came into force in October 2000. The main analysis of the Act and the Convention, and its modus operandi in domestic law, is discussed in full in Chapter 1. The focus in this chapter is on the development of certain Convention provisions as tools for environmental protection.

"Environmental" Rights in the Convention

Those Convention rights which have been enlisted in environmental dis-   4–082
putes—to greater or lesser effect—are set out on pages 84 to 89. The rights to private life (Article 8) and to property (Protocol 1, Article 1) are clear candidates for development of claimable positive obligations on the part of signatory states to the Convention in the context of environmental harm. In more extreme cases, the right to life under Article 2 has been invoked, and the right to due process and its various components under Article 6 is also relevant in this context. The right of freedom to receive information under Article 10 is of obvious importance to environmental NGOs and pressure groups.

The "reading down" obligations on the courts under section 3 of the HRA[249] may prove to be a useful environmental tool, so that for example a private law right clashing with a public law authorisation like planning permission or an environmental licence means that the courts must, so far as they are able, read and give effect to this legislation so as to make it compatible with the Convention. This means, for example, that where a

---

[247] *Watkins v Home Office and Others* [2006] UKHL 17.
[248] See the discussion on exemplary damages in para.4–080 above.
[249] See Chapter 1, para.1–081.

statutory authority is likely to defeat a common law nuisance claim, and that claim is backed up by the invocation of Article 8 (breach of private and home life), that statutory authority should be relaxed.

Before considering the individual provisions and their past and future utility in environmental actions, it is worth mentioning two general caveats with respect to the Convention as a vehicle for environmental enforcement. Whilst acknowledging that environmental rights may be implied by the Convention[250] the European Court of Human Rights (ECtHR) has set the bar high for complaints about environmental harm by allowing a very wide margin for signatory states to set economic and other interests against the claims of individuals to a safe and healthy environment. Secondly, by virtue of section 7(3) of the HRA and Article 34 of the Convention, claims can only be brought by a person who is, or would be, a victim of a violation of the Convention; in other words even though an environmental pressure group may have standing to take judicial review proceedings, this "victim" test for human rights claims effectively prevents them from bringing a Convention claim which might allow for the development of any general ecological protection.[251] There is as yet no legal right under the Convention or the HRA to sue for damage to a natural habitat.

Strasbourg Case Law

4-083   Before considering the impact of the Convention on domestic case law via the HRA, it is worth looking at some of the environmental challenges brought before the ECtHR in terms of the choice of Convention rights invoked.[252]

Article 8[253] is one of the most open-ended and rapidly developing provisions in the Convention; more implied rights have been found to exist within its protective scope than any other of the Convention provisions. For this reason Article 8 has proved the most successful basis for environmental actions. Most of the cases considered below have therefore been based on this provision.

---

[250] See para.96 of the Grand Chamber judgment in *Hatton v United Kingdom*, discussed below at para.4–088.

[251] See Chapter 1 para.1–085 for the discussion on standing.

[252] Article 41 of the Convention and the formulation of remedies by the ECtHR are discussed in detail in Chapter 1.

[253] Set out in full on pp.86, 87.

Pollution

In *Lopez Ostra v Spain*[254] the applicant complained under Article 8 that the noise, smell and fumes emanating from a nearby waste treatment facility breached her right to respect for private and family life. The Court upheld her claim. As always, in Article 8 cases, it had to consider the justification advanced by the respondent state under Article 8(2), that certain measures are necessary for its economic well being—in this case, the waste treatment facility was needed to reduce the pollution emanating from a concentration of tanneries in the area. But the Court did not accept that the Spanish government had struck the correct balance between the town having a waste treatment facility and the applicant and her family's individual rights under Article 8. It was probably significant that the applicant's daughter's health had appreciably deteriorated and there was proven depreciation to the value of her home.

4–084

In *Guerra v Italy*[255] the ECtHR heard a complaint under Article 8 concerning emissions from a chemical factory. The Court noted that the applicants had not been physically injured by the fumes but considered it significant that in 1976 an explosion had occurred at the plant, leading to the release of several tonnes of toxic pollutants and resulting in the hospitalisation of large numbers of neighbouring residents. The Court concluded that the Italian authorities had failed in their duty to warn the applicants of this danger, thereby breaching their right to respect for family and home life by depriving them of the opportunity to take appropriate action. It is an interesting feature of this case that although the Court based its judgment solely on Article 8, the applicants had chosen also to invoke the separate provision protecting the right to life under Article 2(1). Judge Jambrek highlighted this in a concurring opinion, saying that information withheld about circumstances which present a real risk of danger to health and physical integrity could form grounds for a complaint under Article 2.

In *Taskin and Others v Turkey*[256] the applicants complained about a decision taken by the authorities to grant a permit to operate a goldmine in the vicinity of their town. The permit authorised use of the cyanide leaching process for gold extraction. The applicants applied successfully to get this permit annulled by the Supreme Court, but such was the inertia of the ministers concerned, no measures were taken to prevent the continued operation of the cyanidation process, despite evidence of the dangers involved and the risks of pollution of the underlying aquifers and destruction of the local ecosystem. Before the ECtHR the applicants alleged that both the granting of the permit and the related decision-making process had infringed their rights under Articles 2 and 8 of the

---

[254] (1995) 20 EHRR 277.
[255] (1998) 26 EHRR 357.
[256] Application no. 46117/99, November 10, 2004.

Convention. The ECtHR upheld this complaint. In view of the fact that the local Supreme Administrative Court had annulled the authorities' decision to issue the permit on environmental grounds, it found that the state had exceeded the margin of discretion generally allowed to the national authorities in this area.

4–085 Unsurprisingly there are a number of cases from the former Soviet Union involving hazardous pollution from industrial works. In *Fedayeva v Russia*[257] the applicant lived 450 metres from a huge steelworks which emitted various polluting substances in excess of "safe levels" identified by domestic legislation. It was also very noisy. Attempts by the applicant to seek re-housing failed. Before the ECtHR she brought proceedings under Article 8 seeking damages and an order that the state offer her new housing outside the zone. The Court upheld the claim in respect of damages. It accepted that the applicant was inevitably made more vulnerable to disease as a result of the emissions. The quality of life at her home was adversely affected.[258] The state was therefore in breach of its positive obligations in that it authorised the operation of the plant in the middle of a densely populated town. Despite the wide margin of appreciation in matters of environmental policy, the state had failed to strike a fair balance between public and private interest.

This was followed by *Ledyayeva*[259]: in all respects this was identical to *Fedayeva*, except here there were a number of applicants. The Court noted that the Government had not put forward any new fact or argument capable of persuading it to reach a conclusion different from that of the *Fedayeva* case, and that the failure of the authorities to take appropriate measures in order to protect the applicants' right to respect for their homes and private lives against serious environmental nuisances could not be justified by any economic interest in the steelworks. In particular, the authorities had neither resettled the applicants outside the dangerous zone, nor had they provided compensation for those seeking the resettlement. Furthermore, it appeared that the authorities had failed to develop and implement an efficient public policy which would induce the steel-plant to reduce its emissions to the safe levels within a reasonable time. The Court accordingly found a violation of Article 8 of the Convention and granted modest amounts of non-pecuniary damages to the applicants.

In *Giacomelli v Italy*[260] the applicant lived within thirty metres of a processing plant that had been built and designed for the storage and treatment of hazardous and non-hazardous waste. Following three EIAs

---

[257] (2005) 41 EHRR 376.

[258] There was another issue concerning attributability to the state, as the steelworks was at the time of the application in private hands. The Court noted that the state had originally built the steelworks, which malfunctioned from the start. Post-privatisation, it continued to exercise control via the imposition of operating conditions and supervision of the works.

[259] (Applications nos. 53157/99, 53247/99, 53695/00 and 56850/00) First Section, October 26, 2006.

[260] (Application No. 59909/00) November 2, 2006.

carried out in 2000, it was found that there was a risk that the toxic chemical residue generated by the detoxification operations at the plant might
contaminate the ground water, a source of drinking water for the inhabitants of the neighbouring villages. However the relevant state department
eventually concluded that since the company processed 27 per cent of the
waste generated in northern Italy and 23 per cent nationwide, it was in
favour of the continued operation of the plant. Detoxification continued
despite subsequent findings by the regional health authority that there were
abnormal concentrations of carbon and other organic substances in the
atmosphere. The applicant complained under Article 8 that the persistent
noise and harmful emissions from the plant entailed severe disturbance to
her environment and a permanent risk to her health and home. The Court
held that there had been a violation of Article 8.

In particular, it observed that this provision may apply in environmental
cases whether the pollution is directly caused by the State or whether State
responsibility arises from the failure to regulate private-sector activities
properly. It does not matter, in other words, whether the case is analysed in
terms of a positive duty on the State to take reasonable and appropriate
measures to secure the applicants' rights under paragraph 1 of Article 8 or
in terms of an interference by a public authority to be justified in accordance with paragraph 2. The principle remains the same; a fair balance has
to be struck between the competing interests of the individual and of the
community as a whole.

Öneryildiz v Turkey[261] is one of those rare cases where a challenge has   **4–086**
succeeded under Article 2. Here the applicants were residents of slum
dwellings on the outskirts of Istanbul that abutted a huge rubbish tip. The
authorities were responsible for this site and there was evidence that local
regulations regarding ventilation had not been complied with. The
resulting build-up of methane and other gases caused an explosion, which
in turn provoked a landslide which engulfed part of the shanty-town,
resulting in widespread damage and loss of life. In its conclusion that
Article 2 had been breached, the Court declared that the obligation under
Article 2, to take appropriate steps to safeguard lives within the state's
jurisdiction, must be construed as applying in the context of any activity,
whether public or not, in which the right to life may be at stake.

Noise

So much for the protection provided by the Convention to victims of   **4–087**
hazardous substances, airborne or otherwise. Less promising for claimants

---

[261] (2005) 41 EHRR 325.

seeking to rely on the Convention for environmental protection are the air noise cases, *Powell and Rayner v UK*[262] and *Hatton v UK*.[263]

Most of these claimants invoked Article 8. But in *S v France*[264] an early noise case (albeit only an admissibility decision by the European Commission of Human Rights (EComHR), whose preliminary rulings on admissibility determined whether a case was worth adjudicating in the main Court[265]) the claim was articulated as a complaint under Article 1 Protocol 1 as well as Article 8. The claimant invoked the right to peaceful enjoyment of possessions in respect of the effect of noise from a neighbouring nuclear power station on the market value of his property. In this case it was not in dispute that the Laurent des Eaux EDF nuclear power station had been lawfully built and brought into service and the Commission (then part of the European Court of Human Rights) had no doubt that it served the interests of the economic well-being of the country. But the correct balance had to be struck and the person concerned should not have to bear an "unreasonable burden." Although this particular case was rejected on the grounds that the applicant had already obtained compensation from the French courts, it was signficant that the Commission accepted that noise nuisance which is "particularly severe in both intensity and frequency" may seriously affect the value of real property or even render it unsaleable or unusable and thus amount to a partial expropriation.[266] As for the complaint under Article 8, the Commission came up with the now fairly stock response that

> "Considerable noise and other types of nuisance can undoubtedly affect the physical well-being of a person and thus interfere with his private life. They may also deprive a person of the possibility of enjoying the amenities of his home."

In *Powell v Rayner* the applicants complained of breaches of the right to due process under Article 6(1), failure to respect private and home life under Article 8 and breach of the right to a judicial remedy under 13, because of their inability to persuade the national courts to abate the noise nuisance they suffered from the flight paths from Heathrow Airport. All claims were dismissed. The Court agreed that Article 8 was engaged, but found that a fair balance had been struck by the respondent government between the competing interests of the individual and the economic interests of the community as a whole, served by an international hub airport. The other claims—on due process and access to justice—were dismissed since the Article 8 argument was defeated. The Court took the view that the UK government had proceeded correctly by keeping aircraft

---

[262] (1990) 12 EHRR 395.
[263] (2003) 37 EHRR 28.
[264] Application no. 13728/88, [1990] 65 D & R 250.
[265] See Chapter 1 fn.2.
[266] See para.1 of the Commission's decision.

noise out of the courts and dealing with instead via specific regulatory measures.

In the light of this the initial Chamber judgment in *Hatton* was perhaps **4–088** surprising. The ECtHR concluded that a "mere reference to economic well-being of the country" is insufficient in the overriding of individual rights in the "particularly sensitive field of environmental protection.[267] However, the UK government pressed for a referral to the Grand Chamber. By an approximate two-thirds majority the Grand Chamber held that the UK's system of restrictions on flights to and from Heathrow Airport, which allowed a certain number of night flights, did not breach the applicants' rights under Article 8:

"Environmental protection should be taken into consideration by governments in acting within their margin of appreciation and by the Court in its review of that margin ... it would not be appropriate for the Court to adopt a special approach in this respect by reference to a special status of environmental rights".

Stated as such, *Hatton* was something of a body blow to those who were hoping that the Convention might turn out to be a useful tool for environmental regulation. Not entirely unexpectedly, there were strongly worded dissenting opinions attached to the judgement, to the effect that the majority had failed to take on board the "growing concern over environmental issues, all over Europe and the world".

Nevertheless, the majority in the Court distinguished the situation obtaining in *Hatton* from previous cases where it had accepted environmental claims; in those, it said, the violation was predicated on a failure by the national authorities to comply with some aspect of the domestic regime. Thus, in *López Ostra*, the waste-treatment plant at issue was illegal in that it operated without the necessary licence, and was eventually closed down; in *Guerra* the violation was also founded on an irregular position at the domestic level, as the applicants had been unable to obtain information that the State was under a statutory obligation to provide. *Taskin* disclosed serious procedural shortcomings amounting to failure of the rule of law. This element of domestic irregularity was, in the Court's words, "wholly absent" in the present case.[268]

But such "domestic irregularity" did not obtain in *Gomez v Spain*.[269] Here the applicant complained that the Spanish authorities were responsible for the licensing regime allowing a number of bars and discos to open in the vicinity of residential dwellings. She alleged that the resulting onslaught of sound constituted a violation of her right to respect for her home, as guaranteed by Article 8. The Court upheld her complaint. In

[267] *Hatton v UK* (Application 36022/97) October 2001.
[268] para.120.
[269] (2005) 41 EHRR 40.

view of the volume of the noise—at night and beyond permitted levels—and the fact that it continued over a number of years, the Court found that the Spanish government had not discharged its positive obligation to protect the applicant's private and home life by failing to enforce noise abatement regulations.

4–089   The apparent discrepancy between the outcome of this case and that of *Powell and Rayner* and *Hatton* may be explained by the relative insignificance of night-life to the economic well-being of a country when compared to its network of international airports. Environmental lawyers waiting to assess the long-term effects of the decision of the Grand Chamber in *Hatton v UK* upon Article 8 claims may glean some hope from *Gomez*, as with the *Fadeyeva* case. Whilst the Court reiterated that a wide margin of appreciation be allowed to states where environmental policies were in issue, this does not necessarily mean that claims under the Convention for environmental harm will necessarily be met with failure in Strasbourg. *Gomez*, *Fadeyeva*, and *Taskin* all seem to suggest that the ECtHR is perfectly willing to find violations in cases where the state has shown apathy in the presence of an obvious environmental hazard caused by private enterprise.

That said, all these decisions express themselves in rather more cautious terms than *Guerra* and the initial decision in *Hatton* did, with its trailblazing announcement that:

> "in the particularly sensitive field of environmental protection, mere reference to the economic well-being of the country is not sufficient to outweigh the rights of others".[270]

The cases following the overturning of this judgment in the Grand Chamber reflect a definite reluctance to interfere with signatory states' economic and industrial priorities.

Another air noise complaint was considered in *Ashworth and Others v the United Kingdom*.[271] Again, the applicants lived close to an aerodrome, but this time it was privately owned. However the Court accepted, and the government did not contest, that it was responsible for the regulatory regime which governed the frequency of flights and the aviation activity generally. The application was unsuccessful; the Court observed that the impact of the flying, which was confined to the daylight hours and further restricted at weekends, was "markedly less serious than that of the night flights which were the subject of the Hatton case." The ECtHR also considered it reasonable to take into account the individual's ability to leave the area. This might seem somewhat harsh given the negative impact of the aerodrome activity on the value of the applicants' properties—they estimated that it had dropped by about a third as a result of the existence of

---

[270] para.97.
[271] (Application no. 39561/98) January 20, 2004.

the airfield and activity at current levels. But they were not able to produce any evidence to show the effect, if any, of the noise disturbance from the aerodrome on house prices in general or the value of the applicants' properties in particular, or to establish that there existed no realistic prospect of being able to move. As a result the Court declared the application manifestly ill-founded.

Similar lack of success awaited complaints regarding a wind farm in *Lars* **4–090** *and Astrid Fagerskiold v Sweden*.[272] The applicants argued that noises measured at approximately 40 decibels from a wind turbine in the vicinity of their property infringed their Article 8 rights or proprietary interests under Article 1 Protocol 1. The Court rejected the claim as manifestly ill-founded, observing that the applicants had not furnished the Court, or the national authorities, with any medical certificates to substantiate that their health had been adversely affected by the noise or the light reflections.

Justification

In order to draw out some general principles from this body of Strasbourg **4–091** case law to form a sensible prediction in respect to environmental litigation under the Convention it is necessary to consider not only the rights themselves but the arguments advanced in defence of an alleged inter-eference. As was pointed out in Chapter 1, once an interference with a Convention right is made out, the evidential burden shifts from the claimant to a defendant once an interference is made out. In environmental cases this means that the public authority in question has to satisfy the court that the steps or decision taken was proportionate.

The key issue regarding justification under Article 8(2) in the environmental context is whether the steps or lacks of steps taken by the state, and hence the interference, are "necessary in a democratic society". The ECtHR accords a wide margin of appreciation to signatory states in matters of environmental policy, particularly under the long shadow cast by *Hatton*. Even in *Fadeyeva v Russia*,[273] where the claim ultimately succeeded, the ECtHR observed that environmental policy-making was a "difficult technical and social sphere"; that the "complexity of the issues" made the Court's role primarily a "subsidiary one", and "only in exceptional circumstances may [the Court] revise the material conclusions of the domestic authorities."

The arguments referring to difficult questions of resource allocation and scientific complexity are familiar defences in environmental cases; and in addition to these respondent states often point to the various measures they have undertaken to regulate the offending operation. In air noise cases it

---

[272] (Application no. 37664/04) February 26, 2008.
[273] (2005) 41 EHRR 376.

seems the Court is inclined to accept these. In circumstances such as those obtaining in *Fadeyeva* the Court was all too ready to draw an adverse inference and was also robust in its rejection of the state's argument that the applicant voluntarily moved into the area, knowing of the pollution, and equally could move out. Housing shortages were such that she had little choice but to move there, and did not have the resources to move out. The Court stressed that in assessing whether the state gave consideration to all competing interests "... the onus is on the state to justify using detailed and rigorous data, a situation in which certain individuals bear a heavy burden on behalf of the rest of the community".[274]

Conclusion

4-092   Despite the wide margin of appreciation allowed to states in environmental matters it is clear that in hazardous pollution cases the ECtHR is willing to find exceptional circumstances amounting to a violation of applicants' rights in cases where the industry or operation concerned does not have a significant role to play in the economic functioning of the country. The appeals to economic necessity in the Russian cases obviously appeared to the Court to be something of an anachronism, however crucial the installations may have appeared to be in the days of the Soviet command economy. The noise pollution cases are somewhat discouraging, but the fact that only a handful of them have been rejected as inadmissible suggests that noise nuisance is still considered a potentially actionable right under the protective umbrella under Article 8 in Strasbourg, and hence domestically under the Human Rights Act.

Human Rights Act—Domestic Case Law

4-093   Under the HRA, courts must have regard to judgments and opinions of the ECtHR, both in terms of the Convention rights invoked, and in terms of the remedies granted by that Court under Article 41 of the Convention. However the existing channels for civil liability claims have inevitably influenced the manner in which these relatively new Convention rights have developed in domestic law as a mechanism for environmental protection.

The case of *Marcic*, dealing with private nuisance,[275] also involved claims under the Human Rights Act. The claimant argued that the defendant water authority had breached Article 8 and Article 1 of the First Protocol. But ECtHR authorities such as *Hatton v UK* militated against him, since

---

[274] para.28.
[275] Discussed in para.4–019 above.

they accord the Convention a subsidiary role in respect of the implementation of social and economic policies by state legislatures, giving them a "wide margin of appreciation".

So, in the end, Mr Marcic's human rights claims availed him no better than his claims in common law. The House of Lords concluded that, in relation to his human rights claims as well as all the others, precedence should be given to the prescribed statutory scheme for enforcement. Parliament had struck the balance between the competing interests of the individual and the community by means of a statutory scheme administered by an independent expert regulator, whose decisions are subject to judicial review. Particular significance was attached to the heavy financial implications of requiring Thames Water to carry out remedial work (essentially, to build new sewers).[276]

In *Dennis*[277] the claimant's invocation of Article 8 and Article 1 of **4–094** Protocol 1 in respect of air noise from Harrier jets over his property was successful and he was awarded damages, even though the judge declined to make an order abating the nuisance because of the public interest in training Harrier pilots. The granting of a remedy for breach of Convention rights in the absence of a remedy for common law rights was an important (and bold) step in developing the remedial provisions of the Human Rights Act, at that time relatively in its infancy. Currently the position is that no action in nuisance will arise if the activity complained of is characteristic of the locality, or has so altered the nature of the locality that it is no longer exceptional.[278] The fact that the claimant was successful in *Dennis* suggests that the locality rule worked in his favour; indeed the judge observed that if the next generation of fighter plane, projected to be twice as noisy, were to operate from that base, then even in an already noisy environment it could form the basis of a new claim in nuisance. It may well be that this locality rule in ordinary nuisance actions may itself run counter to the right to respect for private life under Article 8, in conjunction with Article 14, which requires that the substantive Convention rights must be enjoyed without discrimination, irrespective of whether the claimant lives in a noisy industrial area or a protected greenbelt zone.[279]

The trial of a number of preliminary issues in *Dobson*[280] is a neat demonstration of the overlap between common law actions and HRA claims in environmental litigation. The claim was brought as a group action by a large number of residents who live near a sewage treatment works run by Thames Water. Their complaint was that odours and mosquitoes from

---

[276] The House of Lords took into account a report by the Director of Ofwat which estimated the cost at £50–70,000 per property, amounting to a total of £1 billion, without taking into account future house building.

[277] See para.4–023 above.

[278] *St. Helens Smelting Co. v Tipping* (1865) 11 HL Cas 642.

[279] As was discussed earlier in the section on nuisance; see para.4–010.

[280] [2007] EWHC 2021 (TCC); March 19, 2007.

the works had caused them a nuisance, and their case was that the cause of that nuisance was Thames Water's negligence in failing to treat the sewage properly. In addition to nuisance and negligence, they sought damages under the Human Rights Act for breach of their rights under Article 8.

Ramsey J found that the claimants were seeking to enforce duties which arose under the statutory regime. Therefore, absent any negligence, the claimants were precluded from bringing a claim in nuisance, by reason of the principle in *Marcic*. However, he did conclude that there was a distinction to be drawn in this case so that certain causes of action in nuisance based on negligence could exist alongside the duties under statutory scheme:

> "Whilst the principle in Marcic precludes the Claimants from bringing claims which require the court to embark on a process which is inconsistent and conflicts with the statutory process under the WIA, it does not preclude the Claimants from bringing a claim in nuisance involving allegations of negligence where, as a matter of fact and degree, the exercise of adjudicating on that cause of action is not inconsistent and does not involve conflicts with the statutory process under the WIA".[281]

4–095   Similarly, in answer to the HRA claims, the judge ruled that the claimants were not precluded by Marcic from bringing a claim based on negligence under the HRA where, as a matter of fact and degree, the exercise of adjudicating on that cause of action was not inconsistent and did not involve conflicts with the statutory scheme.

CONCLUSION

4–096   At the outset of this chapter, we set ourselves the task of surveying the systems of civil liability under common law, Community law and human rights law in order to assess their respective efficacy in protecting environmental interests. Any conclusion laid out here will be something of a hostage to fortune as the interplay between these three systems and their ultimate development in the light of future legislation, particularly on the Community level, is fluid and unpredictable. But if any forecast can be derived from the current situation, it is this: that the common law actions in nuisance and, to a lesser degree, negligence are still the most popular avenues for claimants wishing to turn to the courts for redress for environmental harm, and there is a modest enhancement on their success rate if they can be combined with human rights claims.

Claims against the state or public authorities via the *Francovich* action on the other hand are barely discernible; as we have seen from the foregoing

---

[281] para.148.

paragraphs, the one claim in *Francovich* which was successful before the UK courts in the environmental context never came to trial. This is not to say that *Francovich* will not have its day, particularly in view of the multiplicity of environmental directives whose aims uncontestably include the grant of "individual rights". But at the moment anyway the reliance on Community law in domestic courts is an uncertain, if not perilous business, for the non-legally aided or even legally aided claimant (public funding can be withdrawn at any time); the complicated jurisprudence surrounding the notion of "individual rights" makes the whole thing an unpredictable business with an uncertain outcome. Perhaps the time is ripe for another such landmark in the jurisprudence of the ECJ, that will lay to rest, for ever, the controversy over whether directives aimed at protecting the environment are really aimed at protecting individual human interests.

Chapter 5

THE ENVIRONMENTAL LIABILITY DIRECTIVE

Introduction

The Environmental Liability Directive (ELD)[1] introduced a new liability   **5–001**
regime for preventing, remediating and restoring environmental damage
into English law.[2] Some of the liabilities imposed by the ELD already
existed, albeit often with significant differences. Other ELD liabilities, in
particular, liability for restoring protected species and natural habitats,
have substantially increased the scope of existing environmental liabilities
under English law.

The ELD is the first "polluter pays" legislation enacted by the European
Union and the first pure environmental liability—as opposed to regulatory—
law to enter English law from the EU. As such, the ELD has superimposed
EU law on to an area of law that was, until its enactment, traditional English
statutory law.[3] This means in practice that English environmental liability
law has become much more complex and now includes many more overlapping provisions than before the ELD's enactment.

This chapter briefly reviews the history of the ELD, examines the liability regime imposed by it and comments on the changes that it has made,
or will make, to existing English environmental liability law. The chapter
focuses on the Directive itself, with references, as appropriate, to the draft
Environmental Damage (Prevention and Remediation) Regulations 2008
(Draft Regulations) and the Draft guidance (Draft Guidance) issued by the
Department for Environment, Food and Rural Affairs (Defra) as appendices to its second consultation[4] in February 2008.

---

[1] Directive 2004/35/CE of the European Parliament and of the Council on environmental
liability with regard to the prevention and remedying of damage, as amended [2004] OJ
L143/56.
[2] Defra's website when this book went to print stated that the ELD is "likely to be transposed [in England] by December 2008". See fn.4 regarding the status in Wales, Scotland
and Northern Ireland.
[3] As discussed in para.5–037, the ELD does not impose tort liability for property damage,
bodily injury or economic loss.
[4] Defra and Welsh Assembly Government, Environmental Liability Directive: Consultation
on the draft regulations and guidance implementing Directive 2004/35 on environmental
liability with regard to the prevention and remedying of environmental damage (February
2008) (Consultation). The Consultation also includes draft regulations for Wales. Scotland and Northern Ireland are carrying out separate consultations. The Scottish Executive
issued its second consultation on the ELD on May 16, 2008. The Northern Ireland
Department of Environment had not issued its second consultation when this book went to
print.

History

5–002   The ELD has had a long and controversial history. This history began in the 1970s when the European Commission, the Council and the European Parliament first considered introducing a liability regime to remediate environmental damage. The first proposals focused on liability for waste and were then gradually extended to cover liability for harm from other pollutants.

The Commission submitted the first proposal concerning liability for harm caused by waste on July 28, 1976 when it proposed establishing liability for bodily injury caused by toxic waste in its proposal for a Directive on toxic and dangerous wastes.[5] The liability clause was deleted from the final version of the Directive, however.

On June 24, 1983, the Commission again proposed establishing liability for harm caused by waste in its proposal for a Directive on the supervision and control of transfrontier shipment of hazardous wastes within the European Community.[6] Although the proposed liability clause did not survive, the Council included a statement in the Directive that it would

"determine not later than 30 September 1988 the conditions for implementing the civil liability of the producer in the case of damage or that of any other person who may be accountable for the same damage and shall also determine a system of insurance".[7]

In 1986, following the pollution of the Rhine by fire-fighting water mixed with chemicals from the Sandoz facility at Basel, Switzerland, the Council[8] and the European Parliament[9] adopted resolutions calling for the Commission to propose civil liability for environmental damage. There then followed a period in which the Commission worked on an eventual proposal for a civil liability regime as well as continuing its proposals for establishing liability for harm from waste.

5–003   On September 15, 1989, the Commission submitted a proposal for a Directive on civil liability for damage caused by waste.[10] The proposal, which included provisions imposing strict as well as joint and several liability on a producer of waste for bodily injury, property damage, remediation costs and restoration of the damaged environment, was amended in 1991 to include a requirement for producers and persons who disposed of

---

[5] [1976] OJ C 194/2.
[6] [1983] OJ C 186/3, C 186/9.
[7] Council Directive on the supervision and control within the European Community of the transfrontier shipment of hazardous waste. [1983] OJ C 186/3.
[8] See L. Krämer, *Focus on European Environmental Law* 2nd edition (Sweet & Maxwell, 1997) p.147 (citing European Commission, Bulletin of the European Communities No. 11/1986, para.2.1.146).
[9] [1987] OJ C 7/116.
[10] COM (89) 282, [1989] OJ C 251/3.

the waste to obtain financial security for their actions.[11] Later that year, however, the Commission abandoned the proposal.

Also in 1991, the Commission proposed provisions establishing civil liability for environmental damage caused by waste and financial security requirements for closure and post-closure costs in its proposal for a Directive on the landfill of waste. The financial security requirements were to be backed up by funds to enable governmental authorities to prevent or remedy environmental damage caused by waste if an operator lacked sufficient funds to do so.[12] The final version of the Directive included the financial security requirements but not the provisions that would have established civil liability and funding.

The Commission's first document pursuant to the Council's and the Parliament's resolutions that it should propose civil liability for more general environmental damage than that caused by waste also appeared in 1991, when a draft green paper that was being prepared by the Commission on remedying environmental damage was leaked. The paper discussed the establishment of civil liability for environmental damage together with industry-funded joint compensation schemes to fund the clean ups. The leaked draft resulted in the business and insurance communities opposing the introduction of such liability, particularly because the draft mentioned, among other things, the potential for the imposition of retrospective liability. This opposition continued throughout the ELD's remaining history and, as a result, substantially lengthened the legislative process.

On March 17, 1993, the Commission issued its green paper on reme-   5–004
dying environmental damage.[13] The paper appeared to favour establishing strict liability together with the joint compensation schemes mentioned in the leaked draft. It noted, however, that several issues had to be resolved before a liability system could be established. The issues included:

- the definition of environmental damage;
- the scope of persons who would be liable;
- the scope of actions for which such persons would be liable; and
- the level to which the environment must be restored.

Between 1993 and 2000, the Commission continued work on the proposals to establish civil liability for environmental damage. Activities carried out by the Commission included holding workshops, hosting a joint hearing with the European Parliament and awarding various contracts for background work on a system of civil liability for environmental damage.[14]

[11] COM (91) 219 final, [1991] OJ C 192/6.
[12] [1990] OJ C 190/1.
[13] COM (93) 47 final.
[14] See, e.g. *Study of Civil Liability Systems for Remedying Environmental Damage* (Contract B4/ 3040/94/000665/MAR/H1, June 1996); *Economic Prospects of Liability and Joint Compensation Systems for Remedying Environmental Damage* (Reference 3066, March 1996); see *http://europa.eu.int/comm/environment/liability*, *http://ec.europa.eu/environment/liability/follo-wup.htm* and *http://ec.europa.eu/environment/liability/background.htm*).

In addition, the Economic and Social Committee issued an opinion supporting the liability regime,[15] and the European Parliament issued a resolution requesting the Commission to submit a proposal for a Directive on civil liability for future environmental damage.[16]

On February 9, 2000, spurred in part by the December 1999 oil spill from the *Erika* off the coast of Brittany and following various leaked versions, the Commission issued a White Paper on Environmental Liability.[17] The White Paper stated that a Directive to establish strict liability for traditional damage (bodily injury and property damage) and environmental damage (remediation costs and biodiversity damage) was the most appropriate way forward in establishing a liability regime for environmental damage. In reaching its conclusion, the Commission had also considered the alternatives of (a) imposing liability only for remediating contamination and restoring environmental damage, and (b) acceding to the Convention on civil liability for damage resulting from activities dangerous to the environment—known as the Lugano Convention[18]—as a potential first step prior to submitting a proposal for a Directive.

On July 30, 2001, after having commissioned further background studies, the Commission issued a new working paper entitled "Environment Directorate General Working Paper on Prevention and Restoration of Significant Environmental Damage (Environmental Liability)". The paper set out the Commission's new approach, which was to forgo establishing a civil liability regime for traditional environmental damage and the Lugano Convention approach in lieu of a public law regime.

5–005   On February 21, 2002, the final stage of this long history began with the Commission submitting a proposal for a Directive of the European Parliament and of the Council on environmental liability with regard to the prevention and restoration of environmental damage (Proposed Directive).[19] The Council took a much more active role in shaping the final version of the ELD than the European Parliament, holding over 30 working party meetings on the Proposed Directive by mid-2003. The Legal Affairs and Internal Market Committee of the Parliament, meanwhile, held its first public hearing on the Proposed Directive on May 21, 2002. That committee had been involved in a dispute with the Environment, Public Health and Consumer Policy Committee over which of them should be

---

[15] [1994] OJ C 133/8.
[16] [1994] OJ C 128/165, C 128/166.
[17] COM (2000) 66 final.
[18] The Lugano Convention has never entered into force. Although nine states have signed it since the Council of Europe opened it for signature on June 21, 1993, none have ratified it. It would have imposed strict liability on the operator of a dangerous activity for personal injury, property damage, remediating environmental damage and the cost of preventive measures in respect of damage caused by the operator.
[19] COM (2002) 17 final, OJ C 151 E/132 (June 25, 2002).

lead committee; the Environment Committee having been appointed as lead committee when the Green Paper was issued in 1993.[20] On June 13, 2002, the Legal Affairs Committee was confirmed as the lead committee subject to considering the views of the Environment Committee.

The dispute between the two parliamentary committees delayed, not only Parliament's consideration of the Proposed Directive, but the entire legislative process. This was because the co-decision procedure requires the European Parliament to hold its first reading before the Council can hold its first reading.

On May 14, 2003, the Parliament finally held its first reading of the Proposed Directive and made various amendments to it. The amendments that were to prove the most contentious between the Parliament and the Council were:

- to impose liability for environmental damage, not only for species and natural habitats that are protected under EU law, but also for those that have equivalent protection under the domestic law of the Member States;
- to delete the exceptions to liability for state-of-the-art and an operator's compliance with a permit and, instead, to require a competent authority to consider the initially proposed exceptions as mitigating factors in determining the costs for which an operator was to be liable, with the authority that granted the permit to share such costs;
- to authorise non-governmental organisations (NGOs) and other relevant persons to submit comments when there is an imminent threat of environmental harm as well as when there is actual environmental harm; and
- to establish a deadline of three years after the transposition deadline for the Directive for Member States to ensure the introduction of mandatory financial responsibility for installations with IPPC[21] permits, with a six-year deadline for mandatory financial security for operational activities under other listed EU legislation; Member States were to be given an option to exempt low risk activities.

On September 18, 2003, the Council finalised its first reading of the Directive by adopting its common position.[22] The common position deleted a controversial requirement that Member States must ensure that preventive and remedial measures were carried out even if no operator

---

[20] C. Clarke, *The Proposed EC Liability Directive: Half-Way Through Co-Decision*, RECIEL, vol. 12(3), p.254 (2003).

[21] Directive 2008/1/EC of the European Parliament and of the Council concerning integrated pollution prevention and control. [2008] OJ L 24/8.

[22] Common Position (EC) No 58/2003 adopted by the Council on September 18, 2003, with a view to the adoption of a Directive 2003/ . . . /EC of the European Parliament and of the Council on environmental liability with regard to the prevention and remedying of environmental damage. OJ C 277 E/10 (November 18, 2003).

could be found or the operator had insufficient financial resources to pay for the measures.

5–006 The Council reached a compromise with the Parliament on some of the amendments by providing Member States with the option to adopt specified measures rather than requiring Member States to take the measures or deleting such requirements from the Directive. In particular, the common position provided Member States with the option:

- to impose liability for remediating environmental damage to species and natural habitats that are protected under the domestic law of the Member States that is equivalent to EU law;
- to include the compliance-with-a-permit and state-of-the-art defences;
- to allocate costs in respect of environmental damage caused by multiple operators in accordance with domestic legislation—thus avoiding a decision on whether to impose joint and several or proportionate liability;[23] and
- to authorise NGOs and other relevant persons to provide comments in situations in which there is an imminent threat of environmental damage.

The Council's common position did not include mandatory financial security provisions but instead "encouraged" Member States to develop financial security instruments and markets so as to enable operators to use such instruments to cover potential ELD liabilities. In addition, the common position directed the European Commission to carry out a study regarding the availability of insurance and other types of financial security for activities carried out under EU legislation that is listed in what became Annex III of the ELD, with the potential to submit a proposal for mandatory financial security. The Commission was to submit the report and, potentially, the proposal eight years after the ELD had entered into force.

On December 17, 2003, the European Parliament held its second reading of the Directive and made four amendments to the Council's common position. The amendments stated that:

- the Directive should be without prejudice to an operator's right to limit liability in accordance with various marine conventions;
- competent authorities should carry out preventive or remedial measures but only "as a last resort" if the operator could not be identified, failed to carry them out or was not required to do so by the Directive;

---

[23] Under joint and several liability, all persons who cause indivisible environmental damage are liable to the claimant for the entire damage. Thus, if three persons cause environmental damage and two cannot be found, the remaining person is liable for the entire damage. Under proportionate liability, each person who causes indivisible environmental damage is liable only for the proportion caused by it.

- the Commission was to submit proposals for mandatory financial security five years after the Directive entered into force and prescribed various rules for the financial security requirements; and
- the Commission was directed to report on the implementation of the Directive in respect of the relationship between shipowners' liability and civil receivers' contributions.[24]

The Council did not accept all four of the Parliament's amendments, resulting in the formation of a conciliation committee. On February 20, 2004, the committee reached agreement on the final version of the ELD following a trialogue between the Parliament, the Council and the Commission. The ELD was then adopted by the Parliament and the Council and published in the *Official Journal*, leading to its entry into force on April 30, 2004.[25] The deadline for Member States to transpose the ELD was April 30, 2007.[26]

The Environmental Liability Directive

The ELD is the first EU law that is specifically based on the polluter pays principle.[27] As will be described, it imposes strict liability on persons who carry out various operations that are subject to EU law if such persons cause an imminent threat of, or actual, environmental damage to natural resources; it also imposes fault-based liability on other persons who cause damage to protected species and natural habitats by operations that are not subject to EU law.

5–007

Persons who are liable

The ELD channels liability for preventing and remediating environmental damage to the "operator" of an "occupational activity". The term "operator" is broadly defined to include individuals, organisations, companies and other forms of "legal, private or public person[s]" as well as "the holder of a permit or authorisation for such an activity or the person

5–008

---

[24] European Parliament legislative resolution on the Council common position for adopting a European Parliament and Council directive on environmental liability with regard to the prevention and remedying of environmental damage. COM (2004) 55 final (January 26, 2004).

[25] [2004] OJ L 143/56.

[26] ELD, art.19(1). On June 26, 2008, the Commission announced that it had decided to refer nine Member States to the European Court of Justice for failing to transpose the ELD. See European Commission Press Release IP/08/1025.

[27] See European Commission, *Environmental Liability: Commission welcomes agreement on new Directive* (IP/04/246, February 20, 2004). The polluter pays principle, which is in article 174 of the Treaty on European Union, states that the person who is responsible for polluting the environment should pay the costs of such pollution.

registering or notifying such an activity".[28] The term "occupational activity" is also broadly defined to mean "any activity carried out in the course of an economic activity, a business or an undertaking, irrespectively of its private or public, profit or non-profit character".[29]

An operator is either (a) strictly liable or (b) liable if it is negligent or at fault, depending on the activity carried out by it when an imminent threat of, or actual, environmental damage occurs. If the operator was carrying out an activity under EU legislation listed in Annex III of the ELD, the operator is strictly liable.[30] Annex III includes the integrated pollution prevention and control Directive,[31] waste management operations, specified discharges into inland surface water and groundwater, water abstraction and the transboundary shipment of waste into and out of the EU. Following a lengthy controversy regarding the creation of liability for harm caused by genetically modified organisms, Annex III also includes the Directives on the contained use of genetically modified micro-organisms[32] and the deliberate release into the environment of genetically modified organisms.[33]

The strict liability imposed on Annex III operators is "very strict indeed", veering "towards absolute". There is no need for a competent authority to show that a direct causal link exists between an operator and the environmental damage; the necessary link is between the activity carried out by the operator and the damage.[34]

5–009   If the operator was carrying out an activity that is not controlled by the EU legislation listed in Annex III when the activity caused environmental damage and was not negligent in carrying out the activity, it is not liable under the Directive.[35] In addition, non-Annex III operators are liable only for environmental damage caused to a protected species or natural habitat, as discussed below. In contrast, an Annex III operator is strictly liable for environmental damage to land and water in addition to protected species and natural habitats.[36]

In addition to imposing liability on operators, the ELD also refers, somewhat obscurely, to the liability of a "third party". For example, it provides that "Member States shall ensure that the competent authority

---

[28] ELD, art.2(6).
[29] ibid., art.2(7).
[30] ibid., art.3(1)(a).
[31] Directive 2008/1/EC of the European Parliament and of the Council concerning integrated pollution prevention and control. [2008] OJ L24/8.
[32] Council Directive 90/219/EEC on the contained use of genetically modified micro-organisms. [1990] OJ L117/1.
[33] Directive 2001/18/EC of the European Parliament and of the Council on the deliberate release into the environment of genetically modified organisms. [2001] OJ L106/1.
[34] A. Waite, *The Quest for Environmental Law Equilibrium*, p.49 at 71 in *Environmental Liability in the EU: The 2004 Directive Compared with US and Member State Law* (Cameron May London 2006, G. Betlem & E. Brans (eds)).
[35] ELD, art.3(1)(b).
[36] ibid.

may empower or require third parties to carry out the necessary preventive or remedial measures".[37] It further authorises a competent authority to "initiate cost recovery proceedings against the operator, or if appropriate, a third party who has caused the damage or imminent threat of damage".[38]

The term "third party" appears to include a person who is authorised by a competent authority to act on its behalf.[39] It is less clear, however, how a competent authority could require a third party to carry out preventive or remedial measures or to seek to recover costs incurred for such measures from a third person because, as described above, the focus of the ELD is on the liability of only one category of person; the operator. For example, the ELD states that the "fundamental principle of this Directive should . . . be that an operator whose activity has caused the environmental damage or the imminent threat of such damage is to be held financially liable".[40] There are no provisions setting out the standard of liability or otherwise describing the nature of liability for third persons.

The ELD's channelling of liability to an operator—or third party— **5–010** contrasts with existing English law under which relatively large numbers of persons may be liable for remediating indivisible damage to land or water. For example, under sections 161 to 161D of the Water Resources Act 1991, more than one person may "cause" a pollutant to enter "controlled waters",[41] that is, surface, ground and coastal waters.[42] In addition, Part 2A of the Environmental Protection Act 1990 requires an enforcing authority to consider a broad range of persons who could be liable for having caused or knowingly permitted a substance to be in, on or under land such that the land is "contaminated land". The enforcing authority must then exclude persons according to complex tests in order to determine the persons who remain as appropriate persons for a liability group for each significant pollutant linkage at a contaminated site.[43]

---

[37] ibid., art.11(3).
[38] ibid., art.10.
[39] See, e.g., Proposed Directive, recital 14 ("In cases where a competent authority has to act itself or through a third party in the place of an operator, that authority should ensure that the cost incurred by it is recovered from the operator"); Proposal for a Directive of the European Parliament and of the Council on environmental liability with regard to the prevention and restoration of environmental damage, COM (2002) 17 final (January 23, 2002) s.2, p.2 ("The proposal leaves it open to Member States to decide when the measures should be taken by the relevant operator or by the competent authorities or by a third party on their behalf").
[40] ELD, recital 2.
[41] Water Resources Act 1991, s.104.
[42] See *Empress Car Company (Abertillery) Ltd v National Rivers Authority* [1999] 2 A.C. 22, [1998] 2 W.L.R. 350, [1998] 1 All E.R. 481 (HL) (person may cause water pollution even when act of another person is immediate cause).
[43] See Chapter 16.

Environmental damage to natural resources

5–011   Operators may be liable for causing an imminent threat of, or actual, environmental damage to natural resources. There are three types of natural resources: water, protected species and natural habitats, and land.[44] Thresholds of liability apply in respect of actual environmental damage but (obviously) not for the imminent threat of such damage.

Water

5–012   The ELD imposes liability for remediating environmental damage to waters specified in the Water Framework Directive,[45] that is, surface, transitional, coastal and ground water. The threshold for liability is "damage that significantly adversely affects the ecological, chemical and/or quantitative status and/or ecological potential" of such waters.[46]

The ELD thus overlaps with sections 161 to 161D of the Water Resources Act 1991 in that if an operator causes water pollution subject to liability under the ELD, that person is also subject to liability for the same water pollution under the 1991 Act. All water pollution subject to liability under the 1991 Act is not, however, necessarily subject to liability under the ELD due to the much lower threshold in the former and the channelling of liability to an operator in the latter.[47]

Protected species and natural habitats

5–013   The ELD established liability for harming species and natural habitats that are protected under the Birds[48] and Habitats[49] Directives. Areas protected by the Birds Directive are called special protection areas. Areas protected by the Habitats Directive are called special areas of conservation. Together the two types of areas, collectively known as European sites, form the Natura 2000 network which covers about 15 per cent of the land area of the EU. The ELD also imposes liability for damaging protected species, such as migratory birds, outside such areas.

The establishment of liability for harming protected species and natural habitats was a major reason for the enactment of the ELD. Although most Member States had already enacted legislation imposing liability for

---

[44] ELD, art.2(12).
[45] Directive 2000/60/EC of the European Parliament and of the Council establishing a framework for Community action in the field of water policy. [2000] OJ L327/1.
[46] ELD, art.2(1)(b).
[47] See Chapter 11.
[48] Council Directive 79/409/EEC on the conservation of wild birds. [1979] OJ L103/1.
[49] Directive 2000/60/EC of the European Parliament and of the Council establishing a framework for Community action in the field of water policy. [2000] OJ L327/1.

remediating damage to land and water, only a few had enacted legislation imposing liability for remediating damage to protected species and natural habitats and restoring them to their previous condition.[50]

English law imposed some liability for remediating and restoring natural resources, but only to a substantially lesser extent than imposed by the ELD. For example, English law provides that a person who is convicted of contravening a special nature conservation order may be liable for restoring a European site to its condition before the damage.[51] It also provides that a person who caused or knowingly permitted controlled waters to be polluted may be liable not only for the remediation of the waters but, so far as reasonably practicable, for restoring "flora and fauna dependent on the aquatic environment of the waters, to their state immediately before the [polluting] matter became present in the waters".[52] Further, the statutory guidance under Part 2A imposes liability for remediating European sites and other designated ecological areas such as sites of special scientific interest (SSSIs), and national and marine nature reserves.[53] The guidance does not, however, set out details on remedial or restoration works to be carried out on such sites and does not require them to be remediated to their condition immediately before the damage occurred.

The threshold for liability for damage to a protected species or natural habitat is damage that has "significant adverse effects on reaching or maintaining the favourable conservation status" of the species or habitat.[54] The terms "conservation status"[55] and "favourable"[56] in respect of protected species and natural habitats have the same or similar definitions to those in the Habitats Directive. Annex I of the ELD sets out detailed criteria for determining when the threshold has been reached.

5–014

The Draft Regulations, which have gone beyond the minimum required by the ELD by including all SSSIs as protected natural habitats for purposes of the ELD, propose an additional threshold of "site integrity" in respect of protected species and natural habitats that are located in a SSSI.[57] The site integrity test involves a determination that the environ-

---

[50] See C. Clarke, Update Comparative Legal Study; Study Contract No. 201919/MAR/B3, p.27: available on *http://ec.europa.eu/environment/liability/pdf/legalstudy_full.pdf*.

[51] Conservation (Natural Habitats) Regulations 1994, SI 1994/2716, reg.26(1); see Chapter 10.

[52] Water Resources Act 1991, ss.161(3), 161A(1), 161A(2); Anti-Pollution Works Regulations 1999, SI 1999/1006, reg.2; see Chapter 11.

[53] Defra Circular 01/2006, Annex 3, table A(2).

[54] ELD, art.2(1)(a).

[55] ibid., art.2(4)(a); Council Directive 92/43/EEC on the conservation of natural habitats and of wild fauna and flora (Habitats Directive), art.1(e) (conservation status for natural habitat), art.1(i) (conservation status for protected species). OJ L206/7.

[56] ELD, art.2(4)(b); Habitats Directive, art.1(e) (natural habitat), art.1(i) (protected species).

[57] Draft Regulations, Schedule 1; see Draft Guidance, Chapter 3; Consultation, para.117. See ELD, art.2(1)(a) (Member States may apply ELD to habitats and species not covered by EU law in accordance with equivalent provisions of national law on nature conservation).

mental damage has "an adverse effect on the integrity of the site (that is, the coherence of its ecological structure and function, across its whole area, that enables it to sustain the habitat, complex of habitats or the levels of populations of the species affected)".[58] As such, it differs from the threshold test for protected species and natural habitats described above.

Land

5–015   The ELD imposes liability for damage to land provided that the land is contaminated due to the direct or indirect introduction of "substances, preparations, organisms or micro-organisms" and further provided that the contamination "creates a significant risk of human health being adversely affected".[59] Unlike water and protected species and natural habitats, environmental damage to land is not linked to specific EU legislation. This is because no EU legislation to protect land, or soil, existed when the ELD was enacted. Although the European Commission has since proposed a Directive on soil protection,[60] that Directive had not been enacted when this book went to print, and seems unlikely to be enacted in the reasonably foreseeable future, due to strong opposition to it by some Member States including the United Kingdom.

Much of the land that may be required to be remediated under the ELD is subject to liability for remediation under Part 2A of the Environmental Protection Act 1990. There are significant differences between the two regimes, however. These differences include an absence of detailed consultation processes under the ELD, the focus of the ELD on only human health compared with the wider focus of Part 2A, an absence of defences under Part 2A, the retrospective nature of liability under Part 2A as opposed to the ELD, the inclusion of genetically modified organisms and micro-organisms in the ELD but not Part 2A, and a difference in the threshold for remediation. In respect of the threshold, Defra considers that the ELD threshold for harm to human health "is probably somewhat wider than 'significant harm' in [Part 2A]".[61]

Notification requirements

5–016   The ELD requires operators to notify a competent authority if there is an imminent threat of, or actual, environmental damage. If there is an imminent threat of such damage, the operator must notify the relevant competent authority "as soon as possible" if preventive measures carried

---

[58] Draft Regulations, Sch.1, para.4.
[59] ELD, art.2(1)(c).
[60] Proposal for a Directive of the European Parliament and of the Council establishing a framework for the protection of soil. COM (2006) 232 final (September 22, 2006).
[61] Consultation, para.43. "Wider" presumably means "lower" in this context.

out to dispel the threat fail to do so.[62] The ELD defines the term "imminent threat of damage" as "a sufficient likelihood that environmental damage will occur in the near future".[63] If there is actual environmental damage, the operator has a duty to notify the competent authority "without delay".[64] A competent authority may require an operator who has caused an imminent threat of, or actual, environmental damage to provide supplementary information regarding the threatened or actual damage at any time.[65]

The duty on a person who causes environmental damage to notify a competent authority reflects a growing trend towards the introduction of such requirements. Such duties already exist in respect of the integrated pollution prevention and control Directive[66] and of hazardous waste.[67]

Remediation requirements

There are four types of preventive and remedial actions: preventive measures; emergency remedial actions; remedial measures for water and protected species and natural habitats; and remedial measures for land. Remedial actions for water, protected species and natural habitats are substantially different from those for land.   **5–017**

Preventive measures

If there is an imminent threat of, or actual, environmental damage, an operator must carry out necessary remedial measures "without delay".[68] The term "preventive measures" is defined to mean "any measures taken in response to an event, act or omission that has created an imminent threat of environmental damage, with a view to preventing or minimising that damage".[69]   **5–018**

---

[62] ELD, art.5(2).
[63] ibid., art.2(9).
[64] ibid., art.6(1).
[65] ibid., art.6(2)(a).
[66] Directive 2008/1/EC of the European Parliament and of the Council concerning integrated pollution prevention and control, art.14(b) (operator of installation must notify competent authority "without delay of any incident or accident significantly affecting the environment"). [2008] OJ L 24/8.
[67] Hazardous Waste (England and Wales) Regulations 2005, SI 2005/894, reg.62(3) (person who holds hazardous waste must notify Environment Agency "as soon as reasonably practicable [if] he knows or has reasonable grounds to believe that an emergency or grave danger has arisen").
[68] ELD, art.5(1).
[69] ibid., art.2(10).

Emergency remedial actions

5–019   The ELD has an unusual structure for remediation regimes in that it includes self-executing provisions.[70] That is, an operator who causes environmental damage has an immediate duty to carry out emergency actions to limit and prevent further damage;[71] there is no need for a competent authority to intervene in order to request or require the operator to do so. In contrast, the vast majority of remediation regimes do not require a responsible person to carry out preventive or remedial actions until a competent authority acts according to its duties or powers to require it to do so.

If an operator's activity causes environmental damage, the emergency actions it must take are:

"all practicable steps to immediately control, contain, remove or otherwise manage the relevant contaminants and/or any other damage factors in order to limit or to prevent further environmental damage and adverse effects on human health or further impairment of services".[72]

It thus appears that the duty to carry out such actions continues to exist from the time that the damage occurs until it is fully remediated. This is the approach taken by the Draft Regulations which do not limit a competent authority's power to require an operator to carry out emergency remedial actions to the commencement of environmental damage but rather, provide the authority with such power during the entire time that the damage continues to exist.[73]

The existence of a duty to carry out emergency actions creates a potential problem in that it may take several months—in some cases even longer—for a competent authority to assess whether the damage reaches the threshold under the ELD for a natural resource, in particular a protected species or natural habitat. An operator has a duty, however, to carry out emergency actions immediately. In order to alleviate the problem of knowing whether the damage reaches the threshold in the ELD, the Draft

---

[70] Most remediation regimes provide an enforcing authority with powers to require responsible persons to remediate contaminated land and water pollution; they do not direct the enforcing authority to do so. Examples include section 161 of the Water Resources Act 1991 and the Comprehensive Environmental Response, Compensation and Liability Act (Superfund) in the United States. Some remediation regimes place a duty on enforcing authorities to act if the authority determines that a site meets the threshold for remediating contamination. An example is Part 2A of the Environmental Protection Act 1990. Even when such a duty exists, the authority still has discretion because there is generally no duty to enforce the regime immediately in respect of a specific site.

[71] ELD, art.6(1)(a).

[72] ibid.

[73] Draft Regulations, reg.12. See Consultation, para.82: "[t]his power will exist all the way through until remedial measures are carried out. If, during the course of identifying the right remedial package, it becomes clear that some further emergency action is needed to contain the damage, then the enforcing authority will be able to require the operator to do this".

Regulations require an operator to carry out emergency actions "immediately" that "reasonable grounds" exist to believe that the damage is or will become environmental damage,[74] i.e. damage above the threshold.

Remedial measures for water and protected species and natural habitats

The term "remedial measures" is defined to mean;   5–020

> "any action, or combination of actions, including mitigating or interim measures to restore, rehabilitate or replace damaged natural resources and/or impaired services, or to provide an equivalent alternative to those resources or services as foreseen in Annex II".[75]

The services provided by a natural resource are services that benefit another natural resource or the public.[76]

There is likely to be an overlap between preventive measures and remedial measures. For example, the removal of deteriorating drums and barrels, and the stabilisation of the banks of a dyke to prevent contaminants entering a stream, are measures that may be taken to prevent or minimise environmental damage, as well as being measures to remediate such damage.

Annex II provides that the remedying of environmental damage to water and protected species and natural habitats should be achieved by restoring the environment to its baseline condition by means of primary, complementary and compensatory remediation. The baseline condition is the condition of the relevant natural resource immediately before it was damaged. In recognising that documentary information regarding the baseline may not exist, the ELD states that the condition should be estimated on the basis of the best information available.[77]

The ELD describes primary remediation as "any remedial measure   5–021
which returns the damaged natural resources and/or impaired services to, or towards, baseline condition".[78] This definition does not differentiate between measures to clean up contamination and measures to restore damaged natural resources to their baseline condition. The two types of measures tend, however, to be distinct. For example, a pollutant such as hydrocarbons may need to be removed from the water and banks of a pond in a protected natural habitat. Restoration of the flora and fauna of the

---

[74] Draft Regulations, reg.12(1).
[75] ELD, art.2(11).
[76] ibid., art.2(13). The definition of "remedial measures" also applies to land, as discussed below.
[77] ELD, art.2(14).
[78] ibid., Annex II, para.1(a).

pond, however, is a distinct series of works for which separate expertise is required.

"Complementary remediation" is described as "any remedial measure taken in relation to natural resources and/or services to compensate for the fact that primary remediation does not result in fully restoring the damaged natural resources and/or services".[79] The purpose of complementary remediation is to provide a similar level of services by the natural resource as existed before the resource was damaged. Complementary remediation thus includes the restoration of an alternative site if the damaged site cannot be fully restored. The ELD states that the alternative site should be geographically linked to the damaged site, if possible and appropriate, after taking the interests of the affected population into account.[80]

"Compensatory remediation" is described as "any action taken to compensate for interim losses of natural resources and/or services that occur from the date of damage occurring until primary remediation has achieved its full effect".[81] "Interim losses" are losses that result from the damaged natural resources being unable to perform their ecological functions or to provide services to another natural resource or the public until the primary or complementary measures have taken effect. The term does not include financial compensation to members of the public.[82] Instead, compensatory measures consist of "additional improvements" to the water or protected species or natural habitat.[83]

5–022   The concepts of complementary and compensatory remediation are new to the EU. They have, however, been part of the federal—and state—statutory law of the United States since the early 1970s.[84] The key statutes there are the Comprehensive Environmental Response, Compensation and Liability Act of 1980, also known as CERCLA or Superfund,[85] and the Oil Pollution Act of 1990.[86] The legislative framework for actions for complementary and compensatory remediation in CERCLA and the Oil Pollution Act differs substantially from the ELD. The concept of assessing and quantifying complementary and compensatory remediation, however, has marked similarities in both jurisdictions. Thus, although such actions are in their infancy in the EU, a wealth of regulations, guidance and claims

---

[79] ibid., Annex II, para.1(b).
[80] ibid., Annex II, para.1.1.2.
[81] ibid., Annex II, para.1(c).
[82] ibid., Annex II, para.1(d).
[83] ibid., Annex II, para.1.1.3.
[84] See Trans-Alaska Pipeline Authorization Act of 1973, 43 United States Code (USC) s.1653(c)(1) (repealed); Deepwater Port Act of 1974, 33 USC s.1517(m) (repealed); Clean Water Act, 33 USC 1321(f).
[85] 42 USC ss.9601 et seq.
[86] 33 USC ss.2701 et seq.

experience already exists on which competent authorities and operators in the EU may draw.[87]

Remedial measures for land

Remedial measures for land are less stringent than those for water and protected species and natural habitats. The applicable standard of remediation is the current or approved future use of the land at the time it was damaged rather than a requirement to return land to its baseline condition. If no land use or other regulations exist, the ELD states that the use of a damaged area shall be determined by taking into account its expected development. In order to effect the remediation, the operator whose activity caused the damage must carry out a risk assessment and remove, control, contain or diminish the relevant contaminants, so that the land ceases to pose a significant risk of adversely affecting human health.[88]

Annex II states, among other things, that all necessary measures shall be taken to prevent adverse effects on human health if the land use is subsequently changed. The provision does not appear to subject an operator to indeterminate liability for remediating land if, say, the operator remediates the land to its commercial state and the land is subsequently developed for residences.[89] It would seem beneficial, however, for Member States to ensure that further remediation is carried out during development of the land to a higher use. There are, however, no provisions in the ELD for a public register of damaged natural resources so as to ensure that planning authorities are aware of the potential presence of further contaminants that require remediation. Defra has stated that planning authorities should take the need for further remediation into account when proposed development would change the use of a remediated site. It further stated that the United Kingdom Government does not consider it reasonable to expect operators to carry out further remediation in such a case.[90]

5–023

---

[87] See, e.g. 43 Code of Federal Regulations (CFR) part 11 (US Department of Interior regulations under CERCLA); 15 CFR part 990 (National Oceanic and Atmospheric Administration regulations under Oil Pollution Act). See Fogleman, *Liability for Damage to Natural Resources; A Landmark US Case Provides Guidance on its Scope*, Environmental Liability 15 (2007), p.11. Much excellent work has already been carried out in the EU to quantify remedial measures, in particular, the *Remede* toolkit commissioned by the European Commission to provide information and case studies on the use of resource equivalency methods. See Guidance, para.7.21.

[88] ELD, Annex II, para.2.

[89] ibid.

[90] Consultation, para.125.

Scope of liability

5–024　If more than one operator causes the same environmental damage, a Member State may apply either joint and several or proportionate liability according to its national legislation.[91] The scope of liability to be applied in England, according to the Draft Regulations, is joint and several liability.[92]

The joint and several liability system is the same as that imposed, albeit tacitly, by sections 161 to 161D of the Water Resources Act 1991. In addition, Part 2A imposes modified joint and several liability in that an appropriate person who remains in a liability group after the enforcing authority has excluded other persons from the group is liable, not only for the harm caused by that person but also for the harm caused by the excluded persons.[93]

Prospective liability

5–025　Article 17 of the ELD provides that the ELD does not apply to environmental damage that was "caused by an emission, event or incident":

- "that took place before [April 30, 2007]; or
- "which takes place subsequent to [April 30, 2007] when it derives from a specific activity that took place and finished before the said date".[94]

An "emission" is defined by the ELD to mean "the release into the environment, as a result of human activities, of substances, preparations, organisms or micro-organisms".[95] The ELD does not define the words "event" or "incident".

The word "event" appears in the ELD in:

- the phrase "taken in response to an event, act or omission that has created an imminent threat of environmental damage" in the definition of "preventive measures";[96]

---

[91] ELD, art.9. Article 9 states that the allocation of costs is especially applicable to multiple party causation concerning the apportionment of liability between the producer and the user of a product.

[92] The Draft Regulations do not specifically state that the applicable scope of liability is joint and several liability but section 10.2 of the Draft Guidance states that an enforcing authority may enforce requirements and reclaim its costs from "any one of the operators responsible for causing them". Section 10.2 further states that the operator from whom the costs are sought may then pursue other responsible operators for a contribution for their share of liability. See also Consultation, para.27 (UK Government does not intend to require enforcing authorities to apportion liability before requiring responsible operators to act or before seeking the recovery of costs; operators may claim contribution or indemnity from other liable persons in civil proceedings).

[93] The apportionment criteria in the statutory guidance under Part 2A applies only to persons who are not excluded from a liability group. See Chapter 16.

[94] ELD, art.17.

[95] ibid., art.2(8).

[96] ibid., art.2(10).

- a recital that refers to environmental damage from an "event or emission";[97] and
- the permit defence, which refers to "an emission or event expressly authorised by" a permit.[98]

The meaning of an "event" is thus not entirely clear except that it can be an activity carried out by an operator as part of its occupational activity and may be carried out pursuant to a permit condition.

The word "incident" appears in the ELD in respect of:

- the exclusion of liability under specified conventions;[99]
- the report directed to be carried out by the European Commission on genetically modified organisms, which refers to "incidents of environmental damage";[100] and
- the provision stating that an operator shall not be required to bear the cost of preventive or remedial actions that result from compliance with a compulsory order or instruction from a public authority "other than an order or instruction consequent upon an emission or incident caused by the operator's own activities".[101]

An "incident" thus appears to mean the act or omission that caused the environmental damage in question.

Defra has stated that regulations to implement the ELD will not apply to an emission or incident that occurred prior to their effective date.[102] Whilst no competent authority will have been empowered to enforce the regulations under the ELD until they are effective, this approach is contrary to article 17 of the ELD, as quoted above. This is because article 17 states that the ELD shall not apply to environmental damage that occurred prior to April 30, 2007. The corollary is that the ELD does apply to all relevant environmental damage that occurs after that date—not only damage that occurs after a Member State has belatedly transposed the ELD into domestic law in breach of EU law. The issue will be academic unless an operator causes environmental damage under the ELD after April 30, 2007 but before the regulations become effective. If this occurs, the operator

5–026

---

[97] ibid., recital 20.
[98] ibid., art.8(4)(a).
[99] ibid., arts 4(2), (4). There are various definitions of the word "incident" in the conventions. For example, article I(1) of the International Convention on civil liability for oil pollution defines it as "any occurrence, or series of occurrences having the same origin, which causes pollution damage or creates a grave and imminent threat of causing such damage". The other conventions also use the phrase "any occurrence or series of occurrences having the same origin". E.g. International Convention on civil liability for bunker oil pollution damage, art.1(8); International Convention on Liability and Compensation for Damage in Connection with the Carriage of Hazardous and Noxious Substances by Sea, art.1(8).
[100] ELD, art.18(3)(b).
[101] ibid., art.8(3).
[102] Draft Regulations, reg.7(1); see Consultation, paras 56–58.

would be liable for interim costs from the time that the environmental damage occurred, not the time that the regulations became effective.

Limitations

5–027 The ELD does not apply to environmental damage that results from an "emission, event or incident" if over 30 years have passed since the emission, event or incident occurred.[103] In contrast, there is no statute of limitations for the costs of remediating contamination in Part 2A of the Environmental Protection Act 1990 or the Water Resources Act 1991. The difference in limitations could result in operators continuing to be liable after the 30-year period if, say, environmental damage which meets the threshold under the ELD occurs and liability for such damage also exists in respect of the same damage by Part 2A or the Water Resources Act 1991. This is because Defra has said that transposition of the ELD will not diminish the protection offered by existing environmental legislation.[104]

Defra has also stated that it expects operators and enforcing authorities to deal with incidents of threatened and actual damage to which the ELD and other environmental legislation applies, by looking first at the regulations transposing the ELD, because the ELD imposes duties on operators rather than empowering them to act.[105] This approach is sensible, particularly because the United Kingdom could not, as a practical matter, have issued regulations to transpose the ELD which also re-drafted and superseded provisions of the Water Resources Act 1991, the Environmental Protection Act 1990 and other environmental legislation and thus rewrote many years of existing environmental law. If Defra had taken that approach, businesses would have been kept in limbo regarding the imposition and extent of liability for their activities under existing environmental law whilst Defra drafted the regulations. The overlap is bound to lead to complications, however. For example, the ELD, sections 161 to 161D of the Water Resources Act and Part 2A of the Environmental Protection Act 1990 will inevitably all apply to some of the same incidents of environmental damage.

Exclusions

5–028 The ELD excludes liability for specified instances of environmental damage. The exclusions apply to:

- acts of war, including terrorism;
- acts of God, described by the ELD as "a natural phenomenon of exceptional, inevitable and irresistible character";

[103] ELD, art.17.
[104] Consultation, para.51.
[105] ibid., para.55.

- liability or compensation falling under specified marine and nuclear conventions and the convention on civil liability for damage during carriage of dangerous goods by road, rail and inland navigation vessels;
- diffuse pollution when it is not possible to establish a causal link between individual operators and the environmental damage;
- activities, the main purpose of which is to serve national defence or international security; and
- activities, the sole purpose of which is to protect from natural disasters.[106]

Defences to liability

The ELD establishes various "defences" to the financial liability of an **5–029** operator for the costs of remediating and restoring environmental damage. There are two mandatory defences—in the sense that Member States must adopt them—and two optional defences.

Mandatory defences

An operator has a defence in respect of an imminent threat of, or actual, **5–030** environmental damage if the operator shows that the damage:

- was caused by a third party and occurred despite appropriate safety measures having been in place; or
- results from the operator's compliance with a compulsory order or instruction by a public authority provided that the order or instruction is not in relation to an emission or incident caused by the operator's own activities.[107]

The ELD provides that "[i]n such cases, Member States shall take the appropriate measures to enable the operator to recover the costs incurred".

Establishing the second defence should be straightforward, so long as an operator can show that the environmental damage was, indeed, caused by its compliance with a public authority's mandatory order or instruction. In such cases, it is unlikely that a competent authority would require an operator to remediate the environmental damage instead of the authority.

The first defence could, however, lead to problems. The ELD strongly implies that an operator whose activity causes the damage due to the actions of a third party must carry out appropriate remedial measures and then seek to recover its costs from the third party. Not only does the ELD require Member States to take appropriate measures to enable an operator

---

[106] ELD, art.4.
[107] ibid., art.8(3).

to recover its costs but the word "taken" in the phrase "[a]n operator shall not be required to bear the cost of preventive or remedial actions *taken* pursuant to [the ELD] if he can prove that the environmental damage or imminent threat of such damage . . . was caused by a third party" is in the past tense. The ELD thus implies that the operator must have carried out the requisite measures before it can seek to recover its costs. It also implies that the operator can seek to recover its costs only from the third party and not from the competent authority.

5–031   If the above reading of the ELD is correct, an operator would be liable to remediate environmental damage at its own cost, even though the damage was due to, say, a vandal opening a valve and letting oil leak from a storage tank into a river, thereby causing substantial damage to a protected natural habitat through which the river flows. This result would be the same under the Water Resources Act 1991. For example, in the *Empress Car Company* case, the owner of the storage tank that leaked oil into a river, after having been vandalised, could not escape liability under the 1991 Act for any remedial actions requested or required by the National Rivers Authority.[108]

Defra has, however, classified the defence as a defence against the operator's liability and has included it in the grounds of an appeal to a notification that the authority intends to serve a remediation notice on the operator.[109] Arguably, Defra has failed to follow its approach of not diminishing the protection offered by existing environmental law[110] in making such a classification. For example, if the operator's defence succeeds, the damage may not be remediated because neither the operator nor the vandal would remediate it and the competent authority has no duty to do so.

The defence may lead to further problems because the operator must show that its safety measures were "appropriate". This could be read to require the operator to show that it took all reasonable precautions, and that, even though these were in place, the environmental damage occurred through, and only through, the actions of the third party.

Optional defences

5–032   The optional defences provide an operator with a defence if the operator proves that it was not negligent and that the environmental damage was caused by:

---

[108] *Empress Car Company (Abertillery) Ltd v National Rivers Authority* [1999] 2 A.C. 22, [1998] 2 W.L.R. 350, [1998] 1 All E.R. 481 (HL).
[109] Draft Regulations, reg.14(4)(g).
[110] Consultation, para.51.

- an emission or event that is expressly authorised by, and fully in accordance with, the conditions of a permit that was issued under domestic law implementing legislation listed in Annex III; or
- an emission or activity which is demonstrated by the operator as not considered likely to cause environmental damage according to the state of scientific and technical knowledge at the time that the emission was released or the activity took place.[111]

These so-called permit and state-of-the-art defences apply only to remedial, not preventive, actions.

The United Kingdom has proposed including the defences in its transposition of the ELD. The Draft Regulations list both as grounds of appeal to a notification by a competent authority that it intends to serve a remediation notice.[112] The Draft Regulations apply the grounds of appeal only to remedial measures, however, and not to emergency remedial actions. Their scope is thus limited. For example, assume that an operator is not required to carry out remedial measures due to operation of either defence. Assume further that the competent authority does not carry out the remedial measures at the expense of the public purse. In such a case, the operator could, depending on the circumstances, be under a duty to carry out emergency remedial actions to prevent further environmental damage in perpetuity.

In respect of the permit defence, the Draft Regulations do not include activities under all EU legislation listed in Annex III. Defra has stated that this is because permits do not exist for: the transboundary shipment of waste; the transport of dangerous or polluting goods by road, rail, inland waterways, sea or air; or the manufacture, use, storage, processing, filling, release into the environment and on-site transport of dangerous substances and preparations (unless permitted under other Annex III legislation).[113]

Competent authorities

The ELD directs Member States to designate competent authorities to implement and enforce it.[114] The Draft Regulations designate the following competent authorities: **5–033**

- Environment Agency: damage to water; damage to sites for which the Agency has granted a permit; damage to protected species and natural habitats, including all SSSIs for environmental damage to water but not to the sea;

---

[111] ELD, art.8(4).
[112] Draft Regulations, reg.14(4)(d), (e). Schedule 3 of the Draft Regulations list the permits to which the permit defence applies.
[113] Consultation, para.120.
[114] ELD, art.11(1).

259

- Natural England: damage to protected species and natural habitats on land; damage to other flora and fauna on a SSSI;
- local authorities: damage to land; and
- the Secretary of State: damage at the continental shelf or in the sea up to the limit of the renewable energy zone.[115]

Due to the overlap in duties, more than one competent authority may have responsibilities at some sites.

Competent authorities have various duties under the ELD. If an operator fails to carry out preventive measures, emergency remedial actions or remedial measures, the competent authority has a duty to order the operator to carry them out.[116] An operator has a duty to identify and submit potential remedial measures to the competent authority.[117] The authority, not the operator, is however responsible for assessing the significance of the damage that has been caused and determining the remedial measures that should be carried out. In doing so, the authority should invite NGOs and other relevant persons as well as the owner of the land on which the remediation is being carried out to submit comments and should take any such comments into account.[118] If the competent authority serves an order on an operator to carry out remedial measures, the order should set out the precise grounds on which the authority has based its decision, the time limits for carrying out the specified remedies and the remedies available to the operator.[119]

Competent authorities' duties are supplemented by the following powers:

- to issue information orders[120] on an operator whose activity has caused actual, or an imminent threat of, environmental damage;
- to issue orders requiring the operator to carry out preventive measures, emergency remedial actions and remedial measures as instructed by the competent authority;
- to issue orders requiring the operator to assess environmental damage, including the provision of information and data necessary for such an assessment; and

---

[115] Draft Regulations, regs 9, 10. Defra intends the enforcing authority to be created under the Marine Bill to become the competent authority for damage to the marine area when that Bill becomes law. In the meantime, the Secretary of State acting through the Marine and Fisheries Agency will be the competent authority. Consultation, para.73.

[116] ELD, arts 5(3)(b), 6(2)(c).

[117] ibid., art.7(1).

[118] ibid., art.7(4); see ibid., art.12(1).

[119] ibid., arts 5(4), 6(1)(b), 7(2).

[120] An information order or notice is a written demand from a competent authority seeking specified information. For example, section 71 of the Environmental Protection Act 1990 authorises the Environment Agency to serve a notice that requires the recipient to provide specified information that the Agency "reasonably considers" is needed.

- to carry out necessary preventive and remedial measures itself, with the proviso that remedial measures should be carried out by competent authorities only "as a means of last resort".[121]

Costs

The ELD sets out the costs for which an operator may be liable. It does so   **5–034** by defining the word "costs" broadly to mean:

> "costs which are justified by the need to ensure the proper and effective implementation of this Directive including the costs of assessing environmental damage, an imminent threat of such damage, alternatives for action as well as the administrative, legal, and enforcement costs, the costs of data collection and other general costs, monitoring and supervision costs".[122]

Member States may calculate administrative, legal, enforcement and other general costs sought for recovery by a competent authority by a flat rate.[123]

The above categories of costs are substantially larger than the costs traditionally sought by English regulatory authorities. For example, an authority that successfully prosecutes a person for an environmental or health and safety offence traditionally seeks to recover its investigatory and legal costs as well as other costs incurred in bringing the prosecution.[124] Most works to remediate contamination in the United Kingdom, however, are carried out in the absence of a prosecution. For example, most incidents of water pollution do not involve a prosecution by the Environment Agency. Instead, they involve the Agency, acting under authority of sections 161 to 161D of the Water Resources Act 1991, requesting the person who caused or knowingly permitted a pollutant to enter ground or surface water, or to be seeping through the soil towards groundwater, to clean up the pollution. The Agency may serve a works notice in such cases but there is rarely a need for it to do so because polluters generally remediate the pollution following the Agency's request to do so. The remedial works are, therefore, generally completed in the absence of any formal proceedings.

In contrast to the above actions under the Water Resources Act 1991, a competent authority is authorised by the ELD to charge costs that it incurs in requesting or requiring an operator who causes environmental damage to remediate the pollution. There is no need for a link with a criminal

---

[121] ELD, arts 5(3), (4), 6(2), (3).
[122] ibid., art.2(16).
[123] ibid., recital 19.
[124] See *R v Associated Octel Ltd (Costs)* [1997] 1 Cr.App.R.(S.) Crim.L.R. 144 (CA) (prosecuting authority may recover investigatory costs; Environment Agency, Enforcement and Prosecution Policy para.27 (Agency "will always seek to recover the costs of investigation and Court proceedings")).

offence or a formal civil administrative or judicial proceeding before the competent authority may seek to recover such costs.

Further, although an enforcing authority may recover its "reasonable costs" for carrying out emergency remedial works under Part 2A of the Environmental Protection Act 1990,[125] neither Part 2A nor the guidance provides the enforcing authority with the power to recover its monitoring, supervision and general costs.

Cost recovery actions by competent authorities

5–035   If a competent authority carries out preventive or remedial actions, it may bring a cost-recovery action against the responsible operator or operators. The ELD imposes a limitation period of five years from the date that the authority completes the measures for which it is seeking costs or has identified the liable operator or third party, whichever is later.[126]

Charging notices

5–036   A competent authority that has carried out preventive or remedial actions may also place a charge on property or seek other appropriate guarantees in order to recover its costs from the responsible operator.[127] Professor Bocken has commented that such actions will not assist a competent authority if the operator has insufficient funds to reimburse the authority. He further comments that the only way to ensure that an operator has sufficient funds is to require the operator to have a dedicated source of funding prior to the imminent threat of, or actual, environmental damage.[128]

Liability for bodily injury and property damage

5–037   The ELD does not impose liability for personal injury, damage to private property or economic loss. Neither does it affect any rights regarding such damages.[129] The absence of such liability follows the change in the nature of the proposed ELD in the working paper, issued in 2001, from a civil law to a public law regime. The ELD provides that a Member State may adopt appropriate measures to ensure that there is not a double recovery of costs in a situation when a competent authority acts under the ELD and a

---

[125] Environmental Protection Act 1990, s.78P(1); Defra Circular 01/2006, Annex 2, paras 11.8, 13.7; see Chapter 16.

[126] ELD, art.10.

[127] ibid., art.8(2).

[128] H. Bocken, *Financial Guarantees in the Environmental Liability Directive: Next Time Better*, European Env. Liability Rev. 13–32 (January 2006).

[129] ELD, recital 14.

private person whose property is affected by environmental damage also brings an action.[130]

An operator who causes environmental damage to a privately-owned natural habitat will thus be liable for compensatory damages for property damage suffered by the owner as well as the costs of remediating the damage together, as appropriate, with compensatory and complementary remediation costs. The extent of the compensatory damages will depend on the domestic law of Member States. In England, the owner could bring a claim for private nuisance and, perhaps, trespass to include the loss of use of the natural habitat during its remediation. An action could be quite complex because it could include negotiating an access agreement together with, presumably, payment for access.

The absence of statutory provisions authorising persons to bring actions for personal injury or property damage in legislation that establishes a regime for remediating contaminated land is the norm in common law jurisdictions such as England and Wales, where such actions traditionally lie under the common law rather than statutory law.[131] The situation differs in continental Europe due to civil liability for environmental damage being imposed by Code law rather than common law.

Non-governmental organisations

The ELD specifically authorises natural and legal persons, including qualifying NGOs, to submit comments to a competent authority, if they consider that environmental damage has occurred and to request the authority to take action in respect of the damage. The comments must be accompanied by information and data to support them.[132] If the competent authority considers that it is plausible that environmental damage has occurred, it provides the operator with an opportunity to comment on the request for action and the submitted comments.[133] The competent authority must notify the person who submitted comments "as soon as

5–038

---

[130] ibid., art.16(2).

[131] There are, for example, no such provisions in Part 2A of the Environmental Protection Act 1990 or the Water Resources Act 1991. Indeed, s.100 of the latter specifically bars such a cause of action. The English law provisions that authorise such actions in respect of environmental damage are: s.73(6) of the Environmental Protection Act 1990 (cause of action by person who suffers "damage" caused by unlawfully deposited waste"); s.153(1) of the Merchant Shipping Act 1995 (cause of action for "damage ... by contamination resulting from the discharge or escape" of "oil" from tanker in territory of United Kingdom); and s.12 of the Nuclear Installations Act 1965 (cause of action for compensation if claimant has suffered injury or "damage to any property" from radioactive, toxic, explosive or hazardous characteristics of nuclear matter at nuclear installation or from any ionising radiation that is emitted from anything at installation or from any waste discharged on or from it).

[132] ELD, art.12.

[133] ibid., art.12(3).

possible" of its decision whether to agree with, or refuse, the request. The authority's decision must be accompanied by the reasons for it.[134]

If the competent authority refuses the request, the person submitting the comments may request a court or other independent and impartial public body "to review the procedural and substantive legality of the [competent authority's] decisions, acts or failure to act".[135] The person submitting comments may be required by a Member State's domestic law to exhaust administrative review procedures before instituting judicial proceedings.[136]

The ELD sets out the qualifications of a person who may submit comments. The person must:

- be, or be likely to be, affected by the environmental damage; or
- have a "sufficient interest" in environmental decision making relating to the damage; or
- allege that there has been an "impairment of a right", if a Member State's administrative procedural law requires such impairment to be a precondition to submitting comments.[137]

A Member State may, at its option, decide not to authorise comments in the case of an imminent threat of environmental damage.[138] The Draft Regulations authorise comments in such a case.[139]

Cross-border environmental damage

5–039　The ELD provides that Member States shall co-operate if environmental damage affects or is likely to affect more than one Member State. The co-operation is to include the appropriate exchange of information in order to ensure that preventive and remedial actions are taken.[140] The Member State in which the damage originates shall provide sufficient information to any Member States that are potentially affected by the damage.[141] Conversely, if a Member State discovers environmental damage within its jurisdiction which originates from outside the Member State, it may report the damage to the European Commission and any other relevant Member State and recommend preventive or remedial measures. The Member State may seek recovery of any costs incurred in carrying out the preventive or remedial measures.[142]

---

[134] ibid., art.12(4).
[135] ibid., art.13(1).
[136] ibid., art.13(2).
[137] ibid., art.12(1). The ELD states that Member States shall determine what constitutes a "sufficient interest" and an "impairment of a right".
[138] ibid., art.12(5).
[139] Draft Regulations, reg.18(1); Consultation, para.30.
[140] ELD, art.15(1).
[141] ibid., art.15(2).
[142] ibid., art.15(3).

Financial security requirements

The ELD does not contain any financial security requirements, that is, any   5–040
requirements for an operator to provide evidence to a competent authority
that it has sufficient assets to pay the cost of preventive or remedial measures if its occupational activity results in an imminent threat of, or actual,
environmental damage. As noted earlier in this chapter, the issue of
mandatory financial security was one of the most contentious issues in the
passage of the ELD and, as a compromise, the European Parliament and
the Council agreed to direct Member States to "encourage" the development of financial security instruments and markets in order to enable
operators to protect themselves from liabilities under the ELD. The
instruments were to include financial mechanisms in case an operator
became insolvent.

In addition, the ELD directed the European Commission to submit a
report on the availability of affordable financial security instruments,
including insurance, for the activities covered by Annex III legislation. The
Commission's report is required to consider the following aspects of
financial security: a gradual approach to its introduction; a ceiling for the
limit of the financial security instrument; and the exclusion of low-risk
activities. If the Commission decides that it is appropriate in light of the
report and an extended impact assessment including a cost-benefit analysis, it must submit proposals for a system of harmonised mandatory
financial security. The deadline for the Commission's report is April 30,
2010.[143]

This deadline, which results from a compromise between the European
Parliament and the Council, is however too early to enable the Commission to determine whether to introduce mandatory financial security. Many
Member States missed the deadline of April 30, 2007, for transposing the
ELD. Even those that met the deadline have little history of incidents of
environmental damage under it. It seems likely, therefore, that the Commission will not be able to determine whether to propose a system of
harmonised mandatory financial security before it submits its second—and
more wide-ranging—report in April 30, 2014.[144]

Reports

In addition to the report on financial security, the ELD directed the   5–041
European Commission to prepare reports on the exclusion of liability for
pollution covered by marine and nuclear conventions, application of the
ELD to protected species and natural habitats; and application of the ELD
to environmental damage caused by genetically modified organisms together with the results of any incidents of environmental damage caused by

---

[143] ibid., art.14.
[144] ibid., art.18.

such organisms. The reports are to be prepared, in part, from reports to be submitted on the same topics by Member States to the Commission by April 30, 2013.[145]

More stringent measures

5–042 A Member State may maintain or adopt more stringent provisions than those set out in the ELD. In particular, a Member State may identify additional activities that are subject to the prevention and remediation requirements as well as additional responsible persons.[146]

[145] ibid.
[146] ibid., art.16.

Chapter 6

PUBLIC ACCOUNTABILITY: PUBLIC LAW, PUBLIC PARTICIPATION AND ACCESS TO INFORMATION

INTRODUCTION

In 1992 the United Nations Conference on Environment and Develop- 6–001
ment met in Rio de Janeiro at what has become known as the "Rio Earth
Summit": the Rio Declaration was the result. Principle 10 of that
Declaration reads:

"Principle 10

Environmental issues are best handled with participation of all concerned citizens, at the relevant level. At the national level, each individual shall have appropriate access to information concerning the
environment that is held by public authorities, including information
on hazardous materials and activities in their communities, and
the opportunity to participate in decision-making processes. States
shall facilitate and encourage public awareness and participation by
making information widely available. Effective access to judicial and
administrative proceedings, including redress and remedy, shall be
provided."

The principle outlines four means by which public participation in the
handling of environmental issues should be secured:

   (i) **Access to information** held by public authorities;
  (ii) **Participation** in decision-making processes;
 (iii) The **dissemination** of environmental information;
 (iv) Access to **judicial and administrative** proceedings.

This chapter deals with each of these matters.

It addresses, first, the administrative and judicial means by which the
public are able to monitor and challenge environmental decision-making in
the UK. The section begins with a general rehearsal of public law principles, including an examination of the practice and procedure of judicial

267

review together with the grounds and remedies available.[1] It draws examples and illustrations from the environmental law field where appropriate. This section also examines the case law and practice surrounding the participation by the public in environmental decision-making by means of public consultation.

The remainder of the chapter addresses access to environmental information, which has an indispensable role in enabling and informing the processes of challenge and consultation.

Aarhus Convention

6–002　On June 25, 1998, the Aarhus Convention on Access to Information, Public Participation in Decision-Making and Access to Justice in Environmental Matters ("the Aarhus Convention") was adopted by the United Nations Economic Commission for Europe (UNECE). The EC and the UK were early signatories, although neither ratified the treaty until 2005. It has three main strands: access to environmental information, public participation in environmental decision-making, and access to justice. The Convention's influence on environmental law at the European and domestic level has been felt in several areas and the European Union has adopted directives in relation to the first two of these strands. This influence will be discussed in the body of this chapter.

Detailed guidance on each Article of the Convention is given in the Aarhus Implementation Guide published by the UNECE and the Regional Environmental Centre and may be useful when seeking to interpret the European and domestic law intended to implement it.[1A]

PUBLIC LAW AND PUBLIC PARTICIPATION

General Principles of Public Law

6–003　Public law principles have been, and remain, key to the developments in environmental public law. Their relevance also lies in their applicability to all decision-makers acting in a public, or quasi-judicial, capacity. It is

---

[1] For further reading on Judicial review see *De Smith's Judicial Review*, 6th edition (Sweet & Maxwell, 2008), and Michael Fordham *Judicial Review Handbook*, 4th edition (Hart Publishing, 2004).

[1A] The Aarhus Convention: An Implementation Guide ECE/CEP/72, accessible at *http://www.unece.org/env/pp/acig.htm*. The UNECE also maintains a portal to a comprehensive and regularly updated range of material (arranged by resource type, topic, source and region) relating to the Aarhus Convention and its implementation at *http://aarhus clearinghouse.unece.org/resources.cfm*.

therefore useful to outline the fundamental principles that underscore much of this area of law.[2]

Rule of law

The principle of the rule of law[3] requires that all actions taken by public bodies be subject to the law. The principle is aimed at ensuring that the State operates within legal boundaries, and seeks to prevent State power being exercised in an arbitrary, oppressive or abusive manner.[4] As such, it "enforces minimum standards of [procedural and substantive] fairness".[5]

In order to ensure that the State adheres to the rule of law, the Courts are charged with acting in an independent supervisory capacity. Judicial independence stems from the separation of powers between the courts and the executive, and is an important check on legislative authority.

6–004

Legislative sovereignty

Notwithstanding the rule of law, Parliament is entitled to legislate as it chooses.[6] By standard legislative procedure it may revoke or amend (expressly or by necessary implication) any statute, even those containing fundamental rights such as the Human Rights Act 1998.[7] However, there is a judicial presumption that Parliament legislates in accordance with the rule of law.[8] In other words, legislation is to be regarded as lawful until the contrary is shown. Without this presumption, individuals could not act in reliance of any legislative instrument.

The courts may, though, declare that legislation is incompatible with the European Convention of Human Rights, which has been incorporated into domestic law by the Human Rights Act. However, there is no obligation on Parliament to amend the offending legislation, though this often follows

6–005

---

[2] For further analysis and case law see Michael Fordham *Judicial Review Handbook*, 4th edition, (Hart Publishing, 2004), Part 7, and Wade and Forsyth, *Administrative Law*, 9th edition, (Oxford University Press, 2004), Chapter 2.

[3] The rule of law was recently acknowledged within statute: see section 1 Constitutional Reform Act 2005.

[4] *A v Secretary of State for the Home Department* [2004] EWCA Civ 1123 August 11, 2004, unreported, at [248], cited by Fordham at Pt 12, op cit at 12.1.14.

[5] *R v Home Secretary ex p. Pierson* [1998] AC 539 at 591, per Lord Steyn.

[6] "[B]oth the courts and the executive will treat the authority of Parliament, duly exercised, as absolute. Another aspect, upon which both democratic governance and the rule of law depend, is that the courts will respect all acts of the executive within its lawful province, and that the executive will respect all decisions of the courts as to what its lawful province is". *M v Home Office* [1992] Q.B. 270, 314, per Nolan L.J., cited in Bradley & Ewing, *Constitutional and Administrative Law*, 14th ed (2006), p 90. *R (Bancoult) v Secretary of State for Foreign and Commonwealth Affairs* [2007] EWCA 498 per Sedley L.J. at [35].

[7] This is in contrast to countries with Constitutions which can only be amended in strictly limited circumstances or through the adoption of special legislative procedures: Wade and Forsyth, op cit, p.27.

[8] *R v Home Secretary ex p. Pierson* [1998] A.C. 539 at 591, per Lord Steyn.

such a declaration. The approach to directly effective Community Law is different, due to its supremacy over domestic law; the Courts (as noted under Illegality at paragraph 6–022 below, and discussed in Chapters 1 and 4[8A]) simply disapply domestic legislation in so far as it is inconsistent with Community law.

Principle of legality

6–006   Under this principle, the government can only exercise powers where there is legal authority to do so. Where certain actions would interfere with the ordinary rights of individuals, the government must be able to justify that interference with reference to law. As such, the government remains answerable for its actions before the courts.

One aspect of the principle ensures that statutory powers are subject to fundamental rights, unless there are clear indications to the contrary. This latter point was summarised by Lightman J. as meaning:

> "[I]n the absence of express words or necessary implications to the contrary, even the most general words in an Act of Parliament and in subordinate legislation must be presumed to be intended to be subject to the basic rights of the individual, and accordingly ... regulations expressed in general language are presumed to be subject to fundamental rights, a presumption which enables them to be valid."[9]

The courts are therefore called upon to interpret the legislation in accordance with the fundamental rights where possible.

Access to justice

6–007   Access to justice is a fundamental right recognised by the common law legal system.[10] As highlighted in the Aarhus Convention, this right is also considered to be a key principle of international environmental law. Further, it is now also embodied in EU law.[11]

Given the importance of the principle of access to justice, the way in which it is secured in practice is of paramount importance, in particular in relation to such issues as legal standing and funding. While the right is crucial, it is not absolute or unlimited.[12] To what extent, therefore should a person, association, or interest group be allowed to institute judicial review proceedings? Should funding be provided even where the impecunious

---

[8A] See paras 1–029ff and 4–059ff.

[9] *R v Governor of Frankland Prison ex p Russell* [2000] 1 W.L.R. 2027 at para.11.

[10] *R v Secretary of State for the Home Department, ex parte Anufrijeva* [2003] UKHL 36, (2004) 1 AC 604: (2003) 3 W.L.R. 252: (2003) 3 All E.R. 827 per Lord Steyn at para.26.

[11] art.10A of the Directive 85/337/EEC on the assessment of the effects of certain public and private projects on the environment, as amended by Directives 97/11/EC and 2003/35/EC; art.15A of Directive 96/61/EC concerning integrated pollution prevention and control.

[12] *R v Legal Aid Board, ex parte Duncan* [2000] COD 159, at para.456.

person fronting the claim is supported by people with means? These questions are discussed further below.[13]

Basic fairness (natural justice)

Basic fairness, also known as natural justice, does not easily lend itself to definition. It was once described as "fair play in action",[14] and is usually associated with procedural fairness. It includes such rights as a fair hearing and the expectation that public bodies will perform their "functions fairly and honestly and to the best of their ability".[15]   **6–008**

Principle of equality

It is a "cardinal principle of good administration that all persons in a similar position should be treated similarly".[16] A decision-making body should not treat persons differently unless there are good, justifiable reasons for so doing.[17] This is particularly relevant where a precedent has been set, such as in planning applications.[18]   **6–009**

The Relevant Rules

Judicial review is the procedure by which courts determine whether a public body has acted in accordance with law and public law principles. Judicial review proceedings are defined in Part 54(1)(2)(a) of the Civil Procedure Rules ("CPR") as "a claim to review the lawfulness of an enactment; or a decision, action or failure to act in relation to the exercise of a public function." As this definition indicates, the proceedings are not a review of the merits of the decision but of the decision-making process: the court will scrutinise the public body's powers, the procedures it is required to follow, and the factors it took into account when acting or failing to act. However, the court will not interfere with a decision unless the decision-maker has breached the law or public law principles in carrying out its functions.   **6–010**

Judicial review proceedings can only be brought against public bodies

---

[13] See paras 6–051ff on standing and 6–075ff on costs and funding.
[14] *Wiseman v Borneman* [1971] AC 297, per Lord Morris at para.309B.
[15] *Bushell v Secretary of State for the Environment* [1981] AC 75, per Lord Diplock at p.95B.
[16] *R v Hertfordshire CC ex parte Cheung*, The Times, April 4, 1986.
[17] *R (on the application of Munjaz) v Mersey Health Care NHS Trust et al* [2006] 2 AC 148: [2005] 3 W.L.R. 793.
[18] See *North Wiltshire DC v Secretary of State for the Environment* [1992] JPL 955, CA, referred to below under "Irrationality (unreasonableness): Breach of public law principles" para.6–032.

that are exercising public functions. A public body is generally identifiable by the fact that its powers or duties are derived from statute or the royal prerogative.[19] Typical "public bodies" will therefore include government departments and local authorities. However, the definition is not restrictive: as long as there is a sufficient "public element"[20] to the powers, then the body is amenable to review.[21] Examples falling into this latter category include the Environment Agency and Natural England, the nature conservation body.

In determining whether an enactment, decision, action or failure to act falls within the remit of "the exercise of a public function", the courts have taken a liberal approach. Where the matter has the potential to impact upon a person's rights or interests, then it will be vulnerable to judicial review. Consequently, the courts have not limited themselves to the review of acts done under specific statutory powers and duties, but have held, for example, that non-statutory recommendations, guidance notes and consultation processes are open to judicial review where they have a (potentially) prejudicial effect on individuals.[22]

6–011   An applicant will only be able to bring judicial review proceedings if they can demonstrate that they have "standing".[23] Under section 31(3) of the Supreme Court Act 1981 the court will not grant permission to proceed to a substantive hearing unless the applicant can show that they have "sufficient interest" in the matter.[24] However, the threshold for standing has been lowered over the past few decades, such that applicants are not required to have a personal stake in the outcome provided that the matter is of public importance and they are not motivated by any ill will.

Generally an applicant challenges a public body on the basis that it has acted irrationally, illegally or in a manner that was procedurally unfair.[25] These grounds are not mutually exclusive or finite, but they have stood the test of time and encapsulate broadly the grounds for most judicial review challenges.

---

[19] A body whose authority is derived from the prerogative is one whose powers are endowed by the Crown, albeit that the powers are exercised by her ministers. See AV Dicey, *Introduction to the Study of the Law of the Constitution* (8th Ed.) 1915, p.421.

[20] *R v Panel on Take-overs and Mergers, ex parte Datafin Plc* [1987] Q.B. 815, at 838E per Sir John Donaldson M.R.

[21] CPR 54.1.2.

[22] See, for example, *R v Secretary of State for the Environment, ex parte. Lancashire County Council* [1994] 4 All E.R. 165 and *R (on the application of Greenpeace) v Secretary of State for Trade and Industry* [2007] EWHC 311 (Admin), (2007) Env. L.R. 29: see below, "Grounds of review" at 6–026 for further discussion.

[23] See further below at para.6–051ff.

[24] Judicial review proceedings comprise two stages: a claimant must first seek permission to bring a judicial review claim, and only when permission has been granted will the "substantive" judicial review claim be heard.

[25] *Council of Civil Service Unions v Minister for the Civil Service* [1985] A.C. 374. See below "Grounds of Review" paras 6–020ff for further discussion

Judicial review is a remedy of last resort. An applicant is therefore usually required to exhaust all alternative remedies before applying to the court for relief.[26] This is of substantial importance in environmental proceedings, as many statutes in this area contain appeal procedures or deal with matters of complexity that are more suited to a hearing before a specialist tribunal.[27] In *R v Falmouth and Truro Port Health Authority, ex parte South West Water*[28] the Court of Appeal held that permission to apply for judicial review had been inappropriately granted in relation to a complex issue in the case because the appellant had failed to exhaust the statutory right of appeal to the Magistrates' Court. Simon Brown L.J. noted that:

> "If the applicant has a statutory right of appeal, permission should only exceptionally be given; rarer still will permission be appropriate in a case concerning public safety. The judge should, however, have regard to all relevant circumstances which typically will include, besides any public health consideration, the comparative speed, expense and finality of the alternative processes, the need and scope for fact finding, the desirability of an authoritative ruling on any point of law arising, and (perhaps) the apparent strength of the applicant's substantive challenge."[29]

As indicated by Simon Brown L.J., where there is a discrete point of law **6–012** and limited dispute on issues of evidence, judicial review proceedings may exceptionally be appropriate to resolve the matter, even though an alternative right of appeal may exist. This arose in *Falmouth* where there was a discrete issue of statutory construction which the Court said was appropriate for resolution by judicial review. In *R (on the application of Anti-Waste Ltd) v Environment Agency*,[30] by way of further example, the parties sought declarations from the court on two specific legal issues so that the statutory appeal before a specialist tribunal could be heard in the light of the court's decision.[31]

Procedure under CPR 54

The judicial review procedure is regulated by CPR Part 54, its accom- **6–013** panying Practice Direction and the Pre-Action Protocol.[32] A separate procedure exists where the matter is urgent.[33] The Administrative Court

[26] para.2, Pre-Action Protocol; *R v Secretary of State for the Home Department, ex p Capti-Mehmet* [1997] COD 61.
[27] See, for example, s.80(3) of the Environmental Protection Act 1990 and the Statutory Nuisance (Appeals) Regulations 1995/2644 as amended by the Statutory Nuisance (Appeals)(Amendment) (England) Regulations 2006/771.
[28] (2001) Q.B. 445, (2000) 3 W.L.R. 1464.
[29] (2001) Q.B. 445; at 473D.
[30] (2008) Env. L.R. 18; (2007) NPC 135; (2008) 1 W.L.R. 923.
[31] See para.4.
[32] The CPR Judicial Review Pre-Action Protocol (PAP), March 4, 2002. See M. Fordham, *Judicial Review Handbook*, p.1.5.
[33] See below at 6–018.

Office also produces Notes for Guidance which provide explanations of each stage of the process.[34]

Time limit

6-014   A claim must be lodged promptly and in any event not later than three months after the grounds to make the claim first arose.[35] The courts are strict in relation to this time limit, and may dismiss a claim if it has not been made "promptly" even if it is lodged within three months. However, the courts have a discretion to extend time under CPR Part 3.1(2)(a) where there are very good grounds for doing so, such as where the matter is of public importance[36] or the claimant has reasonably tried to resolve the matter by means other than litigation.[37]

Pre-action protocol

6-015   Where there is sufficient time, the pre-action protocol (PAP) should be followed.[38] Before applying for permission, the applicant sends a letter before claim which identifies the decision, act or omission which is being challenged. It should also provide a summary of the facts on which the claim is based and identify any interested parties. The defendant is given 14 days to respond. Both the applicant and defendant are required to send their protocol letters to the interested parties identified by the applicant.[39] An interested party is "any person (other than the claimant or defendant) who is directly affected by the outcome of the claim";[40] this typically includes developers where the grant of planning permission is challenged. Standard pro forma protocol letters are appended to the protocol.

The protocol does not affect the time limit for judicial review proceedings. Should there be insufficient time to comply with the protocol, the applicant should file and serve the claim form with an explanation of their inability to comply with the protocol.

Where, following the pre-action protocol letter, the matter remains contested, the applicant files the claim form with the Administrative Court

---

[34] Available via *http://www.hmcourts-service.gov.uk/cms/1220.htm.*
[35] CPR 54.5(1). See section on "delay" below at paras 6–057 to 6–064 for further discussion on time limits.
[36] *R v Secretary of State for Trade and Industry ex p Greenpeace* [2000] Env. L.R. 221.
[37] *R v Oxford City Council ex parte Young* [2002] EWCA Civ 990; see "Delay: Good reason for extension of time" below at paras 6–060 to 6–064.
[38] It does not apply when the defendant (for example a statutory tribunal) does not have the power to change the decision under challenge: para.6 of the PAP.
[39] PAP paras 10–17.
[40] CPR 54.1(2)(f). For example, where a claimant challenges a local authority's decision to grant planning permission or a permit, the group or individual who applied for permission or the permit should be joined as the Interested Party.

Office. The claim form must then be served on the defendant and interested parties within seven days after the date of issue.[41] Any party served with a claim form who wishes to take part in proceedings must file an acknowledgment of service on the relevant practice form.[42] This should set out a summary of the grounds for contesting the claim. The acknowledgment must be filed within 21 days after service of the claim form: a person who fails to file in time may not take part in the hearing without the court's permission.[43]

Judicial review procedure

The judicial review procedure is made up of two separate stages. First, a **6–016** claimant must obtain permission to apply for judicial review.[44] In order to gain permission, the claimant has to demonstrate that he or she has standing and that there is an arguable case for seeking judicial review. The "arguable case" threshold is not high, and the permission stage is aimed principally at eradicating vexatious or fruitless claims.[44A] Whilst there is no statutory test for unarguability, it is in practice similar to that governing applications for summary judgment in other types of claim, namely that there is "no real prospect of succeeding on the claim or issue."[45] Permission is usually determined initially on the papers. If it is refused, the claimant may request an oral hearing.

Once permission is granted, the claim proceeds to the second stage, namely consideration of the judicial review claim. While this may be done on the papers if all parties agree, it normally takes the form of a full ("substantive") hearing. In some instances both stages (the permission and the substantive case) are heard together, known as a "rolled-up" hearing. This often happens where the matter requires an urgent decision, or where the case is so complex that permission cannot be granted without hearing detailed submissions.[46]

Where the claimant alleges that the challenged act, omission or decision is currently causing, or may cause, irreversible harm, the claimant can apply for an interim injunction restraining, or requiring, further activity

---

[41] CPR 54.7.
[42] CPR 54.8.
[43] CPR 54.9.
[44] CPR 54.4.
[44A] See, for example, *R (Baker) v Environment Agency* [2008] EWHC 2404 (Admin) where permission to apply for judicial review was refused on the grounds that there was "no basis" on which it was arguable that the EA had acted irrationally in accepting risk assessments carried out by a third party (albeit on the instructions of the interested party) instead of undertaking its own assessments: para.8 per Burnett J.
[45] *De Smith's Judicial Review*, 6th edition (Sweet & Maxwell, 2007) para.16–047 referring to the provisions of CPR 24.2.
[46] See, for example, *R v Secretary of State for Trade and Industry and others, ex parte Greenpeace Ltd* (2000) Env. L.R. 221.

until the substantive hearing is held. In those circumstances the court will generally order that a cross-undertaking in damages be made to the defendant should the claim be successfully resisted.[47] Should the court find in favour of the applicant, it can grant a declaration, injunction, orders of various kinds (such as mandatory, prohibitory or quashing orders) and/or damages.[48]

Interveners

6–017 Any person may apply for permission to "intervene", namely to file evidence or to make oral or written representations at the substantive hearing.[49] This is particularly important for groups that have an interest in the matter, such as lobby groups or non-governmental organisations (NGOs), but who are not "interested parties" and would not therefore be automatically entitled to participate in proceedings. This provision indirectly circumvents the hurdle of standing in some instances, and provides interest groups with an opportunity to add to the legal debate even though the formal legal issue may only arise between the original parties to the claim. Though there is no set time period, any application for permission to intervene should be made to the court promptly, namely at the earliest reasonable opportunity, so as not to delay the hearing.[50] Failure to intervene promptly risks the court deciding not to allow the intervention.

Cases of urgency

6–018 Where the matter is urgent because, for example, there is a need for an injunction, a separate set of rules known as the "Procedure for Urgent Applications"[51] (also known as the "Urgent Cases Procedure") is used instead of the pre-action protocol.[52] Under this Procedure the claimant is required to fill in form N463, indicating the need for urgency and the timescale requested for the consideration of the permission application. Where an interim injunction is requested (for instance, to stop development said to be in breach of an environmental provision), the claimant should also provide a draft order and the grounds for the injunction. The defendant and interested parties must be served with the claim form, the

---

[47] It has been doubted whether ordering a cross-undertaking of damages in environmental cases is in accordance with the Aarhus Convention: see further below at para.6–073.

[48] See further below at paras 6–065 to 6–071. Ultra vires acts per se do not give rise to damages; a claimant must establish that the defendant's acts or omissions amount to a tort or a breach of the Human Rights Act.

[49] CPR 54.17.

[50] CPR 54.17(2); CPR 54 Practice Direction 13(5).

[51] Practice Statement (Administrative Court: Annual Statement) 2001/2 [2002] 1 All E.R. 633, Annex B, per Scott-Baker J.

[52] PAP, para.6.

N463 form and, if relevant, the draft order and grounds for the injunction both by fax and post, informing them of the application and their right to make representations. The Administrative judge will then allocate the papers to the "Urgent Judge" who will seek to consider the application within the timescale requested by the Claimant. He may also order an oral hearing.

Application for injunction to prevent environmental harm

There are times when a local authority will wish to seek an injunction to prevent actual or apprehended harm to the environment, but the identity of the person regarded as the perpetrator is unknown. Under the Practice Direction ("PD") to Part 8 CPR, where an application for an injunction to prevent environmental harm is made under one of the listed legislative provisions,[53] the responsible authority may make the application even though the defendant's identity is not known.[54] However, in the claim form the applicant must describe the defendant by reference to a photograph, an item belonging to or in the possession of the defendant or some other evidence.[55] The description must be sufficiently clear to enable the defendant to be served with proceedings.[56] The court may, though, dispense with service or make an order permitting service by an alternative method.

6–019

Grounds of Review

The substantive grounds for seeking judicial review of a decision are generally referred to as falling within one or other of three broad categories, as outlined by Lord Diplock in *Council of Civil Service Unions v Minister for the Civil Service*[57] ("the *GCHQ* case"): illegality, irrationality and procedural impropriety. However, these grounds are not mutually exclusive, the boundaries between them are not always clear, and nothing ultimately turns on whether a successful argument falls within one category rather than another. As such, categorising the breach as irrational, illegal or procedurally unfair "is an important matter of legal taxonomy but not critical to the finding of legal fault."[58]

6–020

---

[53] s.187B or 214A Town and Country Planning Act 1990; s.44A Planning (Listed Buildings and Conservation Areas) Act 1990; s.26AA Planning (Hazardous Substances) Act 1990.

[54] CPR 8 PD20(1) and (2).

[55] CPR 8 PD20(4).

[56] Though not pertaining to CPR 8, for similar cases under CPR 19.6 see *Huntingdon Life Sciences Group plc et al v Stop Huntingdon Animal Cruelty* [2007] EWHC 522 (Q.B. and *RWE NPower plc et al v Carrol et al* [2007] EWHC 947 (Q.B.).

[57] [1985] AC 374. at 410D–411B.

[58] *R (Bancoult) v Secretary of State for Foreign and Commonwealth Affairs (No. 2)* [2007] 3 W.L.R. 768, per Sedley L.J. at para.61.

Illegality (unlawfulness)

6–021   Lord Diplock noted that:

> "By 'illegality' as a ground of judicial review I mean that the decision-maker must understand correctly the law that regulates his decision-making power and must give effect to it."[59]

The decision-maker must therefore act within the remit of the applicable legislation. In addition, he or she must only base decisions on relevant considerations and disregard any irrelevant matters.

Acting outside remit/legislative aims

6–022   A decision-maker who exceeds the remit of his or her authority acts unlawfully.[60] Were a planning authority, for example, to involve itself in the running of the local hospital, clearly it would be straying outside its remit and area of expertise. Further, where a person acts fraudulently or for improper gain, he or she is patently acting outside their remit.[61] However, these situations are rare: generally a person will be found to have acted unlawfully because he or she has breached mandatory rules or pursued aims other than those laid down by the legislation.

It is clear that when exercising their powers decision-makers must act not only in accordance with domestic law but also with EU principles. In so far as a rule of EU environmental law may be directly effective under EU law it should be regarded by the national court as taking precedence.[62] For example, in *R v Secretary of State for Trade and Industry, ex parte Greenpeace*[63] ["*Greenpeace* [2000]"] the government had granted offshore exploration licences for oil drilling within the UK Continental Shelf, but outside the 12 mile limit of the UK's territorial waters. In granting the licences, the Secretary of State had not had regard to the EU Habitats Directive[64] on the grounds that under the provisions of domestic legislation—which implemented the Habitats Directive—the Directive was not applicable outside the UK's territorial waters. The Claimant argued that

---

[59] *Council of Civil Service Unions v Minister for the Civil Service* [1985] AC 374 at 410D.

[60] *R (Bancoult) v Secretary of State for the Foreign and Commonwealth Affairs* [2001] Q.B. 1067, at para.54, upheld by the Court of Appeal in *R (Bancoult) v Secretary of State for Foreign and Commonwealth Affairs (No. 2)* [2007] 3 W.L.R. 768.

[61] See, for example, the Scottish case of *Lothian Borders & Angus Co-operative Society Ltd v Scottish Borders Council et al* Times, March 10, 1999, where the petitioner unsuccessfully contended that the grant of planning permission was unlawful because the respondent had a pecuniary interest in the outcome.

[62] For the concepts of "direct effect" and the primacy of EU law, see paras 1–029ff and 4–059ff.

[63] [2000] Env. L.R. 221.

[64] Council Directive 92/43/EEC on the conservation of natural habitats, implemented by the Conservation (Natural Habitats etc) Regulations 1994 SI 1994/2716.

the Directive extended to the UK Continental Shelf, and the Secretary of State's failure to carry out his licensing function in accordance with the Directive rendered the decision illegal. Maurice Kay J., upholding the claim, declared that the Directive applied to the entire UK Continental Shelf, and that the Secretary of State's failure to consider and apply the Habitats Directive rendered the decision to grant the licences unlawful.[65]

A decision-maker's omission to exercise a lawful power may be just as damning as acting entirely outside its remit. In *R(Barker) v Bromley London Borough Council*,[66] no environmental impact assessment (EIA) was carried out at the outline planning permission stage of a development proposal. After outline planning permission had been given, the developer submitted an application for the approval of reserved matters, namely a cinema and car park. Consequently, a number of councillors then requested an EIA; however, the council was advised that an assessment could only be carried out at the outline planning stage. The application was therefore approved. The claimant sought a declaration that the council's failure to seek an EIA at the reserved matters stage of the planning permission process was unlawful. Following a referral to the European Court of Justice,[67] the House of Lords held that where it becomes apparent after outline planning permission had been granted that an EIA is necessary, an assessment should be carried out at the reserved matters stage and before such consent is given. The court therefore held that the Council had misdirected itself in determining that it had no power to require an environmental impact assessment at that stage.

Attempting to avoid a legal obligation will also be unlawful. In *Leeds City Council v Spencer*,[68] the council had ordered Mr Spencer to remove rubbish from his property. When he failed to do so on the grounds that it was the council's duty to clear the rubbish, the council removed the rubbish and sought to recover its costs. Though successful at first instance, the claimants lost on appeal: the Court of Appeal held that the council had acted illegally in seeking to impose its statutory obligation to collect and remove rubbish on to Mr Spencer.   6–023

Relevant and irrelevant considerations

A decision-maker is required to consider all relevant matters and ignore   6–024
those that are irrelevant.[69] Determining what amounts to a "relevant consideration" can be problematic but generally the applicable legislation

---

[65] [2000] Env. L.R. at 263–264.
[66] [2007] 1 AC 470.
[67] *R(Barker) v Bromley London Borough Council* Case C-290/03 [2006] Q.B. 764.
[68] (2000) LGR 68; (1999) EGCS 69.
[69] *Associated Provincial Picture Houses Ltd v Wednesbury Corporation* [1948] 1 KB 223.

will provide guidance as to the pertinent matters, either expressly (through its provisions) or implicitly (through its aims).

In terms of explicit guidance, a statute may stipulate that certain matters be taken into consideration. Section 70(2) of the Town and Planning Act 1990 requires that where an application is made for planning permission the local authority shall have regard not only to the provisions of the development plan but also to "any other material considerations". Under section 131 of the Environmental Protection Act 1990, Natural England[70] is under a duty to take appropriate account of actual or possible ecological changes when discharging its conservation functions.[71]

In many cases, though, the legislation does not provide such specific guidance. The courts are then called upon to determine by implication from the statutory provisions read as a whole whether a matter amounts to a "relevant consideration". In *R v Secretary of State for the Environment ex parte Royal Society for the Protection of Birds*[72] the respondent, in accordance with the Birds Directive,[73] designated the Medway Estuary and Marshes as a special protection area because of its international importance as a breeding site for birds. However, he excluded an area known as Lappel Bank on the grounds that economic considerations, namely the expansion of the nearby Port of Sheerness into Lappel Bank, took precedence over conservation matters.

6-025   Following a request for a preliminary ruling from the House of Lords, the European Court of Justice held that economic requirements cannot be taken into account when designating a special protection area under the Birds Directive. Having regard to the aims of the Directive, which seeks to provide a targeted protection regime for endangered birds, ecological requirements should not be balanced against economic considerations when considering whether an area should be so designated.[74] The Secretary of State's intention of promoting the national and local economy was therefore held to be an irrelevant consideration.

Policy and guidance documents

6-026   Relevant considerations may also be garnered by the court from guidance or policy documents. However, an issue may arise as to the weight that such documents should carry. In *R (on the application of Munjaz) v Mersey Health Care NHS Trust et al*,[75] the issue arose in relation to a Code of Practice that provided guidance to hospital staff treating psychiatric

---

[70] Also formerly known as English Nature.

[71] *Fisher and others v English Nature* [2003] EWHC 1599 (Admin), at [14].

[72] Case C-44/95 [1997] Q.B. 206.

[73] Council Directive (79/409/EEC).

[74] Although economic considerations may properly come into play when determining whether or not to permit a development which may have adverse effects on such a designated site.

[75] (2006) 2 AC 148 : (2005) 3 W.L.R. 793.

patients. In determining the status of the Code, the House of Lords held that, whilst the Code was not compulsory, it "cannot be divorced from its statutory background, from the process of consultation and from the parliamentary procedure that must be gone through before it is published ...".[76] Consequently "the Code is something that those to whom it is addressed are expected to follow unless they have good reason for not doing so."[77] Nothwithstanding an apparent power in the hospital to act as it saw fit,[78] the court held that the hospital was required to have regard to any considerations outlined as relevant in such documents.

In *R (on the application of the Council for National Parks Ltd) v Pembrokeshire Coast National Park Authority and others*[79] the issue arose as to the weight to be accorded to a policy document. In determining whether to grant planning permission under section 54A TCPA 1990, the respondent local authority was required to follow the local development plan unless material considerations indicated otherwise. A developer applied for planning permission for a holiday village. The development control officer recommended that the development be rejected on the grounds that it was contrary to the statutory purposes of TCPA 1990 and contrary to the relevant planning policies. The respondent authority nonetheless granted planning permission. The claimant argued that the respondent's decision was unlawful because they had rejected the development control officer's advice and recommendations. The Court of Appeal held that the respondent was not obliged to follow the recommendation of its planning officer. Instead, it had taken account of other "material considerations", namely a policy document which post-dated the relevant development plan. That later policy document allowed the respondent to take account of local economic matters, and this had formed the basis of the respondent's decision to grant permission.

Where a decision-maker does not take account of relevant considerations, or gives weight to irrelevant matters, then the decision will generally be quashed, unless the court is satisfied that the decision-maker would have reached the same decision in any event.[80] In other words, the fact that the decision-maker considered irrelevant matters will not be detrimental if these matters did not affect the outcome.[81] Conversely, where the decision-maker has failed to consider a relevant consideration, the decision may be struck down where the decision maker might have reached a different conclusion if he had taken account of it.[82]

---

[76] *R (on the application of Munjaz) v Mersey Health Care NHS Trust et al* at para.68.
[77] ibid. para.69.
[78] ibid. para.69.
[79] [2005] EWCA Civ 888.
[80] See *Fisher*, para.33 [Lightman J.] citing *Simplex v Secretary of State* [1998] 3 PLR 25.
[81] *R v London (Bishop)* (1890) 24 QBD 213 at 226–227 (cited by De Smith, op cit, at 5–111).
[82] *R v Parliamentary Commissioner for Administration, ex parte Balchin* [1998] 1 PLR 1, per Dyson J. at 15C.

Irrationality (unreasonableness)

6–027   Although a decision-maker may

> "have kept within the four corners of the matters which they ought to consider, they [may] nevertheless come to a conclusion so unreasonable that no reasonable authority could ever have come to it."[83]

Error of this kind, known as *"Wednesbury* unreasonableness", was re-described by Lord Diplock in the *GCHQ* case, who stated that an irrational decision is one that

> "is so outrageous in its defiance of logic or accepted moral standards that no sensible person who had applied his mind to the question to be decided could have arrived at it."[84]

As the language of both these tests suggest, the claimant faces a high threshold in proving that a decision was irrational, because the decision-maker will be afforded a wide discretion: the view of the reviewing court should be that if the decision is one that was reasonably open to him or her, then it will be upheld.[84A] In short, reasonable people may come to a variety of different decisions in respect of a particular matter without any necessarily forfeiting the description of being reasonable. For the courts to intervene other than in extreme cases risks straying from the legitimate realm of judicial "review" to that of substituting its own view of the "merits"

A further consequence of judicial review proceedings involving an examination of the decision-making process, and not constituting a form of appeal, relates to the reviewing courts' reluctance to interfere with expert opinion. In judicial review, claimants face an uphill battle in seeking to undermine expert findings. In *R (on the application of Malster) v Ipswich Borough Council*,[85] the respondent council, on the planning officer's recommendation, had not carried out an environmental impact assessment on the basis that the proposed development would not have a significant effect on the environment. The court was asked to hold that the likelihood of the development having a significant effect on the environment was a question of jurisdictional fact, so that a correct decision on this issue was a pre-condition of the decision-maker having the power in question. In rejecting that proposition, Sullivan J. stated:

---

[83] *Associated Provincial Picture Houses Ltd v Wednesbury Corporation* [1948] 1 KB 223 per Lord Greene at 233.

[84] *GCHQ* [1985] A.C. 374 per Lord Diplock at 411.

[84A] For a recent example of a judicial review claim where the claimant failed to establish irrationality, see *West Midlands International Airport Ltd v Secretary of State for Communities and Local Government et al* [2008] EWHC 2309 (Admin).

[85] [2001] EWHC 711 (Admin); [2002] PLCR 251.

"A detailed knowledge of the locality and expertise in assessing the environmental effects of different kinds of development are both essential in answering that question, which is pre-eminently a matter of judgment and degree rather than a question of fact. Unlike the local planning authority, the court does not possess such knowledge or expertise."[86]

Examples of unreasonable decisions

Notwithstanding the difficulties faced by claimants, there are a number of circumstances in which unreasonableness has been found by the courts. **6–028**

Mistake of fact

Some commentators have held that "a mistake of fact in and of itself renders a decision irrational or unreasonable."[87] This would provide an exception to the rule that judicial review proceedings are solely concerned with the decision-making process. Certainly recent case law indicates a movement towards accepting such a basis for finding irrationality but, as will emerge, the law is far from recognising that every mistake of fact justifies quashing the decision under challenge. In *E v Secretary of State for the Home Department*,[88] Carnwath L.J. stated: **6–029**

"The time has now come to accept that a mistake of fact giving rise to unfairness is a separate head of challenge in an appeal on a point of law, at least in those statutory contexts where the parties share an interest in co-operating to achieve the correct result. The ordinary requirements for a finding of unfairness are apparent from the above analysis of the Criminal Injuries Compensation Board[89] case. First, there must have been a mistake as to an existing fact, including a mistake as to the availability of evidence on a particular matter. Secondly, the fact or evidence must have been 'established', in the sense that it was uncontentious and objectively verifiable. Thirdly, the appellant (or his advisers) must not been have been responsible for the mistake. Fourthly, the mistake must have played a material (not necessarily decisive) part in the tribunal's reasoning."[90]

In *E* the Immigration Appeals Tribunal had refused to take account of new evidence which undermined the basis of their conclusions that had come to

---

[86] para.61. See also *Levy v Environment Agency* (2003) Env. L.R. 245; *Fisher v English Nature* [2004] EWCA Civ 663.
[87] See *De Smith's Judicial Review*, paras 11–041 to 11–056, in particular para.11–056.
[88] [2004] Q.B. 1044; [2004] 2 W.L.R. 1351.
[89] *R v Criminal Injuries Compensation Board, ex p A* [1999] 2 A.C. 330, HL.
[90] ibid., para.66.

light following the hearing but before promulgation of its decision. The Court of Appeal held that justice required that it be taken into account and the Tribunal had been wrong in law to refuse to do so.

The current test in relation to error of fact was laid down in *Shaheen v Secretary of State for the Home Department*[91] by Brooke L.J.[92] Though this case related to an asylum claim, the principles are relevant across all areas of law:

> "i. Proof or admission that the tribunal of fact misapprehended a potentially decisive element of the evidence before it discloses an error of law (as held in the *E* case);
>
> ii. Proof or admission of a subsequently discovered fact permits an appellate court to set aside a decision for fraud, provided that it was potentially decisive and it can be shown that the defendant was responsible for its concealment;
>
> iii. The emergence of any other class of new fact, whether contested or not, has either to be processed [within the Immigration Rules in this case] or simply lived with. In any other case, finality prevails."

A factual error was central to the case of *Belize Alliance of Conservation Non-Governmental Organisations v The Department of the Environment*[93] ("the '*BACONGO*' case"). The claimants challenged the grant of approval for a hydro-electric dam on the Macal River in Belize. One of their grounds for challenge related a geological error contained in the Environmental Impact Assessment report: the report stated that the floor of the valley was granite, when it was in fact sandstone. This error did not come to light until after the decision was taken by the Department of the Environment to grant environmental clearance to the project. Two members of the Privy Council held that the decision should be quashed on the ground that the EIA was

> "so flawed by important errors about the geology of the site as to be incapable of satisfying the requirements of the [Belize Environmental Protection Act 1992] and the [Environmental Impact Assessment Regulations 1995]".[94]

However, the majority held that the geological error was not so significant as to prevent the EIA from fulfilling the Act's requirements. They placed weight in particular on expert opinion that the classification of the rock did not make any material difference: both sandstone and granite were equally suitable for construction purposes.[95] The Privy Council also adopted the following comments regarding EIAs:

---

[91] [2005] EWCA Civ 1294.
[92] ibid., para.29.
[93] [2004] UKPC 6.
[94] Per Lord Walker, at para.118.
[95] ibid., paras 47–48.

"The fact that the environmental impact statement does not cover every topic and explore every avenue advocated by experts does not necessarily invalidate it or require a finding that it does not substantially comply with the statute and the regulations."[96]

This introduces an element of reasonableness into the content of the EIA: as long as the EIA is comprehensive and objective, and alerts the public and decision-makers to the impact of the development on the environment, even a significant error will not necessarily be detrimental.

Given that there is growing recognition of a need for a remedy where there is a serious error of fact in a decision-maker's understanding of a matter, it is contended that this exception to the general rule that judicial review proceedings are solely concerned with the decision-making process, should be supported. It would be wrong for a decision to have to stand where it is based upon flawed evidence that substantially impacts upon the grounds for the decision. **6–030**

Oppressive consequences[97]

Where the decision-maker fails to have regard to the overly-oppressive consequences of its decision, the decision may be overturned.[98] This often arises in relation to planning conditions imposed on developers. In the well-known case *R v Hillingdon LBC Ex p. Royco Homes*, granting planning permission on the condition that the properties be let to people on the council's waiting list was held to be unreasonable because it was contrary to ownership rights.[99] However *Royco* was distinguished in *R v Tower Hamlets London Borough Council, ex p Barratt Homes Ltd 2*;[100] Sullivan J. held that the requirement that 25 per cent of a housing development should consist of affordable housing was not regarded as unlawful: the need for affordable housing was so substantial that the release of the site for development, without a contribution to that need, would be bound to have an adverse effect on that need, and, on the facts, the council was not trying to transfer any of its own obligations on to the housing developer. **6–031**

---

[96] per Cripps J. in *Prineas v Foresty Commission of New South Wales* (1983) 49 LBRA 402, at 417, cited at para.69.

[97] For further analysis and case law see *DeSmith's Judicial Review*, at paras 11–070 to 11–072.

[98] See *R(Khatun) v London Borough of Newham* [2004] EWCA Civ 55 [2004] 3 W.L.R. 417 at [41].

[99] [1974] 1 Q.B. 720.

[100] 2/3/2000. This outcome is usually achieved by the developer entering into a s.106 TCPA planning agreement promising such affordable housing.

Breach of public law principles

6–032   Under the principle of equality, people in similar positions should be treated similarly.[101] A failure to abide by this principle amounts to a discrepancy in treatment, which is judicially reviewable as being unreasonable. As a result of *North Wiltshire DC v Secretary of State for the Environment*[102] the past decisions of planning officers amount to a "material consideration" for the purposes of considering planning applications under section 70(2) TCPA, and therefore equate loosely to non-binding "precedents". As such, a decision-maker must at least have regard to previous, factually similar, applications.[103] Conversely, a local authority may refuse permission where, by granting the permission, a bad precedent would be set which would be difficult to refute when considering similar applications.[104]

Weight attributed to relevant matters

6–033   As long as a decision maker considers all relevant matters, the weight attributed to each matter is usually for the decision-maker alone to determine. In *Tesco Stores Ltd v Secretary of State for the Environment*[105] Lord Keith noted:

> "It is for the courts, if the matter is brought before them, to decide what is a relevant consideration. If the decision maker wrongly takes the view that some consideration is not relevant, and therefore has no regard to it, his decision cannot stand and he must be required to think again. But it is entirely for the decision maker to attribute to the relevant considerations such weight as he thinks fit, and the courts will not interfere unless he has acted unreasonably in the *Wednesbury* sense (*Associated Provincial Picture Houses Ltd. v. Wednesbury Corporation* [1948] 1 K.B. 223)".[106]

In that case, Tesco's application for planning permission had been rejected by the Secretary of State in favour of a competing application. Tesco alleged that the Secretary of State had failed to treat their offer of funding for a link road as a material consideration when determining the applications. The House of Lords held that the Secretary of State had given careful consideration to the offer, but that he was entitled to reject it. Lord Hoffman concluded:

---

[101] See "Public law principles", above.
[102] [1992] JPL 955, CA.
[103] *North Wiltshire DC v Secretary of State for the Environment* [1992] JPL 955, CA at pp.13–14.
[104] *Rumsey v Secretary of State for the Environment, Transport and the Regions* (2000) 81 P & CR 465, [2000] All E.R. (D) 1357.
[105] [1995] 1 W.L.R. 759.
[106] ibid., at p.764G-H.

"The law has always made a clear distinction between the question of whether something is a material consideration and the weight which it should be given. The former is a question of law and the latter is a question of planning judgment, which is entirely a matter for the planning authority. Provided that the planning authority has regard to all material considerations, it is at liberty (provided that it does not lapse into *Wednesbury* irrationality) to give them whatever weight the planning authority thinks fit or no weight at all. The fact that the law regards something as a material consideration therefore involves no view about the part, if any, which it should play in the decision-making process."[107]

However, this distinction is not always easy to apply in practice. There have been occasions where the courts have struck down a decision because the decision-maker failed to accord sufficient weight to relevant matters which statute regards as of particular importance. So the Court of Appeal has stated that:

"The principle that the weight to be given to ... facts is a matter for the decision-maker ... does not mean that the latter is free to dismiss or marginalise things to which the structure and policy of the [relevant] Act attach obvious importance."[108]

The case of *George Wimpey UK Ltd v Tewkesbury Borough Council*[109] is indicative of a decision-maker's marginalisation of relevant considerations. The respondent local authority had approved a plan which allocated two controversial sites for housing development. However, the judge held that the local authority had acted unreasonably in its allocation because there was no evidence to indicate that either site would receive planning permission, or that the housing allocations would be implemented within the relevant time period. The relevant parts of the plan were therefore quashed.

Proportionality[110]

As mentioned above, the three grounds of review listed in *GCHQ* are not finite. The main potential contender as a fourth ground is the principle of proportionality.[111] Proportionality is a principle of European law which is used in a variety of contexts, including the determination of whether an

6–034

---

[107] ibid., at p.780F-H.
[108] *R (von Brandenburg) East London and The City Mental Health NHS Trust* [2001] EWCA Civ 239, [2002] Q.B. 235 (CA) per Sedley L.J. at [41].
[109] [2007] EWHC 628 (Admin).
[110] For further discussion see *De Smith's Judicial Review*, 6th Ed., especially paras 11–073 to 11–085.
[111] Indeed, as far back as 1985 Lord Diplock in *GCHQ* [1985] AC 374 at 410 noted that the principle of proportionality might in the future be adopted as an additional judicial review ground.

interference with an individual's right is justifiable as necessary in a democratic society. It is an established principle adopted by both the European Court of Justice and the European Court of Human Rights, and increasingly by domestic courts in environmental and planning cases following the coming into force of the Human Rights Act 1998.[112] The principle has been expressed in a number of ways. The traditional questions to be asked, in deciding whether a measure is proportionate, are:

"whether (i) the legislative objective is sufficiently important to justify limiting a fundamental right; (ii) the measures designed to meet the legislative objective are rationally connected to it; and (iii) the means used to impair the right or freedom are no more than is necessary to accomplish the object".[113]

However, as Lord Bingham has pointed out more recently in *Huang*,[114] there needs to be added a fourth issue, namely the need to balance the interests of society with those of interests and groups.

Whilst these formulations appear to put a considerable distance between proportionality and traditional irrationality, in practice application of the concepts of proportionality and unreasonableness leads to the same result most of the time. It has, for example, been rightly said that the "standards of proportionality...and unreasonableness are inextricably intertwined."[115] So, where a local authority has failed fairly to balance competing interests, or where a decision places an overly onerous burden on one individual without consideration of less oppressive alternatives, those decisions can be described equally as "disproportionate" or "unreasonable".[116]

Procedural impropriety (unfairness)

6–035   Procedural impropriety arises not only where the decision maker has not adhered to relevant legislative procedures but also where there is a "failure to observe basic rules of natural justice or failure to act with procedural fairness towards the person who will be affected by the decision".[117] This ground of review is an elastic concept, the content of which depends to some extent on the nature of the decision-making body, the decision being made and the statutory framework within which it operates.[118]

---

[112] See, for example, *South Buckinghamshire District Council v Porter* [2003] 2 W.L.R. 1547 and *Walker v Secretary of State for Communities and Local Government et al* [2008] EWHC 62 (Q.B.).

[113] *De Freitas v Ministry of Agriculture* [1999] 1 A.C. 69,80, per Lord Clyde.

[114] *Huang v Home Secretary* [2007] 2 W.L.R. 581.

[115] *De Smith's Judicial Review*, 6th Ed., para.11–084 and see *R. v Ministry of Defence ex p. Walker* [2000] 1 W.L.R. 806.

[116] See *De Smith*, paras 11–084 to 11–085, referring to *Brown v Secretary of State for the Environment* (1978) 40 P & CR 285.

[117] *GCHQ* [1985] A.C. 374 per Lord Diplock at 411.

[118] *Lloyd v McMahon* [1987] A.C. 625 per Lord Bridge at 702.

a. Legislative procedures

A number of legislative instruments contain strict procedures that decision-   **6–036**
makers are required to follow. This is particularly the case with matters
related to planning applications: the Town and Country Planning
(Environmental Impact Assessment) Regulations 1999,[119] for example, lay
down procedures that the Secretary of State and local planning authority
should adhere to. Other examples are:

a)   Under s.71 TCPA 1990, local authorities shall have regard to any
     representations before making a determination on a planning
     application;
b)   The Town and Country Planning (Environmental Impact Assess-
     ment) Regulations 1999[120] require that an Environmental Impact
     Assessment be completed where the development falls within
     Schedule 1 of the Regulations;
c)   Under section 28 of the Environment Protection Act 1990, where
     Natural England, the principal governmental nature conservation
     body, holds that an area fulfils the criteria for an area of special
     scientific interest, they must notify or confirm this to the planning
     authorities, land owners and Secretary of State.

A failure to abide by statutory procedures can lead to a quashing of the
decision, where the failure would cause prejudice to those impacted by the
decision. In *Berkeley v Secretary of State for the Environment*,[121] the Secretary
of State for the Environment granted conditional planning permission for
the rebuilding of the Fulham football stadium. The development would
inevitably have a significant impact on the surrounding environment. As
such, under regulation 4(2) of the Town and Country Planning (Assessment of Environmental Effects) Regulations 1988 then in force, the
Secretary was required to take into consideration an environmental impact
assessment, which should have been submitted by the developers, before
granting planning permission. He failed to do so, and the grant of planning
permission was therefore overturned. In this case the procedural breach
was sufficiently serious to warrant the quashing of the decision: not all
breaches of procedural obligations will lead to successful judicial review
proceedings, but generally only those that will have a detrimental impact
upon parties.

b. Procedural fairness

The principle of natural justice has led to the development of a number of   **6–037**
standards regarding procedural fairness. In summary they are as follows:

---

[119] SI 1999/293 as amended by SI 2008/1556.
[120] SI 1999/293.
[121] [2001] 2 A.C. 603.

- The rule against bias;
- Legitimate expectation;[121A]
- The right to make representations;[121B]
- The right to adequate consultation;[121C]
- The right to reasons;[121D]
- The right to a fair hearing.[121E]

Many of these standards are explored in detail elsewhere in this chapter, but a couple remain to be discussed at this stage.

Bias

6–038   The basic premise is that a man may not be a judge of his own cause.[122] Bias is defined as "a predisposition or prejudice against one party's case or evidence on an issue for reasons unconnected with the merits of the issue."[123] Where a person has a direct personal or pecuniary interest (actual bias)[124] in an outcome, he or she is disqualified from participating in the decision itself.

A party may also be disqualified by virtue of apparent bias. The general test is whether a fair-minded and informed observer would conclude that there is a real possibility of bias.[125] The question arose in the recent case of *R (on the application of Lewis) v Persimmon Homes Teesside Ltd*[126] as to how this test should be applied to elected decision-makers. Two days before a local election, a planning committee voted in favour of a controversial planning application from the respondent. Following the election there was a change of political control. The claimant, who had objected to the application, alleged that the project was likely to have been an issue in the forthcoming election. As such, the real reason for members supporting the proposal appeared to be political advantage rather than planning merits, and the decision—it was argued—was therefore vitiated by bias. The claim was upheld at first instance, but overturned on appeal. The Court of Appeal held that the test was whether there was an appearance of pre-determination, in the sense of a closed mind to the planning application. It was for the court to put itself in the position of a fair-minded observer and

---

[121A] See paras 6–042 to 6–046.

[121B] See paras 6–083ff.

[121C] ibid.

[121D] See paras 6–047 to 6–050.

[121E] See paras 6–039 and 6–040.

[122] See, for example, *R v Bow Street Metropolitan Stipendiary Magistrate, ex parte Pinochet Ugarte (No. 2)* [2000] 1 AC 119, per Lord Browne-Wilkinson at 132G–133C.

[123] *Flaherty v National Greyhound Racing Club* [2005] EWCA Civ 1117 per Scott-Baker L.J. at para.28.

[124] *Davidson v Scottish Ministers* [2004] UKHL 34, (2004) HRLR 34; (2004) UKHRR 1079 at para.6.

[125] *Flaherty v National Greyhound Racing Club* [2005] EWCA Civ 1117 at [27]; see also *Magill v Porter* [2001] UKHL 67; [2002] 2 AC 357 at [103].

[126] [2008] EWCA Civ 746.

determine whether there was a real possibility of bias. Evidence of political affiliation or the adoption of policies regarding planning proposals was insufficient to prove a closed mind.[127] The Court recognised that the councillors were not acting in a judicial role, and were elected to pursue policies. As such, it was expected that they would have formed views on planning issues. It was necessary, though, to distinguish a mere predisposition towards granting the application as opposed to a predetermination. In the present case, there was insufficient evidence of predetermination, and therefore the claim of bias was unsubstantiated.

The distinction between a legitimate predisposition to an outcome, where the decision-maker retains an open mind, and an illegitimate predetermination of the outcome, where the person involved will not consider relevant factors, is a common theme in planning cases.[128] At times there is a fine line between the two, and it would seem that the courts tend to defer to decision-makers. In *National Assembly for Wales v Elizabeth Condron* it was held on appeal that a chance comment by the chairman of a planning decision committee, who was alleged to have said that he was "going to go with the report of the inspector" the day before the committee granted permission for an opencast mining application, did not amount to bias.[129] Similarly, in the *BACONGO* case, the fact that the Belize government and the Department of the Environment had acted as though the decision to approve the dam had already been made—by entering into a further agreement with the construction company and building an access road to the site—was insufficient to demonstrate that they had closed their minds to any further evidence or representations.[130] However, in *Georgiou v Enfield London Borough Council*[131] the planning committee's grant of permission was vitiated by the appearance of bias because half its members had also been on a board that had advised the planning committee to accept the proposal.[132]

The right to a fair hearing

The right to a fair hearing is not only protected under the common law principle of natural justice, but also by Article 6 ECHR. Article 6 provides:

6–039

---

[127] ibid., paras 68 and 96.

[128] See *R v Amber Valley District Council ex parte Jackson* [1985] 1 W.L.R. 298, *(Alconbury Ltd) v Secretary of State for the Environment* [2003] 2 AC 312; *National Assembly for Wales v Elizabeth Condron et al* [2006] EWCA Civ 1573; (2007) BLGR 87, esp. para.43; *R v Secretary of State for the Environment ex p Kirkstall Valley Campaign Ltd* [1996] 3 All E.R. 304; and *R(Island Farm Development Ltd) v Bridgend County Borough Council* [2006] EWHC 2189 (Admin).

[129] *National Assembly for Wales v Elizabeth Condron et al* [2006] EWCA Civ 1573 at para.42.

[130] *Belize Alliance of Conservation Non-Governmental Organisations v The Department of the Environment* [2004] UKPC 6, especially paras 81–82.

[131] [2004] LGR 497.

[132] Though some doubts were expressed as to the test of bias applied in this case: see *R (on the application of Lewis) v Persimmon Homes Teesside Ltd* [2008] EWCA Civ 746 at para.66.

"In the determination of his civil rights and obligations or of any criminal charge against him, everyone is entitled to a fair and public hearing within a reasonable time by an independent and impartial tribunal established by law."

The European Court of Human Rights has held that Article 6 ECHR applies to planning decisions.[133] The question, though, arises as to the substance of Article 6 in such matters. Numerous statutory procedures allow for planning decisions to be taken by a planning inspector or the Secretary of State. Do they amount to an "independent and impartial tribunal" for the purposes of the ECHR?

This matter was raised in *R (Alconbury Ltd) v Secretary of State for the Environment*.[134] The claimants contended inter alia that sections 77, 78 and 79 TCPA 1990 (which allow the Secretary of State or someone acting on his or her behalf to make decisions on planning applications) were incompatible with Article 6(1) ECHR. The claimants argued that the Secretary of State, as policy maker, could not be regarded as an independent and impartial tribunal because he had a vested interest in achieving outcomes in accordance with his policies and his view of the public interest.

The House of Lords considered *Bryan v UK*,[135] in which the claimant had appealed a planning inspector's determination on the ground that the determination procedures did not comply with Article 6(1) ECHR, arguing that the inspector was not an "independent and impartial tribunal" when determining whether a breach of planning permission had occurred. The European Court of Human Rights had held in *Bryan* that the review by an inspector did not of itself satisfy Article 6 because he was not sufficiently independent: he was "still a creature of the Secretary of State, whose own policies were in issue and who could remove him at any time".[136] However, the existence of judicial review mechanisms satisfied Article 6 ECHR because the High Court could examine and set aside the inspector's finding of fact on grounds of irrationality.[137] The European Court therefore dismissed his claim.

6–040   On the basis of this and other related ECHR decisions,[138] the House of Lords in *Alconbury* held that, although the Secretary of State was not independent and impartial, his decisions were compatible with Article 6(1) ECHR provided those decisions were themselves subject to review by an

---

[133] *Fredin v Sweden* (1991) 13 EHRR 784; *Bryan v UK* (1995) 21 EHRR 342.

[134] [2003] 2 AC 312.

[135] (1995) 21 EHRR 342.

[136] ibid., para.38.

[137] ibid., para.47.

[138] *ISKCON v United Kingdom* (1994) 18 EHRR CD 133; *Chapman v United Kingdom* (2001) 33 EHRR 399; *Varrey v United Kingdom* The Times January 30, 2001.

independent and impartial tribunal.[139] As judicial review proceedings satisfied the review requirement, the claim was dismissed.

Procedural unfairness and policy decisions

The courts have also begun to target procedural steps that impact upon **6–041** high level policy decisions. Recently, the court has held that consultation documents related to the formulation of Government policy are also vulnerable to judicial review. In *R (on the application of Greenpeace) v Secretary of State for Trade and Industry*[140] ("*Greenpeace* [2007]"), the respondent had indicated that it was not minded to support nuclear power plants as a means of producing energy, but that if it were to reverse its position it would undertake "the fullest public consultation" before doing so. A few years later the Government announced a review of its energy policy, and issued a consultation paper seeking opinions from all interested parties. Following the consultation the Secretary of State issued an Energy Review report which indicated that he would support nuclear new build as part of the UK's future electricity generating mix.

The claimant challenged the decision, in part on the ground that the respondent had misinformed it as to the status of the review. It was argued that the consultation document had not been put forward as a consultation on the substantive issue, namely whether nuclear new build should be supported; rather, it had been put out as an "Issues Paper" which sought views on the broad issues that should be addressed when deciding whether to support nuclear new build. The consultation was therefore not the "fullest public consultation" that had been promised, but merely one of the steps in such a consultation process. In addition, the public had not been provided with all the relevant information upon which to provide informed responses.

Sullivan J. struck down the consultation exercise as procedurally unfair and in breach of the claimant's legitimate expectation, holding that the consultation exercise was "very seriously flawed".[141] He recognised that consultation leading to the decision to support nuclear new build was not a statutory requirement, and that the decision itself was not a statutory decision but a step towards forming Government policy; however, he held that the decision was critical because it would materially affect the approach of local authorities and the Secretary of State to applications for planning permission for nuclear plants. He noted:[142]

"It would be surprising if the procedural steps leading to a decision of such planning and environmental significance were immune from legal

---

[139] *R (Alconbury Ltd) v Secretary of State for the Environment* [2003] 2 A.C. 312.
[140] [2007] EWHC 311 (Admin); (2007) Env. L.R. 29.
[141] ibid., para.116.
[142] ibid., para.51.

scrutiny, so that the Government could promise consultation in a White Paper and then renege on that promise in a subsequent policy document upon the basis that the latter was a "high level" or "strategic" decision for which it was politically, but not legally, accountable.

I readily accept the proposition that in the absence of any statutory or other well-established procedural rules for taking such strategic decisions it may be very difficult for a claimant to establish procedural impropriety. Similarly, given the judgmental nature of "high-level, strategic" decisions it may be impossible to mount a *"Wednesbury* irrationality" challenge absent bad faith or manifest absurdity: see *R (London Borough of Wandsworth and others) v Secretary of State for Transport* [2005] EWHC 20 (Admin) para.58 (the "Airports White Paper case"). These practical considerations do not mean that decisions such as those contained in the Energy policy are unreviewable simply because they are matters of "high policy."

Legitimate Expectation

6–042　One of the elements of fairness is honouring legitimate expectations. A legitimate expectation arises when an individual is objectively led to believe, either as a result of a promise or continuing practice, that a benefit will be attained or continued. The promise or practice may be express or implied[143] and it can relate to either a procedural or substantive benefit.[144] A failure to uphold a legitimate expectation may not only be a breach of procedural fairness but also amount to an abuse of power.

Who can claim legitimate expectation?

6–043　Legitimate expectation arguments are not limited to specific individuals or groups. In *Greenpeace* [2007][145] Sullivan J., in holding that the claimant's legitimate expectation, as regards consultation prior to a broad energy policy decision being announced, had been breached, noted that

"this was not a consultation with an individual consultee, or a closed group of consultees ... the promise of 'the fullest public consultation' was extended to the adult population of the United Kingdom ...".[146]

Consequently, any member of the adult population could have lodged a claim on the grounds of a breach of legitimate expectation. However, the

---

[143] *Council of Civil Service Unions v Minister for the Civil Service* [1985] A.C. 374.
[144] *R v Department of Education and Employment ex parte Begbie* [2000] 1 W.L.R. 118; *Rowland v Environment Agency* [2003] EWCA Civ 1885.
[145] [2007] EWHC 311 (Admin).
[146] ibid., para.88.

likelihood of succeeding, in particular when seeking a substantive benefit, is likely to be greater if the number of affected people is limited.[147] In relation to a substantive benefit, it is unlikely that the government will be held to be bound by a representation or undertaking made to a large, diverse group; "the broader the class claiming the expectation's benefit, the more likely that a supervening public interest will be held to justify the change of position complained of."[148]

The claimant does not have to prove that he or she suffered a detriment by relying on the legitimate expectation.[149] However, if detriment can be shown, it is likely to strengthen the claimant's case.[150]

Forms of legitimate expectation

There are several categories of legitimate expectation, depending on the nature of the promise or practice. In the seminal case of *R v North and East Devon Health Authority ex parte Coughlan*,[151] Lord Woolf identified three kinds of legitimate expectation:[152]   **6–044**

(a) That the public authority will bear in mind its previous policy or representation, giving it the weight it believes is right, but no more, before deciding whether to change course. In these circumstances, the court can only review the decision on grounds of rationality and whether the decision-maker took into account the implications of not fulfilling its promise;

(b) That the decision-maker will provide a procedural benefit before making a decision, such as by consulting affected parties. Here the legitimate expectation is of procedural fairness in reaching the decision rather than of any substantive benefit as a result of the decision. A party may, for example, be entitled to expect that they will be consulted, but not that the decision will be made in their favour. The court will therefore have to decide whether the decision is procedurally unfair, having regard to the representations made. In *Greenpeace* [2007][153] the claimants contended that the government, contrary to its White Paper, had failed to carry out the "fullest public consultation" on the use of nuclear energy before announcing its support for nuclear new-build. It was held that the consultation

---

[147] see, for example, *R v North and East Devon Health Authority ex parte Coughlan* [2001] Q.B. 213 where only a small group of people were affected by the closure of a care home.

[148] *R (on the application of Bhatt Murphy) v Independent Assessor* [2008] EWCA 755 per Laws L.J. at para.46.

[149] *R v Newham LBC Ex p Bibi* [2001] EWCA Civ 607.

[150] *R v Newham LBC Ex p Bibi* [2001] EWCA Civ 607 at paras 29–31.

[151] [2001] Q.B. 213.

[152] ibid., paras 57–58.

[153] [EWHC] 311 (Admin).

exercise had been flawed and was therefore procedurally unfair and in breach of the claimant's legitimate expectations.

Claimants are also entitled to rely on guidance documents as giving rise to legitimate expectations. In *R(on the application of Jeeves and Baker) v Gravesham Borough Council*,[154] the claimant applied for planning permission for use of a caravan on a site in the greenbelt area. The respondent declined to consider the application pursuant to s.70A Town and Country Planning Act 1990 on the ground that there had been a previous application by a former resident which had been dismissed within the past two years and there was no significant change of circumstances.[155] The claimant contended that the council had failed to have regard to the guidance issued in a circular, which indicated that local authorities should only refuse to determine an application where they believed that the process was being abused by the submission of repetitive planning applications. Collins J. noted that the circular was a material consideration which the authority could not ignore. Consequently the claimant had a legitimate expectation that the circular would be considered by the respondent in the course of determining the claimant's application, and its failure to do so had breached that expectation.

(c) That the decision-maker will grant, or continue to provide, a substantive benefit. A substantive legitimate expectation arises where a claimant is entitled "to enforce the continuing enjoyment of the content—the substance—of an existing practice or policy, in the face of the decision-maker's ambition to change or abolish it".[156] The claimant's right will only be established if there is a clear and unambiguous representation upon which it is reasonable for him or her to rely.[157] The court will be called upon to determine whether the frustration of the expectation would be so unfair as to amount to an abuse of power. If the court holds that there has been a breach of a legitimate expectation, it must then ask whether there is a sufficiently overriding public interest to justify a departure from the promise.[158]

---

[154] [2006] EWHC 1249.

[155] s.70A(1) TCPA 1990 reads: "A local planning authority may decline to determine an application for planning permission for the development of any land if—(a) within the period of two years ending with the date on which the application is received, the Secretary of State has refused a similar application referred to him under section 77 or has dismissed an appeal against the refusal of a similar application; and (b) in the opinion of the authority there has been no significant change since the refusal or, as the case may be, dismissal mentioned in paragraph (a) in the development plan, so far as material to the application, or in any other material considerations."

[156] *R (on the application of Bhatt Murphy) v Independent Assessor* [2008] EWCA 755 per Laws L.J. at para.32.

[157] *R v Devon County Council, ex parte Baker and another* [1995] 1 All E.R. 73, at 88 per Simon Brown L.J.

[158] *Coughlan*, [2001] Q.B. 213 at para.58.

In *Rowland v Environment Agency*,[159] notwithstanding the claimant's legitimate expectation the court held that it could not be enforced because of the unlawfulness of the representations by the authorities and the overriding public interest. The claimant and relevant navigation authorities had for many years treated a stretch of water on the River Thames, known as Hedsor Water, as the claimant's private property. In 2000 the defendant, as the relevant authority, reconsidered their position and contended that public rights of navigation ("PRN") existed over Hedsor Water. The claimant argued inter alia that she had a legitimate expectation at common law or under the ECHR that Hedsor Water had become permanently private. The Court of Appeal held that the representations of the navigation authorities had given rise to a legitimate expectation that Hedsor Water was private property.[160] However, the Court found that the expectation was unenforceable: an expectation could only be based on a lawful representation or practice, but the navigation authorities did not have authority to expressly or impliedly extinguish public rights of navigation because these rights were embodied in statute. As such, they could only be removed by legislation, not by the actions of the defendant. In addition, there was an overriding public interest in protecting PRN such that the respondent was not required to adhere to its previous representations

In contrast, in *R v Brent London Borough Council, ex p MacDonagh*[161] the claimants succeeded through legitimate expectation in showing an "entitlement" to a substantive benefit. The claimants were gypsies who had been expressly informed in a letter from the council that they would not be evicted from their unauthorised site until an alternative location was found. The council then evicted them. It was held that the letter amounted to an express promise which gave rise to a legitimate expectation. The council was therefore wrong, in the absence of overriding public interest factors, to have resiled from the letter's undertaking.

Legitimate expectations relating to property are also protected under the ECHR. In *Pine Valley Developments v Ireland*[162] the European Court of Human Rights held that a legitimate expectation relating to property may constitute a possession, even though the authority did not have the powers to realise that expectation. In *Rowland* Peter Gibson L.J. cited the decision with approval and noted that "an expectation may amount to a possession for the purposes of Article 1 [of Protocol No.1 ECHR] even though it

---

[159] [2004] 3 W.L.R. 249.
[160] ibid., para.73.
[161] (1989) 21 HLR 494, [1990] COD 3.
[162] [1991] 14 EHRR 319.

arises from an act unlawful under the domestic law".[163] As such, the right is protected from interference unless the interference is justified and proportionate. However, as we have seen, the interference with Mrs Rowland's right was justified having regard to the public interest.

The precise grounds of legitimate expectation, albeit well accepted by domestic courts, remain undefined. The extent to which an expectation is justifiable and enforceable is still being explored. However, notwithstanding this proviso, Laws L.J. in *Bhatt Murphy* summarised the principles of legitimate expectation as they currently stand as follows:

> "A very broad summary of the place of legitimate expectations in public law might be expressed as follows. The power of public authorities to change policy is constrained by the legal duty to be fair (and other constraints which the law imposes). A change of policy which would otherwise be legally unexceptionable may be held unfair by reason of prior action, or inaction, by the authority. If it has distinctly promised to consult those affected or potentially affected, then ordinarily it must consult (the paradigm case of procedural expectation). If it has distinctly promised to preserve existing policy for a specific person or group who would be substantially affected by the change, then ordinarily it must keep its promise (substantive expectation). If, without any promise, it has established a policy distinctly and substantially affecting a specific person or group who in the circumstances was in reason entitled to rely on its continuance and did so, then ordinarily it must consult before effecting any change (the secondary case of procedural expectation). To do otherwise, in any of these instances, would be to act so unfairly as to perpetrate an abuse of power."[164]

Whose acts or omissions can give rise to a legitimate expectation?

6-045   As a rule, a public body can only be held to the terms of a representation where the person making the representation has actual or ostensible authority to act on behalf of the public body.[165] As such, the courts will generally not allow a claimant to rely on an unlawful representation made by a person who they were justifiably, but mistakenly, led to believe was authorised to do so.

These principles have evolved over time: 30 years ago, when the concept of legitimate expectation was still in its infancy, the courts originally accepted that a public official's representations could bind a local authority even when he did not have the authority to do so. In *Lever (Finance) Ltd v*

---

[163] [2004] 3 W.L.R. 249, at para.91.
[164] *R (on the application of Bhatt Murphy) v Independent Assessor* [2008] EWCA 755 at para.50.
[165] *Flanagan v South Bucks District Council* [2002] 1 W.L.R. 2601 para.18 per Keene L.J.

Westminster (City) London Borough Council,[166] the Council's planning officer wrongly informed the claimant that additional planning permission for amendments to their building plans was not required. In fact, this was incorrect, and the officer did not have the delegated authority to decide this issue. The Court, though, held that it had been the Council's practice to allow its planning officers to inform applicants whether a variation was material such as to require planning permission. Since the applicant had acted in good faith and on the ostensible authority of the planning officer, the Council was bound by the misrepresentation.

However, *Lever Finance* was the high water mark for claimant's legitimate expectations, and has not been followed.[167] The current approach is that the mistaken and/or unlawful conduct of public officials cannot lead to an extension of a public body's statutory powers or responsibilities. In *Henry Boot Homes Ltd v Bassetlaw District Council*,[168] the claimant failed to prove a legitimate expectation had arisen. Under the TCPA 1990, planning permissions expire if no "material operations" are begun within a certain time frame, "material operations" being defined to include construction work.[169] However, work carried out in breach of a planning condition cannot be relied upon as a "material operation": as such, it is not capable of "stopping the clock" for the purposes of the time limitation. The claimant development company obtained outline planning permission subject to a number of conditions. Notwithstanding its failure to fulfil those conditions, it began construction work. The respondent local planning authority later held that there had been no lawful commencement of the development: as the work had been carried out in breach of conditions, there had been no "material operation". The claimant contended that, in the past, the respondent local planning authority had treated the commencement of works as "stopping the clock", even if those works were in breach of the conditions. They therefore argued that the respondent's previous behaviour and representations gave rise to a legitimate expectation that the development would be treated as having commenced before the permission expired.

The Court of Appeal held that no legitimate expectation had arisen. It **6–046** emphasised the importance of adhering to planning law requirements because of the effect of any development on third parties and the public. It was therefore found that, although in the past the respondent had not required the claimant to fulfil the planning conditions before recognising lawful commencement, the respondent could not lawfully waive any planning conditions because it did not have the authority to do so. How-

---

[166] (1971) 1 Q.B. 222.
[167] See *Brooks and Burton Ltd v Secretary of State for the Environment* (1976) 75 L.G.R 285 at 296 where *Lever Finance* was held to be "the most advanced case of the application of the estoppel doctrine, and one not to be repeated".
[168] [2002] EWCA Civ 983.
[169] s.93(4)(a) and 56(4).

ever, in a departure from the rule, the Court accepted that there may be circumstances where a legitimate expectation may arise from the local authority's conduct or representations if there was no third party or public interest. It was, though, asserted that such occasions would be rare.[170]

The *Rowland* judgment, discussed above,[171] in which the Court of Appeal held that a legitimate expectation arising from wrongful representations that were contrary to the public interest could not be upheld,[172] therefore seems to extend the obiter comments in *Henry Boot Homes*. Consequently, the exception may be summarised as follows: a public body's misrepresentations may give rise to a legitimate expectation; however, it is open to a respondent to argue that, although a legitimate expectation has been established, the greater public interest justifies their refusal to honour it. Should, though, the claimant be able to demonstrate that there is no overriding public interest or repercussions on third parties in the exceptional departure from statutorily derived powers and duties, the legitimate expectation may be honoured. Such cases, though, would be rare, and it remains to be seen whether the courts actually apply this approach.

Reasons

6–047   There is no general common law duty on a decision-maker in every instance to provide reasons for its decision.[173] However, it is increasingly being judicially acknowledged that the principle of procedural fairness requires decision-makers to give adequate reasons, where failure to do so could cause prejudice to affected parties.[174] Further, pursuant to Article 6 ECHR "adequate and intelligible reasons [must] be given for judicial decisions".[175]

This limited duty to give adequate reasons, which may be either express or implied, generally arises in two situations: either because it is an express statutory procedural requirement or, more generally, to prevent unfairness. Where Parliament stipulates that reasons should be given, they must be "proper, adequate ... intelligible ... [and] deal with substantial points that have been raised".[176] Should a decision-maker fail to provide reasons when legally obliged to do so, not only will the breach amount to procedural

---

[170] [2002] EWCA Civ 983, at para.56.
[171] At para.6–044.
[172] For commentary see *De Smith*, para.12–071ff.
[173] *Stefan v General Medical Council* [1999] 1 W.L.R. 1293 at 1300, per Lord Clyde.
[174] See, for example, *R v Secretary of State for Education ex P G* [1995] E.L.R. 58 at 67E-F; *R v Ministry of Defence ex p. Murray* [1998] COD 134; *North Range Shipping Ltd v Seatrans Shipping Corp* [2002] 1 W.L.R. 2397 at [15].
[175] *Anya v University of Oxford* [2001] EWCA Civ 405.
[176] *Re Poyser and Mill's Arbitration* [1963] 1 All E.R. 612 at 616, per Megaw J.

unfairness, but it is likely that the Court will infer that the decision-maker did not deal lawfully with the issues.[177]

What amounts to "adequate reasons"? This was subject to extensive discussion in *South Bucks District Council and another v Porter (No. 2)*.[178] In this case an inspector had exceptionally granted planning permission on the Green Belt area to a gypsy. He concluded that the applicant's gypsy status, the lack of an alternative site in the area and her chronic ill health constituted very special circumstances which were sufficient to override Green Belt policies. He granted planning permission, which was personal to her, in that the caravan could only remain on the site for as long as she lived there. The Council challenged his decision on the ground, amongst others, that he had failed to provide adequate reasons for his decision.

The House of Lords held that the reasons given by the inspector had in fact been clear and ample. Lord Steyn, having analysed the relevant authorities, provided a summary of the principles that should govern the proper approach to a "reasons" challenge in a planning context:

6–048

"The reasons for a decision must be intelligible and they must be adequate. They must enable the reader to understand why the matter was decided as it was and what conclusions were reached on the 'principal important controversial issues', disclosing how any issue of law or fact was resolved. Reasons can be briefly stated, the degree of particularity required depending entirely on the nature of the issues falling for decision. The reasoning must not give rise to a substantial doubt as to whether the decision-maker erred in law, for example by misunderstanding some relevant policy or some other important matter or by failing to reach a rational decision on relevant grounds. But such adverse inference will not readily be drawn. The reasons need refer only to the main issues in the dispute, not to every material consideration. They should enable disappointed developers to assess their prospects of obtaining some alternative development permission, or, as the case may be, their unsuccessful opponents to understand how the policy or approach underlying the grant of permission may impact upon future such applications. Decision letters must be read in a straightforward manner, recognising that they are addressed to parties well aware of the issues involved and the arguments advanced. A reasons challenge will only succeed if the party aggrieved can satisfy the court that he has genuinely been substantially prejudiced by the failure to provide an adequately reasoned decision."[179]

---

[177] *R(on the application of Nash) v Chelsea College of Art and Design* [2001] EWHC Admin 538 at [28] per Stanley Burton J.
[178] [2004] UKHL 33, at para.36.
[179] ibid.

In *Save Britain's Heritage v Number 1 Poultry Ltd*,[180] Lord Bridge cited three circumstances in which a lack of reasons will cause substantial prejudice:

"[F]irst . . . where the reasons are so inadequately or obscurely expressed as to raise a substantial doubt whether the decision was taken within the powers of the [Town and Country Planning] Act. Secondly . . . where the planning considerations on which decision is based are not explained sufficiently clearly to enable [a developer] to reasonably assess the prospects of succeeding in an application for some alternative form of development. Thirdly, an opponent of development may be prejudiced by a decision to grant permission in which the planning considerations on which the decision is based, particularly if they relate to planning policy, are not explained sufficiently clearly to indicate what, if any, impact they may have in relation to the decision of future applications."[181]

In that case the claimant appealed against the Secretary of State's decision to allow the demolition of certain listed buildings, contrary to the Secretary's stated policy, in favour of the erection of a new building. The claimant argued that the Secretary of State had failed to give sufficient reasons for his decision, as required by the Town and Country Planning (Inquiries Procedure) Rules 1988.[182] The House of Lords disagreed, holding that although the reasons lacked particularity the decision letter had adequately outlined the reasons for his conclusion and the circumstances which had warranted a departure from his policy.

It is notable that the onus is on the applicant to demonstrate "substantial prejudice": the threshold is therefore set high. In this respect there is a degree of overlap between procedural unfairness and irrationality because in both of these judicial review grounds the courts give decision-makers wide discretion before striking down the decision. However, the "standard" of reasons required does not vary depending on the importance of the issue; rather, as seen in *Save Britain's Heritage*, the nature of the issues will dictate the degree of particularity that is required.[183]

Remedy for lack of reasons

6–049   Where the decision-maker has failed to provide reasons, or any adequate reasons, the applicant is entitled to have the decision quashed as unlawful.[184] The matter will then be remitted for fresh consideration. Upon

---

[180] [1991] 2 All E.R. 10.
[181] ibid., at 24, cited with approval in *South Bucks District Council and another v Porter (No. 2)* [2004] UKHL 33 at para.30.
[182] Rule 17(1).
[183] *Save Britain's Heritage* [1991] 2 All E.R. 10 at p.23 per Lord Bridge, cited with approval in *Porter (No 2)* at para.28.
[184] *R v Westminster City Council, ex p Ermakov* [1996] 2 All E.R. 302 at 325 per Hutchinson L.J.

quashing the decision, the court may order that the matter not only be reconsidered but also that the authority reach a reasoned decision in accordance with the court's findings.[185]

Retrospective reasons

Occasionally, where the reasons are inadequate the court may accept reasons provided retrospectively, but only if the court considers that the reasons later given were those which existed at the time of the decision, and not simply a later attempt to justify the decision. Where there is a statutory duty on a decision-maker to provide reasons it is only in very exceptional circumstances that the court will accept subsequent evidence of reasons because the adequacy of the reasons is generally a condition precedent to the legality of the decision.[186]

6–050

The courts will accept evidence to clarify or, exceptionally, correct or add reasons for a decision, but will be extremely cautious about doing so.[187] Where, for example, there has been an error in a transcript or an ambiguous word has been used, then the evidence may be allowed to clarify the document. However, the evidence should merely elucidate and confirm the reasons, not fundamentally alter them: the court will not admit evidence which seeks to correct patently flawed reasoning.[188]

When asked to accept additional reasons, the court will take the following considerations into account:

(a) Whether the new reasons are consistent with the original reasons;
(b) Whether it is clear that the new reasons are indeed the original reasons of the whole committee;
(c) Whether there is a real risk that the later reasons have been composed subsequently in order to support the tribunal's decision, or are a retrospective justification of the original decision. This consideration is really an aspect of (b);
(d) The delay before the later reasons were put forward;
(e) The circumstances in which the later reasons were put forward. In particular, reasons put forward after the commencement of proceedings must be treated especially carefully. Conversely, reasons put forward during correspondence in which the parties are seeking to elucidate the decision should be approached more tolerantly.[189]

---

[185] *R v City of London Corporation, ex p Matson* [1997] 1 W.L.R. 765 at 777F per Neil L.J.
[186] *R(on the application of Nash) v Chelsea College of Art and Design* [2001] EWHC Admin 538 at paras 28 and 34, per Stanley Burnton J., citing *Northamptonshire County Council ex p D* [1998] ED CR 14; *R v Westminster City Council, ex p Ermakov* [1996] 2 All E.R. 302.
[187] *R v Westminster City Council, ex p Ermakov* [1996] 2 All E.R. 302 at 315, per Hutchinson L.J.
[188] ibid.
[189] *R(on the application of Nash) v Chelsea College of Art and Design* [2001] EWHC Admin 538 at para.34 per Stanley Burnton J.

Standing

6–051   It is a prerequisite to obtaining permission for judicial review proceedings that the applicant has standing before the court. Under section 31(3) of the Supreme Court Act 1981 the court shall not grant leave to make an application for judicial review "unless it considers that the applicant has sufficient interest in the matter to which it relates". This is wider than the "persons aggrieved" definition, found in a number of environmental or planning statutes,[190] and the "victim" requirement of the Human Rights Act,[191] because it does not require that the person bringing the claim be directly affected by the subject matter of the claim.

"Sufficient interest"

6–052   Since at least the mid 1980s the standing requirement has become easier to meet, as courts have widened the definition of "sufficient interest": it is now the position that an applicant does not need to have a personal stake in the issue as long as it is a matter of public importance and he or she is not motivated by any ill purpose. In *R v Somerset County Council and ARC Southern, ex p Dixon*[192] the applicant, a local resident and parish councillor, challenged the county council's grant of conditional planning permission to the company, ARC Southern, which allowed the company to extend their quarrying activities. It was not disputed that the quarrying would have extensive environmental impact. The applicant argued that the grant of permission was illegal and the council had failed to take relevant considerations into account. The council contended that the applicant had no standing as he was not a landowner of any potentially affected land and had no personal right or interest that would be threatened by the quarrying.

Sedley J. held that the applicant had sufficient interest to have standing. He noted that:

> "Public law is not at base about rights ... it is about wrongs—that is to say misuses of public power; and the courts have always been alive to the fact that a person or organisation with no particular stake in the issue or outcome may, without in any sense being a mere meddler, wish and be well placed to call the attention of the court to an apparent misuse of public power."[193]

---

[190] For example, s.82(1) Environmental Protection Act 1990, ss.287 and 288 Town and Country Planning Act.
[191] s.7(1) Human Rights Act 1998.
[192] [1998] Env. L.R. 111, disapproving the earlier case of *Rose Theatre Trust Co Ltd* [1990] 1 Q.B. 504.
[193] ibid., para.28.

Since the applicant was neither a "busybody" nor motivated by any ill will, he was entitled, as a concerned citizen, to institute proceedings regarding an alleged illegality that would impact upon the environment.[194]

Even where the applicant has not played an active role until instituting proceedings, he or she may be allowed to proceed where he is likely to be adversely affected by the outcome. In *R(Edwards) v Environment Agency and First Secretary of State*,[195] the respondent argued that the homeless applicant had no standing. It was contended that the applicant had not been active in the campaign against the granting of a permit to a cement factory or the associated consultation process. The court found that, notwithstanding his homelessness, the applicant was a local resident who had sufficient interest to bring the claim. Keith J. held that a person should not be debarred from challenging a decision "simply because [he] chose not to participate in the consultation exercise, provided that [he is] affected by its outcome."[195A] The fact that he was put up to front a claim on behalf of an interest group with the aim of obtaining legal aid on account of his personal financial circumstances was not a bar to his application.

"Applicant"

Further, with the relaxation of the "sufficient interest" requirement, the rules on who may lodge proceedings have also been extended. Interest groups and non-governmental organisations may have standing even if the outcome does not affect their members. The Aarhus Convention specifically states that "non-governmental organisations promoting environmental protection and meeting any requirements under national law shall be deemed to have an interest."[196] An advantage of "responsible specialist organisations"[197] bringing judicial review proceedings on behalf of others lies in their access to resources and expertise with which to launch a comprehensive challenge in an area of law that can be technically complex and prohibitively expensive to the individual acting alone. In *R v Inspectorate of Pollution, ex parte Greenpeace*[198] ("*Greenpeace* [1994]"), Greenpeace sought to challenge the Inspectorate's decision to grant applications to British Nuclear Fuels Plc (BNFL) for variations of authorisations under the Radioactive Substances Act 1960 to discharge radioactive waste from

6–053

---

[194] ibid., para.29. Ill will is difficult to prove or define, but is likely to include circumstances where the proceedings are brought out of spite or in revenge. See Dyson L.J., in *R (on the application of Robert Feakins) v Secretary of State for the Environment, Food and Rural Affairs* at para.23.

[195] [2004] EWHC 736.

[195A] ibid., para.16.

[196] Article 2(5). See also art.9(2).

[197] R *(Dixon) v Somerset County Council* [1997] EWHC Admin 393, at para.17 per Sedley J.

[198] *Greenpeace Ltd (No. 2)* [1994] 4 All E.R. 329.

BNFL's premises at Sellafield, Cumbria. It was contended that Greenpeace did not have sufficient interest.

Otton J. held that Greenpeace had standing to bring the judicial review claim on behalf of the residents of Cumbria, of whom 2,500 were members of Greenpeace. He noted that "if I were to deny standing to Greenpeace those they represent may not have an effective way to bring the issues before the court".[199] He recognised Greenpeace as "an entirely responsible and respected body"[200] who would be able to mount a well-informed legal challenge and would be able to pay the legal costs of the respondent and interested parties.

Where the subject matter is of public importance, the courts have allowed organisations to bring judicial review proceedings even when none of their members will be affected by the outcome. In *R v Secretary of State for Foreign Affairs ex p World Development Movement Ltd*,[201] the applicant pressure group (WDM) brought an application to quash the respondent's grant of financial aid to build a dam for the generation of hydro-electric power on the Pergau River in Malaysia. Notwithstanding that the WDM was British-based, with no members in Malaysia, the Court of Appeal held that it had sufficient interest. The fact that there were merits in the challenge was considered the dominant factor in granting standing: the Court held that the Secretary of State had acted unlawfully because, contrary to the Overseas Development and Co-operation Act 1980, the aid was given for political purposes and not for the developmental reasons required by the 1980 Act. However, the Court also held that there were several other factors which supported a finding of "sufficient interest", namely: (i) the importance of vindicating the rule of law; (ii) the importance of the issue raised; (iii) the likely absence of any other responsible challenger; (iv) the nature of the breach of duty against which relief was sought; and (v) the prominent role of the claimants in giving advice, guidance and assistance regarding aid.[202]

6–054   It is also now recognised that companies which have been formed in order to bring judicial review proceedings have standing. This often occurs where local residents establish a company so as to challenge the grant of planning permission.[203] The fact that, technically, the company does not have a relevant interest of its own is usually not an obstacle to standing, because in essence the company represents the interests of its members, many of whom will have sufficient interest.[204]

---

[199] ibid., at 350E.
[200] ibid., at 350C.
[201] ibid., see [1995] 1 W.L.R. 386.
[202] See headnote and pp.395–396.
[203] See *Residents Against Waste Ltd v Lancashire County Council* (2008) Env. L.R. 27. This will naturally have repercussions in terms of costs: see below under "Costs" at para.6–077.
[204] *R v Leicestershire County Council ex p Blackfordby and Boothorpe Action Group Limited* [2001] Env. L.R. 35.

Threshold at permission and substantive stages

At the permission stage, the threshold for fulfilling the standing require- **6–055** ment is low: it is only set at the height "necessary to prevent abuse".[205] As long as the applicant can show that he or she is not a "meddlesome busybody" and the application appears to be arguable, permission will be granted unless there are good grounds (such as delay) for not doing so.[206] Often it is difficult to determine the issue of standing without considering all issues relevant to the claim. As such, the House of Lords has indicated that the question of sufficient interest should not be dealt with as a preliminary issue because the matter cannot "be considered in the abstract, or as an isolated point: it must be taken together with legal and factual context".[207] Consequently, unless the standing point can be taken as a distinct issue or is relatively straightforward, any proper consideration of the matter should be left until the substantive hearing.

At the substantive hearing the court can, at its own discretion, reconsider the question of standing.[208] The strength of the applicant's interest in the issue will be just one of the factors taken into account in determining the question of standing.[209] However, it is rare that the courts will find for the applicant on the merits but then dismiss the case on a technicality, namely for lack of sufficient interest.[210] By virtue of finding for the applicant, there is a recognition that the respondent has acted unlawfully, irrationally or illegally: it is therefore unsurprising that the courts are then reluctant to refuse an appropriate remedy simply on technical grounds of lack of standing.

Human Rights Act 1998

Under section 7 of HRA 1998, a person may only claim that their Con- **6–056** vention rights been infringed if they are, or would be, a "victim". A "victim" is an applicant who is, or is likely to be, directly affected by a measure. This requirement prevents interest groups or NGOs from bringing HRA claims in their own right as they rarely fulfil the victim requirement and cannot argue a legal point in the abstract.[211]

---

[205] *Dixon*, para.12.
[206] *R v Monopolies and Mergers Commission ex p Argyll Group plc* [1986] 1 W.L.R. 763 at 773.
[207] *Inland Revenue Commissioners v National Federation of Self Employed and Small Businesses* [1982] AC 617 at 630, per Lord Wilberforce.
[208] *Argyll Group*, p.773.
[209] *Dixon* [1997] EWHC Admin 393, para.12(d).
[210] *De Smith's Judicial Review*, para.2–020.
[211] Karen Reid "Admissibility Criteria" in J. Simor, *Human Rights Practice*, (Sweet and Maxwell, 2000), at 20.052. For criticism of victim requirement of the HRA, see *De Smith's Judicial Review*, para.2–054.

Delay

6–057 Under CPR 54.5, a claim for judicial review must be filed promptly and in any event no later than three months after the grounds for making the claim first arose. Where the court considers that there has been undue delay in making the application, it may either (a) refuse permission to make the application; or (b) refuse the relief sought if it considers that the granting of relief would be likely to cause substantial hardship to, or substantially prejudice the rights of, any person or be detrimental to good administration.[212]

The courts have laid great stress on the need to act promptly because of the impact of the decision on third parties.[213] As Keene L.J. stated in *Hardy v Pembrokeshire County Council*:[214]

> "A public law decision by a public body in almost all cases affects the rights of parties other than the decision maker and the applicant seeking to challenge such a decision. It is important that those parties, and indeed the public generally, should be able to proceed on the basis that the decision is valid and can be relied on, and that they can plan their lives and make personal and business decisions accordingly."

Such is the emphasis on the need to act promptly that even filing within the three months "limit" may be insufficient to meet this requirement.[215] Further, the issuing of a pre-action protocol letter does not stop time running against the applicant.

It was argued in *Hardy v Pembrokeshire County Council*[216] that the lack of precision in the term "promptly" offends the principle of legal certainty in European Community law. This argument was rejected by the Court of Appeal, which held European law does not require absolute certainty but rather that "a citizen should be able to foresee to a reasonable degree the consequences of his actions."[217] Further, the degree of promptness required will vary from case to case.[218]

6–058 The courts will have regard to all relevant circumstances when assessing delay: where, for example, further information is needed,[219] legal advice is

---

[212] Supreme Court Act 1981, s.31(6).

[213] *R v Independent Television Commission, ex parte TV Northern Ireland Limited* [1996] JR 60.

[214] [2006] EWCA Civ 240, at para.10.

[215] *R (Young) v Oxford City Council* [2002] EWCA Civ 990, at para.38 per Pill L.J.: "Those who seek to challenge the lawfulness of planning permissions should not assume, whether as a delaying tactic or for some other reason, that they can defer filing their claim form until near the end of the three-month period in the expectation that the word 'promptly' in the rule is a dead letter." See also *R v Cotswold DC ex parte Barrington Parish Council* (1997) 75 P & CR 515 at 523 and *R v West Berkshire District Council* [2002] EWHC 1828.

[216] [2006] EWCA Civ 240.

[217] ibid., at para.14 per Keene LJ.

[218] ibid., at para.15.

[219] See *R v Licensing Authority ex p Novartis Pharmaceuticals Ltd* [2000] COD 232.

required to determine the strength of the claim,[220] or there is an excusable delay in securing legal aid,[221] the courts are likely to be more flexible. However, where there are pressing time constraints this will militate towards the court taking a stricter view of any delay.[222] This would be likely to occur where, for example, a claimant wished to halt construction works due to begin shortly after planning permission had been granted. As we will see below, the court will balance the delay against any effects on the defendant and affected third parties such as developers.

The time limit for bringing a claim under the Human Rights Act 1998 is one year, but this is subject to any rule imposing a stricter time period in relation to the procedure in question.[223] Given that the judicial review time limit is shorter, and claims under the HRA are often intertwined with grounds for judicial review, it is imperative to lodge any human rights claim at the same time as any judicial review proceedings.

Time begins to run when the grounds for making the claim first arise. However, the point at which the grounds are sufficiently concrete for a claim to be lodged has not always been clear. This is particularly the case where preliminary decisions, especially in planning matters, are not necessarily determinative of the final outcome. In *R v Hammersmith and Fulham LBC ex p Burkett*,[224] the respondent council passed a resolution in September 1999 to grant planning permission for a development subject to two conditions. The applicant, who lived beside the area of the proposed development, challenged the resolution in February 2000. In May 2000 the developer met the two conditions and planning permission was granted. The question therefore arose as to whether time ran from the date of the resolution to grant planning permission or the date of the actual grant of planning permission.

The House of Lords held that the resolution had created no legal rights: **6–059** it was only once the two planning conditions had been fulfilled that the planning permission lawfully existed.[225] Time therefore ran from the date that the planning permission was granted.[226] Lord Steyn noted that an applicant could challenge a preliminary decision if he wished, but that he was not required to do so, being entitled to "hold fire" until the substantive planning permission—which might never have been given—was granted. To determine otherwise would be at odds with the principle that judicial

---

[220] See *R v Oxford City Council ex parte Young* [2002] EWCA Civ 990.
[221] *R v Stratford-on-Avon District Council, ex p Jackson* [1985] 1 W.L.R. 1319
[222] See *R v Rochdale Metropolitan Borough Council ex parte P,B, C and K* [2000] Ed CR 117, where a decision by an education authority affecting where a child should attend school was challenged, and the onus was on the claimants to bring proceedings promptly and before the school term started.
[223] HRA, s.7(5).
[224] [2002] UKHL 23.
[225] ibid., at para.32.
[226] ibid., at para.51.

review is an avenue of last resort, and would tend to lead to expenditure and effort on a matter that might never come to fruition.[227]

The position, therefore, is that time will start running when a decision has been made that has concrete legal consequences, but an applicant may challenge a decision that *could* lead to such consequences. An application should, however, not be brought unless there is some evidence to support the claim, otherwise the court is likely to refuse permission on the ground that it is premature.[228]

Extension of time limit[228A]

6–060 Notwithstanding the apparently strict rules described above, the courts do have a discretion to extend time under CPR 3(1)(2)(a) where there is good reason to do so and no substantial hardship, prejudice or detriment to good administration will be caused. It will be for the applicant to prove that there was a "reasonable objective excuse" for the late application.[229] While the courts will look at each case on its facts, the cases suggest a number of reasons which may be accepted as justifying an extension of time.

Public importance

6–061 Where the matter is of public importance, such that it is in the public interest that the matter proceeds, an extension may be granted. In *Greenpeace* [2000][230] Maurice Kay J. held that Greenpeace had not acted "promptly", and there had been no reasonable objective excuse in their failure to do so. However, he held it was "plain" that they were correct on the substantive issue of the case, namely that the Habitats Directive applied to the UK Continental Shelf.[231] As such, the fact that the Habitats Directive had not been lawfully implemented and that the approach of the Secretary of State was legally erroneous, were matters of "substantial public importance" that justified the extension of time.

---

[227] ibid., at paras 38 and 42.
[228] See for example *R (on the application of Rackham Ltd) v Swaffham Magistrates's Court* [2004] EWHC 1417 (Admin).
[228A] For further analysis and case law see Fordham, *Judicial Review Handbook*, 4th edition, at para.26.3ff.
[229] *R v Secretary of State for Trade and Industry ex p Greenpeace* [2000] Env. L.R. 221 at paras 261–264, per Maurice Kay J.
[230] *R v Secretary of State for Trade and Industry ex p Greenpeace* [2000] Env. L.R. 221: for facts see under "Illegality" above.
[231] ibid., p.263.

Avenue of last resort

Where the applicant, acting reasonably, has sought other means of resol- 6–062
ving the issue before resorting to litigation he or she may not be penalised
where those means of redress fail.[232] In *R v Oxford City Council ex parte
Young*[233] the applicant had made numerous requests, over several months,
seeking information from the respondent council regarding the procedures
it had followed when granting the contested planning permission. The
council had delayed in providing any information. The Court of Appeal
held that the council was at fault for the applicant's lack of promptness,
and it should not benefit from its failure to respond. Lord Justice Potter
noted:

> "[I]t is undesirable for a litigant to proceed blindly towards challenge of
> a decision in relation to which he suspects a fault or omission susceptible
> of review in a case where, for the purposes of clarification, he reasonably
> requires further information from the decision-making body so that he
> can consider in an informed manner whether proceedings are justified or
> worthwhile. Not only is he entitled to consider the wisdom of embarking
> on the trouble and expense of litigation from his own point of view, it is
> also undesirable that the machinery of litigation and the engagement of
> the court process be set in motion before there has been an effort to
> resolve the matter in pre-trial correspondence."[234]

Substantial prejudice, hardship or detriment to good administration

In cases of undue delay, the court will refuse to grant relief where it "would 6–063
be likely to cause substantial hardship to, or substantially prejudice the
rights of, any person or be detrimental to good administration."[235] The
courts have taken a case-by-case approach to these terms, but again themes
have emerged that provide some guidance.

Where considerable sums have already been spent on the basis of a
decision, this may be a factor against granting an extension of time. In *R v
North West Leicestershire District Council, ex p Moses*,[236] the claimant challenged the construction of an airport runway on the grounds that it breached domestic and EU law because the initial planning permission had
been invalidly granted. By the time of the hearing, six years after the initial
planning permission was given, the interested party had spent over £67

---

[232] *R v Hammersmith and Fulham London Borough Council, ex p Burkett* [2001] Env. L.R. 684
(CA) at [14].
[233] [2002] EWCA Civ 990.
[234] ibid., para.43.
[235] Supreme Court Act 1981, s.31(6).
[236] [2000] Env. L.R. 443.

million on the construction of the runway. The applicant contended that she had not known of any basis for challenging the grant of planning permission until at least four years after it was granted. The Court of Appeal held that where both prejudice and extreme delay had been shown the Court was entitled to apply s.31(6) SCA 1981 even where there was an alleged breach of Community law.[237]

However, in *R v Hammersmith and Fulham London Borough Council ex p Burkett*[238] the court cautioned against the amount of expenditure already incurred being determinative in judicial review proceedings, on the ground that it would "distort the ends of justice" if developers were led to believe that the more money they spent on a project, the more likely they were successfully to resist judicial review proceedings.

6–064   Where the respondent or interested party is made aware at the time of the decision, or shortly after it, that the applicant may lodge proceedings, it will not be in a position to argue reliance in resisting judicial review proceedings. In the case of *Greenpeace* [2000][239] the respondents knew that the claimants were lodging proceedings. As such, their argument that the applicant had delayed, causing them prejudice, was rejected.

While the terms "prejudice" and "hardship" overlap, "good administration" is regarded as a distinct issue.[240] The term lacks a clear definition, but it includes administration in accordance with the law and the implementation of properly reached decisions. It rarely arises, as it only comes into play where neither hardship nor prejudice is sufficient to refuse an extension of time. In those circumstances, it is "rarely, if ever ... in the interests of good administration to leave an abuse of public power uncorrected."[241]

Remedies

6–065   In judicial review proceedings, the court has a number of potential remedies available to them.[242] Under section 31(1) SCA 1981 an applicant can apply for an order or declaration or seek an injunction.[243] The court also

---

[237] See also *R v Hammersmith and Fulham London Borough Council, ex parte Council for the Protection of Rural England, London Branch* (1999) CA (Swinton, Thomas L.J., Singer L.J.) 21/12/99), where the court refused permission, notwithstanding an arguable breach of Community law, because the applicant had delayed for three years without good reason.

[238] [2001] Env. L.R. 684 (CA) at [28].

[239] *R v Secretary of State for Trade and industry ex p Greenpeace* [2000] Env. L.R. 221.

[240] *R v Newbury District Council ex p Chieveley Parish Council* [1999] PLCR 51 at 67 per Pill L.J.

[241] *R v Lichfield District Council ex parte Lichfield Securities Ltd* [2001] EWCA Civ 304 at 39 per Sedley L.J.

[242] The main provisions relating to remedies are found in section 31 Supreme Court Act 1981 and CPR 54.

[243] This is also iterated in CPR 54.3, which allows a claimant to seek a declaration or injunction.

has the power to award damages under section 31(4) or where a claim is brought under the Human Rights Act. The obligation to provide a remedy in environmental cases is also enshrined in the Aarhus Convention, which requires signatories to "provide adequate and effective remedies, including injunctive relief as appropriate, and be fair, equitable, timely and not prohibitively expensive".[244] However, relief is not automatic as "the grant or refusal of the remedy sought by way of judicial review is, in the ultimate analysis, discretionary".[245]

Forms of Remedies

Declaration

A declaration is the most flexible of all the remedies. It essentially provides a statement of law, "so as to make it clear to all the world what [the claimant's] position is in the eyes of the law".[246] Unlike a prerogative order[247] a declaration is not legally enforceable, but it is an authoritative statement which carries the weight of the court's endorsement. **6–066**

The test for granting a declaration is whether it would be "just and convenient" to do so.[248] In reaching its decision, the court will have regard to:

"(a) the nature of the matters in respect of which the relief may be granted by order of mandamus, prohibition or certiorari;
(b) the nature of the persons and bodies against whom relief may be granted by such orders; and
(c) all the circumstances of the case."[249]

The court is entitled to make a declaration whether or not any other remedy is claimed.[250] While the applicants in *Greenpeace* [2007][251] had sought a quashing order, Sullivan J. opted instead to make a declaration which stated that the respondent's consultation process had been procedurally unfair, and that the decision to support nuclear new-build as a means of generating energy was unlawful.[252]

---

[244] Article 9(4).
[245] *Inland Revenue Commissioners v National Federation of Self-Employed and Small Businesses Ltd* [1982] AC 617, at 656 per Lord Roskill, cited with approval by Lord Hoffman in *R(on the application of Edwards) v Environment Agency and others* [2008] UKHL 22, at para.63.
[246] *Vine v National Dock Labour Board* [1957] AC 488, at 504 per Lord Morton.
[247] See para.6–069 below for further discussion.
[248] s.31(4) SCA.
[249] s.31(2) SCA.
[250] CPR 40.20.
[251] [2007] EWHC 311 (Admin).
[252] ibid., para.120.

Injunction

6–067 An injunction can either take the form of an interim or a final injunction, and may be either prohibitory or mandatory. The test is the same as that for declarations, namely whether it would be "just and convenient" to grant the injunction, having regard to the matters outlined in s.31(2)(a) to (c) SCA 1981 (as set out above).

A final injunction, while in substance comparable to the orders discussed below, is in form more flexible because it can be time-limited or lifted when certain conditions are fulfilled.[253] Injunctions, though, are particularly valuable in the form of an interim remedy. They are often sought at the permission stage by the applicant with a view to preventing irreversible damage prior to the substantive hearing. However, the court will usually require a cross-undertaking in damages to compensate the defendant should the injunction be lifted following the final hearing.[254]

Orders[254A]

6–068 Pursuant to section 31(1) SCA 1981 and CPR 54.2 an applicant can seek a mandatory order, a prohibiting order or a quashing order collectively known as prerogative remedies.[255]

A mandatory order requires the defendant to act as ordered by the court. Such orders are rarely made in respect of substantial decisions because this arrogates to the court the role of the decision-maker under challenge; hence, such an order will only be made where the outcome inevitably follows from the court's ruling of law. The commonest instance is when the decision-maker has wrongly decided that it had no jurisdiction to determine a case, but decisions on procedural issues not requiring any expert judgment may equally fall into this category. Prohibiting orders and quashing orders are in many respects similar. A prohibiting order prevents a body from acting in a manner that is unlawful. A quashing order, which is the most common form of order, overturns the challenged decision or act. It essentially achieves the same aim as a prohibiting order in that the decision or act can no longer take place.

Where a court makes a quashing order, it may remit the matter to the decision-maker and direct that he or she reconsider the matter and make a decision in accordance with the court's judgment.[256] However, the court may also make the decision itself if it believes that no purpose would be served in remitting the matter to the decision-maker.[257]

---

[253] De Smith 18–036.
[254] For further discussion, see below under "Access to Justice" at para.6–073.
[254A] See Fordham; *Judicial Review Handbook*, at para.24 for further analysis and case law.
[255] Formerly mandamus, prohibition or certiorari.
[256] CPR 54.19(2).
[257] CPR 54.19(3).

Damages[257A]

An applicant may seek "damages, restitution or recovery of a sum due" but **6–069** he or she cannot seek this remedy alone.[258] A court has a discretion to award damages if

"(a) [the applicant] has joined with his application a claim for damages arising from any matter to which the application relates; and

(b) the court is satisfied that, if the claim had been made in an action begun by the applicant at the time of making his application, he would have been awarded damages."[259]

This provision allows an applicant to claim damages without having to lodge multiple parallel claims. However, there is no common law right to damages for maladministration, and an applicant will have bring himself within the scope of an existing tort or have a claim under the Human Rights Act.[260]

Where a claim is brought under the Human Rights Act 1998, an **6–070** applicant can seek damages where public bodies have acted unlawfully under s.6(1) HRA 1998.[261] Section 8 gives the court a discretionary power to "grant such relief or remedy, or make such order, within its powers as it considers just and appropriate."[262] However, the court will not award damages unless it is "satisfied that the award is necessary to afford just satisfaction" to the claimant. In determining whether to grant a monetary remedy, the court seeks to place the claimant in the position he or she would have been in had the infringement not incurred.[263] Sums awarded under the HRA 1998 are modest, and the court will have regard to any other relief or remedy awarded when determining the amount.

Nature of the court's discretion

The court will generally exercise its discretion and refuse relief in a number **6–071** of situations:

(i) As we have seen when considering extensions of time, under section 31(6) SCA 1981, the court may deny relief where the claimant's delay would mean that, were relief to be granted, the defendant would suffer hardship or prejudice or it would be contrary to good administration.

[257A] For a more extensive analysis of monetary remedies see Fordham, para.25.
[258] CPR 54.3(2).
[259] s.31(4) SCA 1981.
[260] *R v Secretary of State for Transport, ex parte Factortame Ltd (No.2)* [1991] 1 A.C. 603 per Lord Goff at 672H.
[261] s.8(6) HRA 1998. "Unlawful" means unlawful under s.6(1) HRA 1998.
[262] s.8(1) HRA 1998.
[263] See *Anufrijeva v London Borough of Southwark* [2004] 2 W.L.R. 603 at para.59.

(ii) Where events have overtaken the subject matter of the claim. In *R (on the application of Edwards) v Environment Agency and others*,[264] the Agency had granted a permit to a cement plant in Rugby that allowed it to burn tyres as a form of substitute fuel. The claimants contended that the Agency should have carried out a consultation as to whether the burning of tyres would cause significant pollution contrary to the Pollution Prevention and Control (England and Wales) Regulations 1999.[265] In particular, it was alleged that the public had a right to make representations on two Air Quality Monitoring Assessment Unit (AQMAU) reports which had been commissioned by the Agency but had not been made available to the public. These internal reports indicated that environmental quality standards (EQS) in Rugby might be breached if the permission was granted, but that this was unlikely to occur. The Court of Appeal,[266] upholding the decision at first instance, held that the failure to publish these reports was procedurally unfair.[267] However, by the time of the Court of Appeal hearing two AQMAU reports had been produced on the actual emissions from the plant, which concluded that the EQS had not been exceeded. The Court of Appeal therefore refused relief on that basis that "it would be pointless to quash the permit simply to enable the public to be consulted on out-of date data".[268] The House of Lords, approving this decision, held that "the relevance of the [initial, unpublished] AQMAU reports been completely overtaken by events".[269]

(iii) Relief may be refused where the outcome would have been the same had the unlawful breach not occurred.[270] In these circumstances, the claimant has suffered no prejudice, and therefore is not entitled to a remedy. In *R (on the application of Jones) v Swansea City and County Council*,[271] the applicants challenged the grant of planning permission for their neighbours' extension. The court accepted that, in granting the permission, the respondents had been in breach of their policy guidelines on the minimum distance between windows. However, Wyn Williams J. refused relief on the grounds that, were a quashing order granted, "it is virtually inconceivable that the [respondent] would [on a reapplication] do other than grant plan-

---

[264] [2008] UKHL 22. For further discussion, see below under "Public Consultation".
[265] SI 2000/1973.
[266] [2006] EWCA Civ 877.
[267] While this finding was not challenged before the House of Lords, Lord Hoffman noted *obiter* that he would not have reached this conclusion: para.44.
[268] per Auld LJ, at [126].
[269] per Lord Hoffman, *R(ex p Edwards) v Environment Agency and others* [2008] UKHL 22 at [65].
[270] *R v Monopolies & Mergers Commission, ex p Argyll Group Plc* [1986] 1 W.L.R. 763.
[271] [2007] EWHC 213 (Admin).

ning permission".[272] As such, nothing was to be achieved by a quashing order.

The above grounds are not exhaustive, but are merely some of the more common reasons for withholding a remedy. Other notable reasons for refusing relief include circumstances where it is in the public interest to do so,[273] or on grounds relating to good public administration.[274] However, where unlawfulness has been shown, the nature of the court's discretion is very narrow, and it is only in exceptional cases that the court will refuse relief.[275] The discretion is even narrower where the obligation originates from an EU directive, because EU member states are required to take all appropriate measures to ensure fulfilment of Treaty obligations,[276] and national courts are obliged to ensure that Community rights are "fully and effectively enforced".[277]

Access to Justice

Legal principles

As we have seen, under common law, European and international legal principles, access to justice[278] is a fundamental right and a key public law principle. Further, it has been enshrined in statute as a result of the incorporation of the ECHR into domestic law.[279]   **6–072**

In terms of environmental law, the strongest statement of the principle is found in international law. The Aarhus Convention entered into force in October 2001 and was ratified by the UK in February 2005. Under Article 1, each Party shall guarantee access to justice in environmental matters in accordance with the Convention. Article 9, entitled "Access to justice" states:

"(2) Each Party shall, within the framework of its national legislation, ensure that members of the public concerned

---

[272] para.31.
[273] "The court has an ultimate discretion whether to set [public law decisions] aside and may refuse to do so in the public interest, notwithstanding that it holds and declares the decision to have been made ultra vires": see, for example, *Reg. v Monopolies and Mergers Commission, Ex parte Argyll Group Plc.* [1986] 1 W.L.R. 763 *R v Panel on Take-overs and Mergers, ex p Datafin Plc* [1987] Q.B. 815 at 840B per Sir Donaldson MR.
[274] *R v Monopolies & Mergers Commission, ex p Argyll Group Plc* [1986] 1 W.L.R. 763, pp.7744C–775B.
[275] *Berkeley v Secretary of State for the Environment* [2001] 2 AC 603, at pp.608D and 616F.
[276] European Community Treaty, Article 10 (ex Article 5).
[277] *Berkeley v Secretary of State for the Environment* [2001] 2 AC 603, at p.608D per Lord Bingham.
[278] See definition and discussion of this principle above, under "general principles of public law" at para.6–007.
[279] See the Human Rights Act 1998, and Article 6 of the ECHR.

(a) having a sufficient interest or, alternatively,

(b) maintaining impairment of a right, where the administrative procedural law of a Party requires this as a precondition,

have access to a review procedure before a court of law and/or another independent and impartial body established by law, to challenge the substantive and procedural legality of any decision, act or omission subject to the provisions of article 6 and, where so provided for under national law and without prejudice to paragraph 3 below, of other relevant provisions of this Convention.

(3) In addition, and without prejudice to the review procedures referred to in paragraphs 1 and 2 above, each Party shall ensure that, where they meet the criteria, if any, laid down in its national law, members of the public have access to administrative or judicial procedures to challenge acts and omissions by private persons and public authorities which contravene provisions of its national law relating to the environment."

Provisions regarding access to justice have been specifically incorporated into EU law as a result of additional articles to two important directives, the Directive on Environmental Assessment[280] and Directive 96/61/EC (now 2008/1) concerning Integrated Pollution Prevention and Control.[281]

Access to justice via judicial review?

6–073   The United kingdom relies heavily on judicial review procedures to meet their legal obligations in respect of access to justice under the Aarhus Convention.[282] Notwithstanding the fact that the number of environmental judicial review challenges has grown steadily in recent years (albeit that the total numbers are still small[283]), there remain serious practical difficulties in accessing justice on environmental matters because of the risk of high costs and the lack of sufficient legal aid. In the case of *R (ex p Sonia Burkett) v London Borough of Hammersmith and Fulham*,[284] where the claimant challenged the adequacy of an environmental impact assessment, Brooke L.J. expressed serious concern at the level of costs involved in environmental judicial review proceedings:

---

[280] art.10A of the Directive 85/337/EEC on the assessment of the effects of certain public and private projects on the environment, as amended by Directives 97/11/EC and 2003/35/EC.

[281] art.15A of Directive 96/61/EC concerning integrated pollution prevention and control; now codified into Directive 2008/1.

[282] Ensuring access to environmental justice in England and Wales" Report of the Working Group on Access to Environmental Justice, May 2008, (the "Sullivan Report") at para.14. The public participation elements of the Aarhus Convention are separately transposed into domestic law, by, e.g. the Environmental Permitting Regulations SI 2007/3538.

[283] As is pointed out in the Sullivan Report.

[284] [2004] Civ 1342.

"[I]f the figures revealed by this case were in any sense typical of the costs reasonably incurred in litigating such cases up to the highest level, very serious questions would be raised as to the possibility of ever living up to the Aarhus ideals within our present legal system. And if these costs [totalling £35,000] were upheld on detailed assessment, the outcome would cast serious doubts on the cost-effectiveness of the courts as a means of resolving environmental disputes."[285]

A Working Group was set up in 2006 under Sullivan J. "to consider whether current law and practice creates barriers to access to justice in environmental matters in the context of the Aarhus Convention". The Group's report,[286] published in May 2008 (the "Sullivan Report"), concluded that "the key issue limiting access to environmental justice and inhibiting compliance with Article 9(4) of Aarhus is that of costs and the potential exposure to costs."[287] The problem arises due to the application of general costs principles to environmental judicial review claims. The rule that "the loser pays"[288] leaves individuals and small interest groups vulnerable to paying the legal costs of the public authority and potentially those of the interested party.[289]

In addition, the granting of an interim injunction usually requires a cross-undertaking in damages. However, an undertaking is usually not feasible because of the prohibitive potential cost: often the interested party or defendant is a construction company whose deadlines are subject to financial penalty clauses, which the claimant will be expected to pay should the defendant be successful. As such, individuals or NGOs rarely seek an injunction, yet in not doing so they run the risk that, by the time the case comes before the courts for a substantive hearing, the damage may have been irreparably inflicted. In *R v Secretary of State for the Environment ex p RSPB*[290] the judicial review claim to prevent destruction of a wildlife habitat succeeded before the European Court of Justice, but became a moot point because the damage had occurred prior to the final hearing.

In response to these difficulties, the Sullivan Group made a number of recommendations regarding costs and funding in environmental cases, which are discussed below.[291] In addition, the Group recommended that the requirement for a cross-undertaking in damages be lifted "where the court is satisfied that an injunction is required to prevent significant environmental damage and to preserve the factual basis for the proceed-

6–074

---

[285] para.76.
[286] "Ensuring access to environmental justice in England and Wales": Report of the Working Group on Access to Environmental Justice, May 2008.
[287] ibid., para.25.
[288] Civil Procedure Rules Pt.44.3.
[289] Notably where the interested party and the defendant have differing interests which require separate representation: *Bolton MDC v SoS for the Environment* [1995] 1 W.L.R. 1176.
[290] [1997] Env. L.R. 431.
[291] See paras 6–081 and 6–082.

ings".[292] It remains to be seen whether these recommendations will be followed by the courts.

Costs

General rules on costs in JR

6–075 The court has a discretion as to the award of costs.[293] The general principle is "the loser pays"; however, the court will not usually require an unsuccessful claimant to pay the costs of both the defendant and a separate interested party who intervenes unless they had disparate interests requiring separate representation.[294] In *Bolton v Metropolitan District Council v Secretary of the State for the Environment*[295], a planning case involving multiple parties and overlapping issues, the House of Lords outlined the following propositions in relation to costs in such circumstances:

> "(1) The Secretary of State, when successful in defending his decision, will normally be entitled to the whole of his costs. He should not be required to share his award of costs...
>
> (2) The developer will not normally be entitled to his costs unless he can show that there was likely to be a separate issue on which he was entitled to be heard, that is to say an issue not covered by counsel for the Secretary of State; or unless he has an interest which requires separate representation. The mere fact that he is the developer will not of itself justify a second set of costs in every case.
>
> (3) A second set of costs is more likely to be awarded at first instance, than in the Court of Appeal or House of Lords, by which time the issues should have crystallised, and the extent to which there are indeed separate interests should have been clarified.
>
> (4) An award of a third set of costs will rarely be justified, even if there are in theory three or more separate interests."[296]

Costs usually "follow the event" and are thus payable by the loser. In judicial review costs of both the permission and substantive stages (assuming permission is given) are normally awarded only following the final hearing.

Public funding from the Legal Services Commission can be obtained for judicial review proceedings. It is available to applicants who fulfil the

---

[292] The Sullivan Report, summary of key recommendations, p.36(8).
[293] SCA 1985, s.51.
[294] *MDC v SoS for the Environment* [1995] 1 W.L.R. 1176 per Lord Lloyd at pp.1178.
[295] [1995] 1 W.L.R. 1176.
[296] *Bolton MDC v SoS for the Environment* [1995] 1 W.L.R. 1176 per Lord Lloyd at pp.1178–1179.

Funding Code criteria, which assess both the claimant's means[297] and the merits of the case.[298] In order to obtain funding, the applicant must show that:[299]

(i) the act or decision appears susceptible to challenge – funding may be refused where there are other alternatives to legal proceedings which have not been pursued;

(ii) the proposed respondent has had an opportunity to respond or deal with the complaint—this is designed to filter out premature claims;

(iii) the prospects of success are 50 per cent or above, or the case has significant wider public interest or is of overwhelming importance to the client or raises significant human rights issues; and

(iv) the likely costs are proportionate to the likely benefit of the proceedings.

Where permission has been obtained, there is a presumption that funding will be granted where the case has significant wider public interest, is of overwhelming importance to the client or raises significant human rights issues.[300]

The funding of public interest cases is a fairly recent addition: until April 2000 the Legal Services Commission (LSC) determined the granting of funding on the basis of the impact of the outcome for the private client. It now will provide funding where the issue has a wider public interest, defined as "the potential of the proceedings to produce real benefits for individuals other than the client (other than benefits to the public at large which normally flow from proceedings of the type in question)".[301] Where this criterion is met, the applicant is only required to demonstrate that there is a "borderline" prospect of success, rather than a 50 per cent chance. The LSC now recognises that environmental cases may be of wider public interest.[302]

---

[297] Both income and capital are taken into account.

[298] Legal Services Commission Funding Code Criteria, (July 2007), para.7.5.2 (available at *http://www.legalservices.gov.uk/docs/civil_contracting/Funding_code_criteria_Jul07.pdf*. See also Volume 2F (Financial Eligibility) of the LSC Manual, available at *http://calculator.communitylegaladvice.org.uk/ecalc/guidance.asp*).

[299] See Legal Services Commission Funding Code Criteria, (July 2007), para.7.4.

[300] Legal Services Commission Funding Code Criteria, para.7.5.2.

[301] Legal Services Commission Funding Code Criteria, s.2.4.

[302] See the reports of the LSC's Public Interest Advisory Panel which refer specifically to environmental cases; Sullivan Report, para.32.

Costs and environmental cases

6–076   Article 9(4) of the Aarhus Convention also requires that legal procedures regarding environmental matters should be "not prohibitively expensive".[303] In addition, Article 9(5) of the Aarhus Convention signatories "shall consider the establishment of appropriate assistance mechanisms to remove or reduce financial or other barriers to access to justice." There is therefore an onus on the Government to ensure that costs are not an insurmountable obstacle to the lodging of environmental claims.

However, the cost of bringing an environmental claim remains a major barrier to claimants' access to justice in environmental proceedings. Although legal aid is available it is limited, and there is a lack of alternative funding mechanisms.[304] Of greater significance are potential costs liabilities to other parties. Protective Cost Orders[305] have hitherto not been available for most cases. While the *Bolton* principles[306] may assist a claimant with limited means, they do not rule out the possibility of a substantial costs order against the claimant in favour of several parties.[307] The difficulties facing applicants were made starkly clear following the case of *R (ex p Sonia Burkett) v London Borough of Hammersmith and Fulham.*[308] As we have seen, the claimant lost the substantive hearing in the High Court, and was ordered to pay costs claimed at £35,000. Though the Court of Appeal upheld the judge's exercise of discretion on the question of costs, Brooke L.J., in an addendum, expressed concern that the considerable costs involved in litigating environmental matters seriously inhibit access to justice as required under the Aarhus Convention.[309]

Interest groups have therefore sought to circumvent the costs issue by bringing the claim in the name of an impecunious applicant. In *R (Edwards) v Environment Agency and First Secretary of State,*[310] the claim was brought in the name of a homeless man who had been successful in obtaining public funding. The defendants argued that this was an abuse of process. They contended that Mr Edwards had been chosen to front the claim for a campaign group because he qualified for public funding. Keith J. held that it was not an abuse of process to bring proceedings in Mr

---

[303] Article 9(2). The Sullivan Group concluded that this requirement should apply to all judicial review proceedings, including those for interim relief. It also recommended that proceedings should be regarded as "prohibitively expensive" if an ordinary member of the public would be prevented from bringing a claim by the costs involved. The Group defined an "ordinary" member of the public as one who is "neither very rich nor very poor, and who would not be entitled to legal aid." (see paras 20 (4) and(6) of "Ensuring access to environmental justice in England and Wales" Report of the Working Group on Access to Environmental Justice, May 2008).

[304] Sullivan report, para.33.

[305] Discussed below.

[306] Listed above at para.6–075.

[307] See the Sullivan report, para.14.

[308] [2004] Civ 1342. See above at para.6–073.

[309] [2004] Civ 1342, para.76.

[310] [2004] EWHC 736: for further discussion see "Standing".

Edward's name. The LSC had been aware of the facts when granting the funding certificate, and must therefore have considered the matter. It therefore appears that an impecunious litigant may in this way bring a claim on behalf of a group. However, it should be noted that it is likely that in such cases the LSC will have regard to the financial circumstances of the other members of the group, and then opt either to refuse funding where proceedings can be privately funded,[311] or grant an amount limited to a percentage of the total sum on the basis that others may be able to contribute.

Interest groups have also created limited liability companies so as to   **6–077** establish a costs protection. This occurred in *Residents Against Waste Ltd v Lancashire County Council*,[312] where the claimant association was established by the concerned residents two days before the claim was issued. The courts have accepted that there is nothing wrong in principle with this approach:

> "In my view the incorporation of a local action group ought not to be a bar to the bringing of an application for judicial review ... It is true that [an] advantage [of incorporation] is the avoidance of substantial personal liability of members for the costs of unsuccessful legal proceedings. But that should not preclude the use of a corporate vehicle, at least where incorporation is not for the sole purpose of escaping the direct impact of an adverse costs order (and possibly even where it is for that purpose). The costs position can be dealt with adequately by requiring the provision of security for costs in a realistically large sum ... It is, however, the right approach in principle."[313]

The court will also take a practical approach to the question of funding at the permission stage. Where the subject matter of a case no longer exists, the court will take account of the applicant's ability to finance the claim when considering whether to grant permission. In *R (on the application of England) v Tower Hamlets London Borough Council*,[314] a campaigner objected to the local authority's decision to grant planning permission for a housing development on the site of the historic Suttons Wharf in London. Mr England sought to protect the wharf, which was the only one of its kind left in London. The application for permission was dismissed by the Administrative Court,[315] and by the time of the appeal on the question of permission the building had been substantially demolished. At the hearing, it was unclear how the applicant was going to fund the case: he requested that a PCO be granted, but no application had been made and the request

---

[311] Legal Services Commission Funding Code Criteria, para.11.12.7.
[312] [2008] Env. L.R. 27.
[313] *R v Leicestershire County Council ex p Blackfordby and Boothorpe Action Group Limited* [2001] Env. L.R. 35 per Richards J. at para.37.
[314] [2006] EWCA Civ 1742.
[315] (2006) EWHC 1801 (Admin).

was rejected. The Court of Appeal held that while an applicant's means of funding a claim is not normally an issue where there is otherwise an arguable case, it is a factor that may be taken into account when the main practical purpose of the claim no longer exists.[316] Permission was therefore refused.

Protective Costs Orders

6–078 A Protective Costs Order ("PCO") is an order which caps the amount of costs that a party (or parties) will have to pay at or near the outset of the case. It gives parties the certainty of knowing their costs risk, and prevents the costs being "prohibitively expensive". An application for a PCO should preferably be made at the same time as the permission stage of judicial review proceedings.

In *R (Corner House Research) v Secretary of State for Trade & Industry*,[317] the seminal case on PCOs, the Court of Appeal stated that "no PCO should be granted unless the judge considers that the application for judicial review has a real prospect of success and that it is in the public interest to make the order".[318] It noted also that PCOs should only be granted in exceptional cases. The Court then laid down a number of principles regarding the granting of such orders:

"(1) A protective costs order may be made at any stage of the proceedings, on such conditions as the court thinks fit, provided that the court is satisfied that:

(i) the issues raised are of general public importance;
(ii) the public interest requires that those issues should be resolved;
(iii) the applicant has no private interest in the outcome of the case;
(iv) having regard to the financial resources of the applicant and the respondent(s) and to the amount of costs that are likely to be involved, it is fair and just to make the order; and
(v) if the order is not made the applicant will probably discontinue the proceedings and will be acting reasonably in so doing.

(2) If those acting for the applicant are doing so pro bono this will be likely to enhance the merits of the application for a PCO.
(3) It is for the court, in its discretion, to decide whether it is fair and just to make the order in the light of the considerations set out above."[319]

However, in relation to environmental law the *Corner House* principles have been criticised as being incompatible with the Aarhus Convention on two

---

[316] [2006] EWCA Civ 1742, per Carnwath L.J. at para.12.
[317] [2005] 1 W.L.R. 2600.
[318] para.73.
[319] para.74.

main grounds, namely the requirements that (i) the claimant have no private interest, and (ii) the matter must be of "general public importance". There is also the difficulty that the case must be "exceptional"[320] to justify granting a PCO.

As regards the first requirement, this has been heavily criticised as unrealistic. Many claimants wishing to bring environmental judicial review proceedings will have a direct, private interest in the outcome due to the impact it will have on their homes, businesses or local environment. Further, a private interest is often inimical to getting permission to bring judicial review proceedings. The courts have recognised these difficulties and have taken a flexible approach towards this requirement. Sir Mark Potter in *Wilkinson v Kitzinger and Attorney General and Lord Chancellor*[321] noted:

"As to (1)(iii) [of the *Corner House* criteria], I find the requirement that the Applicant should have 'no private interest in the outcome' a somewhat elusive concept to apply in any case in which the Applicant, either in private or public law proceedings is pursuing a personal remedy, albeit his or her purpose is essentially representative of a number of persons with a similar interest. In such a case, it is difficult to see why, if a PCO is otherwise appropriate, the existence of the Applicant's private or personal interest should disqualify him or her from the benefit of such an order. I consider that the nature and extent of the 'private interest' and its weight or importance in the overall context should be treated as a flexible element in the court's consideration of the question whether it is fair and just to make the order. Were I to be persuaded that the remaining criteria are satisfied, I would not regard requirement 1(iii) as fatal to this application."[322]

These sentiments were shared by the Court of Appeal in *England*,[323] and were also recently approved in *Compton v Wiltshire Primary Care Trust*.[324]

The second issue, namely the requirement that the matter must be of **6–079** "general public importance" inevitably severely restricts the availability of PCOs. To qualify under this criterion, the matter must either raise a new point of law or have an impact on a large swathe of the population.[325] In these circumstances, it will be extremely difficult to qualify unless the matter will have a substantial impact on environmental law as a whole. Yet

[320] See *R (Corner House Research) v Secretary of State for Trade & Industry* [2005] 1 W.L.R. 2600 at para.74.
[321] [2006] EWHC 2022.
[322] ibid., para.54.
[323] *R (on the application of England) v Tower Hamlets London Borough Council* [2006] EWCA 1742.
[324] [2008] EWCA Civ 749.
[325] See, for example, *R (on the application of Bullmore) v West Hertfordshire Hospitals NHS Trust* [2007] EWHC 1350 (Admin) where an application for a PCO was refused because the case concerned the closure of a hospital which only affected a particular constituency.

this criterion undermines the notion inherent in the Aarhus Convention that environmental matters are of "general public importance",[326] and therefore each individual has both the right to an adequate environment and a duty to protect and improve it.

However, in the very recent case of *Compton v Wiltshire Primary Care Trust*,[327] the Court of Appeal clarified the principles in *Corner House*, essentially relaxing the criteria the "general public importance" test. The claimant, acting on behalf of a campaign group, was seeking to prevent the closure of facilities at her local hospital. The closure would have affected the 30,000 to 50,000 people who lived in the catchment area. In the two judicial review proceedings lodged against the decision to close the facilities, the claimant had been granted PCOs. The Trust appealed against the decision to grant the PCOs. It was argued that the claimant did not fulfil the *Corner House* criteria because the closure of a local hospital did not raise an issue of "general public importance", nor did the public interest require that the matter be resolved. It also contended that the case was not "exceptional" such as to justify granting a PCO.

The Court of Appeal, by a majority, dismissed the appeals. Waller L.J. held that the two stage test (outlined in *Corner House*) of general public importance and public interest in the issue were difficult to separate.[328] He noted that:

"Where someone in the position of Mrs Compton is bringing an action to obtain resolution of issues as to the closure of parts of a hospital which affects a wide community, and where that community has a real interest in the issues that arise being resolved, my view is that it is certainly open to a judge to hold that there is a public interest in resolution of the issues and that the issues are ones of general public importance. The paragraphs in *Corner House* are not, in my view, to be read as statutory provisions, nor to be read in an over-restrictive way...

Furthermore, I would agree with Holman J that "exceptionality" was not seen in *Corner House* as some additional criteria to the principles set out in paragraph 74 but a prediction as to the effect of applying the principles. Finally I do not read the word "general" as meaning that it must be of interest to all the public nationally. On the other hand I would accept that a local group may be so small that issues in which they alone might be interested would not be issues of "general public importance". It is a question of degree and a question which *Corner House* would expect judges to be able to resolve."[329]

[326] Sullivan report, para.46.
[327] [2008] EWCA Civ 749.
[328] ibid., para.21.
[329] ibid., paras 23–24. See also the very recent case of *R. (on the application of Buglife) v Thurrock Thames Gateway Development Corporation* [2008] EWCA Civ 1209.

However, notwithstanding this relaxation of the *Corner House* approach, the Court in *Compton* indicated that the procedural guidance given in *Corner House* should be followed as far as possible.[330]

Following the cases of *Wilkinson*, *England* and *Compton* the effect of the **6–080** two criticised requirements outlined above have been mitigated, although they still remain. However, the "public interest" requirement is still a potential barrier to claimants. In *McCaw v Middlesex SARL*,[331] the claimant, acting on behalf of other complainants, sought to challenge a decision taken by a magistrate in the claimant's statutory nuisance proceedings against a developer. The magistrate had ruled that the addition of other complainants amounted to multiple charges, and that the complaint was therefore duplicitous. The claimant, relying, inter alia, on the Sullivan report, sought a PCO in order to judicially review the decision. While recognising that the *environmental* issue was not of general public importance, the claimant argued that the *procedural* issue, namely whether a statutory nuisance affecting a number of people amounted to a single charge or multiple charges, fulfilled the "public importance" criteria. However, the application was rejected on the grounds that the claimant had an alternative remedy open to her via proceedings in the magistrates' court and that, contrary to the claimant's arguments, the issues were not sufficiently important to be resolved in the public interest.

It is arguable that this decision is incorrect in that the court sidestepped the issue: the claimant was seeking a decision on a procedural matter of general public importance which would impact upon countless other statutory nuisance claims. It would therefore seem that the fact that the matter is an important legal question which will potentially affect many people is in itself insufficient to justify granting a PCO; rather, the claimant must show that, on the facts of their particular case, the resolution of the issue will directly affect a large number of individuals.

The Sullivan Group's recommendations

In its report, the Sullivan Group examined the issue of costs and the dif- **6–081** ficulties posed by the lack of funding. It then made a number of recommendations aimed at ameliorating these problems, which included the following:

1. Alternative methods of funding should be developed, such as a partnership between non-governmental organisations and legal aid;
2. That while the general "loser pays" principle should remain the norm, Aarhus principles should be taken into account by the court when determining whether to exercise its discretion;

[330] ibid., para.47. The Court also laid down some procedural rules in relation to PCOs: see paras 48–49.
[331] [2008] EWHC 1504 (Admin).

3. Where a claimant is substantially successful, but denied relief on discretionary grounds, he or she should be regarded as having "won" for costs purposes;

4. A claimant should not be expected to pay a defendant's costs of resisting an injunction at the permission stage where such costs are regarded as prohibitively expensive.[332]

The Group also considered PCOs as a means of curtailing costs and thereby increasing access to justice. It held that while they may assist in ensuring access, "the current judicial principles on PCOs were not developed with Aarhus in mind, and contain constraints that are not consistent with Aarhus."[333] In particular the Group criticised the "no private interest" and "general public importance" requirements because they were too restrictive and did not comply with the principles in the Aarhus Convention.[334]

The Sullivan Group therefore proposed a form of PCO, particular to environmental matters, which would comply with the Aarhus principles.[335] In particular, it suggested that the two contentious requirements ("private interest" and general "public importance") be removed, and that a claimant who acts reasonably[336] should be entitled to a PCO where he would otherwise be prevented from bringing the case because of his potential exposure to costs. It was also noted that the costs of applying for a PCO should be limited to a maximum figure of £500.[337] In addition, the Group recommended that there should not be any risk of paying third party costs unless there are exceptional circumstances.

The suggestions in the Sullivan Report have since been judicially acknowledged as relevant when considering PCOs in environmental matters. In *R (on the application of McCaw) v City of Westminster Magistrate's Court*,[338] Latham J. noted that the *Corner House* principles:

"... must be applied in environmental case contexts in the light of the Aarhus Convention. I accept that in general terms, without wishing to seek to tie the hands of any court that considers the matter hereafter, the suggestions of the Sullivan working party should be taken into account by the court."[339]

The issue of PCOs in environmental law is relatively recent. The recommendations in the Sullivan report are likely to impact upon decisions

---

[332] See paras 35 and 36.
[333] ibid., para.9.
[334] ibid., paras 45–48.
[335] ibid., Appendix 4.
[336] "Reasonable conduct" is not defined in the report.
[337] In *England*, (see fn.32), the Court of Appeal noted that the process of applying for a PCO should not "itself become a source of additional cost." (para.14).
[338] [2008] EWHC 1504 (Admin).
[339] ibid., at para.9.

in this area, but until the rules committee codify procedure relating to PCOs the law is likely to remain uncertain for some time to come.[340]

Costs and the ECHR

It has been held by the European Court of Human Rights that the costs of proceedings may violate the right to a fair trial under Article 6(1) because it undermines the equality of arms. In *Affaire Collectif National d'Information d'Opposition à l'Usine Melox—Collectif Stop Melox et Mox c.* France,[340A] the applicant was an association that sought, by legal means, to oppose the making, use and recycling of Mox, a nuclear material. It brought a claim against the State to prevent the building of a plant processing Mox, and France invited the owner of the plant to intervene as a third party. The claim failed, and costs were awarded against the applicant in favour of the plant's owner, a multinational company. The applicant claimed that the costs order breached its rights to a fair trial under Article 6(1) ECHR. It alleged in particular that there was an inequality of arms, as it had been required to fight both the state and the multinational company. The Court dismissed the case on the grounds that the costs bill had been moderate (€762); however, it recognised that the weakest party had been penalised, such that the organisation was likely to be discouraged from pursuing its aims because of limited resources. Further, it did not rule out the possibility that such circumstances may conflict with rights protected under Article 6(1). **6–082**

Consultation

The requirements for consultation and public involvement before the taking of environmental decisions are widely distributed throughout the law, and hence consequently throughout this book. Public involvement before planning decisions are taken is described in Chapters 8 (Planning) and 9 (EIA), and Chapter 9 also looks at environmental plans and projects the subject of Directive 2001/42 on Strategic Environmental Assessment. Public involvement in decisions affecting IPPC installations is considered in Chapter 14; by way of example, the IPPC Directive[341] requires member states "to ensure that the public is given early and effective opportunities to participate in the procedure" for new permits and substantial changes to existing permitted installations. **6–083**

---

[340] The issue of costs generally in environmental challenges is likely to return to the CA in January 2009: *R (Morgan) v Hinton Organics*, in which permission was granted by Carnwath L.J. on Aarhus issues.

[340A] Application no.75218/01, September 12, 2007.

[341] SI 2008/1, at art.15.

The purpose of this section is to look at public consultation, and indeed consultation more generally, in order to see how and when lack of such consultation may give rise to successful judicial review challenges. Hence, we will be concentrating on the common law, although statutory provisions may determine, or provide important context for, the scope of such consultation duties. Its principal subject is *public* consultation, though we will examine the need for consultation of a slightly different sort, namely that which arises out of general fairness when a decision is being taken which directly affects a party, such as a decision to grant or refuse an application made by that party, or a ruling made against them. The common law has in the past more readily recognised the obligations of fairness owned to such applicants than it has any wider obligations of public consultation owed to third parties (whether on specific decisions, or indeed on decisions of policy taken by government), but as we shall see, the approaches of the courts to each of these categories have come closer in recent years.

Essential elements of consultation

6–084   Where a decision-maker is obliged to consult, the requirements of the consultation process, in particular the extent of the consultation and the methods used, will vary according to the circumstances.[342] However, there are some essential elements to any consultation:

> "[T]o be proper, consultation must be undertaken at a time when proposals are still in a formative stage; it must include sufficient reasons for particular proposals to allow those consulted to give intelligent consideration and an intelligent response; adequate time must be given for this purpose; and the product of consultation must be conscientiously taken into account when the ultimate decision is taken."[343]

It is important that consultation documents are clear as to their purpose,[344] so that the consultees will be able to provide a response specific to the issues raised. Notwithstanding any urgency, sufficient time must be given to allow the consultees to provide informed, considered opinions.[345] Consequently, in *R (on the application of Amvac Chemical UK Ltd) v SoS for Environment, Food and Rural Affairs*,[346] an urgent decision to suspend regulatory approval of a pesticide on health grounds was quashed because the claimant company, which used the pesticide, had only been given two days to provide any comment.

[342] *R v Devon County Council, ex p Baker* [1995] 1 All E.R. 73, at 88 per Simon Brown L.J.
[343] *Coughlan*, para.109 per Lord Woolf, citing *R v Brent London Borough Council, ex p Gunning* (1985) 84 LGR 168.
[344] *Greenpeace* [2007] EWHC 311 (Admin) para.74.
[345] *R v Secretary of State for Social Services ex parte Association of Metropolitan Authorities* [1986] 1 W.L.R. 1, at p.14.
[346] [2001] EWHC Admin 1011, paras 61–63.

The obligation to consult and its scope

It is far from necessary to carry out a consultation process for every deci-   6–085
sion, but the duty to consult can arise under statute,[347] or under the
common law duty of fairness[348] where individuals are likely to be affected
by the outcome. Traditionally the common law imposed no such general
requirement in relation to decisions affecting the public generally, though,
in harmony with the relaxation of the standing rules, decisions are now
more readily held to affect individuals. Hence, whether an obligation to
consult arises, and if so its scope, can be contentious.

The interplay of common law and statute can be seen in *Edwards v
Environment Agency*.[349] It was alleged that the Agency had breached its
statutory and common law duties by failing to carry out a public consultation on two internal Air Quality Monitoring Assessment Unit
(AQMAU) reports which not been made available to the public. It was
asserted that the Agency had been legally obliged to consult the public on
these reports as a result of the relevant EU Directive,[350] the 1999 Regulations[351] implementing the IPPC Directive, and under the common law
duty of fairness. By failing to publish these reports, it was said that the
Agency had breached its legal duty and the permit was therefore vitiated by
procedural irregularity. It was also alleged that, pursuant to the 1999
Regulations, informal communications between the cement plant and the
Agency should have been published because they had been part of the
permit application.

The House of Lords held that there had been no requirement to carry
out a consultation on these documents. One issue arose as whether there
was such a duty under the Regulations. Although they required the publication of all documents relevant to the application,[352] this did not extend
to the AQMAUs or informal correspondence. The AQMAUs were internal
documents which were generated by the Agency while processing the
application and were therefore "not particulars of the application".[353]
Further, there was no restriction in the Regulations on obtaining information by informal inquiry, and to prevent the Agency from commu-
nicating informally with an applicant would be extremely inhibiting.[354]

As to the common law duty of consultation, it had previously been held   6–086
by the Court of Appeal that the failure to publish the AQMAUs was

---

[347] See *R v Secretary of State for Social Services ex parte Association of Metropolitan Authorities* [1986] 1 W.L.R. 1.
[348] *Edwards v Environment Agency* [2008] UKHL 22, paras 26 and 44–45.
[349] [2008] UKHL 22, see above under "Remedies" at para.6–066.
[350] European Council Directive 96/61/EC of September 24, 1996, concerning integrated pollution prevention and control (the "IPPC Directive").
[351] Pollution Prevention and Control (England and Wales) Regulations 1999 SI 2000/1973.
[352] Regulation 9 and sch.9, para.1.
[353] Sch.9, para.31.
[354] Sch.9, paras 41 and 42.

procedurally unfair. This finding was not challenged in the House of Lords, but Lord Hoffman indicated that he would not have reached the same conclusion, in part because he was unpersuaded that the common law duty should go any wider than the statute.[355] As the AQMAUs were internal working documents, the Agency should not be under a duty to disclose them, otherwise the consultation process would be never-ending. However, even though the Court of Appeal held that there had been a breach of the common law duty of consultation, it refused to grant relief because more recent reports had indicated that the EQS had not been exceeded, and the AQMAUs had therefore been overtaken by events. The House of Lords upheld this finding and dismissed the appeal.[356]

An issue which often materialises is whether a duty to consult arises between a regulator investigating whether to commence proceedings and the body under investigation. A good example of this is the *Falmouth*[357] case. The defendant authority served an abatement notice on the sewerage undertaker. The undertaker sought judicial review of the decision to serve the abatement notice, arguing, inter alia, that the defendant was under a duty to consult the undertaker before serving the notice. This ground was dismissed. Harrison J. concluded that there was no such duty; it was ultimately a matter of discretion for the enforcing authority whether to consult or not but, as a matter of commonsense and good administration, it would usually be reasonable for it to do so. The Court of Appeal agreed. In each case, the underlying rationale was that such a duty was inconsistent with the statutory scheme in the EPA, and with the policy reasons which might require swift action by a regulator.

Public consultations may relate to general policy decisions rather than the specific decision at stake in *Edwards*. In environmental law, the importance of consultation is evident, as decisions dealing with controversial matters (such as nuclear power, expansion of airports or waste incineration) can have a wide-ranging impact on planning, conservation and health issues at all levels, whether local, national or global. Under the Aarhus Convention each signatory "shall endeavour to provide opportunities for public participation in the preparation of policies relating to the environment".[358] The Government is therefore obliged to provide the public with a means of contributing to discussions on environmental pol-

---

[355] Sch.9, para.44.
[356] Sch.9, para.65. However, Lord Mance, though agreeing with the conclusion dissented regarding the remit of the Regulations: see para.80.
[357] [1999] EWHC Admin 349, Harrison J, and [2001] Q.B. 445, CA. A claim based upon a legitimate expectation of consultation arising out of initial correspondence from the defendant was also dismissed.
[358] Article 7. See *Greenpeace* [2007] para.51; in which Sullivan J. added "Given the importance of the decision under challenge—whether new nuclear build should now be supported—it is difficult to see how a promise of anything less than "the fullest public consultation" would have been consistent with the Government's obligations under the Aarhus Convention."

icy. Traditionally, policy decisions were not subject to a common law or other duty to consult; however, where the Government's conduct gives rise to a legitimate expectation that consultation will be carried out, it cannot renege on this duty.[359] The typical example of this is where a public authority has provided an unequivocal assurance, whether by means of an express promise or an established practice, that it will give notice or embark upon consultation before it changes an existing substantive policy.[360] In the absence of such an assurance there can generally be no objection raised to a policy change made without prior consultation, because there has been no abuse of power.

The Cabinet Office Code of Practice on Consultation,[361] which came into force on January 1, 2001, applies to all public consultations by English government departments and agencies, including consultations on EU Directives. It lists six criteria that must be followed:

6–087

1. Consult widely throughout the process, allowing a minimum of 12 weeks for written consultation at least once during the development of the policy;
2. Be clear about what your proposals are, who may be affected, what questions are being asked and the timescale for responses;
3. Ensure that your consultation is clear, concise and widely accessible.
4. Give feedback regarding the responses received and how the consultation process influenced the policy
5. Monitor your department's effectiveness at consultation, including through the use of a designated consultation co-ordinator.
6. Ensure your consultation follows better regulation best practice, including carrying out a Regulatory Impact Assessment if appropriate.

The effect of the Code on the obligation to consult has been considered recently in *Bhatt Murphy*. In a passage approved by the Court of Appeal, the Divisional Court stated:

"The Introduction states that the Code and the criteria apply to all public consultations by government departments and agencies. [Counsel for the Secretary of State] submits, correctly in my view, that this means that the Code is to apply whenever it is decided as a matter of policy to have a public consultation; not that public consultation is a required prelude to every policy change. The Code states that it does not have legal force but should generally be regarded as binding on United Kingdom departments and their agencies unless Ministers conclude that

---

[359] *R (on the application of Greenpeace) v Secretary of State for Trade and Industry* [2007] EWHC 311 (Admin); (2007) Env. L.R. 29.
[360] See *CCSU* [1985] AC 374 at 408, *ex p Baker* [1995] 1 AER 73 at 89, and *ex p Coughlan* at para.57, p.242.
[361] November 2000, last published in September 2005 (available at *http://www.berr.gov.uk/files/file44364.pdf*).

exceptional circumstances require a departure from it. ... I do not consider that it is possible to read this document as any form of governmental promise or undertaking that policy changes will never be made without consultation. It would be very surprising if it could be so read, not least because a decision in a particular case whether to consult is itself a policy decision. Rather the Code prescribes how generally public consultation should be conducted if there is to be public consultation."

Requirements of fairness in the consultation process

6-088 Irrespective of the methods used or the form employed, it is crucial that the concept of fairness underlie any consultation process.[362] As stated in *R v Secretary of State for Transport, ex parte Medway Council*, "it is axiomatic that consultation, whether it is a matter of obligation or undertaken voluntarily, requires fairness".[363] What fairness will require will vary according to the situation; however, precedent indicates that where the process is flawed, such as in the circumstances outlined below, this may vitiate the fairness of the consultation.

Misleading as to its aim

6-089 Where the decision-makers give a wrong impression as to the aim of the consultation or the matters being consulted upon, the process will be flawed. In *Greenpeace* [2007],[364] the Government promised that there would be the "fullest public consultation" before any policy decision to support the use of nuclear energy. A Consultation Document was released which "gave every appearance"[365] of being a paper on the issues surrounding the use of nuclear energy. It gave the impression that it would be followed by a consultation paper containing proposals regarding nuclear new build. However, following the consultation the Government announced that it would support nuclear energy. When the decision was challenged, Mr Justice Sullivan held that the consultation process had been "very seriously flawed" because, among other defects, the Consultation Document had been misleading as to its aims.

In *Wandsworth*,[366] the Secretary of State for Transport put forward two proposals for the expansion of Luton airport. However, a third option, namely the extension of the existing runway, was not consulted upon.

---

[362] *R v Devon County Council, ex parte Baker* [1995] 1 All E.R. 73 at 88 per Simon Brown L.J.
[363] *R v Secretary of State for Transport, ex parte Medway Council et al* [2002] EWHC 2516 (Admin) para.29 per Maurice Kay J.
[364] [2007] EWHC 311 (Admin); (2007) Env. L.R. 29.
[365] para.16.
[366] *R (London Borough of Wandsworth and others) v Secretary of State for Transport* [2005] EWHC 20 (Admin).

Although there had been an oblique reference to this option in one of the consultation documents, no further clarification was provided when such was sought by one of the consultees. Following the consultation a White Paper was published which was construed as supporting this third option. The decision-making process was challenged on the basis that the consultees had not been given the opportunity to respond to this proposal; as such, it was unfair of the Secretary of State to give policy support to that option. It was held that the White Paper had unfairly conveyed the impression that the proposal to extend the runway

"had been consulted upon, and that it ... was supported in policy terms, when fairness required a clear acknowledgement that since it had not been consulted upon, any decision as to whether or not it should have policy support would have to be the subject of full consultation."[367]

Relevant information provided

Where the decision-maker fails to provide sufficient relevant information, **6–090** not only is the process misleading but it also prevents consultees responding appropriately to the consultation exercise. In *Greenpeace* [2007] the Consultation Paper contained very little substantive information on two critical issues regarding nuclear new build: the cost of using nuclear energy and the disposal of nuclear waste. Relevant information on these matters only came to light after the consultation exercise was finished. It was held that *"elementary fairness"* required that the consultees be given an opportunity to respond to the new material produced before any decision was taken on the role of nuclear new build.[368] As there had been no proper consultation on the substance of these issues, the process had been procedurally unfair. Consultation should be by reference to proposals, rather than merely a bland generality, so as to permit intelligent consideration and response to those proposals.[369]

Remit of consultation too narrow

Where a decision-maker rules out a possible option without reasonable **6–091** justification, the consultation may be struck down as irrational. In *Medway*,[370] the Secretary of State issued a consultation document on the future development of air transport. However, he excluded Gatwick airport as an alternative for additional runway capacity on the ground that the British Airports Authority had agreed in 1979 not to construct a second runway there before 2019. The claimants challenged this exclusion on the basis

---

[367] Per Sullivan J. at para.312(2).
[368] ibid., para.117.
[369] *De Smith's Judicial Review*, at 7–054.
[370] *R v Secretary of State for Transport, ex parte Medway Council et al* [2002] EWHC 2516 (Admin).

that it would stymie any consideration of Gatwick as an expansion option in the future. It was held that the exclusion was plainly irrational. Following the consultation procedure, governmental policy would be formed without consideration of Gatwick as an option. It would then be almost impossible for those proposing development at Gatwick (by way of alternatives to other airports) to challenge that policy and present itself as a viable alternative for expansion in the future. The consultation process was therefore found to be irrational and procedurally unfair.[371]

Consultation need not be flawless

6–092   The courts have recognised that a consultation process need not be flawless. As Sullivan J. put it in *Greenpeace* [2007]:

> "In reality, a conclusion that a consultation exercise was unlawful on the ground of unfairness will be based upon a finding by the court, not merely that something went wrong, but that something went "clearly and radically" wrong.".[372]

It is for the regulators to determine whether the information is adequate, albeit not complete.[373] In *Edwards* the House of Lords held that the following judicial statement on environmental statements was equally applicable to applications for a permit under the 1999 PPC Regulations:

> "In an imperfect world it is an unrealistic counsel of perfection to expect that an applicant's environmental statement will always contain the 'full information' about the environmental impact of a project. The regulations are not based upon such an unrealistic expectation. They recognise that an environmental statement may well be deficient, and make provision through the publicity and consultation processes for any deficiencies to be identified so that the resulting 'environmental information' provides the local planning authority with as full a picture as possible. There will be cases where the document purporting to be an environmental statement is so deficient that it could not reasonably be described as an environmental statement by the Regulations ... but they are likely to be few and far between."[374]

This approach is consistent with the discretionary nature of remedies: even where a flaw is found, it will not necessarily vitiate the whole consultation process.

There is generally no duty to carry out additional rounds of consultation after the first, unless there is a "fundamental difference" between the

---

[371] para.32.
[372] *Greenpeace* [2007], [2007] Env. L.R. 29, at para.63.
[373] *Edwards*, para.38.
[374] *R(Blewitt) v Derbyshire County Council* [2004] Env. L.R. 29, para.41 per Sullivan J., cited with approval in Edwards at para.38.

proposals initially consulted on and those which the decision-maker wishes to adopt,[375] or if the decision-maker comes upon a factor of potential significance to the decision to be made, which fairness requires needs to be disclosed to the affected party.[376]

ACCESS TO ENVIRONMENTAL INFORMATION

Introduction

As Principle 10 of the Rio Declaration makes clear,[377] access to environ- **6–093**
mental information is a vital component in public participation in the development of environmental policy and in environmental decision-making by governments and public authorities, and in the potential for review of the outcome of that decision-making by judicial and administrative means. As noted by the Information Commissioner in a decision relating to the development of liquefied natural gas terminals in Milford Haven, "there is an inherent public interest in individuals having access to information that helps them to understand the decisions made by public bodies".[378]

As is also clear from Principle 10, public access to environmental information may be effected in two ways: firstly, the active dissemination of environmental information by the State ("active" provision of information) and, secondly, the supplying of environmental information to those who request it ("reactive" provision of information). This section will address both types of information provision.

Development of Access to Environmental Information

Prior to the development of European legislation in the field, there had **6–094**
never been a general right of access to environmental information in the UK.

Directive 90/313/EEC and the EIR 1992

Directive 90/313/EEC[379] on the Freedom of Access to Information on the **6–095**
Environment was adopted on June 7, 1990, and was transposed into

---

[375] *R (Smith) v E. Kent Hospital NHS Trust* [2002] EWHC 2640 at para.45.
[376] *Edwards*, CA, [2006] EWHC 877, para.103, a statement of principle unaffected by the decision in the HL.
[377] See introduction to this chapter.
[378] Decision FER0072936 (March 28, 2007).
[379] OJ L 158, 23.6.1990, p.56–58.

English law by the Environmental Information Regulations 1992.[380] These provided for the first time for an environmental information regime ensuring a general right to access to information subject only to certain categories of exemption.

Aarhus Convention

6–096   The Aarhus Convention was adopted in June 25, 1998. Article 4 of the Convention sets out in detail the principles to be adhered to by the Parties in relation to requests for access to environmental information; Article 5 deals with the collection and dissemination of environmental information, including the publication of public registers of environmental information, national reports on the environment, and of pollution inventories or registers. Article 9 requires that the refusal of a request for information be reviewable before an independent court or other forum, with the procedure free or inexpensive.

The development of Freedom of Information in the UK

6–097   Meanwhile, in 1997 the UK Government had published its White Paper on Freedom of Information, *"Your Right to Know"*, which established the principle that all information held by public bodies would be made available unless it would cause harm to various interests, and provided that the decision to release the information satisfied tests to ensure that it was consistent with the public interest. However, the Freedom of Information Act 2000 (the FOIA) expressly excluded environmental information, defined as information which a public authority was obliged to release under Regulations enacted for the purpose of implementing the Aarhus Convention (or which it would have been obliged to release were it not for the exemptions contained within those regulations).[381] At the time the FOIA was passed, however, these regulations had not yet been issued.

Directive 2003/4/EC

6–098   Directive 2003/4/EC[382] ("the Directive") was developed in response both to the perceived flaws in Directive 90/313/EC and to the Aarhus Convention. Its stated aims were to clarify the definition of environmental information so as to encompass

> "information in any form on the state of the environment, on factors, measures of activities affecting or likely to affect the environment or designed to protect it, on cost-benefit and economic analyses used within

---

[380] SI 1992/3240.
[381] ss.39 and 74, Freedom of Information Act 2000.
[382] [2003] OJ L41, pp.26–32.

the framework of such measures or activities and also information of the state of human health and safety . . ."

It also expanded the definition of a public authority.

The Directive deals, not only with the provision of environmental information on request, but also the dissemination of environmental information to the public "as a matter of course".[383]

Environmental Information Regulations 2004

The Environmental Information Regulations 2004[384] (EIR 2004) imple-   **6–099**
mented the Directive and came into force on January 1, 2005. They differ from the preceding 1992 Regulations in several respects:

(a) the definition of environmental information;
(b) the definition of the bodies affected;
(c) the time limit for response;
(d) the introduction of a public interest test to the decision-making process;
(e) the introduction of the reviewing role of the Information Commissioner and the Information Tribunal.

The Regulations provide a highly detailed regime dealing with the reactive provision of information in response to requests, and a rather looser duty in relation to the active dissemination of environmental information. The Regulations are accompanied by "Guidance to the Environmental Information Regulations 2004" ("the Guidance").[385] Whilst it does not have statutory force, it is a useful insight into the government's approach to and interpretation of the EIR. Part of the Guidance was updated in January 2006 but it must be read in conjunction with the most recent case law. It is available from the Defra website.[386]

A Code of Practice for decision-makers, also available from the Defra website, was issued in February 2005 pursuant to regulation 16 of the EIR 2004.[387]

The Information Commission website also includes a useful collection of guidance documents on the time for compliance with a request, what advice and assistance should be afforded to a member of the public requesting information, and public authorities' duties actively to disseminate information (all of which are discussed below). It also provides an archive of all Commissioner and Information Tribunal decisions.

---

[383] art.1(b), Directive 2003/04/EC.
[384] SI 2004/3391.
[385] Defra, March 2005.
[386] At *http://www.defra.gov.uk/corporate/opengov/eir/guidance/full-guidance/index.htm.*
[387] See *http://www.defra.gov.uk/corporate/opengov/eir/pdf/cop-eir.pdf.*

Freedom of Information (FOI) and Environmental Information Regulations (EIR)

6–100 Whilst the Freedom of Information Act was solely a domestic matter, the development of access rights to environmental information was constrained by the EU framework. The regimes are broadly similar but contain significant differences; as discussed below, whether information is categorised as "environmental" or not may thus be of decisive importance.

6–101 The table below summarises the main differences between the FOIA and the EIR. The provisions of the EIR will be covered in more detail below.[388]

Table 6/I

	EIR	FOI
Format of request	Request need not be in writing.	Request must be in writing.
Time limits	Allows an extension of the time limit for response for a further 20 days, but only if the request is complex and voluminous.	Allows an extension beyond 20 working days to allow time to consider the public interest test.
Charging	Requests cannot be refused on cost alone. A charge may be made if it is reasonable and the rates published.	Requests can be charged or refused if over a certain limit.
Holding information	The public authority holds information if it is in its possession and has been produced or received by it.	Excludes information held by the authority on behalf of another person.
Definition of public authority	All authorities covered by the FOI plus any authority under the control of a public authority and have responsibilities, exercise functions or provide public services relating to the environment.	Public authorities as listed in the Schedule to the Act.

[388] For an outline of the differences between the FOIA regime and the EIR 2004 regime—including helpful summaries of the differences in the exceptions—see the guidance on the boundaries between EIR and FOI published by Defra and the then DCA available at *http://www.defra.gov.uk/corporate/opengov/eir/pdf/boundaries.pdf.*

	EIR	**FOI**
Public interest test	All exceptions are subject to a public interest test.	Some absolute exemptions.
Confirm or deny	A public authority may only refuse to confirm or deny that it holds information on the grounds of international relations, defence, national security or public safety.	FOI may refuse to confirm or deny whether it holds information falling within any of the exemptions.

Regulation 20 of EIR 2004 amended section 39 of the FOIA in order to exempt from the FOIA procedures any information which a public authority would be obliged to disclose under "environmental information regulations", defined as regulations made not only in response to the Aarhus Convention but also any regulations made for the purpose of implementing any European obligations "relating to public access to, and the dissemination of, information on the environment".

Other sources of access to environmental information

It should be noted that there are mechanisms within other regimes, such as **6–102** the planning and health and safety regimes, which will also allow for access to certain environmental information.

In addition, the Royal Commission on Environmental Pollution (RCEP) was established by Royal Warrant in 1970. Its remit is to advise on matters concerning pollution in the environment; its advice mainly takes the form of reports which are submitted to the Crown and presented to Parliament. Its publication policy was developed in response to the requirements of the FOIA, and has not been amended in response to the EIR 2004.[389] However, it is interesting that the Information Commissioner has taken into account the publication cycle of RCEP reports when considering the public interest in disclosing certain environmental information, stating in connection with information requested in relation to pesticide spraying that "access to the required information may have allowed the public to engage more meaningfully in public debate in advance of the publication of RCEP's findings [on crop spraying and health]."[390]

---

[389] It remains to be seen whether the EIR regime might force disclosure of information held by the RCEP which it does not disclose under the FOIA publication policy, in particular in relation to interim drafts of reports and confidential responses to consultation: see s.3 of the RCEP Publication Scheme, available at *http://www.rcep.org.uk/about/RCEP PublicationScheme.pdf.*

[390] *Pesticides Safety Directorate*, ICO Decision FER0082566, October 11, 2007.

Active provision of information: public registers

6–103   Article 5 of the Aarhus Convention imposes a duty on governments to collect and to disseminate environmental information: that is, not only to provide environmental information in response to specific requests, but actively to update and publish both environmental information itself, and information about the type and scope of information held by public authorities.

Article 7 of the Directive reflects that duty by imposing the duty on public authorities to organise the environmental information relevant to their functions "with a view" to its active and systematic dissemination to the public.

The duty as contained within the EIR 2004 merely requires that public authorities "progressively make the information [they hold] available to the public" and "take reasonable steps" to organise the information relevant to their functions "with a view" to its active and systematic dissemination to the public.[391] Understandably, there is no such duty in relation to information which the public authority would be entitled to refuse to release under the regulations.[392] The type of information to be subject to active dissemination includes at least the information listed in Article 7(2) of the Directive: that is, not only information relating to international and national legislation and policy reports relating to the environment, but also any data derived from activities "likely to affect the environment", any authorisations "with a significant impact on the environment and environmental agreements", and any environmental impact studies and risk assessments. Alternatively, in the case of the latter two, the government must indicate where such information can be requested or obtained.

6–104   There is, of course, a vast amount of similar environmental information which will be held not only by public but also by private bodies and persons, including industrial and commercial actors. Although under Article 7 of the Directive the government is obliged to disseminate any data derived from the monitoring of activities carried out by such actors which affect or are likely to affect the environment, there is no specific obligation on the State to collect such information in the first place.

The Guidance points out that organisations subject to the FOIA will already be subject to the requirements under that Act to produce a "Publication Scheme" for all the information they publish or envisage publishing, and recommends that authorities not subject to the FOIA consult the guidance on Publication Schemes and record keeping under the FOIA.

Defra has published a detailed "register of registers" that lists all the registers of environmental information published by public authorities.[393]

[391] reg.4(1), EIR 2004.
[392] reg.4(3), EIR 2004.
[393] *http://www.defra.gov.uk/corporate/opengov/eir/pdf/registers.pdf.*

This should be the first port of call in a search for any environmental information which may already be in the public domain.

Decision-making under EIR 2004: requests, enforcement and appeals

Requests. Anyone may make a request for environmental information to a **6–105**
public authority.[394] In contrast to the FOIA regime, a request for environmental information does not need to be in writing.

The authority to which it is directed must provide the information requested, or notify the applicant of its decision to refuse the request within 20 days (subject, of course, the exceptions below).[395] This may be extended to 40 days if it notifies the applicant that it reasonably believes that 20 days will be impracticable.[396] If the public authority does not hold the information, it must either transfer the request to the public authority which it believes does hold it or provide the name and address of that authority to the applicant.[397] It may levy a reasonable charge for providing any information not contained within public registers or lists held by it, and if that charge is demanded in advance, need not provide the information until it is paid.[398]

A public authority has a duty under regulation 9 to provide reasonable "advice and assistance" to applicants. Where the public authority has complied with the Code of Practice, there is a presumption that it has complied with that duty.[399] Where a public authority considers that the request has been made in too general a manner, it must ask the applicant to provide more particulars within 20 days and assist him in the particularisation of the information request.[400]

A public authority must ensure that that any information it releases **6–106**
which it has itself compiled is "up to date, accurate and comparable" (presumably as compared with the original data), so far as it reasonably believes.[401] The Guidance recommends that if it consists of opinion rather than fact, this should be made clear.[402] It also points out that information could come from a third party and be of unspecified reliability, or slanted

---

[394] It should be noted that where the information requested can be classified as "personal data" relating to the applicant, the duty to disclose it does not apply under EIR 2004, and the request will have to be dealt with under the other statutory information regime provided by the Data Protection Act 1998. Where the personal data relates to a third party the EIRs will govern, but there will be an exemption from disclosure under reg.12(3).

[395] reg.5(2), EIR 2004.

[396] reg.7, EIR 2004.

[397] reg.10(1), EIR 2004.

[398] reg.8, EIR 2004.

[399] reg.9(1) and 9(3), EIR 2004.

[400] reg.9(2), EIR 2004.

[401] reg.5(4), EIR 2004.

[402] para.3.7, *Guidance to the Environmental Information Regulations 2004*, March 2005 (updated December 2006).

to support a particular point of view; it therefore recommends that authorities protect themselves by issuing a disclaimer relating to the accuracy, source, reliability or any other limitation on the usefulness of the information. It goes on to emphasise that whilst the authority may give guidance as to the information's accuracy, "it is not required to interpret the information itself, to draw its own conclusions or recommend action."[403]

Reconsideration. If the applicant considers that the public authority has failed to comply with the requirements in the EIR 2004, he may make written representations to that effect which the public authority must consider and respond to free of charge and within 40 days.[404]

Enforcement and appeals. The enforcement and appeal processes under the EIRs have been closely aligned with the FOIA enforcement provisions: Regulation 18(1) provides that the relevant provisions in the FOIA also apply for the purposes of the EIR 2004. The summary of the process which follows will therefore also apply to the corresponding process in relation to requests made under the FOIA.

(1) An initial complaint to the Information Commissioner may be made by the applicant if the decision has been refused, or if he considers that the request has not been handled in accordance with the EIR 2004 (for example, if the fee charged or the time taken to reply has been excessive).[405] A complaint will only normally be considered by the Commissioner if the applicant has already exhausted the internal review or complaints procedure.

(2) The Commissioner may issue an Information Notice requesting any information, including unrecorded information, reasonably required by him in order to make a decision regarding the complaint.[406] The public authority may appeal against the Information Notice to the Information Tribunal.[407] The Information Commissioner also has powers of entry, search and seizure.

(3) If satisfied that the public authority has failed to comply with any of the requirements of the EIR 2004, the Commissioner will issue a Decision Notice setting out the steps needed to rectify its actions.[408]

---

[403] ibid.
[404] reg.11, EIR 2004.
[405] Enforcement by the Commissioner can be excluded if the Secretary of State uses the power conferred on him by regulation 15 to issue a certificate stating that disclosure of the information would "adversely affect national security" and is not in the public interest: reg.18(3) EIR 2004. Either the applicant or the Commissioner himself may challenge the decision to issue the certificate before the Information Tribunal: s.60 FOIA and reg.18(7) EIR 2004.
[406] s.51, FOIA 2000.
[407] s.57(2), FOIA 2000.
[408] s.50(3) and (4), FOIA 2000.

The Commissioner may also issue an Enforcement Notice requiring the authority to take such steps.[409]

(4) If either the complainant or the public authority is dissatisfied with the Information Commissioner's response, an appeal lies to the Information Tribunal.[410] The Information Tribunal's procedure is governed by Schedule 6 to the Data Protection Act 1998.[411]

(5) Appeal lies from the Tribunal to the High Court on a point of law.

Definition of "environmental information"

The gatekeeper to the EIR 2004 is the categorising of the information **6–107** requested as "environmental information". The ambit of the definition is important, given that the range of authorities to which the EIR 2004 applies is considerably broader, and the exceptions narrower, than those which apply in the framework of the FOIA. Moreover, the EIR 2004 provides that any rule of law or enactment which would prevent the disclosure of information does not apply to environmental information.[412]

It is important to note that there is no requirement for the applicant to identify the legislation (be it FOIA or EIR) under which he seeks the disclosure of the information requested: it is for the public authority to identify whether or not that information is environmental information and, if it is, to deal with it under the EIR 2004. If it fails to do so, or wrongly identifies the request as falling within the FOIA, the Information Commissioner—or, on appeal, the Tribunal—will consider whether, if the correct law had been applied, the relevant public authority should have come to a different conclusion.

The Tribunal also recognises that "often, a person seeking information will not be able to identify or describe precisely the document containing the information he is seeking". In that case, he should frame his request by reference to the information he is seeking, and rely on the public authority to identify the documents containing the information, or to seek clarification pursuant to its duty to assist and advise.[413]

The definition of environmental information in the EIR 2004 is identical **6–108** to that contained within Article 2(1) of Directive 2003/4/EC, which itself expands very slightly on the definition contained within Article 2(3) of the Aarhus Convention.

---

[409] s.52, FOIA 2000.

[410] s.57(1), FOIA 2000.

[411] s.53 FOIA 2000, which allows the "executive override" of the decision of the Commissioner or the Tribunal by means of a certificate laid before Parliament, also applies in the framework of the EIR 2004.

[412] Regulation 5(6), EIR 2004. The same is not true of information falling under the FOIA, where the statutory prohibition on disclosure will prevail over the FOIA.

[413] *Benjamin Archer v Information Commissioner and Salisbury District Council* (EA/2006/0037, May 9, 2007) at para.22.

Environmental information is defined in regulation 2(1) EIR 2004 as follows:

'environmental information' has the same meaning as in Article 2(1) of the Directive, namely any information in written, visual, aural, electronic or any other material form on—namely any information in written, visual, aural, electronic or any other material form on—

(a) the state of the elements of the environment, such as air and atmosphere, water, soil, land, landscape and natural sites including wetlands, coastal and marine areas, biological diversity and its components, including genetically modified organisms, and the interaction among these elements;

(b) factors, such as substances, energy, noise, radiation or waste, including radioactive waste, emissions, discharges and other releases into the environment, affecting or likely to affect the elements of the environment referred to in (a);

(c) measures (including administrative measures), such as policies, legislation, plans, programmes, environmental agreements, and activities affecting or likely to affect the elements and factors referred to in (a) and (b) as well as measures or activities designed to protect those elements;

(d) reports on the implementation of environmental legislation;

(e) cost-benefit and other economic analyses and assumptions used within the framework of the measures and activities referred to in (c); and

(f) the state of human health and safety, including the contamination of the food chain, where relevant, conditions of human life, cultural sites and built structures inasmuch as they are or may be affected by the state of the elements of the environment referred to in (a) or, through those elements, by any of the matters referred to in (b) and (c).

The definition is therefore itself extremely broad. As the Aarhus Implementation Guide[414] points out, "information" is intended to cover not only finished documentation, but any information even in its "raw and unprocessed" state, and any new form of information or information storage which might developed in the future.

Both the Information Commissioner and the Information Tribunal have adopted a generally expansive approach to the definition of environmental information, as the following cases demonstrate.

6–109 (a) **State of elements of the environment.** It is clear, for example, that any information relating to planning will be information on the

---

[414] Aarhus Convention: An Implementation Guide ECE/CEP/72, accessible at *http://www.unece.org/env/pp/acig.htm.*

landscape: for example, in *Benjamin Archer v Information Commissioner and Salisbury District Council*,[415] the applicant sought the joint report of the council's solicitor and planning officer relating to "possible prosecution or enforcement for breaches of planning legislation". That information was regarded as "environmental information". Information sought in relation to rights of way is also information on the landscape: *Dainton v Info Commissioner and Lincolnshire County Council*.[416] In *Network Rail v Information Commissioner*,[417] it was assumed that information relating to work carried out by Network Rail and flooding near the applicant's home was environmental information. It is also clear that legal advice containing a view on the matters in this subsection, or any of the others, will constitute environmental information: see *Decision FER0069117* (Re Staffordshire Moorlands District Council, February 12, 2007), which stated that "the definition ... is broad in that it specifies '**any** information ... **on**" the items set out in regulation 2(a).

(b) Factors likely to affect elements of the environment. In *Ofcom v Information Commissioner and T-Mobile (UK) Ltd*,[418] the Tribunal also adopted a non-technical approach to the definition of the term "emissions", stating that it should be given its "plain and natural meaning and not the artificially narrow one set out in the IPPC Directive".[419] The Tribunal also cited the purpose of Directive 2003/4/EC, as set out in its first recital, "to achieve '... a greater awareness of environmental matters, a free exchange of views [and] more effective participation by the public in environmental decision making ...'" in order to support its decision that the names of the mobile network operators who owned radiation-emitting base stations could themselves be classed as "information on energy, radiation or emissions" under regulation 2(1)(b).

(c) Measures and activities likely to affect (a) and (b). It is clear that advice provided in relation to any of these will also be environmental information. In *Burgess v Information Commissioner and Stafford Borough Council*,[420] the Tribunal considered that counsel's advice in relation to a planning appeal, as it "concern[ed] the landscape and it w[ould] affect the Council's policy towards the issues it addresses", should be considered environmental information.[421] Similarly, in *Kirkaldie v Information Commissioner and Thanet District Council*,[422] legal advice concerning an agree-

---

[415] EA/2006/0037, May 9 2007.
[416] EA/2007/0020, September 10, 2007.
[417] EA/2006/0061 and 0062, July 17, 2007.
[418] EA/2006/0078, September 4, 2007.
[419] The IPPC Directive is Directive 96/61/EC on Integrated Pollution Prevention and Control.
[420] EA/2206/0091, June 7, 2007.
[421] At para.29.
[422] EA/2006/0001, July 4, 2006.

ment regarding land usage under the Town and Country Planning Act 1990 fell within regulation 2(1)(c).[423] Advice provided to the Deputy Prime Minister by his officials relating to planning permission for the Vauxhall Tower was also agreed to be environmental information in *Rt Hon Lord Baker of Dorking v Information Commissioner and Department for Communities and Local Government*.[424] In *Robinson v Information Commissioner and East Ridings of Yorkshire Council*,[425] the applicant sought various items of information relating to the Council's decision not to implement two highway schemes and to reduce the contribution to the schemes from Tesco, including information both on the decision-making process and the evidence which was before the Council. Such information was regarded as "environmental information".

6–110   **(d) reports on the implementation of environmental legislation.** It is likely that many of these will already be published and in the public domain pursuant to the public authority's duty actively to disseminate information under regulation 4.

(e) economic analyses used in the framework of (c). The Guidance states that these "could include financial analyses".

(f) Information on the state of human health or safety. The decision in *Ofcom v Information Commissioner and T-Mobile* demonstrates the careful manner in which the Tribunal approaches the definition of 'environmental information. It pointed out that the sought-after data could not qualify as information on the state of human health or safety under reg 2(1)(f), as it was information on a factor which *might affect* human health or a built structure, and not information on the state of human health itself.

Indivisibility of information

6–111   In *Decision FER0099394* (East Sussex County Council, November 14, 2007) the Commissioner addressed the question of whether the whole of a contract for waste management, including its pricing and financial aspects, should be considered environmental information, and determined that the entire contract

"materially relates to, and is inextricably linked to the fundamental nature of the contract (i.e. to manage waste), such that it would be a false

---

[423] In *Kirkaldie*, the legal advice was provided to the Tribunal in confidence in order for it to make its decision. See below for the application of legal professional privilege in relation to exceptions to the duty to disclose. In the first of these cases, legal professional privilege was held to apply; in the second, privilege was found to have been waived.
[424] EA/2006/0043, June 1, 2007.
[425] EA/2007/0012, October 9, 2007.

distinction to consider such information as not being environmental in nature."

He then considered each and every part of the contract to assess the applicability of various exemptions to disclosure.

"Possession" of information by public authorities

It should be noted that (in contrast to the FOIA regime) as soon as any   **6–112** information comes into the "possession" of an authority subject to the EIR 2004 (or is held by any person on that authority's behalf), that information also becomes subject to its provisions, whether or not it was received from a third party or in fact obtained as a result of that authority's environmental responsibilities.

Whether or not a public authority is in fact in possession of the information requested is a matter which will be determined by the Information Commissioner and the Tribunal on the balance of probabilities (see discussion of Regulation 12(4) below).

Definition of a public authority

The definition of a public authority under the EIR 2004 is contained   **6–113** within regulation 2(2) as follows:

(a) government departments;
(b) any public authority which is defined as such by section 3(1) of the FOIA (with certain exceptions);
(c) any other body or person which carries out functions of public administration;
(d) any other body or person which is under the control of a person falling within (a), (b) or (c)and who in addition has one of the following environmental aspects:

   (i) has public responsibilities relating to the environment;
   (ii) exercises functions of a public nature relating to the environment; or
   (iii) provides public services relating to the environment.

Meaning of 'functions of public administration"

The phrase has its origin in the Aarhus Convention.[426] This category brings   **6–114** within the scope of the EIR 2004 executive agencies and other bodies which carry out functions which were previously undertaken by central government. Those functions need not be in any way environmental.

---

[426] Article 2(2)(b) of the Aarhus Convention.

However, it is the administrative nature of those functions themselves which bring the body within the definition, not whether or not it is a "public body" or "performs functions of a public nature". As pointed out by the Tribunal, "public functions clearly extend beyond administration",[427] but only those that are administrative count for the purpose of bringing a body within the definition of an EIR public authority.

As for what kind of functions should be considered administrative, the Tribunal determined that Network Rail, even if it carried out public functions, was not a body which carried out "public administrative functions". It was guided by the decision in *Griffin v South West Water Services Limited*[427A] in relation to whether the defendant was a "public administrative body", in which Blackburne J. observed that

"SWW is no more an administrative body because it administers a service (the supply of water and sewerage services) than is a company carrying on a business, manufacturing and distributing sweets because such a company 'administers' that enterprise".

The same sort of reasoning applied to Network Rail, which the Tribunal said

"runs a railway system, just as SWW ran a water supply and sewage service. It does not administer anything, save in the sense that it runs its own business. ... Whatever the position in 1947, running a railway is not seen nowadays in the United Kingdom as a function normally performed by a public authority".[428]

By way of contrast, in *Port of London Authority v Information Commissioner and John Hibbert*,[429] the PLA argued that an organisation may be a public body in respect of some of the information it holds and not others.[430] The Tribunal had regard to the statutory provisions establishing the Port of London Authority to find that the PLA was subject to a degree of governmental control and regulation and that the PLA was entitled under statute to regulate others. It therefore carried out functions of public administration and, importantly, was a non-profit making organisation bound by statute to use any profit in the performance of its duties and

---

[427] *Network Rail Limited v Information Commissioner* (EA/2006/0061 and EA/2006/0062, July 17, 2007).

[427A] [1995] IRLR 15 (ChD).

[428] Perhaps the most interesting aspect of this case is the postscript added by the Tribunal, which expressed its dissatisfaction that "a major landowner whose estate is intensively visited by many people and, in the words of its website, includes 'many sites of great environmental, geological, historical and architectural importance' as well as much contaminated land" would not be subject to any duty to provide information under the EIR, and suggested that Defra and/or the Department of Transport might consider whether Network Rail should be brought within the EIR so it is required to supply information. No such moves have yet been made.

[429] EA/2006/0083.

[430] Citing *Environmental Resource Management Ltd FER0090259*.

powers. It found that the allegedly private activities it carried out over-lapped with its public functions, and that the public and commercial aspects of the body could not therefore be separated. Accordingly, it was a public authority in respect of all the information it held.

Exceptions

Under regulation 12, a public authority is entitled (but is not required) to refuse a request for information only if   **6–115**

(a) one of the exceptions set out in regulation 12(4) or (5) applies; *and*
(b) in all the circumstances of the case, the public interest in main-taining the exception outweighs the public interest in disclosing the information.

This means that the public interest criterion must be at the heart of the public authority's decision-making process. It is important to note also that the public authority must "apply a presumption in favour of disclosure". As the Tribunal explained in *Archer v Information Commissioner and Salis-bury District Council*,[431] "the result, in short, is that that the threshold to justify non-disclosure is a high one".

It should be noted that when considering the balance of public interest, the Tribunal will address the public interest in each exception relied upon separately, and will not "supplement" or "aggregate" the public interest in maintaining each of the exceptions relied upon. In other words, two weak exceptions cannot be considered equal to one strong one.[432]

Regulation 12(5): adverse effect

Under Regulation 12(5), the public authority must consider the public   **6–116** interest in terms of non-disclosure and in terms of disclosure in any case where it is argued that disclosure would *adversely affect* one of the following exceptions:

(a) International relations, defence, national security or public safety;
(b) The course of justice, the ability of a person to receive a fair trial or the ability of the public authority to conduct a criminal or dis-ciplinary inquiry;
(c) Intellectual property rights;
(d) The confidentiality of any public authority's proceedings;
(e) The confidentiality of commercial or industrial information which is provided by law to protect a legitimate economic interest;
(f) The interests of the person who provided the information to the public authority where that person

---

[431] EA/2006/0037, May 9, 2007.
[432] See paras 56–58, *Ofcom v Information Commissioner and T-Mobile*. EA/2006/0078.

(i) was not, and could not have been put under, any legal obligation to supply it,

(ii) did not supply in circumstances such that the public authority or any other public authority would be entitled to disclose it in any event; and

(iii) has not consented to its disclosure;

(g) the protection of the environment to which the information relates.

In other words, the public authority must first consider whether the exemption applies in relation to the information requested because it would "adversely affect" one of the interests listed; if that is the case, it must then apply the test of public interest to both disclosure and non-disclosure of the information requested.

5(a). National security. A ministerial certificate that disclosure will adversely affect public safety, and is not in the public interest, will be conclusive of the matter.[433] In *Ofcom v Information Commissioner v T-Mobile*, the Tribunal accepted the argument that disclosing the location of mobile phone stations would expose them to the actions of criminals and so adversely affect public safety. However, although the exception "applied", the public interest in maintaining the disclosure did not outweigh the public interest in disclosure, and so disclosure was ordered.[434]

5(b). The course of justice, fair trials and the ability to conduct criminal or disciplinary inquiries. It should be noted that the EIR 2004 do not apply to any public authority when it is acting in a judicial or legislative capacity.[435] This exception will therefore only apply where a public authority is not acting in that capacity. The Guidance states that "the course of justice" includes "law enforcement" and so that it includes information whose disclosure could prejudice the "prevention, investigation or detection of crime, or the apprehension or prosecution of offenders"—and "the proceedings of a coroner's court". It should be noted that the exemption has also been held to cover legal advice covered by legal professional privilege: see *Kirkaldie v Information Commissioner and Thanet District Council*,[436] where this was said to be particularly so "where a public authority is, or is likely to be, involved in litigation". In *Burgess v Information Commissioner and Stafford District Council*,[437] the Information Tribunal held that the exception was equally applicable even after the legal proceedings in relation to which the advice sought by the local authority

---

[433] See reg.15(1) and 15(3) and above.
[434] See para.11, *Ofcom v Information Commissioner v T-Mobile* (EA/2006/0078, September 4, 2007).
[435] reg.3(3) EIR.
[436] EA/2006/001, July 4, 2006.
[437] EA/2006/0091, June 7, 2007.

had been concluded. There could still be an adverse effect in that, essentially, disclosure of counsel's advice might restrict the local authority's freedom of argument in relation to similar future circumstances. However, the Tribunal emphasised that although there is a strong element of public interest inbuilt into legal professional privilege,[438] "legal privilege is not an absolute exception."[439]

5(c). Intellectual property rights. This was also one of the exceptions **6–117** addressed in *Ofcom v Information Commissioner and T-Mobile*, where it was argued that disclosure would violate database right and copyright.[440] The Tribunal accepted that the mobile phone operators' intellectual property would be infringed by the disclosure of the requested information. However, it found that its duty to interpret the exception restrictively meant that it would only apply if the infringement was "more than a purely technical infringement": it must be one which would result in "some degree of loss or harm to the right holder", and that harm must be "actual harm". Anything less could not constitute an "adverse effect".

5(d). Confidentiality of proceedings. In *Decision FS 50094124*[441] the Commissioner upheld the non-disclosure of information by Bolton Metropolitan Borough Council to the complainant in a maladministration investigation by the local government ombudsman. The disclosure of such information is barred under the Local Government Act 1974 section 32(2). However, owing to section 5(6) of the EIR 2004, such statutory bars are not determinative of the matter and the Commissioner, like the authority, was bound to consider the balance of public interest. The balance was in this case in favour of non-disclosure.[442]

5(e). Commercial or industrial confidentiality. This exception requires that the information be protected under the law of confidentiality; that is, that the information has the necessary quality of confidence, that it was communicated to or from a third party in circumstances that give rise to a reasonable expectation that confidentiality would be maintained and that unauthorised disclosure is either threatened or has occurred.[443] In *Ofcom v Information Commissioner and T-Mobile* the Tribunal found that the first of these requirements was not fulfilled in relation to the data sought, as it had already been released by the mobile phone operators to local

---

[438] See *Burgess* at para.44, citing *Bellamy v Information Commissioner and DTI* (EA/2005/0023, April 4, 2006) at para.35.
[439] In *Burgess* the Tribunal determined that on the facts the public interest in maintaining the exception outweighed the public interest in disclosure, "notwithstanding the presumption in favour of disclosure".
[440] See para.43.
[441] May 22, 2007.
[442] Contrast the position under the FOIA.
[443] *Ofcom v Information Commissioner and T-Mobile* at para.64.

authorities without any obligation of confidentiality having been imposed. This was despite the fact that it would take much "time and effort" to extract the information sought from that released: a less easily accessed form of the requested information does not retain confidentiality where the request is for the information in a form which would be "significantly easier to access".[444] In *Decision FER0072936* (March 28, 2007) (relating to risk assessments of two liquefied natural gas terminals at Milford Haven) the Information Commissioner recognised that there is an "inherent public interest in maintaining the confidentiality of commercial information": in other words, the decision-maker may well have to balance competing public interests. However, he determined that the adverse effect of disclosure on that confidentiality would not outweigh the "considerable public interest in providing information about issues of public safety and environmental concern".

6–118 Conjoined *Decisions FER0073984* and *FER0099394* (November 14, 2007), relating to a request to disclose the entirety of a PFI waste contract entered into by two local councils, give a useful example of how the Commissioner will approach the disclosure of commercial information. Each and every item of information contained within the contract was analysed in two stages to determine (i) whether or not it fell within the ambit of the exemption; and (ii) if it did, whether the public interest in maintaining the exception outweighed the public interest in disclosure. With regard to (i), the Commissioner found that the mere presence of a confidentiality clause does not necessarily render the information caught by it confidential: it must have been "imparted in circumstances which created an obligation of confidence" and must have the necessary "quality" of confidence—and that as regards the latter, information could retain that quality of confidence even after the elapse of some years, as long as it has not entered the public domain and remained commercially significant.

5(f). Interests of the provider of information. In *Dainton v Information Commissioner and Lincolnshire County Council*,[445] the Council argued, in support of non-disclosure, that the anonymous providers of the information sought would be identifiable by their handwriting. The Tribunal pointed out that the exception would not apply as the Council could release the information by means of a typed transcript. In *Decision FER0072936* the Information Commissioner determined that although the exception applied, no adverse effect on the provider of risk assessments relating to proposed liquefied natural gas terminals at Milford Haven had been demonstrated—and that even if there had been any adverse effect, the public interest would have favoured disclosure. There have, on the other hand, been several decisions by the Commissioner where the adverse effect

---

[444] ibid. at para.65.
[445] EA2007/0020, September 10, 2007.

on the provider of the information has been held to outweigh the public interest in disclosure. In *Decision FER0125285*[446] the Commissioner found that the release of the minutes of liaison meetings between the local authority and the National Trust would be adverse to the Trust's interests as it would discourage the Trust from being open with the council about the strengths and weaknesses of its arguments, and the pressure of immediate public scrutiny would have made the consultation process more adversarial instead of constructive and cooperative. In *Decision FER0066999*[447] the Commissioner agreed that "given the emotive nature of local planning issues" the public's perception of the FE College which provided the information would be influenced by its knowledge of that information and upheld the local authority's decision not to disclose the information. In *Decision FS50062329* (July 12, 2005) Bridgnorth District Council instituted an investigation into the state of a piece of land after receiving a complaint from the member of the public. The owner of the land complained that he had not been allowed access to information in the enforcement file. The council was ordered to disclose the documents sought, except the parts which would reveal the identities of those providing the information.

5(g). Protection of the environment. The Guidance states, for example, that information about Sites of Special Scientific Interest "should not normally be made available until a formal notice is served" and that the location of sensitive areas may need to be withheld to avoid the risk of damage or disturbance.[448] It should be noted that if release might damage some other aspect of the environment to that which is the subject of the particular request for disclosure, disclosure cannot be resisted within this exception, which only extends protection to the specific environment to which the information relates.

The standard of proof to be applied to the question of whether disclosure **6–119** "would adversely affect" one of the above interests is the civil standard of the balance of probabilities.[449] "Would", that is, means "more likely than not" and the adverse effect must be "real, actual and of substance".[450]

---

[446] Gloucester City Council, October 8, 2007.

[447] Redcar and Cleveland Borough Council, September 17, 2007.

[448] Guidance provided by the National Biodiversity Network also states that the exception may be used to prevent "damage to important partnerships with landowners or volunteer recorders": see the Countryside Agencies' Open Information Network's *Environmental Information Regulations Guidance Note No 1: The "Environmental Exception" and access to information on sensitive features* (Version V1.3.2). All three Guidance Notes issued by the Network are currently available at *http://www.english-nature.org.uk/about/access/docs/sensitiveinformation.pdf*. See also the Network website at *http://www.nbn.org.uk*; at the time of writing this site was undergoing reconstruction.

[449] para.35, *Ofcom v Information Commissioner and T-Mobile*. (EA/2006/0078, September 4, 2007).

[450] *Burgess v Information Commissioner and Stafford Borough Council* (EA/2206/0091, June 7, 2007).

Emissions: the exception to the exception

6–120   Under regulation 12(9), exceptions 5(d) to 5(g) do not apply where the information to be disclosed relates to "emissions". In *Ofcom v Information Commissioner and T-Mobile* the Tribunal considered the scope of this "exception to the exception" and determined that the term "emissions" should be given its "plain and natural meaning" and not any artificially narrow one determined by any other Directive.[451] In so doing it cut across the approach which appears to have been taken by the Aarhus Implementation Guide, which states that "some international agreements may be relevant in delineating the scope of the elements of the environment" and notes the technical definition of "emissions" contained within the IPCC Directive.

Regulation 12(4): the "catch-all" exemptions

6–121   There are also five "catch-all" exceptions under regulation 12(4) which entitle the public authority to refuse to disclose the information if it;

(a) does not hold the information when the applicant's request is received;[452]

(b) the request for information is manifestly unreasonable;

(c) the request is formulated in too general a manner and the public authority has complied with its obligations of advice and assistance under regulation 9;

(d) the request relates to material still in the course of completion, to unfinished documents or incomplete data;

(e) the request involves the disclosure of internal communications.

In each of these cases also, the public authority must balance the test of public interest in favour of disclosure and non-disclosure.

4(a). The local authority does not hold the information requested. Where this is so, the authority nevertheless has an obligation under regulation 10(1) to pass on the request to the public authority which it believes does hold the information, or to supply the applicant with that authority's name and address. As pointed out above, the Information Commissioner will make a finding on the balance of probabilities as to whether the authority holds the information or not. This does not mean, of course, that this is something which the applicant is required to prove when making his request, but is simply a response to the fact that a large orga-

---

[451] See also, in relation to the definition of "emissions" in relation to the definition of environmental information in reg.2(1)(b), above.

[452] The phrasing of this exception means that a public authority will not be under an obligation to contact the applicant and supply him with the information if at some point in the future it comes into possession of the information he requested.

nisation cannot necessarily be certain that "information relevant to a request does not remain undiscovered somewhere within [its] records." In determining whether or not the public authority may in fact hold information which has not been disclosed, the Tribunal will consider

"the quality of the public authority's initial analysis of the request, the scope of the search that it decided to make on the basis of that analysis and the rigour and efficiency with which the search was then conducted".

It may also take into account "the discovery of materials elsewhere whose existence or content point to the existence of further information" which has not been brought to light.[453]

4(b). Request is manifestly unreasonable. The Information Commissioner has produced guidance on vexatious and unreasonable requests, Part D of which applies to the EIR 2004.[454] It points out that, as there is no cost limit, unlike under the FOIA, a request may be deemed manifestly unreasonable because of the cost and work needed to comply with it. Before a public authority does so, however, it must fulfil its obligations under regulation 9 to assist the applicant to amend his request in order to reduce to manageable proportions the cost and effort involved in responding. The public authority can also, under Regulation 7, extend the time for responding to requests that are complex or voluminous. If the applicant refuses to amend his request, the authority can argue that the work and cost involved renders it manifestly unreasonable.

4(c). Request is too general. Again, the public authority must comply   **6–122** with its obligations of advice and assistance under regulation 9 before it can rely on this exception.

4(d). Information is unfinished or incomplete. The Guidance points out that a public authority should not be able to evade its obligation simply by labelling its documents "draft". Regulation 14(4) imposes a duty to specify the name of the authority preparing the information and when it is likely to be completed. In *Decision FER0069925* (March 2, 2006) the Information Commissioner held that an interim safety report into a pedestrian crossing, even though it was not in the form of the final docu-

---

[453] *Bromley v Information Commissioner* (EA/2006/0072, August 31, 2007), para.13. There is also a case where the Commissioner found that the information in question did not in fact exist which at the time of writing was under appeal to the Tribunal: see *Decision FER0162211* (under appeal as *Hardiman v Information Commissioner and Sutton and East Surrey Water*).

[454] *Freedom of Information Act Awareness Guidance No 22: Vexatious and repeated requests* (Version 3.0, July 23, 2007, accessible at *http://www.ico.gov.uk/upload/documents/library/ freedom_of_information/detailed_specialist_guides/awareness_guidance_22_vexatious_and_repeated _requests_final.pdf*).

ment that would be produced, was not "material in the course of completion" as it was a separate document produced at the end of a distinct stage of the investigation.

4(e). Internal communications. Regulation 12(8) provides that this includes communications between government departments as well as within a government department.[455] This exception will, of course, cover a very great number of the documents sought from public authorities. However, in each case the authority must prove the public interest in resisting disclosure. In *Decision FER0082566* (October 11, 2007) the Information Commissioner commented that he

"recognises that frank and honest debate is necessary for high quality policy formulation and that there is *a public interest, in certain circumstances, maintaining private space for such discussions away from public scrutiny*" [emphasis added].

In *Friends of the Earth v Information Commissioner and Export Credits Guarantee Department* (the *"Sakhalin II"* case),[456] the ECGD relied on both the need to "ensure that full and frank provision of discussions and advice within Government was not inhibited" and that "the principle of Government collective responsibility not be undermined": both grounds protect the notion of a "safe space" for governmental decision-making.[457]

6–123   However, it should be remembered that there is a legal presumption in favour of disclosure in regulation 12(2) and that, according to the Directive, the grounds for refusal of disclosure are to be interpreted restrictively.[458] This means that in each case the onus rests on the public authority to "specify clearly and precisely the harm or harms that would be caused were disclosure to be ordered",[459] and to present evidence of how such harm would be caused.[460]

In the *Sakhalin II* case, the Tribunal expressly rejected the general submission that disclosure of information would have an adverse impact, or some sort of chilling effect, on record keeping.[461] In *Rt Hon Lord Baker*

---

[455] In *Friends of the Earth v Information Commissioner and Export Credits Guarantee Department* (EA/2006/0073, August 20, 2007) the Tribunal determined that this provision was not contrary to the provisions of the Directive which it was intended to implement: see paras 44–48 of the decision.

[456] (EA/2006/0073, August 20, 2007). The applicant sought inter-departmental correspondence in relation to an application for export credit for the "politically sensitive" Sakhalin II oil and gas project.

[457] The Tribunal also adopted the principle (as reflected in its FOIA decision in *Office of Government Commerce v Information Commissioner* (EA/2006/0068 and 0080)) that the justification for protecting safe space was stronger in the "early stages of policy formulation and development": ibid at para.57.

[458] Recital 16, Directive 2003/4/EC.

[459] *Friends of the Earth v Information Commissioner and Export Credits Guarantee Department* at para.53.

[460] See, for example, ibid. at para.74.

[461] ibid at para.61.

of Dorking v Information Commissioner and Department of Communications and Local Government, the government department argued that disclosing advice submitted to the Minister by his officials was against the public interest, as civil servants would be "less frank and impartial in their advice, and less punctilious in recording it" if they knew they would be exposed to public attention and possible criticism. The Tribunal stated, somewhat easily, that "effective management guidance" should be enough to deal with any bad practice that might develop in the way that advice was given, and to ensure that complete advice was properly recorded.[462]

It should be noted, however, that in a speech given in September 2007 the Information Commissioner listed various situations where a "chilling effect" is likely to be "self-evident", which included informal exchanges at the "embryonic" stage of policy development or where policy development remains "live"; "genuinely and necessarily private" exchanges where there is an "obvious expectation of private space" and where disclosure would inhibit such meetings or a written record of them; or subject matters relating to national security, defence, diplomatic or economic issues where disclosure would be damaging.[463]

With regard to the timing of the request, it is interesting to note that the Tribunal has adopted the principle (as reflected in its FOIA decision in *Office of Government Commerce v Information Commissioner*[464]) that the justification for protecting safe space is stronger in the "early stages of policy formulation and development".[465] Similarly, in *Rt Hon Lord Baker of Dorking v Information Commissioner and Department of Communications and Local Government* the Tribunal agreed that once the relevant decision had been published by the government department in question, the public interest shifted in favour of disclosure of internal advice tendered in relation to it.[466] **6–124**

[462] EA/2006/0043, 1 June 2007 at para.18.
[463] "Open Government is Good Government", speech by Richard Thomas, Information Commissioner, at Northumbria University (September 20, 2007), para.36. Decisions under the FOIA where the risk of such has been found to mean that the balance of public interest was in favour of withholding the information include *FS50085374*, where an email documenting discussions over an informal lunch between the Minister and the Chairman of the BBC; and *FS50091442* where a distinction was made between communications between officials, where non-disclosure was permitted, and submissions from officials to Ministers, or communication between Ministers, where disclosure was ordered. At the time of writing, the latter decision was under appeal to the Tribunal.
[464] EA/2006/0068 and EA/2006/0080.
[465] ibid at para.57.
[466] FA/2006/0043, June 1, 2007, at paras 29–30.

Personal data

6–125   The EIR 2004 do not apply at all where the applicant is the data subject of the information: his request must be dealt with under the Data Protection Act 1998 ("the DPA").[467]

The situation is more complicated where the applicant requests information where it contains personal data relating to another individual. In such a case, the EIR 2004 replicate some of the protections provided by the DPA. Personal data is defined in section 1(1) of the DPA. For a case in which the definition was considered in relation to the EIR 2004, see *Dainton v Information Commissioner and Lincolnshire County Council* (EA2007/0020), where correspondence relating to the route of a footpath was considered personal data because it recorded the writer's views and information about individuals.

Regulation 13(1) provides that the public authority must not disclose the personal data unless either of two conditions is satisfied, as follows:

(a)   The first of the conditions applies to data which falls within the first four categories of information in section 1(1) of the DPA,[468] and includes situations where;

   (i)   the disclosure of the data would contravene one of the "data protection principles" in the DPA;[469] or

   (ii)   the processing of the data will cause damage and distress contrary to section 10 of the DPA, and the public interest in not disclosing the information outweighs the public interest in disclosing it.

(b)   The second condition is that the information falls within any of the exemptions in Part IV of the Data Protection Act (which remove the right of access of a data subject to data held about him) *and*, in all the circumstances of the case, the public interest in not disclosing it outweighs the public interest in disclosing. In other words, the EIR 2004 adopt the categories of information set out by the DPA which relieve a public authority of its duty to release personal data under that Act. In other words, the public authority must first determine

---

[467]   See reg.5(3) EIR 2004.

[468]   That is, data (a) processed by means of equipment operating automatically in response to instructions given for that purpose, (b) recorded with the intention that it should be processed by means of such equipment, (c) recorded as part of a relevant filing system or with the intention that it should form part of a relevant filing system (d) which forms part of an accessible record as defined by section 68 (that is, health records, educational records, or an accessible public record.

[469]   The data protection principles can be found in Schedule 1 to the DPA. Some manual data held by public authorities are exempt from some of the data protection principles. Regulation 13(2)(b) ensures that, when it comes to environmental information, the data protection principles will continue to apply in relation to that information for the purpose of the prevention of disclosure under regulation 13.

whether an exemption under the DPA applies, then apply the public interest test required by the EIR.[470]

---

[470] See DPA1998, ss.28–37, for a list of the categories of exemption. It should be noted that each category carries with it its own test for determining whether or not the exemption should apply.

Chapter 7

CLIMATE CHANGE LAW

Introduction

The "greenhouse effect" which is brought about by certain gases, notably   7–001
carbon dioxide, in the upper atmosphere, is a natural phenomenon without
which life on the planet would not have evolved as it has. However, the
major concern is that, as a result of man-made (anthropogenic) activities,
the increase in these gases since the start of the industrial revolution, and
especially in the past half century, has enhanced the greenhouse effect, and
caused an unprecedented degree of global warming in recent years.[1] The
work of the Intergovernmental Panel on Climate Change (IPCC) has been
instrumental in our understanding of this phenomenon.[2] The First IPCC
Assessment Report in 1990 provided the scientific basis for the action
endorsed by the international community of states in the 1992 United
Nations Framework Convention on Climate Change ("Climate Change
Convention").[3] The association established between the IPCC and the
Climate Change Convention regime has rightly been described as "a
model for interaction between science and decision makers."[4] The Second
Assessment IPCC was published in 1995 and indeed proved an important
milestone in international efforts to negotiate the Climate Change Convention's 1997 Kyoto Protocol. The findings of the Third Assessment
Report were published in 2001, and the most recent—the Fourth Assessment—in 2007.[5]

The IPCC's Fourth Assessment report indicates that 11 of the 12 years

---

[1] There are of course those who dispute that there is any causal link between anthropogenic
activities and global warming, and others who dispute the existence of global warming as a
long-term phenomenon at all. It is not the intention in this Chapter to enter that debate,
but merely to record the implications of interest to lawyers of the international consensus
that global warming is both happening and that, if not checked and eventually reversed,
there will be massive adverse consequences across much of the globe.

[2] The IPCC was established in 1988 by the World Meteorological Organization (WMO)
and the United Nations Environment Programme (UNEP). It is an intergovernmental
scientific body with a remit to provide policy-makers with an objective assessment of the
scientific, technical and socio-economic literature on the risk of climate change as caused
by human activity, the impact of such change and the potential for adaption to and
mitigation of such impact.

[3] 31 ILM 849 (1992).

[4] IPCC, *Sixteen Years of Scientific Assessment in Support of the Climate Convention* (2004),
foreword.

[5] IPCC, *Climate Change 2007 Synthesis report* (2007).

363

in the period 1995–2006 proved to be "among the twelve warmest years" since records began in 1850.[6] Average temperatures in the Northern Hemisphere in the latter half of the 20th century were "very likely higher than during any other 50-year period in the last 500 years."[7] Furthermore, the report notes that;

> "[t]here is very high confidence that the net effect of human activities since 1750 has been one of warming. Most of the observed increase in global average temperatures since the mid-20th century is very likely due to the observed increase in anthropogenic [greenhouse gas] concentrations."[8]

Projected negative impacts in certain regions include water shortage and consequent impact on food security (particularly in areas of Africa), sea level rise, coastal area flooding, increased frequency of droughts and floods, destruction of coral reefs and biodiversity loss.[9] With particular reference to Europe, the 2007 Fourth Assessment specifically notes that the following consequences are envisaged:

- "Climate change is expected to magnify regional differences in Europe's natural resources and assets. Negative impacts will include increased risk of inland flash floods and more frequent coastal flooding and increased erosion (due to storminess and sea level rise).
- Mountainous areas will face glacier retreat, reduced snow cover and winter tourism, and extensive species losses (in some areas up to 60% under high emissions scenarios by 2080).
- In southern Europe, climate change is projected to worsen conditions (high temperatures and drought) in a region already vulnerable to climate variability, and to reduce water availability, hydropower potential, summer tourism and, in general, crop productivity.
- Climate change is also projected to increase the health risks due to heat waves and the frequency of wildfires."[10]

Set up by the UK Government to assess the economic implications of the move to a global low-carbon economy and the options available to adapt to climate change, the Stern Review, which reported in 2006, referred to climate change as the "greatest market failure the world has ever seen".[11] It

---

[6] IPCC, *Climate Change 2007 Synthesis report: Summary for policymakers* (2007), p.2.
[7] ibid.
[8] ibid, p.5.
[9] ibid, pp.11–12.
[10] Quoted from ibid, p.11. See also "IPCC warns time is short to head off climate change" ENDS Report 388 (May 2007) pp.10–11. On the role of scientists in predicting climate change, see discussion between Erin Gill and Dave Griggs (Director of the Hadley Centre for Climate Prediction and Research) entitled "Climate Prophet" ENDS Climate Review 2006/07 pp.10–13.
[11] *The Stern Review—Report on the Economics of Climate Change* (2006), Summary of Conclusions at viii.

also highlighted the economic impact of climate change noting that "the overall costs and risks of climate change will be equivalent to losing at least 5% of global GDP each year, now and forever".[12]

It is against this backdrop that discussion will focus in this chapter on international, regional and national responses to the climate change phenomenon. An overview of the approaches adopted by the international community of states, the European Union and the UK Government will be followed by a discussion of the flexible mechanisms established by the Kyoto Protocol (Joint Implementation (JI); the Clean Development Mechanism (CDM); and emissions trading). Key regional and national approaches impacting upon the business sector and designed to reduce fossil fuel emissions will then be addressed: the EU's Emissions Trading Scheme; the Climate Change Levy; Climate Change Agreements; and the Carbon Reduction Commitment. Discussion will then focus on the supply of energy including the role of the Renewables Obligation and the Carbon Emission Reduction Target. Finally, efforts in the transport sector to reduce emissions from cars will be addressed including the Renewable Transport Fuel Obligation.

The Response of the International Community

The 1992 Climate Change Convention

Adopted in May 1992 at the United Nations Conference on Environment   7–002
and Development in Rio de Janeiro, the United Nations Framework Convention on Climate Change (hereinafter "Climate Change Convention") entered into force on March 21, 1994.[13] There are more than 190 Parties to the Climate Change Convention including the United Kingdom and the European Community itself. One of the essential elements of the negotiating process was not to alienate the most polluting states, but instead to tie such states into a legal binding framework of international co-operation to address the problem over time. It was therefore always acknowledged that the Climate Change Convention was merely a first step along a long path. The Climate Change Convention failed to introduce a timetable for greenhouse gas emission reductions despite the wishes of the European Community[14] and those states thought likely to be most affected by the impact of global warming (in particular those within AOSIS, the Alliance of Small Island States). Such a timetable was in particular never going to be acceptable to the USA, the world's largest emitter of green-

---

[12] ibid at vi. In relation to some scientific and economic criticism of the Stern Review see "Stern fights back against critics" ENDS Report 385 (February 2007) pp.6–7.

[13] The text of the Climate Change Convention is available at *http://unfccc.int*.

[14] For an introduction to early European policy relating to climate change see Haigh, *Manual of Environmental Policy: the EU and Britain* (looseleaf) at paras 14.2-1–14.2-5.

house gas emissions, or to members of the Organisation of Petroleum Exporting Countries (OPEC). Instead, the treaty makes reference to an ultimate objective "to achieve ... stabilisation of greenhouse gas concentrations in the atmosphere at a level that would prevent dangerous anthropogenic interference with the climate system."[15] The ambiguity in this objective was clear for all to see.

The principle of "common but differentiated responsibilities" is expressly endorsed in the treaty's text.[16] As such all Parties take on certain common obligations: to publish national inventories of greenhouse gas emissions; to implement programmes to address the global warming phenomenon; to cooperate in the development of environmentally-friendly technologies, the dissemination of relevant information, and in preparing for adaptation to the impacts of climate change; to promote scientific research; and to promote the sustainable management of sinks and reservoirs of greenhouse gases.[17] However, developed states take on more onerous obligations bearing in mind that

"the largest share of historical and current global emissions of greenhouse gases has originated in developed countries, that per capita emissions in developing countries are still relatively low and that the share of global emissions originating in developing countries will grow to meet their social and developmental needs".[18]

Those developed country Parties in Annex I (Annex I states) are obliged to adopt such policies and measures to limit emissions that would "demonstrate that developed countries are taking the lead in modifying longer-term trends in anthropogenic emissions consistent with the objective" of the Climate Change Convention.[19] Additionally such States are obliged to report on their policies and measures "with the aim of returning individually or jointly to their 1990 levels" of greenhouse gas emissions.[20] It should however be noted that this was little more than a mere reporting requirement and certainly far from a firm commitment to reduce emissions by a certain time to 1990 levels.[21]

The richer Annex I Parties noted in Annex II (including the UK)[22] are additionally committed to the provision of financial assistance to developing countries to enable them to establish and publish national emission inventories,[23] to finance the "agreed full incremental costs" of transferring

---

[15] Climate Change Convention, art.2.
[16] Climate Change Convention, art.3(1).
[17] Climate Change Convention, art.4(1).
[18] Climate Change Convention, preamble.
[19] Climate Change Convention, article 4(2)a.
[20] Climate Change Convention, art.4(2)b.
[21] See Sands, *Principles of International Environmental Law* (1995), p.277.
[22] Annex II includes all Annex I countries with the exception of countries undergoing the process of transition to a market economy.
[23] Climate Change Convention, art.4(3).

environmentally sound technology to the developing world,[24] and to "take all practicable steps to promote, facilitate and finance, as appropriate, the transfer of, or access to, environmentally sound technologies and know-how to other Parties, particularly to developing country Parties ...".[25] In essence, the richer developing countries had agreed to finance at least part of the costs to be incurred by developing states in meeting their own obligations under the treaty.

Importantly a "Conference of the Parties" (COP) was established,[26] as 7-003 well as a full-time Secretariat which is now located in Bonn, Germany. These key institutions are vital elements in the treaty regime. The Secretariat is a permanent feature and acts as the bureaucracy of the regime. It essentially makes arrangement for the COPs, prepares reports, generally coordinates activities and provides a focus for treaty activities while the COP is not in session. The COP on the other hand is the supreme decision-making body of the treaty and comprises those states that have ratified the treaty. It promotes the exchange of information between Parties, facilitates the coordination of measures and adopts reports on implementation. Most importantly it is at the annual COPs that Parties are reminded of their responsibilities and where the treaty itself is made the subject of review. It was clear that the obligations within the Climate Change Convention would need to be reviewed if real progress was to be made to reduce greenhouse gas emissions. It was at the third COP (COP 3) in Kyoto in 1997 that the Parties agreed on a protocol to supplement the treaty; the Kyoto Protocol.[27] The international legal regime is far from perfect but the IPCC in its Fourth Report noted that there is:

> "high agreement and much evidence that notable achievements of the [Climate Change Convention] and its Kyoto Protocol are the establishment of a global response to climate change, stimulation of an array of national policies, and the creation of an international carbon market and new institutional mechanisms that may provide the foundation for future mitigation efforts."

The 1997 Kyoto Protocol

Although agreement had been reached on the key features of the Protocol 7-004 when adopted in December 1997, detailed rules were only established in the "Marrakesh Accords" in November 2001 at COP 7. The Kyoto

---

[24] ibid.
[25] Climate Change Convention, art.4(5).
[26] Climate Change Convention, article 7.
[27] 37 ILM 22 (1998). The text of the Kyoto Protocol is also available at *http://unfccc.int*.

Protocol entered into force on February 16, 2005, on Russian ratification.[28] Although a signatory, the USA is not bound by the Protocol due to the Bush Administration's refusal to ratify. In part this is due to the fact that the Protocol sets emission reduction targets for the developed world only.[29] Annex I states in the Protocol committed themselves to reducing their collective emissions of six greenhouse gases[30] by an average of at least 5 per cent over the five-year period from 2008 to 2012 when compared to their 1990 levels of emissions.[31] No targets are set for any developing states. Individual targets for Annex I States are noted in Annex B of the Kyoto Protocol:[32] all EC Member States in 1997 (the EC-15) and the EC itself, as a regional economic organization, agreed to reduce emissions by 8 per cent.

The Protocol allows industrialised States to take joint action to reach their reduction commitments. If State A and State B wish to pool their resources they can do so by indicating that their joint emissions will not exceed their combined individual emission targets.[33] The EC-15 grouping has made use of this opportunity and in essence has agreed to burden-share its collective commitment within the so-called "EC Bubble". When ratifying the Protocol the EC noted the following emission commitments.

---

[28] On the Kyoto Protocol regime see Grubb, Vrolijk and Brack, *The Kyoto Protocol: a guide and assessment* (Royal Institute of International Affairs, 1999), Oberthur and Ott, *The Kyoto Protocol: International Climate policy for the 21st century* (Springer, 1999), French, "1997 Kyoto Protocol to the 1992 UN Framework Convention on Climate Change" 10 Journal of Environmental Law 227 (1998), and Freestone and Streck (eds.), *Legal Aspects of Implementing the Kyoto Protocol Mechanisms: making Kyoto work* (Oxford University Press, 2005).

[29] The Bush Administration has taken the view that this would have given some of its major competitors, such as India and China, a commercial advantage over its own industry had the USA ratified the Protocol.

[30] Carbon dioxide, methane, nitrous oxide, hydrofluorocarbons, perfluorocarbons and sulphur hexafluoride. It is important to note that, although carbon dioxide is the main greenhouse gas contributing to climate change due to the large amount of global emissions of this gas, other greenhouse gases have more of a global warming potential (GWP). For example, hydrofluorocarbons have between 140 and 11,700 times the GWP of carbon dioxide, while perfluorocarbons have between 6,500 to 9,200 times the GWP of carbon dioxide. Sulphur hexafluoride has 22,900 times the GWP of carbon dioxide; Defra, "Guidelines to Defra's GHG Conversion Factors" (2008) [available from Defra's website] which also notes that "to compute the carbon dioxide equivalent of the emission of any gas, we multiply its emission by the GWP." In effect, for example, the emission of one tonne of sulphur hexafluoride is $1 \times 22,900 = 22,900$ carbon dioxide equivalent.

[31] Kyoto Protocol, art.3(1).

[32] Targets are established in Annex B for Australia, Austria, Belgium, Bulgaria, Canada, Croatia, Czech Republic, Denmark, Estonia, the EC, Finland, France, Germany, Greece, Hungary, Iceland, Ireland, Italy, Japan, Latvia, Liechtenstein, Lithuania, Luxembourg, Monaco, the Netherlands, New Zealand, Norway, Poland, Portugal, Romania, Russian Federation, Slovakia, Slovenia, Spain, Sweden, Switzerland, Ukraine, and the United Kingdom. Decision 10/CMP2 was adopted at the second session of the Conference of the Parties serving as the meeting of the Parties to the Kyoto Protocol in 2006 and provides for the inclusion of Belarus in Annex B. At the time of writing this amendment to the Kyoto Protocol has not as yet entered into force.

[33] Kyoto Protocol, art.4(1).

Table 7/I

Belgium	−7.5%
Denmark	−21%
Germany	−21%
Greece	+25%
Spain	+15%
France	0%
Ireland	+13%
Italy	−6.5%
Luxembourg	−28%
The Netherlands	−6%
Austria	−13%
Portugal	+27%
Finland	0%
Sweden	+4%
United Kingdom	−12.5%

The Protocol allows emission reductions to be achieved from activities in a **7–006** variety of sectors including, controversially, the land use, land-use change and forestry sector (LULUCF). If commenced on or after January 1, 1990, net changes in emissions brought about by afforestation, reforestation and deforestation projects can be utilised to achieve targets.[34] Forestry projects of this type can assist in reducing emissions as forests act as "carbon sinks". However, there is little consensus on the extent to which such projects actually reduce the level of emissions to the atmosphere. Nevertheless LULUCF activity can generate Removal Units (RMUs—see below) although these units must be validated by expert review teams.

There is little doubt that agreement at Kyoto would have been very difficult to achieve without the inclusion of the so-called "flexible mechanisms": Joint Implementation (JI);[35] the Clean Development Mechanism (CDM);[36] and emissions trading.[37] These highly important mechanisms will be addressed in depth later in this chapter.

[34] Kyoto Protocol, art.3(3). Furthermore the Marrakesh Accords to a certain extent allow States to utilise revegetation, forest management, cropland management and grazing land management where afforestation, reforestation and deforestation activities increase a given country's overall emissions.

[35] Kyoto Protocol, art.6.

[36] Kyoto Protocol, art.12.

[37] Kyoto Protocol, art.17.

Particularly bearing in mind the 2007 IPCC Fourth Assessment, the obligations taken on by the international community in relation to the Kyoto Protocol's 2008–12 commitment period can only be regarded as one further step to establish an effective international legal regime to combat climate change. There is now a pressing need to agree on additional emissions reductions and mitigation measures beyond 2012.[38] Parties to the Climate Change Agreement met in December 2007 and agreed a "Bali Roadmap" with the aim of completing negotiations for an international agreement to cover the period beyond the Kyoto Protocol's initial 2008–12 commitment period. The roadmap envisages the completion of negotiations in 2009.

The Response of the European Union

7–007 Mindful of the need for policy development and implementation to ensure its Kyoto Protocol obligations are met following its ratification of the Kyoto Protocol in 2002,[39] the EU launched the European Climate Change Programme (ECCP) in March 2000.[40] The ECCP established a consultative process facilitating discussion between the European Commission and key stakeholders. Working groups were set up with remits to examine proposals for instruments and policy in a number of areas: energy supply, demand and efficiency; the transport sector; industry; the Kyoto Protocol's flexible mechanisms; research; agriculture; and carbon sinks (forest-related as well as agricultural soils). These working groups comprised a variety of parties including representatives from the European Commission, industry, national governments and environmental pressure groups. The objective was to identify cost-effective measures to ensure compliance with international obligations. A large number of possibilities were discussed and eventually recommendations were relayed to the European Commission. The ECCP has been instrumental in the development of a number of initiatives the most important of which were the EU's Emissions Trading Scheme and adoption of the Linking Directive both of which are discussed later in this chapter.[41] A second ECCP (ECCP II) was launched in October 2005 with a view to assessing opportunities to make further emission reductions once the Kyoto Protocol's initial emission reduction period comes to an end in 2012. Six working groups were established: one

---

[38] On the future of the international system see Tyrell, "Where next for global climate policy?" ENDS Climate Review 2006/07 pp.8–9.

[39] Council Decision 2002/358/EC concerning the approval, on behalf of the European Community, of the Kyoto Protocol to the UN Framework Convention on Climate Change and the joint fulfilment of commitments thereunder, [2002] OJ L130/1.

[40] On EU climate change policy since 2000 see Haigh, *Manual of Environmental Policy: the EU and Britain* (looseleaf) at paras 14.2-6–14.2-9.

[41] See generally European Commission, *The European Climate Change Programme—EU Action against Climate Change* (2006).

to review the first ECCP whilst new groups were tasked to assess opportunities in relation to aviation, carbon dioxide and cars, carbon capture and storage, adaptation to climate change. The focus of the final group has been on a review of the EU Emissions Trading Scheme.

Key measures adopted by the EU in this field include the following:[42]

- Decision No. 280/2004/EC concerning a mechanism for monitoring Community greenhouse gas emissions and for implementing the Kyoto Protocol;[43]
- Directive 2001/77/EC on the promotion of electricity produced from renewable energy sources in the internal electricity market;[44]
- Directive 2003/30/EC on the promotion of the use of biofuels or other renewable fuels for transport ("2003 Biofuels Directive");[45]
- Directive 2004/8/EC on the promotion of cogeneration based on a useful heat demand in the internal energy market;[46]
- Directive 2002/91/EC on the energy performance of buildings;[47]
- Voluntary agreements adopted in 1998 and 1999 with European, Japanese and Korean car manufacturers to reduce carbon dioxide emissions from new passenger cars;[48]
- Directive 2006/32 on energy end use efficiency and energy services;[49]
- Regulation 842/2006 on certain fluorinated greenhouse gases;[50]

[42] For more detailed analyis of key EU instruments in the field see Haigh, *Manual of Environmental Policy: the EU and Britain* (looseleaf) at paras 14.3–14.15.

[43] OJ 2004 L49/1. The measure established a mechanism for monitoring greenhouse gas emissions, evaluating progress on reduction commitments, implementing the Kyoto Protocol in relation to inter alia national programmes and emissions inventories, and facilitating accurate reporting to the UN Climate Change Convention's Secretariat.

[44] OJ 2001 L282/33. The measure established a framework to facilitate increases in electricity generated by renewables and seeks to facilitate market access for such energy.

[45] OJ 2003 L123/42. Intended to promote the use of biofuels or other renewable fuels and thereby replace in part the usage of petrol and diesel in transportation. Members must ensure that a minimum proportion of biofuels and other "renewables fuels" (as defined by Directive 2001/77 and used for transport purposes) are placed on the market. National indicative targets must be set: reference value for these targets must be 2 per cent of all petrol/ diesel placed on a given Member State's market by 31/12/2005; another reference value for national targets is 5.75 per cent of all petrol/ diesel placed on the market by 31/12/2010.

[46] OJ 2004 L52/50. Establishes a framework for the promotion and development of cogeneration of heat and power. "Guarantees of origin" of CHP-produced electricity are established. Cogeneration is otherwise referred to as "Combined Heat and Power" (CHP).

[47] OJ 2003 L1/65. The directive establishes actions to improve the energy performance of buildings. For example, minimum requirements are established in relation to the energy performance of new buildings and of large existing buildings which are undergoing renovation. Energy certification of buildings is required when buildings are sold.

[48] COM (1998) 495 and COM (1999) 446 final; these voluntary agreements are addressed later in this chapter.

[49] OJ 2006 L114/64. The measure establishes indicative national energy savings targets and seeks to promote a market for energy efficiency services. It also aims to remove barriers to the market for energy efficiency services.

[50] OJ 2006 L161/1. Designed to prevent and minimize emissions of the fluorinated greenhouse gas emissions that fall within the Kyoto Protocol's remit.

- Directive 1999/31 on the landfill of waste;[51]
- Directive 91/676 concerning the protection of waters against pollution caused by nitrates from agricultural sources.[52]

In January 2007 the European Commission presented a package of measures designed to limit climate change to a rise of just two degrees Celsius above pre-industrial temperatures.[53] The European Commission noted that confining temperature rise to such an extent would "limit the impacts of climate change and the likelihood of massive and irreversible disruptions of the global ecosystem."[54] The subsequent European Council in March 2007 established a reduction target of at least 20 per cent in greenhouse gases by 2020 compared to 1990 levels.[55] This target would increase to 30 per cent if international negotiations post-Bali led to the adoption of an internationally binding agreement placing obligations on other developed countries to comparable reductions, as well as placing an onus on richer countries in the developing world (such as China and India) to make an appropriate contribution in accordance with their responsibilities and capabilities.[56] Additionally, in relation to energy consumption, the European Council committed the EU to a 20 per cent target share of renewable energy by 2020.[57]

A package of measures proposed by the European Commission in January 2008 seeks to ensure these ambitious targets are reached.[58] Key future instruments envisaged include an updated EU Emissions Trading System, and proposals in this respect will be discussed later in this chapter. Additionally, a 10 per cent cut in emissions is proposed by 2020, when compared to 2005 levels, from sectors (such as agriculture, transport, housing and waste) that do not fall within this trading scheme. The European Commission proposes that Member States will play a part in the attaining of this particular goal by assuming individual reduction targets of up to 20 per cent for richer countries thereby allowing poorer Member States to emit as much as 20 per cent more.[59] Further proposals put forward by the

---

[51] OJ 1999 L182/1. The measure seeks to reduce the amount of biodegradable municipal waste disposed of in landfill thereby reducing methane emissions. It obliges Member States to reduce the total amount of biodegradable waste disposed in this way by 2016 to 35 per cent of the amount of such waste produced in 1995.

[52] OJ 1991 L373/1. Fertilisers made from nitrogen are sources of nitrous oxide (a potent greenhouse gas). This measure is designed to reduce water pollution by nitrates from the agricultural sector.

[53] European Commission, "Limiting Global Climate Change to 2 degrees Celsius—the way ahead for 2020 and beyond" COM (2007) 2 final.

[54] ibid, p. 3.

[55] "EU backs 20% emissions cut by 2020" ENDS Report 386 (March 2007) pp.52–53.

[56] COM (2008) 30 final, p.2.

[57] ibid.

[58] ibid.

[59] European Commission, "Proposal for a Decision on the effort of Member States to reduce their greenhouse gas emissions to meet the Community's greenhouse gas emission reduction commitments up to 2020" COM (2008) 17 final.

European Commission in January 2008 include a proposal to promote the use of energy from renewable sources (to establish a 20 per cent share of renewables in overall energy use and a 10 per cent minimum share in transport for biofuels),[60] and a proposal on the geological storage of carbon dioxide (to regulate carbon storage and remove legislative hindrances to such storage).[61]

The Response of the UK

The UK first adopted a Climate Change Programme in 2000.[62] The **7–008** Programme was designed to not only ensure that the 12.5 per cent "EC Bubble" target for the UK was met but also the UK Government's own unilateral commitment to reduce carbon dioxide emissions by 20 per cent below 1990 levels by 2010. Key elements of the programme included the Climate Change Levy, Climate Change Agreements, emissions trading, implementation of the Integrated Pollution Prevention and Control Directive, increased use of renewables, and EU voluntary agreements with car manufacturers on carbon dioxide. All of these initiatives will be addressed in this chapter. In 2006 a further Climate Change Programme was adopted.[63] An important element of the latter to be discussed in this chapter includes the Renewable Transport Fuel Obligation. Another sig-

---

[60] COM (2008) 19 final. The proposal in its present form is intended to repeal Directive 2001/77/EC on the promotion of electricity produced from renewable energy sources in the internal electricity market from January 2012. In its "Biomass Strategy" the UK Government notes the significant role that biomass (such as agricultural crops, oil-bearing plants, and forestry) will have in meeting targets that will be established once this EU proposal is formally adopted as a legally binding directive; DET and Defra, *UK Biomass Strategy* (May 2007), p.8.

[61] COM (2008) 18 final. This was the European Commission's response to the decision of the European Council in March 2007 to ensure that all EU fossil fuel power stations built after 2020 are equipped with carbon capture and storage (CCS) technology. The UK Government issued a consultation document in June 2008 encouraging the submission of views on this proposed directive; Department for Business Enterprise and Regulatory Reform, *Towards Carbon Capture and Storage* (2008). Describing CCS as having the potential "to reduce emissions from fossil fuel power stations by up to 90%" the Government takes the view that the geology of the North Sea is "thought to be particularly well suited to the storage of carbon dioxide"; ibid, p.3. Globally there are very few carbon capture projects in operation; see "Carbon Capture and Storage around the World" ENDS Climate Review 2006/7 pp.22–23. However, there are high hopes for this new technology in the future; Chapman, "CCS fast becoming technology of choice" ENDS Climate Review 2006/7 pp.24–26. The UK Government has been criticized for perceived tardiness in endorsing CCS; "CCS network planned to capture 10% of UK carbon dioxide" ENDS Report 390 (June 2007) p.12.

[62] Department of the Environment, Transport and the Regions, *Climate Change—the UK Programme* (2000).

[63] Department for the Environment, Food and Rural Affairs, *Climate Change—the UK Programme 2006* (2006). The programme divides activity into certain sectors: energy supply; business; transport; domestic; agriculture, forestry and land use management; public sector; and the stimulation of action by individuals. It is the first three of these sectors which form the main focus of discussion in this chapter.

nificant aspect of both programmes included action to improve energy efficiency by strengthening building regulations requirements, an issue addressed in the chapter on the planning system.[64]

In November 2007 the Government introduced the Climate Change Bill in Parliament. Key aspects of the draft Climate Change Bill[65] include:

- The setting in statute of the UK target to reduce carbon dioxide emissions by at least 80 per cent by 2050, when compared to 1990 levels.
- The introduction of carbon budgets covering five year periods. Three such budgets (to cover 15 years) will always be established at any given time. Carbon budgets will set binding carbon dioxide emission limits.
- The establishment of the Committee on Climate Change to advise the Government on meeting the UK's targets and the setting of carbon budgets. By December 1, 2008, the new Committee is to provide advice on the carbon budgets for the 2008–12, 2013–17 and 2018–22 periods; such advice will address the level of the budgets and the extent to which the budget for a given period is to be met by reducing domestic emissions of greenhouse gases or by using carbon credits obtained from activities abroad. The Committee will additionally report annually to Parliament on meeting targets and budgets and the Government must respond to any such report.
- Enabling powers to introduce new trading schemes (like the Carbon Reduction Commitment discussed later in this chapter).
- A requirement on the Government to assess the impact on the UK of climate change and to adopt a programme to minimise such impacts.

Described in March 2007 by Secretary of State Miliband as putting the "UK at the very front of global efforts to tackle climate change ... [and establishing the UK as] the first country in the world to establish such a legal framework",[66] the bill is expected to become law in the autumn of 2008.[67]

The Kyoto Protocol's Flexible Mechanisms

7–009 Innovative features of the Kyoto Protocol were its "flexible mechanisms": joint implementation (JI); the Clean Development Mechanism (CDM);

---

[64] The chapter on the planning system also addresses the pursuit of Zero Carbon Homes, and action on the Energy Performance of Buildings.

[65] Originally a 60 per cent target was to be established to cover just carbon dioxide emissions but, following the Committee on Climate Change's interim advice to the Government on October 7, 2008, this was increased to 80 per cent of all Kyoto greenhouse gas emissions.

[66] Draft Climate Change Bill (March 2007) Cm 7040, p.5.

[67] At the time of writing this Bill is being considered by the House of Commons and it is intended that the Bill receives the Royal Assent in the autumn of 2008.

and emissions trading. The flexibility these mechanisms introduce ensures that not only action taken domestically by a given Annex I State is capable of contributing to the meeting of that country's Kyoto Protocol emission reduction commitments as, in essence, action taken abroad can create credits that may also be utilised. Moreover it may often be feasible to obtain significantly greater emission reductions for a given expenditure where this is incurred in relatively under-developed countries, rather than in seeking to make efficiency improvements to a relatively modern domestic plant. Nevertheless, it is of much importance to note that the Marrakesh Accords indicate use of the flexible mechanisms will be "supplemental to domestic action" and that domestic action will "constitute a significant element" of a given Annex I State's efforts to reduce emissions.[68]

Both JI and the CDM are project-based. Governments can themselves choose to fund JI or CDM projects without the involvement of the private sector by undertaking to buy credits generated by overseas projects. However, the private sector is intended to be a key player in these mechanisms. If, for example, a private company is obliged by its own government to make emission reductions at home, it may well be inclined to take part in JI or CDM projects abroad if it knows that any reductions made abroad can be used to offset its own domestic reduction obligations. Alternatively it can decide to engage in projects overseas with a view to selling the credits raised or to be raised on the carbon market. In the UK the Climate Change Projects Office (CCPO) has been established to provide advice, guidance and support to UK organisations that wish to engage in climate change projects pursuant to the Kyoto Protocol.[69]

Entities involved in both CDM and JI projects generate carbon credits and these credits can be traded on the international carbon market.[70] They will need an appropriate contract to do so. Both the World Bank and the International Emissions Trading Association (IETA) have taken steps to provide guidance as to the form of carbon contracts for CDM projects, the

---

[68] Report of the Conference of the Parties on its seventh session (Marrakesh) from October 29 to November 10 2001, Decision 15./CP.7, para.1. Concerned that Annex I states would make use of the flexibility introduced by these mechanisms to negate the need to take action at home, the EU had wanted to see put in place a "concrete ceiling" which would have allowed no more than 50% of a given Annex I state's reduction commitment to be achieved by using the flexible mechanisms. This was not politically possible in 2001 when the Marrakesh Accords were adopted.

[69] *http://www.berr.gov.uk/sectors/ccpo/index.html.* It is jointly funded by the Department for Business, Enterprise and Regulatory Reform (BERR) and Defra.

[70] London has been said to have "consolidated its position as the dominant hub for the international carbon market; "Global carbon market alive and well, says World Bank" ENDS Report 388 (May 2007) p. 11.

former producing the Emission Reduction Purchase Agreement (ERPA) and the latter their own form of such an agreement (IETA ERPAs).[71] It is to be noted however that "both models have been developed by institutions that represent mostly buyers (IETA) or act as buyers themselves (World Bank)."[72] More recently, the Inter-American Investment Corporation has sponsored efforts to produce a template agreement known as the Certified Emission Reduction Sale and Purchase Agreement (CER-SPA) specifically designed to assist small and medium sized project developers to draft appropriate carbon agreements.[73] At the time of writing, template JI carbon contracts have as yet not been adopted.[74]

Joint implementation

7–010 Under this project-based mechanism developed countries noted in the Kyoto Protocol's Annex B (Annex I states) can obtain "emission reduction units" (ERUs) by participating/investing in projects in other Annex I states which reduce greenhouse gases or enhance carbon sinks. Only Annex I states can participate in JI projects and the issuance of ERUs could only take place from 2008. The host Annex I nation gains investment from abroad while the sponsor Annex I country can use the ERUs gained towards its Kyoto Protocol reduction commitment. The mechanism allows the more technologically advanced and wealthier Annex I countries to gain credit for sponsoring projects in less technologically-efficient Annex I countries (such as those in Central and Eastern Europe). It may well be possible to make reductions more cheaply this way than at home where industry may already be using the latest technology. A JI project can only proceed with the consent of the Annex I countries involved.[75] It must lead to reduced emissions, or an enhancement of removals by sinks, additional

---

[71] On the IETA ERPA see Zaman and de Witt Wijnen, "Primary market carbon purchase contracts for CDM and JI" [2007] 2 Env. Liability 108–113. More generally as to ERPAs see Wilder and Willis, "Carbon contracts, structuring transactions: practical experiences" [2007] 2 Env. Liability 101–107, and Streck, "Marketing CERS: legal and contractual issues for sellers" in Douma, Massai, Montini (eds.) *The Kyoto Protocol and Beyond: Legal and Policy Challenges of Climate Change* (2007), pp.79–92. The websites of the World Bank's Carbon Finance Unit (*http://carbonfinance.org*) and IETA (*http://www.ieta.org*) provide extensive coverage of developments and template carbon agreements.

[72] Robert O'Sullivan, "CERSPA: a new template agreement for the sale and purchase of CERs" [2007] 2 Environmental Liability pp.120–124. Can be found at *http://www.cerspa.org*.

[73] ibid.

[74] This is symptomatic of the fact that the CDM market has been more active to date than the JI market. The reader is particularly directed to the websites noted in the previous footnotes for any future developments in relation to the possible adoption of templates for JI projects.

[75] Kyoto Protocol, art.6(1)a.

376

to that which would otherwise have taken place without the input of the sponsor nation (the so-called "additionality" issue).[76]

There are two different procedures for JI. Under "Track 1" host Annex I countries can verify that emission reductions are over and above that which would otherwise have occurred, issue ERUs and transfer them to sponsor nations. In essence the host country supervises the JI project in question. However, Track 1 only applies when the host country meets particular eligibility requirements.[77] These requirements include the need for the host country to be a Party to the Kyoto Protocol, to have in place a national system for the estimation of emissions, to have established a national registry to track the creation and movement of credits generated under the Kyoto Protocol's flexible mechanisms, and to have submitted annual inventories of emissions. If the host country does not comply with these requirements the assessment of JI projects must be made in accordance with the verification procedures overseen by the Joint Implementation Supervisory Committee, an international body established in 2005 by the Parties to the Kyoto Protocol.[78] The UK's Climate Change Projects Office stipulated in April 2008 that "at present most countries are unable to meet all the eligibility requirements for Track 1 [and that] it is most likely that JI projects will follow Track 2 procedures."[79] The key difference between the procedures for the two tracks is that under Track 2 the Joint Implementation Supervisory Committee accredits an "independent entity" to determine whether a project meets the JI requirements.[80] The independent entity must ascertain that the project has the approval of the Parties involved, that reductions in emissions would be additional to any that would otherwise have occurred, that a suitable monitoring plan is in place, and that project participants have submitted a suitable environmental impact assessment. It also determines the reduction in emissions or enhancements of removals by sinks made by the project in question.[81] Only then can the host country issue and transfer ERUs.[82]

---

[76] ibid, art.6(1)b.
[77] The full eligibility requirements are set out in the Annex (para.21) of Decision 9/CMP.1 adopted at the Conference of the Parties serving as the meeting of the Parties to the Kyoto Protocol on its first session in Montreal from November 28 to December 10, 2005 (available at *http://unfccc.int*).
[78] Decision 10/CMP.1 adopted at the Conference of the Parties serving as the meeting of the Parties to the Kyoto Protocol on its first session in Montreal from November 28 to December 10 2005, para.24. The verification procedure is established in paras 30–45 of Decision 9/CMP.1 above fn.76.
[79] CCPO, *A Beginners Guide to Joint Implementation* (2008), p.5.
[80] See Appendix A of Decision 10/CMP.1 adopted at the Conference of the Parties serving as the meeting of the Parties to the Kyoto Protocol on its first session in Montreal from November 28 to December 10 2005 in relation to standards and procedures for the accreditation of independent entities.
[81] See ibid, Appendix B of Decision 10/CMP.1 in relation to criteria for baseline setting and monitoring of JI projects.
[82] To receive ERUs in the UK Registry companies must have a Personal Holding Account with the UK Emissions Trading Scheme Registry; *http://emissionsregistry.gov.uk*.

The UK Government is not at present authorising the hosting of JI projects in the UK. However, guidance has been issued by Defra as to the approval and authorisation of proposed overseas JI projects.[83] Defra is the UK's Designated Focal Point and both approval for and authorisation of participation should be made to the Secretary of State for the Environment, Food and Rural Affairs.[84] Application for a so-called "Letter of Approval" can be made only after receipt of the host country's formal approval of the JI project activity. The Secretary of State determines whether or not to approve the project or authorise participation and may attach conditions in relation to any such approval or authorisation.[85] An appeal to the Secretary of State is allowed against any refusal of an application or to conditions attached to any approval.[86]

Clean Development Mechanism

7–011   This mechanism is also project-based but the key difference from JI is that the project is hosted by a developing non-Annex I country.[87] Annex I countries which sponsor these projects obtain "certified emission reductions" (CERS) to offset their individual reduction commitments.[88] Just like JI, Annex I Governments can directly sponsor Clean Development Mechanism (CDM) projects. They can also encourage the private sector to play a role. Companies would wish to play such a role for the same reasons as they would in relation to JI projects as previously discussed. Participation requirements have been established:[89] CDM project participation must be voluntary, involved Parties must have designated a CDM national authority, and non-Annex I Parties must be a Party to the Kyoto Protocol. Additionally, other requirements include that the host country be a Party to the Kyoto Protocol, to have in place a national system for the estimation of emissions, to have established a national registry to track the creation and movement of credits generated under the Kyoto Protocol's flexible mechanisms, and to have submitted annual inventories of emissions.[90]

---

[83] Defra, "UK Guidance on Project Approval and Authorisation to Participate in Joint Implementation" (November 2005) available online at *http://www.defra.gov.uk/environment/climatechange/internat/kyotomech/ji.htm*.

[84] The Greenhouse Gas Emissions Trading Scheme (Amendment) and National Emissions Inventory Regulations 2005 (SI 2005 No.2903), regs.5(1) and 5(2). In the case of Scottish, Northern Irish or Welsh applicants Defra must ensure that a decision made by the Secretary of State is agreed with by the devolved authority; reg.8. Applications can be sent by email to the Designated Focal Point Team at Defra (jifp@defra.gsi.gov.uk) or by mail.

[85] ibid, reg.7.

[86] ibid, reg.9.

[87] For an in-depth analysis and exploration of the CDM see the "CDM Rulebook" developed by Baker and McKenzie made freely available at *http://cdmrulebook.org*.

[88] Kyoto Protocol, art.12(3)b.

[89] Decision 3/CMP.1 adopted at the Conference of the Parties serving as the meeting of the Parties to the Kyoto Protocol on its first session in Montreal from November 28 to December 10 2005, paras 28–30 (available at *http://unfccc.int*).

[90] See more particularly ibid, para.31.

The CDM mechanism is intended to facilitate activities that contribute to sustainable development in developing countries by providing a new source of investment that brings about greenhouse gas emissions reductions. Annex I countries on the other hand benefit by being given the opportunity to invest abroad in cost effective projects and thereby obtain CERs to offset Kyoto Protocol targets. It is also of interest to note that developing states may themselves in fact decide to finance CDM projects in their own country and then sell the accrued CERs on the international carbon market, so-called "unilateral CDM".[91]

The CDM is supervised by the CDM's "Executive Board"[92] and the applicable procedure certainly has a resemblance to the procedure for Track 2 JI projects supervised by the Joint Implementation Supervisory Committee.[93] The Executive Board accredits independent organisations known as "operational entities"[94] which validate projects under the CDM.[95] To validate a project activity a designated operational entity must, for example, be sure that states fulfil the participation requirements already outlined, ensure that local stakeholders have been invited to comment and due account taken of such comments, that project participants have carried out an environmental impact analysis, and that the project "is expected to result in a reduction in anthropogenic emissions ... that are additional to any that would occur in the absence of the proposed project activity".[96] Projects must satisfy specified baseline and monitoring methodologies and the operational entity must ensure appropriate provision has been made for monitoring, verification and reporting.[97] Simplified modalities and procedures have been established for small-scale CDM projects.[98]

Details of validated projects are forwarded to the Executive Board for **7–012** formal registration. "Verification" of the monitored emission reductions is carried out by the operational entity.[99] Formal and written "certification" of actual emission reductions under CDM projects will be made by the

---

[91] CCPO, *A Beginners Guide to the Clean Development Mechanism* (2008), p.4.

[92] On the rules of procedure for the Executive Board see Decision 4/CMP.1 adopted at the Conference of the Parties serving as the meeting of the Parties to the Kyoto Protocol on its first session in Montreal from November 28 to December 10 2005, Annex I.

[93] CCPO above fn.91, p.4.

[94] Decision 3/CMP.1 above fn.89 paras 20–25. See ibid, Appendix A for the standards relevant to this accreditation process.

[95] A "project design project" must be prepared; see Appendix B of Decision 3/CMP.1 above fn.88 for an indication of the information required in this document.

[96] See Decision 3/CMP.1 above fn.89, para.37.

[97] ibid, para.53. Article 12(5) of the Kyoto Protocol, in addition to noting that participation in CDM projects must be voluntary and that reductions must be additional to that which would otherwise occur, stipulates that operational entities shall certify emission reductions on the basis of "real, measurable, and long-term benefits related to the mitigation of climate change."

[98] Decision 4/CMP.1 above fn.92, Annex II at paras 9–39.

[99] Decision 3/CMP.1 above fn.89, paras 61–63.

relevant operational entity and accrued CERs then issued by the Executive Board.[100] CERs can be issued in relation to emission reductions made from January 1, 2000 and used in the Kyoto Protocol 2008–12 commitment period. As regards LULUCF projects, only those relating to afforestation and reforestation are to be eligible under the CDM.[101]

One commentator has noted that the CDM "has been recognized as the most effective mechanism in promoting the widest possible mitigation measures in developing countries in the present and for the future."[102] The Secretariat to the Climate Change Convention has noted that over 1000 projects have been registered under the CDM and that this flexible mechanism "is anticipated to produce CERs amounting to more than 2.7 billion tonnes of carbon dioxide equivalent" in the 2008–2012 commitment period.[103] Defra is the UK's Designated National Authority for this flexible mechanism and has issued guidance on CDM project approval and authorisation.[104] Approval for CDM project activity must be made to the Secretary of State for the Environment, Food and Rural Affairs.[105] As with JI projects, applications for a "Letter of Approval" can be made only after receipt of the host country's formal approval of the CDM project activity. There is a right of appeal against a decision of the Secretary of State.[106]

---

[100] Decision 3/CMP.1 above fn.89, para.64–66. To receive CERs in the UK Registry companies must have a Personal Holding Account with the UK Emissions Trading Scheme Registry; *http://emissionsregistry.gov.uk*.

[101] See Decision 5/CMP.1 adopted at the Conference of the Parties serving as the meeting of the Parties to the Kyoto Protocol on its first session in Montreal from November 28 to December 10 2005 for the modalities and procedures for afforestation and reforestation projects under the CDM. Decision 6/CMP.1 establishes simplified procedures and modalities for small-scale afforestation and reforestation projects under the CDM.

[102] Gao, "The International Climate Regime: Where do we Stand?" in Douma, Massai, Montini (eds.) *The Kyoto Protocol and Beyond: Legal and Policy Challenges of Climate Change* (2007), p.6. However, on perceived difficulties in implementation of the CDM in India see Gupta, "India struggles with the CDM" ENDS Climate Review 2006/07 pp.38–41.

[103] *http://unfccc.int/kyoto_protocol/mechanisms/clean_development_mechanism/items/2718.php*.

[104] Defra, "UK Guidance on Approval and Authorisation to Participate in Clean Development Mechanism project activities" (March 2008) available at *http://www.defra.gov.uk/environment/climatechange/internat/kyotomech/cdm.htm*.

[105] The Greenhouse Gas Emissions Trading Scheme (Amendment) and National Emissions Inventory Regulations 2005 (SI 2005/2903), regulation 5(1). In the case of Scottish, Northern Irish or Welsh applicants Defra must ensure that a decision made by the Secretary of State is agreed with by the devolved authority; Regulation 8. Applications can be sent by email to the Designated National Authority at Defra (dna@defra.gsi.gov.uk).

[106] ibid, reg.9.

Emissions trading

This third flexible mechanism allows Annex I states to trade in "assigned   **7–013** amount units" (AAUs)[107] between themselves, subject to satisfying eligibility requirements.[108] International emission trading under the Kyoto Protocol was possible from January 1, 2008, and enables unused Annex I greenhouse gas quotas to be bought and sold. If an Annex I state knows that it will pollute less than its Kyoto Protocol target, it can sell its unused quota as AAUs to a fellow Annex I country which has taken the view that it will pollute in excess of its target. Any AAUs can be used by the purchasing Annex I state to contribute to the meeting of its Kyoto Protocol emission reduction commitment. It was agreed in the Marrakesh Accords that Annex I countries could also purchase CERs and ERUs from other Annex I states, and also RMUs obtained in LULUCF forestry management and agriculture projects.

Tradable units (AAUs, CERs, ERUs, and RMUs) are to be logged and tracked within a system of registries established pursuant to the Kyoto Protocol regime. All Annex I countries with established Kyoto Protocol emission reduction targets have or are establishing national registries to record tradable units. The key role of these registries is therefore to maintain a record of transactions between entities in the carbon market. The Environment Agency has responsibility for the maintenance of the UK's Greenhouse Gas Emissions Trading Scheme Registry.[109] All national registries will eventually be linked to the International Transaction Log (ITL) which is administered by the Secretariat of the UN Framework Convention on Climate Change. It is the role of the ITL to verify that planned transactions notified by national registries are in accordance with the rules established under the Kyoto Protocol. Planned transactions are to be either approved or rejected electronically by the ITL. If approved, national registries can finalise the transaction. The ITL became operational in November 2007. Japan became the first county to be linked to the ITL and was followed by Switzerland, New Zealand and the Russian Federation. The EU's Community Independent Transaction Log which, as will be addressed later, was established in 2005 and records trading under the EU's regional Emissions Trading System has been linked to the ITL since October 2008, as have EU national registries. The ITL carries out checks verifying transactions as they relate to Kyoto Protocol requirements, but

---

[107] AAUs are units of the quantity of emissions that an Annex I state is allowed to emit in a given year in the 2008–12 Kyoto Protocol commitment period.

[108] Contained in paragraph 2 of the Annex to Decision 11/CMP.1 of the Conference of the Parties serving as the meeting of the Parties to the Kyoto Protocol. These include the need for the Annex I state to be a Party to the Kyoto Protocol, to have in place a national system for the estimation of emissions, to have established a national registry to track the creation and movement of credits generated under Kyoto's flexible mechanisms, and to have submitted annual inventories of emissions.

[109] The UK registry's website is located at *http://emissionsregistry.gov.uk*. Details of all national registry's can be found at *http://unfccc.int*.

with regard to transactions proposed by EU national registries will also forward details of such planned trades to the Community Independent Transaction Log to allow the latter to check compliance with EU emissions trading rules.

CDM credits are issued into a separate "CDM Registry" set up and administered by the Secretariat of the UN Framework Convention on Climate Change. Once a given national registry is connected with the ITL these CERs will be sent to the national registry in question and can be traded within the Kyoto Protocol's emissions trading system.

The EU's Emissions Trading System

7–014   The EU's Emission Trading System (ETS), the world's first international trading system for carbon dioxide, was established on January 1, 2005, pursuant to Directive 2003/87/EC (the Emissions Trading Directive).[110] The latter is currently implemented by the Greenhouse Gas Emissions Trading Scheme Regulations 2005 as amended (Greenhouse Gas Emissions Trading Scheme Regulations 2005).[111] The ETS is the cornerstone of the EU's strategy to comply with its international commitments and applies to more than 10,000 installations "collectively responsible for close to half of the EU's emissions of carbon dioxide and 40% of its total greenhouse gas emissions."[112] The Emissions Trading Directive notes that the scheme is designed "to promote reductions of greenhouse gas emissions in a cost-effective and economically efficient manner."[113] It does so by introducing a "cap-and-trade" scheme. The first trading period ran from the beginning of 2005 to the end of 2007. The second phase commenced on January 1, 2008 and will run until the end of 2012 (in parallel with the first commitment period under the Kyoto Protocol). Member

---

[110] Directive 2003/87 establishing a scheme for greenhouse gas emissions allowance trading within the Community and amending Council Directive 96/61/EC; [2003] OJ L275/32. For a lucid and meticulous analysis of the ETS and its particular relevance in the UK, see Robinson, Barton, Dodwell, Heydon and Milton, *Climate Change Law: Emissions Trading in the EU and the UK* (Cameron May, 2007). See also Hare, "Understanding the EU emissions trading scheme" ENDS Climate Review 2006/7 pp.30–33.

[111] Greenhouse Gas Emissions Trading Scheme Regulations 2005 (SI 2005/925) came into force on April 21, 2005 and have subsequently been amended by the following: the Greenhouse Gas Emissions Trading Scheme (Amendment) and National Emissions Inventory Regulations (SI 2005/2903); the Greenhouse Gas Emissions Trading Scheme (Amendment) Regulations (SI 2006/737); the Greenhouse Gas Emissions Trading Scheme (Amendment) Regulations (SI 2007/465); the Greenhouse Gas Emissions Trading Scheme (Miscellaneous Provisions) Regulations (SI 2007/1096); and the Greenhouse Gas Emissions Trading Scheme (Amendment No.2) Regulations (SI 2007/3433). Hereinafter reference to the "Greenhouse Gas Emissions Trading Scheme Regulations 2005" refers to the 2005 regulations as so amended.

[112] EUROPA Press Release, Ref: MEMO/08/35, January 23, 2008.

[113] Emissions Trading Directive, art.1.

States have adopted National Allocation Plans (NAPs) for each of these phases. Subsequent trading periods from 2013 are envisaged.

NAPs establish a national cap or limit detailing the total amount of carbon dioxide which can be emitted by the Member State in question in a certain time period. National caps take into account the given Member State's need to make emission reductions to fulfil Kyoto Protocol obligations. Once NAPs have been established by agreement with the European Commission, allowances are distributed nationally to "operators"[114] of participating "installations"[115] up to but not exceeding the national cap. Each allowance represents the right to emit one metric tonne of carbon dioxide equivalent,[116] and these allowances can be bought and sold within the ETS. Allowances are the common currency of the ETS. Operators of participating installations must annually surrender a sufficient number of allowances to competent national authorities to cover that installation's emissions in the time period concerned; by April 30 in each year operators have to surrender allowances equal to the total emissions from a given installation in the previous calendar year.[117]

If an installation has insufficient allowances to surrender, the operator in question will face penalties for exceeding its capped limit. However, if an installation has more allowances than it needs, it may sell them on the open market to an operator of an installation in danger of not having enough allowances. Any purchased allowances can be used by the purchasing operator to cover excess emissions from its industrial plant. The free market determines the price for these allowances. In effect, the operator in danger of having insufficient allowances has one of three business choices to make: either to enter the market to buy up sufficient allowances; make changes in the installation's operation which reduce the overall volume of carbon dioxide emitted; or adopt a combination of these approaches. Logically if the cost of buying allowances on the open market exceeds the cost of, for example, installing new technology to reduce carbon dioxide emissions, the operator in question will opt to renovate the relevant plant by purchasing such technology. On the other hand, if the cost of altering the installation by introducing new greener technology exceeds the cost of buying allowances on the open market, the operator may well decide to

---

[114] An operator "means any person who operates or controls and installation or, where this is provided for in national legislation, to whom decisive economic power over the technical functioning of the installation has been delegated"; Emissions Trading Directive, art.3(f).

[115] An installation "means a stationary technical unit where one of more activities listed in Annex I are carried out and any other directly associated activities which have a technical connection with the activities carried out on that site and which could have an effect on emissions and pollution"; Emissions Trading Directive, art.3(e). This definition is reflected in Greenhouse Gas Emissions Trading Scheme Regulations 2005.

[116] A "tonne of carbon dioxide equivalent" is defined in the Directive as "one metric tonne of carbon dioxide or an amount of any other greenhouse gas listed in Annex II with an equivalent global-warming potential"; Emissions Trading Directive, art.3(j). This definition is also used in the Greenhouse Gas Emissions Trading Scheme Regulations 2005.

[117] Emissions Trading Directive, art.6(2)e.

simply enter the market to purchase much needed allowances. However if the reduction in emissions is significantly beyond the minimum needed to comply with the limit, the surplus can be sold and the proceeds used to offset the cost of the new technology. As such the ETS operates to bring down emissions in the most cost-effective and economically efficient manner. Allowances become scarce commodities and the price of an allowance will solely reflect supply and demand in the market place. Any natural or legal person may trade in allowances;[118] individuals and even non-governmental organisations can for example become active in the market.

Activities that fall within the remit of the Emissions Trading Directive

7–015   The ETS currently covers the following activities which are listed in Annex I of the Directive and are also noted in the Greenhouse Gas Emissions Trading Scheme Regulations 2005, Schedule 1:

Table 7/II

Activities
Energy activities Combustion installations with a rated thermal input exceeding 20 MW (except hazardous or municipal waste installations). Mineral oil refineries. Coke ovens.
Production and processing of ferrous metals Metal ore (including sulphide ore) roasting or sintering installations. Installations for the production of pig iron or steel (primary or secondary fusion) including continuing casting, with a capacity exceeding 2.5 tonnes per hour.

---

[118] Emissions Trading Directive, art.12(1)a.

Mineral industry

Installations for the production of cement clinker in rotary kilns with a production capacity exceeding 500 tonnes per day or lime in rotary kilns with a production capacity exceeding 50 tonnes per day or in other furnaces with a production capacity exceeding 50 tonnes per day.

Installations for the manufacture of glass including glass fibre with a melting capacity exceeding 20 tonnes per day.

Installations for the manufacture of ceramic products by firing, in particular roofing tiles, bricks, refractory bricks, tiles, stoneware or porcelain, with a production capacity exceeding 75 tones per day, and/or with a kiln capacity exceeding 4 m^3 with a setting density per kiln of 300 kg/m^3.

Other activities

Industrial plants for the production of;
(a) pulp from timber or other fibrous materials;
(b) paper and board with a production capacity exceeding 20 tonnes per day.

In December 2006 the European Commission put forward a proposal to amend the ETS Directive to also include aviation activities within the ETS.[119]

Annex I activities reflect the major industrial sources of greenhouse gas emissions and, with the exception of the excluded chemicals and waste incineration sectors,[120] broadly reflect the key activities covered by the Integrated Pollution Prevention and Control Directive (IPPC Directive).[121] As far as particular gases are concerned, the Emissions Trading   **7–016**

---

[119] COM (2006) 818. At the time of writing the proposal has not as yet been adopted, but in July 2008 the European Parliament gave its approval to the Common Position adopted by the Council in April 2008. The Common Position envisages aviation activities being included in the ETS from 2012. On the issue of including aviation in the ETS see also European Commission, *Reducing the Climate Change Impact of Aviation* COM (2005) 459 final. See also "Aviation to come under EU ETS from 2011" ENDS REPORT 364 (January 2007) p.45. On the impact of aviation see Gazzard, "Time to fly less" in ENDS Climate Review 2006/07 pp.46–49.

[120] The European Commission noted in 2001 that the chemical sector was not included for two reasons: it was not responsible for particularly significant levels of carbon dioxide emissions; and the administrative burden that the inclusion of approximately 34,000 chemical plants would have brought upon the ETS would have been very significant [COM (2001) 581 final (OJ 2002 C75E/33), para.11]. The waste incineration sector was not included "due to the complexities of measuring the carbon content of the waste material that is being burnt"; ibid.

[121] The original measure Directive 96/61/EC (OJ 1996 L257/26) has now been repealed by the codifying Directive 2008/1 concerning Integrated Pollution Prevention and Control (OJ 2008 L24/8).

Directive covers in principle all the greenhouse gases noted in Annex II of the Directive (carbon dioxide, methane, nitrous oxide, hydro-fluorocarbons, perfluorocarbons and sulphur hexafluoride).[122] However, in fact only carbon dioxide emissions from Annex I activities currently fall within the scheme as the Directive notes that greenhouse gas emission permits are only required for "any activity listed in Annex I resulting in emissions specified in relation to that activity ...";[123] Annex I presently only makes reference to carbon dioxide emissions. The limited scope of the scheme will allow for experience to be gained in trading which could then be utilized to expand the scheme at a later date to other activities and the other Annex II greenhouse gases. It is also clear that the future inclusion in the ETS of any of the Annex II gases other than carbon dioxide will be dependent upon improving the accuracy of monitoring for these gases, the European Commission noting in 2001 that "monitoring uncertainties are still too great for greenhouse gases other than carbon dioxide."[124]

Unilateral inclusion of additional activities, installations and gases

7–017   By virtue of Article 24 Member States from 2005 were allowed to uni-laterally include additional installations in the ETS where such installations carried out Annex I activities but fell below the Annex I capacity limits. Sweden, Austria, Finland, Latvia and Slovenia all made successful appli-cations to the European Commission in this respect in relation to the 2005–07 phase.[125] In making these decisions the Directive required the European Commission to "take into account all relevant criteria, in par-ticular effects on the internal market, potential distortions of competition, the environmental integrity of the scheme and reliability of the planned monitoring and reporting system."[126] From 2008 Member States may include within the ETS other activities or installations even if not men-tioned in Annex I.[127] Additionally, a Member State can unilaterally opt to include greenhouse gases other than carbon dioxide.[128] The European Commission's consent is still required for any such unilateral action and in the making of a decision the European Commission is obliged to take into account the same criteria as in the 2005–07 initial phase.[129]

---

[122] Annex II gases reflect the greenhouse gases covered by the Kyoto Protocol.
[123] Emissions Trading Directive, art.4.
[124] COM (2001) 581 final (OJ 2002 C75E/33), para.10.
[125] These European Commission decisions are all reproduced at *http://europa.eu/environment/climat/first_phase_ep.htm*.
[126] Emissions Trading Directive, art.24(1).
[127] ibid.
[128] ibid.
[129] ibid.

Temporary exclusion of installations

The Directive also indicated that certain installations could be temporarily **7–018** excluded from the ETS but only until the end of 2007 at the latest.[130] Applications were made by just three Member States; Belgium, the United Kingdom and the Netherlands.[131] In granting its approval to these applications, the European Commission had to be satisfied that there would be no distortion of the internal market, and that the installations in question would be subject to equivalent monitoring, reporting and verification requirements, a system of penalties at least equivalent to that imposed by the Directive, and would "as a result of national policies, limit their emissions as much as would be the case if they were subject [to the Directive]".[132] In making the decisions in relation to the UK's applications factors taken into account included the fact that certain installations were subject to the UK Emissions Trading System (UK ETS) and that others were subject to Climate Change Agreements (CCAs).[133] Both the UK ETS and CCAs are to be addressed later. If an installation has been temporarily excluded by the European Commission an obligation is placed on the Secretary of State for the Environment, Food and Rural Affairs to publish the European Commission's decision within seven days of notification.[134] Once the decision is so published, the operator of the installation then has a period of two months to apply for a certificate of temporary exclusion.[135] Any such certificate will stipulate conditions applicable to the temporary exclusion.[136]

Greenhouse gas emission permits

Member States are obliged to ensure that from the beginning of 2005 any **7–019** operator of an installation carrying out an Annex I activity resulting in the emission of carbon dioxide holds a greenhouse gas emissions permit issued by the respective Member State's competent authority.[137] In accordance

---

[130] See Emissions Trading Directive, art.27(2) and also Greenhouse Gas Emissions Trading Scheme Regulations 2005, reg.11.

[131] These European Commission decisions are all reproduced at *http://europa.eu/environment/climat/first_phase_ep.htm*.

[132] Emissions Trading Directive, art.27.

[133] In 2007 59 installations that had opted out of the EU trading scheme in 2005 and 2006 due to their involvement in the UK ETS entered the EU ETS following the conclusion of the UK ETS scheme; "UK emissions covered by Euro-carbon trading rises as coverage widens" ENDS Report 399 (April 2008) pp.10–11.

[134] Greenhouse Gas Emissions Trading Scheme Regulations 2005, reg.11(2).

[135] Greenhouse Gas Emissions Trading Scheme Regulations 2005, regs 11(1) and 11(3).

[136] A greenhouse gas emissions permit under the EU ETS will still be required for a temporarily excluded installation but any such permit will stipulate that the installation is deemed to be in compliance with both monitoring and reporting requirements and the need to surrender sufficient allowances under the EU ETS; Greenhouse Gas Emissions Trading Scheme Regulations 2005, reg.10(6).

[137] Emissions Trading Directive, art.4. See also Greenhouse Gas Emissions Trading Scheme Regulations 2005, reg.7.

with Article 5 of the Emissions Trading Directive the application for a permit must include the following:

- a description of the installation and its activities including the technology used;
- the raw and auxiliary materials, the use of which is likely to lead to emissions of gases listed in Annex I;
- the sources of emissions of gases listed in Annex I from the installation;
- the measures planned to monitor and report emissions in accordance with those guidelines noted below.[138]

In the UK applications for permits are to be made by a given installation's operator to the relevant national regulator. The Environment Agency is the regulator for installations situated in England and Wales; the Scottish Environment Protection Agency if the installation is located in Scotland; and the Chief Inspector if situated in Northern Ireland.[139] Applications are to be made to the Secretary of State for Environment, Food and Rural Affairs for offshore installations.[140] The operator's application will be accompanied by the relevant fee.[141] An application must be determined by the regulator within two months.[142] A regulator must refuse to grant a permit when it takes the view that the applicant will not actually be the operator of the installation after the permit is granted,[143] or is not satisfied that the applicant will operate the installation in such a way to comply with monitoring and reporting requirements.[144]

---

[138] Greenhouse Gas Emissions Trading Scheme Regulations 2005, reg.8(2)a additionally inter alia notes that the applicant's details, the postal address of the installation's site and national grid reference, and a description of any applicable IPPC license must be included.

[139] Greenhouse Gas Emissions Trading Scheme Regulations 2005, reg.8(1).

[140] ibid.

[141] ibid; operators of installations must include with their application a fee as established in the Greenhouse Gas Emissions Trading Scheme Regulations 2005, Schedule 5. Applications to the regulator can be made electronically and fees may then be sent to the regulator separately from the application but the application will not be regarded as having been received until the fee is received; Greenhouse Gas Emissions Trading Scheme Regulations 2005, reg.5(5).

[142] Greenhouse Gas Emissions Trading Scheme Regulations 2005, reg.9(1). After an application has been received the regulator may request further information; reg.8(5). If so, in calculating the two months period of time no account will be taken of the time beginning with the date on which the notice requiring further information was served and ending with the day on which the applicant provided this further information; reg.9(2).

[143] Greenhouse Gas Emissions Trading Scheme Regulations 2005, reg.9(6)a.

[144] Greenhouse Gas Emissions Trading Scheme Regulations 2005, reg.9(6)b.

When a permit is granted it "may cover one or more installations on the same site operated by the same operator",[145] and the operator is obliged to keep the national competent authority informed of any changes to the nature and functioning of the plant which may require the permit to be updated by variation.[146] The permit will include conditions that must inter alia contain monitoring and reporting requirements,[147] and an obligation to surrender allowances "equal to the total emissions of the installation in each calendar year ... within four months following the end of that year."[148] Other conditions may be added to the permit as the regulator deems appropriate.[149] Permit holders are obliged to pay a subsistence charge for the period covered by the permit to cover the regulator's administrative costs.[150] When an operator no longer carries out Annex I/ Schedule 1 activities it is obliged to surrender its permit.[151] The regulator has the power to revoke a permit at any time by serving a notice on the operator.[152] When activities covered by the Directive are also regulated under the Integrated Pollution Prevention and Control Directive (IPPC Directive), the conditions of and procedure for the issuing of greenhouse gas emissions permits must be coordinated with those relating to the issuance of an IPPC permit.[153]

Appeals

Appeals against decisions made by the regulator or registry administrator   **7–020** may be made under the Greenhouse Gas Emissions Trading Scheme Regulations 2005.[154] So, for example, a person whose application for a greenhouse gas emissions permit has been rejected, or wishes to object to

---

[145] Emissions Trading Directive, art.6.
[146] Emissions Trading Directive, art.7. Greenhouse gas emission permits can be varied in accordance with the Greenhouse Gas Emissions Trading Scheme Regulations 2005, reg.14. There is a right to appeal against any such variation; Greenhouse Gas Emissions Trading Scheme Regulations, reg.32(1)b. Where an operator intends to transfer the management of an installation to another, a joint application must be made to transfer the permit by the operator and the operator-to-be; Greenhouse Gas Emissions Trading Scheme Regulations 2005, reg.15.
[147] Emissions Trading Directive, art.6(2)c&d; Greenhouse Gas Emissions Trading Scheme Regulations, reg.10(2).
[148] Emissions Trading Directive, art.6(2)e. The Greenhouse Gas Emissions Trading Scheme Regulations 2005 stipulate that "a greenhouse gas emissions permit shall contain conditions to ensure that the operator surrenders allowances equal to the annual reportable emissions from the installation within four months of the end of the scheme year during which those emissions arose"; reg.10(3).
[149] Greenhouse Gas Emissions Trading Scheme Regulations 2005, reg.10(1). Regulators are obliged to review permit conditions periodically and "may do so at any time"; reg.10(9).
[150] Greenhouse Gas Emissions Trading Scheme Regulations 2005, reg.18(1). The subsistence charge is established in Sch.5, paras 4–5.
[151] Greenhouse Gas Emissions Trading Scheme Regulations 2005, reg.16.
[152] Greenhouse Gas Emissions Trading Scheme Regulations 2005, reg.17.
[153] Emissions Trading Directive, article 8. The provisions of article 5–7 of the Emissions Trading Directive may be integrated into the procedures under the IPPC Directive.
[154] Greenhouse Gas Emissions Trading Scheme Regulations 2005, reg.32.

the provisions of any such permit, may lodge an appeal. Schedule 2 of the Regulations establishes the procedure for any such appeals. Appeals are to be made to the "appropriate authority" which in relation to an installation in England is the Secretary of State for the Environment, Food and Rural Affairs.[155] The Secretary of State may delegate power in this regard by appointing a person to act on his/her behalf,[156] or by referring a matter involved in an appeal to a person so that the latter can then report back to him/her.[157] Any person appointed by the Secretary of State can hold a local inquiry or other such hearing,[158] and must hold such an inquiry if the Secretary of State so directs.[159] Where a local or other inquiry is held, the Secretary of State can appoint an assessor to sit with the appointed person to provide the latter with advice.[160]

Monitoring and reporting

7–021   No greenhouse gas emissions permit can be issued by a competent authority unless the latter is "satisfied that the operator is capable of monitoring and reporting emissions."[161] The Emissions Trading Directive obliges the European Commission to issue guidelines for the monitoring and also the reporting of emissions and Annex IV of the directive establishes principles which the European Commission is to base those guidelines upon. In 2004 the European Commission adopted its first set of guidelines.[162] From January 1, 2008, these have been repealed by the current guidelines established in Commission Decision 2007/589 ("the Monitoring and Reporting Decision").[163] Member States are required to ensure that emissions are monitored in accordance with the guidelines,[164] and that each operator of a relevant installation reports the emissions from that plant "during each calendar year to the competent authority after the end of that year in accordance with the guidelines."[165] These emissions reports have to be verified in accordance with the criteria noted in Annex V of the Directive.[166] If an operator's report has not been verified as being

---

[155] Greenhouse Gas Emissions Trading Scheme Regulations 2005, reg.32(1). In Scotland an appeal would be made to the Scottish Ministers, in Wales to the National Assembly for Wales; see ibid and reg.2 in relation to the definition of "appropriate authority". In Northern Ireland appeals are to be made to the Planning Appeals Commission; reg.32(14).

[156] Greenhouse Gas Emissions Trading Scheme Regulations 2005, reg.34(2)a.

[157] Greenhouse Gas Emissions Trading Scheme Regulations 2005, reg.34(2)b.

[158] Greenhouse Gas Emissions Trading Scheme Regulations 2005, Sch.3, para.4(2)a.

[159] Greenhouse Gas Emissions Trading Scheme Regulations 2005, Sch.3, para.4(2)b.

[160] Greenhouse Gas Emissions Trading Scheme Regulations 2005, Sch.3, para.4(3).

[161] Emissions Trading Directive, art.6(1). Regulation 10(2) notes that the greenhouse gas emissions permit will include conditions to ensure emissions are monitored and reported in accordance with the Monitoring and Reporting Decision.

[162] Commission Decision 2004/156/EC OJ 2004 L59/1.

[163] OJ 2007 L229/1.

[164] Emissions Trading Directive, art.14(2).

[165] Emissions Trading Directive, art.14(3).

[166] Emissions Trading Directive, art.15.

satisfactory by March 31 in each year in respect of emissions in the preceding year the operator in question is not allowed to make transfers of allowances until a report has indeed been appropriately verified.[167] Regulators in the UK are obliged to enforce compliance with monitoring and reporting conditions,[168] and may serve enforcement notices where the operator of a given installation has contravened or is likely to contravene such conditions.[169]

ETS and the IPPC regime

Greenhouse gas emissions from heavy industry were subject to regulation under the IPPC Directive prior to the entry into force of the Emissions Trading Directive.[170] Under the IPPC Directive Member States are obliged to establish emission limit values based on Best Available Techniques,[171] and the measure further stipulates that installations are to be operated in such a way that "energy is used efficiently".[172] The IPPC Directive in its own right must therefore be seen as an important instrument in both EU and UK programmes to reduce greenhouse gas emissions. On entry into force the Emissions Trading Directive made important changes to the IPPC Directive. Article 9(3) of the latter now notes the following:-

7–022

> "Where emissions of a greenhouse gas from an installation are specified in Annex I to [the Emissions Trading Directive] in relation to an activity carried out in that installation, the permit shall not include an emission limit value for direct emissions of that gas unless it is necessary to ensure that no significant local pollution is covered."[173]

This amendment was necessary as otherwise one of the key aims of the Emissions Trading Directive, namely to ensure that greenhouse gas emissions are reduced in the most economically efficient manner, would have been undermined;

---

[167] ibid.
[168] Greenhouse Gas Emissions Trading Scheme Regulations 2005, reg.28.
[169] Greenhouse Gas Emissions Trading Scheme Regulations 2005, reg.29.
[170] See further Robinson et al, above fn.110, p.107.
[171] arts 9(3) and 9(4) IPPC Directive.
[172] art.3(1)d IPPC Directive.
[173] It has been noted that installations under the IPPC Directive are to be operated in such a way that "energy is used efficiently" (art.3(1)d IPPC Directive). Note however that a further amendment to the IPPC Directive introduced by the Emissions Trading Directives inserts the following into art.9(3) of the IPPC Directive: "[f]or activities listed in Annex I to [the Emissions Trading Directive], Member States may choose not to impose requirements relating to energy efficiency in respect of combustion units or other units emitting carbon dioxide on the site."

"[t]he scope for reductions in greenhouse gas emissions to be made in the most economically efficient location ... would be compromised if the relevant installation were simultaneously subject under the IPPC Directive to inflexible emission limit values for those gases."[174]

Emissions of greenhouse gases from installations covered by the IPPC Directive which do not fall within the operations listed in Annex I of the Emissions Trading Directive will still be regulated under the IPPC Directive. So, for example, any greenhouse gas emissions from the chemical sector remain subject to IPPC regulation. Furthermore, as only carbon dioxide emissions are currently tradable under the Emissions Trading Directive, if an Annex I installation emitted greenhouse gases other than carbon dioxide (methane for example), they would remain subject to IPPC regulation until such time as the Emissions Trading Directive is amended to include additional greenhouse gases other than carbon dioxide in its Annex I.[175]

National Allocation Plans

7–023 It will be recalled that NAPs are to be developed by each Member State detailing the number of allowances it intends to allocate nationally in a particular phase of the ETS, as well as how it intends to allocate these allowances.[176] All NAPs need to be approved by the European Commission which is obliged to make a decision on a given NAP within three months of been notified of it by the Member State in question.[177]

Member States were obliged to ensure that NAPs for both the first and second phase are "based on objective and transparent criteria, including those listed in Annex III, taking due account of comments from the public."[178] Eleven criteria noted in Annex III were relevant to first phase NAPs and these included the need to ensure non-discrimination between companies, to indicate how new entrants can begin their participation in the

---

[174] Robinson et al, above fn.110, p.107.
[175] ibid, pp.109–110.
[176] Emissions Trading Directive, art.9(1). The obligation to develop a NAP falls on the Secretary of State for Environment, Food and Rural Affairs; Greenhouse Gas Emissions Trading Scheme Regulations 2005, reg.20(1).
[177] Emissions Trading Directive, art.9(3). In Case T 178–05 *UK v Commission* [2005] ECR II–4807 the Court of First Instance indicated that "if the Commission does not react to the NAP in the three months following notification, the plan must be considered as approved by the Commission and may not then be amended unless the proposed amendments are accepted by the Commission in accordance with Article 9(3) of the Directive"; para.55.
[178] Emissions Trading Directive, art.9(1).

trading scheme,[179] to provide relevant information on the way in which clean technology has been taken into account, and to indicate the way in which the public can comment on the plan before a final decision is made on the allocation of allowances. Most importantly, NAPs also had to be consistent with the need of the particular Member State in question to comply with its international obligations under the Kyoto Protocol and the "EC Bubble". Emission reductions facilitated by the Emissions Trading Directive will not be the only reductions that contribute to the needed reductions to satisfy Kyoto Protocol obligations; NAPs therefore, on the one hand, had to take into account the proportion of overall national emissions which allowances represented "in comparison with sources not covered by this Directive"[180] and, on the other hand, relevant national energy policies.[181]

Member States were obliged to publish and submit NAPs for the 2005–07 phase by the end of March 2004 detailing the number of allowances to be allocated in this first phase and the way in which allowances would be distributed nationally to industrial sectors and industrial installations.[182] All were scrutinised by the European Commission and eventually approved. Nonetheless the last plan was not given approval until June 2005 and this delay inevitably led to a period of uncertainty in the market. The European Commission approved the allocation of 657 billion allowances in the first trading period.[183] Twenty-five NAPs were submitted and the European Commission required reductions in the granting of allowances in 14 cases.[184] Overall, NAPs were more likely to place more onerous

---

[179] The Emissions Trading Directive defines "new entrant" as "any installation carrying out one or more of the activities indicated in Annex I, which has obtained a greenhouse gas emissions permit or an update of its greenhouse gas emissions permit because of a change in the nature or functioning or an extension of the installation, subsequent to the notification to the Commission of the national allocation plan"; art.3. Article 11(3) of the Directive notes that "[w]hen deciding upon allocation, Member States shall take into account the need to provide access to allowances for new entrants." The UK has set aside allowances to be allocated for free to such new entrants that begin or extend such activities after the end of 2007 but before the end of 2012; see Appendix D of the UK's Phase II NAP available online at *http://www.defra.gov.uk/environment/climatechange/trading/eu/operators/phase-2.htm*. On the allocation and issue of allowances from the UK's new entrant reserve see Greenhouse Gas Emissions Trading Scheme Regulations 2005, reg.22. The relevant UK regulator is responsible for the allocation of allowances to new entrants; ibid.

[180] Emissions Trading Directive, Annex III(1). Other particularly significant sources are road transport and boilers used in domestic heating.

[181] ibid.

[182] Emissions Trading Directive, art.9(1). All European Commission decisions on first phase NAPs are available online at *http://ec.europa/environment/climat/first_phase_ep.htm*.

[183] European Commission Press Release, "Emissions Trading: Commission approves last allocation plan ending NAP marathon", IP/05/762, June 20, 2005.

[184] ibid.

restrictions on operators in the power generation industry than others operators.[185]

7-024 The results for 2005 indicated that "aggregate ... emissions, at just over 2 billion tonnes, were significantly below the annual average allocation for the first period of close to 2.2 billion tonnes."[186] It is also of interest to note results for 2006 as installations in the 25 Member States again emitted less than the total number of allowances issued to them in 2006;[187] the Community Independent Transaction Log stipulates that 2,027 million tonnes of carbon dioxide were emitted, a level of emissions of 51.7 million tonnes less than allowances issued.[188] Nineteen Member States had surpluses of allowances in 2006:

> "Poland had the highest surplus in absolute terms, followed by France, Germany, the Czech Republic and the Netherlands. The highest surpluses in percentage terms came from Lithuania, Estonia, Latvia and France. The UK, Italy, Spain, Denmark, Ireland and Slovenia all had deficits of allowances."[189]

Bearing in mind that the European Commission in late 2006 noted that some Member States needed to take further action if the EU as a whole was to meet its international commitments, it issued a word of warning in relation to the second phase of the ETS:

> "[If] more allowances were to be issued by Member States than the likely quantity of actual emissions in 2008 to 2012 from the installations covered, meeting the Kyoto Protocol commitments would be severely compromised and little or no environmental benefit would be provided by the EU ETS. The development of existing and new clean technologies would stall, and the evolution of a dynamic and liquid global market would be seriously undermined."[190]

---

[185] ibid. In Case T-130/06 *Drax Power and others v European Commission* [2007] ECR II–67 the Court of First Instance denied key entities in the UK power industry the opportunity to challenge a rejection by the European Commission of a proposed change by the UK to its NAP due to the entities lack of standing under Article 230 EC Treaty; see Macrory, "European Court of Justice dismisses challenge to UK Greenhouse gas plans" ENDS Report 392 (September 2007) pp.54–55.

[186] COM(2006)725 final. See "Most UK EU ETS sites had allowance surpluses" ENDS Report 385 (February 2007) p.44.

[187] See "UK EU ETS over-allocation increased in 2002" ENDS Report 389 (June 2007) p.12.

[188] Defra, "EU Emissions Trading Scheme: UK Results 2006 Report" (2008), pp.2–3 (this publication is available on the Defra website).

[189] ibid, p.3. The UK deficit has been attributed to coal-powered power stations emitting 45.9 million tonnes more than their allocation due to an increase in electricity generation from these installations rather than from gas-fired installations; "[a]lthough coal use produces more emissions, the cost of gas has been too high and the cost of carbon too low to produce a price that will lead to fuel switching"; ibid. In effect, operators of coal-powered power stations had to enter the market to acquire allowances.

[190] COM(2006)725 final, para.1.

In effect, when taken as a whole NAPs covering the initial 2005–07 period had been too generous as far as the number of allowances granted was concerned and valuable lessons had to be learned. More stringent emission caps had to be established for the ETS 2008–12 trading period, a point underlined by the fact that verified emissions from EU ETS businesses in 2007 showed an increase in carbon dioxide emissions of 0.68% compared to 2006.[191] Commenting on these results European Environment Commissioner Stavros Dimas stipulated that;

"[e]missions trading is yielding results. Studies show that emissions would most likely have been significantly higher without the EU ETS. However, the small rise last year further confirms the need for a strict emission cap for the second trading period."[192]

Bearing experience gained in the first phase in mind, the European Commission acknowledged that NAPs covering the second phase (2008–12) had to be assessed in a way;

"which ensures a correct and consistent application of the [Annex III criteria] and sufficient scarcity of allowances in the EU ETS, thereby in turn ensuring that emission reductions are delivered and that the emerging carbon market is strengthened."[193]

NAPs covering the 2008–12 period had to published and notified by the end of June 2006.[194] The vast majority of Member States failed to comply with this deadline. The UK in fact submitted its NAP to the European Commission on August 28, 2006. The European Commission's guidance for the second phase indicated that Member States could not increase their respective caps over that that which applied in the 2005–07 first phase period.[195] Additionally, those Member States which were on path with their Kyoto Protocol obligations could retain their national cap but those in danger of failing to meet their international commitments had to decrease their national cap. This methodology would lead to an overall lowering of the EU-wide cap in the second phase by 6 per cent when compared to the 2005–07 period cap. Such a reduction by the end of the second phase would ensure that the EU and its Member States comply with their Kyoto Protocol obligations.[196]

[191] EUROPA Press Release IP/08/787, "Emissions Trading: 2007 verified emissions from EU ETS businesses", May 23, 2008.
[192] ibid. Only 68 of the 11,186 installations involved in the EU ETS failed to surrender sufficient allowances to cover their 2007 emissions; ibid.
[193] COM(2006)725 final, para.1.
[194] European Commission decisions on second phase NAPs are available online at *http://ec/ europa/environment/climat/2nd_phase_ep.htm.*
[195] See generally COM(2005) 703 final. In 2003 the European Commission issued guidance relating to first phase NAPs; COM(2003)830 final.
[196] European Commission, "Questions and answers on NAPs for 2008–12"; Press Release Memo/06/2, January 9, 2006.

7–025   The European Commission indicated on November 29, 2006, that no objections would be raised in relation to the UK's second phase NAP as long as it was amended to bring installations on Gibraltar within the NAP.[197] Once European Commission conditional approval had been given, the UK was obliged by the Directive to make a formal decision by the end of December 2006 as to the quantity of allowances it would allocate in the five-year period, and to begin the process of allocating allowances to operators in accordance with its NAP (but bearing in mind the European Commission's comments concerning Gibraltar).[198]

The total average annual number of allowances of 246.2 million tonnes to be allocated to installations listed in the UK's NAP and to any new entrants must not be exceeded.[199] This amounts to a cap in the 2008–12 second phase of 1,231 million tonnes in aggregate. As in the first phase, the "reduction in allowances against the business as usual will be borne entirely by the Large Electricity Producers sector".[200] The NAP indicates that the heavy burden placed on these electricity generators is justified due to the fact that the sector "is relatively insulated from international competition and can pass on the cost of carbon to consumers."[201] All other sectors within the ETS are allocated allowances to match business as usual emission projections.

Allocating allowances

7–026   The Secretary of State enjoys the power to allocate allowances,[202] but such allocation must be based on the applicable NAP approved by the European Commission.[203] In relation to the 2005–07 period the Directive required Member States to allocate at least 95 per cent of allowances free of

---

[197] Commission Decision of November 29, 2006 concerning the national allocation plan for the allocation of greenhouse gas emission allowances notified by United Kingdom in accordance with Directive 2003/87/EC, para.2 (available at *http://ec/europa/environment/climat/2nd_phase_ep.htm*).

[198] Emissions Trading Directive, art.11(2).

[199] Commission Decision of November 29, 2006, above fn.197, para.3.

[200] Defra, EU Emissions Trading Scheme: Approved Phase II NAP 2008–2012 (2007), p.10 (available on Defra website). "Large Electricity Producers" are defined in the following terms in the NAP (see p.19):

"[A]ny operator of a combustion installation (except a hazardous or municipal waste installation):
  (a) which has a thermal rated input of above 20 megawatts; and
  (b) which generates electricity and is normally capable of exporting more than 100 megawatts of electrical power to either the total system in Great Britain or the total system in Northern Ireland; and
  (c) for which the operator is not exempted under section 5 of the Electricity Act 1989 or, as the case may be, Article 9(1) of the Electricity (Northern Ireland) Order 1992 from the requirement to hold a generation licence."

[201] ibid, p.10.

[202] See Greenhouse Gas Emissions Trading Scheme Regulations 2005, reg.21(1)a.

[203] Greenhouse Gas Emissions Trading Scheme Regulations 2005, reg.21(2)a.

charge.[204] Operators of installations can emit free of cost in such situations. In the 2008–12 period at least 90 per cent of allowances must be allocated free of charge.[205] The United Kingdom has determined that 93 per cent of allowances will be allocated for free, but that 7 per cent will indeed be auctioned or otherwise sold.[206] The allowances to be auctioned will be deducted from the total number of allowances for the Large Electricity Producers sector. Defra takes the view that this sector has a greater abatement potential than other sectors. The auctioning of allowances is in line with the polluter-pays principle. There are powerful economic arguments for auctioning all allowances, without exception, and in the long term this may well occur. There are however unresolved questions over how the Government should properly apply the potentially substantial revenues it would receive as a result.

Penalties for non-compliance

It will be recalled that Member States must make sure that operators surrender sufficient allowances to cover emissions from installations during the preceding calendar year by the following April 30 at the latest.[207] Should any operator fail to do so, they will incur in the 2008–12 phase an excess emissions penalty of €100 for every tonne of carbon dioxide equivalent emitted for which the operator has failed to surrender allowances.[208] In the first phase the penalty was €40 for each tonne of carbon dioxide equivalent.[209] The payment of any such civil penalty does not absolve the operator of further responsibility regarding the excess emissions; sufficient allowances covering the excess must be surrendered by April 30 in the following year.

7–027

The Greenhouse Gas Emissions Trading Scheme Regulations 2005 make it a criminal offence not to be in compliance with certain stipulations in the regulations.[210] For example, it is an offence to operate an installation carrying out an Annex I/Schedule 1 activity without an EU ETS greenhouse gas emissions permit, to fail to abide by any condition in such a permit, to fail without reasonable excuse to provide information when required to do so by service of notice by a regulator, and to make a false or misleading statement in a material matter to obtain a permit or recklessly to

---

[204] Emissions Trading Directive, art.10.
[205] ibid.
[206] Defra, EU Emissions Trading Scheme: Approved Phase II NAP 2008–2012 (2007), p.10. On the allocation and issue of allowances see Greenhouse Gas Emissions Trading Scheme Regulations 2005, regs 21–25, and also "Options set out for EU ETS auction" ENDS Report 396 (January 2008) pp.37–38.
[207] Emissions Trading Directive, art.12(3).
[208] Emissions Trading Directive, art.16(3). See the Greenhouse Gas Emissions Trading Scheme Regulations 2005, reg.39(3)(b)ii.
[209] Emissions Trading Directive, art.16(4). See the Greenhouse Gas Emissions Trading Scheme Regulations 2005, reg.39(3)(b)i.
[210] Greenhouse Gas Emissions Trading Scheme Regulations 2005, reg.38.

make such a statement. A person found guilty of such an offence would be liable on summary conviction to a fine not exceeding the statutory maximum or to a prison term of not more than three months.[211] On conviction on indictment, any fine can be imposed and/or a term of imprisonment not exceeding two years.[212]

Pooling of installations

7–028　Operators can apply to create a "pool of installations from the same activity".[213] A pooling of this sort would, for example, therefore allow two or more combustion installations to trade within the ETS as a unit. Applications to pool are to be made to the competent national authority but the Member State in question must send the application to the European Commission to ensure it complies with the Directive's requirements. If the European Commission rejects the application, it cannot proceed unless proposed amendments made by the European Commission are implemented. The opportunity to pool was inserted into the Emissions Trading Directive at the insistence of Germany to ensure ETS compatibility with its national agreements which have adopted a sectoral approach.[214]

Allowance registries

7–029　Every Member State is obliged to establish a national registry which keeps electronic records of allowances in holding accounts. The EU national registries form part of an integrated system tracking the issuing, holding, transfer and cancellation of allowances.[215] National registries are open to the public[216] and accessible through the internet.[217] It will be recalled that all Annex I countries with established Kyoto Protocol emission reduction targets must also establish a national registry. The EU Member State's national registries established under the EU ETS therefore have a dual purpose as they also act as national registries pursuant to the Kyoto Protocol's international regime. The Environment Agency has responsibility for the maintenance of the UK's Greenhouse Gas Emissions Trading

---

[211] Greenhouse Gas Emissions Trading Scheme Regulations 2005, reg.38(2)a.
[212] Greenhouse Gas Emissions Trading Scheme Regulations 2005, reg.38(2)b.
[213] Emissions Trading Directive, article 28(1). See Greenhouse Gas Emissions Trading Scheme Regulations 2005, reg.27 on pooling.
[214] Haigh, *Manual of Environmental Policy: the EU and Britain*, (Maney Publishing: looseleaf) 14.13–4.
[215] Emissions Trading Directive, art.19(1).
[216] Emissions Trading Directive, art.19(2).
[217] Regulation 2216/2004 for a standardised and secured system of registries pursuant to Directive 2003/87 OJ 2004 L386/1, art.3(2). This Regulation specifies general provisions, specifications and requirements for the integrated system of registries and also for a communication system with the CITL. It was amended by regulation 916/2007 OJ 2007 L200/5.

Scheme Registry.[218] Now that EU national registries are linked to the International Transaction Log (ITL) administered by the Secretariat of the UN Framework Convention on Climate Change, the ITL carries out checks to verify transactions in relation to Kyoto Protocol rules and then passes on details of transactions proposed by those EU national registries to the Community Independent Transaction Log (CITL) to allow the latter to check compliance with EU emissions trading rules. Before connection to the ITL, the CITL was linked to EU national registries and simply checked for irregularities under the EU ETS. The CITL is accessible via the internet.[219]

The Linking Directive

By virtue of the "Linking Directive"[220] credits obtained through the Kyoto Protocol project-based mechanisms, JI and the CDM, can be drawn upon by companies to assist them in achieving compliance under the ETS.[221] In effect, credits achieved abroad under these mechanisms can be traded within the ETS. As such, the private sector has been given a further incentive to participate in these project-based mechanisms which facilitate the transfer of environmentally sound technology to the developed (JI) and developing world (CDM). Moreover, the cost effectiveness of the EU's trading scheme is improved as achieving emission reductions abroad may well be realised at a lower price than the costs involved in making reductions at home.

7–030

The Emissions Trading Directive has been amended by the Linking Directive and now notes that one EU ETS allowance is the equivalent of one CER achieved under a CDM project or one ERU achieved under a JI project.[222] CERs (CDM credits) can be used in the ETS from 2005 and ERUs (JI credits) from 2008. Article 11a(1) of the Emissions Trading Directive now notes that;

"Member States may allow operators to use CERs and ERUs from project activities in the Community scheme up to a percentage of the

---

[218] The UK registry's website is located at *http://emissionsregistry.gov.uk*.

[219] *http://europa.eu.int/comm/environment/ets/*. A delay in linking the CITL to the ITL led to Defra's decision to postpone the allocation of EU ETS allowances for the period 2008–2012; "UK delays on phase 2 EU ETS allowances" ENDS Report 398 (March 2008) pp.15–16.

[220] Directive 2004/101 amending Directive 2003/87 establishing a scheme for greenhouse gas emission allowances trading within the Community, in respect of the Kyoto Protocol's project mechanisms OJ 2004 L338/18. On the application of the Linking Directive specifically in relation to JI projects, see Massai, "Joint Implementation in an enlarged EU: recent developments and outstanding legal issues" [2007] Environmental Liability 65.

[221] Reg.27A of the Greenhouse Gas Emissions Trading Scheme Regulations 2005 was inserted to reflect this.

[222] Emissions Trading Directive, art.11a(1).

allocation of allowances to each installation, to be specified by each Member State in its national allocation plan for that period."[223]

However, in assessing NAPs for the 2008–12 period, the European Commission has taken the view that;

"as a general rule, installations should be allowed to use JI and CDM credits to supplement their allowance allocation by up to 10%. In assessing proposed limits that are greater than 10%, the European Commission has taken into account the effort a Member State has to undertake to respect its Kyoto target."[224]

This approach is in line with the Marrakesh Accords which it will be recalled note that use of the flexible mechanisms will be "supplemental to domestic action" and that domestic action will "constitute a significant element" of a given Annex I State's efforts to reduce emissions. In their NAPs for the 2008–12 and subsequent periods, Member States are obliged to indicate the extent to which they intend to use CERs and ERUs.[225] The UK in its 2008–12 NAP has established an 8 per cent limit on the use of CERs and ERUs at an installation level.[226] This is approximately equal to two-thirds of the difference between business as usual projections and the UK national cap.[227] The UK's NAP allows for the banking of project credits ensuring that installations that do not utilise their full entitlement in a particular year can use these credits to fulfil obligations in the following year.

The ability to use credits gained from projects abroad within the EU ETS is subject to the following exceptions:

- Nuclear facilities.
  This limitation is required under the Kyoto Protocol regime. At present the limitation applies in the first and second phase of the ETS only.[228]
- Land use, land use change and forestry activities.[229]
  This limitation on the use of carbon sinks reflects scientific uncer-

---

[223] The same 11 criteria that had applied in relation to the setting of the first phase NAPs applied to the establishment of second phase NAPS. However, in relation to the latter an additional criteria was added by the Linking Directive: NAPS had to specify the "maximum amount of CERS and ERUs which may be used by operators ... as a percentage of the allocation of the allowances to each installation"; Emissions Trading Directive, Annex III(12).

[224] European Commission, "Questions and Answers on Emissions Trading and NAPs for 2008–2012" MEMO/06/452, 29/11/06, p.4.

[225] Emissions Trading Directive, art.30(3) as amended.

[226] Note however that limits for Large Electricity Producer (LEP) installations will be 9.3 per cent of their free allocation as the 8 per cent limit applies to LEPs before allowances are deducted for auctioning.

[227] Defra, *EU Emissions Trading Scheme: Approved Phase II NAP 2008–2012* (2007), p.6.

[228] Emissions Trading Directive, art.11a(3)a.

[229] Emissions Trading Directive, art.11a(3)b.

tainty as to the actual contribution of such activities to the absorption of carbon dioxide from the atmosphere.

It is also important to note that in relation to hydroelectric power projects with a generating capacity exceeding 20MW Member States must ensure when approving such projects that "relevant international criteria and guidelines" must be respected during the project's development.[230] This requirement seeks to ensure that the environmental and social impact of such projects is kept to a minimum.

Linking the ETS to other trading schemes

The Emissions Trading Directive envisages agreements being signed with third countries thereby linking the ETS to other trading schemes. In October 2007 it was announced that Norway, Iceland and Liechtenstein would join the ETS to raise the number of countries participating to thirty.[231] It is of interest to note that other countries such as Canada and Japan now have national trading schemes which may at some stage in the future be linked to the ETS. The European Commission has indicated that it sees the ETS **7–031**

> "as an important building block for the development of a global network of emissions trading schemes. Linking other national or regional cap-and-trade emissions trading systems to the EU ETS can create a bigger market, potentially lowering the aggregate cost of reducing greenhouse gas emissions."[232]

The future of the ETS: beyond 2012

The Emissions Trading Directive stipulates that a review of the ETS was to have been concluded by June 2002.[233] The review was late but finally published by the European Commission in November 2006.[234] It noted that "for reasons of regulatory stability and predictability, any changes to the Directive emanating from this review should take effect at the start of **7–032**

---

[230] Emissions Trading Directive, art.11b(6). The Directive specifically refers to the World Commission for Dams November 2000 Report entitled "Dams and Development: A New Framework for Decision Making".

[231] These three countries are members of the European Economic Area. Such membership allows them to participate in the EU's internal market but without becoming full members of the EU. By virtue of Article 25 of the Emissions Trading Directive agreement can be made with non-EU countries which have reduction targets under the Kyoto Protocol to "provide for the mutual recognition of allowances between the Community scheme and other greenhouse has emissions trading schemes."

[232] EUROPA Press Release, "Questions and Answers on the Commission's proposal to revise the EU Emissions Trading System" MEMO/08/35, 23/01/08, p.8.

[233] Emissions Trading Directive, art.30.

[234] COM (2006) 676.

the third trading period in 2013."[235] In January 2008 the European Commission duly put forward a proposal to improve and extend the ETS for the period after 2012.[236] The European Commission would wish to see this proposal formally adopted during the course of 2009. Key modifications to the ETS would include one single EU cap instead of the setting of individual national caps.[237] This change of approach reflects the European Commission's view that the NAP approach "has generated significant differences in allocation rules, creating an incentive for each Member State to favour its own industry, and has led to great complexity."[238] Allocations would be reduced each year allowing for an overall reduction in emissions by installations within the ETS amounting to 21 per cent by 2020 when compared to 2005 levels. In addition, the proposal envisages a substantially increased level of allowance auctioning as opposed to allowances being issued free of charge (perhaps as much as 60 per cent in 2013),[239] new industrial sectors being brought within the ETS (such as ammonia and aluminium producers), and the addition of two new greenhouse gases (nitrous oxide and perfluorocarbons).

The Climate Change Levy

7–033   An important part of the original UK Climate Change Programme, the Climate Change Levy (CCL) became applicable on April 1, 2001.[240] The CCL is an economic instrument introduced by the Finance Act 2000.[241] In effect, it is a tax on the business and public sector use of energy and its introduction followed recommendations made by Lord Marshall's report in 1998.[242] The aim of the CCL is to assist the UK in meeting its Kyoto Protocol targets and to encourage the more efficient use of energy. Tax paid under the levy is offset by reductions in the rate of employers' National Insurance contributions.

The CCL is charged on the supply of electricity, gas supplied by a gas utility, petroleum gas in a liquid state, coal and lignite, and coke.[243] Hydrocarbon oil or road fuel gas are not taxable as they are already subject

---

[235] ibid, p.5.
[236] COM (2008) 16 final.
[237] See "Support grows for EU-wide EU ETS cap" ENDS REPORT 389 (June 2007) pp.48–49.
[238] EUROPA Press Release, "Questions and Answers on the Commission's proposal to revise the EU ETS" MEMO/08/35 (January 23, 2008), p.4.
[239] ibid.
[240] For an accomplished account of the levy and Climate Change Agreements see Robinson et al, above fn.110, p.361–408.
[241] Part II of the Act (section 30) and Schs 6 and 7.
[242] Marshall, *Economic Instruments and the Business Use of Energy: a report by Lord Marshall* (1998).
[243] Finance Act 2000, Sch.6 para.3(1).

to fuel duties.[244] The smallest of organisations are effectively excluded from the tax if they fall within the de minimis rule.[245] The tax does not apply to the supply of fuel to the domestic sector, or to charities when fuel is used for non-business purposes.[246] A number of exemptions also apply. These exemptions include the use of energy by Good Quality Combined Heat and Power (CHP) stations,[247] the supply of electricity from renewable sources,[248] and the supply of energy used in certain modes of transport (rail industry).[249]

The CCL has partly funded the operations of the Carbon Trust which was established by the Government in 2001.[250] The Carbon Trust's task is to work with organisations to facilitate emission reductions and foster use of environmental friendly technology. It manages the Energy Technology List which identifies a range of energy-saving equipment which, if invested in by a given company, would allow it to claim tax relief under the Enhanced Capital Allowances scheme (ECA).[251]

Climate Change Agreements

The 2000 Finance Act provided for the CCL to be paid at a vastly reduced rate (80 per cent discount) if an agreement known as a Climate Change Agreement (CCA) has been agreed between applicable sector trade associations (for the companies in the given sector) and the Secretary of State for Environment, Food and Rural Affairs.[252] CCAs establish energy efficiency objectives and are designed to provide an incentive to "energy intensive" sectors to reduce emissions or make advances in energy efficiency. An "energy intensive" sector is a sector carrying out an activity listed in Part A1 or A2 of Part 1 of Schedule 1 of the Pollution Prevention and Control (England and Wales) Regulations 2000[253] as amended by the Pollution Prevention and Control (England and Wales) (Amendment) Regulations 2001.[254] Small sites carrying out operations listed in Part A1 or   7–034

---

[244] ibid, Sch.6 para.3(2).
[245] ibid, Sch.8 para.9.
[246] ibid, Sch.6 para.8.
[247] ibid, para.14–15. The Government has established a target of attaining a minimum of 10,000MWe of Good Quality Combined Heat and Power (CHP) capacity by 2010. "Good quality" is energy efficient as set out in the CHP Quality Assurance Programme; see Defra's website on CHP and *http://www.chpqa.com*. See the Government's current CHP strategy; Defra, *The Government Strategy for Combined Heat and Power to 2010* (2004).
[248] ibid, para.19.
[249] ibid, para.12.
[250] *http://www.carbon.trust.co.uk*.
[251] The ECAS provides for the cost of equipment to be written off against taxable profits. The ECA website is located at *http://www.eca.gov.uk/etl*.
[252] Finance Act 2000, Sch.6 paras 44–51.
[253] SI 2000/1973.
[254] SI 2001/503. The types of installation that could form an eligible facility were expanded by the Climate Change (Eligible Facilities) Regulations 2006 (SI 2006/59).

A2 of these regulations but which are exempt from Pollution Prevention and Control regulation due to their size are eligible to be covered by the relevant sector Climate Change Agreement.[255] Under the "90/10" rule if 90 per cent of a given site's total energy use is utilised by the energy intensive facility itself, all other operations on that site will also be eligible to the CCL discount (including, for example, manager's offices).[256]

So-called "Umbrella Agreements", which run until March 31, 2013, are negotiated between trade bodies, representing energy intensive sectors, and the Secretary of State. These are public documents which are made available on the Defra website. Each agreement lists the facilities to which the agreement applies, targets for the sector and other relevant conditions. Over 50 umbrella agreements have been signed with specific trade associations which include the Aluminium Federation, the British Ceramic Confederation, the British Leather Confederation, and the British Glass Manufacturers Confederation. In combination with these umbrella agreements, so-called "Underlying Agreements" are also entered into between either the Secretary of State and the operator of a given eligible facility (Option 2 Agreements) or between the sector association and the operator in question with the approval of the Secretary of State (Option 3 Agreements).[257] These underlying agreements also set targets which must be met.

Targets under CCAs have been set for the years 2002, 2004, 2006, 2008 and 2010. Eligibility for a discount to the CCL is conditional on the established targets being met; where the Secretary of State takes the view that satisfactory progress on meeting targets is not being made, he/she has the ability to refuse re-certification and the facility loses its CCL discount.[258] The latest results show that the vast majority of facilities were re-certified at the end of the third target period.[259]

7-035   The UK launched is own national emissions trading scheme in 2002 (UK ETS). As the scheme came to an end in December 2006 it will not be addressed in detail.[260] However, it was a highly innovative arrangement and, like the EU's ETS, was designed to bring about cost-effective emis-

---

[255] On eligibility see Defra Paper PP8, "Guidance on Eligibility" available online at *http://www.defra.gov.uk/environment/climatechange/uk/business/ccl/papers.htm*.

[256] See Defra Paper PP6, "Guidance on Eligibility" available online at *http://www.defra.gov.uk/environment/climatechange/uk/business/ccl/papers.htm*.

[257] Finance Act 2000, Sch.6 para.48.

[258] Finance Act 2000, Sch.6 para.49(3)b.

[259] Defra, *Climate Change Agreements: results of the Third Target Period Assessment* (2007), p.8.

[260] See however Robinson et al, above fn.109 pp.319–360. Towards the end of this five year pilot project a report commissioned by DEFRA concluded that it was hard to "prove exactly which changes have occurred as a direct result of the scheme and some have argued that industry has been rewarded for decisions and investment that were little different to those that would have been made in its absence"; Defra, "Appraisal of Years 1–4 of the UK Emissions Trading Scheme" (December 2006), p.3. However, there is little doubt that important lessons were learnt by participants; "[t]he majority of organisations agree that the scheme has provided a valuable opportunity to learn about the way an emissions trading scheme operates and the steps required to participate"; ibid, p.1.

sion reductions. Additionally, it provided an opportunity for firms in the UK to gain experience in trading prior to the introduction of the EU Emissions Trading Scheme. The UK ETS was a voluntary scheme in which the private and public sector were eligible to participate. Emission targets were taken on by "Direct Participants" in return for a financial incentive paid for by the Government. Thirty-three Direct Participants committed themselves to making emission reductions when compared to their 1998–2000 levels (a reduction commitment of 3.96 million tonnes of carbon dioxide equivalent by the end of 2006). Participants also included those who had entered into Climate Change Agreements (CCA); if such a company experienced difficulties in meeting their CCA obligation they could enter the UK ETS to purchase allowances to offset their deficit under their CCA. Alternatively, companies could sell allowances within the UK ETS if they had achieved a level of reductions that created a surplus. Although the UK ETS ended in December 2006, CCAs obviously continue beyond that time. As a result, organisations with CCAs can still trade in the UK's Emissions Trading Registry (ETR) established to facilitate trading under the UK ETS.[261] Figures for 2006 emissions show that due to the fact "most facilities managed to perform well against their [CCA] targets there was little trading even though the price of allowances has been low" prompting speculation that targets in CCAs could have been established at a lower level by the Government.[262]

The Carbon Reduction Commitment

The EU ETS, the Climate Change Levy and Climate Change Agreements are intended to bring about emissions reductions and energy savings in energy intensive industries. The Government has additionally announced plans to introduce the Carbon Reduction Commitment (CRC) at the beginning of 2010 in an attempt to reduce emissions from other industries which are not so energy intensive. The Climate Change Bill placed before Parliament in 2007 provides enabling powers to allow the Government to do so. The CRC is a key part of the Government's commitment to reduce carbon emissions from large non-energy intensive sectors (including the services and public sectors) by 1.2 million tonnes each year by 2020.[263]   7–036

---

[261] The website of the ETR is located at *http://etr.defra.gov.uk*. Since the introduction of the EU ETS some installations are covered by both the latter and the CCA scheme. Arrangements have been put into place to avoid double counting between the CCA and the EU ETS; Defra, Paper CCA 23 "Avoiding double counting between CCA and EU ETS" (March 2006); available from Defra's website.

[262] See "Emission results increase pressure for tighter CCA targets" ENDS Report 391 (August 2007) pp.49–50, and "CCA Targets fail to stretch firms, says NAO" ENDS Report 392 (September 2007) pp.11–12.

[263] Department of Trade and Industry (DTI), "Meeting the Energy Challenge: A White Paper on Energy" (May 2007), p.52.

The CRC is intended to bring about approximately 80 per cent of the intended reduction, with the rest reflecting projected reductions to be made pursuant to implementation of the EU's Energy Performance of Buildings Directive.[264]

The introduction of a new and compulsory emissions trading scheme is envisaged once the CRC is established. It will apply to energy use emissions not covered by the EU ETS or CCAs, and current plans anticipate that 5000 large business and public sectors organisations (including, for example, hotels, banks, local authorities, universities and supermarket chains) will be brought within the scheme.[265] Defra has announced that an introductory phase will run from January 2010 with allowances being sold at a fixed price.[266] The year 2013 will see the introduction of a capped phase in which allowances will be auctioned.[267] A league table is to be established indicating those organisations that have performed the best and worst under the scheme, and a system of self certification introduced to minimise administrative burdens.[268] The CRC will apply to organisations with yearly half-hourly metered electricity consumption of more than 6,000 megawatt hours (typically with electricity bills of more than £500,000).[269]

The Supply of Energy

7–037   The UK Government in January 2008 announced that the future construction of new nuclear power plants by energy companies was in the public interest due to the low-carbon nature of the nuclear industry and the need to ensure the UK's energy security. Continued dependence on nuclear power in future years is therefore a chosen policy option, but the Government also stressed that "new nuclear power stations should have a role to play in this country's future energy mix *alongside other low-carbon sources*".[270] Consideration now turns to those initiatives in place to promote the generation of energy from such low-carbon sources.

---

[264] ibid. The impact of the EU's Directive 2002/91/EC on the Energy Performance of Buildings (OJ 2003 L1/65) is highlighted in the chapter on the Planning System.

[265] *http://www.defra.gov.uk/environment/climatechange/uk/business/crc/quanda.htm.*

[266] ibid. See also "Details fleshed out on trading scheme" ENDS Report 390 (July 2007) pp.41–42, and "Carbon Reduction Commitment to include government departments" ENDS Report 398 (March 2008) pp.46–47.

[267] ibid.

[268] ibid.

[269] Department of Trade and Industry (DTI), above fn.263, p.53.

[270] Secretary of State Hutton in *Meeting the Energy Challenge: A White Paper on Nuclear Power* (January 2008) CM 7296, p.7 (emphasis added).

The Renewables Obligation

The Renewables Obligation (RO) is a market mechanism which was **7–038** introduced in 2002 and is administered by the Office of Gas and Electricity Markets (Ofgem). The current RO Order came into force on April 1, 2006[271] and was subsequently amended by the Renewables Obligation Order 2006 (Amendment) Order 2007.[272] The RO is designed to advance the generation of electricity from renewable sources by placing an obligation on electricity suppliers to obtain an increasing percentage of their electricity from renewables. In 2007/08 the percentage is 7.9 per cent and rises to 9.1 per cent in 2008/09. By 2015/16 the percentage will have risen to 15.4 per cent and that obligation will remain in place for each subsequent year until the end of 2027.[273]

Electricity generators apply to Ofgem for formal accreditation confirming that the electricity they generate is indeed from eligible renewable sources.[274] Sources deemed eligible include onshore and off shore wind power, biomass, co-firing of biomass with fossil fuels, wave and tidal power, landfill and sewage gas, and power from hydro-electric power stations with a declared net capacity of 20 megawatts or less.[275] Larger hydro-electric power stations are excluded unless they were first commissioned after April 1, 2002.[276] Once accredited, Ofgem issues the operator of an electricity generating station with the appropriate number of Renewables

[271] Renewables Obligation Order 2006, SI 2006/1004 (Renewables Obligation Order 2006).
[272] SI 2007/1078. Amendments include a new reg.15A allowing an operator of a generating station with a declared net capacity of 50 kilowatts or less to appoint an agent to receive ROCs (Renewables Obligation Certificates) on his behalf. In effect, agents can act for such small generators in relation to the Order; this is of particular relevance to microgenerators. The term "microgeneration" refers to the small scale generation of electricity of production of heat from energy or technologies such as biomass, biofuels, fuel cells, photovoltaics, water, wind, solar power, geothermal sources, and CHP (see more particularly the definition provided in s.82 of the Energy Act 2004). Microgeneration is therefore a process which generates electricity and heat from low-carbon sources. Agents can now "amalgamate the output of several microgenerators which could make it more worthwhile for microgenerators to get involved even where they generate very small amounts of electricity"; Department of Trade and Industry, "Microgeneration and the Renewables Obligation" (2007), p.1. In April 2006 the Government established the "Low Carbon Buildings Programme" which now makes available grants for the promotion of microgeneration technologies in households, the public sector and charities. The programme is administered by the Department for Business Enterprise and Regulatory Reform. By virtue of s.4 of the Climate Change and Sustainable Energy Act 2006 the Government during the period November 1, 2008–March 31, 2009 is obliged to consider whether microgeneration targets are appropriate and to designate such targets if so appropriate. Article 7 of the 2006 Act provides the Secretary of State with the power to alter distribution and supply licenses with a view to increasing the take-up of electricity generated by microgeneration.
[273] Renewables Obligation Order 2006, Sch.1.
[274] On accreditation (grant and withdrawal) see Renewables Obligation Order 2006, art.31. See also Ofgem, *Renewables Obligation: Guidance for generators over 50kw* (2007), pp.12–20.
[275] Ofgem, *Renewables Obligation: Guidance for generators over 50kw* (2007), pp.4–5. In the year 2006/07 landfill gas and on shore wind generation were responsible for over 56 per cent of ROCs issued; Ofgem "The Renewables Obligation 2006–7: Facts and Figures" Factsheet 75 (May 2008), p.2 (available online at *http://www.ofgem.gov.uk*).
[276] Renewables Obligation Order 2006, art.5(2)a.

Obligation Certificates (ROCs). The relevant electricity generator will receive one ROC for every megawatt hour of energy generated from renewables. ROCs are electronic certificates and are issued into the Renewables and CHP Register.[277] ROCs can be sold to electricity suppliers with the generated electricity from renewable sources. However, Ofgem has indicated that "ROCs can be traded separately from the electricity in respect of which they are issued".[278] In effect, ROCs can therefore be sold to electricity suppliers either with or separately from the electricity generated by the accredited electricity generators. Alternatively, ROCs can be sold by eligible electricity generators to traders and brokers who in turn may sell to electricity suppliers.[279] Electricity generators therefore benefit not only by selling renewable electricity but also by being able to sell ROCs at a price set by the market.

Electricity suppliers must provide Ofgem with sufficient ROCs to cover their annual obligation by September 1 after the obligation period in question.[280] The obligation period runs from April 1 to the following March 31. If suppliers have insufficient ROCs, they can pay a "buy-out" price to make up the shortfall. The "buy-out" price rises with the retail price index and amounts to £35.76 per megawatt hour in 2008/09. Monies obtained in payment of the "buy-out" price are placed in the "buy-out fund" and distributed at the end of an obligation period to electricity suppliers in proportion to the ROCs they provided in that period.[281] By providing the appropriate number of ROCs to Ofgem electricity suppliers therefore avoid having to pay "buy-out" prices and also gain a proportion of the "buy-out fund" at the expense of fellow suppliers who failed to meet their obligation.

7–039 The Energy White Paper 2007 was published on May 23, 2007, and set out key reforms of the RO.[282] It confirms the Government's plan to increase the RO to 20 per cent when the generation of renewables validates such a mandatory target. Additionally, the Government intends to introduce "banding" of the RO to provide differentiated degrees of support to particular technologies promoting renewables and in this way "encourage the increased development and deployment of a broader set of renewable technologies."[283] In essence, one ROC will no longer necessarily represent one megawatt hour of renewable energy produced. A statutory consultation on a Renewables Obligation Order 2009 was published in June 2008

---

[277] *https://renewablesandchp.ofgem.gov.uk*. On accreditation by Ofgem electricity generators become registered holders in this register. Ofgem requires licensed electricity suppliers to establish an account on this register.

[278] Ofgem, *Renewables Obligation: Guidance for generators over 50kw* (2007), p.37.

[279] It is important to note that Ofgem has no responsibility in relation to the traded market in ROCs; ibid.

[280] Renewables Obligation Order 2006, art.3.

[281] Renewables Obligation Order 2006, art.22.

[282] Department of Trade and Industry (DTI), above fn.263.

[283] ibid, p.14.

to advance the banding proposals with a view to providing "more support to technologies which are currently further from commercial deployment in order to drive development."[284] Banding will seek to advance higher risk technologies (offshore wind, wave, tidal stream, solar photovoltaic, and electricity generated from biomass by a CHP generating station) by giving generators more than one ROC per megawatt hour produced ("banding up"). More advanced and/or low-risk renewable technologies (landfill gas and sewage gas) will be subject to a "banding down" process. It is expected that the current 10 per cent cap on the share of a given organisation's RO that can be realised by biomass co-firing will be eliminated.[285] Any changes to the RO are not expected to be in place before April 2009 at the earliest.

Carbon Emission Reduction Target

The Carbon Emission Reduction Target (CERT) commenced in April 2008 pursuant to the Electricity and Gas (Carbon Emissions Reduction) Order 2008.[286] CERT is an obligation placed on those who supply energy (gas and electric) to the household sector to ensure carbon emissions from this sector are reduced. Ofgem administers CERT and establishes individual targets for each supplier.[287] Suppliers must achieve their obligations by promoting the following activities:[288]   **7–040**

- Energy efficiency improvements.
- Increased electricity generated or heat production from microgeneration.
- Increased heat production by plant relying wholly or mainly on wood.
- Reduction of energy consumption.

The overall CERT is 154 million lifetime tonnes of carbon dioxide for the three years from April 1, 2008, to 31 March 2011.[289] A minimum of 40 per cent of a given supplier's CERT is to be achieved by targeting carbon emission reductions in "priority group" households (in receipt of those benefits and credits noted in Schedule 2 of the Order, or aged 70 or over).[290] Suppliers are obliged to inform Ofgem of the number and type of

---

[284] Department for Business Enterprise and Regulatory Reform, "*Statutory Consultation on the Renewables Obligation Order 2009: Reform of the Renewables Obligation*" (June 2008), p.4. Amendments to the RO will require the granting of the Royal Assent to the Energy Bill 2007–2008. See generally "Banding of renewables obligation favours wind" ENDS Report 389 (June 2007) pp.42–43.

[285] See ENDS Report 389 (June 2007) p.43.

[286] SI 2008/188. CERT is in fact the third phase of what had previously been known as the Energy Efficiency Commitment (EEF). CERT is likely to double the amount of energy saved under EEF 2005–08.

[287] Electricity and Gas (Carbon Emissions Reduction) Order 2008, art.6.

[288] Electricity and Gas (Carbon Emissions Reduction) Order 2008, art.10.

[289] Electricity and Gas (Carbon Emissions Reduction) Order 2008, art.3(1).

[290] Electricity and Gas (Carbon Emissions Reduction) Order 2008, art.13.

activities they have completed to enable Ofgem to determine the reduction in emissions these activities have brought about.[291]

Transport

7–041   The chapter has so far provided a focus on key initiatives to save energy and improve energy efficiency in the business sector and in relation to the supply of energy. However, given that the transport sector is responsible for more than 20 per cent of total EU greenhouse gas emissions[292] and that these emissions continue to rise,[293] it is important to also provide an overview of approaches to reduce emissions from road transport.

Voluntary agreements with car manufacturers

7–042   The European Commission has for some time sought to address the issue of carbon dioxide emissions from cars. In 1998 it entered into a voluntary agreement with the European Automobile Manufacturers' Association (ACEA) in relation to cars with a view to reducing carbon dioxide emissions from new cars sold in the EC in 2008 by 25 per cent when compared to 1995 levels.[294] Similar agreements were subsequently signed with the Japanese Automobile Manufacturers' Association (JAMA) and the Korean Automobile Manufacturer's Association (KAMA).[295] These agreements were key elements of the EU's approach to reduce carbon dioxide emissions from new cars to 120g/km by 2005, and at the latest by 2010.[296] The envisaged reductions in emissions were most likely to come from the development and application of new technologies. However the detail of these technologies had not at the time been determined and the European Commission therefore took the view that a voluntary agreement would be the most appropriate form of instrument especially as a binding agreement in the form of a directive or regulation would have taken several years to conclude.[297]

The voluntary agreements have proved inadequate. Between 1995 and 2004 emissions from those new cars sold in the EC-15 did in fact decrease

---

[291] Electricity and Gas (Carbon Emissions Reduction) Order 2008, art.19.

[292] European Commission, "Questions and Answers on Emissions Trading and NAPs for 2008–2012" MEMO/06/452, 29/11/06, p.2.

[293] Emissions from road transport increased between 1990 and 2004 by 26 per cent; European Commission, "Questions and Answers on the proposed regulation to reduce Carbon Dioxide emissions from cars" MEMO/07/597, 19/12/2007, p.1.

[294] COM (1998) 495.

[295] COM (1999) 446 final. Targets are to be met by 2009.

[296] The strategy was supported by the adoption of Directive 1999/94/EC relating to the Availability of Consumer Information on Fuel Economy and Carbon Dioxide Emissions in respect of the Marketing of New Passenger Cars, OJ 2000 L12/16.

[297] Bongaerts, "Carbon Dioxide Emissions from Cars: the EU implementing the Kyoto Protocol" (1999) 8(4) EELR 101, at p.103.

from 186g/km to 163g/km,[298] but the European Commission has noted that "given the slower than expected progress to date, the 120g/km carbon dioxide target will not be met ... without additional measures."[299] With this in mind the European Commission has made a proposal for a regulation to reduce emissions from new passenger cars and light-duty vehicles.[300] It envisages the adoption of a legally binding, directly applicable measure placing a given manufacturer under an obligation from 2012 to ensure that the average emissions of all new cars it builds and which it registers in the EU is no more than 130g/km.[301] Efficiency requirements for car components would complement this target and are intended to make sure that the 120g/km target is reached by 2012. Those manufacturers who fail to meet the target will be liable to pay a penalty premium based on the amount by which a given manufacturer has failed to reach the target and the number of cars sold by that manufacturer in the year in question.

Renewable Transport Fuel Obligation

In the UK fiscal incentives have been introduced to encourage the use of vehicles with lower carbon dioxide emissions,[302] but the most important instrument in this field is the Renewable Transport Fuel Obligation (RTFO) which has been fashioned on the Renewables Obligation. The Renewable Transport Fuel Obligations Order 2007[303] places an obligation on transport fuel suppliers to ensure renewable fuels make up 5 per cent of their sales in the period April 15 2010–April 14 2011 and in all subsequent years thereafter.[304] The Office of the Renewable Fuels Agency (RFA) was established by the 2007 RTFO Order to administer the obligation.[305] The RTFO applies from April 15, 2008, and seeks to assist in meeting targets for biofuel use established in the 2003 Biofuels Directive.

The RFA awards Renewable Transport Fuel Certificates (RTF certifi-

7–043

---

[298] Emissions from road transport increased between 1990 and 2004 by 26 per cent; European Commission, "Questions and Answers on the proposed regulation to reduce Carbon Dioxide emissions from cars" MEMO/07/597, 19/12/2007, p.2.

[299] ibid.

[300] COM (2007) 856 final. See "Car industry keeps its head in the sand over carbon emissions" ENDS Report 387 (April 2007) p.11.

[301] For vans the envisaged targets are 175g/km by 2012 and 160g/km by 2015.

[302] Fiscal initiatives include lower Company Car Tax and Vehicle Excise Duty for vehicles which emit less emissions.

[303] SI 2007/3072. This Order was enacted pursuant to section 124 of the Energy Act 2004.

[304] Renewable Transport Fuel Obligations Order 2007, art.4. The precise percentage from 2010 is 5.2632 per cent. In 2008/09 the obligation is 2.5641 per cent and in 2009/10 that obligation is increased to 3.8961 per cent. The RTFO does not apply to a transport fuel supplier who supplies less than 450,000 litres of fuel in a given year; ibid, art.4(2).

[305] Renewable Transport Fuel Obligations Order 2007, art.6. The RFA has its own website; *http://www.dft.gov.uk/rfa*. The RFA is funded by the Department of Transport and is obliged to oversee compliance with the RTFO, report on its performance and also to provide guidance to road fuel suppliers. The following guidance on the RTFO is available from the RFA website: Renewable Fuels Agency, *Guide to RFA Operating Processes for Fossil Fuel Suppliers* (December 2007).

cates) for the supply of renewable fuels (biodiesel, bioethanol, and natural road fuel gas produced wholly by biomass). The annual obligation period runs from April 15 to the following April 14, and by October 5 after a given obligation period has ended a road fuel supplier must have submitted sufficient RTF certificates to the RFA to cover their obligation.[306] Road fuel suppliers must make monthly returns in respect of their supply volumes and also provide evidence of net greenhouse gas emission reductions provided by such fuels and the sustainability of such fuels.[307] The RFA will then determine the certificates to be awarded and duly issue them.[308] The number of certificates a given company has accumulated is recorded on the RFA's Operating System (ROS). One certificate is awarded per litre of renewable fuel supplied or per kilogram of natural road fuel gas.[309] RTF certificates can then be traded within the ROS system at a price set by those involved in the trade.[310] If suppliers are unable to provide sufficient RTF certificates to cover their RTFO, they must "buy-out" the remainder of that obligation by paying the sum of 15p for every litre of their obligation not covered by a RTF certificate. The RFA is obliged to then pay back "buy-out" funds to road fuel suppliers in proportion to the number of certificates presented.[311]

---

[306] Renewable Transport Fuel Obligations Order 2007, art.4(3).
[307] Renewable Transport Fuel Obligations Order 2007, art.13(4).
[308] Renewable Transport Fuel Obligations Order 2007, art.17.
[309] Renewable Transport Fuel Obligations Order 2007, art.17.
[310] Renewable Transport Fuel Obligations Order 2007, art.18.
[311] Renewable Transport Fuel Obligations Order 2007, art.22.

Chapter 8

THE PLANNING SYSTEM AND ENVIRONMENTAL PROTECTION

Introduction

Planning as "environmental law"[1]

For most individuals, the aspects of their environment of which they are **8–001** likely to be most immediately aware consist of the physical appearance of their surroundings and of the impacts of the activities of other people, whether at work, at home, at recreation, or travelling. If an environment is to be attractive, controls are necessary, at least in a crowded island such as Great Britain, to seek to preserve, and where possible to enhance, the visual amenities of the towns and countryside, and to limit the adverse effects on people of the way in which other members of the community lead their lives.

Inevitably, many activities that are considered desirable, or indeed essential, in a modern society are liable to damage the environment. At least where no irreparable harm is involved, controls designed to limit the damage from such activities must achieve an acceptable compromise between those adverse effects and maintaining or improving the external environment.

This chapter reviews the controls under our system of town and country planning which enable the human environment to be protected from adverse impacts, and the natural environment from activities liable to destroy it or materially change its character. Whether, and if so the manner in which, these controls are in fact exercised in any particular instances is usually a matter for political decision on a case by case basis. Their purpose is not automatically to restrain activities that may damage the environment, or even those that are bound to do so, but to try to ensure that such damage as otherwise desirable developments are likely to cause is on balance acceptable, and is no more than is reasonably unavoidable in achieving their benefits. The planning system has in this way, alongside other legislation relating for example to nature conservation, water

---

[1] Many of the acronyms used within this Chapter may be unfamiliar to lawyers who are not regularly involved in planning matters. Any readers needing assistance in this respect are directed to the Table of Abbreviations at the front of the book.

abstraction, climate change, land drainage and flood defence, an important contribution to make to environmental protection.

8–002   For that reason this chapter presents an outline[2] of those aspects of the planning system most relevant to environmental protection. Also, the discussion below of the law relating to environmental impact assessments[3] necessarily requires a background knowledge of the planning law of which, in Great Britain, it is an integral part.

The sequence in which matters will be discussed in this chapter are as follows:

1. The Planning System—a general introduction;
2. Environmental Protection through Planning Controls and Guidance;
3. The "New" Development Plan Structure;
4. Environmental Considerations and the Development Plan;
5. Policy specific examples;
6. Inter-relationship between Planning and other Controls;
7. Statutory and Other Consultees;
8. The General Permitted Development Order and the Use Classes Order;
9. Applications for Planning Permission;
10. Call-in of Applications;
11. Appeals;
12. Costs; and
13. Enforcement.

It should be noted that the development control regime in Northern Ireland, although it generally follows that of England and Wales, constitutes a separate legislative system. The main difference is that the Department of the Environment for Northern Ireland is the planning authority. Likewise the Scottish system is based on separate legislation and guidance separate from that of England and Wales, although the main principles are the same. This chapter does not deal with the detail of the Northern Ireland or Scottish system.

---

[2] For specialist texts on the planning system see e.g. V. Moore, *A Practical Approach to Planning Law*, 10th edition (Oxford University Press: 2007); L. Stein, *Principles of Planning Law*, (Oxford University Press, 2007); Telling and Duxbury's *Planning Law and Procedure*, 13th edition (Oxford University Press, 2005); Blackhall, *Planning Law and Practice*, (Routledge-Cavendish, 2005); C. Lockhart-Mummery, J. Harper and D. Elvin, *Encyclopedia of Planning Law and Practice* (Sweet & Maxwell loose-leaf with regular updates).
[3] Chapter 9.

The Planning System—General

"Planning control" is the regime of control over the use of land operated   **8–003**
primarily by local planning authorities. It has three distinct components:

(i)   The statutory framework;
(ii) Planning policies issued by the Department of Communities and
      Local Government (DCLG);
(iii) The exercise of discretion by local planning authorities in their
      preparation of local plans and when considering and determining
      individual planning applications, imposing conditions on planning
      permissions, and negotiating agreements with landowners governing
      the use of land.

Planning control is therefore the product of a mixture of law, policy
documents, and individual decisions by planning authorities; it is implemented at three levels, namely national, county and district.[4]

The modern planning system dates from July 1947 when the Town and
Country Planning Act of that year came into force. This brought under
control all new development by requiring that prior planning permission
should be obtained for any "material change of use" of land or any
"operations" on or under land. Unlike previous legislative attempts to
control development, which had tackled matters on a piecemeal basis, the
1947 Act was much more comprehensive. Agriculture and forestry were,
and remain, the only significant forms of activity which were left outside its
control. The primary statute is currently the Town and Country Planning
Act 1990 (the TCPA), which consolidates earlier legislation.[5]

Planning permission does not necessarily deal with all aspects of a
development; other consents may also be required, for example under the
Environmental Protection Act 1990, the Planning (Hazardous Substances)
Act 1990, the Planning (Listed Building and Conservation Areas) Act
1990, the Ancient Monuments and Archaeological Areas Act 1979, and, in
the case of tree preservation orders, under Part VIII of the TCPA.

Applications for planning permission are determined by the local plan-   **8–004**
ning authority for the site in question, this generally being the district
council. An applicant who is dissatisfied with the decision on this appli-

---

[4] In some parts of the country, for example the Lake District, there are special planning
authorities whose jurisdiction extends across administrative boundaries; the following
comments do not deal with those special cases.
[5] See para.8–007 below for a fuller discussion of the TCPA as well as the current Planning
Bill which introduces a new system for approving major infrastructure of national
importance, such as harbours and waste facilities, and replaces current regimes under
several pieces of legislation. The objective is to streamline these decisions and avoid long
public inquiries.

cation can appeal to the Secretary of State for the Environment. There is no right of appeal in respect of the grant of planning permission[6] (except to the extent that an applicant can appeal in respect of conditions attached to a permission). Decisions in well over 90 per cent of appeals are delegated by the Secretary of State to Planning Inspectors, who are full time officials of the Planning Inspectorate, an Executive Agency in the DCLG.

The role of the courts in the planning process is quite circumscribed. The courts will not, save in very exceptional circumstances, review the merits of a planning authority's decision. Their role is restricted to reviewing alleged errors of law and procedure underlying the decision-making process. Even if a court, either on appeal or in a judicial review, overturns a planning decision, this does not mean that the decision is reversed, turning a grant of planning permission into a refusal of planning permission or vice versa. The effect of a successful legal challenge is that the application is sent back to the authority to be re-determined. Anyone mounting a legal challenge to a planning decision, with a view to having it reversed, must therefore consider the practical prospects of persuading the relevant authority to reach a different decision when it re-determines the application. In some cases guidance from the court as regards the proper meaning of the relevant planning policy governing the matter may assist such prospects.

The courts have a role in the enforcement of planning control, but generally only as a last resort. If all other remedies have failed, the planning authority can take court proceedings either to restrain action by an injunction or to prosecute a person for any offence under the planning legislation that may have been committed.

Environmental Protection through Planning Controls and Guidance

Introduction

8–005 The help which the basic planning system can give to the protection of the natural environment lies mainly in controlling new development by the requirement of the TCPA that development shall not take place without planning permission.[7] The TCPA defines development as:

"the carrying out of building, engineering, mining or other operations in, on, over or under land, or the making of any material change in the use of any buildings or other land."[8]

---

[6] For example, for the benefit of objectors. Note, however, that objectors may be able to challenge the legality of the grant of planning permission by way of judicial review: see Chapter 6 above.

[7] TCPA, s.57.

[8] TCPA, s.55.

There are thus two essentially distinct limbs to the control: over "operations" and over "material changes of use".

Despite this comprehensive definition there are significant exceptions from the potential scope of the controls. First, certain operations and uses are specifically excluded from the definition of development, e.g. interior works and use of land for agriculture or forestry.[9] Secondly, some development has the benefit of general planning permissions, notably under the General Permitted Development Order.[10] Sometimes extensive development can be undertaken under these general permissions and, hence, effectively without public scrutiny or control. Thirdly, development on the seabed is normally outside planning control because local authority jurisdiction extends only as far as the low water mark.[11]

Additionally, not all changes of use require planning permission: only a "material" change. It is often difficult to know when a change (which, for example, could include mere intensification of an existing use without any other alteration in its nature) becomes so marked as to amount to a material change of use.[12] In practice, extensive changes can take place in this way without being effectively controlled by the planning system. Moreover, the Use Classes Order permits extensive changes between various types of use without the need to apply for planning permission.[13] A factory might change from one producing effectively no emissions, save those from its heating system, and generating 10 vehicle movements per day, to a use producing large quantities of unpleasant, unsightly and perhaps noxious emissions, and generating perhaps 50 vehicle movements per day, and it is entirely possible that this would not amount to development requiring planning permission, nor involve any breach of planning control (e.g. breach of a planning condition). Such a change might perhaps be regulated by controls under other legislation, and in severe cases it could give rise to liability at common law, for example enabling a neighbour to

---

[9] TCPA, s.55(2).

[10] See paras 8–051 to 8–054 below.

[11] Local Government Act 1972, s.72. Other controls also apply.

[12] Intensification of an existing use may itself be a material change of use. However, for that to take place, there must be a change in the character of the use—so the use before the change and the use after the change must be materially different. See *Kensington and Chelsea BC v Secretary of State for the Environment* [1981] JPL 50 (Div Court) where the Borough Council had served an enforcement notice alleging a material change of use of a garden adjacent to a restaurant for the purposes of a restaurant. On appeal, the Planning Inspector decided that the planning unit was the garden and the restaurant and so there was no breach of planning control in using the garden as ancillary to the restaurant. There was no material change of use by intensification as there were just more cars coming and going when the private garage changed to a commercial garage. Compare this to *R(on the application of John Childs) v First Secretary of State and Test Valley Borough Council)* [2005] EWCH 2368, where the judge decided that a single increase in the number of caravans from four to eight on land which was devoid of any development involved a change in the character of the land and amounted to development.

[13] See explanation further on in this chapter.

take action for nuisance. It might also amount to a statutory nuisance, but the planning system itself might be ineffective to prevent it.

8–006 Nevertheless, the planning system is unquestionably important in at least two ways. First, it provides legal control over significant new development and significant changes of use. For example, planning permission will be required to build a new factory or a major factory extension. Planning permission is also generally required to change the use of an existing factory from light industrial use, i.e. a use which could take place within a residential area, to general industrial use, and from general industrial use to special industrial use (i.e. involving particularly unpleasant processes). This is because, firstly, such a change of use will be "material"; and, secondly, these changes do not fall within the Use Classes Order. Planning therefore has a role to play in the protection of the natural environment, but impact on the environment is only one of the factors which must be taken into account in determining a planning application: the planning authority must balance the protection of the natural environment with factors such as the needs for housing and employment and for a proper system of infrastructure, e.g. roads and power lines, and the legitimate requirements of businesses.

There is no general presumption that planning authorities should favour protection of the natural environment over the other considerations such as, for example, economic needs for a particular development. It is more often stressed that the planning system should deliver sustainable economic development in the context of the pressures of a growing population, rising incomes, changing demographics, climate change and the competitive challenges of rapid changes in the global economy. This is why the current Planning Bill, which is discussed further on in this chapter, is being put forward to implement proposals for a new single consent regime for major infrastructure projects.[14] The objective is to speed up controversial planning decisions on the ground that more timely and predictable decisions on infrastructure projects are needed because these are key to economic growth, international competitiveness, tackling climate change, energy security and improving the quality of life.

A second significant feature of the planning system lies in its persuasive rather than legal force. National and local policy guidance can give indications of the weight to be given to the protection of the natural environment.[15] Local Development Frameworks ("local plans"), in particular, can give importance to nature conservation in particular areas and in particular ways. Accordingly, if the local plan makes it clear that environmental considerations are to be given weight in certain areas, and this is reflected

---

[14] The Planning Reform Bill, the Energy Bill and the Climate Change Bill are the three legislative pillars of the Government's strategy to secure long-term prosperity and quality of life for all.

[15] e.g. PPS1: *Delivering Sustainable Development.*

in the treatment of planning applications, this will be a potent influence on developers and landowners when preparing their development projects.

The statutory framework

The TCPA 1990 was the result of the consolidation of a large number of   **8–007** legislative measures. It did not of itself introduce any major reforms, but in the following year, the Planning and Compensation Act 1991 introduced some significant changes, most notably in the field of enforcement, in providing for breach of condition notices and planning contravention notices. Other relevant statutes are the Planning (Listed Buildings and Conservation Areas) Act 1990; the Planning (Hazardous Substances) Act 1990; the Planning (Consequential Provisions) Act 1990; the Greater London Authority Act 1999; and the Planning and Compulsory Purchase Act 2004 (PCPA) and the Planning Bill, which was introduced to Parliament on November 27, 2007.

The PCPA introduced important changes to many areas of planning law, including both the development plan system and planning control. Many of the provisions in the PCPA are free-standing, in that they contain provisions additional to those found in the TCPA. Other provisions in the PCPA, however, operate by repealing or amending, or by the substitution of existing provisions in the TCPA.

The Planning Bill[16] introduces a new system for approving major infrastructure of national importance, such as harbours and waste facilities, and replaces current regimes under several pieces of legislation. The objective is to streamline these procedures and avoid long public inquiries. It's key proposals are as follows:

- Decisions would be taken by a new Infrastructure Planning Commission;
- Decisions would be based on new national policy statements;
- The hearing and decision-making process by the Commission would be timetabled;
- The new regime would be used for energy developments, and in particular new nuclear power facilities;
- The Secretary of State would no longer have the final say on infrastructure decisions covered by the new regime;

---

[16] The Planning and Reform Bill is one of three pieces of legislation which are central to the Government's aspirations. The other two Bills are the Climate Change Bill and the Energy Bill. The Planning Bill's importance rests pre-eminently on the fact that it sets out a new single regime for handling key infrastructure projects: power stations, reservoirs, airports, railways, wind farms, waste projects etc. and establishes a new body, called the Infrastructure Planning Commission. The Planning Bill also provides the enabling powers to establish the Community Infrastructure Levy which will give local authorities the ability to "charge" developers to help fund new infrastructure provision.

- There would be a new Community Infrastructure Levy on developments to finance infrastructure. The idea of this would be to raise money from developers to pay for facilities needed as a consequence of new developments, such as schools, hospitals and sewage plants; and
- Planning appeals for minor developments would be heard by a panel of local councillors, rather than by a planning inspector.

The political process

8–008   The planning of both town and country is a political process. The DCLG is the Government Department responsible for planning policy and building regulations in England. Its planning role is to set national planning policy, to simplify the planning system and to get communities involved. DCLG also has a role to protect and enhance the environment through the planning system, e.g. measures to tackle climate change such as gradually tightening up building regulations up to 2016 to increase the energy efficiency of new homes and eventually make them zero carbon; a Code for Sustainable Homes to give homeowners more information about how green their property is; and a Planning Policy Statement (PPS) on Climate Change.

The role of the Secretary of State

8–009   The duties and powers granted to the Secretary of State can be summarised as follows:

(i)   to ensure that local planning authorities carry out the strategic planning[17] duties placed[18] upon them by the TCPA as amended by the PCPA;

(ii) to approve and publish the guidance in the form of Regional Policy Guidance (RPG) after consultation with the constituent, local

---

[17] Strategic (or "forward") planning means planning to allow land use, economic, social, environmental, and other issues that transcend the locality to be debated in terms of the broader forces that will largely shape them, thus permitting more appropriate and practical solutions to be found. In terms of the most basic characteristics, the TCPA is based on a belief that strategic planning should be: visionary as well as practical; aimed at long-term viability in terms of "sustainable development" criteria; prescriptive, not solely informative; binding, not just advisory; a combination of top-down and bottom-up approaches; spatial, i.e. relating to specific locations; sectoral, i.e. relating to specific sectors and areas of activity; achievable, in terms of resources and processes of implementation; well founded in terms of research and understanding; comprehensive in terms of the range of coverage, but not too detailed; consistent in content and application; open and accessible, with wide consultation, public participation, and direct involvement of the stakeholders; cyclical, through monitoring and review; medium and long term in timescale; and accountable to an elected authority, assembly, or parliament at national/regional level.

[18] Under TCPA, Part II.

planning authorities and other agencies likely to be involved in future development;

(iii) to provide local planning authorities and others involved in the process of development with statements of current government planning policies and formulate planning policies;

(iv) to make delegated legislation—such as the General Permitted Development Order[19]—and make rules and orders in respect of the administrative process of planning;

(v) to call in planning applications for her own determination rather than that of the local planning authority; and

(vi) a quasi-judicial function in the determination of appeals against decisions made by local planning authorities.

The Secretary of State also has responsibilities to declare Urban Development Corporations or Simplified Planning Zones; create a single body as the county planning authority for areas of two or more shire counties; and constitute a joint planning board for any two or more district councils.

National Planning Policy

DCLG issues national guidance from time to time in the form of the new 8–010 style Planning Policy Statements (PPS), which are gradually replacing Planning Policy Guidance Notes (PPG). National policies are also laid out in Minerals Planning Statements and Minerals Policy Guidance Notes (MPS/MPG), Marine Minerals Guidance Notes (MMG) and Circulars. These do not have the force of law, nor are they subject to independent scrutiny in the way in which, for example, local plans are scrutinised. Nevertheless, as relevant considerations in the exercise of discretionary planning control functions, they exercise an enormous influence on the manner in which planning control is exercised in practice. Effectively, they are centrally-determined ground rules within which planning authorities must operate.

In addition, national policy may be developed and promulgated through decisions by the Secretary of State on planning appeals and also through formal statements from time to time on particular policy issues.

Regional policy may be developed both by the Secretary of State at national level and also by groups of local authorities in a particular region. Thus the government issues RPGs. The main thrust of government policy is towards sustainable development, the protection of the environment and amenity, and the need to minimise the need to travel. Urban regeneration

---

[19] This order is discussed at paras 8–051 and 8–052 below. In essence, the order specifies in 39 separate parts various classes of development which may be undertaken upon land without the permission of the local planning authority or the Secretary of State. Each part may itself include a number of classes of development. Development falling within the classes is known as "permitted development".

remains an important objective, as this is intended to re-use previously developed land (brown field sites) which will assist in creating a more sustainable pattern of development, coupled with an increased density of housing. This emphasis on re-use is complemented by policies which are designed to ensure that the amount of agricultural land (green field sites) required for development is kept to a minimum. The planning function in rural areas is to integrate development necessary to sustain economic activity with the protection of the countryside.

Two-tier and one-tier planning

8–011   In parts of England the powers conferred by the TCPA on the local planning authority are exercisable by two local authorities: the county council as the county planning authority for their area and by the district council as the district planning authority for their area. In the Greater London and the metropolitan areas, it used to be the case that the only local authorities with power to act as the local planning authority in those areas were the London Boroughs and the metropolitan districts respectively. However, London regained a two-tier system with the setting up of the Greater London Authority (GLA) in April 2000. The Local Government Act 1992 has now also led to the dismemberment of much of the two-tier system of local government in England and the replacement of many authorities by newly created "unitary authorities", each exercising within their own area the planning powers previously exercised separately by the county council as county planning authority and by the district council as district planning authority for the area.

The GLA is made up of the Mayor of London, the London Assembly and a team of over 600 staff supporting their work. Created by the Greater London Authority Act 1999, the Mayor of London and the London Assembly constitute a unique form of strategic citywide government for London. The Mayor and the Assembly have different but linked roles.

The Mayor of London;

(i)   is the capital's spokesperson and champion, at home and abroad;
(ii) draws up policies for London's social, economic and environmental development;
(iii) works closely with and sets budgets for Transport for London (TfL), the London Development Agency (LDA), the Metropolitan Police Authority (MPA), and the London Fire and Emergency Planning Authority (LFEPA); and
(iv) works with local boroughs to tackle London's issues and the capital's future.

The Greater London Authority Act 1999 places responsibility for strategic planning in London on the Mayor, and requires him to produce a Spatial

Development Strategy for London which he has called the London Plan. The Mayor is also required to keep it under review.

The London Assembly keeps a check on what the Mayor is doing. It;

(i) closely examines—or scrutinises—mayoral activities, decisions and policies;

(ii) questions the Mayor monthly in public at the Mayor's Question Time;

(iii) must approve the Mayor's proposed budget before it can be finalised; and

(iv) investigates issues of importance to Londoners, making proposals and recommendations to the relevant organisations, and publishes its findings.

The Greater London Authority Act 2007 has recently extended the **8–012** scope of the Mayor's planning role. Under it, the Mayor will:

- Publish a London housing strategy, setting out his strategic housing investment priorities for London;
- Be able to determine planning applications of strategic importance in London;
- Publish a strategy for reducing health inequalities between Londoners; and
- Be subject to a duty to address climate change, and publish London strategies for climate change mitigation and energy, and for climate change adaptation.

From April 6, 2008, the Mayor of London's planning powers were extended so that he can grant or refuse planning permission in certain circumstances, so giving him significantly greater influence than before over the face of development in London.[20] In granting additional planning powers to the Mayor, the Government wished to reinforce his ability to implement the regional policies set out in the London Plan.

There are two key strands to the recent changes to the Mayor's planning powers: the first extends the scope of the Mayor's powers; the second increases the categories of applications to which he can apply his new powers. Also from April 6, 2008, the Mayor has been able to direct that for an application of potential strategic importance ("PSI application") he will become the local planning authority himself and will have the power to refuse or grant planning permission. This is different from his previous powers whereby he was only able to direct refusal of permission.[21]

---

[20] See Greater London Authority Act 2007 and The Town and Country Planning (Mayor of London) Order 2008 (SI 2008/580) ("the 2008 Order"). The Mayor's previous powers, which were primarily just based on the power to "veto" certain developments (if they met the specific criteria) were to be found in the Greater London Authority Act 1999 and the Town and Country Planning (Mayor of London) Order 2000.

[21] See Town and Country Planning (Mayor of London) Order 2000 (SI 2000/1493), s.5.

The Mayor's extended planning powers will only apply to applications for large scale development or for major infrastructure which are defined in the 2008 Order as "PSI applications". PSI applications are those where the development exceeds certain thresholds that are set out in the Schedule to the 2008 Order. Many of the thresholds remain as drafted in previous legislation,[22] but there are certain changes of note. The two main areas where the Mayor will have significant additional controls are in respect of waste management facilities and housing where the new thresholds are lower than before. Conversely, in the City of London, the Mayor's powers in respect of large-scale development are being reduced: specifically, the 2008 Order raises the thresholds so that, in the City, a non-residential development will only constitute a PSI application if it is over 100,000sq m (increased from 30,000sq m) or if it is over 150m high (increased from 75m), assuming none of the other thresholds apply. The new higher thresholds in the City reflect the scale of development in that part of London and also Government and Mayoral confidence in the high level of experience and performance in the City in respect of large and, particularly, tall buildings.

8–013   The Mayor must apply a policy test in deciding whether to direct that he will take over a PSI application; and the Government of London Circular[23] emphasises that all three limbs of the test must be satisfied:

- The development would have significant impact on the implementation of the London Plan;
- The development would have significant effects that are likely to affect more than one London borough (except where the PSI application is for more than 150 houses or flats); and
- There are sound planning reasons[24] for issuing the direction.

The Mayor must also take into account the local authority's performance, i.e. the extent to which the local authority has reached any relevant targets set out in its development plan (including new housing and affordable housing development plan targets when the application is for large housing development).

---

[22] See the Greater London Authority Act 1999 and the Town and Country Planning (Mayor of London) Order 2000.
[23] The Government Office for London Circular 1/2008 is the DCLG's guidance on the arrangements for strategic planning in London, which was published on April 4, 2008.
[24] This deals with the reason's for the Mayor's intervention, taking into account the borough's draft decision on the application.

Where the Mayor directs that he will determine a PSI application, it will also be the Mayor who will agree the package of planning obligations to be negotiated in any Section 106 Agreement[25] required in connection with the proposed development (although the relevant local authority must be consulted before any planning obligation is agreed). He will also be empowered to determine connected applications such as an application for listed building consent.

English Partnerships

It is worth mentioning here the role of English Partnerships.[26] English   **8–014**
Partnerships is the national regeneration agency for England, performing a similar role on a national level to that fulfilled by Regional Development Agencies on a regional level.[27] It is responsible for land acquisition and assembly and major development projects, alone or in partnership with private sector developers. It is particularly active in major regeneration areas such as the Thames Gateway and in expansion areas such as Milton

---

[25] Section 106 agreements are legal agreements between local authorities and developers, which are linked to a planning permission. These are also known as planning gain, planning benefits, community benefits or planning obligations. Section 106 legal agreements are associated with a particular development and as they are a legal charge on the land, they transfer automatically with any change in ownership. Section 106 agreements are drawn up when it is considered that a development will have negative impacts that cannot be dealt with through conditions in the planning permission. For example, a new residential development places additional pressure on the existing social, physical and economic infrastructure in the surrounding area. Planning obligations aim to balance the extra pressure from development with improvements to the surrounding area, and so procure that a development makes a positive contribution to the local area.

[26] On January 17, 2007, Ruth Kelly, the Secretary of State for Communities and Local Government, announced proposals to bring together the delivery functions of the Housing Corporation, English Partnerships and parts of DCLG to form a new unified housing and regeneration agency, the Homes and Communities Agency (initially announced as "Communities England"), which is likely to become operational during 2008 or 2009.

[27] English Partnerships is legally two entirely independent bodies set up under separate statutes. One is the Commission for New Towns, launched in October 1961, which was responsible for the Development Corporation established by the New Towns Act 1959, and the other is the Urban Regeneration Agency set up by the Leasehold Reform, Housing and Urban Development Act 1993.

Keynes, where the Deputy Prime Minister (acting as Environment Minister) removed planning from local control and appointed it as the statutory planning authority.[28]

English Partnerships work with a wide range of partners including local authorities, the Housing Corporation, regional development agencies and the Commission for the Built Environment (CABE). Its overall aim is to achieve high-quality, well-designed, sustainable places for people to live, work and enjoy. Its programmes are designed to:

(i) Increase the supply of high-quality affordable housing, and housing for key workers, in areas experiencing housing pressure in the wider south-east;

(ii) Make best use of the nation's scarce supply of land by identifying previously-developed land and increasing its supply for development, particularly in the wider south-east;

(iii) Reduce the stock of low demand and abandoned housing in the Market Renewal Pathfinder areas and other areas suffering low demand for housing, whilst increasing the supply of new and refurbished high quality housing and amenities in those areas;

(iv) Deliver high-quality sustainable urban regeneration in areas experiencing economic restructuring;

(v) Increase the quality and quantity of private-sector investment in housing and regeneration;

(vi) Set and promote best practice in urban design and construction standards across the regeneration and development industry;

(vii) Promote the use of modern methods of construction where appropriate; and

(viii) Improve regeneration skills.

English Partnerships focuses on three core areas of work to deliver its business objectives:

(i) Unlocking and increasing the supply of land to meet housing and other growth needs.

[28] Milton Keynes Partnership Committee (MKPC) brings together Milton Keynes Council, English Partnerships, Local Strategic Partnership representatives from the health, community and business sectors and independent representation. The day to day activities of MKPC are carried out by Milton Keynes Partnership. Milton Keynes Partnership works with a range of organisations to help make projects happen and to secure money for schemes that will benefit the whole of Milton Keynes. They are the local planning authority responsible for determining major planning applications in the eastern, western and northern expansion areas of Milton Keynes. Milton Keynes Council, remains in charge of determining planning applications in the rest of the borough and for determining minor applications in the expansion areas. The Council is also responsible for plan making for the whole borough and for creating policy on all issues including transport, parking and open spaces that MKP and other organisations must pay regard to. Milton Keynes Partnership's statutory remit is set out in the Milton Keynes (Urban Area and Planning Functions) Order 2004 (SI 2004/932).

(ii) Creating and sustaining well-served mixed communities where people enjoy living and working.
(iii) Improving quality of life and enhancing the environment through innovation and raising standards.

The "New" Development Plan Structure

The PCPA 2004 introduced a sea-change to the previous development **8–015** plan system. It provided for the replacement of (non-statutory) regional guidance, structure plans, local plans, waste plans, mineral plans and unitary development plans by regional spatial strategies (RSSs) and local development documents (LDDs).[29] Part I of the PCPA provided for the new statutory RSSs; Part II provided for LDDs. The new system also requires the preparation of Local Development Frameworks (LDFs) designed to integrate with strategies having relevant implications outside traditional land use planning.

The LDF, which is a portfolio of documents which implements the new planning procedure, contains the following:

(i) Local Development Scheme (LDS);
(ii) Local Development Documents (LDDs);
(iii) a Statement of Community Involvement (SCI);
(iv) Annual Monitoring Report;

and may also include:

(v) Area Action Plans (AAPs);
(vi) Supplementary Planning Guidance (SPGs);
(vii) Simplified Planning Zones (SPZs);
(viii) Local Development Orders (LDOs); and
(ix) Other Development Plan Documents (DPDs).[30]

The new system is meant to provide greater predictability for developers on decisions on particular applications, and also to allow for flexibility in delivering regeneration priorities as well as achieving sustainable development.

Regional planning

Regional Spatial Strategies (RSS) are prepared in draft for the relevant **8–016** Regional Planning Boards (RPB) for each of the eight English regions by the regional chambers, whether elected or non-elected. The RSSs are

---

[29] Section 39(2) of the PCPA imposes a new duty on persons and bodies responsible for preparing RSSs and LDDs in England.
[30] Each of these documents will be explained further on in the chapter.

427

intended to provide a broad development strategy for each region for a 15–20 year period. In the preparation of an RSS, the RPB must seek the advice of each planning authority in the region.[31] Once the RPB has prepared a draft RSS, it publishes it for at least 12 weeks public consultation.

Following public consultation, an Examination in Public is held to debate and test the RPB's proposals. A Panel formed by the Planning Inspectorate—independent of the RPB and central Government—oversees this process. Following the Examination in Public, the Panel prepares a report of findings and recommendations to the Secretary of State on how the draft RSS might be improved. The Secretary of State then issues Proposed Changes to the draft strategy, taking account of the Panel's recommendations and representations on any matters not considered at the Examination in Public. The Secretary of State then makes any final amendments in the light of the responses to the Proposed Changes consultation, and issues the final "Regional Spatial Strategy".

Local authorities then prepare Local Development Documents (LDDs), which are consistent with the RSS, identifying specific locations for development and conservation, and establishing local policies for managing development. Collectively, the LDDs will set out the spatial planning strategy for the area and will comprise Development Plan Documents (DPDs) including a Core Strategy, a Statement of Community Involvement (SCI) and Supplementary Planning Documents (SPDs).[32]

8–017   RSSs are expected to;

(i) establish a "spatial" vision and strategy specific to the region—for example, identifying in general terms areas for development or regeneration for a period of about 20 years ahead;

(ii) contribute to the achievement of sustainable development;

(iii) establish regionally specific policies, which are expected to add to rather than replicate national ones;

(iv) address regional or sub-regional issues that may cross county, unitary authority or district boundaries;

(v) outline housing figures for district and unitary authorities to take forward in their LDFs;

(vi) establish priorities for environmental protection and enhancement, and define the "general extent" of areas of green belt;

(vii) produce a regional Transport Strategy as part of the wider spatial strategy;

(viii) outline key priorities for investment, particularly in infrastructure, and identify delivery mechanisms, in order to support development;

---

[31] Namely the county council; metropolitan district council; district council; and a National Parks authority. In London, the RSS is known as the Spatial Development Strategy (SDS) or London Plan which is prepared by the Mayor of London; the London boroughs have responsibility for the preparation of their own DPDs.

[32] LDDs are explained further below in this chapter.

(ix) identify how the region's waste should be dealt with; and
(x) be consistent with and supportive of other regional frameworks and strategies.

Local planning

The PCPA required local planning authorities to submit to the Secretary of   **8–018**
State, and also the RPB, a Local Development Scheme (LDS) within six months of the commencement date of Part II of the PCPA.[33] The LDS is a public statement of the local planning authorities' three year programme for the preparation of LDDs which will form the LDF. Once prepared, the LDS must be kept under review by the local planning authority and revised as appropriate.

The Town and Country Planning (Local Development) (England) Regulations 2004[34] prescribe the form and content of the LDS and the procedure to be followed to bring it into effect. A LDS must specify:

(i) the documents which are to be local development documents;
(ii) the subject matter and geographical area to which each document is to relate;
(iii) which documents are to be development plan documents;
(iv) which documents (if any) are to be prepared jointly with one or more other local planning authorities;
(v) any matter or area in respect of which the authority have agreed (or propose to agree) to the constitution of a joint committee;
(vi) the timetable for the preparation and revision of the documents;
(vii) such other matters as are prescribed.

LDDs set out the spatial strategy and comprise development plan documents (DPDs) and supplementary planning documents (SPDs). DPDs are the basis upon which all development control planning permission decisions are made. DPDs will progressively replace any currently adopted local plans. SPDs, unlike DPDs, are not subject to independent testing and whilst they do not have development plan status they should be the subject of rigorous procedures of community involvement.[35] Local planning authorities also have to prepare and publish a statement of community involvement (SCI) which specifies how the authority intends to involve stakeholders and communities in the process of producing the LDDs. The proposed statement of community involvement is subject to independent examination by an Inspector appointed on behalf of the Secretary of State.

---

[33] March 28, 2005.
[34] SI 2004/2204.
[35] Guidance on this aspect is given in PPS1 under heading "Principles of Community Involvement in Planning". The guidance has been expanded in a document "Community Involvement in Planning: The Government's Objectives" issued in February 2004.

Annual monitoring reports set out the progress in terms of producing LDDs, and also the implementation of their policies.

In terms of how the LDS is examined and adopted, local planning authorities must submit the DPDs, the Statement of Compliance with the Statement of Community Involvement and the Final Sustainability Report to the Secretary of State, who will publish all three documents. There follows a formal 6 week consultation period. The local planning authority is then required to prepare a summary of the representations, and where such representations include proposals for alternative site allocations, the local planning authority is required to publish these and invite representations in a similar manner to the submitted DPD. An independent examination then takes place to determine whether the DPD satisfies the requirements of the PCPA with regard to its preparation and "whether it is sound".[36] The examination will be carried out by an Inspector drawn from the Planning Inspectorate. After the examination, the Inspector is responsible for producing a report that is binding on the local planning authority.

Legal challenges to the development plan

8–019 The dominance of the development plan in determining proposals likely to gain planning permission has led inevitably to a number of legal challenges to the way in which particular plans have been prepared and adopted by the local planning authority.[37]

The courts are not concerned with the "merits" on planning grounds but solely with the question of legality—which may be substantive or procedural. To mount such a challenge, the objector must act within six weeks from the date of adoption of the plan by way of an application to the High Court under section 287 of the TCPA. The starting date is determined from the date the Notice to Adopt was published.

There are two grounds for questioning the validity of the development plan:

(i) It is not within the power conferred in Part II of the TCPA; or
(ii) Any requirement of that Part of the TCPA or any regulations made under it has not been complied with for the approval or adoption of

---

[36] The criteria for assessing soundness is found in PPS12.
[37] For example, on March 31, 2006, Tewkesbury Borough Council adopted The Tewkesbury Borough Local Plan, which was made up of several distinct policies, to guide development within the Borough during the period to 2011. The adopted plan was challenged during the six week period following advertisement of its adoption. On April 3, 2007, the High Court quashed policies BA1 and SD2, the parts of policy HOU1 which specifically related to certain housing sites, and the part of policy GRB2 which specifically related to the BA1 site. The remaining part of the Tewkesbury Borough Local Plan to 2011 is now part of the Statutory Development Plan for the area.

the development plan, or as the case may be, its alteration or replacement.

Following such an application, the High Court may either (i) suspend wholly or in part the operation of the development plan generally, or in so far as it affects the applicant, until the proceedings are finally determined; or (ii) if it is outside the powers of the TCPA, or if the interests of the applicant have been substantially prejudiced by a failure to comply with the TCPA or regulations made under it, the court may quash the whole of the development plan or any part of it, or so much of the development plan as affects the property of the applicant.

A challenge is also available to the Secretary of State's direction, and **8–020** there may also be challenges arising from the Inspector's recommendations. The Secretary of State, like all other Ministers, is subject to general requirements that she must undertake her official duties in a way that upholds the highest standards of propriety. This is found in the Ministerial Code,[38] which sets out a number of principles that Ministers should observe in order to comply with that general requirements. Of particular importance in relation to the handling of planning casework is that Ministers "must ensure that no conflict arises, or appears to arise, between their public duties and their private interests". They must also "keep separate their role as Minister and constituency Member".

On October 8, 2008, DCLG issued conduct guidance for Planning Ministers.[39] This guidance deals with the propriety issues that can arise in connection with the Secretary of State exercising decision-making functions under the Town and Country Planning Acts, principally in individual planning cases, and with respect to RSS and LDDs. The objective is to ensure that decisions are properly taken and to avoid, as far as possible, the risk of successful legal challenge to decisions. The note provides advice for Ministers in the DCLG charged with making those decisions, considers the position of Ministers in other Departments, and that of Parliamentary Private Secretaries, Ministerial Special Advisers and officials. Overall, the guidance sets out general principles that Planning Ministers should observe and offers specific advice on: recovered planning appeals and called-in planning applications, RSS; and LDDs.[40]

---

[38] July 2007.
[39] Guidance on Planning Propriety Issues. "Planning Ministers" refers collectively to the Secretary of State and other Ministers in the DCLG exercising planning decision making responsibilities on her behalf.
[40] Appendix A of the Guidance contains the text of a Government statement detailing the planning appeal recovery criteria. Appendix B sets out a Government policy statement on called-in planning applications.

Environmental Considerations and the Development Plan

8–021 All policies and proposals in the development plan are subject to Sustainability Appraisal and Strategic Environmental Assessment to ensure that they reflect sustainable development principles.

Sustainability Appraisal and Strategic Environmental Assessment

8–022 Sustainable development is central to the reformed planning system. The purpose of Sustainability Appraisal, mandatory under the PCPA, is to promote sustainable development through the integration of social, environmental and economic considerations into the preparation of revisions of RSS and for new or revised DPDs and SPDs.

In addition, when preparing RSS revisions or new and revised DPDs and SPDs, Regional Planning Bodies and Local Planning Authorities must also conduct an environmental assessment in accordance with the requirements of European Directive 2001/42/EC "on the assessment of the effects of certain plans and programmes on the environment" (the Strategic Environmental Assessment or "SEA Directive"), transposed by the Environmental Assessment of Plans and Programmes Regulations 2004.[41] The aim of SEA is to:

"provide for a high level of protection of the environment and to contribute to the integration of environmental considerations into the preparation of and adoption of plans and programmes with a view to promoting sustainable development".

Whilst the requirements to carry out a Sustainability Appraisal and a Strategic Environmental Assessment are distinct, it is possible to satisfy both through a single appraisal process. Guidance has been produced to ensure that Sustainability Appraisals meet the requirements of the SEA Directive, and to assist authorities in carrying out such appraisals.[42]

[41] SI 2004/1633.
[42] "Sustainability Appraisal of Regional Spatial Strategies and Local Development Documents". This guidance supersedes the Interim Advice Note on Frequently Asked Questions (April 2005); the Sustainability Appraisal of Regional Spatial Strategies and Local Development Frameworks Consultation Paper (September 2004) and The Environmental Assessment Directive: Guidance for Planning Authorities (October 2003).

Planning White Paper and Planning Bill

1. Infrastructure reform: proposals for a unified consent regime for major infrastructure projects

The Planning Bill, introduced to the House of Commons on November 27, **8–023**
2007, implements proposals advanced in the Planning White Paper, *Planning for a Sustainable Future*, for a new, single consent regime for major infrastructure projects. The new regime is expected to be in place by April 2009.

Prior to the Bill, different types of infrastructure project were regulated by a number of different consent regimes. The proposals simplify matters by requiring a single development consent order for development projects for energy, transport, water, waste water and waste. Projects will be caught by the regime if they satisfy the criteria for "national significance" for that type of project as set out in the Bill. Greenpeace and Friends of the Earth have criticised the criteria. They say that many renewables projects would be too small to qualify so would not benefit from the speedier approval process offered by the new regime, but proposals for large controversial projects such as a third runway at Heathrow or nuclear power stations could be processed rapidly through the new streamlined procedures despite opposition from local communities and others.

A new body, the Infrastructure Project Commission (IPC) will be responsible for considering applications for development consent under the new regime. The Government has emphasised that the IPC commissioners will be impartial "politically" (they will be barred from holding any outside interests that might compromise that impartiality) and will be drawn from a variety of specialist fields (engineering, planning, law, environmental etc.) However, the commissioners will be appointed by Ministers, and for some this in itself gives rise to questions about their independence.

It is also proposed that Ministers will appoint individual panels of three or **8–024**
five commissioners for each infrastructure project, the particular composition being tailored to an individual application. Again, this could give rise to criticism about the composition of individual panels, and might be an area for potential legal challenge, should there be evidence of any ulterior purpose, or should the administrative law principles regarding apparent bias be infringed.[43]

The IPC will have a dual role: it will be responsible for substantive planning decisions but it is also to be required to give "front-end" pre-application advice on procedural matters, and to ensure that applications are complete and adequate before they enter the determination process. There are concerns, however, that this may lead to resources constraints,

---

[43] As to which see, above, at para.8–020. If the decision-making process of the IPC is fully transparent, it will be easier for the commissioners to demonstrate their impartiality. However, it is not known how the IPC will determine its applications or how its decisions will be framed. Will it reach its decisions by consensus or majority (where there is an odd number of commissioners)? Will it produce a single report on its decisions? Will minority opinions be aired? it is assumed that rules/guidance will be issued to clarify these questions.

resulting in delays in hearing and deciding substantive matters. Against this it is argued that "front end" scrutiny and advice can reduce the range of controversial issues later to be considered by the IPC.

Notwithstanding the creation of the IPC, the policy framework for decision-making will be set by Government. The Secretary of State will issue "national policy statements" in respect of different types of projects. The Secretary of State has a wide discretion as to how prescriptive national policy statements can be. Proposals for national policy statements must be subject to consultation but the extent of consultation will be at the discretion of the Secretary of State. In drawing up the national statements, the Secretary of State must consider the sustainability of the policy. However, she is not subject to any explicit duty to promote sustainable development, despite calls to that effect during passage of the Bill. The Planning Bill allows the Secretary of State to designate existing documents such as *The Future of Air Transport (2003)*, as national policy statements, even though they were published before the relevant provisions of the Bill come into force.

8–025   The IPC will be required to decide applications "in accordance with" the relevant national policy statement, except where it would be "unlawful", "in breach of duty" or where policy suggests refusal, the benefits may be outweighed the harm caused by the development.

The new process is intended to continue to enable local communities and others who will be affected by the development to be involved at each stage of the process. The regime requires developers to carry out pre-application consultation with local authorities, land owners, tenants and occupiers, and others who are interested in the land affected. Developers must also carry out a separate consultation exercise with the broader local community.

Once the IPC receives the application for development consent, it will hold a preliminary meeting to assess how best to proceed. The IPC will invite the applicant, relevant local authorities and other interested parties (to be specified in future regulations) to attend this preliminary meeting. Thereafter, the new regime favours written representations over oral representations, primarily with a view to increasing the speed of the process. The Government expects the average time for decisions on major infrastructure projects to be reduced to less than a year.

8–026   The IPC will be able to decide to hold a hearing on specific issues if it decides it needs oral representations to ensure adequate examination of a specific issue. Also, an open floor hearing will have to be held if at least one interested party wishes to be heard within the deadline notified by the IPC. Practically, this means that open floor hearings are likely to be held in almost every case, despite the attempt to focus on written representations rather than oral hearings. This will slow the process down considerably, particularly for large or controversial projects. Any interested party can make oral representations on the application.

The IPC will have considerable discretion over how a hearing should be conducted. It will be able to:

- Set limits on the time allowed for representations by an individual;
- Set limits on cross-examination of people who make representations (limits may relate to time or subject);
- Carry out all cross-examinations itself;
- Prevent representations which it judges to be frivolous, repetitive or which simply refer to policy in a national policy statement; and
- Exclude disruptive persons.

It will be interesting to see whether objectors to applications will be satisfied with a hearing where the IPC limits or prevents cross-examination, or carries out all cross-examination itself. Cross-examination is considered by many to be a vital part of thrashing out the key issues. The IPC will need to be careful in the limits it sets on calling evidence and cross-examination lest it fall foul of Article 6(1) of the European Convention on Human Rights which protects the right to a fair trial.[44]

The IPC will ordinarily have six months from submission to consider the application. It will then have a further three months in which to make its decision. The IPC will be able to extend these deadlines but will have to notify the Secretary of State of any delay and provide justification. Any challenge to its decision can only be made by way of judicial review to the High Court within six weeks of publication of the decision, or, if it is later, the publication of the statement of reasons for the decision.

2. Proposals for a community infrastructure levy

The Planning Bill also provides for a new tax on development, the "community infrastructure levy" (CIL), replacing unpopular earlier proposals for a planning gain supplement (PGS). The Planning Bill only sets out the basic structure of the CIL and much of the important detail of how it will work is to be set out in future regulations. It is generally thought that the CIL will be a tariff-based mechanism.[45] The CIL is not expected to apply until 2009.   8–027

The proposals for a CIL are set out in Part 10 of the Planning Bill. The purpose of the CIL must be:

"to ensure that costs incurred in providing infrastructure to support the development of an area can be funded (wholly or partly) by owners of land the value of which increases due to permission for development."

---

[44] Reasonable limitation periods and time limits can be lawful. See *Stubbings v UK*, 23 EHRR 24.
[45] An example of such a mechanism is where residential developments may be charged a fixed fee per dwelling, with commercial development charged a fixed fee according to developable area (e.g. £X per square foot).

There are several interesting aspects to this statement. Firstly, the CIL is to be tied specifically to infrastructure costs, leaving open the question of what will happen to other contributions currently secured by planning obligations to go towards needs such as public art, employment, affordable housing. The Planning Bill leaves it to the regulations to define "infrastructure" for this purpose. They may also require local authorities to set out a list of specific projects in their area which can benefit from the CIL.

8–028   Secondly, the CIL, like the earlier PGS proposals, will be connected to the value of land increasing as a result of planning permission being granted. Unlike the PGS, there is (at this stage) no suggestion that the CIL should be calculated by reference to the size of the increase in value. CIL will be payable by the owner of the land at the time development commences.; and the amount of CIL payable will be calculated by reference to, or at, the date at which the relevant planning permission is granted.

3. Improving the Town and Country Planning system

8–029   The Government stated in its Planning White Paper of May 2007 that further change to the planning system is needed in terms of providing a positive framework for delivering sustainable development, supporting local government in its place-shaping role and improving speed, efficiency and customer focus. The Government's proposals for improving planning fall into three main areas:

- Delivering Sustainable Development;
- Positive Strategic Planning; and
- Streamlining Applications and the Appeal Process.

The Government's proposals for delivering sustainable development include:

- New legislation to set out the role of local planning authorities in tackling energy efficiency and climate change and to reflect the ambition of achieving zero carbon development in 10 years;[46]

---

[46] There are several recent pieces of legislation and policy affecting a local planning authority's leadership roles and responsibilities in tackling climate change. Examples include: the Local Government Performance Framework, pursuant to which from 2008 all local authorities are required to report against a new and streamlined set of 198 national performance indicators, of which three are directly relevant to climate change, and a number of others to transport and local environmental issues; the Carbon Reduction Commitment, which is an emissions trading scheme affecting large non-energy intensive organisations, and which will be effective from 2009; Energy Certificates, whereby from October 2008 the EU Energy Performance of Buildings Directive will require all council occupied public-accessed buildings (offices, libraries and schools) over 1000m^2 to display a Display Energy Certificate similar to those used for white goods; and the new PPS on Climate Change which was published in December 2007, which requires new development to be planned to minimise carbon emissions, to make good use of renewable energy and to minimise vulnerability to climate impacts.

- Making it easier for households to use renewable energy by permitting all forms of householder microgeneration without the need to apply for planning permission subject to certain limitations on noise, vibration and visual amenity;[47]
- Extending permitted development rights for microgeneration equipment to commercial land uses;
- Using land efficiently by prioritising the use of vacant and derelict land and buildings and increasing the supply of brownfield and commercial land;
- Paying full regard to the economic as well as the environmental and social benefits of sustainable new development and ensuring that any future changes to planning policy do not unduly add to the burden of regulation for business;
- Having clear and proactive visions for town centres and replacing the "need test" in PPS6 with an "impact test", having a strong focus on the town centre first and also promoting competition and consumer choice; and
- Reviewing the suite of Planning Policy Statements and Planning Policy Guidance notes and other relevant key policy material in order to better manage existing policy by separating out supplementary guidance.

In terms of Positive Strategic Planning, the Government proposes to:

- Make the Local Development Framework Core Strategy (i.e. one of the policy documents replacing Unitary Development Plans which sets out the general spatial vision, objectives and core policies for future development in each area) a key part of the Sustainable Community Strategy, which a local authority is required to produce for promoting or improving the economic, social and environmental well-being of its area, and contributing to the achievement of sustainable development in the UK;
- Develop a more comprehensive community engagement strategy, including a new statutory best value duty (a "duty to involve") imposed on local authorities to ensure high levels of consultation;
- Use the Planning Delivery Grant (which is a performance-based grant regime for local planning authorities) to incentivise the timely production of sound development plan documents in line with an agreed timetable;
- Introduce a more effective and tailored process of plan preparation with more flexibility about the number and type of plans and how

---

[47] From April 6, 2008, microgeneration technologies became permitted development which means householders will be able to take up microgeneration, within sensible limits, without having to apply for planning permission. See The Town and Country Planning (General Permitted Development) (Amendment) Order 2008 (SI 2008/675).

they are produced, and to encourage a more meaningful, engaged level of community involvement in plan making;

- Introduce Local Area Agreements (LAAs) where local authorities and other key stakeholders and public bodies work together;[48]
- Introduce Planning Performance Agreements (formerly Planning Delivery Agreements). Local authorities will be strongly encouraged to seek to agree with the developer all the information required for, and the timetable for delivering decisions on planning applications for major development proposals;[49]
- Increase planning fees from April 1, 2008;[50]
- Require Government Offices to form a view on what further intervention may be required where under-performance in planning by local authorities against national indicators is apparent. If this does not produce the desired results, the Secretary of State would be able to take action; and
- Increase skills and capacity to deliver the new planning system by giving student bursaries; by private sector partnerships and local authorities joining forces to deliver planning services; by extending the Advisory Team for Large Applications ("ATLAS", an advisory team which offers direct support to individual local authorities to deliver planning decision on large-scale housing developments or regeneration projects) in geographic coverage and also to commercial schemes where these form part of large mixed use developments; and by increasing the focus on the use of the online "e-planning" programme.

---

[48] The Local Government White Paper, *Strong and Prosperous Communities* published in October 2007 set out fundamentally different arrangements for LAAs. LAAs will continue to be three-year agreements with priorities agreed between all the main public sector agencies working in the area and with central Government. This will mean everyone working together to develop appropriate evidence to determine what these priorities should be. There will be: more emphasis on area based service delivery; more freedom in spending decisions; and fewer central targets and reporting systems. The major changes are being made in 2008 with the remaining architecture of the new performance framework in place by 2009. In addition, the passage of the Local Government and Public Involvement in Health Bill will place a statutory requirement on the local authority to develop an LAA and duties on named partners to co-operate with the authority. Councils will also be able to agree local targets with partners that will not need to be reported to central government but which will have the same status as targets negotiated with central government.

[49] These were formally introduced into the planning system from April 6, 2008. They can be used for any major planning application, but are primarily aimed at complex development proposals requiring significant pre-application activity.

[50] Introduced by the Town and Country Planning (Fees for Applications and Deemed Applications) (Amendment) (England) Regulations 2008 (SI 2008/958). The Regulations came into force on April 6, 2008. They are a further amendment of the Town and Country Planning (Fees for Applications and Deemed Applications) Regulations 1989 (SI 1989/193). A new Circular on Planning-related fees has also been prepared and came into force on April 6, replacing Department of the Environment Circular 31/92, The Town and Country Planning (Fees for Applications and Deemed Applications) (Amendment) (No.2) Regulations 1992 (SI 1992/3052).

The Government believes that the current planning regime is considered to be overly complex, resulting in a waste of resources and unnecessary delay. To address these concerns, the Government proposes to:

- Introduce a new approach to householder development that assesses the impact on others, to determine what type of householder development is permitted without the need to seek the specific approval of the local planning authority;
- Apply this "impact approach" primarily to permitted development rights for householder development. However, this approach may also be extended to industrial and commercial development as appropriate, subject to limitations and conditions;
- Allow minor amendments to be made to a planning permission without the need for a full planning application;
- Unify consenting regimes in conjunction with the Heritage Protection White Paper published in March 2007. Multiple consents should be brought into a single process, thus reducing complexity, time and costs incurred by those seeking planning permission;
- Streamline information requirements for all applications. A standard application form was introduced from October 1, 2007, with advance publication of associated guidance on required information in Summer 2007;[51]
- Introduce a package of measures aimed at reducing the Secretary of State's involvement in casework;
- Implement fast tracked processes for householder and tree preservation order appeals;[52]
- Establish Local Member Review Bodies to determine minor appeals at local level;[53]
- Enable the Planning Inspectorate, acting on behalf of the Secretary of State, to determine the appeal method (be it an inquiry, hearing or

[51] The National Standard Planning Application form (1APP) is now in use by every local authority in England; effective from April 6, 2008. The new form provides a consistent format and set of questions with the aim of helping to make the process of applying for planning permission more straightforward for applicants. 1APP has replaced all existing planning application forms (with the exception of minerals forms). The requirements follow guidance provided in the DCLG guidance issued in December 2007, "The Validation of Planning Applications—Guidance for Local Planning Authorities".

[52] A new fast track appeals process for tree preservation order appeals and tree replacement notice appeals is in force as from October 1, 2008. See the Town and Country Planning (Trees) (Amendment) (England) Regulations 2008, SI 2008/2260. There is a "pilot" fast track householder appeal currently taking place. It proposes to speed up the way householder appeals submitted via the "written representations" method are dealt with by providing a "fast track" process i.e. appellants will receive a decision on their appeal to around 12 weeks. These changes are being trialed with a limited number of local planning authorities. This trial does not include appeals where the local planning authority has failed to decide an application within the agreed timescales (eight weeks).

[53] This was dropped from the Planning Bill at Committee stage as the Government concluded that while it may bring some benefit, it risks distracting local authorities, particularly at a time when there is an urgent need for them to focus on strategic plans and issues.

written representation) by applying ministerially approved and published indicative criteria;

- Update the provisions for awards of costs;
- Reduce the time limit for planning appeals when the same development is the subject of an enforcement notice;
- Introduce measures to place enforcement appeals and lawful development certificate appeals on the same footing as that for planning appeals; and
- Introduce an appeal fee to improve resourcing of the appeals service.

Policy Specific Examples

Climate change

8–030   Climate change is firmly now on the political agenda. The land use planning system is seen as having a significant role in the UK programme to tackle climate change. The national policy framework starting point is PPS1 (*Delivering Sustainable Development*), which sets out the Government's overarching planning policies on the delivery of sustainable development through the planning system. Alongside PPS1 is "The Planning System: General Principles". This provides a general description of key elements of the planning system, including its structure, the determination of planning applications and the Secretary of State's role. There should also be noted the Planning and Climate Change supplement to PPS1,[54] which states that climate change considerations will become material considerations in all planning applications and across all spatial planning areas.

The Planning and Climate Change supplement makes its primary focus the need to reduce emissions but also stresses the need to minimise vulnerability to the effects of climate change by adapting to its expected consequences, where practicable. Paragraph 9 sets out key planning objectives that should be pursued not only in the preparation, but also in the delivery, of spatial strategies. These include:

- to secure the highest viable resource and energy efficiency and reduction in emissions in providing for the homes, jobs, services and infrastructure needed by communities, and in renewing and shaping the places where they live and work;
- deliver patters of urban growth and sustainable rural developments that help secure the fullest possible use of sustainable transport for moving freight, public transport, cycling and walking; and which, overall, reduce the need to travel, especially by car;

[54] Published on December 17, 2007.

- secure new development and shape places that minimise vulnerability, and provide resilience, to climate change; and in ways that are consistent with social cohesion and inclusion; and
- conserve and enhance biodiversity, recognising that the distribution of habitats and species will be affected by climate change.

A particular focus is on securing new development powered by local, renewable sources of energy.

There are a number of items of legislation, codes of practice, interested bodies and other initiatives relating to the built environment and the drive to reduce its emissions of carbon dioxide and other greenhouse gases. Some examples include the following:

- The Climate Change Bill. The UK Government is committed to addressing both the causes and consequences of climate change and has therefore introduced a Climate Change Bill. The Bill will create a new approach to managing and responding to climate change in the UK through: setting ambitious legally binding targets, taking powers to help achieve them, strengthening the institutional framework, enhancing the UK's ability to adapt to the impact of climate change and establishing clear and regular accountability to the UK Parliament and the devolved legislatures.[55]
- Energy efficiency of buildings. DCLG is introducing measures in England and Wales to improve the energy efficiency of our buildings, including: introducing energy performance certificates (EPC) for properties, providing A-G efficiency ratings and recommendations for improvement; requiring public buildings to display energy certificates; requiring inspections for air conditioning systems; and giving advice and guidance for boiler users. The reforms are currently being rolled out. Since October 1, 2008, all properties—homes, commercial and public buildings—when bought, sold, built or rented, need an EPC.
- Zero Carbon Homes. The DCLG published "Building a Greener Future: Policy Statement" in July 2007. This policy statement confirmed the government's intention for all new homes to be zero carbon by 2016, with a progressive tightening of the energy efficiency building regulations—by 25 per cent in 2010 and by 44 per cent in 2013—up to the 100 per cent zero carbon target in 2016.[56]
- Code for Sustainable Homes. This Code, which came into effect on May 1, 2008, requires the sustainability of a new home to be assessed against nine categories of sustainable design, so rating the "whole home" as a complete package. The Code uses a 1 to 6 star rating

[55] See Chapter 7.
[56] The term zero-carbon refers to an economy where there are no carbon dioxide emissions from the use of fossil fuels (coal, gas and oil, etc.).

system to communicate the overall sustainability performance of a new home. The Code sets minimum standards for energy and water use at each level and, within England, replaces the EcoHomes scheme, developed by the Building Research Establishment (BRE).

- The London Plan.[57] This is the Spatial Development Strategy for London which sets out strategic planning guidance for London. The aim of the London Plan is to provide a framework for all other plans and programmes (which are produced by the boroughs in London and the City of London) in order to ensure consistency. Local development documents prepared by local authorities must be "in general conformity" with it. Furthermore, the London Plan is a material consideration for local authorities to take into account when determining planning applications. Policies in the London Plan relating to green buildings include:

  — The Mayor and local authorities are to require major new developments to demonstrate on-site renewable energy technologies wherever feasible;
  — The Mayor expects planning applications referred to him to include combined heat and power (CHP) and community heating wherever feasible; and
  — The Mayor and local authorities are to request an assessment of the energy demand of major new developments and demonstration of the application of the Mayor's energy hierarchy.[58]

The London Plan will be current until 2020 but is subject to review from time to time. Draft "Further Alterations to the London Plan" were published in September 2006 for consultation. The proposals were subject to an Examination in Public in summer 2007 and the Panel submitted its report on the EIP in October 2007. In light of this the Mayor incorporated both the Early and Further Alterations in the current London Plan published in February 2008. Significant changes include:

  — The Mayor and local authorities are to require all developments to show that heating, cooling and power systems have been chosen to minimise carbon emissions;
  — The Mayor and local authorities are to require developments to supply 20 per cent of their energy needs from on-site renewables.

---

[57] This was published on February 10, 2004.
[58] The Mayor has developed an Energy Hierarchy as a tool to aid business in making decisions, including on building specifications, internal energy management strategy and procurement. The hierarchy is as follows: i) use energy efficiently; ii) use renewable energy; and iii) supply remaining energy efficiently using technologies such as combined heat and power and efficient boilers.

- Draft Strategy for Sustainable Construction. The DBERR consulted **8–031** both Government and industry in 2007 on a Draft Strategy for Sustainable Construction with a view to improving the sustainability of the built environment. The aim is not to introduce new legislation but to "make existing regulation work better". The Draft Strategy sets targets for both the public and private sectors of the industry. Many of these have already been introduced in other policies and initiatives (e.g. all new homes to be zero carbon by 2016), but other targets are new, for example, 20 per cent of projects with a value in excess of £1m are to achieve an "excellent" BREEAM rating[59] or equivalent by 2008. In addition under the Draft Strategy DBERR is to "set a clear timetable and action plan to deliver significant reductions in carbon emissions from new commercial buildings within the next 10 years". A number of the targets are outline proposals only. Much of the focus is directed at the use of the Government's procurement power (40 per cent of construction output is for the public sector) to drive the sustainability agenda. The Government is committed to agreeing a new set of public service agreements, incorporating the principles of sustainable development and the Office of Government Commerce (OGC) is to embed further within such procurement the use of the Common Minimum Standards and the requirement for a BREEAM (or equivalent) assessment for buildings. In relation to design, the Government has called for all public bodies to appoint a "design champion" to provide leadership and motivation for delivering good design. There is a drive to promote offsite construction on the basis that it "can deliver measurable improvements in quality, cost and time predictability and improved health and safety of construction projects in both the private and public sector".[60]

---

[59] BREEAM (Building Research Establishmnt Environmental Assessment Method) assesses the performance of buildings in the following areas—management: overall management policy, commissioning site management and procedural issues; energy use: operational energy and carbon dioxide (CO_2) issues; health and well-being: indoor and external issues affecting health and well-being; pollution: air and water pollution issues; transport: transport-related CO_2 and location-related factors; land use: greenfield and brownfield sites; ecology: ecological value conservation and enhancement of the site; materials: environmental implication of building materials, including life-cycle impacts; water: consumption and water efficiency. Credits are awarded in each category according to performance. A set of environmental weightings then enables the credits to be added together to produce a single overall score. The building is then rated on a scale of Pass, Good, Very Good, Excellent or Outstanding, and a certificate awarded.

[60] As noted in Chapter 2 above, in October 2008, a new Department of Energy and Climate Change (DECC) was set up, merging the energy functions of DBERR with the Climate Change functions of Defra.

Biodiversity and Geological Conservation

8–032   PPS9 (*Bio-diversity and Geological Conservation*),[61] sets out policies on protection of biodiversity and geological conservation through the planning system. Circular 06/05 (*Biodiversity and Geographical Conservation—Statutory Obligations and Their Impact Within the Planning System*) provides administrative guidance on application of the law in England relating to planning and nature conservation. As PPS9 indicates, a separate Defra document, "Working with the grain of nature: a biodiversity strategy for England",[62] sets out the Government's broader vision for conserving and enhancing biological diversity in England, together with a programme of work to achieve it. It includes the broad aim that planning, construction, development and regeneration should have minimal impacts on biodiversity and enhance it wherever possible. In moving towards this goal, the Government's objectives for planning are stated to be:

> "— to promote sustainable development by ensuring that biological and geological diversity are conserved and enhanced as an integral part of social, environmental and economic development, so that policies and decisions about the development and use of land integrate biodiversity and geological diversity with other considerations;
> — to conserve, enhance and restore the diversity of England's wildlife and geology by sustaining, and where possible improving, the quality and extent of natural habitat and geological and geomorphological sites; the natural physical processes on which they depend; and the populations of naturally occurring species which they support;.
> — to contribute to rural renewal and urban renaissance by:
>> (i)   enhancing biodiversity in green spaces and among developments so that they are used by wildlife and valued by people, recognising that healthy functional ecosystems can contribute to a better quality of life and to people's sense of well-being; and
>> (ii) ensuring that developments take account of the role and value of biodiversity in supporting economic diversification and contributing to a high quality environment.
>
> The planning system has a significant part to play in meeting the Government's international commitments and domestic policies for habitats, species and ecosystems."[63]

PPS9 states that "the aim of planning decisions should be to prevent harm to biodiversity and geological conservation interests." Note that the statement refers to "biodiversity", not just protected species. A species may be of biodiversity interest, but the animal and/or its habitat may not be

---

[61] Published August 16, 2005.
[62] Defra (2002).
[63] PPS9, p.2.

formally protected under current wildlife legislation. One of the key principles of PPS9 includes the following statement:

"Where granting planning permission would result in significant harm to
those interests, local planning authorities will need to be satisfied that the
development cannot reasonably be located on any alternative sites that
would result in less or no harm. In the absence of any such alternatives,
local planning authorities should ensure that, before planning permission
is granted, adequate mitigation measures are put in place. Where a
planning decision would result in significant harm to biodiversity and
geological interests which cannot be prevented or adequately mitigated
against, appropriate compensation measures should be sought."

Without suitable mitigation and/or compensation being proposed to offset
potential damage to biodiversity interest, PPS9 directs local authorities to
refuse planning permission: "If that significant harm cannot be prevented,
adequately mitigated against, or compensated for, then planning permission should be refused."

In order to satisfy the requirements of PPS9, it is vital that appropriate
survey work is undertaken and mitigation measures are proposed before a
developer submits a planning application. If planning permission is granted
without these requirements being met, the decision could be challenged as
there may be some potential for objectors to lodge a successful judicial
review.

It should also be noted that, under the European Habitats Directive,[64] **8–033**
local authorities are required to produce an Appropriate Assessment to
determine any potential impacts of an individual development or strategic
level plan on any Special Area of Conservation or Special Protected Areas
(as well as species outlined in Regulation 10 of the Habitats Regulations
1994). The purpose of an Appropriate Assessment is to assess the impacts
of a strategic plan or a proposed project against the conservation objectives
of the European Site. The assessment must determine whether the plan or
development would adversely affect the integrity of the site in terms of its
nature conservation objectives. Where significant negative effects are
identified, alternative options should be examined to avoid any potential
damaging effects. Part IV of the Conservation (Natural Habitats, &c)
Regulations 1994 implements this for specified planning and other similar
consents. In October 2005 the European Court of Justice ruled[65] that this
"Appropriate Assessment" requirement extends also to land use plans.
This has now been provided for in the Conservation (Natural Habitats &c)

---

[64] Directive 92/43/EEC (the Habitats Directive) on the Conservation of Natural Habitats
and of Wild Fauna and Flora.
[65] Case C-6/04. *Commission of the European Communities v United Kingdom of Great Britain
and Northern Ireland.*

(Amendment) (England and Wales) Regulations 2007,[66] which insert a new Part IVA into the 1994 Regulations, effective from August 21, 2007.

Waste Management

8–034   PPS10 (Planning for Sustainable Waste Management[67]) sets out the Government's policy to be taken into account by waste planning authorities and forms part of the national waste management plan for the UK. PPS10 requires regional authorities to include waste management as part of a RSS and states that this should look forward for a 15 to 20 year period. Waste planning authorities are defined as the local authority with responsibility for land-use planning control for waste management. In County Councils where there is a District Council, responsibility for waste management remains with the County Council, except where a District Council proposes to develop a waste management facility on its own land. For unitary planning authorities the responsibility is with that authority. In London, the Greater London Authority is required to produce a Waste Management Strategy.

The core strategy of a waste planning authority should set out policies and proposals on waste management in line with the RSS and ensure sufficient opportunities for the provision of waste management facilities in appropriate locations, including for waste disposal. It should look forward for a period of at least 10 years and be reviewed and rolled forward at least every five.

There are some key principles and tools in PPS10, namely the waste hierarchy,[68] the proximity principle,[69] the cumulative impacts of waste

---

[66] SI 2007/1843.
[67] Published July 21, 2005.
[68] Commented on further below. See also para.15–002.
[69] The proximity principle advocates that waste should be disposed of (or otherwise managed) close to the point at which it is generated, thus aiming to achieve responsible self-sufficiency at a regional or sub-regional level. Where this is not possible priority should be given to transportation by rail or water.

disposal,[70] the health impacts,[71] demonstrating need,[72] and sustainable appraisal.[73] Emphasis is given in PPS10 to the need for more sustainable waste management, moving the management of waste up the "waste hierarchy". The waste hierarchy is a tool which ranks different waste management options according to their impact on the environment. Waste reduction is the most environmentally beneficial option, followed by re-use, recycling or composting, energy recovery then finally, as an option of last resort, disposal. PPS10 contains the new principle of "driving waste management up the hierarchy" which means that waste planning authorities should always try to ensure that waste is managed by the best possible environmental means, represented by the highest levels of the hierarchy i.e. waste reduction, re-use and recycling.

Renewable Energy

The key policies in this area are PPS22 (Renewable Energy); the Supplementary Planning Guidance; and the Energy Statement (2004). PPS22[74] sets out the Government's policies for renewable energy, which planning authorities should have regard to when preparing local development documents and when taking planning decisions. The wording of PPS22 encourages local planning authorities and regional planning bodies to accommodate and promote, where technically viable, renewable energy developments (e.g. wind farms, etc.) and place requirements on building developments to provide a proportion of the site-wide energy from renewable sources. With regard to new building developments, paragraph 8 of PPS22 specifically states: **8–035**

---

[70] Paragraph 21 of PPS10 states that in deciding which sites and areas to identify for waste management facilities, waste planning authorities should take into account "the cumulative effect of previous waste disposal facilities on the well-being of the local community, including any significant adverse impacts on environmental quality, social cohesion or economic potential." This is an important clause which should help ensure that the most deprived communities are not saddled with more and more waste facilities, while wealthier communities send all their waste elsewhere.

[71] Paragraph 31 of PPS10 states that "Where concerns about health are raised" waste planning authorities should draw on Government advice and research, and consult with the relevant health authorities and agencies to obtain advice on health implications. They should also consider the "locational implications" of such advice when determining planning applications. In effect this clause acknowledges that some waste facilities may have a bigger health impact in some communities than others.

[72] Paragraph 22 of PPS10 emphasises that waste companies should not have to demonstrate the need for a waste facility as long as the proposal is consistent with an up-to-date waste development plan.

[73] Sustainability Appraisal is now required of all plans, including Regional Waste Strategies and Waste Development Frameworks. The Practice Guidance that is published to support PPS10 is expected to emphasise the benefits of involving the local community in waste plans and strategies even earlier than required under the Strategic Environmental Assessment.

[74] Published August 10, 2004.

"Local planning authorities may include policies in local development documents that require a percentage of the energy to be used in new residential, commercial or industrial developments to come from on-site renewable energy developments. Such policies:

(i) should ensure that requirement to generate on-site renewable energy is only applied to developments where the installation of renewable energy generation equipment is viable given the type of development proposed, its location, and design;

(ii) should not be framed in such a way as to place an undue burden on developers, for example, by specifying that all energy to be used in a development should come from on-site renewable generation."

Following the publication of PPS22 in 2004, the London Borough of Merton was the first local authority to formalise the government's renewable energy targets, setting a target which requires the use of 10 per cent renewable energy on-site to reduce annual carbon dioxide (CO_2) emissions in the built environment. The first project to comply with this target—10 light industrial units—was completed in June 2005 at Willow Lane, Mitcham, using micro turbines and solar PV to meet the requirement. Croydon was quick to follow Merton's lead, and its first project designed to reach a "10 per cent target" was completed in July 2005. North Devon has chosen to demand 15 per cent CO_2 reduction from renewables and Kirklees Council has proposed that by 2011, 30 per cent of energy consumption in every one of its new buildings is from renewable sources. A large number of planning authorities now have similar policies on renewables, some of which may impose higher targets. The Mayor of London is seeking a 20 per cent renewables requirement in the revisions to the London Plan (up from 10 per cent in the current Plan/Energy Strategy).

There was press speculation in August 2007 that the Government would abolish the "Merton Rule", with The Guardian claiming that a leaked version of a draft for the PPS on Planning and Climate Change would overturn it. However, the DCLG has since denied that this is the case, and has stated instead that the local authorities will be expected to promote a greater use of renewable energy.

Indeed, the Supplement to PPS1 states that planning authorities

"should have an evidence-based understanding of the local feasibility and potential for renewable and low-carbon technologies, including microgeneration, to supply new development in their area. This may require them, working closely with industry and drawing in other appropriate expertise, to make their own assessments. Drawing from this evidence base, and ensuring consistency with housing and economic objectives, planning authorities should:

(i) set out a target percentage of the energy to be used in new development to come from decentralised and renewable or low-

448

carbon energy sources where it is viable. The target should avoid prescription on technologies and be flexible in how carbon savings from local energy supplies are to be secured;

(ii) where there are particular and demonstrable opportunities for greater use of decentralised and renewable or low-carbon energy than the target percentage, bring forward development area or site-specific targets to secure this potential; and, in bringing forward targets,

(iii) set out the type and size of development to which the target will be applied; and

(iv) ensure there is a clear rationale for the target and it is properly tested."[75]

The Mayor is working with London Renewables to produce an SPG on renewable energy which will set out guidelines for locations where stand-alone renewable energy schemes would be appropriate, and set criteria for the assessment of those schemes (Supplementary Planning Guidance on Renewable Energy)[76]. London Renewables has published "Integrating renewable energy into new development: toolkit for planners, developers and consultants", which will inform the SPG on renewable energy.

The Mayor's energy strategy: "Green light to clean power" (2004), aims to minimise the impacts on health and on the local and global environment of meeting the essential energy needs of all those living and working in London. Specifically, it aims to reduce London's contribution to global climate change, tackle the problem of fuel poverty and at the same time promote London's economic development through renewable and energy efficient technologies. The Mayor expects: **8–036**

- planning applications referred to him to supply at least 10 per cent of the development's energy needs from on-site renewables where feasible, and to incorporate energy efficient technologies where feasible;
- local authorities to have at least one zero carbon development;
- local authorities to identify Energy Action Areas where there will be imposed higher energy efficiency standards for new build and retrofit;
- national targets to reduce carbon emissions by 60 per cent from 1990 levels by 2050 to be adopted for London.

Pollution control

PPS23 (*Planning and Pollution Control*)[77] was intended to complement the pollution control framework under the Pollution Prevention and Control **8–037**

---

[75] Supplement to PPS1, page 16.
[76] SPG documents provide detailed advice on some of the policies in the London Plan.
[77] Published November 3, 2004.

(PPC) Act 1999 and the related PPC Regulations 2000.[78] PPS23 and its two annexes (covering pollution control, air and water and development of land affected by contamination) provide guidance on how systems for pollution control and the management of contaminated land should be taken into account when considering proposals for development.[79] The key policy aims of PPS23 are to facilitate planning for good quality, sustainable development that takes appropriate account of pollution control and contamination issues. Local planning authorities should have regard to the policies in PPS23 in preparing local development documents, as well as in determining individual planning applications.

PPS23 advises that:

- any consideration of the quality of land, air or water and potential impacts arising from development, possibly leading to impacts on health, is capable of being a material planning consideration, in so far as it arises or may arise from or may affect any land use;
- the planning system plays a key role in determining the location of development which may give rise to pollution, either directly or indirectly, and in ensuring that other uses and developments are not, as far as possible, affected by major existing or potential sources of pollution;
- the controls under the planning and pollution control regimes should complement rather than duplicate each other;[80]
- the presence of contamination in land can present risks to human health and the environment, which adversely affect or restrict the beneficial use of land but development presents an opportunity to deal with these risks successfully;

---

[78] These Regulations have now been superseded by the Environmental Permitting (England & Wales) Regulations 2007, SI 2007/3538.

[79] There was also a letter sent to Chief Planning Officers on May 30, 2008 to circulate a new set of model planning conditions intended for use during the development on land affected by contamination. They replace Appendix 2B of Annex 2 of PPS23 and paragraphs 56 to 59 of Appendix A of Circular 11/95: Use of conditions in planning permission.

[80] Pollution control and licensing is usually a matter for the Environment Agency, dealt with separately from planning considerations. The relationship between planning controls and pollution controls has caused many difficulties for objectors. The basic position was established in a ruling by the High Court and Court of Appeal in a case involving a proposal for an incinerator in Gateshead. See *Gateshead MBC v Secretary of State for the Environment and Northumbrian Water Group plc* [1994] JPL 255, and Court of Appeal [1994] EGCS 92. The case decided that the environmental impact of emissions is a material consideration at the planning stage; the existence of a stringent pollution control regime under the Environmental Protection Act 1990 is also a material consideration at the planning stage; if there are residual difficulties or uncertainties, the question of whether they can be overcome is a matter of judgment on the facts of each case. Thus, under PPS23, those making planning decisions need to assume that the pollution control regime will work effectively, and to take advice from the pollution control authorities, i.e. the Environment Agency, on the associated risks.

- contamination is not restricted to land with previous industrial uses, it can occur on greenfield as well as previously developed land and it can arise from natural sources as well as from human activities;
- where pollution issues are likely to arise, intending developers should hold informal pre-application discussions with the local planning authority, the relevant pollution control authority and/or the environmental health departments of local authorities, and other authorities and stakeholders with a legitimate interest; and
- where it will save time and money, consideration should be given to submitting applications for planning permission and pollution control permits in parallel and co-ordinating their consideration by the relevant authorities.

With regard to contaminated land, when considering the redevelopment of previously developed land a balanced approach is required which addresses the risk of pollution, whilst recognising the benefits of recycling previously developed land and the damage to community and business confidence caused by failing to remediate contaminated land. PPS23 Annex 2—"Development on Land Affected by Contamination" gives brief details of the roles of the different parties in the development process, on the relationship between planning control and the contaminated land regime and on the requirements and good practice in dealing with these issues through planning control.

Flood risk

The PPS in this area is PPS25 (*Development and Flood Risk*),[81] the primary   8–038
objective of which is to ensure that flood risk is considered at all stages of the planning process and that inappropriate development is avoided in areas which are at risk of flooding.

Currently, the Government is under no statutory duty to protect land or property against flooding. Likewise, certain authorities such as the Environment Agency, local authorities and internal drainage boards have permissive powers but no statutory duty to carry out or maintain flood defence works in the public interest. The onus for protecting property against natural hazards and maintaining the drainage of their land lies with the landowner/developer. PPS25 lays down policies which the developers must bear in mind if they want to secure planning permission. Under PPS25, the Environment Agency is now a statutory consultee for all planning applications in flood risk areas, and for the development of flood risk policies in LDDs. In the case of a major application where the local planning authority is likely to grant permission, discussions may need to take place with the Environment Agency to agree on an acceptable course of action,

---

[81] Published December 2006.

and thereby persuade it to withdraw, or not to raise, any objection. If following such discussions, the Environment Agency maintains an objection and the local planning authority has not moved on its intention to grant permission for the major development, the recent Flooding Direction[82] requires the local planning authority to notify the Secretary of State of the proposal. This gives the Secretary of State the opportunity to review the application's general compliance with PPS25's policies and consider whether it should be called-in by the Secretary of State for her determination. The Flooding Direction came into force on January 1, 2007.

PPG20 on coastal planning deals with the character of the coast, designated areas, heritage coasts and the international dimension. It discusses types of coasts, policies for their conservation and development and policies covering risks of flooding, erosion and land instability, as well as coastal protection and defence. It outlines policies for developments which may specifically require a coastal location, including tourism, recreation, mineral extraction, energy generation and waste water and sewage treatment plants. It indicates that it is the role of the planning system to reconcile development requirements with the need to protect, conserve and, where appropriate, improve the landscape, environmental quality, wildlife habitats and recreational opportunities of the coast.

8–039   On May 14, 2008, it was announced that the Government intends to publish a draft Floods and Water Bill for consultation in 2009.[83] The current timetable is for a consultation draft of the Bill to be published in Spring 2009, with the Bill then being available for introduction in a later Parliamentary Session. The detailed provisions of the Bill are currently being scoped, and there will be opportunity for stakeholder engagement throughout the process. This Bill was proposed following the devastating floods which affected large parts of the country in the summer of 2007. Sir Michael Pitt was asked to lead an independent "lessons learned" review, examining both how to reduce the risk and impact of such flooding, and the emergency response itself. Sir Michael Pitt's Interim Report, published in December 2007, stated that flooding legislation should be updated and streamlined under a single unifying Act of Parliament that, amongst other outcomes, addresses all sources of flooding, clarifies responsibilities, and facilitates flood risk management. The Government agreed with that interim conclusion and awaits the final recommendations of Sir Michael Pitt's full report

Local planning authorities in England have to consult the Environment

---

[82] Town and Country Planning (Flooding) (England) Direction 2007, which is made under the Town and Country Planning (General Development Procedure) Order 1995 (SI 1995/419). See Circular 04/06 (Communities and Local Government): The Town and Country Planning (Flooding) (England) Direction 2007.

[83] This follows both the Pitt Review into the 2007 floods and the Government's Water Strategy, Future Water, which launched a review of competition and innovation in the water industry and water charging and metering.

Agency on most development proposals at risk from flooding. PPS25 and its associated Practice Guide set out Government policy and advice on the subject. The Environment Agency provides technical advice to the local planning authorities and developers on how best to avoid, manage and reduce the adverse impacts of flooding. When commenting on spatial plans and sustainability appraisals, the Environment Agency aims to ensure they are "sound" by encouraging decision-makers to;

(i) carry out regional and strategic assessments of flood risk as part of sustainability appraisal;

(ii) include suitable flood risk objectives and indicators;

(iii) correctly apply the sequential test—steering new development to the lowest risk flood zone appropriate to the proposed use—and the exception test—only appropriate for use when there are large areas in certain flood zones but where some continuing development is necessary for wider sustainable development reasons, taking into account the need to avoid social or economic blight and the need for essential civil infrastructure to remain operational during floods;

(iv) reduce flood risk through making space for water;

(v) when climate change is expected to mean that some existing development may not be sustainable in the long-term, use regeneration to help relocate existing development to lower risk locations; and

(vi) include policies that reflect PPS25's key planning objectives.

The Environment Agency may object to planning applications on the following grounds:

(i) the proposed development is not consistent with Government planning policy;

(ii) lack of evidence that the sequential test and (where needed) the exception test have been applied correctly;

(iii) it is not supported by a flood risk assessment; and

(iv) the flood risk assessment does not demonstrate that the development and its occupants/users will be safe for the lifetime of the development, does not increase flood risk elsewhere and does not seek to reduce risk overall.

The local planning authority is the final decision-maker, but if it grants permission for a major development which the Environment Agency have advised against, it has to notify the Secretary of State.

Minerals

There are two Minerals Planning Statements and one Minerals Planning Guidance Note which are of relevance. Minerals Planning Guidance Notes (MPGs) and their replacements, Minerals Policy Statements (MPSs), set

8–040

out the government's policy on minerals and planning issues and provide advice and guidance to local authorities and the minerals industry on policies and the operation of the planning system with regard to minerals. Mineral planning authorities must take their contents into account in preparing their development plans. The guidance may also be material to decisions on individual planning applications and appeals.

MPS1 (*Planning and Minerals*[84]) is the overarching planning policy document for all minerals development in England. It aims to ensure that the need by society and the economy for minerals is managed in an integrated way against its impact on the environment and communities. MPS2 (*Controlling and mitigating the environmental effects of mineral extraction in England*[85]) sets out how Minerals Planning Authorities (MPAs) should minimise any significant adverse environmental effects that may arise from minerals extraction. Local authorities can achieve this through framing policies in development plans, their consideration of planning applications and through reviews of planning consents under the provisions of the Environment Act 1995. MPS1 states that when considering planning applications "applications which are in accordance with the relevant development plan should be allowed unless material considerations indicate otherwise".

MPAs should have regard to all material considerations, including the policies outlined in PPGs and MPGs, and their successor PPSs and MPSs. Developers should consider whether the development proposed would be in accordance with the development plan and, if not, whether other material considerations might be used to justify the development proceeding nonetheless. MPAs should take into account the full range of social, community, economic and environmental issues relevant to the planning decision. When preparing the application and in proposing any necessary mitigation measures, the developer should demonstrate that any potential adverse effects have been properly and competently considered. Any adverse effects on local communities, environmental damage or loss of amenity must be kept to an acceptable minimum through the design of the proposals, including the use of planning obligation agreements where appropriate and the attachment of conditions. Where effective mitigation of unacceptable impact by those means is not possible, permission should be refused.[86] The guidance makes it clear that industries involving similar processes to mineral extraction, for example recycling, construction and waste disposal, should take into account the relevant elements of the Statement in planning their own development proposals.

8–041   The Marine Mineral Guidance 1 (MMG1, *Extraction by dredging from the English seabed*)[87] provides a statement of the Government's policies on the

[84] Published November 13, 2006.
[85] Published March 2005.
[86] MPS1, p.14, paras 17–18.
[87] Published July 31, 2002.

extraction of marine sand and gravel and other minerals from the English seabed.

Water

Progress has been made by Government in recent years in driving water **8–042** efficiency improvements in new homes and buildings in England and Wales. It has brought water efficiency into the Building Regulations in England and Wales[88] (at a tight, whole-building standard of 125 litres per person per day), and instituted a Code for Sustainable Homes in England. Compliance with this code is compulsory for all new homes receiving Government funding (at a level of 105 litres per person per day), and is being extended to new MoD and NHS homes.

The Government issued a consultation document in 2007 called "Mandating Water Efficiency in New Buildings—A Consultation". This sought views on proposals to make minimum standards of water efficiency performance mandatory in all new homes and new commercial developments. These standards aimed to underpin those set out in the Code for Sustainable Homes. The document sought opinions on various options, and set out the costs and benefits (reduced consumer demand for water supply, carbon savings, etc.) that would result.

Furthermore, The Water Supply (Water Fittings) Regulations 1999[89] currently set minimum levels of water efficiency performance for key water using appliances such as WCs, urinals, dishwashers and washing machines. These Regulations will be reviewed with a view to setting new performance standards for key water using fittings. Through the Regulations it would also be possible to regulate high water volume fittings such as wet rooms, spa baths, etc. to make such appliances notifiable to the local water company. This would enable them to exercise discretionary powers to install a water meter and hence reflect the true cost of the water being used. These measures will apply to individual appliances installed in both new and existing houses and non-domestic buildings, and are intended to complement the overall performance standard set within building regulations.

---

[88] The legislative framework of the "Building Regulations" is principally made up of The Building Regulations 2000 and The Building (Approved Inspectors etc.) Regulations 2000. Both have been amended several times since 2000, the most recent being on September 9, 2008. The latest amendments were delivered through: Energy Performance of Buildings (Certificates and Inspections) (England and Wales) (Amendment No.2) Regulations 2008 (SI 2008/2363); Housing and Regeneration Act 2008 section 317: Time Limit for Prosecutions of Breaches of Building Regulations; the Housing and Regeneration Act 2008 (Commencement No.1 and Transitional Provision) Order 2008, SI 2008/2358; and The Building (Electronic Communications) Order 2008 (SI 2008/2334).
[89] SI 1999/1148.

Contaminated land

8–043   The planning system has for some years been an important way in which contaminated land issues may be addressed by local authorities in the context of planning applications to develop land. The presence of contamination on any land is a material consideration that planning authorities must take into account when considering any proposal for the development of that land. It is government policy that upon redevelopment land which is contaminated should be brought to a standard where it is suitable for its intended use. Guidance on the approach that planning authorities should take to contaminated land is contained in Annex 2 of PPS23,[90] and in the letter sent to Chief Planning Officers on May 30, 2008, circulating a new set of model planning conditions intended for use during the development on land affected by contamination. These model conditions replace Appendix 2B of Annex 2 of PPS23 and paragraphs 56 to 59 of Appendix A of Circular 11/95. The Annex expands on the policy considerations the Government expects Regional Planning Bodies and local planning authorities to have regard to in preparing policies in development plans and taking decisions on applications in relation to development on land affected by contamination. It gives necessary legislative and technical background and some examples of good practice to assist authorities in implementing the policies contained in PPS23.

The contaminated land regime in EPA 1990 Part 2A[91] was introduced specifically to address the historical legacy of land contamination. It focuses on the identification and remediation of land which is in such a condition by reason of contamination that it gives rise to significant harm or the significant possibility of significant harm to certain identifiable receptors, or gives rise to pollution of controlled waters or the likelihood of such pollution. It applies where there is unacceptable risk, assessed on the basis of the current use (including any use that already has the benefit of planning permission but might not yet be implemented, including development permitted under the General Permitted Development Order 1995) and the circumstances of the land. If such land is identified, Part 2A is intended to ensure that where it is reasonable, given the costs and benefits of risk reduction, and practicable, remediation is carried out so that the land no longer presents an unacceptable risk. It is not directed to assessing risks in relation to a future use of the land that would require a specific grant of planning permission. This is primarily a task for the planning system, which aims to control development and land use in the future. Consequently, for planning purposes, the assessment of risks arising from contamination and remediation requirements should be considered on the basis of both the current use and circumstances and its proposed new use.

---

[90] PPS23 Planning and Pollution Control—Annex 2: Development on Land Affected by contamination.
[91] For further detail, see Chapter 16.

In addition, land under redevelopment will be cleaned up under the planning regime, leaving Part 2A only applicable in practice to land which is a serious environmental problem and for which there are no immediate development plans.

In considering planning applications, the potential for there to be contamination or pollution on the site has to be considered together with any contamination which the proposed use itself may produce. PPS23 provides that where development is proposed, the developer is responsible for ensuring that:

"development is safe and suitable for use for the purpose for which it is intended. The developer is thus responsible for determining whether land is suitable for a particular development or can be made so by remedial action. In particular, the developer should carry out an adequate investigation to inform a risk assessment to determine:

— whether the land in question is already affected by contamination through source—pathway—receptor pollutant linkages and how those linkages are represented in a conceptual model;
— whether the development proposed will create new linkages, e.g. new pathways by which existing contaminants might reach existing or proposed receptors and whether it will introduce new vulnerable receptors; and
— what action is needed to break those linkages and avoid new ones, deal with any unacceptable risks and enable safe development and future occupancy of the site and neighbouring land."

Where there is any significant likelihood of contamination being present, a developer would be most imprudent not to inform himself/herself about the nature and extent of any contamination that may be present, since it is likely to affect whether or not spoil from the site is hazardous waste, whether particular precautions need be taken by those working on the site to meet health and safety requirements, whether local surface waters and ground-water may become polluted in the course of the development, and whether he can subsequently respond satisfactorily to inquiries by potential purchasers and/or occupiers, and their financiers, as to absence of contamination. Serious contamination is quite capable of causing a site to have negative asset value.

The local planning authority's role is to identify contaminated land **8–044** within their area and, except for certain categories, to decide what remediation is required and ensure that it takes place. The local planning authority has to satisfy itself that the development proposed incorporates any necessary remediation and management measures to deal with unacceptable risks (and any continuing monitoring programme which may be required). Pre-application discussions are encouraged. A potential developer will need to satisfy the local authority that unacceptable risk from contamination will be successfully addressed through remediation without undue environmental impact during and following the development. Most often, the grant of planning consent is likely to be subject to remediation conditions. Where the likelihood of contamination is less strong, or where it is known that there is only modest contamination, the authority may not insist on a prior investigation by the developer, but simply include conditions in the planning consent prohibiting the development from proceeding until the investigation and assessment of risks have been carried out, and the development adapted as necessary to incorporate remedial measures. Planning consent may be given subject to conditions requiring the developer to notify the authority of the presence of any significant contamination that comes to light in the course of development.

Planning limitations, e.g. conditions or agreements, requiring the remediation of land will normally either set specific clean-up standards or require remediation to the satisfaction of the planning authority in consultation with some other body, normally the Environment Agency.

Inter-relationship between Planning and Other Controls

8-045   The planning regime is only one of several that protect the environment, and there is inevitably considerable potential overlap between them. It is Government policy, reflected in its guidance to the relevant authorities, that duplication of controls over any particular matter is to be avoided. The areas of competence of the various authorities are to be determined by reference to the specific objectives of the different control regimes, and each authority must exercise its powers with a view to achieving its relevant objectives only. Thus, as a matter of law, a planning authority in the exercise of its planning functions is required to have regard to all relevant planning considerations, but to exclude from its mind all non-planning matters.

There is no clear definition of planning matters for these purposes but, historically, this has been interpreted as relating to land uses. The fact that a local planning authority may have other duties as housing authority or as waste disposal authority is not relevant to the land use planning issues, so that a local planning authority cannot use the powers given to it as planning authority to discharge functions given to it in another capacity.

The various forms of environmental control have developed in a piecemeal fashion. Separate tasks are allocated to a variety of bodies but there has hitherto been no clarity on their proper inter-relationship and, except in special areas of the country such as National Parks, no formal co-ordination of the various interests in the preparation of their structure and local plans. This is exemplified in PPS9 (*Biodiversity and Geological Con-*

servation), which invites planning authorities to have policies about nature conservation, but gives them no effective guidance on how to formulate these policies, nor on how they should conduct their consultations. For example, regional planning bodies and local planning authorities are invited to consult with English Nature, the Environment Agency and the British Geological Survey, but no indication is given on the extent to which, if at all, they should consult with neighbouring local authorities. It appears from this that local planning authorities are not expected to perform a co-ordinating role, but nor is any other body.

There is potential for overlap and conflict between planning and environmental regulation. Legislation does not provide a clear-cut dividing line and the courts themselves have avoided trying to fill this statutory omission. It is long established policy[92] that planning authorities should not seek to control matters that are the subject of other regulation. See also the following two cases as to how *Gateshead* was applied: *R (on the application of J Bailey, A Norman and P Wilson) v Secretary of State for Business, Enterprise and Regulatory Reform* [2008] EWHC 1257 (Admin), and *R (on the application of Lewes District Friends of the Earth Ltd v East Sussex County Council* [2008] EWHC 1981 (Admin).

8–046

The three main consenting systems of interest are: development control and development planning; pollution prevention and control (PPC); and discharge consenting. The differing requirements that may impose on a proposed new development may well be inconsistent;[93] nevertheless liaison between the authorities can eliminate avoidable inconsistencies and unnecessary prejudice to the development.

However, there are still areas of weakness which lead to inappropriate standards of environmental protection, delays in resolution of consents, unnecessary burdens on all participants, and public uncertainty and lack of confidence in the working of the regimes. In particular:

---

[92] See PPS23, (*Planning and Pollution Control*), page 6, paragraph 14. The controls under the planning and pollution control regimes should complement rather than duplicate each other. Planning authorities should work on the assumption that the relevant pollution control regime will be properly applied and enforced. See also *Gateshead MBC v Secretary of State for the Environment and another* [1995] JPL 432. This was a case involving a planning application for a clinical waste incinerator which also required an IPC authorisation for its operation. The case illustrated that there was no clear dividing line between planning controls and a pollution control licensing system such as IPC, but as the grant of planning permission will precede the grant of an environmental permit, it inevitably shifts the burden of responsibility for deciding whether the process can become operational over to the environmental regulator. See also the following two cases as to how *Gateshead* was applied: *R (on the application of J Bailey, A Norman and P Wilson) v Secretary of State for Business, Enterprise and Regulatory Reform* [2008] EWHC 1257 (Admin), and *R (on the application of Lewes District Friends of the Earth Ltd v East Sussex County Council* [2008] EWHC 1981 (Admin).

[93] A typical example is a chimney stack, that to preserve visual amenity should be short, but to avoid local pollution must have a substantial height.

(i) lack of understanding between the regulators about each others' regimes means there is uncertainty about what each can and should regulate, particularly in respect of health effects;

(ii) effective consultation at the planning stage is often hindered by lack of the necessary information from applicants;

(iii) environmental impact assessment provides a useful tool for making information available at the planning stage, but it is not always used as effectively as it might be to inform consultation and decision-making;

(iv) planning authorities and the Environment Agency do not always communicate as well as they might, leading to gaps in the information each authority needs if it is to provide useful comment to the other, to consultation responses which are less useful than they might be, and to failure to exchange information which would be of assistance in deciding later consents;

(v) consultation and communication practices vary considerably around England and Wales, sometimes sensibly in response to differing circumstances e.g. between urban and rural areas, but at other times for no obvious reason.

A key way to overcome such problems would be to deliver better implementation of current legislation rather than changing or introducing new statutory duties and powers. This can be done by forming closer working relationships and more effective communication between planning authorities and other departments or agencies such as the Environment Agency. Some recent examples where this is taking place are in flood prevention, discussed above, and waste management permitting.

8–047   As already noted, the interface between planning and pollution control regimes is complex and developers/operators can be subject to overlapping requirements—adding unnecessary burdens to both industry and the regulators, and increasing the costs of development.

Many protocols exist between local planning authorities and Government departments and agencies. One such protocol is "the Local Government Association and Environment Agency Land Use Planning Protocol",[94] which promotes effective collaboration and partnership in all activities of mutual interest. Local authorities are being encouraged to sign up to the plan. It is intended to encourage local authorities and the Environment Agency to work more closely together to achieve sustainable development, best practice and best value within a modern planning system. The Protocol consists of nationally written and agreed working arrangements, and further guidance to be interpreted locally. The protocols are not binding on local authorities or the Environment Agency, and are suggested as models that may be modified to fit local circumstances[95].

---

[94] "Working Better Together in Town and Country Planning" (2003).

[95] See *http://www.environment-agency.gov.uk/aboutus/512398/908812/1351053/1351353/?lang=_e.*

Hazardous installations

One other regime which shows quite clearly the inter-relationship between 8–048 land use and environmental regulations is the control of major accident hazards. There are a number of mechanisms for controlling the risks from hazardous installations. The first is on the siting of new hazardous installations; the primary control is under the Health and Safety at Work etc. Act 1974 (HSWA) via the Control of Major Accident Hazards Regulations 1999 (COMAH).[96] In 1999 the COMAH Regulations were introduced in Great Britain, replacing earlier legislation, with the aim of preventing major accidents involving dangerous substances and limiting the consequences to people and the environment of any which do occur. The COMAH Regulations 1999 set out in detail the scope of the duties imposed by the legislation on the operators of establishments making and/or holding significant quantities of dangerous substances, and also on the emergency services and local authorities. The HSWA and the COMAH Regulations require operators to submit a pre-construction safety report to HSE before construction can begin. Operators must also apply for a hazardous substances consent from the hazardous substance authority (HSA—usually the planning authority—see next paragraph below for further detail). On application, the HSA is required to consult the Health and Safety Executive (HSE) as to the advisability or otherwise of the location of the installation. HSE will then advise on the residual risk that still remains when all reasonably practicable steps have been taken to ensure safety. HSE's role is purely advisory: it is for the HSA to take into account other economic or social factors that should be considered. If the consent is granted, HSE notifies to the local planning authority, a consultation zone around the installation within which it must be consulted on any further proposals for development such as housing, shops, schools, hospitals and the like.

The Planning (Hazardous Substances) Regulations 1992[97] implement the Planning (Hazardous Substances) Act 1990 in England and Wales. Schedule 1 to the 1992 Regulations lists the substances for which consent is required. This list of 71 substances contains all the substances identified in Schedule 1 of the Notification of Installations Handling Hazardous Substances Regulations 1982 as amended[98] and also certain other substances listed in Schedule 3 of the COMAH Regulations, however the threshold levels are not the same in all cases. The 1992 Regulations require persons to apply for a consent from the HSA (usually the local authority) if they propose to have present on their land hazardous substances at or above specified controlled quantities. Any consent granted will identify the hazardous substances, their location on site, and define certain conditions

[96] SI 1999/743.
[97] SI 1992/656.
[98] SI 1982/1357; amended by SI 1996/825 and SI 2002/2979.

of use such as maximum size, temperature and pressure of storage vessels. There is a public register containing full details of applications, consents and conditions etc.

The second mechanism for controlling risks around hazardous installations is the siting of other developments. All applications for planning permission beyond a certain size are required to be notified to HSE by the local planning authority for advice as to their suitability in the vicinity of a major hazard site. This is required by the Town and Country Planning (General Development Procedure) Order 1995, Article 10(d) and (zb). As noted above, HSE advises on the basis of the residual risk that remains after all reasonably practicable steps have been taken to ensure safety in compliance with HSWA. Again, HSE's role is purely advisory: it is for the local planning authority to take into account other economic or social factors that should be considered.

8–049   COMAH applies mainly to the chemical industry, but also to some storage activities, explosives and nuclear sites, and other industries where threshold quantities of dangerous substances identified in the Regulations are kept or used. The COMAH Regulations are enforced by a "Competent Authority (CA)", which consists of both the Health & Safety Executive and the Environment Agency. COMAH establishments are graded by the Competent Authority as either "Top-Tier" or "Lower-Tier", dependent on the quantities and types of substances they produce and/or store. Regulation 5 of COMAH requires lower-tier operators to prepare a document setting out their policy for preventing major accidents (a major accident prevention policy or MAPP.[99]) Top-tier operators have to also comply with the requirement for a MAPP, except that they do not have to prepare a separate document—their safety reports have to include the information that lower-tier operators provide in their MAPPs. A safety report is a document prepared by the site operator and provides information to demonstrate to the CA that all measures necessary for the prevention and mitigation of major accidents have been taken. The purposes and contents of a safety report are set out in Schedule 4 to the COMAH Regulations. Top-tier operators must prepare an emergency plan to deal with the on-site consequences of a major accident.

The local authority has to prepare an off-site emergency plan which specifies the co-ordinated response of partner agencies to an emergency which has any off-site effects. There is also a requirement for the local authorities to review and update the adequacy and effectiveness of the components of these plans and how they dovetail together. Local autho-

---

[99] The MAPP will usually be a short and simple document setting down what is to be achieved, but it should also include a summary and further references to the safety management system that will be used to put the policy into action. The detail will be contained in other documentation relating to the establishment, e.g. plant operating procedures, training records, job descriptions, audit reports, to which the MAPP can refer. The MAPP also has to address issues relating to the safety management system.

rities play a key role by preparing, reviewing, revising and testing "on" and "off-site" plans. Some of the testing involves the actual response of the resources and personnel from the emergency services as if the exercise scenario was a real incident, whilst others take the form of simulations without the need for the deployment of actual resources. In every case a full de-brief takes place and any lessons learned are put into the revised plans. Enforcement of COMAH is the responsibility of the CA. Enforcement of the Planning (Hazardous Substances) Act 1990 and its Regulations 1992 are the responsibility of the appropriate HSA.

Incidents like Buncefield have highlighted deficiencies in the containment measures at existing sites and the harm these incidents can cause; and also the importance of the different departments and agencies working closely together. In December 2005, a number of explosions occurred at the Buncefield Oil Storage Depot, Hertfordshire. A fire burned for several days, destroying part of the site and emitting clouds of black smoke into the atmosphere. Since the incident, the Competent Authority (the Environment Agency and the Health and Safety Executive in England and Wales and the Scottish Environment Protection Agency in Scotland) have reviewed all similar COMAH sites across the UK and revised the COMAH Containment Policy. This policy is a response to recommendations made by the Buncefield Major Incident Investigation Board in their Design and Operations report, published in March 2007, and the Competent Authority Report on the Findings of the Oil/Fuel Depot Safety and Environmental Reviews.[100] The new policy reflects the comments made by both industry, the general public and other interested parties. The policy takes a risk based approach, which means that:

(i) the Environment Agency expects the highest standards where risks to people and environment are greatest;
(ii) it will be site specific, depending on the hazards of the substances present;
(iii) it takes into account the situation, community and environment where sites are located; and
(iv) the measures will be implemented according to hazard and risk as soon as reasonably practicable.

This policy applies to oil and fuel storage installations across Britain covered by the COMAH Regulations.

Statutory and Other Consultees

Many statutory procedures require that prior to a decision being taken there shall be consultation with certain specified bodies. Some of these are **8–050**

---

[100] See: *http://www.environment-agency.gov.uk/commondata/acrobat/comahsafety__1769905.pdf.*

statutory consultees on account of their responsibilities for aspects of the environment or public health (and safety). No special procedural advantages beyond the right to be consulted and to express a view are afforded to such environmental interests.

Of particular note are the consultation requirements with the following consultees:

(1) the Health and Safety Executive: on any proposed development on land which lies within an area which the HSE has notified to the local planning authority because of the presence in the vicinity of toxic, highly reactive, explosive or inflammable substances, and which involves the provision of:

    (i) residential accommodation;
    (ii) more than 250 metres of retail floorspace;
    (iii) more than 500 metres of office floorspace; or
    (iv) more than 750 metres of floorspace to be used for an industrial process;[101]

or which is otherwise likely to result in a material increase in the number of persons working within or visiting the notified area;

(2) the Environment Agency: on development involving mining operations, works or operations in the bed of or on the banks of a river or stream, development for refining or storing mineral oils and their derivatives, development involving deposit of refuse or waste, development relating to sewage or waste treatment retention or disposal, development relating to use of land as a cemetery and development for the purposes of fish farming and development in flood-risk areas;[102] [103]

(3) the relevant waste regulation authority: on development within 250 metres of land which has been used for the deposit of waste or refuse within the previous 30 years, and in respect of which the waste regulation authority notifies the planning authority that it wishes to be consulted;[104]

(4) the Nature Conservancy Council or the Countryside Council for Wales: on development in or likely to affect a site of special scientific interest (an "SSSI"), or development within an area notified to the local authority by the relevant Council which lies within 2 kilometres of an SSSI; and[105]

(5) Defra or the Secretary of State for Wales: on development not for agricultural purposes and not in accordance with the development

[101] The Town and Country Planning (General Development Procedure Order) 1995 (GDPO) (SI 1995/419) art.10(d).
[102] See PPS25.
[103] GDPO, 10(p) to (t) and (y).
[104] GDPO, art.10(x).
[105] GDPO, art.10(u).

plan which will involve or lead to a loss of 20 hectares or more of grade 1, 2 or 3a agricultural land.[106]

The General Permitted Development Order and the Use Classes Order

As indicated earlier, section 57(1) of the TCPA provides that planning **8–051** permission is required for the carrying out of any "development" of land. A development may have the benefit of planning permission in three main ways: by development order without the need for any application to be made; by a deemed grant of planning permission; or as a result of an express (and successful) application for planning permission made to the local planning authority.

The TCPA empowers the Secretary of State[107] to issue development orders and directions relating to planning control. These can include orders and directions granting planning permission generally, or deeming planning permission to exist, in relation to specified categories of development. The best known and most extensive of these are the two orders known as the General Permitted Development Order (the GPDO) and the Use Classes Order (the UCO).

The General Permitted Development Order

The Town and Country Planning (General Permitted Development) **8–052** Order 1995[108] (GPDO) grants permission for development falling within the various categories set out in the Order subject to conditions set out in relation to each type of development. By way of example, the GPDO grants permission to enlarge, improve or otherwise alter a dwelling house, subject to certain conditions and limitations. It permits certain changes of use. It allows temporary use of land for any purpose ("temporary" generally meaning not more than 28 days, with a maximum of 14 days in certain cases). It permits the extension or alteration of an industrial building or warehouse, within certain limitations and subject to conditions.

This general permitted planning permission can be withdrawn by a direction, by the Secretary of State or the appropriate local planning authority, made under Article 4 of the GPDO, and which can be related either to a particular site or to a locality. Where such an Article 4 direction has been made, its effect is to require an application for planning permission to be made for the development specified in the direction, which, if

---

[106] GDPO, art.10(w).
[107] TCPA, ss.58–60 and 74(1).
[108] SI 1995/418. It replaced and re-enacted with amendments part of the GDO/988 which was then repealed.

development were to take place elsewhere, would not be required. The normal rights of the GPDO can also be limited by conditions attached to a planning permission or by a planning agreement or undertaking. One should not therefore automatically assume that the rights exist, and the position needs to be checked in each case. In most circumstances, where it applies, the GPDO authorises the development which it describes, without any reference to the planning authority being required. There are, however, a number of contexts in which, before exercising the GPDO rights, a person must give notice to the planning authority, to give it the opportunity to make an Article 4 direction requiring that an application for express planning permission should be made.

The Use Classes Order

8–053   The Town and Country Planning (Use Classes) Order 1987[109] (UCO), as amended,[110] deems specified changes of use of land not to be "material" changes of use, and so not to require planning permission. The rights to change use under the UCO cannot be removed either generally or in relation to specific localities or sites by direction (by contrast with the GPDO) although revisions, amendments or revocation of the UCO may be made by the Secretary of State by order, i.e. in the same way as the UCO itself was made.[111] However UCO rights can be excluded or modified by conditions attached to an individual planning permission or by the terms of a planning agreement or undertaking. The UCO enables changes of use to take place between uses within the same class of the UCO (the GPDO, in specific limited circumstances, grants permitted development rights for change between uses in certain different classes) without the need for express planning permission. For example, Class B1 includes (a) office use, (b) research and development use, and (c) industrial use—provided that in each case the use can be carried out in any residential area without detriment to the amenity of that area by reason of noise, vibration, smell, fumes, smoke, soot, ash, dust or grit. Industrial use falling within that type is colloquially known as "light industrial use". Clearly, these forms of development could have wholly different impacts on the environment in terms of traffic, water requirements (both intake and discharge), power and heat requirements, noise and discharges to the atmosphere.

The UCO does not authorise any physical operations: only a change of use. However, works which affect only the interior of a building or which do not materially affect the external appearance (save works underground) are expressly excluded from the definition of development, and so do not

---

[109] SI 1987/764.
[110] In particular by the Town and Country Planning (Use Classes) (Amendment) Order 1995 (SI 1995/297), which added to the "development" which can be undertaken without first gaining planning consent and by the Amendment Order 2005 (SI 2005/84).
[111] Under s.55(2)(f) of the TCPA.

require planning permission in any event.[112] It is therefore normally possible for substantial physical adaptation to premises to take place for the purpose of a change of use, without planning permission being required.

As a matter of planning law, a use includes all ancillary uses. This has been accepted in numerous court decisions.[113] Thus, permission to use a building as an office would include permission to park the cars of the office workers and genuine visitors within the curtilage around it. The right to use a building as a factory would include the right to store outside it and within the curtilage of the premises materials used or produced in the factory. These ancillary uses may be controlled by, for example, planning conditions, but in the absence of express restrictions, no genuinely ancillary uses will breach planning control, regardless of their environmental consequences.

The rationale for the UCO grouping is: (a) that the uses contained   8–054
within them are similar in planning terms; and (b) that the flexibility to change from one class to another on the basis that new class is more acceptable in planning terms. The flexibility affected by the UCO and the GPDO reduces the number of planning applications which would otherwise fall to be determined by the local planning authority.

Applications for Planning Permission

The procedure for making applications for planning permission and sub-   8–055
sequent appeals is contained in a mixture of statute,[114] secondary legislation[115] and central Government guidance.[116] The Standard Planning Application Form (1APP) was introduced by Communities and Local Government and the Welsh Assembly Government from October 1, 2008, to replace all existing types of planning application forms (except minerals) within England and Wales.[117] There are broadly two types of planning

---

[112] s.55(2)(a); but note the Planning (Listed Building and Conservation Areas) Act 1990, which prohibits works (including interior works) for demolition, alteration or extension to any listed building which would affect its character as a building or its special architectural or historic interest, unless those works are authorised.

[113] See e.g. *Vickers Armstrong Ltd v Central Land Board* (1958) 9 P & CR 33; *G. Percy Trentham Ltd v Gloucestershire County Council* [1966] 1 W.L.R. 506; *Brazil Concrete Ltd v Amersham Rural District* (1967) 18 P & CR 396.

[114] Part III of the TCPA.

[115] The main procedural provisions are set out in the GPDO; Town and Country Planning (Fees for Applications and Deemed Applications) Regulations 1989, SI 1989/193, as amended; Town and Country Planning (Applications) Regulations 1988, SI 1988/1912; Town and Country Planning (Inquiries Procedure) Rules 1992, SI 1992/2039, as amended.

[116] Circulars 04/08; 02/08; 03/07; 02/06; 01/06; 08/05; 03/05; 05/00; 10/97; 11/95; 15/92 etc.

[117] Previously, local planning authorities produced their own planning application forms, which often differed from one another and were inconsistent in the information they asked for from applicants.

application: (i) for outline planning permission and (ii) for full planning permission.

Outline permission is available only in relation to building operations, e.g. erection of a building. An outline application enables the applicant to ask the planning authority to determine the principle of the development, while reserving for later approval all or any of specified "reserved matters", which are the layout, scale, appearance, access and landscaping. The grant of outline planning permission constitutes the planning permission. The subsequent approval of details on the matters reserved in the outline planning permission is not technically the grant of permission but simply approval of details. Depending on the terms of the permission and the wording of any conditions that have been imposed generally, the grant of outline permission will not put the developer in a position where he may proceed with construction or preparatory work. It is usual in practice for the conditions attached to the permission to require that key details be approved by the local planning authority before development can begin.

A consequence of the outline permission being the grant of planning permission is that it is not open to a planning authority when approving reserved matters to derogate from that grant (except on payment of compensation). If the planning authority has for any reason failed to impose a planning condition at the outline stage relevant to what has been approved (as opposed to any reserved matters), then it will be too late for it to do so at the detailed stage. An application for full planning permission does not ask for matters to be reserved for subsequent approval, although in practice this sometimes happens, as where the planning authority imposes conditions requiring the subsequent approval of certain details of the scheme. For a discussion of environmental impact assessment in the context of outline planning permission and reserved matters approval see Chapter 9 below.

8-056   Planning applications should be determined within a prescribed period, although it is not unusual for planning authorities to request and receive extensions of time from the applicant.[118] The prescribed period is eight weeks from the time of receipt of a valid application and fee by the local planning authority,[119] extended to 16 weeks from receipt of those papers and the environmental statement where one is required.[120] These periods may be extended by agreement with the applicant.[121] Applications may still be considered outside those periods, and valid permissions granted by the local planning authority. An applicant's remedy, if a decision is not made within the prescribed period, is his/her option to treat that non-determination as a refusal (usually called a deemed refusal), and to submit

---

[118]   TCPA, s.78(2).
[119]   art.23, GPDO.
[120]   Town and Country Planning (Environmental Impact Assessment) Regulations 1999 (SI 1999/293), as amended.
[121]   art.23, GPDO.

an appeal to the Secretary of State.[122] However, section 50 of the Planning and Compulsory Purchase Act 2004 inserts a new section 78A into the Town and Country Planning Act 1990, which allows a short period of dual jurisdiction between the Secretary of State and the local planning authority where an appeal has been made against non-determination of a planning application by that authority. This provision applies where an applicant appeals to the Secretary of State on the ground that the local planning authority has not determined his planning application within the pre-scribed period (eight weeks). Once an appeal has been made, jurisdiction to decide whether to grant planning permission passes to the Secretary of State. The local planning authority cannot determine the application, even in circumstances where the local planning authority would have been in a position to do so shortly after the prescribed period. The purpose of this new section is to allow an additional period of time in which the local planning authority could still issue its decision even though an appeal has been lodged. In such cases the appeal will progress under the usual pro-cedures—for example if the local planning authority refuses planning permission, then the appeal (against non-determination) would become an appeal against refusal. If the local planning authority grants permission, the appellant may withdraw the appeal, proceed with the appeal or revise the grounds of appeal.

Every application for planning permission must be accompanied by a certificate either confirming that no-one other than the applicant is an owner of the relevant land, or confirming that notice of the application has been served on every person other than the applicant who is an owner[123] of the land, or confirming that an advertisement of the application has been put in the local press, where it has not been possible to trace all owners.[124] Similarly, every applicant must certify whether or not there is an agri-cultural tenancy on all or any part of the land and, if so, he must serve notice of the application on every agricultural tenant.[125] Those served with notices are given a period of 21 days from the date the notice was served in which to submit comments to the local authority. Submission of comments within that period gives certain limited procedural rights. As a matter of practice local authorities will almost certainly take into account repre-sentations made outside the statutory period, so long as they are received before the authority considers the application.

All planning applications are also publicised by the local planning authority.[126] At the discretion of the authority, this can take the form either

---

[122] s.78 of the TCPA.
[123] Owner is defined as "a person who for the time being is (a) the estate owner in respect of the fee simple in the land, or (b) entitled to a tenancy of the land granted or extended for a term of years certain of which not less than 7 years remain unexpired". TCPA, s.65(8).
[124] TCPA, s.65 and GPDO arts 12 and 12A (substituted by SI 1992/1493).
[125] TCPA, s.5 and GPDO arts 12 and 12A.
[126] TCPA, s.65 and GPDO, art.12B (substituted by SI 1992/1493).

of a site notice or of notification to neighbours, save for an application accompanied by an environmental statement, or one which does not accord with the development plan, or which affects a right of way, in which cases the local authority must publicise the application by posting a site notice and by local advertisement. Local advertisement is also required for any major development, i.e. minerals workings or deposit, waste development, or development of more than 10 dwellings, or more than 1000 square metres floorspace or with a site area of more than one hectare (0.5 hectares if residential). The legal definition of neighbours for this purpose is somewhat limited and, broadly, involves only those whose land actually adjoins the application site. In practice, planning authorities often choose to notify applications more widely. There is no statutory obligation to publicise changes to applications or the submission of details pursuant to conditions, although as a matter of practice authorities do so where they think it desirable. However, where this discretion is not exercised quite significant alterations may be made that may adversely affect neighbours, without their being aware of them.

8–057   Guidance and advice on the scheme for publicity is set out in Circular 15/92. There are additional requirements for publicity in special cases such as applications for planning permission which affect the setting of a listed building or which fall within a conservation area.[127]

On receipt of the planning application, the local planning authority is statutorily obliged to consult various public bodies on the application depending on the description of development,[128] for example, the local highway authority for development involving a new or altered access to a highway (other than a trunk road), or the Environment Agency for development involving the deposit of waste or refuse or if the development proposed is in a flood-risk area. It is the normal practice of most local authority planning departments to circulate details of applications to other departments of the same local authority who may wish to make observations on it. The planning authority may not determine the planning application until at least 14 days after the statutory consultees have been notified,[129] and it is obliged to take into account any representations made by these consultees.[130]

There is no obligation on applicants to supply details of their application to third parties, save that an applicant (or appellant) who has submitted an environmental statement must ensure that a reasonable number of copies are available, for which a reasonable charge may be made. Details of planning applications are placed on a public register at the local authority's

[127] ss.67, 73 of the Planning (Listed Buildings and Conservation Areas) Act 1990 and DoE Circular 8/87.
[128] GPDO, art.18(1).
[129] GPDO, art.18(4).
[130] GPDO, art.18(5).

offices and the contents of that register are open to inspection by members of the public.[131]

Some local authorities delegate decisions on certain types of planning application to the chief planning officer. Normally, however, the planning officer will prepare a report to the authority's planning committee which will determine the application. It can approve the application, with or without conditions; refuse the application, in which case it must give reasons for doing so; defer consideration, for example if it requires further information; or resolve that it will grant planning permission subject to completion of a planning agreement or subject to some other matter. **8–058**

It is worth noting that the Crown is no longer immune from planning law as from June 7, 2006.[132] The Crown has to apply for planning permission from the relevant local planning authority just like any other developer. The Crown is also subject to the same rights of appeal.

When it comes to the role of environmental issues in dealing with planning applications, environmental impact is simply one of a number of relevant considerations to be taken into account, and that the weight to be afforded to it as a relevant consideration is a matter for the planning authority (having regard to guidance in national, regional and local strategic planning documents). It is the duty of a local planning authority to take into account all material considerations, which certainly include environmental issues, before coming to a final decision on a planning application. Section 70 of the TCPA requires the local authority to have regard to all material considerations;[133] no further guidance is given in the TCPA as to what constitutes a "material consideration" but the issue has been considered by the courts of numerous occasions. It is normally interpreted broadly: thus in *Stinger v Minster of Housing and Local Government*:

"... any consideration which relates to the use and development of land is capable of being a planning consideration. Whether a particular consideration falling within that broad category is material in any given case will depend on the circumstances."[134]

There is no right for third parties to appeal in respect of the grant of planning permission or of conditions attached to it. Third parties can only

---

[131] TCPA, s.69.
[132] See Planning and Compulsory Purchase Act 2004 and The Town and Country Planning (Application of Subordinate Legislation to the Crown) Order 2006 (SI 2006/1286). The changes include a revision to application procedures, a new use class for secure residential accommodation (prisons etc.) and a change to the General Permitted Development Order, which gives the Crown a new set of permitted development rights similar to those enjoyed by local authorities and relevant statutory undertakers. There are also special provisions for emergencies and national security development.
[133] ss.77 and 79 of the TCPA apply that section to decisions by or on behalf of the Secretary of State on decisions that are subject to call-in and appeal respectively.
[134] [1971] 1 All E.R. 65 at 77, per Cooke J.

challenge the grant of planning permission by way of an application for judicial review, for which leave must be obtained, and hence only on the limited grounds available in such proceedings.[135] Even where such grounds can be substantiated, which is comparatively rare, the court has discretion whether or not to quash the decision and, for example, might choose not to do so if it decided that the error of law or procedural defect was not material. Anyone wishing to challenge a planning decision in the courts in this way must act with great promptness and apply to the High Court under RSC Order 53 as soon as possible and in any event within three months, for leave to challenge the decision. The need for prompt action cannot be overestimated and the courts will readily refuse an application for leave to challenge, or later exercise their discretion not to quash a planning decision, unless an applicant takes immediate action.

Call-in of Applications

8–059   Section 77 of the TCPA gives the Secretary of State power exercisable by direction to call-in applications for her own decision, thereby removing jurisdiction from the local planning authority to herself. Such directions are rare and used mainly where planning issues of more than local importance arise. The calling-in of an application is normally the result of representations by interested parties or following notification to the Secretary of State by the relevant local planning authority. The main criteria and procedures for the calling-in of an application are set out in the Town and Country Planning (Development Plans and Consultation) (Departures) Directions 1999 (reproduced at Annex 1 of Circular 07/99). Local planning authorities are required to notify the Secretary of State of any application not in accordance with the development plan, which they do not propose to refuse and which involves:

(i)   more than 150 houses or flats;
(ii) more than 5,000 square metres of gross retail, leisure, office or mixed commercial floorspace;
(iii) development of land belonging to a planning authority or any other party, or for the development of any land by such an authority, whether alone or jointly with any other person; or
(iv) any other development which, by reason of its scale or nature or the location of the land, would significantly prejudice the implementation of the development plan's policies and proposals.

The other notification requirements are set out in the Town and Country Planning (Shopping Development) (England and Wales) (No.2) Direction 1993 whereby local authorities must notify the Secretary of State of any

---

[135] An error of law, procedural impropriety or manifest unreasonableness.

applications in relation to development involving more than 20,000 square metres gross shopping floorspace, whether or not it is consistent with the development plan, or lesser amounts which would exceed 20,000 square metres when aggregated with other shopping floorspace.

When an application is "called-in", this will lead to a public local inquiry being arranged by the Secretary of State before she takes her decision. It is theoretically possible for the application to be considered by way of written representations or at an informal hearing, as with appeals (see below), but if a case is important enough to be called-in, it will in practice be dealt with by public inquiry. Those entitled to appear at such an inquiry are the same as those entitled to be heard at appeals by way of public inquiry.[136]

The Secretary of State can also issue directions under Article 14 of the GPDO restricting the right of a local authority to grant planning permission, either in respect of a particular development proposal or in relation to developments of a specified type or class, either for a specified period or indefinitely. She may, for example, require that before granting permission the local authority must refer the papers to the DCLG so that it can decide whether to call-in the application. If she later decides not to call-in the application it remains with the local planning authority for decision in the usual way.

Appeals

The applicant for planning permission is entitled to appeal to the Secretary   **8–060** of State in respect of the refusal of planning permission, the imposition of conditions on the grant of planning permission, or the failure by the planning authority to determine the application within a period of eight weeks (16 weeks where an environmental statement has been provided) or such extended period as the applicant may have agreed with the planning authority.[137] An appeal should be lodged within six months of the date of the decision notice "or such period as the Secretary of State may allow".[138]

An appeal to the Secretary of State can be dealt with by public local inquiry, by written representations, or by informal hearing. The written representations procedure can be used only if both the planning authority and the applicant so agree; in other words, either can elect not to proceed in this way.[139] An informal hearing takes place where either party (or both)

[136] See further Circular 05/00: Planning appeal procedures (including inquiries into called-in planning applications).

[137] TCPA, s.78. There are no provisions for the owner or a third party to lodge an appeal, hence the significance of legal challenges under s.288 TCPA 1990 (a High Court Challenge) or by judicial review.

[138] art.23 Town and Country Planning (General Development Procedure) Order (GDPO) 1995.

[139] The right to a hearing for the appellant or local planning authority is conferred by s.79(2) of the TCPA, or Sch.6, para.2(4) for called-in applications.

elects for a public inquiry, but in the opinion of the Secretary of State the issues are relatively straightforward and can be dealt with by informal hearing. Both parties must however agree to a hearing before this procedure can be used. It generally takes the form of a round table discussion chaired by an independent Inspector from the Planning Inspectorate.[140]

The written representations procedure, as its title suggests, involves the exchange of written submissions between the applicant and the planning authority. The planning authority may notify third parties of a written representations appeal, so that they have the opportunity of submitting representations, but whether it does so is a matter entirely within its discretion; many planning authorities do not. Where they do not, third parties have no other right to participate.[141] Any written representations submitted would be considered by the inspector.

8–061   Procedure by public local inquiry is somewhat more elaborate. There are special rules for major inquiries[142] (not considered here), and the following comments deal with the rules for ordinary inquiries.[143] Shortly after the appeal documents are received by the Planning Inspectorate, it will fix a timescale for submission of statements of case. From that time ("the relevant date"), the planning authority has six weeks in which to submit a statement of its case and the appellant nine weeks (i.e. three weeks longer than the planning authority) to submit a statement of its case to the Planning Inspectorate, local planning authority and any other parties indicated by the Inspectorate. The statements must be accompanied by a list of the documents to which reference may be made. The time limits for submission of statements of case are not always observed and in practice sanctions are rarely applied to defaulters.

An inquiry date will be fixed by the Planning Inspectorate, in consultation with the appellants and the planning authority. Normally this will be several months after the appeal documents have been submitted. The actual date for the inquiry should not be later than 20 weeks from the relevant date for appeals to be decided by inspectors (and 22 weeks if

---

[140] The Town and Country Planning (Hearings Procedure) (England) Rules 2000 (SI 2000/1626).

[141] Town and Country Planning (Appeals) (Written Representations Procedure) (England) Regulations 2000, (SI 2000/1628).

[142] See Town and Country Planning (Major Infrastructure Project Inquiry Rules Procedure) (England) Rules 2002 (SI 2002/1223) and Circular 07/05: Planning Inquiries into Major Infrastructure Projects Procedures. Also note the proposals in the Planning Bill regarding major infrastructure projects. See paras 8–007 and 8–023 to 8–026.

[143] See the Town and Country Planning (Inquiries Procedure) Rules 2000, (SI 2000/1624). See the Town and Country Planning (Determination by Inspectors) (Inquiries Procedure) (England) Rules 2000, (SI 2000/1625) and Circular 5/2000. All references to Rules in this section are to these Inquiries Procedure Rules.

decided by the Secretary of State).[144] Either of the main parties will normally be allowed to refuse one date and are entitled to at least, 28 days notice of the inquiry arrangements. Three weeks before the inquiry date, the appellant and the planning authority must serve copies of their evidence on the Planning Inspectorate and on each other. Generally, third parties are not entitled to copies of the statements of case or evidence, although there are limited exceptions in special cases, e.g. owners or agricultural tenants of the site who have made representations to the planning authority in response to a formal notice of the application, or any person from whom the Secretary of State requires a statement of case under Rule 6(6). Where statements of case are to be served, they need to be served four weeks prior to the inquiry.

Inquiries normally proceed in an adversarial manner, with witnesses being called to give evidence and to be cross-examined in turn. Each inquiry is conducted by an independent inspector from the Planning Inspectorate. He will control the procedure and decide who may appear in addition to those who are entitled to do so. The appellant (or applicant for called-in applications) and the local planning authority have the right to appear at an inquiry,[145] to call witnesses to give evidence and to cross-examine other witnesses.[146] The appellant also has the right to give an opening statement and to make the final submissions; the order in which anyone else appears at the inquiry is in the inspector's discretion.[147] It is usual in practice for the local planning authority to be the first party to cross-examine the appellants' witnesses and to follow the appellants in presenting their case. The part other parties play at the inquiry depends upon the category into which they fall:

(i) Statutory parties. Anyone who is an owner or agricultural tenant of the land to which an appeal relates and who responded to the notification within the prescribed 21 day period is a statutory party.[148] As such, they are entitled to appear, to call evidence and to cross-examine other witnesses.[149] The statutory right to appear includes an implied right to be heard and to have representations

---

[144] However, where it is impracticable to fix a date in accordance with this rule, then the date fixed shall be the earliest date after. In addition, unless the Secretary of State agrees a lesser period of notice with the applicant and the local planning authority, she shall give not less than 4 weeks written notice of the date, time and place fixed by her for the holding of an inquiry to every person entitled to appear at the inquiry. See The Town and Country Planning (Inquiries Procedure) (England) Rules 2000, SI 2000/1624.

[145] r.11(1)(a) and (b).

[146] r.15(5).

[147] r.15(4).

[148] s.79(4) of the TCPA applying s.71(2) of the TCPA to appeals. See also the Inquiries Procedure Rules, r.2. and r.15(5).

[149] r.15(5).

properly considered by the Inspector or Secretary of State in coming to a decision.

(ii) Parties entitled to appear under Rule 11(1) if the appeal site is situated in their area. These include county and district councils and other statutory bodies, e.g. an enterprise zone authority, the Broads Authority and a housing action trust. Anyone else has a statutory right to appear at the inquiry who has given notice of a wish to do so in accordance with Rule 6, has been required by the Secretary of State under Rule 6(6) to serve a statement of case, and has done so within the four weeks allowed. All in this category have the right to be heard, to call witnesses, and to have their case considered. They can cross-examine at the Inspector's discretion, which must be exercised fairly, and in particular must take into account the risk of injustice or unfairness. An objector would normally be given the right to cross-examine witnesses who had given evidence contrary to his case, provided his questions are directed to that evidence and are not repetitive, irrelevant or outside the purpose of the statute being considered.

(iii) Other parties. Anyone may attend an inquiry and may listen to all oral evidence, which must be given in public, and may inspect any documentary evidence.[150] They may take part in the inquiry with the permission of the Inspector, but have no right to do so. The Inspector has a discretion whether or not to allow any party to appear, but permission to do so must not be unreasonably withheld.[151]

Anyone entitled or permitted to appear may present their case themselves, or may be represented by counsel, a solicitor or some other person.[152]

8–062 In practice, it is likely that all those who have a legitimate interest in the proposal will be allowed to present their views, even if not entitled as a matter of legal right to appear, although the extent to which they will be allowed to participate, for example in cross-examination, will be a matter for the Inspector. The Inspector will always have in mind that a refusal to allow a person to make representations may provoke a subsequent application for judicial review of the decision for failing to have had regard to a material consideration. He/she will not readily risk this, and as the principal participants will also generally prefer third parties not to have cause to challenge the outcome, inquiries are more likely to allow in time-wasting irrelevant material than to exclude anything pertinent. In any event, anyone may make representations in writing to the Inspector before the end of the inquiry even where the Inspector has refused to hear such evidence

---

[150] TCPA, s.321.
[151] r.11(2).
[152] r.11(3).

orally.[153] Following the close of the inquiry the Inspector will make a formal inspection of the site and surrounding area, but no representations are permissible at that stage.

The determination of all planning appeals (and enforcement notice appeals) is delegated to the Inspector except appeals by statutory undertakers relating to operational land.[154] However the Secretary of State retains the power to direct that she should recover jurisdiction to decide the appeal, and this is in practice done in a small minority of planning appeals (under 10 per cent), which are of particular significance, either in planning terms or politically.[155]

The decision on an appeal determined by an Inspector is given by letter which will normally be available some weeks after the close of the procedure, i.e. inquiry, written representations or informal hearing. In other cases, where the Inspector sends a report to the Secretary of State for determination of the appeal, the Secretary of State will send out the decision letter. Where the decision is that of the Secretary of State the time taken before decision will tend to be rather longer: running to a good many months and in some cases to more than a year.

There is a right of appeal from a decision of the Secretary of State or of a **8–063** planning Inspector on a point of law. The appeal lies to the High Court and must be lodged within six weeks from the decision.[156] Where grounds exist, an application for judicial review may of course be made.[157] For further discussion of judicial review, see Chapter 6 above.

Costs

The normal rule as to costs incurred on a planning inquiry relating to an **8–064** appeal or a called-in application, or to a hearing on an appeal, is that each party must bear its own. However, there are provisions for the Secretary of State, on the application of one party to an inquiry or hearing,[158] to make an order for costs against another party on the basis that the latter's unreasonable conduct has led to additional, unnecessary costs being incurred.[159]

The power to award appeal costs also applies following the late cancel-

---

[153] r.15(12).
[154] Sch.6 of the TCPA and the Town and Country Planning (Determination of Appeals by Appointed Persons) (Prescribed Classes) Regulations 1997 (SI 1997/420) as amended.
[155] See the reference above (para.8–020) to the DCLG guidance issued on October 8, 2008, for Planning Ministers.
[156] TCPA, ss.284, 288.
[157] Though leave to apply will not normally be granted in respect of a point of law which may be the subject of the statutory appeal procedure.
[158] s.250(5) of the Local Government Act 1972 and s.320 and Sch.6 of the TCPA (costs awards at inquiries); s.322 and para.6(5), Sch.6 of the TCPA (costs awards at hearings).
[159] Policy guidance set out in DoE Circular 8/93.

lation of an inquiry or hearing by either of the principal parties.[160] This could apply, for example, if an appellant withdraws an appeal without reasonable cause or if a local authority is forced to concede that a particular objection is not sustainable. There is at the moment no power to award costs in written representation appeals, with the exception of enforcement appeals dealt with by this method and cases in which the appeal is not determined because of the withdrawal of one party during proceedings.

Applications for costs should normally be submitted to the inspector at the inquiry or hearing, and this will not affect the Inspector's appeal decision in any way, for example, the appellant may have his appeal dismissed but be awarded partial costs against the local planning authority or vice versa.

Enforcement

8–065   Enforcement of the planning system is almost entirely in the hands of public authorities. In general, a member of the public or a neighbour is powerless to initiate direct action in the courts to enforce planning control. Breach of planning control is not in itself a criminal act liable to a penalty. It is open to the planning authority to take action in respect of that breach of planning control, but the authority has a broad discretion whether or not to do so. There is extensive policy guidance in PPG 18 (*Enforcing Planning Control*[161]) on the approach which planning authorities should adopt, which emphasises that formal action to enforce planning control should not be taken unless it is essential and unless there is no other means available.

A breach of planning control only becomes an illegal action, giving rise to possible prosecution, when the planning authority has already taken steps in relation to that breach—typically by serving an enforcement notice or breach of condition notice—and when there has been non-compliance by those against whom action has been taken. Although prosecution of the offence is not limited to the local authority, in practical terms it will only be the planning authority which will have the information needed to mount a prosecution.

The regime of enforcement of planning control has been the subject of much disquiet over its technicality and the delays in taking effective action. A number of statutory reforms were introduced by the Planning and Compensation Act 2004, largely implementing recommendations in a Government commissioned review, "the Carnwath Report".[162] The principal means now of enforcing planning control are enforcement notices

---

[160] TCPA, s.322A, DoE Circular 8/93.
[161] Published December 20, 1991.
[162] "Enforcing Planning Control" (HMSO), 1989.

and breach of condition notices. Other remedies are a stop notice or a court order for an injunction, although these remedies are seldom used.

Enforcement notice

An enforcement notice may apply to any breach of planning control.[163] It **8–066** must (i) state the matters which constitute the alleged breach of planning control, where it is sufficient if "it enables any person on whom a copy of the notice is served to know what those matters [i.e. the matters constituting the breach] are"; (ii) state whether the breach is the carrying out of development without permission or the failure to comply with a condition; (iii) specify the steps required to be taken to remedy the breach or any injury to amenity caused by the breach; (iv) specify the date on which the notice is to take effect; (v) specify the period for compliance; (vi) specify the reasons why the authority considers it expedient to issue the notice; (vii) specify the precise boundaries of the land to which the notice relates/ whether by plan or otherwise; and (viii) be accompanied by an explanatory note including a copy of relevant sections of the TCPA, or a summary setting out the rights of appeal and the requirement to submit grounds of appeal.[164] A copy of the enforcement notice must be served not later than 28 days after the date of its issue and not less than 28 days before the date on which it is to take effect. It is important to note that the notice must specify two dates: the date of issue; and the date on which it is to come into effect.

There is no restriction on what an enforcement notice may require in order to achieve its purposes, namely to remedy the breach complained of, provided it is not unreasonable. It may for example demand the discontinuance of any use, the restoration of the land to its condition before the breach took place,[165] or the remedying of any injury to amenity caused by the breach.[166] Other requirements may be the alteration or removal of any buildings or works; the carrying out of any building or other operations; the ceasing of any activity, save to the extent specified in the notice; and (where the breach complained of is demolition) construction of a replacement building.[167]

An appeal may be made to the Secretary of State for the Environment against an enforcement notice by anyone having an interest in the land to which the notice relates, or by anyone occupying the land by virtue of a

---

[163] TCPA, s.172.
[164] TCPA, s.173 and the Town and Country Planning (Enforcement Notices and Appeals) Regulations 2002, (SI 2002/2682), regs (3) and (4).
[165] TCPA, s.173(5)(a).
[166] TCPA, s.173(4)(b).
[167] TCPA, s.173(5) and (6).

licence, whether or not a copy of the notice has been served on them.[168] The appeal may be on one or more of seven statutory grounds:[169]

(i) that planning permission ought to be granted for the breach complained of;

(ii) that the matters alleged have not occurred;

(iii) that the matters alleged do not constitute a breach of planning control;

(iv) that no enforcement action could be taken in respect of any breach caused by the matters complained of at the time the notice was served;[170]

(v) that copies of the notice were not properly served;

(vi) that the steps required by the notice are excessive; and

(vii) that any period specified for compliance is too short.

An appeal must be made to the Secretary of State before the date for compliance specified in the enforcement notice.[171]

8–067 Both the appellant and the local planning authority have a right to be heard at an appeal[172] save where either party fails to comply with certain procedural requirements.[173] That right is exercisable through a public local inquiry.[174] Inquiries procedure is set out in the Town and Country Planning (Enforcement) (Inquiries Procedure) (England) Rules 2002,[175] which are largely similar in operation to the planning appeals inquiries procedure rules. Both parties may agree that the appeal should be dealt with by way of written representations, although in practice an appeal in respect of an enforcement notice is almost invariably heard at a public local inquiry. The operation of the enforcement notice is suspended while the appeal is outstanding, and this can sometimes involve a substantial period of time.

As with decisions on planning applications, there can be no appeal from the decision of the Secretary of State on a contravention notice appeal except on a point of law, and again the appeal must be lodged within six weeks of the decision.[176] In this case however leave of the court to pursue the appeal must first be obtained.

Once the enforcement notice takes effect, there is a period for compliance, which varies from case to case. If an enforcement notice has not been fully complied with at the end of the period for compliance then the

---

[168] TCPA, s.174(1).

[169] TCPA, s.174(2).

[170] Enforcement action in respect of all breaches of planning control is subject to time limits—4 years for operational development and 10 years for change of use.

[171] TCPA, s.174(4).

[172] TCPA, s.175(3).

[173] TCPA, s.176(4).

[174] TCPA, s.320 and Local Government Act 1972, s.250.

[175] SI 2002/2686.

[176] TCPA, ss.285, 289.

owner of the land at that time is in breach of the notice[177] and therefore guilty of an offence.[178] Anyone who has control of or an interest in the land who continues, or permits or causes to continue, any activity which is required by the notice to cease, after the end of the compliance period is also guilty of an offence.[179] Such offences are triable either summarily (where the maximum fine is £50,000) or on indictment (where there is no limit: to any fine that may be imposed).[180] In determining the level of the fine any financial benefit arising from the offence must be taken into account.[181]

Alternatively, the local authority is empowered to enter on to the land, **8–068** take any necessary steps to end the non-compliance and to recover its costs from the owner.[182] However this is usually an unattractive option, not least because of uncertainties on whether costs will in practice be recoverable from the owner.

Compliance with the terms of an enforcement notice does not discharge the notice.[183] Any attempt to resume the use after that use has been discontinued in compliance with a notice will constitute a further contravention. Similarly, where the notice requires the reinstating or restoration of buildings which have been demolished or altered, the enforcement notice is deemed to continue to apply to such reinstated buildings or works.

Breach of condition notice

A breach of condition notice (BCN) does not apply to all breaches of **8–069** planning control but, as the title suggests, only to breaches of conditions or limitations contained in a planning permission.[184] Where it applies, a breach of condition notice is an exceptionally powerful weapon since, unlike enforcement notices, there is no right of appeal to the Secretary of State. A BCN may be served on anyone who is carrying out or has carried out the development or anyone in control of the land, and may require that person (known as "the person responsible") to secure compliance with the conditions specified[185] by the carrying out of specified steps or stopping of specified activities. If this is not done by the end of the period allowed (which must be at least 28 days) then the person responsible is in breach of the notice[186] and liable on summary conviction to a maximum fine of level 3 on the standard scale (currently £1,000) and may also be subject to

---

[177] TCPA, s.179(1).
[178] TCPA, s.179(2).
[179] TCPA, s.179(4) and (5).
[180] TCPA, s.179(8).
[181] TCPA, s.179(9).
[182] TCPA, s.178.
[183] TCPA, s.181(1).
[184] TCPA, s.187A.
[185] TCPA, s.187A(1) and (2).
[186] TCPA, s.187A(9).

continuing fines.[187] There are two statutory defences to prosecution; that the defendant took all reasonable measures to secure compliance with the conditions in the notice[188] or, where the defendant was served with the notice on the ground that he had control over the land, that he no longer has control.[189] The notice will cease to have effect when, after a BCN has been served, the person has complied with the requirements of the notice. However, the fact that the BCN has wholly or partly ceased to have effect does not affect the liability of any person for an offence in respect of previous failure to comply, or to secure compliance with the notice.[190] A challenge to the validity of a BCN, or the local authority's decision to serve it, may be made by way of a judicial review or by defence submissions in the magistrates' court.[191]

Planning contravention notice

8–070   A supplementary remedy for a planning authority is the service of a planning contravention notice.[192] This does not enforce planning control, but it is a formal notice alerting the recipient to the possible breach of planning control (and, hence, the possibility of enforcement action), requiring the recipient to provide information about current and previous activities on the land, and inviting the recipient to come forward with proposals for regularising the alleged breach of planning control. The notice is served on the owner or occupier of land, or any person who has an interest in it, and may also be served on any person carrying out operations on the land or using it for any purposes.[193] Service of the planning contravention notice does not give rise to any penalties in itself, but it is a criminal offence not to respond properly to the notice, by failing either to answer or to comply with any requirement in the notice.[194] It is a separate offence knowingly or recklessly to make a false statement in response.[195] Both offences are triable summarily with a maximum fine at level 3 on the standard scale.

---

[187] TCPA, s.187A(10 and (11).
[188] TCPA, s.187A(ll)(a).
[189] TCPA, s.187A(ll)(b).
[190] TCPA, s.180(1) (2) and (3).
[191] e.g. *East Hampshire DC v SLV Buildings Properties Ltd* [1996] (Lands Tribunal), the company successfully argued before the Magistrates Court that they had not been in breach of a condition in a planning permission which had restricted use of "working machinery" to specified hours, by using a "forklift truck" on the site outside those hours. The Council appealed to the High Court, but the High Court upheld those findings.
[192] TCPA, s.171C.
[193] TCPA, s.171c(1).
[194] TCPA, s.171D.
[195] TCPA, s.171D(8).

Stop notice

A stop notice can only be served where an enforcement notice has already 8–071
been served. It has the advantage of producing an effectively instantaneous
enforcement of planning control, but it has two disadvantages, at least as
regards the planning authority. Firstly, the authority may be liable to pay
compensation where the preceding enforcement notice is quashed, withdrawn or varied (except in consequence of a later grant of planning permission), or where the stop notice itself is withdrawn.[196] The compensation
payable must relate to any loss or damage directly attributable to the
prohibition in the stop notice and includes (by statute[197]) any sum in
breach of contract caused by the taking of action necessary to comply with
the prohibition.[198] Secondly, it is not generally possible to use a stop notice
just to limit a breach (i.e. tame it) as the stop notice stops it completely. In
many instances a planning authority may not wish to stop an activity
completely but simply to control it, and a stop notice is inappropriate for
that.

Procedurally, a stop notice can be served at the same time as an enforcement notice or at any time thereafter but before the enforcement notice
takes effect.[199] The Planning and Compulsory Purchase Act 2004, section
52, provided a new power to local planning authorities, whereby they may
issue temporary stop notices which have effect for up to 28 days. Temporary stop notices take effect immediately, and there is no requirement to
serve an enforcement notice beforehand. However, similar provisions to
those contained in the TCPA exist relating to compensation if activities
prevented by the temporary stop notice are in fact lawful. Temporary stop
notices may not relate to the use of a building as a dwelling house, or an
activity which has been carried out (whether or not continuously) for a
period of four years ending with the day on which the notice is displayed. A
second or subsequent temporary stop notice must not be issued for the
same activity unless the local planning authority has first taken enforcement action in relation to the activity alleged to be a breach of planning
control.

Any person who contravenes the provision of a stop notice is guilty of an
offence and is liable to a fine not exceeding £50,000, or on conviction on
indictment to a fine of an unlimited amount.[200] The only defence available
is that the person was not served with the stop notice and that he did not
know, or could not reasonably be expected to know, of its existence.[201]

---

[196] TCPA, s.186.
[197] TCPA, s.186(4).
[198] See *Graysmark v South Hams District Council* [1989] 03 E.G. 75, for basis of assessment of
compensation.
[199] TCPA, s.183.
[200] TCPA, s.187(1A).
[201] TCPA, s.187(3).

Injunctions

8–072 Section 187B of the TCPA[202] enables the local planning authority, where they consider it expedient for any actual or apprehended breach of planning control to be restrained, to apply to the High Court or County Court for an injunction. An application can be made whether or not the local planning authority have exercised, or propose to exercise, any of their other powers to enforce planning control.[203] Most applications are initiated by Originating Summons in the Queen's Bench Division of the High Court. An injunction may be sought by the local planning authority in the absence of the person against whom it is sought ("ex parte"); or proceedings may take place in which the parties are represented ("inter partes").

Applications to the court for injunctions to enforce planning control are seldom made, partly because the courts are reluctant to intervene, except in a clear-cut case, and partly because an injunction is in any event a discretionary remedy and will not necessarily be granted, even in the face of a flagrant breach of planning control. The grant of injunctions in respect of breaches of planning controls has now been put on a statutory footing, and they are an important addition to other enforcement powers in cases where urgent action is required, for example in circumstances where the continuing breach might cause permanent harm to land. Provision is expressly made for injunctions against unidentified persons, specifically to prevent environmental harm.[204] It is in the court's discretion whether or not an undertaking in damages will be required from the local authority seeking an interlocutory injunction.[205]

Obtaining information

8–073 Quite apart from the constraints of the legal framework, it is frequently a difficult question of fact as to whether there has been a breach of planning control. In relation to changes of use, in particular, it is not every change which involves a breach of planning control but only a "material" change of use. The question whether a use can be carried out in a residential area without significant environmental detriment is necessarily a subjective one. In many cases there may be problems in finding out what exactly is happening on a piece of land, despite various powers available to local authorities to discover the relevant information. These powers include, in

---

[202] Inserted by section 3 of the Planning and Compensation Act 1991. Paragraph 7 of Schedule 3 to the 1991 Act inserted section 44A into the Planning (Listed Buildings and Conservation Areas) Act 1990. This section corresponds to the provisions of section 187B for the purpose of enforcing listed building control.

[203] Similarly, under section 214A of the TCPA, the local planning authority may apply for an injunction to restrain an actual or apprehended offence under section 210 (work on trees in contravention of a tree preservation order) or section 211 (prohibited work on trees in conservation areas).

[204] TCPA, s.187B(3); R.S.C, Ord. 110 inserted by SI 1992/638.

[205] *Kirklees Borough Council v Wickes Building Supplies Limited* [1992] 3 All E.R. 717 (HL).

particular, the new provisions for use of a planning contravention notice; the power to require an occupier or person receiving rent in respect of premises to provide certain information as to ownership and use of land, so as to enable a local authority (or the Secretary of State) to make, issue or serve any order, notice or other document under the TCPA,[206] and the more limited power to obtain particulars of any person's interests in land from any owner, occupier or managing agent, which are required by a local authority for the purpose of carrying out any of its statutory functions.[207]

Local planning authorities (and the Secretary of State) also have the power to gain entry on to any land at all reasonable hours on production of appropriate written authority to investigate any alleged breach of planning control on that or any adjoining land, to establish what action should be taken to remedy the position, or generally in pursuance of the authority's role in the enforcement of planning control.[208] This is in effect a general power to enter on land for the purpose of finding information and may be supported by warrant from a justice of the peace. Compensation is payable by the local authority (or Secretary of State) for damage to any land or chattels. The disclosure of any information as to any manufacturing process or trade secret by anyone exercising this right of entry is a criminal offence (which can be tried summarily or on indictment with a maximum penalty of two years imprisonment and an unlimited fine) save where such disclosure was made for enforcement purposes.

---

[206] TCPA, s.330—the matters on which information may be required are: (a) the recipient's interest in the land; (b) the name and address of anyone else with an interest in the land; (c) the purpose for which the premises are being used; (d) the time that use began; and (e) the name and address of anyone who has used the premises for the existing purpose. Failure to respond or to respond properly are also offences carrying the same scale fine (level 3) on summary convention as under planning contravention notices.

[207] Local Government (Miscellaneous Provisions) Act 1976, s.16—the maximum fine in this case is set at level 5, again on summary conviction.

[208] TCPA, ss.196A, 196B and 196C.

Chapter 9

ENVIRONMENTAL IMPACT ASSESSMENTS

INTRODUCTION, HISTORY AND PURPOSES OF REGIME

The Environmental Assessment procedure was introduced by the Eur- **9–001**
opean Council Directive[1] of June 1985 on the Assessment of the Effects of
Certain Public and Private Projects on the Environment. Its first recital sets
out that:

> "the best environmental policy consists in preventing the creation of
> pollution or nuisances at source, rather than subsequently trying to
> counteract their effects ... [and] affirm[s] the need to take effects on the
> environment into account at the earliest possible stage in all technical
> planning and decision-making processes ..."

The basic philosophy behind the Directive was to ensure that pollution and
environmental harm were addressed at source before development was
done. What it imposed in order to achieve this was a system whereby there
would be a rigorous procedure undertaken by the developer for providing
certain information so that the environmental effects of a project could be
properly assessed before a decision was taken as to whether it should be
allowed.

This Directive was originally implemented in England and Wales, so far
as the planning system is concerned, by the Town and Country Planning
(Assessment of Environmental Effects) Regulations 1988.[2] Other regulations were produced to cover types of activity outside the planning system
but within the scope of the directive such as for afforestation, land drainage
and transport works. The details of these are set out later in this chapter.

On March 3, 1997 the directive was amended by Directive 97/11/EC[3]
which both extended the range of projects to which the directive applied
and amended the procedure. However the objective remained of ensuring
that importance of the predicted effects, and the scope for reducing them,
are properly understood by the public and the relevant competent
authority before it makes its decision.[4]

The procedure involves an initial or screening stage and then three main **9–002**

[1] 85/337/EEC [1985] OJ L175/40.
[2] SI 1988/1199.
[3] [1997] OJ L223/9.
[4] See Circular 2/99 at para.9.

stages. The "screening" assessment of the proposed project is to decide whether it is EIA development[5] and so must be subject to assessment. This is covered below. The three main stages necessary if the project is subject to the process of environmental assessment are as follows:

- First the developer must compile detailed information about the likely main environmental effects. To help this part of the process the developer can require public authorities to provide information and ask the competent authority for their opinion as to what should be included. This information compiled by the developer is known as an "Environmental Statement" (ES).
- The second stage is that the ES must be publicised and input received. Public authorities and the public must be given the opportunity to give their views about the project and the ES.
- The third stage is that all the environmental information which will include the ES and comments and representations on it must be taken into account by the competent authority deciding whether to give consent to the development. The public must be informed of the decision and the main reasons for it.[6]

The revised EIA Directive is implemented by the Town and Country Planning (Environmental Impact Assessment) Regulations 1999[7] (the EIA Regulations). These regulations consolidate and supersede the various previously applicable regulations and are explained by Circular 02/99. A brief overview is provided below.

Hard Edged European Law

9–003   The EIA Regulations impose a hard edged requirement under Regulation 3(2) that planning permission shall not be granted unless the "Environmental Information"[8] has first been considered. The British Courts have from a relatively early stage treated it as mandatory to have full compliance with the EIA Regulations. In *Berkeley v Environment Secretary* (HL)[9] Lord Hoffmann refused to exercise a discretion under section 288 Town and Country Planning Act 1990 not to quash a planning permission granted when there had been a failure to produce an ES. His conclusion was that the directive required a particular procedure to be followed, and that the

---

[5] Defined in regulation 2(1) Town and Country Planning (Environmental Impact Assessment) Regulations 1999.
[6] See Circular 2/99 para.11.
[7] SI 1999/293.
[8] Defined in the EIA Regulations as being the ES, further information and representations made – see 2.23 et seq. below.
[9] [2001] 2 AC 603.

ambit of the discretion not to quash was very narrow when it came to a requirement imposed by an EU directive. He said:

"The Directive requires not merely that the planning authority should have the necessary information, but that it should have been obtained by means of a particular procedure, namely that of an EIA. And an essential element in this procedure is that what the Regulations call the 'environmental statement' by the developer should have been 'made available to the public' and that the public should have been 'given the opportunity to express an opinion' in accordance with article 6.2 of the Directive."[10] [...]

"I doubt whether, consistently with its obligations under European law, the court may exercise that discretion to uphold a planning permission which has been granted contrary to the provisions of the Directive. To do so would seem to conflict with the duty of the court under article 10 (ex article 5) of the EC Treaty to ensure fulfilment of the United Kingdom's obligations under the Treaty."[11]

Direct Effect and Transposition Failure

The ECJ has found that the EIA Directive has direct effect. This has been **9–004** confirmed in *World Wildlife Fund v Bozen*[12] and in *R (Delena Wells) v Secretary of State for Transport, Local Government and the Regions*.[13] The domestic courts have now also accepted that the Directive has direct effect. This was stated to be the case in *R v North Yorkshire County Council Ex. p Brown*[14] and in *Berkeley* above. However it was confirmed in a case where it was a critical part of the reasoning of the decision in *R v Durham CC Ex p. Huddleston*.[15] Huddleston was a case where the UK had failed to transpose the Directive fully in omitting the revival of old mining permissions from the process of environmental impact assessment. On those facts the Court of Appeal held the citizen claiming rights under the directive was entitled to insist that the national courts should disapply national law in so far as this was necessary to comply with the Directive. In *Huddleston* the Court held that the statutory default provision (i.e. deemed grant of permission) was ineffective. This approach of the Court of Appeal was endorsed by the ECJ in *R. (Delena Wells) v Secretary of State for Transport, Local Government and the Regions*.[16]

[10] p.615.
[11] p.616.
[12] [2000] 2 PLR 1.
[13] [2004] 1 CMLR 31.
[14] [1999] 1 PLR 116.
[15] [2000] 1 W.L.R. 1484.
[16] [2004] 1 CMLR 31.

However once it is accepted that a directive is correctly transposed the domestic courts have consistently held that an individual cannot sue for breach of rights under a directive. People's rights are then contained within the Regulations in this case within the EIA Regulations and do not include the right to enforce the directive directly in the national courts. This was held in *R v Hammersmith and Fulham LBC Ex p. CPRE*[17] which followed *Marks and Spencer Plc v Commissioners of Customs and Excise.*[18]

So the scope for challenges to decisions based on direct effect of the EIA Directive will lie in the areas where there is likely to be a realistic argument that the EIA Regulations do not fully transpose the requirements of the EIA Directive. The most obvious example which is covered later in this chapter is in the case of multi-stage consents and in particular whether further environmental statements are required at later stages in multi-stage consents.

Overview of the Regulations

Derivation and Purpose

9–005 As noted above, the original Directive on Environmental Assessment (the Directive)[19] was amended in 1997 by the Directive on the Assessment of the Effects of Certain Public and Private Projects on the Environment.[20] In England and Wales transposition of both directives into domestic legislation was achieved through a series of statutory instruments made under s.2(2) European Communities Act 1972 and, in the case of the main planning regulations discussed here, under s.71A Town & Country Planning Act 1990. Development projects which fall within planning control (i.e. where there is a need for planning permission) are currently subject to the Town & Country Planning (Environmental Impact Assessment) (England and Wales) Regulations 1999 (the EIA Regulations)[21] as amended.[22] An informal consolidation of the various amendments to the EIA Regulations, in so far as they apply within England, was published in July 2008 as an annex to the explanatory memorandum issued in support of the Town & Country Planning (Environmental Impact Assessment) (Amendment) (England) Regulations 2008 ("the EIA Amendment Regulations 2008").[23]

---

[17] [2000] Env. L.R. 565.
[18] [2000] 1 CMLR 256.
[19] Directive 85/337/EEC.
[20] Directive 97/11.
[21] SI 1999/293.
[22] See SI 2000/2867; SI 2006/3295; SI 2008/1556; and SI 2008/2093.
[23] SI 2008/2093.

Various projects which are excluded from planning control are subject to their own special regimes. These cover activities related to forestry,[24] fish-farming,[25] uncultivated land,[26] land drainage,[27] harbour works,[28] electricity works,[29] pipeline works,[30] gas transporter pipelines,[31] off-shore petroleum works,[32] nuclear reactor decommissioning works,[33] transport and works projects,[34] highways works,[35] and the Channel Tunnel Rail Link.[36] The details of these regulations are not discussed here.

The EIA Regulations revoked and replaced the Town & Country Planning (Assessment of Environmental Effects) Regulations 1988[37] in relation to planning applications received on or after March 14, 1999. The EIA Regulations have been amended by the Town & Country Planning (Environmental Impact Assessment) (England and Wales) (Amendment) Regulations 2000[38] in relation to applications falling within the special regime controlling the registration of old mining permissions. The EIA Regulations have also been amended by the Town & Country Planning (Environmental Impact Assessment) (Amendment) Regulations 2006[39] in relation to the procedures for submitting environmental information and other minor modifications.[40] Further amendments in relation to old mining permissions were made by the Town & Country Planning (Environmental Impact Assessment) (Minerals Permissions and Amendment) (England) Regulations 2008.[41] Additional amendments to extend the scope of EIA to the later stages of a multi-stage consent (i.e. where a planning permission imposes conditions requiring further details to be approved before any or some part of the development can begin) were introduced by the EIA Amendment Regulations 2008.[42] These amendments were introduced as a result of the European Court finding that the EIA Regulations had failed to fully transpose the Directive.

The purpose of the EIA Regulations is to provide a regulatory framework **9–006** to fulfil the requirement of Article 2(1) of the Directive (as amended) that:

[24] SI 1999/2228.
[25] SI 1999/367.
[26] SI 2001/3966.
[27] SI 1999/1783.
[28] SI 1999/3445.
[29] SI 2000/1927.
[30] SI 2000/1928.
[31] SI 1999/1672.
[32] SI 1999/360.
[33] SI 1999/2892.
[34] SI 2000/3199.
[35] SI 1999/369.
[36] SI 1999/107.
[37] SI 1988/1199.
[38] SI 2000/2867.
[39] SI 2006/3295.
[40] See Part 4 below.
[41] SI 2008/1556.
[42] SI 2008/2093; discussed in section 3 below.

"Member States shall adopt all measures necessary to ensure that before consent is given projects likely to have significant effects on the environment by virtue, inter alia, of their nature, size or location are made subject to a requirement for development consent and an assessment with regard to their effects. These projects are defined in Article 4."

Under Article 4 of the Directive (as amended) all projects listed in Annex I must be subject to an assessment of their effects on the environment. For projects listed in Annex II, Article 4 provides that Member States must determine, either by case-by-case examination or by thresholds or criteria set by the Member State (having regard to the selection criteria in Annex III), whether these projects should be made subject to an assessment of their effects on the environment.

The EIA Regulations achieve this requirement by identifying in Schedule 1 certain projects which (unless they involve exempt development)[43] must always be subject to environmental impact assessment (EIA) and in Schedule 2 projects which (unless they involve exempt development) may require EIA depending on the application of specified criteria.

Schedule 1 Development

9–007 All development (other than exempt development) listed in Schedule 1 is defined as "Schedule 1 development" and all Schedule 1 development is defined as "EIA development".[44] Schedule 1 sets out 21 different descriptions of types of development. These cover various forms of energy generation and distribution, particular industrial processes, transport infrastructure projects, water treatment and management, waste treatment and disposal, intensive pig and poultry rearing, the storage of petroleum and chemical products, and changes to Schedule 1 developments.

The descriptions reflect the categories in Annex I of the Directive (as amended) save that the EIA Regulations do not include the construction of 200kV overhead electrical power lines, which are within Annex I, because they are subject to separate regulatory control. The descriptions relate not only to types of development but also in most cases include some requirement as to scale. These are minimum thresholds for inclusion as Schedule 1 development, with smaller scale development of the same type falling to be considered instead under Schedule 2 of the EIA Regulations.

The thresholds in Schedule 1 are variously expressed by site size (for example 25 hectares in the case of quarries and open-cast mining), by

---

[43] "Exempt development" is defined by reg.2(1) of the EIA Regulations (as amended by SI 2006/3295) as development which is the subject of a direction by the Secretary of State under reg.4(4). Development for national defence purposes is no longer automatically exempt development.
[44] reg.2(1).

absolute capacity (for example 200,000 tonnes for petroleum storage installations), by daily output (for example 500,000 cubic metres in the case of natural gas extraction), or by annual output (for example 10 million cubic metres in the case of water abstraction).

As all Schedule 1 development is EIA development, it must be subject to **9–008** EIA prior to the grant of planning permission.[45] This is irrespective of the location of the development and irrespective of whether there is in fact likely to be any effects on the environment. The application of Schedule 1 is therefore a fairly straight-forward exercise.

Changes or extensions to an existing or approved Schedule 1 development will also be Schedule 1 development in their own right if by reference to the scale of the change or extension alone they satisfy Schedule 1.[46] Changes or extensions to a Schedule 1 development which are of a lesser scale are addressed by Schedule 2.[47]

Schedule 2 Development

Development (other than exempt development) listed in Schedule 2 is **9–009** defined as "Schedule 2 development" only if it falls within a description in Column 1 of Schedule 2 and either it (or any part of it) is in a defined sensitive area or it exceeds or meets respectively any applicable threshold or criterion in Column 2 of Schedule 2.[48] Sensitive areas are defined to include Sites of Special Scientific Interest, certain other designated nature conservation sites or areas, Scheduled Ancient Monuments, National Parks, the Broads, World Heritage Sites, Areas of Outstanding Natural Beauty, and European Sites (i.e. Special Protection Areas and Special Areas of Conservation).[49]

Column 1 of Schedule 2 identifies 13 categories of development. The first 12, which reflect 12 of the categories in Annex II of the Directive, are described under the following headings:

   (i) Agriculture and aquaculture;
  (ii) Extractive industry;
 (iii) Energy industry;
 (iv) Production and processing of metals;
  (v) Mineral industry;
 (vi) Chemical industry (unless included in Schedule 1);
 (vii) Food industry;
(viii) Textile, leather, wood and paper industries;

[45] reg.3(2).
[46] para.21 of Sch.1 as inserted by SI 2006/3295.
[47] para.13(a) of Sch.2.
[48] reg.2(1).
[49] reg.2(1).

    (ix) Rubber industry;

    (x) Infrastructure projects;

    (xi) Other projects;

    (xii) Tourism and leisure.

In relation to these 12 categories, Column 1 of Schedule 2 identifies various further sub-categories and Column 2 of Schedule 2 sets out applicable thresholds and criteria. These variously relate to site size, floorspace, operational capacity, or output. These thresholds have, in accordance with the Directive, been determined at national level and are not themselves directly referable to the terms of Annex II of the Directive.

The thirteenth category has no heading but embraces in paragraph 13(a): (i) changes and extensions to Schedule 1 development (other than those which are Schedule 1 development in their own right),[50] and (ii) changes or extensions to development in any of the preceding categories in Schedule 2. In both cases this is only where the change or extension may have significant adverse effects on the environment and the specified thresholds or criteria in Column 2 of paragraph 13 are exceeded or met, as appropriate. The thirteenth category also includes, in paragraph 13(b), development of a description mentioned in Schedule 1 which is undertaken mainly or exclusively for the development and testing of new methods or products and not used for more than two years. If the development satisfies the applicable scale thresholds in Schedule 1 then on a literal interpretation of Regulation 2(1) of the EIA Regulations it will be Schedule 1 development in any event. This suggests that the scope of paragraph 13(b) is limited to development where, despite being a type of development described in Schedule 1, its temporary nature means that the thresholds are not exceeded so that it is not in fact Schedule 1 development. In such a case it will fall within paragraph 13(b) of Schedule 2.

9–010   However, if reference is made to the equivalent provision in paragraph 13 of Annex II of the Directive, this suggests that development which actually is Annex I development will fall into Annex II if it is for testing/development purposes and is only to be used for a limited two year period. In such a case it falls within paragraph 13 of Annex II and by necessary implication is not Annex I development. Since Annex II does not prescribe thresholds or criteria and also only requires EIA where there is a likelihood of significant effects on the environment, this could potentially result in the development not being subject to EIA. This exclusion does not sit easily with Article 4(1) of the Directive, which requires projects listed in Annex I to be subject to EIA (unless they are exempt development), and does not cross-refer to the exclusion in paragraph 13 of Annex II. There is, therefore, a tension between these two parts of the Directive.

Under the EIA Regulations, all development falling within paragraph

[50] para.21 of Sch.1.

13(b) is automatically Schedule 2 development and there are no thresholds or criteria to be applied. The development therefore has to be assessed in every case to determine whether it is likely to have significant effects on the environment. Thus it would appear that the EIA Regulations have been drawn more tightly than the Directive, since the Directive arguably allows what would otherwise be Annex I development to be treated as Annex II development, whereas the EIA Regulations do not allow Schedule 1 development to be treated as Schedule 2 development, even if it is only undertaken for testing purposes for a temporary two year period. The EIA Regulations have therefore more closely followed the requirements of Article 4(1) of the Directive rather than the wording in paragraph 13 of Annex II.

Development which is Schedule 2 development and which is "likely to have significant effects on the environment by virtue of factors such as its nature, size or location" is defined as "EIA development".[51] In determining whether a particular Schedule 2 development is likely to have such effects, the decision maker has to have regard to the selection criteria in Schedule 3 of the EIA Regulations.[52] These criteria relate to the characteristics of the development, the location where it is to take place, and the characteristics of the potential impacts.[53]

Procedure for Dealing with EIA Development

Any application for planning permission for development which is EIA development is defined as an "EIA application". In addition, as a result of the EIA Amendment Regulations 2008, the submission of an application for the approval of details which are required under a planning condition before the whole or part of an approved development can begin is also defined as an "EIA application".[54] Such an application is termed a "subsequent application" and any consent which results from it is termed a "subsequent consent".[55] Regulation 3(2) of the EIA Regulations applies to all EIA applications and (as amended) provides that: 9–011

"The relevant authority or the Secretary of State or an inspector shall not grant planning permission or subsequent consent pursuant to an application to which this regulation applies unless they have first taken the environmental information into consideration and they shall state in their decision that they have done so."

---

[51] reg.2(1).
[52] reg.4(5).
[53] Sch.3 of the EIA Regulations.
[54] reg.3(1)(b) EIA Amendment Regulations 2008; SI 2008/2093.
[55] reg.3(1)(a) SI 2008/2093.

The environmental information which has to be taken into account comprises the Environmental Statement (ES) submitted with the relevant planning application, any further information required by the decision maker or other information subsequently submitted by the applicant and any representations made by those consultees entitled to be consulted or otherwise invited to make representations about the environmental effects of the development.[56]

As discussed below, the EIA Regulations set out "screening" provisions to determine whether a particular development project is EIA development. Where it is EIA development an ES is required. The contents of an ES are discussed in Part 4, together with the "scoping" process which can be used to identify the required content of the ES.

9–012 Once an ES has been submitted, it must be subject to consultation and publicity as set out in Regulations 13 and 14 (where the decision maker is the local planning authority (LPA)) or in Regulation 16 (where the decision maker is the Secretary of State (SoS)). Regulations 17 and 18 make provision for the availability of copies of the ES and charging for copies. Regulation 19 allows the decision maker to require the submission of further information. This provision has been amended by the Town & Country Planning (Environmental Impact Assessment) (Amendment) Regulations 2006[57] to allow developers to submit additional information to supplement an ES on a voluntary basis. This is discussed further below.

The prohibition in Regulation 3(2) of the EIA Regulations ensures that all the relevant environmental information is taken into account by the decision maker before a decision is made on the application for EIA development.

Once the decision has been made the decision maker is required to give publicity to the decision and set out the main reasons and considerations on which the decision was based, together with a description of the main measures to mitigate major adverse environmental impacts.[58] If this duty is not performed the decision is not necessarily invalid, but the decision maker can be required to perform the duty by means of an application for judicial review.[59] However, where there is no proper recording of the main reasons for the decision, the decision maker may find it harder to demonstrate that all of the environmental information was taken into account, and its decision may therefore be susceptible to challenge on this ground.

---

[56] reg.2(1).
[57] SI 2006/3295.
[58] reg.21.
[59] *R(Richardson) v North Yorkshire County Council* [2003] EWCA Civ 1860.

SCREENING PROCEDURES

What is Screening?

Screening is the formal process whereby a planning decision maker, which **9–013** may be the Local Planning Authority (LPA) or the Secretary of State (SoS), decides whether or not the development under consideration is EIA development.[60] If it is, then an Environmental Statement[61] (ES) is required and there is a prohibition[62] on the grant of planning permission without consideration of the ES and other environmental information.[63]

Screening involves an assessment of the development proposal against the criteria in Schedules 1 and 2 of the EIA Regulations[64] to see if it is either Schedule 1 or Schedule 2 development[65] and, in the case of Schedule 2 development, assessment against the further test of whether the proposal is likely to have significant effects on the environment by virtue of factors such as its nature, size or location. In carrying out these assessments decision makers are expected to have regard to relevant advice, including that currently set out in Circular 02/99. In the case of Schedule 2 development they are required to have regard to the selection criteria in Schedule 3 to the extent relevant to the development.[66]

Where a screening decision is made by the LPA it is termed a "screening opinion",[67] and where it is made by the SoS it is termed a "screening direction".[68] However, the issues to be decided are the same in both cases, save that the SoS has wider powers to determine that development is or is not EIA development.[69] The SoS can, for example, direct that development is exempt development and so not subject to EIA.[70] The SoS can also direct that development is EIA development when it falls within a description in Schedule 2 of the EIA Regulations but does not meet any of the relevant thresholds/criteria.[71]

Defects in screening procedures have been a fruitful avenue for judicial review,[72] and even where the challenge is ultimately unsuccessful the delay

---

[60] As defined by reg.2(1).
[61] As defined by reg.2(1).
[62] reg.3(2).
[63] As defined by reg.2(1).
[64] SI 1999/293 as amended in England by SI 2006/3295.
[65] As defined by reg.2(1); see further the discussion in Chapter 3 above.
[66] reg.4(5).
[67] As defined by reg.2(1).
[68] As defined by reg.2(1).
[69] See reg.4(4) and reg.4(8).
[70] reg.4(4).
[71] reg.4(8).
[72] See for example *Berkeley v SSETR* [2001] 2 AC 603; *R(Wells) v SSTLR* [2004] 1 CMLR 31.

and uncertainty caused can be sufficient to frustrate the development proposal.[73]

When is Screening Required?

EIA development—Schedule 1 or Schedule 2?

9–014 If Schedule 1 development is proposed it will always be EIA development and will therefore require the submission of an ES.[74] Invariably, given the nature of projects that fall within Schedule 1,[75] this will be readily apparent to the applicant and an ES will be submitted with (or in advance of) the application. A failure to do so would simply delay the determination of the application whilst an ES is requested.[76] Provided that the ES describes itself as an ES for the purposes of the EIA Regulations, then no screening decision will be required by the LPA because the self-description in the ES automatically makes the development EIA development[77] (unless the self-description is over-ridden by a screening direction made by the SoS).[78] It is in practice difficult to conceive of a type of development that an applicant might reasonably consider falls within Schedule 1 (and so submits an ES which describes itself as an ES for the purposes of the EIA Regulations) but which the SoS takes the view is not even within Schedule 2 and so makes a screening direction that the development is not EIA development.

If Schedule 2 development is proposed, the applicant may choose to take the view that the decision maker is bound to conclude that it is EIA development, and so similarly submit an ES at the outset. If the ES describes itself as an ES for the purposes of the EIA Regulations, the decision maker could and invariably would take that as determinative that the development is EIA development. In such a case no screening decision would be required and the development will be EIA development by reason of the submission of the ES.[79]

In theory, if not often in practice, the decision maker might query whether a development the applicant regards as EIA development and has accompanied by an ES[80] is in fact EIA development. Usually, given the potential for a third party legal challenge on the ground of a failure to require an ES, the decision maker would defer to the applicant's view of the matter. However, in a clear-cut case, the decision maker may take the

---

[73] See for example the Crystal Palace scheme considered in *R v Bromley LBC ex parte Barker* [2006] 3 W.L.R. 1209 and *Commission v UK* [2006] 1 Q.B. 764.
[74] reg.2(1) and reg.3(1).
[75] See Chapter 3 above.
[76] reg.7(2).
[77] reg.4(2)(a).
[78] reg.4(3) and para.1.7 below.
[79] reg.4(2)(b).
[80] Provided that the ES is referred to by the applicant as an ES for the purposes of the EIA regulations.

view that the applicant is simply wrong. In such a case if the decision maker is the LPA it would not be able to make a screening decision,[81] but could apply to the SoS for a screening direction.[82] The SoS would then be in a position to make a screening direction.[83] Such a decision would be determinative and would over-ride the applicant's view of the matter.[84]

Occasionally it may not be clear whether the environmental information submitted with the application is being referred to by the applicant as an ES for the purposes of the EIA Regulations. This may be so even if the information is collated in a document calling itself an ES (but not expressly saying it is an ES for the purposes of the Regulations). Only an ES which describes itself as an ES for the purposes of the EIA Regulations ousts the decision maker's obligation to make a screening decision. In a case where the status of the submitted environmental information is unclear, the LPA may ask the applicant to clarify its status, but if this is not done or the position remains unclear then the LPA must make a screening decision.[85]

9–015

Apart from those cases where an application is accompanied (or preceded) by an ES referred to as an ES for the purposes of the EIA Regulations, the LPA will have to make a screening decision for every application for Schedule 1 or Schedule 2 development to ascertain whether it is or is not EIA development.[86]

It follows that the LPA should, as a matter of good practice,[87] establish an administrative procedure to identify whether each individual application is or is not Schedule 1 or Schedule 2 development. For Schedule 1 developments this will usually be self-evident (assuming that the applicant has not already pre-empted the matter by the submission of an appropriate ES). For Schedule 2 developments this will be determined by reference to the descriptions of development[88] in Schedule 2 coupled with the applicable thresholds and criteria[89] for those descriptions. In many cases the threshold relates to the size of the development, unless[90] the development

---

[81] The submission of an ES which satisfies reg.4(2)(a) is determinative (subject to reg.4(3) and 4(4)) and so removes the LPA's power to make a screening opinion under reg.4(2)(b). However, there is no similar exclusion of the SoS's power to make a screening direction.

[82] reg.4(3) and reg.4(7).

[83] Unlike requests for a screening direction received from the applicant, the EIA Regulations do not impose a duty on the SoS to act on requests from the LPA, but given that the SoS has the power to make a screening direction with or without a request, it is hard to see that the SoS could lawfully ignore a request from the LPA.

[84] reg.4(1) and reg.4(3).

[85] reg.7(1).

[86] This is the practical consequence of the prohibition in reg.3(2) on the determination of EIA applications but it should be noted that there is no requirement to make a screening decision for every application but only those which are for Schedule 2 development.

[87] This is not a requirement of the EIA Regulations as such.

[88] In column 1 of Schedule 2.

[89] In column 2 of Schedule 2.

[90] See definition of Schedule 2 development in reg.2(1).

is located in whole or part in a sensitive area as defined by the EIA Regulations[91].

9-016   In *R(Goodman) v Lewisham LBC*[92] Buxton L.J., relying on the speech of Lord Hoffman in *Berkeley v SoSE*,[93] considered that:

> "The authority is bound to enter upon consideration of whether the application is for Schedule 2 development unless it can be said that no reasonable authority could think that to be the case...".[94]

This suggests a positive duty to consider all applications to see whether they might be Schedule 2 development unless it would be *Wednesbury* unreasonable to think that they might be. This appears to put something of a gloss on the requirements of the EIA Regulations.

Where development is not in a sensitive area[95] and the relevant threshold or criteria for the description of development is not exceeded,[96] the LPA need do no more than assess the application against the relevant threshold or criteria to conclude that it is not Schedule 2 development. Indeed, even if the LPA does not do this, or does so in a way which is deficient, but the objective facts are that the development does not exceed the relevant threshold or criteria, there is no requirement for the LPA to make a screening decision. If the development is not Schedule 2 development there is no requirement to screen it or to adopt a screening opinion.

In *R(Horner) v Lancashire County Council & Castle Cement Ltd*[97] a proposal for a storage silo and ancillary facilities to handle animal waste derived fuel, prior to its burning in a previously approved cement kiln, was granted planning permission. The LPA did not give proper consideration to the question of whether the proposal was Schedule 2 development.[98] However, the objective facts, which did not call for the exercise of any judgment, showed that the development was not Schedule 2 development because for the applicable description of development[99] the relevant threshold was a floorspace which exceeded 1000m^2 and the silo had a floorspace of 1000m^2. The Court of Appeal rejected the argument that the LPA in such circumstances had to adopt an individual evaluation of the proposal and its consequences to determine whether it was EIA development. The CA held that it would undermine the basis of the Regulations and the inclusion of criteria and thresholds if applications had to be indi-

---

[91] reg.2(1).
[92] [2003] EWCA Civ 140.
[93] [2001] 2 AC 603.
[94] para.7.
[95] As defined by reg.2(1).
[96] See columns 1 and 2 of Schedule 2.
[97] [2007] EWCA Civ 784.
[98] At first instance Ouseley J. accepted that the officers had considered the issue but found that if the application was Schedule 2 development their consideration would have been legally deficient. In the CA Auld L.J. proceeded on the basis that the LPA had failed to consider the issue at all.
[99] paras 13 and 5(b) of Schedule 2.

vidually assessed when the relevant criteria or thresholds were not exceeded.[100]

In such circumstances it would be open to the LPA to request the SoS to make a screening direction on a case by case basis that the development was EIA development even though the threshold was not exceeded, but there is no obligation on the LPA to consider this option. If such a request was made, the SoS could determine that the development was EIA development.[101]

9–017

Screening opinions and decisions

Screening decisions can be made at various stages in dealing with an application. A person proposing to carry out development can request a screening opinion from the LPA before or at the time that the application is submitted.[102] The request will need to include a brief description of the nature and purpose of the development and its possible effects on the environment.[103] The LPA can require additional information before adopting a screening opinion,[104] but unless the person making the request agrees an extension of time, the LPA only has 21 days to deal with the request.[105] If the LPA does not make a decision in 21 days (or within any agreed time extension) the person making the request can request the SoS[106] to make a screening direction,[107] even if the LPA has required additional information and this has not been supplied.[108]

9–018

If the LPA adopts a screening opinion to the effect that the development is EIA development, the person making the request can request the SoS to make a screening direction in the hope of a different decision.[109] This could also happen if the LPA decision is that the development is *not* EIA development,[110] but this is only likely where the issue of whether the development is EIA development is unclear and the developer wants a more authoritative determination from the SoS as, perhaps, a better safeguard against potential judicial review challenges. If a developer already considers its proposal is EIA development it is likely that an ES will be submitted with or before the application and no screening opinion will be sought. It follows that, in practice, where the developer has sought a

---

[100] Per Auld L.J. at paras 44–47.
[101] reg.4(8).
[102] reg.5(1).
[103] reg.5(2).
[104] reg.5(3).
[105] reg.5(4).
[106] The request should be made in the first instance to the relevant Government Office (see para.59 of Circular.2/99).
[107] reg.5(6)(a).
[108] reg.5(7).
[109] reg.5(6)(b).
[110] In reliance on the SoS's power in reg.4(7).

screening opinion, then the developer either considers the development is not EIA development or considers the issue is unclear.

There is no appeal against a screening opinion but, as indicated above, the person requesting it can request the SoS to make a screening direction which will over-ride the opinion.[111] Usually that will be a quicker and more effective remedy for that person than judicial review. Other persons interested in the application can also request the SoS to make a screening direction if they are dissatisfied with the LPA's screening opinion.[112] Such a request can be made at any time prior to determination of the substantive application for permission to go ahead with the particular project. Even after the substantive planning decision has been taken there may, however, be a remedy to objectors by way of judicial review, arguing in those proceedings that an erroneous or defective screening opinion has been adopted.[113]

9–019   If a screening direction is sought by a person who requested a screening opinion from the LPA the SoS has 21 days to make the direction but this time limit can be unilaterally extended by the SoS to such period as the SoS reasonably requires.[114] The SoS also has the power to require additional information from either the person making the request or from the LPA before making a screening direction.[115]

There is no appeal against a screening direction but it may be challenged by means of judicial review. A challenge to the screening direction could also be included in a judicial review of a decision to grant planning permission for the development.[116]

If no screening opinion is sought before or in conjunction with the submission of an application, and the application is not accompanied by an ES which is referred to by the applicant as an ES for the purposes of the EIA Regulations, the LPA will have to consider whether the development is for Schedule 1 or Schedule 2 development. If it appears to the LPA that the application is for Schedule 1 or Schedule 2 development, the submission of the application is treated as a request for a screening opinion[117] and the 21 day period in Regulation 5(4) then applies for the LPA to adopt a screening opinion. If the LPA decides that the application is for EIA development it must then require an ES to be submitted.[118] The applicant then has the same right to request a screening direction from the SoS as if a

---

[111] reg.5(6)(b).
[112] There is no express provision for this in the EIA Regulations but it is implicit from the SoS's power to make a screening direction whether or not there has been a request (reg.4(7)).
[113] *R(Catt) Brighton & Hove City Council* [2007] EWCA Civ 298.
[114] reg.6(4).
[115] reg.6(3).
[116] see for example *R(Gillespie) v FSoS* [2003] EWCA Civ 400.
[117] reg.7(1).
[118] reg.7(2).

screening opinion had in fact been requested.[119] If the applicant does not do so and does not write to the LPA within 21 days to indicate that an ES is being provided, then the application is deemed to be refused at the end of the 21 day period and there is no right of appeal.[120] If the applicant indicates that an ES is being provided but does not submit one, the LPA must refuse the application (unless a screening direction is made by the SoS that the development is not EIA development).[121] If the LPA does not adopt a screening opinion in such circumstances, its decision is susceptible to judicial review.

If an application is not the subject of a screening opinion or a screening direction, and is not accompanied by an ES which is referred to by the applicant as an ES for the purposes of the EIA Regulations, and the application is referred to the SoS under one of the "call-in" provisions, then the SoS has to consider whether the application appears to be for Schedule 1 or Schedule 2 development.[122] If it appears to the SoS that the development is Schedule 1 or Schedule 2 development then the referral is treated as a request for a screening direction and the SoS has similar obligations as are placed on the LPA under Regulation 7.[123] If the SoS concludes that the application is for EIA development but no ES is submitted after a requirement has been issued for the same then the SoS must refuse the application.[124]

9–020

If an application is not the subject of a screening opinion or a screening direction and is not accompanied by an ES which is referred to by the applicant as an ES for the purposes of the EIA Regulations, and the application is appealed (either because of non-determination by the LPA or because of the LPA refuses permission), then the SoS has to consider whether the appeal appears to be for Schedule 1 or Schedule 2 development.[125] Initially, this is dealt with administratively by the Planning Inspectorate on behalf of the SoS. If it appears to the SoS that the appeal is for Schedule 1 or Schedule 2 development, then the lodging of the appeal is treated as a request for a screening direction, and the SoS has similar obligations as are placed on the LPA under Regulation 7, with similar restrictions on the grant of permission where there is no ES.[126]

If, in the context of an appeal, the SoS makes a screening direction, that will be determinative of whether the development is or is not EIA development.[127] If there is no screening direction (by implication because it did not appear to the SoS that the development is Schedule 1 or Schedule 2

---

[119] reg.7(4).
[120] reg.7(5).
[121] reg.7(6).
[122] reg.8(1).
[123] reg.8(1).
[124] reg.8(6).
[125] reg.9(1).
[126] regs 9(10) and 9(7).
[127] reg.4(3).

development), but an Inspector questions whether the development may be EIA development, the Inspector must refer that question to the SoS for a screening direction and can only refuse permission if the appeal is determined before a screening direction is received.[128]

Cancelling and varying screening decisions

9–021   Whilst the EIA Regulations provide that a screening direction is determinative, the SoS considers that there is a power for the SoS to cancel or vary a screening direction where there is good reason to do so.[129] There is no express power to this effect but to imply such a power would be consistent with the underlying intention of the EIA Regulations (and the Directive) not only that all EIA development should be the subject of EIA but also that only EIA development should be the subject of EIA. If an initial screening direction was erroneous, or has become overtaken by subsequent events or new information concerning either the development or the receiving environment, then the purpose of the EIA Regulations (and Directive) is better served by allowing the SoS to cancel or vary the direction to reflect this, than by allowing an incorrect or out of date direction to stand. Such an implied power is necessary to avoid a breach of the prohibition in Regulation 3(2) if the initial direction is that the development is not EIA development when as a matter of objective fact it is. The existence of this power was accepted, obiter, by the CA in *Evans v FSoS*.[130]

The SoS recognises that it is open to the LPA to request the cancellation or variation of a screening direction.[131] Logically, there is no reason why an applicant/appellant could not also do so, nor an interested party, nor indeed an Inspector dealing with an appeal. In *Evans v FSoS*, Simon Brown L.J., gave consideration, obiter, to the circumstances when an Inspector might make such a request. He first noted that once a screening direction was made, it was decisive, and the Inspector had no obligation to reconsider the issue. The requirement placed on an Inspector by Regulation 9(2) could not arise whilst the direction stood. However, if the Inspector were to discover during the appeal that the direction was based on an important misapprehension about the development or if material facts come to light which appear to invalidate it, an Inspector should be regarded as having power to invite the SoS to reconsider the direction.

The SoS also takes the view that where the LPA considers that its screening opinion has been superseded by subsequent information, it is open to the LPA to deal with the application as if no screening opinion had

---

[128] reg.9(2).
[129] See para.66 of C.2/99.
[130] [2004] EWCA Civ 1523.
[131] para.66 of C.2/99.

been made.[132] In *R(Fernback) v Harrow LBC*[133] the High Court considered this advice and concluded that since a screening opinion was dependent on a request or a deemed request from the person proposing the development,[134] there was no power unilaterally to adopt a further screening opinion. However, if the initial screening opinion was that the development was not EIA development, the LPA could, if it changed its mind, invoke Regulation 7(2) to require the submission of an ES, provided that it does so within 21 days of the lodging of the application.[135] Thereafter the LPA had no power to require an ES but it would be open to it to request the SoS to make a screening direction which over-rode its opinion. If the initial screening opinion was that the development was EIA development but the LPA subsequently considered this was not the case, it is not open to the LPA to reverse this decision, even in the 21 day period.[136] It could, however, request the SoS to make a screening direction to over-ride its opinion.

Screening and multi-stage consents

Since the decision of the European Court in *Commission v UK*,[137] screening may now be required for some applications even after the grant of planning permission. The European Court found that, in circumstances where the applicable domestic legislation allows for the grant of consents through a multi-stage process, the failure of the EIA Regulations to provide for EIA to be considered at any time other than the initial application for planning permission was an incorrect transposition of the Directive. *Commission v UK* involved outline planning permissions and reserved matters approvals, but the Government has recognised that full permissions which are subject to pre-commencement conditions, which must be satisfied before the development can proceed, are also likely to constitute a multi-stage development consent for this purpose.[138]

    Where at the initial stage (whether an outline application or a full application) there was not a full consideration of the environmental consequences of the development (including the likely impacts of matters dealt with by conditions), the LPA will need to consider later, when dealing with applications for the approval of matters under the conditions (whether

9–022

---

[132] paras 66–70 of Circular 2/99.
[133] [2001] EWHC 278 Admin.
[134] Under either reg.5(1) or reg.7(1).
[135] Or any extended period agreed under reg.7(3).
[136] Because such an opinion was determinative, subject to the SoS's powers to make a direction: reg.4(1) and reg.4(2)(b).
[137] [2006] JPL 1673.
[138] para.3.10 of CLG Consultation Paper on the TCP (EIA) (England) (Amendment) Regulations 2007, October 2007.

reserved matters or other pre-commencement conditions), whether the development is or is not EIA development.[139]

In October 2007 the Government published draft regulations for consultation to address the need for EIA of multi-stage consents. These were then followed in England on July 30, 2008 by the Town & Country Planning (Environmental Impact Assessment) (England) (Amendment) Regulations 2008,[140] which came into force on September 1, 2008 (the EIA Amendment Regulations). The Welsh Assembly Government published similar draft regulations for consultation in November 2007 but to date no final regulations have been made.

9–023   The EIA Amendment Regulations incorporate multi-stage consents into the screening procedures to the same extent as an initial application for planning permission in two cases. These are where either there has been no prior screening opinion or screening direction, or any such opinion or direction was that the development was not EIA development. They do this by expanding the definitions of "EIA application", "Schedule 1 application" and "Schedule 2 application" in the EIA Regulations[141] to include a "subsequent application" in relation to these matters.

A "subsequent application" is defined in the EIA Amendment Regulations[142] as:

"an application for approval of a matter where the approval—(a) is required by or under a condition to which a planning permission is subject; and (b) must be obtained before all or part of the development permitted by the planning permission may be begun."

The requirement for screening in the case of subsequent applications in relation to a multi-stage consent is then achieved by amendments to Regulation 7 of the EIA Regulations.[143] In the case of a subsequent application, there is a requirement for screening if either the development in question has not been the subject of a screening opinion or screening direction, or there was a screening opinion or screening direction to the effect that the development was not EIA development. In either such case, every application for consent as part of the multi-stage consent which appears to the relevant planning authority to be a Schedule 1 or Schedule 2 application must be subject to screening to the same extent as a planning application. Regulation 7 does not apply to applications which were the subject of a screening opinion or direction to the effect that the development was EIA development but where the resulting ES either did not assess particular effects because at the time of determination there was insufficient information to allow proper assessment, or did assess those

[139] *R v Bromley LBC ex parte Barker* [2006] UKHL 52.
[140] SI 2008/2093.
[141] reg.2(1) of SI 1999/293.
[142] reg.3(1) of the EIA Amendment Regulations.
[143] reg.5(10 of the EIA Amendment Regulations.

effects but did not include the full effects now apparent from the information available from the latest application for consent. However, the power under Regulation 19 to require additional information is now available in relation to a subsequent application and so by this means the local planning authority can address any need to revisit the earlier ES.[144] It remains to be seen whether the Commission or in due course the European Court will regard the amending regulations as sufficient to achieve complete transposition of the Directive.

What Does Screening Involve?

If the development is Schedule 1 development, screening (if required) is a simple matter for the LPA, involving nothing more than checking that the description of the development falls within one of the specified categories in Schedule 1, including the application of, usually quantitative, thresholds.

9–024

If the development is Schedule 2 development, the first stage of screening is a check to ascertain the relevant description of development and (unless the site is within a sensitive area[145]) the applicable thresholds or criteria. The LPA's decision at this stage is not simply a finding of fact and nor is it a matter of discretionary judgment. The LPA has to correctly understand the meaning of the terms used in Schedule 2 and apply those terms to the facts. If it errs in its approach its decision can be challenged by way of judicial review.[146] A development might satisfy more than one description of development.

If this initial exercise confirms that the development is indeed Schedule 2 development then the decision maker must apply its judgement to ascertain whether the development is "likely to have significant effects on the environment by virtue of factors such as its nature, size or location".[147]

In forming this judgement the decision maker must have regard to the selection criteria in Schedule 3 to the extent relevant.[148] These cover in more detail the characteristics of the development, its location, and the characteristics of the potential impacts.

Circular 2/99 gives further guidance, including in Annex A indicative thresholds and criteria to assist when judging whether particular types of Schedule 2 development would be likely to have significant environmental effects. However, the Circular stresses that these thresholds and criteria are only indicative and cannot be used as a substitute for a proper judgement looking at the particular proposal and its location.

9–025

[144] reg.7(5) of the EIA Amendment Regulations.
[145] As defined by reg.2(1).
[146] *R(Goodman) v Lewisham LBC* [2003] EWCA Civ 140.
[147] reg.2(1).
[148] reg.4(5).

In order to make an informed judgement as to whether significant environmental effects are likely, the decision maker needs sufficient information about the development and its likely consequences. The decision maker does not need complete information on every aspect of the development, but must have sufficient information on those aspects with the likely potential to have significant environmental effects.[149]

In its screening decision the decision maker is not required to ignore the scope for mitigation or avoidance measures which seek to address effects or reduce them to an insignificant level.[150] This is so whether the mitigation or avoidance is proposed as part of the application or is envisaged by the decision maker as a measure that could be secured by a condition on the grant of permission. However, not every such measure will be accompanied by sufficient certainty as to its efficacy for the decision maker to be able to rely on it at the screening stage. There will be cases where the availability of such measures will be sufficient to enable the decision maker to conclude that significant environmental effects are not likely.[151] There will be other cases where the information about the measures and their effectiveness at the screening stage is insufficient to support such a conclusion.[152] The judgment to be made is very fact-sensitive.

What Documentation is Needed for a Screening Decision?

9–026 Where the screening decision is made by the LPA the EIA Regulations require it to "adopt a screening opinion".[153] The definition of a screening opinion requires it to be "a written statement of the opinion of the relevant planning authority as to whether development is EIA development".[154] If the screening opinion is that the development is EIA development the LPA must accompany its opinion with "a written statement giving clearly and precisely the full reasons for that conclusion."[155] The EIA Regulations impose no similar obligation for an opinion that the development is not EIA development.

For most LPAs most screening decisions are in practice made by officers. It is therefore good administrative practice to ensure that the scheme of delegation to officers specifically deals with this function and identifies the officer(s) who have been given delegated authority to form the LPA's

---

[149] *R(Jones) v Mansfield DC* [2003] EWCA Civ1408 at para 39.
[150] *R(Catt) v Brighton & Hove City Council* [2007] EWCA Civ 298.
[151] As in *Catt.*
[152] As in *R(Gillespie) v FSoS* [2003] EWCA Civ 400.
[153] reg.4(2)(b) and reg.5(1).
[154] reg.2(1).
[155] reg.4(6)(i).

screening opinion. In *R v St Edmundsbury BC ex parte Walton*[156] the High Court quashed a planning permission and a purported officer decision that the development did not require EIA, inter alia on the ground that there had been no delegation of this function to officers. In *R(Lebus) v South Cambridgeshire DC*[157] the High Court quashed a permission where the officer with delegated authority had considered the question of screening, and had concluded that the development, whilst Schedule 2 development, was not EIA development, but the officer had not produced any written statement of this decision which could constitute a screening opinion. Sullivan J. regarded this as a complete failure to comply with the requirements of Regulation 7, and that the LPA had failed to recognise that screening decisions cannot be made informally.[158]

Conversely, in *Younger Homes (Northern) Ltd v FSoS*[159] the CA upheld as a valid screening opinion an unsigned manuscript note (subsequently lost) by an officer on the staff of the chief officer with delegated powers to make screening decisions. The chief officer with delegated powers was empowered to authorise officers on his staff to act on his behalf, but only where the decisions they made were taken in the name of the chief officer. This had not happened with the manuscript note. Nonetheless, Laws L.J. was satisfied that the officer who wrote the note had delegated authority to make the screening decision and that his note fell within the statutory definition of a screening opinion.[160]

It is not easy to reconcile the differing approach of these authorities, **9–027** although on their facts it can be said that in *St Edmundsbury* there was no delegation at all, in *Lebus* there was no written statement, but in *Younger* there was delegation of sorts and a written statement of sorts. In *R(Goodman) v Lewisham LBC*,[161] where the screening decision had been made by an authorised officer but not recorded, the grant of planning permission was quashed on other grounds, but Buxton L.J. said, in an obiter passage, that decisions of such importance should be properly recorded, and that the case should bring home to LPAs generally the importance of the processes of formal and transparent consideration of environmental issues that are required by the Directive.[162]

Screening directions are subject to similar procedural requirements[163] but do not appear to have given rise to similar difficulties in demonstrating that a valid direction has been made. This may be due to the better record

---

[156] [1999] 3 PLR 51.
[157] [2002] EWHC 2009 Admin.
[158] para.53.
[159] [2004] EWCA Civ 1060.
[160] At paras 35–38.
[161] [2003] EWCA Civ 140.
[162] At paras 17–18.
[163] reg.4(6)(i). Note, there is no express requirement for the direction to be in writing but this must be implicit from the terms of reg.4(6)(ii).

keeping of the SoS or to the fact that the SoS has a more opaque procedure for authorising officials to act on the SoS's behalf.[164]

Where the screening opinion or direction is that the development is not EIA development, domestic law has held that the opinion or direction need not give any reasons for this decision.[165] This accords with the terms of the EIA Regulations.[166] However, in a preliminary decision in *Mellor v SSCLG*,[167] the CA has referred to the European Court the question of whether the SoS must, in order to comply with the Directive, give reasons for a decision that Annex II[168] development is not EIA development and if so what are the principles governing that requirement to give reasons. If the European Court considers that there is such a requirement in the case of screening directions, it is inevitable that the same will also be true for screening opinions.

9–028 Hitherto, the approach of the European Court has been that the substantive requirements of the Directive are only applicable to development which is EIA development. However, the Directive and the EIA Regulations do impose some procedural obligations[169] in relation to Annex II/Schedule 2 development, even if it is not EIA development, and it could be said that a requirement to explain why Annex II/Schedule 2 development is not EIA development would be consistent with this position.

CONTENT AND SUBSTANTIVE PROVISIONS

Introduction

9–029 Having considered when a developer will have to embark upon the EIA process, either by voluntarily submitting an ES or by there being a positive screening decision the next logical consideration is what does the ES need to contain and what are the substantive provisions relating the process.

There is a heightened importance of complying with the substantive provisions because of the mandatory requirement in Regulation 3(2) of the EIA Regulations which provides that planning permission cannot be granted before the "environmental information" is taken into consideration. The requirements imposed by the Regulations, giving effect to the

---

[164] There is no equivalent of a published scheme of arrangements for decisions made by officials on behalf of the SoS.
[165] *Marson v SSETR* [1998] 3 PLR 90; *R v St Edmundsbury BC ex parte Walton* [1999] 3 PLR 51; *Probyn v FSoS* [2005] EWHC 398 (Admin).
[166] reg.4(6).
[167] [2008] EWCA Civ 213.
[168] i.e. development within Schedule 2 of the Regulations.
[169] Specifically in relation to screening.

Directive, can be regarded as relating to a process rather than a single document.

General Requirements as to Content from the Regulations

There are two categories of information that are required of an ES by the definition in Regulation 2(1). The first is the information that is reasonably required to assess the environmental effects of the development and which the applicant can, having regard in particular to current knowledge and methods of assessment, reasonably be required to compile. The second is the mandatory information contained within Part II of Schedule 4.

9–030

The mandatory information within Part II of Schedule 4 is:

"1. A description of the development comprising information on the site, design and size of the development.

2. A description of the measures envisaged in order to avoid, reduce and, if possible, remedy significant adverse effects.

3. The data required to identify and assess the main effects which the development is likely to have on the environment.

4. An outline of the main alternatives studied by the applicant or appellant and an indication of the main reasons for his choice, taking into account the environmental effects.

5. A non-technical summary of the information provided under paragraphs 1 to 4 of this Part."

In *R v Cornwall CC Ex p. Hardy*[170], Harrison J. set out the correct order to look at these questions as being:

"(1) the environmental statement must contain a description of the development (para.1);

(2) it must contain the data required to identify and assess the main effects which the development was likely to have on the environment (para.3);

(3) it must contain a description of the measures envisaged to avoid, reduce and, if possible, remedy significant adverse effects (para.2)."

Under Part 1 of Schedule 4 of the EIA Regulations the information that must be provided is subject to the caveats within the definition of "environmental statement" in Regulation 2(1). This requires only whatever is reasonably required to assess the environmental effects and which can reasonably be required having regard to the state of knowledge and methods of assessment. Subject to that caveat it comprises the following:

[170] [2001] JPL 786.

1. Description of the development, including in particular—

    (a) a description of the physical characteristics of the whole development and the land-use requirements during the construction and operational phases;

    (b) a description of the main characteristics of the production processes, for instance, nature and quantity of the materials used;

    (c) an estimate, by type and quantity, of expected residues and emissions (water, air and soil pollution, noise, vibration, light, heat, radiation, etc.) resulting from the operation of the proposed development.

2. An outline of the main alternatives studied by the applicant or appellant and an indication of the main reasons for his choice, taking into account the environmental effects.

3. A description of the aspects of the environment likely to be significantly affected by the development, including, in particular, population, fauna, flora, soil, water, air, climatic factors, material assets, including the architectural and archaeological heritage, landscape and the inter-relationship between the above factors.

4. A description of the likely significant effects of the development on the environment, which should cover the direct effects and any indirect, secondary, cumulative, short, medium and long-term, permanent and temporary, positive and negative effects of the development, resulting from:

    (a) the existence of the development;

    (b) the use of natural resources;

    (c) the emission of pollutants, the creation of nuisances and the elimination of waste,
    and the description by the applicant of the forecasting methods used to assess the effects on the environment.

5. A description of the measures envisaged to prevent, reduce and where possible offset any significant adverse effects on the environment.

6. A non-technical summary of the information provided under paragraphs 1 to 5 of this Part.

7. An indication of any difficulties (technical deficiences or lack of know-how) encountered by the applicant in compiling the required information.

The list of information contained within Part 1 of Schedule 4 only needs to be read to appreciate how widely it is drawn. In the case of large developments it is interpreted by most developers to require a considerable volume of work to be produced to cover all the effects. For a complex development there will often be the need to pull together tens of experts to do reports on traffic, ecology, air quality, noise, architecture, landscape, archaeology, built heritage and flooding. Very often one of the areas is dependent upon the studies of others for example noise and air quality is often dependent upon traffic data so there is a considerable skill in putting together the studies that are mutually consistent and robust.

The Scoping Process

Part IV of the EIA Regulations provides a procedure whereby a person who is minded to make an EIA application may ask the relevant planning authority to provide a "scoping opinion". This is a written document that records the authority's views as to the matters that should be included in the environmental statement.

9–031

A request for such an opinion must include:

"(a) a plan sufficient to identify the land;
(b) a brief description of the nature and purpose of the development and of its possible effects on the environment; and
(c) such other information or representations as the person making the request may wish to provide or make."[171]

Faced with a request the authority must respond within five weeks from the date of receipt of the request unless a different period is agreed in writing with the person making the request. In the case of a request for a scoping opinion being made at the same time as a request for a screening opinion the request runs from the date of adoption of the positive opinion that it is EIA development.[172] If the authority fails to give a scoping opinion within the relevant time the developer may ask the Secretary of State for a scoping direction under Regulation 11.

The authority, in completing the scoping opinion, must consult the person making the request in addition to the various consultation bodies. Circular 2/99 calls for local planning authorities to consult Environmental Impact Assessment "Guidance on Scoping" published by the European Commission.[173]

Whilst the scoping opinion is helpful it is not the case that if the information is not provided as required by the scoping opinion that the ES will necessarily be a defective.[174] There is no mechanism for the requirement of a scoping opinion to be challenged if the developer takes the view that its requirements are excessive. Similarly the authority is not bound by the limits of its scoping opinion. They are not precluded from requiring

9–032

[171] EIA reg.10(2).
[172] EIA reg.10(5).
[173] May 1996.
[174] See Circular 2/99 at para.95.

additional information on top of what the scoping opinion required.[175] The matters which the authority is formally required to take into account in coming to their scoping opinion are:

"(a) the specific characteristics of the particular development;
(b) the specific characteristics of development of the type concerned; and
(c) the environmental features likely to be affected by the development."[176]

Procedure to facilitate preparation

9–033   There is a procedure under Regulation 12 that is aimed at assisting developers to prepare the ES. They may, under Regulation 12(1), serve a notice on the relevant planning authority or Secretary of State who will in turn notify the consultation bodies. The consultation bodies and the planning authority must then enter into consultation to see whether they have any information relevant to the preparation of the ES. If they do, they must make it available unless it is confidential information under Regulation 12 of the Environmental Information Regulations.[177]

General Approach of the Courts to Content

9–034   It is important to remember that Regulation 3(2) prohibits the grant of planning permission before the "environmental information" is taken into account. This is defined as not just the ES but also the representations on it.

In terms of content the courts have been clear that it is for the authority to judge whether the information satisfies Schedule 4 of the Regulations on traditional Wednesbury reasonableness grounds.[178] In *R (Blewett) v Derbyshire County Council*[179] Sullivan J. formulated a robust test to be applied before finding that an ES was legally defective:

"It would be of no advantage to anyone concerned with the development process–applicants, objectors or local authorities–if environmental statements were drafted on a purely "defensive basis", mentioning every possible scrap of environmental information just in case someone might

---

[175] EIA Regulation 10(9).
[176] EIA reg.10(6).
[177] SI 2004/3391.
[178] *R. v Rochdale MBC Ex p. Milne (No.1)* [2000] Env. L.R. 1; *R. v Rochdale MBC Ex p. Milne (No.2)* [2001] Env. L.R. 22; *R (Blewett) v Derbyshire County Council* [2004] Env. L.R. 29 (the Court of Appeal dismissed an appeal at [2004] Env. L.R. 15 but did not deal with the EIA issue since permission to appeal had not been give in respect of them); *R (Jones) v Mansfield BC* [2004] Env. L.R. 21.
[179] [2004] Env. L.R. 29.

consider it significant at a later stage. Such documents would be a hindrance, not an aid to sound decision-making by the local planning authority, since they would obscure the principal issues with a welter of detail".[paragraph 42]

He also took the view that challenges on this basis to ES documents would not succeed often, and adopted a formulation that for an application to succeed it would in effect have to say that the document submitted did not amount to an ES at all. At paragraphs 41 and 68 Sullivan J. said:

"41.   There will be cases where the document purporting to be an environmental statement is so deficient that it could not reasonably be described as an environmental statement as defined by the Regulations ..., but they are likely to be few and far between.
68.   I have dealt with it in some detail because it does illustrate a tendency on the part of claimants opposed to the grant of planning permission to focus upon deficiencies in environmental statements, as revealed by the consultation process prescribed by the Regulations, and to contend that because the document did not contain all the information required by Sch.4 it was therefore not an environmental statement and the local planning authority had no power to grant planning permission. Unless it can be said that the deficiencies are so serious that the document cannot be described as, in substance, an environmental statement for the purposes of the Regulations, such an approach is in my judgment misconceived. It is important that decisions on EIA applications are made on the basis of 'full information', but the Regulations are not based on the premise that the environmental statement will necessarily contain the full information. The process is designed to identify any deficiencies in the environmental statement so that the local planning authority has the full picture, so far as it can be ascertained, when it comes to consider the 'environmental information' of which the statement will be but a part."

Practical Problems: Traps to Avoid

Lack of information vital to assessment

There is, however, one area where uncorrected ES deficiencies can give rise   **9–035**
to planning permissions being quashed by the Courts and where developers must take particular care. This will occur where the authority simply lacks information which is vital to assess whether significant effects are likely. If that is so, it cannot lawfully leave that matter to be investigated and dealt with under a condition after planning permission has been granted.

In *R. v Cornwall CC Ex p. Hardy*[180] the flaw was that the Council had accepted advice from English Nature and the Cornish Wildlife Trust that further surveys should be carried out to ensure that bats would not be adversely affected by the development. The bats were a European-protected species. They and their roosts were subject to strict protection under the Habitats Directive. If their presence were found by the surveys and if it were thought they were likely to be adversely affected by the proposed development, it was an inescapable conclusion that such a finding would constitute a "significant adverse effect" and a "main effect" within paragraphs 2 and 3 of Part 11 of Schedule 4. Thus the decision was defective because it did not contain the data required to identify and assess the main effects which the development was likely to have.

The information required by those two paragraphs should have been contained in the ES and considered by the planning committee before deciding whether to grant planning permission. This meant that the grant of planning permission was not lawful, because the council could not rationally have concluded that there were no significant nature conservation effects prior to having data from the surveys.

A paper chase

9–036　What needs to be avoided in terms of the production of an ES is a paper chase such as that those looking at the document have to go to several documents in order to find the information that is required.

In *Berkeley v Secretary of State for the Environment*[181] a permission was quashed on the basis that there was no ES. The fact that the information was available in a variety of different documents produced at different times by different people for the planning inquiry and referenced in the statement of case was not sufficient to satisfy the requirements. It was thus an extreme case in which there was no ES at all. However Lord Hoffmann set out what is a fairly strict test for the requirements for an ES. He held:

"Mr. Elvin says that the equivalent of the applicant's environmental statement can be found in its statement of case under the Inquiry Procedure Rules, read (by virtue of cross-referencing) with the planning authority's statement of case, which in turn incorporated the comprehensive officers' report to the planning sub-committee, which in turn incorporated the background papers such as the letters from the National Rivers Authority and the London Ecology Unit and was supplemented by the proofs of evidence made available at the inquiry. Members of the public had access to all these documents and the right to express their opinions upon them at the inquiry.

---

[180] [2001] Env. L.R. 25.
[181] [2001] 2 AC 603.

My Lords, I do not accept that this paper chase can be treated as the equivalent of an environmental statement. In the first place, I do not think it complies with the terms of the Directive. The point about the environmental statement contemplated by the Directive is that it constitutes a single and accessible compilation, produced by the applicant at the very start of the application process, of the relevant environmental information and the summary in non-technical language. It is true that article 6.3 gives member states a discretion as to the places where the information can be consulted, the way in which the public may be informed and the manner in which the public is to be consulted. But I do not think it allows member states to treat a disparate collection of documents produced by parties other than the developer and traceable only by a person with a good deal of energy and persistence as satisfying the requirement to make available to the public the Annex III information which should have been provided by the developer."[182]

In practice there are often significant difficulties in avoiding this paper chase where further information is produced.[183] What is required is to know with some precision what the ES consists of in a manner that would be apparent to a member of the public who wants to understand and comment on the application.

Outline applications

In applications for outline planning permission, particular care needs to be taken to ensure there is compliance with the Directive and Regulations. The cases of *R v Rochdale MBC ex parte Tew*.[184] [1999] 3 PLR 74 and *R v Rochdale MBC ex parte Milne*[185] [2001] 81 P&CR27 set out the approach that needs to be taken to EIA development in this context of an application for outline planning permission if they are to comply with the Directive and the Regulations.   **9–037**

Both cases dealt with a legal challenge to a decision of the authority to grant outline planning permission for a business park in Rochdale on largely the same site. In both cases an ES was provided. In *ex parte Tew* the Court upheld a challenge to the decision and quashed the planning permission. The developer, having learned lessons from the first challenge, amended the scheme and ES. The court in the second case *ex parte Milne* the Court rejected the challenge and upheld the authority's decision to grant planning permission.

In *ex parte Tew*, the authority authorised a scheme based on an illustrative masterplan showing how the development might be developed, but

---

[182] See ibid at p.617C ff per Lord Hoffmann.
[183] This is covered below.
[184] [1999] 3 PLR 74.
[185] [2001] 81 P&CR 27.

with all details left to reserved matters approval. The ES assessed the likely environmental effects of the scheme by reference to the illustrative masterplan. However, there was no requirement for the scheme to be developed in accordance with the masterplan and in fact a very different scheme could have been built, the environmental effects of which the ES would not have properly assessed. The Court held that the description of the scheme was therefore not sufficient to enable the main effects of the scheme to be properly assessed, in breach of Schedule 4 of the EIA Regulations.

9–038   In *ex parte Milne*, the ES was more detailed; a Schedule of Development set out the details of the buildings and their likely environmental effects, and the masterplan was no longer merely illustrative. Conditions were attached to the permission "to tie the outline permission for the business park to the documents which comprise the application". The outline permission was restricted so that the development that could take place would have to be within the parameters of the matters assessed in the ES. Reserved matters would be restricted to matters that had previously been assessed in the ES. This mechanism was sufficiently compliant with the requirements in the Regulations.

Sullivan J. emphasised that the Directive and Regulations required the permission to be granted in the full knowledge of the likely significant effects on the environment. This did not mean that developers would have no flexibility in developing a scheme. But such flexibility would have to be properly assessed and taken into account prior to granting outline planning permission. He also commented that the ES need not contain information about every single environmental effect. The Directive refers only to those that are likely and significant. To ensure it complied with the Directive the authority would have to ensure that these were identified and assessed before it could grant planning permission.

There are a number of practical lessons to be learned from these cases:

(i) First an application for a "bare" outline permission with all matters reserved for later approval is extremely unlikely to comply with the requirements of the EIA Regulations;

(ii) When granting outline consent, the permission must be "tied" to the environmental information provided in the ES, and considered and assessed by the authority prior to approval. This can be usually done by conditions, although it is also possible to achieve this by a section 106 agreement.[186] An example of such a condition was referred to in *ex parte Milne*.

---

[186] An agreement under s.106 Town and Country Planning Act 1990 binds the land and can be made by agreement with the local planning authority or unilaterally. This is covered in more detail in Chapter 8 on planning.

"The development on this site shall be carried out in substantial accordance with the layout included within the Development Framework document submitted as part of the application and shown on (a) drawing entitled 'Master Plan with Building Layouts'"

The stated reason for this condition was given as:

"The layout of the proposed Business Park is the subject of an Environmental Impact Assessment and any material alteration to the layout may have an impact which has not been assessed by that process." (see paras 28 and 131 of the judgment);

(iii) Developers are not precluded from having a degree of flexibility in how a scheme may be developed. But each option will need to have been properly assessed and be within the remit of the outline permission. Some degree of flexibility can be built into the ES if it assesses a range of possible options. For example in visual terms it could assess the effect of having a range of heights of building.

(iv) The case of *R (Barker) v Bromley LBC*[187] and when an additional ES is required for the approval of the reserved matters application, is considered above.[188]

Other practical points

One of the principal difficulties that emerges in the production of an ES is **9–039** that it must be co-ordinated between the different parts of the team that produce it. As has been mentioned above there are often very many consultants producing chapters of the ES on traffic, landscape, noise, air quality, and ecology to name but a few. Often one part will be dependent on the work of others.

The requirement in Schedule 4 Part 1 is to assess the likely significant effects of the development; and in Part II a mandatory requirement is to describe the development. Thus where there are amendments to the application there needs to be central co-ordination to ensure that what is assessed and described is the most up-to-date proposal.

The Regulations and Directive require the likely significant effects to be described. This does not of course mean the worst case scenario. There will often be situations where a range of possible outcomes needs to be assessed but what should always be ensured is that the likely significant effects which are assessed.

---

[187] [2006] 3 W.L.R. 1209.
[188] See above.

Revisions and Amendments

9–040 Revisions and amendments to environmental statements have caused considerable problems in practice because of the hard edged rule in Regulation 3(2) that without the environmental information being taken into account applications have to be refused. If the ES becomes out of date or it is realised that there are omissions; the developer is faced with a problem.

There has been recent revision to Regulation 19 to provide in the Regulations for what had become the established practice. There was always a power enabling the Local Planning Authority or the Secretary of State to request further information when they were dealing with the application, and there are rules in Regulation 19 as to how this is to be publicised. What was not clear is what was to happen where information that was provided voluntarily.

Regulation 19 was amended by the EIA (Amendment Regulations 2006)[189] to ensure that voluntary information (called "other information") provided by the developer was to be treated in the same way as that provided on request of the Local Planning Authority or Secretary of State. This was the established practice that built up in any event. These amending regulations also provide however that if further and other information was provided for the purpose of an inquiry or hearing, it would not be subject to those same requirements as to the advertising and service of the information. In such a case where the information was provided for a hearing or inquiry a timetable for publication would have to be arrived at to enable representations to be made although there is flexibility under the Regulations as to what this shall be.

9–041 If extensive amendments are made it will be important to ensure that there is a document or documents that comply with the test that Lord Hoffmann put forward in *Berkeley* of not being a paper trail. Members of the public and consultees must clearly be able to tell what is being consulted upon. There are a variety of methods of doing this from producing a corrected revised ES to producing just an updating document that must be read with the rest of the ES. What is appropriate will depend upon the further or other information that is being added.

---

[189] SI 2006/3295.

Chapter 10

NATURE CONSERVATION

Introduction

Historical background[1]

Although statutory protection has been given to various individual species **10–001** and groups since Norman times, nature conservation, as it is now practised, originated in a resurgence of interest in the natural environment which began in the United States in about 1865 and then spread to much of Europe towards the close of the nineteenth century. In Britain, this led to the establishment of voluntary organisations, such as the (Royal) Society for the Protection of Birds in 1889 and the National Trust in 1895, which aroused public interest and pressure for legislation to protect both habitats and species.

The movement towards statutory protection for wildlife and its natural surroundings took a major step forward with the National Parks and Access to the Countryside Act 1949, giving powers and responsibilities to the newly-established Nature Conservancy. The 1949 Act having laid the foundations, upon which much followed, up until the coming into force of the Wildlife and Countryside Act 1981, was aimed at remedying perceived inadequacies in the law in achieving the effective conservation of endangered species (especially when these were mobile) and in conserving fauna and flora in the face of operations, such as farming and forestry, which were exempt from planning control.

The Countryside and Rights of Way Act 2000 (CROWA) sought to open up the countryside by means of its "right to roam" provisions as well as providing for a much-needed overhaul of the Sites of Special Scientific Interest regime and of the procedures for designating sites as Areas of Outstanding Natural Beauty. The Natural Environment and Rural Communities Act 2006 further promoted the interests of nature conservation with a re-organisation of the UK nature conservation bodies and the creation of a Joint Nature Conservation Committee. The 2006 Act also extends to all public bodies the existing duty under section 74 of CROWA to have regard to biodiversity as far as is consistent with the proper exercise of their functions.

Looking forward, the draft Marine Bill, published in April 2008, pro-

---

[1] The previous edition of this work provides a fuller account.

mises to increase the protection of marine habitats and, through them, of species for which the land-oriented measures of the previous statutes had afforded only partial protection.

The main types of nature conservation

10–002 Nature conservation may be considered under two broad headings: Habitat Conservation and Species Protection.

Habitat conservation: overview

10–003 Habitat conservation is achieved mainly by means of designating sites as meriting special consideration or protection. The various forms of designation carry different consequences and will be the subject of extended discussion below. For present purposes, they can be divided into three groups: those created under international law by specific treaty; those having EU legislation (whether Regulation or Directive) as their origin; and those originating in purely domestic UK legislation.[2]

In general terms, the designation of sites pursuant to "traditional" (i.e. non-EU) international law does not of itself confer any direct protection on the habitat within that site. For example, sites included in the UK's list of wetlands of international importance drawn up pursuant to its obligations under the Ramsar Convention[3] are protected by virtue of their designation under EU or national legislation, rather than by virtue of their Ramsar designation. However, once selected, there is at least a powerful political impetus on the UK to ensure these sites' protection. Likewise the UK's obligations under the Bern Convention[4] are met through the mechanisms established under Part I of the Wildlife and Countryside Act 1981. Similarly, sites included in the UK Biodiversity Action Plan (UKBAP), drawn up by virtue of the UK being a signatory to the Biodiversity Convention,[5] are protected by national or EU designations.

The main classifications introduced as a result of the UK's membership of the European Union are the Special Protection Area for Birds (SPA), introduced by Directive 79/409/EEC on the Conservation of Wild Birds

---

[2] The website of the Joint Nature Conservation Committee at *http://www.jncc.gov.uk/page-1527* sets out a "Protected sites designations directory", summarising 42 different designations which may apply in part or all of the United Kingdom, the majority of which have some form of statutory basis or means of enforcement.

[3] The Ramsar Convention on Wetlands of International Importance; made in February 1971, signed by UK 1973, ratified 1976, amended 1982 (as a result of changes brought about by the Birds Directive—Dir 79/409/EEC).

[4] Bern Convention on the Conservation of European Wildlife and Natural Habitats; agreed by the Committee Members of the Council of Europe in June 1979, came into force June 1, 1982.

[5] Rio Convention on Biodiversity ("Biodiversity Convention" or "CBD"), adopted at the Earth Summit in Rio de Janeiro, Brazil in June 1992, entered into force in December 1993.

(the Birds Directive) and, second, the Special Area of Conservation (SAC) introduced by Directive 92/43/EEC on the Conservation of Natural Habitats and of Wild Fauna and Flora (the Habitats Directive). Mention should also be made of two further pieces of EU legislation impacting in this field. The first, Directive 85/337/EEC, required Member States to put in place arrangements for an environmental assessment to be carried out before the decision is taken to grant permission for a project which is likely to have significant environmental effects. Amended by Directive 97/11/EC, the obligations referred to are now met, inter alia, by the Town and Country Planning (Environmental Impact Assessment) (England and Wales) Regulations 1999.[6] The second, Directive 2004/35/CE on environmental liability with regard to the prevention and remedying of environmental damage, has not yet been transposed into UK law, but Regulations imposing obligations on operators of activities which cause or threaten to cause environmental damage are likely to come into force in late 2008.[7]

Of the UK designations, by far the most pervasive is the Site of Special **10–004** Scientific Interest (SSSI). In its present form deriving from section 28 of the Wildlife and Countryside Act 1981 (as amended), an SSSI is an area of land of which the use is compulsorily restricted in the interests of nature conservation. However, SSSI status does not confer automatic and absolute protection against development; the purpose of the designation is to ensure that conservation considerations are taken into account before any decision affecting the future of an SSSI is made.

The 1949 Act provided for the creation of nature reserves, which are now subdivided into National and Local (NNRs and LNRs), dependent on the scope of their importance. Further, there exist Marine Nature Reserves (MNRs), introduced by sections 36 and 37 of the 1981 Act, designated by the Secretary of State directly. A further mechanism for protecting habitats is the Limestone Pavement Order (LPO), which, as the name suggests, gives special protection to one particular, narrowly specified habitat.

As we shall see below, there is a frequent and substantial overlap between these various forms of designation, both within and across the three categories (international, EU and national) identified above.

Species protection: overview

Alongside, and at times overlapping, the above-mentioned habitat-based **10–005** designations, are provisions aimed at the preservation or promotion of individual species, often in association with anti-cruelty measures.

---

[6] See Chapter 9—Environmental Impact Assessment.
[7] See Chapter 5—The Environmental Liability Directive. Details of the draft regulations can be found at *http://www.defra.gov.uk/environment/liability/index.htm.*

Dating back to the Seabirds Act of 1869, there have been numerous interventions and occasional consolidations aimed at species protection. Provisions protecting wild species of economic or "sporting" value have a much longer history. Much of the current law is to be found in Part I of the Wildlife and Countryside Act 1981, which provides for the protection of wild birds, their nests and their eggs; for the protection of specified wild animals and plants; for the control of the introduction of non-indigenous species into the wild; and for the establishment of a licensing system to permit actions which would otherwise be illegal.

The EU-derived legislation implements a system of protection that in large measure overlaps with the provision of domestic origin. The upshot is that the totality of the legislation aimed at the protection of species is rather incoherent and derived from a bewildering multiplicity of statutory sources. This incoherence is reflected both in the individual species protected and the level of protection afforded to those species. Both the domestic and European measures for species protection are considered in greater detail below.

Other arrangements of benefit to nature conservation

10–006   In addition to "purpose-built" legislation on nature conservation of the kind outlined above, there is a wide range of ongoing schemes and projects which have an important practical impact on nature conservation in the UK. For example, the Environmental Stewardship Scheme (introduced on March 3, 2005, replacing the Environmentally Sensitive Areas and Countryside Stewardship schemes) provides government funding to farmers and other land managers in England who deliver effective environmental management on their land. Similarly, the "Leader+" programme is a European Community funded initiative for assisting rural communities in improving the quality of life and economic prosperity in their local area, applying in part the criterion of sustainable development.[8]

The Authorities Responsible for Nature Conservation

10–007   The category of bodies which can be said to have an impact on nature conservation in the UK is perhaps unlimited, including as it does everything from international and supranational institutions to unincorporated associations and charities.[9] What will be attempted here is merely a survey

---

[8] See generally *http://www.defra.gov.uk/environment/index.htm.*

[9] A useful list of environmental charities may be found at *http://www.britishcouncil.org/environmentuk/charities.htm.*

of what may be said to be the key actors in terms of the making and implementing of primary and secondary legislation in the field.

Government

EU

The European Union in its various guises has long been a major source of   **10–008** policies impacting on the environment generally, and nature conservation specifically, particularly through its systems of agricultural subsidy. The Single European Act, which took effect in 1987, gave the European Community a specific competence in the field of the Environment, contained in the new Title XIX to the Treaty. Previously, Community action was based on the somewhat shakier ground of the internal market harmonisation powers pursuant to Article 100 of the EEC Treaty and the reserve powers under Article 235 permitting measures to be taken for the attainment of the Community's objectives where the Treaty had not specifically provided the necessary powers.

At an administrative level, the Environment Directorate-General of the European Commission has responsibility for initiating new environmental legislation and ensuring that agreed measures are put into practice in the EU Member States.

National government

National government clearly has wide-ranging (if not unlimited) policy-   **10–009** making powers as well as the responsibility for translating those policies into legislation. In addition, it is central government which negotiates and is signatory to international treaties.

More specifically, the Secretary of State (in practice the relevant Minister in the Department for Environment Food and Rural Affairs—Defra[10]) exercises a wide range of powers in the field of nature conservation, such as the making of Nature Conservation Orders[11] and Limestone Pavement Orders[12], the inclusion of species within the Schedules of protected creatures[13], the creation of sanctuary areas for seals[14] and the designation of Marine Nature Reserves[15], to name but a few.

In addition to the above powers, the government is under an often-

---

[10] *http://www.defra.gov.uk/.*
[11] Pursuant to sections 29–32 and Sch.11 of the 1981 Act.
[12] s.34 of the 1981 Act.
[13] s.22 of the 1981 Act.
[14] s.3 of the Conservation of Seals Act 1970.
[15] ss.36 and 37 of the 1981 Act.

overlooked duty imposed by section 11 of the Countryside Act 1968, namely that:

"In the exercise of their functions under any enactment every Minister, government department and public body shall have regard to the desirability of conserving the natural beauty and amenity of the countryside".

10–010 Following devolution, the term "national government" has taken on a variable meaning depending on context. Whereas (presently) it is the UK as a whole which is signatory to international treaties, much policy-making power and legislative initiative has passed to devolved bodies. As a consequence of the Scotland Act (Commencement Order) 1998,[16] all powers exercised by the Secretary of State were transferred to the Scottish Executive (including planning and other land use matters), save for those retained under Schedule 5 to the Scotland Act 1998. Schedule 2 to the Government of Wales Act 1998 and The National Assembly of Wales (Transfer of Functions) Order 1999[17] effect the transfer of the functions in respect of (amongst other things) planning and the environment from the Secretary of State for Wales to the Assembly.

Local government

10–011 Without doubt the decisions of local government can have a major impact on matters of nature conservation. It is however beyond the scope of this work to set out the intricacies of the structure of local government in the United Kingdom or comprehensively to describe the full range of such decision-making power. In broad terms, local government may be viewed as a single tier in Scotland and Wales, whereas both unitary and two-tier arrangements exist in England. The picture is complicated further by the separate arrangements made for London pursuant to the Greater London Authority Act 1999.

All local authorities play a role in balancing the demands of nature conservation against pressures on land use for housing, education and social services, all of which are in competition for scarce resources. The most significant role of local government for present purposes is in the operation of the town and country planning regime, including the making of development plans for their area and the approval of individual appli-

---

[16] SI 1998/3178.
[17] SI 1999/672.

cations for permission to carry out building, engineering or mining operations or to change the use of any land.[18] It is worth bearing in mind that the grant of planning permission can in effect "trump" restrictions placed on activities within an SSSI.

Local authorities also have power to create local nature reserves, enter into management agreements, and in certain instances to make byelaws. Their powers in respect of highway building and public health also lend significance to the role of local authorities in this area.

Statutory conservation bodies

Introduction

A certain amount of historical background in necessary in order to understand the role of the various conservation bodies which now exist in the UK and to distinguish the current bodies from the numerous similarly-titled earlier bodies referred to in case law and texts.　　　　　　　　　　　　　　　　　　　　　**10–012**

In the period 1949 to the present day, there have been two broad trends: first, a removal of the somewhat artificial distinction which existed between bodies charged with wildlife conservation activities and those responsible for landscape conservation and, second, an increasing geographical division in responsibility to bodies in each of the territories comprising the UK.

The modern era in nature conservation commenced with the establishment by Royal Charter on March 23, 1949, of the Nature Conservancy. This body had the functions of providing scientific advice on the conservation and control of the natural flora and fauna of Great Britain, establishing and managing nature reserves and the organisation and development of related research and scientific services.

On the landscape side, 1949 also saw the passage of the National Parks and Access to the Countryside Act 1949, creating the National Parks Commission, a body whose remit for the promotion of amenity-based landscape conservation extended to England and Wales only. The 1949 Act also conferred certain statutory responsibilities in respect of wildlife conservation on the Nature Conservancy, thus entrenching the wildlife/landscape division.　　　　　　　　　　　　　　　　　　　　**10–013**

The Nature Conservancy's Royal Charter status was superseded by the Science and Technology Act 1965, under which the Nature Conservancy was incorporated within the newly formed Natural Environment Research Council (NERC) of the Department for Education and Science.

---

[18] The determination of such applications is now based on the criteria set out in Planning Policy Statement 9: *Biodiversity and Geological Conservation* ("PPS 9") and ODPM Circular 06/05: *Biodiversity and Geographical Conservation—Statutory Obligations and Their Impact Within the Planning System*, both published August 16, 2005. These replace the 1994 Planning Policy Guidance Note: Nature Conservation ("PPG 9"). See further Chapter 8 of this work—The Planning System and Environmental Protection.

Soon afterwards, the Countryside (Scotland) Act 1967 established the Countryside Commission for Scotland. This was itself shortly followed south of the border by a name change for the National Parks Commission to become the Countryside Commission by virtue of the Countryside Act 1968, retaining responsibility for landscape matters in England and Wales.

10–014 Returning to wildlife matters, the Nature Conservancy Council Act 1973 created (as the name suggests) a Nature Conservancy Council, which was to take over the NERC's nature conservation functions. The Council was in effect a quango, overseen by, rather than contained within, the Department of the Environment, thus enjoying a greater degree of independence than its former incarnation. It continued to have GB-wide responsibility, although for practical reasons three territorial headquarters were established by 1976.

Aside from a restructuring of the Countryside Commission consequent on the Wildlife and Countryside Act 1981, the identity of the GB conservation bodies remained stable throughout the 1980s. Northern Ireland however, saw the creation of the Committee for Nature Conservation established under Article 5 of the Nature Conservation and Amenity Lands (Northern Ireland) Order 1985[19], to sit alongside the Ulster Countryside Committee. The Nature Conservation and Amenity Lands (Amendment) (Northern Ireland) Order 1989[20] kick-started the process of merger between UK wildlife and landscape conservation bodies by abolishing both these bodies and setting up in their stead the Council for Nature Conservation and the Countryside to advise on both of these areas of expertise within the territory of Northern Ireland.

A seismic shift took place on April 1, 1991 with the coming into force of Part 7 of the Environmental Protection Act 1990. This Act dismembered the Nature Conservancy Council into its three "country" units, setting up in its stead the Nature Conservancy Council for England, the Nature Conservancy Council for Scotland and the Countryside Council for Wales (CCW). The last of these also assumed the responsibilities of the Welsh branch of the Countryside Commission. By way of balance, the 1990 Act also set up the Joint Nature Conservation Committee (JNCC) to provide a perspective over the whole of the United Kingdom bringing in, for the first time, (non-voting) representation from Northern Ireland. The remit of the JNCC is largely defined by section 133 of the 1990 Act, which sets out various "special functions" of the three Councils exercisable only through the JNCC.

10–015 The merger between wildlife and landscape responsibilities continued with the coming into force on April 1, 1992, of provisions of the Natural Heritage (Scotland) Act 1991, creating Scottish Natural Heritage (SNH), an analogous body to the CCW, taking on the functions of the Nature

---

[19] SI 1985/170 (NI 1).
[20] SI 1989/492 (NI 3).

Conservancy Council for Scotland and the Countryside Commission for Scotland. The 1991 Act can also be seen as attaining a greater degree of sophistication than the 1990 Act, providing as it did for appeals against decisions by SNH and reinforcing a requirement, originally made in part in section 37 of the Countryside Act 1968, that those responsible for the administration of nature conservation should take into account the needs of agriculture, fisheries and forestry, the need for social and economic development, the interests of the owners and occupiers of land, and the interests of local communities.[21] These requirements have been reflected in the decentralised internal structure adopted by SNH.

This left England something of an "odd man out", holding steadfastly to the wildlife/landscape distinction. This situation remained unresolved by two name changes of the relevant English bodies, the Countryside Commission becoming the Countryside Agency in 1999[22] and the Nature Conservancy Council officially assuming the title of "English Nature" in 2000.[23] It was not until October 1, 2006, when section 1 of the Natural Environment and Rural Communities Act 2006 gained full force that the wildlife/landscape schism was removed and symmetry restored by a new body, Natural England, taking on the functions of the dissolved English Nature and Countryside Agency. The 2006 Act also reconstituted the JNCC to comprise the four UK conservation bodies, thus bringing the CNCC fully into the fold, as well as amending those parts of the 1990 Act concerning the constitution of the CCW.

Natural England

Natural England (NE) was established on May 2, 2006,[24] pursuant to section 1 of the Natural Environment and Rural Communities Act 2006 ("the 2006 Act"), taking over the functions of English Nature and the Countryside Agency as from October 1, 2006.[25]   **10–016**

NE is a non-departmental public body, established as a body corporate, not to be regarded as a servant or agent of the Crown nor as enjoying any status, privilege or immunity of the Crown, nor as holding property on behalf of the Crown.[26] It cannot however be said to be wholly independent of government, bearing in mind the fact that the Chairman and board of NE are appointed by the Secretary of State.[27] Further, while NE is obliged only to have regard to guidance issued by the Secretary of State as to the

---

[21] s.3(1) of the 1991 Act.
[22] Pursuant to the Development Commission (Transfer of Functions and Miscellaneous Provisions) Order 1999, SI 1999/416.
[23] Pursuant to s.73 of the Countryside and Rights of Way Act 2000.
[24] SI 2006/1176.
[25] SI 2006/2541.
[26] para.1 of Sch.1 to the 2006 Act.
[27] See para.3 of Sch.1 to the 2006 Act.

exercise of its functions (section 15), it must comply with any general or specific directions (section 16).

NE's general purpose is stated at section 2 of the 2006 Act: "to ensure that the natural environment is conserved, enhanced and managed for the benefit of present and future generations, thereby contributing to sustainable development." This purpose includes: promoting nature conservation[28] and protecting biodiversity, conserving and enhancing the landscape, securing the provision and improvement of facilities for the study, understanding and enjoyment of the natural environment, promoting access to the countryside and open spaces and encouraging open-air recreation and contributing in other ways to social and economic well-being through the management of the natural environment (a purpose which may, in particular, be carried out by working with local communities).

10–017   Some useful commentary on the scope of these purposes is to be found in NE's "Management Statement", drawn up by Defra in consultation with NE.[29] In particular, the purpose of conserving and enhancing the landscape is stated to include, but go wider than, conserving the natural beauty of the landscape. It could for example cover conserving field boundaries (such as hedgerows and dry stone walls), and monuments, buildings and sub-surface archaeological features which contribute to the landscape. NE's powers to conserve and enhance the English landscape are stated to be exercisable for aesthetic, cultural and historic purposes as well as for habitat protection purposes.

NE may itself institute criminal proceedings, even using its own "in-house" prosecutors (section 12), an innovation which it is thought is likely to increase the number of prosecutions undertaken.

The 2006 Act sets out in some detail the composition of NE (at Schedule 1) as well as its functions and powers. In particular, NE's advisory functions (sections 3 to 4) point to its integration with the decision-making process across a range of public authorities, from government Minsters to statutory undertakers.[30]

---

[28] Defined by s.30(1) of the 2006 Act as the conservation of flora, fauna or geological or physiographical features.
[29] *http://www.naturalengland.org.uk/about/docs/governance/BG-A2-ManagementStatement.pdf.*
[30] See s.30(2) of the 2006 Act for the definition of "public authority" in this context.

Other UK conservation bodies

The Countryside Council for Wales (CCW) was established under Part 7[31]   **10–018**
of the Environmental Protection Act 1990 at section 128. It is, like its
English counterpart which post-dates it, a body corporate, not to be
regarded as the servant or agent of the Crown, nor as enjoying any status,
immunity or privilege of the Crown, nor as holding property on behalf of
the Crown.[32] Again, like NE, it cannot be regarded as completely independent of the state, bearing in mind the powers of appointment which,
since 2007, have lain with the Welsh Ministers, previously being in the
hands of the Secretary of State.[33] Detailed provision for the composition
and functioning of the CCW is made at Schedule 6 to the 1990 Act.

Scottish Natural Heritage (SNH) is the successor body to both the
Nature Conservancy Council for Scotland and the Countryside Commission for Scotland, established by the Natural Heritage (Scotland) Act
1991. It is a government body responsible to Scottish Government Ministers and through them to the Scottish Parliament. Its general aims and
purposes are set out at section 1 of the 1991 Act and its functions at section
2. In carrying out its role, SNH is enjoined to have regard to the desirability
of securing that anything done, whether by SNH or any other person, in
relation to the natural heritage of Scotland is undertaken in a manner
which is sustainable. One particular innovation of the 1991 Act is the
concept of "natural heritage", defined to include the flora and fauna of
Scotland, its geological and physiographical features and its natural beauty
and amenity.

The Council for Nature Conservation and the Countryside (CNCC)
was set up in Northern Ireland by the Nature Conservation and Amenity
Lands (Amendment) (Northern Ireland) Order 1989[34] and can be seen as
something of a pioneer body, being the first of the UK conservation bodies
to combine both conservation and countryside-related functions, inherited
from the Committee for Nature Conservation and the Ulster Countryside
Committee respectively. The CNCC differs from the other UK con-

---

[31] Part 7 of the 1990 Act, entitled 'Nature Conservation in Great Britain and Countryside
Matters in Wales' originally provided for the establishment of nature conservation councils
for England and Scotland, the Countryside Council for Wales and the Joint Nature
Conservation Committee (see above). Since the coming into force of the relevant parts of
the Natural Environment and Rural Communities Act 2006 on October 1 2006, Part 7 of
the 1990 Act now concerns only the Countryside Council for Wales.

[32] paras 2–3 of Schedule 6 to the 1990 Act.

[33] From July 1, 1999 the functions of the Secretary of State under Part 7 of the 1990 Act were
transferred to the National Assembly for Wales so far as relating to the CCW, and
s.132(1)(c) had effect so that reference to "the Secretary of State or any other minister"
included a reference to the National Assembly for Wales: SI 1999/672. In 2007 the
functions exercisable by the Assembly under the 1999 Order and the 1990 Act were
transferred to the Welsh Ministers under the Government of Wales Act 2006. For further
information see the note at page ix–x of *A Manual of Nature Conservation Law* 2nd edition,
(NCWG Publishing Ltd, 2008), Fry, NCWG Publishing Ltd (2008).

[34] SI 1989/492 (N.I. 3).

servation bodies in that it has no executive function—it does not, for example, itself notify areas of land as Sites of Special Scientific Interest (or, rather, Areas of Special Scientific Interest, as they are called in Northern Ireland[35]). Its role is purely consultative or advisory, reporting to the Department of the Environment. The constitution of the CNCC is provided for in the Schedule to the 1989 Order.

Joint Nature Conservation Council

10–019   The Joint Nature Conservation Council (JNCC) was established under Part 7 of the Environmental Protection Act 1990 but has since been reconstituted under section 31 of the Natural Environment and Rural Communities Act 2006 as a truly UK-wide body as from October 1, 2006.[36] The aim in setting up the JNCC was to some extent to re-introduce an element of co-ordination which might otherwise have been missing following the break-up of the Nature Conservancy Council. This co-ordination was seen as necessary at both a national (i.e. UK) level but also internationally, providing a single body to deal with the many cross-border issues involved in nature conservation, arising not least from the UK's membership of the European Union.

The JNCC's broad purpose of "nature conservation and fostering the understanding of nature conservation" is served by the carrying out of certain "co-ordinated functions" (sometimes referred to as "special functions"). These co-ordinated functions are set out at sections 34 to 37 of the 2006 Act and involve, in the main, providing advice and disseminating knowledge in relation to any nature conservation matter which (i) arises throughout the United Kingdom and raises issues common to England, Wales, Scotland and Northern Ireland, (ii) arises in one or more (but not all) of those places and affects the interests of the United Kingdom as a whole, or (iii) arises outside the United Kingdom. In addition, the JNCC is charged with establishing common standards throughout the UK for monitoring/research into nature conservation, including commissioning or supporting such research. A more specific function of the JNCC is the review of, and proposal of variation to, the lists of wild plants and animals given protection by virtue of Schedules 5 and 8 to the Wildlife and Countryside Act 1981 and the commissioning of research for the purpose (see section 36 of the 2006 Act). The composition of the JNCC is described at Schedule 4 to the 2006 Act.

[35] See para.28 of SI 2002/3153 (N.I. 7).
[36] SI 2006/2541.

Marine Management Organisation (proposed)

On April 3, 2008 Defra published a Draft Marine Bill,[37] one of the key features of which is the creation of a Marine Management Organisation (MMO). The MMO will be an independent non-departmental public body and is intended to be the government's regulator of most activities in the marine environment. Its general objective is stated to be "to carry out its functions with the objective of making a contribution to the achievement of sustainable development" (Clause 2). As such, it will have wide functions and responsibilities, in particular in relation to marine licensing and planning, of which marine nature conservation forms only part.

10–020

Part of the MMO's functions will include contributing to the selection by the Secretary of State of Marine Conservation Zones (MCZs, of which see more below). It will then, in its planning and licensing capacity, consider applications with the interests of MCZs and conservation objectives generally in mind. The MMO will also have power to make conservation orders (and interim orders where urgent action is needed) to regulate otherwise unregulated activities when this is necessary to further the conservation objectives for a MCZ (or a potential MCZ). It is intended that the MMO will undertake a similar role in respect of European marine sites also.

The MMO is to exercise its functions in the waters around England and also in the offshore area of the UK for matters that are not devolved. A Scottish Marine Management Organisation is planned to deal with matters inside Scottish territorial waters and devolved matters in the offshore area.

Other bodies

Environment Agency

The Environment Agency of England and Wales ("the Agency") came into existence on April 1, 1996, pursuant to the Environment Act 1995, which also created the Scottish Environment Protection Agency. The Agency is a body corporate which is funded by but largely independent of government, though overseen by the Secretary of State for Environment, Food and Rural Affairs. It took over the roles and responsibilities of the National Rivers Authority (NRA), Her Majesty's Inspectorate of Pollution (HMIP) and the waste regulation authorities in England and Wales. The Agency thus has a broad remit, including the management of water resources, control of pollution, flood control, land drainage, fisheries and navigation, all of which have implications for nature conservation. The Agency is

10–021

---

[37] For the full Draft Marine Bill, along with extensive explanatory notes and accompanied by a policy Paper and Impact Assessment, see *http://www.official-documents.gov.uk/document/cm73/7351/7351.pdf*.

subject to specific duties in the exercise of its powers, including the promotion of conservation in the aquatic environment (section 6), and to have regard to the desirability of conserving and enhancing natural beauty and of conserving flora, fauna and geological or physiographical features (section 7). Special provision is also made in relation to the Agency's duties with respect to SSSIs (section 8).

Forestry Commission

10–022   The Forestry Commission came into existence on September 1, 1919, as a response to the long decline in woodland resources, the gravity of which had been highlighted by the wartime need for indigenous timber. It has in the intervening period enjoyed some degree of success in reversing the decline in forestation and, as the body with ownership or management of approximately 827,000 hectares of woodland in the UK (representing 29 per cent of the total area of woodland in the UK)[38] is of major importance in the promotion of nature conservation. It is subject to a statutory duty to endeavour to achieve a reasonable balance between, on the one hand, the interests of forestry, afforestation and timber supply and, on the other, "the conservation and enhancement of natural beauty and the conservation of flora, fauna, and geological or physiographical features of special interest".[39] The Commission has a regulatory role as regards the private sector, requiring a felling licence to be obtained before any significant felling is carried out but also offering a range of grants for woodland creation, woodland management and other related activities.[40]

Crown Estate Commissioners

10–023   The Crown Estate Commissioners constitute a body corporate charged on behalf of the Crown with the function of managing and turning to account land and other property, rights and interests known as the Crown Estate.[41] The majority (by value) of the Crown Estate is urban, including a large number of properties in central London, but the Estate also owns 110,000 hectares (272,000 acres) of agricultural land and forest, more than 55 per cent of the UK's foreshore and tidal river-beds and almost all of the seabed

---

[38] Forestry Statistics 2007: *http://www.forestry.gov.uk/forestry/infd-7aqdgc.*
[39] Forestry Act 1967, s.1(3A). See further the Environmental Impact Assessment (Forestry) (England and Wales) Regulations 1999 (SI 1999/2228) and the Environmental Impact Assessment (Forestry) (Scotland) Regulations 1999 (SSI 1999/43), implementing Council Directive 85/337/EEC on the assessment of the effects of certain public and private projects on the environment.
[40] See generally *http://www.forestry.gov.uk/.*
[41] Crown Estate Act 1961, s.1(1).

within the 12 nautical miles limit; over 400 Sites of Special Scientific Interest are included within the Crown Estate.[42]

The Crown Estate Act 1961 Act does not impose any specific conservation duties (except in so far as these may be included within "the requirements of good management", to which the Commissioners are to have regard[43]) but the general balancing duties owed by all public bodies will apply.[44]

Natural Environment Research Council

The Natural Environment Research Council (NERC) was established under section 1(3) of the Science and Technology Act 1965 to carry out or support research into the earth sciences and ecology and the provision of advice on matters related to its activities. NERC's remit also originally included the establishment, maintenance and management of nature reserves but this function was transferred to the Nature Conservancy Council in 1973.[45]   10–024

NERC retains a key role in the co-ordination of research in the environmental field, supporting several research institutes including the British Antarctic Survey, British Geological Survey, National Marine Facilities (part of the National Oceanography Centre, Southampton) and the Centre for Ecology and Hydrology. Whilst the NERC has no legal powers to intervene directly for the benefit of nature conservation, it has a consultative role in relation to proposals made by government and other organisations.[46]

Habitat Conservation: EU Law

Introduction

The conservation of wildlife is clearly an area in which there are strong arguments in favour of a co-ordinated, international or supra-national approach. Yet for some time the competence of the European Community to intervene in this area remained uncertain, peripheral as it was (or was seen to be) to the internal market goal which formed the motor of European integration over the latter half of the twentieth century. Hence, the first major piece of European legislation in the field, the Birds Directive, was required to be passed by unanimous vote of the Council, pursuant to   10–025

---

[42] *http://www.thecrownestate.co.uk.*
[43] Crown Estate Act 1961, s.1(3).
[44] See Countryside Act 1968, s.11; Countryside (Scotland) Act 1967, s.66.
[45] Nature Conservancy Council Act 1973, sections 1(3), 1(7), 5(2), 5(3), Sch.2, para.1 & Sch.4.
[46] For further information see *http://www.nerc.ac.uk/.*

the reserve power under Article 235 (now 308) of the EC Treaty to attain one of the objectives of the Community where the Treaty has not provided the necessary powers.

The Birds Directive lays down general rules on the conservation of species[47] of naturally occurring wild birds[48] in the European territory of Member States.[49] Individual Member States are not permitted to give protection only to such species as occur in their own territory—the territory in question is the European territory of all Member States combined.[50] Member States are obliged by Article 2 of the Directive to take the requisite measures to maintain the population of the species in question.[51] A number of "special conservation measures" are referred to in the Directive as methods of achieving this objective, including the creation of protected areas (referred to as Special Protection Areas or SPAs, of which more below), the upkeep and management of land both inside and outside the specially protected zones in accordance with the ecological needs of habitats in the zones, the re-establishment of destroyed biotopes and the creation of biotopes.[52]

The current Title XIX (formerly XVI) of the Treaty, a product of the Single European Act which took effect in 1987, provides explicit competence in the field of the environment, with measures to be passed by either qualified majority in the Council or unanimity where they are primarily of a fiscal nature or they affect planning, water resources, land use (with the exception of waste management) or they significantly affect a Member State's choice between different energy sources and the general structure of its energy supply.[53] It was under this explicit power that the second major intervention in the field of nature conservation was passed—the Habitats Directive.

---

[47] See however Case C-202/94 *Van der Feesten* [1996] ECR I-355 at para.18, where the Court determined that the Directive also applies to bird subspecies which occur naturally in the wild only outside the European territory of the Member States if the species to which they belong or other subspecies of that species occur naturally in the wild within the territory in question.

[48] As opposed to birds born and reared in captivity—see Case C-149/94 *Vergy* [1996] ECR I-299.

[49] For an explanation of the concept of "European territory of Member States", see *R v Secretary of State for Trade and Industry and others, ex parte Greenpeace Ltd (No. 2)* [2002] Env. L.R. 221.

[50] See Case 247/85 *Commission v Belgium* [1987] ECR 3029, Case C-149/94 *Vergy* [1996] ECR I-299 and Case 262/85 *Commission v Italy* [1987] ECR 3073.

[51] The qualification applied to this of "taking account of economic and recreational requirements" has been held not to constitute an independent derogation from the general requirements of the Directive: see, in particular, Case C-44/95 *Royal Society for the Protection of Birds* [1996] ECR I-3805.

[52] According to the second edition of the Oxford English Dictionary, a biotope is "the smallest sub-division of a habitat, characterised by a high degree of uniformity in its environmental conditions and in its plant and animal life". This definition was cited with apparent approval by Wall L.J. in *R (Fisher) v English Nature* [2004] EWCA Civ 663 at para.20.

[53] See Chapter 1—Sources of Environmental Law.

The major mechanism for protection introduced by the Habitats   10–026
Directive is the Special Area of Conservation (SAC), which applies to areas
containing the natural habitat types listed in Annex I of that Directive
(such as coastal lagoons) and sites containing the habitats of species listed
in Annex II (such as the *Rhinolophus blasii* or Blasius' Horseshoe Bat).

The Birds and Habitats Directives, though 13 years apart, share certain
structural and substantive features; in particular each includes both measures to protect individual species and measures concerned with the conservation of habitats.[54] Further, Article 3 of the Habitats Directive creates a
Community-wide network of protected sites known as "Natura 2000",
comprising those sites designated as SPAs under the Birds Directive and
those designated as SACs under the Habitats Directive. The coherence of
the Natura 2000 network is maintained by the application of a common
standard of protection across sites of either designation.[55] Indeed, this
distinction between the process of designation (which differs between the
Directives) and method of protection (which is essentially the same in
each) is key to understanding the operation of this area of nature conservation law.[56]

Designating European sites

The fundamental contrast between designation of SPAs and SACs is that   10–027
the selection and designation of SPAs is within the control of the Member
States (though subject to review by the European Court of Justice, usually
on application by the Commission, for compliance with the States' obligations under the Birds Directive). Designation of SACs on the other hand
is essentially a two-stage process under which the Member States provide
an exhaustive list of candidate SACs, from which the Commission selects a
number to form a coherent network (deemed Sites of Community
Importance—SCIs), which the Member States are then obliged to designate as SACs.[57]

---

[54] The species-specific measures of the Birds Directive and Habitats Directive are dealt with
below at para.10–077ff.

[55] Article 7 of the Habitats Directive provides that any obligations arising under Article 4(4)
of the Birds Directive shall be replaced by Article 6(2), (3) and (4) of the Habitats
Directive from the date of its implementation. The deadline for national implementation
was May 21, 1994 (two years from its notification) whereas the main implementing provisions in the UK, the Conservation (Natural Habitats, &c.) Regulations 1994 did not
come into force until October 30, 1994.

[56] The European Commission in 2006 published a useful document summarising the provisions of each of these two major Directives and key case law, entitled "Nature and
Biodiversity Cases—Rulings of the European Court of Justice" which may be found at
http://ec.europa.eu/environment/nature/info/pubs/docs/others/ecj_rulings_en.pdf.

[57] See Case C-244/05, *Bund Naturschutz in Bayern eV and others v Freistaat Bayern* [2006]
ECR I-08445, at para.39ff.

Special protection areas

10–028   Article 1 of the Birds Directive provides that in respect of wild birds "Member States shall take the requisite measures to preserve, maintain or re-establish a sufficient diversity and area of habitats". Article 4 provides:

> "The species mentioned in Annex I shall be the subject of special conservation measures concerning their habitat in order to ensure their survival and reproduction in their area of distribution . . . Member States shall classify in particular the most suitable territories in number and size as special protection areas for the conservation of these species, taking into account their protection requirements in the geographical sea and land area where this Directive applies."

In addition, Member States are obliged to take "similar measures" in relation to migratory birds not listed at Annex I (Article 4(2)).

The classification of SPAs is a matter for the Secretary of State, not any of the conservation bodies, though they of course have an important role in assessing and suggesting possible sites and consulting with interested parties.[58] The question of upon what criteria national authorities are to determine which areas are "most suitable in number and size" to be classified as SPAs has been the subject of judicial determination on several occasions. In particular, in Case C-355/90 *Commission v Spain*[59] (the "*Santoña Marshes*" case), the European Court of Justice determined that the Spanish government was in breach of Article 4 by failing to designate an important wetland area as an SPA. The principle underlying the Court's decision was that once an area is determined to fulfil the objective ornithological criteria laid down in the Directive, a Member State is under an obligation to designate.

This approach was followed in Case C-44/95 *R v Secretary of State for the Environment, ex parte Royal Society for the Protection of Birds*[60] (the "*Lappel Bank*" case). In that case, the RSPB challenged the Secretary of State's decision to exclude an area known as Lappel Bank from land to be designated as an SPA on the Medway Estuary and Marshes in Kent. The area did not itself host Annex I or migratory species but its loss would likely affect the overall integrity of the ecosystem. The background to the decision not to designate was that the area in question adjoined the port of Sheerness, which was looking to expand by reclaiming the area. The UK government argued that the economic considerations created by this planned expansion were relevant, particularly on the basis that economic considerations were mentioned in the preamble to the Directive. The

---

[58] See *R(Aggregate Industries UK Limited) v English Nature & Secretary of State for the Environment, Food and Rural Affairs* [2002] EWHC 908 (Admin), April 24, 2002.

[59] Case C-355/90 *Commission v Spain* [1993] ECR I-4221.

[60] Case C-44/95 *R v Secretary of State for the Environment, ex parte Royal Society for the Protection of Birds* [1997] QB 206.

Court nonetheless held that the duty to designate was not affected by economic considerations.[61] Of interest is also the recent judgment in Case C-418/04 *Commission v Ireland*,[62] where the Court, in finding Ireland to be in breach of its designation obligations under the Birds Directive, also found that in the absence of scientific studies capable of rebutting the results of BirdLife International's inventory of important bird areas in Europe, published in 2000 ("IBA 2000"), that inventory is the most up-to-date and accurate reference for identifying the most suitable sites in number and in size for the conservation of the species listed in Annex I to the Birds Directive and for the regularly occurring migratory species not listed in that annex.

On the question of how boundaries to SPAs are to be drawn, in *R v Secretary of State for Scotland & ors, ex parte WWF U.K. Ltd and RSPB*[63] the Court of Session held that the Secretary of State had unduly fettered his discretion (already strictly limited by the terms of the *Santoña Marshes* judgment) by using the boundaries of existing, domestically designated, Sites of Special Scientific Interest as the starting point for drawing the boundaries of SPAs. The drawing of boundaries should be based on ornithological criteria alone. However, the ecological or ornithological grounds on which the boundary-drawing discretion was to be exercised did not need to be so objective as to enable a court to rule on them. Provided it was within the bounds of reasonableness, the court would not interfere.

10–029

As at August 31, 2007, 253 sites in the UK had been classified as SPAs, covering a total area of 1,583,928 hectares.[64]

Special areas of conservation

The Habitats Directive sets up a more prescriptive process for the designation of protected sites, essentially involving a dialogue between the national authorities of the individual Member States and the Commission. The first stage is for Member States to send to the Commission a list of candidate sites, drawn up by reference to the criteria laid down in Annex III to the Directive. Then, stage two, the Commission must draw up a draft list of "sites of Community importance" (SCIs), again by reference to the criteria set out in Annex III. The Commission then adopts a final list, having taken advice from a committee of independent experts. The Commission also produces a separate list of those sites which it considers

10–030

---

[61] In the event, and to the regret of many, the planned expansion went ahead anyway owing to the House of Lords' refusal to grant interim relief by way of an injunction pending the ECJ's decision.

[62] Case C-418/04 *Commission v Ireland*, Judgment of the Court (Second Chamber) December 12, 2007.

[63] *WWF U.K. Ltd v Secretary of State for Scotland* [1999] 1 CMLR 1021.

[64] *http://www.jncc.gov.uk/page-1399*.

host one or more of the priority habitat types or species listed in Annexes I and II. The Directive also provides, at Article 5, for a consultation mechanism between Member States and the Commission where the Commission considers that a priority site has not been included in the Member State's list of proposed sites; where a dispute remains, resolution is the responsibility of the Council. Once the Commission has adopted the list of sites of Community importance (SCIs), Member States are under a duty to designate any site on the list as a Special Area of Conservation (SAC).

At the time of writing, there are 608 SACs in the United Kingdom, covering an area of over 2.5 million hectares (over half of which is in Scotland).[65] There are an additional six candidate SACs, i.e. sites which have been submitted to the European Commission but not yet formally adopted.[66] The most recent tranche of candidate SACs (Tranche 35) was submitted to the Commission on August 31, 2007. As a matter of policy and law, these candidate sites are treated as if they have already achieved SAC status.[67]

In Case C-71/99 *Commission v Germany*,[68] the Court held that a Member State may be in breach of its obligations under the Habitats Directive where it submits a list of candidate SACs which is "manifestly inadequate".[69] The enforcement of Member States' obligations by the Commission on this basis may present advantages as compared with a multiplicity of actions aimed at gaining the inclusion of individual sites, but there are yet to be laid down any clear criteria for determining when a list of proposals is manifestly inadequate.

As with SPAs, considerable controversy has surrounded the UK's application of the designation criteria. In Case C371/98 *R v Secretary of State for the Environment, Transport and the Regions, ex parte First Corporate Shipping Ltd*,[70] the ECJ held that Member States may not take economic, social or cultural requirements into account in order to remove sites of ecological interest at national level from the list of proposed sites sent to the

---

[65] *http://www.jncc.gov.uk/page-1456.*
[66] In addition, there are a further nine possible SACs (pSACs), i.e. sites which the relevant conservation bodies have advised the UK government are suitable for designation but which have not yet been put forward to the Commission and 1 draft SAC (dSAC), which is an area that has been formally advised to UK government as suitable for selection an SAC, but has not yet been approved by government for public consultation.
[67] See PPS 9 and ODPM Circular 06/05 and *Habitats and Birds Directive: June 2000* (Scottish Executive) and Case C-117/03 *Società Italiana Dragaggi SpA and Others v Ministero delle Infrastrutture e dei Trasporti and Another*, Judgment of the Court (Second Chamber) January 13, 2005, at para.27; Case C-244/05, *Bund Naturschutz in Bayern eV and others v Freistaat Bayern*, at para.46.
[68] Case C-71/99 *Commission v Germany* [2001] ECR I-5811.
[69] See also Case C-3/96 *Commission v Netherlands* [1999] Env LR 147 in which the designation of an insufficient number and total area of sites was held to constitute a breach of the Netherlands' obligations under the Directive.
[70] Case C371/98 *R v Secretary of State for the Environment, Transport and the Regions, ex parte First Corporate Shipping Ltd* [2000] ECR I-9253.

Commission. The requirement under Article 3 of the Directive to set up a "coherent European ecological network" could only be satisfied if all eligible sites were nominated at the first stage. Only if all sites that met the ecological criteria set out in the Directive were put forward would the Commission have an exhaustive list from which to ensure that the coherent network was established.

In *R v Secretary of State for Trade and Industry and others, ex parte Greenpeace Ltd (No. 2)*,[71] the High Court examined the government's interpretation of the Habitats Directive's geographical scope, specified in the Directive as "the European territory of Member States", as referring only to areas within the 12-mile limit of UK territorial waters. The court, persuaded by references to distant water species in the Directive, took the view that the Directive applies to the entirety of the UK's continental shelf.   **10–031**

Protecting European sites

Originally, the obligation on Member States under the Birds Directive in relation to designated SPAs was to take appropriate steps to avoid significant pollution or deterioration of the habitat or disturbance of the birds within it (Article 4(4)). However, the strict interpretation applied to this provision by the ECJ in Case C-57/89 *Commission v Germany*[72] (the "*Leybucht Dykes*" case) amongst others, to the effect that reducing the area of an SPA was justified only where the works were necessary for reasons of public health or public safety and not for merely economic or recreational reasons, led for some while to significant unease among Member States. This was resolved by Article 6 of the Habitats Directive, which established a more flexible approach towards economic considerations for both SPAs and SACs.   **10–032**

The requirements of Article 6 of the Habitats Directive

In broad terms, the Article 6 regime requires, in relation to SPAs, SCIs and SACs, the following: **10–033**

1. The Member State must take appropriate steps to avoid the deterioration of the sites and significant disturbance of the species for which the areas have been designated (Article 6(2));

---

[71] *R v Secretary of State for Trade and Industry and others, ex parte Greenpeace Ltd (No. 2)* [2002] Env. L.R. 221.
[72] Case C-57/89 *Commission v Germany* [1991] ECR I-883.

2. Any plan or project[73] not directly connected with the management of the site but which is likely to have a significant effect on it, is to be subjected to an appropriate assessment of its implications, and the plan or project may be permitted to go ahead only if it will not adversely affect the integrity of the site concerned (Article 6(3));

3. Qualifying 2 above, in the absence of a viable alternative solution, a plan or project may be carried out if there are imperative reasons of overriding public interest, including those of a social or economic nature (Article 6(4)) but compensatory measures must be taken to ensure the overall coherence of the Natura 2000 network.[74]

In addition, there are parallel obligations under Article 4(1) and (2) of the Birds Directive and Article 6(1) of the Habitats Directive to adopt "special" or "necessary" conservation measures, such as management plans or other appropriate statutory, administrative or contractual measures.

Consistent with the principle that Directives shall be binding on Member States as to the result to be achieved but shall leave to the national authorities the choice of form and methods (enshrined in Article 249 of the Treaty), the precise manner in which Member States are to afford the relevant protection to European Sites designated under the Birds and Habitats Directives is largely a matter for their discretion. However, unless legislation is "made to measure", it is unlikely fully to meet the Member States' obligations; for example, in Case C-418/04 *Commission v Ireland* the Court noted that existing directives mandating Environmental Impact Assessments and Strategic Environmental Assessments contained rules on the decision-making procedure but Member States were not bound to accept the decision, whereas under Article 6(3) of the Habitats Directive a plan or project may be agreed to only if the integrity of the site concerned will not be adversely affected, with only limited exceptions on grounds of overriding public interest; subjecting projects to EIAs and SEAs was

---

[73] In Case C-127/02 *Landelijke Vereniging tot Behoud van de Waddenzee and Another v Staatssecretaris van Landbouw, Natuurbeheer en Visserij*, Judgment of the Court (Grand Chamber), 7 September 2004, [2005] All ER (EC) 353, (the "*Waddenzee*" case) the Court determined that mechanical cockle fishing which had been carried on for many years but for which a licence was granted annually for a limited period, with each licence entailing a new assessment both of the possibility of carrying on that activity and of the site where it may take place, fell within the meaning of "plan or project" in Article 6(3). Moreover, even if a project passed the assessment required by Article 6(3), there was still an ongoing duty to avoid deterioration of the site under Article 6(2).

[74] For instructive guidance on the application of the provisions of Article 6, including a review of the relevant case law, see the Commission documents "Managing Natura 2000 sites. The provisions of Article 6 of the 'Habitats' Directive 92/43/EEC" (2000), as supplemented by "Assessment of plans and projects significantly affecting Natura 2000 sites" (November 2001) and "Guidance document on Article 6(4) of the 'Habitats' Directive 92/43/EEC" (January 2007), available from *http://ec.europa.eu/environment/nature/natura2000/management/guidance_en.htm*.

therefore no substitute for the strict criterion laid down by the Birds Directive.[75]

UK fulfilment of obligations to protect European sites

Initially, in the UK the preferred approach to implementation of both the 10–034 Birds and Habitats Directives was simply through the pre-existing mechanisms of the town planning and SSSI systems. However, in the light of the *Leybucht Dykes* and *Santoña Marshes* cases it became clear that the shortcomings of the town planning and SSSI systems (insufficiently strict protection from interference, inapplicability to areas—particularly SPAs and Ramsar sites—which lay below the low-water mark), required a more tailor-made approach in the form of the Conservation (Natural Habitats etc.) Regulations 1994 (SI 1994/2716) ("the 1994 Regulations").[76]

The 1994 Regulations provide that within Great Britain the Minister is under a duty to keep a register of European Sites[77] and to notify the appropriate statutory conservation body when an entry is made or amended. That body is then obliged to notify the owners and occupiers of the land within the site, the relevant local planning authority and anyone else that the Minister directs. The entry on the register is a local land charge in England and Wales. In Scotland, the planning authority is obliged to maintain a register of European Sites of which it has been notified.[78]

The Minister and the relevant nature conservation bodies are required to exercise their functions under the main conservation legislation so as to secure compliance with obligations contained in Article 6 of the Habitats Directive (see above). All other "competent authorities", which includes Ministers, government departments, public or statutory undertakers, public bodies and holders of public office[79] must simply "have regard to" the requirements of the Habitats Directive.

The 1994 Regulations, reflecting a long-standing preference for a 10–035 voluntary co-operation in the field of nature conservation, provide for the management agreement as the first means of ensuring the protection of European Sites.[80] These agreements are between the appropriate nature conservation body and the owner, lessee or occupier of the land in question

---

[75] Case C-418/04 *Commission v Ireland*, Judgment of the Court (Second Chamber) December 12, 2007, para.231; see also the Opinion of Advocate-General Kokott at para.148.

[76] This implementation has, however, itself been determined to be imperfect: see Case C-6/04 *Commission v UK*, Judgment of the Court (Second Chamber) October 20, 2005, and the consequent Offshore Marine Conservation (Natural Habitats, &c.) Regulations 2007 (discussed below).

[77] Defined under Regulation 10 of the 1994 Regulations (as amended) as a SAC, SCI, SPA, site subject to consultation under Article 5 of the Habitats Directive or a candidate SAC.

[78] regs 11 to 15 of the 1994 Regulations.

[79] reg.6(1) of the 1994 Regulations.

[80] reg.16 of the 1994 Regulations.

and may provide for its management, conservation, restoration or protection. Agreements may also be made in respect of land outside but adjacent to a European Site, where activities on the land could have an impact within the designated area. Such agreements may be enforceable as restrictive covenants against successors in title to the land. Provision is made for existing management agreements, orders, notifications and bylaws to continue to have effect as if made under the European Sites provisions.

In addition to management agreements, the 1994 Regulations also provided for the strengthening of the SSSI regime where an area of land was also designated as a European Site, taking advantage of the fact that in the vast majority of cases, the national designation was already in place. Regulation 18 provides that any notification as an SSSI in force in relation to a European site shall have effect for the purposes of the Regulations and empowers the appropriate nature conservation body to amend the notification for the purposes of securing compliance with the Habitats Directive. Regulation 22 gives the Secretary of State power to make a still further designation of any land within a European site by making what is called a "Special Nature Conservation Order" specifying operations which appear to him to be likely to destroy or damage the flora, fauna or geological or physio-geographical features by reason of which the land is a European site. Before making such an order, the Secretary of State is required to consult the appropriate conservation body.

In view, however, of the further strengthening of the regime applicable to all SSSIs by virtue of the Countryside and Rights of Way Act 2000 (see below), it is doubtful whether those SSSIs which also have a European designation enjoy any substantial extra protection.

10–036   The robustness of the protection offered by, in particular, Parts 4 and 4A of the Regulations, transposing the requirements of Articles 6(3) and (4) of the Habitats Directive, was put to the test in the context of an Inquiry (or more strictly a series of concurrent Inquiries) into various applications made by Associated British Ports in connection with their proposal to develop a new deep-water container terminal at Dibden Bay, Hampshire. Four planning applications were originally made to the New Forest District Council as local planning authority, but were called in by the Secretary of State for his own determination under Section 77 of the Town and Country Planning Act 1990.

A total of 6,141 persons or organisations objected to the proposed development. In particular, objection was taken to the likely effect of the development on the Solent and Southampton Water Ramsar site and SPA and the Solent Maritime and River Itchen candidate SACs. The Inspector charged with making recommendations to the Secretary of State found that there would be direct impacts on sites of local and national conservation importance and on these internationally-protected sites. The creation of conservation areas outside the affected areas did not mean that the integrity of the areas themselves was not adversely affected. The Inspector queried whether the proposed development was justified by "Imperative Reasons of Overriding Public Interest" as required under Regulation 49 (adopting the language of Article 6(4)). In particular, referring to the Commission document "Managing Natura 2000",[81] he considered that short-term economic or other benefits would not be sufficient to outweigh the long-term conservation interests protected by the Habitats Directive.[82] The Inspector accepted that there was no "alternative solution"[83] within the meaning of Article 6(4), but found that the proposed compensatory measures were "grossly inadequate", bearing in mind that the starting point should be that replacement habitat should be equivalent in area and form to the habitat destroyed.[84]

The Secretary of State's decision letter of April 20, 2004, refusing to make the orders necessary for continuation of the development, endorses in large part the reasoning and conclusions of the Inspector, particularly as to the impact of the project on wildlife and habitats in the area. The approach of the Secretary of State was perhaps even stricter in that following Commission guidance and ODPM Circular 06/2005, the consideration of "alternative solutions" was not confined to the locality in question but rather "alternative solutions could be located in different regions or countries".[85]

An argument that no project at all should be undertaken may be considered either as an "alternative solution" within the meaning of Article 6(4)[86] or as an argument that there does not exist an imperative reason of overriding public interest for the project to be carried out.[87]

---

[81] "Managing Natura 2000 sites. The provisions of Article 6 of the 'Habitats' Directive 92/43/EEC" (2000).

[82] The analysis of the question of imperative reasons of overriding public interest was among the matters going to the appropriateness of the assessment required under Regulation 48. See also *R(Lewis) v Redcar and Cleveland Borough Council* [2007] EWHC 3166 (Admin), at paras 113 to 131 and on appeal *sub nom. Persimmon Homes Teesside Limited v R(Lewis)* [2008] EWCA Civ 746 at para.73 to 87 of the judgment of Pill L.J.

[83] Article 6(4), as a derogation from Article 6(3) and the general protection offered by the Directive, must be interpreted strictly: see Case C-239/04 *Commission v Portugal*, (the "Castro Verde" case) Judgment of the Court (Second Chamber), October 26, 2006 at para.35 and the Opinion of Advocate-General Kokott. See also Case C-304/05 *Commission v Italy*, (the "Ski run" case) Judgment of the Court (Fourth Chamber), September 20, 2007.

[84] The requirement that the compensatory measures should safeguard the coherence of the Natura 2000 network was emphasised at paragraph 54 of the Opinion of Advocate-General Kokott in Case C-239/04 *Commission v Portugal*.

[85] Both the Inspector's Report (over 700 pages) and the Secretary of State's decision letter are available at *http://www.dft.gov.uk*.

[86] This was the approach of the Commission in its Tenerife port opinion of 2006, which may be found at *http://ec.europa.eu/environment/nature/info/pubs/docs/others/ecj_rulings_en.pdf*.

[87] This was the approach of Ouseley J. when interpreting Regulation 49 of the 1994 Regulations in *Humber Sea Terminal Limited v Secretary of State for Transport* [2005] EWHC 1289.

UK protection of European marine sites

10–037 The 1994 Regulations (discussed above) are applicable only within the land area of Great Britain and UK territorial waters. All of the existing marine Natura 2000 sites are coastal or associated with small islands/islets, although several do have substantial subtidal areas. This left the problem of implementation of Article 6 of Habitats Directive beyond the 12 nautical mile limit, i.e. to the remainder of the UK's Exclusive Economic Zone which, in Case C-6/04 *Commission v UK*,[88] the UK acknowledged it had failed to carry out.

On August 21, 2007 the Offshore Marine Conservation (Natural Habitats, & c.) Regulations 2007 entered into force, extending the area over which SACs and SPAs need to be designated to the UK offshore marine area (those waters, beyond 12 nautical miles, within British fishery limits and the seabed within the UK Continental Shelf Designated Area). To date, JNCC has identified seven possible offshore SACs, which have been put out to a public consultation (December 2007 to March 2008).

Although the UK has SPAs with marine components, only one entirely marine SPA has so far been designated in British waters; Carmarthen Bay was classified in 2003 for its non-breeding aggregations of common scoter.

10–038 It is yet to be made clear to what extent the new designation of Marine Conservation Zone (MCZ), proposed in the Draft Marine Bill (see below) will overlap with the areas to be designated as Marine European Sites (either SPA or SAC) under the 2007 Regulations.

Habitat Conservation: UK Measures

SSSIs—England and Wales[89]

Introduction

10–039 A Site of Special Scientific Interest (SSSI) is defined in section 52 of the Wildlife and Countryside Act 1981 ("the 1981 Act") as an area of land notified by a conservation body under section 28 as being of "special interest by reason of any of its flora, fauna, or geological or physiographical features."

---

[88] Case C-6/04 *Commission v UK*, Judgment of the Court (Second Chamber) October 20, 2005, [2005] ECR I-09017.

[89] The details of the legislative framework relating to Sites of Special Scientific Interest in Scotland (to which the changes brought about by the Countryside and Rights of Way Act 2000 do not apply) and Areas of Special Scientific Interest in Northern Ireland are outside the scope of this work. Readers are referred to the website of Scottish Natural Heritage at *http://www.snh.org.uk* and the website of Northern Ireland's Council for Nature Conservation and the Countryside at *http://www.cnccni.gov.uk*.

SSSIs comprise land,[90] the use of which is compulsorily restricted in the interest of nature conservation. With the exception of those SSSIs which are also National Nature Reserves, SSSIs are not held by any conservation body. One of the innovations of the Countryside and Rights of Way Act 2000 (CROWA) is to introduce a regime under which the owner or occupier of land may also be required to take positive steps to maintain the land in the interest of nature conservation.

SSSIs are by far the most widespread of the statutory nature conservation designations in England and Wales.[91] They are by no means confined to the countryside, for many are found in urban and suburban areas. Despite the common misconception, SSSI status does not confer automatic and absolute protection against development; the purpose of the designation is, and has always been, to ensure that nature conservation considerations are taken into account before any decision affecting the future of an SSSI is made.

The SSSI system in England and Wales

The Countryside and Rights of Way Act 2000 provided a radical overhaul **10–040** of the system of SSSIs in England and Wales,[92] strengthening controls on owners and occupiers of land notified as being of special scientific interest, including the introduction of a power for the nature conservation body to require positive steps to be taken to maintain the site. Provision is also made to extend the SSSI regime to prevent damaging activities by those other than owners or occupiers, such as public authorities and statutory undertakers.

The new sections 28 to 28R of the 1981 Act nonetheless maintain the same basic pattern to the operation of SSSIs, namely notification of sites by the relevant nature conservation body with consequent measures largely tailored to protect the features for which the notification was made.

---

[90] "Land" is defined by section 114 of the 1949 Act as including land covered by water; this definition applies by virtue of section 52(4) of the 1981 Act.

[91] There are over 4,000 Sites of Special Scientific Interest (SSSIs) in England, covering around 7 per cent of the country's land area. Over half of these sites, by area, are internationally important for their wildlife, and designated as Special Areas of Conservation (SACs), Special Protection Areas (SPAs) or Ramsar sites. Many SSSIs are also National Nature Reserves (NNRs) or Local Nature Reserves (LNRs). In Wales, the figure is over 1,000 SSSIs, covering just over 12 per cent of the country's land surface.

[92] CROWA does not apply to Scotland, where the 1981 Act (with minor amendments) continued to apply until the coming into force of the Nature Conservation (Scotland) Act 2004 on November 29, 2004. The 2004 Act adopts a very similar approach to CROWA in its stronger but more flexible protection of Scottish SSSIs.

The duty to notify

10–041   By section 28(1) of the 1981 Act, if Natural England[93] "are of the opinion that any area of land is of special interest by reason of any of its flora, fauna or geographical or physiographical features", they must "notify" that fact to the local planning authority, the owner and occupier of the land and the Secretary of State. Section 28(4) requires any such notification to specify (a) the relevant features of the land and (b) "any operations appearing to Natural England to be likely to damage ... those features."

A novel feature post-CROWA is that the notification is required to;

"contain a statement of Natural England's views about the management of the land (including any views Natural England may have about the conservation and enhancement of ... those features)."

This statement ties in with the shift towards positive management of sites and also the requirement for management plans under the Habitats Directive.[94] Paragraph 6 of Schedule 11 to CROWA requires similar statements of views to be produced in respect of pre-existing SSSIs.

Modification and denotification

10–042   Previously, notification of an SSSI was a "one-shot" process, which in some instances created difficulties on both sides in terms of any adjustments which might be required. Particularly, an over-inclusive approach was often taken to the specification of operations considered likely to damage the relevant features ("Potentially Damaging Operations" or "PDOs"), with the result that owners and occupiers were faced with a list of PDOs which appeared to exclude any exploitation of the land at all. Section 28A now provides for the making of variation notices by Natural England, which may "vary the matters specified or stated in the confirmed notification (whether by adding to them, changing them, or removing matter from them)" but which may not themselves vary the area of land affected.

Extension of the area of land affected may be achieved under two different bases: notification of additional land pursuant to section 28B or enlargement of the SSSI pursuant to section 28C. Notification of additional land applies where the conservation body is of the opinion that if extra land adjacent to an SSSI were combined with the SSSI, the combined area of land would be of special scientific interest. This may be the case particularly where the extra land would act as a "buffer zone", protecting the original area's features. Enlargement of the SSSI is appropriate where the conservation body is of the opinion that any area of land which includes, but also extends beyond, an SSSI is of special interest.

---

[93] Or, as the case may be, the Countryside Council for Wales—see s.27AA of the 1981 Act.
[94] See art.6(1) of Directive 92/43.

Section 28D provides a mechanism by which land which is no longer considered to be of special interest may be denotified. The procedure is similar to that which applies in respect of notification, save that the Environment Agency and relevant statutory undertakers must also be notified.

The consequences of notification

The primary consequence of notification of an area of land as an SSSI is **10–043** that the owner or occupier must not carry out on that land any PDO specified in that notification unless notice of a proposal to carry out the PDO has been given to the relevant conservation body and one of three further criteria is fulfilled, namely that the PDO is carried out with the conservation body's written consent, it is carried out in accordance with a pre-existing management agreement or in accordance with a management scheme or management notice. Importantly, this does away with the previous system under which an owner or occupier could simply tell the conservation body that a PDO was to be carried out and wait three (or, after 1985, four[95]) months, after which it could be carried out lawfully, regardless of the opposition of the conservation body.[96] The system now in fact works in the opposite way; if the conservation body does not respond within four months of being notified of an intention to carry out a PDO, then it is deemed to have refused consent—section 28F(2).

The consent of the relevant nature conservation body is therefore key, whether granted in advance pursuant to a management agreement, scheme or notice (see further below), or on an ad hoc basis in relation to an individual proposal. Section 28P provides that a person who fails to comply with consent provisions of section 28E without reasonable excuse commits an offence. A reasonable excuse includes authorisation by planning permission and the carrying out of operations in an emergency (provided that particulars of those operations are provided to the conservation body as soon as practicable after their commencement).

In terms of sanctions, it is frequently noted in the context of planning law that penalties for breach of an enforcement notice have not always had a deterrent effect. However, in a case before Durham Crown Court heard on January 28, 2008, Wemmergill Moor Ltd, a shooting estate company, was fined £50,000 and ordered to pay costs of £237,548 after pleading guilty to three offences under section 28P relating to the construction of a new

---

[95] Following an amendment introduced by the Wildlife and Countryside (Amendment) Act 1985.
[96] This situation was the subject of criticism from Lord Mustill in *Southern Water Authority v Nature Conservancy Council* [1992] 1 WLR 775. He said, at 778B, that "it needs only a moment to see that this regime is toothless, for it demands no more from the owner or occupier of an SSSI than a little patience", unless the Secretary of State could be persuaded to make a Nature Conservation Order under the old section 29, which Lord Mustill described as "a "task rarely accomplished".

track, car park and associated drainage on the moorland Lune Forest SSSI. Further, the court exercised its power under section 31 to order restoration of the land to its former state. The overall financial cost to the defendant was estimated at over £500,000.[97]

10–044　The new regime, whilst more flexible, is therefore potentially more onerous, in so far as it may impose mandatory obligations with genuine "teeth" for their enforcement. It is therefore to be welcomed that an appeal mechanism is introduced by CROWA to ensure fairness (and compliance with Article 6 of the European Convention on Human Rights). Section 28F provides owners and occupiers with a right of appeal to the Secretary of State against a decision by the relevant conservation body either refusing consent to carry out a PDO or attaching unwanted conditions, modifying or withdrawing such consent.

Extension of provisions to visitors, public authorities and statutory undertakers

10–045　A further novel feature of the scheme introduced by CROWA is the extension of liability for damage to features of special scientific interest to individuals other than owners or occupiers of the land.

Pursuant to section 28R, the relevant conservation bodies may make byelaws for the protection of an SSSI, adopting the mechanism which had been provided by the 1949 Act in relation to the making of byelaws for nature reserves. Such byelaws are a means of regulating the activities of visitors as well as owners and occupiers. Section 28P creates two distinct offences in relation to visitors. The first, under section 28P(6), applies where an individual has intentionally or recklessly destroyed, damaged or disturbed features for which a site is designated, and he knew that what he destroyed, damaged or disturbed was within an SSSI. The sanction is a fine not exceeding £20,000 on summary conviction or an unlimited fine if convicted on indictment. The second offence, under section 28P(6A),[98] is committed in the same way, save that the individual need not know that what he has damaged, etc. was within an SSSI. In such a case, the sanction is a fine not exceeding level 4 on the standard scale[99] on summary conviction.

As regards public authorities and statutory undertakers, section 28G imposes a duty to take reasonable steps, consistent with the proper exercise of the authority's functions, to further the conservation and enhancement of the features by reason of which a site is of special scientific interest. Framed in this way, the duty is obviously not a trump card, to be played when a development with environmental consequences is being con-

---

[97]　*http://www.naturalengland.org.uk/press/news2008/280108.htm.*
[98]　Introduced by Part 4 of the Natural Environment and Rural Communities Act 2006.
[99]　Currently £2,500—see section 17 of the Criminal Justice Act 1991.

sidered. However, it does at least make the effect on an SSSI of such a development a relevant and therefore lawful consideration.

Further, section 28H provides for a more specific duty in relation to **10–046** operations to be carried out by a statutory undertaker where such operations are likely to damage the designated features of a site, whether or not the operations are to be carried out on the site itself. The section provides for the giving of notice of such operations to the relevant conservation body. If assent is given then the operations may go ahead; if not, they may still go ahead provided that the authority notifies the conservation body of how it has taken account of any advice received from the conservation body. In any event, the works must be carried out in such a way as to give rise to as little damage as is reasonably practicable in all the circumstances; if any damage does occur, the site must be restored to its former condition, so far as is reasonably practicable. Similar provisions apply under section 28I in relation to the authorisation by a public authority or statutory undertaker of operations. Failure to meet these obligations may constitute a criminal offence—see section 28P(2) to (3).

Management agreements, statements, schemes and notices

Some explanation is required of these four similarly-named concepts.[100] A **10–047** *management agreement* is a contract between the owner or occupier of land and the relevant conservation body (entered into pursuant to powers under section 15 of the Countryside Act 1968 and section 16 of the National Parks and Access to the Countryside Act 1949), setting out obligations for maintaining or in some cases enhancing the value of a site, in return for which payment may be made.[101]

Under section 28(4), every notification of an SSSI must contain a statement of the relevant conservation body's views about the management of the land (hence *management statement*). This requirement is in part intended to fit with Article 6(1) of the Habitats Directive, requiring Member States to establish the necessary conservation measures for special areas of conservation, involving, if need be, appropriate management plans specifically designed for the site. This marks a shift in focus from pure prohibition of unwanted activities to a more active management of designated land.

A very similar concept is that of the *management scheme*, which is prepared by the relevant conservation body under s.28J, describing how best to conserve, and/or restore, the special features of an SSSI. This will be drawn up in discussion with the owners or occupiers. The aim is for all owners and occupiers of the land to be aware of the preferred methods of

---

[100] See, generally, Sites of Special Scientific Interest: Encouraging positive partnerships (Defra, 2003) *http://www.defra.gov.uk/wildlife-countryside/ewd/sssi/sssi-code.pdf*.
[101] See Guidelines on Management Agreement Payments and Other Related Matters (DETR, February 2001) *http://www.defra.gov.uk/wildlife-countryside/cl/gmapay/pdf/payments.pdf*.

managing the land to conserve or restore the special features for which the site was notified. Payment for compliance with the scheme is provided for at section 28M.

10–048   A *management notice* may be issued by a conservation body pursuant to section 28K if it has been unable to conclude, on reasonable terms, arrangements for implementing a management scheme, and if the special features for which the land was notified are being inadequately conserved. The notice requires the owner or occupier to carry out specific works within a specified time or allows the conservation body to enter the land and carry out work itself.

When all else fails, section 28N provides the power (by reference to section 103 of the 1949 Act) to make a compulsory purchase of all or part of an SSSI provided that the relevant conservation body is satisfied that it is unable to conclude, on reasonable terms, an agreement with the owner or occupier as to the management of the land or that it has entered into such an agreement but is satisfied that it has been breached in such a way that the land is not being managed satisfactorily. A dispute about whether there has been a breach of a management agreement is to be determined by an arbitrator appointed by the Lord Chancellor.

National Nature Reserves

10–049   The acquisition of rights in land so that it can be managed in the interests of wildlife has a long history, through which the underlying motive has gradually changed from field sports to nature conservation. Reserves specifically for the conservation of all nature (rather than a few game species) date back over 120 years[102] but, until the passage of the 1949 Act, their establishment fell to various private bodies set up for this purpose.

The 1949 Act allowed the establishment of what are now known as National Nature Reserves (NNRs) by the government's conservation bodies. There are currently 222 reserves in England, 66 in Wales and 55 in Scotland. All NNRs also carry the SSSI designation.

The powers given to the conservation bodies for the establishment of NNRs derive almost entirely from sections 15 to 21 of the 1949 Act. Over the years, these sections have been much amended by subsequent legislation, including the Science and Technology Act 1965, the Nature Conservancy Council Act 1973, the Environmental Protection Act 1990, and the Natural Heritage (Scotland) Act 1991, but such amendments are principally concerned with the transfer of powers following organisational changes affecting the Nature Conservancy and its successor bodies. A more significant amendment, however, is to be found in section 35 of the 1981

---

[102] The first were private ventures, with conservation organisations entering the field somewhat later. The National Trust, for example, acquired its first nature reserve at Wicken Fen, Cambridgeshire, in 1899.

Act which extends the powers of the conservation bodies under section 19 of the 1949 Act to declare as an NNR land[103] which they do not control, but which is held and managed as a nature reserve by an "approved body" (e.g. a County Naturalists' Trust or the Royal Society for the Protection of Birds (RSPB)).

The definition of "Nature Reserve"

The expression "Nature Reserve" is defined in section 15 of the 1949 Act **10–050** as meaning land managed for a conservation purpose with or without an additional recreational purpose (provided that the recreational purpose does not compromise its management for the conservation purpose). Land is "managed for a conservation purpose" if it is managed for the purpose of:

(a) providing under suitable conditions and control special opportunities for the study of, and research into, matters relating to the fauna and flora of Great Britain and the physical conditions in which they live, and for the study of geological and physiographical features of special interest in the area; or

(b) preserving flora and fauna or geological or physiographical features of special interest in the area;

or for both these purposes.

The 1949 Act refers only to "nature reserves", and although the term "National Nature Reserve" was much employed by the Nature Conservancy and its successor bodies, it did not receive statutory recognition until the 1981 Act. As mentioned below, section 21 of the 1949 Act also gave powers to local authorities to establish their own separate nature reserves, thus creating the distinction between "National" and "Local" nature reserves.

The 1949 Act set no qualitative standards for eligibility as an NNR; its sole requirement is that the area declared should be managed for scientific research and study and/or for the conservation of its features of special interest. What was meant by "special interest" was nowhere defined. Although Nature Reserve Agreements could only be concluded for land which the Nature Conservancy considered should in the national interest be managed as a nature reserve, there appears to have been no restraint on the Nature Conservancy if it chose to declare any land it owned or leased as an NNR. Indeed, by section 19(2), a declaration by the appropriate conservation body that land is being managed as a Nature Reserve is to be taken as conclusive of the matters declared.

---

[103] "Land" is currently defined by s.114 of the 1949 Act. Clause 136 of the Draft Marine Bill proposes an amendment to s.35 of the 1981 Act in order to clarify the circumstances in which NNRs may extend beyond mean low water mark or estuarial waters.

This lack of criteria was to some extent made good by the 1981 Act which, in section 35, stipulates in effect that the appropriate conservation body must be satisfied that land is of national importance before it can be declared an NNR, whether it is owned, leased or established by agreement. There is thus a presumption that NNRs will be of higher quality than Sites of Special Scientific Interest, since section 28 of the 1981 Act does not require the latter to be of national importance (although the contrary has often been argued by the conservation bodies).[104]

Management of NNRs

10–051 Given that all NNRs (at least in England and Wales) now also have SSSI status, which post-CROWA enables the making of byelaws, management agreements etc, the mechanism for management of NNRs set out at sections 15 to 21 of the 1949 Act is now largely redundant.

Local Nature Reserves

10–052 In addition to permitting the national Government's conservation body to establish (national) nature reserves, the 1949 Act, by section 21, also gave counties and county boroughs in England and Wales, and burghs in Scotland, the power to provide, or to secure the provision of, nature reserves on any land in their area—not being land held by the Nature Conservancy or subject to an NRA—which they thought expedient to manage as a nature reserve. Before exercising this power, councils had first to consult with the Nature Conservancy. County districts received similar powers, but could only exercise these with the consent of both the relevant county council and the Nature Conservancy.

Section 194 of the Local Government Act 1972 equalised the powers of district, county and local planning authorities and Schedule 30 to the same Act removed the need for the county districts to obtain the consent of their county and of the Nature Conservancy; in consequence of these changes, and of the re-organisation of the nature conservation agencies, district councils and county councils now have powers to establish nature reserves under section 21 of the 1949 Act, having first consulted the appropriate conservation body.

Such nature reserves are customarily known as "Local Nature Reserves" (LNRs) to distinguish them from the "National Nature Reserves" (NNRs) established by the relevant national conservation body. Both types of reserve are governed by sections 15 to 21 of the 1949 Act but, in the case of LNRs, references in sections 16(1) and 17(1) to the national interest are to

---

[104] The need for an NNR to possess "national importance" was demonstrated in 1990 when the Tring Reservoirs NNR, established in 1955, was "de-declared" as no longer meeting the required standard (17th Annual Report of the Nature Conservancy Council (for 1990–91), p.12).

be taken to include references to the interests of the locality.[105] The requirements in section 35 of the 1981 Act that new NNRs are to be of national importance does not apply to LNRs, so there is no explicit constraint on a council, other than the need to consult the appropriate conservation body, as to the quality in nature conservation terms of any land that it may choose to declare as an LNR. In comparison with NNRs, the typical LNR is much smaller, much more likely to be found in an urban than in a rural setting, and much more likely to lie in lowland than in upland Britain.[106]

The statutory provisions for LNRs are *mutatis mutandis* the same as for **10–053** NNRs. Thus the same definition of "nature reserve" in section 15 of the 1949 Act applies to both types, namely land managed to provide special opportunities for study and research, or to preserve the flora and fauna and/or geological features of special interest. Powers for the compulsory purchase of land to be managed as an LNR are provided, as a last resort, in sections 17 and 18 and are subject to dispute procedures.[107] LNRs are likewise declared under the provisions of section 19; they may be established without any need for outside approval or consultation, although, in the case of LNRs, the appropriate conservation body must be consulted; and councils may introduce byelaws for any LNR under section 20.

As noted above, section 25 of the 1981 Act extended the powers of the conservation bodies to enable them to declare as an NNR land held by an approved body and managed as a "nature reserve". A local authority could well be "approved" in this sense, so that land already declared as an LNR could also be declared as an NNR by a conservation body. However, the reverse procedure is not possible, as the power to do this is expressly excluded by the terms of section 21(1) of the 1949 Act.

LNRs are evaluated and chosen in a purely local context and many do not attain the standards set for SSSIs. In these circumstances, it has been impracticable for the conservation bodies to notify all LNRs as SSSIs under the 1981 Act. Rather than seeking to conserve natural interests of high value, which is the function of the SSSI, the role of LNRs is seen as providing facilities for education and research, or for the informal enjoyment of nature by the public, on land which, while not necessarily of high value, is managed so that its biological or geological interests are preserved or enhanced or interpreted.

---

[105] s.21(4).
[106] At the time of writing, the latest figures for LNRs are 1,280 in England, 53 in Wales and 51 in Scotland.
[107] s.18(3),(4).

Marine Nature Reserves

10–054 Marine Nature Reserves (MNRs)[108] were introduced by sections 36 and 37 of the 1981 Act. They are unique among British nature conservation designations in their physical coverage, and may comprise any land covered, whether continuously or intermittently, by tidal waters or parts of the sea up to the seaward limits of British territorial waters.[109] By contrast all other domestic conservation areas or sites are land-based and extend seaward only as far as the low water mark of neap tides in England and Wales, and of spring tides in Scotland.

MNRs are also unique among British nature conservation designations in that they are designated, not by a conservation body, but by the appropriate Secretary of State; in all other cases, the conservation bodies have sufficient powers to notify or declare conservation areas without the need to seek outside authority.

Under section 36(1), the Secretary of State may by order designate a MNR if he thinks it expedient that the land and water over it be managed by the relevant conservation body for the purpose of conserving marine flora or fauna or geological or physiographical features of special interest in the area, or providing, under suitable conditions and control, special opportunities for the study of, and research into matters relating to this flora and fauna and these features. Following designation, the Agency must manage the MNR for either or both of these purposes.

10–055 The procedure has to be initiated by an application from the conservation body, whereupon the steps set out in Schedule 12 must be followed. A draft of the order is prepared, published and served on every relevant authority[110] in whose area the proposed MNR lies and, at the Secretary of State's discretion, on every person with an interest in the proposed MNR, and on such other bodies as he considers appropriate. If the draft order is unopposed, it can be made without delay; if, however, the draft order is opposed, a local inquiry ensues.

Section 37 of the 1981 Act gives the conservation body powers to make byelaws for the protection of the MNRs, subject to the consent of the Secretary of State. Section 36(2) requires that a copy of any bye-laws proposed at the time of the initial application for the MNR order, and of any byelaws made or proposed by any relevant authority, must accompany the application; such byelaws, as approved or modified by the Secretary of State, are confirmed as part of the order. Any subsequently proposed are made in accordance with the procedures of section 236 to 238 of the Local Government Act 1972 in relation to England and Wales as though the

---

[108] It is intended that the proposed Marine Conservation Zone (see below) proposed in the Draft Marine Bill will supersede the Marine Nature Reserve designation.

[109] s.36(1).

[110] "Relevant authority" is defined in s.36(7), and includes a local authority; the National Rivers Authority and a River Purification Board; navigation, harbour pilotage and lighthouse authorities; and a local fisheries committee.

conservation body were a local authority, subject to any modifications as may be made to those sections by statutory instrument.[111]

Byelaws made under section 37 can prevent entry into the MNR, prohibit any interference with fauna, flora and any object within the MNR, and introduce a permit system. They cannot, however, interfere with the right of passage of any vessel other than a pleasure boat, and even pleasure boats cannot be excluded from all of the reserve for all of the year. They may not prohibit anything done for reasons of safety or preventing damage to vessels or cargo; discharges from vessels; or anything done more than 30 metres below the sea bed. Enforcement may only be undertaken by the conservation body, unless the Director of Public Prosecution otherwise directs.

In practice, the procedures for the establishment of MNRs (set out in Schedule 12 of the 1981 Act) have proved so difficult to complete that only one in England (Lundy), one in Wales (Skomer) and one in Northern Ireland (Stranford Lough) have been designated within almost 30 years of the provision of the relevant powers. In view of the Draft Marine Bill, the MNR designation is now on the verge of becoming a dead letter.

10–056

Marine Conservation Zones (proposed)

Part 4 of the draft Marine Bill[112] sets out a new site designation in respect of marine sites—the Marine Conservation Zone (MCZ). The background to the new designation is the perceived inadequacy of the present means available for protecting the marine environment. In particular, the European Site designations of Special Protection Areas and Special Areas of Conservation are limited to the protection of habitats and species of European, rather than national, importance. Equally, Marine Nature Reserves (to be replaced by MCZs) are limited in their power to protect the marine environment and can only be designated up to three nautical miles from the coast.

10–057

MCZs are intended to assist in meeting the UK's obligations under a range of international convention, including the United Nations Convention on Law of the Sea (UNCLOS), the World Summit on Sustainable Development, the Convention on Biological Diversity and the Oslo-Paris Convention for Protection of the Marine Environment of the North East Atlantic (OSPAR). Immediately, the EU Marine Strategy Directive[113] includes the requirement that Member States implement programmes of measures including the establishment of protected areas covering the range of marine habitats. A further spur to action may also have been provided by

---

[111] s.37(5).
[112] For the full draft Marine Bill, along with extensive explanatory notes and accompanied by a policy Paper and Impact Assessment, see *http://www.official-documents.gov.uk/document/cm73/7351/7351.pdf*.
[113] [2008] OJ L164/19.

the decision of the High Court in *R v Secretary of State for Trade and Industry, ex parte Greenpeace Ltd*,[114] in which it was decided that, as the Habitats Directive concerns habitats and species that are sea-based as well as land-based, the aims of the Directive could only be achieved if its operation extended beyond territorial waters to the continental shelf and its waters. The government undertook to apply this finding to its implementation of the Birds Directive also.

The Secretary of State (or Welsh Ministers where appropriate) will be able to designate as an MCZ an area falling within the seaward limits of the territorial sea adjacent to the UK (save those adjacent to Scotland or Northern Ireland), an area within the limits of a renewable energy zone or an area of the seabed or subsoil within the limits of the UK sector of the continental shelf. The grounds for designation of an MCZ will be that the appropriate authority considers it desirable to do so for the purpose of conserving marine flora or fauna, habitats or types of habitat or features of geological or geomorphological interest.

10–058   Protection of MCZs will be through the imposition of duties on public authorities in respect of decisions which may impact on an MCZ, the planning and licensing functions of the proposed MMO and also the possibility of the MMO[115] making a conservation order in respect of the zone.

The intended timescale is for statutory conservation bodies to develop programmes to enable designation of MCZs by the end of 2012.

Limestone Pavement Orders

10–059   Under the provisions of section 34 of the 1981 Act, Limestone Pavement Orders (LPOs) are made, modified, revoked and confirmed by Secretary of State or by a local planning authority, following notification by the relevant conservation body of the presence of a limestone pavement in the local planning authority's area. These Orders are unique in conservation legislation in that they give special protection to one particular, narrowly specified habitat; no other habitat is singled out in this way.

The origin of LPOs dates back to the 1960s when a "grey area" in planning law became apparent. Stone merchants removing water-worn rockery limestone piece-meal from limestone pavements were required to apply for planning permission and, on their applications being refused, appealed on the grounds that the removal of "loose stone" from grazing land was not only a traditional agricultural practice but was also permitted development. In contesting these appeals, considerable difficulty was experienced in deciding how "loose stone" should be defined. Matters were not clarified by the 1977 General Development Order so that, when

---

[114] *R v Secretary of State for Trade and Industry, ex parte Greenpeace Ltd* (2000) Env. L.R. 221.
[115] See above at para.10–020.

the 1981 Act came to be drafted, the working of "water-worn" rockery stone from limestone pavements was placed under specific controls.[116]

Prior to its amendment by the Natural Environment and Rural Communities Act 2006, section 34 of the 1981 Act imposed a duty on the conservation bodies to notify the local planning authority of any area of limestone pavement in the countryside which in their opinion "is of special interest by reason of its flora, fauna or geological or physiographical features". A scientific criterion, identical to that imposed in relation to SSSIs, was therefore applied. As amended, no such criterion applies and the duty to notify extends to any limestone pavement, the obvious inference being that limestone pavements are now assumed to be of sufficient importance (scientific or otherwise) to merit at least the chance of protection by order. To assist them in their responsibilities, conservation agencies have power, under section 51 of the 1981 Act, to enter land to ascertain whether an LPO should be made, or whether an LPO is being or has been breached.

The making of LPOs differs, however, from the notification of SSSIs in   **10–060**
that it is a two stage process, the second stage of which lies outside the competence of the conservation body. By section 34(2) if either the Secretary of state or the relevant local planning authority consider that the "character or appearance" of land notified as just described under section 34(1) would be likely to be adversely affected by the removal of the limestone or its disturbance in any way whatever, either of them may make an LPO designating that land. Such endorsement brings the provisions of Schedule 11 to the 1981 Act into play. These provisions allow for appeals against the imposition of LPOs.

Any person removing or disturbing limestone without reasonable excuse on a site covered by an LPO commits an offence under section 34(4), rendering him liable to either a fine not exceeding £20,000 on summary conviction or an unlimited fine on conviction on indictment. As in the case of SSSIs, a grant of planning permission provides a "reasonable excuse" and so is effective to overcome an LPO; section 34, however, makes no provision for emergencies.

There is no explicit statutory link between LPOs and SSSIs; areas of pavement covered by LPOs do not have to be SSSIs, and SSSI status can be given to areas of pavement which are not covered by LPOs. On the other hand, given the identical qualifying grounds which until recently existed (see above) it is difficult to envisage a conservation body coming to the opinion that some particular area of limestone pavement fulfils the requirements of section 28(1) but not the requirements of section 34(1) or vice versa. It is clear from section 34(2), however, that the main purpose of an LPO is to retain, not the scientific values, but the "character and appearance" of the pavement. In other words, areas subject to LPOs may

---

[116] "Limestone pavement" is defined in s.34(6) as an area of limestone which lies wholly or partly exposed on the surface of the ground and has been fissured by natural erosion.

be chosen for scientific merit but are to be conserved to preserve their visual amenity. Little confusion is likely to result, however, for it is understood that it is the intention of the conservation bodies that all limestone pavement SSSIs will also be covered by LPOs, although it remains unclear whether LPOs will be extended over areas which are not to be notified as SSSIs.

10–061   Because of the overlapping provisions of the two designations, such application of LPOs to sites already designated as SSSIs, will largely repeat, but will also to some extent reinforce, the constraints imposed by the SSSI notification. In particular, designation as an LPO invokes significant considerations of visual amenity in addition to the essentially science-based considerations which underlie SSSIs.

National Parks

10–062   In England and Wales, the purpose of National Parks is to conserve and enhance landscapes within the countryside whilst promoting public enjoyment of them and having regard for the social and economic well-being of those living within them. There are 8 National Parks in England, covering 7 per cent of the land area, whereas there are 3 in Wales, covering 20 per cent. The earliest designations took place in 1951 and the most recent, the New Forest, was in 2005. The South Downs have been proposed as a National Park but are yet to be so designated.[117]

Part 2 of the National Parks and Access to the Countryside Act 1949 established the National Park designation in England and Wales. In addition, Part III of the Environment Act 1995 introduced a range of amendments to the 1949 Act, including a new section 11A, requiring relevant authorities to have regard to nature conservation when performing any task which may impact on a National Park. Special Acts of Parliament may be used to establish statutory authorities for the management of National Parks (e.g. the Broads Authority was set up through the Norfolk and Suffolk Broads Act 1988).

The National Parks (Scotland) Act 2000 enabled the establishment of National Parks in Scotland. In addition to the purposes described above, National Parks in Scotland are designated to promote the sustainable use of the natural resources of the area and the sustainable social and economic development of its communities. These purposes have equal weight and are to be pursued collectively unless conservation interests are threatened.

---

[117] Further information about National Parks in the UK can be found at *http://www.national parks.gov.uk/learningabout/factsandfigures.htm.*

Areas of Outstanding Natural Beauty

The primary purpose of the designation as an Area of Outstanding Natural   **10–063**
Beauty (AONB) is to conserve wildlife, physiographic features and cultural
heritage which go to make up that beauty, as well as the more conventional
concepts of landscape and scenery.

AONBs were established under the National Parks and Access to the
Countryside Act 1949, though Part 4 of CROWA[118] now contains the
main provisions as to designation and its effect, which is mainly to require
the consultation of the relevant conservation bodies in any planning process the outcome of which may affect an AONB. There are 40 AONBs in
England and Wales (35 wholly in England, 4 wholly in Wales and 1 which
straddles the border); the designation does not apply to Scotland, where
the National Scenic Area is the broad equivalent.

Account is taken of the need to safeguard agriculture, forestry and other
rural industries and the economic and social needs of local communities.
AONBs have equivalent status to National Parks as far as conservation is
concerned but, according to section 82(1) of CROWA, may not overlap
with National Parks.[119]

Areas of Special Protection

Sanctuary Areas, originally designated under the Protection of Birds Acts   **10–064**
1954, were replaced under section 3 of the Wildlife and Countryside Act
1981 with Areas of Special Protection (AoSPs—not to be confused with
the European designation of Special Protection Area). These may be
designated with view to preventing disturbance or destruction of birds in
the areas concerned. AoSPs are discussed further in paragraph 10–080
below.

Species Protection

Introduction

Common law and historical background

Statutory measures for species protection have been enacted against the   **10–065**
background of the common law, in particular property rights relating to
animals and plants.[120] All plants growing in the ground, including wild
plants and fungi, belong to the owner of the land subject to any other

---

[118] The relevant provisions came into force on April 1, 2001, in England and May 1, 2001, in
Wales.
[119] For more information, see *http://www.aonb.org.uk/*.
[120] For a more comprehensive treatment of the common law position, see Reid, *Nature
Conservation Law*, 2nd ed, 2002.

relevant interest in the property. Thus, in theory, a landowner will have common law rights against anyone removing or destroying wild plants on land, with remedies in damages (likely to be minimal) or by injunction. The law of theft is, however, not very protective of these property rights. Under section 4(3) of the Theft Act 1968 a person who picks wild flowers, fruit, foliage, or fungi on another's land does not steal what he picks, unless it is for a commercial purpose. Thus, the gathering of holly or mistletoe on private land will not constitute theft, unless it is for sale. However, in theory, such activity will nevertheless be a tort actionable at common law. It may be seen that the common law provides no protection for wild plants from the activities of the owner of the land on which they are growing.

The ownership of wild animals is more complex, but the broad principle at common law is that there is no property in a wild animal (*ferae naturae*) until it is caught or killed, whereupon it becomes the property of the person taking it. This is subject to the qualification that, if the person taking the animal has done so contrary to the rights of the land owner (i.e. the animal has been poached), property in that animal vests in the owner of the land. In terms of the criminal law, this is now subject to section 4(4) of the Theft Act 1968, which provides that wild animals are to be regarded as property. However a person cannot steal a wild creature (not tamed nor ordinarily kept in captivity) or its carcase unless it has been, or is in the course of being, "reduced into possession" of another—and possession of it has not since been lost or abandoned. Ownership of a wild creature for the purposes of the offence of theft is therefore not dependent on the ownership of the property from which the animal was taken, but the identity of the person taking it into ownership by killing or catching it.

It may therefore be seen that the common law, and law of theft, provide very limited protection to wild animals or plants. In particular, there is no protection at all from the actions of the owner of the land (or relevant property right) on which the species happens to be. Against this background, from the fifteenth century, legislation aimed at species protection was mainly directed to the protection of species serving human interests (in particular game and other quarry species), and the destruction of "pests" inimical to those species, so as to facilitate their effective exploitation. This principally benefited of the owner of the relevant interest in the land (through criminalising the taking of such species by those not entitled to do so), and more generally (for example, through the provision of a "close season" to enable the species to reproduce). In terms of nature conservation, the activities which such legislation was designed to support may be seen to have had incidental benefits to other species and the environment. Notably, however, management for the purposes of hunting and game shooting historically involved the persecution of various predator species (leading to the extinction of some, such as wolves). Whether the control of, for example, corvids and some raptor species, serves a wider conservation interest is a matter of continuing and heated debate amongst a range of interested parties, even today. This is an example of an area on which modern legislation directed at nature conservation generally, rather than the conservation of specific quarry species, has impacted.

Since Victorian times, legislation aimed at species protection has had a **10–066** broader aim, initially directed against cruelty and over-exploitation, and into the twentieth century reflecting a heightened value placed on the value of the natural world for its own sake. The law has therefore developed so as to seek to provide protection for a range of species, which is otherwise lacking in the common law and criminal law—as well as being absent from the early legislation directed at the protection and promotion of specific commercial or "sporting" value to humans. In doing so, nature conservation law (in the protection of species as well as habitats) has increasingly come to override the common law rights of landowners and other commercial interests, so engaging policy issues in determining where the balance of those conflicting issues should lie. The policy objectives of biological diversity (biodiversity)[121] since the early 1990s have also impacted on the role and extent of species conservation law. Nevertheless, even now, it will be seen that species conservation is frequently subverted by conflicting commercial or other interests in the operation of legislation designed to protect species. Although its importance as a policy consideration enshrined in legislation has increased hugely over the last century (accompanying a degradation of the natural environment), the interests of the natural world often ultimately lose out to those of environmentally destructive commercial activity.

The development of an integrated policy approach?

A Wildlife Management Strategy for Defra is under development which **10–067** "aims to achieve more effective management of the impacts of wildlife on man's activities, and vice versa". This was the subject of public consultation in summer 2008. The Government's stated intention is that this strategy "will enable better achievement of our biodiversity objectives while fully taking into account species conservation and welfare issues as well as human or socio-economic activities." It may perhaps be thought surprising that no such integrated strategy has existed before, in the modern era.

Statutory means

The statutory mechanism adopted for the protection of animal species has **10–068** been the establishment of criminal offences variously prohibiting activities that may be categorised as follows:

---

[121] Pursuant to the UK Biodiversity Action Plan (UKBAP), adopted in 1994.

(a) causing direct harm by capturing, killing or injuring (or in the case of plants, picking, uprooting) a protected species;
(b) taking or destroying a protected species' eggs;
(c) disturbance of a protected animal;
(d) activities which harm a site used by a protected animal, such as a nest or roost;
(e) possession of a protected animal, live or dead;
(f) commercial activity involving a protected animal, live or dead; and
(g) activities liable to release or disperse species that are perceived to be harmful.

An additional feature of the national law of species conservation is that it is inter-woven with measures that are principally concerned with welfare and avoiding cruelty, such as the prohibition of the use of various inhumane traps. Further, provisions to enhance the ability to enforce the principal provisions have been enacted; for example requirements to ring and register certain captive birds so as to discourage untruthful (but otherwise hard to disprove) claims that a bird in captivity had been captive-bred, rather than taken from the wild.

Principal legislative measures

10–069 The principal legislative measure enacting species protection is Part 1 of the Wildlife and Countryside Act 1981 (WCA 1981). This both consolidated previous legislation, and implemented the EC Birds Directive 79/409. The 1981 Act has since been amended several times, in particular by the Wildlife and Countryside (Amendment) Act 1991 as well as a series of orders amending the schedules listing species to which provisions of Part 1 relate, and the Countryside and Rights of Way Act 2000. With this legislative history, particular care is necessary in ascertaining the provisions of the WCA 1981 at any relevant time.

A parallel, and significantly overlapping, regime is provided by Part 3 of the Conservation (Natural Habitats, etc.) Regulations 1994 (the Habitats Regulations 1994), by which the Habitats Directive was implemented. Principally as a result of judgments of the European Court[122] which held that the Habitats Directive had not been fully transposed in relation to species protection provisions, the Habitats Regulations were extensively amended with effect from August 21, 2007.[123]

Somewhat confusingly, therefore, any general consideration of the application of the law of species conservation (other than for birds, the protection of which is dealt with comprehensively under the WCA 1981) requires examination of these separate statutory regimes, even aside from the specific regimes applicable to, for example, badgers, deer, and seals.

---

[122] Case C-6/04, *Commission v UK* and Case C-131/05, *Commission v UK*.
[123] SI 2007/1843.

SPECIES PROTECTION

Thus, for an otter (a European protected species) to be lawfully live-trapped for the purposes of scientific research, licences under both the WCA 1981 and the Habitats Regulations 1994 would be required, yet the requirements for the issue of a licence under the respective regimes is almost identical. Such activity in the absence of a licence would constitute a criminal offence under both regimes.

The Offshore Marine Conservation (Natural Habitats, &c) Regulations   **10–070**
2007 (the Offshore Marine Regulations 2007) implement the Habitats Directive and Birds Directive in offshore marine areas,[124] providing equivalent provisions to those protecting birds in Part 1 of the WCA 1981, and other animals and plants in the Habitats Regulations 1994.

The structure of Part 1 of the WCA 1981

Protection of birds is dealt with in sections 1 to 8 of the WCA 1981, other   **10–071**
animals at sections 9 to 12, and plants at section 13. There are considerable similarities in the principal offences provided for the protection of each group, and the specified exemptions. Sections 14 to 15 make miscellaneous provisions relating to introductions, non-native species, and trade in endangered species. Section 16 provides the power to grant licences, considered below. Sections 17 to 21 make provision relating to the investigation and enforcement of the preceding measures.

Much of the protection afforded to individual species by the WCA 1981 depends on their inclusion in the Schedules to that Act. Under section 22, species can be added to, or withdrawn from these Schedules by order of the Secretary of State. For example since 1981, over 70 species of animal have been added to Schedule 5, and over 125 species of plant have been added to Schedule 8. The extent of the protection afforded to species named in the Schedules may vary geographically, and by dates. It is therefore necessary to confirm exactly what species are currently protected, and the extent of that protection, before attempting to apply the Act. Sections 23 to 25 set out the functions of various bodies under the Act.

The Act makes provision for various activities to be performed by an "authorised person", defined at s.27(1). Essentially, this means the owner or occupier of land on which the action occurs, or anyone authorised by him; or someone authorised by the local authority; or someone authorised by a relevant conservation body (as specified).

[124] As defined in reg.2(2).

565

Standard exemptions

10–072 Exemptions from the offences created by the principal provisions protecting each group[125] appear in section 4 (birds); section 10 (other animals); and section 13(3) (plants). These are essentially very similar and include:

- Cases where Ministers, under other legislation, require action to prevent damage to agriculture or the spread of disease: s.4(1) (birds) and s.10(1) (animals).
- Provisions to allow the treatment and mercy killing of injured creatures: s.4(2)(a) and (b) (birds) and s.10(3)(a) and (b) (animals).
- Acts which are the "incidental result of a lawful operation and could not reasonably be avoided" do not generally constitute offences under the Act: see s.4(2)(c) (birds); s.10(3)(c) (animals); and s.13(3) (plants). In relation to birds only (curiously), it is provided that to rely upon this provision it must be shown that there was no other satisfactory solution.
- Emergency measures to protect public or economic interests: s.4(3) and s.10(4). The scope of these provisions is rather different, but in both cases the exemption does not apply if beforehand it was apparent that the action would prove necessary and a licence had not been applied for as soon as reasonably practical, or an application for a licence had been determined (s.4(5) and s.10(6)).

Offences of possession

10–073 The WCA includes offences constituted by the possession of a protected species or part thereof: e.g. s.1(2) (birds and birds eggs), s.9(2) (animals in Schedule 5). In each case it is not an offence if the item had been obtained lawfully. This gives rise to considerable evidential difficulties in any prosecution, as an item will have been obtained lawfully if legislation prohibiting the action involved in obtaining the specimen was not in force at the relevant time. Likewise, there may be a variety of other plausible explanations as to how an item had been lawfully obtained. However, in each case, the burden is on the person in possession to establish that the item had been obtained lawfully.[126]

---

[125] i.e. in relation to birds, ss.1 and 3; animals at s.10; and plants at s.13. These general exemptions are not applicable to the prohibitions in ss.5 and s.11 on the means of killing or taking birds or other animals.

[126] See also *Hughes v DPP* [2003] EWHC 2470 (Admin), [2004] Env. L.R. 28 at footnote 131 below.

Licensing

Many of the actions defined as offences in Part 1 of the WCA 1981 and the   **10–074**
Habitats Regulations 1994 (as well as other, more specific, legislation for
the protection of species[127]) can be carried out legally if the appropriate
licence has first been obtained: in the case of the WCA 1981 under section
16, and the Habitats Regulations 1994 under regulation 44. In most cases
it is a requirement that the activity is for a specified purpose; thus, for
example, an activity that would be contrary to section 1 of the WCA 1981
if performed without a licence must be for one of the purposes specified in
section 16(1). Such purposes are varied, and include scientific, research or
education purposes; photography; preserving public health; and preventing
serious damage to (inter alia) crops, fruit, fisheries, or inland waters.
Section 16 sets out the legal basis of the issue of such licences, and the
attachment of conditions to them.

Various activities which would be illegal without a licence (including, in
some circumstances, the sale, exhibition and possession of protected species, the investigation of wildlife crimes, the rehabilitation of injured animals and the control of certain species that are, at times, in conflict with
people's interests—such as air safety, damage to crops and the conservation of other species) do not require a specific application for a licence.
Standard form licences are available to carry out such activities, with
conditions: these are known as "general licences" and may be freely
obtained (including by downloading from Natural England's website).

It has been held that the mere possession of a licence does not authorise
the activity it purports to permit: it must still be shown that the activity is
for a relevant purpose under section 16.[128] This is particularly significant in
assessing the legality of activity covered by "general licences". So, for
example, the shooting of a woodpigeon (a species generally recognised as
an agricultural pest) would constitute an offence if done without a licence.
However, woodpigeons are one of the species named on the freely available
standard general licence "to kill or take certain birds to prevent serious
damage or disease". The activity will nevertheless be an offence (under
section 1) if it was not pursuant to a statutory purposes set out at section
16(1) or the activity has not been carried out in accordance with the terms
of the general licence. Notably, one of those terms is that the licence can
only be relied on in circumstances where the authorised person is satisfied
that "appropriate non-lethal methods of control such as scaring are either
ineffective or impracticable".[129]

---

[127] The Protection of Badgers Act 1992, s.10; the Deer Act 1991, s.8; the Conservation of
   Seals Act 1970, s.10, and the Destructive Imported Animals Act 1932, s.8.
[128] *Royal Society for the Prevention of Cruelty to Animals v Cundey* [2002] EWHC Admin 906,
   Silber J. See also *RSPCA v Shinton* [2003] EWHC 1696 Admin.
[129] This reflects the restriction on the power to grant a licence under s.16(1A) unless the
   appropriate authority "is satisfied that, as regards that purpose, there is no other satisfactory solution".

10–075 Obtaining a licence through making false statements is an offence contrary to section 17 of the WCA 1981 (and regulation 46 of the Habitats Regulations 1994). Statistics on the licences issued, and their purposes, are published by Natural England, the body which now administers the licensing regime on behalf of the Secretary of State.[130]

Evidential presumptions

10–076 An evidential issue liable to arise in the enforcement of the WCA 1981 is whether a particular specimen alleged to be the subject of an offence was in fact wild within the meaning of the Act, or whether it had been bred in captivity (or cultivated, in the case of plants). In all cases the legislation creates a presumption in favour of the former, placing the burden of proof on a defendant to establish the contrary on the balance of probabilities: s.1(6) (birds[131]), s.9(6) (animals); s.13(4) (plants).

Birds

10–077 There is a marked disparity between the strength of the protection afforded to birds, as compared with non-avian vertebrates, invertebrates, plants, and fungi. The reasons for this are probably more historical and emotive, rather than founded in ecological principle. Voluntary organisations concerned with wild birds, in particular the Royal Society for the Protection of Birds (RSPB) in the United Kingdom, have been particularly influential, and this in turn led to European legislation, the Birds Directive, to protect birds emerging earlier than for any other group.

Sections 1 to 8 of the WCA 1981 protect wild birds. Notably, in relation to birds, the protection is inclusive; in other words the Act applies to all wild birds unless a species is exempted by the Act or its Schedules. By contrast, as will be seen below, protection in relation to non-avian animals and plants is dependent upon a species being expressly identified.

---

[130] Natural England administers the licensing regime on behalf of the Secretary of State pursuant to an agreement under s.78 of the Natural Environment and Rural Communities Act 2006. Statistics are in relation to licences granted appear on the website of Natural England: *http://www.naturalengland.org.uk/conservation/wildlife-management-licensing/statistics. htm.*

[131] The evidential presumption arising from the wording of s.1(6) was confirmed in *Hughes v. DPP* [2003] EWHC 2470 (Admin), [2004] Env. L.R. 28, Stanley Burnton J. at para.17: "it is the defendant who must show, on a balance of probabilities, that the bird has been bred in captivity". The judge in this case also held that the court was entitled to take judicial notice that a species (in that case goldfinches) is ordinarily resident in or a visitor to the United Kingdom (as the definition of wild bird then required, prior to amendment of s.27(1) expanding the area to the European territory of any member state).

Wild birds

Wild birds are defined by section 27(1) to be "any bird of a species which is   **10–078** ordinarily resident in or is a visitor to the European territory of any member State in a wild state", but not poultry nor, generally, various specified game birds.[132] By this definition, a bird is wild by reference to its species, rather than whether it is in fact living in a wild state. However, for the purposes of section 1, "wild bird" does not include any bird which is shown to have been bred in captivity,[133] thus a captive bird cannot become wild following escape for the purposes of this section.

Section 1 of the WCA 1981

Section 1(1) prohibits intentional or reckless killing, injury or capture of   **10–079** any wild bird, or its nest (while in use, and in some circumstances even when not in use), or the taking or destroying[134] of its eggs. Section 1(2) prohibits the possession of any wild bird, living or dead (or part thereof), or its egg (or part thereof), but is subject to broad exceptions in subsection (3)—essentially if the bird or egg had been lawfully killed or taken. Section 2 makes exceptions to section 1 in relation to birds identified in Schedule 2 (quarry species outside the close season[135]). Enhanced penalties apply in relation to offences involving species listed in Schedule 1.

    Prosecutions for offences under section 1 are regularly reported in the press. Many of those accused are, not unexpectedly, individuals with specialist interests that run counter to the purpose of the legislation, such as egg collectors, taxidermists, and falconers. Game-keepers are also fairly regularly prosecuted and convicted of such offences.

Areas of special protection under section 3 (AoSPs, not SPAs)

Designation as an Area of Special Protection[136] under section 3 of the 1981   **10–080** Act aims to prevent the disturbance and destruction of the birds for which the area was identified, by making it unlawful to damage or destroy either

---

[132] "Game bird" is defined at s.27(1) as "any pheasant, partridge, grouse (or moor game), black (or heath) game or ptarmigan". The regime applying to game birds, by this definition, is outside the scope of this work. The principal act is the Game Act 1831. As from August 1, 2007, a game licence under the Game Licences Act 1860 is no longer required to kill or deal in game.

[133] s.1(6), which also brings back into the definition of wild bird for the purposes of s.1, a bird that has been lawfully released to the wild as part of a re-population or re-introduction programme.

[134] "destroy" in relation to an egg includes doing anything to it which is calculated to prevent it from hatching: see s.27(1)—and so includes pricking and oiling.

[135] For most species the close season runs from February 1, to August 31, inclusive: s.2(4).

[136] Areas of special protection under s.3 are not to be confused with "Special Protection Areas" ("SPAs") for birds under the Birds Directive (see above).

the birds or their nests and in some cases by prohibiting or restricting access to the site.

Offences mirroring those in section 1(1) are provided in section 3 in an AoSP, but the exceptions provided in section 2 are inapplicable in this instance. Therefore, in such an area, the killing of quarry species specified in Schedule 2 even in the open season will be unlawful. Designation of an area by order under section 3 requires the consent of all owners and occupiers of the land concerned, and is subject to the rights of that owner and occupier (s.3(3) to (5)), which substantially restricts their utility in practice. Nevertheless, orders under section 3 have the advantage (unlike land-based SSSIs or sea-based MNRs) that they can be made over areas consisting partly of land and partly of sea; so they may be of use where the coastline is mobile.

Other provisions

10–081 Certain methods of killing or taking wild birds are prohibited by section 5. In respect of such actions knowingly causing or permitting them is also an offence. Trade in wild birds, live and dead, and their eggs (as well as the exhibition of wild birds) is regulated by section 6. The registration and ringing of captive birds belonging to the species listed in Schedule 4, which includes the species normally used in falconry, is required by section 7. Section 8 prescribes minimum standards for the keeping of all captive birds, except poultry.

Other animals

10–082 Sections 9 to 11 provide protection to those wild animals listed in Schedule 5, subject to the defences in section 9 itself and section 10. "Wild animal" is defined at section 27(1) as any animal other than a bird which is (or was before it was killed or taken) living wild. Under section 9(6) an animal is presumed to be wild unless the contrary is shown. However, "animal" itself is not further defined, but may be seen from the Schedules to include all non-avian vertebrates and invertebrates (so, including, for example, insects, worms, slugs, jellyfish, and sea anemones). As noted above, eggs and all immature stages are included within the definition of animal in the Act, unless the context otherwise requires. In terms of biological classification, it is questionable whether single-celled organisms and sponges would be capable of constituting animals, so as to be eligible for inclusion in the Schedule of protected animals.

Under section 9, the following actions are generally prohibited in relation to any wild animal included in Schedule 5:

- intentionally to kill, injure or take any such animal: s.9(1)
- possession of such an animal, live or dead, or any part thereof: s.9(2)

570

- intentionally or recklessly to damage or destroy a structure or place that a wild animal uses for shelter or protection; or the disturbance of an animal while it is occupying such a place; or obstructing its access to such a place: s.9(4)
- commercial activity, including advertising, involving any live or dead wild animal, or anything derived from it: s.9(5)

In addition, intentional or reckless disturbance of a dolphin, whale, or basking shark included in Schedule 5 is prohibited: section 9(4A).[137]

Reference to Schedule 5 reveals a wide range in the degree of protection afforded to animals included. For many animals (for example the common frog and toad, and some of the rarer butterflies) the only prohibition is under section 9(5)—commercial activity—so killing such animals is permitted under the Act. For others (such as the slow worm, adder, and grass snake) the prohibition is under section 9(1), but only in so far as it relates to killing and injuring, as well as under section 9(5)—so capturing and keeping these species is permitted.

The scope of section 9, in particular section 9(4), is much less precisely **10–083** defined than that of the equivalent protection for birds under s.1. Birds' nests are generally recognisable entities and their protection under section 1 relates to an equally recognisable period when they are being built or are in use. In contrast the "structures and places" used by animals for shelter vary greatly with the species and are virtually impossible to define, as appears to be acknowledged in the 1981 Act by the absence of any general attempt to do so and the doubtful effect of some of such legislative attempts as have been made. For example, it is hard to see how section 9(4) could be applied to a basking shark, which is free ranging yet the Act purports to do so (although now no longer does in relation to cetaceans). The manner in which an animal has to "use" a "structure or place" for "shelter and protection" is also unclear. Many species will use a structure or place transiently, or even ephemerally or opportunistically, and this may be dependent upon the season, the stage in its life cycle, or the immediate environmental conditions.

In view of the fluid nature of Schedule 5 and the range of permutations in the degree of protection it affords to individual species at any time, it is necessary to confirm its current contents at any relevant time before any potentially unlawful action is taken, or advising as to whether an offence has been committed. Even then, significant uncertainty may remain as to the application of section 9(4).

---

[137] There is an oddity in that porpoises (which are cetaceans) are not expressly included in ss.9(4A), which refers to "a dolphin or whale (cetacea)". Porpoises are listed separately from dolphins in Sch.5. It therefore appears that intentional disturbance of a porpoise could not be an offence under ss.9(4A).

Development liable to infringe section 9 and planning control

10–084   Under the Habitats Regulations 1994 a planning authority[138] is required to "have regard to" the requirements of the Habitats Directive so far as they may be affected by the exercise of its functions. Thus the impact on a European protected species will be relevant to, but not determinative of, the outcome of a planning application.

However, the grant of planning consent does not carry any right to contravene the provisions of Part 1 of the WCA 1981 and the planning authority does not have power to authorise any action in contravention of section 9. Action prohibited by section 9 may be licensed under section 16(3), but only for the purposes set out in that subsection; in practice, in the face of a development, this would be for the purposes of conservation (section 16(3)(c)). While a licence might properly be granted where the site used by a species was already under threat, such that the survival of that population was at risk, it would not be proper to do so if the sole threat were posed by the development itself.

Bats

10–085   By way of illustration of the complexity and confusion liable to arise from the overlapping protection regimes, but the need to consider both, the case of bats is considered. All bats have protection under section 9(4)(b) (disturbance while occupying a place used for shelter or protection) and section 9(4)(c) (obstruction of their access to any such place), as well as under section 9(5)—but not otherwise under the WCA 1981. Notably, it is not an offence under WCA 1981 to kill or capture a bat, as the provisions of section 9(1) do not apply.

Defences under section 10(2) (disapplying section 9(4) in relation to anything done within a dwelling house) and section 10(3)(c) (disapplying section 9 in relation to an act which was the incidental result of a lawful operation which could not reasonably have been avoided) are generally not available in relation to bats, other than in the living area of a dwelling house, as a result of section 10(5), unless the relevant conservation body[139] has been notified and given a reasonable time to advise whether that act should be carried out and if so how. The role of the conservation body is simply to offer advice. There is no obligation on the householder to follow that advice. The purpose of the provision is particularly directed to protecting bats from the effects of chemical wood treatments and preservatives applied in roof-spaces where bats may be roosting. The effectiveness of the measure is dependent upon the goodwill of the householder towards the

---

[138] Being a "competent authority" within the meaning of reg.6.
[139] Natural England, the Countryside Council for Wales, or Scottish Natural Heritage: s.27(3A).

bats—once he has given the conservation body the opportunity to offer advice, the statutory defences become available to him.

However, significant further protection is afforded to bats through the Habitats Regulations 1994. All bats are European protected species under the Habitats Directive, and Schedule 2 to the 1994 Regulations. As such they receive protection under regulation 39 which makes it an offence to deliberately capture, injure or kill a bat, as well as providing for a range of other offences that in many respects are co-terminous with those under the WCA 1981. In the Habitats Regulations as originally enacted there were equivalent provisions to those in the WCA 1981 providing a defence in relation to actions taken in a dwelling house, provided appropriate advice had been taken.[140] Those equivalent provisions have now been removed, by amendment of the 1994 Regulations.[141]

Other provisions of the WCA 1981

Certain methods of taking or killing wild animals are prohibited by section 11. This is not restricted in its application to species listed in Schedule 5. "Knowingly causing or permitting" such acts also constitutes an offence. **10–086**

Badgers

Badgers are protected by the Badgers Act 1992, which consolidated pre- **10–087** vious legislation. They are not a species listed in Schedule 5 of the WCA 1981, nor are they a European proteced species. Indeed, badgers are nei- ther rare nor threatened in Britain, and the intent behind the legislation is more to avoid cruelty than to protect them in the interests of nature con- servation. The Act contains provisions equivalent to the WCA 1981, as well as other specific welfare-related offences. Licences may be issued to carry out activities which would otherwise constitute an offence. A more detailed consideration of the Act is contained in the previous edition of this work.

Seals

There are two species of seal found in British waters: the grey seal and the **10–088** common seal. Both are European protected species, so the Habitats Reg- ulations apply. The Conservation of Seals Act 1970 also provides legal protection to seals. Although seals are not listed in Schedule 5 of the WCA 1981, many of the provisions of the 1970 Act are equivalent to those encountered in WCA 1981, including restriction on the methods that may be used to kill seals; in particular poisoning, and the use of all firearms

---

[140] regs 40(2), (3)(c), and (4), prior to substitution.
[141] See reg.40, as substituted by SI 2007/1843.

except rifles of a minimum specification are prohibited (section 1). The possession of poison or prohibited firearms or ammunition with intent to kill or take a seal is itself an offence under section 8(2). For each species a close season is specified under section 2, which may be extended by orders made by the minister where considered necessary for the proper conservation of seals. There is currently in force an order prohibiting the killing, injuring or taking of either species of seal on the eastern coast of England and adjacent territorial waters.[142]

Various defences are specified, including in the case of an injured seal, mercy killing, and the unavoidable killing or injuring of a seal as an incidental result of a lawful action, or the killing or injuring of a seal in order to prevent damage to a fishing net or tackle, or to fish in a net (section 9). Licences to kill or take seals may be issued by the Secretary of State for specified purposes, under the provisions of section 10, after consultation with the conservation agencies.

The 1970 Act and its predecessors have been uniquely effective among national conservation legislation, in achieving their objective. The grey seal population in British waters has risen from about 500 animals at the end of the nineteenth century; in 1986 it was estimated to be over 20,000, and current estimates exceed 125,000.[143] As early as the 1960s, it was considered that control over numbers was required in order to keep the seal population in balance with the competing fishery and other interests.[144] The culling that was authorised in 1963 triggered adverse public reactions. A proposed cull in 1978, on the advice of the NERC,[145] was drastically curtailed in the face of a public campaign, a long-term consequence of which has been a reluctance to license action to prevent damage to fisheries, as provided for by section 10. It is a sadly unusual dilemma for the government to be confronted with problems created by the success of nature conservation measures.

Cetaceans

10–089   All species of whale, dolphin, and porpoise are protected under both Schedule 5 of the WCA 1981 and the Habitats Regulations 1994.

Deer

10–090   Deer are not protected under the WCA 1981 or the Habitats Regulations 1994. The legislation is now consolidated in the Deer Act 1991, which

---

[142] Conservation of Seals (England) Order 1999, SI 1999/3052.
[143] Sea Mammal Research Unit, St Andrew's. Population estimates, both currently and historically, vary widely.
[144] Report of the Nature Conservancy for the year ended September 30, 1962.
[145] The NERC advised that the grey seal population would increase to 140,000 in the next 10 years if measures were not then taken.

provides close seasons for different species, and specifies the circumstances in which killing deer outside the close season is permitted. Various methods of killing deer are prohibited, and the prohibitions in the Deer Act 1991 must now be read together with the Hunting Act 2004.

Fish

Some species of fish, including the basking shark, are protected under Schedule 5 of the WCA 1981. The sturgeon is the only sea fish which is a European protected species named in Schedule 2 of the Habitats Regulations 1994 and the Offshore Marine Regulations 2007 (as well as being protected under Schedule 5 of the WCA 1981). Several species of fish are listed in Schedule 3 to the Habitat Regulations 1994 and so benefit from the prohibition on the use of poisons and explosives, although these were largely protected under the WCA 1981 already. **10–091**

The conservation of freshwater fish may be seen, to a significant extent, as an aspect of the control of water pollution, and the exercise by the Environment Agency of its powers and duties, which include the duty to maintain, improve and develop salmon fisheries, trout fisheries, freshwater fisheries and eel fisheries.[146]

The Salmon and Freshwater Fisheries Act 1975 is concerned principally with controlling the fishing of salmon, trout, eels and freshwater fish,[147] including by the grant of fishing licences, prohibiting certain methods of taking fish, setting close seasons and making provision for the sale and transport of fish in such a manner as to facilitate the control of poaching. Under section 4(1), subject to section 4(2), it is an offence to cause or knowingly permit matter to be added to waters containing fish which causes those waters to be poisonous or injurious to fish (or their spawning grounds, spawn, or food). In addition, this will amount to an offence under section 85 of the Water Resources Act 1991. Entry of matter into controlled waters (as defined in the 1991 Act) which are under and in accordance with a discharge consent under the WRA 1991 are exempted from s.4(1).[148]

Sea fish

Generally, however, the conservation of marine fish stocks is also largely based on commercial considerations and international quota agreements that are outside the scope of this book. In passing, the provisions of the Sea Fisheries (Wildlife Conservation) Act 1992 are noted. Section 1(1) requires ministers and bodies exercising functions by virtue of the Sea **10–092**

[146] s.6(6) of the Environment Act 1995.
[147] "Freshwater fish" are defined in s.41(1) as excluding salmon, trout, eels and any other fish migrating between fresh and tidal waters.
[148] Water Consolidation (Consequential Provisions) Act 1991, Sch.1, para.30.

Fisheries Acts[149] to have regard to the conservation of marine flora and fauna; and "to endeavour to achieve a reasonable balance between that consideration and any others to which they must have regard".

Plants

10–093   In contrast to the provisions for the protection of wild birds and other animals, those for the protection of plants are relatively simple. Section 13 of the WCA 1981 makes it an offence for any person intentionally to pick, uproot or destroy any of the wild plants listed in Schedule 8, or for anyone other than an authorised person[150] intentionally to uproot any other wild plant.[151] It is also an offence to possess, transport, trade, or attempt to trade in any Schedule 8 plant, any parts of one, or anything derived from one. To "pick" is defined as "to gather or pluck any part of the plant without uprooting it", so includes removal of seeds from a plant. Schedule 8 has been greatly extended under the provisions of section 22(3) so now applies to many more species than the 62 originally listed in 1981.

Introduced species

10–094   Under s.14(1) it is an offence to release or allow to escape into the wild an animal of a species that is not ordinarily resident in and is not a regular visitor to Great Britain in a wild state or one listed in Part 1 of Schedule 9 (which consists of non-native species now established in the wild). Under s.14(2) it is an offence to plant or otherwise cause to grow in the wild any plant included in Part 2 of Schedule 9 (which consists of various noxious or invasive species, such as giant hogweed and Japanese knotweed). It is also an offence to sell (or offer for sale, or transport for the purposes of a sale) an animal or plant to which section 14 applies: section 14ZA.

Trade in endangered species

10–095   The desire for ownership or use of certain wild animals or parts of them, has had devastating effects on some species. The efforts to supply such markets can destroy populations of certain animals, with tigers, elephants and rhinoceroses obvious and striking examples from a depressingly long list. Plant species may be similarly at risk. However, properly regulated trade in a species may, theoretically at least, assist its prospects of survival,

---

[149] Sea Fisheries Acts is defined widely and flexibly in s.1(2) as any enactments for the time being in force relating to sea-fishing, including fishing in the sea for shellfish, salmon, or migratory trout.
[150] "authorised person" is defined at s.27(1); see above.
[151] "'wild plant' means any plant [(including fungi)] which is or (before it was picked, uprooted or destroyed) was growing wild and is of a kind which ordinarily grows in Great Britain in a wild state": s.27(1).

although the strength of this argument and the validity of its application to individual cases, is highly controversial. In any event, the scale of the problem has led to international action, in particular through the Convention on International Trade in Endangered Species of Wild Fauna and Flora (CITES).[152] The treaty attempts to regulate international trade, either by a total prohibition in some cases, or requiring licences to be granted before animal or plant specimens or items derived from them can be imported or exported. Relevant species are placed in three Appendices depending on the severity of the threat of extinction, with Appendix I being for those "threatened with extinction which are or may be affected by trade" (for example tigers).

At the European level, CITES has been implemented by Regulation EC 338/97,[153] which requires member states to comply with the provisions of the Convention, as well as imposing some additional obligations and procedures. The principal domestic provisions are the Endangered Species (Import and Export) Act 1976 and the Control of Trade in Endangered Species (Enforcement) Regulations 1997.[154]

---

[152] Convention on International Trade in Endangered Species of Wild Fauna and Flora, Signed at Washington, D.C., on March 3, 1973; amended at Bonn, on June 22, 1979.
[153] [1997] OJ, L61/1.
[154] SI 1997/1372.

Chapter 11

THE WATER FRAMEWORK DIRECTIVE AND WATER POLLUTION

INTRODUCTION

In England, water pollution was for centuries controlled, if at all, under the **11–001** common law of nuisance. This proved wholly inadequate to prevent massive water pollution from occurring during the industrial revolution, continuing throughout the nineteenth century and into the twentieth century. The first attempts in modern times to impose statutory controls were the Salmon Fishery Act 1861 and the Rivers Pollution Prevention Act 1876. However, the bodies empowered to enforce these provisions often had little incentive to do so, especially as the statutes included defences calculated to avoid industrial activities being substantially prejudiced. Moreover, as with the bulk of early "environmental" legislation, the objective was in fact solely to control threats to public health—a very pressing fear in the early days of this legislation.

The modern controls on water pollution derive from a series of European Community Directives dating from 1975 onwards, implemented initially under the Water Act 1973 and the Control of Pollution Act 1974, and via administrative directions to the (then) publicly controlled water authorities. Privatisation of the water industry led to the Water Act 1989, involving the division of responsibilities between the new water and sewerage undertakers, and the National Rivers Authorities who took over the bulk[1] of the regulatory functions previously exercised by the water authorities. The Water Act 1989 was rapidly followed by consolidated legislation considered in this and the following two chapters, namely the Water Industry Act, the Water Resources Act, the Land Drainage Act, the Statutory Water Companies Act, and the Water Consolidation (Consequential Provisions) Act, all of which date from 1991.

Though the day-to-day procedures involved in enforcement and discharge consents are home-grown, policy and standards in respect of surface water, groundwater, drinking water, coastal waters, together with discharges from agriculture, industry and sewage works all derive from a quite

---

[1] The exception being trade effluent consents which remain under the control of the water companies: see below.

579

confusing mass of European legislation developed over the last 30 years. However, the Water Framework Directive of 2000[2] and its daughter directives are likely to steer EU law and policy, and domestic responses, over the next 20 years, in a potentially more coherent fashion than hitherto. So, before we examine the detail of water pollution in the rest of this Chapter, and turn to resources management and flood protection in the following Chapters, it is worth summarising the provisions of the Water Framework Directive and its implementation.

The Water Framework Directive 2000/60 (WFD)

11–002   The WFD applies to all water bodies, namely groundwater, and all surface waters (defined as rivers, canals, lakes, reservoirs, estuaries and coastal waters up to one nautical mile from the shore). It says that water planning must be done by reference to river basins, and hence not some political unit which may have little relevance to hydrology. It requires the production of strategic management plans for each river basin setting out how the objectives set for the water bodies within that river basin are to be achieved. River basins can be considerable areas of land, as can be seen from the fact that England and Wales have been divided into only 11 basins, with two of these straddling the English-Scottish border. These river basin management plans must be based on a detailed analysis of the pressures on the water bodies within the river basin and an assessment of their impact. The idea is that a comprehensive programme of measures should be identifed by reference to that particular river basin,[3] in order to focus improvements and monitoring efforts upon those water bodies that are most at risk of failing to meet their objectives.

Article 1 of the WFD 2000 sets out its main purposes, namely the protection and enhancement of these waters. In particular, it aims;

(a) to prevent further deterioration of waters, and to protect and enhance aquatic eco-systems,
(b) to promote sustainable water use based upon long-term protection of available water resources,
(c) to reduce discharges, emissions and losses of priority substances, and to cease or phase out discharges, emissions and losses of priority hazardous substances into the aquatic environment,
(d) to reduce and prevent groundwater pollution, and
(e) to contribute to mitigating the effects of floods and droughts.

Priority, and priority hazardous, substances are substances specifically identified as being of particular concern, and, as we shall see, they are

---

[2] Directive 2000/60, [2000] OJ L327/1.
[3] art.11.

governed by a combination of the WFD and a daughter directive, the Environmental Quality Standards Directive[4] which is about to be made law.

The objective of "good" status

The core of the WFD 2000 is Article 4 which sets environmental objectives **11–003**
to be addressed by the measures set out in the river basin plans. The objectives vary depending on the water body in question. Member States are to "aim" at achieving "good" surface water status,[5] which comprises good chemical status *and* good ecological status—failure on either score forfeits that status.[6] For artificial surface water bodies or bodies which have been heavily modified by man, the aim is to achieve good status by good ecological *potential* and good chemical status. For groundwater, good status is measured in terms of its quantity and chemical status, and both need to be good for the water body to qualify for that status.[7] All these objectives are to be achieved by December 22, 2015, via the measures for each river basin prescribed in accordance with Article 11. These measures must address both point source[8] and diffuse pollution.[9] There are additional obligations with a view to reducing pollution and in particular reducing discharges etc of priority or priority hazardous substances.

Member States must establish a register of protected areas, namely areas designated under other Community legislation, for the abstraction of drinking water, for the protection of economically significant aquatic species, recreational waters, nitrate-vulnerable zones and nutrient-sensitive areas, and Natura 2000 sites under the Birds and Habitats Directives.[10] The register was to have been completed by December 2004.[11] In those protected areas, Member States shall achieve compliance with any standards and objectives by 2015 at the latest, unless otherwise specified under that other Community legislation.[12]

Article 4 also contains important exemptions from these objectives. The deadlines may be extended for up to two further updates of river basin plans (namely to 2021 or 2027), if this delay is sufficiently justified in the plan.[13] Alternatively, Member States may aim at less stringent environmental objectives, where the water body is so affected by human activity, or is naturally in such a condition, as to render achievement of the objectives

---

[4] Shortly to be adopted.
[5] art.4(1)(ii)
[6] art.2(18).
[7] art.2(19).
[8] art.11(3)(g).
[9] art.11(3)(h).
[10] art.6 and Annex IV.
[11] This work has been completed in England and Wales.
[12] art.4(1)(c).
[13] art.4(4).

"infeasible or disproportionately expensive." Member States must also establish that the needs served by these particular human activities cannot be achieved by other means, that no further deterioration will occur, and they must justify this position in every new version of the plan. There are also exemptions for temporary deteriorations caused by "circumstances of natural cause" or *force majeure*, for failures caused by modifications or alterations of overriding public interest or other environmental benefit, which cannot be achieved by other means. Significantly, all such exemptions, in one form or another, bring in the possibility of economic justification for such exemptions. However, notwithstanding this breadth, there are express restrictions on the applicability of all these exemptions. They may not permanently exclude or compromise other bodies or water, and Member States must also take steps to ensure that the application of the Directive guarantees at least the same level of protection as existing Community legislation. In addition, there is a principle of Community law whereby such derogations are construed restrictively, so that the exception does not swallow the rule.[14] Given the width of the exemptions in this case, this principle may be important in the future implementation of the Directive.

11–004   Good groundwater status involves quantity, as well as quality, and the former is addressed for the first time at Community level in this Directive. Quantitative status is defined in terms of groundwater levels being such that the available groundwater resource is not exceeded by the long-term annual average rate of abstraction.[15] Resources are to be protected by ensuring a balance between abstraction and recharge,[16] and groundwater levels must be regularly monitored.[17] All of this will have implications for future grants, and revocations, of abstraction licences by the EA, as set out in Chapter 12.

The WFD also requires Member States to identify within their river basin plans all those water bodies used for human consumption providing more than 10 cubic metres a day or serving more than 50 persons. In addition, Member States shall ensure that those water bodies meet the separate obligations laid down in the Drinking Water Directive, taking into account the treatment in fact received by water taken from those water bodies.[18]

Unlike much previous Community environmental legislation considered later in this Chapter, the WFD does not set out a detailed definition of good status, though its Annexes, in particular Annex V, contain lengthy provisions specifying what must be addressed in the river basin management plans. Hence good status may vary in its definition from water body

[14] C-6/04 *Commission v United Kingdom*, ECJ, October 20 2005, at para.112.
[15] art.2(28) calling up table 2.1.2 of Annex V.
[16] art.4(1)(b)(ii).
[17] art.8, with details in 2.2 of Annex V.
[18] art.7. The Drinking Water Directive is 80/778, as amended by 98/83.

to water body, basin to basin, let alone Member State to Member State. Thus "good" in Brussels may be "poor" in Bristol. It is no coincidence that the Directive arose out of the Commission's original proposals made in late 1993[19] shortly after conclusion of the Maastricht Treaty on European Union with its emphasis on subsidiarity.

At first sight, the language is broad, even imprecise—what exactly does a   **11–005** Member State have to do to "aim" at a given water status, and how enforceable is that obligation, either by the Commission or an affected party? That said, the apparent imprecision may not be as much a hurdle as the language may suggest. Indeed, the European Court of Justice has already ruled in *Commission v Luxembourg*[20] that Articles 2 and 4 impose "on Member States precise obligations to be implemented within the precise timescales in order to prevent deterioration of the status of all bodies of surface water and groundwater."[21]

We are still some years from the first application of the Community-wide test of "good status," which arises in 2015. So it is too early to tell whether the lack of numerical parameters, coupled with a positive invitation to determine river-basin-specific standards and measures, will torpedo this ambitious attempt to improve Community waters. However, Member States may find it more difficult than the sceptics fear to avoid setting realistic standards for their water bodies which meet the requirements of the potentially demanding Annex V. Certainly preliminary indications from the United Kingdom are that very substantial expenditure is anticipated in order to meet its obligation under the Directive. To take one example, additional phosphate stripping from sewage treatment works (phosphates are a significant cause of eutrophication in water bodies) is being seen as one significant financial consequence of compliance with the WFD.[22] More generally, there is considerable concern that, unless addressed more vigorously than to date, diffuse water pollution will prevent widespread attainment of "good status" in England and Wales. Up to 82 per cent of rivers, 53 per cent of lakes, 25 per cent of estuaries, 24 per cent of coastal waters, and 75 per cent of groundwaters are at risk of not achieving good status because of diffuse water pollution.[23]

---

[19] [1994] OJ C222/6, explanatory memorandum COM(93)680 of June 15 1994.

[20] *Case 32/05*, [2007] Env. L.R. 467.

[21] Para.63 of the judgment. In paras 75 and 86 of her opinion, Advocate-General Sharpston added that arguably arts 2 and 4, and art.7(2) (water used for the abstraction of drinking water) may grant rights to individuals.

[22] Report for Ofwat by Ove Arup/Oxera, *Water Framework Directive, Economic Analysis of Water Industry Costs*, November 2005 (on Ofwat website).

[23] This emerged from the EA's risk assessment under art.5 of the WFD: see the EA website, under water quality.

Economic instruments

11–006 There are attempts to minimise pressure on water resources by use of economic instruments, albeit in a somewhat oblique fashion. The first sentence of Article 9(1) of the WFD 2000 requires Member States to take account of the principle of the costs of water services, including environmental and resource costs, in accordance in particular with the polluter pays principle. Water services include abstraction, storage, treatment, and distribution of water, and waste water collection and treatment facilities which discharge into surface waters.[24] Article 9(1), by its second sentence, also requires that by 2010; (a) water-pricing policies provide adequate incentives for users to use water resources efficiently, and (b) different water uses (at least industry, households and agriculture) shall contribute to the recovery of the costs of water services, though there may be a derogation from these obligations if the Member States act in accordance with established practices and this can be justified in the applicable river basin management plans.

Defra's "provisional" view[25] was that the only pollution to be taken account of in the "polluter pays" principle mentioned in the first sentence of Article 9(1) is that related to the costs of over-abstraction or the treatment of waste water; hence the more general environmental impact of, say, agricultural or industrial polluters could not be reflected in abstraction charges, water prices or discharge consents costs placed on agriculture or industry. This appears overly narrow, particularly in the light of the "polluter pays" principle being invoked in the second sentence of Article 9(1), and the broad justification for economic instruments as set out in recital (38) to the Directive.

Public participation

11–007 As is typical of post-Aarhus[26] Community legislation, the WFD provides for public information and consultation in respect of the plan-making process.[27] This involves setting out the consultation measures at least three years before the plan period, provision of an overview of the significant issues identified in the particular basin at least two years before the plan period, and draft copies of the plan at least one year before the plan period. Consultation periods must be at least six months. Access to all background documents and information should be available on request.[28]

---

[24] art.2(38).
[25] As reported in NERA Group Consulting's report, *CRP Project 1C*, of May 2006 (DEFRA website)
[26] See Chapter 6.
[27] art.14
[28] art.14(1), last sentence.

Transition, transposition and implementation

The WFD entered into force on December 22, 2000. Transposition into **11–008** domestic law was required by December 22, 2003. This was effected by the Water Environment (Water Framework Directive) (England & Wales) Regulations 2003[29], which unsurprisingly made the EA the prime mover towards implementation. The EA has the role of making proposals for the environmental objectives to be attained in the various river basins and it is for Defra to confirm these.[30] There is an intermediate stage under the WFD towards preparation of the river basin plans, namely an analysis of each basin's characteristics, a review of the impact of man upon water bodies, and an economic analysis of water use.[31] There is also a general obligation upon Defra and the EA to exercise their functions so as to secure compliance with the requirements of the Directive.[32] The WFD's deadline for submission of the river basin management plans themselves is December 2009, with 6-yearly reviews thereafter. The Regulations set an intermediate timetable for achievement between transposition and that deadline. As we have seen, good status is to be achieved by December 22, 2015, and significant effort and investment is expected to be made over the next years in order to maximise the number of water bodies which qualify for good status.

The Regulations also set out a detailed timetable for public participation as required by the WFD. They require publication of the river basin management plan and any revisions on the EA's website.[33] The various background documents leading to the plans need to be made available at the EA's head office, but do not need to be put on the EA's website.[34] The justification for the latter appears questionable, given that all the information will surely exist in electronic form.

The WFD will also be implemented in a number of ways considered in detail below, including implementation of its daughter Directives, and domestic provisions designed to enlarge the scope of Water Protection Zones, for which see paragraph 11–044 below.

Daughter Directives

The WFD 2000 was always intended to set a framework, and no more, and **11–009** more precise measures are expressly required by its Article 16 in respect of priority substances, and by Article 17 in respect of groundwater. New Directives in terms of priority substances (replacing the Dangerous Sub-

---

[29] SI 2003/3242.
[30] reg.10 of the 2003 Regulations.
[31] art.5, and the technical specifications in Annexes II and III.
[32] reg.3(1) of the 2003 Regulations. A generalised obligation of this sort found in the Habitats Directive did not find favour with the ECJ in C-6/04 *Commission v United Kingdom*.
[33] reg.13, and reg.15(3) for revisions.
[34] reg.18.

stances Directive 2006/11[35] and Groundwater Directive 2006/118[36] are examined below. The Water Framework Directive also repealed the Surface Water Directive 75/440[37] from December 2007, and the Freshwaters Fish Directive 78/659[38] and Shellfish Waters Directive 79/923[39] from 2013.

However, the WFD leaves in place certain sectoral legislation affecting water such as the Urban Waste Water Treatment Directive 91/271,[40] the Nitrates Directive 91/676[41] and the Drinking Water Quality Directive 98/83.[42] The Bathing Water Directive 76/160[43] was also unaffected but has been repealed as from 2014 by a replacement Directive on bathing waters 2006/7.[44]

EC SPECIFIC WATER POLLUTION LEGISLATION

11–010 As is apparent from the above overview, EC legislation concerning water pollution is at a transitional stage between initiatives pre-dating the WFD, and those which are inspired by it. Hence it is necessary to look at the first steps made into the area, as well as more recent enactments. Hence below is a table of current or recently repealed Directives, involving a first phase passed during the 1970s and 1980s together with the new generation of Directives which follow on from the WFD.

---

[35] [2006] OJ L64/52.
[36] [2006] OJ L372/19.
[37] [1975] OJ L194/26.
[38] [1978] OJ L194/26.
[39] [1979] OJ L281/47.
[40] [1991] OJ L135/40.
[41] [1991] OJ L375/1.
[42] [1998] OJ L330/32.
[43] [1976] OJ L31/1.
[44] [2006] OJ L64/37.

Table 11/I

Summary of Water Pollution Directives   11–011

No & OJ	Short Title	Transposition Date	Substantive compliance	Repeals/ repealed
	Framework & Daughters			
2000/60 [2000] OJ L327/1	**Water Framework**	12.2003	Good status by 2015	Repeals: Dangerous Substances, Fresh Fish, Shellfish & Surface Water Abstraction Dirs.
2006/118 draft[45]	*Groundwater Surface Water EQS*	03.2009		Repeals: Groundwater Dir. 80/68 from 12.2013 Repeals: DSD daughter Dirs.
2006/11	**Dangerous Substances**	Original DSD from 7.1983, 2006/11 from 3.2006		Consolidates & repeals: DSD 76/464. To be repealed by WFD from 12.2013
82/176 [1982] OJ L229	*Limit values for mercury from clor-alkali electrolysis industry—daughter to old DSD*			To be repealed with effect from 12.2012 by Surface EQS
83/513 [1983] OJ L91	*Cadmium— daughter*			To be repealed with effect from 12.2012 by Surface EQS.

[45] See footnote 58 for progress.

No & OJ	Short Title	Transposition Date	Substantive compliance	Repeals/ repealed
84/156 [1984] OJ L74	*Mercury from elsewhere— daughter*			To be repealed with effect from 12.2012 by Surface EQS.
84/156 [1984] OJ L491	*Hexachloro-cyclo-hexane*			To be repealed with effect from 12.2012 by Surface EQS.
86/280 [1986] OJ L158	*Carbon tetrachloride, DDT, pentachlorophenol*			To be repealed with effect from 12.2012 by Surface EQS.
88/347 [1988] OJ L158	*Drins, hexachloro-benzene & - butadiene, chloroform,* amending 86/280			To be repealed with effect from 12.2012 by Surface EQS.
90/415 [1990] OJ L219	*1,2-dichloroethane, TCE, PCE & trichlorobenzene,* further amending 86/280			To be repealed with effect from 12.2012 by Surface EQS.
Sectoral				
2006/7 [2006] OJ L64/37	Bathing Waters	03.2008	2015	Repeals previous BWD 76/160 from 2014
2006/44 [2006] OJ L264/40	Fresh Fish Waters	1978	1980s	Consolidates and repeals previous 78/659, repealed by WFD as from 12.2013
2006/113 [2006] OJ L376/4	Shellfish Waters	1979	1980s	Consolidates and repeals previous 79/923, repealed by WFD from 12.2013

No & OJ	Short Title	Transposition Date	Substantive compliance	Repeals/ repealed
98/83 [1998] OJ L330/32	Drinking Water (repealing 80/ 778)	Original 7.1982 98/83 from 12.2000	Original 7.1985 98/83 from 12.2003	Repealed 80/778 from 2003; consultation on replacement underway
91/676 OJ L375/1	Nitrates Directive	12.1993	1993–1995	
91/271 OJ L135/40	Urban Waste Water Treatment	6.1993	1998–2005	
	Other repealed			
75/440	Surface Water Abstraction			Repealed in 12.2007 by WFD

With the exception of the WFD, these water Directives fall into three **11–012** categories:

(i) Directives controlling the discharge of specific dangerous sub-stances to surface waters or to groundwater;
(ii) Directives specifying quality standards for waters to be used for specific purposes;
(iii) Controls over specific polluting activities, which as will be seen are essentially unaffected by the WFD and its progeny.

(i) Dangerous Substances

Surface water

The recently enacted Dangerous Substance Directive 2006/11 is in fact **11–013** simply a codification of 76/464[46], and for reasons which will emerge, its days are numbered. Directive 76/464 was one of the early and ambitious manifestations of Community water policy. As originally enacted, it applied to all waters, but from the coming into force of the Groundwater Directive 80/68[47] it was limited to surface waters, widely defined as including inland, coastal and territorial, whereas groundwaters became separately regulated.[48]

[46] [1976] OJ L129/23.
[47] [1980] OJ L20/43.
[48] art.21(3) of 80/68.

This system of separate regulation between surface and groundwaters was retained in the 2006 Dangerous Substances Directive.[49] It requires Member States to *eliminate* pollution of *surface* waters by List I substances (known as the black list) and to *reduce* pollution by List II substances (known as the grey list).[50] There must be prior authorisation of all discharges of black list substances, setting emission standards, including where appropriate, standards for discharges to sewers.[51] "Discharges" under the Directive have been interpreted widely by the ECJ as including "any act attributable to a person by which [such a substance] is directly or indirectly introduced into the waters."[52] Hence the term applied to pollution caused by creosote-impregnated shoring posts and by contaminated steam which later condensed into waters.[53] The standards set under the 2006 Directive must specify both the maximum permitted concentration in the discharge and the maximum quantity that may be discharged over prescribed periods, either in absolute terms or by reference to the production levels of the activity giving rise to the discharge.[54] As for grey list substances, Member States were obliged to establish programmes to implement the reduction in these substances, involving authorisations based on environmental quality standards, either to be fixed by the Member States or by Community legislation where it exists.[55]

The long process of fixing emission standards, quality objectives for black-list substances and of adding to the list, all via daughter Directives, stalled in the 1980s, as can be seen from Table 11/I above. Domestically, the old Dangerous Substances Directive was been implemented by a combination of individual discharge consents imposed by the EA (considered later in this Chapter) coupled with domestic Regulations, the Surface Waters (Dangerous Substances)(Classification) Regulations 1989 which set out the standards contained in such daughter Directives as were enacted.

11–014 The Dangerous Substances Directive, even the 2006 version, is being overtaken by events. It is to be repealed by the Water Framework Directive, with effect from December 22, 2013. This is because the WFD has set out its own way of identifying and regulating dangerous substances. Article 4(1)(a)(iv) of the WFD, applicable to "emissions, discharges or losses" into surface waters, contains obligations upon Member States in respect of priority substances (which must be progressively reduced), and priority hazardous substances (which must be ceased or phased out)—echoing the

[49] art.1.
[50] Annex 1.
[51] art.4.
[52] *C-232 Nederhoff*, at para.37 of the judgment.
[53] *Nederhoof* and *C-231 A.M.L van Rooij* respectively.
[54] art.5.
[55] art.6.

obligations in respect of grey list/List II and black list/List I substances respectively.

Despite these obligations being embedded in its Article 4, the WFD as originally enacted contained no list of priority or priority hazardous substances. It did contain an obligation upon the Commission to submit proposals in respect of such substances.[56] The first step in this process was taken by a Decision in 2001,[57] which identified 33 priority substances, including certain herbicides, insecticides, chlorinated solvents, lead mercury, nickel, and tributylin tin. Of these, 14 were identified as possible priority *hazardous* substances. Both lists differ significantly from either black or grey list substances.

The Surface Water EQS Directive

The second step towards identifying priority, and priority hazardous, substances occurred more recently, in the form of a draft Directive on Environmental Quality Standards.[58] This lists the 33 priority substances or groups of substances as identified in the Decision, identifying 20 of them as priority hazardous substances, and setting environmental quality standards for all 33. So, by way of example, mercury must be present at less than 0.05μg/l in inland surface waters, 0.05μg/l in other surface waters, each on an annual basis, with a maximum allowable concentration in inland surface waters of 0.07 μg/l. Member states have the option of applying standards to sediment or biota instead of to waters.[59] There is an important qualification to these standards, namely that Member States may designate mixing zones, namely areas close to specific discharges where the standards may be exceeded[60] before dilution takes place and the concentrations of pollutants fall to acceptable standards. The EQS Directive also requires the preparation of an inventory of emissions, discharges and losses within each river basin, which are to be published in the river basin management plans, and also are designed to demonstrate to the Commission that progress is being made toward reducing or ceasing discharges of the substances in question.

Pending repeal in 2012 of the daughter Directives to the old Dangerous Substances Directive, Member States may monitor and report in accor-

11–015

---

[56] art.16(2) for priority substances, and art.16(3) for priority hazardous substances.

[57] Decision No. 2455/2001 of the European Parliament and of the Council, of November 20, 2001.

[58] At the time of writing, this is near adoption. The Commission Proposal is at COM (2006) 398 final. A more recent Commission Communication to Parliament is at COM (2007) 871 final. On June 17, 2008, the European Parliament agreed a text (P6-TA(2008)0283), and on July 17, 2008, the Commission agreed to the amendments proposed by the EP (COM(2008) 587 final).

[59] art.3.

[60] art.4.

dance with the new regime instead. As noted above, the new Dangerous Substances Directive will in turn be replaced by the EQS Directive.

Groundwater

11-016 Slightly different rules apply to groundwater, for understandable reasons. It is in the nature of groundwater that normally it travels very slowly through the permeable strata in which it lies (the aquifer), and it is highly susceptible to contamination from both point and diffuse sources, depending on the permeability of the strata lying between these sources and the aquifer. Once contaminated, groundwater is exceptionally difficult, and in some circumstances virtually impossible, to clean up. Groundwater provides around one third of demand in England and Wales, and in some areas is the only available future resource. Over the EU as a whole, the proportion is higher, with some 75 per cent of the population depending upon groundwater. The pressures on water resources are now such that it is vital to protect reserves of groundwater to ensure that they are available for future use, even if they are not in use currently. In practice, however, despite their separate treatment in these Directives, groundwater impacts upon surface water, and vice versa. This is because surface water may flow or seep into groundwater, and groundwater springs may likewise feed rivers or other surface water bodies.

The first Groundwater Directive 80/68

11-017 The Groundwater Directive currently applicable is 80/68, though it is in the course of replacement by 2006/118, and it will be necessary to look at both texts. The purpose of 80/68 is to prevent or minimise the discharges of certain dangerous substances. To that end it established two lists, List I, the black list, and List II, the grey list. These are, not surprisingly, very similar to the lists forming part of the original Dangerous Substances Directive which previously governed both surface and groundwater. The main differences are that all mineral oils and hydrocarbons are in the black list of the Groundwater Directive, whether persistent or not, and cyanides are in the black list of the Groundwater Directive, but in the grey list of the Dangerous Substances Directive.

Articles 4, 5 and 7 of the 1980 Directive required a prior hydrogeological survey before landfilling could be permitted. This underpinned the first domestic legislative obligation (transposed as late as 1994) to prevent or minimise pollution caused by landfills. This was to be implemented by making the grant of a waste management licence dependant on the applicant demonstrating that there were adequate measures to prevent contamination by black or grey list substances.[61] Hence applicants were

---

[61] Waste Management Licensing Regulations 1994, reg.15, and now in reg.7 of the Groundwater Regulations 1998.

required to produce such a survey in support of their application for a licence.

The 1980 Directive contains an exception from its scope in Article 2(1)(b), namely;

"discharges which are <u>found</u> by the competent authority of the Member State concerned to contain substances in lists I or II in a quantity and concentration so small as to obviate any present or future danger of deterioration in the quality of the receiving groundwater."[62]

So there is a threshold before a discharge becomes subject to the Directive, but it is a low one. In *Commission v Germany*[63] the ECJ pointed out that substances in lists I or II contained in such discharges must be present in quantities "sufficiently small as to obviate prima facie without there being a need for any evaluation, all risk of pollution of the groundwater". As the ECJ said elsewhere in their judgment, if a risk of pollution cannot automatically be excluded, the Directive must apply.

The new Groundwater Directive 2006/118 contains a similar provision **11–018** in Article 6(3)(b): Member States may exempt from the measures required to prevent or limit inputs, inputs that are considered by the authorities to be of a quantity and concentration so small as to obviate any present or future risk of deterioration in the quality of the receiving water.

Further exceptions are to be found in Article 4 of Directive 80/68.[64] A discharge of a black list substance may be authorised after prior investigation if that investigation reveals that the groundwater is permanently unsuitable for other uses (especially domestic or agricultural uses), presence of the substance does not impede exploitation of ground resources and conditions are imposed which require all technical precautions to prevent that substance reaching other aquatic systems or harming other ecosystems. A discharge may also be made if it amounts to re-injection into the same aquifer of water drawn for geothermal purposes, minewater or quarry water, or water pumped out for civil engineering works. Similar, if expanded, exceptions in respect of re-injection etc are to be found in Article 11(3)(j) of the WFD.

Implementation of the first Groundwater Directive

Wider domestic implementation came many years after the adoption of **11–019** Directive 80/68, when its provisions were finally transposed outside the waste management licensing regime. Since the Groundwater Regulations 1998,[65] the Directive's obligations have been applied directly to PPC permits (now Environmental Permits), and to discharge consents granted

---

[62] Transposed by reg.2(1)(c) of the Groundwater Regulations 1998.
[63] Case *C-131/88*, [1991] 1 ECR 825.
[64] Now in reg.4(5) of the Groundwater Regulations 1998.
[65] SI 1998/2746.

by the EA under Part III of the Water Resources Act 1991.[66] Finally, the Groundwater Regulations were in turn consolidated and amended in 2006[67] to include waste management operations which had hitherto been separately regulated.

The replacement Groundwater Directive 2006/118

11–020   As with the Dangerous Substances Directive, a replacement Groundwater Directive, 2006/118, has been enacted by way of a daughter directive to the WFD 2000. It came into force at an EC level on January 1, 2007, requires transposition into domestic law by January 16, 2009, but only operates as to repeal the old Groundwater Directive from December 2013. Instead of the black and grey lists, it contains specific parameters for two substances only, namely nitrates with a quality standard of 50 mg/l, and pesticides standards of 0.1 μg/l per pesticide and 0.5 μg/l for total pesticides.[68] These parameters are intended to set good chemical status for groundwater. They are subject to review by the Commission by 2013.[69]

The 2006 Groundwater Directive does not contain provisions (as in 80/68 and transposed in the 1998 Regulations) specifically requiring prior hydrogeological surveys. Such obligations have been swept into the more general obligations to be found in the Water Framework Directive concerning inputs into groundwaters, and the more specific rules concerning the construction and maintenance of landfills to be found in the Landfill Directive, and which are considered at paragraph 15–080.

The approach in the new Groundwater Directive mirrors that of the WFD and the river-basin-specific policies which it pursues. The rest of the parameters for groundwater, other than pesticides and nitrates, are to be set by Member States in respect of specific water bodies. There is an obligation[70] to set threshold values for further pollutants such as arsenic, cadmium, lead, mercury, ammonium, chloride, trichloroethylene and tetrachloroethylene (industrial solvents),[71] and to set thresholds for conductivity as a indicator of saline intrusion, as a minimum, by December 22, 2008. Such threshold values establish a groundwater quality standard for purposes of assessing groundwater chemical status.

11–021   Article 4 of the new Groundwater Directive summarises the criteria applicable to good chemical status. Groundwater must either comply with

---

[66] reg.1 of the Groundwater Regulations.
[67] By repeal of reg.15 of the Waste Management Licensing Regulations and of the matching waste licensing exclusion in the original Groundwater Regulations (SI 1998/2746).
[68] Annex I.
[69] art.10.
[70] art.3(1)(b) and Annex II, Part B. The pollutants on this list are also subject to review by the Commission by 2013: art.10.
[71] The offending substances in the *Cambridge Water* case. It was sampling carried for the initial implementation of the Groundwater Directive which detected the substances, put the borehole out of use, and hence triggered the claim.

Table 2.3.2.of Annex V to the Water Framework Directive or comply with the parameters of the Groundwater Directive (nitrates, pesticides and the thresholds levels), or, if not, any exceedences must be shown not to present a significant environmental risk.[72] In addition, the new Groundwater Directive requires studies to be carried out to identify significant and sustained upward trends in pollution, and these are to be included in the river basin management plans.[73]

Finally, Article 6 of 2006/118 requires measures to limit the inputs of pollution into groundwater, in particular preventing hazardous substances. The Directive exhorts Member States "to take account" of hazardous substances listed in 1–6 of Annex VIII to the WFD 2000 (organohalogens, organophosphorus compounds, organotin compounds, substances with carcinogenic or other mutagenic properties, persistent hydrocarbons, and cyanides), as well as such other substances in Annex VIII which are considered to be hazardous (these includes metals and compounds, arsenic, biocides, substances which contribute to eutrophication, and which affect the oxygen balance of water. Article 6 therefore is the groundwater equivalent of the provisions regarding priority substances and priority hazardous substances set out in the EQS Directive governing surface waters. Although Article 6 may appear to be less prescriptive than its surface water equivalent, the difference may be more apparent than real. It will be very difficult indeed for a Member State to set a completely minimalist course through this Directive, given the nature of its obligations, without a cogent scientific case that a particular substance is in fact of no concern in the aquifer or aquifers under consideration. Subsidiarity may be more in the form than the substance of the main provisions of this Directive.

There are however exemptions[74] enabling Member States to exclude various pollutants including immaterial ones, those that result from accidents or exceptional circumstances of natural cause, those which cannot be avoided without environmental, human health or disproportionate cost consequences, or those which result from necessary interventions in surface waters to mitigate the effects of floods or droughts, or for other water management purposes—only where authorised by general binding rules. Again Member States must record these exemptions, and notify the Commission of them, on request.[75] Such derogations will, no doubt, be interpreted by the ECJ strictly.

[72] Summarising the complex terms of art.4(2)(c)(i)–(iv).
[73] art.5.
[74] art.6(3).
[75] art.6(4).

Domestic implementation of the Groundwater Directives

11–022 The piecemeal implementation of the current Groundwater Directive has been noted above. The main provision now covering the field is the Groundwater Regulations 1998 as amended which transpose Directive 80/68. The deadline for transposition of the new Directive, 2006/118, is not until March 2009, and transposition will be effected by amending the scope of the 1998 Regulations. Once amended, DEFRA intends to include the groundwater permitting regime within the EP system. In the interim, however, the Secretary of State gave the EA a Direction (the Groundwater (Water Framework Directive) Direction 2006) in which the EA was to prepare proposals for threshold values in accordance with Annexes I and II of the draft Directive as it then stood.[76]

(ii) Quality standards for specific purposes

Drinking water

11–023 It might be thought that, with the combination of Directives protecting surface waters and groundwaters, there was limited room for the EC to make separate provision for drinking water. Far from it. Until very recently, there were two separate Directives governing drinking water, the first being 75/440, the Surface Water Abstraction for Drinking Directive,[77] and the second being 98/83 (replacing 80/778), the Drinking Water Directive.[78] Mercifully, 75/440 has recently been repealed with effect from December 2007.[79] However, more change is afoot, with consultation underway on a replacement for the current Drinking Water Directive 98/83.[80]

The old surface water abstraction Directive 75/440 can quickly be dealt with, even though one can see some of the policy approaches in this very early Directive reproduced in the WFD. This required member states to divide surface waters into three categories, with class 3 not allowed to be used for drinking. Member States were to set quality values for various pollutants set in the Directive, and to ensure continuing improvement of surface water quality within 10 years. The Directive was conspicuously ignored by most Member states, and the Commission, despite a few belated attempts to pursue defaulting Member states, turned its attention to the enforcement of the first Drinking Water Directive, 80/778.[81] In any

---

[76] The Common Position adopted by the Council on November 9, 16062/05.
[77] [1975] OJ L194/26.
[78] [1998] OJ L330/32.
[79] By art.22 of the Water Framework Directive.
[80] There is little indication as to the likely areas of reform, though the Commission flags up issues raised by EU enlargement.
[81] It was transposed in the United Kingdom by the Surface Waters (Abstraction for Drinking Water) (Classification) Regulations 1996 made under s.82 of the WRA, and the Water Supply (Water Quality) Regulations 2000 which are examined below.

event, the obligations to identify and protect drinking water catchments remain under Article 7 of the WFD.

The Drinking Water Directive, 80/778, was of importance, both at an EC level and domestically.[82] It limited the presence of undesirable substances in drinking water, by fixing 62 Maximum Admissible Concentrations or MACs for substances, and giving non-mandatory guide values for some of these. So, for example, the MAC for ammonium was 0.5 mg/l, whereas the guide value was 0.05 mg/l. Member States were expected to fix values at or less than the MAC, but had to "take as a basis" the guide values. Monitoring was to be carried out at the point where the water was available to the user, namely at the tap.[83] Specific derogations were allowed. In *Commission v United Kingdom*,[84] it was argued before the European Court of Justice, in a case concerning nitrate levels not meeting the MAC of 50 mg/l, that the Directive only required member states to take all practicable steps to comply with the standards set by it. The ECJ disagreed, stating that member states were not only obliged to make an effort, but were obliged to reach the specific result required by the Directive. Concern thereafter about the implications led to the inclusion of a domestic regime covering nitrate vulnerable zones, for which see paragraph 11–033.

As noted above, the Drinking Water Directive currently in force is 98/83.   **11–024** This requires drinking water to be "wholesome and clean."[85] Drinking water excludes natural mineral waters which are separately regulated, and member states may exclude small domestic supplies from its scope.[86] To be wholesome and clean, drinking water must be free from any micro-organisms and parasites and from any substances which, in numbers and concentrations, constitute a potential danger to health, and it must also meet some 28 microbiological and chemical parameters set out in Annex I(A) and (B).[87] The lead concentration is reduced from 50 μg/l to 25 μg/l with effect from the end of 2003, and then down to 10 μg/l from the end of 2013. The point of compliance for mains water is stated to be the tap, but compliance may be deemed if it is shown that non-compliance was caused, not by the standard of the raw water, but by the domestic distribution system itself—lead pipes being the obvious example. The Directive provides for derogations in respect of particular parameters, for up to two periods of three years, and, in exceptional circumstances, for a third three-year period.

---

[82] It was to be transposed by 1982, and enforced by 1985. The transposing regulations were the Water Supply (Water Quality) Regulations 1989, SI 1989/1147.

[83] art.12(2).

[84] [1992] ECR 1–6103.

[85] art.1(2).

[86] art.3.

[87] art.4.

Domestic provisions concerning drinking water quality

11–025 Now to domestic implementation of these drinking water obligations, for which it is necessary to review the statutory structure before looking at the transposing regulations. The supply of drinking water to the general public is the responsibility of the statutory water undertakers appointed by the Secretary of State under section 6 of the Water Industry Act 1991. For many parts of England and Wales, these undertakers are the same as the sewerage undertakers who succeeded to the 10 regional water authorities upon privatisation. There had also been statutory water companies operating within defined areas in these regions under a highly regulated monopoly for the supply of drinking water to the public. They acquired the water themselves from sources they had developed or acquired themselves, or they purchased water from the local regional water authority. Currently there are 24 water undertakers of which 10 are combined water and sewerage undertakers. Essentially the same structure for the water supply industry—with a few refinements introduced by the Water Act 2003[88]—has continued since privatisation in September 1989. Controls over the quality of drinking water are enforced by the Drinking Water Inspectorate, which is an independent arm of Defra.[89]

Under section 68 of the WIA, the primary duty on water undertakers,[90] when supplying water to any premises for domestic or food production purposes, is to supply only water which is wholesome at the time of supply. They must also ensure so far as is reasonably practicable that there is no deterioration in the quality of the water in respect of each source or combination of sources from which water is so supplied.[91] The requirement to supply wholesome water continues up until the water leaves the undertaker's pipes. The undertaker must also seek to minimise the risk of the water becoming unwholesome thereafter whilst in the mains, which in practice is achieved by controlling the pH of the water so that it does not become over-acidic and so liable to attack lead, copper or zinc pipes and hence to fail the standards for those metals.

What is to be understood as "wholesome" for these purposes is defined in the Water Supply (Water Quality) Regulations 2000, as amended,[92] which transposed Directive 98/83 as summarised above. In particular, regulation 4 (read with Schedule 1 containing the various parameters) sets out the meaning of wholesome as contained in Article 4 of the Directive. It also specifies the compliance points, which are variously the point at which

---

[88] These enable major purchasers of water (requiring more than 50 megalitres a year) to switch suppliers.
[89] s.86 WIA as amended.
[90] And licensed water suppliers under the Water Act 2003.
[91] s.61(1)(b) WIA.
[92] SI 2000/3184, applicable to England only. These have been amended in 2001, 2002 and 2005, and most recently amended with effect from December 2007 by the Water Supply (Water Quality) 2000 Amendment Regulations 2007 SI 2007/2734.

the water emerges from a tanker, the point at which the water first emerges from any bottle or container collected from a local distribution point, and in any other case, the consumer's tap. But regulation 4(4) sets an additional requirement for wholesomeness other than that laid down in the Directive, namely that water on transfer from a treatment works meets the prescribed coliform bacteria or *E. Coli* parameter or contains nitrite in excess of 0.1mg/l. Regulation 4(6) applies these bacterial standards to water being transferred from service reservoirs—if more than 5 per cent of samples taken in a year exceed those standards. The Regulations also address "departures", a procedure under which the Secretary of State may authorise undertakers to supply water which does not meet wholesomeness as defined. The Secretary of State must be satisfied that continued supply is necessary, there is no other reasonable means of achieving that supply, and that the water supplied does not constitute a potential danger to public health.[93]

The primary enforcement body in respect of these Regulations is the **11–026** Drinking Water Inspectorate. The DWI may prosecute water companies for supplying water which is unfit for human consumption under section 70 of the WIA.[94] In such proceedings, it is a defence to show that the supplier had no reasonable grounds for suspecting that the water would be used for human consumption; or took all reasonable steps and exercised all due diligence for securing that the water was fit for human consumption on leaving the undertaker's pipes or that it was not used for human consumption.

It has powers of entry, powers to carry out inspections and tests, and powers to require production of records.[95] It also provides guidance on the application of the Regulations.[96] Most prosecutions have been for discoloured water, though two high-profile cases have been brought in respect of cryptosporidium pollution. The first, against South West Water, failed because the prosecution could not prove the underlying elements making up epidemiological evidence upon which it relied.[97] The second, against Dwr Cymru, arising out of 231 cases of illness in November 2005, led to a guilty plea on October 11, 2007, and fines of £15,000 on each of four specimen counts.[98] Guidance has been given by the Court of Appeal as to the level of fines in section 70 cases, with fines for each count ranging from £2,800 to £6,000 depending on culpability, with the total fines for each incident of between £14,000 and £30,000.[99]

---

[93] reg.20.
[94] Proceedings may be brought in the DWI's name: s.86 WIA, as amended. There are more specific water quality offences under the 2000 Regulations.
[95] s.70(4) WIA.
[96] See, e.g. Guidance of May 2005 on the DWI website.
[97] HHJ Bursell, Bristol Crown Court, unreported, but see reference on DWI website.
[98] DWI website press release.
[99] *Secretary of State for the Environment, Transport & the Regions v Yorkshire Water Services* [2002] Env. L.R. 449.

The duties of the water undertakers as to wholesomeness are also enforceable under section 18 of the WIA by the Secretary of State,[100] again in practice the DWI. Sections 18 to 21 prescribe a procedure for enforcing a variety of obligations under the WIA, including both water and sewerage obligations. Initially, this may involve an enforcement order, which may be either a final or provisional order, which requires action by the undertaker. The undertaker has the right to make representations. There is no obligation to make an enforcement order if any contraventions or apprehended contraventions are trivial, or if a company has given a suitable undertaking in respect of its compliance. If an order is made, the undertaker may challenge the order in the High Court on the basis that it is ultra vires section 18 or that the procedural requirements of section 20 have not been complied with and the undertaker has been substantially prejudiced by the non-compliance. Otherwise, the validity of such an order shall not be questioned in any legal proceedings whatsoever. There is also provision for imposition of penalties for breaches enforceable under section 18, with an appeal to the High Court in the event of the making of such penalties.[101]

11–027   Undertakings in respect of drinking water breaches have given rise to difficulties in the past. Water companies were supplying water in breach of the pesticide standard in Directive 80/778. The Secretary of State accepted undertakings from them instead of making an enforcement order. This decision was challenged in the *Friends of the Earth* case,[102] for lack of conformity with the terms of the Directive but the challenge was rejected by the Court of Appeal. However, the European Commission pursued the matter, and the ECJ decided in due course that the use of such undertakings was indeed not consistent with the requirements of the Directive.[103] The response to this was the Drinking Water (Undertakings) (England & Wales) Regulations[104] which require undertakings only to be entered into for the shortest period of time and if no reasonable alternatives exist. Whether this ultimately meets the ECJ's point must be open to question. Undertakings continue to be used, and are drafted by the water undertakers for consideration by the DWI.

Private Water Supplies

11–028   We have seen that small private water supplies are not caught by the Drinking Water Directive, though there is a duty on member states to provide information to those using such supplies if a danger to health

---

[100] s.68(5) WIA.
[101] ss.22A to 22F WIA inserted by the Water Act 2003.
[102] *R v Secretary of State for the Environment, ex.p Friends of the Earth* [1995] Env L.R. 11.
[103] C-340/96 *Commission v United Kingdom* [1999] ECR I-2023.
[104] SI 2000/1297. There is DWI guidance, for which see its Information Letter 15/2000 on their website.

becomes apparent.[105] However, domestically they are subject to the Private Water Supplies Regulations 1991[106] and the WIA, which impose similar standards as arise in respect of public supplies. The requirements of the regulations are enforced by local authorities under the WIA,[107] who may serve a private supply notice requiring action in response, and who may do the works themselves and recover the costs, if the occupier fails to respond.

Bathing Water Directives

As with many of the Directives considered in this Chapter, Community and domestic legislation is in transition. Directive 76/160[108] on the quality of bathing water has governed the position since the 1970s, but Directive 2006/7[109] repeals it with effect from 2014. A summary of both old and new is therefore needed.   **11–029**

The present Directive, 76/160, fixes quality requirements for bathing waters, including both coastal and inland waters. However, neither the old nor the new Directive applies to *all* coastal or inland waters. 76/160 applies to areas where bathing was either expressly authorised *or* not prohibited and traditionally practised by a large number of bathers. The United Kingdom adopted the latter definition.[110] The new Directive 2006/7 applies to any element of surface water where Member States expect a large number of people to bathe, judged by past trends and measures taken to promote bathing, and where no permanent bathing prohibition or contrary advice has been issued.[111] Neither applies to swimming pools. The scope of both Directives is thus similar. After some debate, the new Directive was not extended to areas involving the recreational use of waters such as surfing or kayaking, however much water exposure these sports may entail.[112]

The quality requirements under 76/160 fixed mandatory parameters for total coliforms, faecal coliforms, mineral oils, surface active substances, phenols and a number of other substances, with guideline parameters set in other instances. In all, 19 different substances or parameters are addressed in the Annex, which also set a minimum sampling frequency during the

---

[105] art.3(3) of 98/83.

[106] SI 1991/2790.

[107] ss.80–83 WIA.

[108] [1976] OJ L31/1.

[109] [2006] OJ L64/37.

[110] Even the Commission acknowledged that the "interpretation of [this] notion ... is not easily practicable" and gave guidance via a written answer in the European Parliament on September 10, 1985, as to objective criteria pointing towards established bathing: OJ Annex 2–239 Debates 1985/86, reports of proceedings September 9–13 1985.

[111] arts 1(3) and 2(4). This slightly expanded wording is consistent with the Commission guidance given in respect of 76/160.

[112] This is consistent with settled interpretation of 76/160, for which see *Moase v SSETR* [2001] Env. L.R. 227 (CA), a challenge to a compulsory purchase order on the basis that the proposed scheme was insufficiently engineered to meet, and hence inconsistent with the terms of, the Directive.

bathing season. Not every sample had to meet the parameters in order to achieve compliance; 95 per cent of the samples must meet the mandatory parameters in the Annex.[113] Subject to those limits, and exemptions for "abnormal weather conditions", the European Court of Justice ruled that the requirements of 76/160 are absolute, in that they do not allow Member States to assert compliance by establishing that they have taken all practicable steps to comply.[114] In addition, bathing must be banned if exceedences under the Directive amount to a health hazard.[115]

11–030   After initial minimalist implementation, both in the United Kingdom[116] and in the rest of the Community, the Bathing Water Directive 76/160 has had a very significant beneficial effect on marine water quality, predominantly via very significant investment in improving the standard of discharges from waste water treatment plants using marine outfalls.[117] It has been implemented domestically via ss.82 and 83 of the Water Resources Act 1991 and the Bathing Waters (Classification) (England) Regulations 2003,[118] and via the terms of individual discharge consents.[119] According to the Court of Appeal in *Bowden v South West Water*,[120] the Bathing Water Directive does not confer enforceable rights on anyone (in that case, a shellfisherman) affected by a breach of its terms.[121]

The new Bathing Waters Directive, 2006/7, pursues a different approach, albeit one consistent with the line taken by the Water Framework Directive in the direction of greater subsidiarity. The Directive was to be transposed by March 2008,[122] though compliance with its substantive obligations is not required until 2015, in line with the WFD. In the event it was transposed in April 2008 by the Bathing Water Regulations 2008.[123] Member States are required to make a bathing water quality assessment after the end of each bathing season,[124] under which each bathing water is placed into "poor", "sufficient", "good" and "excellent" categories[125] as a result of monitoring during that season and the four previous seasons.

---

[113] art.5(1).
[114] C-56/90 *Commission v United Kingdom* [1993] ECR I-4109, concerning Blackpool and Southport beaches.
[115] C-307/98 *Commission v Belgium* [2000] ECR I-3933, ECJ, at para.62.
[116] At one stage during the 1980s the United Kingdom had designated fewer bathing waters than Luxembourg, and no inland waters at all were designated until 1998.
[117] Often improvement schemes were designed to meet both 76/160 and the obligations under 91/271, namely the Urban Waste Water Treatment Directive.
[118] SI 2003/1238, re-enacting the Bathing Waters (Classification) Regulations 1991 (SI 1991/1597).
[119] See, for an unsuccessful attempt to quash a decision by the EA not to revoke a discharge consent for alleged inconsistency with 76/160, *Moase & Lomas (R on the Application of) v Environment Agency* [2001] EWHC Admin 231, Richards J—by way of sequel to the CPO challenge.
[120] [1999] Env. L.R. 438.
[121] See Chapter 4 for further discussion of the case.
[122] art.18.
[123] SI 2008/1097.
[124] art.4, and art.2(10).
[125] Annex II.

However, mandatory monitoring is limited to just two microbiological parameters, namely intestinal enterococci and E.coli, with different concentrations of these contaminants[126] leading to different categorisations. These standards (called Faecal Indicator Organism or FIO standards in the literature) are in practice tighter than their equivalents under the old Directive; Defra and the EA estimate that whereas bathing water compliance is currently 99 per cent, it will fall to 92 per cent if no action is taken to reduce current levels of pollution. Most of the other parameters under the existing Directive had already fallen into disuse, and had become regarded as irrelevant. Short-term pollution, of up to three days, may be ignored, as long as the Member State addresses its causes.[127]

The first such classification under this new Directive must be carried out by the end of the 2015 bathing season, and Member States shall ensure that by then all bathing waters are at least "sufficient."[128] There is however an exemption which may swallow this rule in the hands of a less than enthusiastic Member State. This enables bathing wasters to be "temporarily" classified as "poor", as long as Member States ensure identification of the causes, and the taking of adequate remedial measures, together with the rather defeatist "management" step of banning or advising against bathing.[129] But even this temporary status may be declared permanent after five consecutive years if the Member State considers that the achievement of sufficient quality would be infeasible or disproportionately expensive.[130]

Though the net effect of the change in standards, if enforced, may be to lead to an improvement in water quality, concerns have been also expressed about its enforceability and transparency once in force.[131] Its effect is certainly to reverse the absolute obligations confirmed in the Blackpool beach case, and, given this, its timing is curious—30 years after the original Directive, 20 years after the due date for its implementation, and at a point when belatedly most Member States had brought most of their designated waters into effective compliance most of the time.[132] **11–031**

[126] Annex I.
[127] art.2(8).
[128] art.5.(1)–(3).
[129] art.5(4).
[130] art.5(5).
[131] See Kramer, *EC Environmental Law*, 6th edition, (Sweet & Maxwell, 2006) pp.7–15.
[132] The Commission report for 2005 stated that in the EU 3.9 per cent of coastal bathing and 14.4 per cent of freshwater bathing did not comply with 76/160. The EA predicts that only 34 out of 486 designated waters in England and Wales will fall into the "poor" category, assuming no improvement between now and 2015: see DEFRA's list of March 19, 2007 on its website.

Fresh Fish Water & Shellfish Waters Directives

11–032 Both these Directives, namely 78/659 on fresh fish water (consolidated by 2006/44), and 79/923[133] (consolidated by 2006/113) on shellfish waters are due to be repealed by the WFD in 2013, and are not to be replaced. Both set quality standards with mandatory and guideline values in similar form to that in the Bathing Water Directive, and directed Member States to designate fresh water fish and shellfish areas. Neither was systematically enforced by Member States or the Commission, particularly during the early years of the Directives. This was despite the ECJ holding that there were sufficient objective criteria set out in the Shellfish Waters Directive to mandate designation if those criteria applied.[134] The Court of Appeal in *Bowden v SWW*[135] held it was arguable that the Shellfish Waters Directive (in contrast to the result reached for the Bathing Water Directive) conferred rights on affected shellfishermen enabling them to sue a public authority responsible for a breach of the Directive for any losses caused by such breaches. The European Commission,[136] however, more recently has considered that Directive 91/942, on Shellfish Hygiene, has made the Shellfish Waters Directive redundant, even though the Hygiene Directive plainly does not grant any rights to shellfishermen whose stocks may be contaminated by sewage discharges.

In England, 98 shellfish waters were designated under the Shellfish Waters Directive, and some 31,000km of rivers and canals have been designated across England and Wales under the Fresh Fish Water Directive. Defra intends that these sites will become protected areas under the Water Framework Directive.[137]

(iii) Controls over specific polluting activities

The Nitrates Directive

11–033 The Nitrates Directive (91/676) is aimed at protecting waters "against pollution caused by nitrates from agricultural sources", as its title suggests, and was the first significant Directive to address agricultural pollution. Nitrates cause eutrophication i.e. an excess of nutrients. This leads in turn

---

[133] Currently transposed by the Surface Water (Shellfish) (Classification) Regulations 1997 (SI 1997/1332).

[134] Case C-225/96 *Commission v Italy* [1998] Env. LR 370, at paras 24–5 of the judgment of the ECJ. See also C-298/95 *Commission v Germany* [1997] ECR I-6747 on both shellfish and fresh fish water.

[135] [1999] Env. L.R., relying on *Italy* and also C-298/95 *Commission v Germany* [1997] ECR I-6747 (on both shellfish and fresh fish waters Directives). Contrast the finding on the Bathing Water Directive referred to above. See Ch. 4 for a full discussion of the case.

[136] Commission, COM(96)59, Annex point 1.6.

[137] See art.6 and Annex IV of the WFD, and Defra's Consultation on Diffuse Sources in England, August 2007, at para.1.17.

to excessive growth of algae and other plant life, with consequent de-oxygenation of the water affecting fish and insect life. The Directive applies to all waters capable of being affected by such pollution, and hence includes coastal and marine areas.[138] Member States had to designate vulnerable zones by reference to criteria set by Annex I of the Directive, namely zones with (a) waters affected by pollution of more than 50mg/l of nitrates[139] or which could be affected by such pollution if not designated, or with (b) eutrophic or potentially eutrophic waters.[140] For these zones, Member States had to establish action programmes, covering rules relating to fertiliser application, and including a provision that after certain transitional periods livestock manure containing no more than 170 kg of nitrogen could be applied per hectare.[141] In addition, Member States were obliged to establish codes of good agricultural practice to be implemented on a voluntary basis, save when its terms were incorporated into action programmes.[142]

Member States did not cover themselves with glory in the implementation of this Directive. Indeed, the Commission started 56 sets of proceedings under Article 226 of the Treaty for failing to transpose or implement the Directive properly.

Domestic implementation has been via a raft of statutory instruments,[143] reflecting certain of those proceedings brought against the United Kingdom. Initially, 68 Nitrate Vulnerable Zones (NVZs), totalling only some 8 per cent of England, were designated, expressly on the basis that nitrate concentrations in those areas had been found in surface water or groundwater used from drinking water purposes over the Drinking Water Directive limit of 50mg/l. This led to proceedings against the United Kingdom,[144] in which it was eventually conceded that the United Kingdom should have designated all surface and groundwater with nitrates con-

---

[138] There is no definition, but these areas are expressly referred to in Annex I.
[139] The definition calls up the limit for surface waters in the original Drinking Water Directive 75/440 of 50mg/l, which is reproduced in 98/83. The groundwater limit is expressly set out at 50mg/l, the same limit as set out in Groundwater Directives 80/778 and 2006/118.
[140] art.3(1) and Annex I. For detailed discussion of what is meant by eutrophication in this context, see C-258/00 *Commission v France* [2002] ECR I-5959, and see also C-280/02 *Commission v France* in the context of sensitive areas under the Urban Waste Water Treatment Directive.
[141] art.5 and Annex III. The limit applies to the amount of nitrogen spread on or otherwise introduced into on the land, not the amount actually penetrating into the land: Case C-161/00 *Commission v Germany* [2002] ECR I-2753.
[142] art.4, Annex II, when read with art.5(4)(b).
[143] The Protection of Water against Agricultural and Nitrate Pollution (England & Wales) Regulations 1996 (SI 1996/88), the Action Programmes for Nitrate Vulnerable Zones (England & Wales) Regulations 1998 (SI 1998/1202), The Nitrate Vulnerable Zones (Additional Designations) (England) (No. 2) Regulations 2002 (SI 2002/2614), and the Protection of Water Against Agricultural Nitrate Pollution (England and Wales) (Amendment) Regulations 2006 (SI 2006/1289) entrenching public participation rights in the process, and the draft Action Programme for Nitrate Vulnerable Zones Regulations 2008, which, if enacted, would operate so as to repeal all previous provisions.
[144] Case C-69/99 *Commission v UK* [2000] ECR I-10979.

centrations falling within Annex I, not simply those used for drinking water. Similarly, it has been decided in *Standley*,[145] a reference to the ECJ, that it is irrelevant that nitrate concentrations which lead to designation of an NVZ may have been contributed to by non-agricultural sources, as long as the agricultural component makes a significant contribution to the pollution of the relevant waters which is the trigger for designation under Article 3(1).

11-034 Since 2002, the position has been that about 55 per cent of England has been designated as Nitrate Vulnerable Zones, though this coverage still lags behind the Netherlands, Denmark and Germany, where the whole land mass is covered by measures adopted pursuant to the Directive.[146] This percentage is likely to increase in response to continued pressure from the Commission to the effect that the NVZs designated in England do not fairly represent the areas in fact impacted by nitrate concentrations. There is also the difficulty posed by the fact that existing nitrates contamination may leach through strata at such a slow rate that recent changes in agricultural practice will have only a long-term impact on monitored nitrate levels. Consultation by Defra[147] proposes raising the percentage coverage to "about 70% of England."

Defra's action programmes for England prohibited applications of livestock manure providing more than 170kg of nitrogen per hectare per year to arable land and 250kg to grassland, but intends (subject to consultation) to reduce the grassland figure to 170kg.

The Nitrate Vulnerable Zones designated as a result of the Nitrates Directive should be distinguished from the previous system of Nitrate Sensitive Areas, designated under section 94 of the WRA 1991. This compensated farmers for changing practices designed to reduce nitrate pollution, but was closed to new entrants with effect from 1998. In future, and for reasons explained in the context of Water Protection Zones, NVZs and Water Protection Zones are likely to become integrated.

The Urban Waste Water Treatment Directive

11-035 It is no coincidence that the Urban Waste Water Treatment Directive 91/271 (UWWT Directive) was adopted in the same year as the Nitrates Directive. Their primary aims are very similar, namely to reduce the amount of nutrients being discharged into receiving waters, though they operate in different sectors. The UWWT Directive applies to sewage, and in particular to domestic waste water, both on its own and mixed with industrial waste waters and/or run-off rainwater. It required Member

---

[145] Case C-293/97 *Standley and others* [1999] 3 WLR 744, paras 31 and 35. This was an unsuccessful attempt to annul the designation of certain NVZs in East Anglia. The principle was followed in Case C-416/02 *Commission v Spain* ECJ, September 8, 2005, at para.69 and in Case C-221/03 *Commission v Belgium*, ECJ, September 22, 2005.

[146] Under art.3(5).

[147] August 2007.

States to provide, by the end of 2000, a sewerage system for "agglomerations" of more than 15,000 people and, by the end of 2005, such a system for agglomerations of more than 2,000 people. In each case the system must be capable of carrying out secondary or biological treatment of the waste water entering collecting systems (i.e. sewers) before discharge,[148] thus reducing its nutrient load. Secondary treatment shall comply with the requirements of Table 1 concerning Biological Oxygen Demand or equivalent, Chemical Oxygen Demand, and suspended solids. The point of discharge from the works should be chosen, so far as possible, to minimise the effects on receiving waters.[149] There are also more general obligations in the UWWT Directive that the works be designed, constructed and maintained in accordance with best technical knowledge not entailing excessive costs, so as to prevent leaks and limit pollution due to storm water overflows.[150]

There are additional obligations in the UWWT Directive applicable to sensitive and less sensitive areas. Sensitive areas are those sensitive to eutrophication of water bodies[151] and Member States must designate these. Applicable criteria are similar but not identical to NVZs under the Nitrates Directive, namely eutrophic areas, those where concentrations of more than 50mg/l nitrates are found in drinking waters, and areas where further treatment is required to fulfil other Directives.[152] In such areas, treatment must additionally address total phosphorus and/or total nitrogen levels. As for less sensitive areas, Member States may identify marine areas as less sensitive if the waste water discharges do not adversely affect the environment as a result of specific conditions applicable to those areas, and in such areas only primary treatment (i.e. screening and initial settlement) of waste waters is required.[153]

The UWWT Directive also obliges Member States to regulate industrial **11–036** waste water from specified sectors[154] (e.g. brewing and certain food industries) in accordance with general obligations set out in Annex I, which include a duty to pre-treat where necessary to ensure that any consequent discharges do not adversely affect the environment. Member States were also required to stop dumping sewage sludge at sea by the end of 1998.

---

[148] art.4 read with art.2(8). In *Application by Friends of the Earth for judicial review*, June 28, 2006, Weatherup J., sitting in the High Court in Northern Ireland, decided that the Directive did not impose an obligation on a public authority to prevent the entry of sewage into sewers feeding works which did not comply with other provisions of the Directive. The obligation under art.4 only applied to sewage once in the system. This appears to be an overly narrow reading of art.4. The policy of the authority to allow connections was however quashed on another ground, considered below.
[149] Annex I, at B.5.
[150] Annex I, at A.
[151] Defined in art.2(11).
[152] Annex II. "A water body" within Annex II included groundwater as well as surface water: Case C-416/02 *Commission v Spain* at para.54.
[153] art.6.
[154] Annex III.

Transposition and implementation

11–037 The Directive was transposed domestically by the Urban Waste Water Treatment (England & Wales) Regulations 1994.[155] The principal method of implementation was to impose upon sewerage undertakers an additional duty under section 94 of the Water Industry Act 1991 to comply with the terms of the Regulations.[156] This means that Ofwat may pursue the undertaker under section 18 of the WIA for any breaches of the UWWT Regulations, in the same way as we have seen in the drinking water context. In addition to this, there is the existing system of discharge consents administered by the EA under the Water Resources Act 1991, which is applicable to waste water treatment works and direct industrial discharges. There are also trade effluent consents administered by sewerage undertakers under the WIA. Both are considered later in this chapter. For present purposes, one should note that the EA is enjoined by regs 6 and 8 of the 1994 Regulations to exercise its discharge consent functions in accordance with those Regulations, and a similar duty is imposed by reg.7 upon sewerage undertakers in respect of trade effluent consents.

Differences in the transposing Regulations were slight; less sensitive areas were termed accurately, if wordily, as areas of high natural dispersion or HNDA. This accurate transposition did not however prevent the Secretary of State from designating all of the Humber and Severn estuaries as HNDA but impermissibly taking into account the extra costs of secondary treatment which would be saved by such a designation. Hardly surprisingly, this decision was quashed in *R. v Secretary of State ex p. Kingston upon Hull CC*,[157] and the re-determination drew a rather less generous HNDA. Indeed, shortly thereafter, in 1998, all HNDAs in England and Wales were revoked.

Consonant with this trend towards more rigorous implementation of the UWWT Directive, the number of sensitive areas has been significantly increased by DEFRA over the years; in 1994, there were 33 areas, whereas by October 2007 there was a total of 367 sensitive areas in England designated as requiring additional measures to combat eutrophication. The aim is explicitly to assist in the achievement of "good" ecological status for purposes of the Water Framework Directive.

11–038 The Directive has had a very significant effect on the quality of discharges from sewage works, albeit at a considerable cost—estimated in 2004 at €152 billion across the Community. Not every Member State implemented it with vigour. In 1999 and 2000, "agglomerations" as large as Brussels and Milan were still without a compliant sewerage system.

---

[155] SI 1994/2841.
[156] reg.4.
[157] [1996] Env.L.R. 248, Harrison J.

Interrelationship with the Waste Framework Directive

Waste waters regulated by the UWWTD are not waste for the purposes of the Waste Framework Directive.[158] The margins of this definition have been explored in two recent cases. In *R. (Thames Water) v South East London Division, Bromley Magistrates' Court*[159] the ECJ held that sewage which had escaped from an undertaker's sewers before arriving at its sewage works had ceased to be waste waters within the jurisdiction of the UWWTD once it escaped. The UWWTD did not manage such waste waters after its escape. The sewage had therefore become waste for the purposes of the Waste Framework Directive.[160] In *United Utilities v Environment Agency*[161] sewage sludge, once drawn off from waste waters into the sludge handling processes within the undertaker's works, had similarly ceased being waste waters, and had become waste for the purposes of the Waste Framework Directive. This conclusion led to these processes being regulated by the Integrated Pollution Prevention & Control Directive 96/61, as discussed in Chapter 14 on Environmental Permitting. **11–039**

WATER QUALITY

It is necessary to draw together certain domestic provisions which address water quality issues, not all of which derive from European legislation. The first is institutional responsibility. The EA has a responsibility for devising policies for maintaining and improving the quality of "controlled waters", for monitoring that quality and for enforcing statutory controls.[162] Defra then must decide between strategic options presented to them, and this broad division of responsibilities is reproduced in the 2003 Regulations which implement the Water Framework Directive. **11–040**

The phrase "controlled waters" within these domestic provisions, including section 85 of the Water Resources Act 1991 discussed below, is defined in section 104 of the WRA. It includes virtually all inland and coastal waters, namely territorial waters to a line three miles from the shore, coastal waters, inland waters and groundwaters. A river bed may form part of controlled waters,[163] as may a man-made ditch if it drains into

---

[158] art.2(1)(b)(iv) of the Waste Framework Directive, 2006/12.
[159] Case C-252/05, May 10, 2007, [2007] 1 WLR 1945. See also the Divisional Court judgment at [2008] EWHC 1763 (QB) confirming this result by reference to domestic legislation.
[160] Unless regulated by other provisions of domestic legislation: see discussion in Chapter 15 on Waste.
[161] [2006] Env. L.R. 849, Nelson J., unaffected in CA or HL.
[162] s.6 Environment Act 1995 and s.84 WRA 1991.
[163] *NRA v Biffa* [1996] Env. L.R. 227.

controlled waters.[164] The definition extends to waters which have diverted from their usual course.[165]

In addition to the general functions of the EA in respect of water pollution, it has more specific functions that include the protection against pollution of any waters belonging to it or any water undertaker or from which any of them may take water, including reservoirs and underground strata.[166] Its strategy in relation to water quality involves setting water quality objectives for surface and groundwater, coupled with policies for the siting of actually or potentially polluting activities, and for the imposition of controls over such activities so that water quality objectives may be met.

11–041   Domestically, surface waters have been categorised by various schemes in the past, essentially by reference to their values for biological oxygen demand, dissolved oxygen, and ammonia, and more recently incorporating minimum and maximum pH, dissolved copper, and total zinc. This whole process will inevitably evolve as the EA works towards achieving compliance with the river-basin based requirements of the Water Framework Directive.

PROTECTIVE MEASURES

11–042   In addition to the system for consenting discharges to controlled waters backed by criminal sanctions as described later in this chapter at paragraphs 11–048 and 11–064, there are a number of precautionary and other administrative measures available for reducing both the risk of pollution occurring at all, and also the amount of pollution in cases where the risks materialise or the pollution is authorised.

These include in particular (i) powers to require works to be carried out and precautions to be taken in relation to those holding matter that will pollute if it escapes; (ii) the designation of Water Protection Zones in which prescribed activities may be prohibited or restricted; (iii) controls over municipal and other waste waters in accordance with the Urban Waste Water Treatment Directive as explained above.

Precautionary works

11–043   The Secretary of State has power under section 92 of the WRA to prohibit any person from having custody or control of any poisonous, noxious or polluting matters unless such works and precautionary measures as may be

[164] *Environment Agency v Brock* [1998] Env. L.R. 607.
[165] *R v Dovermoss* [1995] Env. L.R. 258.
[166] s.10(2) Environment Act 1995.

prescribed are taken to prevent or control that matter entering controlled waters. Under this section there have been made:

(i) the Control of Pollution (Oil Storage) (England) Regulations 2001,[167] which set minimum standards for above ground[168] oil storage facilities at industrial, commercial, institutional and large domestic premises; such facilities include tanks and the fuel lines which lead to and from them; the Regulations were fully applicable from 2005;

(ii) the Control of Pollution (Silage, Slurry and Agricultural Fuel Oil) Regulations 1991,[169] as amended, which address agricultural fuel oil storage, and required all new tanks to be bunded since 1991. As the name suggests, they provide for crops in the course of forming silage being compressed into sealed bales at least 10m away from controlled waters, and for technical requirements for slurry storage and fuel oil.

Under both sets of Regulations, it is an offence not to comply, punishable by a fine of £5,000 on summary conviction or an unlimited fine on indictment.

In addition, there is a Statutory Code of Practice for underground tanks at petrol stations and other fuel dispensing facilities, outlining operational and management practices for underground oil storage at such facilities. This was made under the Groundwater Regulations 1998 and introduced in November 2002.

Water protection zones

As we will see in Chapter 12, the EA has responsibility for the granting, varying and revocation of discharge consents, and abstraction licences, and of the conditions attached to them. It must have regard to the current likely future quality of the surface and ground waters of the relevant catchment, to river flows, and to the present and likely future demands for abstraction of water in that area. It is further able to have a positive, and not merely reactive, role as statutory consultee under planning legislation, and so exert influence on both development plans and individual applications. The EA must have regard not only to the impact of activities operating in compliance with applicable permits, but also to the consequences of accidents and spillages.

11–044

---

[167] SI 2001/2954.
[168] Underground tanks are regulated by the Groundwater Regulations 1998.
[169] SI 1991/324, as amended by SI 1997/547.

Policy: source protection zones

11–045 Hence the EA has developed a policy of source protection zones (SPZs), each designed to protect a specific source of groundwater, and from which it is able to develop a coherent set of rules as to the appropriate location of industrial and other potentially polluting activities. Some 2,000 such zones have been defined. The EA divides groundwater source catchments into four zones, as follows:

Zone 1 (Inner protection zone)
Any pollution that can travel to the borehole within 50 days from any point within the zone is classified as being inside zone 1. This applies at and below the water table. This zone also has a minimum 50m protection radius around the borehole. These criteria are designed to protect against the transmission of toxic chemicals and water-borne disease.

Zone 2 (Outer protection zone)
The outer zone covers pollution that takes up to 400 days to travel to the borehole, or 25 per cent of the total catchment area, whichever area is the greater. This travel time is the minimum amount of time for which it is thought that pollutants need to be diluted, reduced in strength or delayed by the time they reach the borehole.

Zone 3 (Total catchment)
The total catchment is the total area needed to support removal of water from the borehole, and to support any discharge from the borehole.

Zone of special interest
Sometimes, the EA defines a fourth zone. This is usually where local conditions mean that industrial sites and other polluters could affect the groundwater source even though they are outside the normal catchment area.

In determining whether operation of a potentially polluting activity is acceptable at a particular proposed site, and if so on what conditions, consideration of its location in relation to any relevant source protection zone enables the EA better to assess the degree of risk it poses, and to act in a consistent manner on the basis of coherent policies. These policies are largely contained in the EA's revised Groundwater Protection: Policy and Practice (GP3).

Law: water protection zones

11–046 While the impact of new development on water resources can be controlled under standard planning and regulatory procedures, existing activities cannot be so readily modified in the same way in a manner that will be perceived as operating fairly on all actual or potential polluters. Any attempt to achieve a significant upgrading of an area with many industrial sites on an individual basis is likely to lead to numerous appeals and be most laborious.

Accordingly section 93 of the WRA enables the Secretary of State to designate certain areas as water protection zones (WPZs), and to prohibit or restrict specified activities within that area. To do so, the Minister must be satisfied that it is appropriate to do so with a view to preventing or controlling the entry of any poisonous, noxious or polluting matter into controlled waters. This now applies to all types of polluting matter, including nitrates.

To date only one WPZ has ever been designated, namely the River Dee Catchment, and that only after a six year run-up.[170] This WPZ covers an area of 2,251km^2 of north-east Wales, Cheshire, Shropshire and the Wirral. It consists of a single river basin; that of the River Dee, its tributaries and estuary. The designation provides for a specialist consenting regime within the zone to regulate the storage and use of certain controlled substances by industrial and other processes.

However, a more wide-ranging use of WPZs has been proposed by Defra. As noted when considering the impact of the WFD, diffuse water pollution, particularly from agriculture, is a major obstacle to the attaining of "good" status under the WFD by 2015, and the programme of measures to be devised by Member States must address this.[171] Defra has somewhat tentatively decided that the principal way of doing so is via an extension of WPZs, and it intends to give the EA specific statutory guidance to that effect.[172] So it appears that the EA must propose the designation of specific areas as WPZs where further controls are needed to prevent or minimise the entry of diffuse pollutants, including phosphorus, Faecal Indicator Organisms and sediment into controlled waters as a result of agricultural activities.[173] WPZs are not intended to be used for the *primary* purpose of tackling diffuse nitrate pollution, as this falls within the scope of the Nitrate Vulnerable Zones, and Defra has apparently shelved any idea of merging WPZs and NVZs. Legislation on WPZs and accompanying guidance is promised for 2009.

11–047

---

[170] The Water Protection Zone (River Dee Catchment) Designation Order 1999 SI 1999/915 and the Water Protection Zone (River Dee Catchment) (Procedural and Other Provisions) Regulations 1999, 1999/916.

[171] art.11(3)(h).

[172] Defra website.

[173] para.3.1 of the draft Guidance forming part of Defra's consultation.

POLLUTION OFFENCES AND CONSENTS

11-048 The other major method of water pollution regulation is via the principal water pollution offences coupled with the system of discharge consents, compliance with which is a defence to those offences. The main offences, which are central to the legislation, are contained in section 85 of the WRA 1991, and can be summarised as follows. A person contravenes the section if he causes or knowingly permits:

(1) any poisonous, noxious or polluting matter or any solid waste matter to enter any controlled waters; this is the most commonly used offence;

(2) any matter, other than trade effluent or sewage effluent, to enter controlled waters by being discharged from a drain or sewer in contravention of a prohibition notice imposed under section 86;

(3) any trade effluent or sewage effluent to be discharged:
  (a) into any controlled waters; or
  (b) from land in England and Wales, through a pipe, into the sea outside the seaward limits of controlled waters

(4) any trade effluent or sewage effluent to be discharged, in contravention of any prohibition, from a building or fixed plant:
  (a) on to or into any land, or
  (b) into any waters of a lake or pond which are not inland freshwaters

(5) any matter whatever to enter any inland freshwaters so as to tend (either directly or in combination with other matter which he or another person causes or permits to enter those waters) to impede the proper flow of the waters in a manner leading, or likely to lead to a substantial aggravation of
  (a) pollution due to other causes; or
  (b) the consequences of such pollution.

Section 85 is extended via the Groundwater Regulations 1998, reg.14, which makes it an offence to cause or knowingly permit (a) the disposal or tipping for the purposes of disposal of any substance in list I or II in circumstances which might lead to an indirect discharge of that substance into groundwater unless authorised under those Regulations; (b) any activity in contravention of such an authorisation.

Importantly, it is also an offence under section 85(6) to contravene the conditions of any discharge consent – irrespective of whether that contravention amounts to a breach of section 85(1). "Contravention" is defined under section 221 as including a failure to comply, and so offences under section 85 may be committed by a person even though he had taken no positive step with regard to the offending act.[174]

The offences most commonly charged are those under sections 85(1), (3)(a) and (6)—indeed an offence under section 85(3)(a) will almost invariably be an offence under section 85(1) also. The converse is not necessarily so, even in relation to, for example, trade effluent, in that a distinction can be drawn between *permitting* entry of matter into waters, which could be committed though the offender was entirely passive, and a *discharge* of the same matter, which requires some sort of operation, however, defined,[175] conducted by the defendant.

The offences of sections 85(2) and (4) are only committed where there is a relevant prohibition under section 86. If there is such a prohibition, the matter entering waters (for instance surface water) need not be poisonous, noxious or polluting for these offences to be made out. One should note that the offence in section 85(4) applies to discharges into waters other than controlled waters, as well as on to land. **11–049**

It is an offence under section 4 of the Salmon and Freshwater Fisheries Act 1975 to cause or knowingly permit to flow, or to put or knowingly permit to be put, into any waters containing fish, or into any tributaries to such waters, any liquid or solid matter to such an extent to cause the water to be poisonous or injurious to fish or the spawning grounds, spawn or food or fish. This offence, unlike section 85 which may be prosecuted by anyone, may be prosecuted only by the EA or a person who has obtained a certificate that he has a material interest in the waters concerned. It is also subject to a statutory defence of lawfulness coupled with the use of best practicable means.[176] It is infrequently prosecuted today, with most major fish kills being pursued under section 85(1) of the WRA.

Section 90 of the WRA contains related offences, of (a) removing accumulated deposits held back by a dam or similar by causing them to be carried downstream and (b) causing vegetation to fall into waters and failing to remove such vegetation, in each case without consent of the EA.

"Poisonous, noxious or polluting matter"

"Poisonous, noxious or polluting matter" within section 85(1) WRA must "enter" controlled waters. There is no definition of these adjectives in the Act, and hence they must be given their natural meaning. The word "polluting" has however been addressed in two relatively recent cases, and **11–050**

---

[174] *Taylor Woodrow Property Management v NRA* [1995] Env.L.R. 52.
[175] See *Rooij* and *Nederhoff* for ECJ learning on *"discharge"*, at para.11–013 above. *Quaere* the successful argument in *NRA v Coal Products* ENDS December 1993, Vol. 227, p.45 which persuaded the Chesterfield Magistrates that seepage from a tip or lagoon through land into controlled waters was not a "discharge". The outcome appears to have been a fortunate one for the polluter.
[176] s.4(2).

as will emerge the generous ambit of "polluting" includes in practice both "poisonous" and "noxious" matter within it.

The first case was *R v Dovermoss*.[177] Slurry was placed on a farmer's field. A stream became diverted from its usual course, and ran across the field, thus becoming contaminated with ammonia from the slurry. The levels of ammonia in the water exceeded the EC drinking water standard. The Court of Appeal held that "polluting" requires simply that a likelihood or capability of harm exists as a result of the contamination, not proof that such harm has occurred. The second was *Express Ltd v Environment Agency*.[178] Small quantities of spilt cream contaminated a stream. There was no evidence of "harm". The justices considered that this was "polluting matter", and the Divisional Court agreed. Hence, even discolouration of a stream may be sufficient to amount to polluting matter. Both *Dovermoss* and *Express* approved the dictionary definition of "pollute" in this context, namely "to make physically impure, foul, filthy, to dirty, stain, taint, befoul." However, there was a limit to this principle, as the Court in *Dovermoss* explained. Not every entry of potentially polluting matter would pollute the receiving waters:

> "Obviously a very small quantity poured into a large watercourse may have no polluting effect at all. It is so diluted that it does not make it impure, foul or filthy. That is a question for the jury."[179]

As noted, it is not enough that the defendant causes contamination of the waters in question. He must cause the *entry* of the contaminating matter. Hence, a defendant who drove excavators and the like through the bed of a stream, stirring up sediment and causing discolouration of the waters, was not guilty of a section 85(1) offence.[180] He had not caused anything to *enter* waters; the sediment was already there in the stream, and it had simply moved from forming part of the bed to being in suspension.

11-051   Since this part of the WRA was used to implement obligations under EC legislation, the definition of "pollution" in the EC Groundwater Directive 80/68 is also potentially relevant to the interpretation of section 85(1), on *Marleasing* principles[181] even though the wording of section 85, including the word "polluting", can be traced back into nineteenth century legislation. The Directive defines "pollution" as "the discharge by man ... of substances or energy into waters, the results of which are to endanger

---

[177] [1995] Env. L.R. 258.
[178] [2005] Env. L.R. 7. See for discussion of an earlier case on discolouration, *NRA v Egger UK Ltd*, June 17, 1992, Newcastle-upon-Tyne Crown Court, at 8–098 of the 1st edition of this work.
[179] Per Stuart-Smith J. in *Dovermoss*.
[180] *NRA v Biffa Waste Services* [1996] Env. L.R. 227.
[181] See Chapter 1. An implementing provision must be interpreted, so far as possible, in accordance with the directive it seeks to transpose, whether the provision of domestic law was passed before or after the EC measure in question. *Marleasing* is reported at [1990] ECR I-4135.

human health, or water supplies, harm living resources and the aquatic eco-system, interfere with the other legitimate uses of water."[182] This would tend to support a contention that "polluting" should be generously construed.

"Causing"

The offences under section 85 of the WRA are committed by a person who **11–052** *"causes* or knowingly permits" pollution of controlled waters. The framing of water pollution offences in this way dates back to the Salmon Fishery Act 1861; it was repeated in the Rivers Pollution Prevention Act 1876, and it is to be found in all subsequent legislation on the topic. Nevertheless, it was not until over 100 years later, in *Alphacell v Woodward*[183] that the House of Lords pronounced definitively on what is needed to make good a charge of "causing" pollution, and specifically on the relevance, if any, of the defendant's knowledge and intent, and the nature of his conduct. *Alphacell* was followed by *Empress Cars v Environment Agency*.[184] Their upshot, discussed in detail below, is that section 85 is an offence of strict liability; no degree of intention or negligence is required. Additionally, the defendant does not need to be the only, or indeed the dominant, cause of the pollution; all he needs to be is *a* cause.

Alphacell Limited were paper manufacturers with premises on the banks of a river. Polluted washing water from the paper making process entered the river, despite a series of tanks and pumps designed to prevent this. Unbeknownst to Alphacell, brambles, leaves and ferns had entered the pumps, thereby disabling them. Alphacell was convicted of causing polluting matter to enter the river.[185] It appealed on the ground that a person cannot be said to cause matter to enter a river if he is ignorant that he is doing so and has not been negligent in any respect, or alternatively that to cause something to happen denotes both knowledge and some positive act, or at least some positive omission.

The case proceeded in the House of Lords on the basis that Alphacell had not been negligent in any respect. Nevertheless the conviction was upheld on the ground that Alphacell, by locating and operating its factory where and in the way it did had undertaken a positive act which led to the pollution, and that knowledge of the mechanism of the pollution was not a necessary ingredient of the offence. The House approved and applied statements taken from related contexts concerning offences which are "not criminal in any real sense, but are acts which in the public interest are

---

[182] art.1(2)(d).
[183] [1972] AC 824.
[184] [1999] AC 22.
[185] The offence was under the Rivers (Prevention of Pollution) Act 1951, which was in identical terms to s.85(1) WRA.

prohibited under a penalty."[186] In such cases, and unlike the general criminal law, there was no presumption that *mens rea* or intent was an element of the offence. Policy reasons were to the fore. It was said that there would be "an impossible onus of proving that the pollution was caused intentionally or negligently" if the law were different, and that a "great deal of pollution would go unpunished and undeterred to the relief of many factory owners." The section "encourages riparian factory owners not only to take reasonable steps to prevent pollution but to do everything possible to ensure that they do not cause it."[187]

11–053   Having established that no mental element was called for, the question resolved into whether Alphacell had "caused" the pollution. "Caused" must be given its ordinary and natural meaning and it consequently covers causing something not only intentionally or negligently, but inadvertently without negligence or intention. Lord Salmon stated:

> "It seems plain to me that the appellants caused the pollution by the active operation of their plant. They certainly did not intend to cause pollution but they intended to do the acts which caused it."

Lord Cross deduced from the contrast between the "causing" and "knowing permitting" limbs of the offence that a man cannot be guilty of causing pollution unless he does some positive act in the chain of acts and events leading to that result.

It is said that hard cases make bad law, and it might be said that the hardest of them is *R v CPC*.[188] CPC bought a factory. Pipework failed. This had been installed by a negligent sub-contractor engaged by CPC's predecessor, and the underlying defect was undetectable even at a carefully carried out audit of the factory by CPC at the time of acquisition. Polluting matter ended in the local stream. It was held by the Court of Appeal that, despite all this, CPC had caused the entry of the pollution, by reason of the operation of the factory. The result follows inexorably on from the decision in *Alphacell*, and was expressly approved by the House of Lords in *Empress Cars*.

11–054   The next step in the development of the law was the *Empress Cars* case. The defendant owned a bunded diesel oil tank, though the bund had been effectively overridden by the defendant via provision of a pipe leading from the tank to a drum outside the bund. Vandals opened the unlocked valve on the tank, causing the contents of the tank to flow out through the pipe into the river. The defendant said that the vandals had caused the pollution to enter the river. The House of Lords did not dissent from this, but ruled that the defendant had also caused the pollution. They accepted the submission that the pollution must be caused by something which the

[186] Lord Salmon at 848–9, approving *Sherras v De Rutzen* [1895] 1 QB 918, 922.
[187] All per Lord Salmon at 849.
[188] CA, [1995] Env. L.R. 131. It is telling that CPC received an absolute discharge from the magistrates.

defendant did, rather than something that he did not do.[189] But the something which the defendant had done did not need to be the immediate cause of the escape. Hence, on the facts, the escape was caused by the way the company maintained its oil tank.

The Lords then turned to the far from easy question of when *would* a subsequent event lead to a finding that the factory owner's operations had *not* caused the pollution. In the leading speech, Lord Hoffmann put it thus:

"The true common sense distinction is, in my view, between acts and events which, although not necessarily foreseeable in the particular case, are in the generality a normal and familiar fact of life, and acts and events which are abnormal and extraordinary ... There is nothing extraordinary about leaky pipes or lagoons ... There is nothing unusual about people putting unlawful substances into the sewage system and the same is, regrettably, true of ordinary vandalism. On the other hand, the example I gave of terrorist attack would be something so unusual that one would not regard the defendant's conduct as having caused the escape at all."[190]

According to Lord Hoffmann, deliberate acts of arson by a workman or a lightning strike,[191] or by a terrorist attack breaching lagoon walls[192] would fall into the latter category. Since *Empress*, it has been decided that the sequence of events by which a tyre blow-out on a milk tanker ultimately led to the outlet valve sheering off the tanker and hence milk entering into a local brook would not be sufficient to break the chain of causation between operating a milk lorry and the pollution.[193]

The distinction envisaged by Lord Hoffmann between the intentional act of a vandal opening a valve and the intentional act of a workman igniting a tank of vapour seems a fine one, though the underlying decision of the Lords to spread the net of causation widely is evident. It follows that two or more parties involved in a particular incident, say an employer and his contractor, or a main contractor and his sub-contractor, may be both responsible under section 85(1) as concurrent causers, and it will not usually amount to a defence for one party to say that the other party caused it.

An example of this problem is presented by the facts of *Northwest Water*   **11–055**

---

[189] At 27H.
[190] At 34F. Pre-*Empress Car* cases need to be read with great care. The House of Lords expressly disapproved of reasoning in *Impress (Worcester) Ltd v Rees* [1971] 2 All ER 357, *Price v Cromack* [1975] 1 WLR 988, *Wychavon DC v NRA* [1993] 1 WLR 125, and *NRA v Wright Engineering* [1994] 4 All E.R. 281.
[191] At 31A.
[192] At 33E. Very heavy rain would almost certainly not break the chain of causation: *Southern Water Authority v Pegrum* [1981] Crim LR 442.
[193] *Express Ltd v Environment Agency* [2003] Env. L.R. 29, though the company was acquitted under section 89, for which see para.11–062.

Authority v McTay Construction Ltd.[194] McTay was a main contractor contracted to Greater Manchester Council. McTay sub-contracted vibro-flotation works to a sub-contractor (from a list selected by the Council), and the sub-contractor caused slurry to enter a stream. The magistrates acquitted. They found that McTay had no control over and were not in charge of the vibro-flotation process, although the process was specified by McTay to the sub-contractor, and McTay would be most probably have been liable in contract to the Council for the sub-contractor's defaults. The Divisional Court upheld the acquittal, but it is questionable whether the outcome would be the same in the light of *Empress Car*. It is plain that careful analysis of the contracts between all parties is required in order to decide whether in any meaningful sense the operations which caused the pollution can be said to be those carried out by the main contractor.[195]

The reference quoted above in Lord Hoffmann's speech to unlawful substances in the sewage system is to the third leading House of Lords case, *NRA v Yorkshire Water Services*.[196] A third party discharged iso-octanol, a dangerous pollutant, illegally into its trade effluent. The iso-octanol passed through the defendant's sewage works, and then into controlled waters, and the defendant's consent from the NRA did not allow its discharge. Yorkshire Water was guilty of causing iso-octanol to enter the waters, though, as noted later, it had a statutory defence to the charge because it was an authorised sewerage undertaker. The conviction was reached despite the fact that it specifically banned discharge of any iso-octanol into its sewers.

The final issue which arises under this limb of section 85(1) concerns a defendant who has been carrying on a set of operations and then ceases them. After cessation, does the defendant remain a causer? The answer is that he may well do. A good example is the Scottish case of *Lockhart v National Coal Board*.[197] The Coal Board was held liable for causing polluting matter to enter a stream, by its failure to continue pumping and treating minewater accumulating in its workings after the mine had been closed. The court adopted the argument of the Procurator Fiscal that everything stemmed from the original sinking of the mine in 1951. The ingress of air caused pyrite (iron sulphide—a very common mineral) in the workings to become oxidised. Constant pumping was necessary to remove water which otherwise inevitably accumulated in the mine. When the mine closed, the pumping ceased, allowing the mine to fill with water that brought to the surface the oxidised pyrite, which then spilt into local

---

[194] QBD April 1986, unreported, discussed in the 1st edition at p.364.
[195] Compare *Environment Agency v Biffa* [2006] EWHC 1102 (Admin), considered below, and in particular para.23 on the importance of the contractual relationship. For an example where a landfill operator, a contractor, and a consultant were all prosecuted and fined under s.85, see ENDS 319, August 2001, p.53.
[196] [1995] 1 AC 444.
[197] 1981 SLT 161.

streams. Thus there was a continuous chain of events carried out by the Coal Board which caused pollution of the streams. This pollution was bound to occur unless there were pumps of sufficient capacity to prevent it. The Coal Board's decision to cease operating was held by the court to be a positive act.[198] It was no defence that the lease had expired, so that the Coal Board was not in a legal position to continue the pumping. A person could not be heard to say that he had put himself in a position where he could do nothing about a danger which he had created. The outcome in the *Lockhart* case was approved by Lord Clyde in *Empress Car*. As he observed: "In many cases an omission may be analysed as the provision or operation of a deficient system."[199]

On the other hand, in a case involving a mine in South Wales[200] where **11–056** the mechanism of the pollution was similar, the successor entity British Coal was acquitted, on the ground that the original sinking of the mine was by a third party, prior to nationalisation of the coal industry, and that the polluting water from the mine came from workings other than those developed since nationalisation. If British Coal had acquired the mine and had done nothing further with it other than to stop pumping, then it would be *prima facie* liable for knowingly permitting pollution, though an exception in sections 89(3) and (3A)-(3B) of the WRA limits such a charge where it arises out of a mine abandoned before December 31, 1999.

"Knowingly permitting"

This is the alternative limb of criminal liability under section 85(1), namely **11–057** that the defendant knowingly permitted the pollutant to enter controlled waters. Unlike "causing", there is relatively limited case law on what the words mean, even though, as we will see, both "knowingly" and "permitting" give rise to issues of some difficulty.

The starting point, again, is *Alphacell*, and Lord Wilberforce's dictum that knowingly permitting "involves a failure to prevent the pollution, which failure, however, must be accompanied by knowledge". Lord Salmon added that the offence "was probably included in the section so as to deal with the type of case in which a man knows that contaminated effluent is escaping over his land into a river and does nothing more to prevent it."

The test was considered in *Price v Cromack*[201] where the defendant allowed effluent from a neighbouring abattoir (in which he had an interest) to flow into lagoons on his own land which lagoons had been built by the abattoir. The pollution occurred when effluent overflowed from the lagoons. The Divisional Court ruled that the defendant had not *caused* the

---

[198] *Quaere* this, though this may not necessarily be the critical question since *Empress Car*, per Lord Clyde.
[199] At 37E.
[200] *R v British Coal Corporation* ENDS, December 1993, Vol. 227, p.44.
[201] [1975] 2 All E.R. 119.

pollution, a conclusion with which the House of Lords disagreed in *Empress Cars*. However, the original Divisional Court added that they could not see that the defendant had a defence to a charge that he had knowingly permitted the pollution.

"Permitting"

11–058 Some assistance as to the meaning of "permitting" can be gained from *Bromsgrove District Council v Carthy*.[202] The offence was not under section 85, but was under an entirely unrelated regime whereby permitting land to be used as a caravan site without a licence was an offence. Lord Widgery C.J., summarising earlier authority,[203] said this:

> "What we get from that authority is, first the proposition that 'permitting', when related to a failure to take steps, must take into account the reasonable or other character of those steps. Failure to take steps by refusing to take reasonable means may amount to permitting. A failure to take steps which on the facts are unreasonable does not amount to permitting".

This is important guidance when the defendant wishes to contend that the steps which were necessary to forestall the pollution are unreasonable.[204] Plainly not every step which could theoretically have been taken amounts to "permitting" within the section.

A problem arises in the *McTay* type of case where there are a number of parties with some involvement in the state of affairs which leads to the pollution. Can they all be charged with "knowingly permitting"? *Environment Agency v Biffa & Eurotech*[205] is a good example. A sewer belonging to Severn Trent Water became blocked, causing sewage to leak into controlled waters. Severn Trent asked Biffa to "jet" the blockage free. This did not work. Severn Trent had men on site, and they then appointed contractors, Morgan Est, to clear the blockage. Biffa asked Eurotech to "tanker" escaping sewage away. Eurotech did this overnight as instructed. Biffa and Eurotech were criticised by the EA for leaving the scene, and for failing to do more to address the problem. The Divisional Court upheld both acquittals. The court acknowledged that responsibility under section 85(1) *could* attach to a contractor who comes across a state of affairs where pollution is already occurring, but said that "in each such case, it will be necessary for there to be a careful analysis of the extent of the responsibility which the contractor has assumed for preventing the pollution from occurring."[206] So on the facts, Severn Trent were still in control of the

[202] [1975] 30 P &CR 34.
[203] At 36.
[204] See the discussion of this issue in Chapter 16 on Contaminated Land, where the knowingly permitting test arises.
[205] [2006] EWHC 1102 (Admin).
[206] para.3. See also para.39.

incident, and unless Biffa or Eurotech were told, but failed, to carry out a specific task, they could not be found liable for knowingly permitting the pollution to continue. "The criminal liability under the Act of causing or permitting can, it seems to me, rarely, if ever, be incurred in circumstances where a contractor simply fulfils a specific contractual obligation."[207] So a theoretical ability to remedy a problem is not enough unless there is some expectation (contractual or otherwise) as between those involved with an incident that the given defendant will sort the problem out, albeit that he may not have been the original causer of the problem.

"Knowingly"

More contentious is the precise scope of the requirement that the defendant "knowingly" permitted the entry of pollution within the section, and in particular the circumstances where knowledge can be imputed to the defendant. In *Schulmans v National Rivers Authority*[208] the court found that knowledge in a section 85(1) case may be proved either by actual knowledge or by showing that the defendants had "deliberately shut their eyes to the obvious, or refrained from inquiry because they suspected the truth but did not want their suspicions confirmed." The case is often cited as authority for a general principle of *constructive* knowledge, but the judgments do not support this. Constructive knowledge involves imputing knowledge of facts to someone who does not actually know them. It is a difficult and important question, which is likely to occur both in the present context and the Part IIA test for responsibility for contaminated land.

11–059

To see what is in fact within the scope of constructive knowledge, it is necessary to travel outside the cases on section 85. The leading authorities include the decision of the House of Lords in *Vehicle Inspectorate v Nuttall*,[209] in which Lord Steyn cited a celebrated dictum of Devlin J. in *Roper v Taylors Central Garage*[210] regarding three types of knowledge which may arise in cases:

1. actual knowledge;
2. where a defendant shuts his eyes to an obvious means of knowledge; that is, where he deliberately refrains from making inquiries the result of which he might not care to have;[211]
3. where the defendant had in effect the means of knowledge but "merely neglect[ed] to make such inquiries as a reasonable and prudent person would make": in other words, he negligently fails to make such inquiries.

---

[207] para.40, per Burnton J.
[208] See a summary at [1993] Env. L.R. D1, but otherwise unreported.
[209] [1999] 1 WLR 629.
[210] [1951] WN 385.
[211] Typified in *Westminster CC v Croyalgrange* [1986] 2 All E.R. 353.

It is suggested that for "knowledge" to arise for the purposes of section 85(1), there must be either actual knowledge (Devlin J's category 1); or the person must have deliberately refrained from making enquiries the results of which he might not care to have (Devlin J's category 2), in other words, wilful blindness. By contrast, Devlin J's category 3 does not give rise to "knowledge" under the section. After all, the section incriminates knowledge (plus permitting), and not what the defendant ought to have known.

The other closely connected issue is whether knowledge held by an agent may be imputed to the principal who is being charged with the offence—irrespective of the conduct of the principal. This arose in *Circular Facilities (London) v Sevenoaks DC*[212], a Part IIA EPA contaminated land case. In that case Circular Facilities had been designated an appropriate person on the basis of a soil report which was on the planning register and so, the council contended, was within the knowledge of Circular Facilities. The planning application had been carried out by an individual whom, as found by Newman J. (at paragraph 35), the evidence showed was the agent of Circular Facilities. Simply saying that there is knowledge in the agent does not automatically lead to the principal being imputed with all knowledge which his agent (say, his environmental consultants) knew or ought to have known. Newman J. ruled that the presence of the report on the planning register which was placed there by the agent "in itself was insufficient to impute knowledge of the contents of the report to [Circular Facilities]".[213]

11–060 Case law drawn from general principles of the law of agency demonstrates that knowledge—even if actual knowledge—on the part of an agent cannot be automatically attributed to the principal. In *Sevenoaks* the court cited the leading decision of the Court of Appeal in *El-Ajou v Dollar Holdings Plc*.[214] In that case Hoffmann L.J. set out three categories of case where an agent's knowledge may be imputed to a principal: one is where an agent is authorised to enter into a contract on behalf of a principal where that agent's own knowledge is material; the second is where a principal has a statutory, contractual or tortious duty to investigate or make disclosure about something and employs an agent to discharge that duty; and the third is where an agent has authority to receive communications on behalf of his principal. Hoffmann LJ's decision also makes it clear that even where information is known to the agent, and that agent has a duty to disclose such information to his principal but does not do so, knowledge of that information cannot, without more, be imputed to the principal.

Some of these issues about the meaning of "knowingly permit" and constructive knowledge were debated in two contaminated land appeals, heard in April 2007, concerning land in Sandridge, near St Albans. The

---

[212] [2005] EWHC 865.
[213] At para.38.
[214] [1994] 2 All E.R. 685, especially at 702.

appeals were called in and the Secretary of State's conclusions are still awaited in October 2008.

Breach of conditions or prohibition notice

Where the water pollution offence involves knowingly permitting a discharge in breach of a prohibition under section 85(4) or in breach of a condition of a discharge consent under section 85(6), it seems that the knowledge need only extend to the discharge, not to the prohibition or condition which has been breached.[215]   **11–061**

Responsibility for others

A more general topic which arises under many environmental offences is whether a company can be prosecuted for the acts or omissions of its employees or agents.[216] This is considered in Chapter 3, together with the circumstances in which a director or officer of a company may be prosecuted for an offence committed by the company. However the provisions of section 217(2) of the WRA should be noted here. In summary, where an offence is committed by any person but the offence is due to the act or default of another person, then the latter may be charged as well as, or indeed instead of, the former. The scope of the section is well illustrated by *Express Ltd v Environment Agency*[217] where Pardys carried out a regular operation for Express on Express's land whereby cream was manoeuvred in a manner so that it spilt. Pardys pleaded guilty to causing pollution under section 85. Express were prosecuted under section 217(2) for their act or default, in permitting an operation on their land without carrying out a prior risk assessment and without responding to the results of such an assessment. The Divisional Court upheld their conviction.   **11–062**

Sewerage undertakers

Sewerage undertakers are naturally held responsible for the compliance of discharges from their sewage works with applicable consents. Nonetheless, though they have some control over what they receive into their works through the sewage system by way of trade effluent consents, and general controls on what may or may not be discharged to sewer, inevitably they will receive from time to time substances, or unexpected volumes of substances, which the works cannot neutralise, and which will put the works in breach of the terms of its discharge consents. The starting point under the   **11–063**

---

[215] *Ashcroft v Cambro* [1981] 1 WLR 1349, an offence under COPA s.3(1) of knowingly permitting waste to be deposited in breach of a waste disposal licence.
[216] See, e.g. *NRA v Alfred McAlpine Homes* [1994] Env. L.R. 198: site manager and site agent responsible for s.85 purposes, and *Moore Stephens v Stone & Rolls* [2008] EWCA Civ 644 concerning the one-man company.
[217] [2004] EWHC 1710 (Admin).

WRA is to place total responsibility upon the sewerage undertaker for treating matter arriving at its works in so far as he is bound to receive it—if the matter is included in the subsequent discharge, he is deemed to have caused that discharge for the purpose of any offence under section 85.[218] In such circumstances, where a sewerage undertaker is bound to receive any matter, the person discharging it to the sewer is relieved of any criminal liability which he might otherwise have had, were the receiving waters to be polluted by his discharge—as long as he has observed any conditions under which his original discharge was made.

We have already seen when discussing "causing" that a sewerage undertaker may cause the entry of polluting matter from his works, even if he was unaware that the polluting matter was being discharged into sewers for which he is responsible: *NRA v Yorkshire Water Services*.[219] However, the undertaker is provided with a statutory defence in section 87(2) which will absolve him if the discharge was attributable to another person (e.g. the original discharger of the iso-octanol), the undertaker was not bound to receive that discharge or was bound to receive it subject to conditions which were not observed, and the undertaker could not reasonably have expected to prevent the discharge into the sewer or works.

Statutory defences

11–064 The principal statutory defence to an offence under section 85 is where the discharge is consented by the EA. More precisely, section 88(1) provides a defence "if the entry occurs or the discharge is made *under and in accordance with*" various consents, including discharge consents under the WRA, and permits or licences granted under the Environmental Permitting Regulations.

A defence under section 89(1) is also available in respect of all of the offences under section 85 where:

(a) the entry of any matter into any waters is caused or permitted, or any discharge is made, in an emergency in order to avoid danger to life or health;

(b) the defendant takes all such steps as are reasonably practicable in all the circumstances for minimising the extent of the entry or discharge or of its polluting effects; and

(c) particulars of the entry or discharge are furnished to the Agency as soon as is reasonably practicable after the entry occurs.

This defence is not however a "due diligence" defence comparable to that contained in section 33(7) of the EPA concerned with the deposit of waste. It is limited to emergencies involving danger to life or health, and has no

---

[218] s.87(1).
[219] [1995] 1 AC 444.

application to an inadvertent discharge despite all reasonable precautions and the exercise of all due diligence to avoid it. It has been examined in one case, *Express Ltd v Environment Agency*,[220] noted above, in which a milk tanker from which milk was pouring as a result of a blown out tyre pulled over onto the hard shoulder. The Divisional Court held that in those circumstances the *entry* was capable of being caused by the driver pulling over onto the hard shoulder for the purposes of this section, namely for emergency reasons. The justices had concentrated on the different question of whether the *discharge* was as a result of an emergency, and hence the case was remitted to them.

There is also a defence available in section 89(4) WRA where a person has deposited solid mine and quarry waste such that it is carried into inland freshwaters. However, this does apply if the waste amounts to poisonous, noxious or polluting matter within section 85(1), and also it must be shown that the deposit on land must be with the consent of the Agency, there is no other reasonably practicable site, and the person depositing the waste takes all reasonable steps to prevent the refuse from entering those waters.

Consents to discharge to controlled waters

The procedures for applying for a discharge consent, and for the revocation and variation of consents and conditions, are set out in Schedule 10 to the WRA, supplemented by the Control of Pollution (Application, Appeals and Registers) Regulations 1996.[221] The following section addresses this freestanding procedure, but it should not be forgotten that many of the more potentially polluting discharges these days are regulated as one element of Environmental Permits which are the subject of Chapter 14. Indeed, Defra is proposing to bring the discharge consent system within the EP regime during 2009.   **11–065**

An application for a discharge consent shall be made to the EA on the appropriate form, and must be accompanied or supplemented by such information as the EA shall reasonably require. Applications shall be advertised, unless the EA considers that the discharge will have "no appreciable effect" on the receiving waters[222] and a minimum period of six weeks is to be allowed for representations in response. The EA is duty-bound to consult with water undertakers and statutory bodies with responsibilities for the receiving waters in question. It is also bound to consider the conservation implications of the proposals under the Conservation (Natural Habitats, etc.) Regulations on any European site which may be affected. In most cases[223] where sufficient information has been provided, the EA is required to determine the application within 4 months,

---

[220] [2003] EWHC 448 (Admin).
[221] SI 1996/2971.
[222] regs 2 and 3, and 4(b).
[223] See reg.3 for the exceptions.

and the application will be deemed to be refused if not determined within this period unless an extension is agreed between the parties. The Secretary of State may call in any application.

A grant of consent will invariably be made subject to conditions. These typically extend to (a) the point of discharge, and the design and construction of the discharge, (b) the nature, origin, composition, temperature, volume and rate of the discharge, and the period during which they may be made; (c) any treatment or process which should be applied to minimise the polluting effects of the discharge; (d) the provision of sampling facilities, metering, and keeping of records; and (e) the making of returns to the EA.[224] The most common conditions address the biological oxygen demand of the discharge, as well as levels of toxic or dangerous materials, and suspended solids. Industrial discharge consents normally include absolute numerical limits on the parameters included in the consents. Consents may also specify the time within which the EA will not seek to revoke them or otherwise modify them, which, unless the applicant agrees, shall be not less than four years.

11–066 The EA may also regularise existing unconsented discharges by serving a discharge consent upon the discharger. A discharge consent now needs transferring to a new owner,[225] and new and old owners need to give notice to the EA of this.[226]

Revocation and variation of consents

11–067 The EA may review any consents granted under these provisions, and any conditions attached to them. By serving a notice on a discharger, it may revoke, modify, or add to the conditions attaching to his consent on expiry of such period as may be specified in the notice.[227] If no discharge has been made within the previous 12 months, the EA may revoke the consent.[228] The Secretary of State also has an independent power to direct the EA to revoke a consent, or to modify or add to its conditions, if it is appropriate (a) to do so to give effect to EC obligations or any international agreement, (b) to protect public health or of flora or fauna dependent upon the aquatic environment, or (c) in consequence of any representations or objections which may be made.[229]

There is a limited right of compensation, if the notice of revocation is served as a result of a direction from the Secretary of State to protect public health, flora and fauna, within the four year minimum period, and arises as a result of circumstances which were foreseeable by the EA at the begin-

---

[224] See para.3(4) of Sch.10 to WRA.
[225] para.11(1) of Sch.10.
[226] para.11(6) as substituted by the Water Act 2003.
[227] WRA Sch.10, paras 6, 7.
[228] WRA Sch.10, para.6(3).
[229] WRA Sch.10, para.6(4).

ning of the period or where material information underlying the Secretary of State's direction was not reasonably available at that time.[230]

Appeals

Appeals may be made to the Secretary of State against a refusal of a **11–068** consent, or in respect of the conditions attached, and against any revocation or variation of a consent under section 91 of WRA. An appeal in these respects may only be made by the applicant; there is no right of appeal for objectors, and hence their remedies, if any, will only lie by way of judicial review of the EA's decision (or the Secretary of State's decision if the applicant appeals). The procedure is laid down in the Control of Pollution (Applications, Appeals and Registers) Regulations 1996, and allows three months for the service of a notice of appeal, running from the notification of, or deeming of, the EA's refusal. There is discretion in the Secretary of State to extend time. The EA's decision does not operate pending appeal, unless the EA concludes that this is necessary for the purpose of preventing or minimising the entry into controlled waters of any poisonous, noxious or polluting matter or any solid waste matter, or harm to human health. If the EA reaches that conclusion unreasonably, then the applicant will be entitled to compensation for the period since it reached that conclusion.[231]

Careful consideration should be given to the terms of any conditions when set, and whether an appeal should be mounted to the Secretary of State. This is because in any prosecution for a breach of condition under section 85, it is unlikely that a defendant will be able to challenge the condition upon which the prosecution is based. Such a challenge (whether by statutory appeal or judicial review) may only be open to the defendant in response to the original imposition of the condition. This principle, prohibiting "collateral challenge", is illustrated by *R v Ettrick Trout Co.*[232] The company was in breach of a condition of a discharge consent which limited flows to 10 million gallons a day. One day, it discharged 24.9 million gallons. It argued in the Crown Court that the condition was invalid, not having been imposed for purposes of pollution control, but in order to limit the amount of water the company was allowed to abstract. The Crown Court, and the Court of Appeal, held that such an argument was impermissible. However, it should not be assumed that all such challenges are invalid, as *Ettrick* may need revisiting in the light of later decisions of the House of Lords, namely *R v Wicks*[233] (no challenge to planning enforce-

---

[230] WRA Sch.10, para.6(5).
[231] s.91(2H) of WRA.
[232] [1994] Env. L.R. 165.
[233] [1998] AC 92.

ment notice permissible in Crown Court) and *Boddington v British Transport Police*[234] (bye-law challenge: it depends on the precise statutory framework whether a defendant is permitted to challenge the *vires* of an administrative act). However, in the case of any doubt, a consent-holder should pursue an appeal against the terms of a condition when imposed, rather than expect that such arguments may be advanced in defence to any prosecution.

Enforcement of Pollution Controls

11–069 Summary offences under Part III of the WRA may be tried if the relevant information is laid within 12 months of the commission of the offence.[235] This contrasts with the normal six months maximum for laying an information in the case of summary proceedings.[236] A person guilty of any of these offences is liable on summary conviction of a fine of up to £20,000 and/or imprisonment of up to three months. Upon conviction on indictment, an unlimited fine may be imposed and imprisonment of up to two years. The offences under section 90 are subject to a fine on summary conviction of up to £2,500.

Information to form the basis of a prosecution may be obtained either by direct sampling, normally by the EA, or on the basis of information provided by the discharger and recorded by him in accordance with the provisions attached to his consent. The EA may request this information either under section 202 of the WRA or under section 108 of the Environment Act 1995, and failure to provide it is an offence under each section. Any other person may commence proceedings for offences under Part III of the WRA.[237] Wide powers of entry are granted under section 169 of the WRA and under the general enforcement powers of section 108 of the 1995 Act. The powers include the right to carry out experimental borings and to install and to keep monitoring and other apparatus on any premises.

Anti-pollution works by the EA

11–070 Independently of any criminal proceedings, the EA may take appropriate pre-emptive or remedial works under section 161 with a view to preventing any poisonous, noxious or polluting matter, or any solid waste matter, from

[234] [1999] 2 AC 143. See also *Dilieto v Ealing London Borough Council* [1998] 2 All E.R. 885, which suggests that not every planning matter will be decided the same way as *Wicks*; a challenge may be made to a notice in the course of a prosecution dependent upon that notice, on grounds of uncertainty.
[235] s.101.
[236] s.127 of the Magistrates Court Act 1980.
[237] A notable example of this is *R v Anglian Water Services* [2004] Env. L.R. 10, which prosecution was initiated by a member of the public. Anglian Water was originally fined £200,000, which was reduced to £60,000 on appeal to the Court of Appeal.

entering any controlled waters. Similarly, where such matter appears to be or to have been present in any controlled waters, the EA may undertake remedial work to remove or dispose of the matter, to remedy or mitigate any pollution it has caused and, so far as reasonably practicable, to restore the waters, including any flora and fauna dependent upon the aquatic environment of the waters, to their state immediately before the pollution became present in the waters. Where it carries out this work, it may recover its expenses from the polluter under section 161(3). In practice this power was rarely exercised in respect of significant remedial works, not least because the EA and the NRA as its predecessor simply did not have the funding to enable substantial works to be carried out on such sites without being sufficiently confident of recovering that expenditure from the polluter.

Works notices

These powers were significantly expanded by the Environment Act 1995,[238] which inserted section 161A into the WRA, giving the EA power to serve a "works notice" on appropriate parties. At the same time, the EA's section 161 powers became exercisable only if the EA considers that it is necessary to carry out works forthwith under that section or if there is no suitable recipient of a section 161A notice. Hence the EA's section 161A powers became far more important in practice. These enabled the EA, instead of carrying out the works itself, to serve a notice upon those who caused or knowingly permitted the matter in question to be (a) in a place from which it is likely to enter any controlled waters (b) present in controlled waters. There is no reason to believe that the requirements under (a) will be construed any differently from those in section 85 of the WRA, and *Bartoline v Royal Sun Alliance*[239] confirms this. The procedure governing the content of such works notices, and for appeals to the Secretary of State from such notices, is set out in the Anti-Pollution Works Regulations 1999.[240]

11–071

Section 161A is designed to mesh in with the contaminated land provisions in Part 2A of the EPA as amended, so that measures taken to clean up *offsite* controlled waters will be pursued against the polluter under section 161A (and if necessary via the EA's own powers under section 161) whereas measures necessary to clean up the source of the potential contamination within the contaminated land itself are to be exercised under

---

[238] EA 1995, Sch.22, para.162.
[239] [2007] Env. Liability, His Honour Judge Hegarty QC. This decision also contains an interesting comparison of the powers under these provisions and criteria for tortious liability.
[240] SI 1999/1006.

the Part 2A regime by local authorities or the EA, if the land amounts to a special site.[241]

One other overlap may be important in the future in limiting the occasions upon which such works powers are exercised. This overlap is between the scope of the section 161A powers and the Environmental Liability Directive.[242] As described in the Chapter on the Directive, there will be occasions when there is water pollution warranting a works notice and which also exceeds the ELD threshold for water damage. At the time of writing, there are no transposing Regulations in force, though Defra has produced a Second Consultation draft together with draft Guidance.[243] From the Guidance, it appears to be Defra's intention that in such an overlap the Regulations should apply rather than the EA serving a works notice; it is only when the Regulations do not apply because the operator can invoke one of the "defences" under the Regulations, because, say, he acted in accordance with a permit, that it would be appropriate to serve a works notice.

Civil liability implications

11–072   Apart from these specific provisions, no civil liability arises directly out of any breach of the pollution control provisions of the WRA, though the WRA does not affect any other right, including any claims in common law nuisance, which may be available to those affected by water pollution.[244]

Pollution Control Registers

11–073   The EA is required under section 190 of the WRA to keep a pollution control register containing various information concerning matters contained in Part III of the WRA, including applications for discharge consents, the consents granted, samples taken by the EA, applications for revocation made by the EA, enforcement notices, revocations, convictions, and orders made under sections 161 and 161A of the WRA. The obligation to keep such information must also be read in the light of the obligations upon the EA to provide environmental information on request pursuant to the Environmental Information Regulations, for which see Chapter 6.

---

[241] See Chapter 16 on Contaminated Land.
[242] 2004/35, [2004] OJ L143/56.
[243] Defra, February 2008, website.
[244] s.100 of WRA.

Trade Effluent to Sewer

Under section 106 of the WIA there is a general entitlement for the owner **11–074** or occupier of premises, and the owner of any private sewer, to have the premises or sewer connected with the public sewers owned by the relevant sewerage undertaker for the discharge of foul water and surface water. However, this does not entitle any person to discharge directly or indirectly into any public sewer any liquid from a factory or manufacturing process (other than domestic sewage, surface or storm water) or any liquid which is otherwise prohibited. Similarly, one cannot discharge foul water into surface water sewer, or vice versa, nor may one discharge the contents of drains or sewers into any storm water overflow sewer.

Hence, the structure of the WIA is that there is a general right to discharge trade effluent into sewers subject to the consent of the relevant sewerage undertaker. There is a prohibition on damaging effluent streams. So, unless expressly authorised, no person shall throw, empty or turn or suffer or permit to be thrown or emptied any matter (a) likely to injure the sewer or drain, to interfere with the free flow of its contents or to affect prejudicially the treatment and disposal of its contents, or (b) anything at a temperature higher than 100°F (43°C), if it is dangerous, a cause of a nuisance or injurious or likely to cause injury to health; (c) any petroleum spirit as defined in section 111(5) of the WIA and (d) calcium carbide.

Trade effluent, and trade premises from which trade effluent may be discharged, are defined by section 141 of WIA. Discharge of such effluent without consent is an offence subject to a fine of £5,000 on summary conviction and an unlimited fine on conviction on indictment.[245] The system of regulation of trade effluent administered by the sewerage undertakers amounts to domestic transposition of parts of the Urban Waste Water Treatment Directive, as discussed in paragraphs 11–035 to 11–038 above.

Deemed consents

There is provision for deemed consent under the Public Health (Drainage **11–075** of Trade Premises) Act 1937 for processes that were operating before the coming into force of that Act. These continue in effect under the WIA, though sewerage undertakers may submit the users to an actual consent if appropriate.[246] Any disputes concerning this go to Ofwat, or thereafter to the High Court on a point of law.

---

[245] s.118(5) WIA.
[246] WIA, s.140, Sch.8, para.2(2).

"Special category" effluent

11–076   Ordinarily, a sewerage undertaker will be expected to accept trade effluent, subject to payment of appropriate charges. The charges are computed by reference to the Mogden formula, to cover the costs of treating the trade effluent to a standard allowing discharge from the sewage treatment works which in turn must comply with its discharge consent. However, when trade effluent contains certain highly toxic substances, it is designated "special category effluent", and not only can the sewerage undertaker refuse to receive it, but he may not do so unless the matter has been referred to the EA for its determination, and it has determined not to prohibit the discharge.[247] Special category effluent is any trade effluent which contains, in a concentration greater than background concentrations, any of the substances listed in Schedule 1 to the Trade Effluents (Prescribed Processes and Substances) Regulations as amended,[248] or which derive from the processes listed in Schedule 2, if either asbestos or chloroform is present in a concentration greater than background.

There is a significant exception to this. Trade effluent from a PPC installation (or, now, premises subject to an Environmental Permit involving the IPPC Directive) otherwise falling within the regulations is not to be regarded as special category effluent, since it will have been considered as part of the permitting process itself.[249] As time goes on, the EP process will reduce the numbers of processes which require the application of the special category effluent procedure.

Consent procedure

11–077   Except where it is proposed to enter an agreement in relation to the discharge of trade effluent under section 129 of the WIA, the person wishing to make the discharge must serve upon the sewerage undertaker a "trade effluent notice" stating the nature and composition of the trade effluent to be discharged, the maximum daily quantity, and the highest intended rate of discharge.[250] The undertaker may make enquiries as to the sewers and other drains etc which it is proposed to use for discharging the trade effluent, including production of all relevant plans and other information. Any consent will be subject to conditions as to the nature of the effluent and as to the sewers into which the effluent is to be discharged, and as to elimination or diminution of any specific constituent which may injure or obstruct the sewer, or make treatment or disposal especially difficult or expensive. Conditions will also stipulate the charges payable for the

---

[247] s.120 WIA.
[248] SI 1989/1156 (including mercury, cadmium, various pesticides, PCP, and PCBs), as amended by SI 1990/1629, and SI 1992/1939 (adding trichloroethylene and perchloroethylene).
[249] s.138(1A) WIA.
[250] s.119 WIA.

effluent, and in determining those charges the undertaker shall have regard to the matters stipulated in section 121(4) WIA, including any additional expense incurred or likely to be incurred by the undertaker in connection with the reception or disposal of that trade effluent.

Evidence and enforcement

Meters or other apparatus provided in any trade premises for measuring, recording or determining the volume, rate of discharge, nature or composition of any trade effluent discharged, will be assumed to be accurate unless the contrary is shown. **11–078**

Quite apart from any remedy which may be available in civil proceedings brought by the undertaker, any contravention of a condition attached to a trade effluent consent constitutes an offence by the occupier of the premises concerned, who is liable on summary conviction to a fine of up to £5,000 and an unlimited fine on indictment.[251]

Appeals and charges

There is a right of appeal to Ofwat in the event of a refusal of an application for trade effluent consent, or the failure to grant one within two months of the date of the application, and also in respect of any condition attached to the consent.[252] The two month period in a case of special category effluent runs from the day after the EA receives the application.[253] **11–079**

The approach of Ofwat to appeal is contained in an Information Note of May 1993, as revised in September 2001. Most disputes arise over the practical implications of the consent conditions imposed, the timescale in which such conditions must be met, or the costs which meeting the conditions imposes on the discharger. Before considering any appeal the sewerage company should have fully explained the reasons for any special conditions or costs to the discharger, and for the discharger to have discussed the matter with the undertaker and explained why he feels unable to accept the conditions.

Once an appeal is received, Ofwat will seek representations from both parties. If the dispute is not capable of informal resolution, then Ofwat will (after consultation) decide whether the appeal will be dealt with by written representations, a private hearing, or a private enquiry

Within legal constraints, appeals will normally be decided in the light of Ofwat's understanding of the practical and financial consequences for both sewerage undertaker and discharger. Health and safety requirements will be taken into account, and consideration given to any substances likely to **11–080**

---

[251] s.121(5) WIA.
[252] s.122 WIA.
[253] s.123(1) WIA.

damage sewers, or cause special difficulty (or expense) in treatment. As well as a general duty to protect customer interests, Ofwat has a specific duty, in deciding trade effluent appeals, to have regard to the desirability of a sewerage company recovering costs incurred, including a reasonable return on capital. Therefore, Ofwat must be satisfied that a new or amended condition is justified, and that the conditions imposed by the sewerage company should be related to the discharge conditions imposed on it by the Environment Agency, to meet environmental obligations in respect of sewage treatment works and storm overflows. Ofwat will also consider the long-term cost implications, for the discharger and sewerage company respectively, of treating the effluent at minimum cost to meet environmental obligations. The estimates will have to take account of all of the consequences of the new or revised requirements, especially changes in necessary processes. Evidence will also be required about sensible time-tables for the achievement of these changes.

If the disputed condition is justified on its merits, Ofwat will judge whether the discharger's long-term costs of complying with the standards imposed upon him are less than those reasonably estimated by the sewerage company to treat the discharge to the same environmental standard at their works. If they are, Ofwat will normally dismiss the discharger's appeal. If the discharger's costs are more than those of the sewerage company, then Ofwat will normally uphold the appeal. Costings prepared by a sewerage undertaker may be averaged across a region and may not be based exclusively on costs incurred at any one treatment works. Charges may be reduced if a discharger contributes to the sewerage company's capital costs.

Variation of consents

11–081 The conditions of a trade effluent consent may be varied at any time; however if this is done within two years from when the consent was granted or from the latest of any variations on the initiative of the sewerage undertaker, then the owner or occupier of the trade premises may be entitled to compensation.[254] Any variation made outside the two year limit may not come into effect earlier than two months from when the notice of variation has been served upon the owner or occupier. This notice must include information as to the right of appeal to Ofwat under section 126(1), within the two month period or any later time allowed by Ofwat. If an appeal is brought within those two months, the variation does not taken effect until the appeal is withdrawn or finally disposed of, with the exception of a variation as to charges which may take effect on any date inside or outside of the two months.[255]

[254] ss.124 and 125 WIA.
[255] s.126(3) WIA.

Even though a sewerage undertaker directs that a variation is to take place earlier than two years from the initial consent or last variation, compensation will not be payable if the undertaker considers the variation to be in consequence of a change in circumstances since the beginning of the two years that could not have been reasonably foreseen at the beginning of the period, and that it is required for reasons other than in consequence of other consents for discharges given since the beginning of that period.[256]

Where a consent relates to special category effluent, the EA may additionally review it as to whether the discharges authorised should be prohibited altogether or, if not, whether any conditions as to the discharges should be imposed. Such a review may be undertaken at any time, if carried out to enable the United Kingdom to give effect to any international agreement to which it is a party, or for the protection of public health, or of flora and fauna dependent upon an aquatic environment. Except in these situations, the circumstances in which a review may be carried out are limited to those specified in section 127(2)—these require two years to have elapsed since the time or the last time when notice of a determination by the EA of any reference or review relating to the consent was served.

Trade effluent agreements

Instead of applying for a trade effluent consent, the owner or occupier may enter into an agreement with the sewerage undertaker for the discharge of trade effluent. Under section 129(3) of the WIA, this agreement has the effect of a consent granted under the notice procedure. An agreement may be typically preferred where the sewerage undertaker has had to install additional or special effluent treatment facilities to cater for the specific discharge in question, thus relieving the discharger of the obligation of the need to install suitable effluent treatment plant on his own premises. In such a case there is generally a need for commercial arrangements to cover payment by the discharger for the installation and for a longer period than the two years to which it would be committed under a standard discharge consent. Any proposed agreement relating to special category effluent must be referred to the EA.[257] No binding agreement is to be made unless the EA determines that the discharge be allowed. The EA may review such agreements as if they were consents to discharge special category effluent.[258] The EA also has wide powers under section 132 of the WIA to prohibit such discharges, to vary conditions, and to revoke any applicable consent or agreement. No compensation is payable in consequence. However, compensation is payable under section 134 on grounds similar to

11–082

---

[256] s.125(2) WIA.
[257] s.130 WIA.
[258] s.131 WIA.

those applicable under section 127(2) in respect of special category effluent consents.

Trade effluent registers

11–083 Sewerage undertakers are required to keep available at their offices for inspection by the public copies of every consent and direction given by the undertaker, every trade effluent agreement, and every notice served by the EA. Nevertheless, by section 206 of WIA, no information in respect of any particular business or any individual may be disclosed. This protection as to information does not apply to trade effluent subject to PPC or EP permits, where there are EC provisions as to the availability of such information.

MARINE POLLUTION

11–084 We have seen how the Water Framework Directive applies to estuaries and coastal waters up to one mile from the shore, and the definition of "controlled waters" under domestic legislation[259] extends to territorial waters to a line three miles from the shore. We have also seen particular regimes which bear on coastal waters, such as discharges to sea governed by the Urban Waste Water Directive, and which also involve consideration of the Bathing Waters and Shellfish Waters Directive. In addition, rules concerning marine conservation are considered in Chapter 10.

There are specific and voluminous provisions concerning marine pollution, though there is space here only to touch on the most important of these rules which affect the United Kingdom.

First, one should note that both the United Kingdom and the EU are party to a number of the major international conventions concerning the marine environment. At the general level, these include the Montego Bay Convention on the Law of the Sea or UNCLOS,[260] which aims to codify, clarify and develop the rules of general international law relating to the peaceful cooperation of the international community when exploring, using and exploiting marine areas, and which has been adopted by the European Community. The main specific provisions applicable to the United Kingdom are summarised below.

---

[259] s.104 WRA
[260] December 10, 1982, into force on November 16, 1994, and approved by the European Council Decision 98/392/EC [1998] OJ L179/1. The UK acceded to UNCLOS in 1997.

Dumping etc. at Sea

This is currently governed at an international level by the 1992 Paris **11–085**
(OSPAR) Convention to which the EU was a signatory, and which was
approved by the EU in its Decision of October 7 1997 (98/249/EC).[261]
This bans incineration at sea (Article 2 of Annex II of OSPAR), which
therefore renders D11 to Annex IIA to Waste Framework Directive,
Incineration at Sea, an unlawful operation from that date. Article 3 of
Annex II of OSPAR prohibits "dumping of all wastes or other matter" at
sea, save for the following (i) dredged material, (ii) inert natural material,
(iii) sewage sludge until December 31, 1998, (iv) fish waste, and (v) waste
from vessels and aircraft until December 31, 2004. This in practice very
substantially reduces the lawful application of D7 of the Waste Framework
Directive: "Release into seas/oceans including sea-bed insertion". Sea-bed
insertion within D7 is also included within the scope of OSPAR; see the
definitions at Article 1 of Maritime Area and Dumping, and the provisions
prohibiting placement of matter in the maritime area under Article 5 of
Annex 2 of the Convention.

The rules under the OSPAR Convention bear directly on the legality of
Carbon Capture and Storage in the seabed, and to that end the EU is in the
course of considering a specific proposal for a directive dedicated to that
subject.[262]

Food & Environmental Protection Act 1985

The OSPAR Convention is in practice enforced in the United Kingdom by **11–086**
the Food and Environmental Protection Act 1985 (FEPA). FEPA in fact
implemented OSPAR's predecessors, the Oslo and London Conventions,[263] in banning uncontrolled dumping at sea. It requires licences for
the deposit of substances and articles by anyone in UK territorial waters,
and by UK vessels, wherever they may be.[264] Defra is the body responsible
for granting such licences. There is provision for the licensing of incineration at sea, but in fact no such licences have been granted since the
United Kingdom became party to OSPAR. Similarly, no such licence
would be granted for the discharge of sewage sludge, as this is now forbidden by the OSPAR Convention and the Urban Waste Water Treatment
Directive. More generally, Defra is required to have regard to the need to
protect the marine environment, the living resources which it supports, and

---

[261] [1998] OJ L014/1.
[262] (COM) 2008/018 final.
[263] The Convention for the Prevention of Marine Pollution by Dumping from Ships and
Aircraft, Oslo 1972, Cmnd. 6228 and the Convention on the Prevention of Marine Pollution by the Dumping of Waste and Other Matter, London, 1972, Cmnd. 6486.
[264] s.5. For example, offshore wind farms require a s.5 license.

human health, as well as to prevent interference with legitimate uses of the sea.[265]

Pollution by Ships

11–087   There are two further areas which should be considered, namely (a) international, Community and domestic instruments governing pollution from ships, and criminal liabilities therefor; and (b) compensation applicable to damage caused by spills of oil at sea.

Preventing pollution from ships

11–088   At the international level, there is, in addition to UNCLOS, the 1973 International Convention for the Prevention of Pollution from Ships and the 1978 Protocol thereto (Marpol 73/78). Marpol 73/78 restricts discharges of oil or oily mixtures in special areas within a minimum distance from land, or at more than a specific quantity of oil per nautical mile.[266] There are then exceptions to this in the case of damage to the vessel, which apply where all reasonable precautions have been taken to prevent or minise the discharge and where the owner or master had not acted with intent, or recklessly and with knowledge that damage would probably result.[267] Marpol 73/78 applies similar provisions to "noxious liquid substances or mixtures".[268] Discharges of garbage and sewage are also regulated. Marpol 73/78 also regulates the design, construction and maintenance of oil tankers.

The Community has itself sought to intervene in a similar area, via Directive 2005/35[269] on Ship-Source Pollution and on the Introduction of Penalties for Infringements. This applies to discharges in all marine waters.[270] Members States shall ensure that ship-source discharges of polluting substances are regarded as infringements if committed with intent, recklessly, or by serious negligence.[271] However, the Marpol exceptions (including those summarised above) then apply.[272]

The date for transposition of Directive 2005/35 was March 1, 2007. No separate transposing measure has yet been notified by the United Kingdom to the European Commission. However, much of the substance of the Directive, and Marpol 73/78 itself, is covered by the existing regime of domestic pollution offences under Part VI of the Merchant Shipping Act

---

[265] FEPA, s.8.
[266] Annex I, regs 9 and 10.
[267] Annex I, reg.11.
[268] Annex II, regs 5 and 6.
[269] [2005] OJ L255/11.
[270] This is the upshot of art.3(1).
[271] art.4.
[272] art.5.

1995 when coupled with the Merchant Shipping (Prevention of Oil Pollution) Regulations 1996.[273]

Compensation for marine oil pollution

There are in addition specific conventions concerning compensation for oil damage at sea caused by oil tankers. These lay down a strict liability regime for such damage, with certain limitations on the amount of that liability by reference to the tonnage of the vessel. That regime is also backed by a substantial compensation fund. The main conventions are (a) the International Convention on Civil Liability for Oil Pollution Damage adopted at Brussels, as amended by the Protocol signed in London on November 27, 1992 (known as the Liability Convention);[274] (b) the International Convention of the Establishment of an International Fund for Compensation for Oil Pollution Damage adopted at Brussels on December 18, 1971, as amended by the Protocol signed in the London on November 27, 1992 (known as the Fund Convention);[275] and (c) the Protocol of 2003 to the Fund Convention,[276] creating "an International Oil Pollution Compensation Supplementary Fund" and applicable to incidents after November 1 2003.

11–089

The EU has not acceded to these conventions, but it has come as close as it can to doing so, as can be seen from Council Decision 2004/246/EC[277] authorising Member States to sign, ratify or accede to these conventions, and "to use their best endeavours to ensure that [the conventions] are amended in order to allow the Community to become a Contracting Party to them."

These conventions are transposed into domestic law by sections 152 to 182 of the Merchant Shipping Act 1995, and, in the case of the 2003 Protocol, by the Merchant Shipping (Pollution) Act 2006. Sections 153 and 154 imposes strict liability for any damage caused by tankers and other ships.

The purpose of these oil pollution conventions is to channel liability to the owners of the vessel in question, and then to back the strict liability thereby imposed with a compensation fund. Other instruments, such as the Environmental Liability Directive,[278] contain provisions disapplying the terms of the ELD when these conventions apply. However, as the ECJ has recently ruled in *Commune de Mesquer v Total France SA & Total International Ltd*,[279] the conventions do not necessarily override the provisions of

11–090

---

[273] 996/2154.
[274] [2004] OJ L78/32.
[275] [2004] OJ L78/40.
[276] [2004] OJ L78/24.
[277] [2004] OJ L78/22.
[278] 2004/35, [2004] L143/56.
[279] *C-188/07*, June 24, 2008.

other Community instruments, in that case the polluter-pays principle in the Waste Framework Directive.

The Marine Strategy Directive

11–091 Finally, one should note the Marine Strategy Framework Directive.[280] It establishes a framework, within which, as Article 1 provides, "Member States shall take the necessary measures to achieve or maintain good environmental status by the year 2020 at the latest." It applies to waters not covered by the Water Framework Directive, and coastal waters insofar as particular elements of their environmental status are not otherwise provided for in Community legislation.[281] Environmental status includes consideration of marine ecosystems, taking account of physical, acoustic and chemical conditions, including those resulting from human activities in and outside the area concerned.[282] Good environmental status includes consideration of the sustainability of the use of the marine environment.[283] The primary obligation under the Directive is to develop a marine strategy for its marine waters, including a programme of measures by 2015 in order to achieve good status by 2020.[284]

[280] 2008/56/EC, [2008] OJ L164/19.
[281] art.3(1).
[282] art.3(4).
[283] art.3(5).
[284] art.5.

Chapter 12

WATER ABSTRACTION

Introduction

In the last chapter, we have been treating water as a resource worthy of **12–001** protection, and we shall continue to do so in this chapter, before turning to water as a threat in the next. But preventing water pollution is only one way of regulating that resource, and the focus of this chapter is the provision of sufficient supplies of water of satisfactory quality for drinking, industrial, agricultural and other purposes, and the way in which the law enforces the sharing of water between these various interests. It is an area of law with a long history in water-scarce societies or societies with highly complex agricultural systems. Elaborate codes concerning water use can be found in a number of areas in the Fertile Crescent such as the Levant, Ancient Mesopotamia and Ancient Egypt.[1]

We have seen a general review of the Water Framework Directive in Chapter 11, including reference to its "quantitative" status. This status is defined in the WFD; groundwater levels must be such that the available groundwater resource is not exceeded by the long-term annual average rate of abstraction.[2] Resources are to be protected by ensuring a balance between abstraction and recharge.[3] Groundwater levels must be regularly monitored.[4] We shall return to these themes in the course of reviewing the present law of water abstraction.

Water Abstraction

From this modern framework legislation, we need to go briefly to domestic **12–002** common law principles for the background against which the law of water abstraction must be understood. Traditionally, a landowner could extract

---

[1] See, e.g. Caponera, *Principles of Water Law and Administration* 2nd edition, (Taylor and Francis, 2007), Chapter 2, citing the following, at p.17, "Let him not entertain at a [dinner] ... he who diverts watercourses and he who delights in obstructing them" from Chapter III, section 151 of the Code of Manu, the ancient Hindu codes of law.
[2] art.2(28) calling up table 2.1.2 of Annex V.
[3] art.4(1)(b)(ii).
[4] art.8, with details in 2.2 of Annex V.

groundwater to his heart's content, irrespective of the interests of his downstream neighbour.[5] By contrast, a riparian owner could use water from his neighbouring watercourse only to the extent that his use did not prejudice the quantity (or indeed quality) of the watercourse downstream.[6] These riparian principles were carefully worked out against the background of water power being critical to mediaeval trade and later industrialisation.[7]

Whilst the common law position may have a residual role to play between landowners,[8] the law concerning abstraction is now almost entirely the province of statute, which not only prohibits most unlicensed abstractions but also, as we shall see, sets out basic rules governing civil liability between rival landowners, and also between landowners and the EA.

Licensing

12–003   The right to abstract water in England and Wales first came under comprehensive statutory control through the Water Resources Act 1963, which introduced the requirement that abstraction be licensed. Those who had been abstracting in the five years immediately preceding the coming into force of the 1963 Act were entitled to a licence of right, whereas all new abstractors had to apply for a licence. The licensing provisions of the 1963 Act were re-enacted by the Water Act 1989, and are now contained in the Water Resources Act 1991 as significantly amended by the Water Act 2003. The licensor is the EA.

There is a general prohibition on unlicensed abstraction of water from any source of supply.[9] Source of supply includes watercourses and groundwater.[10] It is similarly prohibited, in relation to water contained in any underground strata, (i) to begin, or to cause or permit any other person to begin, to construct any well or borehole for abstraction purposes; (ii) to extend such borehole or well; or (iii) to install or modify any machine or apparatus for abstracting additional quantities of water.[11] Breach of any of these prohibitions in the absence of a licence, or breach of the terms of any licence, is an offence subject to a fine of up to £20,000 on summary conviction or an unlimited fine upon conviction on indictment.[12] The EA

---

[5] *Chasemore v Richards* (1859) 7 HL Cas. 349. Long use by the claimant did not help him, as the right to draw on groundwater was held not to be capable of giving rise to an easement.

[6] *Mason v Hill* (1833) 5 B & A 1. For a scholarly account of the history of the common law, see Getzler, *A History of Water Rights at Common Law*, Oxford, 2004.

[7] By 1700, there were between 10,000 and 20,000 watermills in Britain, and up to five watermills could be found for every mile of usable stream near industrial towns such as Sheffield: Getzler, p.22.

[8] It still forms an important part of the law underlying civil liability for flooding, for which see Chapter 13.

[9] s.24(1) WRA 1991.

[10] s.221(1) WRA 1991.

[11] s.24(2) WRA 1991.

[12] s.24(5) WRA 1991.

can also serve an enforcement notice in respect of such breaches, with criminal enforcement if its terms are not observed.[13] An appeal lies against an enforcement notice to the Secretary of State. Any such breach does not confer, of itself, any right of action in civil proceedings.[14]

Similar restrictions, and enforcement mechanisms, apply to unlicensed impounding works, namely those involved in constructing a dam, weir or other works designed to impound inland waters, or to divert flows to that end.[15] However, in respect of impounding works, there is an additional power upon the EA, namely that of serving a works notice upon anyone who appears to the EA to have responsibility for unlicensed impounding works. This notice should specify such works as may be required for the protection of the environment or for the performance of the EA's functions in connection with its management of water resources.[16]

There are however the following important exceptions to these prohibitions on unlicensed abstractions: **12–004**

(a) Abstractions under licences of right, whether deriving from the Water Resources Act 1963 (giving existing users a licence) or via Schedule 26 to the Water Act 1989.[17]

(b) Abstractions in the course of or resulting from land drainage operations.[18]

(c) At present, abstractions in the course of mining, quarrying, engineering, building or other operations, or to prevent damage to works resulting from any such operations;[19] however, if a well or borehole is to be constructed or extended for this purpose, notice of the intention to do so must be given to the EA, and the EA may serve a conservation notice in response requiring reasonable measures to be taken to conserve water. There is a right of appeal against the terms of such a notice. However, this exception will disappear upon the coming into force of amendments to section 29 of the WRA via section 7 of the Water Act 2003. Thereafter all such operations will need a licence, except where an emergency arises and an abstraction is necessary to prevent immediate danger to such operations or an

---

[13] s.25A and 25C WRA as amended. The required content of such notices is set out in reg.27 of the Water Resources (Abstraction & Impounding) Regulations 2006, SI 2006/64, but is similar in form to the details required under the waste management licence regime (now part of the EP regime).

[14] s.70 WRA 1991. But see para.12–005 below.

[15] s.25 WRA 1991, as amended.

[16] s.4 of WA 2003 for works notices, s.3(12) for the definition of "relevant person". Required content is again set out in the 2006 Regulations, this time at reg.27.

[17] s.48, Sch.7.

[18] s.29(1) WRA 1991; "land drainage" includes coast protection, warping and irrigation, other than spray irrigation (s.29(5)). Spray irrigation is itself defined by the Spray Irrigation (Definition) Order 1992 (SI 1992/1096) as excluding spraying where nutrients or pesticides are combined with water.

[19] s.29(2) WRA 1991, pending repeal by s.7 WA 2003, which is not yet in force.

immediate risk to health. Even in that instance, the abstractor must give notice of the abstraction within five days of commencement.[20]

(d) The abstraction of small quantities, namely less than 20 cubic metres a day.[21] This figure may be varied locally by statutory instrument.[22] This threshold was increased by the WA 2003 and has had a very significant effect on the number of licence holders; some 23,000 licence holders ceased to be licence-holders as a result, leaving 21,000 remaining licence-holders.[23]

(e) Miscellaneous exemptions in section 26 of the WRA 1991 (navigation, harbour and conservancy authorities) and section 32, namely abstractions for use aboard a vessel, for fire-fighting, and for exploratory activities concerning potential future abstractions.

(f) there is a possibility of further exemptions being made by statutory instrument under s.33A of the WRA as amended, though no such regulations have yet been made.

The statutory regime of civil liability

12–005 A licence, apart from conferring immunity from prosecution, also confers a "right" to abstract water upon its holder, and hence a defence to any civil action brought against the licence-holder, in each case as long as the abstraction is within the scope of the licence.[24] Those who do not have a licence but "are in a position to carry out an abstraction" of small quantities of water within s.27 also have a similar "protected right" to the extent of the maximum they may abstract under section 27 or under any statutory instrument under section 27A.[25] However, protected rights under this exemption (*i.e.* those who have rights other than via a licence) may in future become subject to a compulsory duty to register them with the Secretary of State, failing which these rights will have no effect.[26] The existence of rights under the legislation also obliges the EA not to derogate from such rights when considering licence applications by others,[27] and if the EA does so derogate, the affected licence-holder has a claim for damages against the EA for breach of statutory duty.[28]

The final component of the civil abstraction regime is the statutory claim

---

[20] s.29(2A) and (2B) WRA 1991, as amended.
[21] s.27 as amended by WA 2003. The previous more detailed s.27 also exempted regular domestic and agricultural operations (except spray irrigation) abstracting less than 20 cubic metres.
[22] s.27A as amended by WA 2003.
[23] See the EA's *Developing Our Water Resources Strategy for England & Wales*, July 2007, EA website.
[24] ss.48(1)–(2) WRA 1991.
[25] s.39A WRA 1991, as amended by WA 2003.
[26] s.39B WRA 1991; s.39B(4) for the loss of protection on non-registration.
[27] s.39(1) WRA 1991.
[28] s.60 WRA 1991: unless the derogation is caused by exceptional shortage of rain or accident or other unforeseen act or event outside the control of the EA: s.60(5).

(for breach of statutory duty) conferred by section 48A of the WRA on those who suffer loss and damage after April 1, 2005,[29] as a result of abstractions from inland waters or underground strata. This ousts all other claims (i.e. in nuisance) save for those based upon common law negligence or breach of contract.[30] No claim under section 48A arises in respect of a drought order (there is a separate regime for that considered below). A section 48A claim against another abstractor is also precluded by (a) the abstractor having his own licence and (b) the claimant having a claim for damages against the EA for derogation.

Summarising, therefore, the claimant therefore has a section 48A claim against the abstractor where the abstractor has no licence, and has a section 60 claim against the EA where the abstractor does have a licence (and hence a defence) where that licence derogates from the claimant's rights.

Applications for licences

Applications for abstraction licences may be for a full licence (namely one covering 28 days or more of abstractions), a transfer licence, covering the transfer of water from one point to another, or a temporary licence, for less than 28 days.[31] To apply for an abstraction licence, the applicant must, by the time of the proposed licence comes into effect, have a right of access to land contiguous to the inland waters, or access to the underground strata, as the case may be. In each case, that right of access must be for at least one year after the coming into effect of the proposed licence.[32]

12–006

The procedures governing licence applications are contained in the Water Resources (Abstracting and Impounding) Regulations 2006.[33] Applications are made to the EA and must, in most cases, be published by the Agency.[34] A period of at least 28 days is allowed for objections. The Secretary of State may "call in" licence applications, either on an individual basis or by reference to any class which may be specified, with the procedure (including hearings or a local inquiry) being set out in section 42 WRA. Appeals in other cases lie to the Secretary of State[35] and thereafter by way of appeal under section 69 WRA.[36]

Applications for abstracting and impounding licences may also require an Environmental Impact Assessment, if they involve a water management

---

[29] The commencement date of the relevant amendments to the WRA made by s.24(1) of the WA 2003.

[30] s.48A(5)–(6) WRA 1991.

[31] s.21A WRA, 1991, as amended.

[32] s.35 WRA, as amended.

[33] SI 2006/641.

[34] s.37 WRA as amended; power to dispense is under s.37A as amended, and the specific exemptions are in reg.7 of the 2006 Regulations.

[35] The procedure is set out in ss.43–45, and in regs 12–13 of the 2006 Regulations.

[36] For an unsuccessful challenge under this section, see *Ettrick Trout Co. v Secretary Of State & NRA* [1995] Env. L.R. 269.

project for agriculture with abstractions of more than 20 cubic metres a day which would be likely to have significant effects on the environment by virtue inter alia of its nature, size or location.[37]

Legal criteria on determination of licence applications

12–007   On determining such applications, the EA is under an express, albeit unrevealing, duty under s.38 of the WRA to "have regard to all the relevant circumstances", including any representations and any reasonable requirements of the applicant. The EA is also under additional duties laid down by the WRA and elsewhere. First of all, there is the general duty under section 6(2) of the Environment Act 1995[38] to conserve, redistribute or otherwise augment water resources, and to secure the proper and efficient use of water resources. Low flows may impact on fish stocks, and a duty to have regard to fisheries is imposed on the EA by section 6(6) of the 1995 Act. We have already seen one specific obligation owed by the EA when determining such applications for licences, namely its duty not to derogate from existing licences under section 39 of the WRA. Other mandatory requirements upon the EA include the duty to take river flows into account under section 40 of the WRA. It is also duty-bound by section 39 of the Environment Act 1995 to have regard to costs and benefits. The EA has a separate statutory duty, either of its own accord or under direction of the Secretary of State,[39] to address low river flows caused by existing abstractions, and shall have regard to its general environmental functions[40] in determining the minimum acceptable flows in such rivers. If it has so determined the flows in the course of this procedure before the licence application, then it has to have regard to the need to secure those flows on the licence application. If it has not so determined the flows, then it must decide what the flows would have been had it carried out the exercise in advance of the licence application.

The Agency is also under a duty[41] as a competent authority to secure compliance with the provisions of the Water Framework Directive, which, as noted above, includes ensuring a balance between abstraction and recharge of groundwater, with the aim of achieving good groundwater status by December 2015.[42]

---

[37] Water Resources (Environmental Impact Assessment) (England and Wales) Regulations 2003 (as amended by the 2006 regs (SI 2006/3124)), especially reg.3. See Ch.9 for consideration of these words which are taken from the EIA Directive. The procedure is modelled on the planning EIA process, albeit with the EA as decision-maker.

[38] As amended by s.72 of the Water Act 2003.

[39] s.21–22 WRA.

[40] Under its conservation duties under s.6 EA 1995 (as amended by s.72 of the Water Act 2003), its general environmental duties under s.7 EA 1995, and its duties in respect of SSSIs under s.8 EA 1995: see s.21(4) WRA.

[41] reg.3 of the Water Environment (Water Framework Directive) (England and Wales) Regulations 2003, as amended.

[42] art.4(b)(ii) of the Water Framework Directive.

The EA also owes overarching duties as a competent authority under the Habitats Directive, including the duty to avoid causing deterioration of natural habitats in Special Areas of Conservation;[43] an obvious example of this would be considering the effect of the grant of any licence upon nearby wetlands, and, as we shall see, the EA owes a similar duty to review extant licences which are causing deterioration in habitats. Where the application proposals may affect a Site of Special Scientific Interest, a SAC or a Special Protection Area, the EA will consult Natural England or the Countryside Commission for Wales. Decisions concerning water abstraction licences (as with other water abstraction plans and projects) are now expressly subject, via regulations 48 to 51 of the Habitats Regulations,[44] to the obligations contained in Article 6(3) and (4) of the Habitats Directive in respect of European sites. These provisions cover assessment of the implications of decisions for European sites, considerations of overriding public interest and consideration of existing decisions and consents.

Policy criteria on abstraction licensing

Since 1999, and in response to the Government's own policy statement, **12–008** *Taking Water Responsibly,*[45] the EA has been developing Catchment Abstraction Management Strategies (CAMS) for individual catchments. It set out its water licensing policies, including CAMS and their relationship to abstraction licensing in *Managing Water Abstraction.*[46] England and Wales has been divided up into 129 catchments, based primarily on surface water catchments, with the rivers Severn, Trent and Thames as corridor catchments. Individual assessments based on each catchment are then prepared, identifying whether water is available, not available, over-licensed or over-abstracted within that catchment, and hence the likelihood or otherwise of a new licence being granted within that catchment. The underlying principle in the CAMS process is to make information on the availability of water resources, and hence the EA's policies towards licensing, more publicly available. Important policy elements are that all licences should be time-limited, with a normal renewal period of 12 years. Recent policy statements from DEFRA in *Future Water*[47] are to the same effect, though the timescale proposed for a full transfer to such licences is

---

[43] art.6(2) of Directive 92/43. Note *C-6/04 Commission v UK*, a decision of the ECJ to the effect that the previous regime was non-compliant. The detail concerning this important Directive obligation is to be found in Ch.10.

[44] As amended by reg.84B inserted by the Conservation (Natural Habitats, &c.) Amendment Regulations 2007, SI 2007/1843, made in response to *C-6/04 Commission v UK*, a decision of the ECJ to the effect that the previous regulations did not sufficiently implement the requirements of the Directive.

[45] DEFRA, 1999.

[46] Revised version July 2002 available on EA website.

[47] February 2008, p.36.

an unambitious 2021 to 2027. These policy moves contrast with the pre-WA 2003 position, in which most licences were not time-limited.

Managing Water Abstraction contains a helpful decision tree on determining licence applications, summarising the legal and policy obligations considered above. The first question is Resource Assessment: is there enough water? The second is Proposal Assessment: are the applicant's requirements reasonable? Is the proposal acceptable? The third is Impact Assessment: on resources, on water-dependent conservation sites, existing abstractors and other interests. Finally, there is Mitigation Assessment, via potential mitigation of any impacts, conditions or any environmental enhancement.

The information generated by the CAMS process is facilitating the formulation of river basin management plans as required by the Water Framework Directive.

Form and content of licences

12–009   Licences must contain provisions as to the quantities of water to be abstracted, the means of abstraction, the purpose for which the water is to be abstracted, and the start date and expiry date of the licence.[48] The EA may attach such conditions as it thinks fit to any licences. To protect river flows, an abstraction licence may include conditions prescribing flows for neighbouring rivers at or below which there may be no abstraction. This may include a "hands off" condition which means that an appropriate structure of weirs or sluices has been put in place that automatically ensures that water is not abstracted when the flow or level falls below the prescribed level. Such a condition is preferred because it is more reliable than a system involving human intervention to prevent abstraction. Finally, the licence will bring an obligation to pay charges under the EA's scheme applicable to such applications, which is usually based upon the annual amount of water capable of being abstracted under the licence.

Modification and revocation of licences

12–010   Licences may be revoked or varied on the application of the holder. An application to vary a licence will be treated in essentially the same way as a new application for a licence, save that where the variation is by way of reduction of the amount of water to be abstracted, the provisions for publicity and consideration of representations do not apply.[49]

The EA may revoke or vary licences on its own initiative or pursuant to a direction given by the Secretary of State.[50] All such proposals must be

[48] s.46 WRA as amended.
[49] s.51(4).
[50] s.52(1)–(3).

published, and notice of them must be served on the licence holder. Any person may make representations with respect to the proposals and the holder may serve notice of objection. If the holder raises no objection, the EA may determine the matter itself in the light of such representations as it may have received, but if he does object, the matter must be referred to the Secretary of State.[51] The Secretary of State may, if he thinks fit, set up a local inquiry or otherwise arrange for a hearing of the matter. His decision is declared by section 54(6) of the WRA to be final, but on ordinary public law principles it will be challengeable by way of judicial review for error of law.

Where fishing rights have been affected by a licensed abstraction of water, and one year or more has elapsed since grant of the licence, the owner of those rights may be entitled to apply under section 55 for the relevant abstraction licence to be revoked or varied. "Fishing rights" for this purpose are rights which constitute or are included in an interest in land, or which are exercisable by virtue of an exclusive licence granted for valuable consideration, including rights held in common with one or more persons.[52] An application under section 55 may however only be made where no minimum acceptable flow has been determined[53] in respect of the waters in question. Applications under section 55 are determined by the Secretary of State on local inquiry or hearing, if he so directs. The licence may not be revoked or varied if he is satisfied that any loss or damage caused to the applicant by abstraction was wholly or mainly attributable to exceptional shortage of rain or to an accident or other unforeseen act or event not caused by and outside the control of the EA.[54] Even when he does determine that a licence should be varied, the variation is to be limited to that which is requisite have regard to the loss and damage sustained by the applicant that is directly attributable to the abstraction of water. Again the Secretary of State's decision on the application is said to be final.

Compensation on revocation or variation of a licence

The basic rule is that revocation or variation of a licence under sections 54 **12–011** and 56 of the WRA entitles the licence holder to compensation in respect of any directly attributable loss or damage, including wasted expenditure carrying out work which has been rendered abortive.[55] No compensation will be payable if there has in fact been no abstraction under the licence during the four years immediately preceding service of the notice of the proposals for revocation or variation. This provision enables the EA to extinguish old unused licences without redress. Disputes about compen-

---

[51] s.53(3)–(4).
[52] s.55(5).
[53] s.55(1).
[54] s.56(4). These matters also excuse the EA from liability to the abstractor under s.60.
[55] s.61(1).

sation are referred to the Lands Tribunal in accordance with the Land Compensation Act 1961.[56] If the owner of fishing rights establishes that he has suffered loss and damage, but the abstraction licence is nevertheless not revoked or varied, he is entitled to compensation unless within six months the EA has served a notice to treat for their acquisition, or has offered to acquire them on compulsory purchase terms.[57]

Potentially a more important withdrawal of the right to compensation arises under section 27 of the WA 2003. If a licence is revoked or varied after July 15, 2012 on direction from the Secretary of State under section 54 or 56 of the WRA, on the ground that the revocation or variation is necessary in order to prevent serious damage to any inland waters, groundwater, or underground strata, or flora or fauna dependent upon such waters or strata, no compensation is payable. This means that the Secretary of State, doubtless on prompting from the EA, can terminate valuable rights to water abstraction without compensation—but only where there is real environmental benefit in doing so. In practice, and prior to the coming into force of this removal of the right to compensation, the EA has been reviewing all licences in areas designated under the Habitats and Birds Directives in order to assess the impact of abstraction licences on those habitats.[58]

Succession to licences and water rights trading

12–012 The complicated provisions for succession in the case of abstraction licences in sections 49 and 50 of the WRA have been replaced via the WA 2003 by a simpler regime applicable to both abstraction and impounding licences. Section 59A of the WRA as amended by the 2003 Act enables transfers to be effected via notice to the EA (and such information as the EA may reasonably require), and section 59B vests licences on the death of the holder in his personal representatives, and on bankruptcy, in the trustee in bankruptcy. Licences can also be apportioned between two successors.[59]

This regime as modified by the WA 2003 is designed to facilitate water rights trading. This is of particular benefit in areas where all the available water is currently licensed but where some licensees do not require their full licensed amount[60] and are therefore in a position to transfer part of their entitlement to others.

---

[56] ss.61(5)–(6).
[57] s.62(3).
[58] *Managing Water Abstraction*, Annex 1.
[59] s.59C-D of WRA as amended by WA 2003.
[60] See *Accessing Water Resources: A Guide to Trading Water Rights*, March 2007, and *Managing Water Abstraction*, pp.25ff, both on the EA website.

Registers of abstraction and impounding licences

Section 189 of the WRA contains a requirement for the EA to maintain **12–013** public registers of abstraction and impounding licences. Regulation 34 of the Water Resources (Abstraction & Impounding) Regulations 2006[61] sets out the particulars required of this register, which include details of applications, decisions made upon them, and details of revocations, variations, and transfers of such licences. There is also the possibility of a separate register of protected rights (mostly those under the volumetric threshold and hence not requiring a licence) if the Secretary of State makes regulations under that provision;[62] this is certainly contemplated by the Agency as a response to the significant increase in protected non-licenced abstractions caused by the recent raising of the abstraction thresholds.

Water resources management

We have examined the EA's general duties in respect of water resources in **12–014** the context of abstraction licensing. However, the WRA, WIA and WA 2003 make specific provisions in respect of one set of major water abstractors, namely water undertakers.[63] First, section 20 of the WRA requires the EA to enter into and maintain arrangements with water undertakers to secure the proper management or operation of the waters available to be used by those undertakers, as well as reservoirs and other works operated by the water undertakers. Such arrangements, once entered into, then become enforceable as against the water undertakers under the general enforcement mechanism under section 18 of the WIA administered by Ofwat. Section 20A[64] of the WRA provides for similar schemes in respect of other major abstractors,[65] and in such cases Ofwat is to determine any questions arising between EA and abstractor. There is also power to refer disputes about proposed arrangements between EA and undertaker or other abstractor to the Secretary of State.[66]

The WA 2003, via new sections 37A-D of the WIA, also imposed new duties upon water undertakers to produce water resources management plans. These plans must demonstrate how the undertaker will manage and develop water resources in order to perform its own water supply duties under section 37 WIA (including the duty to provide an "efficient and economical system"), and are prepared after consultation with the EA and pursuant to directions from the Secretary of State as to the form of the

---

[61] SI 2006/241.
[62] s.39B of WRA.
[63] 45.5 per cent of all non-tidal abstractions in 2004/2005 are by water undertakers, according to the EA.
[64] Inserted by WA 2003.
[65] Other major abstractors are the electricity supply industry (30.6 per cent of the whole as at 2004/5).
[66] s.20B WRA, as inserted by WA 2003.

plan. Regulations[67] address the publication and consultation obligations upon the undertakers, and an initial Direction[68] sets the first plan period at 25 years starting on April 1, 2010.

One should note the EA's own national strategy documents. The current, 2001, version is *Water Resources for the Future—a Strategy for England & Wales*, but consultation for a new strategy is ongoing, with a new strategy expected by the end of 2008. It poses a number of challenging questions as to how the current pressure on water resources, particularly in the south-east of England, can be managed for the future, including the controversial issue of pipe leakage addressed below. It will also have to mesh in with ongoing preparations for the river basin management plans required by the Water Framework Directive.

Water Conservation

Specific measures

12–015   There are various statutory provisions aimed at conserving water other than through the mechanism of an abstraction licence. It is an offence to cause or allow groundwater to go to waste or to abstract more than one's reasonable requirements.[69] There are limited exceptions concerning water used to test the water supply or for various cleaning and maintenance purposes, and for disposing of water that would otherwise interfere or threaten to interfere with underground works. In addition to fining the defendant, the court on conviction may order the well or borehole to be sealed up, with further sanctions including costs recovery in the event of non-compliance.[70]

Similar criminal provisions are aimed at owners or occupiers of land who intentionally or negligently cause water fittings to be, or to remain to be, out of order or in need of repair.[71] There are also regulations seeking to enforce the provision of appropriate water fittings in works to water apparatus carried out after July 1, 1999.[72]

Water losses caused by these types of defect will in practice be dwarfed by the amount lost through leaking water supply pipes. It is estimated that nearly one-quarter of all water supplies (3,418 million litres a day in 2006–07) is lost via leakage from undertakers' or consumers' pipes. However, there is no easy answer to these losses, with large quantities of nineteenth century pipework requiring replacement at vast cost, ultimately to be borne by the consumer. The current method of enforcement against undertakers

---

[67] Water Resources Management Plan Regulations 2007, SI 2007/727.
[68] Water Resources Management Plan Direction 2007.
[69] s.71(1) WIA 1991.
[70] s.71(6) WIA 1991.
[71] s.73(1) WIA 1991.
[72] Water Fittings Regulations 1999 made under s.74 WIA.

is by Ofwat relying upon a breach of the undertaker's section 37 WIA duty of economic and efficient supply, and proceeding via section 18 WIA for an enforcement order in respect of that duty. Threats of such enforcement action in respect of failed leakage targets led recently to Thames Water undertaking[73] under section 19 WIA to carry out further replacement works estimated at an extra cost of £150m. On the principles laid down in *Marcic v Thames Water*[74] such enforcement action may be the only remedy available for such a breach of section 37. The EA's consultation draft strategy seeks a more onerous set of targets, doubtless with an attendant increase in water prices. The extent to which this "pay now, save later" strategy will be politically acceptable remains to be seen.

General obligations

There are general[75] and specific obligations on the EA and water under-   **12–016** takers to conserve water. However, the WA 2003 imposes more general duties on all public authorities to encourage water conservation. The Secretary of State or Minister of the Welsh Assembly Government is under a duty to take steps to encourage the conservation of water.[76] All public authorities (including Government departments, local authorities and statutory undertakers) are additionally under a duty to take account the desirability of conserving water supplied or to be supplied to premises.[77]

Droughts

We are here concerned with the various regulatory steps which may be   **12–017** sought in response to droughts which will have the effect of abrogating, to a greater or lesser degree, other licensing and discharge regimes during the drought.

The first and least onerous step is for the water undertaker to impose a temporary hosepipe ban under section 76 of the WIA, if it is of the opinion that there is a serious deficiency of water available for distribution by that undertaker. The undertaker must publicise the proposed ban before it comes into force. Contravention of the ban amounts to a criminal offence. This step will be familiar to those living in the South-East of the United Kingdom.

A more significant step is a drought order, which comes in ordinary and

---

[73] July 3, 2006, letter of undertaking at Ofwat website.
[74] [2004] AC 42.
[75] s.6(2) EA 1995 for the EA, s.3(2)(a) WIA 1991 as amended for water and sewerage undertakers.
[76] s.81 WA 2003.
[77] s.83 WA 2003.

emergency forms.[78] It is made by the Secretary of State on application from the EA or a water undertaker. An ordinary drought order requires the Secretary of State to be satisfied that there is either a serious deficiency of water supplies (as per a hosepipe ban) or such a deficiency in the flow or level of water in any inland waters as to pose a serious threat to any of the flora or fauna which are dependent upon those waters. An emergency order requires the Secretary of State to be satisfied that by reason of an exceptional shortage of rain, a serious deficiency exists or is threatened, and that the deficiency is such as to be likely to impair the economic or social well-being of persons in the area of the deficiency.

12–018   An ordinary drought order can be in many different forms,[79] and they may depend on the status of the applicant. If the applicant is the EA, it may enable the EA or a person authorised by the EA to take water from a certain source or to discharge water (typically under a Part III WRA discharge consent) to a specified place. It may prohibit an abstraction if the source in question seriously affects the supplies available to EA, water undertaker or other abstractor. Equally, it may relax a restriction or obligation otherwise preventing someone else (who may be abstractor, discharger or water supplier or treater) from abstracting, discharging or treating, as the case may be. If the applicant is a water undertaker, a similar wide set of powers are laid out, including modifying the terms of any trade effluent discharge granted by them. An ordinary drought order may last six months, but is extendable by the Secretary of State to a maximum of 12 months.

An emergency drought order may be in similar (but not identical) forms to an ordinary drought order. It may additionally empower a water undertaker to supply water via stand-pipes or water. It may only last three months, extendable to five months.

Any proposed drought order (which must be published and served on interested parties[80]) may lead to objections, and if it does the Secretary of State will either direct a hearing or a local inquiry. The procedures are expedited.[81]

12–019   Drought orders come at a cost, namely a liability to pay compensation for loss and damage sustained as a result of anything done or omitted in pursuance of an ordinary drought order. Compensation arising out of the entry upon land or occupation of the land is payable in respect of ordinary and emergency drought orders. Any such claim is referred to the Lands

---

[78] ss.73–80 WRA 1991.

[79] s.74 WRA 1991.

[80] This will depend on the precise nature of the order sought: see Sch.8 to the WRA for the details.

[81] Drought Order (Inquiries Procedures) Rules 1984.

Tribunal in default of agreement.[82] All claims must be made within six months of the end of any ordinary drought order.

The WA 2003 also introduced an abbreviated procedure[83] by which the EA may issue a drought permit to a water undertaker without involving the Secretary of State or the Welsh Assembly. Under such a permit, the EA may enable the undertaker either to take water from a specified source or modify any restrictions to which the undertaker is otherwise subject in respect of that source. A permit cannot be obtained via this procedure to protect wildlife. Procedure and compensation is essentially as for a drought order. Contraventions against drought orders or the terms of a drought permit is a criminal offence under section 80 WRA.

Finally, a licence to abstract water for spray irrigation may be varied in a period of exceptional shortage of rain or other emergency so as to reduce the amount of water that may be abstracted.[84] However this will only apply in the case of underground strata if this is likely to affect the flow, level or volume of any inland waters. If there are two or more such licences for abstraction from the same point or from points which are "not far distant", proportionate reductions are to be required of each licence holder.[85] No compensation is payable in this event.

Community action on water scarcity and droughts

In July 2007, the European Commission issued a Communication on **12–020** water scarcity and droughts, with a view to examine the need for action at EU level. The Communication appears even-handed as to whether action is or is not required, and little can be gathered as to the likely scope of any action, if required. In any event, the lead time before the implementation of any action which may be recommended in due course is considerable; no official steps were taken by the Commission between July 2007 and July 2008.

---

[82] Sch.9 to the WRA. Interest is payable on compensation: s.80 Planning & Compensation Act 1991.
[83] s.79A WRA 1991.
[84] s.57.
[85] s.57(4).

Chapter 13

LAND DRAINAGE, FLOOD DEFENCE AND COAST PROTECTION

Introduction

It is difficult to exaggerate the economic importance of flood risk, both in **13–001** the United Kingdom and more widely. One estimate has some £250 billion of assets in the United Kingdom at risk of flooding and coastal erosion. It is also said that 10 per cent of existing homes, housing five million people, are located in areas at substantial risk of flood. And to take one example of recent costs incurred, the floods of summer 2007 led the United Kingdom to claim £2.7 billion from the European Union Solidarity Fund in respect of losses suffered as a result. And the risk of flooding will only increase as a result of climate change over the next century.

The law on the topic goes back to the Middle Ages. Statutes governing land drainage or flood defence (phrases which are for present purposes, synonymous) can be traced back to the Commissioners of Sewers Act of 1427, which despatched Commissioners on a one-off basis to survey sea defences and flood alleviation in rivers and repair the same. The first semi-permanent act was passed in 1531 during the reign of Henry VIII, and empowered the Crown to create Commissioners of Sewers.[1] That act and numerous subsequent statutes[2] continued in force until comprehensive new legislation was brought into effect by the Land Drainage Act 1930.

The broad structure of the 1930 Act has been repeated in succeeding Acts (Land Drainage Acts of 1961, 1976 and 1991[3]). In 1991, the legislative provisions were divided between local drainage and its administra-

---

[1] The word "sewers" bore a much broader meaning then than in current usage. One definition (that of Mr Sergeant Callis) held it to be the diminutive of river, being a freshwater trench encompassed in on both sides with a bank: see *Coulson & Forbes, on Waters & Land Drainage* 6th edition, 1952 (Sweet & Maxwell, p.788.

[2] Including a further one passed under Henry VIII, and others under Edward VI (rendering the original Act perpetual), Mary Stuart, Elizabeth I and James I. There were also more recently Acts of 1833 and 1861. Much of the terminology in the current legislation is taken from past Acts, especially that of 1861 and they are therefore of more than historical interest.

[3] There was a bewildering array of different bodies primarily responsible for flood defence matters during this period; catchment boards became river boards in 1948, which became river authorities in 1965, which became water authorities in 1974, which became the NRA in 1989.

tion (via the Land Drainage Act 1991) and national responsibilities vested in the National Rivers Authority (Water Resources Act 1991). The Environment Agency (EA) succeeded to the NRA's responsibilities in 1996, at which time certain minor amendments were made to its duties and powers. Legislative change is afoot, with Defra promising a consolidated Floods and Water Bill in 2009.[4]

Institutional Overview

13–002   The position remains institutionally complicated, and an overview may assist before turning to the detail of the fragmented responsibilities of the public bodies in question. Much of local drainage is in the hands of Internal Drainage Boards (IDBs), which are locally elected and financed, but which do not cover the whole of England and Wales. National flood defence is in the hands of the EA, and of the regional flood defence committees through which the EA acts. The broad demarcation between their respective areas of responsibility is that the EA is responsible for "main rivers", which include estuaries, whereas the IDBs concern themselves with other watercourses—"ordinary" watercourses in LDA terminology. Local authorities are responsible for local drainage where there is no IDB, and have powers to maintain smaller watercourses. In due course the EA will be given responsibility for taking a strategic overview of all flooding within England.[5]

Currently, there is a separate statutory regime covering coastal protection under the Coast Protection Act 1949, under the control of coastal protection authorities who are in practice the relevant councils of the districts adjoining the sea. The demarcation between the responsibility of the EA and of coastal protection authorities is between flood defence and protection against coastal erosion respectively. However in June 2007[6] the Government announced changes intended to enable the EA to oversee management of coastal erosion as well as coastal flooding, and ministerial powers to make grants under both the LDA and the Coastal Protection Act 1949 have now also been delegated to the EA.

The lines of demarcation for primary flood defence responsibilities are cut across by various supervisory responsibilities. The EA has a general supervisory role in respect of the IDBs. The EA is itself in turn under the supervision of the Secretary of State for Defra or the relevant Minister of the Welsh Assembly Government. The EA[7] and IDBs[8] may receive grants from Defra for flood defences works, though in practice approval for grant

---

[4] Speech by Phil Woolas MP, June 17, 2008, Defra website.
[5] ibid.
[6] News Release, June 22, 2007, Defra website.
[7] s.47 EA 1995, enabling the provision of grant-in-aid for all purposes.
[8] s.59 LDA 1991.

aid to many projects has been delegated by Defra to the EA. Defra has an open-ended discretion as to the circumstances in which these grants may be conferred on the EA, and may be satisfied of the environmental acceptability of a given project by relying on the fact that planning permission had been granted, and without carrying out its own investigations.[9]

Finally, we should briefly note the responsibilities of two sets of under-   **13–003**
takers in respect of surface water which can be a major component in flooding, namely highway authorities as being responsible for highway drains, and sewerage undertakers who are duty-bound effectually to drain their areas by means of public sewers.[10] Many sewers ("combined" sewers) carry substantial flows of surface run-off rainwater in addition to foul flows, and therefore may be overloaded at times of heavy rainfall. Both undertakers are often sued in respect of damage caused by flooding, as described below. Again changes are afoot here, with proposals that local authorities take over responsibility for surface water flooding in their areas, with the benefit of EA guidance.[11]

Terminology

"Drainage" as used in the LDA, "includes defence against water   **13–004**
(including sea water) irrigation, other than spray irrigation, and warping".[12]

"Flood defence" is defined in the WRA as meaning "the drainage of land and the provision of flood warning systems";[13] "drainage" in the same section of the WRA is given the same definition as in the LDA. In practice, the EA uses the term "flood risk management" today, as this rightly emphasises the rather wider set of responses by the EA and others to flooding risks, other than pure "defence".

"Main rivers" are those rivers, or stretches of rivers, shown as such on a "main river map".[14] Such maps are open to public inspection, and may be varied by adding or removing rivers or stretches of rivers, from them[15]—a process sometimes referred to as "maining" and "de-maining". As noted above, the significance of whether a watercourse is a main river or not is that drainage functions relating to main rivers may only be performed by

---

[9] *Isaac v Defra & EA* [2002] EWHC 1983 (Admin) concerning the provision of grants under s.147 WRA 1991, now repealed.
[10] s.94 WIA 1991.
[11] Speech by Phil Woolas, June 17, 2008.
[12] s.72 LDA 1991. Warping is a term used for the deliberate flooding of low lying land by adjacent rivers and streams, with a view to receiving alluvial sediments that improve its quality.
[13] s.113(1) WRA.
[14] s.113(1) WRA, derived from the LDA 1930. A similar distinction is found in the *Lex Visigothorum's flumina maiora* and *flumina minora*.
[15] s.194 WRA. Defra initiate such amendments.

the EA, and not by IDBs, except by agreement. Main rivers also includes watercourses subject to works schemes under section 137(4) WRA, as mentioned below.

"Watercourse" is defined in the Acts relating to drainage[16] to include "all rivers, streams, ditches, drains, cuts, culverts, dykes, sluices, sewers and passages through which water flows, except a public sewer."

Drainage Authorities

13–005   The EA has a general supervisory duty over all national and local flood defence matters.[17] It is expressly required to arrange for all its functions relating to flood defence under both the WRA and LDA to be carried out by regional flood committees appointed for their respective areas. Those areas largely correspond to those of the water authorities before privatisation and of the sewerage undertakers upon privatisation.[18] The EA may nevertheless give directions to those committees where their operations seem likely to affect the EA's management of water for purposes other than flood defence.[19] The EA (in conjunction with Defra) also provides a methodology to assess proposals for major flood defence works. The regional flood defence committees, though acting on behalf of the EA, are primarily under the control of the "relevant Minister", who is the Secretary of State for Defra or the relevant Welsh Assembly Minister.[20] A majority of each committee must be appointees of the relevant councils for the area, two members are appointed by the EA and the remainder by the relevant Minister. Regional flood defence committees are also likely to take over responsibilities in respect of coastal erosion if Defra's proposals of June 2007 are implemented.

Drainage of land is administered at local level through IDBs, each of which is the drainage board for a corresponding "internal drainage district". The latter are such areas within those of the regional flood defence committees "as will derive benefit, or avoid danger, as a result of drainage operations."[21] The principles applied, in determining whether an area falls within this description were established in a decision given in relation to a scheme for setting up the River Medway Catchment Board in 1933, known as "the Medway letter". These entail ascertaining the highest known flood level in an area under consideration; outside tidal areas, agricultural land up to eight feet above that area may be brought within a district, while in

---

[16] s.113(1) WRA when read with s.221(1) WRA, and 72(1) LDA 1991 which is in effectively identical terms. The difference lies in the exception.
[17] s.6(4) EA 1995.
[18] s.106(1) WRA.
[19] s.106(3) WRA.
[20] s.221(1) WRA as amended.
[21] s.1(1) LDA.

urban areas only land below the flood level will be so treated, save for areas that would otherwise be cut off by floods. In tidal areas, a district will normally include agricultural land lying five feet or less above spring tides, urban land being brought in where it is at or below the level of spring tides.

IDBs exercise a general supervision over all drainage matters within their district.[22] The EA may take over the powers and responsibilities of an IDB,[23] it may itself be a drainage board for an internal drainage district,[24] and any functions that it may have as such may be transferred from the EA to an IDB.[25]

The EA is entitled to give any directions it considers reasonable to guide **13–006** IDBs in relation to their powers and duties, so as to ensure efficient working and maintenance of existing drainage works and the construction of any necessary ones.[26] The powers of the IDBs are circumscribed,[27] in that they may not, except with the consent of the EA, construct or alter any drainage works if this would affect any other drainage board, nor may they, otherwise than by maintenance, construct or alter any structure, appliance, or channel for the discharge of water from their districts into a main river, except on terms agreed with the EA. Such consent from the EA must not be unreasonably withheld, though it can be granted subject to reasonable conditions. In the event of any breach of these obligations, the EA may take action to restore the situation, and to recover any costs incurred from the person occupying the property. If the IDB fails to exercise its drainage powers adequately or at all, the EA[28] (or a local authority with the agreement of the EA[29]) may exercise all or any of them itself, provided the IDB has had at least 30 days notice of this intention.

In the exercise of their functions under the LDA, the IDBs and local authorities must comply with the same environmental and recreational duties, and with those relating to Sites of Special Scientific Interest, as are imposed upon the EA,[30] and likewise must observe relevant codes of practice, as discussed in Chapter 2 on regulators.

---

[22] s.1(2) LDA.
[23] s.108 WRA.
[24] s.4 LDA.
[25] s.5 LDA.
[26] s.7(1), (2) LDA.
[27] By s.7(2).
[28] s.9(1) LDA.
[29] s.10(1).
[30] s.61A–D LDA 1991, as inserted by the LDA 1994. The EA is under these duties under s.6–8 EA 1995.

Flood Defence Works Powers

13–007 The main objectives of the EA in relation to flood defence are to provide effective defence against flooding both from rivers and from the sea, and adequate arrangements for flood forecasting and warning.

The principal flood defence works powers

13–008 Both EA and IDBs have similar underlying works powers in respect of flood defences. They may maintain existing works, improve existing works, and construct new works for flood defence purposes, in respect of watercourses falling within their respective competencies.[31] The EA also has the power to maintain, improve or construct drainage works for the purpose of defence against sea water or tidal water, in the sea or in any estuary.

It is important to note that these functions are expressly described as *powers*, and so the EA or IDB does not have a statutory duty to construct or maintain flood defences, to a particular standard, or indeed at all. This lack of a duty is critical to the availability of any challenge to the EA's flood defence policies, whether by way of public law challenge or private law action for damages as discussed further below. The only exception to this permissive regime are the duties which arises under European conservation legislation, namely the Birds Directive and the Habitats Directive (considered in Chapter 10) under which flood defence and coastal protection agencies are bound by Community law to protect conservation sites from flooding or erosion. As a result habitats implications have become in practice a very significant factor when flood defence schemes are under consideration.

Another curiosity may be evident from the above summary of the powers held by EA and IDBs. There is no express works power to remove, in whole or in part, or abandon existing flood defence works. Despite this, that the EA or IDB must have such powers cannot seriously be in doubt. This must follow from the fact that the EA has permissive powers only (i.e. cannot be obliged to maintain existing defences *ad infinitum*). Alternatively, such powers may arise from the incidental general functions vested in the EA by section 37 of the Environment Act 1995 to do anything to facilitate, or which is conducive or incidental to its carrying out of it functions, including carrying out engineering and building works as it considers appropriate.

13–009 This issue is important in that the EA has been faced with the upkeep of increasingly indefensible and unsustainable flood defences threatened by rises in river and sea levels, and the rational approach has been to abandon or modify the existing defences and/or to build new defences inland of the

---

[31] s.165(1) WRA for the EA and s.14(2) for the LDA.

old.[32] Often, instead of straightforward abandonment, it is preferable to move back from the existing defences in a controlled way, and this process is termed Managed Realignment or Managed Retreat and is now well embedded in Government policy.[33] This process may involve affected landowners taking over maintenance of the defences themselves, though in order to do so they need apply to the EA for consent under applicable bye-laws[34] to enable this lawfully to be done.

Part of the same issue involves whether flood defences can be lawfully abandoned by the EA or other responsible bodies. For it has been argued in the past[35] that there is a prerogative duty upon the Crown to maintain sea defences, based upon dicta in cases such as *Attorney-General v Tomline*. However, it is clear from later cases that the present law does not impose a prerogative duty on the Crown in respect of flood defences. That is because, as we have seen, Parliament on repeated occasions has legislated in respect of flood defence, and it is a general principle of constitutional law that, where Parliament has legislated, any residual prerogative powers or duties will have been deemed to been swept up into such legislation.[36] The fact that legislation is couched in terms of permissive powers is inconsistent with there being a duty in respect of the same subject-matter.

The New Zealand coastal erosion case of *Falkner v Gisborne DC* is of particular relevance to the policy of managed realignment. Local beach residents sued their council for failing to protect their properties, and also sought to challenge a ruling by the Minister of Conservation that their own privately-sponsored proposed sea defences required consent. Neither plea was successful. Any challenge would be limited to circumstances where the Crown had entirely neglected to act, rather than where it had genuinely decided as a matter of public policy not to erect of maintain a particular sea wall.[37] A similar approach would be likely to be adopted by the English courts were such a challenge be mounted to managed realignment.

---

[32] See, e.g. Defra's *Maintenance of Uneconomic Sea Defences: A Way Forward*, of April 2004.

[33] See, e.g. Defra's guidance *Shoreline Management Plans—A Guide for Coastal Defence. Authorities* (2005) and its consultation paper *Managed Realignment—Land Purchase, Compensation & Payment for Alternative Beneficial Use* (2001).

[34] Either made by the EA under s.210 and Sch.25(5) WRA 1991, or more commonly under existing bye-laws inherited from the EA's statutory predecessors, including water authorities.

[35] *Coulson & Forbes*, p.44, adopted by counsel in the New Zealand case of *Falkner v Gisborne DC* [1995] 3 NZLR 622. See also Lord Coke in *Isle of Ely* at p.141, citing *Tomline* [1879] 12 Ch 214 (Fry J.) and [1880] 14 Ch 58 (CA), and *Attorney-General v De Keyser's Royal Hotel* [1920] A.C. 508 and *Symes & Jaywick v Essex Rivers Catchment Board* [1937] 1 KB 548 on the prerogative.

[36] See *De Keyser's Hotel* and *Symes*, above.

[37] At p.628.

Compensation under the main works powers

13–010   The WRA and LDA[38] make provision for compensation where "injury" is sustained by any person by reason of the exercise by the relevant authority of its flood defence or drainage powers. These apparently straightforward provisions are not as simple as they sound. First, compensation is only payable for what arises out of the exercise of the authority's powers, and hence this provision cannot be used to obtain compensation for those injured by the authority deciding not to exercise its powers to protect a given individual. Secondly, compensation is only payable where the act for which compensation is sought would have been actionable in the absence of the statutory authority.[39] Hence, if at common law, the authority would have been entitled to do what it did without incurring liability, then it cannot be liable under the statute. Perhaps the best example of this is the authority's ability (in common with any riparian owners) to protect its own land against flooding even though such works may cause flooding downstream;[40] this, as will be explained further below, is not actionable at common law, and therefore does not give rise to a claim to compensation. On the other hand, works carried out by the EA or an IDB on the river bed itself which cause damage would give rise to a claim for compensation.

Defra has given guidance on the circumstances in which compensation may be payable in cases where productive use of land has been lost as a result of Managed Realignment. These include where the land seaward of the new defence line is to be used in effect as part of the new defence (because, for example the intervening land reduces wave action) or the land improves discharge capacity or reduced flood levels, or provides compensatory habitat for a scheme carried out elsewhere.[41]

Ancillary works powers

13–011   Section 23 of the LDA makes it unlawful to obstruct a watercourse or construct a culvert likely to affect flows without consent, and in default, any such obstruction shall constitute a nuisance, and may be the subject of an abatement notice.[42] Consent for such works, including construction of a culvert, is to be obtained from either the IDB or, in any other case including an applicant local authority, the EA.[43] The EA also has powers to

---

[38] s.177 and Sch.21 of the WRA for the EA, and s.14(5) LDA for IDBs. The wording dates back to the LDA 1861.

[39] *Marriage v East Norfolk Rivers Catchment Board* [1950] 1 KB 284 on the LDA 1930, based upon a long line of nineteenth century statutory authority cases including *New River Co v Johnson* which preceded the LDA 1861.

[40] See *R v Commissioners of Sewers for Pagham* [1828] 108 ER 1075, as applied in *Arscott v Coal Authority* [2004] EWCA Civ 892.

[41] *Managed Realignment—Land Purchase, Compensation & Payment for Alternative Beneficial Use* (2001).

[42] s.24 LDA 1991.

[43] s.23(8) LDA 1991.

make by-laws concerning works carried out near a main river. Typically, these prohibit works carried within eight metres of a main river without consent of the EA.[44] These enable the EA to limit the circumstances in which one landowner, in pursuit of his own flood protection interests, may increase flood risks to others. This regime tempers the common law position (touched on above, and considered below) under which the landowner has a broad autonomy as to what he may do in pursuit of his own interests. The effective decision-maker therefore becomes the EA (subject of course to judicial review) rather than the landowner.

All relevant drainage bodies have separate powers to secure the maintenance of flows in watercourses and, where these are obstructed, may to that end serve an abatement notice on riparian owners responsible for the length of watercourse in question or the person causing the obstruction a notice requiring its removal.[45] There is an appeal to the magistrates court against such a notice.[46]

Culverting works may additionally be carried out as part of the IDBs' or local authorities' general drainage powers under section 14 of the LDA. Often the precise ownership of culverts is obscure, and responsibility in law may lie with local councils,[47] if, as they often do, they assume responsibility for clearing culverts and the trash screens which are designed to minimise the risk of blockage.

In respect of watercourses, riparian owners, as owners of the bank or bed   **13–012**
of any watercourse abutting their land, have their own powers and duties to maintain the watercourse over the length under their ownership, and may, as noted above, be subject to works orders and similar served by the local drainage body so as to prevent the obstruction of the watercourse. Finally there is a separate regime applicable to ditches under which the Agricultural Land Tribunal may order remedial works against the owner or occupier of the relevant land.[48]

As with the main works powers, these various provisions vest permissive powers in the relevant authorities.

---

[44] e.g. Thames Region Land Drainage Byelaws 1981, bye-law 4(b). Most regions have similar pre-privatisation provisions which are still in force, albeit now enforced by the EA. In November 2007, magistrates fined a Mr Payrani £2,000, and ordered him to pay the EA's costs of £1,500, under this bye-law, for unconsented flood protection works, which he had refused to remove.

[45] s.25 LDA 1991.

[46] s.27 LDA 1991.

[47] See, e.g., the conclusion in *AF Plc v Northumberland CC & Tyndale DC*, 1997 A No. 09128 (Bell J., April 13, 2000, unreported) that the county council was the occupier of culverts and screens in Hexham, for the purpose of any liability in nuisance.

[48] ss.28–29 LDA.

Powers of entry and compensation

13–013 Both WRA and LDA vest powers of entry for enforcement, works and other purposes in the EA[49] and IDBs respectively. Compensation is also payable for damage caused by such entry or works. There is also the power compulsorily to acquire land[50] or to obtain a compulsory works order to enable the carrying out of engineering or building operations or discharging waters.[51]

Coast protection

13–014 Coast protection is subject to separate legislation from that concerning flood defence, though inevitably there is potential overlap between the regimes. The statutory controls are currently contained in the Coast Protection Act 1949, which applies throughout Great Britain (i.e. excluding Northern Ireland). These controls are exercised by "coast protection authorities" which are the councils of each "maritime district", that is, a district any part of which adjoins the sea, though as we have seen the EA will be overseeing the management of coastal erosion by these authorities.

To avoid conflict with the flood defence provisions of the WRA and the LDA, the Coast Protection Act defines "sea" as excluding all the waters specified in the Fourth Schedule to the Act, and references to the seashore exclude the bed and shore of those waters. The Fourth Schedule sets out an extensive list of tidal waters, defining in each case the point below which the relevant coast protection authority has responsibility. Coast protection authorities have general powers under the Act to carry out coast protection work (both inside and outside their area) "as may appear to them to be necessary or expedient" in order to protect any land in their area against erosion or encroachment by the sea.[52] To this end, they may maintain and repair existing coastal defences; if they propose any further coast protection work, they must publicise such intentions.[53] Notice of the proposed works must be served on neighbouring authorities, and they and any other person have the right to object. A hearing or a local inquiry must be held to hear objections on the grounds that the proposed work will be detrimental to the protection of any land specified in the notice, or will interfere with the exercise by the objector of any statutory functions laid on him (otherwise by the Coast Protection Act 1949 itself). The Minister must make a determination, following expiry of the time for receipt of objections, and

---

[49] s.169–173 and Sch.20 WRA, and s.64 LDA 1991.
[50] s.154 WRA 1991.
[51] s.168 WRA 1991.
[52] s.4(1) CPA. The definition of coast protection work is to be found in s.49(1).
[53] Coastal Protection (Notices) (England) Regulations 2002, SI 2002/1278 and Coastal Protection (Notices) (Wales) Regulations 2003 W.197.

any subsequent hearing or inquiry.[54] This procedure need not be followed in an emergency, but in such a case, the coastal protection authority must give notice to the EA and any relevant internal drainage board (in so far as these bodies are not represented on the Coast Protection Authority) of the nature of the work before it commences, or as soon as possible thereafter.

Where a person is subject to obligations to carry out coast protection work independently of the coast protection authority, by reason of tenure, custom, prescription or otherwise, the authority may require him by notice to carry out such work as it considers desirable.[55] If he fails to do what is required within the period stipulated the authority may carry out the work itself and recover its reasonable expenses from him. Essentially the same provisions apply in relation to sea defence commissioners who have powers or duties to carry out any coast protection work that is considered by the coast protection authority to be necessary or desirable, and they have failed to exercise or perform them. In such a case, the Minister must give the commissioners an opportunity to make representations, but subject to that he may make an order authorising the coast protection authority to carry out the work and to recover its reasonable expenses from them.

If compulsory powers are needed for coast protection work, or it is **13–015** considered by the coast protection authority that persons with interests in land that would be benefited by carrying out coast protection work should pay charges under the Act, then the authority may prepare a "works scheme".[56] Such a scheme must indicate the nature of the work to be carried out by the authority on its own land or land that it proposes to acquire for the purpose, and also any work to be carried out on any other land and specify the estimated cost of all the work to be undertaken. It may indicate "contributory land" in respect of which charges should be payable on the grounds that it will be benefited by the work to be carried out.[57] A works scheme may only take effect when it has been confirmed by the Minister.

As with other coastal works, publicity must be given to works schemes. Copies of the scheme must be served on all affected parties.[58] A period of at least 28 days must be allowed for objections to be made to the scheme, and if any are made on any of five stipulated grounds[59] (including that the scheme is unnecessary, would cause hardship to the objector, or that any charges would be unduly onerous), there must be a hearing or a local inquiry. The Minister may either confirm the scheme or quash it; he may also modify it, but if he does so in a way that introduces additional contributory land or further persons upon whom a coast protection charge may

---

[54] s.5 CPA.
[55] s.15 CPA.
[56] s.6 CPA.
[57] s.7 CPA.
[58] s.8 CPA.
[59] s.8(4) CPA.

be levied, then the procedure must be repeated to allow the owners of that land or those further persons to lodge objections.

A scheme that has been confirmed by the Minister provides full powers to the coast protection authority to carry out the works concerned.[60] Nevertheless, if any owner of land that is neither vested in the authority nor proposed to be acquired by it, notifies the authority that he proposes to do the work himself, then the authority may not do it. However, if the owner then fails to do it, the authority may set a time limit on him to complete it, failing which it may do it itself.[61]

13–016   Coast protection charges may be imposed followed implementation of a works scheme, and in any other case by serving on the person to be charged a notice specifying its amount.[62]

Coast protection works constructed, altered or improved under a works scheme will be subject to specific obligations regarding their maintenance and repair in accordance with that scheme. In relation to other works, coast protection authorities have powers under section 12 of the 1949 Act to maintain and repair them and to recover their reasonable costs from the owner or occupier of the land on which the work is situated. Except in an emergency, prior notice of the proposal to carry out the works must be served on the owner, and on the occupier if different, specifying both the work to be done and a period after which the authority will carry out the work if it has not already been completed.[63]

If at the end of that period the work has still not been done, the authority may take all necessary steps for to do it itself and recover its reasonable costs from the owner or occupier concerned. Where the owner and occupier are different persons the original notice must have specified from which of them the authority proposed to recover its costs. Within 21 days of service of the notice, either of them may refer the matter by way of complaint to the magistrates on a variety of grounds, including that the other should pay the whole or some part of the costs, or that the coast protection authority itself should do so. The complaint may also be based on the grounds that the work is not maintenance or repair at all, or that in all the circumstances the work should be done under a scheme. If the court holds that a scheme is the appropriate procedure for the works, then essentially the same procedure as set out above applies, save that the only grounds of objection that may be made are that any provision as to the charges is inequitable or unduly onerous.[64]

13–017   It is an offence to carry out any coast protection work, other than maintenance or repair, without the written consent of the relevant coast protection authority, or to carry out such work in contravention of any

[60] s.9(1) CPA.
[61] s.9(3) CPA.
[62] s.10(1) CPA. Details of the recovery of such charges are set out in the rest of s.10.
[63] s.12(1) CPA.
[64] s.13(6) CPA.

conditions to which any consent may have been granted.[65] Where any such offence has been committed, the coast protection authority may require the person concerned to remove the works or to alter them in such matter as it may specify, and stipulate a period of not less than 30 days for this. If the requirements of the notice are not complied with in due time the authority may do the work itself and recover its expenses from the person concerned.

Excavation or other removal of materials from the sea shore may result in erosion, and hence powers are provided under section 18 to enable coast protection authorities to counter this. Authorities may make an order (in accordance with the provisions of Schedule 2 to the Act) applying that section to any portions of the sea shore within their area, including any portions of the sea shore within the three mile limit. The effect of an order is to make it unlawful to excavate or remove any materials (other than minerals more than 50 feet below the surface) on, under or forming part of any portion of the sea shore concerned, save to the extent that any exceptions to the prohibition are contained in the order. The statute is silent as to the criteria upon which such an order can be made, but case law has established that the authority need only have reasonable apprehension that the extraction of the materials might cause erosion or encroachment, and it is not necessary for there to be conclusive proof of the same.[66] For the purposes of such an order, "materials" includes minerals and turf, but not seaweed.[67]

Where any portion of a sea shore is subject to such an order, a coast protection authority may grant licences to do anything that would otherwise contravene it, imposing such conditions as it thinks fit. There are no provisions for public involvement in this process save only that a drainage authority concerned with any relevant part must be consulted before any licence is granted. It is made an express duty of coast protection authorities to enforce the provisions of section 18;[68] consequently, any failure to take steps against a person offending against the prohibition may be made the subject of an action in the courts against the authority requiring it to perform its statutory duty.

Compensation for coast protection works

Where any interest in land has been depreciated, or where a person's **13–018** enjoyment of land has been disturbed, causing him damage, as a result of carrying out coast protection work by a coast protection authority under

---

[65] s.16(1) CPA. This provision does not however apply to certain statutory bodies as defined in s.17.

[66] *British Dredging (Services) Ltd v Secretary of State for Wales and Monmouthshire* [1975] 1 WLR 687. See also *R v Secretary of State for the Environment et al ex parte Bryant*, QBD, unreported July 30, 1996, noted [1997] *Water Law* 93.

[67] s.49(1) CPA.

[68] s.18(8) CPA.

the Act, the authority is liable to compensate him for that depreciation or damage under section 19(1). Compensation is expressly stated to be subject to the requirement that the act or omission would be actionable at common law, and hence what it is implicit in the flood defence regime is explicit in the coastal protection statute. In addition, where a person has applied for consent to carry out protection work and the consent has been refused, or where conditions imposed on any such consent have caused him loss, he may seek compensation for any reduction in the value of his interest. Any such claim must be made within 12 months of the completion of the relevant work or the refusal of consent or the imposition of conditions, as the case may be.[69] Disputes in respect of such claims must be determined by arbitration.

There is however one significant difference in the wording of the compensation provisions for coastal protection and flood defence works. Compensation in respect of coastal protection works is payable in respect of damage caused "in consequence of the *carrying out* of coast protection work", whereas compensation in respect of flood defence is payable for injury caused "by reason of the *exercise*" of those powers. The Lands Tribunal in *Earle v East Riding of Yorkshire Council*[70] was concerned with the consequences of a scheme of breakwaters constructed by a coast protection authority which the claimants alleged had caused an acceleration of erosion on their land. It construed the words of section 19(1) as applying only to the effects of the construction work, and not to the erosive consequences of the scheme once in operation. Whether this outcome was intended by the draftsman of the 1949 Act must be seriously in doubt. The Lands Tribunal took its lead from one of the leading nineteenth century railway cases, *Hammersmith & City Ry v Brand*[71] which was concerned with very similar language, and which drew this distinction. It must however be arguable that since the coming into force of the Human Rights Act and the interpretative obligations under section 3 of that Act, the compensation provisions would be read in the same way as the flood defence provisions. Other aspects of the *Earle* decision are considered below.

Flood warnings and civil contingencies

13–019   The EA has specific functions in respect of the giving of flood warnings. It must take such steps as appear to be reasonable and practicable to provide flood warnings, and must keep a record at its area offices a record of such arrangements.[72] Since January 2006, it has operated an automatic flood

[69] s.19(2) CPA.
[70] (1999) LCA/143/95, unreported.
[71] (1869–70) LR 4 HL 171.
[72] Ministerial Direction to the NRA, March 1996.

warning system known as Flood Warning Direct, and is in the course of extending its coverage to as many households and businesses as possible.

But this flood warning system is now underpinned by a far wider-ranging duty on the EA. Under section 2 of the Civil Contingencies Act 2004 it shall maintain arrangements to warn the public, and to provide information and advice to the public, if an emergency is likely to occur or has occurred.[73] Floods or threatened flooding fall within the definition of emergency within section 1 of the Act. Section 2 also requires the EA also to assess the risk of flooding, and maintain plans to respond to it if it occurs.

Civil claims in respect of flooding or erosion

There exist a number of potential claims at common law in respect of   **13–020** flooding or erosion. These will include claims by private landowners against other private landowners, and in such cases the statutes considered above will play little part in resolving the dispute. However claims against public bodies must always be assessed against the statute or other legal relationship under which the body has been acting or omitting to act. It will therefore be necessary briefly to consider the common law position, before turning to some of the more typical situations in which a landowner might be seeking redress against a public body whom he seeks to blame for flooding or erosion.

Common law absent the statute

Riparian and coastal owners

Slightly different rules apply as between riparian owners on the one hand   **13–021** and those affected by groundwater or surface water on the other. Any riparian owner, namely the owner of land next to a watercourse, is entitled to receive flows down the watercourse in their natural state in terms of quantity and quality. With that right also comes the duty on that owner to accept such flow. The flow he is entitled and obliged to accept is the natural flow alone, and not any artificial flows introduced by an upper riparian owner. He cannot obstruct natural flows in the watercourse so as to cause water to back up and affect his upper neighbour. Equally, he cannot complain about the erosive or flooding consequences of natural flows. However, he may guard himself against such consequences by carrying out works on his own land so as to prevent flooding, even if he knows that such works might cause his opposite or downstream neighbour to

---

[73] s.2(1)(g). Specific powers—applicable to the acquisition and provision of information between emergency bodies (responders, in the jargon of the Act)—are to be found in the Civil Contingencies Act 2004 (Contingency Planning) Regulations 2005, SI 2005/2042.

flood. On a similar principle, a coastal owner (subject to any statutory limitations)[74] may carry out coastal defence works, even if he knows that such works may lead to greater impact of the sea upon his neighbours. The principle in both riparian and coastal contexts is known as the "common enemy" rule, and it is explained with characteristic clarity in the judgement of Laws L.J. in *Arscott v Coal Authority*[75] a river flooding case. This confirms that the rule still subsists, and reflects a degree of autonomy and self-help in the law which is still consistent with the rights between neighbours.

As *Arscott* also illustrates, the common enemy rule only goes so far. First, the riparian owner's activities must not be unreasonable, or in the words of Baron Bramwell in *Nield v London & NW Rly*[76] the owner must be acting within the scope of its "reasonable selfishness" in so doing. Secondly, if the riparian owner modifies the bed of the river (called the *alveus* in the old cases) or an established flood channel, then he will be liable for any consequences, because such activities fall outside the scope of those permitted by reason of his status as riparian owner. Thirdly, such works may well be subject to statutory or byelaw regulation by the EA, though the fact that such works may be unlawful under such a regime is *by itself* unlikely, on ordinary tortious principles, to confer a remedy on any private landowner affected by the breach: unlawful action identified under public or criminal law principles does not without more confer any private law claim.

A similar principle to the "common enemy" rule underlies a further traditional rule which, unlike *Arscott*, has most probably been affected by more recent developments in the law of nuisance. A riparian owner has always had the right to remove silt or vegetation from the watercourse in question. But traditionally he has not been under any duty to do so.[77] Similarly, the nineteenth century landowner was able to allow his own sea defences to fall into disrepair even though that disrepair caused his neighbour to flood, without recourse.[78] The traditional dichotomy was—if the damage arises as a result of nature, then there was no liability; if it arose as a result of man, then strict liability followed.

13-022   This traditional rule as between riparian owners has been modified by the well-known line of cases starting with *Sedleigh-Denfield*,[79] continuing

---

[74] As explained above, he will need the consent of the relevant authority before constructing such defences.

[75] [2004] EWCA Civ 892, following *R v Commisioners of Sewers for the levels of Pagham* (1828) 8 B&C 355 and *Gerrard v Crowe* [1921] 1 AC 395.

[76] [1874] LR 10 Exch 4.

[77] *Hudson v York Corporation* (1873) 28 LT 836.

[78] *Hudson v Tabor* (1877) 2 QBD 290.

[79] [1940] AC 880.

with *Goldman v Hargrave*,[80] *Leakey v National Trust*,[81] *Bybrook Barn Centre v Kent CC*,[82] and *Holbeck Hall*[83] and culminating in *Green v Somerleyton*.[84] This has established a measured duty of care owed in such circumstances by the riparian owner, even though the hazard arises out of the forces of nature.[85] The owner, whether private (*Sedleigh-Denfield* and *Green*) or public (the highway authority in *Bybrook*), must take reasonable steps to keep his culvert or watercourse in good repair; he must take reasonable steps to mitigate any hazard arising on his land, whether by fire (*Goldman*), or by instability affecting his lower (*Leakey*) or upper (*Holbeck*) neighbour. The duty is measured because it must reflect (broadly) the financial positions of the parties and the costs to each of them of remedying the defect in question. Any duty may also be discharged in appropriate cases by the defendant providing information (if the defect is latent—*Holbeck*) or allowing the claimant to carry out remedial works on the defendant's land.

Though the concept goes back to *Goldman*, the courts have been cautious about the first issue (the financial position of the parties), not wishing to get drawn into a protected means enquiry or indeed to pay too much attention to their means.[86] The second question, the cost of repairs in terms of reasonability, is critically important. We see this illustrated in the land drainage case of *Green* where it was held that the costs of clearing the blocked watercourse were disproportionate to the cost of the damage likely to be caused to the lower land were the watercourse to remain blocked.

Because of the nature and scope of the duty, there can be no hard and fast rules; we are in the territory of seeking to achieve "a fair sharing of expense" (*Leakey*), "a just result" which is *Caparo*-style "fair, just and reasonable" (*Holbeck*), and involving "reasonableness between neighbours" (*Delaware*[87]). The general willingness or otherwise of the parties to negotiate and seek to solve underlying problems is also taken into account, as the Court of Appeal confirmed in *Green*. Foreseeability of the harm in

---

[80] [1967] AC 645: duty to abate fire accidentally caused.
[81] [1980] 1 QB 485: a claim by a lower owner in respect of landslip naturally coming from an upper owner.
[82] [2000] Env. L.R. 543: flooding claim in respect of an inadequately sized culvert.
[83] *Holbeck Hall v Scarborough BC* [2000] QB 836, a claim by a higher owner against a lower owner for loss of support.
[84] [2004] 1 P&CR 33: flooding claim in respect of drainage channel which the upper owner said had been inadequately maintained. The principle of law was accepted by the Court of Appeal, but the claimant lost on application of the reasonability principle.
[85] The other element of the dichotomy, strict liability for man-made hazards, has also been modified over the years by the principle that any damage, to be actionable, must be a foreseeable consequence of the conduct complained of.
[86] The problems of this are well illustrated in a different but related context, as between upper freeholder and lower flat owner in *Abbahall v Smee* [2003] 1 WLR 1472. The judge at first instance held that the defendant on state benefits was held to be liable to contribute only 25 per cent of the cost of the roof repairs benefiting both her upper and the claimant's lower properties. This was reversed by the Court of Appeal who imposed a 50 per cent–50 per cent outcome.
[87] [2002] 1 AC 321.

675

question will also temper the extent of a defendant's liability to contribute where damage has taken place by the time of the enquiry by the court: this can be seen in *Holbeck*, where it was held that there was no duty on the lower owner to spend large sums of money on geological investigations to ascertain whether the danger was substantially greater than appeared upon reasonable investigation to be the case.

13–023 The above rules apply both to natural watercourses and to artificial watercourses in the absence of specific agreement as to rights and responsibilities between those whose land borders such watercourses.

Ground/surface unconfined water

13–024 Flooding may of course occur in the absence of a defined channel, and the similar but not identical rules governing such surface water and ground-water should also be noted.

An upper owner may allow his land to drain naturally onto his lower owner's land, even if this foreseeably could flood his lower owner's land.[88] Any different prima facie rule, and his landowner's autonomy would be unduly affected. He may be liable for artificially modifying his land so as to concentrate flows onto his lower neighbour's land, but again subject to the damage being a reasonably foreseeable consequence of his activities.[89]

As for the lower owner, he may prevent such water from draining onto his land by constructing a barrier between upper and lower land, as long as he acts reasonably in so doing.[90] He may also block up existing *artificial* drainage channels on his own land, even if the effect of this is to aggravate drainage problems on his neighbours' lands.[91] He may not however cause water already on his land to go onto the upper owner's land.[92]

13–025 Subject to these slightly different starting points, the *Leakey* principle otherwise operates between higher and lower owners as it does between riparian owners. Both upper and lower owners must ultimately act reasonably in respect of the other. An obvious manifestation of that reasonableness would be for one owner to give notice to the other of an intention to change the status quo in circumstances where it would be open to the other owner to mitigate any losses which might be suffered as a result of that change.

---

[88] *Home Brewery plc v Davis & Co* [1987] Q.B., approved by the CA in *Palmer v Bowman* [2000] 1 WLR 842.

[89] *Ellison v Ministry of Defence* (1996) 81 BLR 101 (HHJ Bowsher Q.C.). The case went to the CA on a pleading point, and the ruling below is unaffected.

[90] *Home Brewery*, above (infilling of clay pits on lower land), following *Gartner v Kidman* (1961) 108 CLR 12 *Home Brewery* was followed by *Ryeford Homes v Sevenoaks DC* (1989) 16 Con L.R. (lower landowner constructs embankment causing waterlogging and flooding of upper land; reasonable, and therefore not liable). The CA in *Palmer* expressed no view on this conclusion in *Home Brewery*.

[91] *Elston v Dore* (1982) ALR 577.

[92] *Home Brewery*, above.

The impact of statute

This topic is considered generally in Civil Liabilities in Chapter 4, but it is **13–026** of particular importance in the context of flooding liabilities. A statute may help or hinder a civil claim. It may help a claim if it imposes an enforceable duty on the public authority. It may hinder a claim if the statutory authority conferred by the Act renders the authority immune from some or all civil claims. There is a presumption against the statute conferring total immunity; far more commonly, the courts have found that the statute may prevent claims being brought in "simple" nuisance but does not affect claims alleging negligence or negligent nuisance.[93] However, a claim may fail if it is held to be inconsistent with the statutory scheme laid down by the Act, either because there is an existing statutory compensation scheme or because the Act requires a complaint to be brought in a particular form, and not by civil action. Finally, a public authority is in no better position simply because it is a public body; there are many cases where the statute neither confers a cause of action nor precludes it, and liabilities are determined as they would be between private landowners.[94]

As explained above, the vast bulk of flood defence and coastal protection powers are permissive. It is thus extremely difficult to sue a flood defence authority simply for failing to exercise its powers, as the authority enjoys a wide discretion as to the circumstances under which it may exercise those powers. The well-known case of *East Sussex Rivers Catchment Board v Kent*[95] demonstrates this well. A very high tide breached defences on the River Deben. The Board as flood defence authority was very slow in repairing the damage, and the claimants' land was flooded for longer than necessary. The House of Lords held that no action lay, because the Board was under no duty to repair the wall or indeed to complete the work after beginning it. However, there are cases, as *Kent* itself acknowledges, where the authority has exercised its powers in such a way as to add to the damage caused to the claimant over and above that which would have been caused had the authority not acted at all. Similarly, the authority will owe a duty not to implement any decisions in a negligent way which increases unnecessarily the flooding risk, as recognised in the coastal protection case of *Fellowes v Rother DC*.[96] In those circumstances, a common law claim in negligence or nuisance may lie even in the presence of the statute, and would certainly lie in the absence of the statute. An example of such facts might be *Adcock v Norfolk Line et al*[97] where the water authority negligently oversaw the construction of an incompetently constructed temporary sandbag wall.

---

[93] In the *Allen v Gulf Oil* ([1981] AC 1001) sense.
[94] *Bybrook Barn Centre v Kent CC* [2001] Env. L.R. 30.
[95] [1941] AC 74, considered with approval in *Stovin v Wise* [1996] AC 923.
[96] [1983] 1 All ER 513. See *Earle* (above) which also recognises this duty.
[97] CA, unreported, May 28, 1993. The case is no authority on public authority liability, as the water authority then responsible for flood defence admitted liability for its negligence.

A further complication in suing a flood defence or coastal protection authority is the effect of the statutory compensation schemes under the WRA, LDA, and CPA. In *Marriage v East Norfolk Rivers Catchment Board*[98] the Court of Appeal held that the only remedy for a flood caused by the Board raising one bank of the river was via compensation under the Land Drainage Act, which, as noted above, requires demonstrating that the flooding would be actionable at common law in the absence of statutory authority.

13–027   A similar, if not more restrictive, rule applies in the case of a claim against a sewerage undertaker for flooding from its sewers due to their lack of capacity. On the face of it, the claim might be thought to be assisted by the fact that there is at least a *duty* upon the undertaker effectually to drain the area,[99] rather than the *powers* we have been concerned with above. However, that has not availed claimants because the courts have found that any civil remedy has been found to be inconsistent with the statutory scheme. The leading case is *Marcic v Thames Water*[100] where a *Leakey*-type claim arising out of sewer flooding was held to be excluded by the statute which enabled complaint to be made to Ofwat. The rationale is that decisions about priorities in respect of remedial works on sewers should be taken not by the courts but by the statutory body whose task it is and who can bring wider economic considerations (such as water pricing or other environmental funding issues) to bear on its determination. Precisely the same considerations defeated Mr Marcic's Human Rights Act claims for breaches of the claimant's rights under Article 8 (private and family life) and Article 1 of the 1st Protocol to the European Convention. However, where the flooding occurred not because the sewers were too small but because they were insufficiently maintained, there may be a remedy.[101] This latter ruling may have considerable implications for flood damage which arose out of equipment failure.

    Suing a local authority for negligently granting planning permission for a development likely to flood, or the EA for their input on such a decision is likely to be a difficult course to pursue, given the broad nature of the functions invoked, when coupled with the increasing wariness of the Courts to extend liability to such public authorities in these circumstances.[102] However, leaving aside the legal difficulties of such a claim, this is increasingly unlikely to occur in the future as it is standard practice for any developer to obtain his own flood risk assessment before proceeding with any development application.

---

[98] [1950] 1 KB 284.
[99] s.94(1) WIA.
[100] [2004] 2 AC 42.
[101] *Dobson v Thames Water* [2007] EWHC 2021 (TCC), Ramsey J.
[102] See *Ryeford Homes Ltd v Sevenoaks DC* (1989) 16 Con L.R. 75: claim against planning authority for negligently allowing a neighbouring development struck out.

Prevention of unsuitable development

An essential element of the EA's flood defence responsibilities is the need 13–028 to control development in flood plains, and the EA, though not the decision-maker, is a statutory consultee[103] to the Local Planning Authority on any such development proposals. A recent Ministerial Direction[104] requires an LPA to tell the Secretary of State of any major development in a designated flood risk zone where the LPA is minded to grant against the advice of the EA. Major development is defined in the Direction as 10 houses or 0.5 ha of residential development, or floorspace of 1000m^3 or site area of 1ha if non-residential.

Inappropriate development may be subject to unacceptable risks of flooding and, by increasing the developed fraction of the catchment, may also heighten the risks to those already living and working within the catchment.

Policy for England[105] in this regard is set out in the Secretary of State's Planning Policy Statement 25 of 2006. PPS25 requires a sequential test of flood risk to be applied to development decisions. The sequential test identifies three "Flood Zones" applicable to any proposed development. The zones are based upon flood maps prepared by the EA, and in assessing probabilities of flooding they ignore any existing flood defences—by way of application of the precautionary principle.[106] The critical obligation under the sequential test is upon local planning authorities to satisfy themselves, when drawing up Local Development Documents or assessing proposed developments, that there are no reasonably available sites in areas of a lower probability of flooding suitable for the type of development proposed—in over-simplified terms, that there are no sites higher up available for development.

Flood Zone 1 is where there is a low probability of river or tidal 13–029 flooding, with an annual probability less than 0.1 per cent (i.e. 1 in 1000 years). There are no special planning constraints in this zone, and all land except that within zones 2 and 3 fits into this category.

Flood Zone 2 is where there is medium probability of such flooding, with an annual probability of river flooding of 0.1–1.0 per cent, and of tidal & coastal of 0.1–0.5 per cent. This zone is suitable for most development, but will require a Flood Risk Assessment appropriate to the scale and

---

[103] art.10 of the TCP (General Development Procedure) Order 1995, as amended in October 2006 by SI 2006/2375.

[104] The Town and Country Planning (Flooding) (England) Direction 2007.

[105] For Wales, see Technical Advice Note 15 of 2004, and a Ministerial letter from Carwyn Jones of November 10, 2006, seeking to temper some of the perceived rigidity of TAN 15.

[106] See, for an unsuccessful challenge to an Inspector's decision on the basis that he should have taken into account existing flood defences when applying the sequential test in PPG 25 (PPS 25's predecessor), *R (Thomas Bates) v Secretary of State* [2004] EWHC 1818 (Admin), Harrison J.

nature of the development. Warning and evacuation procedures should be considered.

Flood Zone 3 is where there is a high probability of flooding, with an annual probability of more than 1 per cent river flooding or 0.5 per cent tidal or coastal flooding. Whether development should be permitted will depend on its nature and whether the proposed development is on a functional flood plain.

13–030   Zone 3A land is not on a functional flood plain. This is suitable for residential, commercial & industrial development, provided that the exception test is satisfied. This test is satisfied where it is demonstrated that (a) the development provides wider sustainability benefits to the community which outweigh the flood risk, (b) the development must be on developable previously-developed land or there are no reasonable alternative sites on such land, and (c) a flood risk assessment must demonstrate that the development will be safe without increasing flood risk elsewhere, and where possible will reduce flood risk overall.[107] Zone 3B consists of functional floodplains. Only water-compatible development and essential services should be allowed there.

PPG 25, PPS 25's predecessor setting out a similar structure for decision-making, has been considered on occasion by the courts. In *R (Environment Agency) v Tonbridge & Malling DC*,[108] Lloyd-Jones J rejected an argument from the Council that it was entitled only to apply the sequential test at the policy stage, as opposed to when dealing with individual development proposals. On this basis, and in the absence of consideration of the test in the case under consideration, the Council's grant of planning permission was quashed.

Policy, if anything, is likely to become stricter in terms of development in areas of flood risk. That is certainly the message of Sir Michael Pitt's final report[109] on the floods of 2007, which, though it does not recommend any specific changes to the terms of PPS 25, seeks to instigate a wide-ranging review of the system in practice.

Other Strategic Documents

13–031   Defra has over the years encouraged the preparation of large-scale and long-term (50 to 100 years) policy documents covering individual sections of the coastline, known as Shoreline Management Plans. The first batch of these plans was prepared in 1996 to 1999, and revised plans are in preparation. In addition, Catchment Flood Management Plans, based around rivers, are being prepared. Neither have a statutory basis though this is

---

[107] D9 in Annex D to PPS 25.
[108] [2005] EWHC 3261 (Admin).
[109] Cabinet Office website.

likely to change upon transposition of the EU Floods Directive discussed below. However, since the decision in *Commission v UK*,[110] Defra has recognised[111] that such flood management plans must be assessed against any significant effects which the plans may have on Special Areas of Conservation pursuant to the obligation under Article 6(3) of the Habitats Directive.[112]

The Future

As noted above, there are indications from Government that flood defence statutes will be subject to consolidation and amendment via a bill proposed for 2009. Little indication has been given to date of the substance of these amendments, but it would be surprising if it did not address the following issues. The first is the realisation that the current statutory framework is not designed to reflect the reality of current flood risk management under which flood defence (in the sense of engineering structures) is only one of a series of responses to rising sea levels and increasing urbanisation. The second is that the EA's increasing role in managing flooding (both strategic and day-to-day) needs reflecting in a newly-drafted statute. The third is likely to be a response to the 2007 floods, and the Independent Government Review carried out by Sir Michael Pitt[113] in which a number of new measures, both practical and legislative, are proposed. The fourth may be a response to the Floods Directive summarised below.

13–032

The Floods Directive

The European Community has recently adopted the Floods Directive[114] on the assessment and management of flood risks. This is avowedly a directive to establish a "framework" for such policies.[115] It requires transposition two years after coming into force, namely by November 2009. It covers inland areas and coastal flooding, but "may" exclude floods from sewerage systems.[116] It sets out obligations on member states to carry out preliminary flood risk assessments for each of the river basins[117] within

13–033

---

[110] *C-6/04.*
[111] See a note to that effect *Flood Management Plans and the implications of C-6/04 Commission v United Kingdom* on the Defra website.
[112] 92/43/EEC.
[113] His Interim Report has been published.
[114] 2007/60, OJ L 6.11.07.
[115] art.1.
[116] art.2.
[117] Which may be those identified under the Water Framework Directive or if different need notifying to the Commission: art.3(2).

its territory by 2011, and then to prepare flood hazard and flood risk maps by 2013,[118] and completed flood management plans by 2015.[119] Flood risk and flood hazard maps require some considerable level of detail, with the extent of flooding, water depths and flow velocities being required for each of extreme event floods, floods with a return period of 100 years or or more, and floods with a high probability.[120] Flood risk maps require indicative numbers of people who might be flooded, details of economic activities affected, and a list of installations covered by the IPPC Directive which might cause pollution if flooded. There is provision for review of these assessments, maps and plans thereafter.[121]

Domestic transposition and implementation of this Directive is unlikely to pose much of a challenge to Defra and the EA. By a combination of current flood risk maps, Shore Management Plans and Catchment Flood Management Plans, much of the ground work has been done, and any remaining provisions necessary may be found in the promised Floods and Water Bill.

[118] art.6.
[119] art.7.
[120] art.6(3)–(5)
[121] art.14

Chapter 14

THE ENVIRONMENTAL PERMITTING REGIME
AND AIR POLLUTION

Introduction

The Environmental Permitting (EP) regime which came into force in April   **14–001**
2008 is designed to regulate many of the more polluting industries in a
consistent and uniform way. It already combines some of the regulatory
regimes previously applicable to different sectors of industry. The process
of bringing additional consent regimes within one umbrella will continue.
However, like a good deal of environmental regulation, it is a mixture of
home-grown law, both traditional and more recent, and European Directives. So it remains to be seen how the EP regime now transposes the
European Integrated Pollution and Control regime, which had some of its
roots in the domestic Integrated Pollution Control system. That system
was itself based on its exclusively air pollutant-regulating predecessors
(although it sought to remedy some of their faults).

This chapter focuses principally on the Environmental Permitting
regime, which provides a common structure to a number of different
industrial activities. It also considers additional air pollution measures
which are not implemented through the EP Regulations. But before doing
so, and to provide some context, it is necessary to sketch a little of how the
law got to where it is.

Domestic History of Air Pollution Control

The control of pollution to the air, both by statute and the common law,   **14–002**
has a lengthy history in Britain. Regulatory control in a form recognisable
to modern eyes dates from the second half of the nineteenth century. The
experience of the intervening 150 years ago remains relevant—some of the
problems encountered in earlier phases of industrial development continue
to trouble regulators. Significant parts of the current regulatory apparatus
can best be understood in terms of the deficiencies of its predecessors.

Air pollution controls developed, like other areas of environmental law,
incrementally—step by step, responsive to particular problems as and when
they arose, and not always in an entirely coherent fashion. Shortly before

Rylands v Fletcher[1] and *St Helen's Smelting Co v Tipping*[2] crystallised private law remedies for escapes for land and nuisances, Parliament passed the Alkali Works Act 1863. This was a response to air pollution by emissions of hydrogen chloride and hydrogen sulphide arising from the production of caustic soda by the Leblanc process. The Act created a national regulator with responsibility for air pollution, the Alkali Inspectorate, and imposed on factories producing alkali a limit value on their hydrochloric acid[3] gas emissions to reduce the quantity of harmful releases from their works. However, as the number of plants increased, with each new one producing more pollution, the Inspectorate's powers under the act were of only limited use.[4] Moreover, some operators appear to have responded to the new rules by merely changing the medium of their emissions from air to water. Doing this kept them within the letter of the law, but simply shunted the problem elsewhere.

The creation of the national Alkali Inspectorate was, however, an exception to the emerging trends of the time. These were to create local level regimes that typically had powers relating to emissions into a particular medium. These local agencies were, like the Alkali Inspectorate, often created in response to a particular problem of the moment, usually triggered by worries about public health. See for example the Rivers Pollution Prevention Act of 1876. This forbade water pollution and created criminal offences for enforcement. However, there was no national prosecutor, and launching proceedings required the consent of the relevant local government board.

14–003   The early approach to pollution control can be characterized as being concerned with specific human problems, usually involving public health, and directed at emissions into a particular medium, such as air or water. This may reflect the fact that there was then no clear concept of "the Environment" as an entire, holistic entity. This medium-specific and rather ad hoc method was to continue for over 100 years. The post-war concern with air quality is well documented. In the late 1940s and early 50s, emissions from low grade fuel burnt domestically and in power stations would combine with other prevailing weather conditions to cause the problems of urban smog—for example the London "pea-soupers" which were estimated to have caused or expedited several thousands of deaths. These led to the passage of the Clean Air Acts, first in 1956 and then 1968.

---

[1] (1868) LR 3 HL 330.
[2] (1865) 11 HLC 642.
[3] Referred to in the Act as "muriatic acid". The limit value was however one fifth of a grain of HCl per cubic foot of emissions, which is equivalent to approximately 458 mg HCl/m^3, compared with a typical ELV for HCl today of 10mg/m^3.
[4] There is an ongoing, unresolved tension in achieving a fair balance between overall environmental protection on the one hand, and the rights of an operator whose plant has comparatively low emissions but which raise the overall level of pollution above an acceptable level. See the judgment of Lord Hoffmann in *R (Edwards) v Environment Agency* [2008] UKHL 22, at para.8.

They gave new powers to local authorities to deal with this form of air pollution, and they certainly led to improvements in local air quality. However, many industries responded to the demands of the new regime with a simple solution—build taller chimneys. This moved the problem on, but did little to resolve it.

The first signs of a less medium-specific and more holistic attitude to pollution came with the creation of the Department of the Environment, in Edward Heath's 1970 Conservative Government. This also represented a move towards centralised control and away from enforcement at the local level. The Control of Pollution Act 1974, now replaced by later legislation, continued the traditional approach of trying to deal with pollution by sector rather than as a whole. Despite this shortcoming, it did put together in one Act measures concerning water, waste and air. Nonetheless, in 1976 the Royal Commission on Environmental Protection reported that pollution control was fragmented and unsatisfactory.[5] It proposed a single regulatory system with power to consider releases into multiple media. This was not to be achieved immediately. Her Majesty's Inspectorate of Pollution was created in 1987, amalgamating different agencies[6] into a single body under the control of the Department for the Environment. The National Rivers Authority was created shortly afterwards, in 1989. The names of these two bodies suggests a continuation of the trend towards medium-specific regulation. However, it represented progress in a different direction. Until then, much water pollution control was under the control of local authorities. These bodies had responsibility for highly polluting activities, like sewage and waste disposal, creating conflicts of interest which seriously inhibited vigorous enforcement.[7]

The most important development for the regulation of air pollution was the passing of the Environmental Protection Act 1990 (EPA). This implemented a number of European Directives, including the Air Framework Directive (84/360 EEC[8]). The Directive created a system of categories of industrial activity which had to be subject to a system of permits from the appropriate regulator. A number of the key concepts of the air pollution regime are contained in it. It required all appropriate preventative measures to be taken to reduce air pollution, and specifically the use of the "Best Available Technology Not Entailing Excessive Cost" (BATNEEC). It specified various air pollutants, such as sulphur dioxide, NOx and particulates, as requiring specific attention and control, to avoid undue air

---

[5] January 1976, *Air Pollution Control: An Integrated Approach*.
[6] The Alkali Inspectorate, the Radiochemical Inspectorate and the Hazardous Waste Inspectorate.
[7] It is open to question what would have happened for example in the case of *Secretary of State for the Environment v Yorkshire Water Services Ltd* (2001) EWCA Crim 2635, (an authority on sentencing for supplying water unfit for human consumption and other environmental offences), if the body with responsibility for enforcing water standards was the same as the utility that was prosecuted.
[8] [1984] OJ L188.

pollution. The EPA replaced the sector and medium-specific concerns of earlier regulation, and instituted the system of Integrated Pollution Control (IPC). Part 1 of the Act created two separate systems of control. One, the IPC regime, was common to all three media (air, water, land), and as such represented a properly integrated approach. It applied to a substantial list of potentially polluting processes, mostly being operated on a large scale. Her Majesty's Inspectorate of Pollution was the body with responsibility for enforcing IPC. The other part of the system was the Local Authority Air Pollution Control (LAAPC) regime. This part of the system aimed to control emissions to air from smaller operations, and was enforced by local authorities—in many respects as an extension of their responsibilities to control statutory nuisances, which is how air pollution from such operations would generally have been dealt with previously.

14-004   In both the IPC and LAAPC, the system of control was broadly the same. Permits were required, with restrictions on their transfer and variation (although not, at this stage, on their surrender). The IPC regime covered Part A processes. These were the minority of the most hardcore polluting activities. These were to be controlled by applying BATNEEC, with the overriding aim of achieving BPEO (Best Practicable Environmental Option). This latter concept was another expression of the integrated approach. It required a holistic view of the effect on the environment as a whole, and so was a great step away from the medium-specific concerns of previous attempts at regulation. In the case of LAAPC regulation, BATNEEC was to be applied but not with BPEO in mind, as the LAAPC regime was only concerned with emissions to air. Part 2 of the EPA was the successor to the much criticized Control of Pollution Air 1974. It implemented the then current Waste Framework Directive (75/442), and controlled the management of waste in, on or under land. The management of waste will be addressed in the following chapter.

The EPA was a major step in the history of air pollution regulation. It retained local level regulation for the majority of less complex and less polluting activities that were to come under LAAPC. However, it also took the significant step of centralising control of the most seriously polluting installations in the hands of what is now the Environment Agency. It was the means of introducing parts of the conceptual framework, such as BATNEEC and BPEO which underpin the modern integrated approach to pollution. These concepts were at the core of the system for air pollution control that developed under the Integrated Pollution Prevention and Control Directive 96/61,[9] which with subsequent amendments has recently been consolidated into Directive 2008/01,[10] namely the Pollution Prevention and Control Regulations 2000[11] ("the old, or PPC, regulations")

---

[9] [1996] OJ L257/26.
[10] [2008] OJ L24/8.
[11] SI 2000/1973.

and the Environmental Permitting (England & Wales) Regulations 2007[12] ("the EP regulations").

IPPC Directive

As its name suggests, the IPPC Directive relied significantly upon the British experience of regulation across different environmental media under the IPC. However, its scope was considerably greater. Rather than dealing with specific processes, it was concerned with particular "activities" carried out at "installations". It brought within its scope a wider range of installations than had been covered by the IPC—for example, landfill was a new addition. The full list of activities covered by the current Directive is set out in its Annex I, and can be conveniently summarised as follows: **14–005**

(i)   the energy industry;
(ii) metal production and processing;
(iii) the mineral industry;
(iv) the chemical industry;
(v)   certain waste management activities, including landfill; and
(vi) "other activities", a catch-all category including pulp and paper works, textile treating, tanning hides, slaughterhouses, food processing, milk processing, animal waste disposal and recycling, poultry and piggeries, plus installations for treatment with organic solvents and for the production of carbon and electrographite.

In many instances, there is a specified minimum capacity threshold which determines whether an installation is within the scope of the Directive. Where an operator carries out several activities of the same type in the same installation, they are treated cumulatively, so that the capacities are combined for permitting purposes. The Directive also goes further than the IPC regime, covering a wider range of environmental impacts.

The recitals set out the regulatory background to the Directive, and its objectives. Perhaps most significant is the ninth recital, which states that the primary purpose of the integrated approach is "to prevent emissions into air, water or soil wherever this is practicable", failing which "to minimise them in order to achieve a high level of protection for the environment as a whole". One of the principal tools to achieve this is the requirement[13] that permits include Emission Limit Values (ELVs) for pollutants, including but not limited to a list of specific air and water emissions listed in Annex 3 to the Directive. These values are to be determined by reference to the "best available techniques". This concept is the successor to BATNEEC as defined in the IPC regime. In Annex 4 to

---

[12] SI 2007/3538.
[13] art.9(3).

the Directive, there is a list of specific principles to be considered in determining the BAT, including the use of low waste technology and the recovery and recycling of waste. The individual terms of the acronym are themselves specified, as discussed below.[14]

The Directive can be seen to operate more by way of guiding principles than specific, prescriptive rules. One striking instance is recital 19, which explicitly does not state that it seeks to set out rules for specific installations, but rather:

> "It is for the Member States to determine how the technical characteristics of the installation concerned, its geographical location and local environmental conditions can, where appropriate, be taken into consideration."

One example is that the ELVs determine what are acceptable levels of emissions from an installation, but they do so by prescribing process standards rather than by seeking to apply uniform emissions levels. At the time of the drafting of the Directive, there was considerable disagreement about the correct approach. The representatives of some member states argued that a system based on guiding principles rather than defined limits would not be fair, and indeed could be abused, and that a harmonised system was preferable. To take the example of a river along the border between two member states, if an operator on one side was subject to less stringent limits than its competitor on the other, it would have a useful but arguably unfair competitive advantage. This objection is open to the criticism that total fairness of this kind is in any case impossible, since the availability of technology is likely to vary rather than be uniform. Although the Directive was expressed in terms of principles to be achieved, there is some compromise. Under Article 19, there is provision for setting ELVs with community-wide application, where the information-sharing processes have identified a need for it. However, the application of Article 19 has been limited. There are various possible reasons for this. The dynamic nature of BAT is clearly a significant one. Where technology develops rapidly and these developments are communicated between member states and industries, centrally set limits are liable to be outpaced by change.

14–006 Following its initial implementation, the original IPPC Directive was amended four times and consolidated on January 29, 2008, into 2008/1/EC. The four amendments included reinforcing public participation rights in accordance with the Aarhus convention, and setting out the relationship between the Directive and the EU's separate greenhouse gas emissions trading scheme.

---

[14] art.2(12) (a) to (c). See para.14–017.

Installations—summary of terms and scope

The most important term in the Directive is "installation". This is the   **14–007**
basic unit of permitting, and it is expansively defined at Article 2(3):

> "Installation means a stationary technical unit where one or more
> activities listed in Annex I are carried out, and any directly associated
> activities which have a technical connection with the activities carried on
> at that site and which could have an effect on emissions and pollution."

The Commission's Directorate-General for Environment has published
guidance specifically on the definition of installation and of the related
concept, operator.[15] Although the guidance does not have official status, it
is nonetheless of some help as a guide to interpretation.

Installation

The term can be read in one of two ways. The first is as a "stationary   **14–008**
technical unit" in which an Annex I activity takes place, with other directly
associated activities potentially but not necessarily part of that unit. The
alternative is that the entire installation, comprising both Annex I activity
and directly associated activity, is a stationary unit. The different transla-
tions of the Directive can be used to support either view. However, reading
across to the Waste Incineration Directive (2000/76/EC[16]) would tend to
support the latter; this states that "plant" in that context means any
technical unit and equipment which includes the site and the whole plant.
Under this approach, the installation equals the technical unit. To determine an installation, therefore, first identify the Annex I activities on the
site, then identify any directly associated activities with a technical connection and which could have an effect on emissions and pollution. The
unit is accordingly the sum of all the activities. This latter reading would
tend to be supported by the Commission's current proposals[17] for the
replacement Directive in which "installation" is to mean

> "a stationary technical unit within which one or more activities listed in
> Annex I or in Part 1 of Annex VII are carried out, and any other directly
> associated activities on the same site which have a technical connection
> with the activities carried out on that site listed in those Annexes and
> which could have an effect on emissions and pollution."

---

[15] *Guidance on Interpretation of "Installation" and "Operator" for the purposes of the IPPC
Directive*, April 2007.
[16] [2000] OJ L337.
[17] COM (2007) 844 final.

The emphasised words are inserted to exclude offsite directly associated activities from the definition of "installation" and hence to confirm that "installation" equals a stationary technical unit and no more.

Stationary: the guidance acknowledges the omission of mobile units from the defining phrase "stationary". However, the guidance does not support a purposive reading that, like the EPA, would include mobile units. It gives the examples of mobile plant for incineration or land decontamination, stating that if the equipment "will operate at a particular location for a significant period . . . it should be considered stationary for the purposes of the Directive." As we will see, such plant is regulated domestically by the EP Regulations.

Technical unit

14–009 "Technical" is perhaps one of the less problematic terms, although the guidance notes that it is not necessary for all the activities within the technical unit to be technically sophisticated. "Unit" does not signify that the permitted operations are confined to a single structure. With both terms, there is considerable breadth to the definition.[18]

Directly associated activities which have a technical connection

14–010 This phrase was considered by the lower courts in *United Utilities v Environment Agency*[19] (the House of Lords proceedings did not involve the interpretation of this specific phrase). Both at first instance and in the Court of Appeal, the judges expressed considerable difficulty in defining what was meant by this phrase. The installations in question were a plant operated by United Utilities, a sewerage undertaker, in which effluent from a separately-operated brewery was pre-treated and mixed with water, and another United Utilities plant which treated the effluent of a milk processing plant. In both cases the treating plant was connected to the main plant by a pipeline, at distances of 800 and 700 metres respectively. The question before the Court was whether they could be said to be directly associated activities. The case was not decided on the point, but giving the judgment of the Court of Appeal, Laws LJ summarised the arguments as follows:[20] There was a direct, dedicated pipeline from the main plant to the

---

[18] There is a useful discussion of the phrase in the context of landfill to be found in *R (Anti-Waste) v Environment Agency* [2007] EWCA Civ 1377 at paras 13–27. The issue arose whether a "piggy-backing" landfill on its own was a stationary technical unit, independent of another older landfill on the same site, and therefore could be permitted without reference to the other landfill.

[19] [2007] UKHL 41.

[20] See *United Utilities v Environment Agency* [2006] EWCA Civ 633 at para.36ff, and specifically 40–41.

treating plant; the pipeline enabled the operator to treat the effluent from its main plant; and the treatment was essential to the main processes. These facts were also said to establish a direct association. In what is clearly obiter dicta, the Court expressed a "marginal preference" for the view that the three factors set out above made it a directly associated activity with a technical connection. However, in the same passage the Court expressed "grave doubts" about the drafting of the legislation, noting that "technical connection" is undefined, and yet the construction of the phrase could determine guilt in criminal proceedings. It considered the phrase so vague that a prosecution brought under it would be likely to raise issues about compliance with the human right to a fair trial.

The European Commission guidance leaves the question little more certain. It states that a "direct association" must in some sense be operational, such as an auxiliary unit performing a function which would not happen on that site without the main installation. Technical connection does not, according to the guidance, require a physical connection such as pipework or wiring, but where either is present technical connection is therefore "automatic". This conclusion is in agreement with that of Laws LJ, albeit expressed with much greater confidence. The guidance states that "technical" means "a link in terms of intended process operation and materials flow". In giving a broad definition of "technical connection", it is suggested that if direct association is established, a connection by means of a fork-lift truck or even manual handling would be enough to satisfy the other part of the definition. A dedicated relationship between an Annex I activity and a non-Annex I activity would normally mean that they both come within the definition. Where the non-Annex I activity is not dedicated and can relate to other facilities, then the question of direct association will be a matter of judgment.

Site

"Site" has been differently interpreted in different member states. Meanings include: the geographical location; installation and site understood as strictly connected, i.e. one installation-one site; a fenced area around an installation; and the area owned or controlled by the operator. Article 2(9) of the Directive states that a permit may authorize multiple installations on one site. Therefore multiple installations on one site may come within one permit, but multiple sites would require multiple permits. Ownership and fencing both seem somewhat arbitrary ways to determine what is a site, and ones which do not take into account the particular characteristics of different installations. The guidance gives the example of a chemical plant with raw materials stored in tanks which are connected by a pipeline but not located in the same complex. That case would be a matter for judgment. As we have seen, part of the *United Utilities* decision concerned

14–011

whether treatment plants connected to the milk processing plant and brewery by 700 and 800 metres of pipeline were on the same site as them. Although the Court expressed great difficulty with interpreting other parts of the definition, it had no difficulty in stating that no sensible interpretation of "same site" could cover this. The Court did not accept the submission that a broad interpretation of the phrase should be adopted, and explicitly rejected a one mile limit. This suggests that a principled definition may prove elusive, and that this is another part of the definition where in practice regulator discretion will be extensive.

Could have an effect on emissions and pollution

14–012   This phrase only requires a *potential* rather than an actual effect, and it does not require emissions and pollution, merely an effect on them. As such, it is widely drafted so that few installations or related activities could readily come outside its scope.

Differences in UK implementation

14–013   Domestic regulation, unlike the IPPC Directive, has always applied to mobile units, both under the old PPC regulations and the new EP regulations; they are within the definition of "regulated facility" under reg.8(1) of the latter. Their inclusion is inherited from the EPA 1990 regime of IPC and Local Authority Air Pollution Control permitting. Questions of the definition of mobile plant can be answered from these sources, but not the Directive. As with installations,[21] mobile plant is divided into categories which are defined by Schedule 1 of both the PPC and the IPPC regulations. These are Part A(1), Part A(2) and Part B. Part A(1) are former IPC activities, whether within the scope of the Directive or not. Part A(2) are former LAAPC activities that were within the Directive's scope; Part B—former LAAPC activities that were not within the Directive's scope. Part A mobile plant was typically of the more "hardcore", heavily polluting type. It was therefore less mobile, and less likely to move.

Operator

14–014   This is defined at Article 2(13) of the Directive as meaning

"any natural or legal person who operates or controls the installation or, where this is provided for in the national legislation, to whom decisive

---

[21] Mobile plant is defined to exclude installations: reg.2(1).

economic power over the technical functioning of the installation has been given".

The guidance highlights the potential anomaly that there is no express provision for more than one person to be the operator, so that it is arguable under the present text that if two individuals operated an installation of the requisite size only one of them could be the operator for permitting purposes. The underlying purpose behind this is certainty of operator to secure enforcement. Article 5 of the Commission's proposals[22] for a replacement directive provides expressly for joint operators of installations or parts of installations, without materially amending the equivalent of Article 2(13).

Which regulator—Parts A(1), A(2) and B?

Responsibility for permitting installations is divided between the Agency and the relevant local authority. The division of competence goes back to the IPC regime under the EPA 1990, and in some respects is not much changed. The rule of thumb is that the Agency is responsible for the potentially most serious hardcore polluting installations, principally those deriving from the IPPC Directive itself, while local authorities are competent for the potentially less polluting installations and those which only emit to air.

14–015

Regulation 3 of the new EP Regulations defines Part A(1), A(2) and B activities as those activities which fall within the relevant section of Part 2 of Schedule 1. In essence, the Part A(1) category is for the largest and most serious types of installation, Part B for the smallest and least serious, and Part A(2) is an intervening category between the two. It should be noted that for certain types of activity, there is no Part A(2). See for example asbestos, at section 3.2 of Part 2 of Schedule 1; and organic chemicals at section 4.1. Having determined which of the three is the relevant category, Regulation 32 states that functions relating to Part A(1) installations and mobile plant are exercisable by the Agency, and functions relating to Part A(2) and B activities are exercisable by the local authority in whose area the activity will be operated.

The correct way for the regulator to exercise its functions is set by Schedules 7 and 8. Paragraph 3 of Schedule 7 requires that when exercising functions relating to a Part A installation, the regulator must seek to achieve "a high level of protection of the environment taken as a whole by ... preventing or ... reducing emissions into air water and land." However, Paragraph 3 of Schedule 8 limits the Local Authority regulator's concerns as regards Part B installations to emissions into the air. The division of labour between the Agency and local authority regulators is that the latter are mostly concerned with emissions to air, save for any Part A(2) instal-

[22] Above.

lations in respect of which the local authority will be concerned with emission to all three media.

14-016 In some cases, however, the roles may be reversed. The "appropriate authority", which is defined as either the Secretary of State or the relevant Welsh Minister, has power under Regulation 33(1)(a) and (b) to direct either that the Agency will exercise certain local authority functions, or vice versa. The direction may relate to a specific facility or to facilities of a particular description. There is a further residual power under regulation 61 whereby the appropriate authority may give directions to the regulator to exercise or not to exercise certain of its powers, in certain ways or in certain circumstances.

Some types of installation will be capable of being categorised in more than one Part. The rules in Part 1 of Schedule 1 cover this situation. The general approach within the section is that where there is doubt, a facility should be subject to the more onerous regime, i.e. move up the regulatory hierarchy rather than down. Paragraph 2 of Part 1, Schedule 1 provides that where an activity comes within Parts A(1) and B, or within A(2) and B, then it should be deemed to fall only within the Part A regime. This avoids regulatory duplication, and keeps installations within the more onerous regime. Where an activity comes within Parts A(1) and (2), it should be deemed to fall only within the one that "fits it most aptly". Similarly, where there are several activities of the same description in different parts of the same unit, or different units on the same site, paragraph 4 of Part 1 requires that determining the Part A(1) or A(2) status should be done cumulatively, that is by adding together the different capacities and attributing them to each Part. The effect of this will be to raise rather than lower the deemed capacity, and move it into the A(1) category. Paragraph 5 contains a further rule to the effect that if an installation carries on activities which are defined by a threshold, such as a capacity threshold, the installation will not cease to have the relevant Part A(1), A(2) or (B) status because it is operated below the threshold. The effect of this is that operators cannot evade the permitting regime by running below capacity.

Outline of conditions, BAT and BREF, EQS

14-017 When regulators set permit conditions they are required to give effect to the general principles set out in Article 3 of the Directive. These are: using preventive techniques against pollution, especially through BAT; causing no significant pollution; waste avoidance; energy efficiency; accident prevention and limitation; and site restoration so that pollution risk is avoided. Defra's March 2008 guidance[23] states that the use of BAT in setting permit

---

[23] *Environmental Permitting Guidance: The IPPC Directive: Part A(1) Installations and Part A(1) Mobile Plant.*

conditions is "the essence" of the integrated approach.[24] ELVs are to be set using a combination of BAT on the general level, and the specific technical characteristics of the installation and its location. The general aims of Article 3 are given specific form in Article 9(1)–(6). This requires the minimisation of long distance and transboundary pollution,[25] proper waste management and ensuring the protection of soil and groundwater,[26] that there should be measures covering abnormal situations such as malfunctions and stoppages,[27] and that the operator should monitor emissions properly and provide the regulator with data to enable compliance with the condition. Article 12 requires the regulator to ensure that the operator informs it of proposed changes. This is separate from the Regulation 20 requirement that operators apply to the regulator to vary their conditions.

BAT is defined by reference to a number of principles. Thus Article 2(12) of the Directive states:

> " 'best available techniques' means the most effective and advanced stage in the development of activities and their methods of operation which indicate the practical suitability of particular techniques for providing in principle the basis for emission limit values designed to prevent and, where that is not practicable, generally to reduce emissions and the impact on the environment as a whole".

It goes on to define techniques[28] as including both the specific technology, for example the method of producing clinker for cement,[29] and also the way the installation is designed, built, maintained, operated and de-commissioned. "Available technique"[30] is that which is economically and technically viable having regard to its costs and advantages, and subject to it being "reasonably accessible" to the operator. The definition of "best"[31] recalls the recital's objectives – it is that which is most effective in "achieving a high level of protection for the environment as a whole". But, as noted above, "best" is qualified by cost considerations. The BAT concept is expressed in terms of principles partly because it applies to all manner of different installations, operating in different locations and sectors. It may be indicated in guidance from a regulator, but for many installations with unique characteristics, the BAT for that installation can only be determined after detailed consideration of that particular installation. Defra's March 2008 Guidance states[32] that BAT will mean the best overall technique as long as it is available. Determining availability involves

[24] March 2008 Guidance, para.3.10.
[25] art.9(4).
[26] art.9(3).
[27] art.9(6).
[28] art.2(12)(a).
[29] Annex I, 3.1.
[30] art.2(12)(b).
[31] art.2(12)(c).
[32] para.3.18–20.

a two stage test: first, what are its costs and advantages? Excessive cost is one reason for not deeming as BAT a technology which otherwise has considerable environmental benefits. Secondly, is it reasonably accessible? Accessibility is a comparatively low test. The technique need not be widely used, and can still be deemed accessible where it has only been tested as a pilot scheme.

Though the principles provide the background, BAT is often set in practice by reference to national and European guidance—the Agency has produced a wealth of sector specific guidance notes. Many of these come from the Directive requirement[33] that the Commission facilitate a process of information exchange between member states and industry on BAT and monitoring techniques, and publish the products every three years. This process is organised by the European IPPC Bureau (EIPPCB), which is based in Seville. The Bureau has established a number of technical working groups on specific sectors. Each one gathers and assesses information, creating a BAT reference document (BREF). The Bureau acts as a neutral secretariat for the working groups. The process varies considerably according to the sector. However, according to the EIPPCB Guidance,[34] where there is a new BREF to be written, the process typically involves two plenary meetings before the creation of a draft BREF, which is reviewed and then finalised. This typically takes between two and three years for each BREF. The purpose of the BREF is not to eliminate the need for regulators to take specific decisions at local and national level, but rather to provide information that will assist the making of decisions.

14–018   The format of BREFs is broadly speaking as follows:

- **General information**. Taking the example of the BREF for the food, drink and milk industries (FDM) published in December 2005, this section sets out industry characteristics, such as its diversity and broad spread across Europe, the fact that it is separately regulated by food safety standards and laws, and that the most significant environmental issues are water consumption and contamination, energy consumption, and waste minimisation.

- **Applied processes and techniques**. This describes the processes currently used in the sector, including changing trends and alternatives being developed. This may include the chemical and materials consumed in the processes, including energy, the preparation, process and manufacture, product storage and the method of dealing with by-products.

- **Emission and consumption levels**. This will cover energy, water and raw material use, as well as emissions to air, water and land. The FDM industries' BREF explains that the sector uses very considerable amounts of water, both as an ingredient and as a cleaning agent.

[33] art.17(2).
[34] *IPPC BREF Outline and Guide*, December 2005.

- **Techniques to consider in the determination of BAT**. This will often comprise a large number of techniques—more than 370 for FDM—including pollution prevention ("process integrated") and pollution control techniques ("end-of-the-pipe"). Very detailed guidance is produced in respect of each technique explaining what information may be required as part of a permit application.

- **BAT**. The conclusions on BAT are expressed in general terms. In the case of the FDM BREF, the BAT are often operational, and so can be implemented by training and maintenance rather than major capital investment. The BREF will often describe achievable consumption and emission levels for particular techniques, without actually setting ELVs. Minimising water consumption is a common BAT for the FDM sector, for example by dry methods of cleaning. As well as generalised forms of BAT, there are sector specific BAT. These can be highly specialised. The BAT for the commercial thawing of mackerel is to achieve water consumption below 2 cubic metres per tonne of mackerel.

- **Emerging techniques**. This might include information about potential efficiencies achievable with a particular technique, plus costs and the time in which it might be available.

- **Conclusion**. This typically describes the process of information exchange in producing the BREF, for example how long it took, and its scope.

Environmental quality standards

Decisions on the appropriate ELVs to be included in a permit are typically made by reference to BAT. However, there will be situations where a more stringent standard is applied by virtue of Article 10 of the Directive. This requires that where an environmental quality standard (EQS) requires stricter conditions than would be achieved by the application of BAT, they shall be achieved by stricter conditions in the permit. EQSs are set by other Directives,[35] and are expressed in terms of maximum levels for concentrations of particular substances. There are specific EQSs for air that set limits for benzene, carbon monoxide, ozone, poly-aromatic hydrocarbons, cadmium, arsenic and nickel. EQSs can be breached either by the emissions of a single installation or as a result of a combination of multiple installations and other sources. If an EQS is already being breached in a particular area, the Guidance[36] states that "a permit should not be issued to any new installation that would cause anything beyond a negligible increase". Where there is a breach of an EQS because of a particular installation, the regulator can use its power of review in order to reset the

14–019

---

[35] For example 99/30/EC, [1999] OJ L163/41.
[36] March 2008 guidance, para.3.51.

relevant ELVs in the existing permit. EQSs set by European legislation are recognised by the EP regulations.[37] However, there are also EQSs set at national level, for example the standards set by the Air Quality Strategy by virtue of the Environment Act 1995, though these are not within the EQS definition in the IPPC Directive, which only applies to those set by Community legislation.[38]

Application procedure

14–020   The process of applying for a permit under the new EP regulations is very much a technical matter, where issues of environmental policy generally play a minor role. In that respect the new procedure resembles that under the old regulations. The rules governing permit applications under the new regime are codified in Chapter 2 and Schedule 5 of the Regulations. The requirements are that[39]: it should be made by the applicant for the permit; it should be on the form provided by the regulator; it should include the information which the form specifies; and it should be accompanied by the appropriate fee. The Agency has published its *Environmental Permitting Core Guidance* ("The Core Guidance"), which expands on the formal requirements of Schedule 5. The regulator is only required to determine applications which are "duly made."[40] In assessing whether an application is duly made, the guidance makes it clear that normal standards of reasonableness and common sense will be used, and that the regulator should always explain why it does not consider an application to have been properly made. Examples include: not using the correct form; seeking a permit for an activity which is outside the regulations; applying to the wrong regulator; not paying the correct fee; and failing to address "a key point in the application form".[41]

The Core Guidance makes it clear that if there is uncertainty about the above issues or any others, the operator can request a pre-application discussion. The purpose of the discussion is to see if a permit is in fact needed, and if so for the regulator to advise about the likely issues and draw attention to the available guidance. Public consultees may be invited to attend the meeting. The guidance states "good engagement with ... interested parties at the pre-application stage can be beneficial to all sides". This is particularly relevant to controversial cases.

It is expected that applications will be made when full designs of plant and machinery are ready. An operator can start building before applying for a permit, but this is done at the operator's risk, as it will bear the costs of any changes required by the permit conditions. If the application is parti-

---

[37] Schedule 7, para.5(c), giving effect to art.10 of the Directive.
[38] art.2(7).
[39] Sch.5, Part 1, paras 1 and 2.
[40] Sch.5, Part 1, para.12.
[41] Core Guidance, para.5.4.

cularly unusual or complicated, or has a long lead time, the regulator and the operator may agree to a staged process.

Once an application has been submitted, the regulator is expected to acknowledge it.[42] An applicant may withdraw the application at any point before it is determined, although the regulator is not obliged to return the fees paid.[43] Although it is clearly preferable to submit the application in a complete final state, the Guidance makes it clear that amendments may be accepted after submission. These can include substantial changes, such as a change in the operator. However, if the proposed change is too significant, the regulator will require a new application.[44] **14–021**

As the EP Regulations are derived from the IPPC Directive, applicants for permits bear the same requirement as before to set out the necessary technical information in their application. This concerns the nature of the installation, foreseeable emissions and waste, plus a non-technical summary. See Article 6(1) of the Directive for the full list. The Core Guidance puts particular emphasis on the assessment of environmental risk. Regulators are explicitly referred to the 2000 *Guidelines for Environmental Risk Assessment and Management*,[45] and applicants would be well advised to do the same. If appropriate, the application should include an assessment of the risks under both normal and abnormal conditions. Applicants are required to justify their assumptions, while regulators are specifically directed to consider whether risks and impacts are matched by appropriate control measures.

Regulators continue to be able to require further information from applicants. Failure to comply with a regulator's request means the regulator can serve a further notice, whereby the permit application is deemed to be withdrawn. The relevant sections of the old and new rules[46] set out what is a broad and apparently unfettered discretion. However, the Core Guidance indicates that requests should be used sparingly—only where "essential" to determine the application, by reference to the requirements of the Directive or the conditions to be imposed.[47] Requests for information should be issued as early in the process as possible, should clearly set out what is required and why, and give the applicant a reasonable period in which to answer. The request has the effect of "stopping the clock" for the purposes of calculating the regulator's deadline for its determination.[48] If an applicant has not answered a request, the regulator should not immediately serve the notice deeming the application to be withdrawn. Before

---

[42] Core Guidance, para.5.7.

[43] Sch.5, Part 1, para.3.

[44] Core Guidance, para.5.8.

[45] Jointly published by the Department of the Environment, Transport and the Regions, as it was then, the Agency and the Institute for Environment & Health.

[46] Compare Sch.4, Part 1, para.4 of the old regulations and Sch.5, Part 1, para.4 of the new regulations.

[47] Core Guidance, para.5.16.

[48] Sch.5, Part 1, para.16(3)(a).

doing so, it should review the decision to require further information. If, after a review, it still proposes to serve the further notice deeming withdrawal, the regulator should give the applicant a last chance and an opportunity for a face to face meeting.[49]

14–022   The Guidance makes it clear that operator competence is one of the most important considerations for the regulator—the lack of it is perhaps the most likely reason for refusal to grant a permit. An applicant will need to demonstrate good management systems, technical competence, that it does not have a poor compliance record, and that it has adequate financial resources. The guidance suggests that operators of complex facilities obtain external certification for their management system, such as the European Union's Eco Management and Audit Scheme (EMAS). Showing a robust system may also give the operator the benefit of fewer inspections after the grant of a permit. External accreditation is also likely to assist in demonstrating technical competence. The guidance on compliance states that any offence relating to the environment will be taken into account, and that deliberate disregard for the environment, illustrated by repeated convictions or making false statements, may lead to refusal of a permit. Financial competence will only be relevant in certain circumstance, where for example there are high running costs relative to potential profits.

The regulator is required to consider representations from public consultees, third parties with property rights who will be affected by the proposed permit, and other EU member states. The consultation process is considered at greater length in the section below entitled *Public Participation.*

The basic time limit for the regulator to make its determination is three months from when it receives a duly made application. If there is public participation the limit is six months. These time limits can be extended with the operator's consent. The clock is stopped where there is a request for further information, where there is consultation with affected third parties (i.e. a separate consultation from the standard one with public consultees), where there is consideration of national security or other, commercially confidential issues, or where the public is informed about certain draft decisions.

14–023   A permit application must involve consultation with another member state, if the regulator considers that the operation is likely to have a significant negative effect on the environment of another member state, or if another member state requests information about an application. If so, the clock does not start to run until the consultation with that country has finished. In the case of an application to vary an existing permit, the time limit is two months.

An application must be refused in two situations: where the regulator considers that the applicant will not be the operator of the facility, or that

---

[49] Core Guidance, paras 5.20–21.

the applicant will not operate it according to the conditions of the permit.[50]

The regulator can impose any conditions it sees fit. Under the old regulations, the regulator was required either to grant a permit subject to conditions or to refuse it.[51]

The requirement that conditions must be imposed in every case appears to have been removed—the new rules give the regulator a discretion to impose none, although it is unlikely that this would ever happen. Conditions may be imposed which require the consent of third parties. This consent must be given, but there is a scheme for compensation along the model of compulsory purchase.[52]

Public participation, confidentiality, public registers

Public participation is an area of the new regime where there have been **14–024** some significant changes. Broadly speaking, the trend is towards a less exacting regime of consultation and public participation, in which the regulator has various discretions. These include whom to consult, and the means by which the consultation is carried out.

The old rules required[53] that after an application had been made, the applicant was to advertise in the London Gazette or in one or more local newspapers, and in the case of Part A mobile plant in both. The advertisement was required to state the applicant's name, the site address, the activities, the foreseeable significant effects of emissions, where the register could be inspected and the means of making representations.

In place of this prescriptive method, the new system allows the regulator to use its discretion in deciding the means of consultation. The guidance states that the effect of this is to enable "proportionate and flexible approaches to public participation".[54] The new rules are set out in Schedule 5, Part 1 of the new regulations. All permit applications are governed by the consultation rules, except for standard facilities which are not Part A installations, and mobile plant. In the former case, the rationale for the exemption from the rules is that there is a separate consultation process for installations to which the new standard rules permit provisions apply. In this situation consultation takes place at the time of production of the generally applicable rules and also on their review, and this replaces consultation for subsequent specific applications. Applications for mobile plant permits are also exempt from the consultation requirements. The guidance explains that this is because they can operate in different locations, and so "local involvement cannot be meaningfully provided at the application stage". This is a striking development from the old rules.

---

[50] Sch.5, Part 1, para.13.
[51] reg.10(2).
[52] Sch.5, Part 2.
[53] Sch.4, Part 1, paras 5 and 6.
[54] Core Guidance, para.9.3.

14–025   Under the new rules, there continues to be a de minimis exemption from the consultation requirements. The exempt activities are burning waste oil below a certain thermal input level, motor refuelling and petrol unloading at service stations. Dry cleaning has been added to the exempt list, while odorising and blending odorant appear no longer to be exempt.[55]

Substantial change

14–026   The consultation requirements are also triggered by variations to the permitted operations involving a substantial change, and other variations where the regulator decides that the requirements should apply. The language of the regulations makes it clear that whether something is a substantial change is a question for the regulator alone[56]—the definition states that

> "substantial change means a change in the operation of an installation which *in the regulator's opinion* [emphasis added] may have significant negative effects on human beings or the environment".

If the regulator does not consider that an application involves a substantial change, it still retains a discretion to require public participation.[57] The regulations themselves give two examples of substantial changes,[58] a change in the operation of a Part A installation which itself meets a relevant threshold in Schedule 1; and, in relation to waste plant for incineration or co-incineration, a change involving hazardous waste. The examination of what is substantial is described in the guidance as fact based, and requires a consideration of all impacts, positive and negative, rather than just the net effect of the change.[59] In addition to the release of emissions, heat vibrations and noise emissions are also relevant, as are impacts like the production of waste, the consumption of energy and the risk of accidents. If having considered the effect of a change it is thought to be negative, the next step is to determine if it is "significant". The regulator will consider whether the change justifies a consultation, having regard to the extent of the effect in terms of area and affected population, effects on protected areas, any transboundary effect, the magnitude, complexity and probability of the impact, and its duration, frequency and reversibility.[60] The guidance concludes that the decision is solely for the regulator to make, and should be taken on the basis of the facts and common sense.

Assuming that a proposed installation meets the consultation criteria, the regulator must inform the public consultees of the application and how to

---

[55] Compare Sch.4, Part 1, para.8 of the old rules and Sch.5, Part 1, para.5(4) of the new.
[56] Sch.5, Part 1, para.5(5).
[57] Sch.5, Part 1, para.5(2) and (3).
[58] Sch.5, Part 1, para.5(5).
[59] March 2008 Defra guidance on IPPC Directive, para.4.23.
[60] March 2008 guidance, para.4.24.

inspect the register. "Public consultee" is defined as a person who in the regulator's view is or is likely to be affected by an application, or has an interest in it. To inform consultees of the application, the regulator must "take the steps it considers appropriate."[61] The regulator may intend to impose a condition which will require the operator to do things involving the consent of third parties. The third party, who can be the owner, leasee or occupier of the affected land, must be consulted.

The regulator must also invite representations from the consultees, and set out the means of doing so. In the consultation process, regulators are prohibited from revealing information that is kept off the register for national security reasons, unless the Secretary of State or relevant Welsh Minister directs otherwise. Commercially confidential information is also not to be published, except where the consultee is a public authority which needs the information to exercise its functions, or if the consultee is a sewerage undertaker into whose sewer a substance may be released.

The Agency is required to publish a statement of its policies for com- **14–027**
plying with its public participation duties. The statement itself will be the product of consultation with affected parties, and must be kept under review. The Agency is also required to act consistently with the statement when consulting about standard permits and certain waste-related matters.

Regulators must maintain for public inspection a register of information about permitted facilities. This duty binds both the Agency and local authority regulators, and the Agency is required to provide the local authority with information (which the latter will keep on its register) about facilities which the Agency regulates but which are in the authority's area. The register can be in any form, including electronic form. There is a detailed list of the information to be recorded on the register. This includes applications for every kind of permit, convictions and cautions for per-mitting offences, requests for further information, all determinations, notices and appeals, as well as representations made to the regulator about a permit. The regulator may exclude representations from the register at the request of the party that made them. If so, the register must state that representations were made which were requested to be kept from the register. Information that is no longer relevant for public participation may be removed from the register, and information about formal cautions must be removed after five years.

Information can be excluded from the register for reasons of national security and commercial confidentiality. In the former case, the Secretary of State or Welsh Minister will direct the regulator to keep specific infor-mation or information of a particular type off the register, and the regulator must then notify the Secretary of State of the specific information excluded as a result of complying with the direction Alternatively, the Secretary or Minister can require a category of information to be referred to it for a

---

[61] Sch.5, Part 1, para.6(1)(a).

decision before it is published on the register. Any person may notify the regulator and the Secretary or Minister that he considers that information should be excluded for reasons of national security. The information then may not be published until a decision has been made to do so.

14–028   The process for keeping confidential information (defined as being "commercially or industrially confidential in relation to any person"[62]) from the register can start in two ways, either with the regulator deciding that information may be confidential, or with an information holder serving the regulator with an objection notice. In the former case, the information holder must respond either by a consent to the information notice, or by an objection notice. The regulator must then make a determination.

An operator's objection will in most cases be the trigger for the process. The guidance states that objections should be made at the time information is submitted to the regulator and should include a justification for each item to be kept confidential. It is suggested that the information should be presented so that it can be easily removed if the request for confidentiality is granted.

Regulators are required to operate a presumption in favour of making information public, and it is clear that restrictions will not be made just because the operator requests it. Commercial prejudice alone will not justify a restriction. An operator must show that the information is commercial or industrial, that "confidentiality is provided by law to protect a legitimate economic interest" and that in all the circumstances the interest in confidentiality outweighs the interest in inclusion on the register.[63] Information to be excluded should be kept to a minimum. In as much as the information relates to emissions, the regulator must keep it on the public register despite its confidentiality.

14–029   The regulator must within 20 working days of an application decide whether to keep information confidential (unless an extension is agreed with the operator). If it decides to publish, the information must still be restricted for a further 15 working days, which is the time limit for an appeal to the Secretary of State or Welsh Minister, after which it must be published absent a notice of appeal. If the regulator fails to decide within the 20 day period, the information subject (usually the applicant) may notify the regulator that it is deemed to have decided in favour of publication. This triggers the appeal process.

An appeal to the Secretary of State or Welsh Minister is as of right and should be by written notice setting out the grounds. The regulator cannot publish the information until the appeal has been decided. The appeal can be by written submissions or by hearing. A hearing can be held in any case, and must be held where the notice of appeal requests it. The regulator is then bound by the decision of the Secretary or Minister, from which there

[62] reg.45.
[63] reg.52(2).

704

is no appeal. Information deemed to be confidential remains so for four years, or a shorter period if agreed. The information subject can notify the regulator if it still objects to the information being published at the end of that period, and the process outlined above then starts again.

Determination of permits, grounds for challenge

Under both the previous permitting regimes and under the new one, there **14–030** has been a procedurally sophisticated mechanism for regulators to follow in making their decisions. Technical considerations are paramount. Objectors have attempted various different challenges, with limited success. According to one study, fewer than 10 per cent of environmental judicial reviews have succeeded in getting the decision overturned.[64] The reason for this is not clear—perhaps a combination of good decision-making by regulators and over-optimism on the part of objectors. However, judicial caution in interfering in technical decisions reached by expert bodies may be a further significant factor.

The challenge brought in *Levy v Environment Agency*[65] was to a variation to an IPC authorisation under the EPA 1990. Among the grounds advanced was that the Agency had failed to ensure that emissions would be minimised by applying BATNEEC and that the Agency had failed to consider whether in light of the cost savings associated with the variation, a more expensive but potentially cleaner technology might be BATNEEC. Silber J rejected all the grounds. He held[66] that the margin of appreciation would be wider than normal: firstly, in cases where the decision-maker was a specialised body entrusted by Parliament to make technical judgments, and secondly where the decision involved a balance of considerations. In those circumstances, the margin would be "substantially greater" than normal. There are similar powers under the new regime as under the IPC regime, and so the same arguments about leaving the Agency a wide margin of discretion would remain available in future challenges

The High Court considered the issue of the extent to which likely compliance with conditions should be considered at the application stage in *R v Secretary of State for the Environment and R.J. Compton ex parte West Wiltshire DC*.[67] In that case, a permit application by Crompton for a piggery and animal rendering business had been refused by the applicant District Council under section 6(4) of the EPA 1990. This states that the enforcing authority shall not grant an application unless it considers that the applicant will be able to carry on the process applied for so as to comply with the conditions of the permit. Compton had a history of operational

---

[64] *Modernising Environmental Justice: Regulation and the Role of an Environmental Tribunal* (London (UCL) 2003).
[65] [2002] EWHC 1663 (Admin).
[66] See paras 76–81 of the judgment.
[67] [1996] Env. L.R. 312.

failures, including poor record keeping and making an unpleasant smell. The Secretary of State had overruled the district council's refusal. The Court held that in so overruling, the Secretary had applied the wrong test. The test was not whether it was *possible in theory* for the operator to comply, but rather whether that particular operator would in fact be *able* to comply, given his history of incompetence. The distinction is between the theoretical and the practical, and the judgment came down firmly in favour of practicality.

14–031   Since the Court in *Levy* was reluctant to interfere with a decision on scientific/technical grounds, it might be thought that a challenge made on procedural grounds would be one which the Court might consider came more naturally within its competence. The House of Lords considered this issue in *R (Edwards) v Environment Agency*.[68] The case concerned a permit granted in August 2003 for a cement works in Rugby. Following a public consultation, the Agency requested further information from the company about the emissions of dust, and did not disclose certain internal reports on air quality to the consultation process. Lindsay J at first instance held that the question of whether there was adequate information provided in an application was one for the regulator, as long as the application was bona fide and did not fall so far short of the requirements as no longer to be truly an application. This could be said to be deference to a technical body of the kind to be expected after *Levy*. However, he further found that although the Agency was not in breach of the requirements of the PPC regulations, there was a breach of the common law duty of fairness. He nonetheless used his discretion to withhold relief. The point was taken before the House of Lords that the regulator had a formal power to request further information, with a corresponding duty to publish the request and its answer. Therefore, it was argued, it would be improper for a regulator to make a decision on the basis of informally obtained, unpublished information, or else the publication requirements could be circumvented. Lord Hoffmann gave the majority judgment and decisively rejected this, stating at paragraph 44 that if the Court imposed a duty requiring the regulator to publish all its internal documents and consult on them, the process would never end. However, Lord Mance dissented on the latter issue, stating at paragraph 80 that the power to request further information was a "last resort", and that a regulator would ordinarily receive information through other, informal channels, which should be published.

By contrast with the *Levy/Edwards*-type challenge, where a concerned resident or similar claimant objects, there are cases in which one operator challenges the grant of a permit to its rival, often for commercial reasons. See for example *R (Rockware Glass Ltd) v Chester CC*.[69] In that case, the Claimant manufacturer of glass brought proceedings to review the grant of

---

[68] [2008] UKHL 22.
[69] [2005] EWHC 2250 (Admin) and, on appeal, [2006] EWCA Civ 992.

a permit to Quinn Glass. The challenge succeeded both at first instance and in the Court of Appeal. It was held that in its consideration of BAT, the local authority regulator had improperly had regard to irrelevant matters, i.e. the emission levels set at other plants. It had therefore failed to consider whether a different design would reduce the emissions of nitrogen oxide and other pollutants, and consequently had set emission limits that were more generous to the operator than they should have been. The permit was quashed, pending the consideration of a new permit.

Applying BAT in practice

There is a wealth of guidance from the Agency and Defra to expand upon   **14–032** the basic Directive principles underpinning BAT. Defra's March 2008 guidance puts into context the determining of BAT for a specific permit application. The process can be summarised: setting out the options; considering the environmental effects of each one; and looking at the economic costs.

The starting point for BAT is likely to be the Agency's sector guidance, and any relevant BREF documents. These should make clear which option will eliminate pollution or best reduce it; and, more broadly, which will have the best overall impact on the environment. The guidance gives the example[70] of the iron and steel industry, in which there might be a choice between traditional blast furnaces and more recent technologies which do not use coke.[71] Depending on the type of operation the subject of the application, there may be a range of technologies or little choice at all.

Having established the range of options, each one's environmental effects must be considered. Annex 4 of the Directive sets out 12 specific factors which constitute a non-exhaustive list of considerations when determining BAT, of which a number directly concern environmental effects. These include low waste technology, recovery and recycling of waste, and the likely emissions from the process. All 12 are to be considered in light of "the likely costs and benefits of a measure and the principles of precaution and prevention". The guidance[72] draws particular attention to:

- The consumption and nature of raw materials, including water. The use of fewer resources is to be preferred. The assessment should consider the specific requirements for raw materials of each option.
- Energy efficiency: this is a part of the BAT assessment in which there may be a tension between minimising emissions and minimising energy consumption. The example given is of pollution abatement

---

[70] March 2008 guidance, para.3.22.
[71] Also see the new regulations, Sch.1, Part 2, section 2.1 (1).
[72] March 2008 guidance, para.3.28.

systems which consume a lot of energy, creating a tension between releases of carbon dioxide and other substances.

- Waste minimisation: the goal is to eliminate waste, failing which to reduce it to the lowest level.
- Accidents: the operation of installations under abnormal conditions is a relevant factor, and how an accidental release would be dealt with.
- Site restoration: it is because of site restoration that permit applicants are required to set out the base-line condition of the proposed site.[73] If a particular technology will improve the chances of restoring the site to its previous condition, for example the placing of pipelines above ground rather than in the ground, then it may be preferred.

The object of this exercise is to create a hierarchy of techniques in terms of their overall effects. In addition to the Annex 4 matters, Article 2(5) states that "emissions" extends to include vibrations, heat and noise released into any environmental medium, in addition to particular substances. There is at Annex 3 a further non-exhaustive list, of substances to be taken into account when setting ELVs. Those relevant to emissions to air are: sulphur dioxide and compounds; nitrogen oxides and compounds; carbon monoxide; volatile organic compounds; metals; dust; asbestos; chlorine; fluorine; arsenic; cyanides; carcinogenic or mutagenic substances; and polychlorinated dibenzodioxins and dibenzofurans.

14–033   Having established a hierarchy of options, the final stage of the process is to consider the economic assessment. This will only affect the ranking if the technology with the minimal environmental impact is unavailable for economic reasons. Other than this, the guidance is clear that "the lack of profitability of a particular business should not affect the assessment [of BAT]". An operator's lack of resources would not justify lower standards any more than significant financial resources would support higher ones. It was said for the claimant in *Levy* that cost savings arising from a change in technology would make possible a suggested BATNEEC involving an expensive abatement technique that used "sulphur scrubbers". Silber J noted that the limits for sulphur dioxide emissions were in any case being retained in the permit and that, at a cost of £5–6 million, the challenger's suggested additional abatement technique was excessively expensive.

The final decision on BAT should be made having regard to the site itself and the relevant local factors.[74] These include the existing land use; the site's natural resources; the sensitivity of local environmental receptors; and the absorption capacity of the natural environment. These may in exceptional circumstances justify not meeting the indicative guidance on BAT.

---

[73] art.6(1) (d) of the Directive.
[74] March 2008 guidance, para.3.40.

Changes to permits: review, transfer and surrender of environmental permits

On these matters there is a big change between the old PPC regulations **14–034** and the new EP regulations in the provisions requiring regulators to review environmental permits, but substantial continuity otherwise. Under regulation 15 of the old rules, regulators were required to review conditions "periodically", and had a discretion to review at any time. A body of technical guidance was produced on the frequency of review. For example, industry sectors which had been subject to IPC or waste management licensing were to be reviewed every six years, whereas the period was four years for others such as food and farming. The old regulation 15(2) also required reviews in certain prescribed situations—where the pollution caused was so significant that the permit needed emission limit values to be added, or existing ones needed to be revised; where there were substantial changes in BAT; or where operational safety required other techniques. Mandatory review on grounds of pollution or safety would most likely be triggered by a specific, "one-off" incident, whereas review for reasons of BAT would more properly be part of the regulator's continuing role. The new review provision, Regulation 34, makes the striking change of removing the three mandatory grounds of review, and simply states that regulators must "periodically review" permits. The same word periodically is used in both the old and the new provisions, and it would appear that the frequency of review will continue as before. The Regulation 34(1) duty to review is coupled with the duty to inspect under 34(2).

The new rules governing transfers of permits (Regulation 21, and Part 1 of Schedule 5) remain substantially as they were under the old system (Regulation 18). As previously, applications to transfer must be made jointly by the operator and the proposed transferee. Partial transfer continues to be possible, with a requirement that applications for partial transfer identify the part to be retained by the operator. The two month deadline for the regulator to determine the transfer application is the same as before. As under the old regime, regulators may only vary the conditions on transfer for reasons arising out of that transfer. The grounds for refusal remain two-fold. A transfer application may only be refused if the regulator is not satisfied that the transferee will be the operator of the facility, or else is not satisfied that the transferee will operate in accordance with the permit conditions. There will be consultation if the transfer involves "substantial change", or, more generally, if the regulator considers that consultation should be carried out.[75]

Under the old rules, there were two systems for applications to surrender permits—an easier regime for Part B installations and mobile plant, and a more onerous one for Part A installations and mobile plant. In both cases it

---

[75] para.5 of Sch.5.

was possible to make a total or a partial surrender. Under PPC Regulation 20 for Part B facilities, the operator simply notified the regulator, in the approved form and with certain specified information, of the surrender (or partial surrender). The surrender would take effect on a date not less than 28 days from the date when the regulator was notified. It was thus a straightforward administrative process. The alternative was Regulation 19, for Part A installations and mobile plant. For a surrender application to be accepted, the regulator had to be satisfied that appropriate steps had been taken to avoid pollution risk from the installation and to return the site to a satisfactory state. The regulator could request further information, subject to which there was a three month deadline for decisions. The operator had six months in which to appeal.

14–035   The new rules are set out in Regulations 24 and 25, and Part 1 of Schedule 5. The structure is retained, of administrative surrender for less serious, Part B installations and regulator sanctioned surrender for more serious, Part A installations. The test for approving Part A applications is the same as previously, pollution risk and return of the site to a satisfactory state. The principal change is that the administrative regime has been extended to include all mobile plant, thereby removing Part A mobile plant from the more onerous regime.

The rules on variations to permit conditions are set out in Regulation 20 and Part 1 of Schedule 5 to the EP regulations. The regulator may decide to vary conditions because of a review[76] or notification,[77] or as an enforcement measure if the existing conditions were insufficient to ensure compliance with the aims of Regulations 11 and 12. Having made the decision to vary, the regulator serves a variation notice setting out the conditions[78] and the fees payable.[79] If an operator wished to vary its permit conditions, it was obliged to use an application for variation form, setting out the proposed change and the prescribed information,[80] and including a site map if additional land was to be included on top of the existing area.[81] If the application involved a "substantial change" in the operation of the regulated facility, the regulator was obliged to perform a statutory consultation.[82] The regulator had a discretion to do so even where no substantial change was involved, but it nonetheless determined to consult anyway.[83] The regulator would notify the operator and the statutory consultees within 14 days[84] (not including the time from the service of a

---

[76] reg.15.
[77] reg.13 or 16.
[78] reg.17(5).
[79] reg.17(6).
[80] Sch.7, Part 1, para.1.
[81] Sch.7, Part 1, para.2.
[82] Sch.7, Part 2, para.4(1).
[83] Sch.7, Part 2, para.4(2).
[84] Sch.7, Part 2, para.4(6)(a).

request for further information until it was answered[85]). Subject to national security and commercial confidentiality (Regulations 30 and 31), there was a duty to advertise the variation in the prescribed manner and with the necessary information.[86] There was a 28 day period for representations.[87] The regulator was obliged to consider the representations,[88] and any relevant environmental impact assessments.

Revocation

Regulators' powers to revoke permits are continued in the new regime, with much staying the same. The rules are set out in Regulation 21 of the old regime, and 22–23 of the new. There is the same wide discretion to revoke as before. Without prejudice to the regulator's discretion to revoke, the old Regulation 21(2) gave two examples of situations where the regulator might serve a revocation notice—where the operator of a waste management facility was no longer a fit and proper person, and where the permit holder had ceased to be the operator of a facility. These examples are dispensed with. The power of partial revocation is retained. As before, revocation notices must state: the date on which the revocation takes effect (not less than 20 working days from the service of the notice); in the case of partial revocations, the notice must state the extent of the revocation and any variations. What is new is an explicit requirement for the regulator to give reasons, albeit that this was sometimes done anyway. There is a new power in case of a partial revocation to issue a consolidated permit. The post-revocation remedial powers are substantially the same as before—the question for the regulator to consider is whether, in the case of a part A installation or mobile plant, it is necessary for the operator to act to avoid a pollution risk, or to return the site to a satisfactory state. If the permit had conditions requiring these actions, then the notice should state that the permit remains in force, to the extent necessary for those acts to be performed. Similarly if the acts are not in the permit, the revocation notice should set them out, and they become conditions for compliance and enforcement purposes.

14–036

The regulator's powers to revoke remain much the same as before. The requirement to give reasons is perhaps the single biggest addition, although it remains to be seen how much practical effect it will have. It is expected that revocation will continue to be a measure of last resort. The Environment Agency has previously indicated that it would only be used where other enforcement measures had failed, and the operator was unable to operate in accordance with the conditions.

---

[85] Sch.7, Part 2, para.4(7).
[86] Sch.7, Part 2, para.4(8) and (9).
[87] Sch.7, Part 2, para.4(12).
[88] Sch.7, Part 2, para.4(11).

Standard rules

14–037 One of the most significant innovations of the new rules is the regime for standard rules (SRs) for environmental permits. The new type of permits would have just one condition, which would be to keep to the standard rules for that type of facility. They will replace site specific permit conditions. The Agency has made it clear that it hopes for significant benefits from this new system—it is expected to be cheaper, easier and quicker. Standard permits will have lower application fees, and will be "outcome-focussed", i.e. the standard for the site is set by the conditions, and the operator is then left to find its own method of meeting that standard. However, SRs "must achieve the same high level of environmental protection as site-specific conditions".[89]

The SRs will be available online, and it is hoped that this will eliminate the need for a pre-application meeting with the regulator, and reduce the associated paperwork. They follow the trend discussed elsewhere in this chapter of changing the level of public participation by diminishing the site-specific consultation. The SR regime is voluntary—where SRs exist, the operator may request that a term is included in its permit that the relevant SRs are conditions of that permit.[90] Because the regime is voluntary, there is no appeal in relation to an SR.[91]

The guidance states that SRs are expected to be suitable for sectors where there are several facilities whose hazard characteristics are similar. They may well also be useful to large individual operators with multiple plants of the same type—a single permit can authorise multiple standard facilities under a single operator.[92] If the permit application process can be replicated or reduced to a single application, it will ease the regulatory burden substantially. When the EP regulations came into force in April 2008, there had been consultation on SRs for no less than 28 separate activities that require a permit, from metal recycling to clinical waste to animal incineration.

14–038 The regulator has an obligation to consult those it considers are likely to be affected by the facilities, and those who are representative of the communities likely to affected.[93] The guidance anticipates that this will be a wide consultation, including statutory bodies and industry, and in substance the consultation should take into account the standards of all such facilities. The duty to consult is subject to a de minimis exemption for "minor administrative changes".[94] The regulator has a duty to review SRs

---

[89] Core Guidance 7.3.
[90] reg.27(2).
[91] reg.27(3).
[92] reg.17(d).
[93] reg.26(2)(a) and (b).
[94] reg.26(3).

and when necessary revise them,[95] and to publish all SRs on its website.[96]

If the regulator proposes to revise a particular type of SRs, it has a duty to notify operators holding a relevant permit of the proposed revisions and the date when they will have effect, which must be not less than three months after the notification, and that on the date the revisions take effect the operator's permit will be changed accordingly.[97] Operators should not be caught out by the notification, as the regulator must consult those who "are likely to be affected by or have an interest in"[98] the revision. The regulator has a similar power to revoke SRs, subject to the duty to consult.[99] If the regulator does revoke a set of SRs, the revoked rules continue to apply after the revocation, but as soon as is reasonably practicable the regulator will include in the affected permit(s) the alternative conditions it considers appropriate.[100]

The move from site-specific consultation to generic, national consultation may, it is expected, mean less consultation and fewer objections. The cases indicate that it is often informal, local lobby groups who are the keenest objectors. This should of course be balanced against the fact that facilities under the SR regime will intrinsically be the less controversial ones, where objections should be rare. For example, the guidance anticipates that facilities requiring a site-specific risk assessment will be unsuitable for SRs.[101]

The SR regime is striking for its brevity—it is set out in five fairly concise regulations, whereas the EP Regulations consist in total of seven parts comprising 74 Regulations, with some 23 Schedules. In this context, five Regulations might be thought of as short. The guidance puts some flesh on the bones, but it is still limited given the potentially substantial effect on operators' daily working practices—for example, there is no statutory provision to explain when SRs are appropriate, or to what type of installation. **14–039**

Enforcement

As regards the regulators' enforcement powers there is substantial continuity, although there are a number of fairly minor alterations and one or two significant innovations. The overall structure of the provisions remains much as it was before. The regulator can in certain circumstances serve enforcement and suspension notices on operators.[102] In the former case, this power arises where the regulator thinks an operator has, will or is likely **14–040**

---

[95] reg.26(4).
[96] reg.26(5).
[97] reg.28(2).
[98] reg.26(2)(b).
[99] reg.29.
[100] reg.30.
[101] Core Guidance 7.11.
[102] reg.36 and 37.

to contravene a permit condition. The notice must set out the contravention, the remedial steps and the period in which they are to be complied with. The steps may be to make a facility compliant or to rectify damage already caused. In the case of suspension notices, the structure likewise remains much the same as before—the power is subject to a qualifying test, the notice must specify the pollution risk, the remedial steps and the deadline in which to take them. It must also state the extent to which the permit is suspended. However, the qualifying test has been modified. Under the old Regulation 25(1), the regulator had to be satisfied that the facility was being operated in a way that caused an "imminent" risk of serious pollution. If so, the regulator was obliged, subject to a separate power to act to prevent or reduce the pollution, to serve the notice. The new regulation 37 no longer requires the risk to be imminent, and it replaces the obligation to act ("shall") with a power to do so ("may"). Problems with the term imminent include the possibility of gradual pollution which does not pose sufficient risk of the right type to trigger the notice, and the situation where a regulator has perhaps not acted quickly enough, and there is pollution that is continuing and serious without being imminent.

There is a range of different offences, divided into more and less serious categories and with two sentencing scales. The regulator can seek further enforcement remedies from the High Court where prosecution for failure to comply with a notice has not provided an "effectual remedy". Offences by bodies corporate are provided for, and there are specific rules relating to admissibility of record evidence. There is a new offence of knowingly causing or permitting a regulated facility to be operated without a permit.[103] The offence of failing to notify the regulator of a proposed change has been removed.[104]

The more serious offences are: breaching the obligation to operate under and as authorised by a permit; failing to comply with a condition; and failure to comply with a notice. For these, the maximum sentences are (on summary conviction) a fine of £50,000, 12 months imprisonment, or both, or (on conviction on indictment) an unlimited fine and/or five years imprisonment. The Court of Appeal recently considered the sentencing approach to be taken for an offence contrary to the old regulations in *R v Cemex Cement Ltd.*[105] In that case, the appellant cement manufacturer had failed to comply with a condition to maintain its plant. A kiln door was hanging off its hinges, which allowed cement dust to escape. This emission was potentially harmful to health (although no-one was in fact injured). The Court deemed the eye-catching fine of £400,000 "manifestly excessive", and replaced it with one of £50,000. In doing so, it reiterated its

---

[103] reg.38(1)(a).
[104] Old reg.32(1)(i).
[105] [2007] EWCA Crim 1759, (2008) Env. L.R. 6.

support for the principles stated in *R v F Howe and Son (Engineers) Ltd*,[106] a health and safety prosecution. These principles were applied to environmental crime in *Environment Agency v Milford Haven Port Authority*.[107] Under them, the main aggravating factors are, firstly, failing to heed warnings and, secondly, profiting from the unlawful action. Mitigating factors are prompt admission of guilt and timely plea, acting to remedy the problem, and a good safety record.

A significant development is the introduction of the defence of acts done in an emergency.[108] It only operates against the three more serious offences contrary to Regulation 38(1), namely (a) operating without a permit, (b) contravening a condition and (c) non-compliance with a notice. The operator's defence is narrowly drafted—it must show that all reasonably practicable steps were taken to reduce pollution, and that the regulator was informed as soon as reasonably practicable. There are similarities to the mitigating factors set out above. As this is a common form of best practice in many sectors, it seems likely that the defence will be widely relied on.   **14–041**

Appeals

The rules governing appeals against a regulator's decision are contained in Regulation 31 and Schedule 6 of the EP Regulations. Appeals lie to the "appropriate authority", i.e. the relevant Secretary of State or Welsh Minister, as the case may be. The original regulator must be notified of the appeal at the same time as the appropriate authority. An applicant can appeal against the refusal of its application for the grant, variation, transfer or surrender of a permit. Similarly, a person who is "aggrieved" may appeal against a condition imposed on a permit grant, variation, transfer or surrender. It is also possible to appeal against: a deemed withdrawal of an application following failure to answer a request for further information; a decision not to authorise closure under Article 13 of the Landfill Directive; notices of revocation, enforcement, suspension or landfill closure (except where the notice is served for failure to pay a charge); and confidentiality decisions, i.e. to include information on the public register. In certain cases, there is no appeal—where the appropriate authority gives a direction to a regulator, against the appropriate authority's decision to refer a particular application to itself, or against the direction subsequently given to the regulator.   **14–042**

The form and content required in appeals is specified in Schedule 6, as are the time limits. The standard period is six months from the relevant decision, except for appeals against revocation notices, in which case the appeal must be submitted before the notice takes effect; for confidentiality

---

[106] [1999] 2 All E.R. 249.
[107] [1999] 1 Lloyd's Rep 673.
[108] reg.40.

determinations and for deemed withdrawals following failure to answer a request for further information, where the limit is 15 working days from the regulator's notice; and variation, suspension, enforcement and landfill closure notices, where it is two months from the notice. The appropriate authority has a discretion to extend time, but the Core Guidance states that this will only be exercised "in the most compelling circumstances".[109]

All decisions have effect pending appeal, with the exception of revocations, which do not come into effect until final determination or withdrawal of the appeal. Within 10 days of receiving the notice of appeal, the regulator must notify those who have an interest in or are likely to be affected by the appeal. The notified persons may make representations to the appropriate authority within 15 days of this notification.

14–043   The appropriate authority may appoint another person to administer appeals. This will normally be the Planning Inspectorate. Appeals will be dealt with on paper, unless the appellant or the regulator requests a hearing, or the appropriate authority determines that there should be one. Whether conducted orally or on paper, appeals will be "in the spirit of the rules and regulations for planning appeals."[110] Those entitled to be heard are the appellant, the regulator and any party which has made representations following notification from the regulator. There is a discretion to permit others to be heard, which is not to be unreasonably withheld. An appeal may be dismissed or upheld, in whole or in part. A notice may be upheld, quashed or varied, and directions may be given to a regulator about what permit conditions are to be imposed. Each party will normally bear its own costs. However, there is a discretion to award hearing costs where a party has acted unreasonably. Decisions on appeal can be challenged by judicial review.

Proposals for reform—Industrial Emissions Directive; enlargement of scope of environmental permitting regulations

14–044   Member states were required to implement the Integrated Pollution Prevention and Control Directive (the IPPC Directive) in full across all sectors by not later than October 30, 2007. On that date, the Commission published a document entitled "Questions and Answers on Implementation of the IPPC Directive". It noted[111] that full implementation meant not just that the relevant authorities had issued permits by that date, but also that operators were complying with them. Although there had been significant levels of implementation, by the middle of 2006 only 50 per cent of installations were permitted, out of a total of more than 52,000 installa-

---

[109] Core Guidance 12.2.
[110] Core Guidance 12.12.
[111] At para.3.

tions. This state of affairs was "unacceptable". It was also noted that a substantial proportion of emissions of the most dangerous substances listed in Annex 3 were produced by the small number of very large industrial installations. For example, 83 per cent of sulphur dioxide emissions came from just a small number of operators. The targets for emissions reduction by 2020 set in the Thematic Strategy on Air Pollution would not be met. The Commission reviewed the data submitted in light of these short-comings. It concluded that notwithstanding the problems, the permitting system and integrated approach remained the best option. However, the review had found a number of issues requiring attention. These were that BAT had not been fully implemented; environmental protection and innovation was hindered by limited enforcement; the legal framework was complex and not wholly coherent, which caused administrative burdens; the Directive had insufficient scope; and flexible tools like emissions trading systems were constrained. Commission plans for improvement were fivefold—ensuring full transposition of the legislation; supporting member states in their implementation; enhanced monitoring of permits; improved data collection for BAT review; and seeking to reduce the administrative burden.

Reform of the IPPC Directive will be achieved through the proposed Industrial Emissions Directive. The Commission issued a document on December 21, 2007, setting out its proposals. The seven existing Directives on industrial emissions[112] will be merged into a single Directive. It is suggested that this will reduce the bureaucratic burden and enhance clarity. BAT will be clarified in the new Directive, and limits will be imposed on the circumstances in which conditions can require technology less good than BAT. These will have to be justified. The position of BREFs will be strengthened within the new Directive. The minimum ELVs for large combustion plants will be tightened. The proposal will also require more of regulators by way of inspection, review and enforcement.

Closer to home, as a domestic initiative, it is intended that the permitting regime will expand so that other polluting activities are regulated by EPs. Defra has drawn up plans so that the regime will include other regulated activities, such as discharge consents, groundwater authorisations, water abstraction, radioactive substances, and waste carriage and brokering. The regime may be further extended to include other emissions to air. However, pending that extension, there are other separate regulations governing other types of polluting activity considered elsewhere in this work.

In addition to these separate regimes which may in due course be   **14–045**

---

[112] The three titanium dioxide directives culminating in Council Directive 92/112/EEC of December 15, 1992, [1992] OJ L409/11, as well as (iv) the IPPC Directive, (v), Council Directive 1999/13/EC of March 11, 1999 (Solvent Emissions Directive), [1999] OJ L85/1, (vi) Directive 2000/76/EC of December 4, 2000 on the incineration of waste, OJ L332, 28.12.2000, p.91, and (vii) Directive 2001/80/EC of October 23, 2001 (large combustion plants) [2000] OJ L309/1.

brought within the EP system, there are other polluting activities which are likely to remain outside the scheme. Not all types of polluting activity can readily be regulated by EPs. Some are conceptually and/or technically different, so that a permit would be an inappropriate tool for control. For example, emissions from cars and aeroplanes have a significant effect on air quality, but a permit of the type designed for a cement works would not be appropriate. The third runway at Heathrow airport will necessarily affect air quality in West London, but its regulation cannot be implemented by a traditional environmental permit.

The remainder of this chapter will consider the forms of air pollution control set out in the schedules to the EP regulations and in other legislation, which will come within the EP system. It will also survey these other regimes, such as the Auto Oil Programme, which will remain outside the EP system.

Other Emissions to be Regulated through the EP System

Solvent Emissions Directive (SED) installations

14-046 Schedule 14 of the EP Regulations applies to every SED installation as defined by the Solvent Emissions Directive.[113] Schedule 14 of the Regulations imposes an obligation on the regulator,[114] to exercise his "relevant functions" so as to comply with the Solvent Emissions Directive.[115] The "relevant functions" include the grant and refusal of permits, setting conditions within those permits and securing compliance with such permits. This means that the regulator has to deal with situations where: (i) there is a substantial change to the installation pursuant to Article 4(4), (ii) permit conditions must have regard to the emissions and reduction scheme in accordance with the permitting part of Article 5, (iii) permit condition must have regard to European Guidance pursuant to Article 7(2), (iv) where monitoring is required pursuant to Article 8(1) to 8(4) (v) compliance is needed in accordance with Article 9, and (vi) where non-compliance must be dealt with pursuant to Article 10.

Article 4(4) of Schedule 14 to the Regulations is concerned with a substantial change to an existing SED installation. It also applies where the SED installation falls within the ambit of the Directive for the first time. If, as a result of the substantial change, the Solvent Emissions Directive

---

[113] Council Directive 1999/13/EC on the limitation of emissions of volatile organic compounds due to the use of organic solvents in certain activities and installations. [1999] OJ L85/1, as last amended by Directive 2004/42/EC [2004] OJ L240/24. There are two relevant corrigenda, [1999] OJ L188/54 and [1999] OJ L240/24.

[114] That is either the local authority or the Environment Agency, depending on the nature of the SED installation.

[115] para.3(1) of Sch.14 to the Regulations.

applies, then the installation must comply with the requirements of the Solvent Emissions Directive. Interestingly, the same installation could also fall within the ambit of the IPPC Directive at the same time and so must also comply with the requirements of the IPPC Directive.

Article 5 of Schedule 14 to the EP Regulations is concerned with the Member State's scheme to reduce emissions. The regulator must impose conditions on the face of the permit in order to secure compliance with Article 5 of the Directive (save in so far as it relates to reporting requirements). In order to meet the volatile organic compounds (VOC) emission requirements there are two options: either meeting the VOC limit values and fugitive limit values and continuously or annually submitting monitoring reports, or using a solvent reduction approach to achieve the equivalent of meeting a mass emission limit. Member States must now specify the operating conditions on the face of the permit itself. Member States can no longer make "general binding rules"[116] covering permits. Instead each installation should have its own bespoke conditions, rather than an off the peg set of general rules. In practice, substantially the same conditions are likely to appear repeatedly on individual permits. The regulator must also have regard pursuant to Article 7(2) to the Commission guidance on the least harmful substances and techniques.

The regulator must also set out as a condition of the permit the monitoring requirements for the installation, pursuant to Articles 8(1) to 8(4). The regulator may require an annual monitoring report, but in cases where it is necessary to demonstrate compliance ith VOC emission limits, or where the average emission following abatement exceeds 10kg/h of total organic carbon, then continuous monitoring will be required. **14–047**

Compliance with the requirements of the Solvent Emissions Directive pursuant to Article 9 should be proved to the regulator, who will ensure compliance through the permit conditions. At the very least the permit conditions will require monitoring reports to be provided to the regulator regularly and for the regulator to be notified immediately where there are excessive emissions which are dangerous. In the case of non-compliance, the regulator must suspend the activity where there is an immediate danger to human health, and may suspend the activity even if there is no such risk. The terms in the Regulations must be interpreted consistently with the Solvent Emissions Directive.[117] Finally,[118] the demands of the Solvents Emissions Directive are no longer satisfied merely because "the accrual solvent emission ... plan is less than or equal to the target emission." Schedule 14 of the EP Regulations puts considerable power and responsibility into the hands of the regulator.

---

[116] This phrase is to be given the same meaning as in Article 9 of the IPPC Directive.
[117] See section 2(2) of Schedule 14 to the Regulations.
[118] Point 1 of Annex IIB of the Solvent Emissions Directive as amended.

Large combustion plants

14–048   Since 2001 the Large Combustion Plant Directive[119] aimed to reduce acidification, ground level ozone and dust throughout Europe by controlling emissions of sulphur dioxide, nitrogen oxides and particulate matter from large combustion plants in power stations, petroleum refineries, steelworks and other refineries running on solid, liquid or gaseous fuel. While every new combustion plant was obliged to meet the emission limit values in the Large Combustion Plant Directive, existing combustion plants which had been in operation before 1987 could opt either to comply with the emission limit values for sulphur dioxide, nitrogen oxides and particulate matter, or to operate within a National Emissions Reduction Plan (NERP) which would set an annual level of emissions.[120]

However, in addition, Article 4(4) of the Large Combustion Plants Directive provided an opt out from the obligations under the Directive: operators of existing plants could be exempted from compliance with ELV or a NERP if they made a written declaration by June 30, 2004, to the competent authority not to operate the plant for more than 20,000 operational hours starting from January 1, 2008, and ending no later than December 31, 2015. It follows that the Large Combustion Plants Directive required energy companies either to install flue gas desulphurisation equipment to remove sulphur dioxide and nitrous oxide, or to opt out from this obligation and run for up to a further 20,000 hours between January 2008 and December 31, 2015, before closing down. It was a hard choice. In the UK it prompted concerns about the security of energy supply as the Directive particularly affects coal fired power stations, which make up about a third of the UK's electricity generation.

Against that background Schedule 15 of the EP Regulations[121] was adopted. It applies to all large combustion plants.[122] Unsurprisingly, the terms in the EP Regulations have the same meaning as in the Large Combustion Plants Directive. Schedule 15 of the Regulations effects a number of significant changes. First, the national emissions reduction plan is identified[123] as the emission plan published pursuant to the Large Combustion Plants (National Emission Reduction Plan) Regulations

---

[119] 2001/80, [2001] OJ L309.
[120] These annual limits are calculated by applying the emission limit values approach to existing plants, on the basis of those plants average actual operating hours, fuel used and thermal input over five years.
[121] Regulation 35(i).
[122] As defined by the Large Combustion Plants Directive 2001/80/EC, [2001] OJ L309. See Corrigendum published in [2002] OJ L319.
[123] Section 2(2)(c) of Schedule 15 defines the national emission reduction plan referred to in Article 4(6) of the Large Combustion Plants Directive as the emission plan, as amended from time to time, published under regulation 4(1) of the Large Combustion Plants (National Emission Reduction Plan) Regulations 2007. SI 2007/2325.

2007. Secondly, the Large Combustion Plants Directive is interpreted[124] so that even if plants fulfil the conditions of its operating permit, nevertheless the plants must be included in the NERP, which had not previously been the case. The regulator must ensure compliance with particular obligations under the Large Combustion Plants Directive, namely:

(i) Article 4(1), (2) and (4) which is concerned with constructing plants and limiting emissions;

(ii) Article 5(1) which deals with sulphur dioxide emissions;

(iii) Article 6 which covers the development of new plant;

(iv) Article 7 which addresses the malfunction or breakdown of equipment;

(v) Article 8 which concerns emissions limits for multi firing units;

(vi) Article 9 which addresses the discharge of waste gases by combustion plants;

(vii) Article 10 which deals with Emission Limit Values for extended combustion plants;

(viii) Article 12 which covers monitoring;

(ix) Article 13 which requires the communication of information about measurements; and

(x) Articles 14(1), 14(2) and 14(4) which concern the conditions for compliance with ELVs.

Where an existing plant elects to comply with ELVs and is included in the NERP,[125] the regulator must immediately alert the appropriate authority to any suspension[126] or derogation[127] resulting from a malfunction or breakdown of equipment. Further the regulator must immediately alert the appropriate authority if it considers a judgment needs to be made as to whether there is an overriding need to maintain energy supplies.[128] If the competent authority decides whether or not there is an overriding need to maintain energy supplies, the regulator must ensure compliance with that decision. Future legislation in relation to small combustion plants is anticipated, perhaps by expanding the ambit of the IPPC Directive to combustion sources below 50MWh. Emissions from small combustion plants are not currently regulated at Community level.

---

[124] See s.2(2)(g) of Schedule 15, which requires the words "and from their inclusion in the national emission reduction plan" in Article 4(4) of the Large Combustion Plants Directive to be ignored.

[125] To the extent that compliance with Article 4(3)(b) of the Large Combustion Plants Directive is not ensured by the Large Combustion Plants (National Emission Reduction Plan) Regulations 2007.

[126] Under Article 7(2) of the Large Combustion Plants Directive.

[127] Under Article 7(3) of the Large Combustion Plants Directive.

[128] See Article 7(1) or 7(3) of the Large Combustion Plants Directive.

Asbestos

14–049 Asbestos has for many years been known as a dangerous group of sub-stances liable to cause respiratory illnesses and death unless strictly regu-lated, and the Community's intervention came as long ago as 1987. Schedule 16 of the EP Regulations[129] applies to all regulated facilities within the meaning of the Asbestos Directive[130] and terms in both Sche-dule 16 and the Directive are interpreted consistently. The regulator must ensure compliance with specified provisions of the Asbestos Directive.[131] Schedule 16 imposes an obligation to measure emissions into the air and discharges of aqueous effluent from facilities subject to ELVs every six months.

Titanium Dioxide

14–050 Schedule 17 of the EP Regulations[132] applies to every regulated facility which carries out the chlorine process or the sulphate process,[133] for example, the processes in making paint. The terms in Schedule 17 and the Titanium Dioxide Directive are interpreted consistently and the regulator must ensure compliance with specific provisions of the Titanium Dioxide Directive.[134]

Petrol vapour recovery

14–051 It is thought that the imminent petrol vapour recovery regime will cut petrol station pollution by 85 per cent in the United Kingdom. Defra considered that petrol stations selling more than 3.5 million litres of petrol per annum will prevent 16,000 tonnes a year of petrol fumes from entering the atmosphere. Petrol stations have until January 1, 2010 to install vapour capture equipment. The terms in Schedule 18 of Environmental Permit-

---

[129] reg.35(k).

[130] Council Directive 87/217/EEC on the prevention and reduction of environmental pollu-tion by asbestos. [1987] OJ L85/40, as last amended by Council Regulation (EC) No. 807/2003 ([2003] OJ L122/36).

[131] Namely Article 3; Article 4(1); Article 5; Article 6(1) and 6(2) and Article 8.

[132] reg.35(j).

[133] Section 1 of Schedule 17: "chlorine process" and "sulphate process" have the same meanings as they have in Article 2 of the Titanium Dioxide Directive, that is, Council Directive 92/112/EEC on procedures for harmonizing the programmes for the reduction and eventual elimination of pollution caused by waste from the titanium dioxide industry: [1992] OJ L409/11.

[134] Namely Article 4; Article 6; Article 9; Article 10 and Article 11 of the Directive.

ting (England and Wales) Regulations 2007[135] and the Petrol Vapour Recovery Directive[136] and interpreted consistently and the regulator must ensure compliance with specific provisions of the Directive.[137] The Volatile Organic Compounds (VOC) from fuel significantly contribute to ground level ozone. Schedule 18 allows the UK to derogate from the requirement to paint tanks which reflect 70 per cent of total radiant heat in "special landscape areas" including the Broads, the New Forest and any National Park or Area of Outstanding Natural Beauty.[138] Further, in interpreting the Vapour Recovery Directive for the purpose of exercising his functions, the regulator can ignore the part of the Directive[139] regarding loading conditions and overfill detection control units.[140]

Ambient Air Quality

Air pollution results from substances being emitted into the atmosphere which, either alone or through chemical reaction, can damage human health and/or the environment. Air pollution is both a local and a transboundary problem: emissions from one country can travel large distances in the atmosphere and cause adverse effects in other countries. The pollutants which cause most damage are nitrogen oxides (NOx), sulphur dioxide (SO_2), ammonia (NH_3), ground level ozone and airborne fine dust, known as particulate matter (PM). It is thought that ground-level ozone and particulate matter are the most dangerous to human health. Fine dust can be emitted directly to the air (primary particles) or can be formed in the atmosphere by gases such as sulphur dioxide, nitrogen oxides and ammonia. Ozone is not emitted directly but forms by volatile organic compounds (VOCs) reacting with nitrogen oxides in sunshine. Air pollution harms humans. Its effect ranges from minor problems with the

14–052

---

[135] reg.35(l). Schedule 18 applies to every activity within sub-paragraphs (c) and (d) of Part B of Section 1.2 of Chapter 1 of Part 2 of Schedule 1.

[136] European Parliament and Council Directive 94/63/EC on the control of volatile organic compound (VOC) emissions resulting from the storage of petrol and its distribution from terminals to service stations OJ L 365, 31.12.1994, p.24, as amended by Regulation (EC) No. 1882/2003 (OJ L 284, 31.10.2003, p.1. This was implemented into UK legislation by SI 1996/2678: The Environmental Protection (Prescribed Processes and Substances Etc.) (Amendment) (Petrol Vapour Recovery) Regulations 1996; SI 1996/2095: The Carriage of Dangerous Goods by Road Regulations 1996; SI 1996/2089: The Carriage of Dangerous Goods by Rail Regulations 1996; The Petrol Vapour Recovery (Stage 1) (Local Enforcing Authorities) Direction and Notice 1996; SI : The Petrol Vapour Recovery (Stage 1) (Environment Agency) Direction and Notice 1996; SI 1994/670: The Carriage of Dangerous Goods by Rail Regulations 1994; SI 1992/743: The Road Traffic (Carriage of Dangerous Substances in Road Tankers and Tank Containers) Regulations 1992.

[137] Namely Article 3(1), first paragraph; Article 4(1), first and last paragraphs, Article 4(3) and Article 6(1), first paragraph.

[138] Point 1 of Annex I of the Directive.

[139] Namely points 2.3, 3.2 and 3.5 of Annex IV.

[140] s.3(2)(b) of Schedule 18 of Environmental Permitting (England and Wales) Regulations 2007.

respiratory system to reduced lung function, asthma, chronic bronchitis and reduced life expectancy. Forests, rivers lakes and buildings can also be damaged through acidification, i.e. acid deposits caused by emissions of SO_2, NOx and ammonia. Air pollution damage also occurs through eutrophication: an excess input of nitrogen oxides and ammonia disturbs the structure and function of land-based and aquatic ecosystems which may lead to a loss of biodiversity and to nitrogen leaching into water courses land and aquatic ecosystems.

The EU is keen to prevent the deterioration of ambient air quality and to improve it. It does this in three ways. First, through limiting pollutants by legislation, namely The Air Quality Framework Directive[141] and its four daughter Directives: (1) Directive 1999/30/EC relating to limit values for sulphur dioxide, nitrogen dioxide and oxides of nitrogen, particulate matter and lead in ambient air;[142] (2) Directive 2000/69/EC relating to limit values for benzene and carbon monoxide in ambient air;[143] (3) Directive 2002/3/EC relating to ozone in ambient air;[144] and (4) Directive 2004/107/EC relating to arsenic, cadmium, mercury, nickel and polycyclic aromatic hydrocarbons in ambient air.[145] These directives set concentration limit values or target values for a range of air pollutants and require the pollutants to be monitored. If the target values are exceeded Member States must set up, implement and report on abatement plans. The Air Quality Framework Directive and daughter Directives have evolved over time in response to emerging scientific knowledge. Some limit values are already in force, but others will only come into effect in 2010.

Secondly, air quality is protected and improved by national emissions ceilings. The National Emission Ceilings Directive[146] sets national emission ceilings for sulphur dioxide, nitrogen oxides, ammonia and volatile organic compounds which must be achieved by 2010 through EU and national measures. The ceilings are reviewed periodically.

14–053　　Thirdly, the threats to air quality are tackled according to their source. There are sectoral emission laws which are aimed at emissions from different sources for example vehicles and non-road machinery, large combustion plants and industrial processes (the IPPC Directive), the use of solvents and solvent-containing products and the sulphur content of liquid fuels.

---

[141] Council Directive 96/62/EC on ambient air quality assessment and management, [1996] OJ L296.

[142] [1999] OJ L163/41. This Directive is substantially repealed from 11.06.2010.

[143] [2000] OJ L313/12. This Directive is substantially repealed from 11.06.2010.

[144] [2002] OJ L67/14. This Directive is substantially repealed from 11.06.2010.

[145] [2005] OJ L23/3.

[146] Directive 2001/81/EC on national emission ceilings for certain atmospheric pollutants, [2001] OJ L309.

Air quality framework directive

On November 21, 1996 the Ambient Air Directive[147] was adopted. In an   **14–054**
attempt to identify areas requiring action it directed that the ambient air
quality in the Member States should be assessed according to common
criteria. The assessments should be collated and published. The aim was to
maintain good air quality; and to improve poor air quality. In order to
assess air quality effectively a list of atmospheric pollutants was identified
and annexed to the Directive and guidance was provided for scrutinising
particular air pollutants and identifying the information necessary for
programmes to improve air quality.[148] A five year period of reciprocal
exchange of information from monitoring stations in the Member States
ensued.[149] Directive 99/30/EC established limits in respect of sulphur
dioxide, nitrogen oxide and oxides of nitrogen, particulate matter and lead
in ambient air[150] in accordance with the requirements of the Air Quality
Framework Directive which itself established limit values and alert
thresholds for concentrations of such pollutants.

The implementation of the Air Quality Framework Directive and consequent legislation has been patchy. Air quality standards are demanding
and cannot be met in many Member States. The chances of effective
implementation have been boosted as individuals have been recognized as
having standing to challenge in the domestic courts an omission to draw up
the relevant action plan. In a reference for a preliminary ruling from the
German Bundesverwaltungsgericht in *Janecek v Freistaat Bayern*,[151] the
ECJ held that preventing individuals from relying on the Member State's
obligations in Directive 96/62 would be incompatible with its binding
effect. Where there was a risk of exceeding the specified pollutant limits, a
directly concerned individual can require the Member State concerned to
draw up an action plan. The mere fact that there were alternative legal
remedies under domestic law for requiring the competent authorities to
take measures to combat atmospheric pollution was irrelevant. The content of the action plan need not be particularly onerous. The ECJ noted

---

[147] Council Directive 96/62/EC on ambient air quality assessment and management [1996]
OJ L296. See COM (94) 109 final and COM (96) 311 final. Known as the Air Quality
Framework Directive (see above). This was implemented into UK legislation by SI 2003/
2121: The Air Quality Limit Values Regulations 2003; SI 2002/3183 and SI 2001/2315:
The Air Quality Limit Values Regulations 2001.

[148] This was implemented into UK legislation by SI 2003/2121: The Air Quality Limit Values
Regulations 2003; SI 2002/3183: The Air Quality Limit Values (Wales) Regulations 2002;
and SI 2001/2315: The Air Quality Limit Values Regulations 2001.

[149] Pursuant to Council Decision 97/101/EC of January 27, 1997 there was established a
reciprocal exchange of information and data from networks and individual stations measuring ambient air pollution within the Member States [1997] OJ L35. See COM(94) 345
final.

[150] Council Directive 99/30/EC relating to limit values for sulphur dioxide, nitrogen oxide and
oxides of nitrogen, particulate matter and lead in ambient air [1999] OJ L163. See
COM(99) 93 final, COM(97) 500 final and COM(98) 386 final.

[151] C-237/07 25/07/2008, unreported but the original reference is at [2007] OJ C183/29.

that Member States were not obliged to ensure that the limit values or alert thresholds were never exceeded. They were obliged only to take such short term measures in the action plan which would minimize the risk of exceeding the stated limits, and to ensure a gradual return to the proper levels, in the light of all the circumstances. This case should be read in the context of an increasing regulatory emphasis on public involvement in environmental decision-making.[152]

However, environmental concerns are not always a trump card and do not necessarily outweigh other EU priorities. The demands of good air quality sometimes conflict with the interests of trade. In *Commission v Austria (re Inn Valley Motorway)*[153] the Grand Chamber of the ECJ considered a Tyrolean law banning lorries of over 7.5 tonnes carrying certain goods[154] from using a 46km section of a motorway in the Inn valley in order to improve air quality. The Commission accused Austria of breaching its obligations under Articles 28 to 30 EC Treaty to allow free movement of goods. The ECJ agreed because the lorry ban applied to an important main land route between the south of Germany and the north of Italy. However, the ECJ considered that, in certain circumstances, even the free movement of goods, one of the founding principles of the EC, could be prevented if the need to protect the environment justified it. Although the annual limits for nitrogen dioxide had been exceeded in the zone in 2002 and 2003, and although Austria was obliged to take steps to comply with the limits, the lorry ban was considered to be disproportionate. Before banning lorries from a vital communication link between certain Member States, Austria should have researched the possibility of less restrictive measures, such as alternative road routes or alternative methods of transportation (e.g. rail). The ECJ found that the traffic ban at issue was incompatible with the free movement of goods.

14-055   The Air Quality Standards Regulations 2007[155] implements Directive 2004/107/EC and the other daughter Directives of the Air Quality Framework Directive into domestic law. The Secretary of State is the competent authority for the purposes of Article 3 (implementation and

---

[152] Directive 2003/35/EC [2003] OJ L156, on public participation, derived from the Aarhus Convention, and both discussed in Ch.6.

[153] Case C-320/03.

[154] Namely waste, stone, soil, motor vehicles, timber or cereals.

[155] SI 2007/64 which came into force on February 15, 2007. These Regulations implement the following Directives: Council Directive 96/62/EC on ambient air quality assessment and management ([1996] OJ L296/55); Council Directive 1999/30/EC relating to limit values for sulphur dioxide, nitrogen dioxide and oxides of nitrogen, particulate matter and lead in ambient air ([1999] OJ L163/41); Directive 2000/69/EC of the European Parliament and of the Council relating to limit values for benzene and carbon monoxide in ambient air ([2000] OJ L313/12); Directive 2002/3/EC of the European Parliament and of the Council relating to ozone in ambient air ([2002] OJ L67/14); and Directive 2004/107/EC of the European Parliament and of the Council relating to arsenic, cadmium, mercury, nickel and polycyclic aromatic hydrocarbons in ambient air ([2005 OJ L323/3).

responsibilities) of Council Directive 96/62/EC.[156] Chapter 1 of Part 2 of these Regulations requires a particular standard of air quality to be achieved in respect of the concentration of various pollutants in ambient air. In accordance with Regulation 6, limit values are imposed for "Group A" pollutants (benzene, carbon monoxide, lead, nitrogen dioxide and oxides of nitrogen, particulate matter (PM_{10}) and sulphur dioxide); target values are imposed for "Group B" pollutants (the content of arsenic, benzo(a)pyrene, cadmium and nickel, and their compounds, within the PM_{10} fraction); and target values and long-term objectives are imposed for ozone. Regulation 5 requires the Secretary of State to divide England into zones within which the necessary air quality management and assessment takes place. The measures the Secretary of State is required to take in order to attain the relevant standards are identified.[157] Where benzene or nitrogen dioxide or oxides of nitrogen concentrations or ozone concentrations exceed the limit value plus the margin of tolerance specified, Regulation 8 requires the Secretary of State to prepare and implement an improvement plan. The Secretary of State must take the measures specified in that regulation where concentrations of Group B pollutants exceed the relevant target value where concentrations of ozone comply with the target value but exceed a long-term objective.[158] He must ensure compliance with the limit values and target values and, as far as the factors specified in that regulation allow, the long-term objective for ozone.[159] Action plans indicating the steps to be taken if there is a risk of exceeding the limit value or the alert thresholds for nitrogen dioxide, oxides of nitrogen, sulphur dioxide[160] and ozone must be drawn up and implemented. Regulation 12 requires the Secretary of State to assess the concentration of Group A pollutants, Group B pollutants and ozone within each zone. Regulations 13 to 16 prescribe the assessment methods which are required or permitted (as the case may be), and the detailed requirements in relation to each method (for instance, requirements as to sampling points for fixed measurement). Part 3 of the Regulations (regulations 17 to 19) require the Secretary of State to measure or monitor, respectively, $PM_{2.5}$, ozone precursor substances and certain polycyclic aromatic hydrocarbons. Regulation 20 requires indicative measurements to be taken of the concentration and deposition of Group B pollutants, polycyclic aromatic hydrocarbons and mercury. Part 4 of the Regulations (regulations 21 to 25) require the Secretary of State to disseminate up-to-date information, particularly to public interest groups. An annual report for ozone[161] and details of the

---

[156] Regulation 3.
[157] Chapter 2 of Part 2. The measures ordinarily required are those set out in regulation 7.
[158] reg.9.
[159] reg.10.
[160] reg.11.
[161] reg.26.

action and improvement plans and their implementation must be made available.[162] The Secretary of State must consult the public in preparing, modifying or reviewing improvement plans.[163] Transboundary pollution involving Group A pollutants and ozone is tackled by mandatory measures.[164] The Secretary of State can give the same directions to the London Mayor and local authorities in Greater London as he is able to give to local authorities in England outside Greater London under section 85(5)(a) of the Environment Act 1995.[165]

By Decision 2004/224/EC the Commission required Member States to provide the Commission with information on their national plans to restrict certain pollutants.[166] Guidance was given for national short term action plans to be implemented if ozone levels got too high.[167] Member States have not always adopted this challenge with enthusiasm. In *Commission v Greece*[168] the Commission asked for a declaration that by failing to legislate in accordance with Directive 2002/3/EC relating to ozone in ambient air, Greece was in breach of its obligations.[169] The Commission has taken a robust stand with Member States, for example, the Commission would not grant a derogation in respect of particulate matter, even when exceptional circumstances were alleged in *Netherlands v Commission*.[170]

More recently, on May 21, 2008, Directive 2008/50/EC of the European Parliament and of the Council on ambient air quality and cleaner air for Europe[171] was adopted. It has six principal aims. First, it defines and establishes objectives for ambient air quality which may be summarized as avoiding, preventing or reducing harm to health and to the environment. Secondly, it repeats the requirement to assess national ambient air quality using common methods and criteria. Thirdly, it requires information be provided with the aim of combating air pollution and nuisance. Long-term trends and improvements resulting from national and Community measures should be monitored. Fourthly, Directive 2008/50/EC ensures the publication of information on ambient air quality. Fifthly, it reinforces the commitment to maintain air quality where it is good and to improve it

[162] reg.27.
[163] reg.28.
[164] Part 5, reg.29.
[165] reg.30.
[166] This laid down arrangements for the submission of information on plans or programmes required under Directive 96/62/EC in relation to limit values for certain pollutants in ambient air ([2004] OJ L68/27). The pollutants concerned were sulphur dioxide, nitrogen dioxide and oxides of nitrogen, particulate matter and lead following Directive 99/30/EC and benzene and carbon monoxide following Directive 2000/69/EC.
[167] On March 19, 2004 Commission Decision 2004/279/EC provides guidance for implementing Directive 2002/3/EC of the European Parliament and of the Council relating to ozone in ambient air ([2004] OJ L87/50) was adopted.
[168] Case C-63/05, *Commission of the European Communities v the Hellenic Republic*, 2006/C60/68, C60 p.33 (Removal from the register): 2005/C82/42 (Application) p.21.
[169] The request for a declaration was ultimately not pursued.
[170] Case T-182/06 27/6/2007, 2006/C212/63 (Application).
[171] [2008] OJ L152/1.

where it is not. Finally, it promotes increased cooperation between the Member States in reducing air pollution.

Directive 2008/50/EC effectively merges the four daughter Directives **14–056** and the Council Decision 2004/224/EC[172] set out above into a single Directive on air quality. It sets standards and target dates for reducing concentrations of fine particles ($PM_{2.5}$), which together with coarser particles known as PM_{10} are considered to be among the most dangerous pollutants for human health. The Directive requires Member States to reduce exposure to $PM_{2.5}$ in urban areas by an average of 20 per cent by 2020[173] and to bring exposure levels below 20 micrograms/m³ by 2015. Even in non-urban areas a maximum $PM_{2.5}$ limit of 25 micrograms/m³ must be achieved by 2015, or by 2010 where possible. Although Directive 2008/50/EC is important in that it introduces new restrictions for fine particles, in reality it does not change existing air quality standards. Arguably it even dilutes the impetus for existing standards to be met[174] by allowing Member States an extended deadline for compliance.[175] Significantly, there is also a departure from "bottom line" analysis: when assessing compliance with the standards, all natural contributions are now disregarded whereas previously only certain natural events such as the trans-boundary movement of Saharan sand particles were disregarded.[176] Directive 2008/50/EC came into force on June 11, 2008, and must be implemented by June 11, 2011.

The trend for future environmental regulation is thematic review, rather than prescriptive rules in respect of particular pollutants or economic sectors. The Sixth Environmental Action Programme (the 6EAP) required the Commission to have a thematic strategy for air pollution running to 2012 following analysis undertaken as part of the Commission's Clean Air for Europe (CAFE) programme. As the 6EAP's aim of eradicating air pollution harmful to health and the environment cannot be met by 2020, the Strategy has been forced to prioritise interim measures preventing pollution causing ill-health. The Strategy impacts on agriculture, transport and industry.

In accordance with the thematic strategy for air pollution, the National Emissions Ceilings Directive[177] was adopted. It deals with deposits of acidifying and eutrophying substances at levels which harm the environ-

---

[172] [2004] OJ L68/27.

[173] Relative to 2010 levels.

[174] 25 of the 27 Member States were reportedly unable to comply with the PM_{10} limits in at least part of their territory. See IP/07/1537.

[175] To June 11, 2011, or a maximum extension to June 11, 2013, for nitrogen dioxide and benzene provided that the relevant EU legislation and IPPC is fully implemented and all abatement measures have been taken.

[176] Following the adoption of Directive 2008/50/EC, Directives 96/62/EC, 1999/30/EC, 2000/69/EC and 2002/3/EC are repealed from June 11, 2010, with the exception of certain provisions thereof as outlined in Directive 2008/50/EC.

[177] The European Parliament and Council Directive 2001/81/EC of October 23, 2001 on national emission ceilings for certain atmospheric pollutants. [2001] OJ L309.

ment. Remarkably, in 2001 each and every Member States exceeded the WHO guideline limits for the protection of human health and vegetation from photochemical pollution. Directive 2001/81/EC is not a panacea but does provide a first step to reducing critical levels by setting national emission ceilings, taking years 2010 and 2020 as benchmarks. Successive reviews are required. Annual national emission ceilings of the pollutants sulphur dioxide (SO_2), nitrogen oxides (NOx), volatile organic compounds (VOCs) and ammonia (NH_3), are set out in Annex I. Each Member States has a deadline for compliance of 2010 at the latest. Directive 2001/81/EC covers emissions, irrespective of source, but excludes emissions from international maritime traffic; aircraft emissions (beyond the landing and take-off cycle which are arguably the most polluting activities); and the outermost regions of the Community (the Canary Islands, the French Overseas Departments, Madeira and the Azores). The Directive requires emission inventories and projections; reports by the Member States and the Commission; regular reviews of the Directive; cooperation with third countries; and reports concerning ship and aircraft emissions. The Directive was implemented into UK legislation by SI 2002/3118: The National Emission Ceilings Regulations 2002 and SI 2002/2528: The Pollution Prevention and Control (Designation of Council Directives on Large Combustion Plants, Incineration Waste and National Emission Ceilings) Order 2002.

14–057   The National Emission Ceilings Regulations 2002 requires the Secretary of State to ensure that in 2010, and each subsequent year, emissions from the United Kingdom of sulphur dioxide, nitrogen oxides, VOC and ammonia do not exceed the amounts specified in the Schedule.[178] The Secretary of State will prepare a national programme for the progressive reduction of such pollutants.[179] Regulation 4(3) requires public authorities, if acting in a manner which significantly affects the level of emissions of such pollutants in the UK, to take account of the national programme. Annual inventories of emissions of those pollutants, and projections of emissions of those pollutants in 2010, must be prepared.[180]

The obligation in relation to national emissions ceiling regulations is onerous. Both Greece and the Netherlands were censured for failing to notify the Commission of the relevant laws, regulations and administrative provisions necessary to comply with the national emission ceilings Directive: *Commission v Greece*[181] and *Commission v Netherlands*.[182] Air pollution is such a problem that it has sparked a political impetus to tackle it effectively. The Commission is likely to enforce the obligations on Member States with enthusiasm.

---

[178] reg.3.
[179] reg.4.
[180] reg.5.
[181] Case C-68/04 2004/C94/46 C94 p.22 (Application).
[182] Case C-146/04 2004/C106/75 p.44 (Application).

Ozone Depleting Substances

There has been much legislation to regulate substances that deplete the   **14–058**
ozone layer and the Chapter on Climate Change will put the legislation
into context. Currently ozone depleting substances are controlled by
Regulation 2037/2000.[183] Prior to its adoption there had been a rapid
increase in the availability of alternatives to ozone-depleting substances
such as hydrochlorofluorocarbons (HCFCs) and methyl bromide, and
changes had been made to the Montreal Protocol and the International
Convention on ozone-depleting substances. Regulation 2037/2000
required Member States to phase out ozone-depleting substances by prohibiting the production, marketing and use of chlorofluorocarbons, halons,
carbon tetrachloride, trichloroethane, methyl bromide, hydrobromo-
fluorocarbons and HCFCs. Further, Member States had to establish systems for the recovering, collecting or re-cycling of such substances from
products marketed from September 2000 and report to the Commission by
December 31, 2001, on the systems they have put in place. Regulation
2037/2000 affected the manufacture and marketing of most white goods
such as fridges, freezers, air-conditioning units and water coolers, as well as
products such as aerosols, insecticides and other pesticides, paints, varn-
ishes, and perfumes. Furthermore the imports of such products from third
countries were regulated.[184]

The Environmental Protection (Controls on Ozone-Depleting Substances) (Amendment) Regulations 2008[185] builds on the Environmental
Protection (Controls on Ozone-Depleting Substances) Regulations 2002
by extending the 2002 Regulations to offshore oil and gas installations that
use ozone depleting substances in equipment in the marine area.[186] Various
terms are re-defined, including the "enforcing authority".[187] The Secretary
of State is the competent authority in respect of offshore installations.[188]
The 2008 Regulations require prior authorisation of methyl bromide
fumigations for quarantine and pre-shipment purposes and set out penalties for failure to do so. They replace, update and add to powers for

---

[183] Regulation 2037/2000 on substances that deplete the ozone layer. [2000] OJ L244 29
September 2000. As amended by Regulation 2038/2000, Regulation 2039/2000, Commission Decision 2003/160/EC, Regulation 1804/2003, Decision 2004/232, Commission
Regulation 2077/2004, Commission Regulation 29/2006, Regulation 1366/2006, Commission Regulation 1784/2006 and Commission regulation 899/2007.

[184] The Regulation was implemented into UK legislation by SI 2008/91, The Environmental
Protection (Controls on Ozone-Depleting Substances) (Amendment) Regulations 2008.

[185] Amending the Environmental Protection (Controls on Ozone-Depleting Substances)
Regulations 2002 SI 2002/528.

[186] See new regulation 1A, in the 2002 Regulations, inserted by paragraph 1 of the Schedule to
the 2008 Regulations. "The marine area" is contained in new regulation 2(1) and "offshore installation" is defined in new regulation 2(1A), inserted by paragraph 2 of the
Schedule to these amending Regulations.

[187] reg.2.

[188] reg.3.

enforcement bodies and authorised persons. The 2008 Regulations create new offences and penalties for failing to supply information/records about halon exports or supplying false information about proposed exports and new offences and penalties for producing bromochloromethane or placing bromochloromethane on the market in breach of EU or international bans. Finally, the 2008 Regulations enable the Secretary of State to require persons to dispose of a controlled substance, a product or equipment following an improper export or placing on the market. The failure to dispose of a controlled substance when ordered to do so is an offence.

Member States have had difficulty complying with the rigours of Directive 2037/2000, which has resulted in the Commission taking action against Ireland, Germany, Belgium. Luxembourg, France, Greece, Italy, Spain, Portugal, Netherlands, Austria, Sweden and the UK.

Motor Vehicles: 98/69/EC

14–059   The motor industry has been a significant contributor to air pollution. This has been tackled in a number of different ways: by restricting pollutants in fuel, by type approval and licensing of vehicles for sale in the EU and by requiring technological development (for example, catalytic converters and on-board diagnostic systems) in order to reduce harmful emissions. The environmental legislation relating to motor vehicles is legion and outside the scope of this work but the framework for controlling fuel emissions is found in The Auto Oil Programme which was introduced by 98/69/EC.[189] This controls the quality of petrol and diesel. The limit on emissions from motor vehicles has become ever more exigent as technological developments allow.[190] Vehicles which do not comply with the legislative requirements are not granted a type approval and cannot be marketed in the EU. The Commission and vehicle manufacturers associations have agreed programmes to reduce CO_2 through technological development. In 1999 a series of CO_2 reduction targets for 2008 and 2012 was agreed with

[189] On October 13, 1998 Directive 98/69/EC of the European Parliament and of the Council relating to measures to be taken against air pollution by emissions from motor vehicles and amending Directive 70/220/EEC was adopted. [1998] OJ L350. See COM(97) 77 final, COM(97) 61 final and COM(96) 248 final.
[190] e.g. low temperature emissions of carbon monoxide and hydrocarbons from cars and vans Directive 2001/100/EC, [2002] OJ L16 which was implemented into UK legislation by SI 2002/1835: The Motor Vehicles (EC Type Approval) (Amendment) Regulations 2002.

the European Automobile Manufacturers Association (ACEA)[191] And in 2000 a similar agreement was made with the Association of Korean Automobile Manufacturers (KAMA)[192] and with Association of Japanese Automobile Manufacturers (JAMA)[193] setting CO_2 emission targets for 2009 and 2012.

For over 20 years there have been attempts to limit pollutants such as sulphur, lead and volatile organic compounds from fuels[194] and develop clean fuels with some considerable success. Tax incentives have been permitted by the Commission to encourage the use of cleaner fuels.[195]

The use of fuels in land-based activities is currently controlled under the Sulphur Content of Liquid Fuels Directive (SCLFD) 1999/32/EC.[196] It limits the sulphur content of heavy fuel oil to 1 per cent by mass from January 1, 2003 and gas oil (including marine gas oil) to 0.2 per cent by mass from July 1, 2000 (0.1 per cent by mass from January 1, 2008). However, the SCLFD does not apply to other liquid fuels used by sea-going ships. Emissions of sulphur dioxide (SO_2) from the maritime sector in Europe are projected to surpass total emissions from all land-based sources by 2020.[197] In response to this threat the Sulphur Content of

[191] On February 5, 1999 Commission Recommendation 99/125/EC on the reduction of CO_2 emissions from passenger cars was adopted. [1999] OJ L40. The Commission recommended that the members of the European Automobile Manufacturers Association should collectively achieve a target of 140 g/km CO_2 as measured according to Directive 93/116/EEC, for the average of their new cars sold in the EC, as defined in Annex I to Council Directive 70/156/EEC, by 2008. This would be done by developing technology and marketing the changes linked to these developments. The ACEA had to evaluate the potential for additional fuel efficiency improvements with the aim of a 2012 target of 120 g/km CO_2. The ACEA would cooperate with the Commission in the monitoring this commitment.

[192] On April 13, 2000 Commission Recommendation 2000/303/EC on the reduction of CO_2 emissions from passenger cars was adopted. [2000] OJ L100. It was recommended that KAMA achieve a CO_2 emission target of 140 g/km CO2, (measured according to Directive 93/116/EC) for new passenger cars sold in the EC by 2009. Such targets would be achieved by technological and associated market developments.

[193] On April 13, 2000 Commission Recommendation 2000/304/EC on the reduction of CO2 emissions from passenger cars was adopted [2000] OJ L100. 2000/304/EC. JAMA should collectively to achieve a target of 140 g/km CO_2, (measured according to Directive 93/116/EC) for new cars sold in the EC by 2009, to be achieved by technological developments and associated market developments.

[194] Council Directive 80/1268/EEC [1980] OJ L375, amended by Directive 2004/3/EC.

[195] e.g. On June 29, 2000 by Council Decision 2000/433/EC Germany was allowed to charge differential taxes on fuels according to sulphur content. On November 10, 2000 Council Decision 2000/719/EC authorised France to charge lower taxes for refuse collection vehicles using LPG or natural gas, rather than diesel. On May 15, 2002 Commission Decision 2003/238/EC authorised France to apply differentiated tax rates to biofuels.

[196] Council Directive 99/32/EC of April 26, 1999 relating to a reduction of the sulphur content of certain liquid fuels and amending Directive 93/12/EEC. Its aim is to reduce sulphur dioxide emissions resulting from the combustion of certain types of liquid fuels, in order to reduce harm to health and the environment. The sulphur content in fuel is limited as a condition for their use within the Community. This was implemented into UK law by SI 2000/1460: The Sulphur Content of Liquid Fuels (England and Wales) Regulations 2000.

[197] See CAFÉ emission estimates 1: *http://europa.eu.int/comm/environment/air/cafe/index.htm*.

Marine Fuels Directive (SCMFD – Directive 2005/33/EC)[198] was adopted. It limited sulphur for fuels used by all ships in the SOx Emission Control Areas of the Baltic Sea to 1.5 per cent, from August 11, 2006, and the North Sea and English Channel from either August 11, 2007 or 12 months after the entry into force of the International Maritime Organisation designation, whichever is the earlier. Further, a 1.5 per cent sulphur limit for fuels used by passenger ships on regular services between EU ports was imposed from August 11, 2006. A 0.1 per cent sulphur limit on fuel used by inland waterway vessels and by ships at berth in EU ports, applies from January 1, 2010. In addition, the marketing of marine diesel oils with a sulphur content exceeding 1.5 per cent by mass was banned from August 11, 2006, and the marketing of marine gas oils with a sulphur content exceeding 0.1 per cent by mass was banned from January 1, 2010. Marine fuel with only a 0.5 per cent sulphur content is permitted in port areas. Ships must switch off their engines and use shore-side electricity while at berth in ports. The Directive is implemented by The Sulphur Content of Liquid Fuels (England and Wales) Regulations 2007.[199]

[198] Directive 2005/33/EC of the European Parliament and of the Council of July 6, 2005 amending the Sulphur Content of Liquid Fuels Directive (SCLFD) 1999/32/EC, as regards the sulphur content of marine fuels which came into force on July 6, 2005, [2005] OJ L191/51. Directive 1999/32/EC, which itself amended Directive 93/12/EEC.

[199] SI 2007/79 implementing in part 1999/32/EC and 1882/2003/EC. This SI revokes SI 2000/1460 with savings. It replaces the Sulphur Content of Liquid Fuels (England and Wales) Regulations 2000 (SI 2000/1460), which transposed the Sulphur Content of Liquid Fuels Directive (1999/32/EC). The Sulphur Content of Liquid Fuels (England and Wales) Regulations 2007 also transpose the provisions of Directive 1999/23/EC as amended by Directive 2005/33/EC, except the marine provisions.

Chapter 15

WASTE

Introduction

We have seen in Chapter 14 how there is now a common permitting system **15–001** for a whole range of operations with potential effects on the environment. We now turn to one sector of these operations, namely those handling waste. Before we look at the detail, it is important to see the new system in context. Hence, the structure of this chapter is to look at the policy problems involved, and the domestic responses in the 1970s, before analysing the Waste Framework Directive and the domestic rules which preceded the Environmental Permitting (EP) Regulations but which still remain in force. We then turn to the various other Directives concerned with waste and how they are transposed by the EP and other Regulations.

The Policy Problem

In 2004 around 335 million tonnes of waste were produced annually in the **15–002** United Kingdom. This figure includes waste from municipal (including household), industrial and commercial sources but also from construction and demolition, mining and quarrying, and agriculture. Waste from just the first three sources amounts to approximately 100 million tonnes per year.[1] The production of household waste is amongst the highest in Europe, with each person generating just over half a tonne on average per year. Moreover, the rate at which municipal waste is produced increases by 3–4 per cent per year, again amongst the fastest in Europe.

Every tonne of waste produced becomes an environmental, economic and regulatory problem: an item which is discarded as waste is not only something lost to the economy but something which must be dealt with carefully in order to avoid it damaging the environment. The cost of dealing with those risks, in turn, adds another burden to the economy. It is in response to this problem that the concept of a "waste hierarchy" has developed. The most efficient and effective way of dealing with waste is to prevent it from being created in the first place: at the top of the waste hierarchy is therefore the reduction in the use of natural resources and the

---

[1] Defra Waste Strategy 2007.

prevention of waste creation. If this is impossible, the object or substance which would otherwise become a waste should be re-used wherever possible. If re-use is impossible, the waste material should be recycled. Only if it cannot be recycled should it be used for energy recovery, for example through energy-efficient incineration. Disposal of the waste should be an absolutely last resort.

Diagram 15/I

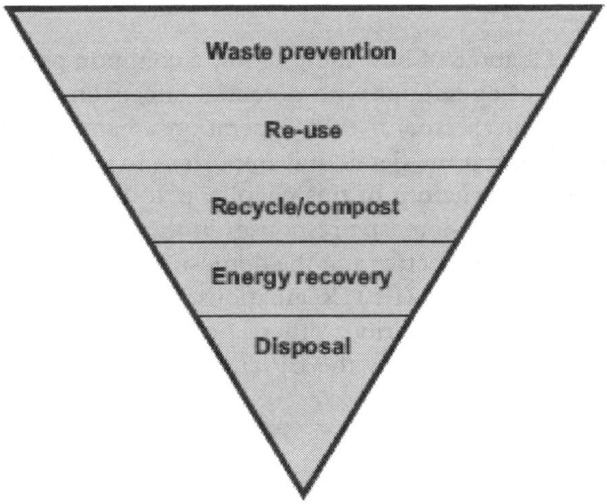

Source: Defra Waste Strategy 2007 Figure B.2[2]

Historically, landfill has been the United Kingdom's disposal method of choice: in 1999 over 80 per cent of its waste was sent to landfill, or around 50 per cent of waste arising from households, commerce and industry (that is, excluding mining or quarrying waste).[3] This has been attributed to the UK's particular geology: traditionally, disused quarries have been used for landfill. However, landfill is increasingly seen as the worst possible option for waste management. Existing landfill sites are reaching capacity. Supply of land for new sites is very limited: not only is there limited new land for the traditional type of landfill site, but land used for landfill will thereby be removed from use as a community amenity, open space or potential development site, for maybe 30 to 50 years. Landfill sites may give rise to problems of methane emissions and surface- and groundwater pollution caused by leachate, as well as forms of pollution more noticeable to nearby residents such as smells, dust, litter, traffic movements, vermin and noise.

[2] Crown copyright.
[3] Sustainable Development Indicator 18: Waste, *http://www.sustainable-development.gov.uk/ progress/national/18.htm.*

The environmental effects of a landfill site last far longer than its operative life. Moreover, all waste buried in landfill is a potential resource wasted which could otherwise have been used in the economy or to replace a raw material. Accordingly, both European and domestic legislation have in recent years been focussed on reducing the proportion and amount of waste sent to landfill. Incineration as a method of waste disposal also carries the risk of air pollution, including toxic pollution and the release of greenhouse gases, and has elicited wide public opposition.

Dealing with waste is no longer a case of removing it from public view, or throwing it away. Underpinning waste management law is the very real truism that there is no "away": every stage in the lifecycle of waste, from production through reuse, recycling and recovery to final disposal, is now covered by some form of control. Moreover, increasingly, waste is seen not just as a problem to be regulated closely, but as an economic resource the handling of which can present environmentally beneficial commercial opportunities. **15–003**

This means that the regulation of the collection, holding, managing, processing and disposal of waste is detailed and complex. Once waste is created, there is an evident environmental interest in controlling it, and controlling it as early as possible and for as long as necessary.

There is no doubt that the rules and regulations are onerous; and this is where a policy conflict emerges, for there is a clear environmental interest in the rules and regulations being such as actively to promote recycling and reuse, and reduce the use of natural resources. The long-term goal, says the European Commission, is for Europe to become an "economically and environmentally efficient recycling society".[4] This means that there must be incentives built into the waste regime to promote such reuse and recycling, and to encourage economic actors to find alternative raw materials to primary natural resources; and when such natural resources must be used, to encourage as resource-efficient a use of it as possible.

In the development of policy on waste key issues include firstly, what is to be considered "waste". Material which is no longer needed by the person who discards it will not necessarily itself cause significant pollution or harm to the environment. Some waste is quite inert; other waste may be highly toxic. Moreover, what is waste to the economic actor who no longer needs it may be a valuable resource for another: posing important questions as regards when matter may become waste, and when waste may cease to be waste. Secondly, there is the question of what type of controls should be imposed on what kinds of waste, and at what stages in the waste life-cycle. Placing insufficiently stringent controls on the disposal of waste may inhibit its recycling or recovery, or fail to prevent its production in the **15–004**

---

[4] Thematic Strategy on the Prevention and Recycling of Waste COM (2005) 666 final, December 21, 2005.

first place.[5] Thirdly, there is the larger question of sustainable development. Even if it is agreed that from a waste-environment policy perspective it is better to re-use than to recover, and better to recover than to discard, each control will have an effect on the use of other resources such as energy, land, labour and capital. This means that in some cases adhering rigidly to the waste hierarchy will not result in the optimum waste solution from a sustainable development point of view. The system of waste control must be flexible enough to deal with these competing environmental objectives.

It is for this reason that the definition of waste is crucially important: and we shall need to ask whether the definition adopted at EU level has meant that the "weight" of the waste regime serves to inhibit the realisation of the European Union's waste, and broader environmental, objectives, Firstly, if the reuse and recycling of waste is to be encouraged, there must come a point when that recycling should be considered to hâve successfully rescued waste from the trash pile and brought it back to be used in the economy on equal terms with the natural resources that would otherwise be exploited. In other words, at some point what fell within the definition of waste must cease to do so: this is the question of what constitutes the "end of waste". Secondly, if the efficient use of resources is to be encouraged, there must be some incentive to ensure that as little as possible of any resource is regarded in law as having gone to "waste": this raises the contentious distinction between non-waste by-products of industrial processes, which can be used or re-used, and "production residues" which are to be considered as waste. These matters are considered in detail later in this chapter.

The Waste Framework Directives

15–005 From the very inception of EU waste policy, there has been a focus on the whole lifecycle of waste creation and management, and not just on controlling how waste is disposed of once created. Council Directive 75/442 on Waste was adopted on July 15, 1975, and was one of the first EU environmental directives.[6] Article 3 stated that:

> "Member States shall take appropriate steps to encourage the prevention, recycling and processing of waste, the extraction of raw materials and possibly of energy therefrom and any other process for the re-use of waste".

---

[5] For example, opponents of economically viable large scale energy from waste ("efw") incineration proposals often point to concerns that such waste recovery processes, requiring large throughputs of material, can divert waste from recycling and re-use processes.

[6] OJ [1975] L194/39.

However, no formal "waste hierarchy" was put in place.

The Directive included for the first time in substantive European legis-lation the principle that the cost of waste disposal should be borne by the waste holder, and/or the previous holders, and/or the producer of the product or waste.[7] The Directive did not, however, provide any further guidance on how this "polluter pays" principle should be applied.

In 1975 the encouragement of prevention and recycling was very much an adjunct to the regulation of waste disposal, which occupied the bulk of the Directive. However, in 1989 the Commission published a Commu-nication on a Community Strategy for Waste Management, COM (89) 934, which stated that "the Community must first address itself to pre-venting waste before considering its (re)use and how it is ultimately to be disposed of."

This Communication formed the basis for the amendments which **15–006** would, by means of Council Directive 91/156, transform the 1975 directive into the Waste Framework Directive (WFD).[8] The WFD, in that form or in its consolidated form 2006/12,[9] presently governs the position (until the coming into force of the proposed new 2008 Waste Framework Directive).

The stated objectives of Directives 91/156 and 2006/12 are to "achieve a high level of environmental protection", particularly by promoting clean technologies and products which can be recycled and re-used.[10] The WFD established a clear hierarchy in waste management, stating that Member States were to encourage "firstly" the prevention or reduction of waste production and "secondly" recovery of waste by means of recycling, re-use or reclamation, or by using it as a source of energy.[11]

In addition, the Waste Framework Directive indicates in its third recital the need for a common terminology and definition of waste. The 1975 Directive defined waste as something which the holder "disposes of or is required to dispose of" under national law. In contrast, the 1991 Directive, for the first time, purported to lay down a Community-wide definition: " 'waste' shall mean any substance or object in the categories set out in Annex I which the holder discards or intends or is required to discard". As we shall see below, harmonisation of the definition across Europe has been far from self-evident. It is clear from the recital, however, that the Com-munity is interested in harmonising practices in the disposal and recovery of waste for the sake of both environmental quality and the functioning of the internal market.

---

[7] Article 11 and eighth recital, Directive 75/442 as enacted.
[8] OJ [1991] L78/32.
[9] OJ [2006], L114/9.
[10] Fourth recital of 91/156, and sixth recital of 2006/12.
[11] Article 3, Directive 91/156.

Objectives

15–007 Articles 3–5 of the 1991 and 2006 WFDs set out the Directive's principal objectives:

Article 3

1. Member States shall take appropriate measures to encourage:

  (a) firstly, the prevention or reduction of waste production and its harmfulness, in particular by
   - the development of clean technologies more sparing in their use of natural resources,
   - the technical development and marketing of products designed so as to make no contribution or to make the smallest possible contribution, by the nature of their manufacture, use or final disposal, to increasing the amount or harmfulness of waste and pollution hazards,
   - the development of appropriate techniques for the final disposal of dangerous substances contained in waste destined for recovery.

  (b) secondly:

   (a) the recovery of waste by means of recycling, re-use or reclamation or any other process with a view to extracting secondary raw materials, or
   (b) the use of waste as a source of energy.

Article 4

Member States shall take the necessary measures to ensure that waste is recovered or disposed of without endangering human health and without using processes or methods which could harm the environment, and in particular:
- without risk to water, air, soil and plants and animals,
- without causing a nuisance through noise or odours,
- without adversely affecting the countryside or places of special interest.

Member States shall also take the necessary measures to prohibit the abandonment, dumping or uncontrolled disposal of waste.

Article 5

i. Member States shall take appropriate measures, in cooperation with other Member States where this is necessary or advisable, to establish an integrated and adequate network of disposal installations, taking account of the best available technology not involving excessive costs. The network must enable the Community as a whole to become self-sufficient in waste disposal and the Member States to move towards that aim individually, taking into account geographical circumstances or the need for specialized installations for certain types of waste.

ii The network must also enable waste to be disposed of in one of the nearest appropriate installations, by means of the most appropriate methods and technologies in order to ensure a high level of protection for the environment and public health.

As can be seen from the above, the WFD extends the focus of the Directive to recovery of waste, and not just its disposal. The WFD also has as one of its stated aims that the Community become "self-sufficient" in waste disposal. Article 5 of the WFD 2006 introduces the ideas (a) of an network of waste disposal installations in order to achieve, first, Community self-sufficiency and, secondly, self-sufficiency within each Member State; (b) of the disposal of waste by means of the "best available technology not entailing excessive costs" (BATNEEC); and (c) that waste should not be transported large distances: waste should be disposed of "in one of the nearest appropriate installations".

The Directive—being essentially a framework measure—does not itself lay down detailed rules the achievement of its aims. However, Article 7 imposes a duty on Member States to draw up "waste management plans" in order to attain the objectives in Articles 3, 4, and 5.

Permitting

The WFD 2006 sets down at European level what would become the regulatory basis for waste management across the EU: the permitting system. Article 9 provides that any establishment or undertaking which carries out a disposal or recovery operation (as specified in Annex II of the WFD 2006) must obtain a permit from the competent national authority. The WFD 2006 lays down what the content of that permit should be when it relates to the *disposal* of waste, as defined in Annex IIA,[12] but not when it relates to waste *recovery* operations as set out in Annex IIB, merely stating   **15–008**

---

[12] Article 9, Directive 91/156.

that a permit is necessary to carry them out.[13] The permitting system will be discussed further below.

In 2001 the Commission brought proceedings against Ireland for persistent failure to comply with its obligations under the Directive.[14] Ireland had been slow to implement any kind of permitting system, and the system it did introduce was so slow, and the measures in place for ensuring that waste facilities became subject to permits so ineffectual, that due to the apathy of the government unauthorised waste activity continued to take place all over Ireland,. The decision of the European Court of Justice (the ECJ) made clear that the objectives set out in the WFD, including the setting up of a network of waste installations and to ensure that waste recovery and disposal is carried out without endangering the environment, can only be achieved by means of an effective permit system.

In the same case, Advocate-General Geelhoed summarised well how the objectives of the Directive were to be achieved by its regulatory scheme:

"5. The core obligation for the Member States under the waste directive is to ensure that waste is recovered or disposed of without endangering human health and without using processes and methods which could harm the environment (Article 4, first paragraph). To this end it requires them to impose certain obligations on all those dealing with waste at various stages. Thus, in what the Commission describes in its application as a 'seamless chain of responsibility', the Directive imposes obligations on holders of waste, collectors and transporters of waste and undertakings which carry out waste disposal or recovery operations. Holders of waste must ensure, where they do not recover or dispose of it themselves, that it is handled by a public or private waste collector or by a disposal or recovery enterprise (Article 8). Dumping and uncontrolled disposal of waste are to be prohibited (Article 4, second paragraph). Undertakings which collect or transport waste on a professional basis must at least be registered with the competent national authorities (Article 12), whereas undertakings carrying out disposal or recovery operations must obtain a permit from these authorities (Articles 9 and 10). These undertakings are to be inspected periodically by the competent authorities (Article 13) and, in order to facilitate these inspections, they must keep records of their activities in respect of waste (Article 14)...".

Exemptions from the Requirement for a Permit

15-009 It is open to Member States to exempt from the permitting system undertakings which dispose of their own waste on site, or any undertakings carrying out any sort of waste recovery, where such an exemption is con-

---

[13] Article 10, Directive 91/156.
[14] *C-494/01 Commission v Ireland* [2005] ECR I-3331.

sistent with the objectives of the Directive contained in Article 4.[15] However, Article 3 of Council Directive 91/189 on hazardous waste (the Hazardous Waste Directive, or HWD) provides that a Member State cannot apply the derogation in Article 11 WFD to someone disposing of hazardous waste. If a Member State wants to exempt an undertaking carrying out a recovery operation from the permitting system, it must lay down general rules for when the exemption applies, listing the type and quantity of waste and laying down specific conditions (listed as "limit values for the content of hazardous substances in the waste, emission limit values, type of activity") for carrying out different forms of recovery. In any event, any undertaking carrying out recovery operations must be registered with the competent national authorities.

Disposal and recovery

The 1991 amendments to the WFD extended controls over waste to its recovery as well as its disposal. It is convenient briefly to summarise the difference between the two. **15–010**

Annex IIA of the WFD 2006 lists 15 disposal operations, in categories D1 to D15, and includes such operations as: deposit into land (ie, landfill) or the treatment of land; release into bodies of water; biological or chemical treatment; incineration or storage; and the mixing, repackaging or storing of waste before it undergoes any of the other disposal operations.

Annex IIB of the WFD 2006 lists 13 recovery operations, from R1 to R13. They cover activities such as: use of waste as a fuel; reclamation, regeneration or recycling of various types of substance; recovery of components; refining of oils; the treatment of land; and the storage of waste before it is subjected to any recovery operation, or its use thereafter.

It can be seen that, very often, the same operation could be classed either as a recovery or as a disposal operation: for example, land treatment or incineration can be classed as either. The distinction is relevant because, as we will see, different rules may apply to a person who manages waste according to whether what he does with it is classed as recovery or disposal. This applies not only to the permitting regime, but also to rules contained within other legislation.[16] In C-6/00 *Abfall Service AG v Bundesminister für Umwelt, Jugend und Familie*[17] the European Court insisted that any treatment of waste under the Directive must be classifiable as one or the other.[18] Any operation capable of falling within either must be assessed on a case- **15–011**

---

[15] Article 11, Directive 2006/12.
[16] See, in particular, the legislation relating to the shipment of waste, below: a Member State can prevent the shipment of waste into its territory if it is destined for disposal, rather than recovery.
[17] [2002] ECR I-1961.
[18] *Abfall,* para.63.

by-case basis;[19] however, the Court, following the suggestion of the Advocate-General, also indicated that the "essential characteristic" of a recovery operation is that its principal objective is that the waste serve a "useful purpose in replacing other materials which would have had to be used for that purpose", thereby conserving natural resources.

In *Abfall Service* the court also pointed out that the operations in Annex II are not intended to be an exhaustive list of recovery or disposal operations, simply a list of the most common ones.[20] This means that new waste operation technologies will also be covered: any waste management operation must either be "recovery" or "disposal", and will be subject to the Directive, even if it resembles none of the operations listed in the Annex.

The European Court has considered the distinction between disposal and recovery in relation to several different types of operation. For example, R1 of Annex IIB lists amongst the recovery operations the use of waste principally as a fuel or other means to generate energy. In C-228/00 *Commission v Germany*[21] the Member State argued that waste which was shipped for use as fuel in cement kilns was intended for recovery, and not disposal. The Court laid down three conditions which must be fulfilled for the incineration of waste to be considered recovery rather than disposal:

(a) the main purpose of the operation must be to use the waste as a means of generating energy;
(b) the conditions in which the operation take place must give reason to believe that it is indeed a means to generate energy and
(c) the waste must be used principally as a fuel or other means of generating energy.

These three conditions translated into three technical requirements when it came to incineration:

(a) the energy generated and recovered from the combustion must be greater than the amount of energy consumed by it;
(b) part of the surplus energy produced must be used immediately; either in the form of heat or electricity;
(c) the waste must be used principally as a fuel: i.e. most of it must be consumed and most of the energy generated must be recovered and used.

15–012   Other matters, such as the calorific value of the waste, or whether it contains harmful substances, are irrelevant. In *SITA EcoService Netherland v VROM*[22] (a case about the transfrontier shipping of waste) the Court reiterated that the three conditions above are both necessary and sufficient.

---

[19] *Abfall*, para.64.
[20] *Abfall*, para.60.
[21] [2003] ECR I-1439.
[22] *C-116/01* [2003] ECR I-2969.

It should be noted that even if some or all of the technical requirements are fulfilled, the *purpose* of the incineration must still be recovery rather than disposal. In C-458/00 *Commission v Luxembourg*[23] (another transhipment case where waste from Luxembourg was intended for an incinerator in Germany),[24] the Court found that the waste had been incinerated in a plant which was designed to dispose of waste, not to recover it, and that the reclamation of the heat generated was merely a secondary effect of the operation. Even if all of the heat produced by combustion was reclaimed, the principal objective was still the disposal of waste, and the operation would have to be classified as such.[25] Proof that the principal objective was the recovery, rather than disposal, of waste might come from evidence that the plant would have had to use a primary energy source if it were not supplied with waste, or that the plant operator had paid rather than been paid for the waste delivered to it.[26] As we shall see, an entirely different, and more technical, approach to this problem is taken in the 2008 WFD.

The Sixth Environmental Action Programme and 2005 Thematic Strategy

On July 22, 2002, the European Parliament and the Council adopted the   **15–013** "Sixth Environmental Action Programme" (the 6EAP). It set out the framework for environmental policy until 2012, and aimed at the "decoupling" of environmental pressures from economic growth. The 6EAP called for the development of Thematic Strategies in four areas of environmental policy, waste and resources being one of them. Article 8 of the EAP deals with the sustainable use and management of natural resources and waste and sets out its aims: to achieve an overall reduction in the volumes of waste generated, and a reduction at the other end of the cycle in the quantity of waste going to disposal; and to encourage the re-use of those wastes which are generated. Preference, it states, should go to recovery and especially to recycling; disposal of waste should be carried out safely and as closely as possible to the place of its generation—but only "to the extent that this does not lead to a decrease in the efficiency in waste treatment options".

In the field of waste and resources, the aim of "decoupling" the historical link between economic growth and environmental damage may be achieved by making policies and practices which are favourable to the environment economically advantageous. The 2005 Thematic Strategy on the Prevention and Recycling of Waste[27] describes waste "an environ-

---

[23] C-458/00 [2003] ECR I-1553.
[24] For more on transhipment, see below.
[25] *Commission v Luxembourg* at paras 41–43.
[26] ibid., at para.44.
[27] COM (2005) 666 (final).

mental, social and economic challenge" and emphasises that waste policy should be integrated into wider thinking about the impact of resource use on the environment. It emphasised that, whilst the "waste hierarchy" should not be thought of as a hard-and-fast rule, since in particular instances different waste treatment methods can have different environmental impacts, there should be a general move away from landfill, as the worst possible option for the environment, towards recycling and recovery. However, this was not enough: the Strategy pointed out that whilst the percentage of overall waste going to landfill had decreased, there had been no reduction in the overall amount of waste sent to the ground because of increased waste generation.

In order to achieve its aims of creating a "recycling society" in Europe, the Thematic Strategy proposed the simplification and consolidation of existing legislation—including the consolidation of legislation on hazardous waste and waste oils into the WFD—and the integration of "lifecycle thinking" into waste policy. It favoured more composting and energy recovery from waste, and promised to increase energy efficiency by introducing efficiency thresholds for waste incinerators to distinguish between waste incineration as recovery and as disposal. It also hinted that clarifying when waste ceased to be waste (for a discussion of which, see below) could simplify the administrative burden on regulators and operators, and proposed that a definition of "recycling" be introduced into the WFD. It also envisaged the clarification of the distinction between disposal and recovery, by focussing attention on the criterion of substituting resources in the wider economy. It expressed concern that the jurisprudence of the Court at the time meant that the vast majority of municipal incinerators were classed as disposal facilities rather than recovery operations, meaning that there was no incentive for municipalities to divert waste from landfill towards energy production. It pointed out the need for incentives for waste recycling and recovery—making special mention of national landfill taxes as a suitable economic instrument for this purpose.

15–014   Despite its talk of "lifecycle thinking", however, the Thematic Strategy fell short of proposing the development of waste prevention policies at EU level, stating that waste prevention would have to take into account consumption patterns and economic growth. It left prevention policies for the national, regional or local level. It did, however, promise to amend the WFD to clarify the obligation on Member States to develop publicly available waste prevention programmes—albeit "in the context of sustainable production and consumption".

In 2006, in preparation for the development of new European waste policy, the WFD was consolidated as Directive 2006/12/EC.

The 2008 Waste Framework Directive

The revision process for the 2008 WFD started with the Commission's **15–015** proposal in December 2005. Since then the proposal has been considered by all the Community institutions, and on October 20, 2008, after significant amendment by the European Parliament, an agreed text was finally adopted by the European Council. It is to be transposed into domestic law within two years, so will come into force by the end of 2010. The main proposed changes will be summarised shortly in the next few paragraphs, and other changes will be noted in the discussion of various central topics below. We make express reference to numbered provisions of the new WFD by reference to the June 2008 text adopted by Council.

In Article 4 the new WFD enshrines the five-step waste hierarchy—prevention, reuse, recycling, recovery and disposal—within EU law. The hierarchy must apply as a priority order in all waste prevention and management legislation. Member States must, nevertheless, take measures to deliver the best overall environmental outcome: this will mean departing from the hierarchy where necessary.

Despite the status of waste prevention at the top of the hierarchy, the new Article 9 on waste prevention is not terribly far-reaching for the moment: it simply mandates the production of reports and the setting of objectives for waste prevention by 2020. Member States are also required to establish waste prevention programmes within five years of the new WFD coming into force. However, no targets have been set.

Although the new WFD sets targets in relation to recycling, the Directive **15–016** merely requires Member States to take "necessary measures designed to achieve" a target to recycle 50 per cent of waste from households by 2020. It is debatable, therefore, how far it will be possible to bring any enforcement proceedings against a Member State whose measures designed to achieve them are demonstrably ineffectual. However, by 2015 member states must set up separate collections for at least paper, metals, plastics and glass, provided this is technically, environmentally and economically feasible.

The new WFD also permits incinerators which reach certain efficiency thresholds to be classed as recovery operations rather than disposal operations: Annex II provides the formula for energy efficiency. The intention is to encourage energy-efficient incineration over landfill. The provision puts the distinction between recovery and disposal in this context on to much more of a scientific footing.

A change is to be made to the principle of waste management self-sufficiency currently to be found in Article 5 of the 2006 WFD. Article 16 extends this beyond the disposal installations currently provided for to recovery installations treating mixed municipal waste. The underlying thinking is to reinforce the proximity principle by encouraging member states to recover their own mixed municipal waste, rather than to export it to elsewhere in the EU.

15–017   The new WFD also includes a definition of by-products which is intended to make the distinction between waste and non-waste rather clearer. This is considered below.

Meaning of waste

15–018   We outlined above the policy reasons why the definition of waste is so crucial. However, despite its centrality to the European system of waste control, and despite the Directive's call for a common definition of waste, a definitive clarification of this key concept has not been achieved, either by the European legislation or through numerous decisions from the European Court.

Is it waste? The intention of the holder

15–019   Article 1(a) of the 2006 Directive defines waste as "any substance or object in the categories set out in Annex I which the holder discards or intends or is required to discard". Annex I provides a list of categories of waste, each designated by the letter "Q". Many of them will be instantly recognisable as substances or objects which could easily become waste: "Q2 Off-specification products"; "Q4 Materials spilled, lost or having undergone other mishap"; "Q6 Unusable parts"; "Q13 Any materials, substances or products whose used has been banned by law"; "Q14 Products for which the holder has no more use". It also includes residues of industrial processes, mining and manufacturing. These categories, each quite specific, are followed by Q16 which provides a catch-all category of "any materials, substance or products which are not contained in the above categories". Anything, therefore, can be a waste, as long as its holder discards or intends to discard it. Those items which are listed in the Q1-Q15 categories, moreover, are not themselves waste unless the holder discards or intends to discard them. In other words, categories Q1-Q15 do not themselves provide any very useful guide to what is and is not a waste under the Directive.

As the European Court has pointed out time and again, this means that the scope of the term waste turns on the meaning of the term "discard".[28] The original Directive used the term to "dispose of".[29] That term would appear to place the focus on the intention of the waste holder: if someone wants to get rid of something, that thing will be a waste. However, the Court considers that placing the emphasis on the intention of the waste holder might jeopardise the essential aim of the Directive, which is to protect human health and safeguard the environment: after all, what one man wishes to get rid of may well be, for another, a useful economic

---

[28] *C-129/96 Inter-Environnement Wallonie* [1997] ECR I-7411, para.26.
[29] Article 1(a), Directive 75/442.

resource. In *Vessoso and Zanetti*[30] the Court dealt with substances that, whilst being disposed of by their original holder, were still capable of economic reutilisation. The Court nevertheless considered them to be waste and so subject to the controls of the Directive. Article 1, the Court said, draws no distinction according to the intentions of the holder disposing of any substance. As pointed out in C-304/94 *Tombesi and Others* [1997] ECR I-3561,[31] the system of supervision and control established by Directive 75/442, as amended, is intended to cover all objects and substances discarded by their owners, even if they have a commercial value and are collected on a commercial basis for recycling, reclamation or reuse. This means that the instant the holder of a substance decides to discard it, the Directive will apply, and will not relinquish control until it has been conclusively shown that the substance should no longer be considered a waste.

The European Court's approach did not change with the amendments brought about by the 1991 Directive.[32] However, the structure of the Directive means that the meaning of the term "discard" is even less clear than that of the term "dispose of". This is because, as pointed out by the Court in C-129/96 *Inter-Environnement Wallonie* [1997] ECR I-7411,[33] the definition of waste in Article 1(a) applies not only to things which undergo disposal operations as listed in Annex IIA of the Directive, but also those which undergo "recovery" operations as listed in Annex IIB. This means that, for example, even such operations as R4 the recycling or reclamation of metals, which in ordinary language could not really be considered the action of someone who intended to discard them, may be considered a discarding. The metals so treated will therefore still be considered waste pending further enquiry. As Advocate-General Jacobs pointed out in his opinion in *Tombesi*, little is to be gained by considering the ordinary meaning of the word "discard".[34]

This expansive definition of the word "discard", which governs the European definition of waste, is reflected in the dicta of the European Court. In *Arco*, the Court insisted that, given that the Directive and the

15–020

---

[30] C-206/88 and C-207/88, [1990] ECR I-1461.
[31] Joined Cases C-304/94, *C-330/94*, C-342/94 and C-224/95 Tombesi and Others [1997] ECR I-3561, para.52.
[32] As the Court itself stated in C-442/92 *Commission v Germany* [1995] ECR I-1097, para.23.
[33] At para.27; see also C-418/97 *Arco Chemie Nederland Ltd Anors* [2000] ECR I-4475 at para.47.
[34] Joined cases C-304/94, C-330/94, C-342/94 and C-224/95 *Criminal proceedings against Euro Tombesi anors* [1997] ECR I-3561, Opinion of AG Jacobs at para.50. AG Jacobs preferred to "bypass" the term discard altogether in favour of a definition which revolved around the concepts of "recovery" and "disposal", an approach known as the "Tombesi bypass". However, the Court has not favoured this approach: as it has said inter alia in *Niselli*, an interpretation of the term "discard" based solely on the disposal or recovery operations listed in Annex II would mean that "a substance or object not subject to a disposal or recovery requirement whose holder discards it by simple abandonment, without subjecting it to such an operation, would not be classified as 'waste' although it would be such within the meaning of Directive 75/442" The illogicality is self-evident.

Treaty aim at achieving a high level of protection for the environment, the "precautionary principle and the principle that preventive action should be taken", the concept of waste "cannot be interpreted restrictively."[35]

Equally cautious is the new WFD, which is discussed further in relation to the definition of the end-of-waste, below. Whilst as a result of the efforts of both the Council and Parliament the text contains attempts to clarify the definitions of the end-of-waste and by-products, there is no change to the definition of waste currently found in Article 1(1). It is as if everyone recognises that the search for meaning is not to be found in this definition but in the other parts of the Directive which apply the definition in practice.

As a caveat to the above, it should be noted that, whilst the intention or inferred intention of the waste holder determines whether or not the material he holds is waste, the same is not true where the holder of a material accidentally spills it. In *Van de Walle*[36] the court pointed out that, whilst Annex I to the WFD 2006 includes as a category of waste "Q4 materials spilled, lost or having undergone other mishap, including any materials, equipment, etc., contaminated as a result of the mishap," that category merely indicated that the spilled material *may* fall within the scope of waste; it did not necessarily mean that it did. The Court nevertheless found that, given that the spilled hydrocarbons could not be used or marketed they had therefore been discarded, "albeit involuntarily".[37] Similarly, in *Thames Water Utilities Ltd v South East London division, Bromley Magistrates' Court*,[38] the Court found that the escape of waste water from a sewerage network constituted an "event by which ... the holder of that waste water 'discards' it": the escaped water was therefore waste, at least in principle.[39]

---

[35] *ARCO* at para.40; whether or not this conclusion necessarily follows will be discussed below.

[36] [2004] ECR I-7613.

[37] The same logic was used in *C-188/07 Commune de Mesquer v Total France SA*, n.y.r, June 2008, in which the Court found that, whilst the heavy fuel oil in question was itself not a waste, when accidentally spilled at the sea its further use was uncertain and hypothetical and would be very costly: it was, therefore, no longer capable of being exploited or marketed without prior processing and the holder had therefore, "albeit involuntarily", discarded it.

[38] [2007] ECR I-3883.

[39] The ECJ nevertheless left open the question of whether the escape of waste water was covered by domestic legislation so as to exclude it from the scope of the Directive pursuant to Article 2(1)(b)(iv). When the case came back to the UK, the Divisional Court determined ([2008] EWHC 1763) that there were no precise provisions governing the management of waste that escaped unintentionally from the sewerage system. Accordingly, the waste water was not "covered by other legislation" and was "controlled waste" for the purposes of the prosecution of the utilities company under s.33 EPA.

The beginning of waste: By-products

Virtually every production process will produce not only the substance, 15–021
material or object which is the primary purpose of that process, but also
secondary products which may or may not be waste. Some of those products may be economically or practically useful, whether to the original
producer or to another economic actor. Despite the "precautionary principle", the European Court has shown itself amenable to preventing the
secondary by-products of production processes from being consigned
immediately to the legal category of "waste". To do so would be to fail to
encourage the reuse of such "by-products" of manufacturing or industry in
the economy.

In *Palin Granit Oy*[40] the Court outlined what might determine whether a
secondary product is in fact waste. As a start it is necessary to distinguish
between what is a product and what is a "production residue". The latter is
a product not in itself sought for a subsequent use, one which is not the
primary objective of its producer, and of which the undertaking seeks to
limit the quantity produced. If the substance is in fact a primary product,
there is no further inquiry: it will not be waste. Likewise when a by-product
is used as part of the production process itself: for example, in *AvestaPolarit
Chrome Oy*,[41] leftover stone was used to fill in underground galleries. It was
therefore being used "as a material in the industrial mining process
proper" and could not be regarded as substances which the holder discards
or intends to discard, "since, on the contrary, he needs them for his
principal activity."[42]

If, however, the substance can be considered a production residue, it
must be considered waste unless certain other criteria are met: after all,
said the Court in *Palin Granit*,

> "according to its ordinary meaning, waste is what falls away when one
> processes a material or an object and is not the end-product which the
> manufacturing process directly seeks to produce".

Further questions must therefore be asked to determine whether or not it is
a waste product.

Amongst these further questions it must be considered whether reuse of 15–022
the secondary materials produced is not a "mere possibility but a certainty". In relation to this criterion, the Court indicated in *Palin Granit* that
where there was a financial advantage to the holder in reusing the by-
product, likelihood of reuse is high and that the "substance in question
must no longer be regarded as a burden which its holder seeks to discard,
but as a genuine product." In the case itself, the leftover stone was to be
stored on site for a considerable length of time pending its foreseeable

---

[40] C-9/00 [2002] I-3533.
[41] C-114/01 [2003] ECR I-8725.
[42] *Avesta* at para.37.

reuse. Those "potentially long-term storage operations ... constitute a burden to the holder" and the stone was therefore to be considered waste.

Equally, reuse must be possible "without any further processing". In *AvestaPolarit* the Court said that if a further recovery process—i.e. one of the operations set out at Annex IIB—is needed before the material can be used, it is evidence that the material is waste, and remains so, until that process is completed. In that case the material in question was leftover rock and ore-dressing sand, which required processing into aggregates before it could be used, and so it was to be considered waste.

Further, the by-product must be reused as "an integral part of the production process".[43] The meaning of this criterion is somewhat obscure. It is clear that when a substance is used by its producer to assist the production of the primary product, or as an integral part of its business, the substance will be a useful by-product and not a waste:. Thus the leftover rock and sand residue from ore-dressing operations in the working of a mine were not classified as waste where their holder used them lawfully for the necessary filling-in of the galleries of the mine.[44] From *Niselli*[45] it seems clear that the product must be reused as an integral part of the *same* process of production or use.[46] The consumption residues which were the subject of that case, and were held to be waste, could be "reused in the same or a similar or different production or consumption cycle" and the Italian law under challenge permitted the substance to escape the definition of waste if "it is or could be reused in any production or consumption cycle". However, in *Commission v Spain*[47] the phrase used was "as part of the continuing process of production"[48] and the Court considered that live-stock effluent from pig farms could be considered a by-product even if it was to be used as fertiliser on land not part of the same agricultural holding as that which generated the slurry.[49] It is, therefore, not clear when the Court considers the process of production to end, and whether the reuse must be an integral part of that production, or whether in fact it is enough that the production of the by-product ready for use be an integral part of the production process.

15–023   In 2007 the Commission issued an Interpretative Communication containing a decision tree for the determination of whether a substance is a

---

[43] *Palin Granit* at para.36.
[44] C-114/01 *AvestaPolarit Chrome*, para.43.
[45] C-457/02 [2004] ECR I-10853.
[46] *Niselli* at para.52.
[47] C-121/03 [2005] I-7569.
[48] C-416/02 [2005] I-7487.
[49] The Court pointed out that in *Saetti and Frediani* (at para.47) the Court had held that it is possible for a substance not to be regarded as waste if it is certain to be used to meet the needs of economic operators other than that which produced it: the petrol coke was to be used as fuel not only in the refinery which produced it but "in other industries". See C-235/02 *Saetti and Frediani* [2004] ECR I-1005, para.47.

product, by-product or waste. This echoes the judgment in *Palin Granit*, and is set out below:[50]

Diagram 15/II

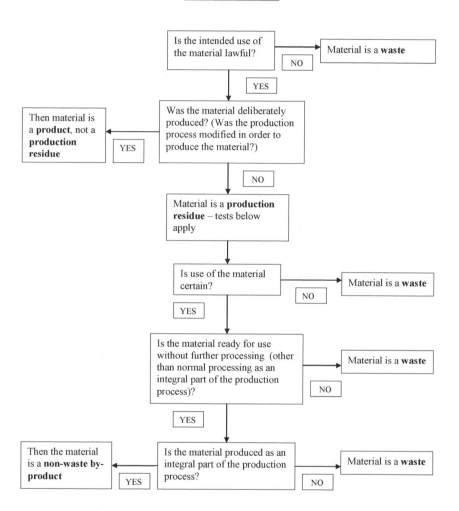

If all these steps are fulfilled, the material will be a by-product and not a waste and will not therefore be subject to the waste controls put in place by the Directive. The Interpretative Communication also provides the Commission's position on the interpretation of all the criteria set out above. It is worth noting that the Commission considers that it is only the

---

[50] Commission Communication on the Interpretative Communication on Waste and By-Products COM (2007) 59 final, Annex II.

production of the by-product that must be an integral part of the production process of the primary material, and not necessarily its re-use, so favouring the position taken by the ECJ in *Commission v Spain*,[51] as described above.

It should also be noted that the risk of harm to human health or of environmental pollution plays no part in determining whether a secondary substance is a production residue which must be considered waste, or is a non-waste by-product. This appears to be because the Court considers that the accumulation, or storage, of material which will not or may not be used is itself a type of environmental pollution,[52] whether or not it can be shown to be harmful.

15–024   The new WFD essentially codifies the principles laid down by the ECJ. Article 5 provides that a substance is a by-product rather than as waste as long as:

(a) Further use of the substance is "certain";
(b) The substance can be used directly without any further processing other than "normal industrial practice";
(c) The substance is produced as an "integral part" of a production process; and
(d) Further use is "lawful", i.e. the substance fulfils all relevant product, environmental and health protection requirements for the specific use and will not lead to overall adverse environmental or human health impacts.

It is to be presumed that the Court's explanations of the phrases such as "certain", without any further processing, and "integral part of a production process" will continue to apply. However, there are potential difficulties in applying the criteria in (d). What does it mean that a substance will not lead to "overall" adverse environmental impacts? May the substance have some adverse impacts, as long as "overall" its impact is acceptable? Further, if the use of a substance can be shown to have an adverse environmental impact yet its use in the Member State in question is not illegal, are the criteria in (d) fulfilled?

There is also provision in Article 5(2) of the 2008 WFD for measures to be laid down in relation to specific substances or materials in order to determine the criteria which must be met for them to be considered by-products rather than waste. Those measures will be proposed by the Commission and overseen by the European Parliament.

---

[51] *C-121/03* [2005] I-7569.
[52] See *Palin Granit* at paras 45–51.

End of waste

In order to encourage the re-use and recycling of waste into useful eco-   **15–025**
nomic products, there must come a point when a substance which has been
considered waste is allowed to escape the burden of regulation and control
imposed by the Directive and compete on equal terms with the natural raw
materials which would otherwise have been used. Unfortunately, once a
substance has come within the system of supervision and control envisaged
by the Directive, it is not always easy to predict when the Court will accept
that the substance has left it.

The conjoined cases in *ARCO* related to two types of substance: in the
first the substance was a petrochemical manufacturing residue which was
to be burned as a fuel; in the second it was wood chip residue from the
construction industry which was to be reduced to powder and burned as a
fuel. The Court determined that the method of treatment or use of a
substance does not determine conclusively whether or not it is to be
classified as waste:[53] a substance will not be a waste just because it has
undergone one of the "recovery" operations in Annex IIB.[54]

However, although not all substances treated by such methods will
necessarily remain waste,[55] it is clear that some will. The parties in *ARCO*
canvassed multiple ways in which the Court might come to a decision that
a substance has ceased to be waste. The national court asked whether the
answer to the question as to whether a substance has ceased to be waste
depends on whether (a) it is commonly regarded as waste; (b) it may be
recovered "in an environmentally responsible manner for use as fuel
without substantial processing"; (c) the use of the substance as a fuel
amounted to a "common method of waste recovery"; (d) the substance
used is a main product or a by-product.

The court reiterated that the method of treatment or use of a substance   **15–026**
does not determine conclusively whether or not it is to be classified as
waste.[56] It also stated that the definition of waste does not exclude substances and objects which are capable of being recovered as fuel in an
environmentally responsible manner and without substantial treatment.[57]
In fact, it stated, somewhat surprisingly, "the environmental impact of the
processing of that substance has no effect on its classification as waste".
However, the court conceded that

> "if the use of a substance as fuel is a common method of recovering
> waste, that use may be evidence that the holder has discarded or intends
> or is required to discard that substance".

[53] *ARCO*, para.67.
[54] *ARCO*, para.49.
[55] *ARCO*, para.45.
[56] *ARCO*, para.64
[57] *ARCO*, para.65.

It also considered that

"the fact that a substance used as fuel is the residue of the manufacturing process of another substance, that no use for that substance other than disposal can be envisaged, that the composition of the substance is not suitable for the use made of it or that special environmental precautions must be taken when it is used may be regarded as evidence"

—but no more than evidence—that the holder discards that substance. Likewise, the fact that a substance has undergone a "complete recovery operation" so as to acquire the same properties and characteristics as a raw material is one of the factors—but only one of those factors, not a determinative one—to be taken into consideration for the purpose of determining whether the substance has ceased to constitute waste. Rather unhelpfully, the court concluded that whether a substance is waste "must be determined in the light of all the circumstances", regard being had to the aim of the directive and the need to ensure that its effectiveness is not undermined.

In *Mayer Parry v Environment Agency*[58] the European Court addressed the question of when packaging waste could be considered to have been recycled.[59] It also dealt with the definition of waste in that it went on to decide that the waste in question, having gone through a recycling process which involved the transformation of the packaging waste into a new product "possessing characteristics comparable to those of the material from which the waste was derived", was no longer to be considered waste.[60] The decision is in apparent contrast to the decision in *ARCO* that the fact that a substance has undergone a complete recovery operation and thus acquired "the same properties and characteristics as a raw material" was not a determining factor in assessing whether the substance had ceased to be waste.

The "end of waste" case law has caused much confusion. This is understandable when it is considered that there may be disputes about what, exactly, the Directive is intended to achieve and at what kind of effectiveness it aims. As discussed above, the Court's stated aim, derived from the Directive, of achieving a "high level of environmental protection" is not necessarily best achieved by giving "waste" the widest possible definition.

15–027   For reasons which will become clear it is worth pointing out here that the OECD definition of waste has focussed, as regards the end of waste issue, on whether the use of that waste is as environmentally sound as the

[58] *C-444/00* [2003] ECR I-6163.
[59] Within the meaning of Article 94/62 on packaging and packaging waste.
[60] See *Mayer Parry* at paras 75 and 91. It may be noted that, when considering what constituted "recycling", the court found it important to point out the ecological aim of the Community legislator: a reduction in the consumption of energy and of primary raw materials.

material it is replacing, and whether it causes no more risk to human health or the environment than the use of the corresponding raw material.[61] Its Waste Management Policy's Group's *Final Document for Distinguishing Waste from Non-Waste* sets out the criteria as follows:

"a waste ceases to be waste when a recovery, or another comparable, process eliminates or sufficiently diminishes the threat posed to the environment by the original material (waste) and yields a material of sufficient beneficial use. In general the recovery of a material (waste) will have taken place when:

(a) it requires no further processing by a [recovery] operation
AND
(b) the recovered material can and will be used in the same way as a material which has not been defined as waste
AND
(c) the recovered material meets all relevant health and environmental requirements."[62]

The Court's reasoning in *ARCO* has been described in the English courts as "Delphic"[63] and "obscure".[64] Stanley Burnton J., in *Castle Cement v Environment Agency*,[65] and Lord Reed, in the Scottish case of *Scottish Power Generation Ltd v Scottish Environment Protection Agency*,[66] each undertook a comprehensive review of the case law as it then stood. Lord Reed enumerated the indicators which might be addressed by the court when determining whether or not a substance remained waste, pointing out that none of them was conclusive in itself.[67] Disagreeing with Stanley Burnton J., he came to the conclusion that the right test to apply, when it is claimed that a substance which was once waste has ceased to be waste, was one similar to that used by the OECD: that is, the test described in *ARCO* of whether the substance has undergone a "complete recovery operation" so as to become "analogous to a raw material, with the same characteristics as a raw material and capable of being used in the same conditions of environmental protection". He adopted the test used by Advocate-General Alber in *ARCO* of whether a substance continued to

---

[61] The approach taken by the OECD is pertinent, as it expresses the common approach in countries beyond the European Union. The OECD has played an important part in harmonising international definitions of waste. It is important to note that it too uses a very similar structure of "recovery" and "disposal" in setting out waste management policy.

[62] *Final Guidance Document for Distinguishing Waste from Non-Waste*, OECD Environment Directorate, Waste Management Policy Group, April 23, 1998 (ENV/EPOC/WMP(98)1/REV1), para.43.

[63] Stanley Burton J. in *Castle Cement* at para.45.

[64] *OSS v Environment Agency* [2007] EWCA Civ 611 at para.43.

[65] [2001] Env. L.R. 46.

[66] [2005] SLT 98.

[67] *Scottish Power* at paras 135–7.

pose a "danger typical of waste".[68] Lord Reed glossed over the fact that the Court in *ARCO* rejected the test of environmental risk by indicating that the Court's conclusion was in fact a caveat, indicating that a substance which would otherwise have reached the stage of no longer being considered waste would nevertheless be waste if the owner discards it.[69]

It appears that when Lord Reed used the term "discard" in this second context he was using it in a subjective sense: that is, in its common meaning of "getting rid of" a substance. There are two problems with this approach: firstly, that his conclusion appears to ignore the plain meaning of the Court's conclusion in *ARCO* at para.65 that the environmental impact of a substance has "no" effect on its classification as waste. Secondly, as Stanley Burnton J. agreed with the Environment Agency in *Castle Cement*, the "environmental risk" test is too uncertain in that it presents the problem of determining which type of raw material is to be compared with the substance that it is claimed has ceased to be waste—some types may be more damaging to the environment than others.[70]

15–028   More recently, in *OSS v Environment Agency*[71] the Court of Appeal relied heavily on the exposition of the case law set out in *Castle Cement* and *Scottish Power*. The case dealt with the question of whether waste lubricating oils, having gone through a decontamination process, could "thereafter be burnt other than as waste". Carnwath L.J. noted with approbation Lord Reed's approach of applying a series of indicative factors to the question of whether a substance had ceased to be waste, none of which was by itself determinative. However, he found himself unable to agree with the interpretation of *ARCO* offered by Lord Reed in *Scottish Power*. He did not think that the Court should have regard to the remote possibility that a waste holder might, having undertaken a costly recovery process, be unable to find a market for the material produced and have to discard it. Neither was he able to accept the explanation offered by the judge at first instance that the decision in *ARCO* meant that a substance which had undergone a complete recovery operation might nevertheless become waste again through undergoing a subsequent recovery operation,[72] and confessed that the Court's decision in *ARCO* remained a mystery to him.[73]

Carnwath L.J. summarised the position thus:

"although the Court continues to pay lip-service to the 'discarding' test, in practice it subordinates the subjective question implicit in that definition to a series of objective indicators derived from the policy of the

[68] *Scottish Power* at para.107.
[69] *Scottish Power* at para.104.
[70] *Castle Cement* at para.47.
[71] [2007] EWCA Civ 611.
[72] *OSS* at para.43.
[73] *OSS* at paras 44 to 47.

Directive. What is required from the national court is a value judgment on the facts of the particular case in the light of those indicators".

However, he also went on to state that "it should be enough" that a waste material has been converted into a "distinct, marketable product, which can be used in exactly the same way as an ordinary fuel, and with no worse environmental effects".[74]

His Lordship went on to encourage Defra and the Environment Agency to formulate some practical guidance for the assistance of waste handlers. They have now done so in the form of the Agency's Waste Protocols Project, which aims to develop a Quality Protocol for several different waste streams on how to recover each one in order to render it non-waste and to remove it from the regulatory regime. For each waste it will provide detailed steps and set out the regulatory requirements with which those who would use that waste must comply. The waste streams under consideration, together with the final uses to they can be put as non-waste, are listed on the Agency's website. A consultation is being launched in turn for each material under consideration for a Quality Protocol.[75]

15–029

Whilst the Waste Protocols Project is in progress, the Agency's position is that a waste remains a waste until the "point of final use". This approach may well be in conflict with the decision in OSS, at least in relation to fuel oils. However, it has stated that it recognises that enforcement action may not be appropriate against those who use one of the relevant wastes for that final use without holding a permit or exemption from permitting—as long as the activity is not mixed with other wastes, is mixed with non-wastes only to improve its use, and the activity is carried out in such a way that it does not, or is unlikely to, cause harm to human health or the environment The Agency is unlikely to take enforcement action unless the activity has caused, or is likely to cause, pollution or harm to health.[76] Wastes which are not being considered for a quality protocol will not benefit from such

---

[74] At the time of writing Advocate General Kokott had just issued her opinion in C-317/07 *Lahti Energia Oy*, September 11, 2008. She stated that treatment and purification of a gas in a gas factory could transform that gas into a substance which has ceased to be waste. A waste could cease to be waste if it is transformed so that it is no longer distinguishable from the primary material or from other products (para.53). It is also necessary to examine whether there is a market for the product and if the "waste" product has comparable characteristics to the primary product in the light of risk to the environment (para.56). In other words, it appears that the European Court is moving in the same direction as the domestic authorities. The judgment of the Court in *Lahti* is awaited.

[75] Those being considered include: anaerobic digestate (for which a Draft Quality Protocol has been produced); blast furnace slag; compost; flat glass (for which a summary report has been produced); non-packaging plastic waste (for which a summary report has been produced); processed fuel oil (a consultation has been launched for such oil produced from waste lubricating oil); pulverised fuel ash (for which a Draft Quality Protocol has been produced with a consultation running from September to December 2008); soils; tyre-derived rubber (for which a Draft Quality Protocol has been produced); "biodiesel" from waste cooking oil (for which a summary report has been produced); and wood waste.

[76] Regulatory position statement: the regulation of materials being considered under the Waste Protocols Project (MWRP017 Version 2), July 2008.

official guidance as regards when they may cease to be waste. That decision will continue to be governed by the, somewhat uncertain, general principles of law outlined above.

In similar vein to the Agency's Waste Protocols Project, the new EU Waste Framework Directive, in Article 6, sets out a test for the end of waste—but only for "specified wastes" yet to be determined. The test states that a specified waste shall cease to be waste only when it has undergone a recovery operation, "including recycling", and complies with specific criteria to be developed in accordance with the following conditions:

(a) the substance or object is commonly used for specific purposes;
(b) a market or demand exists for such a substance or object;
(c) the substance or object fulfils the technical requirements for the specific purposes and meets the existing legislation and standards applicable to products;
(d) the use of the substance or object will not lead to overall adverse environmental or human health impacts.

The criteria are to include "limit values for pollutants where necessary and shall take into account any possible adverse environmental effects of the substance or object."

15–030   In other words, the question of whether certain specified wastes have ceased to be a waste will to a large extent no longer be a question for the judgment of national courts and will very largely be determined by guidance issued at EU level by a technical committee. It can be seen that the European institutions are keen to introduce a technical, product-standard approach to the determination of the end of waste, whilst also preserving the criterion of overall environmental impact.

It will be noted, however, that such environmental impact is not to be measured in comparison with the raw material which the substance is intended to replace, but is a question of "overall" adverse environmental or human health impacts. The problem remains, of course, that there are different types of environmental impact. What does it mean that a substance will "overall" not lead to adverse environmental impacts? It should be noted that this condition is not comparative. Does this mean that a substance has to have no adverse environmental impacts, even though the natural substance which it replaces has some? Or does it mean that a secondary substance may have some adverse impacts, even if they are worse than those produced by the natural product, as long as "overall" its impact is acceptable? There appears to be a consensus that "overall" in fact imports the comparison with the virgin raw material, but this may yet to be determined by the courts. Different criteria will of course apply in the case of each different type of waste and will be the subject of long negotiation.

Although the specified wastes and the criteria which apply to them have yet to be determined, Article 6(2) suggests that: "End-of-waste specific criteria should be considered, among others, at least for aggregates, paper, glass, metal, tyres and textiles". Until such time as the specified wastes and the criteria which apply to them are determined, the existing case law will in all likelihood apply under the new WFD as under the old. The Commission's original proposal[77] for the new WFD stated that in the meantime, and for waste where no criteria have been set out, Member States might decide case by case whether a certain waste has ceased to be waste, "taking into account the applicable case law". This statement is no longer in the proposed WFD, but is in all likelihood how the courts will continue to go about determining when the end of waste is reached—at least for those wastes which are not or not yet governed by a Quality Protocol. It remains to be seen whether the "specified wastes" in line for European technical definition will coincide with those being considered by the UK Waste Protocols Project.

Polluter pays principle

Article 191 (previously Article 174) of the European Treaty states that European environment policy should be based on **15–031**

"the precautionary principle and on the principles that preventive action should be taken, that environmental damage should as a priority be rectified at source and that the polluter should pay".

Article 15 of the WFD 2006 amplifies the "polluter pays" principle by stating that;

"in accordance with the polluter pays principle, the cost of disposing of waste must be borne by the holder who has waste handled by a waste collector and/or the previous holders or the producer of the product from which the waste came."

This was generally thought to amount to no more than a general guiding principle, rather that a mechanism for determining liability in legal proceedings.[78] However, the recent decision in *Mesquer*[79] (the "Erika" case) dealt directly with the question of who should bear the financial cost of disposing of the waste generated by oil spilled in a shipwreck: the producer of the heavy fuel oil spilled at sea, the seller of the fuel and charterer of the ship, or the carrier by sea. The ECJ found that the owner of the ship carrying the hydrocarbons immediately before they became waste may be considered as having produced that waste, and so could be considered its "holder" for the purposes of the Directive.[80] Likewise, if the seller of the

[77] Council document 12463/07 ENV 445 CODEC 869, August 30, 2007.
[78] See, for example, Bell and McGillivray, *Environmental Law* 7th edition, (OUP, 2008), pp.244–5
[79] Above, June 2008.
[80] *Mesquer*, para.73.

hydrocarbons and charterer of the ship contributed in some way to the risk that pollution would occur, or failed to take measures to prevent such an incident (the ECJ gives the example of the choice of ship), he could also be considered the producer of waste. However, the ECJ applied the polluter pays principle to find that national law could not impose the cost of disposing of the accidentally spilled hydrocarbons on the producer of the product from which the waste came unless he had contributed by his conduct to the risk that the pollution caused by the shipwreck would occur.

Article 15 of the new WFD elaborates the principle in several respects. It provides that "in accordance with the polluter-pays principle, the costs of waste management [NB: not just waste disposal] shall be borne by the original waste producer or by the current or previous waste holders". There is no indication of a priority order for liability. However, paragraph 2 of the new Article 15 now allows Member States to decide that the costs of waste management are to be borne "partly or wholly by the producer of the product from which the waste came [NB: not just the producer of the waste itself] and that the distributors of such product may share these costs". The Article is a welcome reflection of the new emphasis on lifecycle thinking in waste management.

Excluded wastes

15–032   There is a relatively wide category of wastes excluded by Article 2 of the WFD 2006 from its scope. This has changed somewhat over time,[81] but the gist is to avoid duplication of controls where a given type of waste is separately regulated. The purpose of this section is therefore to consider these excluded wastes, and to explain briefly the alternative regimes applicable to these specific waste streams.

Article 2(1)(a) of the 2006 WFD unequivocally excluded "gaseous effluents into the atmosphere" from its purview. Then, in Article 2(1)(b), there is a list of types of waste which are excluded from its provisions where they are *already covered by* other legislation:

(i)   radioactive waste;
(ii)   waste resulting from mining and quarries;
(iii) animal carcases and "faecal matter and other natural, non-dangerous substances used in farming";
(iv)   waste waters "with the exception of waste in a liquid form";
(v)   decommissioned explosives.

The new WFD moves radioactive waste and decommissioned explosives into the unequivocally excluded category (i.e. currently Article 2(1)(a)) together with agricultural waste falling within (iii) above. "Land in situ

---

[81] This is well charted in para.50 of the opinion of Advocate-General Kokott in C-252/05, *R (Thames Water) v Bromley MC* [2007] 1 WLR 1945.

(including unexcavated contaminated soil and buildings permanently connected with land" will also be excluded, thereby reversing the result of the *Van de Walle* case.[82] Uncontaminated excavated soil[83] is also to be excluded, a change of some importance given the quantities of construction and demolition waste within the scope of the WFD 2006.[84] Article 2(3) of the new Directive excludes sediments taken from surface waters from its application, but only when it is proved that these sediments are non-hazardous.

The question as to whether a waste falls into the unequivocally excluded category (Article 2(1)(a)) or is only excluded when "covered by other legislation" in Article 2(1)(b) is one of some importance. This is because the European Court has set a quite onerous test in relation to the latter provision. As it observed in *AvestaPolarit*[85] and *Thames* (above),

"to be regarded as 'other legislation' within the meaning of article 2(1)(b) of Directive 75/442, the rules in question must not merely relate to a particular substance, but must contain precise provisions organising its management as waste within the meaning of article 1(d) of the Directive."[86]

Hence, in *Thames*, for a leak from sewers to amount to "waste waters covered by other legislation", it needed to be shown that other legislation (which currently[87] may include both Community and domestic legislation) satisfied the requirements of the 2006 WFD's Articles 4, 8 (proper waste management) and 15 (polluter pays).[88]

Before turning to the specific exclusions, one should note the provisions **15–033** of Article 2(2) of the WFD 2006, repeated in Article 2(4) of the new WFD. This provides that detailed rules may be made by individual directives supplementing those in the WFD. This does not mean that waste falling within those rules is not waste within the meaning of the WFD, even

---

[82] In *Thames*, above, at para.47, Advocate-General Kokott warned that this change "could however substantially weaken the practical effectiveness of European waste law in respect of dealing with infringements, since illegal disposal of waste frequently involves it being mixed with soil. That applies in particular to contamination with liquids, but it may also be the case with the depositing of solid substances on illegal waste tips."

[83] The new exclusion also extends to "other naturally occurring material excavated in the course of construction activities where it is certain that the material will be used for the purposes of construction in its natural state from the site from which it was excavated."

[84] This reverses the result in cases like *Department of Environment & Heritage Service v O'Hare & Phillips* [2007] NICA 45, a decision of the Northern Ireland Court of Appeal.

[85] *C-114/01* [2003] ECR I-8725.

[86] para.33 of the judgment.

[87] This is to be changed by the new WFD, where the other legislation must be Community legislation: art.2(2).

[88] The ECJ had held that this test was not satisfied by the Urban Waste Water Treatment Directive. The matter returned to the Divisional Court ([2008] EWHC 1763 (QB), July 28, 2008), which decided that this test was not satisfied by either domestic sewerage legislation or the EPA 1990, Parts 2A (contaminated land) or Part 3 (statutory nuisance).

though the provisions within those individual directives (as special legislation or *lex specialis*) may prevail over those in the WFD.[89]

Article 2(1)(a)

Gaseous effluents

15–034   The justification for this exclusion is reasonably clear. Either the process creating the gaseous effluents is a waste operation, such as the deliberate evaporation of waste solvents,[90] or landfill or waste incineration,[91] in which event those operations are governed by the WFD or other waste legislation, *or* the effluents will arise from some process which, in the case of any real hazard, is likely to be governed by the IPPC Directive or the EP Regulations.

Radioactive waste

15–035   Comprehensive controls over radioactive waste are contained in the Radioactive Substances Act 1993, and regulations made thereunder (see Chapter 20), as well in Council Directive 96/29/Euratom. This exclusion at Community level is reflected in section 78 of EPA 1990, under which Part 2 of that Act (on waste) does not apply to radioactive waste unless specifically provided for in Regulations.

Faecal matter (new WFD)

15–036   The decision to include this in the category of unequivocally excluded waste material appears to follow decisions of the European Court which have become known as the Spanish Pigs cases.[92] These decided that pig manure spread on farmland was generally speaking, a product, not waste. The decision was legally controversial,[93] but evidently politically welcome to agricultural interests. There is an ambiguity in the wording of the new provision. Is faecal matter[94] excluded in any event, or only where "it is used in farming ... through processes or methods which do not harm the environment or endanger human health", as the closing words of the new Article 2(1)(f) provide? A literal reading would favour the former, but a typically purposive reading by the ECJ would tend towards the latter.

---

[89] *AvestaPolarit*, para.48, and *Thames*, para.57 per A-G Kokott, and para.39 per ECJ.

[90] See, for instance, the wording of D9 of Annex IIA to the current WFD, which includes evaporation as a "physico-chemical treatment."

[91] See A-G Kokott in C-317/07 *Lahti Energia Oy*, September 11, 2008, at para.44.

[92] C-416/02 *Commission v Spain* [2005] ECR I-7487 and C-121/03 *Commission v Spain* [2005] ECR I-7569.

[93] Kramer, *EC Environmental Law*, 6th edition, (Sweet & Maxwell, 2006) para.10.22 and *Brady v EPA* [2007] IEHC 58, High Court of Ireland, Carleton J.

[94] There is a caveat: faecal matter which amounts to animal by-products falls to be regulated by art.2(2), namely to the extent that it is covered by other legislation.

Article 2(1)(b)

Waste Waters (with the exception of waste in liquid form)

The intent here is to exclude waste waters when being collected into sewers   **15–037**
and being treated in sewage works. As we have seen in Chapter 11,[95] the
Urban Waste Water Treatment Directive applies, and hence covers, this
position, unless and until sewage escapes from sewers.

The wording of the WFD 2006 expressly includes "waste in a liquid
form", as a specific subset of, and exclusion from, waste waters in general.
A passage from the first edition of this work was approved by Nelson J. in
United Utilities v Environment Agency.[96] This drew a distinction

> "between (consented) aqueous discharges, whether to controlled waters
> or to sewer, in which the concentration of any pollutants is very low, and
> waste materials and products which are in fact relatively concentrated
> aqueous solutions or suspensions".

Nelson J.,[97] applying this interpretation, concluded that sewage sludge was
"waste in liquid form" within the meaning of this phrase. The former will
be waste waters and so excluded; the latter "liquid waste" and so within
the WFD.

The new WFD deletes the reference to "liquid form". Whether this
makes a material change is doubtful. It might be said that the distinction
identified above is implicit in the definition of waste "waters". It is not
intended to exclude concentrated aqueous solutions from the ambit of the
Directive, let alone non-aqueous liquids. Whether it was sensible to delete
this clarification is another matter.

Household sewage is not commercial waste[98] though it may be industrial   **15–038**
waste, and hence controlled waste, if it is disposed of in or on land.[99] If
disposed of within a sewage works, it is not controlled waste.[100] This
coincides with the distinction drawn at a European level between waste
waters regulated by the UWWT Directive and those subject to the WFD.

When sewage is subject to settlement and other treatment processes
within sewage works, its more concentrated fraction will become sewage
sludge. Whilst being treated, it is subject to the WFD or the IPPC
Directive, depending on the processes and capacities of the plant involved.
However, once it is "used" in agriculture, and to the extent that it remains
"waste waters"[101] then it may become "covered by" the separate regime

---

[95] para.11–039.
[96] [2006] Env. L.R. 849, approving para.11–106.
[97] The point did not arise on appeal.
[98] EPA, s.75(8).
[99] Controlled Waste Regulations 1992 (SI 1992/588), reg. 5(1), and para.7 of Sch.3.
[100] CWR 1992, reg.7(1)(a).
[101] Contra Nelson J. in *United Utilities*, above.

laid down by Council Directive 86/278/EEC concerning Sewage Sludge in Agriculture,[102] as implemented by the Sludge (Use in Agriculture) Regulations 1989, as amended.[103] These seek to ensure safety from toxic substances contained in the sludge, by limiting the concentration of heavy metals in the sludge, and by prohibiting grazing or harvesting within defined periods after application of the sludge to the land.

Animal by-products/carcases

15–039 The WFD 2006 simply refers to animal carcases. The 2008 WFD expands this into animal by-products and animal carcases, thus reversing the outcome of the ECJ's decision in *KVZ Retec v Austria*[104] that meat and bone meal derived from animal carcases did not amount to animal carcases. In either case, the present European position is regulated by the Animal By-products Regulations 1774/2002, governing both carcases and products made from carcases, dividing these into various risk categories, and hence defining the ultimate processing required in the light of those categories. The Advocate-General in *KVZ Retec*, having concluded (contrary to the ultimate decision of the Court) that meat and bone meal did fall within Article 2(1)(b) as then drafted, went on to conclude that the Regulations did contain sufficiently precise provisions governing the management of the material, and hence it was "covered by other legislation" within the meaning of Article 2(1)(b) of the 2006 WFD.

Mineral and quarry waste

15–040 Here there is little change between the 2006 and 2008 WFDs, save the addition in the latter of a reference to Directive 2006/21, on the Management of Waste from Extractive Industries.[105] This Directive arose out of accidents in Aznalcolar in Spain, and Baia Mare in Romania, and the consequent discovery by the Commission that such mining and quarrying activities were largely exempt from existing Community legislation. Directive 2006/21 lays down basic provisions for the storage and treatment of mining waste. It adopts the principle of best available techniques from the IPPC Directive. Its general requirements (as contained in Article 4) are modelled on Article 4 of the 2006 WFD. Article 6 addresses major accident prevention and information, along the lines of the regime applicable, for example, to major chemical works (and implemented in the UK under the COMAH Regulations). Article 7 requires all such operations to have a permit; and public participation in the permitting process is required by Article 8. The technical, financial and aftercare provisions which make up

---

[102] OJ [1986] L181/6.
[103] SI 1989/1263, as amended by SI 1990/880. Advocate-General Kokott left this question open in *Thames*, at para.21.
[104] C-176/05.
[105] [2006] OJ L102/15.

much of the rest of the Directive are similar to those contained in the Landfill Directive, considered below, though, not surprisingly given its genesis, the need for structural safety is emphasised. As for compliance with the polluter-pays principle, such operations are added to the list of activities subject to the preventive, remedial and costs recovery regime imposed by the Environmental Liability Directive 2004/35.[106]

The Directive was due to be transposed into domestic law by May 2008, but this has not yet been done. Defra's proposal is, not surprisingly, to transpose it via a further sub-category to the Environmental Permitting Regulations, discussed above in Chapter 14. This involves a permitting regime common to many activities, with more specific provisions relevant to particular kinds of permitted activity contained in an additional schedule to those Regulations. At the moment, mining and quarry waste is currently defined as "industrial" waste within the meaning of section 75(6)(e) of the EPA, as recently amended. However, it will not qualify as "Directive waste" under the EPA, if it is excluded waste under the WFD.

This discussion has been addressing whether a given material, which would otherwise be waste covered by the WFD, is specifically excluded from its scope. We will later consider various specific provisions of domestic law implemented by the Environmental Permitting Regulations 2007, under which specific waste in specific circumstances may either not require a permit at all (exempt waste operations, which do however need registration), or may be deposited without offending against section 33 of the Environmental Protection Act 1990[107] (excluded activities, which require neither permit nor registration).

The regulation of waste management in the UK

Before going further we should explain the various competent authorities responsible for waste management in the United Kingdom. There are three principal types of authority, each with different functions: (a) the waste regulation authority, which in England and Wales is the Environment Agency; (b) waste collection authorities, which in England and Wales are the district councils or London borough councils; and (c) waste disposal authorities. **15–041**

The waste collection authorities (WCAs) have a duty to arrange for the collection of household waste and, on request, the collection of commercial and industrial waste.[108] They must also provide receptacles for waste.[109] As for recycling, section 5(2) of the Household Waste Recycling Act 2003 (a Private Members Bill) inserted a duty at section 45A EPA 1990 for WCAs

---

[106] For discussion of which, see Chapter 5.
[107] EPA 1990, s.33 contains the main waste offences, including the prohibition upon carrying out waste management activities without a permit.
[108] EPA 1990, s.45.
[109] EPA 1990, s.46.

to arrange for the collection of "at least two types of recyclable waste"[110] unless the cost of so doing would be unreasonably high, or comparable alternative arrangements are available.[111] However, the section is not due to come into force until December 31, 2010.[112]

In the meantime, WCAs may require householders to separate waste into different compartments or receptacles according to whether the waste is to be recycled or not.[113] However, in contrast to the other requirements which may be imposed on a householder by a WCA, no offence is committed by those who fail to comply.

15–042   The WCAs must deliver all waste collected to the place designated by its waste disposal authority (WDA—see below)[114] unless they decide to make arrangements for recycling it.[115] Where a WCA does retain waste for recycling, the relevant WDA must pay the WCA the sum which it would have spent on disposing of the waste; conversely, the WCA must pay to the WDA any sums which it has saved by not having to arrange for the collection of that waste.[116]

The WDAs are the county councils and other local government authorities. In many cases they will be the same local authority as the waste collection authority; in others they may be different.[117] They are under a duty to make arrangements for the disposal of waste collected by the WCAs and for the provision of places to receive, treat and dispose of waste deposited by the public;[118] they also have powers to make arrangements to recycle waste or to use it to generate heat or electricity. Both WDAs and WCAs may buy "or otherwise acquire" waste with a view to it being recycled.[119]

Development of UK waste policy

15–043   Historically, domestic law dealing with waste focussed on controlling the accumulation of waste which might cause harm to human health and the fundamental concern was to remove waste from where it might cause a risk

---

[110] EPA 1990, s.45A(2) and (3). "Recyclable waste is defined as waste which is capable of being recycled or composted": s.45A(6).

[111] EPA 1990, s.45A(2)(a) and (b).

[112] EPA 1990, s.45A(4); unless the date is delayed by the Secretary of State under the power to do so conferred by s.46(5) on the request of a WCA.

[113] EPA s.46(2).

[114] EPA 1990, s.48(1).

[115] EPA 1990, s.48(2).

[116] EPA 1990, s.52. The section also provides that these payments may be disapplied by the Secretary of State or by the agreement of the authorities.

[117] Between 1990 and 2005, local authorities were obliged to contract out the actual running of waste disposal operations to private or privatised companies (the latter being Local Authority Waste Disposal Companies, or "LAWDCs", created by the local authority under s.32 EPA 1990). That requirement was abolished by s.47 of the Clean Neighbourhoods and Environment Act 2005.

[118] EPA 1990, s.51.

[119] EPA 1990, s.52.

of such harm. The Public Health Act 1875 imposed a duty on local authorities to arrange the removal and disposal of household waste every week. As long as waste was removed from population centres, there was little concern for what happened to it; and landfill proved the most convenient option.

Whilst the Town and Country Planning Act 1947 required local councils to conform with planning and development controls when planning new waste sites, existing sites and the disposal of waste by anyone other than the local authorities with statutory waste duties remained uncontrolled. In any event, the planning system could not deal with detailed regulation of the technical operation of a waste management site.

The first concerns relating to uncontrolled disposal of waste related to hazardous waste. The dumping, in February 1972, of 36 drums of cyanide in Nuneaton caused a public outcry, and calls in Parliament and by the Royal Commission on Environmental Pollution (the RCEP)[120] for controls over the tipping of potentially dangerous wastes. The Deposit of Poisonous Waste Act 1972 (the DWPA) was passed within a month in order to provide such controls, albeit in a fairly rudimentary form.

The DPWA 1972 was soon replaced by the Control of Pollution Act 1974, which put in place a comprehensive system for dealing with the disposal of waste generally, not just that immediately recognisable as hazardous. It relied on a system of compulsory licensing for those disposing of waste by landfill or incineration, to be administered by local authorities. However, the focus of waste law was still very much on the final deposit of waste. COPA 1974 did not deal with its storage, treatment or transportation, or with any aspect of waste production or treatment further up the chain. It was also unsatisfactory in other ways, particularly in so far as enforcement was concerned. As soon as a licence holder surrendered his licence, the conditions attached to it would cease to have effect, and although the former holder could no longer work the site, he would escape any further responsibilities under the licence for the site. Equally, there was no offence of failing to comply with a licence condition; and the local authorities in charge of regulating the system were also, for the most part, those who themselves operated the waste disposal sites. **15–044**

Following the Waste Framework Directive in 1975, the first major piece of environmental legislation dealing with waste was Part 2 of the Environmental Protection Act 1990. The EPA 1990 introduced a system of waste *management* licensing. Rather than COPA's focus solely on the disposal of waste, the new system introduced controls over the whole of the waste lifecycle by ensuring also that those who produce or store waste might only do so if licensed, and in compliance with licence conditions.

Waste management licences were issued by what the EPA calls a "waste regulation authority". Originally, the relevant authorities were the London

---

[120] RCEP Second Report: *Three Issues in Industrial Pollution*, March 1972 (Cmnd. 4894).

Waste Regulation Authority and county councils exercising their waste regulation functions. However, the Environment Act 1995, which created the Environment Agency, vested it with the functions of waste regulation authorities under Part 2 EPA 1990—as well as the waste regulation functions conferred by the Control of Pollution Act 1974 and the Control of Pollution (Amendment) Act 1989.[121] Most of Part 2 EPA 1990 was brought into force on May 1, 1994, alongside the Waste Management Licensing Regulations 1994 (WMLR) which governed the operation of the regime until April 2008.

Transposing of the objectives and the development of waste policy

15–045   Schedule 4 to the WMLR transposed the objectives contained in Articles 3 to 5 of the Waste Framework Directive—set out at 15–007 above—by stating that "the competent authorities shall discharge their specified functions, in so far as they relate to the disposal or recovery of waste, with the relevant objectives"—which are then transposed almost verbatim from the WFD. The "competent authorities" are the waste regulatory authorities: the Environment Agency and any local planning authority exercising waste-related functions.

A decision-maker must therefore consider whether the aim of ensuring that waste is disposed of or recovered without endangering human health or harming the environment will be achieved as a consequence of his intended decision.[122] Although it is not incumbent on the decision-maker to ensure that the objective will actually be achieved, the objectives are not, as is usually the position, just one consideration amongst many to be taken into account. In *R v Daventry District Council ex p Thornby Farms; R (Murray) v Derbyshire County Council*[123] the Court of Appeal stated that the objectives were "more than a material consideration". The Court of Appeal considered that there could be circumstances where the decision-maker has arrived at a result that amounts to so flagrant a disregard for the objective that he can be held to have breached its obligations under Article 4.

Waste policy has continued to develop. In accordance with the requirement in Article 7 WFD for the development of national "waste management plans", the Environment Act 1995 introduced, at section 44A of the EPA 1990, a requirement that the Secretary of State produce a national waste strategy. The first, non-statutory, strategy had already been

---

[121] Environment Act 1995, s.2(b) and (c).
[122] *R v Leicester County Council, Hepworth Building Products Ltd and Onyx (UK) Ltd, ex p Blackfordby and Boothcorpe Action Group Ltd* [2001] Env. L.R. 2.
[123] [2002] Env. L.R. 28.

published that year.[124] However, it took until 2000 for the National Waste Strategy, aimed at fulfilling the UK's obligations under Article 7, to appear: *Waste Strategy 2000 for England and Wales*.[125]

The Waste Strategy 2000 contained policies to achieve the environmental objectives contained in Articles 4 and 5 of the Directive, transposed into domestic law in Schedule 2A of the EPA 1990: that is, that Member States take the necessary measures to ensure that waste is recovered or disposed of without endangering human health and without using processes or methods which could harm the environment. The way the Strategy does so is to require that decisions be made "in line with" the "best practicable environmental option" or "BPEO".

15–046

What is the BPEO in any given case may often be a more complex matter than might appear: in *West London Waste Authority v Greater London Authority*[126] the Mayor of London had made a direction to a WDA (pursuant to his powers under section 356 of the Greater London Authority Act 1999 to issue such directions for the purpose of implementing his waste strategy) that a proposed waste disposal operation could only use an incinerator which minimised emissions and generated heat and power, and that waste had to be pre-treated. This rendered operations potentially so expensive that no operator might tender for it and the waste would, in default, continue to be sent to landfill. The court held that a decision-maker cannot exclude any option that might accord with the "strategy taken as a whole"[127] and that in this case the Mayor's direction ignored practicability and cost. What the direction ordered would not, therefore, be the BPEO in the circumstances.

In *R (on the application of Blewett) v Derbyshire County Council*[128] the High Court had held at first instance that a planning authority was required to refuse planning permission unless it was "in line with" the National Waste Strategy; the authority was therefore obliged to assess whether the landfill project was the BPEO for the waste stream in question. The Court of Appeal, on the other hand, held that it was not a pre-condition that the BPEO was achieved: the BPEO, whilst important, was not the overriding consideration. However, like the objectives, the National Waste Strategy was more than a material consideration: "the added focus of waste management calls for particular attention to be given to the objectives of the Waste Framework Directive when considering an application for planning permission for a landfill proposal". On the facts, the local planning authority had failed to demonstrate that it had given sufficient importance

---

[124] *Making Waste Work: A Strategy for Sustainable Waste Management in England and Wales* (Cm 3040, 1995).

[125] Cm 4693, 2000.

[126] [2007] Env. L.R. 27.

[127] Following *R v Secretary of State for Environment, Transport and the Regions, ex p West Sussex County Council* (1997) 77 P& CR 263.

[128] [2005] Env. L.R. 15.

or weight to the BPEO policies. The Strategy also set out targets for the reduction of industrial and commercial waste going to landfill, for the recovery of municipal waste and the recycling of household waste.

15–047   The revised Defra Waste Strategy, issued in 2007, set higher targets for the recycling and composting of household waste and the recovery of municipal waste, and included the objective of "moving waste management up the waste hierarchy" in order to reduce the environmental impact of waste generally. The key objectives of the 2007 Strategy are as follows:

"● Decouple waste growth (in all sectors) from economic growth and put more emphasis on waste prevention and re-use;

● Meet and exceed the Landfill Directive diversion targets for biodegradable municipal waste in 2010, 2013 and 2020;[129]

● Increase diversion from landfill of non-municipal waste and secure better integration of treatment for municipal and non-municipal waste;

● Secure the investment in infrastructure needed to divert waste from landfill and for the management of hazardous waste;

● Get the most environmental benefit from that investment, through increased recycling of resources and recovery of energy from residual waste using a mix of technologies."[130]

At a local level, section 49 EPA 1990 formerly required WCAs to draw up waste recycling plans. That provision was repealed by section 32 of the Waste and Emissions Trading Act 2003. The 2003 Act placed a duty on WCAs and WDAs to produce "joint municipal waste management strategies" where they operate in a "two tier area" i.e. where the WCA and WDA are different authorities.) Oddly, there is no such statutory duty to produce a local plan where the area is not a two-tier area.

The Waste Management Licensing Regulations have now been replaced by the Environmental Permitting (EP) Regulations 2007,[131] of which Schedules 9 and 20 relate to waste operations. The Schedule provides that the regulator must exercise its relevant functions "for the purposes of implementing Article 4 of the Waste Framework Directive"[132] and, in relation to disposal of waste, (a) for the purposes of implementing Article 5 of the WFD; (b) for the purposes of implementing any waste management plan;[133] and (c) so as to ensure that the requirements in Article 9(1) of the WFD are met (that is, the obligation on anyone carrying out waste disposal operations to obtain a permit). The same goes for any authority carrying

---

[129] See, further, below at 15–079.
[130] pp.28–29, *Waste Strategy for England 2007* (Cm 7086).
[131] SI 2007/3538.
[132] para.3(a), Sch.9 to the Environmental Permitting (EP) Regulations 2007.
[133] Including the national strategy formulated under s.44A, EPA 1990.

out its specified functions in relation to waste operations and the disposal of waste.[134]

In other words, any regulator or authority exercising functions in relation to waste must do so "for the purposes" of implementing the objectives in Articles 4 and 5 of the WFD: that is, the objectives of ensuring recovery and disposal of waste without danger to human health and the environment; and of establishing an integrated network of disposal installations. It should be noted that the relevant Articles of the 2006 WFD will change their numbering in the new WFD: Article 4 is now expressed in Article 13; Article 5 is now expressed in Article 16.   **15–048**

Enforcement

The kernel of the enforcement of the waste management system under the EPA 1990 is section 33, which creates the criminal offences of;   **15–049**

(a) depositing of controlled waste on any land, or causing or knowingly permitting such waste to be deposited, without a permit or not in a accordance with any permit held;

(b) subjecting waste to any "listed operation"—that is, any disposal or recovery operation in Annex IIA and IIB of the WFD—without a permit, or not in accordance with a permit (an amendment made by the EP Regulations 2007);

(c) treating, keeping or disposing of such waste in a manner likely to cause pollution of the environment or harm to human health.

"Controlled waste" means household, industrial and commercial waste or "any such waste"[135] (that is, waste similar to the waste produced by households, commerce or industry). Section 75 EPA also incorporates domestically the key definitions of waste and waste operations taken from the WFD.

A section 33 offence, whether tried summarily or on indictment, carries a fine and/or imprisonment, and any person convicted of an offence under section 33 may also have to bear the Agency's costs of investigating the infringement and bringing proceedings,[136] as well as the costs of any clean-up.[137]

The EP Regulations 2007 have also added fixed penalty notices to the Agency's enforcement arsenal. An authorised local authority officer, a constable or the authorised officer of the Agency may issue such a notice where he has reason to believe that someone has committed an offence under section 33(1)(a), depositing controlled waste or knowingly causing or permitting waste to be deposited without a permit or outwith its con-   **15–050**

---

[134] paras 3 and 4, Sch.20 to the EP Regulations 2007.
[135] EPA 1990, s.75(4).
[136] EPA 1990, s.33A.
[137] EPA 1990, s.33B.

ditions, or section 33(1)(c), treating, keeping or disposing of controlled waste in a manner likely to cause pollution of the environment or harm to human health. Any person issued with such a notice may discharge it by paying the fixed penalty within 14 days. Otherwise, he will be issued with proceedings for the relevant offence.[138]

Sections 34B and 34C of the EPA, as amended, contain detailed powers open to the EA and any WCA to search and seize vehicles (and the contents of those vehicles) involved in offences under sections 33 and 34. These new sections were added in 2005 but have not yet been brought into force. There are also duties upon these authorities set out in the draft Waste Control (England and Wales) Regulations 2009 (WCRs)—the subject of consultation at the moment—obliging those authorities to keep, trace, and, if necessary, dispose of such vehicles.

"Knowingly" permit

15–051   The term "knowingly" has been strictly interpreted. In *Shanks v McEwan (Teeside) Ltd v Environment Agency*[139] the court held that the defendant need only know of the deposit of the waste; it did not need to know that it was in breach of the conditions of the licence in order to be convicted of the offence. This means that once the Agency has proved that a deposit of waste was made with the knowledge of the defendant, the burden falls on the defendant to prove that it was in accordance with any condition.

Moreover, the requisite knowledge may be constructive knowledge; the court may infer that the defendant knowingly permitted waste to be deposited where such deposit was obvious. In *Shanks* Mance J. held that as the defendant knowingly operated its site to receive and deposit waste, it must have known of any waste deposited there.

Due diligence

15–052   There is, however, a defence under section 33(7) where the defendant can prove that he took all reasonable precautions and exercised all due diligence to avoid the commission of the offence. The ambit of the defence is fairly narrow: someone who deals with the waste must make very specific enquiries as to whether the waste he is handling, and the manner in which it is handled, is covered by the permit or any exemption.[140] The standard of proof for this defence will be the civil standard, namely on a balance of probabilities.

---

[138] EPA 1990, s.33A.

[139] [1997] Env. L.R. 305.

[140] See *Durham County Council v Peter Connors Industrial Services Ltd* [1993] Env. L.R. 197 in relation to the analogous defence under section 3(4) of the Control of Pollution Act 1974; and *Environment Agency v Short* [1998] Env. L.R. 300.

Emergencies

There is also a defence under section 33(7)(c) where the defendant can **15–053** prove that the acts alleged to constitute the contravention were done in an emergency in order to avoid danger to human health, and where

(i) he took "all such steps as were reasonably practicable in the circumstances" for minimising pollution of the environment and harm to human health; and
(ii) he informed the Agency as to what was done as soon as reasonably practicable.

What constitutes an emergency appears to be an objective matter, not one which relates to how the permit holder perceived the facts (see *Waste Incineration Services Ltd v Dudley Borough Council.*[141]

Duty of care

Section 34 EPA also introduces a "duty of care" on anyone who imports, **15–054** produces, carries, keeps, treats or disposes of controlled waste or, as a broker, has control of it, to;

(a) take "all such measures applicable to him in that capacity as are reasonable in the circumstances" to prevent any other person contravening section 33;
(b) prevent the escape of the waste from his control or that of any other person.

In other words, the onus is put on each person who has any kind of responsibility for waste to ensure that he does not pass it on to, or deal with, others who may not deal with that waste in accordance with the statutory controls. The intent is that the waste disposal system should be self-policing. The duty of care does not, however, apply to domestic householders except in so far as they must take "all measures available ... as are reasonable in the circumstances to ensure that any transfer ... of household waste produced on the property is only to an authorised person".[142]

Section 34 is supplemented by the Environmental Protection (Duty of Care) Regulations 1991, which requires anyone who is subject to the section 34(1) duty of care and who transfers controlled waste to another to complete and keep a transfer note detailing the waste and who is transferring and receiving it, and providing various other details set out in

---

[141] [1993] Env. L.R. 29.
[142] EPA 1990, s.34(2A). An authorised person is, according to s.34(3), a waste collection authority or someone who holds an environmental permit, is registered as a carrier of controlled waste, is carrying on an "exempt" waste operation, or to whom the requirement to hold a permit or licence under s.33 does not apply.

regulation 2(2). Change to these details is proposed in a Defra consultation running at the time of writing.[143]

It is an offence to fail to comply with the duty of care or any requirements imposed by the regulations.[144] However, in contrast to sub-sections 33(8) and (9), the offence attracts a fine only, and not imprisonment. The statutory provisions and the Regulations are supported by the Code of Practice on the Duty of Care (revised several times) issued by the Secretary of State after consultation[145] and laid before Parliament.[146] The Code of Practice is not binding, but must be taken into account if it is relevant to any question in proceedings against a person charged with failing to comply with the duty.[147]

Civil Liability for Waste Deposits

15–055   Section 73(6) of the Environmental Protection Act 1990 establishes strict liability in tort for any damage arising out of the unlawful deposit of waste under section 33(1) discussed above. The defences available in that section (due diligence, acting under instructions, emergency, as discussed above) are equally available under this section. No liability arises if the damage was due wholly to the fault of the Claimant, or if the Claimant voluntarily accepted the risk of the damage being caused.

Brokers and Carriers

15–056   Much of the waste produced here and throughout the Community is transported by, or to the order of, entities other than its original producer. These entities are regulated as either carriers or brokers. There is currently no definition of "broker" in the EPA, or in the Waste Management Licensing Regulations 1994, a surviving part of which still requires their registration.[148] The meaning of the term is to be taken from the Waste Framework Directive 2006/12. Article 12 requires brokers to be registered if not otherwise required to be licensed, in the following terms:

"Article 12
Establishments or undertakings which collect or transport waste on a professional basis or which arrange for the disposal or recovery of waste

---

[143] See the draft Waste Controls (England and Wales) Regulations, reg.10 (WCRs).
[144] EPA 1990, s.34(6).
[145] EPA 1990, s.34(7).
[146] EPA 1990, s.34(9).
[147] EPA 1990, s.34(10).
[148] For the purposes of this section "broker" and "dealer" are synonymous, and "broker" is used exclusively.

on behalf of others (dealers or brokers), where not subject to authorisation shall be registered with the competent authorities."

There are three different categories of people commonly regarded as brokers or dealers:

(i) Companies which buy and sell scrap metal and other recoverables—or which arrange such deals for a commission (traders or dealers);

(ii) Companies which arrange for the disposal of waste to an appropriate facility (usually brokers);

(iii) Companies whose main business is as either a waste operator or carrier, but which may make alternative disposal arrangements for waste which they are unable to accept at their own sites.

The English language version of Article 12 of the Directive is unclear as to whether "on behalf of others" qualifies only "arrange for the disposal or recovery of waste" or also the words earlier in the provision "collect or transport of waste on a professional basis". However, reference to other language versions indicates the former.[149] Consequently, only category (ii) are properly "brokers"; though a waste operator making alternative disposal arrangements for waste that it does not itself hold will also then be acting as a broker. A person buying and selling scrap metal will not on that account alone be a broker as the term is used in Article 12: he will be a dealer.[150] To be a broker, the person should not himself hold the waste on his own account; there must also be an arrangement for waste disposal or recovery—mere buying and selling does not amount to this.

The Article 12 requirement for registration of brokers is given effect by regulation 20(1) of the 1994 Waste Management Licensing Regulations[151] whereby it is an offence for an establishment or undertaking to arrange (as dealer or broker) for the disposal or recovery of waste on behalf of another unless it is registered.

Draft Waste Control Regulations (WCRs) seek to remedy any ambiguity which there may be in these definitions. Draft Regulation 2(2) defines a broker as any person who arranges for the recovery or disposal or controlled waste on behalf of others, and a dealer as any person who buys and sells waste as a principal, and in either case it is irrelevant whether or not that person takes physical possession of the waste.

The requirement to register is declared inapplicable to those who **15–057**

---

[149] The German text leaves no room for doubt on this point: "Die Anlagen oder Unternehmen, die Gewerbemäßig Abfällen einsammeln oder befördern oder *die für die Beseitigung oder Verwertung von Abfällen für andere sorgen* (Händler oder Makler), müssen bei den zuständigen Behörden gemeldet sein, sofern sie keine Genehmigung haben." The Italian test supports this, having a comma following the Italian words for "on a professional basis". The French text is similar in structure and punctuation to the English.

[150] This distinction is drawn in the definition of "dealer" and "broker" to be found in art.2.12 and 2.13 of the recent Waste Shipments Regulations 1013/2006.

[151] One of the few parts of these Regulations still in force since the EP Regulations.

themselves[152] undertake the disposal or recovery under such an arrangement, if they are otherwise licensed for this purpose, or if recovery of the waste is covered by a relevant exemption under schedule 3 of the EP Regulations or the Deposits in the Sea (Exemptions) Order 1985.[153]

Also exempted from registration under regulation 20(1) are charities, certain voluntary organisations[154] and waste collection, disposal and regulation authorities.[155] These bodies still fall within the Article 12 requirement nevertheless, and so are made subject to the simpler registration obligation of Schedule 4, paragraph 12(2), to the WMLR 1994.[156] The procedure for this, and enforcement provisions, are laid down in the remainder of paragraph 12. Registration is simpler in that it is automatic, and not subject to any pre-conditions or possibility of revocation.

Registration under regulation 20(1) of the WMLR 1994 is governed by Schedule 5 to those regulations, and, if implemented in their current form, the draft Waste Control Regulations. The applicable rules, including those relating to refusal to register in the event of conviction or a prescribed offence, duration of registration, revocation and appeals, are in all material respects the same as those governing the registration of carriers of waste. Combined applications for registration as both broker and carrier may be made, and also for renewal of such registrations.[157]

15–058 All establishments and undertakings which act as brokers of controlled waste must be inspected periodically by the EA.[158] The EA has powers to appoint inspectors, to enter premises and to obtain information.[159] Breach of the prohibition in regulation 20(1) is an offence punishable on summary conviction by a fine of up to £5,000. Directors and other similar officers of a company may be criminally liable along with the company, in accordance with section 157 of the EPA, as may its members.[160]

Carriers of Controlled Waste

15–059 Concern about the fly tipping of waste led to the Control of Pollution (Amendment) Act 1989, ahead of the main reforms brought about by the EPA the following year. Detailed provisions for its implementation are contained in the Controlled Waste (Registration of Carriers and Seizure of

---

[152] In reg.20(2) of the WMLR 1994.
[153] SI 1985/1699, made under the Food & Environmental Protection Act 1985.
[154] As defined in s.48(1) of the Local Government Act 1985.
[155] reg.20(4).
[156] Unless they hold an applicable permit under the EP Regulations, under FEPA 1985, Part 2, or WRA, Part 3.
[157] Sch.5, paras 3(8), 3(9).
[158] WMLR Sch.4, para.13(1) or proposed WCR reg.5.
[159] reg.20(8).
[160] reg.20(6).

Vehicles) Regulations 1991[161] ("the 1991 Regulations"), as amended.[162] The 1991 Regulations are due to be repealed by and replaced with the WCRs, when made.

The 1989 Act had two principal objectives: to require registration of all those in the business of carrying waste (with certain limited exceptions), and to provide for the seizure of vehicles used for the illegal disposal of waste. These objectives are not therefore in themselves intended to control the carriage or disposal of waste directly, but to enable the regulatory authorities to establish who is engaged in these activities, so that other controls can be exercised and enforced.

The registration of carriers is made mandatory by section 1(1) of the 1989 Act, applicable to those who "in the course of any business of his or otherwise with a view to profit, ... transport any controlled waste to or from any place in Great Britain." This requirement does not however apply to:

(a) the transport of controlled waste within the same premises between different places in those premises;
(b) the transport to a place in Great Britain of controlled waste imported into it from elsewhere that is not landed in Great Britain until it arrives at that place;
(c) the transport by air or sea of controlled waste from a place in Great Britain to elsewhere outside it.[163]

Various organisations and other persons were exempted from the requirement to register under the 1989 Act[164] including waste collection, waste disposal and waste regulation authorities, charities and certain voluntary organisations. The most important exemption applied to the producer of the relevant controlled waste, except where it is building or demolition waste.[165] However, in the light of Article 12 of the Directive, these bodies (except waste producers disposing of their own waste) must still register,[166] albeit they are subject to a simplified and unconditional procedure. Even the exemption for waste producers carrying their own waste in the course of operating their own businesses (although not professional waste carriers) appears to be inadequate transposition of Article 12 in the light of the decision of the European Court of Justice in *Com-*

---

[161] SI 1991/1624; amended by reg.23 of the 1994 Licensing Regulations, and by reg.19 of the Transfrontier Shipment of Waste Regulations 1994, SI 1994/1137.

[162] Most recently, by the Controlled Waste (Registration of Carriers and Seizure of Vehicles) (Amendment) Regulations 1998, SI 1998/605.

[163] s.1(2).

[164] Exemptions under reg.2.1 of the 1991 Regs. These Regulations were made under s.1(3).

[165] "Building or demolition waste" means waste arising from works of construction or demolition, including waste arising from work preparatory thereto (reg.2(2)); "construction" means improvement, repair or alteration" (as amended bv Controlled Waste Regulations 1992, reg.10(1)).

[166] Sch.4, para.12(1). Unless they hold an applicable environmental permit, or are licensed under FEPA, Part 2; or under WRA, Part 3.

779

mission v Italy[167]. Draft regulation 5 of the WCR takes a middle view: those who do not normally and regularly transport waste do not need to be registered carriers. The rest of Part 3 of the WCR seeks to simplify the registration provisions.

15–060 It is a defence to any offence charged under s.1(1) of the 1989 Act;

(a) that the waste was transported in an emergency of which notice was given as soon as practicable thereafter to the relevant waste regulation authority; or

(b) that the person charged neither knew nor had reasonable grounds for suspecting that what was being transported was controlled waste, and he took all such steps as it was reasonable to take for ascertaining whether it was such waste.[168]

"Emergency" for these purposes means any circumstances in which, in order to avoid, remove or reduce any serious danger to the public or serious risk of damage to the environment, it is necessary for the waste to be transported from one place to another without the use of a registered carrier.

A person guilty of an offence under these provisions is liable on summary conviction to a fine not exceeding £5,000. A conviction under section 1 of the 1989 Act of the holder of a goods vehicle operator's licence, or of the holder's servant or agent, may also lead to the revocation or suspension of that licence, by virtue of section 26 and Schedule 2 of the Goods Vehicles (Licensing of Operators) Act 1995.[169]

In *Hallett Silberman Limited v Cheshire County Council*,[170] it was held that a road haulage company could properly be regarded as the "user" of a vehicle even though it was being driven by a self-employed driver who provided the tractor unit used to tow a trailer. That case was concerned with an offence under section 42(1)(b) of the Road Traffic Act 1988, whereby it is an offence to use on a road a motor vehicle or trailer which does not comply with any regulations made under section 41 of that Act or who causes or permits a vehicle to be so used. While the construction appropriate to one statute cannot of course automatically be applied to another dealing with quite separate subject matter, the reasoning in *Hallett Silberman* indicates that where a person is responsible for selecting the waste to be loaded on a lorry and determining the route to be taken to its destination, that person is transporting the waste, and should therefore be registered as a carrier, even though the vehicle may be driven by a self-employed driver and be owned by the driver or some other third party. It does not however follow that the self-employed driver in such circum-

---

[167] *C-270/03* June 9, 2005.
[168] s.1(4), as amended by the Clean Neighbourhoods and Environment Act 2005.
[169] See draft WCRs, regs 8 and 6(4).
[170] [1993] RTR 32; *The Times*, June 9, 1992.

stances is not also transporting waste; he must himself also be registered as a carrier.

The 1991 Regulations lay down the procedure for applying for regis- **15–061** tration as a carrier and for renewing existing registrations. Except where a registration has been voluntarily terminated or revoked, or where an appeal against revocation is pending, registration lasts for a period of three years (to become one year in all but exceptional cases when the proposed WCRs are made). Applications for renewal may be made at any time within the final six months of the three year period. Applications for renewal are treated on the same basis as initial applications for registration.

Applications for registration are made to the EA.[171] An application on behalf of a partnership must be made by all the partners or prospective partners;[172] if any of the partners ceases to be registered, or if any person who is not registered becomes a partner, the registration automatically ceases to have effect.[173] An application to register a person about to join a partnership that is already registered may be made under regulation 4(5). Changes of circumstances affecting information in a register entry relating to any person, including therefore any resignation or appointment of partners, must be notified under regulation 8.

If the application is duly made, the EA may only refuse to register an applicant if (i) he or another relevant person has been convicted of a "prescribed offence" and (ii) in the opinion of the authority it is undesirable for the applicant to be authorised to transport controlled waste.[174] Accordingly, even where there has been a conviction of a relevant offence, the authority must be of the opinion, arrived at on reasonable grounds, that it is undesirable for the applicant to be placed, or remain, on the register and therefore authorised to transport controlled waste. For individuals the Rehabilitation of Offenders Act 1974 will result in conviction being "spent" after 5 years; bodies corporate have no corresponding relief, though the EA should consider whether conviction of the same offence would have been spent had it been committed by an individual.

The "prescribed offences" are set out in Schedule 1 of the 1991 Reg- **15–062** ulations, as amended. These are environmental offences under the various acts in force over the last 30 or so years, with the sole exception of section 60 of the Transport Act, whereby it is an offence to use a goods vehicle on a road unless the operator is duly licensed.

Who is a "relevant person", whose conviction of a prescribed offence is material for this purpose, is set out below.[175] This applies equally to the registration of waste brokers.

---

[171] 1991 Regulations reg.4(1).
[172] reg.4(4).
[173] reg.11(6).
[174] reg.5(1).
[175] 1989 Act, s.3(5); 1994 Licensing Regs, Sch.5, para.1(3).

Table 15/I

15–063	**Registration of Waste Carriers and Brokers** *Conviction of Relevant Persons*	

Status of applicant/registered carrier or broker at time of offence	Relevant person convicted
Employer	Any employee
Member of partnership (carrying on *any* business)	Any partner or other person convicted of an offence committed in the course of the partnership's business
Director, manager, secretary or other similar officer of a body corporate	That body corporate
Body corporate	(1) Any director, manager, secretary or other similar officer of the body corporate and (2) Any other body corporate of which any person within (1) was a director, manager, secretary or other similar officer at the time of commission of the offence.

An appeals procedure is provided for contesting any refusal to register a person as a carrier or to renew his registration, as the case may be, or any revocation of a registration.[176]

Enforcement

15–064   All establishments and undertakings which collect or transport controlled waste on a professional basis must be inspected periodically by the EA.[177] Powers are also provided under section 5 of the 1989 Act, as amended,[178] to both duly authorised officers of the EA and to any constable to check whether an offence under section 1(1) has been, is being or is about to be committed, if it reasonably appears to any such person that this is so. These revised powers are not in force at the time of writing, but are imminent. In

[176] s.4 and regs 15–18.
[177] 1994 Licensing Regulations, Sch.4, para.13(1). Reg.3 of the draft WCRs.
[178] By the Clean Neighbourhoods and Environment Act 2005.

such a case, the officer or constable may stop any person and require him to produce his authority or his employer's authority for transporting controlled waste. The officer or constable may search any vehicle, carry out tests on anything found on the vehicle and take away samples for testing, and seize the vehicle and its contents.[179] Where a person is required under these provisions to produce authority for transporting controlled waste, and he does not do so forthwith, he must produce it as required.[180]

It is an offence intentionally to obstruct an authorised officer of the EA or constable exercising their powers under section 5 or to fail without reasonable excuse to comply with any requirement that they may impose in exercise of those powers, the burden of proof being on a defendant charged with any such offence to show that there was a reasonable excuse.[181] It is however not an offence to fail to comply with a requirement that may have been imposed, unless it is shown that the waste in question was controlled waste and that the person charged did transport it to or from a place in Great Britain.

The 1989 Act contains the standard provisions whereby in the event of an offence by a body corporate, connivance by any director, etc. is also an offence, and, where the commission of any offence is due to the act or the fault of some other person, that other person is also guilty of the same offence.[182]

Removal of unlawful deposits

Where there has been an unlawful deposit of waste, enforcement may be via section 59 of the EPA 1990 instead of or in addition to a prosecution under section 33 of the EPA. Section 59 gives a waste regulation or waste collection authority the power to demand that the occupier either remove from any land in its area any controlled waste unlawfully deposited on it, or to take steps with a view to eliminating or reducing the consequences of the deposit.[183]   **15–065**

In *Neal Soil Suppliers Ltd v Environment Agency*[184] the Divisional Court found that a notice might lawfully allow the waste to remain on the land, albeit that its deposit breached section 33 of the Act, and the notice might simply require some steps to be taken short of removal. The purpose of section 59 of the Act was remedial and there was no presumption in it to prefer removal of the waste rather than treatment on site.

"Unlawfully" means without an environmental permit, in contravention of section 33(1) or the 2007 EP Regulations. Failure to comply with the

---

[179] s.5(2) as amended.
[180] reg.14(1).
[181] s.5(7).
[182] ss.7(5)–(7).
[183] s.59(1) EPA 1990.
[184] [2007] EWHC 2592 (Admin).

notice without reasonable excuse is a summary offence carrying a fine of up to level 5 on the standard scale. If the defendant continues to defy the notice after conviction the authority may impose a fine of up to one-tenth of level five for every day that he continues to do so.[185] The authority may also, if the occupier fails to comply with the notice, carry out the necessary work itself and recover the expenses from the occupier.[186]

15–066   An appeal from a section 59 notice lies to the magistrates court, which will quash the requirement if it is satisfied that (a) the appellant neither deposited nor knowingly caused nor knowingly permitted the deposit of the waste; or (b) there is a material defect in the notice. In any other case it may either modify the requirement or uphold the notice.[187] It will be noted that in order for a section 59 notice to be imposed, there must be knowledge on the part of the occupier that he caused or permitted the waste to be there.[188]

If there is no occupier of the land (or the occupier cannot be found without the authority incurring unreasonable expense), or the occupier did not himself make or knowingly permit the deposit of the waste, the authority may remove the waste itself or take other steps to eliminate or reduce the consequences of the deposit if it is necessary to remove or prevent pollution of land, water or air or harm to human health.[189] The costs may be recovered from any person who deposited or knowingly caused or knowingly permitted the deposit of any of the waste.[190] The onus is on the occupier to prove that he did not make nor knowingly caused nor knowingly permitted the deposit of the waste.[191] The removed waste belongs to the authority, which may deal with it as it wishes.[192]

Environmental Permits for Waste

15–067   The coming into force of the Environmental Permitting (England & Wales) Regulations 2007[193] means that "waste operations" need an environmental permit, unless they are exempt (in which case they require registration with the EA) or are excluded operations. Existing PPC permits and waste management licences operate automatically as such permits.[194] However,

---

[185] s.59(5) EPA 1990.
[186] s.59(6) EPA 1990.
[187] ss.59(2)–(3) EPA 1990.
[188] Contrast the position under Part 2A (the Contaminated Land regime), where liability may be imposed on a person who caused contaminating substances to be present even without his knowledge.
[189] s.59(7) EPA 1990.
[190] s.59(8) EPA 1990.
[191] s.59(8)(a).
[192] s.59(9).
[193] SI 2007/3538.
[194] reg.69.

environmental permits for waste operations are also subject to rules derived from specific waste Directives. Hence, the Schedules to the EP Regulations set out those requirements in respect of the Waste Framework Directive, the Landfill Directive, the Waste Incineration Directive (WID), the End of Life Vehicles Directive, and the Waste Electrical and Electronic Equipment (WEEE) Directive, all of which are considered in turn below.

The detail of the EP Regulations, and the common procedure they institute for all environmental permits, is discussed in Chapter 14. However, the key terminology of, and interrelationship within, the EP Regulations is as follows. An "activity" or an "installation" relates to operations the subject of the IPPC Directive, and hitherto regulated by a PPC permit. *Some* of those activities are waste operations. A "waste operation" means recovery or disposal of waste. All waste operations require an environmental permit, hitherto known as a waste management licence, unless they are exempt or excluded waste operations. There are special additional rules applicable to landfill waste operations; in addition, most landfills will be subject to the IPPC Directive. Hence many waste operations will need to comply with IPPC rules, as well as rules arising from other waste Directives.

Waste operations

First, then, to waste operations generally, before considering the specific **15–068** regime applicable to landfills. Here, barring the mind-numbing particularity of the exemptions, the scheme of the EP Regulations is quite minimalist. A waste operation (namely any recovery or disposal of waste) needs an environmental permit like any other operation falling under the EP Regulations. A waste operation must also comply with the one-page Schedule 9 to the EP Regulations, most of which transposes provisions of the Waste Framework Directive as obligations to be enforced by the EA, including the objectives set out in Article 4 of the 2006 Waste Framework Directive.

The one substantive further obligation in Schedule 9 is that the EA must not grant an environmental permit for "a relevant waste operation" unless there is an extant planning permission in force (or no need for such permission).[195] A "relevant waste operation" includes the various waste activities regulated by IPPC as well as non-IPPC regulated waste operations. The EA is the primary regulator under the EP Regulations,[196] though, because planning permission must precede the issue of a permit, in practice major issues concerning waste sites are determined as much through the conditions of the planning consent granted (if at all) by the

---

[195] para.2 of Sch.9.
[196] Local authorities have air pollution responsibilities for lesser operations under what was PPC.

planning authority (after consultation with the EA as statutory consultee) as through the conditions of the environmental permit as directly determined by the EA. To that end, Schedule 20 contains further institutional arrangements to bind other public bodies (such as local planning authorities) to exercise functions in accordance with the Waste Framework Directive. Operators are advised to apply for planning permission and environmental permit in parallel.

Operator competence

15–069 Those familiar with the detailed provisions of the EPA 1990 and Waste Management Licensing Regulations concerning "fit and proper person", will look in vain for specific parts of the new waste regime on these subjects. Those provisions (including sections 74 and 36 of the EPA) have been repealed by the EP Regulations. As discussed in Chapter 14, the only statutory provisions on this matter under the new regime are contained in paragraph 13 of Schedule 5, headed "Identity and competence of the operator," under which the EA must refuse any application for any permit if the EA considers that the operator will not operate the facility in accordance with the permit. Defra Guidance, again as discussed above, addresses potential inadequacies in management, technical competence, record, or financial competence.[197]

Exempt waste operations

15–070 Some waste operations that are thought to pose a sufficiently low risk can be exempt from the need to hold a permit, although they must be registered with the EA. Under the Waste Framework Directive, these are recovery operations or disposal operations only where a business produces non-hazardous waste and disposes of it at the place of production.[198] A waste operation must also meet certain general criteria in order to be exempt from requiring an environmental permit. The most important is that it meets the requirements of Regulation 5, which include that the activity must meet the objectives in Article 4 of the 2006 Waste Framework Directive. These require that an operation should be carried out without endangering human health and without using processes or methods likely to harm the environment.

As noted above, exempt waste operations generally must be registered with the regulator.[199] Hence, the regulator is required to maintain a register of establishments and undertakings carrying out exempt waste opera-

---

[197] See Ch.14, above, and Ch.8 of the EP Core Guidance.

[198] art.11 of WFD 2006/12, when read with art.3(1) of the Hazardous Waste Directive 91/689/EEC. This is consolidated into art.24 of the 2008 WFD.

[199] para.3(1) of Sch.2. The regulators for each type of exempt waste operation are identified in para.2 of Sch.2.

tions.[200] However, certain exempted activities that are deemed to pose a somewhat higher risk require notification. These are termed "notifiable exemptions" and must comply with specific notification requirements,[201] e.g. supplying details of the quantities of waste to be handled, and providing plans, documents and other information that may be reasonably required by the regulator, serving a renewal notice every year, and paying an annual charge.[202]

The specific operations which may (and ordinarily will) be exempt operations are listed in Schedule 3 to the EP Regulations. These run to 24 closely typed pages, and can only be summarised in very short form here. The working rule, however, is that small and medium-scale recovery operations may well be found somewhere in Schedule 3, and a general category, namely beneficial uses of waste not requiring further treatment, is expressly provided for within paragraph 15. The more specific listed operations include small-scale burning waste as a fuel,[203] treating land with sludge[204] or other specified wastes,[205] other forms of land reclamation,[206] composting waste,[207] manufacturing timber and other construction products etc from wood and construction wastes[208] and secure storage of wastes (including specified hazardous wastes.[209] However, unless specifically mentioned in Schedule 3 of the Regulations, an operation cannot be an exempt operation if it involves hazardous waste or WEEE.

Various scrap metal recovery operations also qualify as exempt operations within fairly substantial tonnage thresholds,[210] but subject to specific requirements such as an impermeable working surface provided with a sealed drainage system.[211] However, much of the scrap metal industry may become subject to greater regulation if the current European Commission proposals in respect of a new Industrial Emissions Directive are adopted. In effect, such activities will become installations subject to the regulation currently contained in the IPPC Directive, and hence be subject to Schedule 7 of the EP Regulations.

15–071

There is no unconditional right to register an operation which otherwise falls under Schedule 3, as a regulator can refuse to register a notifiable

---

[200] para.4 of Sch.2.
[201] para.8 of Sch.2.
[202] para.10 of Sch.2.
[203] paras 3 and 5.
[204] para.6.
[205] para.7.
[206] para.9.
[207] para.12.
[208] para.13. The predecessor provision was interpreted in *Environment Agency v AES* [2005] Env. L.R. 919: storage of wood waste prior to making into chipboard.
[209] para.17.
[210] para.45. There are specific registration (para.6, Sch.2) and record keeping (para.45(5)) requirements for activities falling within paragraphs 45(1) or 45(3)).
[211] para.45(1)(c) (sorting operations), and para.45(3)(f) (storage operations): see the ELV Directive, Annex I, discussed below.

exemption. There is no right of appeal against this decision but the regulator must provide the reasons for the decision. The commonest such reasons are likely to be that the activity cannot be carried out as it stands (i.e. without imposing conditions on the operation) without offending against the objectives contained in Article 4 of the Waste Framework Directive.

Temporary non-prohibited operations

15–072   There are miscellaneous temporary operations involving waste to which the prohibition in section 33(1)(a) of the EPA (against depositing without a permit) is expressly stated not to apply. These are listed in Part 2 of Schedule 3 to the EP Regulations, and include temporary storage of ship's garbage or ship's tank washings, temporary storage of non-liquid waste not exceeding 50m^3 for no longer than three months, temporary storage of scrap rails not exceeding 10 tonnes, and temporary storage of waste (including WEEE) on the site where it is produced, under certain conditions. This last (set out in paragraph 52) is of importance. It does not apply to scrap yards. Hazardous waste may be kept for no longer than 12 months; if liquid, must be kept in a secure container and must not exceed 23,000 litres, whereas if solid, and kept in a secure container, it must not exceed 80m^3, or if kept in a secure place, must not exceed 50m^3. Vehicles may be stored (albeit not in a scrap yard) if the general requirements of Article 4 are met, and the premises meet the minimum technical requirements imposed by Annex I of the End of Life Vehicles Directive—discussed below. The underlying exemption in paragraph 52 transposes the provision in the Waste Framework Directive whereby "temporary storage, pending collection, on the site where it is produced" is expressly exempted from the list of recovery operations in Annex IIB.

Exemptions in practice

15–073   These exemptions have been far from easy in practice to police, and very considerable quantities of industrial waste has undoubtedly been spread on land in purported compliance with various exemptions in the WMLRs[212] over the years in circumstances where its legality has been, to say the least, doubtful. The EA has tended to monitor exempted activities with a light touch, given the apprehended modest risks which most properly conducted activities involve. *Environment Agency v Newcomb*[213] is a good example of the difficulties which occur in practice. The defendant was constructing a

---

[212] Typically, "beneficial use of waste" under para.15 of Sch.3 of the WMLRs or spreading of waste soil "on land which is used for agriculture" under para.7A(1).
[213] [2003] Env. L.R. 12.

football pitch using construction and demolition wastes.[214] The EA said that biodegradable waste would not be acceptable on site, but the defendant relied on a letter to the effect that because of the difficulty in keeping this segregated from acceptable waste, the EA would allow a 5 per cent tolerance. The EA then found biodegradable waste on site, and prosecuted under section 33 for the deposit of controlled without a waste management licence. The magistrates acquitted on the basis that the waste fell within the 5 per cent tolerance. The High Court allowed the appeal on the basis that, even if the EA letter was to be interpreted as the defendant submitted, it had no power to vary the terms of the exemption. Newman J. also confirmed that the burden remained upon the prosecution at all times to show that there was waste which fell outside the terms of the exemption; it was not a case where the onus was on the defendant under section 101 of the Magistrates Courts Act 1980.[215]

Defra issued a consultation document in July 2008[216] with proposals for a major revision to the system of exemptions; though the objective is to make it simpler and more extensive, and thereby to encourage recycling, nine higher risk notifiable activities would lose their exemptions, and so need to obtain a full environmental permit.[217] If the proposals proceed as planned, they are expected to take effect in October 2009.

Excluded activities

Excluded waste operations neither need a permit (they are not "regulated facilities"[218]) nor registration. This is because they are the subject of other licensing regimes. They are listed in regulation 4 of the EP regulations, and consist of (a) dumping at sea activities licensed or permitted by the Food and Environmental Protection Act 1985, (b) liquid discharges authorised under the Water Resources Act 1991, (c) disposals of agricultural waste authorised by the Groundwater Regulations, and (d) disposal or recovery of sewage, sludge or septic tank sludge within a sewage treatment works, or sludge or septic tank sludge which is supplied or used in accordance with the Sludge (Use in Agriculture) Regulations 1989.[219]

15–074

Whilst not expressly termed "excluded activities", the "disposal or recovery of household waste from a domestic property within the curtilage

---

[214] He relied on paras 13 and 19 of Sch.3 to the WMLRs (now paras 13 and 19 of Sch.3 to the EP Regulations.

[215] See also *Environment Agency v Foley* [2002] EWHC 258, and the discussion under s.33 EPA at 15–049 above.

[216] "Consultation on Revised Waste Exemptions from Environmental Permitting"; issued jointly by Defra, the Welsh Assembly Government and the Environment Agency, July 2008.

[217] The Environment Agency is developing standard permits, with fixed, non-negotiable conditions, for the more straightforward operations, which will be cheaper for the operator than the so-called "bespoke", site-specific permits, which must otherwise be obtained.

[218] reg.8(3)(a) of the EP Regs.

[219] reg.4(d), read with regs 7 and 1(1) of the Controlled Waste Regulations 1992.

of a property by a person other than an establishment or undertaking" is not "a regulated facility".[220] Put simply, the waste controls do not apply to a domestic bonfire or compost heap; though these must not of course cause a nuisance to the neighbours, or constitute a statutory nuisance (for which see Chapter 17).

Hazardous wastes

15–075   Before we turn to other Directives implemented through the EP Regulations, it is necessary to examine the concept of hazardous waste, and to explain how this differs from non-hazardous waste. The matter is far from straightforward. Community and domestic legislation on this has evolved over the years. The original Deposit of Poisonous Wastes Act 1972 was only concerned with poisonous and other dangerous waste, and the procedural rules over consignments of such wastes that it introduced were followed by more detailed rules concerning "special wastes"[221] which were made in 1980 under section 17 of the Control of Pollution 1974. By then the Community had made its first intervention, in the form of Directive 78/319 on Toxic and Dangerous Waste. This set out a variety of requirements for dealing with hazardous waste, including keeping hazardous waste separate from other waste when being collected, transported, stored or deposited, imposed special packaging and labelling rules, and required comprehensive records to be kept of waste disposed of. This Directive explicitly required the "polluter pays" principle" to be applied to the cost of disposing of toxic and dangerous waste. All these provisions have been reproduced in later Community legislation.

The problem of how to define toxic, dangerous, or hazardous waste has bedevilled legislation in this area. The 1978 Directive listed various substances and materials in an Annex, but without specifying the quantities or concentrations at which the substances posed a risk; that, originally, was a matter for Member States. The definitional question became more acute as Community legislation on transboundary movements of waste approached. This (as explained below) originally only applied to hazardous waste, and plainly harmonisation across the EU was required in order to make the system of prior notification work as between Member States. This led to Directive 91/689, drafted in order to cross-refer to the new Waste Framework Directive of that year (91/156).[222]

---

[220] reg.8(3)(b). Household waste is defined by s.75(5) of EPA 1990.
[221] Control of Pollution (Special Waste) Regulation 1980.
[222] [1991] OJ L377/48.

Directive 91/689

This Directive remains in force, although it is due to be incorporated, in **15–076** slightly amended form, into the new Waste Framework Directive adopted in late 2008. By Article 1.4 of Directive 91/689, hazardous waste was to mean wastes featuring on a list to be drawn up by the Commission by reference to (a) Annex I categories or generic types according to their nature or the activity which generated them (for example, spent catalyst materials) or (b) Annex II constituents of the wastes (e.g. cadmium or cadmium compounds). But such wastes, to be hazardous, also had to have one or more of the properties listed in Annex III, which includes explosive, flammable, irritant, harmful, corrosive, toxic, or mutagenic.[223] The definition of "harmful" is particularly wide, namely "substances and preparations which, if they are inhaled or ingested or if they penetrate the skin, may involve limited health risks", thus giving the Commission a very wide scope in drawing up its list. Member States were also permitted to regard other wastes as hazardous if they displayed any of the properties in Annex III, and in this event they were to notify the Commission accordingly, who would consider whether to add that waste stream to the list.[224]

This part of Article 1.4 was considered by the European Court of Justice in *Fornasar*.[225] Isocyanates, which were widely regarded as hazardous, but not then specifically listed on the Commission's list, were found at a waste tip in Fruili. They were traced back to a shipbuilding and demolition works in which the defendants were actively involved, though the expert appointed by the national court could not identify precisely from which process at the works the waste had come. The defendants took two points which ended up before the ECJ. Neither found favour. Firstly, they said that unless the prosecution could prove the specific origin of the wastes, as set out in the Commission's list of hazardous wastes then it could not succeed. Secondly, they also said that the Commission's list was exhaustive. The latter argument fell foul of the terms of the second part of Article 1.4 of the Directive, noted above, which enabled Member States to regard additional wastes as hazardous. The former met with this response:

"It is clear on the wording alone of that provision that the decisive criterion, as regards the definition of 'hazardous waste, is whether the waste displays one or more of the properties listed in Annex III to Directive 91/689. Although the basis for inclusion in the list of 'hazardous waste is indeed the origin of the waste, that does not mean that it is essential for its exact origin to be determined for it to be classified as hazardous. The origin of the waste is not the only criterion for classifying

[223] The terms of Annex III are very similar to those of the Directive on Dangerous Substances and Preparations then in force (67/548, as amended, [1967] OJ L196/1).
[224] art.1.4.
[225] C-318/98 [2000] ECR I-4785.

it as hazardous but constitutes one of the factors which the list of hazardous waste merely takes into account."

So Annex III (including whether the waste was "toxic" or "carcinogenic" or "harmful" as therein defined) was indeed given its full weight as a determinant of whether a given substance was or was not hazardous waste. Of less importance was the ultimate origin of the waste.

The Commission's first list of hazardous wastes was promulgated in 1994,[226] and this was replaced in 2000 by the European Waste Catalogue.[227] The Catalogue merges the two previous lists of hazardous and non-hazardous wastes, with the former being denoted by an asterisk against the given waste stream. It also provides further details[228] (such as applicable concentrations) of the parameters set out in Annex III.

The Hazardous Waste Regulations

15-077　In the United Kingdom, the 1994 list was transposed by the Special Waste Regulations of 1996, and the current 2000 European Waste Catalogue by the List of Wastes (England) Regulations 2005.[229] The current Directive is implemented by the Hazardous Waste (England and Wales) Regulations 2005.[230] Regulation 6 of the latter defines hazardous waste as any waste listed in the List of Wastes, or which is exceptionally classified as hazardous by the Secretary of State, or which is declared hazardous by virtue of any regulations made under section 62 of the Environmental Protection Act 1990. The 2005 Regulations make it an offence for hazardous waste to be collected from a site that has not been notified or is not exempt.[231] All non-exempt sites that produce hazardous waste must be notified to the EA[232] even if they are unlikely to have that waste collected for some time. The effect of the new List of Wastes is that, inter alia, PC monitors, refrigerators, televisions, oily rags and fluorescent tubes are hazardous waste and need separate collection. Certain sites specified in the regulations are exempt if they expect to produce less than 200kgs of hazardous waste a year; these include agricultural premises, office premises, shops, premises where Waste Electrical and Electronic Equipment is collected, dental, veterinary and medical practices and ships.[233]

There is one important exception. Domestic waste (which is not defined in the Regulations) is excluded by regulation 12(2) from the Hazardous

---

[226] Council Decision 94/904/EC, OJ L356/14.
[227] Commission Decision 2000/532/EC, OJ L226/3.
[228] art.2.
[229] SI 2005/895.
[230] SI 2005/894.
[231] reg.65, read with regs 21 and 22.
[232] reg.21.
[233] reg.23 for the premises, and reg.30 for the "qualifying limitation" of 200kg.

Waste Regulations on collection from the domestic property. However, any asbestos[234] or any hazardous waste which is collected separately from domestic premises[235] is subject to the Regulations. Regulation 19 bans the mixing of hazardous wastes with any other non-hazardous wastes or a different category of hazardous waste, unless mixed under a permit, and regulation 20 requires the holder of waste to separate mixed waste if this is technically and economically feasible, and where necessary to comply with the objectives contained in Article 4 of the 2006 Waste Framework Directive.[236]

The Regulations provide for a system of consignment notes designed to track movements of hazardous waste.[237] Before hazardous waste can be removed from premises, a consignment note must be completed, and a copy must accompany the load to the place of final disposal or recovery. This is similar to the Duty of Care transfer note system explained above. A consignment note is required even if the waste is produced at premises which are exempt from the requirement to notify the EA. Records must be kept of these notes, in a register for a minimum of three years,[238] except for carriers where this is limited to 12 months.[239] Consignees must provide the EA with quarterly returns,[240] and must send a return to the producer or holder from whom the waste came.[241] Anyone who tips or disposes of hazardous waste in or on any land,[242] or who recovers it in or on land or at a transfer station,[243] is required to record in a register the location of each deposit, or the nature of the recovery, in the form of site records.

Landfills

The present separate regulation of landfills arises from the Landfill   **15–078** Directive 1999/31,[244] coupled with, in many cases, the provisions of the IPPC Directive.[245] Its transposition and implementation is via the EPA

---

[234] reg.13.
[235] reg.14.
[236] A transposition of art.2.4 of Directive 91/689.
[237] regs 35–38.
[238] reg.49(3), transposing Article 4.3 of Directive 91/689.
[239] reg.50(2).
[240] reg.53.
[241] reg.54.
[242] reg.47 (transposing art.2.1) and reg.48.
[243] reg.48(1)(b)–(c).
[244] [1999] OJ L85/1. The Directive was, even by the standards of the EC, a very long time in the preparation. As early as May 1990 ([1990] OJ C122/2), the Council invited the Commission to propose criteria and standards for landfill, and the Commission did so in July 1991. A Common Position of October 1995 ([1996] OJ C59/1) adopted a text similar to the final, albeit with a derogation for areas of low population density which would have excluded about 50 per cent of the EC territory on this ground alone.
[245] Directive 96/61, [1996] OJ L257/26, as now codified by Directive 2008/1, [2008] OJ L24/8.

1990, and now via the EP Regulations. All landfills, properly so called, are within the scope of the Landfill Directive, though certain activities (sludge spreading, the use of inert waste for restoration and construction purposes in landfills[246] and/or the deposit of inert waste derived from quarries, and the deposit of dredging sludges[247]) are expressly excluded. Landfill is defined by Article 2(g) of the Directive as including any waste disposal site for the deposit of waste on to or into land, other than temporary facilities. "Landfill" also includes the re-injection of contaminated liquids into groundwater at an onshore oil production facility, in circumstances where those liquids will not dissipate beyond the site.[248]

Most landfills will *also* be regulated by the IPPC Directive,[249] which applies to landfills receiving more than 10 tonnes a day or with a total capacity exceeding 25,000 tonnes, but excluding landfills of inert waste.[250] From 2002, the domestic implementation of the IPPC Directive applied the provisions of that Directive to all landfills, not just those over the capacity thresholds, though this extension of the IPPC Directive to all landfills is not repeated in the EP Regulations.[251] The Commission has sought to clarify the interface between the Landfill Directive and the IPPC Directive.[252] It is its view that landfills which meet the technical and other standards laid down in the Landfill Directive will also meet the requirements for Best Available Techniques under the IPPC Directive. However IPPC landfills must also meet the general obligations to be found in Article 3 of the IPPC Directive, including that energy be used efficiently, and that necessary measures are taken on cessation to avoid any pollution risk and return the site of operation to a satisfactory state. Defra is of the view that the application of general BAT requirements may be of importance where the Landfill Directive does not set out specific technical requirements, such as landfill gas utilisation, leachate treatment and odour management.[253]

In general, however, the specific rules and technical standards applicable to landfills are to be found in the Landfill Directive. For the most part,[254] the provisions of the Directive are now transposed verbatim into domestic law by Schedule 10 of the EP Regulations. The Directive ended the British

---

[246] Inert waste used for this purpose will also qualify for exemption from the landfill tax: see ss.43C and 44A of Finance Act 1996, discussed at 15–094 and 15–095 below.

[247] art.3.2.

[248] *Blackland Park Exploration Ltd v Environment Agency* [2004] Env. L.R. 33. Because of the ban on hazardous liquid waste in landfill imposed by art.5.3 of the Landfill Directive, this conclusion was to lead to the cessation of the business: ENDS 397, p.18, February 2008.

[249] 96/61, now codified as 2008/1.

[250] para.5.4 of Annex I to the IPPC Directive.

[251] PPCR 2000, as amended, Sch.1, section 5.2(b), but omitted in EP Regs Sch.1, Part 2, s.5.2.

[252] Guidance on Interpretation and Interpretation of IPPC Directive, at *http://ec.europa.eu/environment/ippc/general_guidance.htm*.

[253] Defra EP Guidance on Landfills, March 2008, para.3.10.

[254] Sch.10 of the EP Regs makes a number of clarifications and minor amendments to the Directive, some of which will be noted below.

practice of disposal of hazardous and non-hazardous waste mixed together, known as co-disposal. Under Article 3 each landfill may only be for hazardous waste, non-hazardous waste, or inert waste. Hazardous waste is defined[255] by reference to the Hazardous Waste Directive 91/689/EEC discussed above.

Article 5.3 of the Landfill Directive contains important prohibitions on landfilling liquid waste,[256] waste which is explosive, corrosive, oxidising, highly flammable or flammable, clinical waste, and whole used tyres. The provision is also tied into a more general set of "waste acceptance criteria" more recently promulgated by the Commission in Annex II of the Directive, as amplified by Council Decision 2003/33/EC and its Annex, and deposits in breach of those criteria are also prohibited. Wastes must be characterised in terms of their composition, leachability, long-term behaviour and general properties. These acceptability criteria confirm that the leachability of a given waste material and/or of its degradation products may matter more than its absolute chemical composition. They also list wastes, particularly certain materials taken from construction and demolition sites, which can be assumed to be inert without testing them.[257] Where testing is required this involves three stages, namely (i) basic testing for each type of waste prior to acceptance of that waste stream, followed by (ii) periodic compliance testing to demonstrate conformity with the results of the basic testing, and finally (iii) on-site verification in respect of (i) and (ii).[258] A landfill operator may justify exceedances of the waste acceptance criteria via an environmental risk assessment, and potentially up to a factor of 3 for specific parameters.[259] Various detailed modifications of the Annex to Decision 2003/33 are to be found in paragraphs 7 to 9 of Schedule 10 to the EP Regulations.

15–079

Article 5 of the Landfill Directive sets targets for reducing the amounts of biodegradable municipal waste going to landfill, stipulating a reduction to 75 per cent of the 1995 tonnages by 2006, to 50 per cent by 2009, and to 35 per cent by 2016.[260] However, Member States, such as the United Kingdom, which sent at least 80 per cent of their municipal waste to landfill in 1995 have been afforded an extension of a further four years to these dates, so deferring compliance with those targets until 2010, 2013,

---

[255] art.2(c).

[256] "including waste waters, but excluding sludge", art.2(q), and also see Defra EP landfill guidance at 3.14–3.20. Similarly mixing liquid wastes with sand or sawdust is not acceptable under the mixing prohibition under art.5.4.

[257] Section 2.1.1 to the Annex to the Decision 2003/33.

[258] Section 3 of Annex II to the Directive, and para.1 of the Annex to the Decision.

[259] Section 2 to the Annex to the Decision.

[260] The ECJ has held that member states may set more onerous targets (in terms of the definition of the biodegradable fraction), given the terms of Article 176 EC which enabled member states to maintain or introduce more stringent protective measures: *Deponiezweckverband v Land Rheinland-Pfalz* [2005] Env 841. Contrast the different approach taken in the transhipment cases (such as *DaimlerChrysler*) considered at para.15–137 below.

and 2020 respectively. These obligations are implemented by the Waste and Emissions Trading Act 2003, and the Landfill Allowances and Trading Scheme (England) Regulations 2004, which allocate to each waste authority a (transferable) reducing landfill allowance, and impose substantial financial penalties if such an allowance is exceeded. Being transferable, an authority that is pro-active and out-performs its compliance targets may sell surplus allowances to others who have failed to reach them. The selling authority may thus recoup some of its investment made to improve its performance, while the buying authority may avoid becoming subject to these penalties.

Under Article 6, all wastes must be subject to "treatment" before being landfilled, treatment being defined[261] as processes which change the characteristics of the waste in order to reduce its volume or hazardous nature, facilitate its handling or enhance recovery. This obligation to carry out pre-treatment does not apply to inert waste for which treatment is not technically feasible or indeed to any other kind of waste where treatment does not assist to achieve the objectives of the Directive.[262]

Technical standards

15–080   All landfills must meet the "general" requirements set out in Annex I to the Directive, wherein lies the substance of the measure. These include assessing potential location under paragraph 1,[263] and water control and leachate management under paragraph 2,[264] and perhaps most importantly, there is the requirement in paragraph 3 that landfills be situated and designed so as to prevent pollution of soil, groundwater or surface water, and to ensure the efficient collection of leachate produced by the landfill. To that end, paragraph 3.1 specifies that there must be a geological barrier (which may be natural or artificial, e.g. made of clay or other minerals meeting permeability standards specified in 3.2, or heavy duty plastic sheeting) and bottom liner during the operational phases of the landfill, together with a geological barrier and top liner covering the landfill post-closure. Under paragraph 3.3, a leachate collection and sealing system must be installed to minimise leachate accumulation. The EA also requires leachate drainage layers across the basal areas of the landfill.[265] Paragraph 3.4 permits a reduction in the requirements for the barrier/liner and the leachate system under 3.2 and 3.3 respectively, if an assessment taking into

---

[261] art.2(h). See Defra EP guidance at 3.35–3.44.
[262] art.6(a). The "may" in "may not apply" in the Directive becomes "does not apply" via para.6(a) of Sch.10 to the EP Regs.
[263] So no landfills should be located within a Source Protection Zone 1: see, for this and other advice, the EP guidance at 3.134–5.
[264] Not for inert landfills: last sentence of para.2 of Annex I, as confirmed in para.6(c) of Sch.10 to the EP Regs.
[265] EP guidance, para.3.157.

account the provisions of the Groundwater Directive 80/68/EEC[266] satis-fies the competent authority that these are not necessary and that the landfill poses no potential hazard to soil, groundwater or surface water. However, this derogation does not on the face of it allow the omission of any of the requirements of paragraph 3.1: there must remain a bottom geological barrier and liner, and a top barrier and liner. That does not necessarily mean that the barrier has to be artificially created. Decision 2003/33 makes it plain that storage in salt mines or hard rock may comply with the obligations of the Landfill Directive, as long as a site-specific risk assessment demonstrates that "the level of isolation from the biosphere is acceptable."[267]

There must also be gas control measures under paragraph 4. Landfill gas must be collected from all landfills receiving biodegradable waste, and it must be treated and used, or flared if energy cannot be generated from it.[268] There are also requirements for measures to be taken against emissions of odours[269] and dust, wind-blown material (i.e. litter), noise, vermin, insects, aerosols, and fires.

We have noted above the one reference to the Groundwater Directive in the Landfill Directive. That fleeting reference belies the importance of the groundwater legislation in the context of landfills. We have traced in Chapter 11 the part played by Directive 80/68 in the evolution of domestic waste management legislation, and in particular the requirement that all landfills required prior hydrogeological survey before permits could be issued. It will also be recalled that the Groundwater Regulations 1998[270] transpose the Groundwater Directive 80/68/EEC, under which there is a division of dangerous substances into List I substances (of which there must be no direct discharge into groundwater), and List II substances where there must be a limitation upon such discharges.

Council Decision 2003/33, which post-dates the Water Framework **15–081** Directive and its anti-pollution measures, well demonstrates the linkage between the water and the landfill regimes. Discussing underground storage, the Decision points out that the Water Framework requirements can be fulfilled only by demonstrating the long-term safety of the installation. Article 11(3)(j) of the Water Framework Directive (and now the new Groundwater Directive 2006/118) generally prohibits direct discharges of pollutants into groundwater. However, deep storage in hard rock,[271]

---

[266] [1980] OJ L20/43.
[267] App.A to 2003/33, 1.1, 2.3, 4.1.
[268] para.4 of Annex I.
[269] A commonly imposed condition requires that "there shall be no odours emitted ... at levels as are likely to cause ... serious detriment to the amenity of the locality outside the permitted installation boundary, as perceived by an authorised officer of the [EA]": a challenge to the validity of such a condition (on *vires* grounds) was rejected in *Environment Agency v Biffa* [2007] Env. L.R. 330, [2006] EWHC 3495 (Admin).
[270] SI 1998/2746.
[271] See Chapter 11.

namely at several hundred metres depth, may still meet the requirements of the Water Framework Directive if

> "any discharges of hazardous substances from the storage will not reach the biosphere, including the upper part of the groundwater system accessible for the biosphere, in amounts or concentrations that will cause adverse effects."[272]

This is a telling reminder that the requirements of the various Water Directives are not absolute. A careful risk assessment may be sufficient to displace any presumptions outlined in those Directives.

A good example of the intersection of water and landfill regimes, coupled with a pragmatic interpretation of the terms of the Landfill Directive, is to be seen in *R (Lewis) v Environment Agency*.[273] The claimant challenged the grant by the EA of a permit for a new landfill in Blackfordby.[274] The landfill, like many, was to extend below the water table. To minimise the risk of contaminated groundwater flowing out through the sides or base of the site, the operator proposed to pump leachate from the base of the site so that the level was always lower than that of the surrounding groundwater. This would maintain a hydraulic gradient into, rather than out of, the site, or, put simply, water, if any quantities were to flow at all, would flow into the site, and only out of it through the pumps, where it could be treated before final discharge. Sullivan J. rejected a submission that "hydraulic containment", as summarised above, was in breach of both Landfill and Groundwater Directive obligations. He held that the obligation in paragraph 2 of Annex I of the Landfill Directive to "prevent surface water and/or groundwater from entering into the landfilled waste" was complied with if a clay barrier was constructed that was otherwise in accordance with the Directive. Any other conclusion would effectively rule out all sub-water table landfills, given that, to some extent, all clay, however low its permeability may be, will allow some groundwater to pass through. Hence the word "prevent" could not be interpreted in absolute terms. Nor was the mixing of waste and incoming groundwater within the landfill a "direct discharge" of list I substances within Article 4 of 80/68, on two grounds: it was not a discharge, nor could the water which had entered the site be described any longer as "groundwater".

Closure

15–082 A landfill may be "closed" within the meaning of Article 13 of the Directive when the permit conditions are met, when the operator requests it and the regulator agrees, or "by reasoned decision of the competent

---

[272] para.4.1 of App.A to 2003/33.
[273] [2006] Env. L.R. 227.
[274] The proposal was the subject to an earlier challenge at the planning stage in *R v Leicestershire CC ex p. Blackfordby & Boothorpe Action Group* [2001] Env. L.R. 2.

authority". As the EP Regulations make clear, this last must be made by a closure notice enclosing the EA's reasoning, and specifying the steps to be taken by the operator, and the period within which they are to be taken.[275] Importantly, closure of a landfill does not relieve the operator of liability under the conditions of the environmental permit.[276] Nor can the operator simply surrender the permit. As we have seen in Chapter 14, an operator cannot surrender *any* environmental permit under the EP Regulations without the EA being satisfied that the necessary measures have been taken to return the site to a satisfactory state,[277] having regard to the state of the site prior to the operation starting. This prevents the problem which used to occur under the Control of Pollution Act 1974, whereby companies owning onerous and severely polluting landfills could simply close the site, cancel the licence, and walk away from their obligations under the licence without further recourse.

Closed sites have also given rise to the question of "piggy-backing", namely the construction of a new landfill site above part or all of an existing closed site. The existing site may have been designed many years before, not on the containment principle required by the Landfill Directive, but on that of "dilute and disperse", whereby contamination would move off from the site in amounts and concentrations which by the standards of the times were thought to be acceptable. This has given rise to problems both for operators and the EA when designing and permitting the new site. The operator may be concerned not to be obliged to carry out remedial or reconstructive works to the old site. The EA has been concerned as to the legality of piggy-backing the new site, as well as more generally with the effects of building a new structure on top of an old structure. This new structure would have to be strong enough to prevent leachate migrating from the new waste, and yet must not exert undue compression on the old structure such as to exacerbate leaching from the latter.

The legal issues came before the courts in *Environment Agency v Anti-Waste*.[278] The EA argued that a permit could not be granted just for the new landfill, because of the degree of "functional interdependence" between old and new. The Court of Appeal disagreed. An application could properly be made for such a permit, although it would be a matter of technical evidence (reviewable by the EA or the Secretary of State on appeal) whether old and new could be separated as the operator claimed they could be. Another point in this case turned on regulation 4(1) of the Groundwater Regulations, which provided that "an authorisation shall not be granted if it would permit the direct discharge of any substance in List

---

[275] paras 10(1) & (2) of Sch 10 to EP Regs.
[276] para.10(4), ibid.
[277] As Defra's Environmental Permitting Core Guidance points out at 6.31, this requirement to return a site to a satisfactory state may be "significantly stricter" than the "suitable for use" test laid down in Part 2A of the EPA 1990 for remediating contaminating land.
[278] [2007] EWCA Civ 1377 (CA) on appeal from Collins J. at [2007] EWHC 717 (Admin).

I". The EA argued that the new permit would have to require the operator to stop any discharges from the old landfill, as failing to so specify would amount to a permission for that discharge. The Court of Appeal disagreed. A permit which does not require the ending and prevention of an old discharge does not "permit" that discharge within the meaning of regulation 4. The Regulations contemplate a discharge which results from the activity to be authorised and its consequences, but not a discharge extraneous in the sense that it is unrelated to the new activity.

Operator competence

15–083   Article 8(a)(ii) of the Landfill Directive requires that the management of the landfill must be in the hands of a person who is technically competent to manage the site and appropriate professional and technical development is provided. This is implemented in two ways; there is a specific duty upon the EA to enforce all Article 8 obligations to be found in paragraph 5 of Schedule 10 (the landfill schedule) to the EP Regulations; there is also a duty on the EA to refuse any application for *any* environmental permit if the EA considers that the operator will not operate the facility in accordance with the permit.[279]

Financial provision

15–084   As we have seen, one problem posed by landfills is that they tend to have a relatively long tipping life, and if they contain biodegradable waste there is a far longer period, typically 30 years or more, during which the site needs monitoring and managing in respect of landfill gas and leachate formation after such tipping has been completed. There are therefore significant provisions requiring inspection by the competent authority before the landfill can be regarded as definitively closed under Article 13 of the Directive, coupled with gas and leachate monitoring thereafter "for as long as the competent authority considers that a landfill is likely to cause a hazard to the environment."[280]

Since the enactment of section 74 of the Environmental Protection 1990,[281] there has been a requirement that the operator make financial provision in respect of any waste management operation until the licence or permit is surrendered. A similar, though as we shall see, potentially more water-tight, provision is to be found in Article 8(a)(iv)[282] of the Landfill Directive. A permit may not be granted until the applicant has satisfied the

---

[279]   para.13 of Schedule 5 to the EP Regs.
[280]   See art.13(c) and (d), and the precise monitoring obligations set out in Annex III.
[281]   Though this specific provision has recently been repealed by Sch.23 to the EP Regs.
[282]   The Directive enables member states not to require financial provision in the case of inert waste landfills, though the EP Regs (Sch.10, reg.6(b)) and Defra Guidance on Landfills, March 2008, at para.3.185, expressly states that this opt-out is to be ignored by the EA.

competent authority that adequate provision "by reason of a financial security or any other equivalent" has been or will be made, prior to commencement of disposal operations, to ensure that the obligations (including after-care provisions) under the permit are discharged and the closure procedure (under Article 13) is followed. These provisions must be kept in place for as long as required by maintenance and after-care of the site.

An important issue arises as to what is meant by "financial security". The term is undoubtedly intended to convey something which makes the performance of the permit obligations more secure than it would otherwise be if one was simply left with the company's promise or obligation to adhere to the terms of the permit. Equally, the "other equivalent" must be to the same effect, whatever its precise legal mechanism. Therefore, what is required is something external to the operator (not simply a promise by the operator, in whatever form) to which recourse may be made, if need be, whatever the ultimate financial fate of the operator. This is supported by the *travaux preparatoires*. The Commission's proposal of March 1997[283] included the following: "adequate provisions, by way of a financial security or any other equivalent (e.g. bank guarantee) . . .", which suggests that the words "any other equivalent" must be interpreted fairly narrowly. One aspect of this provision was considered in *R (Lewis) v Environment Agency*.[284] This case was principally concerned with whether a hydraulic containment system for a landfill complied with the Landfill and/or Groundwater Directives. However, a subsidiary argument challenged the Agency's decision to require the waste company to enter into a bond in a particular form in favour of the Agency. The argument, which failed before Sullivan J., was abstruse in the extreme, namely that because the Agency had required (and could only require) contingency provision in the bond for the period after 60 years,[285] and its ability to access the bond thereafter was not unconditional, the bond was for that later period inadequate, and, as such, was not compliant with Article 8(a)(iv).[286]

The requirement for an independent financial security avoids many of the very considerable problems posed by the intersection of the rules of insolvency with financial obligations emanating from the operating company itself. These were well demonstrated by *Official Receiver (Celtic Extraction Ltd & Bluestone Chemicals Ltd) v Environment Agency*[287] and by *Environment Agency v Hillridge*.[288] In the first case, both licence holders had gone into compulsory liquidation. The licences under which the holders had remedial obligations in respect of landfills remained in force. The

15–085

---

[283] (COM/97/105) at Article 8.1(c), the equivalent of the present Article 8(a)(iv).
[284] [2006] Env. L.R. 227.
[285] It was accepted that there was adequate provision up until the 60-year point.
[286] For the detail of the argument, see paras 71–77 of the judgment.
[287] [2000] Env. L.R. 86.
[288] [2004] Env. L.R. 32.

Official Receiver contended before the court that he was entitled to disclaim the licences as onerous property within the meaning of section 178 of the Insolvency Act 1986. The Court of Appeal held that a licence was property, and could be disclaimed as onerous under section 178, even though this had the effect of terminating the obligations; the polluter pays principle did not operate so as to prevent this. The Court considered that the words of section 35(11) of the Environmental Protection Act 1990 ("the licence shall continue in force until it is revoked ... or its surrender is accepted") were not irreconcilable with the provisions of section 178; the former did not prevent the insolvency statute taking effect. Section 35(11) of the EPA has now been repealed, but has been replaced by regulation 19 of the EP Regulations, which is in similar form. The ruling of the Court of Appeal is therefore likely to be applicable to the new EP legislation.

The *Hillridge* decision took matters one stage further. The operator had made financial provision via a trust fund designed to guarantee the performance of its long-term obligations under the licence. The operator went into liquidation, the liquidators disclaimed the licence, and the court was concerned with the fate of the trust fund, with the Agency contending that it should be used to clean up the land. The High Court ruled that the liquidators were not entitled to the fund, as their disclaimer of the licence operated so as to disclaim their interest in the fund. However the EA was not entitled to the fund either, because it could only be used whilst the licence was in force. The fund therefore became *bona vacantia*,[289] and thus reverted to the Crown.

These problems can be properly avoided if security is given *other* than by assets of the company, such as by a guarantee or bond, as in *Lewis*, above. It is now well established from cases on disclaimers of leases that such a security may be called upon, even though the lease in respect of which the security was given has been disclaimed.[290] This principle is applicable to the obtaining of a permit backed by such security. Hence after the cautionary tales of *Celtic* and *Hillridge*, the EA will be astute to ensure that security is given in guarantee or bond form which cannot be clawed back despite the permit being disclaimed in the event of insolvency.

Costs of landfill

15–086   The Landfill Directive also seeks to encourage financial security through another route, namely Article 10. This requires that "all of the costs involved in the setting up and operation of a landfill site" including the costs of financial security and after care for at least 30 years "shall be covered by the price to be charged by the operator". This aims to ensure that operators charge the market price of a properly run landfill for their

---

[289] Unclaimed property.
[290] [1997] AC 70.

services (to avoid significant under-cutting based upon under-capitalised businesses), which objective coincides with the general principle that cheap landfill should not undermine the economics of other waste operations which are higher in the waste hierarchy.[291]

Article 10[292] was the subject of interpretation in *3C v Mersey Waste Holdings Ltd.*[293] A landfill operator sought to increase the prices he could charge a customer under a long-term fixed-price waste disposal contract. He relied on the unlawfulness of those charges, because the contractual price had fallen below the costs of his landfilling operations, as prohibited by his landfill permit and indeed by Article 10. Hence, he said, the price had to rise to such a point as would cover his costs, and the contract would be unlawful for him to perform until such time as this occurred. One issue was whether the operator's "costs" as referred to in Article 10 had to be covered by the price charged in respect of all deliveries to the site, or whether that computation related just to the waste streams in question. David Steel J. held that the provision did not simply mean that the landfill had to break even as a whole. Income for the particular waste streams under consideration had to meet expenditure, though the operator could not include an element of profit on those charges. However, the landfilling costs so determined were net costs; on another sub-issue, the judge also ruled that any income from electricity generated by the use of landfill gas from the site should be set off against such costs.

Transposition of the Landfill Directive

The Directive was originally transposed by the Landfill (England & Wales) **15–087** Regulations 2002, with effect from June 2002. The waste acceptance criteria in Council Decision 2003/33 were transposed by the Landfill (England & Wales) Amendment Regulations 2004, with effect from July 2004. July 2004 also saw the end of co-disposal. As from July 2007, there could be no more depositing of non-hazardous liquids in landfill; hazardous liquids had been banned from the original coming into force of the Directive in 2001. The requirement for pre-treatment of all non-inert wastes came into force on October 30, 2007.

The Directive applied to new and existing landfills, albeit not those which had closed before its commencement date, only open ones. A set procedure under Article 14 was adopted to bring existing landfills into conformity with the provisions of the Directive, with a long-stop date of 2009.[294]

---

[291] See the Commission's Explanatory Memorandum to the proposal for the Directive to this effect.
[292] And its then transposing regulation, reg.11 of the Landfill (England & Wales) Regulations 2002.
[293] [2006] EWHC 2598 (Comm).
[294] This is now transposed by para.5 of Sch.10 of the EP Regs.

Landfill Tax

Introduction

15–088   The proposal for a Landfill Tax was first announced in 1994. The tax itself was introduced in the UK by Part III of the Finance Act 1996 ("FA 1996"), which remains the governing legislation.[295] It was designed to be "a new and imaginative way to encourage more environmentally friendly ways of waste disposal".[296] The revenue from the tax was designed to reduce employers' national insurance contributions and so it had an economic as well as an environmental purpose. Unlike many policy initiatives in this area the tax is entirely a creature of domestic law and policy, but it fits broadly within the aim of the EU in seeking to shift the burden of taxation from employment to the use of resources.

The charge to tax

15–089   The tax is administered by the Commissioners for Her Majesty's Revenue & Customs (HMRC), previously the Commissioner of Customs and Excise (CCE), and is collected from landfill site operators as the persons liable to pay the tax (section 41(1) FA 1996). It is levied per tonne of waste according to the nature of the material discarded. The amount per tonne is specified on a periodic basis, being relatively high for active waste and much lower for inactive material known as "qualifying material".[297] There is a discretion vested in HMRC to direct that small quantities of non-qualifying material can be included in a disposal without it losing its status as qualifying material. This discretion can be exercised so as to apply either generally or in particular cases (section 63 FA 1996). The determination of weight is in accordance with Regulations made under section 68 FA 1996 which also provides for special methods to be agreed with HMRC.[298]

The trigger for the application of the tax is the making of a "taxable disposal" which is defined in section 40 FA 1996. A disposal is a taxable disposal if it is a disposal of material "as waste", it is made "by way of landfill", is made "at a landfill site" and it is made on or after October 1, 1996. The fulfilment of these cumulative conditions at the same time

---

[295] The main regulations which have been made under the Act and which contain much of the detail of the manner in which the tax operates at a practical level are contained in the Landfill Tax Regulations 1996 SI 1996/1527 ("LTR 1996")

[296] Customs & Excise News Release 51/96 September 30, 1996.

[297] For the year ending March 31, 2009 the rates were £24 per tonne for active waste (rising by £8 per tonne in each succeeding year for at least the next three years) and £2 for qualifying material. What counts as qualifying material is set out in the Landfill Tax (Qualifying Material) Order SI 1996/1528 which groups the material included, subject to various conditions and notes for interpretation.

[298] Regulations 41–44 LTR 1996 – the basic method is, unsurprisingly, to weigh the material at the time of disposal.

brings about the charge to tax (see *Parkwood v Customs and Excise Commissioners*[299]).

Meaning of "as waste"

The meaning of this particular phrase has given rise to some difficulty, It is sometimes less than straightforward to determine whether someone disposes of something as waste. Section 64 assists in defining the scope of this element of a taxable disposal. **15–090**

A disposal is a disposal of material as waste if "the person making the disposal does so with the intention of discarding the material" (section 64(1) FA 1996) but the fact that he (or someone else) could "benefit from or make use of the material is irrelevant" (section 64(2) FA 1996). On the face of it then discarding material is the hallmark of a taxable disposal, irrespective of whether discarding allows the person discarding it or someone else to use the material or to benefit from it. There also seems on the face of the legislation to be at least a potential distinction between the person who disposes of the waste and the person who operates the landfill and it is the intention of the former which is critical.

However, it is clear that where the material is disposed of for the purpose of being used at the landfill site for road making or for daily cover, the material is not being disposed of "as waste" (see *Parkwood*, above and *HMRC v Waste Recycling Group*[300] (*WRG*) at paragraphs 32–34). Those decisions effectively overrule the earlier High Court decision in *CCE v Darfish*[301] where Moses J. held that material used in site engineering had been disposed of not by the person making use of it for site engineering purposes but rather by the person from whom the material had been obtained.

What these cases show is that if one looks to the person who makes the deposit of the material as the person who is disposing of the material, there is real scope for cutting down the ambit of the tax by reference to that person's use of the material in site engineering. Such use is not obviously construed as discarding the material. If one adopts the approach of the Court of Appeal in *WRG*, and looks at who has title in the waste at the time at which it is deposited, that effectively rules out charging the tax on material which, while undoubtedly discarded by someone earlier in the chain, is useful to the landfill operator. At a general level, it is not easy to see how this fits with the overall ethos of the tax; the reason why material is needed for daily cover is that there is a landfill site in operation which is receiving enough waste to require it. Further as is noted below, the only phase in the construction of the landfill which is exempted from the tax is **15–091**

---

[299] [2002] EWCA Civ 1707.
[300] [2008] EWCA Civ 849.
[301] [2000] All ER (D) 361.

site restoration i.e. the final stage of waste disposal when the site has reached its limit. The cap (i.e. the "lid" of the landfill site) is not exempted even though it is clearly a necessary part of site engineering. It is interesting in this respect that *Ebbcliff v CCE* (see below) was not cited by the Court of Appeal in *WRG*.

Meaning of "by way of landfill"

15–092   Section 65 defines the ambit of the phrase "disposal by way of landfill" by employing the concept of material being "deposited" and provides that the disposal of material is by way of landfill if it is deposited on the surface of land or on a structure set into the surface or if it is deposited under the surface of land (section 65(1)(i) and (ii) FA 1996).

Meaning of "landfill site"

15–093   Landfill site has a technical meaning set out in section 66 FA 1996, namely, land which is licensed under various provisions of environmental legislation, principally Part 2 of the Environmental Protection Act 1990. The operator of the landfill site is the person who holds the licence or environmental permit as the case may be.

Exemptions

15–094   The scheme of the legislation is therefore to adopt a broad charging provision which is then made the subject of a series of exemptions which are as follows (i) material removed from water,[302] (ii) contaminated land,[303] (iii) site restoration,[304] (iv) mining and quarrying materials,[305] filling in old quarries[306] and (v) pet cemeteries.[307]

The exemptions broadly reflect an environmental policy goal. For example, the contaminated land exemption applies to certified land reclamation projects. In order to qualify the project has to be carried out

"with the objective of facilitating development, conservation, the provision of a public park or other amenity, or the use of the land for agriculture or forestry" or "with the object of reducing or removing the potential of pollutants to cause harm" (see section 43B(7) FA 1996).

---

[302] s.43 FA 1996.
[303] s.43A FA 1996, and see *Augean Plc v The Commissioners of HM Revenue and Customs* [2008] EWHC 2026 (Ch). This exemption is being phased out: see HMRC's *Revised Notice LFT2*, confirming that applications for certificates of exemption had to be made by November 30, 2008, and waste had to be disposed of by March 31, 2012.
[304] s.43C FA 1996.
[305] s.44 FA 1996.
[306] s.44A FA 1996.
[307] s.45 FA 1996.

Consistently with the objective of reducing the amount of waste deposited at landfill sites, the site restoration exemption in section 43C FA 1996 applies to exempt the final stage of waste disposal at a landfill site known as the restoration layer. In order to qualify the waste has to be inert; this is unsurprising since the purpose of the restoration layer is to return the landfill site in question to some sort of beneficial use at the end of waste disposal operations, i.e. on completion of the restoration process. The capping layer which is usually directly beneath the restoration layer and serves to contain the waste material beneath, is expressly not subject to the exemption. This is presumably because it is more closely connected with the need to contain the waste beneath than it is with bringing waste disposal to an end (see *Ebbcliff v CCE*).[308]

For similar reasons deposits of inert material which are made at current **15–095** or former quarries in order to refill that quarry are exempt under section 44A FA 1996. The fact that former industrial land is being re-filled, and hence will be returned to some sort of use, depending upon the planning consent, is sufficient to justify a potentially wide exemption in respect of all deposits of inert material. This exemption is not confined to the restoration layer (see *Ebbcliff v CCE*).

The mining and quarrying materials exemption contained in section 44 FA 1996 is there to ensure that natural materials which have been not been subject to significant processing so as to change their character are not taxed when they are deposited. The exemption therefore applies even though material has been moved from one place to another. This is presumably on the basis that material which needs to be removed from one place (for legitimate commercial reasons), which is a natural product of the earth and which is simply deposited elsewhere is not seen as an environmentally damaging enough to be targeted by the tax.

Administration

The administration works like the VAT system on the basis of a liability to **15–096** register for the tax on the part of any landfill site operator who carries out taxable activities (section 47(2) FA 1996). Such a person submits returns to HMRC in which they account for the tax, again much the same as the VAT system. The tax is, to that extent self-administered, with the landfill site operator in the role of tax collector.

As with any other tax there is a power of assessment where a person has failed to make returns or to keep necessary documents or to facilitate verification by HMRC of returns or, perhaps most importantly, where it appears to the Commissioners that the returns submitted are incomplete or incorrect. Where the Commissioners assess, the assessment must be made "to the best of their judgment". By analogy with VAT law, where the same

---

[308] [2004] STC 391.

phrase is used, an assessment will not be called into question on these grounds unless it is made in bad faith or is a spurious or vindictive act on the part of the Commissioners missing all elements of judgment.[309] This is a deliberately high hurdle, because if the returns are indeed absent or incorrect then some sort of assessment is justified. Any adjustment to the amount of that assessment can be made at the stage of internal review by the Commissioners themselves, or by the VAT and Duties Tribunal on appeal from such a review under section 55 FA 1996.

There is a prescribed list of decisions contained in section 54(1) FA 1996 which can be challenged by the taxpayer by requesting a review by HMRC. If the taxpayer is dissatisfied with the outcome of that review, then an appeal lies to the Tribunal, but the taxpayer is generally required to pay the amount of any assessment before the appeal will be entertained, subject to considerations of hardship.

Landfill Tax credits

15-097 The LTR 1996 provides for a system of credits to arise against a liability to the tax in a number of circumstances. These include disposals which have been made with the intention of recycling the material or incinerating it where the amount of the credit equals the amount of the tax charged (Regulation 21 LTR 1996). There is also a system of credits for making contributions to approved bodies which have the object of protecting the environment. The specific aims which must be present for a body to be "approved" include land reclamation, the maintenance of public amenities and parks or the promotion of conservation or biodiversity through conservation of natural habitat (see Regulation 33 LTA 1996 (as amended)).

Offences and Penalties

15-098 Parts IV and V of Schedule 5 set out a regime of criminal and civil penalties which can be imposed for culpable conduct, e.g. fraudulent evasion of the tax (criminal penalties set out in paragraphs 15 to 16), dishonesty for the purpose of evading tax (paragraphs 18–19); lesser penalties are incurred for misdeclaration or neglect (paragraph 20).

Waste Incineration Directive

Introduction and summary

15-099 Directive 2000/76/EC[310] on the incineration of waste (widely referred to as WID) is another one in the series of Directives now transposed via the

---

[309] See *Rahman (t/a/Khayam Restaurant) v CCE (No 1)* [1998] STC 826.
[310] [2000] OJ L332/91.

schedules to the EP Regulations. As with several other EP schedules, transposition, via Schedule 13, is done in a minimalist fashion, and it is therefore convenient to follow through the main obligations within the WID itself. The WID replaced predecessor legislation which separately addressed the incineration of municipal waste (89/369[311] and 89/429[312]) and of hazardous waste (94/67[313]). The current Directive addresses the incineration of all waste, not simply hazardous waste. By its nature, and unlike much of the legislation in this Chapter which is concerned with waste on land, it is a measure essentially to reduce air pollution. It seeks to do this by a detailed and prescriptive set of rules, addressing both process (temperature, residence times etc) and outcome (emission limit values). Its main objectives are the reduction of emissions of nitrogen dioxides, sulphur dioxide, heavy metals and dioxins, as well as hydrogen chloride and fluoride (which are typically the product of flue gases as treated by abatement technologies such as scrubbers).

Overlaps

As with many Directives, there are regulatory overlaps, particularly with the IPPC Directive. This arises from the inclusion within IPPC "activities" of installations for the disposal of hazardous waste exceeding 10 tonnes per day, and for the incineration of municipal waste exceeding three tonnes per hour.[314] The domestic equivalent of IPPC in the EP Regulations does not apply any threshold to the incineration or co-incineration of hazardous or non-hazardous waste.[315] So the effect is that WID applies to all waste incineration and co-incineration activities, as does the domestic, more generous, transposition of the IPPC Directive. The Community rule is that compliance with the WID should be regarded as a necessary but not sufficient condition for compliance with any requirements which might be imposed via the IPPC Directive;[316] and therefore it is not impossible that developments in Best Available Techniques may change the obligations arising under the WID, even in the absence of any amendment to WID itself.

15–100

Definitions

The WID applies to all "incineration" and "co-incineration" plant. Neither term is straightforward in its definition. For incineration, there must be a (stationary or mobile) technical unit and equipment dedicated to the

15–101

---

[311] [1989] OJ 163/32.
[312] [1989] OJ L203/50.
[313] [1994] OJ L365/34.
[314] paras 5.1 and 5.2 to Annex 1 of 2008/1.
[315] s.5.1 to Sch.1.
[316] Recital (13) to WID, and, rather less explicitly, art.4 to WID.

thermal treatment of wastes, with or without recovery of the combustion heat[317] generated. This expressly covers pyrolysis, gasification and plasma processes, if their resultant products are then incinerated. All associated plant and equipment is included within the definition. Waste is defined as any solid or liquid waste as defined by the Waste Framework Directive,[318] but this does not exclude the incineration of gases derived from such wastes as the extended meaning of incineration suggests.[319]

In a combined heat and power plant consisting of multiple boilers, some burning non-waste and others burning waste, each boiler is a separate "plant" for purposes of deciding whether it is an incineration or a co-incineration plant.[320] Defra says in its EP guidance on WID[321] that the definition of incineration plant implies a degree of technical sophistication; a device which is no more than a physically contained open bonfire is not "incineration plant". There is probably something in this point (not every bonfire falls within WID), but it seems a risky line of argument to claim that the unsophisticated is not regulated by WID, whereas the sophisticated is, given that the whole point of WID is to require a considerable level of sophistication in all equipment dedicated to the burning of waste. Defra gives helpful guidance on the circumstances in which thermal treatment of waste does not fall within the definition of incineration,[322] with the most obvious examples being the drying of sewage sludge (where no irreversible molecular change happens), or the cleaning of paint from jigs (where the purpose is not incineration, but cleaning the jig for re-use).

"Co-incineration plant" means plant whose main purpose is the generation of energy or production of material products, but which uses wastes as a regular or additional fuel, or in which waste is thermally treated for the purpose of disposal.[323] If the plant's main (but not exclusive) purpose is the thermal treatment of waste, then the element of energy material production does not stop it being "incineration" plant.[324] To decide whether a given plant is incineration or co-incineration plant, one must look at the main purpose of the plant, in the light of the volume of energy created or products produced by the plant as against the quantity of waste incinerated and the stability and continuity of that production.[325]

---

[317] art.3.4. "Heat" must include recovery of heat for energy-generating purposes: see, e.g. art.4.2(b) which suggests that a broad definition is to be adopted.

[318] art.3.1.

[319] Per A-G Kokott in *Lahti* at para.38.

[320] *C-251/07 Gävle Kräftvärme AM v Länsstyrelsen I Gävleborgs Iän*, September 11, 2008. There is a discussion in *Lahti* at para.80 about how the definition of "plant" in WID should be read in the light of the definition of "installation" in the IPPC Directive; this gains force from the fact that, unlike the English texts, the French and German versions of WID and IPPCD use the same word ("installation" and "Anlage" respectively).

[321] para.2.5, and 2.14 giving the example of the waste oil burners providing space heating.

[322] paras 2.15–2.19.

[323] art.3.5.

[324] ibid.

[325] *Gävle*, above.

Expressly excluded from WID are plants only treating (a) vegetable **15–102**
waste from agriculture and forestry, and from the food processing industry,
if the heat generated is recovered; (ii) fibrous waste from the paper
industry, if co-incinerated at the place of production, with heat recovery;
(iii) wood waste (unless treated with preservatives), and cork waste; (iv)
radioactive waste; (v) animal carcases;[326] (vi) waste from oil and gas
exploration,[327] as well as experimental incineration plants treating less than
50 tonnes a year. But exclusion from WID does not exclude wastes from
being regulated by IPPC, as noted under *Overlaps* above.

Technical standards

The main technical requirements vary as between incineration and co- **15–103**
incineration, and hazardous and non-hazardous waste. Common to all is a
requirement that waste is combusted at 850°C for two seconds, to optimise
destruction of the contaminants in the underlying wastes. Hazardous
wastes which include more than 1 per cent of halogenated organic substances must be combusted at 1100°C for two seconds.[328] Such temperatures and residence times must be achieved under the most
unfavourable operating conditions. There must be automatic waste feed
interlocks, i.e. devices to prevent waste being introduced when such temperatures are not met, or when continuous monitoring shows that emission
limit values are not being met.[329] Article 6.4 allows derogations (albeit on
specific terms) for specific wastes or specific processes in respect of temperatures and residence times, but any such derogations must be notified
to the Commission.

Incineration (not co-incineration) plants require at least one auxiliary
burner per line, to be run on fuel or waste which is no more polluting than
gasoil, and to cut in during start up, shut-down, and whenever the combustion gases fall below 850°C or 1100°C, as the case may be. Under
Article 6.1, incineration plants must be operated so as to result in Total
Organic Carbon of less than 3 per cent, and Loss on Ignition of less than 5
per cent. Permits must ensure that residues will be minimised in their
amounts and harmfulness, and shall be recycled where appropriate. Defra
advises that compliance with Article 6.1 and BAT will generally be used to
demonstrate that residues have been minimised.[330] Operators must also
ensure that the specific emission limit values (ELVs) set out in Annex V are
met, for total dust, organic carbon, HCl, HF, SO_2, NOx, for certain
metals, and for dioxins.

---

[326] The complex interrelationship between WID and the Animal By-Products Regulations is
well shown on p.18 of Defra's EP Guidance on WID.
[327] art.2.2.
[328] arts 3.1 & 3.2.
[329] art.6(3).
[330] EP WID Guidance, para.3.18.

Co-incineration plants have different ELVs set out in Annex II, for such plants *simpliciter*, for cement kilns co-incinerating waste, and for combustion plants co-incinerating waste; some of these ELVs reflect the mixing rule (namely how much waste and how much non-waste fuel is used in the process). However, if a co-incineration plant derives more than 40 per cent of its "heat release" from hazardous waste or burns untreated mixed municipal waste,[331] then the incineration rules of Annex V shall apply.

15–104 All plants must meet the ELVs set for discharges of waste water from the cleaning of exhaust gases set out in Annex IV, and meet the other provisions for prevention of water pollution set out in Article 8, including providing storage for contaminated rainwater run-off or fire-fighting water. There are more onerous delivery and reception procedures for hazardous wastes than for non-hazardous wastes set out in Article 5. There are also highly complex measuring requirements set out in Article 11, with a basic rule of continuous monitoring of NOx, CO, total dust, TOC, HCl, HF and SO_2, plus temperature and other reference parameters in the combustion chamber and in exhaust gases. These measurement obligations are then qualified by various lengthy derogations in Articles 11.4–7, and 11.10.[332]

There are also exceptions to the basic operating rules. Article 3.2 (as does recital 16 to WID) recognises that the properties of waste which render it "hazardous" in EU terminology are primarily its pre-incineration qualities, and do not reflect their propensity to cause harmful emissions on incineration. Hence, combustible liquid wastes without PAHs or without other constituents in Annex II of the Hazardous Waste Directive, and with a net calorific value of at least 30 MJ per kg, shall be treated as non-hazardous waste, and combustible liquid wastes which are no more polluting than gasoil are similarly treated. The latter makes the point well; gasoil, if waste, would certainly be "hazardous".

Permits

15–105 Any WID plant requires a permit, and the permit may only be granted if it is established that the plant will meet the technical requirements of the WID.[333] In addition, the heat generated during the processes must be recovered as far as practicable. Defra's EP guidance on WID[334] ranks heat

---

[331] arts 7.2 and 7.4. Note that to be so regarded, the mixed municipal waste must be "untreated". Defra regards treatment as including "any physical, thermal, chemical or biological process, including sorting, that changes the characteristics of waste in order significantly to enhance its combustion qualities in the co-incineration process in which it is to be used: para.3.56 of its guidance. It also declares that it is for the operator to prove that he is not using untreated municipal waste, though does not attribute this reversal of the usual onus of proof to any provision in the WID.

[332] The Defra EP guidance has an equally lengthy treatment of these monitoring obligations at paras 3.83–3.113.

[333] arts 4.1 and 4.2.

[334] paras 3.38–3.44.

recovery operations, in descending order of preference as follows: (a) use of waste heat from boiler water cooling system; (b) use of a boiler for steam generation or electricity generation; (c) use of exhaust steam for process heating or Combined Heat & Power schemes; (d) internal heat exchange for primary air heating and/or flue gas re-heating; and, not surprisingly at the bottom, (e) no heat recovery. It recognises that the high capital and operational costs of electricity generation may not be economical at smaller plants, and that heat recovery objectives may conflict with pollution abatement considerations.

Permits must list the wastes which can be burnt, the (maximum) capacity of the plant, and the applicable sampling and measurement procedures. Those applicable to hazardous wastes must give further details including the maximum and minimum mass flows, and the maximum contents of given pollutants. There are public participation provisions in Article 12 of WID concerning permit applications, which must be made open for public comment in one or more accessible locations. These provisions apply not only to completely new projects, but also to permits for an additional line to an existing incinerator.[335]

Reform

Article 14 of WID required the Commission to report on the application of **15–106** the Directive before December 31, 2008. In fact, the Commission reported in December 2007, in a rather different context, namely the proposal to adopt a new Industrial Emissions Directive covering IPPC and WID (and other air pollution provisions such as the Large Combustion Plant Directive) within one instrument.[336] Rather than move towards a stricter regime, as the terms of Article 14 might have suggested, the proposal seeks to add additional derogations, particularly in terms of monitoring frequencies and requirements.[337] Change may however come from a different part of the proposed Directive governing IPPC, which will apply to all but the smallest incinerators or co-incinerators: a legislative strengthening of the status of BAT Reference documents (or BREFs) is proposed, which means that more onerous standards may be imposed in practice via these technical documents, albeit without any amendments being required to the substantive parts of the WID itself. At the time of writing, the precise method of achieving this intention is a matter of some controversy as between the European Parliament and the Commission, but the Commission proposal involves it formally adopting the BREF documents and then the BREF documents being used as the reference for setting IPPC permit conditions.

---

[335] *C-255/05 Commission v Italy*, July 5, 2007.
[336] COM(2007) 843 final.
[337] Annex VI of the Proposal.

PRODUCER RESPONSIBILITY DIRECTIVES

15–107　The Waste Framework, Waste Incineration, and Landfill Directives are now implemented by the EP Regulations, and so are (at least in part) directives concerning end-of-life motor vehicles and waste electrical and electronic equipment. But it is convenient now to review the first directive raising producer responsibility, namely the Packaging and Packaging Waste Directive 94/62.[338] This involved not only the consumer and the waste operator in the waste handling process, but also those who designed and manufactured the product, primarily in waste prevention measures coupled with recycling targets. We shall also see in later directives explicit schemes compelling producers to collect or make provision for the collection of their products, once they become waste. Article 8 of the proposed new WFD seek to encourage wider use of extended producer responsibility outside these waste-stream specific directives.

The Packaging and Packaging Waste Directive 94/62

15–108　Packaging and its accompanying waste is a relatively small proportion of total Community waste (about 5 per cent), but a rather larger proportion of municipal waste (between 20 per cent and 30 per cent). However, it was rightly identified by the Community as an area in which it was important to reduce waste, not least because of the opportunities to prevent it arising in the first place. This derives from the fact that packaging, unlike most other categories of goods, is rarely an entity wanted in itself. Its prime function is simply to enable us to receive the underlying product in good condition (even if marketing is often an important secondary objective). Therefore any scheme of regulation needs to address the person who produced the packaging, as much as the person who ends up with it when it becomes waste. Waste prevention (a concept to be found in Article 3 of the original Waste Directive of 1975) is in this way at least as important as re-use, recycling and recovery; and requires measures imposing producer responsibility, as distinct from waste handler responsibility. But producer responsibility presents its own difficulties, for the simple reason that by the time the packaging becomes waste, the producer is no longer the holder of it.

Like almost all recent initiatives in the waste field, the current legal picture is defined by Community instruments and their domestic implementation. An initial and modest sortie into the field was made by the Bottles Directive (or more formally, Directive 85/339[339] on containers of liquids for human consumption). However, the trigger for wider inter-

---

[338] [1994] OJ L365/10.
[339] [1985] OJ L176/18.

vention appears to have been the German domestic packaging regulations (encouraged by the Commission) which led to an outflow of packaging waste from Germany into other Member States. The motivation was therefore both trade and environment-related. It led to the Packaging and Packaging Waste Directive 94/62.[340] As will be shown, the bulk of this Directive remains in force, though certain of the critical targets were changed by amendment in 2004.[341]

The objectives of the Directive are well stated in Article 1, namely measures aimed

"as a first priority, at preventing the production of packaging waste and, as additional fundamental principles, at re-using packaging, at recycling and other forms of recovering packaging waste and, hence, at reducing the final disposal of such waste".

The extended scope of the Directive is equally important: it covers "all packaging placed on the market in the Community and all packaging waste". The Directive (unlike most waste regulation) thus regulates *product* and the waste which derives from that product.

The general shape of the Directive is to promote prevention (Article 4, **15–109** and prevention includes reducing the harmfulness of the materials[342]), re-use (Article 5) and recovery and recycling (Article 6). But it is only in Article 6 that the regime gets its teeth. This requires Member States to take the necessary measures to attain certain targets. Hence, by the end of 2008, a minimum of 60 per cent by weight of packaging waste should be recovered or incinerated at waste incineration plants with energy recovery. Similarly, between 55 per cent and 80 per cent should be recycled. There are also specific targets for glass and paper/board (60 per cent), metals (50 per cent), plastics[343] (22.5 per cent), and wood (15 per cent). The Community institutions were also required, by the end of 2007, to fix further targets for 2009–14, though the Commission has taken the view that this is premature prior to the expiry of the first target period. There are also requirements under Article 11 to limit concentrations of lead, cadmium, mercury and hexavalent chromium in packaging or packaging components.

The Directive has, in Article 3, its own definitions of "re-use", "recycling" and "energy recovery". This is of particular importance in respect of energy recovery, which is defined as the use of packaging waste "as a means

---

[340] General targets had in fact been proposed by the European Parliament in the run up to the amendment of 75/442 in 1991, but were rejected by the Commission.
[341] Directive 2004/12/EC.
[342] art.3.4.
[343] There is no obvious legislative impulse (other than the general injunction to prevent waste) for the current movement towards re-usable non-plastic bags, and away from the typical plastic supermarket bag which is used but once before ending up, typically, in landfill. Modbury in Devon seems to have led the way in England towards a plastic bag-free town, but Hay-on-Wye followed swiftly, and supermarkets have more recently reacted nationally to this movement.

to generate energy through direct incineration with or without other waste but with recovery of the heat." It seems reasonably plain that "recovery of the heat" includes recovery of the energy from the heat. However, this form of energy recovery does not necessarily accord with the definitions of recovery to be found in the Waste Framework Directive[344] under which the principal purpose of the incineration must be the generation of energy. This may seem an abstruse point, but a significant contribution towards meeting these specific recovery targets is made by incineration operations which would not necessarily qualify as recovery operations in the terminology of the Waste Framework Directive. This point reminds us that even though the Directive shares much of its terminology with the Waste Framework Directive, it is, in European terms, a "lex specialis" or law containing specific rules, which take priority over those set out in the general provisions laid down in the WFD. This was evident, for example, in *Mayer Parry 2*,[345] involving the question of when scrap metal was ultimately recycled, in which the bulk of the ECJ's judgment considers the specifics of the Packaging Directive, rather than the generalities of the Waste Framework Directive.

The Packaging Directive was initially transposed into domestic law in 1997,[346] but the highly complex Producer Responsibility Obligations (Packaging Waste) Regulations 2007, as amended, now govern.[347] The Regulations seek to achieve the objectives of the Directive by spreading the responsibility for meeting the recovery and recycling targets between all those involved in the waste chain from producers through to retail outlets. The targets apply to recyclable material, namely glass, aluminium, steel, paper/board, plastic,[348] and wood. Those involved with such materials (producers in the terminology of the Regulations) have "producer responsibility obligations". Producers are those who manufacture raw materials for packaging (raw material manufacturers), convert those materials into packaging (converters), pack the goods (packers/fillers), or sell the packaging to the consumer (sellers). Those "producer responsibility obligations" require that the producer (a) register with the EA and supply data on the packaging handled by that entity; (b) recover and recycle a given percentage of the packaging handled in that year; and (c) sign a certificate of compliance verifying the fact that the entity has met the target for that year and send this to the Environment Agency which enforces the scheme.[349] There are exceptions to this rule for businesses

---

[344] R1 of Annex IIB.
[345] *C-444/00, Mayer Parry*, [2004] 1 WLR 538, at para.57.
[346] By the Producer Responsibility Obligations (Packaging Waste) Regulations 1997, SI 1997/642.
[347] SI 2007/871, as amended in terms of the targets in Sch. 2 by Amendment Regulations 2008 SI 2008/413, with effect from March 14, 2008.
[348] Plastic plant pots used by nurseries are packaging: *Davies v Hillier Nurseries Ltd* [2001] EWHC Admin 587.
[349] reg.4(4).

which handle less than 50 tonnes of packaging waste a year, *or* with a turnover of less than £2m.[350] Hence only the larger producers share the burden of meeting United Kingdom targets.

A producer, if its main activity is that of seller, must also provide **15–110** information to consumers of its goods about the return, collection and recovery systems available to them, the role of those consumers in contributing to the reuse, recovery and recycling of packaging and packaging waste, and the meaning of related markings on packaging that it places on the market and that relates to its recovery and recycling obligations, and the relevant part of the national waste strategy.[351]

One key obligation noted above is to register with the EA. This must be done by application in due form. It is for the EA to decide whether to register a given applicant, but must register the application if provided with the requisite information under regulation 7(4). There is an appeal to the Secretary of State.[352] Producers may qualify for compliance under the Regulations either individually, or by joining a compliance scheme under which compliance is met on an aggregate basis reached by its members. Such compliance schemes also must be registered with the EA,[353] and, to be granted unconditionally, schemes applying for such registration must satisfy the EA that they are likely to last for five years, and that the operator of the scheme will meet his recovery obligations over that period. Failure to meet these recovery obligations must be reported to the EA, and must lead to re-application in respect of the compliance scheme in question.

Compliance (whether by individuals or schemes) can be achieved by acquiring Packaging Recovery Notes or Packaging Export Recovery Notes (PRNs or PERNs) in the market and equivalent to the amount of packaging recovered or recycled. The Regulations also make it clear that the only method of proving compliance is by acquiring PRN or PERNs,[354] either by meeting the recovery targets as a "reprocessor" (namely someone who recovers or recycles) or by buying these Notes in the market. The *Mayer Parry* case discussed below shows how this works in practice.

There are criminal sanctions for various offences of failing to comply **15–111** with the obligations under the Regulations.[355] The fines for these offences were initially quite modest. Magistrates were often sympathetic to companies who said that they had misunderstood the highly complex regulations. More recently, fines appear to have become more severe: a fine of £75,000 was meted out to Pizza Express in 2004, and in February 2008 Western Wines Limited were fined £225,000 by Shrewsbury Crown Court

---

[350] para.3 of Sch.1.
[351] reg.4(4)(d).
[352] reg.27.
[353] regs 14 and 15.
[354] reg.4(5).
[355] s.40.

in respect of non-registration between 2003 and 2005 (which had saved the company recovery and recycling costs of £185,059).[356]

The domestic system in operation can be illustrated by the *Mayer Parry* case. The underlying commercial dispute, mediated by the Environment Agency, was between the scrap metal operator Mayer Parry, and steel companies including Corus. Mayer Parry said that, as a result of its works of sorting, cleaning and cutting, crushing, separating and baling, it qualified as a reprocessor within the meaning of the regulations, and was hence entitled to issue PRNs in respect of the steel so recycled under Article 3(7) of the Directive as it underwent "reprocessing in a production process" Corus (and the EA) challenged this position, saying that it was only when the metal became ingots, sheets or coil of steel, that it was recycled. They therefore claimed the right to issue PRNs in respect of the same underlying raw material. The European Court found in favour of the EA and Corus, on the basis that scrap metal had not been reprocessed until it had been melted down in the furnace and turned into product.

The Directive has been the subject of relatively little litigation for such a complex and unprecedented measure. The main issues which have led to cases coming before the ECJ is whether more stringent domestic regulation by Denmark or Germany is consistent with its terms, or whether it amounts to trade barriers contrary to the Treaty.[357]

End-of-Life Vehicles Directive 2000/53

Introduction

15–112 "Every year end of life vehicles in the Community generate between 8 and 9 million tonnes of waste, which must be managed correctly" is the challenge accepted by recital (3) to the End of Life Vehicles Directive 2000/53.[358] An end of life vehicle means simply a vehicle which is waste with the meaning of the Waste Framework Directive.[359] Originally transposed, late, in 2003 into United Kingdom law, the ELV Directive is now transposed via the End of Life Vehicles Regulations 2003,[360] a handful of paragraphs in the EP Regulations (particularly Schedule 11), and via the End-of-Life Vehicles (Producer Responsibility) Regulations 2005.[361] This less than straightforward method of transposition means that we must look at the salient parts of the Directive and domestic legislation in parallel.

---

[356] ENDS Vol. 397, p.60.
[357] Opinion of A-G Colomer in *C-246/99 Commission v Denmark* and judgments of ECJ in *C-463/01 Commission v Germany* and *C-309/02 Radlberger Getrankegesellschaft mbH*.
[358] [2000] OJ L269/34, but amended by Commission and Council Decisions in 2002 and 2005 (x 3). See consolidated text on the Europa website.
[359] art.2.1 of the ELV Directive.
[360] SI 2003/2635.
[361] SI 2005/235.

Producer responsibility

The ELV Directive adopts some of the producer-responsibility methods **15–113** assumed by the earlier Packaging and Packaging Waste Directive. Article 4, on Prevention, tells Member States to encourage vehicle manufacturers to limit the use of hazardous substances and to reduce them "as far as possible from the conception of the vehicle onwards"; similarly, manufacturers are to design and produce vehicles so as to facilitate the dismantling, reuse, recovery and recycling of vehicles. The definition of these key terms found in Article 2 follows that in the Packaging Waste Directive. There are prohibitions in Article 4.2(a) on the use of lead, mercury, cadmium and hexavalent chromium, other than as set out in Annex II.[362]

Article 5 requires collection systems to be introduced for vehicles, and for all end of life vehicles to be transferred to authorised treatment facilities. Member States shall also ensure that producers meet all, or a significant part of, the costs of implementing this Article or take back vehicles themselves. Article 5 is implemented by: (i) Regulation 39 of the 2003 Regulations which requires that cars put on the market on or after July 1, 2002 which have no market value be accepted for destruction free of charge, and (ii) the 2005 Regulations, which require producers (i.e. manufacturers) to register and declare which cars they have produced, and then set up systems for their collection which need approval by the Secretary of State (this time BERR, rather than Defra). Those collection systems needed to be reasonably accessible and capable of treating the expected flow of vehicles as from 2006. There is a compliance notice procedure to enforce these provisions,[363] as well as the usual offence-creating provision.[364] Also, and in a way similar to the Packaging Directive, Article 7[365] sets re-use and recovery targets for post-1980 cars of 85 per cent and re-use and recycling targets of at least 80 per cent by weight per vehicle (i.e. per model) per year from 2006 till December 31, 2014.

Waste handling requirements

The ELV Directive also addresses the minimum standards to be adopted **15–114** by authorised treatment facilities designed to scrap and recycle cars and their component parts. Article 6.1 requires that all end of life vehicles be stored, even temporarily, and treated in accordance with Article 4 of the 2006 Waste Framework Directive *and* meet the standards set out in Annex I.[366] These standards require impermeable surfaces, water treatment equipment, appropriate storage for spare parts, batteries and used tyres,

---

[362] Originally transposed by reg.6 of the 2003 Regs. Note that the most recent version of Annex II derives from a Council Decision 2005/673/EC of September 20, 2005.
[363] reg.16 of the 2005 Regs.
[364] reg.23 of the 2005 Regs.
[365] Transposed by reg.18 of the 2005 Regs.
[366] Together with art.6.3, transposed by para.3 of Sch.11 of the EP Regs.

segregated storage of fluids from vehicles such as oils, antifreeze, brake fluids and battery acids, and treatment facilities to promote recycling. Article 6.3 requires (a) stripping of vehicles before further treatment to reduce any adverse impact on the environment (b) segregation of hazardous materials and components, and (c) the carrying out of stripping and storage in such a way as to ensure the suitability of the components for reuse. All treatment operations are to be carried out as soon as possible.

Article 6.2 requires that all treatment operations require a permit or be registered. Registration under this provision may apply to recovery operations concerning vehicles after they had been treated (namely after removal of batteries, air bags, fuel, oils and liquids, and any components containing mercury). The facility must be inspected before registration in order to assess its compliance with the objectives of Article 4 of the 2006 Waste Framework Directive,[367] and be inspected at least once a year thereafter.[368] This option of registration (rather than a full environmental permit) has been taken up by Defra in setting out the exemptions contained in paragraph 45 of Schedule 3 to the EP regulations.

Waste Electrical and Electronic Equipment Directive 2002/96

15–115   The Waste Electrical and Electronic Equipment Directive 2002/96[369] (the WEEE Directive) is another waste-stream specific Directive which follows the pattern and indeed much of the detail adopted by the ELV Directive. It includes measures aimed at preventing waste, as well as waste management provisions. As with the ELV Directive, it is transposed via two different government departments. The prevention measures are transposed by the WEEE Regulations 2006[370] initiated by BERR, and the waste management provisions are transposed by the EP Regulations and regulated by the EA. The various provisions will be considered together.

The 2006 Regulations and the Directive

15–116   Like many recent provisions, the Regulations are long and complex, running to 75 Regulations and 11 Schedules, and can only be summarised briefly here. Some of the obligations under the WEEE are upon producers (namely manufacturers, importers or re-branding sellers) of WEEE, to finance the costs of collection, treatment, recovery, and environmentally sound disposal of *consumer* WEEE which is either deposited at a collection

---

[367] Transposed by para.2 of Sch.6 of the EP Regs.
[368] Transposed by para.13 of Sch.6 of the EP Regs.
[369] [2003] OJ L37/24, as amended by Directive 2003/103.
[370] SI 2006/3289.

facility by members of the public or which is returned to distributors (i.e. retailers).[371] WEEE is defined in Annexes 1A and 1B of the Directive, and includes all household appliances, IT and telecommunications equipment, lighting equipment, electric and electronic tools, toys, leisure and sports equipment, medical devices, monitoring and control instruments, and automatic dispensers. The cost to each manufacturer of these various arrangements for dealing with WEEE is computed by reference to its market share. Similarly, retailers are obliged to take back, free of charge, and on a one to one basis, equipment equivalent to that which they supply,[372] which they can then pass on to the manufacturers. There is separate provision for the financing in respect of business WEEE, in which producers have to finance costs relating to their own WEEE put on the market since 2005, and in respect of historic WEEE produced by others, accept this in exchange for EEE which the producers are selling to the business customer in question.

The Directive also contains recovery targets in Article 7, applying to various categories of WEEE as listed in Annex IA. Differing percentages are given for the rate of recovery (e.g. 80 per cent by weight in the case of large household appliances) and component, material, and substance reuse and recycling (e.g. 75 per cent by weight for the same appliances). In order to meet these targets, producers (by contrast to the Packaging Directive, under which they may go it alone) *must* join a compliance scheme which will then recover or dispose of the WEEE, as the case may be. The operators of compliance schemes must register individual producers with the EA,[373] and there are elaborate rules in Part 7 of the Regulations concerning approval or withdrawal of approval by the EA of such schemes. An appeal lies against a refusal to approve or withdrawal of approval.[374]

Also in need of approval are Authorised Treatment Facilities (ATFs), whereby an ATF becomes an Approved ATF (AATF)). An ATF must have a permit to operate, as defined in regulation 2(1). Approval must be also forthcoming from the EA under Part 8 of the Regulations, before the ATF operator can issue evidence notes. Similar rules apply to Approved Exporters (AEs). These evidence notes are the key to proving compliance with the targets. Only AATFs and AEs may issue them as evidencing re-use, recovery, or recyling, either when they have carried out these various operations or when the material has been transferred on to and received by a reprocessor—it does not have to have been reprocessed by the recipient.[375]

There is a potentially important provision under which scheme operators **15–117** must prioritise the re-use of whole appliances, though without proper

---

[371] arts 5(2) & 5(4), transposed by reg.8 of the WEEE Regs.
[372] art.5(2)(b), transposed by reg.31.
[373] reg.19.
[374] reg.66.
[375] reg.47(2).

enforcement, this risks being a dead letter, given the commercial considerations of their members. There is no provision in the Directive or the Regulations requiring producers or indeed distributors to promote cost-efficient methods of repairing EEE. This is unfortunate, given that uneconomic repair charges levied by EEE producers are often the trigger for purchase of new EEE, and hence the generation of WEEE.

The Regulations contain a separate enforcement code, under which enforcement notices may be served on the various parties involved in the system (producers, scheme operators, AATF operators),[376] and a multitude of different criminal offences may be charged under Regulation 73.

Waste handling provisions

15–118 The core of the provisions concerning the appropriate handling of the WEEE is to be found in Article 6 of the Directive. Member States are to ensure that producers set up systems to provide for the treatment of WEEE "using best available treatment, recovery and recycling techniques" which generates another acronym, BATRRT, used by Defra in its EP and other guidance.[377] Treatment must involve the removal of all fluids, coupled with selective treatment of a list of substances and components in Annex II of the Directive. So, for example, toner cartridges, cathode ray tubes, and large LCD displays must be selectively treated. Specific direction is also given in Annex II for cathode ray tubes (the fluorescent coating has to be removed), and the removal of ozone-depleting substances from foams and refrigeration circuits. Under Article 6.3, treatment operations are to be carried out in accordance with Annex III which requires premises to have impermeable surfaces, appropriate storage and containers, and water treatment equipment.

Article 6 is transposed by Schedule 12 to the EP Regulations. The only amendment of note[378] is the disapplication of the requirement in Article 6.4 that the permit shall require the achievement of the recovery targets. This is because those targets are to be achieved via the compulsory membership of the compliance schemes which must then meet the targets, as noted above.

Conclusion

15–119 The system as implemented is the subject of considerable criticism, given the disjointed system of enforcement, lying between two government departments, and with a limited role for the EA. That criticism has come from many different quarters, NGOs, producers, the waste industry, and

---

[376] reg.71.
[377] There is separate and specific guidance on BATRRT to be found on the Defra website.
[378] para.3(2)(b).

the head of the EA.[379] Irrespective of this particular division of responsibilities, it is plainly important to integrate in an effective way the provisions concerned with waste prevention addressed at producers (hence the involvement of BERR) with those concerned with waste handling.

Attentive readers will note that there is nothing in the WEEE Directive equivalent to the provisions in the Packaging and ELV Directives concerning the inclusion of hazardous substances in EEE products. This is not because the Community legislature was not attentive; indeed far from it. It was decided that the subject warranted a separate directive, the subject of the next section.

Restriction of Certain Hazardous Substances Directive 2002/95

The Restriction of Certain Hazardous Substances Directive 2002/95[380] **15–120** (synchronous with the WEEE Directive 2002/96, as the numbers reveal) is to be read with the WEEE Directive. It applies to 8 out of the 10 categories of equipment listed in Annex IA of the latter,[381] together with electric light bulbs and household luminaires. It prohibits the putting on to the market on or after July 1, 2006, of such equipment if they contain lead, mercury, cadmium, hexavalent chromium, polybrominated biphenyls (PBB) or polybrominated diphenyl ethers (PDBE).[382] The Annex contains certain excepted, and much amended, specific uses of these substances. Again in amended form, it also contains a threshold of 0.1 per cent for all substances apart from cadmium where the threshold is 0.01 per cent. There is an exemption for spare parts for equipment which went on to the market prior to July 2006. The Directive probably does not apply to equipment supplied as part of another product, such as lighting or entertainment equipment forming part of a vehicle, train or aeroplane.[383] Nor does it apply to batteries, which are the subject of the separate Directive analysed below.

Since adoption, the Commission has struggled with the practical problems posed by the need to develop less hazardous and equally effective materials for use in EEE, leading to many applications by industry for exemptions from its provisions, and the technical progress referred to the Directive has not led to any expansion of its scope.

The Directive was transposed, nearly two years late, by the Restriction of

---

[379] See ENDS 397, February 2008, p.5.
[380] [2003] OJ L37/19.
[381] Those omitted are Medical Devices and Monitoring and Control Instruments. The Commission was charged in the Directive to review these categories, though no proposals have yet been forthcoming.
[382] PBB and PDBE are both flame retardants.
[383] This is the view of BERR and of the Commission's legal department: see the DTI's RoHS Government Guidance Notes of June 2006.

Use of Certain Hazardous Substances in Electrical and Electronic Equipment Regulations 2006. These were replaced with Regulations of the same title made in 2008.[384] These 2008 Regulations follow the Directive closely. They create a system of enforcement and compliance notices, as well as various offences,[385] to which there is a due diligence defence.[386] Businesses must be able to demonstrate compliance by submitting technical documentation or other information on request and retain such information for 4 years after the EEE is placed upon the market. The 2008 regulations contain additional investigative powers. BERR from the start delegated its enforcement functions to the National Weights and Measures Laboratory, an executive agency of that department, and a certain amount of criticism has also been addressed at the low-key way in which enforcement has been addressed to date.

Batteries Directive 2006/66

15–121   Directive 2006/66 "on batteries and accumulators and waste batteries and accumulators" is the most recent in the series of directives addressing individual waste streams.[387] It has been transposed by the Batteries and Accumulators (Placing on the Market) Regulations 2008.[388] It contains what may have become[389] a familiar mixture of measures addressed principally at producers and distributors. It contains collection schemes enabling end-users to discard batteries accessibly,[390] and obliging retailers to accept such on a one-to-one basis. Producers must finance the net costs of these schemes.[391] The Directive prescribes minimum collection rates by 2012 (25 per cent[392]) and by 2016 (45 per cent), and differing recycling efficiency targets by 2010 depending on the batteries in question.[393] There are prohibitions under Article 4 in respect of hazardous substances such as

---

[384] 2008/37: see also RoHS Regulations: government guidance notes of February 2008, URN08/582.

[385] reg.16.

[386] reg.21.

[387] [2006] OJ L266/1, repealing 91/157 [1991] OJ L78/38.

[388] 2008/2164, in force from September 26 2008.

[389] See the various producer responsibility Directives set out above, starting with the Packaging Directive.

[390] Not surprisingly, given the presence of batteries in WEEE, such schemes may be run in tandem with WEEE schemes: art.8.1(d).

[391] art.16.

[392] This may seem very low. However, the current rate of collection of portable batteries is a mere 3 per cent or 600 tonnes in toto: see BERR consultation paper on implementation, at para.4.3. There is currently no full recycling plant for either alkali manganese or zinc carbon batteries in the UK, despite these making up 80 per cent of the market.

[393] art.12.4 and Annex III.

mercury (no more than 0.0005 per cent by weight[394]) or cadmium (no more than 0.002 per cent by weight[395]). The transposing domestic Regulations impose corresponding prohibitions upon manufacturers when placing such products on the market. Batteries must also be readily removable from appliances.[396] Article 12 requires that all batteries and accumulators are recycled as from September 26, 2009 using Best Available Techniques for their Treatment and Recycling. Portable batteries and accumulators may however be landfilled, but waste industrial and automotive batteries may not be landfilled or incinerated.[397] There are provisions under which information is to be made available for end-users and all batteries are to be labelled as not for placing in wheelie-bins.

The domestic Regulations, apart from transposing the above, contain a typical hierarchy of enforcement mechanisms, starting with the compliance notice (to be served in the case of infringement),[398] then moving to an enforcement notice (if the compliance notice is not obeyed),[399] and finally criminal offences.[400] There is a due diligence defence.[401]

MISCELLANEOUS WASTE PROVISIONS

Port Reception Wastes Directive 2000/59

There are a number of specific provisions which are not implemented by **15–122** the EP Regulations and which also are not part of the sequence of producer responsibility directives considered above. For instance, Directive 2000/59[402] on Port Reception facilities for ship-generated waste and cargo residues requires facilities for such discharges to be made available at every port. Ships are required to deliver all such wastes to those facilities. Under Article 8, ships also have to pay a fee irrespective of their actual use of these facilities, in order to prevent discharge occurring before entering port. The Directive was transposed by the Merchant Shipping and Fishing Vessels (Port Waste Reception Facilities) Regulations 2003.[403] Regulation 14, implementing Article 8, directs that waste charges shall be made at such level as will ensure that ships make a significant contribution to the costs of

---

[394] Save for button cells, i.e. watch batteries or similar: art.4.2.
[395] art.4, with exceptions in the case of emergency lighting, medical equipment and cordless power tools.
[396] art.11.
[397] art.12.1, second para, and art.14.
[398] reg.13.
[399] reg.14.
[400] reg.15.
[401] reg.20.
[402] [2000] OJ L332/81.
[403] SI 2003/1809.

waste reception facilities irrespective of actual use of the facilities, and so as to provide no incentive for ships to discharge ship-generated waste into the sea. The Regulation also contains draconian enforcement powers, in addition to the usual series of offences for breaches of its terms: a ship may be detained by an inspector if he is satisfied that wastes or residues have not been delivered in accordance with the Regulations. Provision must be made by the port or the Secretary of State in default, for a waste management plan in respect of the waste reception facilities.[404]

Directive on PCBs/PCTs 96/59

15-123   Wastes containing polychlorinated biphenyls (PCBs) and terphenyls (PCTs) in anything other than minute quantities are hazardous wastes. An initial Community legislative foray, 76/403,[405] addressing these fluids, which were then widely used in transformers and capacitors, has now been replaced with Directive 96/59.[406] Under the latter, which defines PCBs as including PCTs, Member States must ensure that used PCBs are disposed of, and that PCBs and equipment containing PCBs are decontaminated or disposed of. Inventories must be compiled of equipment with any significant quantities of PCBs. The equipment and PCBs contained in the inventories must be decontaminated or disposed of by the end of 2010 at the latest. Member States must prohibit the separation of PCBs from other substances for the purposes of reusing the PCBs, and the topping-up of transformers with PCBs. Member States must take the necessary measures to ensure that PCBs, used PCBs and equipment containing PCBs which is subject to inventory are transferred to licensed undertakings, at the same time ensuring that all necessary precautions are taken to avoid the risk of fire. They must also ensure that any incineration of PCBs or used PCBs on ships is prohibited, and that all undertakings engaged in the decontamination and/or the disposal of PCBs, used PCBs and/or equipment containing PCBs obtain permits. Finally transformers containing more than 0.05 per cent by weight of PCBs are to be decontaminated under the conditions specified by the Directive.

Waste Oils 75/439

15-124   It is perhaps fitting that the Waste Oils Directive 75/439[407] should be addressed as last of the various directives concerned with specific waste streams. It was the first dedicated environmental directive to emerge from

---

[404] regs 6 to 10.
[405] [1976] OJ L108/41.
[406] [1996] OJ L243/31.
[407] [1975] OJ L194/31.

the Community. However, the Directive is now of little and transient significance, as most of its substantive provisions have been overtaken by the WID, and those that have not are due to be submerged into the new Waste Framework Directive currently passing through the Community legislative institutions. It set combustion emission limit values for various metals.[408] Dioxins do not feature in this measure adopted a year before the Seveso explosion. The Directive enjoined Member States to give priority to regeneration of base oils, by which was meant the process of cleaning up and re-using these lubricating oils.[409] This obligation was not entirely aspirational, as Germany, the United Kingdom, and Portugal discovered when found in breach of its terms for failing to take "tangible measures" to implement it.[410]

The new Waste Framework Directive proposes to confine specific provisions about waste oils to one article, Article 21, under which waste oils are to be collected separately, treated according to the objectives which are currently to be found in Article 4 of the 2006 WFD, and also in accordance with the waste hierarchy in which preparing for re-use assumes a high position. The priority hitherto afforded to regeneration has been watered down into a provision which allows, but does not mandate, Member States to prescribe that regeneration should take place if technically feasible.

Transfrontier Movements of Waste Regulations 1013/2006

We have so far described the way in which waste is regulated within the United Kingdom, by a combination of local and EU instruments. We now turn to the way in which movements of waste are regulated when waste is moved between countries, including between EU countries and non-EU countries. As one might expect, all the instruments in this field are derived from EU and wider international rules, and the domestic involvement is no more than a relatively straightforward transposition of those rules. However, the rules are extremely complex, and what follows can only be a brief summary of present legislation, and of certain issues under previous legislation which have come before the courts.

The current principal EU instrument is Regulation 1013/2006[411] on shipments of waste, which is to be read with the domestic Transfrontier Shipment of Waste Regulations 2007, in effect from July 12, 2007. However, before summarising this regime, it is necessary to look briefly at

15–125

---

[408] The Annex.
[409] art.3.1.
[410] Cases *C-102/97 Commission v Germany* [1999] ECR I-5051, *C-424/02 Commission v United Kingdom* [2004] ECR I-0000 and *C-92/03, Commission v Portugal*, 27 January 2005.
[411] [2006] OJ L190/1.

the history of the legislation, as this will help explain why we have ended up with such a complicated set of rules.

History

15-126 The original EEC Hazardous Waste Directive 78/319[412] laid down some general requirements concerning the shipment of hazardous waste. There then followed in the early 1980s deliberations between Community countries and the United States under the aegis of the OECD, which led the Commission to propose a directive on the shipment of hazardous waste[413] within the Community, followed by a directive concerning shipments to non-Community countries.[414] The underlying principle of the first directive to be specifically addressed at transhipment, and which is maintained in current legislation, is a system of prior informed notification and consent for shipments of hazardous waste. Member States had also to make some broad assessment of the ability of the country of destination to dispose of the waste without presenting danger to human health or the environment.

By the end of the 1980s, the focus had moved to the international stage, with the conclusion of the 1989 Basel Convention on transboundary movements of hazardous waste. This came as a response to a number of incidents involving illegal shipments of waste from industrialised to developing countries. The primary purpose of the Convention was to regulate the movement of *hazardous* wastes for *disposal* purposes, though it also touched on movements for recovery purposes. The EEC and most OECD members quickly became signatories to the Basel Convention, and now 170 countries in all are party to the Convention. It was then followed in 1992 by a decision of the OECD on the control of transfrontier movements of *all* wastes destined for *recovery*.[415] This set out a three-tiered structure of wastes (i.e not just hazardous wastes), namely green list (non-hazardous), amber list and red lists, with differing natures of regulation addressed to each list.

The first consolidated Community provision followed in 1993, namely Regulation 259/93,[416] which applied to all waste shipments for all purposes—namely the subject matter of both the Basel Convention and the OECD Decision—and this Regulation (chosen for its simultaneous self-executing nature rather than via a potentially ill-transposed Directive) governed the Community position between 1993 and 2007. It, like the OECD Decision, divided waste into three categories:

---

[412] [1978] OJ L84/43.
[413] 84/631.
[414] 86/279.
[415] C(92)39/Final.
[416] [1993] OJ L30/1.

(a) green (essentially non-hazardous) where prior notification was not required unless the movement was for disposal purposes,

(b) amber where notification was required, but consent was not required, and

(c) red, where notification and consent was required.

Unfortunately, the lists of waste underpinning these categories, drawn from the OECD set of lists, did not coincide with the Community hazardous waste list which, as we have seen, distinguishes between hazardous wastes and ordinary wastes for purposes of the Waste Framework and Hazardous Wastes Directives.

There were two other main distinctions in the 1993 Regulation, reproduced in the present regime, which affected whether waste could be moved across borders, and if so on what terms. The first is whether the transshipment was for disposal or recovery purposes. This accords with the same distinction drawn directly in the Waste Framework Directive.[417] The second is the identity and nature of the destination country, with differing regimes applicable to differing destinations. Part of the complexity arises from the fact that the regime needs to address all permutations of (a) the nature of the waste, (b) the purpose of the shipment and (c) the identity of the destination country.

15–127

The next main step after the 1993 Regulation came in 1995 with an important amendment to the Basel Convention, banning (not just regulating) the export of hazardous wastes from OECD to non-OECD states as from the end of 1997.[418] This was implemented by the EC in 1997[419] via amendments to the 1993 Regulation.

The present Regulation

Provisions common to shipments of all waste

The current Regulation 1013/2006,[420] which came into force in 2007, adopts a similar approach to the 1993 Regulation, though, as we shall see, rather more provisions are addressed to green list shipments for recovery than previously. The new Regulation also merges the amber and red lists, in line with the OECD's 2001 decision to that effect,[421] thus creating a common regime applicable to these more hazardous wastes. After a legislative tussle on the Treaty basis for the measure, it explicitly states in

15–128

---

[417] In practice the 1991 version of the WFD (91/156), which itself adopted the Annexes distinguishing disposal from recovery operations, from the very similar Annex IV to the Basel Convention.

[418] Via a new art.4A introduced by the Third Convention of the Parties to the Basel Convention of 1995.

[419] Council Decision 97/640/EC [1997] OJ L272/45, and Regulation 120/97, amending Regulation 259/93.

[420] Minor amendments to the Annexes have been made by Regulation 1379/2007.

[421] Council Decision C (2001)107.

recital (1) that "the main and predominant objective and component of this Regulation is the protection of the environment, its effect on international trade being only incidental."

Mixed wastes

15–129   As before, green list wastes, if destined for recovery, and if homogeneous, need not be notified. Both caveats are important. We shall return to the problem of recovery versus disposal below, but should note the provisions on homogeneity and mixtures here, as the problem often occurs in practice. Articles 3(1)(b) and 3(2)(b) of the Regulation render all mixtures of green list wastes notifiable, unless the composition of these mixtures does not impair their environmentally sound recovery *and* provided that the mixtures are listed in Annex IIIA. At the moment, this is not a generous proviso, as Annex IIIA is empty.

The problem of mixed wastes has come before the courts on a number of occasions under the 1993 Regulation, though as we shall see the legislative changes between the two Regulations are important. The first case was *R v Environment Agency, ex. p Dockgrange Ltd*,[422] in which Carnwath J. rejected the Agency's contention that a mixture of green wastes amounted to waste unassigned to a particular category and therefore amounted to red list waste. The second case was *Beside*[423] in which the ECJ has applied its own version of the de minimis rule to this problem of mixed wastes: a "small quantity" of non-green waste would not render the complete batch notifiable, unless "it is contaminated by other materials to an extent which increases the risks associated with the waste sufficiently to render it appropriate for inclusion in the amber or red lists, or prevents the recovery of the waste in an environmentally sound manner".[424] The third is *Omni Metal*[425] in which scrap electrical cable (consisting of a copper core covered with PVC sheathing) was under consideration; the Court held that a combination of two materials, both of which were listed as green list wastes, did not render the combination a green list waste. The terms of Article 3 of the present Regulation, as summarised above, confirm this position reached in the European Court. In short, and contrary to *Dockgrange*, most mixtures of green wastes, if separately catalogued in the European list of wastes, will be notifiable under the transshipment rules.

---

[422] QBD, July 22, 1997.
[423] *C-192/96 Beside* [1998] ECR I-4029.
[424] para.33 of *Beside*.
[425] *C-259/05 Omni Metal*, 21.6.07.

Tracking

However, for green list wastes, as well as all notifiable wastes, there is an **15–130** obligation under Article 49 for those involved with the shipment of all wastes to take the necessary steps to

> "ensure that any waste they ship is managed without endangering human health and in an environmentally sound manner throughout the period of shipment and during its recovery and disposal."

This is a far from straightforward obligation on a shipper if, say, the shipper is in the United Kingdom, and the recovery is to be carried out in a series of recovery operations in different parts of China. In addition, all consignments of all wastes must be accompanied by formal tracking documentation under Article 18, to be signed by the person arranging the shipment, as well as by the recovery facility when the waste is received. The contract between the shipper and the consignee must contain an obligation on both shipper and (in the event of the shipper's insolvency) the consignee to take or get the waste back or arrange for its recovery, and provide for its storage in the meantime. Finally, Article 19 contains a prohibition on mixing any wastes at any stage from the start of the shipment until receipt in the disposal or recovery facility.

What is a shipment?

The term "shipment" is used throughout the Regulation, and its trans- **15–131** posing legislation, without definition. The Regulation only applies to movements between countries. When therefore does a shipment start? The ECJ considered this in passing in *EU-Wood Trading*,[426] of which more below. The shipment of waste as a whole was said to be "from the point of departure of the waste in the state of dispatch until the completion of its treatment in the state of destination".[427] This would appear to cover the container-load put on a heavy goods vehicle in country A, even before the container was loaded aboard a vessel, and certainly before it arrived in country B. This is of practical importance as many consignments are inspected by the EA before they are loaded aboard the vessel which will take them outside the United Kingdom.

Prohibitions

Regulation 1013/2006 contains a number of absolute prohibitions on **15–132** movements of waste, the most important of which are (a) all exports of wastes from the Community destined for *disposal* outside the Community,

---

[426] C-277/02 *EU-Wood Trading Gmbh v Sonderabfall-Management-Gesellschaft Rheinland-Pfalz mbH.*
[427] para.46 of the judgment of the ECJ.

other than to EFTA countries which are also parties to the Basel Convention;[428] (b) exports of hazardous wastes destined for *recovery* to non-OECD countries,[429] (c) imports of waste into the Community destined for *disposal* from countries which are not signatories to the Basel Convention and which have not signed similar bilateral or multilateral agreements with the Community or its Member States;[430] (d) imports of wastes destined for *recovery*, unless the 1992 OECD decision discussed above applies to that country of origin, or it is a Basel signatory, or similar.[431]

Objections concerning shipments within the Community

15–133   Articles 11 and 12 of the Regulation set out the grounds upon which a Member State may object to a proposed shipment of waste within the Community. Article 11 is applicable to wastes destined for disposal, and Article 12 to wastes destined for recovery. In each case, both the Member State of dispatch and the Member State of destination may make a reasoned objection to the shipment.[432] The grounds set out in these Articles are plainly intended to be exhaustive of such grounds for objection.[433] They are summarised below, and then some of the more important issues arising will be discussed.

Objections to disposal shipments within the Community

15–134   In the case of shipments for disposal within the Community under Article 11, objections may be made "on the following grounds and in accordance with the Treaty". The first, Article 11.1(a), is that;

> "the planned shipment or disposal would not be in accordance with mesasures taken to implement the principles of proximity, priority for recovery, and self-sufficiency at Community and national levels to prohibit ... shipments of waste".

There is considerable overlap between this and the ground in Article 11.1(g) under which objection may be made if the shipment "is not in accordance with" the WFD, and "in particular, Articles 5 [the requirement for an integrated network of disposal facilities] and 7 thereof [the obligation to draw up waste management plans]". The common theme is that the shipment offends against general principles of European waste law. Unlike the corresponding provision applicable to recovery,[434] there is no express

---

[428] art.34. Iceland, Liechtenstein, Norway and Switzerland qualify.
[429] art.36.
[430] art.41.
[431] art.43.
[432] Transit member states have more limited rights of objection: art.11.2
[433] *C-324/99 DaimlerChrysler AG v Land Baden-Wurttemberg* [2001] ECR I-9897.
[434] art.12.1(a).

reference to Article 4 of the WFD, and its general objectives, in Article 11.1(g). This probably is of no consequence, given that it appears that *any* apprehended breach of the WFD may be relied upon.[435]

The second ground, Article 11.1(b) is that the;

"planned shipment or disposal would not be in accordance with national legislation relating to environmental protection, public order, public safety or health protection concerning actions taken in the objecting country."

The objecting country may be the country of dispatch or the country where the disposal is to take place; in each case, the grounds of objection must relate to "actions taken" in that objecting country, typically the proposed transport arrangements in the country of dispatch and the proposed manner of disposal in the country of destination.

The third and fourth grounds are more straightforward: they address the character of the parties to the transaction. So under Article 11.1(c) and (d) objection may be made if the notifier or consignee has been convicted of illegal shipment, or has repeatedly failed to comply with procedural requirements.

Article 11.1(e) enables the Member State to object to the import of **15–135** hazardous waste or household waste (even if for recovery purposes[436]) or its incineration residues under its right to do so under Article 4(1) of the Basel Convention. Ground (f) is that the planned shipment or disposal conflicts with international conventions. Ground (g) (shipment not in accordance with the WFD) is summarised above. Ground (h) is that the waste will be treated in a facility regulated by the IPPC Directive but which does not apply best available techniques. Ground (i), which is important, and is new to the 2006 Regulation, is that the waste is mixed municipal waste. Ground (j), which is also new, is that the waste will not be treated in accordance with legally binding environmental protection standards in relation to disposal operations established in Community legislation.

Objections to recovery shipments within the Community

The grounds of objection to shipments destined for recovery are listed in **15–136** Article 12.1. Many are common with those in Article 11.1 applicable to shipments for disposal. Those that significantly differ include Articles 12.1.(c), (g), and (k). Article 12.1(c) applies, where the planned shipment or recovery would not be in accordance with the national legislation in the country of dispatch, including where the treatment standards in the recovery facility are lower than those of the country of dispatch. This is

---

[435] The counter argument is that the express inclusion of Article 4 WFD in the recovery provision, without a corresponding reference in the disposal provision, means that a wider standard of review against the WFD is called for in recovery cases than in disposal cases.

[436] This is confirmed by art.3.5.

immediately subject to two caveats: firstly, proper functioning of the internal market must not be prejudiced; secondly, one cannot object if there is corresponding and comparably stringent Community legislation in the country of destination, or the recovery conditions are broadly similar to that prescribed in the legislation of the country of dispatch, or the national legislation of the country of dispatch has not been notified to the Commission. We return to the meaning of this difficult provision below.

Article 12.1(g) enables objection on the grounds that the costs and ratio of recoverable to non-recoverable waste does not justify the recovery: in effect, an objection that the proposed shipment is for "sham" recovery, namely disguised disposal. Closely related is ground (h), namely the objection is that the shipment is in fact for disposal, whatever the shipper may be asserting. There are particular concerns in this respect since the accession of Eastern European Member States in 2004, with widely differing costs of disposal throughout the Community, and hence there arises a great impetus to export waste to take advantage of those lower costs. Finally, Article 12.1(k) applies where the waste will not be treated in accordance with domestic waste management plans drawn up to implement recycling or recovery targets.

Extra-territorial application of environmental standards

15–137   One controversial issue under the 1993 Regulation was the extent to which one Member State could impact on the market in waste shipments by imposing its own environmental standards on shipments destined for other Member States. This issue remains under the 2006 Regulation, though we will need to look at the decided cases before analysing the present position. The first decision of the European Court of Justice was *Dusseldorp*.[437] The Netherlands' waste management plan permitted exports from the country only if the overseas method of processing the waste was superior. Dusseldorp wished to export oil filters to Germany for processing.[438] The ECJ rejected Netherlands' arguments that the grounds of objection were non-exhaustive, and held that the principles of self-sufficiency and proximity were only applicable to shipments for disposal, and hence not to shipments for recovery. Netherlands' attempts to rely upon what is now Article 176 of the EC Treaty (the ability to maintain "more stringent protective measures ... compatible with this Treaty") also failed, on the grounds that the particular measures were not compatible with what is now Article 29 EC (ban on restrictions of exports).

The second ECJ case was *DaimlerChrysler*. DaimlerChrysler wished to export its hazardous wastes produced in Germany for cheaper disposal in Belgium. The applicable *Land* required the waste to be incinerated in

---

[437] *C-203/96 Chemische Afvalstoffen Dusseldorp BV and Others* [1998] ECR 4075.
[438] It is not clear from the judgment whether this was for disposal or recovery purposes.

Hamburg, some 600 to 800km from the factories in question, in a plant co-run by the *Land* and the Hamburg *Land*. It therefore objected to the export, on what it claimed were self-sufficiency grounds, equivalent to the present Article 11.1(a). DaimlerChrysler sought to annul the objection on Article 29 EC grounds. On a preliminary reference, the European Court held that because the Regulation was exhaustive and harmonised shipments in order to protect the environment once it was shown that a measure fell within the scope of ground (a), then it was not necessary to assess that measure against the general EC Treaty obligations such as Article 29. However, the Court further held that the German measure in question did *not* fall within the scope of grounds for objection (a), namely self-sufficiency, priority for recovery, and proximity. It pointed out that the Regulation did not enable a country of despatch to object on the grounds that the disposal abroad would not meet its own environmental standards, if applicable. This ground of objection raised by the *Land* to the proposed export was therefore flawed.

It should be noted that there is still no provision in the 2006 Regulation enabling the country of dispatch to object on grounds that the disposal standards in the country of destination do not meet those in the country of dispatch, although there is now a provision (under Article 12.1(c)) enabling a like objection to be made in the case of shipments for *recovery* purposes in specific circumstances. Objections by the country of dispatch in shipments *for disposal* must therefore still focus on the shipment offending against Community standards as set out in WFD (via grounds (a) or (g)), as opposed to some difference in national standards.

The third case was *EU-Wood-Trading* (above), again still under the 1993 regime. This concerned a proposed shipment of lead-contaminated wood waste from Germany to Italy for recovery purposes. Germany objected on the grounds that the concentrations of lead contamination in the wood exceeded its own domestic guidelines for recovery, and hence the recovery operations and use thereafter of the chipboard to be made from the waste might endanger workers' health. The ECJ held that such an objection *was* capable of falling within a provision similar to Article 12.1(a) of the Regulation,[439] namely that the recovery in Italy might be in breach of the obligations of the Waste Framework Directive, including Article 4 requiring recovery operations to be carried out without endangering human health. So the Court held that for purposes of an objection to a proposed shipment, the state of dispatch may, in assessing the effects on health and the environment of the recovery envisaged at the destination, and provided it complies with the principle of proportionality, rely on the criteria to which the recovery of waste is subject in the state of dispatch,

15–138

---

[439] The old provision enabled objection to be made if the shipment was not "in accordance with [the Waste Framework Directive] in particular Article 7 thereof". The new provision includes express reference to Article 4.

even where those criteria are stricter than those in force in the state of destination.[440] To that extent, stricter standards can—in effect—be exported.

Discussion: disposal

15–139 The current position is this. The drafting of Article 11 applicable to disposal shipments has retained the relatively restrictive grounds on which more onerous standards embedded in the national legislation of the country of dispatch may be applied to the country of destination. Indeed, as we have seen, Article 11.1(b), concerned with national legislation, explicitly states that this only applies to "actions taking place in the objecting country" which excludes *Wood-Trading* type concerns about the standards in the destination country unless they amount to a breach of the WFD. In a disposal case, an objecting country of despatch must therefore invoke a likely breach of obligations under an international Convention in the destination country (under (e)) or identify some breach of the WFD principles under Article 11.1(g).

That said, some of the loose drafting might encourage the more ambitious Member States to attempt a more extra-territorial approach. Article 11.1(j), relating to legally binding standards established in Community legislation, is presumably aimed at the sort of highly prescriptive limits to be found in, for example, Annex V of the Waste Incineration Directive.[441] The other possibility for a wider ground for reviewing shipments for disposal is under (g), applicable to where the shipment is not in accordance with a state's waste management plans drawn up under Article 7 of the Waste Framework Directive or, arguably,[442] reliance upon a breach of the objectives set out in Article 4 of the WFD. However, attempts via over-restrictive waste management plans to police standards abroad will be scrutinised with considerable care by the Court, along the lines of the approach adopted in both *Dusseldorp* and *DaimlerChrysler*.

Discussion: recovery

15–140 The wording in respect of objections to recovery shipments under Article 12 is wider. Objection may certainly be made either because the proposed recovery would be in breach of Article 4 of the Waste Framework Directive (i.e. under Article 12.1(a), as per the ruling in *EU-Wood-Trading*)[443] or because the objecting country can bring its objection within Article

---

[440] para.46.

[441] 2000/76, considered above.

[442] This assumes that reliance may be placed upon Article 4 WFD, even though it is not expressly set out in art.11.1(g), whereas it is expressly included in the corresponding art.12.1(a) on recovery shipments.

[443] See the above discussion as to whether such an objection lies to a disposal shipment.

12.1(c). This last ground, and in particular, its proviso, has no analogue in Article 11. It is far from straightforward to interpret, and was subject to considerable controversy as the measure proceeded through the Community legislative bodies. It envisages an *EU-Wood-Trading* situation of lower standards in the destination country than in the dispatching country's law. However, there is a proviso: the dispatching country cannot object if the destination country has correctly transposed applicable Community legislation, presumably because in that event it is thought that such legislation would set the appropriate standards. The proviso, however, leaves open the anomaly that if the destination country has transposed such laws but systematically does not enforce them, then the country of dispatch may not object. Perhaps, it was thought that such an objection would be too politically controversial, and that enforcement is more properly a matter for domestic courts in the destination state or for the Commission by way of infraction proceedings under Article 226 EC. One other matter should be noted about this provision. Recital (22) explicitly states it to be an interim measure, pending the submission by the Commission of proposed Community-wide standards.

Recovery v disposal

These concepts take their meaning from the Waste Framework Directive.[444] However, the assessment is being made by the Member State of dispatch before the shipment takes place, and issues have arisen as to precisely what is meant by "destined for disposal" as opposed to "destined for recovery". As we have seen, it has been made clear in the *Abfall Service (ASA)*[445] case that the operation which the waste is due to undergo must be either disposal or recovery, but cannot be both. The *SITA*[446] case then addressed the question of what happens if the waste was due to undergo a series of operations. It concerned various waste paints and sediments to be sent for use as fuel in cement kilns. Apart from generating energy, the ash thus produced formed part of the cement clinker. The ECJ held that the "recovery or disposal" question was to be answered by reference to the first operation which the waste undergoes when it arrives at its destination, and not any subsequent processing or disposal of residues from that initial operation.

15–141

---

[444] art.2(4) and 2(6) of the Regulation, calling up art.1 of the WFD.
[445] *C-6/00 Abfall Service AG (ASA)* [2002] ECR I-1961.
[446] *C-116/01 Sita Ecoservice Nederland v Minister van Volkshuisvesting, Ruimtelijke Ordening en Milieubeheer.*

Energy recovery

15–142　As we have seen in the context of the distinction between disposal and recovery,[447] there was a series of cases under the 1993 Regulation concerning the export of waste for use in municipal incinerators and cement kilns, and in particular the attempts by certain Member States to introduce their own criteria such as calorific value of the waste to determine whether the operation was a disposal operation involving incineration or an operation under R1 of Annex IIB to the WFD involving the recovery of energy. The line was in the end drawn by *Commission v Germany*[448] and *Commission v Luxembourg*.[449] To be recovery, the main purpose of the operation needed to be to generate energy, the greater part of the waste must be consumed during the operation, and the greater part of the energy recovered and used. This approach excluded the majority of municipal waste incinerators from being regarded as carrying out recovery operations, though Annex II of the 2008 Waste Framework Directive now determines this issue by application of a specific energy efficiency parameter.

Notifications and procedure

15–143　The procedure concerning notification has been simplified in the 2006 Regulation. The notifier (who may be shipper, producer, dealer or broker[450]) must submit a prior written notification through the competent authority of dispatch (in England and Wales, the EA). Article 4 provides that the notification must be accompanied by; (i) a standard-form movement document, (ii) either a concluded contract with the consignee or evidence of this, and (iii) a declaration that the notifier has established a financial guarantee[451] or equivalent insurance. The guarantee or insurance must cover the costs of transport and storage in the event that the waste needs returning to the country of dispatch.[452] There is also a procedure under Article 13 covering a general notification where the proposed shipments are essentially similar, are made to the same consignee and same facility, and the route of the shipment is the same. Case law on the 1993 Regulation has confirmed that the procedure is harmonised just as much as the substance of the regime.[453]

Once a shipment is validly notified, the authority of dispatch must

---

[447]　para.15–010ff above.
[448]　*C-228/00* [2003] ECR I-1439 (cement kilns).
[449]　*C-458/00* [2003] ECR I-1553 (municipal incinerators), but see also *C-113-02 Commission v Netherlands*, where as late as 2004 the Netherlands was still seeking to justify its previous practice.
[450]　art.2(15).
[451]　For a commercial dispute concerning an importing authority's wrongful assertion that such a guarantee was not in place, see *Catalyst Recycling Ltd v Nickelhütte Aue GmbH* [2008] Env. L.R. 47, and now, unreported, on appeal.
[452]　art.6.
[453]　*DaimlerChrysler* per ECJ at para.67

transmit this to the authority of destination and any authorities of transit, within three days of receipt. Supplemental information may be requested by those recipients, but again within three days of receipt by them, and the authority of destination must acknowledge receipt of a valid notification. The various authorities must decide within 30 days of that acknowledgment via reasoned decisions to consent to the shipment with or without conditions, or to object under Articles 11 or 12. It is plain that it is the duty of all of these bodies to check that the waste has been correctly classified, not just that of the authority of dispatch.[454] It has also been decided that even if the authority of dispatch disagrees with the notifier's classification of the purpose of a given shipment, that authority is duty-bound to transmit the notification to the other authorities and consignee; it is not open to that authority to reclassify the proposed shipment and hence refuse to notify the other parties. The authority's remedy is simply to object to the proposed shipment at the end of the 30 day period on the basis of the mis-classification.[455] Another ECJ case, *Pedersen*, touches on the burden of proof in circumstances where the issue (under Article 12.1) is whether the conditions in the state of destination are of a lower standard than in the state of dispatch.[456] The notifier must supply information concerning those conditions, but it is not incumbent upon him to prove that those conditions will be equivalent to those required by the rules in the state of dispatch. That is a matter for the state of dispatch which must show the risks to human health and the environment which would be entailed in recovery abroad.

Consents to shipment expire one year after being issued. Final recovery or disposal of the waste shall be completed no later than one year after the receipt of the waste,[457] and the facility carrying out such operations shall certify that this has taken place.[458] There are also provisions covering interim recovery and disposal operations, under which there may be a maximum of two years from initial receipt by the interim recoverer or disposer to the point when the final recoverer or disposer had completed the process.[459]

Domestic rules

As noted above, the 2006 Regulation was supplemented by the domestic   **15–144**
Transfrontier Shipment of Waste Regulations 2007. Provisions of note are (a) the definition under regulation 2 of "person who ships waste" as including the notifier, any transporter, any freight-forwarder, and any other

---

[454] *Abfall Service (ASA)* per ECJ at paras 40–42.
[455] *C-472/02 Siomab*, 19.10.04.
[456] *C-215/04 Marius Pedersen A/S v Miljøstyrelsen* [2006] ECR, at paras 32–34.
[457] art.9(7).
[458] art.16(e).
[459] art.15.

person involved in the shipment of waste and (b) the offences of (i) shipping or undertaking the disposal or recovery of waste,[460] contrary to the obligations of Article 49 of the EU Regulation (explained above) and (ii) shipping waste without having followed the procedures set out in the EU Regulation.[461] There are the usual provisions rendering criminally liable those whose act or default led to the offence. Penalties under the 2007 Regulations are in most cases up to the statutory maximum of £5,000 on summary conviction, or on conviction on indictment, up to two years imprisonment and an unlimited fine.

---

[460] reg.16.
[461] reg.18(2).

Chapter 16

CONTAMINATED LAND

Introduction

On April 1, 2000, a new contaminated land regime came into force in **16–001** England. The relevant legislation was set out in Part 2A of the Environmental Protection Act 1990 (the EPA), the Contaminated Land (England) Regulations 2000,[1] and in Circular 02/2000[2]. Part 2A of the EPA applies throughout Great Britain and closely similar regimes were implemented in Scotland on July 14, 2000,[3] and in Wales on September 15, 2001.[4] For convenience the discussion in this chapter relates essentially to the English regime, with material differences elsewhere being mentioned as appropriate. In 2006 the English regime was extended to cover land contaminated by radioactivity,[5] and the Regulations and the Circular were replaced by amended versions.[6]

The Part 2A regime was explicitly modelled on that used for statutory nuisances, and similarly imposes duties on local authorities (i) to inspect their areas for contaminated sites, and (ii) where they find any, and subject to a consultation stage, to serve a "remediation notice" on an "appropriate person" that requires him to deal, at his expense, with any contamination for which the legislation deems him to be responsible. Where there is an appropriate person in existence, the enforcing authority therefore does not need to have substantial resources available to it to make this happen.[7]

The changes brought about by Part 2A were presented as being primarily procedural: the intention was to avoid imposing any liabilities that did not

---

[1] SI 2000/227.

[2] "Implementation of Part 2A of the Environmental Protection Act 1990 in England", March 20, 2000.

[3] SSI 2000/178, The Contaminated Land (Scotland) Regulations 2000, and Scottish Executive Circular 1/2000.

[4] SI 2001/3211.

[5] For which see below, and Chapter 20.

[6] SI 2006/1380, the Contaminated Land (England) Regulations 2006; Circular 01/2006—Environmental Protection Act 1990 Part 2A Contaminated Land. At the same time the way the regime is referred to was changed—what was previously Part IIA is now referred to as Part 2A in the more recent regulations and in the Circular, and this change has been adopted throughout this chapter.

[7] Although the extent of the information needed to designate a site as "contaminated land" is the subject of some guidance in Circular 01/2006 (see paragraphs B.17A and B.37ff) and resources will normally need to be spent by the local authority in order to underpin a designation.

exist before, even though these had been rarely enforced. However, the significance of the new regime lies in the relative ease with which liability can be made to attach to an "appropriate person". Experience to date suggests that the new provisions are less widely employed than anticipated, although the number of sites formally designated as contaminated land is increasing each year, but also that those potentially affected are carrying out effective remediation on a voluntary basis in many more cases than hitherto.[8]

Structure of the legislation

16–002   The provisions of the new regime are to be found in a complex mix of primary and secondary legislation and Ministerial guidance. Part 2A alone consists of 26 sections, ss.78A to 78YC, which set out the statutory framework and are discussed in greater detail below.

These are supplemented by the Contaminated Land (England) Regulations 2006[9] which prescribe:

- which sites should be designated as "special sites";
- the content of remediation notices,[10] and the procedure for their service;
- the rules relating to compensation where an appropriate person must enter on to a third party's land in order to carry out remediation;
- the grounds of appeal against a remediation notice, and the procedures for appealing to the magistrates and to the Secretary of State;
- modification and suspension of remediation notices; and
- the content of remediation registers.

A flow chart setting out the twelve basic steps involved in the process is included in Table 16/I at the end of this chapter.

16–003   Further, a considerable number of issues that are central to the operation of the new regime, including the definition of "contaminated land" and the rules for allocation and apportionment of liability to remediate con-

---

[8] The Environment Agency is required under s.78U(1) of the EPA 1990 to issue a report on the state of contaminated land in England (and Wales). The report published in September 2002 is entitled "Dealing with contaminated land in England". A separate report was intended to be published for Wales, but had not been released at the time of writing. The low figures for the number of sites which had been designated as contaminated land, 33 by the end of March 2002 with 11 of these being "special sites" is stated to be due to local authorities concentrating on their inspection strategies. The next report was intended to be published in 2007–8 although at the time of writing none had materialised. In the Agency's 2005 publication, "Indicators for Land Contamination", it noted that over 12,000 sites still needed treatment for historic land contamination but that 21,000 sites had already undergone remediation work.

[9] SI 2006/1380.

[10] In Scotland the form of the remediation notice is also prescribed—see SSI 2000/178, Sch.2.

tamination, referred to here as "the Guidance", are contained in Circular 01/2006 issued by the Secretary of State.[11]

Notably, on the most significant aspects, those to whom the Guidance is addressed are required by the statute "to act in accordance with" it, and not merely, as is more usual, "to have regard to" it. In such cases the Guidance is therefore mandatory, and not discretionary—indeed styling these aspects of it "guidance" at all is somewhat misleading. The mandatory "guidance" relates to:

- what is to be regarded as "contaminated land"—s.78A(2);
- what "harm" is significant, whether the possibility of causing significant harm is "significant", and whether pollution of controlled waters is being, or is likely to be, caused)—s.78A(5);
- the inspection by local authorities of their land for contamination—s.78B(2);
- the allocation and apportionment of liability among two or more "appropriate persons"—ss.78F(6), (7).

It is convenient to address the Part 2A regime under the headings provided by the Circular.

The Guidance is contained in five Chapters of Annex 3 of the Circular, as follows:

A. The Definition of Contaminated Land.
B. The Identification of Contaminated Land.
C. The Remediation of Contaminated Land.
D. Exclusion from, and Apportionment of, Liability for Remediation.
E. The Recovery of the Costs of Remediation.

The Definition of "Contaminated Land" (Circular Annex 3, Chapter A)

Land is to be regarded as "contaminated" if it appears to the relevant local authority to be in such a condition, by reason of substances in, on or under the land, that: **16–004**

(a) significant harm is being caused or there is a significant possibility of such (i.e. significant) harm being caused; or
(b) pollution of controlled waters is being, or is likely to be, caused.[12]

---

[11] This circular replaces DETR Circular 02/2000.

[12] s.78A(2). It should be noted that this section is to be amended by the Water Act 2003, s.86(2)(a): Section 2(b) will then read: "(b) significant pollution of controlled waters is being caused or there is a significant possibility of such pollution being caused". At the time of writing, no commencement date had been set for this change. See para.16–007 below.

"Harm" is defined broadly in terms closely corresponding to those used elsewhere in the EPA, as "harm to the health of living organisms or other interference with the ecological systems of which they form part and, in the case of man, includes harm to his property".[13]

However, whether land is determined to be "contaminated" within the meaning of Part 2A depends on either of the two quite separate considerations above: firstly, that there be actual significant harm or a significant possibility of significant harm (SPOSH), or, secondly, actual or likely pollution of controlled waters.

The question as to what constitutes "significant harm", whether there is a significant possibility of it being caused, or whether pollution of controlled waters is being caused, must be determined in accordance with the Guidance.[14]

Significant harm

16–005   What constitutes significant harm and SPOSH is covered by Chapter 3, Part A of the Guidance.

Pollution linkages. The Guidance requires that, as a pre-condition of harm being found to be "significant" in any circumstances, there must be all of

(1) a pollutant,
(2) a receptor (or target) that may be harmed by it, for example an ecological system or an aquifer used for drinking water, liable to be harmed by *that* pollutant, and also
(3) one or more "pathways" capable of exposing that receptor to that pollutant.

These three elements, pollutant, receptor and pathway, together constitute what is termed a "pollutant linkage"—if there is no pollutant linkage, land cannot be contaminated land for the purposes of Part 2A.

Type of harm. Section A.23 of the Guidance provides that a local authority may only regard harm as significant if it is (a) to one of the receptors listed; and (b) within the description of harm specified for that type of receptor. The four receptors are;

1. Human beings;
2. Any ecological system or living organism within a "special site" or site protected under one of various legislative provisions;
3. Crops, livestock and wild animals subject to shooting or fishing rights;

---

[13] s.78A(4).
[14] s.78A(5).

4.   Property in the form of buildings.

Notwithstanding the broad definition of "harm", the concern of the Government is essentially harm to human health or to agriculture or silviculture; purely environmental harm is only relevant if it occurs in a Site of Special Scientific Interest or other protected area.[15]

Significant possibility of significant harm

The Guidance also describes the factors which should be taken into account when determining whether there is a significant possibility of such harm occurring. It states that the term "possibility of significant harm being caused refers to a measure of the *probability* or *frequency* of circumstances occurring which would lead to the causing of significant harm".[16] Local authorities (and the Environment Agency where relevant) must also take into account;

16–006

(a) the nature and degree of the harm;
(b) the susceptibility of the receptors to which harm might be caused; and
(c) the timescale within which the harm might occur.

Table B sets out circumstances in which a local authority should regard as significant a possibility of significant harm. These cover the following:

1.   Human health effects from ingesting or bodily contact with a contaminant; there will be SPOSH where the amount of a pollutant would result in an unacceptable intake or exposure by a human being.
2.   Any other human health effects; there will be SPOSH where the probability or frequency of the occurrence of significant harm is unacceptable. When assessing what is unacceptable, the local authority should take into account matters such as whether harm would be irreversible or untreatable, or would affect large numbers of people.
3.   Effects on ecological systems; there will be SPOSH where significant harm from the pollutant linkage is "more likely than not" *or* there is a reasonable possiblity of significant harm and that risk, if it eventuated, would cause damage beyond the practicable restoration.
4.   Effects on animals and crops; for SPOSH the significant harm need only be more likely than not.

---

[15] The descriptions of harm for each receptor are listed in Annex 3, Chapter A, Table A, category 2.
[16] Annex 3, para.A.27.

5. Effects on buildings; there will be SPOSH where significant harm is more likely than not during the economic life of the building (or, if it is an Ancient Monument, the "foreseeable future")

In July 2008 Defra published non-statutory guidance to the "Legal Definition of Contaminated Land", aimed at local authorities carrying out their duties under Part 2A and helping them to determine what constitutes significant harm and SPOSH; it also sets out the policy behind the risk-based approach of the legislation.[17]

Defra and the Environment Agency have published technical documents relevant to the assessment of human health risks arising from long term exposure to contaminants in soil, and which are to assist local authorities in making an assessment of whether significant harm or SPOSH are present. The technical documents consist of the CLEA (Contaminated Land Experience Assessment) package which is made up of the main Contaminated Land Reports (CLRs) 7–10, the CLEA 2002 software, and the Health Criteria Values ("TOX reports") and Soil Guideline Values (SGVs) for individual substances. Previously advice was contained in the ICRCL Guidance Notes.[18] Though some of these have now been withdrawn, others, which contain general information and do not set trigger values, have not. These remain a valid source of information although Defra does not consider that ICRCL notes should be used as the sole source of information on which to base decisions. There is also a specialised Radioactively Contaminated Land Exposure Assessment (RCLEA) Methodology, which is currently in draft form but is available from the Defra website.

Pollution of controlled waters

16–007 The phrase "controlled waters" has the same meaning as that provided in section 104 of the Water Resources Act and so covers both surface waters and groundwater.[19] Section 86(2)(f) of the Water Act 2003 amends the definition of "groundwaters" to exclude waters contained in underground

---

[17] *Guidance on the Legal Definition of Contaminated Land*, Defra, July 2008.

[18] In particular Guidance Note 59/83 which was revised in July 1987 and set out a number of trigger values (threshold inaction concentrations) for contaminants in soil including ten metals, cyanide, sulphates, pHs and phenols. In December 2002, Defra formally withdrew ICRCL 59/83 on the basis that it was technically out of date and its approach was no longer in line with the statutory regime set out in Part 2A.

[19] The Secretary of State also has the power to amend the way any waters are to be treated in terms of the definitions (section 104(4) WRA).

strata but above the saturation zone; no commencement date for this provision has yet been appointed.[20]

Whereas section 78A(2) gives a threshold of "significance" for harm to land, it does not restrict the breadth of "pollution of controlled waters". As noted above, the Guidance substantially curtails what might otherwise be taken to be "significant harm" and "a significant possibility of significant harm", but does not do so in relation to "pollution of controlled waters".[21] In other words, under the current wording of section 78A(2), land can be liable to be designated "contaminated" if any water pollution at all is caused by what is in or on it, however trivial it may be.

This position is to be amended by section 86(2)(a) of the Water Act 2003, which determines that the pollution caused must be significant, or that there must be a significant possibility of such harm being caused; again no commencement date for this provision has yet been appointed.[22]

Special sites

Sites of a description covered by Regulations 2 and 3 and Schedule 1 of the Contaminated Land (England) Regulations 2006 are to be classed as "special sites". These are essentially sites where the contamination present will or may cause *serious* harm or *serious* pollution of controlled waters, or where it is otherwise desirable to call on the Agency's expertise to deal with it.   **16–008**

Responsibility for dealing with the contamination on special sites passes to the Environment Agency. The initial designation is normally to be by the relevant local authority (which must first consult with the Agency[23]), subject to the Agency not having disagreed with its decision within 21 days.[24] The Agency can however itself propose to a local authority that a site should be designated as a special site;[25] if the authority decides against this, the Agency may challenge that decision. Any dispute passes to the Secretary of State for determination.[26] Contaminated land may also

---

[20] Defra Guidance Note CLAN 3/04 (February 2004) and CLAN 5/04 (October 2004) indicate that the implementation would be staged, that new guidance would first need to be formulated, and that they indicate that any such guidance will have to deal with the relationship between that guidance and the implementation of the Water Framework Directive. Moreover, at the time of writing the government had just launched its consultation on the proposed Environmental Damage (Protection and Remediation) Regulations 2008 implementing the Environmental Liability Directive. The commencement date for section 86, if it comes, is likely therefore to be some way off.

[21] Despite the apparent power to do so under s.78A(5)(c).

[22] It should be noted that the changes have already taken place in relation to Scotland, which also replaces references to "*controlled waters*" to "*the water environment*"—which includes surface waters, groundwaters, and "*wetlands*".

[23] s.78C(3).

[24] s.78C(6).

[25] s.78C(4).

[26] under s.78D.

become a special site at any time after a local authority has served a remediation notice, and where this happens the Agency may adopt the notice, without prejudice to the local authority's right to recover its costs under section 78P.[27]

Even where a site is not designated under this procedure as a special site, the Agency always has power to issue site-specific guidance to a local authority in respect of any site, and where it does so the specific guidance prevails over any general guidance that may be inconsistent with it.[28]

Procedure—Circular Annex 3, Chapter B

Local authorities' duties to inspect their land and to serve remediation notices

16–009 Local authorities are under a duty to inspect the land in their area for the presence of contamination,[29] and where they identify any they (or the Agency in the case of a special site) are then under a further duty to serve a "remediation notice" on the "appropriate person", specifying both what action is to be taken by way of remediation and when it must be done.[30] For the purposes of the Act, "remediation" means any or all of three things, namely a site assessment, clean up of contamination, and subsequent monitoring, in appropriate cases, to establish that the clean up has been effective.[31] Authorities have comparatively little discretion in performing their duty to identify contamination: the relevant guidance is mandatory and not discretionary. Moreover, once they have determined that any land is contaminated, they have no discretion to postpone giving effect to the legislation.[32] The Guidance[33] sets out the duty on local authorities to develop a "strategic approach" to the inspection and identification of contaminated land; if an authority follows that guidance, it is unlikely that its approach will be susceptible to legal challenge. However, it must not wait for the development of its strategy before starting its inspection work.[34]

The Guidance stipulates[35] that an authority must be satisfied that "there is a reasonable possibility" that a pollutant linkage exists on the land before it can take action to inspect land it suspects of being contaminated: that is, it must be satisfied that there is "a reasonable possibility" of the presence

---

[27] s.78Q.
[28] s.78V.
[29] s.78B(1).
[30] s.78E(1).
[31] s.78A(7).
[32] cf. *R. v Carrick D.C., ex p. Shelley and anor.*, [1996] Env. L.R. 273.
[33] Annex 3, paras B9–B.15.
[34] Annex 3, para. B.14.
[35] Annex 3, para.B.22.

of a contaminant, a receptor and a pathway, and that "these would together create a pollutant linkage": a mere assumption that land is likely to be
contaminated because of previous activities on it will thus not suffice.
Though desirable in order to discourage over-zealous authorities from
demanding numerous site investigations unnecessarily, such a pre-condition may prove to be a significant brake on implementation of the regime if
significant (and hence costly) work must be carried out in order to identify
contamination in the first place, as there is no provision for local authorities
to recover any of the costs they incur at this preliminary stage.[36]

Initial notice under s.78B

The first step by a local authority that has discovered contamination is to   **16–010**
serve a notice (referred to here as a "78B notice") on all appropriate
persons of this fact, and also on the owner, the occupier(s), and the
Agency.[37] Except in cases of emergency, it may not serve a remediation
notice on anyone until at least three months after that person has received
the 78B notice.[38]

In the meantime, the authority must endeavour to consult with the
person(s) it intends to serve the remediation notice on, as well as the owner
and occupier(s) of the land, to determine what remediation is
appropriate.[39]

Exceptions from duty to serve remediation notice

If a potentially liable person agrees to clean up the land voluntarily to an   **16–011**
appropriate standard, or is already doing so, then the local authority is
expressly prohibited from serving a remediation notice on that person for
so long as it remains satisfied that he is taking suitable steps to achieve an
adequate clean up.[40] There is a presumption throughout the Guidance that
voluntary action, in consultation with the authority, should be the norm.
Service of a remediation notice is to be reserved for where co-operation is
not forthcoming, or where a notice is needed to allocate remedial work or
to apportion liabilities between two or more appropriate persons. Special
provision, primarily designed to help private householders, is also made for

---

[36] By contrast, the costs of preliminary investigations carried out under WRA s.161(1), as
amended by EA s.60(3), are recoverable from the recipient of a works notice by virtue of
s.161A(11) of that Act. Guidance to English Local Authorities from Defra (CLAN 1/06)
on the Contaminated Land Capital Projects Programme (CLPPP) does note at para.2.1(a)
that for "intrusive investigations" prior to investigation funding may be available. The
local authority will need to demonstrate that it is likely—rather than merely reasonably
possible—that a contaminant is actually present and that, given the current use of the land,
a receptor is or is likely to be present.
[37] s.78B(3), (4).
[38] s.78H(3).
[39] s.78H(1).
[40] s.78H(5)(b).

those who may suffer hardship as a result of having to pay for remediation.[41] In such a case, the local authority may proceed to clean up the land without serving a remediation notice,[42] and waive all or part of the costs incurred. Where the authority is itself the appropriate person, then there is self-evidently no purpose in serving a remediation notice and none is required.[43]

Section 78N sets out a variety of circumstances in which remedial work can be carried out without service of a remediation notice, including where:

- there is imminent danger of serious harm or serious pollution of controlled waters;
- a person has failed to comply with requirements of a remediation notice;
- the authority has decided that it will not seek to recover its costs, or will look for only a portion of its costs, from the appropriate person; and
- no person has been found, after reasonable enquiry, who is an appropriate person in relation to any particular "thing"—presumably this will only apply where there is no relevant owner or occupier on whom a remediation notice can be served.[44]

Remediation statement

16–012   If an authority is satisfied that any of its powers under s.78N to carry out remediation itself are exercisable, then it is precluded from serving a remediation notice, and must instead issue and publish a "remediation statement". It must also proceed in this way if it is satisfied either that remediation will be carried out satisfactorily without the service of a remediation notice, or that the person on whom the notice would be served is the authority itself.[45]

The "remediation statement" must state, inter alia, "the things which are being, have been, or are expected to be, done by way of remediation in the particular case", and also who is responsible for them and by when they will be done. It is the authority that is responsible for this where s.78N applies or where the authority is itself the appropriate person. Where a site is being cleaned up voluntarily, whoever is doing it must themselves publish the remediation statement, though if they fail to do so the relevant authority has reserve powers to do it and to recover the costs incurred.[46]

---

[41] s.78P(2). See paras para.16–036 below.
[42] ss.78H(5)(d), 78N(3)(e).
[43] s.78H(5)(c).
[44] s.78N(3).
[45] s.78H(7).
[46] s.78H(8).

Remediation declaration

Where there is nothing the authority can specify in a remediation notice **16–013**
because its cost would be excessive in relation to the seriousness of the
harm or pollution of controlled waters in question,[47] then it may not serve a
remediation notice, but must instead issue and publish a remediation
declaration, setting out what the authority would have specified and why,
and the grounds on which it is satisfied that it is precluded from specifying
it in a remediation notice.[48]

Two or more appropriate persons

Where two (or more) people are each appropriate persons, either (i) **16–014**
because they have been responsible for different substances on a site or (ii)
because they have been responsible at different times for contaminating the
site with the same substance, then the remediation notice served on each
will specify, in the first case, what each must do in relation to the different
substances, and, in the second case, what proportion of the remediation
costs each must bear. The Guidance prescribes in Annex 3, Chapter D,
how these proportions are to be calculated.

The Standard of Remediation—Circular Annex 3, Chapter C

Remediation is only to be required to meet whatever standard is suitable **16–015**
for the current use actually being made of the land concerned, and not any
possible use that might conceivably be made of it.[49] The "current use"
however extends to all other uses to which the land is likely to be put in
practice and also (whether "likely" or not) all uses to which it may be put
without requiring a new or amended grant of planning permission.[50]
"Hard" end uses, such as residential use where vegetables may be grown,
and areas where children may play, will be subject to relatively demanding
standards, but conversely "soft" end uses, where these factors do not
apply, for example car parks, shopping developments, industrial estates
and so on, may be subject to considerably less stringent standards. Indeed
since the *likelihood* of harm or of water pollution from land will suffice to
bring it within the definition of "contaminated", the use to which the land

---

[47] See para.16–017 below.
[48] s.78H(6).
[49] Annex 3, para.C.17. An owner or developer is not of course precluded from remediating to
a higher standard than may be demanded under Part 2A, and may wish to do so to in
preparation for a likely subsequent change of use.
[50] Annex 3, para.A.26.

is or may be put will often be a material factor in determining whether the legislation applies to it at all.[51]

A mere change of use of a site, from a soft use to a harder one, may thus by itself result in the land becoming "contaminated land" as defined. Likewise, although remediation appropriate to an earlier (soft) end use may have already been carried out, the change may itself necessitate further remediation. If so, this will be dealt with under the planning and building control regimes and not Part 2A.[52] Moreover, if the toxic effects of a contaminant are subsequently discovered to be greater than presently thought, further remedial work to deal with the contaminant might be called for at some later date. Local authorities will not therefore be prepared to "sign off" contaminated land as having been cleaned up; they will merely record what has in fact been done.

What is to be done by way of remediation

16–016   There are three forms of "remediation action" which can be required in a remediation notice: "assessment actions", "remedial treatment actions" and "monitoring actions". These are discussed in Chapter C, Part 7 of the Guidance.[53]

The standard of remediation

16–017   The intention of remediation is to bring land into such a condition that, in its current use, it is no longer to be considered "contaminated land": i.e. that it be "suitable for use".[54] The extent of remediation that may be required is limited to what the authority considers reasonable having regard to the likely cost and the seriousness of the harm or the water pollution to be dealt with.[55] In determining what is reasonable, what any person should do, and the standard of remediation, regard must be had to Annex 3, Chapter C, of the Guidance (which in this respect is discretionary only, not mandatory).

The authority should look for the "best practicable technique" to achieve this aim. In order to do so, it should look for a method which is

(a) is reasonable (that is, whose benefits justify incurring the costs)[56]
(b) represents the best combination of the following factors:

---

[51] See discussion of the definition of contaminated land, above.
[52] Annex 1, para.50, and paras A.33, A.34.
[53] See Annex 3, para.C.8 on s.78A(7) EPA and Annex 3, Chapter C, Part 7 (paras C.64 to C.69).
[54] Annex 3, para.C.17.
[55] s.78E(4).
[56] Annex 3, Chapter C Part 5. Paras C.29 to C.43J offer guidance as to the factors which should be taken into account when considering the benefits and costs of a remediation action.

(i) practicability
(ii) effectiveness;
(iii) durability.[57]

In the case of radioactive contamination, the authority must also, when carrying out the cost-benefit analysis, ensure that any intervention that forms part of a remediation scheme is both "justified" and "optimised".[58] "Justification" means ensuring that the reduction in the detriment due to radiation is sufficient to justify any adverse effects and costs, including social costs, of the intervention; "optimisation" means ensuring that the intervention maximises the benefit of the reduction in the detriment to health "less the detriment associated with the intervention".[59]

Whilst the Guidance is explicit that no more remediation can be required than is sufficient to make the site suitable for its *current* use, where a person has breached the conditions of a licensed activity he is, under the "polluter pays" principle, liable to rectify all the consequences.

As mentioned above, prima facie if contaminated land causes any water pollution, however trivial, the Part 2A procedures should be activated. However no useful purpose will be served by issuing a remediation notice in relation to insignificant pollution of controlled waters, since if the costs of any remedial action would be disproportionate to the benefits none can be required. In such cases the enforcing authority should simply issue a remediation declaration.   **16–018**

Who is Liable?—The "Appropriate Person"—Circular Annex 3, Chapter D

The "appropriate person" is defined in Part 2A as: **16–019**

> "any person, or any of the persons, who caused or knowingly permitted the substances, or any of the substances, by reason of which the contaminated land in question is such land to be in, on or under that land".[60]

However if, but only if, no such person—called a "Class A appropriate person"—has been found "after reasonable inquiry", then the owner or occupier for the time being of the contaminated land in question is an appropriate person: a Class B appropriate person.[61]

---

[57] Annex 3, Chapter C, Part 6 offers guidance on the considerations which should be taken into account when assessing all three of these aspects.
[58] Annex 3, paras C.43Bff.
[59] Annex 3, para.C.8(h) to (j); para.C.43Bff.
[60] s.78F(2).
[61] ss.78F(3), 78F(5).

Those who have caused or knowingly permitted part only of the contamination will only be appropriate persons in relation to that part. Responsibility for dealing with the remainder will fall on the other person(s), and if he or they cannot be found, on the current owner or occupier.

"Appropriate person" thus potentially embraces a very wide variety of people, but the Government nevertheless sought to avoid the quantity of litigation created by the joint and several liability regime of the United States Superfund legislation. Specifically, it aimed to avoid the situation where, when several companies are liable, the one with the deepest pocket is made primarily responsible for paying the full costs and must then seek contributions, so far as it can, from other potentially responsible parties. It is thus one of the main functions of the Guidance to set out binding rules for the allocation of responsibility for carrying out remedial work, and for the apportionment of liability where two or more people are held responsible for it.

16–020   There are additional provisions to cover situations where two or more people have contaminated the same land with the same or different substances. Potential appropriate persons must be determined for each significant pollution linkage which renders the site in question contaminated land. Each potential appropriate person forms part of a "liability group" for that significant pollution linkage; the authority must then determine which of the members of the liability group should in fact bear the liability for the remediation action needed for that linkage. The procedure for determining liabilities takes five stages:

First Stage: Identifying potential appropriate persons and liability groups;
Second Stage: Characterising remediation actions
Third Stage: Attributing responsibility between liability groups
Fourth Stage: Excluding members of a liability group
Fifth Stage: Apportioning liability between the (or the remaining) members of a liability group

First stage: causing or knowingly permitting

16–021   The Circular states that:

"it is ultimately for the courts to decide the meaning of 'caused' and 'knowingly permitted' as these terms apply to the Part 2A regime, and whether these tests are met in any particular case."

Causing

The meaning of "causing" has been considered in depth by the House of **16–022**
Lords, most recently in *Empress Car*,[62] the effect of which is that it is to be
construed very widely indeed. If any contamination results from the
operation of a commercial activity, then it will be deemed to have been
caused by that activity unless it was totally unforeseeable, such as an act of
terrorism: mere vandalism by outsiders will still be regarded as the
responsibility of the site operator, who is to be held liable for the
consequences.

The question remains as to whether some positive act is required, or
whether an failure to act can count as "causing" a substance to be present.
The Government certainly considers that an omission on the part of a site
occupier can amount to "causing".[63] However, the matter is yet finally to
be determined in relation to the contaminated land regime.[64]

Knowingly permitting[65]

The question of whether someone knowingly permitted the contaminating **16–023**
substances to be in, on or under the land in question is a difficult one in
both its limbs: firstly, what type and what level of knowledge is needed and,
secondly, what constitutes permitting.

Knowledge. There is uncertainty as to:

- what minimum level of knowledge is necessary as to the nature,
  extent or concentration of the contaminants—a person presumably
  cannot have to have the precise information only obtainable by an
  intrusive survey;
- whether there is any need for knowledge both of a receptor and a
  pathway to it, and whether the receptor is suffering or is likely to
  suffer "significant harm";
- who in a corporate organisation needs to have whatever knowledge is
  requisite. Old cases indicating that it would have to be those constituting its "directing mind and will" are no longer good law[66]—it is
  suggested that it should be the person(s) who in practice has or have
  the authority to prevent or to remedy the pollution in question;

---

[62] *Environment Agency (National Rivers Authority) v Empress Car Company (Abertillery) Ltd.*
[1999] A.C. 22 (H of L).
[63] See Circular Annex 2. para.9.9.
[64] See also cases such as *Environment Agency v Biffa Waste Services and Eurotech Environmental
Ltd* [2006] EWHC 1102, where it was held that a failure to prevent pollution would (in the
circumstances) be an offence of *"knowingly permitting"* pollution to occur, and not an
offence of causing pollution: para.29 of the judgment.
[65] For further discussion of "knowingly permitting", see paras 11–057 to 11–060.
[66] See *Meridian Global Funds Management Asia Ltd. v Securities Commission*, (P.C.) [1995] 3
W.L.R. 413.

- whether "constructive knowledge" will suffice, i.e. where there is reason to suspect the presence of contamination that might need to be dealt with, and a relevant responsible person fails to make the appropriate inquiries that would have revealed it—it seems probable that the courts will not allow people to avoid liabilities by turning a blind eye.[67]

In *Circular Facilities (London) Ltd v Sevenoaks District Council*[68] the Administrative Court considered an appeal from a decision of the Magistrates Court as to whether Circular Facilities (London) Ltd (CFL) should have been the recipient of a remediation notice served by the council. The remediation notice had been served on CFL on the basis that it had caused or knowingly permitted the substances by reason of which the land was contaminated to be in, on or under that land. The District Judge upheld the notice against CFL who then appealed to the Administrative Court.

16–024　　The site, which had been used for residential purposes for approximately 20 years, was an infilled clay pit. In about 2002 the council discovered contamination sufficient to justify it being designated as contaminated land. CFL's role in the development of the site involved acquiring the site and developing it for housing. The issues in the case turned upon what information CFL had available to it that supported a finding that CFL was aware of the contamination at the time it redeveloped the property and allowed the contamination to remain underneath the houses.

The issues turned on knowledge of a 1978 technical report identifying a "black organic layer" which appeared to have been provided to the council on March 27, 1980, by CFL, before the development was finalised. The inference made by the council was that the contents of the report were known to CFL. The "controlling mind" of CFL was a Mr Ketteringham, whose evidence was that he was not aware of the report and only knew that soil samples had been taken and the results passed to the local authority. There was also involvement by a Mr Scott, who was not employed by CFL but may have been their agent, in the day to day technical issues. The District Judge concluded that CFL must have known of the report and the risk posed by sites like this one.

On appeal, the Administrative Court dealt with the matter by sending it back for re-trial on the basis that the critical issue was the knowledge of CFL and the District Judge's reasons for finding that CFL actually had knowledge of the presence of the substances had not been made clear. The case was then settled out of court and the re-trial did not occur.

16–025　　The Administrative Court also offered some obiter comment on whether, in order for a person to "knowingly permit", they need to be aware of both the presence of the substances and the potential harm to which that

---

[67] See also the comments on Test 3 at para.16–033 below.
[68] [2005] All E.R. (D) 126, [2005] EWHC 865 (Admin).

presence could give rise. The view of Newman J was that "there is no basis for limiting the ambit of the section to exclude responsibility ... The knowledge of the substance is taken to be the knowledge of the substance generated by the process", and not knowledge of its harmful potential.

The case deals with the far from uncommon scenario of a residential developer taking on a historically contaminated site on the basis of limited information about the presence of contaminants. Whilst that is, hopefully, far less common now than it was, in particular pre-1987 (when the first planning circular on contaminated land was published), the wording and intention of Part 2A is that developers as well as the original polluter (if they still exist) can be appropriate persons in certain circumstances. The extent to which the District Judge was willing to infer knowledge of a technical report may well be indicative of the reaction to an argument by a developer that they did not know and there was no reason why they should have known of the presence of contamination.

Permitting. What constitutes permitting is difficult to pin down.[69] It must however cover both permitting the original entry of the contaminant on to the land, and also permitting the continued presence of that contaminant. A practical question that is as yet undecided is whether a person can be said to permit the continued presence of a substance, if he does not have the resources to pay for the costs of dealing with it. Can a person be held to permit what he cannot prevent? It is suggested he should be expected to use his "best endeavours", as that term has been defined by the courts, to deal appropriately with any contamination, but no more. This would be consistent with the guidance on apportionment between Class A persons at paragraph D78 of Annex 3.

Owner and occupier where "no [such] person has ... been found"

Where no "causer" or "knowing permitter" has been found "after rea-   **16–026**
sonable inquiry", the owner or the occupier for the time being is to be the appropriate person. This person is referred to as a "Class B" appropriate person,

"Found" is, in this context, problematical. Does it simply mean "identified", or does it require the person also to be in existence (if a company) or alive (if an individual)? If the latter, just when must they be in existence: when the contamination is found, or when the remediation notice is served? There are numerous sites with historic contamination where the original polluter can be precisely identified without any difficulty—Victorian gasworks are typical examples—but has long since ceased

---

[69] *Vehicle Inspectorate v Nuttal* [1999] 1 W.L.R. 629.

to exist. However the language of the statute, coupled with the need to give it practical effect, strongly indicates that the expression excludes defunct companies and the dead.[70]

16–027 The case of *R (National Grid Gas Plc) (previously Transco Plc) v Environment Agency*[71] (often referred to as the "Bawtry" case) was based on a judicial review of the Environment Agency's decision that Transco was an appropriate person for the purposes of Part 2A. The issue turned on liability of a company for the acts of its statutory predecessors.

The claimant was the company that, upon privatisation of the gas industry in 1986, had transferred to it the property, rights and liabilities of the state owned company, British Gas Corporation. A former public gasworks site had operated in Bawtry, Doncaster, from the nineteenth century until it was redeveloped in the 1950s.

The House of Lords found that, given that British Gas' statutory successor was only to take on the liabilities of its predecessor "immediately before" the transfer date, and that liability under the Part 2A regime was not created until many years later, the liability did not exist at the time and could not be passed on. The claimant could not be held to have caused or knowingly permitted the presence of the contaminating substances.

The Guidance offers no help on what "after reasonable inquiry" entails, merely saying that its meaning is ultimately a matter for the Courts to decide.[72]

Owners and occupiers

16–028 Where the owner and the occupier for the time being of the land in question are different people, the statute does not provide for any priority between them, or whether they should be jointly and severally liable.

"Owner" is defined as:

> "a person (other than a mortgagee not in possession) who, whether in his own right or as a trustee for any other person, is entitled to receive the rack rent of the land, or, where the land is not let at a rack rent, would be so entitled if it were so let".[73]

Mortgagees who have gone into possession are owners, therefore, as are lenders who have had assigned to them the right to receive rents as security for, or repayment of, a loan. Depending on the nature and term of his interest, a leaseholder may be an owner as well as the ultimate freeholder.

---

[70] The provisions of the Companies Act 1985 do allow for companies which have been dissolved to be reinstated within 20 years upon application by a company or a member or a creditor. However, a local authority wishing to serve a remediation notice years after dissolution may not be accurately described as a creditor.

[71] [2007] UKHL 30.

[72] Annex 2, para.9.18.

[73] s.78A(9). Note the different language in this sub-section that is applicable in Scotland.

"Occupier" on the other hand is not defined. The only attempt at clarification in the Guidance does little more than re-state the problem:

"The term "occupier" is not defined in the contaminated land legislation and it will therefore carry its ordinary meaning. In the Government's view, it would normally mean the person in occupation and in many cases that will be the tenant or licensee of the premises."[74]

Contamination migrating to other land

There are somewhat complex provisions in s.78K(3) and (4) in relation to innocent owners and occupiers of land that is contaminated by substances that have escaped from elsewhere. In so far as they have not themselves caused or knowingly permitted the contamination of their land, they will not be statutorily liable to remediate any other land or water, either that from which the contaminants first came, or land or water to which they have further escaped, unless they caused or knowingly permitted that further escape.   **16–029**

Allocation and Apportionment of Liability to Remediate—Annex 3, Chapter D

Where there are two or more people within the definition of "appropriate person", the enforcing authority must determine, in accordance with the Guidance, who is *not* to be treated as an appropriate person. Thus *all* appropriate persons are to be held liable for remediation unless so excluded.[75] Chapter D of Annex 3 accordingly sets out a series of six tests for excluding members of a Class A liability group, and rules for apportioning liability where two or more remain after applying these tests. The same Chapter also sets out a test for excluding certain members of a Class B liability group, and further rules for apportioning liability where two or more Class B members remain jointly liable. This guidance is mandatory, and so the authority must comply with it, though a degree of discretion is allowed within prescribed limits.   **16–030**

Application of private rights

Though the purpose of the Guidance is to define who is statutorily liable for the costs of remediation, it in no way precludes the enforcement of private rights whereby a person who is so liable may seek recourse from someone else. The enforcing authority will normally give effect to an   **16–031**

---

[74] Ch.IV, para.28.
[75] s.78F(6), (7).

agreement between two or more potentially liable persons that provides for which of them should bear that liability or how the liability should be shared. The authority will not however get involved in any contentious questions of interpretation, and so it will only implement the agreement if it is given a copy and there is no dispute as to its effect.[76] Even so, if the effect is to make a party liable who is entitled to avoid or reduce payment of remediation costs on grounds of hardship or the other restrictions on cost recovery provided in Chapter E of Annex 3 (see below), and so transfer some or all of the clean-up costs on to the public purse, then the Guidance requires the agreement to be disregarded[77]—even where the circumstances amounting to hardship only arose subsequently to the agreement. Liable parties cannot therefore safely rely on contractual arrangements to give them full protection, although in practice many agreements now contain language indicating a definitive allocation of liabilities.

The Class A "exclusion" tests

16–032   The six Class A tests are very detailed and only a brief summary can be given here.[78] A vital point to note at the outset, however, is that they do not *exempt* anyone from liability, but merely *prioritise* those who are potentially liable—a person who satisfies the criteria of a test is excluded from liability *only* if at least one other person, who is still in existence, does not.

Test 1,[79] which is misleadingly headed "Excluded Activities", lists a large number of normal commercial activities that might in some cases amount to "causing or knowingly permitting" the presence of contaminants on a site, including e.g. lending money, letting property to a (polluting) tenant, and consigning waste to an authorised landfill. The Guidance makes clear, however, that merely because an activity is mentioned in Test 1, there is no presumption that it in fact amounts to "causing or knowingly permitting" contamination in the first place. Nevertheless, in some cases these clearly must amount to "knowingly permitting" the presence of (potentially polluting) substances in, on or under land, e.g. where a waste regulation authority licensed a landfill site, or failed to use enforcement powers available to it to get a contaminated site cleaned up. Employees who pollute in the course of their employment are also "excluded", but the directors and managers of the employing company are not.

Test 2[80] excludes those who have made a payment to another liable person to remediate land. The exclusion will only apply, however, if the

---

[76] Annex 3, para.D38.
[77] Annex 3, para.D39.
[78] They are also discussed in Chapter 21 below, at paras 21–008 to 21–015, with particular reference to their implications for commercial property transactions.
[79] Annex 3, paras D47 to D50.
[80] Annex 3, paras D51 to D56.

payment is sufficient to cover all the costs of making the land no longer "contaminated". The payer must therefore ensure he collects the necessary evidence on this if he wishes to be able to rely on this test many years after the event. Since the payer remains potentially liable he should in fact seek to ensure that the money is applied to effective remediation. A reduction in sale price to reflect potential clean-up costs should always therefore be accompanied by suitable obligations on the buyer, plus recitals evidencing compliance with the Test 2 criteria. It will only extend to the particular remediation contemplated at the time the payment was made.

Test 3[81] excludes a liable seller in an arm's length transaction if the buyer received information, before he became contractually bound, that would reasonably have allowed him to be aware both of the presence of a relevant pollutant or pollutants in or on the land and of "the broad measure" of that presence. For this purpose "sale" includes the grant or assignment of a lease of over 21 years. Test 3 is disapplied if the seller retains any interest in the land after the sale, other than certain limited rights—including however reversions on the expiry of a lease of over 21 years. A "large" buyer in a transaction which took place since the beginning of 1990 who has had permission to investigate for himself is normally to be deemed to have the knowledge that this would have given him, again whether or not he actually undertook the investigation. This test only applies of course if the buyer and seller are both part of the same liability group when relevant appropriate persons are being identified—which means the buyer must by then be a knowing permitter. He can only be a knowing permitter, where he has not in fact taken steps to find out whether there is any contamination, and no-one has informed him of it unilaterally, if constructive knowledge is imputed to him.

16–033

Test 4[82] is concerned with the situation where one person has deposited a contaminant which by itself does not render the land "contaminated", and a second person deposits a second substance which interacts the first in a manner that then makes the land "contaminated".

Test 5[83] deals with liability for land that has become contaminated by substances that another liable person has caused or knowingly permitted to escape from neighbouring land.

Test 6[84] addresses who is liable where a contaminant has been present on land for some time but a "significant pollutant linkage" making the land "contaminated" only exists because a later person has subsequently introduced a pathway or a receptor. Strangely, given the new regime's claimed aim to discourage contamination, under Tests 5 and 6 the original polluter is excluded from liability in favour of someone who may have

---

[81] Annex 3, paras D57 to D61.
[82] Annex 3, paras D62 to D64.
[83] Annex 3, paras D65 to D67.
[84] Annex 3, paras D68 to D72.

allowed the escape, or introduced the pathway or receptor, wholly innocently.

If there are two or more Class B liable persons, there is a single exclusion test, whereby a tenant or licensee who either has no interest in the land that has any marketable value, or who pays a rent equivalent to a rack rent and holds no other beneficial interest in the land, will be excluded in favour of the freeholder and any superior leaseholder. Where two or more Class B persons are jointly liable, then their liability will be apportioned in proportion to the capital values of their respective interests.

16–034   If two or more people (being all Class A persons or all Class B persons) are all within a single liability group that is liable for remediation costs, Chapter D[85] indicates the approach that should be taken to apportioning the liability between them. In the case of Class A persons, the broad aim should be to reflect their relative responsibilities for creating or continuing the problem the contamination has given rise to. If sufficient facts to form a considered view on this are not available, and cannot reasonably be obtained, there is a presumption that the costs should be apportioned in equal shares.

Where one Class A person has "caused" contamination (e.g. original polluter) whilst another Class A person has "knowingly permitted" it (e.g. subsequent landowner), the guidance advises the authority to consider the extent to which the second person had the means and a reasonable opportunity to deal with the presence of the pollutant and reduce the seriousness of the implications of its presence. Where the second person had the necessary means and opportunity to do this, the guidance states that the second person should bear the same responsibility as the first person.[86] In the case of Class B persons, the apportionment will be in relation to the capital values of their respective interests in the land in question (including any buildings or other structures on it).

Yet further apportionment rules are set out in Chapter D[87] to cover a variety of different situations where there are two or more liability groups, due to there being two or more pollutant linkages on the same site. These also address apportionment where there are "orphan linkages". Such linkages arise if (i) no Class A or Class B persons can be found at all, (ii) the pollution linkage in question relates solely to the pollution of controlled waters, but only Class B persons can be found (owners and occupiers are not liable for water pollution, if they have not also caused or knowingly permitted it), or (iii) the persons otherwise liable come under any of the statutory exemptions (which concern water from abandoned mines, owners and occupiers whose neighbouring land is contaminated, and insolvency practitioners, receivers and the like).

---

[85] At paras D73 to D86 for Class A persons, and D91 to D97 for Class B persons.
[86] Annex 3, para.D.78.
[87] At paras D98 to D109.

Recovery of Costs of Remediation—Annex 3, Chapter E

Charges on land for enforcing authority's remediation costs

Where a remediation notice has not been complied with, the authority may   **16–035**
do the work itself. Its costs, with accrued interest, are not only recoverable
from the relevant appropriate person, but may be made the subject of a
charge on the land.[88] (This is not however possible in Scotland.) Applying
previous cases, particularly under public health legislation, such charges
are likely to be given priority over existing non-statutory charges, notably
those of banks by way of security for a loan.[89] The existing water pollution
legislation of course already gives the Agency power to do remedial work,
and to charge its costs to the person responsible,[90] but there is no provision
for making those costs the subject of a charge on any land.

"Hardship"

Where however a liable party would suffer "hardship" if made to bear the   **16–036**
full costs of remediation, and provided the criteria in the Guidance are
satisfied, the enforcing authority is given discretion not to require that party
to undertake the remediation, but to do it itself, and either to bear all the
costs itself or to charge the party concerned such proportion of them as it
considers reasonable. Where there are two or more liable parties and an
authority relieves one party of some or all of its share of the remediation
costs, no other liable party can be required to pay any more than it would
have had to bear anyway. The costs relieved thus fall on the public purse.

"Hardship" is not defined in the legislation, though the Guidance gives
as its ordinary meaning "hardness of fate or circumstance, severe suffering
or privation".[91] It is evidently not intended to cover mere unfairness as a
result of someone with adequate financial means being held liable for
remediation costs when he might reasonably have expected someone else
to be. The Guidance indicates that in the case of a company, a serious
likelihood of its being forced into liquidation may, if it is in an area of high
unemployment, or where there is little alternative employment, represent
"hardship" to which the enforcing authority should have regard. It is
suggested that the authority should nevertheless consider the likelihood of
a "phoenix" company emerging from the liquidation—if that is so, then it
should be more prepared to recover what it can from those who profited
from the contaminating activity. Every authority, and the Agency, is

---

[88] ss.78N(3)(c), 78P.
[89] See e.g. *Birmingham Corporation v Baker*, 17 Ch.D 782; *City of Bristol v Virgin*, [1928] KB
622; *Paddington BC v Finucane*, [1928] 1 Ch.D 567; *Westminster CC v Haymarket Publishing Ltd.*, [1981] 2 All E.R. 555.
[90] WRA s.161.
[91] Annex 2, paras 10.8 to 10.10.

encouraged to develop a policy on "hardship" with a view to ensuring consistent decisions, even though this may result in inconsistent decisions between authorities, and between special and ordinary sites in any one authority's area.

Lender liability

16–037   Banks and other lending institutions have been very concerned about the implications for them of the Act. The Government constantly said that it had no wish to prejudice the normal commercial activities of such organisations, and that it would not consider a lender to be liable as an appropriate person merely by virtue of having made a loan that enables the conduct of the relevant operation. However, it refused to provide expressly that, where a borrower has become insolvent, actions taken by the lender designed simply to preserve the property and to protect the general public should not be regarded as making the lender an owner and potentially liable accordingly.

Special provisions are however made in sections 78X(3) to (5) whereby, for example, insolvency practitioners shall not be personally liable for remediation costs unless the remediation is to any extent referable to contaminating substances the presence of which is the result of any act or omission which it was unreasonable for a person acting as an insolvency practitioner to do or make. The same immunity applies to certain others acting in a similar capacity, such as official receivers. Just what the courts will consider is unreasonable must as yet remain speculative. Insolvency practitioners are typically accountants, who cannot generally be expected to have any experience of hazardous materials that might contaminate land or water, which would suggest a very low standard. Presumably, they will be required to employ (at least if funds permit) suitably qualified people to establish what is on a site and how dangerous it is or might be—the standard could appropriately be that of a non-technical director. To the extent that banks and others making such appointments must in practice give indemnities against liabilities of this sort, this will be of real value to them.

Appeals and Enforcement

16–038   A person served with a remediation notice may appeal against it on any of 19 grounds listed in Regulation 7 of the Contaminated Land (England) Regulations 2000.[92] Any appeal must be duly lodged within 21 days

---

[92] SI 2000/227 in Scotland, Regulation 7 of the Contaminated Land (Scotland) Regulations 2000, SI 2008/178.

(including the day of service) of receiving the notice appealed against.[93] Provided it has been duly made, the notice is suspended until final determination or abandonment of the appeal.[94] Until August 4, 2006, appeals against remediation notices served by local authorities were made to the magistrates' courts by way of a complaint for an order,[95] with a right of further appeal to the High Court.[96] Appeals against remediation notices served by the Environment Agency, on the other hand, were made to the Secretary of State (as with appeals from works notices), who may cause the appeal to proceed in the form of a hearing, in public or in private, or to be dealt with in a public inquiry. All appeals now go to the Secretary of State.

It is worth noting that there is provision for the Secretary of State not only to uphold a remediation notice on appeal but also to make it more onerous for an appellant. No further appeal is available from the decision of the Secretary of State, though judicial review of the decision may of course be applied for in appropriate cases.

These appeal procedures are governed by Regulations 8 and 9 to 12 respectively of the Contaminated Land (England) Regulations. Non-compliance with remediation notices may lead to substantial fines—in the case of industrial, trade or business premises these may be up to £20,000, with a further daily fine of up to £2,000 for so long as the non-compliance continues (£5,000 and £500, respectively, in relation to other premises).[97] Non-compliance with enforcement and works notices, on the other hand, leads to the penalties conventional in the water pollution legislation, i.e. up to £20,000 and/or three months' imprisonment on summary conviction, and an unlimited fine and up to two years' imprisonment on conviction on indictment.[98]

Registers

Local authorities must maintain registers containing details of virtually all **16–039** significant actions taken in respect of contaminated land, including remediation notices served, remediation declarations, remediation state-ments, the designation of special sites, appeals, and several other matters as set out in Schedule 3 to the Contaminated Land (England) Regulations. In Scotland, but not elsewhere, they will also include details of initial notices issued under section 78B(3) advising appropriate persons that the local authority has identified a contaminated site. The registers also include notifications given to the relevant authority by those on whom a reme-

---

[93] s.78L(1).
[94] reg.14(1).
[95] para.48 of Annex 4 says "it is expected that most appeals of this kind will be heard by a stipendiary magistrate".
[96] reg.13.
[97] s.78M(3), (4).
[98] WRA ss.90B(3), 161D(2).

diation statement has been served, and/or by owners and occupiers of land the subject of a remediation notice, stating what has been done by way of remediation; the authority will not however give any guarantee that these particulars are correct.

Once an entry is made on a register, there is no provision for subsequently removing it.[99] There will thus always be a permanent record of a contaminated site dealt with under the Part 2A regime, even though it may have been comprehensively remediated.

Registers must be available at all reasonable times for free inspection by the public. They must not however include information, the publication of which may harm national security (in the view of the Secretary of State)[100] or which is commercially confidential.[101]

Tax Issues

Remediation tax relief

16–040   As part of the policy to encourage more use of brownfield sites and remediation of contaminated land, tax relief on certain costs incurred in remediating contaminated land was provided for in the Finance Act 2001.[102]

Tax relief is available for "qualifying land remediation expenditure" incurred since May 11, 2001. However if the land was contaminated by an act or omission of the polluter or a group company, if the expenditure is subsidised, or if the scheme violates the anti-avoidance provision, then the relief will not be available. The relief available is either a capital deduction of an amount equal to 150 per cent of qualifying remediation expenditure or payable as a tax credit of up to 16 per cent of qualifying remediation expenditure. In addition to incurring the qualifying land remediation expenditure it is also necessary for the land to have been acquired by a company for the purposes of a trade and, at the time of acquisition, all or part of the land is or was in a "contaminated state".

Landfill tax exemption

16–041   An exemption from landfill tax is available when the waste sent to landfill results from the remediation of contaminated land, provided that the

---

[99] It is nevertheless to be expected that the Courts will be willing to order entries wrongly made to be expunged.

[100] s.78S.

[101] s.78T. Information is commercially confidential if its being contained in the register would prejudice to an unreasonable degree the commercial interests of any individual or person. Not every item of information that the common law would protect as confidential will therefore benefit from this provision.

[102] Finance Act 2001, s.70 and Schs.22 and 23.

remediation is carried out with the object of reducing or removing the potential of pollutants to cause harm (mere dereliction will not suffice), or with the object of facilitating development, conservation, the provision of a public park or other amenity, or the use of land for agriculture or forestry.[103] Application needs to be made in advance and if it is approved then a certificate will be issued allowing the waste to be disposed of at the nominated sites (which must be advised to HM Revenue and Customs in advance) without payment of landfill tax.

2007 saw consultation by HM Treasury about the abolition of this exemption and its replacement by another form of remediation tax credit, so as to enhance land remediation relief rather than subsidise landfill. The exemption is planned to be phased out by April 2012.[104]

Overlap with other legislation

With one notable exception, relating to water pollution, overlap of Part 2A with other legislation relevant to contamination is largely avoided. Thus where it appears that the powers of a relevant regulatory body "may" (N.B. not "will") be exercised in relation to (a) contamination from an IPPC process, or (b) under EPA s.59 in relation to an unlawful deposit of waste, no remediation notice may be served.[105]   **16–042**

Waste. The regime does not apply at all to land in respect of which there is a subsisting permit in respect of waste, unless the contamination is caused by something other than the permitted activity, and which is not a breach of the permit conditions.[106] The statutory nuisance provisions of Part III of the EPA do not apply to nuisances to the extent that they consist of, or are caused by, land "in a contaminated state" (which has a closely

---

[103] Finance Act 1996, s.43A and 43B (inserted by the Landfill Tax (Contaminated Land) Order 1996, SI 1996/1529.

[104] Budget Report 8, section 6.78.

[105] s.78YB(1), (3). A very practical link exists between IPPC and Part 2A in the requirement of the Environmental Permitting (England and Wales) Regulations 2007 [SI 2007/3538] that information be provided relating to the condition of the site at the permit application stage. This information could, identify contamination which was unrelated to the PPC process/installation, and which would meet the Part 2A definition of "contaminated land". The Environment Agency was generally entitled to provide copies of site reports submitted for PPC purposes under the IPPC regime to the relevant local authority. However, only when it is no longer possible to take enforcement action under the PPC regime will the local authority be able to issue a remediation notice. See Defra, *Integrated PPC: a practical guide (14th edition, para.14.40)*. Presumably the same principle will apply under the EP Regulations.

[106] s.78YB(2). Nonetheless the Environment Agency appears to be of the view that this provision would entitle, for example, a landfill site with an existing waste permit, which had at some point in its history received wastes of a type not permitted in the permit, to be designated as contaminated land.

similar, though broader, definition to that of "contaminated land" in the Part 2A).[107]

Unlawful deposits of waste that may be dealt with under s.59 of the EPA are also excluded from the scope of Part 2A.[108] It is by no means clear nevertheless where the dividing line between the two regimes lies. Arguably, owners and occupiers of land on which waste contaminants have been deposited after section 59 came into effect,[109] who neither knowingly caused nor knowingly permitted the original deposit, and who could prove this, would be free of any liability to deal with it under either regime. Further, at the time of writing the ECJ's judgment in *Van de Walle*,[110] which determined that soil contaminated by hydrocarbons spilled on to land under a petrol station was waste, and so subject to waste legislation, remains current. The potential for a confusing overlap with the contaminated land regime is obvious. However, the new Waste Framework Directive as adopted by the European Parliament excludes land in situ, including "unexcavated contaminated soil and buildings permanently connected with land" from the scope of the Directive, and so appears to resolve the problem.[111]

16–043   **Water pollution.** Further, for England and Wales, the EA has also introduced new sections 161A to 161D into the Water Resources Act 1991[112] to reinforce the existing provisions[113] for dealing with such cases. These new provisions permit the Environment Agency/SEPA to serve a "works notice" on a person who has caused or knowingly permitted any such situation, requiring him to take appropriate remedial action at his expense. In contrast with the Part 2A regime, there is no statutory duty to serve a works notice, merely a power to do so, but if one is served, none of the complex provisions under the Part 2A Guidance for allocation and apportionment of liability, and for relief in the event of hardship, will

---

[107] EA 1995, Sch.22, para.89. The extra breadth is due to a deliberate failure by the Government to amend the definition of "contaminated land" in EA Schedule 22 to conform with amendments made to the previously corresponding definition in s.78A when the legislation was before Parliament. In practice the difference will not be of major importance very often, since *ex hypothesi* it would only be so if contamination were significant. Nevertheless, as the Guidance on what constitutes "contaminated land" (as to which see below) is expressed very narrowly by objective standards, and excludes some types of contamination that many would consider to be significant in fact, there are now no statutory powers to deal with these situations, unless and to the extent that they create or threaten pollution of controlled waters (and so fall within the relevant controls under the WRA) or are covered by s.76 of the Building Act 1984 (see para.23A–10))
[108] s.78YB(3).
[109] April 1, 1992.
[110] *C-1/03*, [2004] ECR I-7613. A bizarre effect of this decision is that every owner and occupier of a contaminated site is a keeper of waste, and so requires a waste permit, failing which they commit an offence under EPA s.33(1)(a).
[111] Article 2(1)(b) of the proposed new Waste Framework Directive; for more detail on the Directive, see Chapter 15.
[112] Also new s.90B, providing for enforcement notices in respect of actual or potential breaches of discharge consents.
[113] In s.161.

necessarily apply: for example, the allocation of liability where there are two or more incidents of contamination, or as between those who have owned and/or occupied the relevant land at different times. Where land has resulted in pollution of waters but there is no longer a land-based source of the pollutant then if an Agency wishes to take action, the water pollution regime will be the appropriate one.[114]

Radioactive Contaminated Land. A summary of the law in relation to radioactive contaminated land is to be found in Chapter 20, at paragraph 20–028.

Future developments

Environmental Liability Directive. Directive 2004/35 on the preven-   **16–044**
tion and remedying of environmental damage (the Environmental Liability Directive, or ELD) was adopted on April 21, 2004. As it addresses land contamination issues, it will be necessary for the Government to ensure that the Part 2A regime is consistent with the provisions of the ELD. Although the ELD was to have been implemented in all Member States by April 30, 2007, that was not achieved in the UK.

There is no doubt that some elements of the existing regime will need to be amended to enable implementation of the ELD, if only to make the language used consistent with that in the Directive. As the ELD covers water pollution and natural resource damage as well as land contamination, implementation will result in amendment to other legislation dealing with these issues. Areas where the Directive differs from Part 2A are, for example, the definition of damage: Part 2A requires the causing of "significant harm", or a "significant possibility of significant harm"; the ELD, on the other hand, only requires a "significant risk of human health being adversely affected", which appears to be a lower threshold (although it only applies to damage to human health, and not other environmental elements). Damage under the Directive and the Regulations also covers risks to human health by "organisms and micro-organisms", which is not covered by Part 2A, whereas the harm caused under Part 2A must be due to "substances". There is also a duty under the Regulations to notify the relevant authority of any damage and imminent threats of environmental damage, whereas Part 2A relies on identification of contaminated land by the local authority; the duty to require preventative and remedial measures is also, according to the consultation, "more immediate" than that under Part 2A.

On February 29, 2008, Defra published its consultation on the proposed

---

[114] The Anti-Pollution Works Regulations 1999 (SI 1999/1006) set out the procedures for implementing the works notice powers and were accompanied by a non-statutory DETR policy statement stating that when works notices rather than contaminated land powers should be used. This has been replaced by the Environment Agency Policy Guidance on the Use of Anti-Pollution Works Notices.

Environmental Damage (Prevention and Remediation) Regulations intended to implement the ELD, which proposed that the Part 2A regime would continue to apply to all circumstances except where there is a risk to human health, which would be covered by the Regulations. Part 2A would also apply to all damage to land caused before the Regulations come into force, including where there is a risk to health.[115] The responses were summarised in August 2008, and at the time of writing the Government's response was awaited. The responses to the consultation also raised the question of whether Part 2A would continue to be used if, measures having been taken under the ELD, it emerged that contamination was still a risk.[116]

16–045   **Soil Protection Directive.** September 2006 saw the release of the European Commission's draft directive on soil protection,[117] intended to implement a strategy first published for consultation in 2002. This strategy includes a number of elements related to contaminated land aimed at slowing destruction by construction, defining risk areas for erosion, organic matter decline, etc and harmonising identification and management of contaminated land. Defra published its regulatory impact assessment in July 2007 and the results of the resulting consultation on the proposed Directive in January 2008: issues surrounding the treatment of sealing of landfill sites, and the link with the contaminated land regime were of particular concern, with the industry feeling that the proposals relating to soil contamination were far too restrictive and burdensome. At the time of writing the adoption of the Soil Protection Directive looks to be some way off: no political agreement has yet been reached within the EU Environment Council on whether the matters in the proposed Directive should in fact be dealt with at Community level.

---

[115] para.52, *Consultation on draft regulations and guidance implementing the Environmental Liability Directive 2004/35/EC with regard to the prevention and remedying of environmental damage*, Defra February 29, 2008.
[116] The Environmental Liability Directive is discussed in detail, in Chapter 5.
[117] COM(2006) 232 final, 22.9.2006.

Diagram 16/I

Contaminated Land:
A Step by Step Guide to Part 2A

Stage 1:	Inspection of area by local authority – is land contaminated?

Stage 2:	Is the situation governed by other statutory provisions?

Stage 3:	Should the land be designated as a special site?

Stage 4:	Is urgent action needed?

Stage 5:	Preliminary identification of appropriate persons to bear responsibility and Service of notice under s.78B(3) on all relevant appropriate persons and owner

Stage 6:	Consultation as to what is to be done by way of remediation

Stage 7:	Restrictions on service and/or contents of remediation notice

Stage 8:	Service of remediation notice

Stage 9:	Possible appeal against notice

Stage 10:	Prosecution for failure to comply with notice

Stage 11:	Remedial action by authority

Stage 12:	Cost recovery by authority

Chapter 17

STATUTORY NUISANCE AND CONTROLS OVER NOISE

ng history and remains to this **17–001**
ntal law. A duty to deal with
ocal authorities by the Public
missive power that they pre-
nces to which this duty has
d refined over the years, and
ith them. The Environmental
e list of nuisances with minor
amendments and set ou.. are applicable to all of them.
The Noise and Statutory Nuisance 8 added a further category of
statutory nuisance covering noise emitted caused in a street (noise could
previously only be a statutory nuisance where it was emitted from premises), and necessarily created special procedures for dealing with this
particular problem. The EPA 1990 also introduced a more streamlined
system of summary procedures. Table 17/I sets out the main procedural
aspects of statutory nuisance proceedings by both local authorities and
aggrieved individuals.

Statutory nuisance is to be distinguished from the tort of private nuisance, which is restricted to protecting those with sufficient proprietary
interests in land from substantial and unreasonable interference with their
reasonable enjoyment of that land. The House of Lords recently affirmed
this limitation to the entitlement to sue for private nuisance in *Hunter v
Canary Wharf*.[3] It is also distinct from common law public nuisance,
because public nuisance does not operate to protect individuals within that

---

[1] The 1846 Act making provision for "the more speedy removal of certain nuisances" (9&10
Vict. C. 96) gave power to the magistrates upon complaint to make abatement orders
regarding filthy and unwholesome conditions of dwelling houses, accumulation of offensive or noxious matter where the same was likely to be prejudicial to the health of the
occupiers or of the persons whose habitations are in the neighbourhood. That legislation
was renewed by the Nuisance Removal and Diseases Prevention Act 1848 (11&12 Vict. C.
123) and consolidated with amendments by the Nuisances Removal Act 1855 (18&19
Vict. C.121).
[2] In ss.79 to 83.
[3] [1997] AC 659.

community unless there has been an injury suffered to the community or a significant section of it as a whole.[4]

The statutory nuisance regime therefore fills an important gap in the common law as it protects individuals within the community, rather than property, from harm. There is no need for the victim to have property rights in order to benefit from remedies under the statutory nuisance regime. Furthermore, the statutory nuisance regime can be used by local authorities as well as by aggrieved individuals who wish to take action themselves.[5]

17–002   This chapter focuses on the statutory nuisance regime under the EPA and explores both the duties and powers of local authorities as well as the actions that can be taken by individuals. The chapter also examines the other statutory provisions that govern nuisance, with particular emphasis on noise nuisance.

The Statutory Nuisance Regime under the EPA

What constitutes a statutory nuisance under the EPA regime?

17–003   Under section 79(1) of the EPA, the following circumstances constitute a statutory nuisance:

(a) any premises in such a state as to be prejudicial to health or a nuisance;

(b) smoke emitted from premises so as to be prejudicial to health or a nuisance;

(c) fumes or gases emitted from premises so as to be prejudicial to health or a nuisance;

(d) any dust, steam, smell or other effluvia arising on industrial, trade or business premises and being prejudicial to health or a nuisance;

(e) any accumulation or deposit which is prejudicial to health or a nuisance;

(f) any animal kept in such a place or manner as to be prejudicial to health or a nuisance;

---

[4] See for example, *R v Rimmington* [2006] 1 AC 459. Also note decision of the Court of Appeal in *Corby Group Litigation v Corby Borough Council* [2008] EWCA Civ 463.

[5] Although it is important to note that the statutory nuisance regime does not always provide a remedy and it may be necessary to resort to public or private nuisance remedies. See, for example, *Watson & Others v Croft Promo-Sport Ltd* [2008] EWHC 759 (Q.B.), where one of the claimants was pressing the local authority in vain for a number of years to serve abatement notices in relation to what he considered to be a statutory nuisance caused by the defendant's use of its land at the Croft Motor Circuit. The claimants were eventually forced to seek an injunction in the civil court.

(fa) any insects emanating from relevant industrial, trade or business premises and being prejudicial to health or a nuisance;[6]

(fb) artificial light emitted from premises so as to be prejudicial to health or a nuisance;

(g) noise emitted from premises so as to be prejudicial to health or a nuisance;

(ga) noise that is prejudicial to health or a nuisance and is emitted from or caused by a vehicle, machinery or equipment in a street;

(h) any other matter declared by any enactment to be a statutory nuisance.

"Prejudicial to health or a nuisance"

It will be seen that each of the specific nuisances under the EPA statutory regime is qualified by the expression "prejudicial to health *or* a nuisance", thus creating two quite separate limbs, either of which will suffice.[7] One of the most important distinctions between the two limbs is that the latter can only arise in cases where persons other than those occupying the premises where the nuisance takes place are affected.[8] In contrast, under the prejudicial to health limb, occupants of premises can complain of something intrinsic to those very premises that is prejudicial to their health. The distinction is particularly noteworthy in respect of whether the state of particular premises constitutes a statutory nuisance under section 79(1)(a), as discussed further below.

17–004

(a) "Prejudicial to health"

"Prejudicial to health" is defined to mean "injurious, or likely to cause injury, to health", and consequently evidence of actual injury is not needed. However, something liable to injure health is distinct from something liable to injure per se. Therefore a steep and dangerous staircase, liable to cause accidents, was not prejudicial to health.[9] The test is an objective one, and does not vary depending on the characteristics of the particular individual affected. Therefore in *Cunningham v Birmingham City Council* a kitchen, harmful to an autistic child but not otherwise, did not come under this limb.[10]

(b) "A nuisance"

In a case brought under the Public Health Act 1936 (PHA), it was held that a statutory nuisance coming within the meaning of that Act

---

[6] Subsections (fa) and (fb) were added by the Clean Neighbourhoods and Environment Act 2005; subsection (ga) was added by the Noise and Statutory Nuisance Act 1993.

[7] *Bishop Auckland Local Board v Bishop Auckland Iron and Steel Company Ltd* (1882) 10 QBD 138, where it was observed that the 1875 Public Health Act definition did not refer to "an injurious nuisance" but had the two quite distinct limbs.

[8] See *National Coal Board v Neath Borough Council* [1976] 2 All E.R. 478 at 482.

[9] See *R v Bristol City Council ex p Everett* [1999] 2 All E.R. 193 CA.

[10] *Cunningham v Birmingham City Council* [1998] Env. L.R. 1.

must be either a private or a public nuisance as understood by common law.[11] In so deciding, a public nuisance was defined as "an act or omission which materially affects the material comfort and quality of life of a class of Her Majesty's subjects", and it was said that "private nuisances, at least in the vast majority of cases, are interferences for a substantial length of time by owners or occupiers of property with the use or enjoyment of neighbouring property".[12] Hence if what has taken place affects only the person or persons occupying the premises where the nuisance is said to have taken place, this cannot be a statutory nuisance under the *nuisance* limb (though it may be one under the "prejudicial to health" limb as discussed above).

It was also argued in the same case that not only must a statutory nuisance be either of a private or public kind at common law, but the act of nuisance itself must be such as to come within the spirit of the 1936 Act, that is, it must in some way be concerned with the health of the person who claims to be or who has been affected by the nuisance. That proposition was considered attractive, though no decision was called for on the point. However, whereas the long title of the 1936 Act is "an Act to consolidate with amendments certain enactments relating to public health", the EPA 1990 is billed, so far as relevant, as "an Act . . . to *restate* the law defining statutory nuisances and improve the summary procedures for dealing with them". Accordingly, it is probably no longer appropriate, if it ever was, to construe the references to statutory nuisances as necessarily being coloured or driven by public health issues. There seems to be no reason to put any particular gloss on the normal meaning of the words.[13] In so far as the legislative context is material, it must be one of controlling pollution of the environment generally.

The heads of nuisance

(a) "Any premises in such a state as to be prejudicial to health or a nuisance"

17–005 "Premises" is defined to include land and any vessel, with the exclusion of one "powered by steam reciprocating machinery".[14] It

---

[11] *National Coal Board v Neath Borough Council* [1976] 2 All E.R. 478 at 482.
[12] op cit., at 481.
[13] It is notable that in *London Borough of Hounslow v Thames Water Utilities Limited* [2003] EWHC 1197 Admin, the Divisional Court held that section 79(1)(d) was to be given its "plain meaning", rejecting an argument that "premises" was to have the meaning given to it in *Queen v Parlby* [1889] XXII Q.B. 520. At [51], Pitchford J. noted "It seems to me that the definition of statutory nuisance by identification of conditions was completely recast by the Environmental Protection Act 1990. As the preamble to the Act informs, it was Parliament's intention to restate the law".
[14] s.79(12).

follows that if the state of premises only affects its occupants, it can generally only come within section 79(1)(a) if it is prejudicial to health. For example, mould growth caused by condensation ("toxic mould") was held to be a statutory nuisance where the building was subject to a "wholly exceptional vulnerability to condensation" which was "so unusual that there had to be a special form of heating to combat condensation".[15]

In contrast, in *Vella v Lambeth LBC*[16] the Administrative Court held that lack of adequate sound insulation did not mean that the premises were themselves in such a state as to be injurious or likely to cause injury to health ("they are not defective, unwholesome, filthy, verminous etc").

In so doing, the Court referred to the history of the section 79(1)(a) nuisance.[17] However, there was an explicit reference to the policy arguments against finding a lack of soundproofing to be a nuisance, namely:

"[the] immense financial burden that would be imposed on social and private landlords if the court were, by the statutory nuisance route, to require the immediate upgrading of properties

---

[15] *Greater London Council v London Borough of Tower Hamlets* (1983) 15 HLR 54. See also *Birmingham District Council v Kelly* (1985) 17 H.L.R. 572 where the Divisional Court upheld an abatement order which required the Council to install central heating. However, the magistrates did not find that the absence of central heating was prejudicial to health. That finding was based upon the presence of mould growth which was liable to cause health problems and food poisoning. The installation of central heating was a way to remove the threat to health created by the mouldy state of the premises. Compare *Henry Pike v Sefton Metropolitan Borough Council* [2000] D.C., L.T.L. February 29, 2000 (unreported elsewhere) where the justices' finding that the condensation-associated mould growth did not constitute a statutory nuisance was upheld as the cause of the mould growth had been because the appellant was unwilling to use the system of heating provided. Therefore, the justices had been correct on the evidence before them to adopt the approach taken in *Dover District Council v Farrah & Ors* [1980] 2 HLR 35 where the construction of the houses and the method of heating supplied were perfectly proper and adequate and would have maintained the houses in a state which would not have been prejudicial to the health of the occupants, had the systems been used.

[16] [2005] EWHC 2473 (Admin).

[17] Poole J. considered and applied the decision of *R v Bristol City Council ex p. Everett* [1999] 2 All E.R. 193 where the Court of Appeal examined the legislative antecedents of section 79(1)(a) and said that although as a matter of ordinary language it could be said that something which created a risk of accidental injury was prejudicial to health, the history showed that Parliament was concerned solely with the spread of disease. Accidental injury was altogether outside the scope of the mischief at which the legislation was directed. The House of Lords judgment in *Birmingham City Council v Oakley* (2001) 33 HLR 283; (2001) LGR 110, which held that the object of s.79(1)(a) of the 1990 Act and its predecessors was to provide a means for the summary removal of noxious matters, was also considered and applied.

generally to a standard of sound insulation not required when they were constructed or adapted".[18]

Imposing such burdens is a matter for housing management rather than environmental health.[19]

These policy concerns echoed those of the majority in *Birmingham City Council v Oakley*,[20] where the House of Lords held that it was not sufficient to render the house itself "in such a state" as to be prejudicial to health that the WC and basin were in separate rooms and that to get from one to the other it was necessary to pass through the kitchen where food was prepared. The arrangement of the rooms in question, which were otherwise not in themselves unsanitary so as to be prejudicial to health, did not fall within s.79(1)(a) of the 1990 Act. As Lord Hoffman explained:

> "For the courts to give section 79(1)(a) an extended "modern" meaning which required suitable alterations to be made to existing houses would impose a substantial financial burden upon public and private owners and occupiers. ... I do not think that it is either sensible or in accordance with modern notions of democracy to hold that when Parliament re-enacted language going back to the nineteenth century, it authorised the courts to impose upon local authorities and others a huge burden of capital expenditure to which the statutory language had never been held to apply. ...the decision as to whether or not to take such a step should be made by the elected representatives of the people and not by the courts."

(b) "Smoke emitted from premises so as to be prejudicial to health or a nuisance".

17–006   There are a number of exceptions[21] to this head of statutory nuisance in order to avoid overlap with the Clean Air Act 1993. Thus it does not apply to smoke emitted from a chimney of a private dwelling within a smoke control area; dark smoke emitted from a chimney of a building, or a chimney serving the furnace of a boiler or industrial plant either attached to a building or fixed to or

---

[18] Per Poole J. at para.71.
[19] Contrast the earlier decision of the Divisional Court in *Southwark London Borough Council v Ince* (1989) 153 JP 597, which involved the adequacy of sound insulation in a conversion of a block of flats. In that case tenants of a local authority sought an abatement order against it for failing to insulate a block of converted flats adequately against traffic and railway noise. That case was largely based on the penetration of noise being prejudicial to health, and turned on the authority having carried out the conversion of the flats unsatisfactorily.
[20] (2001) 33 HLR 283; (2001) LGR 110.
[21] Spelled out in s.79(3).

installed on land; dark smoke emitted in any other circumstances from industrial or trade premises; or smoke emitted from a railway locomotive steam engine. "Smoke" is defined to include soot, ash, grit and gritty particles emitted in smoke. By implication, from the definition of "dust", (see paragraph (d) below), dust may also amount to smoke, although dust that amounts to smoke may be exempted from section 79(1)(b) when emitted from a chimney for the reasons just given. It is specifically provided that expressions used in the definitions in EPA section 79(7) are to have the same meaning as in the Clean Air Act 1993. Accordingly the definition of industrial or trade premises contained in section 2(6) of the Clean Air Act 1993[22] applies to the exclusion from this head of nuisance, and not the EPA definition of "industrial, trade or business premises". The effect of the exclusions in favour of the Clean Air Act 1993 means that the principal application of this statutory nuisance will be to fires burning on open ground. There is case law to the effect that the smell of smoke can be a statutory nuisance.[23]

(c)   "Fumes or gases emitted from premises so as to be prejudicial to health or a nuisance".

"Fumes" means any airborne solid matter smaller than dust, while   **17–007**
"gas" includes vapour and moisture precipitated from vapour. "Premises" for the purposes of this statutory nuisance are confined to private dwellings only. A private dwelling means any building, or part of a building, used or intended to be used, as a dwelling. The effect of all these definitions is to make a clear distinction between this statutory nuisance and that under (d) below.

(d)   "Any dust, steam, smell or other effluvia rising on industrial, trade or business premises and being prejudicial to health or a nuisance".

In so far as "dust" is an ingredient of smoke emitted from a   **17–008**
chimney, it is excluded from this head of statutory nuisance, and will be controlled under the provisions relating to smoke—in practice under the Clean Air Act 1993.[24] "Industrial, trade or business premises" are broadly defined as premises used for any industrial, trade or business purposes, or premises not so used on which matter is burnt in connection with any industrial, trade or business process. Premises are used for industrial purposes where they are used for the purposes of any treatment or process as well as

---

[22] i.e. premises used for any industrial or trade purposes; or premises not so used on which matter is burnt in connection with any industrial or trade process.

[23] *Griffiths v Pembrokeshire County Council* [2000] 18 LS Gaz R 36, DC.

[24] Smoke from industrial or trade premises that is not dark smoke is potentially under this head, though this seems unlikely to represent a problem in practice.

where they are used for the purposes of manufacturing. Steam from a railway locomotive engine is however excluded.[25]

Soya meal dust falling on cars was held to be outside the scope of the corresponding provision of the Public Health Act 1936 on the grounds that though it might cause inconvenience or diminish the value of the motor car, it did not interfere materially with the residents' personal comfort in the sense of materially affecting their well-being.[26] This decision appears to have relied, to some extent at least, on the fact that the 1936 Act was concerned with public health. Moreover, while every case depends on its facts, significant amounts of dust constantly falling on motor cars would appear to represent a public nuisance within the definition given in *National Coal Board v Neath Borough Council*,[27] namely "an act or omission which materially affects the material comfort and quality of life of a class of Her Majesty's subjects". In 1882 it was held that smells amounting to a nuisance would come within the 1875 Act, irrespective of any actual or potential injury to health.[28]

The definitions in section 79(7) distinguish between "industrial, trade or business premises" on the one hand and a "private dwelling" on the other. In the case of a mixed hereditament, the definition of "private dwelling" clearly is applicable to such part as is used as a dwelling. The definition of "premises" does not necessarily require that the term apply to the entire structure of any building, and consequently given the evident intention of the legislature to distinguish between the two types of property use, it would be appropriate to regard only those parts of a mixed hereditament used for industrial, trade or business purposes as "industrial, trade or business premises" for the purposes of these statutory nuisance provisions.

There has been discussion about whether or not s.79(1)(d) can apply to odour problems at sewage treatment works. In *R v Parlby & Ors*, an 1889 case, sewage works constructed under s.27 of the Public Health Act 1975 were found not to come within the scope of "premises in such a state as to be a nuisance" under s.91 of that Act (the predecessor of s79(1)(a) of the 1990 Act).[29] In a recent case, *London Borough of Hounslow v Thames Water Utilities Limited*, it was argued that they therefore fell outside s.79(1)(d), such that an abatement notice could not properly be served upon a sewage treatment works under that provision. The Divisional Court con-

[25] s.79(5).
[26] *Wivenhoe Port v Colchester Borough Council* [1985] JPL 175 and [1985] JPL 396.
[27] [1976] 2 All E.R. 478.
[28] *Bishop Auckland Local Board v Bishop Auckland Iron and Steel Company Limited*, see fn.5 above.
[29] *R v Parlby and Others* [1889] 22 Q.B. 520.

sidered the legislative history of s.79 and observed that there was no equivalent provision to s.79(1)(d) in the nuisance legislation which preceded the Public Health Act.[30] The Court noted that the EPA 1990 "completely recast" the definition of statutory nuisance by identification of conditions; it did not consider that the legislative intention when framing s.79(1)(d) was to exclude any particular premises from its operation, unless there was express statutory provision to the contrary. The Court went on to note that the policy considerations which assisted the Court to its conclusion in *Parlby* "do not . . . apply in the year 2003 as they did in 1889", and found that sewage works were not excluded from the operation of s.79(1)(d) of the 1990 Act. In contrast, in *East Riding of Yorkshire Council v Yorkshire Water Services Ltd*, the court held that a public sewer could not be "premises" for the purposes of s.79(1)(a).[31] In so doing, Maurice Kay J. held that the current wording of the sub-section is virtually identical to the comparable wording in the 1875 Act, and by re-enacting the old wording Parliament is presumed to have affirmed the decision in *Parlby*. So it would seem that the term "premises" means different things within s.79 depending on the legislative history and precise wording of the particular subsection under consideration.

(e)   "Any accumulation or deposit which is prejudicial to health or a nuisance".

This type of statutory nuisance dates from the 1875 Public Health   **17–009**
Act. A mere accumulation or deposit on land that does not create any physical interference with the legitimate activities of anyone else is not likely to amount to a nuisance except in so far as there may be smells or noxious materials blowing or carried away by rain water on to other land, or where it attracts animals or birds that themselves represent a nuisance or risk to health. Cases are likely to be decided on the issue of whether the accumulation or deposit may properly be held to be prejudicial to health; as to that, much will depend on the particular evidence relating to the extent of danger and the risks posed to those who may have access to it. For example, an accumulation of purely inert matter was held not to amount to a statutory nuisance under this head, even though it may have included broken glass and old tin cans liable to injure children from a nearby school.[32]

(f)   "Any animal kept in such a place or manner as to be prejudicial to health or a nuisance".

---

[30] [2003] EWHC 1197 Admin.
[31] [2000] Env. L.R. 113.
[32] *Coventry City Council v Cartwright* [1975] 1 W.L.R. 845, [1975] 2 All E.R. 99.

17–010 This head is clearly appropriate to the keeping of animals in a manner that gives rise to smells or the risk of disease. It is open to question whether it applies to noise made by animals. The noise made by greyhounds was considered not to fall under this head in *Galer v Morrissey*,[33] though this was doubted, obiter, in *Coventry City Council v Cartwright.*[34]

(fa) "Any insects emanating from relevant industrial, trade or business premises and being prejudicial to health or a nuisance"

17–011 This head was added by the Clean Neighbourhoods and Environment Act 2005 for England and Wales,[35] and came into effect in relation to England on April 6, 2006, and Wales on January 31, 2007. It is intended to provide local authorities with a remedy to nuisances from insect infestations (whether naturally occurring or caused by human activities) on "relevant" industrial, trade or business premises. However, it is not intended to be used against most naturally occurring concentrations of insects on open land or in ways that would adversely affect biodiversity. Accordingly, certain types of land and certain waters are excluded by s.79(7C) and s.79(7D), which for example exclude from the definition of "relevant" industrial, trade and business premises "land used as arable, grazing, meadow or pasture land", and land included in a Site of Special Scientific Interest. Also, the subsection does not apply to insects listed in Schedule 5 to the Wildlife and Countryside Act 1981, unless they are included in that Schedule solely to prevent their trade or sale. It is expected that the most likely sources of complaints will include poultry houses/farms,[36] sewage treatment works, manure/silage storage areas, animal housing, stagnant ditches and drains, landfill sites/refuse tips, waste transfer premises, trade or business premises (e.g. contaminated goods, kitchen areas), slaughterhouses, and used car tyre recycling businesses.[37]

(fb) "Artificial light emitted from premises so as to be prejudicial to health or a nuisance"

17–012 This head was also added by the Clean Neighbourhoods and Environment Act 2005[38] and came into effect at the same time as s.79(1)(fa). Artificial lighting emitted from a broad range of premises are exempted from constituting a statutory nuisance: such premises include those occupied for defence purposes, various

[33] [1955] 1 W.L.R. 110.
[34] [1975] 1 W.L.R. 845, [1975] 2 All E.R. 99.
[35] s.101.
[36] Buildings on agricultural land are not exempt from statutory nuisance from insects, even though the land surrounding them may be.
[37] See DEFRA Guidance at *http://www.defra.gov.uk/environment/localenv/legislation/cnea/statnuisance.pdf.*
[38] s.102.

transport-related premises (such as airports, harbours and railways), and prisons. The most likely causes of complaint under this head are domestic and commercial security lights, sports facilities, domestic decorative lighting,[39] laser shows, light art, and sky beams. Streetlights are not specifically exempt, but because of their location are unlikely to qualify, as generally speaking they are not found on "premises".[40]

(g)   "Noise emitted from premises so as to be prejudicial to health or a nuisance".

By s.79(7), "noise" includes vibration, and "premises" include **17–013** "land" and vessels (hence noise from moored party boats for example can come within the Act). Aircraft however are specifically excluded,[41] with the exception of model aircraft s.79(6). The noise does not have to come from a building; noise coming from a private garden would come from "premises".[42] "Emitted" does not require that the premises themselves generate the noise, simply that the noise comes from the premises.[43]

In terms of satisfying the requirement that the noise be "prejudicial to health or a nuisance", the possibility of noises being prejudicial to health should not be overlooked. For instance, sleeplessness can be injurious to health, and noise can often be responsible for disturbance of sleep.[44]

There is no fixed formula for determining whether noise amounts to a nuisance. The difficulty is that there is no universally accepted system of classification for noise and what constitutes noise is often in practice a highly subjective issue. Therefore, cases will turn on their facts. In *London Borough Hackney v Rottenberg*, David Clarke J. noted:[45]

"When considering whether noise amounts to a nuisance, it is necessary to have regard to a number of factors, which include the nature and context of the neighbourhood; the competing and

---

[39] Christmas lights may potentially come under this regime although this seems unlikely given their short duration.

[40] See DEFRA Guidance at *http://www.defra.gov.uk/environment/localenv/legislation/cnea/stat-nuisance.pdf*. See also Taylor M., "Light pollution and nuisance: the enforcement guidance for light as a statutory nuisance", *Journal of Planning & Environment Law JPL* (2006) August pages 1114–1127 and Taylor M. and Hughes D., *Journal of Planning & Environment Law JPL* (2005) September pages 1131–1144.

[41] Further immunity from action for trespass or nuisance for aircraft noise is contained in the Civil Aviation Act 1982, which creates a reliance on the Secretary of State for Transport to protect from excessive aircraft noise.

[42] For example, in *Godfrey v Conwy BC* [2001] Env. L.R. 38, noise from an outbuilding constituted a nuisance.

[43] *Network Housing Association v Westminster City Council* [1995] Env. L.R. 176.

[44] It is possible that the controversial use of machines that emit high-pitched noise to disperse groups of youths (the "mosquito alarm") will be challenged on this ground, amongst others, according to the campaign group Liberty.

[45] At para.11, [2007] EWHC 166 (Admin).

conflicting interests of adjoining owners and occupants and other people affected; and the fact of any activities in the premises, and whether those are activities permitted by planning permission and the like."

Nature and context of the neighbourhood

17–014   As Lord Westbury pithily expressed it in *St Helen's Smelting Co v Tipping*: "what would be a nuisance in Belgrave Square would not necessarily be so in Bermondsey".[46] Therefore, for example, in *Roper v Tussaud*,[47] it was held that local inhabitants must expect some inconvenience from the site of Alton Towers, which had been a theme park since 1979 and a place of public recreation beforehand. This was in part the reason why the abatement notice that was granted in that case set the maximum noise level from the daily operation of the site as 40dbA, higher than that which the Claimant had sought.[48] In contrast, in *Godfrey v Conwy*,[49] noise from an outbuilding that had been converted for use as a music studio for rock bands in an extremely quiet rural location constituted a nuisance, the only sources of noise in the area being agriculture, wildlife, a river and the weather.

Nature of activity

17–015   The House of Lords held in *Baxter v London Borough of Camden*[50] that the noise of the normal use of a residential flat, audible in a neighbouring dwelling because of a lack of adequate soundproofing, cannot amount to a nuisance. In contrast, in *East Dorset District Council v Eaglebeam*,[51] it was held that the running of motocross activities on land nearby residential property constituted both a statutory and public nuisance. Similarly the breeding of 24 howling Siberian huskies in a predominantly residential area of Southampton was held a nuisance in *Manley v New Forest District Council*.[52]

Other factors

17–016   Other factors relevant to whether a noise amounts to a nuisance include timing, and duration of the noise. Generally speaking, the

[46] (1865) 11 HL Cas 642.
[47] [2007] EWHC 624 (Admin), [2007] Env. L.R. 31.
[48] paras 5 and 15.
[49] (2001) Env. L.R. 38.
[50] [2000] Env. L.R. 112.
[51] [2006] EWHC 2378.
[52] [2000] EHLR 113.

working day is the least sensitive period for noise; night from 11pm to 7am the most sensitive. Hence commercial construction and other noisy activities can generally be carried out in an ordinary working day.[53] Duration can also be relevant. In *Coventry City Council v Harris*,[54] it was held that practice of a brass instrument for up to one hour a day was not a nuisance, but it might be if longer.

Quantification of noise

The quantification of the noise, in terms of decibels, is often sig-   **17–017**
nificant evidence in determining whether it amounts to a nuisance, although such quantification is not necessary.[55] Common measurements taken include the maximum level reached during an individual noise event; the level exceeded for 90 per cent of the time; the level exceeded for 10 per cent of time; and the level of noise if averaged over time. All of these measures have their advantages and disadvantages. For example, in respect of a short but very loud event that occurred just once over the course of an entire night, but which was sufficiently loud to wake a neighbour, the average level of noise over that period might be quite low. A maximum level reading would be more appropriate.

Quantification can take into account context, in so far as the background levels of noise can also be recorded, such that the "additional" volume of the potential nuisance can be assessed. Guidelines include BS 4142 (1997) "Method for rating industrial noise affecting mixed residential and industrial areas", which suggests that, if a development in an area of mixed residential and industrial activity would exceed average background levels by 10dB(A), this would cause an adverse degree of disturbance, whereas a difference of 5dB(A) or more may be of significance in less built-up areas.

However, there are limitations in a purely quantitative approach. In addition to the problems and costs of accurate and objective measurement,[56] there is the fundamental fact that it is not just the volume of noise, but also its nature, that is of relevance in deter-

---

[53] *London Borough of Hammersmith v Magnum Automated Forecourts Ltd* [1978] 1 W.L.R. 50 CA.
[54] (1992) 4 Land Management and Env. L.R. 168.
[55] *Westminster v McDonald* [2003] EWHC 2698 (Admin) [17]; *London Borough Hackney v Rottenberg* [2007] EWHC 166 (Admin) at [10].
[56] Noise can be expensive to monitor, and can be susceptible to manipulation (e.g. monitored at certain times). If a reading is taken, it must note the location at which it was taken, *Ex p. Watney Mann* [1976] 1 W.L.R. 1107.

mining whether it amounts to a nuisance. For example, in *Godfrey v Conwy BC*[57] the court held that noise which "by virtue of its nature is obtrusive, annoying and out of character with the area in which it occurs is capable of amounting to a statutory nuisance", even though, measured by a noise meter, it did not add measurably to the background level of noise.

(ga) "Noise that is prejudicial to health or a nuisance and is emitted from or caused by a vehicle, machinery or equipment in the street".

17–018 In its original form the EPA only dealt with noise emitted from premises under s.79(1)(g). Subsequently, this further head of statutory nuisance s.79(1)(ga) was created by the Noise and Statutory Nuisance Act 1993[58] to cover "noise that is prejudicial to health or a nuisance and is emitted from or caused by a vehicle, machinery or equipment in a street". It pertains to *individual* vehicles, machinery or equipment in the street but by s.79(6A) explicitly does not apply to traffic noise, armed forces or political and campaigning demonstrations. It is likely that the same considerations as set out above in relation to noise from premises will broadly apply.

Action may consequently be taken against noise from, for example, car radios, diesel generators and parked refrigerator vehicles in the street.[59] Equipment is defined as including a musical instrument, and "street" is given the same meaning as it has in the Control of Pollution Act 1974 (COPA) s.62(1).[60] The "person responsible", who may be made the subject of statutory nuisance proceedings in relation to noise in a street, is to include, in relation to a vehicle, the person in whose name it is registered and also any other person who is for the time being its driver, and in relation to machinery or equipment, any person who is for the time being the operator of it. The Noise and Statutory Nuisance Act 1993 includes various consequential provisions for amending Part III of EPA to provide for this additional statutory nuisance, including a requirement to serve the abatement notice by fixing it on the vehicle, machinery or equipment concerned where the person responsible for it cannot be found, or where the local authority in any event determines that this provision shall apply.[61] However, where a notice is served in this way, and the person can be found

---

[57] [2001] Env. L.R. 38. As mentioned above, the noise in that case—from a building that had been converted for use as a music studio for rock bands in an extremely quiet rural location—was held to constitute a nuisance.

[58] As s.79(1)(ga), which came into effect on January 5, 1994.

[59] It was originally intended to cover also noisy political and other demonstrations, but these are now specifically excluded from being a statutory nuisance by EPA, s.79(6A)(c), inserted by s.2(3) of the 1993 Act.

[60] Inserted into EPA, s.79(7) by the 1993 Act, s.2(4).

[61] s.80A(2).

and served with a copy within one hour, it must also be served on him.[62] There are also provisions in relation to the use of loud-speakers on the street contained in COPA, discussed in section C on other statutory frameworks below.

(h) "Any other matter to be declared by any enactment to be a statutory nuisance".

A number of matters have been declared to be statutory nuisances   **17–019**
under this provision including:

- Any well, tank, cistern, or water-butt used for the supply of water for domestic purposes which is so placed, constructed or kept as to render the water therein liable to contamination prejudicial to health—PHA 1936, s.141;
- Any pond, pool, ditch, gutter or watercourse which is so foul or in such a state as to be prejudicial to health or a nuisance; and any part of a watercourse, not being a part ordinarily navigated by vessels employed in the carriage of goods by water, which is so choked or silted up as to obstruct or impede the proper flow of water and thereby to cause a nuisance, or give rise to conditions prejudicial to health—PHA 1936, s.259(1), and the Transport Act 1968, s.108;[63]
- A tent, van, shed or similar structure used for human habitation:

  (a) which is in such a state, or so overcrowded, as to be prejudicial to the health of the inmates; or
  (b) the use of which, by reason of the absence of proper sanitary accommodation or otherwise, gives rise, whether on the site or on other land, to a nuisance or to conditions prejudicial to health—PHA 1936, s.268(2).

- Shafts and outlets of abandoned and discontinued mines, and quarries (whether being worked or not), where inadequately stopped up or without adequate barriers to protect the public—Mines and Quarries Act 1954, s.151(2).[64]

Prior to implementation of Part 2A of the EPA statutory nuisance could, in some circumstances, be used to address land contamination issues. To avoid overlap, Part 3 and the enactments listed above are not available to the extent that a statutory nuisance consists of or is caused by land being in a "contaminated state". It should be noted that the definition of "con-

---

[62] s.80A(3).
[63] As amended by EPA Sch. 15, para.10(1), (3). The decision of Hale L.J. in *R. v Falmouth and Truro Port Health Authority, Ex Parte South West Water Ltd.* [2000] 3 W.L.R. 1464 considered the meaning of "watercourse" in this context and concluded that an estuary is not a watercourse for the purposes of s.259(1)(a).
[64] s.151(2) has been summarised here; it should be referred to for its full terms.

taminated state" is wider than the definition of "contaminated land" in Part 2A, in that there is no reference to the opinion of the local authority and there is no reference to "significant" harm.[65] Therefore there will be circumstances where land has received pollutants sufficient for it to be in a "contaminated state", but not to such an extent that it is "contaminated land" for the purposes of Part 2A. In these cases neither the statutory nuisance regime nor the Part 2A regime are available should the pollution give rise to any problems.[66]

Though not "statutory nuisances" under the EPA, other statutes may adopt the same language to achieve essentially the same object. Thus section 59(1) of the Building Act 1984 provides that if a local authority considers that certain features of a building, for example, a cesspool, private sewer, drain, soil pipe or rain-water pipe, is in such a condition as to be prejudicial to health or a nuisance, then it must serve a notice on the owner or the occupier of the building requiring such work as may be necessary to be done.[67] In the case of a breach in a private sewer, it is sufficient to serve the notice on all those served by the sewer upstream of the breach; it is not necessary to serve it also on those connected downstream of it.[68]

The duty to inspect

17–020   An express duty is placed on every local authority to have its area inspected from time to time to detect any of these statutory nuisances in its area.[69] Such inspections may, for example, include taking decibel measurements by an environmental health officer—and such measurements may, at least if uncontested, be sufficient in itself, without evidence from persons aggrieved, to establish the existence of a nuisance.[70]

Where a local authority is satisfied that a nuisance exists or is likely to occur or recur in its area, it must serve an abatement notice requiring the nuisance to be abated or prohibiting or restricting its occurrence or recurrence.[71] The abatement notice may also require further action to be taken as may be necessary to achieve those ends. In appropriate cases, an

---

[65] s.80(1A)(B).
[66] This is what has come to be called the "statutory gap". The earlier drafts of the Bill that was to become the Environment Act 1995 used identical wording for defining both what was "contaminated land" and what the statutory nuisance regime would not apply to, and hence there was no gap between them. However, in the very last legislative stages the Government, without notice or consultation, narrowed the definition of contaminated land, but (deliberately) did not expand the corresponding wording setting limits on the scope of the statutory nuisance regime.
[67] s.99 and 102 of the Building Act govern the procedures for service of notices and appeals.
[68] *Swansea City Council v Jenkins*, (1994) 158 JP 952.
[69] s.79(1).
[70] *Cooke v Adatia*, (1988) LG Rev 189.
[71] s.80. The authority has no discretion not to act once these circumstances have been found to exist.

abatement notice may be served before a nuisance has in fact arisen, if the authority is satisfied that it is likely to occur.

Additionally, if a complaint of a statutory nuisance is made to a local authority by any person in its area, it must take all reasonably practicable steps to investigate that complaint.[72] Local authorities have extensive powers of entry to any premises at any reasonable time to ascertain whether or not a statutory nuisance exists, as set out in Schedule 3, paragraph 2. At least 24 hours notice must be given where entry is required to premises used wholly or mainly for residential purposes, except in an emergency. In appropriate cases, a magistrate's warrant may be obtained to enter premises, if necessary by force.[73]

If the Secretary of State considers that a local authority has failed to carry **17–021** out its duty to have its area inspected to detect statutory nuisances, he may declare the authority to be in default, and give it directions for the purpose of remedying the default. If the authority fails to comply with the directions as well, the Secretary of State may himself take over the relevant functions of the authority to which the direction related.[74]

Abatement notices and orders

Pursuant to Section 80 EPA, a local authority that has satisfied itself that a **17–022** statutory nuisance[75] either exists or is likely to occur or recur in its area must serve an abatement notice on "the person responsible" for the nuisance. If he cannot be found, or if the nuisance has not yet occurred, it is to be served on the owner or occupier of the relevant premises. Also, where the nuisance arises from any defect of a structural character, the notice is to be served on the owner of the premises. The "person responsible" is defined, as regards statutory nuisances not involving vehicles or machinery or equipment, as the person to whose act, default or sufferance the nuisance is attributable.[76] This can include a person who has acquired or gone into occupation of premises and who has allowed a pre-existing nuisance on them to continue.[77]

An abatement notice either requires the abatement of the nuisance or

---

[72] s.79(1).

[73] Sch.3, para.2(3).

[74] Sch.3, para.4.

[75] The special procedure for dealing with noise nuisances in the street is separate and was dealt with in the section above on s.79(1)(ga). This section is therefore concerned only with that appropriate to the other heads of statutory nuisance (in ss.79(1)(a) to (g), and (h).

[76] s.79(7).

[77] *Clayton v Sale U.D.C.*, [1926] 1 KB 415; cf. *Sedleigh-Denfield v O'Callaghan*, [1940] AC 880 as regards private nuisance. See also *Clydebank District Council v Monaville Estates Ltd*, 1982 SLT 2, as regards the corresponding provision applying in Scotland under the Public Health (Scotland) Act 1897, s.3, which defines the "author of a nuisance" as "the person through whose act or default the nuisance is caused, exists, or is continued, whether he be the owner or occupier or both".

prohibits or restricts its occurrence or recurrence; or alternatively requires the execution of such works, and the taking of such other steps, as may be necessary to abate or restrict the nuisance.[78] It must specify the time or times within which these requirements are to be complied with.[79]

There was a developing line of case law to the effect that an abatement notice which did not specify what works were to be done to abate the nuisance was defective.[80] The rationale for this was essentially that, as the penalty for non-compliance with an abatement notice is criminal, a notice needed to specify the steps to be taken so the recipient would know what was required in order to comply. However, more recent case law supports the proposition that the abatement notice does not need to specify what works are required—the nuisance must be abated, but it is up to the recipient of the notice to decide what method to use to achieve the abatement.[81] There are no specific provisions requiring consultation prior to service of an abatement notice although there could, in some circumstances, be a legitimate expectation that consultation will take place.[82]

17–023   Apart from the issue of abatement notices by local authorities, a separate procedure is available under section 82 to any individual aggrieved by a nuisance, who may make a complaint to the magistrates court seeking an abatement order. The proceedings are taken against the same person or persons as a notice would be served on, as set out above. Not less than 21 days notice must be given of the intention to bring them, specifying what is complained of. However, in the case of noise nuisances within head (g) or (ga) only three days notice is required.[83] If at the hearing of the complaint, it is proved that the alleged nuisance existed when the complaint was made, then the court must order the defendant(s) to pay the complainant his reasonable costs, whether or not at the date of the hearing the nuisance still exists or is likely to recur.

If more than one individual is affected by a nuisance, there would seem to be no need for multiple s.82 complaints. In *McCaw v City of Westminster Magistrates Court (D) and Middlesex SARL*,[84] the Claimant brought a s.82 complaint about the environmental effects caused by a property developer who had permission to develop a site adjacent to the multiple occupancy property in which she resided. The Claimant sought to add to her complaint a number of other potential complainants (most of whom lived in the

---

[78] s.80(1).

[79] ibid.

[80] For example, *Sterling Homes (Midlands) Limited v Birmingham City Council* [1995] Env. L.R. 121.

[81] *Falmouth & Truro Port Health Authority v South West Water Ltd* [2000] EWCA Civ 96, as followed in *Godfrey v Conwy District Council* (Divisional Court, Nov 13, 2000) [2001 Env. L.R. 38.

[82] See *R. v Falmouth and Truro Port Health Authority, ex p. South West Water Services* [2000] 3 All E.R. 306, [2000] 3 W.L.R. 1464 for discussion when a legitimate expectation to consult arises.

[83] s.82(7).

[84] [2008] EWHC 1504 (Admin).

property), but the district judge determined that the consequence of seeking to do so was to produce a complaint which was duplicitous and she was not entitled to add the other complainants in that one information.

Where more than one person is responsible for a nuisance, an abatement notice or proceedings for an order may be served on any one or more of them individually, whether or not what the person served is responsible for would by itself amount to a nuisance.[85]

To avoid duplication of controls over processes that are covered by Part I of the EPA or under regulation under the Pollution Prevention and Control Act 1999, no summary proceedings may be brought by a local authority in respect of a nuisance falling within any of heads (b), (d), (e) or (g) except with the consent of the Secretary of State, if proceedings in respect of it could be brought under the 1999 Act.[86] This does not prevent a person aggrieved applying for an abatement order in any such case, however. **17–024**

Abatement orders under section 82 may be made in respect of essentially the same matters and require much the same action as an abatement notice. However, since anticipatory action is not possible under that section an abatement order cannot prohibit the occurrence of a nuisance, as opposed to its recurrence. Further, there is no power to order that recurrence of a nuisance be merely restricted, as opposed to prohibiting it outright.[87] A further distinction between the two procedures is that the magistrates may, when making an abatement order, also impose a fine of up to £5,000. In contrast, with an abatement notice no penalties can be imposed unless the requirements of the notice are not observed.[88]

Appeals to the magistrates court

A person served with an abatement notice has a right of appeal to the magistrates court within the 21 days following the date of service. The appeals procedure is laid down by the Statutory Nuisance (Appeals) Regulations 1995,[89] and there is a further right of appeal from the magistrates to the Crown court at the instance of any party to the pro- **17–025**

---

[85] ss.81(1), 82(5).
[86] s.79(10).
[87] s.82(2).
[88] This power to fine was inserted in the course of the legislation through Parliament, so as to retain powers previously available under s.99 (taken with s.94) of the Public Health Act 1936, which were frequently relied on by those occupying rented property. Though compensation awards can be made following a conviction, they could not be made in respect of damage suffered earlier, even after the making of an abatement order. Criminal sanctions are in practice frequently more effective than the prospect of having to pay a comparatively modest award of compensation.
[89] SI 1995/2644.

ceedings.[90] The Regulations set out[91] an extensive list of grounds of appeal including:

- the abatement notice was not justified under the Act;
- there has been some material informality, defect or error in or in connection with the notice. If the Court is satisfied the defect or error is not material it may dismiss the appeal;
- the requirements of the notice are unreasonable or unnecessary, or the authority has unreasonably refused to accept alternative requirements;
- times for compliance are not reasonably sufficient;
- in circumstances where use of best practicable means[92] is a legitimate defence, that such means were used to prevent or counteract the effects of the nuisance;
- in cases dealing with noise from vehicles, machinery or equipment then the requirements are more onerous than notices or consents given under other legislation;
- the notice should have been served on someone else;
- the notice might lawfully have been served on someone else instead of or in addition to the appellant, and it would have been equitable to do so. (In this case the appellant must serve a copy of the notice of appeal on the other person or persons referred to.)

The court hearing the appeal may allow it and quash the abatement notice or dismiss it; it may also vary the notice in such a manner as it thinks fit.[93] The court may also, in its discretion, determine who should carry out any work or contribute to its cost, and the proportions in which any recoverable expenses are to be shared between the appellant and anyone else. In making any such determination as between an owner and an occupier, the court must have regard to the terms and conditions of any relevant tenancy, and the nature of the works concerned; it must also be satisfied that any person that it makes subject to any requirement has received a copy of the notice of appeal.

An appeal does not automatically result in an abatement notice being suspended, but it will ordinarily have that effect where compliance with it would require expenditure to be incurred on carrying out any works before the hearing of the appeal (whether by the appellant or anyone else) or in the case of a noise nuisance under s.79(1)(g) or (ga) where the noise is caused in the course of the performance of some duty imposed by law on the appellant.[94] However, suspension of the notice may be over-ridden if the

[90] Sch.3, para.1(3).
[91] In reg.2(2).
[92] The defence of best practicable means is discussed in greater detail below at paras 17–029 and 17–030.
[93] reg.2(5).
[94] reg.3(1).

local authority certifies in the abatement notice that the nuisance concerned is injurious to health, or is likely to be of so short a duration that suspension of the notice would mean that it had no practical effect, or if the expenditure that would be incurred before any appeal has been decided would not be disproportionate to the public benefit to be expected in that period from compliance with the notice in the meantime.[95]

There are no provisions for paying any compensation to the appellant **17–026** where the appeal succeeds, notwithstanding the fact that he may have suffered damage by being required to comply with the terms of the abatement notice.

Failure to comply with abatement notices and orders

Failure to comply with an abatement notice within the prescribed time is **17–027** an offence, subject to a maximum fine on summary conviction of £5000 with daily fines of up to £500 for so long as the non-compliance continues after conviction, save that where the non-compliance relates to action required on industrial, trade or business premises, the maximum fine is £20,000 (in this case, there is no provision for daily penalties in addition).[96] In the case of a failure to comply with an abatement order, no such distinction is made, and the maximum penalties are £5000 and daily fines of £500.

Where the local authority considers that taking proceedings against a person who has failed to comply with an abatement notice would not provide an adequate remedy to the nuisance, it may take proceedings in the High Court for an appropriate injunction to abate, prohibit or restrict the nuisance.[97] Additionally, if an abatement notice has not been complied with, the local authority may itself abate the nuisance and do whatever may be necessary to secure extension of the notice,[98] whether or not it also takes proceedings for the non-compliance.

However, even if an abatement notice has been served the local authority is not obliged to take action to enforce the notice. In these circumstances the section 82 procedure is still available to aggrieved individuals, and there does not appear to be a prohibition on individuals commencing a prosecution for any non-compliance with the local authority's abatement notice.

Unless otherwise stated, an abatement notice or order is of unlimited **17–028** duration. Thus, where a person who was served with a notice in respect of a noise nuisance, prohibiting its recurrence, created a further noise nuisance

---

[95] reg.3(2), (3).
[96] s.80(5), (6).
[97] s.81(5). This is subject to s.81(6) which provides a defence in High Court proceedings in relation to a noise nuisance that the noise was authorised by a notice under COPA, s.60 or a s.61 consent.
[98] s.81(3). The abatement procedure is discussed in greater detail below at paras 17–032 to 17–035.

some three years later, he was convicted of breaching the original notice.[99]

In practice, there will often be discussions with the local authority following service of the abatement notice although there are no specific provisions requiring consultation prior to service. In some cases, it may be felt appropriate for the local authority to withdraw the notice or to vary the notice so that the notice is in a form with which the recipient agrees. However, there is no specific power in Part III to withdraw or vary a notice. In *R v Bristol City Council, ex p. Everett*[100] the Court of Appeal upheld the High Court's decision that there is an implied power for a local authority to withdraw an abatement notice, although the matter has not been tested in the context of a judicial review action of a decision to withdraw.[101]

Defence of "best practicable means"

17–029   In certain scenarios it is a defence to an abatement notice, and to any proceedings for an abatement order, to prove that "best practicable means"[102] were used to prevent, or to counteract the effects of, the nuisance.[103] The drafting of this head of defence is somewhat convoluted, but the effect is that the use of best practicable means may be pleaded as a defence in the following circumstances:

    (i) where any of the following nuisances arise on industrial, trade or business premises[104]

- any premises in such a state,
- any dust, steam, smell or other effluvia,
- any accumulation or deposit,
- any animal kept in such a place or manner,
- any insects emanating from premises,
- noise emitted from premises.

---

[99] *Wellingborough District Council v Gordon*, [1991] JPL 874; also *R. v Birmingham Justices, ex p. Guppy* (1988) 152 J.P. 159. It was held by the House of Lords that a notice served under the corresponding provision of COPA, namely section 58, remains in effect notwithstanding the repeal of that section, and despite the absence of transitional provisions in Part III of the EPA, *Aitken v South Hams District Council*, (1995) 1 AC 262; (1994) 3 W.L.R. 333.

[100] [1999] 2 All E.R. 193 CA.

[101] [1999] 1 W.L.R. 92; [1999] 2 All E.R. 193.

[102] The term "best practicable means" has a long statutory history, appearing in both the Alkali Act 1874 and the Public Health Act 1875. It was a requirement under the air pollution provisions of the HSWA 1974 to use the best practicable means for "preventing the emission into the atmosphere from premises of noxious or offensive substances, and for rendering harmless and inoffensive such substances as may be so emitted".

[103] s.80(7), (8) and 82(9), (10).

[104] In other words, in the case of a nuisance falling within s.79(1)(a), (d), (e), (f), (fa) or (g), where any of the following nuisances arise on industrial, trade or business premises.

(ii) in the case of a nuisance relating to artificial light, where the light is emitted from industrial, trade or business premises or is emitted for the purpose only of illuminating an outdoor sports facility;

(iii) where noise is emitted from or caused by a vehicle, machinery or equipment in a street, if the vehicle, machinery or equipment is being used for industrial, trade or business purposes.

(iv) where smoke is emitted from premises, but only where it is from a chimney.[105]

The use of best practicable means is not available as a defence in relation to head (c) "fumes or gases emitted from premises (in fact private dwellings), nor is it necessarily so in relation to head (h) "any other matter declared by any enactment to be a statutory nuisance". Additionally it is not available as a defence in proceedings for an abatement order where the nuisance is such as to render the premises unfit for human habitation.[106] There is no corresponding provision to this last item in relation to abatement notices—it may be seen as aimed particularly at housing departments of local authorities.

The expression is required[107] to be interpreted by reference to the following provisions:

(a) *"practicable" means reasonably practicable having regard among other things to local conditions and circumstances, to the current state of technical knowledge and to the financial implications.* This is clearly a relatively wide provision, which leaves much to the discretion of the court.

(b) *the means to be employed include the design, installation, maintenance and manner and periods of operation of plant and machinery, and the design, construction and maintenance of buildings and structures.* Hence someone who seeks to rely on the defence of best practicable means faces this wide view of the "means" by which he may be expected to use to avoid or mitigate a nuisance. Hence for example using the quietest machinery on the market might not be sufficient if it is used in a manner and at a time which is not reasonable; conversely, using out-dated and loud machinery might be unreasonable even if used at a reasonable time.

(c) *the test is to apply only so far as compatible with any duty imposed by law.* In other words, the best practicable means defence cannot require an failure to comply with a duty—for example, to have an audible alarm when reversing certain vehicles.

(d) *the test is to apply only so far as compatible with safety and safe working conditions, and with the exigencies of any emergency or unforeseeable*

---

[105] In many circumstances smoke emitted from a chimney will not come under this head of nuisance at all—see para.23–006.

[106] s.82(10)(d).

[107] By s.79(9).

circumstances. This stands to reason: avoiding a statutory nuisance has no net benefit if people's safety is thereby endangered.

Furthermore, in circumstances where a code of practice under section 71 of COPA (noise minimisation) is applicable, regard shall also be had to guidance given in it.

17–030   What constitutes best practicable means is very specific to each particular case, and it is difficult to make generalisations. It does appear, however, that best practicable means does not extend to completely ceasing operations at a particular location.[108] In the 1999 case of *Manley v New Forest DC*,[109] one of the questions on appeal by way of case stated was whether the Court was right to decide that "best practicable means" included moving the Kennels to a non-residential location. Newman J. found that "best practicable means" does not include the relocation of the business involved. He further noted:

> "An important feature of the doctrine or concept has always been that it allowed for flexibility to cater for local and individual circumstances. There are distinctive aspects of the law of nuisance: private nuisance, public nuisance and now, as one sees in this Act, statutory nuisance. Proof of private or public nuisance will generally lead to the cessation of the nuisance, but the provisions of the 1990 Act are penal and they give rise to criminal proceedings in the event that a notice is not complied with. They affect the way in which a permitted lawful business is being carried on. Parliament plainly thought it right to give the operator of a business the benefit of the principle of "best practicable means", otherwise, in my judgment, it would be obvious that great hardship could be caused to businesses with the threat of penal consequences in summary proceedings in the Magistrates' Court."

However, where a defendant resisted the service of an abatement notice the burden was upon the defendant to demonstrate that at the time of the abatement notice he was doing something and that those were the best practicable means to prevent the noise. In later litigation involving the same Howling Dog Kennels, Moses L.J. observed that because Mrs Manley had done nothing to prevent or counteract the nuisance, it did not avail her to complain that the suggestions advanced by the local authority were impracticable.

> "The boot was on quite the other foot. It was for her to demonstrate that she was doing something, and that those were the best practicable means ... she had done nothing, the only way she could succeed in having the abatement notice set aside was to show that nothing could be done."

---

[108] [1999] 4 P.L.R. 36. It was held that the Crown Court had failed to consider whether the appellants could have been said to have used their best practical means if they had reduced the number of dogs at the premises rather than relocating the business entirely.
[109] [1999] EWHC Admin 752.

In that case, it was clear that things could be done to reduce the noise of the dogs, therefore there was no possibility of her demonstrating that the best practicable means had been used.[110]

Defence of reasonable excuse

There is also a general defence of "reasonable excuse" for failure to comply with an abatement notice or order.[111] There is relatively little judicial authority on the applicability of this defence, save that it does not overlap with the statutory defence of using best practicable means,[112] nor does it extend to lack of money to carry out works.[113] The excuse is most likely to be available in connection with procedural matters, such as where the person served with a notice is for some reason physically incapacitated from complying with it or appealing against it (at least if there would have been good grounds for appealing), and possibly where there has been a genuine misunderstanding as to what was required, especially if brought about by officers of the local authority. Avoidable inadequacies in the apparatus or the management of the defendant are therefore unlikely to amount to a reasonable excuse.   **17–031**

Some guidance may be gleaned from *Wellingborough Borough Council v Gordon*,[114] where Taylor L.J. approved the view that:

"...the defence of reasonable excuse is not available to a defendant who contravenes the notice deliberately and intentionally in circumstances wholly under his control. It would have been available, however, if the contravention occurred in an emergency or in circumstances beyond his control. If for example, a man devoted to DIY had made a habit of hammering through the night and notice was served prohibiting noise nuisance of that kind, he could plead reasonable excuse if a window had broken during the night in a storm and, to exclude the elements, he hammered some boarding into position."

Abatement

Where an abatement notice has not been complied with, the local authority has full powers to abate the nuisance itself and to do whatever may be necessary to give effect to its abatement notice, quite independently of whether or not it takes proceedings for the non-compliance.[115] Similarly,   **17–032**

---

[110] *Manley and Another v New Forest District Council* [2007] EWHC 3188 (Admin); (2008) Env. L.R. 26.
[111] ss.80(4), 82(8).
[112] *A. Lambert Flat Management Company v Lomas*, [1981] 2 All E.R. 280.
[113] *Saddleworth Urban District Council v Aggregate and Sand* (1970) 114 SJ 931.
[114] [1993] Env. L.R. 218.
[115] s.81(3).

where a person subject to an abatement order has been convicted of contravening it, the magistrates court may direct the relevant local authority, having first given it an opportunity to be heard, to do anything which the person convicted was required to do by the order.[116] The court may also direct the local authority to do anything which the court might have ordered the person responsible for a nuisance to do, where neither he nor the owner or occupier of the relevant premises can be found,[117] subject to the authority's right to be heard before such a direction is made. In neither of these cases is the authority given any right of recourse against the person responsible for the nuisance to recover its costs.

In exercise of its powers, a local authority may authorise any person to enter any premises at any reasonable time, both to ascertain whether or not a statutory nuisance exists and also for the purpose of taking any action authorised for the purpose of abating a statutory nuisance.[118] Seizure of equipment may be the only practicable way of securing immediate abatement of the nuisance in some cases of noise nuisance—such a step is likely therefore to be justified under EPA s.81(3). Nevertheless, the step can only be taken where an abatement notice has already been served and not complied with.

However, except in an emergency entry to premises used wholly or mainly for residential purposes cannot be demanded as of right without having given 24 hours prior notice to the occupier.[119] An emergency for these purposes is

"a case where the person requiring entry has reasonable cause to believe that circumstances exist which are likely to endanger life or health, *and* that immediate entry is necessary to verify the existence of those circumstances or to ascertain their cause and to effect a remedy".[120]

The second limb of the definition requires immediate entry to be necessary either to find out what is happening or to effect a remedy. In some cases, for example temporarily unoccupied residential premises containing abandoned animals or rotting material attracting pests or creating offensive smells, the need for immediate entry may be very real. However, in the difficult case of neighbourhood noise nuisance, it will be all too clear what is the case, and it may well be impossible to persuade a court that immediate entry is necessary to effect a remedy, except possibly after a series of repeated failures to respond to other legal sanctions.

17–033   In the case of an abatement notice, where an authority has undertaken the appropriate work itself, its reasonable expenses incurred in abating or preventing the recurrence of the nuisance may be recovered from the

---

[116] s.82(11).
[117] s.82(13).
[118] EPA, Sch.3, para.2(1).
[119] EPA, Sch.3, para.2(2).
[120] EPA, Sch.3, para.2(7).

person by whose act or default the nuisance was caused.[121] The person liable to be charged is not necessarily the "person responsible", in that the latter expression includes a person to whose "sufferance" the nuisance is attributable. There will however be few circumstances in which a person may be said to have suffered or permitted a nuisance to be caused, but where he was not also in default in failing to make sure it did not happen. Where the person to be charged with the expenses is the owner of premises, and there is more than one owner, any one or more of them may be held liable. Further, where there are two or more persons whose acts or defaults cause the nuisance, the court may apportion the expenses between them as it thinks fair and reasonable.

For the purposes of these provisions, a definition of "owner" has been inserted into the EPA,[122] whereby it means, in relation to any premises:

"A person (other than a mortgagee not in possession) who, whether in his own right or as trustee for any other person, is entitled to receive the rack rent of the premises or, where the premises are not let at a rack rent, would be so entitled if they were so let."[123]

"Premises" for this purpose does not include a vessel. Liabilities under these provisions may also affect a superior landlord whose immediate tenant, having sub-let the premises, is in arrears—if notice is given for rent to be paid by the under tenant direct to the superior landlord under section 6 of the Law of Distress (Amendment) Act 1908, the latter will become the owner and liable accordingly.

There is no definition of "occupier" in the statute. In *Southern Water* **17–034** *Authority v Nature Conservancy Council* [1992] 1 W.L.R. 775, where one issue was whether the water authority, which was temporarily present on land to carry out drainage work, was an occupier for the purposes of the Wildlife and Countryside Act 1981, Lord Mustill observed:[124]

"No useful progress can be made ... by looking up in dictionaries the words 'occupy' and 'occupier' or by inquiring what meaning the Courts have given to them in reported cases, for they draw their meaning entirely from the purpose for which and the context in which they are used."

He noted that the term even has different meanings in different Parts of that one Act. Nevertheless he considered that, in view of the juxtaposition of "occupier" with "owner" in the provision in question, the occupier was for that purpose "someone who, although lacking the title of an owner, nevertheless stands in a comprehensive and stable relationship with the

---

[121] s.81(4).
[122] By the Noise and Statutory Nuisance Act 1993.
[123] s.81A(9).
[124] [1992] 1 W.L.R., at 781; [1992] 3 All E.R. at 487.

land as to be, in company with the actual owner, someone to whom the [relevant mechanisms of the 1981 Act] can sensibly be made to apply."

A similar relationship is, it is suggested, appropriate if a person is to be an "occupier" for the purposes of Part III of the EPA. This would nevertheless be likely to bring within the term a receiver who, although acting as agent for a company, has the power to manage and control it even though the directors have not been removed.[125] It is this quality of control, in addition to a mere right to be present, that is generally necessary to be an "occupier", though it need not be exclusive.[126]

Where expenses are recoverable from an owner, the local authority may create a charge on the relevant premises for the expenses concerned and accrued interest.[127] To create this charge, the authority must serve a notice on the owner of the premises, and also copies of it on every other person who to the knowledge of the authority has an interest in the premises who may be affected by the charge.[128] The charge takes effect after 21 days from the date of service of the notice, save that if there is an appeal by either the owner or anyone served with a copy of the notice, the charge does not come into effect until the appeal is finally determined. Once it has come into effect, the charge continues until the expenses and accrued interest are recovered. Anyone served with such a notice or with a copy of it may appeal against it to the county court within 21 days; the court may confirm the notice or quash it, or vary the amount specified in it.[129]

17–035 In a case involving premises that were due to be demolished quite shortly,[130] the position of the justices from whom an abatement order was sought was stated as follows:

"Once they were satisfied that the house constituted a statutory nuisance they were bound to make a nuisance order under section 24 [of the PHA 1936] but they have within the framework of this section a considerable tolerance as regards the precise terms which the nuisance order shall take. It must be directed, of course, to the abatement of the nuisance, that is the purpose of the order, but the section makes it clear that the justices have a discretion as to whether to require the owner to do the whole of that work referred to in the abatement notice as opposed to only part of it. Further the section expressly gives a discretion in regard to the time within which the work has to be done, and in my judgment would certainly enable the justices to divide the work into phases or pro-

[125] *Meigh v Wickenden*, [1942] 2 KB 160.
[126] *Wheat v E. Lacon & Co. Ltd.*, [1966] A.C. 522; [1966] 2 W.L.R. 581; [1966] 1 All E.R. 582.
[127] s.81(A), inserted by the Noise and Statutory Nuisance Act 1993, reinstating provisions of the PHA 1936, s.291.
[128] s.81A(3).
[129] s.81A(6), (7).
[130] *Nottingham City District Council v Newton* [1974] 1 W.L.R. 923; [1974] 2 All E.R. 760 (sub nom. *Nottingham Corporation v Newton*).

grammes requiring some to be done quickly and others to be done at a later time ... In deciding within that wide ambit of detailed discretion just what the terms of the nuisance order should be, I have no doubt it is the duty of the justices, as common sense dictates, to look at the whole circumstances of the case and to try and make an order which is in its terms sensible and just having regard to the entire prevailing situation."[131]

The guidance that justices should use discretion and common sense was endorsed by Lord Wilberforce in *Salford City Council v McNally*.[132] In *London Borough of Southwark v Ince*,[133] Woolf L.J. referred to *McNally* and added that

"The obligations which local authorities have to their tenants in general and the extent of their resources are in my view proper considerations to be taken into account in following the guidance given by Lord Wilberforce as to the contents of an abatement notice."[134]

Expenses due to a local authority under these provisions from a person who is the owner of the relevant premises may carry interest, to be calculated at such reasonable rate as the authority may determine, and, with the accrued interest, be the subject of a charge on the premises.[135] To have this effect, the authority must serve notice on the owner specifying the expenses claimed, stating that these with accrued interest shall be a charge on the premises, and setting out the entitlement of the owner to appeal against the notice. The authority must also serve a copy of the notice on every other person who it knows to have an interest in the premises capable of being affected by the charge. The charge takes effect after 21 days from the date of service of the notice; the person served with the notice or with any copy of it has the same period within which to appeal against it. In the event of an appeal, the charge does not take effect until its determination. An appeal is made to the county court, which may confirm the notice as it stands, vary the amount specified in it, or quash the notice.

A local authority seeking to enforce a charge so made has the same powers and remedies as if it were a mortgagee by deed having powers of sale and lease, of accepting surrenders of leases and of appointing a receiver.[136]

Where expenses have been made subject to a charge on premises in this manner, the authority may by order declare them to be payable, with interest, by instalments within such a period of up to 30 years as may be

---

[131] Per Lord Widgery C.J.
[132] [1976] AC 379.
[133] (1989) 21 HLR 504.
[134] 1 (1989) 21 HLR 5. See also *Cunningham v Birmingham City Council* [1997] EWHC Admin 440.
[135] s.81A, inserted by the Noise and Statutory Nuisance Act 1993.
[136] s.81A(8).

specified in the order.[137] These instalments may be recovered from the owner or occupier for the time being of the premises, though where they are recovered from an occupier paying rent for them, he may deduct them from that rent.[138] Further, an occupier is not to be required to pay at any one time more than the rent due to his landlord. It follows that where premises are subject to such a charge, and the owner has leased them to someone who has in turn sublet them to an occupier subject to these provisions, while the occupier has the statutory right to make deductions from the rent payable by him, there is no corresponding statutory right benefiting the landlord leasing the premises from the owner, who must therefore ensure he is appropriately covered by contractual stipulations.

Other Statutory Frameworks Relating to Nuisance and Noise

Noise abatement zones

17–036   Under sections 63 to 67 of COPA, there is provision for local authorities to specify an acceptable level of noise and to declare noise abatement zones.[139] These provisions allow a local authority to designate by order an area as a noise abatement zone. That order will specify the classes of premises to which the noise abatement controls are to apply. These classes should be specified broadly by function, e.g. industrial premises, places of entertainment of assembly, transport installations etc. It is not recommended that domestic premises are classified, since the numbers involved would make enforcement impracticable, and in any event control from domestic premises is more suitably dealt with as a statutory nuisance (or indeed in civil proceedings).[140]

Where an order has been made, the then current levels of the noise from the specified classes of premises in the zone must be measured. These noise measurements are entered in a register of noise levels, and will form the reference levels against which noise from the same premises will be judged

---

[137] s.81B(1).

[138] s.81B(4).

[139] A survey conducted for the Department of the Environment in 1993 concluded that noise abatement zones had failed to meet their objectives and had fallen into virtual disuse. This followed a report by the Noise Review Working Party in 1990 that they were proving difficult to operate. The system is nevertheless in place and being operated by a few local authorities and therefore requires some description here. A DEFRA survey of local authorities' practices regarding noise published in 2008 as part of its Noise Climate Assessment, found that there are at least 45 Noise Abatement Zones (present in about 9 per cent of authorities), but noted that it is unclear if all are actively used or pending de-commissioning. [*http://www.defra.gov.uk/environment/noise/research/climate/chapn4.htm*].

[140] Extensive detailed guidance on the use of the noise abatement zone powers under COPA is set out in Appendix 2 to DoE Circular 2/76 (WO 3/76) "Control of Pollution Act 1974. Implementation of Part III—Noise".

thereafter. The measurement and registration of noise levels are subject to the Control of Noise (Measurement and Registers) Regulations 1976.[141]

It is an offence to emit noise exceeding the noise level as recorded in the register[142] except with the local authority's consent (for example to allow excess noise to be made at certain times of day), or to breach any condition attached to a consent. The grant of a consent will provide a defence in proceedings brought by a local authority for a statutory nuisance under EPA, s.79(1)(g), relating to noise; this defence is not available however in proceedings for a statutory nuisance abatement order under EPA, s.82.[143]

Local authorities also have the power[144] to issue noise reduction notices   **17–037** on the person responsible for any noise where a reduction in that level is practicable at reasonable cost, and would afford a public benefit.[145] The effect of a noise reduction notice is as though the level as recorded in the register has been reduced to the prescribed figure in the noise abatement zone.

Appeals may be made against an initial entry in a noise level register, against a refusal to allow a registered noise level to be exceeded, against a noise reduction notice, and against a determination of the noise level from a new or converted building. Appeals against a noise reduction notice are made to the magistrates' court; all other appeals are made to the Secretary of State. These latter will normally be dealt with in writing, though a public local inquiry can be held if thought appropriate.

Noise Act 1996

The Noise Act 1996, as amended by the Clean Neighbourhoods and   **17–038** Environment Act 2005, provides for speedy action by local authorities in relation to night time noise by creating a summary procedure for dealing with noise from domestic premises based on absolute noise levels.

Under s.2, local authorities must take reasonable steps to investigate a complaint from a person present in a dwelling between the hours of 11pm and 7am that excessive noise is coming from another dwelling or licensed premises. If after investigation, the council officer is satisfied that noise would or might exceed the permitted level set by the Secretary of State under s.5, he may serve a warning notice against the person wholly or partly responsible for the noise.[146] If the noise exceeds the permitted level, as measured from the complainant's dwelling, during the rest of the night[147] that person may be guilty of an offence. Any such offence may be

---

[141] SI 1976/37.
[142] s.65(1).
[143] EPA, s.80(9), COPA, s.65(8).
[144] By s.66.
[145] s.66(1).
[146] s.2(4).
[147] s.3(2): no earlier than 10 minutes after the service of the notice to 7am.

dealt with by way of a fixed penalty notice rather than prosecution.[148] Furthermore, if the council officer has reason to believe that the noise has exceeded the permitted level after a warning notice has been given, the council officer has power under section 10 to enter the dwelling or other premises from which the noise in question is being or has been emitted and may seize and remove any equipment which it appears to him is being or has been used in the emission of the noise.

Control of Pollution Act 1974 on loudspeakers and street noise

17-039   There are additional specific restrictions on the use of loudspeakers on the street contained in COPA. A loudspeaker may only be operated in a street to the extent permitted by section 62 of COPA, as amended by section 7 of the Noise and Statutory Nuisance Act 1993. For this purpose "street" means a highway and any other road, footway, square or court which is for the time being open to the public.[149] Subject to exceptions set out in sections 62(2), (3) and (3A), loudspeakers may not be used for any purpose between 9pm and 8am,[150] nor at any other time for the purpose of advertising any entertainment, trade or business. Nevertheless, a loudspeaker can be used between noon and 7pm where it is fixed to a vehicle used for conveying perishable commodities and is solely operated to inform the public (otherwise than by means of words) that the commodity is on sale from the vehicle, and provided it is operated so as not to give reasonable cause for annoyance. This exemption is principally designed to allow the use of chimes on ice-cream vans. Detailed guidance on the operation of such chimes is contained in the "Code of Practice on Noise from Ice-Cream Van Chimes etc." (1982) issued by the Secretary of State under COPA, section 71.[151]

Exemptions from the general prohibition of section 62(1) allow public authorities, including the police, fire brigade and ambulance services, to operate without this restraint, and also anyone else in case of emergency.[152] Car radios are also exempted, provided they are "so operated as not to give reasonable cause for annoyance to persons in the vicinity".

A number of additional controls over noise in the streets under COPA have been introduced by the Noise and Statutory Nuisance Act 1993.[153] This generally tightens the controls, but at the same time makes them more flexible and capable of modification at the discretion of the local authority.

[148] s.8.
[149] s.62(1).
[150] s.62(1)(a). These times may be amended by the Secretary of State by order under s.62(1A) but not so as to include any time between 9pm and 8am.
[151] Approval for its issue being given under the Control of Noise (Code of Practice on Noise from Ice-Cream Van Chimes etc.) Order 1981, SI 1981/1828.
[152] s.62(2).
[153] With effect from January 5, 1994.

Accordingly, local authority consent may be given to any use of a loud-speaker that would otherwise be in contravention of section 62(1) of COPA, provided it is not for the purpose of advertising any entertainment, trade or business. This additional flexibility is only available to local authorities that have passed a resolution to the effect that Schedule 2 to the Act is to apply to its area. Any such resolution must be published in a local newspaper, and once the provisions of the Schedule have come into effect[154] any person may apply for a consent; the authority must determine any such application within 21 days.

Control of Pollution Act 1974 on construction site noise

Construction sites are inherently liable to create noise nuisance. While this   **17–040**
can be mitigated to some extent by the use of appropriate muffling of equipment, and by requiring the equipment to comply with specific noise emission standards, construction work in built up areas will almost always be inconvenient for neighbours, and often may cause them serious disturbance. Nevertheless, it has been held that if the building work is carried out legitimately and reasonably, with all reasonable and proper steps being taken to ensure that no undue inconvenience is caused to neighbours, then no cause of action in private nuisance will arise at the instance of those neighbours.[155]

Sections 60 and 61 of COPA provide for controls to be imposed on those carrying out construction and demolition work and on any others who may be in control of it or otherwise responsible for it, and also for consents to such work being conducted under prescribed conditions. The types of construction work that the provisions apply to are set out in section 60(1) of COPA, and include demolition and dredging works. Where any construction works are being or going to be carried out, the local authority may serve a "section 60 notice" on the person who appears to be carrying out or about to do so, and also on any other persons that appear to the authority to be responsible for or to have control over the works. Section 60 is essentially permissive, therefore, in contrast with the duty on local authorities to take action in respect of noise amounting to a statutory nuisance. The section 60 notice will impose requirements on now the works are to be carried out, including specifying, for example, the plant or machinery which may or may not be used, the hours of working, and noise levels that may be emitted either generally or at any specified point on the premises or at particular times. The notice must be limited to specific identifiable works in contemplation at the time of the notice, and may not extend to other uncontemplated works at the same premises for which a fresh notice

---

[154] Which must be at least one month after the date of the resolution, s.8(2).
[155] *Andreae v Selfridge & Co Ltd*, [1938] 1 Ch 1 CA.

should be issued if necessary.[156] Where a section 60 notice has been served and is complied with, then that will constitute a defence to any proceedings brought by a local authority under EPA, section 80 or 81 in respect of a statutory nuisance—though not in proceedings brought under EPA, section 82, by persons aggrieved by the existence of a statutory nuisance.

In specifying any particular methods or plant or machinery, the authority must have regard to whether any other methods, plant or machinery would be substantially as effective in minimising noise and more acceptable to those subject to the requirements of the notice.[157] The authority must also have regard to the relevant provisions of any code of practice that may have been issued and approved under section 71 of COPA. The current code in this connection is that approved under the Control of Noise (Codes of Practice for Construction and Open Sites) (England) Order 2002,[158] i.e. British Standard BS 5228. The authority must further have regard to the need for ensuring that best practicable means are employed to minimise noise.[159] Finally, the authority must, in exercising its powers under section 60 have regard to the need to protect any persons in the locality of the construction site from the effects of noise.[160] An HSE publication "Noise in Construction" provides guidance for workers and employers on limiting the effects of noise in the construction industry.

17–041   Any person served with a section 60 notice may appeal against it within 21 days from the date of service. The grounds of appeal and the applicable procedure are contained in the Control of Noise (Appeals) Regulations 1975[161] ("the Appeals Regulations"). The grounds of appeal may include any of the following:[162]

(a) Section 60 does not justify the service of the notice;

(b) There has been some informality, defect or error in the notice;

(c) The authority has refused unreasonably to accept compliance with alternative requirements, or that the requirements with the notice are otherwise unreasonable in character or extent, or are unnecessary;

(d) The time or times given for compliance with the notice is or are not reasonably sufficient;

(e) Notice should not have been served on the appellant but on someone else instead who is carrying out or going to carry out the works

---

[156] *Walter Lilly & Co Ltd v Westminster City Council*, (1994) *The Times*, March 1, 1994.
[157] s.60(4)(c).
[158] SI 2002/461.
[159] For the purposes of these sections in COPA, the relevant definition of best practicable means appears in COPA, s.72. This definition is to all intents and purposes the same as that contained in EPA, s.79(9) (discussed above), which applies to the statutory nuisance provisions in the EPA.
[160] s.60(4).
[161] SI 1975/2116.
[162] reg.5.

or who is responsible for or who has control over the carrying out of the works;

(f) The notice might lawfully have been served not only on the appellant but also on someone else falling with category (e) above, and it would have been equitable for it to have been served on this other person;

(g) The authority has not had regard to some or all of the requirements of section 60(4) (i.e. the Code of Practice, the use of best practicable means, the specifying of other methods plant or machinery that is substantially as effective, and the need to protect persons in the locality).

Where an appeal is based on ground (e) or (f), the appellant must serve a copy for his appeal on the other person referred to. Appeals are made to the local magistrates' court, who may quash the notice the subject of the appeal, vary it or dismiss the appeal.

Where an appeal is made against a section 60 notice, its effect will be suspended until the appeal has been abandoned or determined either (a) if the noise concerned is caused in the course of the performance or some duty imposed by law on the appellant, or (b) if compliance with the notice would require expenditure on the carrying out of any works before the hearing of the appeal.[163] Nevertheless, if in the opinion of the local authority the noise concerned is injurious to health or is likely to last for so short a time that suspension of the notice would make it ineffective in practice, or if the authority considers that the expenditure that would be incurred before determination of any appeal would not be disproportionate to the public benefit from compliance in the meantime, the notice may (and in practice nearly always does) include a statement that is to have effect notwithstanding any appeal.[164] There are no provisions for paying any compensation to the appellant where the appeal succeeds, notwithstanding that he may have been damaged by being required to comply with the terms of the notice.

It was held in *Johnsons News of London Limited v Ealing London Borough Council*[165] (which was concerned with an action for statutory nuisance, but the reasoning of the case is equally applicable to a section 60 notice) that since the statutory provision in issue was administrative and not criminal in nature, the objective of the court should be to seek to secure appropriate conduct and was not to punish wrong-doing. Accordingly, the fact that the service of the notice may have been fully justified as at the date of service is therefore not material, if the appellant has since taken suitable measures to respond to it. Hence, on the hearing of an appeal against a section 60 notice, the magistrates' court should confine its consideration to the

---

[163] The Control of Noise (Appeals) Regulations 1975 reg.10(1).
[164] reg.10(2).
[165] *The Times*, July 26, 1989. Also *Coventry City Corporation v Doyle* [1981] 1 W.L.R. 1325.

situation, including the likelihood of recurrence of any noise nuisance, as it exists at the time of the hearing of the appeal.

17–042   The fact that a local authority may have served a notice under section 60 does not create a defence against proceedings for an injunction to restrain a nuisance, notwithstanding compliance with the conditions of the section 60 notice. In *Lloyds Bank v Guardian Assurance Plc and another*,[166] the plaintiff obtained an injunction against the defendants which prohibited the use of certain drills and other tools during working hours on weekdays. At substantially the same time, the local authority served a section 60 notice prohibiting work within time limits that were somewhat narrower. On appeal against the injunction, the Court of Appeal held that the jurisdiction of the court in the tort proceedings was not ousted by section 60. In the case in point, the difference between the terms of the injunction and the section 60 notice were comparatively narrow, but in principle a court might impose a prohibition on working a construction site at night time so as to protect local residents, while the local authority might see fit, as in the case just referred to, to prohibit operations during working hours so as to protect local business interests. In such a situation, it would appear that both sets of controls might operate simultaneously, effectively making it impossible to carry out any construction work at all. This situation could also arise where a person has sought relief for a statutory nuisance under EPA, section 82, where the existence of a section 60 notice is not relevant.

Breach of the requirements of a section 60 notice is an offence that is triable summarily, and subject to a maximum fine of £5,000 with a possible further daily fine in respect of each day on which the offence continues after the conviction.[167] The costs to a construction company in not meeting a contractual deadline or, for that matter, in remaining any longer on a site than is reasonably necessary, particularly when there is other work to be done, are often many times the size of the fine that it may be subject to for not complying with a section 60 notice served on it, so that the deterrent effect of a fine on the company may be largely lost.

In *City of London Corporation v Bovis Construction Ltd*,[168] a section 60 notice had been served requiring operations causing noise outside the boundaries of the construction site to be limited to 8am to 6pm on weekdays, 8am to 1pm on Saturdays, with no such operations being permitted on Sundays and bank holidays. (Minor exceptions were permitted of no direct relevance to the case). Informations were laid against the contractors for contravention of the section 60 notice without reasonable excuse. The hearing was adjourned on several occasions, and meanwhile the contractors continued to contravene the terms of the notice. The local authority issued a writ for an injunction under section 222 of the Local

---

[166] CA, October 17,1986, unreported.
[167] s.74(1).
[168] CA, [1992] 3 All E.R. 697.

Government Act 1972, and an interlocutory injunction was granted. The contractors appealed on the ground that an injunction should not be granted to prevent a breach of the criminal law unless it had been established both that the person restrained not only had committed an offence but also was deliberately and flagrantly flouting the law, and that the criminal law provided an inadequate remedy. The grounds of the appeal were based on speeches by Lord Templeman and Lord Fraser of Tullybelton in *Stoke-on-Trent City Council v B & Q Retail Limited*,[169] which was concerned with unlawful Sunday trading. The Court of Appeal held unanimously that civil proceedings for an injunction could be resorted to in other circumstances than those contended for by the contractors. Bingham L.J. held that the guiding principles must be:

i. that the jurisdiction to grant an injunction is to be invoked and exercised exceptionally and with great caution;
ii. there must certainly be something more than mere infringement of the criminal law before the assistance of civil proceedings can be invoked and accorded for the protection or promotion of the interests of the inhabitants of the area;
iii. the essential foundation for the exercise of the court's discretion to grant an injunction is not that the offender is deliberately and flagrantly flouting the law, but the need to draw the inference that the defendant's unlawful operations will continue unless and until effectively restrained by the law, and that nothing short of an injunction will be effective to restrain them.[170]

Applying those principles he held that the original grant of an injunction was justified and that the appeal should fail.[171]

To enable contractors to establish in advance with the relevant local **17–043** authority working hours, and other conditions of operations that, if complied with, will avoid the service of any section 60 notices, section 61 entitles any person who intends to carry out construction works to apply to the local authority for a consent ("a section 61 consent"). An application for the consent must be made at the same time as or after the request for Building Regulations approval, and must particularise the works to be undertaken, the methods that will be used, and also the steps that will be taken to minimise noise resulting from the construction works. The local authority must give its consent to the application if it considers that if the

---

[169] [1984] AC 754 at 775 and 767; [1984] 2 All E.R. 332 at 341, 342 and 335, respectively.
[170] [1992] 3 All E.R. at 714 g–j.
[171] The COPA controls here discussed are distinct from injunctive relief that a landowner might seek in nuisance against the those responsible for building works at an adjacent site. In the recent case of *Hiscox v Pinnacle* [2008] EWHC 145, Judge Hodge QC referred to the well-established principle that "the law takes a commonsense view ... if operations' such as demolition and building are reasonably carried on and all proper and reasonable steps are taken to ensure that no undue inconvenience is caused to neighbours, whether from noise, dust or other reasons, the neighbours must put up with it".

works are carried out in accordance with it it would not serve a section 60 notice. In granting the consent, the authority may attach conditions to it, it may limit or qualify the consent to allow for any changes in circumstances, and it may limit the duration of the consent. Anyone who knowingly carries out the works, or permits them to be carried out, in contravention of any conditions attached to a consent commits an offence. Provided however the consent and its conditions are complied with, it constitutes a defence under any proceedings brought by a local authority under EPA sections 80 or 81, in respect of an alleged statutory nuisance.

Applications for a section 61 consent should be dealt with within 28 days from receipt of the relevant application. Where the authority either does not give its consent within that period, or grants a consent subject to conditions that the applicant considers unacceptable, the applicant may appeal within 21 days from the end of the 28 day period. Appeals are subject to the provisions of regulation 6 of the Control of Noise (Appeals) Regulations 1975,[172] and may be based on any of the following grounds:

(a) any condition attached to the consent is not justified under section 61;
(b) there has been some informality, defect or error in or in connection with the consent;
(c) the requirements of any relevant condition are unreasonable in character or extent or are unnecessary;
(d) the time or times within which the requirements of any condition are to be complied with is one not reasonably sufficient.

A practical difficulty in setting conditions on section 61 consents, in so far as these relate to noise levels, is the means by which, and where, these should be measured. The measurement of noise is a technically highly complex subject; where the extent of a condition is in fact uncertain, then an appeal will almost certainly succeed on the grounds that the requirements of the condition are unreasonable in character or extent.

Controls over equipment and commercial/industrial activities

17–044 There are numerous controls over the design and construction of certain equipment to limit noise emissions, in particular motor vehicles, aircraft, construction plant and equipment, industrial machinery, household appliances and lawnmowers, all of which are based on EC directives. The Noise Emission in the Environment by Equipment for use Outdoors

---

[172] SI 1975/2116.

Regulations 2001, implementing Directive 2000/14/EC, provides for permitted noise levels of a wide range of equipment that might be used outdoors, such as compressors, lawnmowers, dozers and so on, revoking prior legislation.[173] Household appliances remain covered by the Household Appliances (Noise Emission) Regulations 1990 as amended.[174]

Motor vehicles

There are two sets of controls over motor vehicles of relevance: these are made under the Road Traffic Act 1988 and consist of "construction and use" regulations, and type approval schemes, which require any manufacturer, before marketing a new type of vehicle in the United Kingdom, to have a sample tested by the Department of Transport. The Road Vehicles (Construction and Use) Regulations 1986[175] as amended, govern permissible noise limits for motor vehicles, which have been progressively reduced.[176]   **17–045**

The applicability of the EC directives was called into question in *Freight Transport Association Limited and Others v London Boroughs Transport Committee*[177] in which conditions laid down by the Greater London Council were challenged, whereby heavy goods were banned from using residential streets in Greater London at night time, unless especially permitted to do so. The grant of special permits included a condition that vehicles over 16.5 tonnes which were capable of being fitted with an air brake noise suppressor must have one. On judicial review, the condition was quashed on the ground that it required technical features of the vehicles beyond those demanded by the relevant EC directives. Though upheld in the Court of Appeal, the decision was reversed by the House of Lords, on the grounds that the condition did not seek to determine the construction requirements of the vehicles, but was merely concerned with the proper regulation of local traffic. Given that the necessary suppressor only cost some £30, the condition could not be said to interfere with the operation of the single market. While this decision must surely be right, it does not constitute justification for widespread regulation of traffic throughout the country by reference to features of vehicle construction, if

---

[173] This revoked the Construction Plant and Equipment (Harmonization of Noise Emission Standards) Regulations 1985, the Construction Plant and Equipment (Harmonisation of Noise Emission Standards) Regulations 1988, and the Lawnmowers (Harmonization of Noise Emission Standards) Regulations 1992.

[174] SI 1990/161, as amended by Household Appliances (Noise Emission) (Amendment) Regulations 1994 SI 1994/1386.

[175] SI 1968/1078.

[176] Regulation 55 sets out noise limits for motor vehicles in general, and 55A applies to those first used after 1 October 1996. There are also noise limits in regards to agricultural motor vehicles and tractors, and motor cycles.

[177] [1991] 3 All E.R. 915; [1991] 1 W.L.R. 828.

this were to present unreasonable obstacles to the use of the vehicles concerned.

Aircraft

17–046   Most types of aircraft[178] may only take-off or land in the UK if they possess a noise certificate appropriate to its aircraft type. The standards that must be met to obtain a noise certificate are set out in the Air Navigation Noise Certification Order 1990, as amended,[179] made under the Civil Aviation Act 1982.

Restrictions on the movement of aircraft, and particularly night landings at airports, are ultimately based on international agreements under the jurisdiction of the International Civil Aviation Organisation (ICAO). The Aeroplane Noise Regulations 1999 as amended replaced the Aeroplane Noise (Limitation on Operation of Aeroplanes) Regulations 1993. These 1999 Regulations set out noise certificate requirements and related provisions, including penalties for those who contravene the requirements, and the power to prevent an aeroplane flying if the Civil Aviation Authority (or an authorised person) has reason to believe that it does not have the requisite noise certificate. It is to be noted that noise from any aircraft except for model aircraft is exempted from the statutory nuisance legislation, by section 79(6) EPA. Moreover, under section 76(1) of the Civil Aviation Act 1982, no action shall lie in respect of trespass or in respect of nuisance, by reason only of the flight of an aircraft over any property at a height above the ground which, having regard to wind, weather and all the circumstances of the case is reasonable, or the ordinary incidents of such flight, so long as the provisions of any Air Navigation Order and of any orders under section 62 have been duly complied with and the aircraft was not flying dangerously under section 81 of the Act.

The effect of this exclusion of liability has been challenged on a number of occasions in the European Court of Human Rights. In *Powell and Rayner v United Kingdom*[180] the applicants, who lived under flight paths from Heathrow airport, chiefly relied on ECHR Article 8. The court dismissed the claims. Under Article 8, regard had to be had to the fair balance that needed to be struck between the competing interests of the individual and of the community as whole. In view of the provisions of Article 8(2), which allow for this balance to be struck, and the fact that relevant noise abatement measures were observed at Heathrow, the claim could not be sustained. More recently the Grand Chamber of the court in *Hatton v United*

---

[178]   The principal exception being those with a take-off distance at maximum authorised weight under standard conditions of not more than 610 metres.
[179]   SI 1990/1514.
[180]   Case No. 3/1989/163/219; *The Times*, February 22, 1990.

Kingdom[181] upheld the UK regime on aircraft noise as being compatible with the Convention.

Injunctions under section 222 of the Local Government Act 1972

A local authority may seek an injunction to prevent or restrict a nuisance either before or, if it is likely to recur, after its creation, under the extensive powers provided by section 222 of the Local Government Act 1972. These entitle local authorities to act as they see fit in the promotion or protection of the interests of the inhabitants of their areas, including, inter alia, to prosecute any legal proceedings. An injunction may therefore be sought under this procedure where a nuisance is feared, and if the authority considers that proceedings for an offence would not afford an adequate remedy; the sanctions that may be imposed for contempt of court resulting from a breach of an injunction being frequently more respected than relatively modest criminal penalties. These powers were used in *City of London Corporation v Bovis Construction Ltd* to restrain builders from causing a noise nuisance outside the permitted hours without reasonable excuse, even though the contravention had not been proved to be a criminal offence.[182]

17–047

Byelaws

Local authorities have powers under section 235 of the Local Government Act 1972 to make byelaws to suppress nuisances, breach of which is a criminal offence. Public use of radios and cassette players, and singing and playing musical instruments in the street, for example, may be controlled in this way.

17–048

---

[181] (2002) 34 EHRR 1, (2003) 37 EHRR 28.
[182] [1992] 3 All E.R. 697. Even though the conduct complained of might not be actionable at the suit of the authority, it was an actionable wrong and there was evidence that the threat of prosecution by the local authority had been ineffective. Therefore the Court of Appeal upheld the grant of an injunction to restrain the contractors from causing a noise nuisance outside the permitted hours without reasonable excuse.

Table 17/I

Procedure under Part III Environmental Protection Act 1990, Statutory Nuisance

Local Authority—England and Wales

17–049

Local authority under a duty to inspect its area to detect statutory nuisances and to investigate complaints (s.79(1)).

↓

Local authority satisfied that a statutory nuisance exists or is likely to occur or recur (s.80(1)).

↓

Service of abatement notice on person responsible or owner or occupier (depending on the circumstances) (s.80(1)).

↓

Person served may appeal to Magistrates within 21 days (s.80(3)).

↓

Failure to comply with abatement notice is an offence. Local authority may:
abate nuisance and recover expenses (ss.80(4), 81(3) and (4)); or
take proceedings in Magistrates' Court for non-compliance.

On conviction a fine may be imposed not exceeding £5,000 plus £500 per day or, if the offence was on industrial, trade or business premises, not exceeding £20,000.

↓

Local authority abatement expenses carry interest and may be made a charge on the premises (s.81A).

Aggrieved Persons

Aggrieved person gives notice of intention to make a complaint to the Magistrates on the ground that he is aggrieved by the existence of a statutory nuisance (s.82(6)).

↓

Aggrieved person makes complaint to the Magistrates' Court against person responsible or owner or occupier of premises (depending on circumstances) (s.82(1)).

↓

The Magistrates' Court will decide if it is satisfied the alleged nuisance exists or is likely to recur. The Court can: (i) make an order requiring defendant to abate the nuisance or prevent its recurrence; and/or (ii) impose a fine not exceeding £5,000 (s.82(2)).

↓

Where neither the person responsible for the nuisance nor the owner or occupier of the premises can be found, the Court may direct the local authority to do anything the Court would have ordered that person to do (s.82(13)).

↓

A person who, without reasonable excuse, contravenes the Magistrates' Order is guilty of an offence, and can be fined up to £5,000 plus £500 per day for each day on which the offence continues (s.82(8)).

↓

Where there has been a conviction for non-compliance with a Magistrates' Order, the Magistrates'. Court may direct the local authority to do anything which the person convicted was required to do (s.82(12)).

Chapter 18

CHEMICALS

Introduction

Throughout most of the twentieth century the chemical industry, in its various forms, was one of the most vigorous participants in economic development world-wide. Major industries have grown up around petro-chemicals and polymers in particular, pharmaceuticals, and agrochemicals, (both bulk fertilisers and pesticides). Numerous other products have been developed, often highly specialised for specific applications. Many are sold for use by the public, for example paints and adhesives, rubber and plastics, aerosols and pesticides, medicines and cosmetics, and food and fuel additives. Many others are used in industrial processes, for example in water treatment and food production, and as emulsifiers and wetting agents, dielectric and hydraulic fluids, degreasing agents and solvents, and pigments and dyes.

The undoubted direct benefits of new chemical products often resulted in a ready take-up by the market, and widespread application; only later were adverse effects on human health and the environment recognised.[1] The growing experience of the adverse aspects of apparently excellent products has led to an increasingly sophisticated regulatory regime, controlling both the introduction of new products, the manner in which they must be labelled when supplied to others, the conditions that must be complied with on their transportation and in certain cases over their actual use, and whether they may be exported to other countries without their prior consent. Several substances have of course long been recognised to be inherently hazardous, whether through their inflammable or explosive nature or through their toxicity, and controls over them have been in place for many years. Nevertheless, this has tended to be on a somewhat piecemeal basis, and in recent decades the whole system of chemical regula-

---

[1] The use of DDT (dichloro-diphenyl-trichloro ethane) as an insecticide, PCBs (poly-chlorinated biphenyls) as a dielectric fluid in transformers and as a hydraulic fluid, tetra-ethyl lead as an anti-knock agent in petrol, and CFCs as refrigerants and in aerosols are perhaps among the most notable examples. All of these were, and indeed still are, excellent for the purposes for which they were intended, but their impact on the environment is such that these benefits are not now considered worthwhile. Nevertheless, the use of substitutes may well bring other disadvantages—the ban on lead in petrol has resulted in reformulations that have markedly higher contents of carcinogens such as benzene, toluene and xylene, as well as lower efficiency, leading to higher emissions of carbon dioxide.

tion, within the EU and in the UK in particular, has become much more coherent and comprehensive.

A full description of the operation of all the controls now in place and to be brought in over coming years would take up disproportionate space in this work. The purpose here is to enable those affected to understand the nature of the various controls that apply to specific circumstances, but not to provide their detail, for which reference should be made to the relevant legislation and the often very extensive official guidance.

18–002 This chapter first describes the current controls over the putting of chemicals on to the market. ("Chemicals" is used here to indicate broadly chemical compounds[2] and mixtures of compounds, and also substances consisting of a single chemical element, such as lead or chlorine.) This is followed by an outline of the specific controls over a number of particularly hazardous chemicals. All these controls are however in the process of being superseded over a period of years by a new comprehensive EU-wide regime, known as REACH,[3] and this is also described, though in view of its massive content, and as the implementing UK regulations are not in final form at the time of going to print, it is only appropriate to give a summary. Finally, the controls specific to asbestos, pesticides and biocides are separately considered. Those over genetically modified organisms and radioactive substances are the subject of Chapters 19 and 20 respectively.

The global trade in chemicals, whether as raw and intermediate materials or as finished products for sale to industry or through retail outlets, is so extensive that its regulation requires international harmonisation if significant distortions of that trade are to be avoided. Thus virtually all the substantive law in the United Kingdom in this area is derived from EU legislation (and significant elements of that are the implementation of global conventions), though much of the administrative structure for applying the law is left to the discretion of the Member States. Accordingly the underlying EU directives and regulations are reviewed first, before considering the implementing UK legislation.

[2] "Compound" is used here to mean a particular chemical substance having a specific molecular structure, as distinct from a composition, which is a mixture of distinct compounds and/or elements, even though there may be some binding of these together, as in the composition of a car tyre.
[3] "The **R**egistration, **E**valuation, **A**uthorisation and restriction of **Ch**emical substances", the name given to EU Regulation 1907/2006 that governs the new regime.

EU LEGISLATION

Classification, Packaging and Labelling Directive 67/548

Any regulation of chemicals must necessarily start by classifying the chemicals that are to be regulated by reference to relevant properties. The basis of EU chemicals regulation is Directive 67/548 concerning the classification, packaging and labelling of dangerous substances—referred to here as the "CPL Directive".[4] This Directive has been subject to numerous amendments whereby, among other changes, it applies in certain respects to all substances and not only those classed as dangerous. The original 1967 Directive provided for the classification of dangerous chemicals by degree of hazard and the nature of the risks entailed, and set out rules for packaging and labelling them appropriate to the physical, chemical and health risk categories into which they had been classified. The 6th Amendment[5] of the CPL Directive, dating from 1979, which replaced all the substantive provisions of the original Directive, referred for the first time to protection of the environment as being among the objectives of the regime, so broadening it from the original purpose of protection of the public, and especially members of the workforce who might use the products it covered. It also added a further risk category to the previous ones, which were essentially concerned with health and safety: "dangerous for the environment". The 7th Amendment,[6] which likewise replaced all the substantive provisions, explicitly refers to the requirement of what was then Article 100A(3) of the Rome Treaty that the internal market measures concerning (among other things) health, safety and environmental protection, must "take as a base a high level of protection".

"Substances" is defined to mean chemical elements and their compounds in the natural state or obtained by any production process, as distinct from "preparations" which means mixtures or solutions composed of two or more substances. "Substances" also includes any additive needed to preserve a product's stability, and any impurity deriving from its production process. In essence the system is intended to cover products as put on the market or used commercially, and not merely their pure constituents. Any solvents that may be present are however excluded, if they can be separated without affecting the stability of the substance or changing its composition in any other respect.[7]

18–003

---

[4] To distinguish it, and the series of amending and adaptation Directives related to it, from Directive 76/769, and its series of related Directives concerning the marketing and use of dangerous substances, referred to in para.18–011ff below.

[5] Directive 79/831, [1979] OJ L259/10.

[6] Directive 92/32, [1992] OJ L154/1.

[7] Directive 92/32, art.2(1).

The 6th Amendment

The 6th Amendment

18-004 The 6th Amendment introduced a new requirement into the classification, packaging and labelling regime that new substances should not be placed on the market either on their own or in admixture with one or more others—mixtures being termed "preparations"—unless the substances had been notified to the appropriate authority in one of the Member States, as well having to be packaged and labelled in the prescribed manner. This requirement took effect on September 18, 1981. The notification procedure required the notifier (any manufacturer or importer into the EU of the substance, or any designated representative of a non-EU manufacturer) to submit to the competent authority, not less than 45 days before the product was placed on the market, a technical dossier containing the information necessary to evaluate the foreseeable risks, setting out detailed information on the substance, a full description of the tests done on it and their results, a declaration as to the unfavourable effects of the substance when used as proposed, the notifier's proposals for its classification and labelling and for any safety precautions to be recommended. To avoid duplication of effort, the 6th Amendment contained an Annex I listing as potentially dangerous a number of chemical substances classified into special risk categories, together with the safety precautions to be applied in each case. Where a substance was on the Annex I list, certain of these notification requirements were waived; where the substance had been notified at least 10 years previously, then a later notifier was merely required to provide a much more limited amount of information relating to the identity of the substance and a limited amount of information on it, but excluding information on its physico-chemical, toxicological and ecotoxicological properties.

EINECS and ELINCS

EINECS and ELINCS

18-005 In addition to having to keep a list of new substances notified after September 18, 1981, the Commission was required to draw up an inventory of "existing" substances that had been on the Community market "for genuine commercial purposes" between January 1, 1971, and September 18, 1981, inclusive; this came to be known as EINECS (the European Inventory of Existing Chemical Substances). EINECS also included monomers from which "polymerisates, polycondensates and polyadducts" had been manufactured and placed on the Community market in that period.[8] The Commission drew up a basic list,[9] which manufacturers and others could supplement by filing declarations relating to additional sub-

---

[8] For the rules on what was to be included in EINECS, see Commission Decision 81/437, [1981] OJ L167/31.
[9] Known as ECOIN, the "European Core Inventory".

stances that were also entitled to be listed on EINECS. Eventually EINECS listed slightly over 100,000 substances.[10]

New substances notified to the competent authorities in the Member States from September 18, 1981, were listed in a separate inventory called ELINCS (the European List of Notified Chemical Substances).[11] The national authorities were required to inform the Commission of all notifications of new substances that they had received, and the Commission, in theory, published by the end of each year an updated version of ELINCS including all new substances notified to national authorities between July 1 of the previous year and the following June 30. In practice the procedure has become seriously delayed, and the sixth update of ELINCS, which is the last to have been published to date, was published on October 29, 2003, and only lists those new chemical substances notified on or before 30 June 1998.[12]

The authority responsible for dealing with notifications of new substances in the United Kingdom has been, and remains, the Health and Safety Executive (the HSE). Under the new REACH regime the competent authority for England is expected to be the Secretary of State, but his functions, and those of the competent authorities in the other jurisdictions are to be delegated to the HSE. Currently notifications are still made under the Notification of New Substances Regulations 1993 (NONS 93) as amended,[13] but this will cease when this aspect of the REACH regime takes effect.

The 7th Amendment

The 7th Amendment[14] strengthened a number of the provisions in the 6th   **18–006** Amendment. In particular, it revised the previous Annex I so that it consisted of a list of chemical substances classified according to the principles outlined in the 7th Amendment, together with their appropriate classification and labelling details. The list includes a substantial number of those in the EINECS inventory and also some taken from ELINCS. The 7th Amendment envisaged that the remaining substances in EINECS were to be reviewed, by methods it prescribed and according to procedures laid down by Regulation 793/93,[15] to assess their properties and the appropriate risk category, and that they should then also be included in its Annex I. It further required, for the first time, that safety data sheets be supplied to industrial users receiving any of the substances listed in Annex I. These

---

[10] [1990] OJ C146A/1.
[11] For the rules on what was to be included in ELINCS, see Commission Decision 85/71, [1985] OJ L30/33.
[12] COM 2003/642 final, October 29, 2003.
[13] SI 1993/3050, as amended by SI 2001/1055.
[14] Directive 92/32, [1992] OJ L154 and 154A.
[15] [1993] OJ L84/1.

were to be prepared in accordance with Directive 91/155.[16] The safety data sheet provisions have been superseded by those in REACH, and have accordingly now been withdrawn.

The effect of the 7th Amendment was to create four classes of substances:

- Substances listed in its Annex I (and also in EINECS or ELINCS);
- Substances in EINECS, but not yet listed in Annex I;
- Substances not contained in EINECS or Annex I, but which have been previously notified—these are either already in ELINCS or due to be included in its next update; and
- Other substances proposed to be placed on the market in the EU but which have not yet been the subject of any notification.

These different categories are subject to different requirements as regards their packaging and labelling. Those already in Annex I must conform with the requirements of that Annex, even though they may have become out of date, or even misleading—Member States are however enabled to prescribe more suitable requirements on a temporary basis, pending a decision at EU level, if they consider this to be necessary.[17] Clearly it is in the interests of those marketing such substances to seek changes to the Annex I requirements if compliance with them fails to draw attention to a known hazard that may give rise to a product liability issues.

There is a presumption that continued marketing of the remaining "existing" substances listed in EINECS is acceptable unless and until such time as review of them indicates otherwise. Those responsible for them must merely make and keep themselves aware of such relevant and accessible data on them as does exist, and package and label them accordingly. Notified substances that are neither in Annex I nor in EINECS must be classified, packaged and labelled in accordance with the requirements of the 7th Amendment Directive. Substances that do not fall into any of the other categories, whether "dangerous" in fact or not, may not be placed on the market until they have been notified in accordance with the Directive, the prescribed period for considering the notification has elapsed, and no action has been taken requiring marketing to be postponed.

Exceptions

18-007 The following products when in the finished state intended for the final user were excluded[18] from the scope of the CPL Directive, either entirely or at least from its notification requirements, being substances and pre-

---

[16] [1991] OJ L76/39.
[17] Directive 92/32, art.31.
[18] By art.1(2), which was amended.

parations that are subject to substantially equivalent regimes providing for risk assessments and official approval:

(a) medicinal products for human or veterinary use;
(b) cosmetic products;
(c) mixtures of substances in the form of waste within the scope of EU waste legislation;
(d) foodstuffs;
(e) animal feeding stuffs;
(f) pesticides, plant protection products and biocides;[19]
(g) radioactive substances;
(h) other substances or preparations for which equivalent Community notification or approval procedures exist.

The CPL Directive has been substantially amended by the REACH Regulation, which has removed from it all the provisions relevant to notification and to safety data sheets, as these matters are now covered by REACH. What is left is essentially concerned with the conduct of risk assessments, and the classification and labelling of substances so assessed.

Dangerous Preparations—Directive 88/379

A Directive closely related to the 7th Amendment Directive is the so-called Preparations Directive 1999/45.[20] This has been amended several times, most recently by the REACH Regulation, which again supersedes, and so has withdrawn, its provisions on safety data sheets. Preparations, being mixtures or solutions of two or more substances, can take an infinite variety of forms,[21] and if each of these were to be required to be tested as though it were a new substance in order to evaluate any dangerous properties, and to classify those it may have, there would not only be a massive amount of duplicated work, which would be both inefficient and time wasting, but also repeated testing on animals which the Commission, as a matter of policy, seeks to avoid.[22] Accordingly the purpose of the Preparations Directive is (i) to set out procedures for establishing, for any preparation, which of the danger categories, as set out in the 7th Amendment, it should be regarded as belonging to, and (ii) to provide a set of principles for deriving the appropriate classification from the properties of the component substances in the preparation, having regard in particular to their concentrations. The Directive sets out various labelling requirements, and

18–008

---

[19] Plant protection products and biocides were excluded from the notification requirements by Directive 2000/21, [2000] OJ L103/70.
[20] [1999] OJ L200/1, replacing the original Preparations Directive 88/379, [1988] OJ L187/14.
[21] Including alloys, the properties of which may differ greatly from those of their individual components. Nevertheless alloys are assessed for the purposes of the Preparations Directive as though they were simple mixtures.
[22] See Recital 8 of Directive 1999/45.

it provides that suppliers must lodge details of their products with an appropriate body that can give advice in the event of medical emergencies.[23] There are also provisions for preserving confidential information, subject to certain limitations and qualifications.

MARKETING AND USE OF DANGEROUS SUBSTANCES AND PREPARATIONS

Enabling Powers

18–009 While broad protection against hazards from chemical products may be obtained by suitable labelling, this does not necessarily ensure adequate protection of all individuals who may directly or indirectly come into contact with them. Further, even though all necessary precautions may be made to avoid harm to human health, other materials, such as PCBs, various heavy metals and their compounds, for example organotin anti-fouling paints and certain wood preservatives, are potentially so damaging to the environment that it is considered desirable to restrict, and in some cases to prohibit, marketing and use of them. Numerous powers are available to the government to impose controls to protect human health, whether at the workplace or elsewhere, and damage to the environment. Among the most significant of these and the most widely used, are the powers under section 15 of the Health and Safety at Work etc. Act 1974 (HSWA) to issue health and safety regulations, of which the Control of Substances Hazardous to Health Regulations 2002[24] are particularly important for those concerned with chemical hazards.

Additionally, safety regulations may be made under section 11(1) of the Consumer Protection Act 1987. These may ban, restrict, or allow subject to prescribed conditions, the importation and marketing of potentially harmful substances and articles. Further wide powers are given by section 140(1) of the Environmental Protection Act (EPA) to the Secretary of State which he may exercise in relation to any substance or article for the purpose of preventing it from causing pollution of the environment or harm to human health or to the health of animals or plants. Under these controls, he may prohibit or restrict the importation into, and the landing and unloading in, the United Kingdom of any specified substance or article, its use or supply for any purpose and its storage.[25] Further, the controls may

---

[23] art.17.
[24] SI 2002/2677.
[25] Although the text of s.140 has not been amended to reflect the subsequent devolution of powers in respect of the environment to the devolved jurisdictions, the Secretary of State would doubtless in practice confer with the relevant authorities before exercising them.

be limited to specific areas and/or persons; they may be made subject to conditions, or contingent on certain circumstances.

Where a particular substance or article has already been produced in or brought into the United Kingdom, section 140(3) of the EPA enables the Secretary of State to procure that it is dealt with and/or disposed of in a suitable fashion. Regulations may be issued pursuant to this section enabling him to direct that the substance or article concerned is to be treated as waste or as any particular description of controlled waste, and he may either apply any provisions of Part 2 of the EPA relating to waste, or simply direct that it be disposed of or treated as he sees fit. Provisions within Part 2 include section 70 which gives an inspector extensive powers to deal with any substance or article which he believes to be a cause of imminent danger of serious pollution of the environment or serious harm to human health. If a substance or article has been imported into the United Kingdom, the Secretary of State may require that it either be disposed of or treated in the United Kingdom or that it be re-exported. Where any other UK statute or any EU legislation imposes a prohibition or restriction on the importation into or the landing and unloading in the United Kingdom of anything, section 140(4) enables the Secretary of State to direct that he may treat such a prohibition or restriction as having been imposed under section 140(1), and thus give himself all the necessary enforcement powers.

Before the Secretary of State may exercise any of the powers available to him under section 140, he must consult an advisory committee set up under section 140(5), and before making any regulations under the section he is also required to consult the public. He may however proceed without these consultations if he considers that holding them would result in an imminent risk of serious pollution of the environment.[26] **18–010**

Since it may not always be immediately apparent whether a substance is liable to cause pollution of the environment or harm to human health, section 142 enables the Secretary of State to issue regulations whereby he may make orders to secure any relevant information relating to such substances as he may specify. He may not do so however in relation to a substance first supplied in the EU on or after September 18, 1981, i.e. a substance which would not have been entitled to be in the EINECS inventory, and required its own specific notification and authorisation. Likewise no order may be made in respect of any substance that is regulated for the purposes of statutes relating to explosives, radioactive substances, medicines and veterinary medicines, fertilisers, and animal feeding stuffs.[27] Except in an emergency, before making any such order the Secretary of State must confer with the advisory committee set up under section 140(5).

---

[26] s.140(6).
[27] s.140(2)(b) and (7).

Marketing and Use Legislation

18–011   The legislative controls over the marketing and use of most dangerous substances and preparations are now contained in the REACH Regulation. However as these largely, and necessarily, maintain the previous controls, a brief survey of the latter is in order. The controls ultimately derive from Directive 76/769.[28] An Annex to that Directive listed substances and preparations which could only be marketed and used in accordance with the conditions prescribed for each of them in that Annex; in some cases marketing and use was prohibited altogether. Quite frequently supply to the general public would be prohibited, while allowing industrial use and/or use to prepare articles containing relatively small quantities for supply, when suitably packaged and labelled, to the general public. The Directive was amended many times over the years to add to and to refine the list of substances and preparations in the Annex, and how they might be marketed and used, if at all.

18–012   There are specific controls of significance over the marketing and use of the following articles and substances.

Table 18/I

Articles / Substances	Principal aspects
Batteries and accumulators Directive 2006/66[29] The Batteries and Accumulators (Placing on the Market) Regulations 2008[30]	Bans, subject to exemptions, the placing on the market of batteries and accumulators containing hazardous substances. Prescribes rules for the design of certain appliances to enable waste batteries to be readily removed, and for the collection, treatment, recycling and disposal of waste batteries and accumulators, with a view to promoting high levels of collection and recycling. (See paragraph 15–121 for further detail.)
Detergents Regulation 648/2004[31]	Harmonises rules on: the biodegradability of surfactants in detergents; restrictions or bans on surfactants on grounds of biodegradability; labelling of detergents, including fragrance allergens; and the information manufacturers must hold at the disposal of competent authorities and medical personnel.

[28] [1976] OJ L262/201.
[29] [2006] OJ L266/1, replacing Directive 91/157, [1991] OJ L78.
[30] SI 2008/2164.
[31] [2004] OJ L104/1.

Persistent Organic Pollutants (POPs) Regulation 850/2004[32]	Prohibits the production, use and placing on the market of twelve POPs listed in its Annex, including DDT, Aldrin, Dieldrin, Endrin and PCBs (polychlorinated biphenyls).
Hazardous substances in Electrical and Electronic Equipment (EEE) Directive 2002/95[33] The Restriction of the Use of Certain Hazardous Substances in Electrical and Electronic Equipment Regulations 2008[34]	Bans the placing on the market of new EEE containing more than permitted levels of lead, cadmium, mercury, hexavalent chromium, and polybrominated biphenyl (PBB) and polybrominated diphenyl ether (PBDE) flame retardants.

The main recent UK legislation implementing Directive 76/769 and its series of amending directives consists of the Dangerous Substances and Preparations (Safety) Regulations 2006 and the Dangerous Substances and Preparations Regulations 2006,[35] coupled with the Chemicals (Hazard Information and Packaging for Supply) Regulations 2002,[36] as amended, so far as relevant. Separate important controls over asbestos and the protection of those liable to be exposed to it, including licensing provisions, are contained in the Control of Asbestos Regulations 2002,[37] discussed below at paragraphs 18–034 to 18–039. The controls over ozone depleting substances are covered in Chapter 14 on Environmental Permitting: IPPC and Air, at paragraph 14–058.

REACH

It quite quickly became apparent that the intended comprehensive review **18–013**
of all the chemicals within EINECS was going to take considerably longer than originally envisaged, largely because of the high costs each assessment entailed, and the reluctance of Governments and industry to incur such

---

[32] [2004] OJ L229/5. The Persistent Organic Pollutants Regulations 2007, SI 2007/3106, provide the administration necessary to enforce the POPs Regulation in the UK, though as a Defra memorandum says, the POP chemicals covered have not been made or used in the UK for quite some time.

[33] [2003] OJ L37/19.

[34] SI 2008/37. See also the official guidance "RoHS Regulations: Government Guidance Notes", DBERR, February 2008, URN 08/582.

[35] SI 2006/2916 and SI 2006/3311 respectively.

[36] SI 2002/1689.

[37] SI 2002/2739.

costs on numerous substances that were in regular use and apparently causing little or no harm to anyone in practice, at least if sensibly handled.[38] How to move forward was addressed in the 6th Community Action Programme on the Environment,[39] which included in its Article 7(1) a list of objectives and priorities:

- aiming to achieve within one generation (2020) that chemicals are only produced and used in ways that do not lead to a significant negative impact on health and the environment, recognising that the present gaps of knowledge on the properties, use, disposal and exposure of chemicals need to be overcome;
- chemicals that are dangerous should be substituted by safer chemicals or safer alternative technologies not entailing the use of chemicals, with the aim of reducing risks to man and the environment; [and]
- reducing the impacts of pesticides on human health and the environment and more generally to achieve a more sustainable use of pesticides as well as a significant overall reduction in risks and of the use of pesticides consistent with the necessary crop protection. Pesticides in use which are persistent or bio-accumulative or toxic or have other properties of concern should be substituted by less dangerous ones where possible.

These objectives were to be pursued by the priority actions of Article 7(2)(b), which provided, as regards chemicals:

- placing the responsibility on manufacturers, importers and downstream users for generating knowledge about all chemicals (duty of care) and assessing risks of their use, including in products, as well as recovery and disposal;
- developing a coherent system based on a tiered approach, excluding chemical substances used in very low quantities, for the testing, risk assessment and risk management of new and existing substances with testing procedures that minimise the need for animal testing and develop alternative testing methods;
- ensuring that the chemical substances of concern are subject to accelerated risk management procedures and that substances of very high concern, including carcinogenic, mutagenic or toxic for reproduction substances and those which have POPs (persistent organic pollutants) characteristics, are used only in justified and well defined cases and must be subject to authorisation before their use;

---

[38] A Defra consultation document of June 2008 on the Enforcement of REACH in the UK— see below—notes that although around 30,000 chemicals are made, sold and used in significant amounts, the current system has generated proper assessments on only a few hundred.
[39] Decision 1600/2002, [2002] OJ L242/1–15.

- ensuring that the results of the risk assessments of chemicals are taken fully into account in all areas of Community legislation where chemicals are regulated and to avoid duplication of work; [and]
- providing criteria for including among the substances of very high concern those that are persistent and bioaccumulating and toxic and substances that are very persistent and very bio-accumulative and envisaging the addition of known endocrine disrupters when agreed test methods and criteria are established.

This led eventually to the REACH Regulation,[40] adopted in 2006. It entered into force on June 1, 2007, though many of the principal measures did not come into effect until a year later, on June 1, 2008. At the time of writing draft Regulations intended to provide the administrative infrastructure for operating REACH in the United Kingdom, entitled "The REACH Enforcement Regulations 2008", (referred to here, to avoid confusion with the EU Regulation, as the "UK Regulations") were published for consultation in June 2008 by Defra.[41] The consultation document[42] accompanying these draft regulations gives considerable detail on REACH and the proposals for operating the regime in the United Kingdom. The following commentary has had to be written on the assumption that the UK Regulations as finally issued will not differ materially from the consultation draft.

The REACH Regulation is a massive document occupying 849 pages of the Official Journal.[43] A description of it in this work can therefore only be by way of a brief summary, focussing on its main features. For the same reason, it is impossible here to indicate all the detailed limitations and qualifications in the legislation. Readers who need to comply with it should make direct reference to it, and also to the guidance available on it, especially from the European Chemicals Agency[44] (the ECHA),[45] and also from Defra.

For the purposes of the following discussion, the definitions below, taken **18-014** from Article 3 of REACH, are to be noted:

---

[40] reg.1907/2006, [2006] OJ L396/1.
[41] Several Government departments are involved in the operation of REACH in the UK. Defra is the lead department.
[42] "Consultation on the enforcement of REACH in the UK", Defra, June 2008.
[43] 394 pages for the body of the Regulation and its Annexes I to XVI, followed by 455 pages for Annex XVII which lists restricted dangerous chemicals.
[44] In particular, "Guidance on Registration: Guidance for the implementation of REACH", ECHA, February 2008. Other REACH guidance documents currently available from the ECHA are on: Substance identification; Downstream users; Requirements for substances in articles; Data sharing; Information Requirements and Chemical Safety Assessment (Part A, Introduction to the Guidance Document, and Part D, Exposure Scenario Building).
[45] The ECHA website is http://echa.europa.eu/home_en.asp. The "H" in ECHA indicates Helsinki, where the Agency is based.

Table 18/II

Substance	A chemical element and its compounds in the natural state or obtained by any manufacturing process, including any additive necessary to preserve its stability and any impurity deriving from the process used, but excluding any solvent which may be separated without affecting the stability of the substance or changing its composition
Preparation	A mixture or solution composed of two or more substances
Placing on the market	Supplying or making available, whether in return for payment or free of charge, to a third party. Import shall be deemed to be placing on the market
Polymer	A substance consisting of molecules characterised by the sequence of one or more types of monomer units. Such molecules must be distributed over a range of molecular weights wherein differences in the molecular weight are primarily attributable to differences in the number of monomer units. A polymer comprises the following: a simple weight majority of molecules containing at least three monomer units which are covalently bound to at least one other monomer unit or other reactant; less than a simple weight majority of molecules of the same molecular weight. In the context of this definition a "monomer unit" means the reacted form of a monomer substance in a polymer
Monomer	a substance which is capable of forming covalent bonds with a sequence of additional like or unlike molecules under the conditions of the relevant polymer-forming reaction used for the particular process
Downstream user	Any natural or legal person established within the Community, other than the manufacturer or the importer, who uses a substance, either on its own or in a preparation, in the course of his industrial or professional activities. A distributor or a consumer is not a downstream user.
Phase-in substance	A substance which meets at least one of the following criteria: (a) it is listed in the European Inventory of Existing Commercial Chemical Substances (EINECS); [or]

	(b) it was manufactured in the Community, or in the countries acceding to the European Union on 1 January 1995 or on 1 May 2004, but not placed on the market by the manufacturer or importer, at least once in the 15 years before the entry into force of this Regulation, provided the manufacturer or importer has documentary evidence of this; [or]
	(c) it was placed on the market in the Community, or in the countries acceding to the European Union on 1 January 1995 or on 1 May 2004, before entry into force of this Regulation by the manufacturer or importer and was considered as having been notified in accordance with the first indent of Article 8(1) of Directive 67/548/EEC but does not meet the definition of a polymer as set out in this Regulation, provided the manufacturer or importer has documentary evidence of this.

REACH is based on the principle that it is for manufacturers, importers **18–015** and downstream users to ensure that they manufacture, place on the market or use substances, whether on their own, in preparations or (in some circumstances) in articles, that do not adversely affect human health or the environment. Its provisions are underpinned by the precautionary principle.[46] Accordingly any substance, whether on its own, in preparations or in articles, that a person (whether an individual or a company) manufactures in, or imports into, the EU in quantities of 1 tonne or more in a calendar year[47] must be registered; a substance that is not registered may not be manufactured or placed on the market in the EU.[48]

The bulk of polymers in everyday use are extremely inert, and so present minimal health risks, unless they happen to contain a significant quantity of unreacted monomer units, which is generally unlikely. Polymers (which as defined include copolymers of two or more different monomer units) are accordingly exempted from registration as such, and so also from any evaluation of their properties under the Regulation's provisions applicable to substances generally.[49] Instead, where a polymer is made or imported in a quantity of 1 tonne a year or more, the manufacturer or importer must

---

[46] art.1(3).
[47] For the purposes of calculating annual quantities of "phase-in substances" (see below) that have been imported or manufactured for at least three consecutive years, quantities per year are to be calculated on the basis of the average for the three preceding calendar years; art.3(30).
[48] arts 5, 6(1).
[49] art.2(9). Recital 41 says that the exemption from registration and evaluation should continue until those that need to be registered due to the risks posed to human health or the environment can be selected in a practicable and cost-efficient way on the basis of sound technical and valid scientific criteria.

register the relevant monomer substance and/or any other substance chemically bound in the polymer if "the polymer consists of 2% or more by weight of such monomer substance(s) or other substance(s) in the form of monomeric units and chemically bound substance(s)", unless these substances have already been registered "by an actor up the supply chain".[50] This is liable to put an impossible burden on many manufacturers and importers who may have no way of ascertaining precisely what the polymer they are concerned with contains, and in what proportions. Simple polymers, such as 100 per cent polyethylene, polystyrene or PVC, present no problems in this respect of course, but in practice many polymers are polymerisates of two more monomers, chosen, and mixed in precisely calculated amounts, so as to optimise the physical properties of the eventual copolymer.

This concern led to a case being brought in the High Court[51] by four claimants, who all represented different interests,[52] challenging the monomer registration requirement of Article 6(3) as being (a) inconsistent with the Article 2(9) exemption of polymers, and so invalid, and (b) contrary to EU law because it is disproportionate and discriminates against importers. Although the claim under heading (b) failed, it was agreed by both sides that there is a real issue over the validity of Article 6(3). Accordingly a reference has been made to the European Court of Justice to seek its opinion on this issue. In the same case the Court was asked to rule on the meaning of the expression in Article 6(3) "that have not already been registered by an actor up the supply chain". The Court held that what the parties had eventually agreed on among themselves was correct, namely that it meant "that have not been already registered by someone who is an actor *in the present supply chain.*"[53]

18–016   Registration of substances in articles is also required if (a) the substance is present in those articles in quantities totalling over 1 tonne per producer or importer per year; and (b) the substance is intended to be released under normal or reasonably foreseeable conditions of use.[54] If a substance is in fact released from articles and presents a risk to human health or the environment, even though this is not intended, so that point (b) does not apply, the ECHA may require the relevant producers and importers to register the substance.[55]

---

[50] art.6(3).

[51] *SPCM SA & Ors, R (on the application of) v Secretary of State for Environment, Food & Rural Affairs*, [2007] EWHC 2610 (Admin) (October 11, 2007).

[52] SPCM SA, a French manufacturer of polymers; CH Erbsloh KG, a German distributor and wholesaler; Lake Chemicals and Minerals Ltd., a UK importer into the EU; and Hercules Inc., a US exporter to the EU.

[53] Emphasis added.

[54] art.7(1).

[55] art.7(5). Examples might be articles that contain a substance that is liable to be released as they wear out, or when discarded.

Exclusions and exemptions

The REACH Regulation does not apply at all to radioactive substances; **18–017** substances under customs supervision, e.g. in transit; non-isolated intermediates; the carriage of dangerous substances and dangerous substances in dangerous preparations by rail, road, inland waterway, sea or air; or to wastes.[56] Its provisions on registration, evaluation and authorisation do not apply to the extent that a substance is used in medicinal products for human or veterinary use, or in food or feedingstuffs, where these are covered by the EU legislation specified in Article 2(5). Further exemptions from particular REACH requirements are listed in Articles 2(6) to (8). Among those exempted by Article 2(7) are the substances in Annexes IV and V—these are well-known substances considered to be of minimal risk, and other substances where registration is considered inappropriate or unnecessary, including oxygen, hydrogen and nitrogen, and the noble (inert) gases.[57] As already mentioned, polymers are exempted from registration and evaluation by Article 2(9).

There is a five year exemption, extendable by up to five further years (or in some case 10), from registration for substances that are made or imported for the purposes of "product and process oriented research and development",[58] provided further quantities are not made or imported for other purposes. Nevertheless the manufacturers and importers have to comply with detailed notification requirements as set out in Regulation 9.

Active substances of plant protection products and biocidal products that have been placed on their respective Annex I or one of Annexes I, IA or IB (see paragraphs 18–040 and 18–050 below), as the case may be, and of products that are in the process of being assessed for inclusion in one of those Annexes, are deemed to have been registered,[59] so no further action is required in this respect. Similarly, a substance that has been notified for the purposes of the CPL Directive 67/548 is to be treated as registered, save that if the annual tonnage reaches the next tonnage threshold for the purposes of completing a dossier (i.e. 10, 100 or 1,000 tonnes), the appropriate additional information must be submitted, in accordance with the relevant Annexes.[60]

Registration dossiers

For all substances (and polymer monomers) manufactured or imported in **18–018** quantities of 1 tonne a year or more, a registration dossier must be lodged

---

[56] art.2(1), (2).
[57] Helium, neon, argon, krypton and xenon.
[58] Being research and development in the course of which pilot plant or production trials are used to develop a production process and/or to test the fields of application of the substance; art.3(22).
[59] art.15(1), (2).
[60] art.24.

with the ECHA. The basic registration information is prescribed in Annex VI, to which must generally be added further information depending on the annual quantities involved, as specified in Annexes VII to X. Annexes VI and VII generally apply to annual quantities of 1 tonne up to 10, Annexes VI to VIII to 10 tonnes up to 100, Annexes VI to IX to 100 tonnes up to 1,000, and Annexes VI to X to 1,000 tonnes or more.[61] Isolated intermediates are subject to registration in accordance with Articles 17 to 19. For all substances, chemical safety assessment must be carried out, and a chemical safety report prepared, where the annual quantities are 10 tonnes or more.[62]

Once three weeks has elapsed after submission of a dossier, the manufacturer or importer may start or continue his activity with the relevant substance, unless he receives an indication from the ECHA that he should not do so within that time.[63] Special provisions apply where a dossier on a "phase-in substance" is submitted within two months of the applicable deadline for doing so under Article 23.

The information in the original dossiers is bound over time to become out of date, with increasing experience of the chemicals, their properties, and their effects on humans and the environment. Registrants are obliged to notify the ECHA, and update the data it holds on them and their chemicals, whenever changes occur rendering the data no longer accurate. This will apply, inter alia, if they become aware of any information relevant to the risks they pose, or may pose in particular circumstances. As a result the ECHA database will constantly develop, and seems likely to become a valuable information resource.

Testing on vertebrate animals

18–019 It is now explicit EU policy to minimise the number of tests carried out on vertebrate animals. Thus it is stated in REACH:

> "In order to avoid animal testing, testing on vertebrate animals for the purposes of this Regulation shall be undertaken only as a last resort. It is also necessary to take measures limiting duplication of other tests".[64]

Accordingly, where a person seeking to register a substance needs to supply data from animal tests in his dossier, and the same substance was already registered within the past 12 years on the basis, inter alia, of animal test data, provisions in Article 27 encourage the parties to reach an agreement on data sharing, by arbitration if appropriate, with the later party paying an appropriate sum to the first party. The ECHA has issued guidance on

---

[61] art.12(1).
[62] art.14. Where the substance is present in preparations at a concentration below all of several maxima specified in art.14(2), this requirement does not apply.
[63] art.21(1).
[64] art.25(1).

"Data Sharing", and parties are recommended to follow this.[65] If no agreement can be reached, then the ECHA has the power to allow the later applicant to have access to and to use the relevant data, on his showing that he has paid the earlier registrant for the data. Provided the earlier registrant makes the full study report available to the potential registrant, he may claim from the later applicant an equal share of the cost incurred by him, and this claim is to be enforceable in the national courts.[66] However, where an earlier registration for the same substance is more than 12 years old, then any "study summaries or robust study summaries of studies" submitted with it can be used freely.[67]

Transitional provisions—phase-in substances

Although the REACH regime amounts to a completely fresh start, it of course builds on 40 years of chemical regulation at European level, and on practical experience of chemicals going back much further than that. There is a mass of accumulated information available on chemicals, and to incorporate this fully into the new regime will inevitably take many years. The approach adopted in REACH is to arrange for so-called "pre-notification" of chemicals already in current use within the EU when the regime came into effect on June 1, 2007, and to assess these over time, alongside assessments of new chemicals that may be introduced. These assessments will enable the determination of what conditions, if any, should be imposed on their manufacture, sale and use, and specifically, in the case of the most hazardous substances, whether they should be permitted to remain on the market at all, if other less hazardous substances are able to perform the same functions at an economic cost. Meanwhile the existing controls over each substance should continue until REACH control conditions have been determined for that substance. Priority is therefore to be given to those substances that appear to represent the greatest risks, while substances representing modest risks, especially if only small quantities of them are involved, will be left to the end of the queue.

18–020

Phase-in substances (see the definition in Table 18/II) are, broadly, (i) those that are already contained in EINECS, (ii) those that were manufactured in the EU, but not placed on the market, at any time in the 15 years before June 1, 2007, and (iii) those (not being polymers) that were placed on the market in the EU and deemed to have been notified for the purposes of the CPL Directive 67/548. They are exempted from the REACH registration requirements for limited periods, provided they were "pre-registered" in the five months ending December 1, 2008, by submitting to the ECHA the information prescribed by Article 28(1). Where

---

[65] art.27(3).
[66] art.27(6).
[67] art.25(3).

this was done, a series of deadlines are set[68] for their full registration, namely:

18-021

Table 18/III

Deadline	Substances affected
December 1, 2010	Substances classified as carcinogenic, mutagenic or toxic to reproduction, category 1 or 2, and manufactured in the EU or imported, in quantities of 1 tonne or more per year per manufacturer or per importer, at least once after June 1, 2007;
	substances classified as very toxic to aquatic organisms which may cause long-term adverse effects in the aquatic environment, and manufactured in the EU or imported in quantities of 100 tonnes or more per year per manufacturer or per importer, at least once after June 1, 2007;
	all other substances manufactured in the EU or imported, in quantities of 1,000 tonnes or more per year per manufacturer or per importer, at least once after June 1, 2007.
June 1, 2013	Substances manufactured in the EU or imported, in quantities of 100 tonnes or more per year per manufacturer or per importer, at least once after 1 June 2007.
June 1, 2018	Substances manufactured in the EU or imported, in quantities of 1 tonne or more per year per manufacturer or per importer, at least once after 1 June 2007.

Registration is permitted at any time before the above deadlines.

18-022 Anyone who manufactures or imports a phase-in substance for the first time after December 1, 2008, and who was not therefore in a position to pre-register, may nevertheless take advantage of the same exemption from registration if he provides the Article 28(1) pre-registration information within 6 months of his first manufacture, import or use of the substance, and at least 12 months before the relevant deadline in Table 18/II.[69]

All potential registrants, downstream users, and third parties who have submitted Article 28(1) pre-registration information to the ECHA on a phase-in substance are automatically included in so-called "Substance Information Exchange Fora", designed to facilitate exchange of relevant information on the substance, so avoiding duplication of studies, and agreement on appropriate classification and labelling for it.[70]

---

[68] art.23.
[69] art.8(6).
[70] art.29.

Safety data sheets and provision of information

Anyone who supplies a substance or preparation must also provide the **18–023** recipient, free of charge and/or electronically, with a safety data sheet (SDS) containing all the information specified in Article 31(6) where the substance or preparation falls within any of the following categories:

(i)   a substance or preparation classified as dangerous in accordance with the relevant CPL Directives 67/548 or 1999/45;

(ii) a substance that is persistent, bioaccumulative and toxic, or very persistent and very bioaccumulative in accordance with the criteria set out in Annex XIII of REACH;

(iii) all other substances within the scope of Article 57 (see below) and listed as a "substance of very high concern" (SVHC) under Article 59(1).[71]

Where a substance or preparation is supplied or offered to the general public, however, an SDS need not be provided (unless one is specifically requested) if sufficient information accompanies it to enable users to take whatever measures may be necessary to protect human health, safety and the environment.[72] Anyone in the supply chain who carries out a chemical safety assessment (see para.18–018) must ensure that the SDS is consistent with that assessment.[73]

Even where an SDS is not required under the above rules, a supplier of a substance or preparation that is subject to authorisation under REACH must provide downstream users with information on it, including whether or not it has been authorised and, if so, the conditions of the authorisation, and any other available and relevant information about it needed to enable appropriate risk management measures to be taken.[74]

Every manufacturer, importer, downstream user and distributor of a **18–024** substance or preparation is obliged to keep all the information required to comply with the SDS and information requirements of REACH for a period of at least 10 years after he last manufactured, imported, supplied or used the substance or preparation. He must also, if so requested, provide it without delay to the competent authority of his Member State or to the ECHA.[75] If he goes into administration or liquidation, or transfers his business to a third party, the administrator, liquidator or transferee becomes subject to the same obligations in his stead.[76]

---

[71] art.31(1).
[72] art.31(4).
[73] art.31(2).
[74] art.32(1).
[75] art.36(1).
[76] art.36(2).

Evaluation of substances

18–025   The ECHA is required to develop criteria for prioritising the evaluation of registered substances, in consultation with the Member States, by reference to (i) the hazards they represent, or may represent, having regard to any similarities with known substances of concern or with substances which are persistent and liable to bio-accumulate, (ii) information on exposure to the substance, and (iii) the tonnages involved, including where appropriate, the aggregated tonnage from registrations submitted by several registrants. It must then compile a draft rolling action plan, covering a period of three years, that specifies the substances to be evaluated in each of those years. The first such plan is due to be submitted by December 1, 2011, with draft updates being submitted by February 28 in each subsequent year. A "Member State Committee", which is a constituent part of the ECHA, takes the final decision on what the programme, and the updates, are to cover, and which Member States are to be responsible for evaluating which substances.[77]

Substances of very high concern and Annex XIV listings

18–026   "Authorisation" is the means by which substances of very high concern (SVHC) are controlled under REACH. Such substances are defined in Article 57 as:

- substances meeting the criteria in Directive 67/548 for classification as carcinogenic category 1 or 2, mutagenic category 1 or 2, or toxic for reproduction category 1 or 2;
- substances which are either (a) persistent, bioaccumulative and toxic, or (b) very persistent and very bioaccumulative, determined in accordance with the criteria set out in Annex XIII of REACH;
- substances, such as those having endocrine disrupting properties or those having either persistent, bioaccumulative and toxic properties, or very persistent and very bioaccumulative properties, but which do not fulfil the relevant criteria of Annex XIII, for which there is scientific evidence of probable serious effects to human health or the environment, where these give rise to an equivalent level of concern to those of the other substances listed above, as identified on a case-by-case basis by the procedure set out in Article 59.

The identification of SVHC may be made either by the ECHA, acting on a request from the Commission, or by any Member State. Those that are so identified are listed in Annex XIV of REACH. In either case a dossier is prepared on the substance in accordance with the requirements of Annex XV (an Annex XV dossier); if this is done by a Member State, it is for-

[77] art.44.

warded to the ECHA for action. The ECHA publishes details of Annex XV dossiers it has prepared or received, and invites comments from interested parties within a specified period. If there are no comments, then the substance is automatically listed in Annex XIV. If comments are received, the Member State Committee considers the case, and where the members are unanimous, its view determines the issue. If there is disagreement, the Commission publishes a proposal for determining the issue that is considered by a different regulatory committee, composed of representatives of the Member States with weighted voting rights, which will decide the matter, by qualified majority if necessary.[78]

A decision to list a substance in Annex XIV must also include transitional arrangements prescribing (i) the date(s) from which the placing on the market and the use of the substance will be prohibited unless an authorisation is granted ("the sunset date(s)"); and (ii) a date or dates at least 18 months before the sunset date(s) by when applications must be received if the applicant wishes to continue to use the substance or place it on the market for certain uses after the sunset date(s). The decision may also provide for review periods for certain uses, and exempt certain uses from the authorisation requirement, if appropriate, coupled with any conditions for such exemptions.[79]

Once a substance is listed in Annex XIV, a manufacturer, importer or downstream user may not place it on the market for any use, or use it himself, unless the relevant use has been authorised, either generally or, in the case of a person placing it on the market, an authorisation has been granted to his immediate downstream user. This prohibition does not apply where the use has been exempted from authorisation under Article 58(2), or to uses that are permitted in the conditions of a listing on Annex XIV for a limited period until the sunset date, and either that period has not expired, or an application for authorisation has been made at least 18 months before the sunset date and no decision has yet been taken on it.[80] There is also a time-limited exemption for product and process orientated research, referred to above.[81]   **18–027**

Authorisation

Authorisation only applies to substances listed in Annex XIV. If one is granted, it will normally be subject to conditions, including monitoring, and be subject to review after a prescribed time.[82] The basic approach is that the use of an Annex XIV substance should be authorised, provided the   **18–028**

---

[78] art.133(3), which applies the procedure of Commission Decision 1999/468, [1999] OJ L184/23.
[79] art.58(1).
[80] art.56(1).
[81] para.18–037.
[82] art.60(8).

risks to human health and the environment that it entails can and will be adequately controlled. When deciding to grant an authorisation, and the conditions to be attached to it, account has to be taken of all discharges, emissions and losses of the substance, including risks arising from diffuse or dispersive uses, known at the time of the decision.[83]

There is however a presumption against any authorisation at all in the case of certain substances, namely those that are:

- within (i) or (iii) of paragraph 18–023, for which it is not possible to determine an acceptable safety threshold;
- within category (ii) of paragraph 18–023;
- within category (iii) of paragraph 18–023 and are persistent, bioaccumulative and toxic properties or are very persistent and very bioaccumulative.[84]

In the case of such substances, and in other cases that are subject to the basic approach where an authorisation would normally be refused, an authorisation may only be granted if it is shown (i) that the socio-economic benefits outweigh the risk to human health or the environment arising from the use of the substance, and (ii) that there are no suitable alternative substances or technologies. In deciding whether or not to grant an authorisation in these circumstances, account has to be taken of, among other matters:

(a) the risks posed by the proposed use(s) of the substance, including the appropriateness and effectiveness of the risk management measures proposed;
(b) the socio-economic benefits arising from its use and the socio-economic implications of a refusal to authorise;
(c) the analysis of the alternatives or of any substitution plan submitted by the applicant, and any third party contributions on this issue, having regard, *inter alia*, to the technical and economic feasibility of alternatives for the applicant; and
(d) any available information on the risks to human health or the environment of any alternative substances or technologies,

Restrictions on manufacturing, placing on the market and use

18–029   REACH contains an Annex XVII consisting of a long list of dangerous substances and preparations, together with, in each case, binding restrictions that have been placed on one or more of their manufacture, placing them on the market, and their use. The restrictions do not apply to scientific research and development, however, and they may also be framed,

---

[83] art.60(2).
[84] art.60(3).

but need not be, so as not to apply to product and process orientated research and development for a limited period.[85] Until June 1, 2013, Member States may maintain any existing restrictions that are more demanding than those in Annex XVII, provided they have been notified to the Commission.

There are extensive provisions in REACH[86] for amending Annex XVII by adding new substances, removing those currently there, and amending the restrictions or adding to them. Thus if a Member State or the Commission considers that the manufacture, placing on the market or use of a substance, whether on its own, in a preparation or in an article, poses a risk to human health or the environment that is not adequately controlled and needs to be addressed, the Member State may notify the ECHA that it proposes to prepare a dossier in accordance with Annex XV, while the Commission must ask the ECHA to prepare one. The dossier, including suggested restrictions, is published on the ECHA's website, with interested parties being invited to provide, within six months, comment on the dossiers and suggested restrictions and/or a socio-economic analysis of the suggested restrictions, or information which can contribute to one.

The ECHA has both a Committee for Risk Assessment and a Committee for Socio-economic Analysis. Each of these committees considers the proposals and any contributions from interested parties, and their opinions are submitted to the Commission. The Commission in turn prepares a formal proposal for amending Annex XVII accordingly, which is voted on by a regulatory committee under the Article 133(3) procedure.[87]

Access to information

The ECHA is required to make publicly available through the internet the information that it holds on substances, whether on their own, in preparations or in articles, as set out in Article 119. This includes basic information on the substance, its classification and labelling, physico-chemical data, and guidance on its safe use. Further information will also be made public in the same way, unless the person who submitted it can show that doing so would be harmful to his, or to a third party's, commercial interests, including: the degree of purity of the substance and the identity of impurities and/or additives which are known to be dangerous; the total tonnage band (e.g. 1–10 tonnes, 10–100 tonnes, etc.) within which a particular substance has been registered; information contained in the safety data sheet; and the trade name(s) of the substance. In addition to what is expressly required to be made public by REACH, Regulation

18–030

---

[85] art.67(1).
[86] arts 68 to 73.
[87] See para.18–026, and fn.78.

1049/2001[88] on public access to European Parliament, Council and Commission documents applies to documents held by the ECHA.[89]

Nevertheless the following categories of information will "normally be deemed to undermine the protection of the commercial interests of the concerned person", and consequently will normally not be made public:

(a) details of the full composition of a preparation;
(b) the precise use, function or application of a substance or preparation, including information about its precise use as an intermediate;
(c) the precise tonnage of the substance or preparation manufactured or placed on the market; and
(d) links between a manufacturer or importer and his distributors or downstream users.

Even so, the ECHA may disclose such information in an emergency.[90]

Appeals

18–031 Within the ECHA is a Board of Appeal that has jurisdiction[91] to hear appeals from certain of its decisions, namely those concerning: exemptions for product and process orientated research and development; completeness checks on registration dossiers; and data sharing. Where an appeal is lodged it has suspensive effect on the decision in question.

Enforcement of REACH in the United Kingdom

18–032 Being an EU Regulation, REACH has direct effect in the United Kingdom, without the need for any implementing legislation. Nevertheless, to ensure that its provisions are complied with, proposed REACH Enforcement Regulations 2008 have been prepared and issued in draft by Defra. Schedule 1 of these consists of a lengthy "Table of REACH provisions", that appoints the enforcing authorities in respect of each provision in England and Wales, Scotland, and Northern Ireland respectively. For the vast majority of the provisions, the enforcing authority in England and Wales is the Health and Safety Executive, though for a few the Environment Agency or local authorities are named. Regulation 11 makes it an offence to contravene a listed REACH provision, or to cause or permit another person to do so, while Regulation 3(1) states that an enforcing authority must enforce a listed REACH provision where it is named against that provision in the Schedule 1 Table.

---

[88] [2001] OJ L145/43.
[89] art.118(1).
[90] art.118(2).
[91] Under art.91.

Leaded paints

Regulation 8 of the UK Regulations provides that the marketing and use of **18–033** leaded paints in compliance with the provisions of Schedule 5 does not breach the marketing and use restrictions provided for in REACH Article 67. Schedule 5 permits the use of leaded paint in the restoration or maintenance of:

(a) historic buildings or their interiors;
(b) scheduled monuments; or
(c) fine or decorative works of art,

where it is required to restore or maintain historic textures or finishes. A person may market leaded paint with a view to its use for these purposes. Further provisions require declarations and notifications to be made and/or supplied to the relevant competent body in advance of the proposed marketing or use of leaded paint. The competent body for England and Wales is English Heritage.

Asbestos

The term "asbestos" is used to refer to a class of fibrous impure magne- **18–034** sium silicates. The most common forms to be used commercially were crocidolite (also known as blue asbestos), amosite (brown asbestos), chrysotile (white asbestos), anthophyllite, tremolite and actinolite. The material itself is highly inert, even at high temperatures, which makes asbestos an attractive product for use in numerous circumstances where the physical and chemical conditions are highly demanding. However a further property of asbestos is that it forms extremely fine dust particles with a particular length to thickness ratio that allows the particles to reach the remoter parts of the human respiratory system and become lodged there. Because of the inertness of the material the particles once lodged remain essentially unchanged, and are liable to cause asbestosis, lung cancer and mesothelioma. The principal, and certainly the most danger-ous, form of ingestion is thus through the air.

The main EU legislation on asbestos and asbestos products comprises the REACH Regulation, in relation to the marketing and use of such materials; Directive 87/217[92] on minimising emissions of asbestos into the environment; Directive 83/477,[93] which was made under the framework Directive 80/1107[94] on protection from risks related to exposure to che-mical, physical and biological agents at work; Directive 90/394/EEC[95] on

---

[92] [1987] OJ L85.
[93] [1983] OJ L263/25, as amended by Directive 91/382/EEC, [1991] OJ L206/16, and Directive 2003/18, [2003] OJ L97/48.
[94] [1980] OJ L307.
[95] [1990] OJ L196/38.

the protection of workers from the risks related to exposure to carcinogens at work; and Directive 98/24/EC[96] on the protection of the health and safety of workers from the risks related to exposure to chemical agents at work.

The UK legislation relating to asbestos has quite recently been consolidated into the Control of Asbestos Regulations 2006,[97] which implement the bulk of the EU legislation just indicated.[98] These are supplemented by a series of guidance notes, published by the HSE, on the safe use and handling of asbestos under the general title of "Asbestos Essentials".[99] The 2006 Regulations have two main substantive parts: Part 2, which imposes a general duty and a series of obligations on those responsible for non-domestic premises, and Part 3, which consists of prohibitions and restrictions on the supply and use of asbestos in its various forms. They are as applicable to self-employed people as they are to employers and employees.

18–035 Certain provisions (relating to licensing, notification of proposed work, arrangements for emergencies and accidents, designation of asbestos areas, and keeping health records) do not however apply where:

(a) the exposure of employees to asbestos is sporadic and of low intensity;

(b) it is clear from a risk assessment that the exposure of any employee to asbestos will not exceed the prescribed control limit; and

(c) the work involves;

(i) short, non-continuous maintenance activities,

(ii) removal of materials in which the asbestos fibres are firmly linked in a matrix,

(iii) encapsulation or sealing of asbestos-containing materials which are in good condition, or

(iv) air monitoring and control, and the collection and analysis of samples to ascertain whether a specific material contains asbestos.[100]

It is to be noted that all of (a), (b) and (c) must be complied with if the Regulations are not to apply; the only alternatives are the four categories within (c).

---

[96] [1993] OJ L131/11.
[97] SI 2006/2739.
[98] Or the predecessors to the REACH Regulation, in the case of marketing and use.
[99] Available on *http://www.hse.gov.uk/pubns/guidance/aseries.htm.*
[100] reg.3(2).

General requirements

Regulation 4 creates a "dutyholder" on whom the burden of complying   **18–036**
with the Regulations falls. He is primarily whoever has a legal obligation
under a contract or tenancy in relation to the maintenance or repair of any
relevant (non-domestic) premises, including all entrances and exits. If
there is no such contract or tenancy, then whoever has any control over any
part of the premises, again including all entrances and exits, will be the
dutyholder. There may well be more than one dutyholder, in which case
their obligations under the Regulations are in proportion to the nature and
extent of their respective maintenance and repair obligations.

The first obligation of the dutyholder is to ensure that a "suitable and
sufficient" assessment is carried out as to whether asbestos is or is liable to
be present in the premises, and to record his conclusions.[101] If he concludes that it is, or is liable to be, present he must assess the risk it
represents, and prepare a plan identifying the relevant parts of the premises
and setting out the measures for managing that risk.

An employer must not undertake any work, whether demolition, maintenance or otherwise, that is liable to expose his employees to any asbestos
unless he has carried out a suitable assessment of whether it is present, and
if so its nature and condition, and of the steps that need to be taken to
comply with the Regulations. If there is doubt as to whether asbestos is
present or not, he must assume that it is, and that it is not chrysotile
asbestos alone, and comply with the Regulations accordingly.[102]

Regulation 6 specifies what is required in carrying out a risk assessment   **18–037**
where there is potential exposure to asbestos, and Regulation 7 stipulates
the contents of the plan of work that must be drawn up where it is proposed
to deal with asbestos. In cases of final demolition or major refurbishment of
premises, the plan of work must, so far as is reasonably practicable, specify
that asbestos is to be removed before any other major works begin, unless
that would cause a greater risk to employees than leaving it in place.[103]

Before carrying out any work with asbestos, an employer must apply to
the HSE for a licence to do so at least 28 days in advance, and give the
HSE (or where relevant such other enforcing authority as is appropriate) at
least 14 days notice of his intention to begin work.[104] These periods may be
reduced with the HSE's consent.

Employers must give those of their employees who are liable to be
exposed to asbestos, and/or those who supervise them, adequate information, instruction and training on its properties, the risks entailed and
how to manage these, in accordance with the requirements of Regulation
10. They must in any event prevent so far as reasonably practicable any

[101] reg.4(3), (7).
[102] reg.5.
[103] reg.7(3).
[104] regs 8, 9.

exposure to asbestos, and minimise it where prevention is not possible, complying in particular with the provisions of Regulations 11 and 14 as regards protective equipment and clothing. Where work entails the use of asbestos or the removal or repair of asbestos-containing materials, then unless the risk of significant exposure is slight, the employer must have accident and emergency procedures ready to deal with any incident.[105] Where there is any risk of exposure to asbestos at work, the employer must designate both "asbestos areas", in which the level of asbestos is more than insignificant, and "respirator zones", in which the level exceeds or is liable to exceed the control limit, and in which respiratory protective equipment must be worn. No-one should be permitted to enter either unless required to do so by his work, and eating drinking and smoking in any designated area or zone must be prohibited.[106] The Regulations prescribe procedures for air monitoring, together with standards for air testing and analysis, the issue of site clearance certificates, and the maintenance of health records and medical surveillance. Suitable washing and changing facilities must be provided for those liable to be exposed to asbestos, with protective clothing being kept separate from clothing worn outside working hours. Raw asbestos and asbestos waste must be kept in sealed containers or other sealed wrapping, labelled in accordance with the Carriage of Dangerous Goods and Use of Transportable Pressure Equipment Regulations 2007,[107] where these apply, or otherwise in accordance with Schedule 2 of the Regulations.

18–038   Where any person is charged with an offence under Part 2 of the Regulations, it is a defence to prove that the defendant took all reasonable precautions and exercised all due diligence to avoid the commission of that offence.

Prohibitions and restrictions

18–039   Part 3 of the Asbestos Regulations contains a series of prohibitions on;

(a) exposing employees to asbestos during the manufacture of asbestos products or of products containing intentionally added asbestos,*
(b) asbestos spraying,
(c) the use of low density insulating or sound proofing materials that contain asbestos,
(d) the import of asbestos or any product to which asbestos has been intentionally added,*
(e) the supply to any person, save for disposal, of asbestos or any product to which asbestos has been intentionally added,*

---

[105] reg.15.
[106] reg.18.
[107] SI 2007/1573.

(f) the use of asbestos or any product to which asbestos has been intentionally added, save in connection with its disposal, subject to exceptions where a product was in use before January 1, 1986, January 1, 1993, or November 24, 1999, depending on the type of asbestos concerned,

(g) the use of asbestos cement,*

(h) the use of any board, panel or tile painted with a paint or covered with a textured finishing plaster that in either case contains chrysotile, unless it is installed in any premises or plant, and has been there since before November 24, 1999.

In the case of the items marked with an asterisk, there are limited exceptions in respect of chrysotile asbestos.

In so far as asbestos may be legitimately supplied to third parties, it must be labelled as prescribed by Schedule 2, unless the amount or article involved is too small for that to be practicable.[108] Exemptions may be granted from several of the obligations imposed by the Regulations, allowing, inter alia, the supply and use of asbestos and asbestos products, and the emergency services to carry out their functions without necessarily complying with the Regulations, provided that the HSE is satisfied that the health or safety of persons who are likely to be affected by any exemption will not be prejudiced.[109]

Pesticides and biocides

Pesticides

For many years the marketing of pesticides in the United Kingdom was **18–040** subject to a Government supported voluntary agreement between the major pesticides manufacturers: the Pesticides Safety Precaution Scheme. This ensured that pesticides were only supplied to approved wholesalers who were competent to, and did, advise farmers on how best to use the pesticides, and on the risks attached. The scheme however made it difficult or impossible for parallel imports of pesticides from elsewhere in the EU to be marketed in the UK, and for this and other reasons it was eventually disbanded, and replaced by statutory controls. These now consist of Part III of the Food and Environment Act 1985 (FEPA)[110] and the Control of Pesticides Regulations 1986 (COPR),[111] made under it, both of which have been considerably amended over the years, together with the Plant Protection Products Regulations 2005 (the PPP Regs),[112] which imple-

---

[108] reg.30.
[109] reg.32.
[110] 1985, c.48.
[111] SI 1986/1510, amended many times, including by the Control of Pesticides (Amendment) Regulations 1997, SI 1997/188.
[112] SI 2005/1435.

ment EU Directive 91/414 on plant protection products,[113] as amended (the PPP Directive).

The effect of these controls is that any substance (other than one already used in an approved pesticide) that is proposed to be used as the active ingredient of a pesticide must be subjected to a rigorous assessment procedure at EU level, before any pesticide product, i.e. a plant protection product, containing that substance may be marketed. The PPP Directive has an Annex I which lists all substances that have been approved following this procedure, and which is therefore constantly being updated. The products themselves must however receive national approval in the UK before they may be marketed here, though parallel imports of essentially comparable products must be permitted provided it is shown that they are indeed comparable.[114] National approval of products containing one or more Annex I substances as their only active ingredients is governed by the UK PPP Regulations. There are of course numerous established pesticide ingredients that were in use before the EU PPP Directive first came into effect, and approvals of these continue to be made under COPR by virtue of transitional provisions in the PPP Directive. Over time, as these existing ingredients are assessed and added to Annex I (or banned), approvals under COPR will no longer be needed. In the UK the controls are exercised by the Pesticides Safety Directorate (the PSD), an agency of the HSE, and extensive guidance on the practical application of the legislation is available from its website.[115] Reference may also usefully be made to the official Code of Practice on pesticides.[116] Accordingly only an outline is given here.

Under Part III of FEPA a pesticide is "any substance, preparation or organism prepared or used for destroying any pest", "pest" being:

(a) any organism harmful to plants or to wood or other plant products;
(b) any undesired plant; and
(c) any undesired creature.[117]

"Creature" means any living organism; other than a human being or a plant; and "plant" is defined as any form of vegetable matter, while it is growing and after it has been harvested, gathered, felled or picked, and includes: agricultural crops; trees and bushes grown for purposes other than those of agriculture; wild plants; and fungi.[118]

18–041　　The definition of "pest" appears to contrast "harmful organism" with "undesired plant" and "harmful creature", which might indicate an

---

[113] [1991] OJ L230/1, amended inter alia by Directive 2005/25, [2005] OJ L90/1.
[114] PPP Regulations, reg.11.
[115] http://www.pesticides.gov.uk/home.asp.
[116] "Pesticides: A Code of Practice on Plant Protection Products" prepared by Defra, the Health and Safety Commission and the Welsh Environment Planning and Countryside Department, pub. Defra, Jan. 2006.
[117] s.16(15).
[118] s.24(1).

intention to limit the term "organism" to micro-organisms, though on the other hand "creature" clearly includes larger organisms, for example slugs, caterpillars and rodents. Since there is no necessary reason to treat the three categories of "pest" as mutually exclusive, the wider meaning appears to be the more appropriate, both there and in the definition of pesticide. COPR, as amended in 1997, defines "organism" as "any animal, plant, fungus or micro-organism capable of carrying on life processes", which is consistent with this view.

The meaning of "pesticide" is effectively broadened by COPR which provides that the Regulations apply, not only to any pesticide, but also to any substance, preparation or organism prepared or used for any of the following purposes as if it were a pesticide:

(i) protecting plants or wood or other plant products from harmful organisms;
(ii) regulating the growth of plants;
(iii) giving protection against harmful creatures;
(iv) controlling organisms with harmful or unwanted effects on water systems (including sewage treatment works), buildings or other structures, or on manufactured products;
(v) protecting animals against ectoparasites.

COPR does not however apply to organisms, other than bacteria, protozoa, fungi, viruses and mycoplasmas, used for destroying or controlling pests.[119] There is also a long list of substances, preparations and organisms, to which it does not apply, including those controlled by other regimes,[120] and a variety of low risk materials within the definition of "pesticide" such as disinfectants, and bleaching and sterilising agents, and insect repellants for human use.[121]

The Control of Pesticides Regulations 1986 (as amended)

To the extent that COPR applies to a product, it prohibits using a pesti-   **18–042** cide, and the advertising, selling, supplying and storing of a pesticide, unless (i) the activity has received approval under Regulation 5, and (ii) the so-called "basic conditions" of this approval and of the relevant consent granted under Regulation 6 are complied with. The basic conditions are set out in Schedules 1 to 3, which relate respectively to advertising (Schedule 1), sale supply and storage (Schedule 2), and use (Schedule 3). Aerial applications of pesticides are subject to the conditions of Schedule 4. Among the Schedule 2 conditions is the requirement that any person who sells, supplies or stores a pesticide must be "competent for the duties which

---

[119] reg.3(2)(a). So though a terrier used for rat catching is a pesticide for the purposes of FEPA, it escapes the controls of COPR.
[120] These include medicines, veterinary medicines, and cosmetics.
[121] reg.3(2)(b) to (i).

that person is called to perform", and that no person may sell, supply or otherwise market to an end-user a pesticide approved for agricultural use unless he has a recognised certificate of competence, or is under the direct supervision of someone who holds one.[122]

The Plant Protection Products Regulations 2005

18–043   The PPP Regulations apply to England and Wales, and are administered by the PSD. At their core is a list of prohibitions in Regulation 3. No new "active substance" may be placed on the market unless it is already in Annex I of the PPP Directive, or has been approved for inclusion in that Annex, or if an application for approval is pending.[123] "Active substance" is defined as any substance or micro-organism, including a virus, having general or specific action against harmful organisms or on plants, parts of plants or plant products; "harmful organisms" being pests of plants or plant products belonging to the animal or plant kingdom, viruses, bacteria and mycoplasmas and other pathogens. "Placed on the market" is appreciably broader than its literal meaning, and extends to any supply, whether for payment or not, within England and Wales, and includes import into England and Wales otherwise than from an EEA state.[124] (Import is however permitted if it is only for storage pending export otherwise than to an EEA state or disposal.) An active substance is "new" as regards England and Wales if it was not marketed here on or before July 26, 1993.[125]

Additionally, no "plant protection product" may be placed on the market or used unless it has been approved under one of the procedures set out in the PPP Regulations (or under "an equivalent provision"[126]) for standard, provisional and emergency approvals, and the marketing and use complies with the conditions of that approval.[127] There is no similar exemption for products that are the subject of a pending application for approval; hence although products of which the active substance is awaiting approval for inclusion in Annex I may be placed on the market, this can only be done with the consent and under the control of the PSD. Further, use of a pesticide must also be in accordance with the principles of good plant protection practice and "whenever possible, be in accordance with the principles of integrated control".[128] However non-compliance with these last requirements is not of itself an offence, though it could well

---

[122] Sch.2, paras 2(1)(b) and 2(4).
[123] reg.3(3).
[124] EEA states are all the EU Member States plus Norway, Iceland and Liechtenstein.
[125] This being the date the original PPP Directive was due to be implemented. Later dates apply to Member States that acceded more recently.
[126] Being an equivalent provision in Regulations implementing the PPP Directive elsewhere in the UK.
[127] reg.3(2)(a), (b).
[128] reg.3(2)(c), (d).

be relevant as a matter of evidence in a prosecution for other offences under the PPP Regulations. "Integrated control" is given a special meaning in this context, namely:

"the rational application of a combination of biological, biotechnological, chemical, cultural or plant-breeding measures whereby the use of chemical plant protection products is limited to the minimum strictly necessary to maintain harmful organisms below levels above which economically unacceptable damage or loss would occur".

The general prohibitions of Regulation 3 are not applicable:

(a) to active substances or products that have been approved for research and development under the separate provisions of Regulation 9; or

(b) so as to impede the production, storage or movement within England and Wales of a plant protection product intended for use in another EEA state, provided that product is authorised for use in that other state, and the inspection requirements laid down in Article 3(1) of the PPP directive are satisfied, these being whatever measures are appropriate to ensure that unauthorised products are not marketed or used in their territory.

To apply to have an active substance approved for inclusion in Annex I **18–044** of the PPP Directive, the applicant must provide dossiers on (i) the active substance, complying with the Directive's Annex II, and (ii) at least one preparation, in practice a plant protection product, containing that substance, complying with Annex III. These dossiers, which are designed to enable a through assessment of the potential risks to human and animal health, groundwater and the environment, from the substance, the product and any pesticide residues, are submitted to the Secretary of State—in fact, the PSD—the competent authorities in the other Member States, and to the European Commission.[129] Thereafter the procedure is as stipulated in Articles 5 and 6 of the Directive. Following approval, the substance will be included in Annex I for a period of at most 10 years, and may be made subject to conditions and limitations relating to e.g. the minimum degree of purity of the active substance, any specific impurities that are liable to be present, the nature of the product incorporating the substance, and the way in which the product is used.[130] Subsequent applications to renew inclusion of the substance in Annex I must be made at least 2 years before the current period is due to expire.[131]

Approval of the placing on the market and of the use of a plant protection product is given by the PSD, on behalf of the Secretary of State,

[129] PPP Regulations, reg.4(1).
[130] PPP Directive, art.5(4).
[131] PPP Directive, art.5(5).

under the "standard" procedure of Regulations 5 and 6, under the "provisional" procedure of Regulation 7, or the "emergency" procedure of Regulation 7. (These procedures only apply to products in which the, or all the, active substances are "new"—if an "old" active substance, i.e. one that is not a "new" active substance, is present, then COPR continues to apply.[132]) The standard procedure is only applicable where the active substance, or all of them if more than one, is or are included in Annex I at the time approval of the product is granted. It requires the applicant to submit information dossiers on the product and on each active substance in it that conform with the requirements of Annexes II and III of the PPP Directive. However, where the active substance is already included in Annex I, the applicant need not supply a dossier on it, provided he can show that in his case the active substance does not differ significantly in purity and the nature of impurities from the composition originally approved for inclusion in Annex I.[133] This information is assessed by reference to the general criteria set out in Regulation 6(3), which relate inter alia to efficacy, and to whether there are harmful effects on human or animal health or on groundwater, unacceptable effects on plants, plant products and the environment generally, and whether unnecessary suffering and pain is caused to vertebrates which are to be controlled. Standard approvals of products are for a period of at most 10 years, and will be made subject to such conditions as are considered appropriate.

Conditions that will necessarily apply are those set out in the Regulations 18 and 19 in respect of packaging and labelling, the labelling requirements being detailed in Schedule 3. The Secretary of State may require the approval holder and, if different, the person(s) responsible for the final packaging and/or labelling of the plant protection product at any time to provide samples, models or drafts of the packaging, labelling and leaflets referred to in that Schedule.

18–045   The grant of provisional approvals is designed to allow a gradual assessment to be made of new active substances and to avoid undue delay in getting new products into agricultural use. They apply where the active substance has been made the subject of an application for inclusion in Annex I, and so the relevant dossiers have been submitted, but final approval has not yet been granted. The Secretary of State must be satisfied that both the active substance and the product can be expected to satisfy the applicable requirements for approval and, if so, he may grant provisional approval of the product for a period of up to 3 years; this period may be extended at the request of the approval holder.

Article 8(4) of the PPP Directive envisages exceptional situations in which a Member State finds that it needs to use an unapproved product to deal with an unforeseen danger that cannot be contained by other means.

---

[132] Sch.4, para.1.
[133] reg.5(5).

It thus allows the placing on the market of an unapproved product for a "limited and controlled use" for a period not exceeding 120 days. The Member State must immediately inform all other Member States and the Commission if it takes action under this provision, and a decision is to be taken collectively on whether the action may be extended for a given period, repeated, or revoked. Regulation 8 of the PPP Regulations gives effect to Article 8(4) by permitting emergency approvals in such situations.

Much research and development relating to pesticides is of course necessarily concerned with active substances and products that have not yet been approved, and possibly never will be. The general prohibition of Regulation 3(3) relating to active substances applies solely to their being placed on the market, and so does not affect laboratory work. However the prohibition of Regulation 3(2) applies to the use of plant protection products, and inevitably covers any trials of them that may be conducted on a significant scale. Regulation 9 expressly prohibits the carrying out of any experiment or test for research or development purposes involving the release into the environment of a plant protection product without an approval under that Regulation. An application must be made to the Secretary of State (i.e. the PSD) that provides all available information relevant to an assessment of possible effects on human or animal health or on the environment from what is proposed to be done. If the experiments or tests are liable to have harmful effects on human or animal health or "an unacceptably adverse influence" on the environment then they may be prohibited altogether, or they may be permitted subject to conditions appropriate to prevent such consequences.

Where (i) a product has been authorised by another Member State to be **18–046** placed on the market and used there, and (ii) its active substance, or all of them if more than one, is or are included in Annex I, any person may apply for approval of that product under Regulation 11. Provided the applicant can satisfy the so-called "comparability requirement" then approval must be granted.[134] This requirement is that the agricultural, plant health and environmental (including climatic) conditions relevant to the use of the product in the other EEA state must be comparable to those of the United Kingdom. Nevertheless, conditions may be imposed to protect the health of those dealing with the product, to keep residues to a safe level, and, with the consent of the applicant, to reflect differences between conditions in the original country and the United Kingdom to enable the comparability requirement to be met.

Transitional Provisions

The Commission is conducting a rolling programme of testing existing **18–047** active substances, with a view to either including them in Annex I or, where

---

[134] reg.11(3).

necessary, banning them.[135] The consequences of decisions taken under this programme are set out in Schedule 4 to the PPP Regulations. This states that, except as provided in the Schedule, COPR, and not the PPP Regulations, will continue to apply to products that contain at least one old active substance, i.e. one that was on the market in the UK on or before July 26, 1993.[136] However after a decision has been taken on an old active substance, from then onwards the PPP Regulations will apply as regards that substance, in lieu of those of COPR, subject to special provisions that apply to holders of approvals for products containing that substance.

If it is decided to refuse to allow an old active substance on to Annex I, the Secretary of State will notify the approval holder of any pesticide containing it, and must revoke the current pesticide approval. As a matter of discretion, but not of right, provisional authorisations under the PPP Regulations may be granted for up to one year from the date of the revocation, to allow at least those other than the approval holder, and if thought fit the approval holder also, to continue to advertise, sell, store, supply and use the pesticide, so allowing an orderly wind down of the relevant business.

Where a decision is taken to include an old active substance in Annex I, the Secretary of State again notifies the approval holder who must, within such period as is specified in the notification, show (i) that the active substance in his product complies with the applicable Annex I conditions, and (ii) that he has access to a dossier on the active substance meeting the requirements of Annex II of the PPP Directive. Provided he does this within the prescribed period, he may continue to market and use his product until the Secretary of State decides whether or not the information provided establishes points (i) and (ii). If it does not, a reasonable time may be allowed for providing additional information, but subject to that the approval will be revoked. In that event, provisional authorisations under the PPP Regulations may be granted, as above, for up to one year from the date of the revocation to allow the business to be wound down. If the information is considered sufficient, then the approval holder must, within such period as the Secretary of State may reasonably determine, apply for authorisation of his product under the PPP Regulations in the normal way.

Data Protection

18–048   Where products must be put through lengthy and costly trials and related procedures before they can obtain regulatory approval, it is inevitably a sensitive issue as to how far, if at all, later competitors, seeking to sell

---

[135] This programme is described in detail on the page of the PSD's website headed "The European Community (EC) review programme for existing active substances", which includes a link to a list, prepared by the PSD, of all existing active substances on Annex I.
[136] The Schedule calls such a product a "relevant plant protection product". Later dates may apply in other Member States—see fn.125 above.

comparable products, should be able to benefit from the pioneering work carried out by the first applicant at his own expense. As mentioned above, where a later applicant intends to use a substance that is for practical purposes the same as one included in Annex I in a new product, when seeking approval of the new product he is exempted from having to supply a duplicate of the relevant dossier on that substance. Nevertheless, Articles 13(3) of the PPP Directive expressly provides that, when granting authorisations of new products, Member States shall not, for a period of 10 years from when the substance was first included in Annex I, make use of the information contained in the previous dossier on the relevant active substance, unless the later applicant has agreed with the first one that this may be done. If there has been a decision, following the provision of additional information on a substance, either to vary the conditions imposed on the substance, or to maintain its inclusion in Annex I unaltered, a five year period from the date of that decision applies, if that will expire after the end of the applicable 10 year period. Similarly, Article 13(4) prohibits Member States from using information in the previous dossier on the product containing that active substance for a period of 10 years from when the product was first authorised in any Member State, unless the two applicants agree otherwise.

It is settled EU policy that testing of substances on animals should be kept to the unavoidable minimum. Regulation 16 reflects this by making provision for where a later applicant for authorisation of a product of which the active substance is in Annex I plans to carry out experiments on vertebrate animals for the purpose of seeking authorisation of that product. He is obliged to enquire whether approval has already been granted for that product and, if so, obtain the name and address of the approval holder; failure to make such an enquiry is an offence. The two parties are obliged to take all reasonable steps to reach agreement on the sharing of information so as to avoid duplicate tests on vertebrate animals. If they cannot agree the Secretary of State may direct that the relevant information be shared, and also determine how the information is to be used and "the reasonable balance of the interests of the parties involved".

There is a general obligation to keep confidential all information submitted pursuant to applications to include an active substance in Annex I or for approval of a plant protection product, to the extent that the Secretary of State considers that it contains industrial or commercial secrets. This is nevertheless subject to the provisions of the Environmental Information Regulations 2004,[137] and is expressly stated not to apply to information as listed in Schedule 2 to the PPP Regulations, namely:

- the name and content of the active substance and the name of the plant protection product;

---

[137] SI 2004/3391.

- the name of other substances present which are regarded as dangerous under either the Dangerous Substances or Dangerous Preparations Directives;
- physico-chemical data concerning the active substance and plant protection product;
- any ways of rendering the active substance or plant protection product harmless;
- a summary of the results of the tests to establish the efficacy and harmlessness to humans, animals, plants and the environment of the active substance or the plant protection product;
- recommended methods and precautions to reduce handling, storage, transport, fire or other hazards;
- relevant methods of analysis;
- methods of disposal of the product and of its packaging;
- decontamination procedures to be followed in the case of accidental spillage or leakage; and
- first aid and medical treatment to be given in the case of injury to persons.

Future Developments

18–049   The EU 6th Environmental Action Programme required[138] a "Thematic Strategy for Pesticides" to be developed that was to address the following issues:

  (i) minimising the hazards and risks to health and environment from the use of pesticides;

 (ii) improved controls on the use and distribution of pesticides;

(iii) reducing the levels of harmful active substances, including by substituting the most dangerous with safer, including non-chemical, alternatives;

(iv) encouragement of the use of low input or pesticide free cultivation through, inter alia, raising users' awareness, promoting the use of codes of good practice, and promoting consideration of the possible application of financial instruments;

 (v) a transparent system for reporting and monitoring progress made in fulfilling the objectives of the strategy including the development of suitable indicators.

This led to the Commission publishing, in 2006, (i) the required thematic strategy, (ii) a proposed "sustainable use" framework directive for Community action to achieve a sustainable use of pesticides, and (iii) a proposed new regulation on the placing of plant protection products on the

---

[138]   In art.7(2)(c) of Decision 1600/2002 [2002] OJ L242/1-15.

market, designed to replace the current Directive 91/414.[139] At the time of writing the draft directive and regulation are still going through the legislative process, but some form of each, after going through the co-decision procedure, seems likely to be adopted during 2009. There will then have to be some further period before they take practical effect.

Among the probable changes is a provision dividing the territory of the EU into several, probably three, "authorisation zones" reflecting the different climates of each, with compulsory mutual recognition of authorisations in Member States belonging to the same zone. There are likely to be specific provisions for substances and products containing substances of low concern. Separately, the Commission has indicated that in the longer term it will seek to incorporate biocides into the definition of "pesticide", and so avoid the present two very similar but distinct regimes (see below).

Biocides

In European parlance biocides used to be called "non-agricultural pesticides" but, having regard to the enormous range of products concerned and their economic importance, they have been given the less negative appellation of "biocidal products".[140] They have been subject to specific EU control since EU Directive 98/8[141] came into effect on May 14, 1998. Implementation in the United Kingdom of this Directive as amended is through the Biocidal Products Regulations 2001, as amended.[142] These Regulations define "biocidal product" as "an active substance or a preparation containing one or more active substances, in the form in which it is supplied to the user, intended to destroy, deter, render harmless, prevent the action of, or otherwise exert a controlling effect on, any harmful organism by chemical or biological means". An "active substance" is "a substance or micro-organism having a general or specific effect on or against harmful organisms". "Harmful organism" is "any organism which has an unwanted presence or a detrimental effect for humans, their activities or the products they use or produce". Biocidal product types are listed exhaustively in Annex V to the Directive and in Schedule 1 to the Regulations, and fall into four "main group" categories: (i) disinfectants and general biocidal products; (ii) preservatives; (iii) pest control (including repellents and attractants); and (iv) other biocidal products.

It will be immediately seen that the definition of "biocidal product"

18–050

---

[139] COM (2006) 372 final, COM (2006) 373 final and COM (2006) 388 final, respectively, all dated July 12, 2006. A related proposal for a Statistics Regulation, COM (2002) 778 final, was published on December 11, 2006.

[140] The term is somewhat of a misnomer, though, as biocides do not necessarily operate by killing, or attempting to kill, anything.

[141] [1998] OJ L123/1; most recently amended by Directive 2008/31, [2008] OJ L81/57.

[142] SI 2001/880, amended most recently, and quite significantly, by the Biocidal Products (Amendment) Regulations 2007, SI 2007/293.

overlaps very substantially with that of "pesticide" in COPR and of "plant protection product" in the PPP Regulations. As compared with a plant protection product, the difference is essentially that the intended application of biocides is not primarily, if at all, the prevention of harm to plants. The Biocidal Products Regulations do not apply to products controlled by any of the numerous regimes listed in Schedule 2, including the Plant Protection Products Regulations. They are also disapplied in respect of medicinal and veterinary medicinal products, medical devices, food additives and flavourings, cosmetic products, and many others, in so far as these are governed by the various relevant EU regimes.

The controls in the Biocidal Products Directive and Regulations follow the general pattern of the PPP Regulations, though they are somewhat more complex, especially as they cater for what are termed "low-risk" biocidal products by a process of registration, rather than the standard pre-authorisation procedure applicable to those of higher risk. The Regulations are made under the European Communities Act and the HSWA, and are administered by the HSE, which provides useful guidance on its website on the legislation and the procedures for obtaining authorisation of active substances and products.[143]

Active substances

18–051　As for pesticides, there are separate controls over the active substances used in biocides, and over the individual biocidal products. When an active substance is approved for use in a product it is assigned to one of Annex I, Annex IA or Annex IB to the Directive. A product of which the only active substance(s) is or are all listed in Annex IA will be deemed a "low-risk biocidal product", that merely requires to be registered before being marketed and used. Substances will not be included in Annex IA if they are classified as carcinogenic, mutagenic, toxic for reproduction or sensitising, or if they are bioaccumulative or not readily biodegradable. Annex IB is for substances whose major use is non-pesticidal, but which has some minor use as a biocide, either directly or in a product that consists of that substance and a simple diluent (which must not be a "substance of concern"[144]) and which is not directly marketed for biocidal use. A substance that does not qualify for Annexes IA or IB will, if approved, be assigned to Annex I.

Transitional provisions apply to "existing" active substances, i.e. those that were on the market for a biocidal purpose on or before May 14, 2000. These had to be notified within a prescribed period in relation to the product types that they were used in; to the extent this was not done, all

---

[143] *http://www.hse.gov.uk/biocides/bpd/index.htm.*
[144] "Substances of concern" are any that have an inherent capacity to cause an adverse effect on humans, animals or the environment, and are present in a product in a sufficient concentration to have such an effect in practice.

products not conforming to those types in respect of which a notification had been made had to be withdrawn from the EU market by September 1, 2006. There is an EU review programme for duly notified existing active substances, designed to determine whether they should be included in any of Annex I, IA or IB.[145] Meanwhile, the biocidal products of the notified types that contain them may continue to be sold and used under the controls of COPR.

An application for authorisation of an active substance is made to the HSE together with the dossiers on it conforming with the requirements of Regulations 5, and a further dossier on at least one biocidal product containing it. Thereafter, provided the application is considered to comply with the formal requirements, it is copied to the Commission and the other Member States. It is then examined, and if accepted in principle the Secretary of State sends a recommendation to the Commission, the other Member States and the applicant as to whether the substance should or should not be included in Annex I, IA or IB. Where the Commission receives a favourable recommendation, it prepares a proposal for inclusion of the substance in the appropriate Annex if it successfully passes the regulatory and scrutiny procedure laid down in the Directive.[146] Inclusion is for an initial period of up to 10 years, and is thereafter renewable for periods of up to 10 years.[147]

Biocidal Products

These are subject to general prohibitions on their being placed on the **18–052** market or used unless (i) they are authorised (if they contain any Annex I substances), (ii) registered (if they only contain Annex IA substances), or (iii) their only active substance(s) is or are in Annex IB.[148] In all cases any applicable conditions must of course be complied with, and use of the product must be kept to the minimum necessary for effectiveness, in line with the requirements of Regulations 8(5) and 8(6)(b). There is an exception for research and development, which requires separate authorisation[149] if it may involve or result in release of a biocidal product into the environment.

Application for the standard authorisation of a biocidal product follows a procedure essentially similar to that for obtaining authorisation of a plant protection product,[150] and a like procedure, though less demanding, applies for registration of a "low-risk" product containing only Annex IA

---

[145] See reg.1451/2007, [2007] OJ L325/3, for the procedure to be followed, Annex II of this Regulation contains a comprehensive list of the active substances to be reviewed.
[146] arts 11, 27 and 28 (4).
[147] art.10(1) and (4).
[148] reg.8(1), (2) and (4).
[149] Under reg.16.
[150] reg.9.

active substances.[151] In each case provisional authorisations and registrations for a period of up to 3 years (extendable by one further year) are available where the active substance has not yet been included in Annex I or IA, but an application for this is pending.[152] Emergency authorisations are permitted for up to 120 days if necessary in exceptional circumstances.[153] "Essential use" authorisations are catered for by Regulation 15A,[154] and allow temporary use of a biocidal product listed in Schedule 5A for the specific use stated in that Schedule until the specified date.[155] Standard product authorisations are initially for a period that expires on the expiry date of the first authorisation to expire of any active substance in the product, and they may thereafter be renewed, assuming the relevant substance authorisation has meanwhile been renewed, for a further period calculated on the same basis. If there is a single active substance, these periods may therefore be for up to 10 years.

The person first responsible for placing a biocidal product on the market in Great Britain is required to provide the National Poisons Information Service (the NPIS) the information on the product specified in Schedule 8 within one month of when the product was first placed on the market.[156] Any changes to this information must also be notified to the NPIS. The NPIS must keep this information confidential, save that it may disclose it to a registered medical practitioner if so requested, or to a person working under the direction of such a practitioner.

Data Protection

18–053   Essentially similar provisions apply in the case of biocidal active substances and products as for plant protection active substances and products.[157] These include provisions for co-operation between parties where one is seeking to obtain an authorisation on the basis of vertebrate animal experiments carried out previously by the other, though the most that can be done is to "encourage" the first to co-operate. There is no power to direct that relevant information be shared. Over-riding these however is a general right to use information relating to existing active substances and products containing them after May 14, 2010, (this being 10 years from the date the Directive was due to be implemented by the Member States,

---

[151] reg.10.
[152] regs 13, 14.
[153] reg.15.
[154] Inserted by SI 2007/293, regs 13 and 23.
[155] This enabled effect to be given to Commission Decision C (2006) 6707 of December 20, 2006, allowing the temporary use of ammonia as a veterinary hygiene biocide for the prevention of certain infections in livestock. The end date of May 14, 2008, has now expired. However it is clearly conceivable that similar circumstances, requiring a similar response, may occur again in the future.
[156] reg.29(3). Reg.29(6) stipulates that the information is to be sent to NPIS Birmingham Centre, City Hospital, Dudley Road, Birmingham B18 7QH.
[157] regs 23 to 27.

and the last date on which an existing active substances could be created), and in some cases sooner. There is also a general right to use information relating to a product containing a "new" active substance after 10 years have elapsed since the first authorisation or registration of that product,[158] and a right to use information relating to a "new" active substance 15 years after its first inclusion in Annex I or IA.[159]

All information submitted pursuant to the Regulations must be kept confidential, to the extent that it is accepted that disclosure might harm the applicant's industrial or commercial position. This is nevertheless subject to the provisions of the Environmental Information Regulations 2004,[160] and is expressly stated not to apply to the information relating to a product listed in Schedule 6 to the Regulations, once that product has been authorised or registered.[161]

EXPORTS, IMPORTS AND CARRIAGE OF DANGEROUS GOODS

The export and import of certain dangerous chemicals, including pesti- **18–054** cides, is subject to an international "prior informed consent" (PIC) procedure established by the 1998 Rotterdam Convention,[162] which lists in its Annex III the chemicals to which it applies, and contains rules for adding to the Annex III list and for removing items from it. The Convention is given effect within the EU by EU Regulation 304/2003, as amended,[163] which however extends beyond the chemicals in the Convention's Annex III, and applies to additional ones that are banned or severely restricted in the EU or a Member State, and also applies generally to the classification packaging and labelling of a wider range of chemicals that are proposed to be exported to territories outside the EU. It does not apply to a variety of materials and articles covered by other EU legislation[164] including radioactive substances, wastes, food, food additives and feedingstuffs, GMOs, and medicinal and veterinary medicinal products, and specifically excludes from its scope chemicals in quantities not likely to affect health or the environment, and in particular quantities of not more than 10kg imported for research or analysis.

---

[158] reg.24(3).
[159] reg.23(3).
[160] SI 2004/3391.
[161] reg.26.
[162] The Rotterdam Convention on the Prior Informed Consent Procedure for Certain Hazardous Chemicals and Pesticides in International Trade, September 10, 1998; Cm 6119.
[163] [2003] OJ L63/1.
[164] Listed in Article 2.

Annex I of the Regulation is divided into three parts, in which are listed chemicals[165] that are subject to one or more of three actions: export notification, PIC notification (a procedure specific to the Regulation), and the international PIC procedure in accordance with the Convention. Part 1 lists chemicals that are subject solely to export notification; Part 2 those that are subject to both export notification and PIC notification; and Part 3 those that are subject to the PIC procedure, being in the Convention's Annex III.[166] Part 2 contains chemicals that are not as yet in the Convention's Annex III but, by reason of their hazardous properties, are considered to qualify for it. Accordingly the Commission liaises with the Secretariat operating the Convention with a view to adding the Part 2 chemicals to that Annex. The Regulation requires Member States to assist the Commission in providing additional information on such chemicals so that a decision on them can be taken.[167]

Export notifications must be made at least 30 days before the first export takes place, to give time for the receiving country to respond to the notification. Thereafter, in each subsequent calendar year, the exporter must notify his intention to export the chemical at least 15 days before the first export of that year.[168] In the case of chemicals in Parts 2 or 3 of Annex I, these may not be exported unless explicit consent from the relevant authority in the importing country to receive them has been sought and received, except where, in the case of a Part 3 chemical, the Convention's Secretariat has issued a circular stating that the importing country consents to the import of that chemical. The Regulation is administered in Great Britain by the Health and Safety Commission, under the provisions of the Export and Import of Dangerous Chemicals Regulations 2005.[169]

Carriage of Dangerous Goods

18–055   The controls over the carriage of dangerous goods have recently been consolidated into the Carriage of Dangerous Goods and Use of Transportable Pressure Equipment Regulations 2007[170] which, unlike the previous 2004 Regulations, now revoked, apply to carriage by both road and rail. They give effect to the so-called ADR[171] (the European Agreement Concerning The International Carriage Of Dangerous Goods By Road), and RID, which is annexed to COTIF, the Convention concerning

---

[165] The Regulation defines "chemicals" as meaning both industrial chemicals and pesticides; art.3(1). "Industrial chemicals" are chemicals for use either by professionals or by the public; art.3(5).
[166] art.6.
[167] art.10(5).
[168] art.7(1).
[169] SI 2005/928.
[170] SI 2007/1573.
[171] Current edition (2007): ISBN 9789211391121.

International Carriage by Rail,[172] and implement Directives 2006/89 and 2006/90,[173] which adopt the 2007 versions of ADR and RID as Annexes to their respective parent Directives 94/55 (on transport by road) and 96/49 (on transport by rail).[174] The provisions of ADR and RID are immensely detailed and require close scrutiny by those affected, but space does not permit that in this work.

---

[172] The ISBN of the 2007 edition of Appendix C to COTIF (which includes the Annex) is 9788086206288.
[173] [2006] OJ L305/4 and [2006] OJ L305/6, respectively.
[174] [1994] OJ L319/7 and [1996] OJ L235/25, respectively.

Chapter 19

GENETICALLY MODIFIED ORGANISMS

Introduction

Micro-organisms have been used by man for thousands of years in the production of food and drink, for example the leavening of bread with yeast, the fermentation of a variety of carbohydrate-containing natural products to give alcohol, and the preparation of yoghurt from milk. The selective breeding and cross-breeding of animals and plants has also for many years been used to promote the production of particularly desired strains of genetic material. It was however only following the discovery of the molecular structure of genetic material (the double helix, that is the principal characteristic of DNA[1]) and establishing the nature of the units of which it is composed, that it became possible to operate on these structures in a controlled way to produce intended changes in the replicating material.[2] The end products of many commercial processes involving genetic engineering are often identical to those found in nature, save that they are in a pure form, and so potentially safer and generally more suitable for commercial use.[3]

Thus, biotechnology may be, and often is, used to obtain no more than what can be achieved by traditional techniques with natural materials, but it does so with more precision and greater efficiency. Even where new products are produced, these are often only what might have been obtained by conventional selective breeding techniques, but the possibility of splicing into genetic material a new gene with an identified property eliminates to a considerable degree the randomness that is an unavoidable part of selective breeding.[4] However, genetic engineering techniques also undeniably make possible the creation of replicating organisms containing wholly novel combinations of genetic material, that would almost certainly

19–001

---

[1] First postulated by James Watson and Francis Crick in 1953.
[2] The now standard DNA splicing techniques used in genetic engineering were first developed by Stanley Cohen and Herbert Boyer in around 1973.
[3] Biotechnology is now widely used in the pharmaceutical industry, for example, to manufacture naturally occurring products, such as hormones, that have previously only been produced by lengthy and expensive purification and concentration processes on naturally occurring raw materials. The ability of genetic engineering techniques to create an identical product without impurities produces far greater predictability of performance and helps to avoid uncertain side effects.
[4] Typical examples of such techniques are the production of plants with increased resistance to particular diseases or to drought.

never occur without human intervention.[5] These raise the inevitable possibility, albeit in the great majority of cases an extremely remote one, that such new organisms might, if allowed to escape, proliferate uncontrollably in the absence of any existing organisms that could compete successfully with them. The consequences could be severe, conceivably even fatal, disturbances to the eco-systems on which they might impinge.

It is this possibility of an adverse and conceivably catastrophic effect on humans and the environment generally from a newly created substance that demands that the handling, and in particular any deliberate release, of genetically modified organisms (GMOs) capable of independent survival and reproduction be conducted with great care.

19–002   Commercial research using recombinant DNA techniques developed rapidly from the mid-1970s onwards. After an initial period when those involved operated voluntary constraints, the first statutory controls in the United Kingdom that directly addressed these concerns were the Health and Safety (Genetic Manipulation) Regulations 1978,[6] which required notification to the Health and Safety Executive (the HSE) of any proposals to carry out genetic manipulation. They were essentially aimed at protecting the health and safety of those working with genetic material; protection of the environment more generally was not their purpose. In the mid-1980s, however, official concern with the risks associated with the release of genetic material into the environment led to the issue of formal guidelines by the Advisory Committee on Genetic Manipulation (the ACGM) that had been set up by the Health and Safety Commission in 1984. The ACGM guidelines were given statutory force in the Genetic Manipulation Regulations 1989.[7]

At much the same time, the European Commission was developing its own proposals for control over genetically modified organisms, and these resulted in Directives 90/219 and 90/220[8] relating respectively to the contained use of genetically modified micro-organisms, and the deliberate release into the environment of genetically modified organisms. The Environmental Protection Bill was also then in the course of its passage through Parliament, and Part VI of the eventual Environmental Protection Act (EPA) represented the first piece of primary legislation in the UK relating to the use of genetically modified organisms and concerned with the protection of the environment as well as human health.

Despite the introduction of the legislation nearly 20 years ago, the uptake in the United Kingdom of genetically modified products outside the pharmaceutical industry has been modest. By contrast, the cultivation of GM crops in e.g. North America, Brazil and China has developed very

---

[5] Such an approach has been used to develop uniquely effective delivery mechanisms for pharmaceuticals for treating specific organisms within the body, typically tumours.
[6] SI 1978/752.
[7] SI 1989/1810.
[8] [1990] OJ L117/1 and [1990] L117/15.

substantially over the same period. Many consumers in the UK, and indeed in much of the EU, appear to remain firmly sceptical as to the benefits to them of the new technology, whatever advantages it may have for those higher up the supply chain. The initial attempts to introduce GM foods and crops into the UK met with strong resistance from a large section of the public, including several invasions of fields where GM crops were being trialled. In particular, there was a general demand that foods containing GM material should always clearly state on their labels that this was so.[9] The view of the supermarkets that any such labelling would be highly detrimental to sales, resulted in the manufacturers and suppliers fairly rapidly withdrawing from the UK market. Although a number of farm-scale evaluations (FSEs) were conducted, the UK Government agreed with the seed manufacturers and suppliers that there should be no commercial scale plantings until the FSEs had been completed. At EU level the political hostility was such that there was a moratorium from October 1998 on the granting of authorisations for new GM crops, pending the setting up of a regime for ensuring appropriate labelling and traceability of GM foods and food ingredients.[10] This was lifted in 2004, on the coming into effect that year of the EU GM Food and Feed Regulation 1829/2003[11] (see below). To date in the UK, some development work has been conducted, mostly on oilseed rape, sugar beet, fodder beet, maize and potatoes, with a view to introducing or enhancing their herbicide tolerance and pest or disease resistance.

EC Legislation

Of the original EC legislation, Directive 90/219 on the contained use of **19–003** micro-organisms (the "Contained Use Directive") remains in effect, though it has been subject to a series of amending directives. Directive 90/220 on the deliberate release into the environment of genetically modified organisms ("the Deliberate Release Directive") has however been revoked and replaced by Directive 2001/18, as amended.[12]

Both the Contained Use and Deliberate Release Directives require the Commission to set up a committee of national "competent authorities" to assist it in implementing the Directives. The UK competent authorities are the HSE and Defra jointly. Prime responsibility for contained use activities is nevertheless taken by the HSE, and for deliberate release activities by Defra. The European Commission itself has also issued guidelines on the

---

[9] As will be seen later in this Chapter, the EU laid down rules requiring such labelling where the GM content is over 0.9 per cent.
[10] The moratorium on authorisations led to a formal complaint to the WTO by the USA, Canada and Argentina that the EU had created an illegal barrier to trade.
[11] [2003] OJ L268/1.
[12] [2001] OJ L106/1.

interpretation of various issues arising under the Directives which have been discussed and agreed in the committee, this guidance being reflected where appropriate in the official guidelines on the UK Contained Use and Deliberate Release Regulations.

EU Regulation 258/1997[13] provides for a consistent EU-wide system for the risk assessment of novel food and food ingredients prior to any approval of them, and for their labelling. Originally it covered, though was not confined to, such food and ingredients as consisted of, contained or were derived from GMOs. However, since April 18, 2004, genetically modified food and feed applications have been regulated in the European Community under EU Regulation 1829/2003,[14] the so-called "Food and Feed Regulation", which provides for a single Community procedure for their authorisation. It covers all of (i) GMOs for food use, (ii) food containing or consisting of GMOs, and (iii) food produced from or containing ingredients produced from GMOs. It amended the earlier Regulation 258/1997, restricting it so as to prevent overlap with the Food and Feed Regulation.

19–004   The Cartagena Protocol on Biosafety, a protocol to the 1993 UN Convention on Biological Diversity, was signed on January 29, 2000, and formally approved by the EU Council of Ministers on June 25, 2002.[15] The Protocol is primarily concerned with the safe transfer, handling and use of GMOs, and led directly to EU Regulation 1946/2003 on transboundary movements of GMOs,[16] on which the Protocol specifically focuses.

UK Legislation

19–005   The substantive UK legislation on GMOs currently consists primarily of:

(i) the bulk of Part VI of the EPA, namely Sections 106 to 127;

(ii) the Genetically Modified Organisms (Contained Use) Regulations 2000, as amended by the Genetically Modified Organisms (Contained Use) (Amendment) Regulations 2002 and 2005[17]—the "Contained Use Regulations";

(iii) the Genetically Modified Organisms (Deliberate Release) Regulations 2002, as amended by the Genetically Modified Organisms (Deliberate Release) (Amendment) Regulations 2004[18]—the "Deliberate Release Regulations"; and

---

[13] [1997] OJ L43/1.
[14] [2003] OJ L268/1.
[15] Council Decision 2002/628; [2002] OJ L201/48, to which the text of the Cartagena Protocol is annexed at pages 50–65.
[16] [2003] OJ L287/1.
[17] SI 2000/2831; SI 2002/63; SI 2005/2466.
[18] SI 2002/2443, SI 2004/2411.

(iv) the Genetically Modified Organisms (Transboundary Movements) (England) Regulations 2004—the "Transboundary Movements Regulations".[19]

It should be noted that since Part VI of the EPA was drafted independently of the 1990 European GMO legislation being introduced at much the same time, some of its original definitions are inconsistent with the latter. The Deliberate Release Regulations 2002 make amendments to Part VI to ensure effective implementation of Directive 2001/18.

The structure of the UK legislation is complicated by the need to implement the two principal EC Directives, which differ as to the GMOs controlled, and also since environmental protection and health and safety are governed in the UK by largely distinct legal regimes with different regulatory authorities. There are separate official committees that advise in relation to issues arising under the two sets of GMO Regulations. The Advisory Committee on Genetic Manipulation (ACGM), which was established in 1984 to advise the HSC and the HSE, and the relevant ministers, on aspects of genetic manipulation, continues to have responsibility for advising on human health and safety standards applicable to activities involving GMOs, and is responsible for advising in relation to the Contained Use Regulations. The Advisory Committee on Releases to the Environment (ACRE) was in existence before Part VI was brought into force, but its membership is now appointed under section 124 of the EPA to advise the Secretary of State on releases to the environment, and on the exercise of other powers available to him under Part VI.

Part VI of the Environmental Protection Act 1990

The purpose of Part VI of the EPA is stated to be to ensure that "all **19–006** appropriate measures are taken to avoid damage to the environment which may arise from the escape or release from human control of GMOs".[20] However, since controls over contained use of micro-organisms are contained in regulations made under the Health and Safety at Work Act (HSWA) 1974, Part VI has been brought into force only so far as appropriate to control the release and marketing of (all) GMOs and the contained use of GMOs other than micro-organisms (for their definition see paragraph 19–007).

---

[19] SI 2004/2692.
[20] s.106(1), as amended by the Deliberate Release Regulations 2002.

The Contained Use Regulations 2000, as amended

19–007 Though the Contained Use Directive applies only to *micro*-organisms, the Contained Use Regulations also apply to other organisms, albeit that the controls over the latter are generally less demanding. The Regulations are made under both the HSWA 1974 and the European Communities Act 1972, but are nevertheless explicitly stated to be also for the protection of the environment as well as from risks to health, though in this respect they are only concerned with activities involving genetic modification of micro-organisms.[21] They cover virtually every likely activity involving GMOs other than deliberate release (and marketing) and, to some extent, transport. Part VI of the E.P.A., which applies, inter alia, to the acquiring and importing of GMOs, is therefore also potentially applicable to some contained use activities. They are administered by the HSE, which has issued guidance on them.[22]

The Contained Use Regulations define "organism" as "a biological entity capable of replication or of transferring genetic material"; the term also includes a micro-organism. "Micro-organism" is defined as being a micro-biological entity, cellular or non-cellular, capable of replication or of transferring genetic material; it is explicitly stated that the term includes a virus, a viroid, and an animal or plant cell in culture. "Genetic modification" is also defined and means the altering of the genetic material in an organism by a way that does not occur naturally by mating or natural recombination or both. To assist in applying this definition, the Regulations set out in Part I of Schedule 2 examples of techniques that do constitute genetic modification, and in Part II of the same Schedule techniques which are considered not to result in genetic modification. Thus genetic modification includes:

(a) recombinant DNA techniques whereby a new combination of genetic material is formed by the insertion of nucleic acid molecules into a vector system which is incorporated into a host organism, so that the whole is capable of continued propagation;

(b) the direct introduction into an organism of heritable material; and

(c) cell fusion or hybridisation techniques using methods that do not occur naturally.

Techniques which are considered not to result in genetic modification are;

(a) *in vitro* fertilisation;

(b) conjugation, transduction, transformation or any other natural process; and

---

[21] reg.3(1)(b).

[22] "A Guide to the Genetically Modified Organisms (Contained Use) Regulations 2000", L29 (HSE Books, 2000).

(c) polyploidy induction,

provided that these do not involve the use of recombinant DNA molecules or GMOs within the scope of the Regulation.

Regulation 3(2) excludes from the scope of the Contained Use Regulations[23] the genetic modification of organisms solely by any techniques listed in Schedule 2, Part III, and also organisms so modified. Provided they do not involve the use of recombinant DNA molecules or GMOs other than any produced by these techniques, they consist of: **19–008**

(a) mutagenesis;
(b) cell fusion (including protoplast fusion) of prokaryotic species which can exchange genetic material through homologous recombination;
(c) cell fusion (including protoplast fusion) of any eukaryotic species, including production of hybridomas and plant cell fusions;
(d) self-cloning,[24] where the resulting organism is unlikely to cause disease or harm to humans, animals or plants.

Under Regulation 25 the "competent authority"—a composite body consisting of the relevant Government Ministers[25] and the HSE, acting jointly—may grant exemptions from any of the requirements and prohibitions of the Regulations, though it may attach conditions to such an exemption if it sees fit. No exemption may however be granted unless the authority is satisfied that, having regard to the particular circumstances and any conditions it proposes to attach to the exemption, it would not prejudice the health and safety of anyone likely to be affected or, where the relevant activity involves a micro-organism, the protection of the environment.

Regulation 4 extends the meaning of "work", as it is understood for the purposes of the HSWA, to include any activity involving genetic modification, irrespective, therefore, of where and the circumstances in which this takes place. Further, regulation 5 modifies, inter alia, section 3(2) of the HSWA, which places general health and safety duties on self-employed persons to seek to avoid risks to themselves or to the public,[26] such that where any activity involving genetic modification is conducted by any person who is neither an employer nor an employee, that person is made subject to the general duties. Thus those conducting private, non-commercial research would also be covered.

---

[23] Except for Regulation 17, laying down general principles of occupational and environmental safety, which therefore still applies.
[24] "Self-cloning" is defined in para.4 of Sch.2.
[25] These vary depending on whether the proposed activity is to be in England and Wales or in Scotland.
[26] HSWA, s.3(2) reads: "It shall be the duty of every self-employed person to conduct his undertaking in such a way as to ensure, so far as is reasonably practicable, that he and other persons (not being his employees) who may be affected thereby are not thereby exposed to risks to their health or safety".

19–009   Before any activity involving genetic modification of micro-organisms is carried out, there must be an assessment of the risks it may create to human health and the environment; this must comply with the provisions of Schedule 3.[27] Before carrying out any activity involving genetic modification of organisms other than micro-organisms, there must be an assessment of the risks it may create to human health (but not to the environment); this must comply with the provisions of Schedule 4.[28] In each case an assessment must be reviewed if there is reason to suspect it is no longer valid or there has been a significant change to the relevant activity.[29] Assessments and any reviews must be kept for at least 10 years after the relevant activity has ceased.[30] Where any premises are to be used for the first time for any activity involving genetic modification, the competent authority must first have been notified in accordance with the requirements of Schedule 5,[31] and it must have acknowledged receipt of that notification before the premises may be used for that activity.[32]

Schedule 1 of the Regulations lists four classes of activity involving genetic modification, graded according to the risk they represent, and against each of these the prescribed containment level appropriate to protect human health and the environment from that risk. Schedule 8 sets out the containment measures needed for each of the distinct containment levels. Thus Class 1 consists of activities of no or negligible risk, for which containment level 1 is prescribed. Classes 2, 3 and 4 are in turn activities of low, moderate and high risk, requiring containment levels 2, 3 and 4 respectively.

A person intending to carry out a Class 2 activity involving micro-organisms must first notify the competent authority, provide the information required by Part I of Schedule 6, and prepare an emergency plan.[33] Similarly, a person intending to carry out a Class 3 or 4 activity involving micro-organisms must also first notify the competent authority, provide the information required by Part II of Schedule 6, and again prepare an emergency plan.[34] A person intending to carry out any activity involving genetic modification of organisms other than micro-organisms must, unless the GMO product (not being a micro-organism) poses no greater risk to humans than the unmodified parental organism, first notify the competent authority and provide the information required by Part III of Schedule 6, but in this case an emergency plan is not necessarily required.[35] In each

[27] reg.6.
[28] reg.7.
[29] reg.8(1).
[30] reg.8(2)(a).
[31] reg.9.
[32] The authority is however obliged to give a receipt within 10 working days of receiving the notification; reg.9(2).
[33] reg.10(1).
[34] reg.11(1).
[35] reg.12(1).

case the authority must send an acknowledgement of receipt of the notification within 10 days, and, depending on the class of activity, the notifier may generally not proceed with the activity until the authority has either given its approval or at least not refused to permit the activity[36]—it must however normally do this within 45 days[37] of sending its initial acknowledgement. However where the authority requests additional information from the notifier, as it is entitled to do under Regulation 14, the 45 day period ceases to run until that additional information has been provided.[38]

The Regulations impose a variety of duties on those carrying out GMO **19–010** activities, including a requirement to notify the authority of any material changes to the way in which or place where the activity is being conducted, and of any cessation of the activity. They must also review the containment measures adopted for their particular activity at regular intervals—forthwith if they suspect they are inadequate or if, in the light of new information, the original risk assessment is no longer valid—and if appropriate modify them in the light of such reviews. They are also subject to the principles of occupational and environmental safety laid down in Regulation 17, and so must ensure both that the exposure of humans and the environment to GM micro-organisms is reduced to the lowest level that is reasonably practicable, and also that harm to humans arising from an activity involving genetic modification of organisms other than micro-organisms is reduced to the lowest level that is reasonably practicable. Schedule 7 sets out general principles of good microbiological practice and of good occupational safety and hygiene, which must be adhered to in the case of activities involving micro-organisms; where an activity involves the genetic modification of other organisms, the Schedule 7 principles are to be applied so far as appropriate.

Emergency plans

An emergency plan must be prepared before an activity involving genetic **19–011** modification begins where a risk assessment shows that, as a result of any reasonably foreseeable accident, the health and safety of persons outside the relevant premises is liable to be seriously affected, or, where the activity involves micro-organisms, there is a risk of serous damage to the environment. Plans must be regularly reviewed and updated as necessary. Local emergency services and other bodies and authorities liable to be affected by an accident must be informed, and the plan must be made publicly available.[39] In the event of an accident the person carrying out the activity must inform the competent authority, giving details of the accident, the GMOs concerned, any information necessary to assess its effect on health

[36] Formal consents are only needed in respect of Class 3 and 4 activities.
[37] 90 days where premises are being used for the first time for a Class 3 or 4 activity.
[38] reg.14(6).
[39] reg.20.

of the general population and on the environment, and the measures taken in response.[40]

Register of notifications

19–012   The competent authority must maintain a publicly available register of notifications containing the details specified in Regulation 24. There were originally lengthy provisions in the 2000 Regulations on the extent of disclosure of information supplied to the competent authority and on publicity. These were supplemented, in the 2002 Amendment Regulations, by provisions on maintaining confidentiality in the interests of national security. However the 2005 Amendment Regulations swept all these away in order to give effect to EU Directive 2003/4 on public access to information on the environment,[41] which has been implemented in England and Wales by the Environmental Information Regulations 2004.[42] These last Regulations now govern public access to the information that is on the register or otherwise supplied to or acquired by the competent authority. In particular if the competent authority decides that information should be kept confidential pursuant to the provisions of the Environmental Information Regulations 2004, then this will not be placed on the register.[43]

Enforcement

19–013   By Regulation 26, sections 16 to 26, 33 to 42, and 47 of the HSWA 1974, which relate respectively to approved codes of practice and enforcement, provisions as to offences, and civil liability, and also the Health and Safety (Training for Employment) Regulations 1990, apply to the Contained Use Regulations as though they were health and safety regulations made under the 1974 Act. The enforcement by criminal sanctions of the provisions of the Contained Use Regulations is liable therefore to be in accordance with normal HSE practice. This frequently involves proceedings against relevant individuals in a company's workforce considered to be responsible for any non-compliance. It is by no means clear that the same position will obtain in relation to offences under the legislation relating to deliberate release and marketing where, historically, prosecutions have rarely been taken against individual members of a workforce, but against the employing organisation, and on occasion its directors under EPA s.157(1).

---

[40] reg.21(1).
[41] OJ L41/26, 14.2.2003.
[42] SI 2004/3391; SSI 2004/520 in Scotland.
[43] reg.24(3), as amended.

The Deliberate Release Regulations 2002, as amended

The Deliberate Release Directive and Regulations both apply to the release 19–014
to the environment of all GMOs (as defined), whether micro-organisms or
not. Deliberate release is one of several activities which the Secretary of
State may prescribe, under Part VI of the EPA, as prohibited unless made
the subject of an express consent, and it is so prescribed in the Deliberate
Release Regulations.[44] "Deliberate release" in this context applies both to
marketing and to other releases, being defined in the Directive as

"any intentional introduction into the environment of a GMO or a
combination of GMOs for which no specific containment measures are
used to limit their contact with and to provide a high level of safety for
the general population and the environment".[45]

The most recent official guidance on this legislation is a draft document
published by Defra in November 2002 "Deliberate Release Of Genetically
Modified Organisms: A Guide", to which anyone proposing to undertake
any such activity should refer. It describes in detail how the Department
intends the various statutory provisions to be operated.

Definitions

"Organism" is defined to mean any acellular, unicellular or multicellular 19–015
entity in any form, other than humans or human embryos, and includes
any article or substance consisting of or including "biological matter".[46]
This latter term means anything consisting of or including tissue, cells,
sub-cellular entities, or genes or other genetic material, capable of replication or of transferring genetic material.[47] These definitions apply equally
to products of natural and of artificial reproduction, and biological matter
does not need to have been part of a whole organism.

Section 106(4), as amended, provides that an organism is "genetically
modified" if its genes or other genetic material have been artificially
modified, or if any of its genes or other genetic material have been derived
in any way, through any number of replications, from genes or other
genetic material which were artificially modified. For this purpose genes or
genetic material are "artificially modified" if they are altered otherwise
than by a process which occurs naturally in mating or natural recombination.[48] Sub-sections 106(4B) and (4C) provide for regulations to be
made that prescribe when genes or genetic material are, or are not, to be
treated as being artificially modified, and when an organism is not to be

---

[44] regs 8, 9.
[45] art.2(4).
[46] s.106(2).
[47] s.106(3).
[48] s.106(4A).

taken as a GMO for the purposes of Part VI. Regulation 5 of the Deliberate Release Regulations so prescribes in terms that correspond closely, but not precisely, with those of Parts I to III of Schedule 2 of the Contained Use Regulations (see paragraphs 19–007 to 19–008 above). There can therefore be no automatic presumption that an organism that is not regarded as genetically modified for the purposes of the Contained Use controls will also fall outside the ambit of the Deliberate Release controls.

"Damage to the environment" is to be understood as being caused by the presence in the environment of GMOs which have (or a single such organism which has) escaped or been released from a person's control and are (or is) capable of causing harm.[49] Organisms are under the "control" of a person where he keeps them contained by measures designed to limit their contact with humans and the environment and to prevent or minimise the risk of harm".[50] "Harm" in turn means "adverse effects as regards the health of humans or the environment,[51] while the "environment" includes "land, air and water and living organisms supported by any of those media".[52]

19–016 An organism under a person's control is "released" if he deliberately causes or permits it to cease to be under his control or the control of any other person and to enter the environment, and it "escapes" if, otherwise than by being released, it ceases to be under his control or that of any other person and enters the environment.[53] GMOs are deemed to be "marketed" by a person when products consisting of or including such organisms are placed on the market by being made available to other persons, whether or not for consideration.[54] To the extent that the Regulations apply to unintended escapes, they go (quite legitimately) beyond the scope of the Deliberate Release Directive. Thus a person operating under a consent issued pursuant to the Contained Use Regulations who is responsible for such an escape may be liable to prosecution under the HSWA for failure to comply with his obligations under those Regulations, and also under section 118(1) of the EPA for making an unconsented release contrary to section 111(1).

The Deliberate Release Control regime—general

19–017 Control over the deliberate release and marketing of GMOs under Part VI of the EPA and the Deliberate Release Regulations follows the normal pattern of a general prohibition of the controlled activities, under subsection 111(1)(a), followed by provisions for licensing prescribed activities

---

[49] s.107(3).
[50] s.107(9).
[51] s.107(6).
[52] s.107(2).
[53] s.107(10).
[54] s.107(11).

within that prohibition subject to conditions. Release and marketing are both prescribed activities for the purposes of that sub-section by virtue of Regulations 8 and 14 respectively of the Deliberate Release Regulations.

Applications for consent to release

Applications for consent to release GMOs are handled somewhat differently from applications for consent to market them. Before applying for a consent to release a GMO, the applicant must advertise his intention to do so in a national newspaper specified by the Secretary of State, giving details of the GMO to be released, and where and when this would occur. The applicant must also carry out an environmental risk assessment in accordance with the requirements of Annex II of the Directive and complying generally with those of Regulation 6. This assessment must in particular identify and evaluate the potential damage to the environment, whether direct or indirect, immediate or delayed, which may arise from the release or marketing of the GMOs in question.[55]   **19–018**

An application for consent to release is made to the Secretary of State (in practice Defra), who is required (a) to invite comments from the public, within a period of not less than 60 days, on the risks that may be involved in the release applied for, and (b) to pass a summary of the application to the European Commission, which in turn circulates this to the competent authorities of the other EU Member States.[56] Before granting any consent, the Secretary of State must take into account any comments that may have been made by members of the public in due time or by these other authorities, and must in any event have the agreement of the HSE to the consent in so far as protection of human health is concerned. There is a general obligation on the Secretary of State to reach a decision on an application within 90 days of receiving it, but this period ceases to run while any further information requested from the applicant remains outstanding, and may be extended by up to 30 days in order to consider representations from the public.[57]

A simplified procedure[58] allows a single notification dossier to be submitted for more than one release of genetically modified plants which have resulted from the same recipient crop plant species but which may differ in any of the inserted/deleted sequences or have the same inserted/deleted sequence but differ in phenotypes. This enables a notifier to submit in a single notification information on several releases of genetically modified crop plants, to be released on several different sites. Where an applicant seeks consent to release any GM higher plant, he must comply with the

---

[55] reg.6(1)(a).
[56] reg.20.
[57] reg.21.
[58] Provided for by the Commission's Decision 94/730, known as the "First Simplified Procedure (crop plants) Decision"; [1994] OJ L31.

information requirements of Schedule 1; in any other case the information requirements of Schedule 2 apply. Should there be any inconsistency between the requirements of the Regulations and those of the First Simplified Procedure (crop plants) Decision,[59] the latter prevail.[60]

Applications for consent to market

19–019 An application for consent to market GMOs is likewise made to the Secretary of State (again, in practice Defra). Consents to market are granted for a limited period not exceeding 10 years,[61] so a distinction is made between first applications and those to renew an existing consent.[62] A first application must comply with the requirements of Regulation 16(2), and include:

(i) information prescribed by either Schedule 1 (for GM higher plants) or Schedule 2 (in all other cases),

(ii) information prescribed by Schedule 3 in all cases,

(iii) information on any other release of the same organisms elsewhere,

(iv) an environmental risk assessment prepared in accordance with Regulation 6,

(v) proposed conditions for marketing the product, its labelling and its packaging,

(vi) a monitoring plan, and

(vii) a proposed period for the consent (of at most 10 years).

An applicant may be excused from submitting some or all of the information in Part II of Schedule 3 if he can show on the basis of actual results or other "substantive, reasoned scientific evidence" that the marketing and use of the GMOs do not pose a risk of damage to the environment.[63] The applicant must also provide a summary of the application in the form prescribed in the Deliberate Release Directive, so that this can be directly forwarded on to the European Commission.

Applications to renew a marketing consent must be made at least nine months before expiry of the existing consent, and include a report on any monitoring results, any other new information relating to the risks of the product causing damage to the environment, and any proposals for amending or extending the previous conditions of the consent.

On receiving an application for consent to market the Secretary of State must forward a summary of the application both to the European Com-

---

[59] Commission Decision 94/730; [1994] OJ L292/31.

[60] reg.10(3).

[61] reg.24(4). Special provisions apply to the period of the first consent for GM plant varieties and forest reproductive material; regs 24(5), (6).

[62] Where a consent to market GMOs had been granted before October 17, 2002, when the 2002 Regulations came into force, an application to renew it had to be made by October 17, 2006, at the latest, failing which it is deemed to have expired on that date; reg.18(3).

[63] reg.16(5).

mission and to the competent authorities of the other EU Member States. The application will be examined by Defra, further information may be requested from the applicant, and an assessment report issued within 90 days of receipt by Defra of the application, stating whether or not marketing of the GMOs should be permitted, and if so on what conditions, or refused.[64] As with release applications, the 90 day period ceases to run while any further information requested from the applicant remains outstanding. Unlike release applications, however, there is no formal provision for inviting comments from the public on an application for a consent to market GMOs.

When the assessment report has been prepared it must be sent to the European Commission,[65] which circulates it to the competent authorities of the other Member States. However before sending the Commission an assessment report favouring the grant of consent to market, the Secretary of State must first consult with the HSE, and is expressly prohibited from sending a favourable opinion on the consent in so far as protection of human health is concerned if the HSE has decided that the application does not fulfil the requirements of the EPA or the Regulations.[66] Where the assessment favours the grant of consent this may be given effect if no objection is received from the Commission or any Member State within 60 days from when the report was circulated by the Commission. If an objection is raised within that time, consent may only be granted if the objection is resolved within 105 days (calculated from the same date),[67] or a favourable decision is given in a Commission decision on the issue under Article 18(1) of the Directive.[68]

19–020

In the case of applications to renew a consent a further assessment report is prepared determining whether or not renewal is favoured, and if so on what conditions, and this is forwarded to the Commission. As before, a favourable decision may be over-ruled by the HSE on human health grounds.[69] The Commission circulates the assessment report to the competent authorities of other Member States and, again, renewal consent may only be granted if no objection is raised within 60 days or, if one is raised, it is resolved within 75 days, or the Commission reaches a favourable decision on the issue under Article 18(1).[70]

---

[64] reg.23(1).
[65] reg.23(2).
[66] reg.23(4).
[67] Time stops running during the final 45 days if any further information requested from the applicant is pending; reg.24(3).
[68] reg.24(1).
[69] reg.25(2).
[70] reg.26(1).

Applications in respect of GM Food and Feed

19–021   Applications in respect of GMOs for food use, food containing or consisting of GMOs, and food produced from or containing ingredients produced from GMOs are now regulated under EU Regulation 1829/2003,[71] the so-called "Food and Feed Regulation". The European Food Safety Authority (EFSA), based in Parma, Italy, is responsible for the scientific assessment of genetically modified food and feed, and itself deals with all applications for consent for such products from Member States. Applications are submitted to the relevant national competent authority in each Member State, which then forwards them on to the EFSA,[72] which decides on whether or not to grant an approval, and if so on what conditions.

Exemptions

19–022   Where a consent to market a GMO or to use a GMO product has been granted, then any release of that GMO that is in accordance with the relevant marketing consent and any use of the product that complies with the conditions and limitations imposed on its use is exempt from the need for any additional consent.[73] Further exemptions are set out in Regulation 15—these include marketing GMOs for use for a consented release and an approved product for its approved use, marketing GM micro-organisms for activities regulated under the Contained Use Regulations and other GMOs for uses where appropriate stringent containment measures are used, and the marketing of GM foods and feeds, and of GM food and feed ingredients, within or authorised under EU Regulation 258/97, as amended,[74] or the EU Food and Feed Regulation 1829/2003.[75]

As genetically modified food and feed applications are now dealt with by the EFSA, the Genetically Modified Organisms (Deliberate Release) (Amendment) Regulations 2004 allow for this by adding to the list of exempt activities in Regulation 15 of the principal 2002 Regulations the marketing of GM food or feed authorised under the Food and Feed Regulation. The 2004 Amendment Regulations also added a further exemption in respect of the marketing of GM novel food or GM novel food ingredients within the scope of EU Regulation 258/97, as amended.

Prohibition notices

19–023   There is a broad power in the Secretary of State under section 110 and Regulation 32 to serve a prohibition notice to stop an act authorised by any

---

[71] [2003] OJ L268/1.
[72] For further information on EFSA see its website: *http://www.efsa.europa.eu/EFSA/efsa_locale-1178620753812_home.htm*.
[73] reg.9.
[74] [1997] OJ L43/1; amended by the Food & Feed Regulation (see next footnote).
[75] [2003] OJ L284/1.

consent if, but only if, it is considered that that act would involve a risk of causing damage to the environment on the basis of either new information made available since the consent was granted or of a reassessment of existing information. Where the risk of damage to the environment is "severe" a prohibition notice may also positively require additional measures to be taken as are considered appropriate. This procedure is subject to the provisions of Article 23 of the Deliberate Release Directive. The Secretary of State must inform the Commission of the steps taken, the issue will normally be passed to the relevant EU scientific committee for its opinion, and a decision will then be taken on it by the Commission. To the extent the notice is inconsistent with that decision it must be withdrawn.[76]

Public register

A public register is maintained containing a wide range of information   **19–024** specified in Regulation 34 of the Regulations. This includes full details of an application to market or release a GMO, including: the locations at which the GMOs are proposed to be released, and also where any are in fact being grown, in so far as the latter information is supplied pursuant to applicable monitoring requirements;[77] a summary of any advice given by ACRE on whether a consent to release should be granted or not; details of consents, including those granted by other EU Member States; decisions taken pursuant Article 18 of the Directive, which provides for objections to be raised by the Commission and other Member States; prohibition notices; and convictions under section 118 of the EPA Regulation 35 lays down maximum time limits for placing the bulk of the prescribed information on the register. Where limits are imposed they are short—either 12 or 14 days from the relevant action.

After a consent to release GMOs has been granted or an application rejected, copies of representations made in connection with that application are to be made publicly available within 28 days of the grant or rejection. However if a representation contains confidential material, and the person making it requests that it be kept confidential, it will not be made public.[78]

GM Food and Feed

As mentioned above, a distinct regime for controlling the marketing of GM   **19–025** foods and feeds has been put in place by EU Regulation 1829/2003.[79] As a

---

[76] reg.32(5).
[77] This has proved contentious as it enables those hostile to GMO activities to take positive action against them. See also ACRE's "Advice on Notification of Locations of GM Crop Releases", December 1, 2000.
[78] reg.36.
[79] [2003] OJ L268/1.

result such material is excluded from the controls of the Deliberate Release Regulations by extending the exemptions of its Regulation 15—see paragraph 19–022 above. There is no space for an extensive discussion of this new regime, but its main objectives are expressed to be:

(a) to provide the basis for ensuring a high level of protection of human life and health, animal health and welfare, environment and consumer interests in relation to genetically modified food and feed, whilst ensuring the effective functioning of the internal market;

(b) to lay down Community procedures for the authorisation and supervision of genetically modified food and feed; and

(c) to lay down provisions for the labelling of genetically modified food and feed.[80]

GM Food and Feed—labelling requirements

19–026   In view of its focus on ensuring effective functioning of the internal market, the labelling requirements of the Food and Feed Regulation are of particular significance. Specifically, Article 13 lays down that products subject to the labelling requirements[81] must be labelled as being or containing GM material. However this does not apply to foods containing material which contains, consists of or is produced from GMOs in a proportion no higher than 0.9 per cent[82] of the food ingredients considered individually, or food consisting of a single ingredient, provided that this presence is adventitious or technically unavoidable. The onus is on the operator to be able to demonstrate that he has taken appropriate steps to avoid the presence of such material.[83] The labelling provisions in respect of GM feeds[84] are expressed in identical terms.[85] Where this exemption does not apply, operators must also comply with the provisions of the related EU Regulation 1830/2003 on the traceability and labelling of genetically modified organisms and the traceability of food and feed products produced from genetically modified organisms.[86]

Transboundary movements of GMOs

19–027   The Cartagena Protocol on Biosafety, mentioned in paragraph 19–004 above, is concerned with the safe transfer, handling and use of GMOs that

---

[80] art.1.

[81] Namely, foods which are to be delivered as such to the final consumer or mass caterers in the Community and which contain or consist of GMOs, or are produced from or contain ingredients produced from GMOs; art.12(1).

[82] Presumably 0.9 per cent by weight, though this is not stated in the Regulation.

[83] art.12(2) and (3).

[84] Namely, GMOs for feed use, feed containing or consisting of GMOs, and feed produced from GMOs.

[85] art.24(2) and (3).

[86] [2003] OJ L268/24.

may have harmful effects on biological diversity, as well as posing risks to human health. In relation to the EU, the legislation already discussed is regarded as sufficient to meet the bulk of the Protocol's requirements, particularly that on deliberate release, coupled with the requirement for risk assessments in respect of GMOs imported into the EU, and the EU legislation on the carriage of dangerous goods. In addition, pharmaceuticals are covered by other international agreements and by extensive EU legislation, and no additional provisions relating to them are considered necessary to comply with the Protocol. Accordingly the main area needing further controls is that of exports of GMOs from the EU; EU Regulation 1946/2003 on transboundary movements of GMOs[87] is designed to fill this gap by setting up a common system within the EU of notification and information for transboundary movements of GMOs from the EU to countries outside the EU. GM pharmaceuticals for humans are excluded from its scope, however, as these are addressed by other international agreements.

A so-called Biosafety Clearing-House (BCH) has been established under the Protocol to receive scientific, technical, environmental and legal information on, and experience with, GMOs, and to share this information with the parties to it. All parties are required to provide the BCH with, among other things, risk assessments on GMOs subject to the Protocol, and any final decisions they take on the importation or release of GMOs.[88]

Regulation 1946/2003 requires a person proposing to export GMOs to notify the competent authority of the importing country in advance of his wish to do so,[89] providing the information listed in its Annex 1 as a minimum. This includes the details of both the exporter and the importer, full information on the GMO or GMO products under consideration and the quantities involved, the results of a risk assessment carried out as though under the Deliberate Release Directive, and the regulatory status of the GMO or GMO product in the exporting country. No intentional transboundary movement may be carried out unless and until the appropriate authority in the importing country has given its prior express written consent.[90] It is expressly provided that no tacit consent may be inferred from any failure to reply to the exporter's notice. The reply from the importing country should conform with the requirements of Articles 9 and 10 of the Protocol, which includes an obligation to inform the BCH of its decision on the application. If there is no reply, the exporter may send a reminder, and copy this to the Commission, which will seek to facilitate effective working of the Protocol.

Regulation 1946/2003 has in turn been implemented in England by the **19–028** Genetically Modified Organisms (Transboundary Movements) (England)

[87] [2003] OJ L287/1.
[88] Protocol, art.20.
[89] reg.1946/2003, art.4.
[90] reg.1946/2003, art.5(1).

Regulations 2004,[91] which provides for the administrative arrangements needed to comply with the Protocol's requirements. In particular, contravention of or non-compliance with any of the scheduled "Specified Community Provisions"—these being obligations under the EU Regulation—is an offence.[92] The more serious offences are breaches of the Community Provisions in Part I of the Schedule, which mostly entail actual export of GMOs otherwise than in accordance with the Regulation. Inspectors may be appointed to enforce the 2004 Regulations. They have extensive powers of access to non-domestic premises and to obtain, inter alia, information and samples.[93] The Secretary of State may also directly require any person who appears to be, to have been, or to be about to be involved in exporting GMOs to provide any specified relevant information.[94] Regulations 9 and 10 set out the standard provisions for an offence due to the act or default of another person, who is thus also potentially criminally liable, and an offence by a body corporate, whereby its directors and other officers may also be held guilty of the offence.

---

[91] SI 2004/2692. Similar regulations have been made in respect of Wales, Scotland and Northern Ireland.
[92] reg.8.
[93] reg.6.
[94] reg.7.

Chapter 20

RADIOACTIVE SUBSTANCES AND NUCLEAR INSTALLATIONS

Introduction

This chapter considers the laws relating to radioactive substances, **20–001** including radioactive waste, and, in particular, the requirements of the Radioactive Substances Act 1993, as amended (the RSA 93), and Regulations made under it. It does not however cover the legislation on the structure of the nuclear industry, and it would also occupy a disproportionate amount of space to discuss in detail the regulatory provisions governing nuclear installations under the Nuclear Installations Act 1965[1] (the NIA). Accordingly this chapter is primarily concerned with the RSA 93, the wide variety of controls over radiation exposure and the use and carriage of radioactive goods and materials, and a summary of the principal provisions of the NIA, as amended, of direct interest to the general public.[2]

Technical Background

Radioactive substances may be broadly described as those that emit **20–002** ionising[3] radiation. This is constantly emitted by radioactive substances (both those which are naturally radioactive and those which have been made so artificially), and also by non-radioactive substances if bombarded with appropriate radiation. The atoms of radioactive substances contain unstable nuclei (radionuclides) that undergo spontaneous transformation, each transformation involving a release of energy in the form of radiation. Ionising radiation may take a variety of forms including:

- Alpha particles, which are positively charged helium atoms, i.e. helium nuclei, consisting of a pair of protons and a pair of neutrons. By comparison with beta particles, they are heavy. Though they may

---

[1] 1965 c.57.
[2] For a more detailed discussion of nuclear installations, see "The Law of Nuclear Installations and Radioactive Substances" by Tromans and FitzGerald, (Sweet & Maxwell, 1997) (now out of print).
[3] i.e. removing electrons from atoms, so producing a charge on the remainder. An ion is a charged atom or group of atoms.

contain considerable energy, they are relatively easily absorbed. A substance emitting alpha particles is losing protons and neutrons from its nucleus, and accordingly changes its chemical character as it decays. Thus radium, on emitting alpha particles is converted into the radioactive inert gas radon.

- Beta particles, which are electrons ejected from the nucleus of a radioactive substance. They have a comparatively short range of just a few centimetres in air.
- X-rays. These are "pure" electromagnetic radiation, having a frequency of around 10^{18} Hz (Hertz).[4] In the conventional depiction of the electromagnetic spectrum, the ultraviolet band stops and the X-ray band starts at around 3×10^{16} Hz.
- Gamma rays, which are also "pure" electromagnetic radiation, having a frequency of approximately 10^{21} Hz. They are capable of penetrating substances for considerable distances, even several centimetres of lead, and accordingly effective screening requires substantial forms of protection.
- Cosmic rays. This is the term given to the forms of radiation that bombard the earth from outer space. They are absorbed to a considerable extent by the atmosphere, but form a significant component of the annual radiation dosage received by those who frequently fly at high altitudes in, for example, commercial passenger aircraft.

All forms of electromagnetic radiation differ from each other only in their frequency and, of wavelength, which always bear a constant inverse relationship to each other.[5] The harm that radiation may do to humans, animals and other living things depends on the sensitivity of their tissues to the wavelength involved, which varies according to the particular tissue. Thus the lower frequencies pass through the tissues of living things without being absorbed, and so cause no perceptible damage. Consequently, in setting standard exposure limits, account needs to be taken both of the radiation energy received, and also of the biological effects of radiation of that particular frequency. The standard measure of radiation is the Becquerel ("Bq"—a unit that has replaced the older unit, Curie), which corresponds to the decay of one radionuclide, i.e. one nuclear transformation, per second.[6] The radioactivity of a substance is expressed in Becquerels per unit weight, normally one gram, of the radioactive substance concerned.

When a person is exposed to radiation, their body absorbs energy. The

---

[4] Frequency in cycles per second (i.e. Hertz) multiplied by the wavelength in centimetres is a constant: 3×10^{10}.

[5] Lower frequency, non-ionising forms of electromagnetic radiation are radio waves used for broadcasting, microwaves as used in microwave ovens and radar, infra-red radiation, which is perceived as heat, and the visible light spectrum. This chapter does not deal with non-ionising radiation or electromagnetic fields.

[6] The Curie is defined by reference to the radioactivity of 1 gm of radium; 1 Curie = 3.7×10^{10} Becquerels.

amount of energy absorbed per unit weight of human tissue—the absorbed dose—is measured in rads or Grays ("Gy").[7] To indicate the risk of harm that a particular dose of radiation may have on a person, yet another measure, the Sievert ("Sv"), is used, which represents the dose of radiation received over a period of time, adjusted by a "quality factor", Q, to take account of the differing biological effects of different types of radiation. Inevitably this adjustment is somewhat arbitrary, since the exact effects of any particular dose of radiation will vary considerably depending on all the relevant circumstances. Nevertheless, as an approximation, the Sievert is accepted as being the appropriate unit when considering the protection of human health.[8] Natural background radiation in the UK provides an annual average dose of around 2 mSv, though the actual dose received by particular individuals may vary widely from this figure, depending on where they live and their occupation. For the purposes of setting acceptable levels of artificial radiation, so-called Generalised Derived Limits (GDLs) have been established, which are considered to represent an insignificant risk to members of the public. These GDLs are calculated such that, on very pessimistic assumptions, the radiation dose of people exposed should be no more than 1 mSv annually (in addition to the average natural dose of 2 mSv). Regulatory thresholds are mostly concerned with when a specific substance is sufficiently radioactive to pose a significant risk of making a material contribution to the dose of radioactivity that any one person may receive; such thresholds are therefore normally expressed in Becquerels per gram.

Guidance on safety standards in respect of radiation is issued by the International Commission on Radiological Protection (the ICRP). Its recommendations are widely accepted, and provide the basis of legislation made under the Euratom Treaty, and in particular European Directive 96/29/Euratom (referred to as the "Basic Safety Standards Directive").[9] However, the ICRP has no formal power to impose its proposals on anyone.

Within the United Kingdom, the Radiation Protection division of the **20–003** Health Protection Agency (the HPA) fulfils a similar role to the ICRP at national level. Previously the National Radiological Protection Board (the NRPB) had this function, but on April 1, 2005, it was absorbed into the newly formed HPA. The Radiation Protection division undertakes research to advance knowledge about protection from the risks of both ionising and non-ionising radiations, provides laboratory and technical services, runs training courses, provides expert information, and has a significant advisory role in the UK. By Directions under the Radiological Protection Act

---

[7] "rad" = Radiation Absorbed Dose. 1 Gy, the SI unit, is 100 rads, and equals 1 joule / kilogram.
[8] The Sievert being a large unit, in practice dosage limits are usually measured in milli-Sieverts (mSv) or even microSieverts (μSv).
[9] OJ L159/1–114, 29.6.1996, replacing Directive 80/836.

1970, the NRPB was specifically required to advise on the acceptability to, and the application within, the United Kingdom of standards recommended by international or intergovernmental bodies, such as the ICRP, and to specify emergency reference levels of dose for limiting radiation doses in accidents. The NRPB consequently published advice on Generalised Derived Constraints and on Generalised Derived Limits, intended to be used as convenience reference levels against which proposed environmental discharges (constraints) or the results of environmental monitoring (limits) can be compared, and these documents, updated as necessary, remain important advice and guidance.[10]

Historical

20–004   The harnessing of nuclear energy for practical purposes dates from the development of the atomic bomb during the last world war. After the war, the Atomic Energy Act 1946 provided for control over the use of and research and development in nuclear energy, which at that time was essentially entirely for military purposes. The Atomic Energy Authority was set up by the Atomic Energy Authority Act 1954 with general powers of research and development in not only the military but also civil fields. The civilian applications of nuclear energy were separated from military applications in the 1970s, with the setting up of the Radiochemical Centre at Amersham, the transfer of other civil operations to British Nuclear Fuels Limited under the Atomic Energy Authority Act 1971, and research on military aspects being transferred to the Ministry of Defence under the Atomic Energy Authority (Weapons Group) Act 1973. The Radioactive Substances Act 1948 was the first to provide regulatory control over the handling of radioactive materials. This was followed by the Radioactive Substances Act 1960 (the RSA 1960), which was variously amended in numerous respects by subsequent legislation, and in particular by the Environmental Protection Act 1990.[11] The legislation has now been consolidated, with minor improvements and corrections, into the Radioactive Substances Act 1993, referred to here as the RSA, or where appropriate for clarity, the RSA 93.[12]

[10]   *Generalised Derived Constraints for Radioisotopes of Strontium, Ruthenium, Iodine, Caesium, Plutonium, Americium and Curium*, documents of the NRPB, 11, No.2, 1–41 (2000) and *Generalised Derived Limits for Radioisotopes of Polonium, Lead, Radium and Uranium*, documents of the NRPB, 11, No.2, 43–71 (2000).
[11]   Namely Part V (ss.100–105) and Sch.5.
[12]   A guide to the RSA 1960 was published in 1982: "Radioactive Substances Act 1960, A guide to administration of the Act", Department of the Environment, HMSO, London. Despite a commitment to update this guidance in the 1995 White Paper on *The Review of Radioactive Waste Management Policy* (Cm 2919, 1995), the guide has still not been updated. Principles for the assessment of prospective public doses is addressed in a December 2002 Environment Agency interim guidance on Authorisation of Discharges of Radioactive Waste to the Environment.

The generation of nuclear power is now primarily governed by the Nuclear Installations Act 1965 (the NIA 1965), regulatory control over nuclear installations being the responsibility of the Nuclear Installations Inspectorate, which is a part of the Health and Safety Executive. The Nuclear Decommissioning Authority (NDA)[13] is responsible for decommissioning and clean-up of the nuclear legacy in the United Kingdom including power stations, fuel reprocessing and UKAEA nuclear research and development facilities.

EU Legislation

EU legislation now forms the basis of the United Kingdom controls. **20–005** Directive 96/29, already mentioned, governs basic safety standards both for those working with radioactive material and also the general public. It has been implemented in the UK mainly through the RSA 93 and Regulations made under it. The so-called "HASS" Directive 2003/122/Euratom on the Control of High Activity Sealed Sources and Orphan Sources[14] strengthens the controls over sealed radioactive sources, being implemented in the United Kingdom with effect from October 20, 2005, by the HASS Regulations 2005,[15] coupled with the Environment Agency's "HASS Guidance".[16]

Although the Environmental Liability Directive 2004/35,[17] discussed in Chapter 5, generally provides a framework for imposing liability for causing environmental damage, its provisions are however disapplied in respect of

"such nuclear risks or environmental damage or imminent threat of such damage as may be caused by the activities covered by the Treaty establishing the European Atomic Energy Community or caused by an incident or activity in respect of which liability or compensation falls within the scope of any of the international instruments listed in Annex V, including any future amendments thereof."[18]

The instruments listed in Annex V are:

(a) the Paris Convention of July 29, 1960, on Third Party Liability in the Field of Nuclear Energy, and the Brussels Supplementary Convention of January 31, 1963;

(b) the Vienna Convention of May 21, 1963, on Civil Liability for Nuclear Damage;

---

[13] Set up on April 1, 2005, under the Energy Act 2004, and in particular directions made under s.3 of that Act.
[14] OJ L 346/57, 31.12.2003.
[15] SI 2005/2686.
[16] Currently version 4, June 2007.
[17] OJ L 143/56, 30.4.2004.
[18] Environmental Liability Directive, art.4(4).

(c) the Convention of September 12, 1997, on Supplementary Compensation for Nuclear Damage;

(d) the Joint Protocol of September 21, 1988, relating to the Application of the Vienna Convention and the Paris Convention;

(e) the Brussels Convention of December 17, 1971, relating to Civil Liability in the Field of Maritime Carriage of Nuclear Material.

Shipments of radioactive waste and spent nuclear fuel are the subject of Directive 2006/117/Euratom (the Shipments Directive).[19]

The Radioactive Substances Act 1993

20-006   The RSA 93 controls the keeping and use of "radioactive material" and of "mobile radioactive apparatus" (as defined in the RSA, in each case) and the accumulation and disposal of radioactive waste. Administration of the Act comes under the Department of the Environment, Food and Rural Affairs with the detailed regulation being the responsibility of the Environment Agency in England and Wales, and the Scottish Environmental Protection Agency in Scotland.

Definitions

20-007   The controls in the RSA over keeping and using radioactive material relate to substances that are either or both of (i) a substance listed in Schedule 1 to the RSA having a radioactivity per gram in excess of the figure prescribed for that substance in the Schedule, or (ii) a substance possessing radioactivity which is:

- wholly or partly attributable to a process of nuclear fission or other process of subjecting a substance to bombardment by neutrons or to ionising radiations (not being a process occurring in the course of nature);
- in consequence of the disposal of radioactive waste; or
- by way of contamination in the course of the application of a process to some other substance.[20]

The elements listed in the Schedule and the prescribed radioactivity for each are set out in Table 20/I.

---

[19] OJ L 337/21–32, 5.12.2006, discussed in para.20–036 below.
[20] s.1(2).

Table 20/I

Radioactive Substances (RSA Schedule 1)   20–008

Element	Becquerels per gram (Bq/g)		
	Solid	Liquid	Gas or Vapour
Actinium	0.37	7.40×10^{-2}	2.59×10^{-6}
Lead	0.74	3.70×10^{-3}	1.11×10^{-4}
Polonium	0.37	2.59×10^{-2}	2.22×10^{-4}
Protoactinium	0.37	3.33×10^{-2}	1.11×10^{-6}
Radium	0.37	3.70×10^{-4}	3.70×10^{-5}
Radon	—	—	3.70×10^{-2}
Thorium	2.59	3.70×10^{-2}	2.22×10^{-5}
Uranium	11.10	0.74	7.40×10^{-5}

"Radioactive material" is defined as anything which, not being waste, is   20–009
any such substance, or an article made wholly or partly from or incorporating such a substance.[21] "Radioactive waste" is waste which consists
wholly or partly of (a) any radioactive material, as defined, or (b) any
substance or article which has been contaminated in the course of the
production, keeping or use of radioactive material, or by contact with or
proximity to other radioactive waste within (a) above.[22] The use of the
words "which consists wholly or partly" means that even if only a very
small component of a consignment of waste consists of radioactive waste as
just described, the whole consignment is to be described as "radioactive
waste". The RSA defines "waste" as including "any substance which
constitutes scrap material or an effluent or other unwanted surplus substance arising from the application of any process, and also includes any
substance or article which requires to be disposed of as being broken, worn
out, contaminated or otherwise spoilt."[23]

Likewise, any substance or article which, in the course of the carrying on
of any undertaking is discharged, discarded or otherwise dealt with as if it
were waste shall, for the purposes of the RSA, be presumed to be waste
unless the contrary is proved.[24] The definition of "Directive waste"
adopted in 1994 for the purposes of the EPA controls over conventional
wastes is not included in the RSA. Article 5 of Directive 96/29 refers to
"disposal, recycling or re-use" of radioactive substances or materials, and

[21] s.1(1).
[22] s.2.
[23] s.47(1).
[24] s.47(4).

also provides scope for Member States to establish "clearance levels" of radioactivity, below which substances or materials may be disposed of, recycled or re-used without needing authorisation. The terms "recycling and re-use" are not used in the RSA. As the RSA 93 uses the pre-amendment definitions the earlier case law on the meaning of disposal, recycling or re-use will be relevant. Nevertheless, one can expect the courts, which are obliged to give effect to the underlying EU legislation so far as practicable, to seek to avoid differences in the meanings of these expressions if they can.

"Mobile radioactive apparatus" means anything which is radioactive material, including but not limited to "apparatus, equipment and appliances" which is constructed or adapted for being transported from place to place, or which is in fact portable and designed or intended to be used for releasing radioactive material into the environment or introducing it into organisms.[25]

Controls over radioactive material and mobile radioactive apparatus

20–010 Section 6 of the RSA imposes a general prohibition whereby no person may, on any premises used for the purposes of any undertaking carried on by him, keep or use, or cause or permit to be kept or used, radioactive material of any description, provided that he knows or has reasonable grounds for believing it to be radioactive material, unless he is registered under the Act in respect both of those premises and of the keeping and use by him on those premises of that radioactive material. There are approximately 6,500 organisations which use radioactive sources registered under the RSA.

However if the radioactive material is mobile radioactive apparatus for which he or anyone else is registered under section 10 or is exempted from registration under that section, then the section 6 prohibition does not apply.[26] This exemption would appear to be entirely general in application, and so extends not only to persons on whose premises the mobile apparatus has been brought or to whom it has been hired out, but also the owner of the apparatus itself. A person who is lending or hiring out mobile radioactive apparatus may well do more than merely keep or use it on his own premises, for example maintenance or repair, and in such circumstances, registration under section 6 will be required.

By virtue of regulation 2 of the Radioactive Substances (Substances of Low Activity) (Exemption) Order 1986,[27] registration is not however

---

[25] s.3.
[26] s.6(c).
[27] SI 1986/1002, as amended by the the Radioactive Substances (Substances of Low Activity) (Exemption) (Amendment) Order 1992, SI 1992/647.

required for the keeping of substantially insoluble solid radioactive material, other than a closed source,[28] with radioactivity not exceeding 0.4 Becquerels per gram, organic liquids which are radioactive solely because of the presence of carbon 14 or tritium (often incorporated into organic molecules for purposes of tracing reactions in which they are involved) with a radioactivity not exceeding four Becquerels per ml, and gases with one or more radionuclides none of which have a half life greater than 100 seconds. There are currently 18 exemption orders under the RSA which also exempt specific articles and uses.[29] A series of exemptions are expressly set out in section 8 covering, subject to specific qualifications and conditions, holders of nuclear site licences under the NIA 1965, and clocks and watches which are radioactive material, other than those manufactured or repaired by processes involving the use of luminous material.

Applications for registration in respect of radioactive material are made **20–011** on prescribed forms obtainable from the appropriate Agency, and must give details of the relevant premises, the activities for which the premises are used, a description of the radioactive material in question and the maximum quantity likely to be kept or used at any one time, and the manner (if any) in which this material is proposed to be used on the premises. Copies are sent by the Environment Agency to the local authority for the area of the relevant premises. The registration may, and invariably will, be made subject to various conditions listed generically in section 7(6). These may relate to the premises, possibly including structural alterations, and to requirements on the person to whom the registration relates to provide information on any movement of radioactive material from the premises, and they may prohibit any supply of radioactive material from the premises unless it is appropriately labelled. When imposing conditions regarding premises, regard may only be had to the amount and character of radioactive waste likely to arise from the keeping or use of the radioactive material in accordance with the registration on those premises.[30] (Safety precautions in respect of radioactive substances are imposed under the Ionising Radiations Regulations 1999 referred to in paragraph 20–035.

Registration in respect of mobile radioactive apparatus is required by section 9, which provides that unless they are registered (or are exempted from registration), no person shall keep, use, lend, or let on hire, any mobile radioactive apparatus, or cause or permit this, for the purposes of investigating (including testing and measuring) any characteristics of

---

[28] i.e., "an object free from patent defect which is radioactive material solely because it consists of one or more radionuclides firmly incorporated on or in, or sealed within, solid inert non-radioactive material so as to prevent in normal use the dispersion of any radioactive material" (1986 Order art.1(3)).

[29] Made under s.8(6). A list of these is available on-line at *http://www.defra.gov.uk/environment/radioactivity/government/legislation/exemption_orders.htm*.

[30] s.7(7).

substances or articles or releasing quantities of radioactive material into the environment or introducing it into organisms. The requirement is waived for certain electronic valves and testing instruments by various exemption orders.[31] The procedure for registering in respect of mobile radioactive apparatus is essentially the same as for radioactive material; the application must specify the apparatus concerned and the manner in which it is proposed to be used, and a copy of the application is sent to each local authority in whose area the apparatus is likely to be kept or used for releasing radioactive material into the environment. In relation to mobile radioactive apparatus, the Environment Agency is entitled to impose such conditions as it thinks fit.

In either case, an application may be treated by the applicant as having been refused if it is not determined within four months or such longer period as may be agreed,[32] so entitling him to invoke the appeals procedure under sections 26 and 27.[33] A registration may be cancelled or varied at any time, by attaching or varying applicable limitations or conditions, without compensation.[34]

20–012   There is a charging scheme, that is regularly revised, which specifies the cost of applications under the RSA 93 for authorisation or registration. There is also an annual subsistence charge for sites where an authorisation is needed.

Registration in respect of radioactive material and mobile radioactive apparatus is personal to the applicant, and there are no provisions for transferring registration from one person to another. Consequently, in the event of any proposed transfer of ownership of radioactive material, whether by physical supply, or by the acquisition of an undertaking that is registered in respect of any radioactive material or mobile radioactive apparatus, the person registered must remain in control of the item until such time as the new owner is appropriately registered, and can take it over.

Records

20–013   Anyone who has been granted an authorisation under any of the provisions of the RSA, may be required to maintain records as specified by the Environment Agency, and to retain these not only throughout the period of the activities or the authorisation, but also for such periods as may be specified thereafter. Additionally, the person may be required to supply the Environment Agency with copies of the records, in the event of his regis-

---

[31] SI 1967/1797, SI 1985/1049.
[32] ss.7(5), 10(4) and 47(1).
[33] See para.20–014.
[34] s.12(1).

tration being cancelled or the authorisation revoked, or in the event of his ceasing to carry on the relevant activities.[35]

Appeals

There is a right of appeal to the Secretary of State in respect of any refusal   **20–014**
of an application for registration or authorisation, of any limitations or conditions attached to one, of any variations that may be made (other than revocations of a limitation or condition), and of any cancellation of a registration or revocation of an authorisation. There is no right of appeal against any decision taken by the Environment Agency pursuant to a direction given by the Secretary of State, either in relation to any application or granted registration or authorisation, or the calling in of any application or applications generally.[36] Appeals are subject to detailed rules as set out in the Radioactive Substances (Appeals) Regulations 1990.[37] These provide, inter alia, that the appeals must generally be brought within two months of the relevant decision appealed against (or of when an application is deemed refused).[38] However an appeal against a decision by the Environment Agency to cancel a registration or to revoke an authorisation must be made within 28 days.[39] An appeal may be required to be advertised before it is dealt with,[40] and if either party so requests it must be in the form of a hearing,[41] otherwise a written procedure will apply. Where it takes the form of a hearing, the person hearing the appeal may decide that it should be held wholly or partly in private. The bringing of an appeal will not affect the enforceability of the decision or notice appealed against, save in the case of a cancellation or revocation of a registration or authorisation, unless the Secretary of State otherwise directs.[42]

The management of radioactive wastes—policy issues

Radioactive wastes were the subject of a 1959 White Paper,[43] and the   **20–015**
Radioactive Substances Act 1960 was based on its recommendations. A review of this White Paper by a group of experts led to a report[44] that

---

[35] s.20.
[36] s.26(3).
[37] SI 1990/2504.
[38] reg.3(1).
[39] reg.3(2).
[40] s.27(2).
[41] s.27(3).
[42] s.27(6).
[43] Cmnd. 884 "The Control of Radioactive Wastes", 1959.
[44] "A Review of Cmnd. 884 'The Control of Radioactive Wastes". A Report by an Expert Group to the Radioactive Waste Management Committee (1979).

recommended that the radiological protection aspects of radioactive waste management practices should be based on the system of dose limitation recommended by the ICRP.[45] These further recommendations were adopted by the government, and formed the basis of the 1982 Guide to the RSA 1960, and specifically its Part II.[46]

Following a report of the Royal Commission on Environmental Pollution,[47] there was set up what became the Radioactive Waste Management Advisory Committee (RWMAC). The Committee's terms of reference were to advise the Secretaries of State for the Environment, for Scotland and for Wales on; (a) the technical and environmental implications of major issues concerning the development and implementation of an overall policy for all aspects of the management of civil radioactive waste, including research and development, and (b) on any such matters referred to it by the Secretaries of State. In September 2001 it published advice to the Government on the way in which it believes future policy for the long-term management of the UK's solid radioactive waste should be decided, and in March 2003 published a report on Management of Low Activity Solid Wastes within the United Kingdom. In 1995, the Department of the Environment, Scottish Office and Welsh Office published the "Review of Radioactive Waste Management Policy—Final Conclusions".[48] Although this remains part of the guidance given to the Environment Agency, it has in large part been superseded by more recent developments. However, in March 1997 it became apparent that "further review" would be needed when the Secretary of State for the Environment did not grant Nirex planning permission for a Rock Characterisation Facility with a view to creating a deep repository for the disposal of radioactive waste. The House of Lords Select Committee on Science and Technology conducted an enquiry into "The Management of Nuclear Waste" from November 1997 until March 1999.[49] The Government's response to this Report promised a detailed and wide-ranging consultation.

In 2001, the Government (DEFRA and the devolved administrations acting jointly) published a consultation paper[50] on a revised policy for radioactive waste management, "Managing Radioactive Waste Safely". This was followed by separate enquiries into the consultation by both the House of Commons Environment, Food and Rural affairs Committee and by the House of Lords Select Committee on Science and Technology.

20–016 In July 2002, as part of the implementation of the 2001 programme, the

---

[45] See Database of Dose Coefficients Publications 68 and 72 (now included in 1 CRP CD Rom 1, Elsevier, January 2002).
[46] This Guide has not yet been revised. See fn.12.
[47] "Nuclear Power and the Environment", 6th report, 1976.
[48] Department of the Environment, Scottish Office and Welsh Office, Cm 2919, HMSO London.
[49] House of Lords Session 1998–99 Third Report of the Select Committee on Science and Technology. "Management of Nuclear Waste" (March 1999).
[50] "Managing Radioactive Waste Safely", September 12, 2001.

Government announced the creation of a new independent advisory body, called the CoRWM (Committee on Radioactive Waste Management), to review the options for safely managing waste and recommend a long term strategy. This resulted in the publication by CoRWM in July 2006 of a package of recommendations that included:

- geological disposal is currently the best form of long term manage-ment for the UK's higher activity radioactive waste;
- there should be a commitment to the safe and secure interim storage of the waste during the period it will take to plan and construct the geological disposal facility; and
- the UK should look to develop partnership arrangements, linked to appropriate involvement and benefit packages, with local authorities and communities as a means of securing the siting of facilities.[51]

In its response,[52] the Government broadly endorsed these recommendations.

In addition to all of the above, the UK Strategy for Radioactive Discharges 2001–2020[53] aims to implement the OSPAR strategy for radio-active substances which was agreed by Ministers of the Contracting Parties at Sintra, Portugal in 1998,[54] and at subsequent meetings. The Strategy focuses on reducing liquid discharges from the major sectors of the nuclear industry, and although there is a presumption that discharges from other diverse minor sources will be highly controlled, discharge profile or targets are set for these other sources. Defra is now consulting on a revised Strategy for Radioactive Discharges for the period 2006–2030,[55] one objective of which is to implement the OSPAR strategy, having regard to the UK Government's change of attitude since 2002 to the use of nuclear power for electricity generation—it now envisages that existing nuclear plants will remain active for longer, and that there is a role for new nuclear plants in the country's energy mix alongside other low-carbon sources. The

---

[51] "Managing our Radioactive Waste Safely", July 2006, CorWM Doc 700.
[52] "Managing Radioactive Waste Safely—A Framework for Implementing Geological Disposal", June 12, 2008.
[53] Department for Environment, Food and Rural Affairs, Scottish Executive, Welsh Assembly Government and Department of Environment, Northern Ireland (2002).
[54] The OSPAR Convention for the protection of the marine environment brought together the Oslo and Paris Conventions—in 1998 radioactive substances was agreed to be a priority area and an initial strategy with objectives and time lines was agreed (reference number 12998-17). This Strategy includes the ultimate aim of, by 2020, additional concentrations in the environment of artificial radioactive substances being "close to zero". A Radioactive Substances Committee was established in 2000 to facilitate implementation of the OSPAR Strategy with regard to Radioactive Substances. See the OSPAR Commission http://website—www.ospar.org.
[55] "UK Strategy for Radioactive Discharges 2006–030", consultation document, June 2008.

revised strategy sets out the principles that regulatory bodies will apply in progressively reducing discharges of radioactive material to the minimum practicable.[56] Targets have been set for discharge reductions for five nuclear sectors and the non-nuclear sector.[57]

Nuclear safety and radioactive waste management may be said to suffer from a plethora of regulators and advisory bodies, including those listed in the following table.[58]

Table 20/II

Regulator / Advisory Body (in alphabetical order)	Main Duties or Powers
BNFL (British Nuclear Fuels)	Established by the Atomic Energy Authority Act 1971, it is the company responsible for power generation from remaining magnox reaction in UK.
CoRWM (Committee on Radioactive Waste Management)	Offers independent advice to Government on the options for safe management of radioactive waste and on a long term strategy.
DEFRA (Department of the Environment, Food and Rural Affairs)	The Department responsible for environment interests in nuclear and radioactive matters including radioactive waste management and also involved in the management and recycling of used reactor fuel— Radioactive Substances Division.
DECC (Department of Energy and Climate Change)	The Department (created in October 2008) responsible for energy matters including nuclear power.
EA (Environment Agency)	Registrations and authorisations in England and Wales under the RSA 93.
FSA (Food Standards Agency)	Statutory consultee on matters relating to the Nuclear Installations Act 1965 authorisations and RSA disposal authorisations.

20–017

---

[56] Related consultations are on "Statutory Guidance to the Environment Agency on the regulation of radioactive discharges into the environment" (Defra, June 2008), and "Public consultation on the radioactive substances regulation environmental principles" (Environment Agency, June 2008).

[57] But omitting potential discharges from nuclear power stations yet to be built.

[58] The position is noted in a May 2003 joint report of the Health and Safety Commission's Nuclear Safety Advisory Committee and the Radioactive Waste Management Advisory Committee.

HPA (Health Protection Agency)	A new agency, incorporating the NRPB, created on April 1, 2005. It undertakes research, provides laboratory and technical services, runs training courses, provides expert information, and has a significant advisory role.
HSC (Health and Safety Commission) and HSE (Health and Safety Executive)	The Nuclear Safety Directorate administers the site licence procedure under the NIA 1965 and the Nuclear Installations Inspectorate deals with safety issues of major nuclear licensees.
IRPB (International Radiological Protection Board)	An international advisory body whose recommendations and guidance are widely accepted and underpin a number of the recommendations of the NRPB and HPA and measures made under the Euratom Treaty.
NDA (Nuclear Decommissioning Authority)	Responsible for decommissioning of the UK's "nuclear legacy" i.e. civil nuclear sites.
NIREX	Examines safe, environmental and economic aspects of deep geological disposal of radioactive waste.
SEPA (Scottish Environment Protection Agency)	Registrations and authorisations in Scotland under the RSA 93.
UKAEA (U.K. Atomic Energy Authority) AEA Technology	Established by the Atomic Energy Authority Act 1954. Privatised in 1996 as AEA Technology, and now responsible for managing the decommissioning of the nuclear reactors and other radioactive facilities used for the U.K.'s nuclear research and development programme.

Exposure to radiation—governing principles

Controls over operations in the UK liable to give rise to exposure to radioactivity are subject to certain basic principles, derived from ICRP publications and NRPB / CoRWM advice, namely that: **20–018**

(a) no practice involving exposures to radiation should be adopted unless it produces sufficient benefit to offset the radiation detriment it causes;

(b) radiation exposure of individuals and the collective dose to the population arising from radioactive wastes must be reduced to levels which are as low as reasonably achievable (ALARA), economic and social factors being taken into account, so that optimisation of protection limits the inequity likely to result from the inherent economic and social judgements; and

(c) the average effective dose equivalent from all sources, excluding natural background radiation and medical procedures, for representative members of a critical group of the general public is not to exceed 5 mSv in any one year.[59]

The 1982 Guide to the RSA 1960 recognised that while the principles it discussed applied primarily to the radiation that may be received by humans, exposure to other living things must also be taken into account. However in the case of other living things, it is the exposure to the population as a whole rather than to individual members of it that is generally of significance, and the ICRP's opinion is quoted that protection arrangements drawn up to ensure the health and safety of man will in general provide sufficient protection for other species.[60]

Apart from the RSA 93, the main domestic legislation giving effect to these criteria is the Nuclear Installations Act 1965,[61] as amended, the Highly Active Sealed Sources (HASS) Regulations 2005,[62] the Justification of Practices Involving Ionising Radiation Regulations 2004,[63] the Ionising Radiations Regulations 1999,[64] the Carriage of Dangerous Goods and Use of High Pressure Equipment Regulations 2007,[65] including in particular Schedule 5 "Radiological Emergencies", and the Radiation (Emergency Preparedness and Public Information) Regulations 2001.[66]

The Basic Safety Standards Directive 96/29 contains a number of provisions which have resulted in a legal obligation being placed on the Environment Agency to ensure that, when granting authorisations under

[59] Authorisation of Discharges of Radioactive Waste to the Environment, Appendix 1 "Law, Policy and Principles: Criteria for decision making", Environment Agency document BX 0237. This maximum figure is considered to represent an average dose related equivalent of less than 1 mSv per year of life-long whole body exposure from all sources, giving a lifetime whole body dose equivalent of not more than 70 mSv, which is regarded as acceptable. However, it may be necessary to pay particular attention to this lifetime dose equivalent in certain cases.

[60] The ICRP is currently reviewing its position with respect to the protection of the environment and there are various international and European initiatives to development a framework for protecting the wider environment. This may lead to additional principles for the assessment of doses to non-human species. Interim methods and data for the assessment of doses to non-human species are provided in the Environment Agency's 2001 publication "Impact Assessment of Ionising Radiation in Wildlife", R&D Report 128.

[61] 1965 c.57.

[62] SI 2005/2686.

[63] SI 2004/1769.

[64] SI 1999/3232.

[65] SI 2007/1573.

[66] SI 2001/2975.

the RSA, any resulting exposure to individuals in the population is kept as low as reasonably achievable, social and economic factors being taking into account. In addition, this Directive prescribes a mandatory dose limit of 1mSv effective dose in a year for members of the public. Although this was the dose limit endorsed by Government, an obligation on the Environment Agency to ensure that as a consequence no member of the public receives a dose in excess of the specified dose limits was required. This was placed on the Environment Agency in the Radioactive Substances (Basic Safety Standards) (England and Wales) Direction 2000 of May 9, 2000.[67]

The HASS Directive and Regulations

The HASS Directive[68] requires the EU member states to ensure that **20–019** effective safety measures are in place in relation to the potentially most harmful sources of radioactivity—highly active sealed sources, being defined as those all sealed sources that contain a radionuclide with an activity level at or above that shown in Annex I to the Directive. If other radionuclides are involved that are not listed in the HASS Directive but in Annex I of the Basic Safety Standards Directive 96/29, the relevant level is one hundredth of that given in the IAEA regulations for the safe transport of those radioactive materials. To ensure the focus is on the most hazardous sources, these levels are above the exemption levels of Directive 96/29. The controls it stipulates apply both to such sources that are properly covered by relevant authorisations, and also to "orphan sources" which are defined as sources which are not under regulatory control, either because they never have been, or because they have been abandoned, lost, misplaced, stolen or transferred, without proper notification of the competent authority, to a new holder or without informing the recipient.

Under the Directive Member States must ensure, before authorising any source or operation involving one, that firstly, adequate arrangements have been made for the safe management of the source, including when it becomes disused. These may provide e.g. for the transfer of a disused source back to the supplier or manufacturer, or its placement in a recognised depositary. Secondly, adequate provision must be made, by way of financial security or any other equivalent means appropriate to that source, for the safe management of the source when it becomes disused, including where the holder becomes insolvent or goes out of business.[69] Additionally, Member States must ensure that each authorisation of a highly active source covers:

(a) responsibilities;
(b) minimum staff competencies, including information and training;

---

[67] The Scottish equivalent is dated May 11, 2000.
[68] 2003/122/Euratom, OJ L 346/57–64, 31.12.2003.
[69] art.3(2).

    (c) minimum source, source container and additional equipment performance criteria;

    (d) requirements for emergency procedures and communication links;

    (e) work procedures to be followed;

    (f) maintenance of equipment, sources and containers;

    (g) adequate management of disused sources, including agreements regarding the transfer, if appropriate, of disused sources to a supplier, another authorised holder or a recognised installation.[70]

Further obligations are imposed on e.g. the keeping of records and the conduct of regular tests to ensure the integrity of the source is maintained.

The Directive obligations are given effect by the HASS Regulations 2005. These came into effect for new sources on January 1, 2006; holders of existing sources had until January 1, 2008, to apply for a variation of their current authorisation to enable this to reflect the requirements of the HASS Directive.

"Regulation Environmental Principles" (REPs)

20–020   The Environment Agency applies a set of principles, known as "Regulation Environmental Principles" (REPs), which set out a framework for the technical assessments and judgments that the Agency has to make when regulating radioactive discharges, and also in its other roles as consultees or advisers. The REPs have recently been updated, principally to reflect the fact that the Agency must now apply BAT (Best Available Techniques) rather than BPM (Best Practicable Means) or BPEO (Best Practicable Environmental Option).[71] The Agency however expects that the level of environmental protection will be the same under BAT as under BPM / BPEO.

"Justification of practices"

20–021   The Justification of Practices Involving Ionising Radiation Regulations 2004 implement the justification requirements of the Basic Safety Standards Directive 96/29, including; (a) Articles 6(1) and 6(2) which deal with justification of new classes or types of practice involving exposure to ionising radiation, and the review of existing practices, and (b) part of Article 6(5) which prohibits the addition of radioactive substances to certain goods and their import or export. Prior to the 1996 Directive, justification decisions were taken on a site-by-site basis by the regulators

---

[70] art.3(3).

[71] A draft of the updated version "Radioactive Substances Regulation Environmental Principles" was published by the Agency for consultation in June 2008.

when considering individual applications under the RSA 93. The 2004 Regulations introduce procedures for justification decisions to be made on a generic basis, and for the review of existing practices in changed circumstances. Detailed Guidance on the Regulations has been issued by Defra.[72]

Applications for a justification decision in England are made to the Secretary of State, and elsewhere to the appropriate devolved administration. Thus all "new practices"[73] must now be shown to be justified by their economic, social or other benefits in relation to the health detriment they may cause before they may be carried out. Similarly a person may apply for a justification decision in respect of an existing practice if either (a) new and important evidence about its efficacy or consequences is acquired; or (b) there has been a justification decision that it is not justified. The relevant authority may also review an existing practice, on its own initiative, if either of these conditions applies. Before taking a justification decision the authority must consult all of the HSE, the FSA, the HPA, and (in England) the Environment Agency, and may consult anyone else.[74] A justification decision may be made subject to conditions.[75]

The authorities have powers of entry on to premises substantially equivalent to those of s.108(4) of the EPA. for the purpose of determining whether a person has committed a relevant breach of the Regulations.[76] Thus if a person carries out a practice that requires but has not received a favourable justification decision, fails to comply with a relevant condition, or commits certain other breaches, they are liable to be served with a contravention notice specifying steps they must take to remedy the breach, and the period within which that must be done. The person served has 14 days to seek a variation or withdrawal of the notice. The notice will not however take effect for 28 days, unless it is considered that it should have immediate effect or be otherwise expedited.[77] It is not an offence to breach the Regulations themselves, but only to fail to comply with a contravention notice. Offences may only be prosecuted by the relevant authority or by those to whom its powers have been delegated under Regulation 27.[78]

The Regulations also contain a specific prohibition on knowingly or recklessly (a) adding any radioactive substance in the production of personal ornaments or toys, or (b) importing or exporting any personal **20–022**

---

[72] The Justification of Practices Involving Ionising Radiation Regulations 2004: Guidance on their application and administration, Defra, May 2008.
[73] A practice is "new" for the purposes of the Regulations if no practice in that class or type was carried out in the United Kingdom before May 13, 2000, and the practice has not been found to be justified. Reg.4(1).
[74] reg.18.
[75] reg.11(1).
[76] reg.23, Sch.1.
[77] reg.22.
[78] reg.26. Scotland is excluded from these provisions, and hence the normal Scots criminal procedure applies.

ornament, toy or cosmetic, to which any radioactive substance has been added in its production.[79]

Controls over the Disposal and Accumulation of Radioactive Waste

20–023 The RSA deals separately with the disposal of radioactive waste, in section 13, and accumulation of radioactive waste with a view to its subsequent disposal, in section 14. In practice, the dividing line between these two procedures is not always clear cut—radioactive wastes are liable to be stored for a long time while attempts are made to organise suitable final disposal sites. In principle, however, storage of such wastes will be deemed to be an accumulation rather than disposal where it involves placing the wastes in a facility, with the intention of taking further action subsequently, in such a way and at such a location that further action is expected to be feasible. The further action might, for example, be recovery of the radioactive material in situ, or it could be a declaration that nothing further needs to be done, and that the material will be left where it is undisturbed, so converting the process into one of disposal.

The "disposal" of waste includes its removal, deposit, destruction, discharge (whether into water or into the air or into a sewer or drain or otherwise) or burial (whether underground or otherwise).[80] The controls over disposal of radioactive waste apply:

- to its disposal on or from any premises which are used by a person for the purposes of any undertaking carried on by him;
- where it is received by a person for disposal by the recipient; and
- where it arises from any mobile radioactive apparatus kept for any of the purposes controlled under the RSA,

provided, in the first two cases (only), he knows or has reasonable grounds for believing it to be radioactive waste. In each case, disposal of the waste (or causing or permitting it to be disposed of) requires prior authorisation under the relevant subsection of section 13, save only that where a person receives waste for disposal he does not need a specific authorisation if the relevant authorisation in respect of the premises or the mobile radioactive apparatus on or from which the waste arose provided for its disposal, and the disposal complies with its terms.

A person may not accumulate any radioactive waste (with a view to its subsequent disposal) on any premises used for an undertaking that he carries on, nor may he cause or permit this accumulation, if he knows or has reasonable grounds for believing it to be radioactive waste, except in

[79] reg.20.
[80] s.47(1).

accordance with an authorisation granted under section 14. A number of exceptions to this are nevertheless provided, namely:

- an authorisation to dispose of radioactive waste under section 13 may provide for its temporary accumulation, in which event no further authorisation under section 14 is needed;
- the prohibition does not apply to the accumulation of radioactive waste on any premises situated on a nuclear site, since this will be controlled by the relevant site licence;
- there are a series of exclusions applying both to accumulation and the disposal of radioactive waste, mentioned below.

Inevitably, where radioactive waste is produced, it cannot always be instantaneously disposed of, and it must in practice be kept for at least a brief period. Nevertheless, if any substance arising from the production, keeping or use of radioactive material is accumulated in a part of the premises appropriated for that purpose and is retained there for a period of not less than three months, the substance will be presumed to be radioactive waste and to be accumulated on the premises with a view to its subsequent disposal, unless the contrary is proved.[81] Exemptions to the prohibitions on disposal and accumulation of radioactive waste, unless appropriately authorised, apply to such waste arising from clocks or watches, except where it arises on premises on which the clocks or watches are manufactured or repaired by processes involving the use of luminous material. Additionally, as already mentioned, there are numerous exemptions from either or both of sections 13 and 14.[82]

Section 16 of the RSA governs the grant of authorisations for the disposal or accumulation of radioactive waste, application for which is made to the appropriate Agency.[83] In England, Wales and Northern Ireland, where an application relates to radioactive waste on or from premises on a nuclear site, the Environment Agency will consult with the Food Standards Agency and the HSE.[84] In any such case, the Minister must consult with such local authorities, relevant water bodies,[85] and other public or local authorities as he thinks it proper to do so. In all cases, the Inspectorate will send a copy of the application to each local authority for the area in which the disposal or accumulation is to take place. Grant of an authorisation may, and invariably will, be made subject to such limitations and conditions as the Environment Agency sees fit. On grant, the Environment Agency must (except where disclosure is restricted on grounds of national

20–024

---

[81] s.14(4).
[82] See para.20–010 and fn.28.
[83] On forms provided by the Agencies.
[84] s.16(3)—repealed—see 16(4a).
[85] i.e. water and sewerage undertakers and fisheries committees in England and Wales; Scottish Water and district salmon fishery boards in Scotland; and the [Fisheries Conservation Board] in Northern Ireland.

security)[86] send a copy to each local authority for the relevant area, and also to any other public or local authority that may have been consulted in respect of waste to be disposed on or from premises on a nuclear site. To give these bodies time to make representations, the authorisation will normally not come into effect until at least 28 days after the various copies have been sent to the local or other public bodies, unless it is considered necessary for it to come into effect sooner.

It was held in *R. v Secretary of State for the Environment, ex p. Greenpeace and Lancashire County Council*[87] that sections 13 and 16 must be construed so as to be consistent with Euratom Directive 80/836 as it was then, as amended, and which the RSA is intended to implement. Article 6 of this Directive sets out certain general principles, including:

"(a) the various types of activity resulting in an exposure to ionising radiation shall have been justified in advance by the advantages which they produce".

Although there is no comparable language in the UK statute, there is thus nevertheless a binding obligation on the Environment Agency under the replacement Directive 96/29 to satisfy itself that any exposure to ionising radiation that would result from any new type of practice is justified before authorising it. This statutory omission has of course now been rectified by the Justification of Practices Regulations discussed above,[88] but the general point remains that the Environment Agency and other "emanations of the State" must give effect to binding EU legislation, whether or not it has yet been the subject of implementing domestic legislation.

The issue was considered further in a case involving a judicial review of authorisations for discharge of radioactive waste from sites managed by the Atomic Weapons Establishment as a contractor for the Ministry of Defence. The matter was initially considered in the Administrative Court where the application for judicial review was dismissed. The Court of Appeal then dismissed an appeal.[89] The activities underlying the need for authorisation included decommissioning of redundant nuclear weapons and production of Trident missiles. The application of the Euratom Treaty to military uses was considered in the High Court and the High Court concluded that although it did regulate civilian commercial uses of nuclear energy, the Treaty did not apply to military uses. In the Court of Appeal, Laws L.J. considered that, reading the Euratom Treaty as a whole, it was not intended to apply to miliary use. The other judges agreed that the appeal should be dismissed, but Moreland J. considered that, although not expressly stated in the Euratom Treaty, Chapter III did apply to military

[86] Under s.25.
[87] [1994] 4 All E.R. 352.
[88] para.20–021.
[89] *R. (on the application of Marchiori) v The Environment Agency* [2002] E.W.C.A. Civ 3; [2002] EU. L.R. 225 (CA).

uses, and Thorpe L.J. stated that he was "less certain" than Laws L.J. that the provisions had no application to military uses.[90]

Another procedural point that was raised was that Article 37 of the Euratom Treaty required notification of the European Commission prior to grant of an authorisation. The Court of Appeal held that a failure in this regard did not make grant of the authorisation unlawful. There did appear to be a possible procedural irregularity in connection with the consultation of the Food Standards Agency, which had actually subsequently approved the proposals. Turner L.J. emphasised the fact that the Food Standards Agency had at all times been aware of the proposal and had not objected and that there were "good and powerful reasons" for proceeding the way the Environment Agency had done.

20–025

Before granting any authorisation in circumstances where it appears that any local or other public authority or any relevant water body may need to take special precautions, there must be consultation with them.[91] Where such special precautions are taken by a local or public authority in accordance with an authorisation or with the prior approval of the Environment Agency (or the Minister where appropriate), the costs of so doing may be recovered from the person authorised.[92] If an authorisation to dispose of radioactive waste requires or permits radioactive waste to be removed to a place provided by a local authority for the deposit of refuse, that authority has an express duty to accept any radioactive waste taken to that place in accordance with the authorisation, and to deal with it in any manner as may be required by the authorisation.[93]

On grant of an authorisation, the Environment Agency must supply the applicant with a certificate containing all the material particulars of it. In so far as it relates to any premises in which radioactive material is kept or used, or used for the disposal or accumulation of radioactive waste, a copy of the certificate must be displayed at all times in a position where it may be conveniently read.

An application for authorisation may be treated by the applicant as having been refused if it is not determined within four months or such

20–026

---

[90] An interesting feature of the decision was the argument that the Trident nuclear weapons programme is contrary to international law and that the Environment Agency had failed to consider this when deciding whether to grant the authorisation. In the High Court, Turner J. held that this was an issue which lay beyond the remit of the Environment Agency as an environmental regulator. In the Court of Appeal the critical finding was that "the law of England will not contemplate what may be called a merits review of any honest decision of government upon matters of national defence policy". Laws L.J. emphasised that there is no legislation (having considered the Human Rights Act 1998 pursuant to which he felt that no points arose) which contains a mandatory provision that "the respondent examine the merits of defence policy, specifically the Trident programme, however remotely. Certainly, the RSA does not do so".

[91] s.18(1).

[92] s.18(2).

[93] s.18(3).

longer period as may be agreed,[94] so entitling him to invoke the appeals procedure under sections 26 and 27.[95] A granted authorisation may at any time be revoked or varied, by attaching or varying applicable limitations or conditions, without compensation.[96]

Where a site is authorised to make discharges under RSA 93 there is a procedure for reporting releases of radioactive substances for the entire site to the Environment Agency for inclusion in its pollution inventory. Information so provided could be made publicly available, although the person supplying it would be entitled to identify any substances or other material which it claims is confidential.

Overlap with Other Statutes

20–027   There is substantial potential overlap between the operation of the RSA and that of various other statutes including Part III of the EPA relating to statutory nuisances, numerous provisions of the Water Resources Act 1991, including those relating to pollution of water, and the provisions in the Water Industry Act 1991 relating to trade effluent. These and other statutory provisions, as listed in Part I of Schedule 3 to the RSA continue to apply to radioactive substances, but in so far as they do apply, no account is to be taken of any radioactivity possessed by any substance or article, or by any part of any premises,[97] while the RSA applies in respect of their radioactivity. Several of these other statutes likewise have provisions designed to avoid the overlap of jurisdiction. Thus, EPA section 78 provides that Part II of that Act (waste on land) does not apply to radioactive waste within the meaning of the RSA, unless regulations otherwise provide. To date no such regulations have been issued. In relation to water pollution, the WRA 1991 has a corresponding provision in section 98, but by virtue of the Control of Pollution (Radioactive Waste) Regulations 1989,[98] made under the corresponding provision of the Water Act 1989, its pollution controls are applied in respect of all matters other than radioactivity. Similarly, controls over the discharge of trade effluent under the Water Industry Act 1991 have been made applicable to matters other than radioactivity.[99]

---

[94] ss.16(7), 47(1).
[95] See para.20–014.
[96] s.17.
[97] RSA, s.40(1), (2).
[98] SI 1989/1158.
[99] SI 1976/959.

Radioactive Contaminated Land

As enacted, section 78Y of the EPA provides that Part 2A (dealing with **20–028** contaminated land) does not apply in relation to harm or pollution of controlled waters so far as attributable to any radioactivity possessed by any substance. However, if the presence of a substance would cause land to meet the definition of "contaminated" irrespective of any radioactive properties, then Part 2A can still apply to the non-radioactive properties of any substance. A corresponding regime has now been set up by the Radioactive Contaminated Land (Modification of Enactments) (England) Regulations 2006,[100] as amended by the Radioactive Contaminated Land (Modification of Enactments) (England) (Amendment) Regulations 2007,[101] which apply Part 2A with modifications to the identification and remediation of radioactive contaminated land. Space does not allow a discussion of this regime in detail, but it is to be noted that the definition of "contaminated land" for this purpose is simply

> "any land which appears to the local authority in whose area it is situated to be in such a condition, by reason of substances in, on or under the land, that (a) harm is being caused; or (b) there is a significant possibility of harm being caused".

"Harm" is defined as "lasting exposure to any person resulting from the after-effects of a radiological emergency, past practice or past work activity". In determining the appropriate person to hold responsible for the remediation, a new subsection 1A has been inserted into section 78F providing that in relation to any land contaminated by a nuclear occurrence, the Secretary of State is deemed to be the appropriate person. "Land contaminated by a nuclear occurrence" is elaborately defined but is primarily land damaged by the presence of substances caused by breaches or deemed breaches of any of sections 7 to 10 of the Nuclear Installations Act 1965. The regime does not however apply to;

- radioactivity on land causing significant harm to the wider environment or the pollution of controlled waters,
- radon gas,
- risks arising from changes in the way land contaminated with radioactivity is used,
- radioactivity on land within the boundary of a nuclear licensed site; where this occurs, it is regarded as an accumulation of radioactive waste and the licensee is required to manage it as such.

As with the normal contaminated land regime, authorities determining the issues of "harm", and whether harm is "significant", in relation to

---

[100] SI 2006/1379.
[101] SI 2007/3245.

radioactive contaminated land must act in accordance with guidance issued by the Secretary of State.[102]

Enforcement

20–029 Enforcement of the provisions of the RSA may take the form of criminal prosecutions for breach of the various requirements of the RSA, or by the service of an enforcement or a prohibition notice under sections 21 and 22 respectively. Offences against the principal provisions of the Act, including a failure to comply with any requirement of an enforcement or prohibition notice, are subject to a fine not exceeding £20,000 and/or imprisonment for up to six months, on summary conviction, and to an unlimited fine and/ or imprisonment for up to five years on indictment. Lesser penalties are provided for failure to display a certificate of registration or authorisation, or to comply with any obligations to retain or produce records.[103] In addition, the Environment Agency may take proceedings in the High Court (and the Scottish Environment Protection Agency in the Court of Session in Scotland) for the purposes of securing compliance with an enforcement notice or prohibition notice.[104] Unlike most other regulatory offences, private prosecutions are excluded by an express prohibition against the taking of proceedings in respect of any offence under the RSA in England and Wales except by the Secretary of State, the Environment Agency, or by or with the consent or the Director of Public Prosecutions.[105]

The standard provisions render directors liable who have consented or connived at an offence by their company or where it has been committed through their negligence.[106] Unusually, however, no corresponding liability is placed on the members of a body corporate that is managed by them, except where it is established by or under any enactment of the purposes of any nationalised industry.[107] The normal provision is provided for any other person to be charged with an offence where this is due to his act or default.[108]

Where a person has failed to comply with any limitation or condition the subject of his registration or authorisation, or if the Environment Agency considers he is likely to do so, he may be served with an enforcement notice.[109] This must state the opinion of the Environment Agency on which the notice is based, specify the matters constituting the relevant

---

[102] Namely Defra Circular 01/2006, September 2006.
[103] ss.32, 33.
[104] s.32(3).
[105] s.38.
[106] s.36.
[107] s.36(2).
[108] s.37.
[109] s.21(1).

failure and also the steps that must be taken to remedy them, and the period in which they must be taken.[110] Where a local authority or other body has been sent copies of a registration or authorisation, a copy of the enforcement notice is to be served on them also.[111]

Where the Environment Agency considers that there is an imminent risk **20–030** of pollution to the environment or of harm to human health due to any person continuing to keep or use radioactive material or mobile radioactive apparatus or to dispose or accumulate radioactive waste, it may serve a prohibition notice on that person.[112] This may be done whether or not the manner of carrying on the relevant activity complies with the requirements of the applicable registration or authorisation;[113] the procedure is not available if there is no registration or authorisation at all. A prohibition notice must likewise set out the opinion of the Environment Agency on which the service of the notice is based, specify the matters giving rise to the risk involved, and the steps that must be taken to remove it, as well as the period in which they must be taken.[114] Additionally, it must direct that the registration or authorisation in question shall cease to have effect, either wholly or in part, until the prohibition notice is withdrawn. If the registration or authorisation is only partially suspended, limitations or conditions may be imposed in relation to the activity or activities that may still be carried on.[115] As with enforcement notices, copies of any prohibition notice must be sent to the relevant local authority and any other public bodies involved.[116] The prohibition notice must be withdrawn when the Environment Agency is satisfied that the risk specified in the notice has been removed, and a copy of this withdrawal notice must likewise be sent to any authority or other body that was sent a copy of the prohibition notice originally.[117]

Anyone on whom an enforcement or prohibition notice has been served and who requests a hearing within the period prescribed by the notice is entitled to be heard by an inspector appointed for the purpose,[118] except where the notice was issued pursuant to a direction by the Secretary of State.[119]

Special powers are given to the Secretary of State to arrange for the safe disposal or accumulation of radioactive waste, if it appears to him that adequate facilities are not available.[120] The Environment Agency has

---

[110] s.21(2).
[111] s.21(4).
[112] s.22.
[113] s.22(2).
[114] s.22(3).
[115] s.22(4).
[116] s.22(6).
[117] s.22(7).
[118] s.26(2).
[119] s.26(3)(b).
[120] s.29.

powers for disposing of radioactive waste on any premises where it is satisfied that it ought to be disposed of, but that it is unlikely for any reason that it will be lawfully disposed of unless extra powers are taken.[121] Where it takes such action, it may recover any expenses reasonably incurred from the occupier of the premises or, where they are unoccupied, from their owner, as defined in section 343 of the Public Health Act 1936 as regards England, Wales and Northern Ireland, and section 3 of the Public Health (Scotland) Act 1897 in relation to premises in Scotland, with certain qualifications.[122]

20–031   Extensive rights of entry and inspection are provided by the Environment Act 1995, section 108. Any intentional obstruction of any person exercising these powers, and any refusal to provide facilities or assistance or any information, or to permit any inspection reasonably required under those powers constitutes an offence.[123] It is also an offence to make false or misleading statement when obtaining a registration or authorisation, when furnishing required information or within any required record. These offences can lead to a fine of up to £5,000 on summary conviction and an unlimited fine on indictment.[124]

Public Access to Documents

20–032   There is a general right of access to all applications made to the Environment Agency under the RSA and to all documents issued by the Environment Agency under it, as well as to any other documents that the Environment Agency may have sent to any local authority in pursuance of directions given by the Secretary of State and records of convictions, except to the extent that this would involve the disclosure of information relating to any relevant process or trade secret or where the Secretary of State has directed restrictions on grounds of national security.[125] Likewise, each local authority must both keep and make available copies of all documents that may be sent to it under any provision of the RSA, unless directed by the chief inspector that all or any part of a document is not to be made available.[126] The public has a right to inspect copies of all such documents and to be provided with copies on payment of a reasonable fee.[127]

---

[121] s.30.
[122] Set out in s.13(3).
[123] s.35.
[124] s.34A.
[125] s.39(1).
[126] s.39(2).
[127] s.39(5).

Territorial Scope

The RSA 93 itself extends throughout the United Kingdom, including any **20–033** activities on the continental shelf. Nevertheless following the devolution of powers to Scotland and Wales, much of the recent secondary legislation is specific to the individual jurisdictions. The Act is binding on the Crown, save in relation to premises occupied for military or other defence purposes or by or for a visiting force.[128] Nevertheless, any contravention by the Crown does not render it itself criminally liable, though the court may, if requested to do so, declare unlawful any contravention that it has found.[129] Though the Crown is not per se criminally liable, any persons in the public service of the Crown are potentially as liable as any other persons.[130]

Radiation Emergency Information

Information is to be supplied to the general public about health protection **20–034** measures required in the event of a "radiological emergency", by virtue of the Radiation (Emergency Preparedness and Public Information) Regulations 2001[131] which implement Euratom Directive 96/29.[132] These impose obligations on operators and carriers who work with ionising radiation or transport radioactive substances to identify hazards and carry out a risk evaluation. Where a radiation risk exists, reasonable steps must be taken to prevent or limit radiation accidents. If a radiation emergency could arise, the operator or carrier must prepare an emergency plan as set out in the Regulations. A "radiation emergency" is any occurrence which is likely to result in any member of the public being exposed to ionising radiation arising from that occurrence in excess of any of the doses set out in Schedule 1 to the Regulations. Schedule 1 sets out separately dose limits for (i) the whole body, and (ii) skin and the lens of the eye. If any one or more of these limits is likely to be exceeded, then there is a potential radiation emergency. An emergency response facility, incorporating automatic monitors connected into an information network, known as the Radioactive Incident Monitoring Network (RIMNET), has been set up to collect data and to raise an alert if any significant increase in radioactivity is detected.

---

[128] s.42(1)(2).
[129] s.42(3).
[130] s.42(4).
[131] SI 2001/2975.
[132] OJ L159 [1996].

Health and Safety at the Workplace

20–035   The health and safety at the workplace of those who may come into contact with ionising radiations is the subject of the Ionising Radiations Regulations 1999,[133] and an Approved Code of Practice: "Work with Ionising Radiation" (L121). These replaced the Ionising Radiations Regulations 1985, except for the requirement for special hazard assessments (regulation 26) and related provisions, and the Ionising Radiations (Outside Workers) Regulations 1993. The 1999 Regulations implemented most of the revised Euratom Directive 96/29 on Basic Safety Standards. They apply to a large range of workplaces where radioactive substances and electrical equipment emitting ionising radiation are used. They also apply to work with natural radiation, including work in which people are exposed to naturally occurring radon gas and its decay products. Any employer who undertakes work with ionising radiation must comply with the Regulations. The Regulations require employers to keep exposure to ionising radiations as low as reasonably practicable. Exposures must not exceed specified dose limits. Restriction of exposure should be achieved first by means of engineering control and design features. Where this is not reasonably practicable employers should introduce safe systems of work and only rely on the provision of personal protective equipment as a last resort. Member States may impose stricter limits than those laid down in the Euratom Directives.[134] Guidance on the regulations has been issued by the HSE.[135]

Transport of Radioactive Substances

20–036   The transport of radioactive substances by both road and rail is now governed in the United Kingdom by the Carriage of Dangerous Goods and Use of Transportable Pressure Equipment Regulations 2007,[136] and specifically Regulation 42 which sets out the requirements relating to the carriage of "Class 7" goods. These 2007 Regulations implement ADR,[137] which is discussed in Chapter 18. Of the ADR classes of dangerous goods, Class 7 relates to "radioactive material".[138] By ADR Section 2.2.7.1.2, six categories of material are excluded from the scope of Class 7, including

---

[133] SI 1999/3232.
[134] ECJ Case 376/90, *European Commission v Kingdom of Belgium*, OJ 337, 17.12.92.
[135] "Work with ionising radiation: Ionising Radiations Regulations 1999, Approved code of practice and guidance", HSE Books 2000.
[136] SI 2007/1573.
[137] The European Agreement Concerning The International Carriage Of Dangerous Goods By Road.
[138] Defined in ADR Section 2.2.7.1.1 as "any material containing radionuclides where both the activity concentration and the total activity in the consignment exceed the values specified in 2.2.7.7.2.1 to 2.2.7.7.2.6". The provisions of ADR are immensely detailed and require close scrutiny by those affected, but they are beyond the scope of this work.

radioactive material moved within an establishment subject to appropriate safety regulations (otherwise than on public roads or railways); radioactive material implanted in a person or live animal for diagnosis or treatment; radioactive material in consumer products that have received regulatory approval, following their sale to the end user; and non-radioactive solid objects with radioactive substances present on their surface within the limit set in the definition for "contamination" in ADR 2.2.7.2.

Shipments of radioactive waste and spent nuclear fuel (whether waste or not) are the subject of Directive 2006/117/Euratom (the Shipments Directive),[139] which replaced Directive 92/3/Euratom with effect from December 25, 2008. Among the changes this introduces are: the controls apply to nuclear fuel being sent for reprocessing (which is not regarded as "radioactive waste"); there is a compulsory automatic consent procedure; and exports of waste and spent fuel require the consent of the receiving country. At the time of writing the Government is consulting on the transposition of the Shipments Directive with a view to implementing it by December 25, 2008.

Nuclear Installations

The use of any site within the United Kingdom for the purpose of installing 20–037 or operating any nuclear reactor or any other prescribed installation for (i) the production or use of atomic energy, (ii) the carrying out of any process which is preparatory or ancillary to the production or use of atomic energy, and which involves or is capable of causing the emission of ionising radiation, or (iii) the storage, processing or disposal of nuclear fuel or of bulk quantities of other radioactive matter produced or irradiated in the course of the production or use of nuclear fuel, requires a licence under the Nuclear Installations Act 1965 (the NIA)[140] a "nuclear site licence". Nuclear site licences may be granted only to a body corporate, and it is expressly provided that such a licence shall not be transferable.[141] Certain amendments were made to the 1965 Act by the Nuclear Installations Act 1969, and further amendments have been made by virtue of powers given to the Secretary of State under section 80 of the Health and Safety at Work Act (HSWA) 1974.

Whether or not a nuclear site licence is in force, no one other than the United Kingdom Atomic Energy Authority (the UKAEA) may extract plutonium or uranium from irradiated matter or treat uranium such as to increase the proportion of uranium 235, except pursuant with a written permit from the UKAEA or relevant government department.[142] Fissile

[139] OJ L 337/21–32, 5.12.2006.
[140] s.1(1).
[141] s.3(1).
[142] s.2(4).

material produced under such a permit may be disposed of only as approved of by the grantor of the permit. Applications for a nuclear site licence are made to the Health and Safety Executive in consultation with the Environment Agency or the Scottish Environmental Protection Agency. The HSE may, where it considers it appropriate, require the applicant to give notice of his application, and such particulars as may be specified, to a variety of public authorities, including local authorities, water undertakers and local fisheries committees.[143] A licence must have attached to it such conditions as the HSE considers necessary or desirable in the interests of safety, whether in normal circumstances or in the event of any accident or other emergency.[144] Further conditions may be added at any time with regard to the handling, treatment and disposal of nuclear matter, and any condition attached to a nuclear licence can be varied or revoked at any time. The HSE is obliged to consider representations that may be made to it by any organisation representing persons having duties upon a site, in respect of which there is a nuclear site licence in force, with a view to the exercise by it of their powers in relation to licence conditions.[145] Copies of any conditions must be kept posted on the site in a manner enabling them to be conveniently read by those having duties on the site who may be affected.[146] Nuclear site licences may at any time be revoked by the HSE, or surrendered by the licensee.[147] Notwithstanding revocation or surrender, a licensee continues to remain responsible under the licence until the HSE gives written notice that there has ceased to be any danger from ionising radiations from anything on the site. This duty will also cease if a new nuclear site licence is issued in respect of the same site, whether to the same licensee or someone else.[148]

Any holder of a nuclear site licence is under an express statutory duty to secure that no occurrence involving nuclear matter causes injury to any person or damage to any property of any person other than the licensee, whether this arises out of or results from the radioactive properties, or a combination of those and any toxic, explosive or other hazardous properties of the nuclear matter.[149] The licensee must also secure that there are no ionising radiations emitted from anything he has caused or permitted to be on the site that is not nuclear matter, or from any waste that may be discharged, in any form, on or from the site, that cause injury to any person or any damage to any property to any person other than the licensee. The duty in relation to nuclear matter applies not only to an occurrence on the site itself, but also, inter alia, to occurrences outside the site involving

---

[143] s.3(3).
[144] s.4.
[145] s.4(4).
[146] s.4(5).
[147] s.5(1).
[148] s.5(3).
[149] s.7—A breach of this duty underpinned the claim in *Blue Circle Industries Plc v Ministry of Defence*; see para.20–039.

nuclear matter other than "excepted matter", and which at the relevant time is in the course of carriage on behalf of the licensee. (There are certain exceptions to this last duty, notably where the matter is on another licensed site in the United Kingdom). The duty does not however create liability in relation to a nuclear installation on the relevant site or other property on it that is there for use in connection with the operation or cessation of the operation of the installation or for constructing one. The same duties as just set out apply equally to the UKAEA in relation to any premises that it currently occupies or has previously occupied.[150] Similarly, if a government department uses any site for a purpose that would require a nuclear site licence if the use were by anyone else, then the Crown becomes subject to the same liability as a nuclear site licensee throughout the duration of its occupation of the relevant site.[151]

A duty is also imposed on foreign operators in certain circumstances to secure that there is no injury to a person or damage to any property other than that of the operator, where this arises out of or results from the radioactive properties or a combination of those and any toxic, explosive or other hazardous properties of that matter.[152] This duty applies principally to nuclear matter, not being excepted matter, which is in the course of carriage on behalf of the foreign operator and is not for the time being "on any relevant site in the United Kingdom". Similar duties are placed on anyone carrying nuclear matter within the territorial limits of the United Kingdom to avoid any occurrence involving that matter that causes injury to any person or property damage.[153]   **20–038**

The duties under these various provisions impose strict liability, irrespective of fault. The only exclusion of liability of general application is where the injury or damage or the causing of it is attributable to hostile action in the course of any armed conflict, including any within the United Kingdom.[154] It is expressly provided that the liability will apply even where the occurrence or the causing of the injury or damage is attributable to a natural disaster "notwithstanding that the disaster is of such an exceptional character that it could not reasonably have been foreseen", i.e. an act of God.[155] Operators must therefore be prepared for earthquakes, or take the consequences. Certain other defences are set out in section 13 where the relevant injury or damage took place in certain other countries, and there is a provision for reduction in the compensation on account of the fault of the claimant, but only if and to the extent that the causing of his injury or damage is attributable to any act of his committed with the intention of causing harm to any person or property or with reckless disregard for the

---

[150] s.8.
[151] s.9.
[152] s.10.
[153] s.11.
[154] s.13(4)(a).
[155] s.13(4)(b).

consequences of his act. This provision would therefore bite on terrorist action or, in some circumstances, anti-nuclear protesters, were they to take direct action against a nuclear installation.

Subject to the defences just indicated, provided that a claim is brought within time and no foreign court has jurisdiction over it under a relevant international agreement, compensation is due by virtue of section 12. There is an overall limit of £140 million capping the liability under these provisions in respect of any one occurrence, excluding payments in respect of interest and costs.[156] The NIA includes detailed provisions aimed at ensuring there is appropriate financial cover for payments that may become due on any claims for breach of the statutory duties it imposes.[157] In general, there is a statutory bar on any claims made under these provisions after 30 years from the date of the relevant occurrence. However, where the occurrence was a continuing one, or was one of a succession, all being attributable to a particular happening on a particular relevant site, or to the carrying out from time to time on a particular relevant site of a particular operation, the date of the last event in the course of that occurrence or succession of occurrences governs the calculation of the 30 year period. Nevertheless, where the occurrence involves nuclear matter that has been stolen from, or lost or abandoned by, the person subject to the duty, the period for bringing a claim is limited to 20 years from when the nuclear matter concerned was stolen, lost or abandoned.[158]

20–039   The compensation available under the NIA is limited to compensation in respect of injury to any person or damage to property. This does not however, extend to mere economic loss. Thus, in *Merlin et al. v British Nuclear Fuels plc*[159] the value of a house had been adversely affected because it was in an area of radioactive fallout resulting from a nuclear accident. However the house was still habitable, and it had not itself suffered damage, and the plaintiffs accordingly failed to recover under their claim brought under the NIA.

Merlin was however distinguished by the Court of Appeal in the case of *Blue Circle Industries plc v Ministry of Defence*.[160] The claim was based on a breach of the duty imposed by section 7(1)(a) of the Nuclear Installations Act 1965 to ensure that no occurrence involving nuclear matter caused damage to any property of any person other than the licensee.

Blue Circle Industries plc owned land adjacent to the Atomic Weapons Establishment at Aldermaston. The plaintiffs wished to sell their site and had had detailed discussions with a purchaser. It emerged during the

---

[156] £10 million maximum in respect of such sites as may be prescribed by the Nuclear Installations (Prescribed Sites) Regulations 1983 (SI 1983/1919).
[157] ss.18–21.
[158] s.15.
[159] [1990] 2 Q.B. 557; [1990] 3 W.L.R. 383; [1990] 3 All E.R. 711.
[160] [1999] Env. L.R. 22, [1998] EGCS 93, [1999] 2 W.L.R. 295, [1999] Ch 289, [1998] EWCA Civ 945, [1998] 3 All E.R. 385.

course of the negotiations that some four years previously that Blue Circle Industries' land was contaminated by radioactive material from an over-flowing pond on the Atomic Weapons Establishment facility. Although the Atomic Weapons Establishment were aware of the contamination in July 1989, Blue Circle was not informed until July 1993 and the negotiations broke off on learning of the contamination. At first instance, Carnworth J. held that there had been a breach of the duty imposed by section 7(1)(a) of the NIA 1965 and the plaintiffs had lost the chance of a sale which he assessed at 75 per cent. He then quantified the plaintiff's loss by reflecting the difference between the value of the estate as it would have been without the contamination and the value at the date of trial (which due to market conditions would actually have decreased).

The Ministry of Defence appealed and the Court of Appeal held that **20–040** physical damage to property contemplated in section 7(1)(a) of the NIA 1965 was not limited to particular types of damage and that it included damage resulting in some alteration of the physical characteristics of the property caused by the radioactive properties of the nuclear material which rendered the property less useful or less valuable. Although the consequence was economic and that the property was worth less and required expenditure of monies to remove contaminated topsoil, the court held that the land had been physically damaged by the radioactive properties of the plutonium which had mixed with the topsoil. *Merlin v British Nuclear Fuels* could thus be distinguished.

Reporting of nuclear incidents

Where any dangerous occurrence occurs on a licensed site or in the course **20–041** of the carriage of nuclear matter subject to any of the statutory duties imposed by the NIA as may be prescribed, the relevant licensee or other person must report the occurrence forthwith to the Inspectorate and to anyone else as may be prescribed.[161] The occurrences subject to this requirement are prescribed in the Nuclear Installations (Dangerous Occurrences) Regulations 1965 as amended by the Nuclear Installation (Dangerous Occurrences) Amendment (Regulations) 1974.[162] Inspectors may be appointed by the Secretary of State in respect of most matters covered by the NIA, who may exercise such of the powers set out in section 20(2) of the HSWA 1974, as may be conferred on them, for example investigating any occurrence and the publication of reports on such investigations.

A system for the international reporting of nuclear incidents was introduced in 1990, with a view to achieving prompt informing of the media and the public on the safety significance of such incidents, graded on the

---

[161] s.22.
[162] SI 1965/1824; SI 1974/2056.

International Nuclear Event Scale (the INES). The HSE is responsible for the United Kingdom's international reporting functions.

Chapter 21

ENVIRONMENTAL ISSUES IN COMMERCIAL PROPERTY TRANSACTIONS

Introduction

Because of the heavy financial impact environmental regulation can have **21–001** on businesses and property owners, it is generally vital to ensure that account is taken of this in commercial transactions. Such transactions are many and varied. Environmental due diligence may take place in the context of a company acquisition, in ensuring that provisions of a commercial lease adequately allocate the responsibility of complying with environmental law and its requirements, or in protecting the interests of a lender by ensuring that the loan agreement pays adequate regard to the borrower's environmental performance. In much of this work, and in spite of differences in context, the task of the environmental lawyer involved in a transaction will have a common core: establishing the level of environmental risk facing the client, and offering necessary comfort and protection by shaping the transaction accordingly. The scope of the work will vary according to the client and the transaction. In certain sectors clients may be well used to coping with such risks and highly experienced in working under the relevant regulations. They may be willing to trade risk for price or income. Moreover, it is unlikely, except *in extremis* that concerns about the environment will shape the transaction. It will be one ancillary species of risk to factor into a deal that will have rather more immediate objectives than compliance with environmental law. Nonetheless if the transaction is to be successful, the environmental lawyer may have a particular role to play in recognising and safeguarding against environmental risks.

The Nature of Environmental Risk

In many senses this book reflects the risks that may arise in the context of **21–002** an environmental transaction. One might begin with exposure to liability to third parties by the acquisition of a company or its physical assets, the occupation of premises or the undertaking of work where these kinds of activity may give rise to a claim, such as an action in nuisance. It is not difficult to see how such liability could arise, since, for example, one may adopt a nuisance[1] or create a nuisance in pursuing the undertaking that is the subject of the commercial agreement. The likelihood of liability will fluctuate in accordance with the type of transaction. As explained below, the general stance of the law is that a vendor of real property owes no duty of care in negligence to an incoming purchaser in relation to the state of the premises, and this would seem to be so notwithstanding the vendor's awareness of the defect.[2] Thus the primary risk here is not that of the vendor but of the purchaser.[3] Similarly although from time to time fears have been expressed as to lender liability for environmental damage, there would seem to be no examples in the UK of a lender being liable only in that capacity (as opposed for example as a mortgagee in possession) for environmental harm. This means that provisions in loan agreements covering such risks can be limited, but it does not mean that a lender should forgo all environmental due diligence prior to the loan, since it may have reason to fear both financial and reputational risks attaching to financing an environmentally damaging activity.[4]

Not all risk is that of third party liability in private law. As indicated above and reflected in this book, the considerable weight of environmental regulation brings with it obvious risk of non-compliance, the result of which may be regulatory intervention and enforcement. Depending on the context, this may mean that a company taking possession or control of premises may face prosecution, or be subject to notices compliance with which could entail significant expenditure on pollution control or process re-engineering. One might expect that the client would wish to factor into the deal such expenditure on the back of effective due diligence and advice on likely regulatory requirements.

In the course of a variety of non-contentious work, the environmental lawyer will need to advise on such risk issues. In order to do so, some broad understanding of pollution is necessary. Even if the lawyer is guided by an environmental consultant, this information has to be interpreted in terms of how environmental shortfalls result in legal obligations or liabilities. This interpretation may be aided by asking simple questions concerning pollutant linkages in the manner adopted within the contaminated land regime under Part 2A of the Environmental Protection Act 1990.[5] Ultimately pollution depends upon a receptor or target being affected, or at risk of being affected, by a source of pollution by means of a pathway linking the source to the target. This source-pathway-target methodology is a useful

---

[1] *Sedleigh-Denfield v O'Callaghan* [1940] AC 880.
[2] *Bottomley v Bannister* [1932] 1 KB 458, though there may be statutory exceptions to this common law rule—see the Defective Premises Act 1972.
[3] See the discussion on the sold with information test under Part 2A of the Environmental Protection Act 1990, above, which places the seller at risk of retaining remediation liabilities if it does not provide the requisite information on the environmental condition of a site to the seller.
[4] See paras 21–026 and 21–027 below.
[5] See Chapter 16 (above).

preliminary approach to risk, as at an early stage in transactions it might be possible to envisage targets in the vicinity of (say) a site scheduled for acquisition that might be adversely affected by hazardous materials traditionally used upon the site. More detailed investigation of the site history and potential pathways is probably then best left to an environmental consultant.

Appointing an Environmental Consultant

Initial survey work by an environmental consultant can take the form of a 21–003
Phase I assessment exploring the historical uses and activities on the site. This is sometimes misleadingly called a desktop study; misleading because although much of the work can be done by reviewing records and documentation in the office, a site inspection is always advisable. After identifying past owners and the property usage during each period of ownership, the consultant will consider issues relevant to environmental conditions at the site, such as its past use and the use or disposal of hazardous substances. This may involve discussions with regulatory agencies and the review of planning and other local records. If the site is being bought together with a business as a going concern, the consultant should check present levels of compliance with environmental permits, not least because upgrades of environmental control systems to a BAT standard[6] can be costly. The Phase I site assessment report should contain some evaluation of environmental conditions at the site and of the degree of environmental risk attaching to site ownership or occupation, with particular indications as to whether hazardous substances remain on the property. However, it cannot reach a position of absolute certainty and greater investigation of environmental risk will require further (Phase II) work.

If following the Phase I investigation there is a medium to high likelihood that pollution on site, or migrating through the site poses or could pose an unacceptable risk, a Phase II report may be advisable. The purpose of this Phase of the work is to gain a better understanding of the precise contaminants on the site, their concentrations, their locations and their behaviour. Achieving this is likely to require intrusive investigation of the site, taking soil and perhaps water (or even gas) samples, and subjecting these to laboratory testing. Both the sampling and the testing methods will depend upon the findings of the Phase I report including the suspected contaminants and their source, together with soil and groundwater conditions at the site. The laboratory test results can be adjudged in line with thresholds in terms of matters such as harm to human health or impact on

---

[6] See the discussion of Best Available Techniques under the IPPC Directive 2008/01 and the UK implementing Regulations at para.14–017 above.

drinking and other water resources. This will help determine whether remediation work (Phase III) is necessary.

There are a number of issues for the lawyer here. The first is that the Phase I report may contain information about potential risks, but it is for the lawyer to evaluate those risks by reference to the potential for the client's legal liability. This may be crucial in determining whether to undertake the more costly Phase II work, and the lawyer will often be asked to advise on this decision. In managing environmental risk, the lawyer will also be expected to manage the process to ensure delivery of reports adequate for the purposes of due diligence. Whether or not Phase II work is possible will depend on site access and the time schedule for the deal. There may also be issues of cost/benefit depending on the value of the transaction. If access to the site is refused, or Phase II work is otherwise not feasible, then the risk equation changes as the assessment is possible only by reference to the Phase I work, with its obvious shortcomings. In such a situation the client may expect greater protection through the contractual documentation, whereas if the Phase II work paints a reasonably clear picture of the site conditions and/or the remediation requirements, there may be a much greater focus on price than on contractual comfort. One crucial element, therefore, which a purchaser needs to factor into his approach to a transaction as early as possible, is whether the time needed for Phase II and any subsequent work is, or can be made, available.

21–004   It used to be common for the solicitor to appoint the consultant, according to client instructions and to commission the relevant reports. This is less so as the market for environmental consultancy services has matured, and it has become easier for clients to gauge the reputation, experience and professionalism of consultants in the market. It is sometimes argued that professional legal privilege would protect an environmental consultant's report from discovery in legal proceedings when commissioned by a solicitor. This stance must now be in doubt following the collapse of BCCI and the "Three Rivers" litigation. Essentially there are two forms of privilege. The first is legal advice privilege—protecting confidential communications between lawyers and clients seeking and giving legal advice in a professional capacity. The second, litigation privilege, arises where those communications are in contemplation of litigation or once litigation is under way, where communication is for the dominant purpose of pursuing that litigation or advising in connection with it. The latter is unlikely in most transactional work, though it is more extensive than the former particularly since it attaches to a wider range of communications—including those between lawyers and third parties. In *Three Rivers DC v Bank of England (No. 5)*,[7] the Court of Appeal held that only

---

[7] *Three Rivers DC v Bank of England (No.5)* [2003] Q.B. 1556; the Court of Appeal and the House of Lords refused leave to appeal this decision and it remained undisturbed by the House of Lords in the later case on privilege *Three Rivers DC v Bank of England (No.6)* [2004] Q.B. 916 (HL).

lawyer/client communications containing advice on the client's legal rights and liabilities is protected by legal advice privilege. Direct communications between the lawyers and third parties, even if connected to client advice, are not so covered.

This largely undermines any legal imperative to commission environmental consultancy services through a solicitor, though any solicitor undertaking transactional work with regularity should be well placed to advise on the selection of consultants, and to assist in negotiating and concluding terms of appointment and instructions for the work. Confidentiality is vital from the outset and may arise even at the tender stage of the appointment (if there is such a stage) so that it may even be necessary to introduce confidentiality obligations at this stage. The brief to the consultant may be crucial, as it is against the scope of this work that the consultant will be judged in the event of any dispute concerning the quality of work undertaken.[8] The standard terms and conditions of most environmental consultants are limited in matters such as the reliance that may be placed on the report and the available indemnity, leaving the solicitor to advise on and seek to negotiate more appropriate contractual protection for the client. For example Phase I work involves information gathering, and consultants may seek to limit liability for negligence where information provided to the consultant is inaccurate. A more appropriate contractual provision might be that the consultant should not rely on information which a reasonably diligent consultant ought to have recognised as unreliable.

The professional indemnity insurance cover of environmental consultants is dealt with in the next chapter of this book.[9] Regard should be had to the points made there. Consultants may be working to low levels of cover, and this is nearly always aggregate cover rather than available cover applicable to "each and every" claim. The insurance cover may even contain pollution exclusion clauses. It may help to know the claims history of the consultancy, and where necessary it may be wise to require the firm to obtain top-up insurance to an appropriate level.

The nature of the transaction will dictate the parties that may wish to rely upon the contents of any report, but developers in particular are likely to want eventual third party purchasers (who will usually be unidentified at that stage) to be able to rely upon the report, necessitating the use of collateral warranties. Even property owners with no current intention to sell should protect the value of their asset by procuring the ability to pass on the benefit of rights in respect of the report to any subsequent owners there may be—and those subsequent owners may wish to be able to do the same in their turn. While it might be argued that the risk of negligent work,   **21–005**

---

[8] *Urban Regeneration Agency v Mott Macdonald Group Ltd* (2000) 12 Envtl. L. & Mgt. 24 (QBD) and *Sutradhar v Natural Environment Research Council* [2006] 4 All E.R. 490.
[9] Chapter 22 (below).

covered by insurance, is no greater as a result of extended reliance on the warranties, the risk of a claim is heightened and the timescale of a claim may increase. Also the warranty adds value to the land. It will be necessary to check that the consultants' insurance policy backing such warranties is sufficient in terms of issues such as time caps on claims or, where the policy extends cover for work already completed, that there are no notification issues in relation to the negligent conduct of that work.[10]

Among the issues to be considered in the deed of appointment are the following:

- the purpose of the report and the reliance to be placed upon it;
- provision for any associated deeds of collateral warranty and rights of assignment;
- the services to be provided and the fee structure for those services;
- the duty of care including its application to sub-contractors;
- rights to terminate the appointment;
- the requirement to insure and any limitation cap on liability under the contract;
- ownership of and rights to use copyright in the documents generated;
- confidentiality provisions; and
- governing law and jurisdiction.

Caveat Emptor and Environmental Negotiations

21–006   Because of traditional notions of caveat emptor, a risk is always attached to buying land which might be contaminated, and which might pose a risk to third parties. However, there is no doubt that this risk has been heightened by the introduction of the regime to remediate contaminated land under Part 2A of the Environmental Protection Act 1990 (as introduced by the Environment Act 1995 with effect from April 1, 2000).[11] There is an irony here. Essentially, Part 2A must be described as a public law framework to regulate potential hazards emanating from contaminated land. In fact, however, its main impact may lie in the private sphere, as parties take into account the risks that attach not only to the buying, but also to the selling of land that is contaminated. It makes obvious sense for parties to seek to offload their liability at the time of land transfer, or where that is not possible, at least to cap their likely liabilities under the regime.

The caveat emptor rule was approved by Lord Atkin in *Bell v Lever Bros*, in which he said:[12]

---

[10] Since the policy will be issued on a claims-made basis, any prospective claims ought to have been notified to the insurer and checking whether such claims are foreseen will help establish the value of any cover especially where there is an aggregate limit on claims—see Chapter 22.

[11] See Chapter 16.

[12] [1932] AC 161 at 227.

"ordinarily the failure to disclose a material fact which might influence the mind of a prudent contractor does not give the right to avoid the contract".

He went on to take the example of property which A buys from B, not knowing it to be uninhabitable. Although the rule may act harshly against A, Lord Atkin states that contractual certainty is in the long run a more important matter than justice, and that parties should regulate their affairs by contracting wisely rather than looking to the law to amend the bargain.

However, since 1932, the law has intervened often in the form of statute to do just that—hence legislation on unfair contract terms (which generally has no application to land sales). Moreover the extent of the caveat emptor rule is largely misunderstood and the extent of the exceptions to it underestimated. Thus in the following circumstances the rule does not apply,[13] namely where:

- the parties are in a relationship of *uberrimae fidei*;
- there is a fiduciary relationship between the parties;
- a positive representation is distorted by later non-disclosure;[14]
- there is a misrepresentation by the vendor, including a false representation by conduct;[15]
- there is a defect to the title of the property, which the vendor failed to disclose, such that the vendor could not sell free from encumbrances of which the purchaser could have no knowledge, since "a liability of uncertain amount at some future time" may constitute "a latent defect which goes to the title of the property";[16]
- there is negligence on the part of an owner who has undertaken work upon the land;[17] and
- conduct by the owner constitutes the tort of deceit;[18]
- where the traditional immunity of the vendor (above) may be lost on account of the dangerous state of the premises following "work of construction, repair, maintenance or demolition or other work done" in accordance with section 3(1) of the Defective Premises Act 1972.

In addition to the above it is worth noting that the Property Misdescriptions Act 1991 renders it a criminal offence to:

"make a false or misleading statement about a prescribed matter in the course of an estate agency business or a property development business. . . ."

[13] Law Commission *Caveat Emptor in Sales of Land* (Consultation Paper, 1988) described caveat emptor as "an unjustifiably ramshackle principle" the foundation of which "may be regarded as suffering from the legal equivalent of subsidence."
[14] See *Laurence v LexCourt Holdings Ltd* [1978] 1 W.L.R. 1128.
[15] *Gordon and Texeira v Selica Ltd* (1986) 11 HLR 219.
[16] *City Towns Ltd v Bohemian Properties* [1986] 2 EGLR 258 at 261.
[17] *Hone v Benson* (1978) 248 EG 1013.
[18] *Downs v Chappell and Stephenson Smart* [1996] 3 All E.R. 344.

A property development business is one concerned "wholly or substantially with the development of land" and a statement can be caught where it is made with a view to disposing of an interest in land. The prescribed matters are sufficiently widely drawn to include most physical attributes of the land including "condition" and "environment".[19]

21–007   It follows that, although there is a starting point of "buyer beware", the seller cannot be completely cavalier in dealings to sell the land. Historically, however, the caveat emptor rule has shaped the pattern of transactions, with the seller seeking to maintain a position in which no representations are made and the buyer then looking to draw the seller into disclosing information about the site. The seller is traditionally evasive in answering enquiries put by the buyer, thus forcing the buyer to seek information from elsewhere (hence the value of Phase I assessments). This information may help smoke out representations, which contractually appear as warranties,[20] or produce disclosures by the seller. This might in certain circumstances lead to agreed indemnification of liability arising out of problems on the site. These matters are dealt with below, but for now what is significant is that these patterns of transaction are less dominant than before, not least because of the exclusionary tests under Part 2A of the Environmental Protection Act 1990.[21] These tests for exclusion actually represent the opportunity for risk transfer between potentially appropriate persons under the liability regime. Because of the strict and retroactive nature of Part 2A, it certainly remains possible for the seller to transfer land while retaining historic liabilities. The exclusionary devices allow the seller to offload this risk, but, as is shown below, this may involve the disclosure of information about the condition of the site.

Contaminated land—exclusion of liability

21–008   Before dealing with particular exclusions of liability, some general points must apply. The exclusions considered here are those relating to Class A persons. There is an exclusion in relation to Class B occupiers which favours those parties who have no capital interest in the land. However, this will not be dealt with further here. For the Class A exclusions to apply, there must be at least two parties in the liability chain. Moreover, having applied these exclusionary tests, at least one Class A party must remain. The Guidance makes it clear that the exclusions cannot be used to absolve all parties from liability. The way in which the Guidance achieves this is to apply the test in relation to each pollutant linkage, in the order in which the

---

[19] Note also that the Fraud Act 2006 introduced a general offence of "fraud" that might be wide enough to catch false representations or by failures to disclose information in connection with property sales.

[20] The reasons for this are explained below—see para.21–018.

[21] These tests are laid down in Part 5 of Defra Circular 01/2006 *Contaminated Land* (hereafter the Guidance) and are considered more fully in Chapter 16 (above).

tests are set out in the Guidance. The tests cease to be applied at the point at which the application of a test would result in the exclusion of the only remaining member(s) of the group. Finally, note that these tests are the only mechanisms to be applied. For example, questions of the financial circumstances of the parties are totally irrelevant at the point at which the tests are applied. Once all exclusions have been applied, liability is apportioned as between remaining members of the group with the enforcing authority being liable for the costs of any party for which it has waived liability due to hardship provisions.

The exclusions are considered in Chapter 16 above, but this Chapter will concentrate on tests 2 and 3 for two reasons. The first is that these are the tests which are overwhelmingly likely to involve some investigation of activity that took place at the point of land transfer. They involve parties expressly, or by implication, accepting some responsibility for the condition of the land in question. Moreover, because this is the case, the effect of the application of these tests is to shift liability from one party to another. The application of tests 2 and 3 is therefore different from that of tests 1, 4, 5 and 6, where the impact of the test is to exclude entirely the relevant party as though they had never fallen within the liability group whatsoever.

Test 1

Having said that, certain issues of relevance for transactional work arise out   **21–009**
of test 1, which sets out a list of excluded activities, some of which are referable to matters that might form part of a commercial property transaction. Examples include:

- providing financial assistance;
- underwriting an insurance policy;
- creating a tenancy over land in favour of a person who subsequently pollutes; and
- providing legal, financial, engineering, scientific or technical advice.

The test is of course only relevant to the above parties, be they banks, insurers, lawyers, site engineers, etc. if they are within the liability chain to begin with, i.e. if they have caused or knowingly permitted substances to be in, on or under the land. This assumes therefore that it is possible for a party such as a banker to (e.g.) knowingly permit substances to be on the land, where the information is apparent, having been reported to the bank, and where the bank has the power under the facility agreement to regulate the affairs of the company. Even if this scenario is found to amount to knowingly permitting, the person providing financial assistance by making the loan would have the benefit of the exclusion under test 1, and presumably would be first-ranked amongst all parties in test 1 (assuming, which is not clear, that test 1 itself is meant to be hierarchical in its application).

Note that the exclusion only applies in so far as the person is undertaking the particular activity outlined in test 1.[22] A bank going beyond the provision of financial assistance and actually taking control of the activities of a company in financial difficulty could, if it were to cause or knowingly permit pollution, find itself outside this exemption altogether.

Test 2

21–010 Test 2 excludes from liability persons who have already made a payment sufficient to pay for the remediation of the land to another member of the liability group. Note the necessity of the person receiving the monies forming part of the liability group. This payment need not be part of a commercial property transaction transferring the ownership of land. It may be paid under some other contract, or on an ex gratia basis. Equally, it may be in settlement of a dispute, perhaps in the aftermath of an earlier transaction. Commonly, it will take place as part of a commercial property transaction in the form of an agreed reduction of the intended purchase price, and in such instances there are certain safeguards that a paying party may wish to take. One obvious safeguard is to ensure, as the guidance demands, that, at the time the payment is made, the payment would be sufficient to meet the remediation requirements on the land, such as to take it outside the definition of "contaminated land". Some ad-hoc reduction in price may not serve the intended purpose. It follows that it is sensible to document the payment, its purpose, and to back it with some technical information regarding the likely cost of remediation.

If the money in question is deployed in effectively remediating the land, then no remediation notice should be served.[23] It follows that the test will only apply where money is paid over but no remediation or inadequate remediation is carried out. Clearly, the paying party will wish to ensure that remediation does take place. However, the exclusion demands that a person making payment should relinquish subsequent control over the condition of the land in question. Although this is said not to apply to the holding of "contractual rights to ensure the proper carrying out of the remediation",[24] it is apparent that care will have to be taken to ensure there is no long-term retention of control. Note also, that where money is paid over and spent on remediation, but at a later date a pollutant linkage is nonetheless found, there is a danger that the test may not apply. This is

---

[22] See para.D.48 of the Guidance.
[23] EPA s.57H(5)(b).
[24] See para.D55(a) of the Guidance.

because there may be an argument here that payment was not sufficient to fund a robust remediation scheme to clear the contamination.

Test 3

Test 3 is probably the most problematic of all of the tests. It excludes from liabilities those who sell land to a purchaser with the benefit of information. The idea here is that the purchaser, armed with this information, has an opportunity to negotiate on price, allowing for the contaminated state of the land. Again, both parties to such a transaction must fall within the liability group. On the face of it, transactions between appropriate persons may be somewhat rare. However, by the time of the service of the remediation notice, it may be that the purchaser can be found to have knowingly permitted the substances to remain on the land, especially, having been informed of their existence.[25]   **21–011**

Those drafting the legislation were obviously wary of the creation of loopholes here. The regulator is required when applying the test to ensure that a sale took place at arm's length in terms of a sale on the open market between willing parties. Moreover, after the date of the sale, the seller must retain no interest in the land in question. For a sale with information to apply, the information must be available to the purchaser prior to any binding sale, and the information must be such as to allow that purchaser awareness of the "broad measure" of the presence of the pollution.[26] Note that if the seller is to take advantage of this exemption, then the seller must have done nothing to materially misrepresent the consequences of the pollution to the purchaser.

Although, the discussion above refers to "sale with information" there are two points to note in relation to this phrase. The first is that the exemption applies to the grant or assignment of long leases as well as to the sale of a freehold. A long lease is defined as a lease or sub-lease granted for a period of more than 21 years.[27] The second point is that as a sale of land will become binding on the exchange of contracts, this will put time pressure on the parties to obtain available information (e.g. through Phase II survey work) prior to exchange. The final point is that the information need not be given by the seller to the purchaser, as it may be sufficient to allow the buyer to carry out its own investigation. This important matter deserves further consideration.

The Guidance says that in transactions since January 1, 1990, where the   **21–012**

---

[25] A situation in part contemplated by para.D59(b) of the Guidance which states that the composition of the liability group should be decided not at date of sale but at date of determination that the land is contaminated.

[26] para.D58(c) of the Guidance.

[27] para.D59(a) of the Guidance and see further definition of "owner" in section 78A EPA 1990.

buyer was a "large commercial organisation" and permission was given by the seller to inspect the condition of the land, then this should be normally taken as a sufficient indication of a sale with information. There are clear problems with this, quite apart from the fact that for more than five years in the early 1990s transactions took place in absolute ignorance of the likelihood that this rule would be brought in. Problems largely surround the lack of definition of both a "large scale organisation"[28] and the notion of what amounts to an investigation "of the condition of the land".[29] Note that it is not necessary that the buyer undertook such investigation, merely that permission was given by the seller. Quite what form this permission should have taken is again not clear; is it a visual inspection for Phase I purposes or intrusive investigation of the land in the form of a Phase II survey? This is likely to depend upon what would have been necessary to raise awareness of the presence of the pollutant forming the pollutant linkage.[30]

Test 4

21–013 Tests 4[31] and 5[32] are less relevant to land transactions, and can be examined briefly. Test 4 assumes that there are at least two appropriate persons—a first person and a later person—who, both, introduce substances, in turn, to the land. For the purposes of this discussion, we will assume the involvement of only two persons in the liability group. However, this test assumes (though it might say so more clearly than it does) that the first substance is safely contained and becomes a contributor to a pollutant linkage only because of the second substance. In other words there is an "intervening change" caused by the presence of the second substance,[33] which was not occasioned by the first person and which that person could not have reasonably foreseen, prior to the introduction of the second substance to the land. Alternatively, it may be sufficient to show that the arrival of the substances themselves could not have been foreseen, or that if either the arrival of the substances or the intervening event was foreseeable, reasonable precautions were taken to avoid such an event. Because the exclusion will only apply where the pollutant linkages results such precautions must have proved inadequate. It follows that this part of the test may operate as almost a "state of the art" defence—i.e. that at the time the precautions seemed reasonable in accordance with the state of technical

---

[28] para.D59(d) of the Guidance.
[29] ibid.
[30] It is enough that the pollutant is known about even though the pollutant linkage was not known: see para.D59(c) of the Guidance and *Circular Facilities (London) Ltd v Sevenoaks DC* [2005] Env. L.R. 35.
[31] para.D62 et seq.
[32] para.D65 et seq.
[33] para.D63(a)(ii) of the Guidance.

know-how. To invoke the exclusion, the first person must not have engaged in any act or omission to bring about the intervening change. It may well be then that where contaminants are left on site in engineered containment, the person responsible for this activity should take steps to regulate future activity in the vicinity of the contaminants to prevent the development of a pollutant linkage.

Test 5

This test applies so as to exclude an appropriate person who is in the liability group as a result of substances that have escaped onto land as a result of the act or omission of another member of the liability group. It does so by wording that is convoluted and less than clear. However, it assumes a liability group made up of at least two parties. For our purpose we will assume two persons only. The source of a pollutant linkage is present on the land only because of an escape from other land. One (first) member of the liability group (A) finds itself within the group only because of "that reason".[34] Assuming this to refer to the escape (and in this respect the wording is ambiguous) it is the second member of the liability group (B) who caused or knowingly permitted the escape that will bear responsibility once the first member is excluded. Note that if this first person (A) is unaware of the escape, there can be no question of liability. For the exclusion to apply, the first person must have at least knowingly permitted the substances to be present on (to remain) on the land. As with all exclusions, this will benefit party A only if party B can be "found".[35] It follows that where land is being purchased that is affected by migrating pollution, a buyer will want greater contractual protection from the vendor than simply the ability to rely on any recourse offered by the workings of test 5.

21–014

Test 6

Test 6 is perhaps the most curious of the tests. It seeks to exempt from liability an appropriate person where another appropriate person has introduced either a pathway or a receptor (a "later action"), which has completed a pollutant linkage where no such linkage would have existed otherwise. The person responsible for the "later action" must be an appropriate person who must have caused or knowingly permitted substances to be present in, on or under the land. Possibly the introduction of

21–015

---

[34] para.D66(b) of the Guidance.
[35] In the Guidance the Oxford English Dictionary definition of "found" is given, namely "discovered, met with, and ascertained". The Guidance also remarks that a person who has ceased to exist cannot logically be found.

a pathway could render someone an appropriate person, but more probably there will be some existing responsibility for the pollution compounded by the introduction of a pathway or receptor.

It is not every action that constitutes a "later action" for the purpose of the exclusion.[36] The action must consist of the carrying out of building, engineering, mining or similar operations and/or the making of a material change in the use of the land, which change of use was subject to the requirement for a specific application for planning permission.[37] However in these cases the development or change of use must relate to the land itself and not to neighbouring or other land. In addition to actions, omissions may also be taken into account. These may consist of failing to take a step which would have ensured that a pollutant linkage did not result from the later action. This may involve the person responsible for that action but also some other party. Alternatively or additionally, an omission may consist of failing to maintain or operate a system installed to manage the risk attaching to the presence of substances on the land and the possible development of a pollutant linkage. Once again, the effect of the exemption is to shift liability to the persons responsible for the relevant acts or omissions. This exclusion may work in a potentially harsh manner since, as the *Circular Facilities case* demonstrates, the person actually responsible for bringing or leaving pollutants on the land may be absolved whereas a developer of the land may attract liability.[38] It follows that when acting for a party such as a house builder, whose planned development of the land will entail bringing receptors to the land, if at all possible, the solicitor should ensure that liability for any contaminants on the land remains with the party or parties responsible for their presence on the land. The Guidance offers one route by which this may be done, which is now reviewed.

Agreements on liability

21–016 Given the uncertainties attaching to the application of the above tests, parties may conclude that it is more beneficial to face the issue of remediation directly, and reach express agreement on how the cost of any remediation might be allocated between them. This might be a particularly appropriate device where it seems likely that only two parties will form the appropriate persons for a pollutant linkage.

Paragraph D38 of the Guidance requires the regulator generally to make determinations on apportionment of liabilities so as to give effect to such agreements except where this would have the effect of evading liability. This seeks to avoid the artificial creation of an agreement to pass liabilities to a party without the requisite capacity to handle the remediation. It does

---

[36] para.D69(a) of the Guidance.
[37] para.D70 (a)(i) and (ii).
[38] See *Circular Facilities (London) Limited v Sevenoaks District Council* [2005] Env. L.R. 35.

mean, also, that any such agreement is only as good as the solvency of the party with whom it is reached. Nonetheless, this may be an appropriate device subject to two provisos. One is that a copy of the agreement must be provided to the authority. The point at which this must be done is not absolutely clear. To do so at the point at which an agreement is reached would seem to invite the attentions of the regulator. It is therefore thought that it must be sufficient to draw an agreement to the attention of the authority in the consultation period following designation of the land as contaminated and running up to the service of remediation notice. In addition, the Guidance suggests that the authority could ignore such an agreement if it is clear that a party to it challenges its application. This is highly problematic, and has led to such agreements incorporating alternative dispute resolution (ADR) mechanisms or forms of wording seeking to exclude the triggering of a disagreement following any notification of likely intervention by a regulator or determination of the land as contaminated.

Such an agreement may be tied in elsewhere to the transaction. The agreement need not pass all liability to one party, but it could draw lines using environmental baseline studies to apportion liability between seller and buyer. It could also be tied into wider indemnity agreements[39] covering risks other than that of regulatory intervention. Depending on the bargaining power of the parties, that indemnity may pass from vendor to purchaser or from purchaser to vendor.[40] There may be some merit in having this backed by an environmental insurance policy. A vendor seeking to reach this form of an agreement with a buyer may wish to know something of the buyer's intentions. For example, if the buyer seeks to sell rapidly on and then cease business, the seller's agreement with the buyer may be worth little. The buyer may not constitute an appropriate person for the purposes of the regime (not having caused and (arguably) not having knowingly permitted within the timescale).[41] The vendor may be left without any recourse against the later incoming purchaser to whom his buyer has sold. Other issues for a seller constructing an agreement with a buyer might also include future access to the land where the vendor retains responsibility for a clean up, and/or agreements with the buyer on future

---

[39] Dealt with below – see para.21–024.
[40] It is quite common for the party accepting liability and therefore giving an indemnity to switch after a period of years from the vendor to the purchaser, on the assumption that, if there is any significant contamination at the time of the sale, this will be discovered within that initial period.
[41] In the first instance case of *R (on the application of National Grid Gas Plc) v Environment Agency* [2006] 1 W.L.R. 3041 the Environment Agency conceded that they would not consider a person holding land for a period of nine months to be an appropriate person, though the company may in any case have been unaware of the pollution. While that is no doubt a sensible working practice, it would be unwise to rely on it in cases where there may be no other solvent appropriate person to be found.

uses of the land, lest contamination become worse, or receptors be introduced to create new pollutant linkages.

Environmental Warranties

21–017 Many asset transactions begin with the buyer's solicitor making preliminary enquiries of the vendor. These may include enquiries concerning the condition of the site. In the case of environmental matters, additional enquiries may continue as information becomes available from environmental assessments. Obviously the seller may bear responsibility for inaccurate responses to these queries, with potential liability in misrepresentation—care must be taken in the wording of any replies to enquiries. It is not uncommon for replies to be rather evasive, but a response that one is not aware of a problem may imply that reasonable steps have been taken to check matters out.[42] Similarly a reply that the seller is unaware and that the buyer should undertake an inspection will amount to a misrepresentation, not rescued by the invitation to inspect, where the seller is aware of the issue forming the subject of the enquiry.[43] Happily for solicitors, the solicitor for the seller is not likely to owe a duty to the buyer to ensure the accuracy of the seller's replies.[44] False, as opposed to merely inaccurate replies to enquiries may open the door to an action in fraudulent misrepresentation.[45]

Role and function of warranties

21–018 Because in an action for misrepresentation it must be shown that the particular representation sued on induced the buyer to enter into the contract, it is often better to ensure that such representations take the form of a warranty. The contractual status of the warranty is of some significance; listing a term as a warranty avoids any confusion as to its status and the difficulties that may arise in relation to innominate terms. It is clear that a warranty is not a condition and there is no suggestion that breach of warranty carries repudiatory rights. If a warranty is breached then the innocent party can sue for damages but cannot terminate the contract. The innocent party does have one advantage here, however, as it is not necessary to prove any element of reliance upon the warranty in order to gain a remedy in damages. It would be for that party to prove the damages flowing from the breach of warranty, but the parties can make some pro-

---

[42] *Clinicare Limited v Orchard Homes and Developments Limited* [2004] EWHC 1694; a response that the seller is not aware is said to carry an implication that the seller has made some reasonable enquiry—*William Sindall Ltd v Cambridgeshire CC* [1994] 1 W.L.R. 1016.
[43] *Morris v Jones* [2002] EWCA Civ 1790, (2003) CILL 1966.
[44] *Gran Gelato Limited v Richcliff Group Limited* [1992] Ch. 560.
[45] See for example *Doe v Skegg* [2006] EWHC 3746 (Ch).

vision for this, not least because a seller will wish to cap the potential liability at some fixed amount.

It is not unusual to look for contractual protection at the first level by the purchaser seeking environmental warranties from the seller, if only to smoke out disclosure of known environmental problems against the warranties sought. By disclosing information, as is explained below, the seller will seek to qualify the warranties. Naturally the seller will look to limit the extent of these warranties to lessen exposure to liability and to restrict disclosures that might affect the price. This can generally be done by attaching qualifying language—such as limiting the warranty in terms of the seller's awareness, or introducing some type of materiality provision. This may seem not unreasonable, but it is important always to remember that negotiations here concern risk allocation. It is not necessarily unreasonable for a buyer to ask that a seller be responsible for events up to the point of completion whether or not the seller is aware of these.

The whole concept of negotiation here is crucial. The buyer wants to use the warranties to smoke out disclosure of potential liability to move on to the next level of protection—indemnification—where this is appropriate. Even where no indemnity is likely, the disclosure of information through the clever use of warranties may be reflected in price reduction or in a restructuring of the transaction itself. The use of warranties to gain, through disclosures, significant background information on the property and the facility on it, may even reveal earlier environmental reports or audits. As a minimum, the buyer will wish to know that there are the necessary environmental approvals in place to run the facility and that operating the facility from day one will not lead to immediate breaches of environmental law. Having said that, in large transactions it may be rare to find that all facilities are in total compliance; hence the perceived need for materiality provisions.

It ought to be clear that the more information that the buyer can command, the more that requests for warranties and/or indemnities may be seen as reasonable. This means that the more that an environmental consultant can provide the buyer's lawyer with risk factors (accompanied by risk evaluation made available to the buyer) the more ammunition can be built up. This is why law firms are generally eager to ensure that they work with consultants that understand the underlying requirements of transactional negotiation. **21–019**

There is a core set of environmental warranties that are generally vital in the transfer of most businesses. These include warranties in relation to:

- compliance with environmental laws[46] and the absence of circumstances that could lead to breach or liability;

---

[46] The phrase "environmental laws" will need to be carefully defined to include (or not) hard and soft law, local, national, regional and international law, laws relating to the environment such as planning or health and safety laws, and present and future laws (with the seller strongly resisting the latter).

- there being no outstanding claims or proceedings for breach of environmental laws;
- there having been no complaints or notices for breach of environmental laws;
- the availability of and compliance with environmental consents;
- there having been no disposal of hazardous waste at the site; and
- the disclosure of any available environmental reports or audits (within an agreed timeframe).

Even for these, however, the seller may wish to qualify the warranty by materiality provisions—e.g. by warranting only material compliance with environmental law.

Quite how ambitious one is in seeking warranties beyond this core will depend on the deal as a whole and the bargaining power of the parties. There is a crucial difference between a share sale in which one is purchasing the company and one in which only the assets are being purchased. In the former case, because the acquisition of the company will transfer existing liabilities, a wider range of warranties is likely to be needed as the purchaser will be concerned with (for example) former sites[47] and any earlier warranties or indemnities given by the company (or its subsidiaries) to previous purchasers of other property assets. Generally these non-core warranties are more specific to the circumstances of the sites or businesses. They can be very wide ranging but for illustrative purposes could cover:

- the presence and escape of hazardous substances;
- underground storage tanks or other underground hazards;
- major upgrades needed to the site;
- the integrity of the site, including matters such as asbestos or drainage; and
- waste and waste management;

In general, however, these non-core warranties will be diverse, and specifically drafted so as to provide assurance on issues of concern arising from the due diligence exercise. There is always a risk of conceding bargaining advantage, however, by the seller asking for too much (at least initially) and in particular by its putting forward standard sets of warranties with no thought applied to their relevance to the transaction at hand. This cedes advantage to the buyer, inviting immediate red lining of the warranties proposed.

21–020   At times lawyers seem to forget that warranties are about risk transfer. If the buyer puts a warranty to the seller, then this is a proposal that the latter retains the risk of not being able to deliver on the warranty. Thus if the buyer asks for a warranty that there is no litigation or events that might give rise to litigation against the company, this is a formula for stating that losses

---

[47] Because of potential liability under Part 2A of the Environmental Protection Act 1990.

from such risks arising during the seller's control of the company should attach to the seller. As stated earlier, it is not necessarily unreasonable therefore for a buyer to resist the qualification of this type of warranty by restricting it to events of which the seller is aware.[48] On the other hand, if this restriction is permitted the buyer will need to be cautious concerning precisely whose awareness counts for these purposes. Main board directors are not always aware of day to day environmental conditions on the company's sites.

Disclosure against warranties

It is standard practice for a disclosure letter to accompany the warranties **21–021** and for the warranties to be qualified by the disclosures made in accordance with the letter, that is, the warranties will be deemed not to be breached by matters that have been disclosed against them in that letter. The letter seeks to restrict the ambit of the warranties given by pointing to information already disclosed or taken to be disclosed (for example where information is in the public domain) of which the buyer can be deemed to have knowledge. Of late the courts have warned that where parties agree a disclosure letter, then the standard of fair disclosure will be in accordance with the strict interpretation of that letter. In the Court of Appeal decision in *Infiniteland Ltd v Artisan Contracting Ltd*[49] the claimants' action was based in misrepresentation and breach of warranty in connection with financial warranties given by a parent company in a share sale agreement involving two subsidiary companies. The first defendant agreed to sell the shares in two companies to the first claimant. Shortly before exchange, the defendants made an adjustment to the group's accounts to make provision for over £1m by way of a fair value adjustment to cover prospective losses on the contracting works of one of the companies being purchased by the claimants. This had the effect of increasing the profitability of that company, but the payment was inadequately identified in the statutory profit and loss account. When the company failed and ceased trading, the claimants refused to meet the balance of payments owing on the sale.

The defendants had given both general and specific warranties making disclosure of papers provided to the claimants' accountants, but there was no specific warranty covering the adjustment to the accounts. The warranties were qualified by the phrase: "save as disclosed in the Disclosure Letter". The agreement itself provided that the claimants' rights in respect of any breach of warranty were not to be affected by any investigation made by it or on its behalf "except to the extent of the Buyer's actual knowl-

---

[48] Though a seller that acquired a property or company at some earlier date may reasonably wish to restrict warranties as to what happened before that date by reference by "so far as the seller is aware", and/or offer merely to pass on the benefit of such warranties and indemnities as it obtained from the earlier seller.

[49] [2005] EWCA 758; (2006) 1 BCLC 632.

edge." The accountants did not draw the attention of the claimants to the adjustment of the accounts though the papers provided in disclosure would have allowed the adjustment to have been tracked. At first instance the High Court held that the accountants had sufficient information to know that the adjusted accounts were misleading and that the accountant's "actual knowledge" could be imputed to the claimants under the type of clause outlined above. Then, however, the disclosure process was held to be inadequate because it failed to offer specific reference to the adjustment to the profit and loss account and to give a true and fair view of the Company's financial position.

Accepting the finding of fact that the accountant knew the accounts to be misleading, the Court of Appeal split, however, on the issue of whether this amounted to actual knowledge for the purposes of the knowledge savings clause. Chadwick and Carnwath L.JJ. both felt that if the documents had intended to include "imputed knowledge" then they should have said so most specifically. Pill L.J. disagreed with this approach, believing that actual knowledge in this context was intended to contrast with constructive knowledge so that if the claimants' advisors knew of an issue, that knowledge was not constructive but actual for the purposes of the transaction. Nonetheless, all three judges found that the knowledge savings clause had no application on the facts, since it was only ever supposed to apply to knowledge not arising from disclosure but which would, if possessed by the buyer, have the effect of limiting claims for breach of warranty. This indicates that, in the absence of such a provision, a buyer aware of facts can nonetheless sue for breach of warranty, and that parties to an agreement must set out carefully the standard of knowledge applicable if that right to sue is to be negated.[50]

21–022 As regards the quality of disclosure, the Court of Appeal held that the disclosure made was adequate. Relevant documents had been provided to the claimants' accountants, allowing them to carry out due diligence in the run up to completion. It was true that no specific disclosure was made but the claimants had made no demands for such disclosure against particular warranties. It had to be assumed that the claimants were content for its accountants to trawl through the documents and advise on issues thought to be of significance. The accountants might fairly be expected to reach conclusions from examination of the documents supplied as these contained ample material alongside other disclosures to indicate the financial adjustment. The warranty that the accounts gave a true and fair view was qualified therefore by the disclosure made in accordance with the dis-

---

[50] While it might seem unfair to allow a claim for breach of a warranty if the claimant was fully aware of the breach before entering into the contract, in practice the extent of the buyer's knowledge is rarely so definite. It is often precisely because the buyer suspects the existence of some unwelcome fact, that it seeks a contractual stipulation that the suspicion is unfounded, so giving it the assurance that it (and its funder) needs in order to proceed with the transaction.

closure letter such that there was no breach of warranty. In the past courts have applied a fairness standard so that:

"mere reference to a source of information ... will not satisfy the requirements of a clause providing for fair disclosure with sufficient details to identify the nature and scope of the matter disclosed."[51]

The better view would now seem to be that, as between commercial parties, the significant factor is the language used by those parties, who will be taken to have carefully drafted the sale and purchase agreement and disclosure letter.

In environmental negotiations, sellers would be happy with a general disclosure standard of the type allowed in this case. There is room for bargaining for more specific disclosure and even for criteria of fairness and sufficiency of disclosure, however, as the seller will also want some assurance that the buyer has no awareness prior to completion of facts relating to environmental compliance that might give rise to a warranty claim. The seller would generally hope that any disclosure made against one warranty will be effective against all other warranties where relevant. It is quite commonly the case in relation to environmental warranties that they are "ring-fenced" such that these warranties must be qualified by schedules which are specific to each warranty. In the light of the case law above this practice may spread.

Claiming on the warranty

Post-completion the buyer may seek to argue that a breach of warranty has occurred. In this event, there may be notice provisions in the contract so that the buyer specifies those events which it is believed amount to a breach of warranty. In such a case the court may apply certain requirements to such notice. In *RWE Nukem Ltd v AEA Technology plc*, Mrs Justice Gloster laid down her expectations of such requirements: **21–023**

"I would expect that a compliant notice would identify the particular warranty that was alleged to have been breached; I would expect that, at least in general terms, the notice would explain why it had been breached, with at least some sort of particularisation of the facts upon which such an allegation was based, and would give at least some sort of indication of what loss had been suffered as a result of the breach of warranty..."[52]

If the agreement does not specify particular mechanisms as to how damages for breach of warranty are to be calculated, the usual contract

---

[51] Per Lord Penrose in *New Hearts Ltd v Cosmopolitan Investments Ltd* [1997] 2 BCLC 249 at 258–9.
[52] [2005] EWHC 78 (Comm) at para.11; see also the appeal hearing in this case at [2005] EWCA Civ 1192.

rules apply. A theoretically sound way to calculate damages flowing from the breach is to attempt to calculate the difference between the market value of the company's shares allowing for the breach of warranty and the market value those shares had the warranty been accurate.[53] This implicitly incorporates a materiality provision since it implies that the breach should be such as to affect the share price. Sellers may prefer, however, to incorporate more precise materiality provisions and buyers may try to insist that damages are assessed on an indemnity basis set out expressly in the agreement. Often damages on an indemnity basis will be resisted by a seller leading to the compromise that only certain specified risks will be the subject of individual indemnity provisions. An indemnity mechanism might allow the buyer to recover against the breach whether or not the share value was affected, the calculation being the money that the buyer would need to spend to remedy the factors amounting to breach of warranty. One can argue that this is perfectly fair. The buyer does not need to show reliance in a warranty claim, is entitled to that which was the subject of the contract and can relatively easily prove and quantify the loss. For these reasons these mechanisms might be preferred and where appropriate can be tied into other forms of indemnification supporting the agreement.

It is also common practice to have a threshold monetary limit and monetary and time caps for a warranty claim. As a general rule, the monetary limits apply to claims under all warranties; usually there are no sub-limits for environmental (or other) warranties except, perhaps, the tax warranties.

Environmental Indemnities

21–024　An environmental indemnity, if well drafted[54] probably offers the best available form of contractual protection to a client worried about environmental risk, not least because it can specify precisely which risks are at issue and what should happen if these materialise. This simple understanding gives the indemnity agreement a shape. To begin with it must have a well defined scope relating to the sort of matters covered by environmental warranties (above). This will be both an issue of concern (such as groundwater contamination) but it will also govern the trigger provisions under the indemnity, the point at which liability to pay under

---

[53] This is not straightforward in practice however. For a quoted company, share prices can fluctuate for all sorts of extraneous reasons related slightly, if at all, to the company's performance, and in the case of a large company even a quite substantial loss may not necessarily have any appreciable impact on its share price in the market. For an unquoted company, calculating its value is inevitably a very subjective exercise, and any impact that a loss may have on the value is probably more simply assessed directly.

[54] It is assumed for our purposes that, notwithstanding any general indemnification in the agreement, the parties choose to conclude a separate indemnity agreement to cover environmental liabilities.

the indemnity will arise (such as the service of a works' notice[55] to remedy water pollution). Agreements as to trigger conditions may not be easy, as indemnifiers will wish to avoid "soft" triggers, such as discovery of contamination, which offers an incentive to investigate and gain betterment through remediation, preferring "hard" triggers, such as the regulatory determination of the land as contaminated. Harder triggers are less likely to engender dispute. In *Bal 1966 Ltd v British Alcan Aluminium Ltd*[56] the parties failed to agree whether a letter from the Environment Agency, pointing to a breach and its available powers to remedy this, represented a "serious" written threat of proceedings. At a preliminary hearing the Technology and Construction Court ruled that a threat did not need to be express in order for it to be serious.

Because a party agreeing to indemnify against loss will not wish to attract unquantifiable liability, the agreement will invariably contain caps, limiting both the amount held out under the indemnity agreement and the time during which this is available. It makes sense for the indemnifier to ensure that the trigger will not be cost free for the indemnified party by including a de minimis threshold below which there can be no claim. This may serve as, or there may be a separate, deductible under the agreement. Finally there may be exclusions from the indemnity agreement, so that specific environmental risks are not covered, or so that there is no requirement to pay out where it is the indemnified party that is the immediate cause of the triggering of the indemnity.

Any indemnity is only as good as the resources of the party providing it. Although given most commonly by the seller, therefore, it may be given by a parent company or another guarantor from inside the seller group. It may be insurance backed[57] to better ensure the available funds, or it might be funded by a retention on the proceeds of sale. It is not impossible, however, that the purchaser may indemnify the seller because as explained above the deal may be constructed to relieve the seller of liability, especially liability under Part 2A of the Environmental Protection Act 1990.[58] It is necessary to consider also which parties precisely are indemnified. In the case of land development a primary purpose of the indemnity may be to assure further incoming purchasers. The seller in such a case may be prepared to go some way down this road in order to realise the purchase price, but will demand that the core of the indemnity remains so that, for example, it covers only liabilities arising out of environmental law as it stands at date of completion of the original sale.

Whereas, in relation to a warranty, a claim can be resisted usually to the   **21–025**

---

[55] Under ss.161A–161D Water Resources Act 1991.
[56] [2006] Env. L.R. 26.
[57] As explained in Chapter 22.
[58] A seller, who has accepted a reduction in price sufficient to cover the costs of remediating his contaminated site, will certainly wish to ensure, by way of an indemnity from the buyer, that he is as free as he can be from any further liabilities on account of that site.

extent that matter giving rise to the claim was disclosed by the seller, the indemnity offers the opportunity to face squarely risks known to both parties. The seller might argue, not unreasonably, that the purchaser could factor these into the price of the deal, but it may be the case that although the risk is known, the potential liability is not. In theory the indemnity can be used to cover unknown risks, but the seller might argue that unless there is some basis upon which a risk can be identified any suggestion of an indemnity is entirely speculative and cannot be considered. Ultimately it is crucial that the indemnified risks are clearly identified; for example if confined to risks "arising out of the businesses" as sold, this may not be adequate to cover historic pollution surfacing as a result of past, discontinued activity. The burden will generally be on the indemnified party as claimant to demonstrate that the indemnity was intended to cover the loss now claimed. Equally in line with *contra proferentem* principles, the party seeking to rely on the agreement will find that it might be strictly construed against it in the event of any ambiguity.[59] It is usual to refer disputes on the agreement to some form of alternative dispute resolution, since it may serve neither party for the claim, or its underlying trigger event, to become public knowledge.

It is no less important to reach clear agreement on the losses that might form the subject of a claim under the agreement. If the trigger for the indemnity is liability to a third party, not only may this not cover statutory liabilities,[60] but it may not cover legal costs. Where losses cover wider issues such as remediation costs, and where the indemnity funding is capable of delivering considerable betterment to the indemnified party by way of improvement of the site, the indemnifier will wish to ensure that such costs are reasonable. This may mean that the indemnifier will seek to retain conduct of claims and even to oversee the necessary work in compliance with the statutory demands. The ability of a party to do so may depend on the timely notification of the trigger event, so requirements for this should be written into the indemnity agreement and will be strictly applied by the courts.[61] Cost sharing agreements can work well in certain circumstances, offering both parties an incentive to produce a cost effective solution. This can be significant in the context of contaminated land where few remediation notices are served, and the matter is generally settled by way of a remediation statement containing the proposed work on the site. Different remediation solutions will have different cost bases, so a structure to produce an efficient workable solution makes sense. Once again,

---

[59] *Hollier v Rambler Motors* [1972] 2 Q.B. 71.

[60] This problem arose in *Bartoline Ltd v Royal Sun Alliance Insurance* [2006] EWHC 3598 (Q.B.) (considered in Chapter 22—below) where an indemnity against "legal liability for damages" was held to cover neither a debt owed under statute to the Environment Agency in respect of its emergency clean-up costs, nor the costs of further clean up carried on in accordance with a works notice.

[61] See *RWE Nukem Ltd v AEA Technology plc* (above fn.52).

devising the appropriate trigger is important, for one might well wish to act in advance of a statutory notice being served.[62]

Lenders and Environmental Risk

It has been argued[63] that lenders face several different species of risk arising out of financing transactions that might be affected by the environmental conditions at the subject property. The first is credit risk: the risk that expenditure necessary to bring the facility up to appropriate environmental standards affects the ability of the borrower to service the loan. The second is security risk: the notion that the value of the property may be adversely affected by the discovery of pollution attaching to it. This may constitute a risk on a particular site or across the whole portfolio of secured properties as better account is taken of the effect of pollution on property prices. The third is liability risk: the risk that the bank itself may become liable for pollution at a facility it has helped fund. Although as we will see there are few examples of this, this risk may align with the security risk as the bank cannot afford to exercise its security and take possession of the site lest, as a mortgagee in possession, it is considered owner of the site[64] and open to liability as a result.[65] Finally, becoming linked with a badly contaminated site might pose reputational risks for the bank. That this is a sensitivity for banks is indicated by the rapid development of the Equator Principles.[66]

21–026

In terms of liability, banks may worry about the possibility that in a situation of financial crisis any operational control of the borrower's business may lead to it causing or knowingly permitting pollution. This type of liability was known in the United States under early interpretations of its statute law.[67] However, in the UK there is no case in which this has occurred, and equally there is no example of this type of conduct leading to the bank's liability as a shadow director.[68] Nonetheless, the other species of

---

[62] An issue which arose in *Eastern Counties Leather Plc v Eastern Counties Leather Group Plc* [2002] Env. L.R. 34.

[63] Lee R G and Egede T "Banking and the Environment: Not Liability but Responsibility" (2007) *Journal of Business Law* (November) pp.868–883.

[64] Section 78A(9) of the Environmental Protection Act 1990 defines an owner as a person "other than a mortgagee not in possession ..." implying that a mortgagee in possession will be considered owner of the property; see also *Maguire v Leigh on Sea UDC* (1906) 95 LT 319.

[65] This may be in the form of common law liability, for example if the site constitutes a nuisance to adjoining owners, or under statute, for example as a class B appropriate person under Part 2A of the Environmental Protection Act 1990.

[66] M Forster et al, "The Equator Principles—Towards Sustainable Banking?" (2005) 20(6) *Buttersworths Journal of International Banking and Financial Law* 217.

[67] See *United States v Fleet Factors Corporation* (1990) 901 F 2d 1550, (1993) 821 F Supp 707 interpreting the Comprehensive Environmental Response, Compensation and Liability Act 1980 (CERCLA).

[68] *Re Hydrodam (Corby) Ltd*, *The Times*, February 19, 1992, and *Triodos Bank NV v Dobbs* (2004) EWHC 845.

risk are sufficient to ensure the bank's due diligence in environmental matters. For example, increasingly where environmental regulators have clean up powers, they have the ability to charge the land in order to recover remediation expenditure[69] and there is a decided risk that this statutory charge will outrank that of the lender.[70]

It follows that the lender, especially in a large transaction, will have as much interest in the due diligence exercise as the borrower, and the bank may wish to see Phase I and other information to assure itself that the environmental risks attaching to the proposed transaction are capable of being effectively managed. Information obtained as a result of environmental due diligence exercises may help shape the loan agreement by the imposition of conditions precedent to ensure that pressing problems have been addressed. It might even be that additional collateral will be required to support the loan if the bank has doubts about the condition of property offered as security. The loan agreement through its covenants and warranties will seek to ensure existing and future[71] compliance with environmental law. As indicated earlier, the presence of warranties in the loan agreement will lead to disclosure from the borrower as the process of due diligence discovers more about the state of the facilities to be purchased.

21–027   The lender has every interest in fixing such terms at the outset of the loan. It is likely that breach of warranty or disclosure of material adverse change in the operation of the facility will constitute an event of default. However, this is a weak remedy for a lender in certain respects since it is likely to involve acceleration of the loan repayments. This may lead to cross-acceleration on the part of other lenders and the bank may be left looking to recover money at a time when a borrower is already hit by the events that caused the default and the costs attaching to these. At best the lender may be able to re-negotiate the agreement seeking additional assurances and/or security. Although the bank could foreclose, as is suggested above, the bank may have no great wish to become a mortgagee in possession of a site beset by environmental problems. It follows that the bank's best opportunity to safeguard its position is in the course of the negotiation of the loan agreement, and hence solicitors acting for a borrower in an environmentally problematic transaction may expect continual contact with the client's bankers.

Commercial Leases

21–028   Where land has been or may be put to potentially contaminative uses, environmental risk is no less applicable to leasehold transactions. The risk

[69] See for example s.78P of the Environmental Protection Act 1990.
[70] See *Westminster City Council v Haymarket Publishing* [1981] 2 All E.R. 555.
[71] Future compliance can be scrutinised as it is likely that the warranties under the loan agreement will need to be repeated during the life time of the agreement.

for the tenant lies in assuming responsibility for historic contamination and for the landlord in assuming liability for the tenant's activity. Issues of due diligence and certain risk management devices such as warranties and insurance are sufficiently well covered in this and the following chapter to allow discussion here to largely focus on the terms of the lease. Before doing so, it is useful to emphasise that site conditions on the property may shape the terms of the lease. We might expect more attention to be given to environmental risk, where there is known contamination on the site (whether or not there is a pollutant linkage) making both parties potential class A persons for the purposes of Part 2A of the Environmental Protection Act 1990.[72] Also attention should be paid to the length of the lease. As a lease with an original term of 21 years (20 in Scotland) or more is to be regarded as a sale for the purposes of allocation of liabilities under Part 2A,[73] it becomes possible for a landlord to take advantage of Test 3 of the Guidance (above) by "selling" with information.

In terms of a commercial "rack rented" lease involving potentially contaminated land, it seems wise to have regard to the provisions of the repairing covenant. The ordinary language with words such as "good and substantial repair and condition" might not easily extend to site remediation because the notion of "repair" does not fit readily with land remediation and because the historic land contamination is not easily described as "disrepair".[74] In addition the very idea of repair denotes some physical deterioration in the hands of the tenant.[75] As there is no requirement on the tenant to hand back a property that is fundamentally different to that let, it is reasonable to conclude that standard repair covenants will not of themselves cover major remediation works. This being the case it makes sense to address the issue directly since if obligations are not to fall on the tenant then logically they should fall on the landlord instead.

Where repair obligations remain with the tenant, it is not uncommon for the landlord to reserve the right to carry out repairs in default, following notice, and undertake the work, thereafter recovering the cost from the tenant. The costs then recovered are likely to be treated as a debt[76] making enforcement procedurally rather easy,[77] and tenants will wish to ensure that this device cannot be used to short circuit the mechanisms under the contaminated land regime. The landlord will also want to consider other rights of entry to the property. Do these allow the carrying out of intrusive site investigation, should this prove necessary to appease the regulators?

[72] See Chapter 16 (above).
[73] See para.D59(a) of the Guidance.
[74] *Post Office v Aquarius Properties Ltd* [1987 1 All E.R. 1055.
[75] *Quick v Taff Ely BC* [1986] Q.B. 809.
[76] *Jervis v Harris* [1996] Ch 195.
[77] Avoiding the application of the Leasehold Property (Repairs) Act 1938 and the restriction otherwise placed on damages in s.18 of the Landlord and Tenant Act 1927.

Where the tenant has expended money in addressing the remediation of pollution, it will wish to ensure that any improvement made to the land is disregarded for purposes of rent reviews and service charges.

21–029   If the concern with land based contamination arises out of regulatory intervention, it may be that the matter could be dealt with through the covenants on statutory compliance. This is a general requirement, ordinarily, to comply with current and future statutes. It may be wide enough to catch any notice served in respect of the property whether served on the tenant or the landlord, which will need to be met at the tenant's expense.[78] As the tenant will not wish to be responsible for historic pollution where a remediation notice is served upon a landlord as an appropriate person, the tenant will wish to restrict the covenant's application to notices served on it directly. This would seem to be reasonable on the assumption that any contamination caused by substances brought on to the land by the tenant will render the tenant an appropriate person, and the apportionment of liability will be a matter for the regulator. Again it may be possible to go further than this with sites beset by known contamination, and make precise provision for dealing with any regulatory intervention. This can then take account of wider matters such as the business interruption suffered by the tenant.

Where the use of the premises by the tenant might give rise to pollution, thought will have to be given to both the user clause and to the covenant not to cause a nuisance. There are a series of issues here including the extent to which the covenant can be used to demand tenant responses to (say) migrating pollutants, and whether, if the user clause accepts a potentially contaminative use, the nuisance provisions can then be employed to restrict this user. Similarly in terms of any alienation provisions, if the landlord is worried about a contaminative use, it may withhold consent to assignment where the tenant is already in breach of environmental obligations under the lease or where an incoming user seems likely to put the property to contaminative use.

Finally, it is open to the parties to make specific provision through covenants and backed by indemnity on a host of matters including: the handling and management of hazardous and waste substances by the tenant; the rights of the landlord to be informed promptly of environmental incidents at the tenanted property and of any later proceedings; precisely what works can be covered by a service charge; and even compliance with appropriate industrial or environmental management standards on the part of a tenant. The lesson for commercial leases is the same as that for

---

[78] Though the courts may be persuaded to apportion the liability for costs as between the parties—see *Horner v Franklin* [1905] 1KB 479 and *Monk v Arnold* [1902] 1KB 761—if it seems that the matter at hand was not within the contemplation of the parties; see also the Statutory Nuisance Appeals Regulations 1995 (SI 1995/2644).

commercial transactions more generally; it is always prudent on the back of information suggesting potential environmental risk for the parties to make express provision in the event that such risk materialises.

Chapter 22

INSURANCE

Introduction

Pollution incidents can be costly for the persons who cause or knowingly   **22–001**
permit, or who are otherwise charged with responsibility for, the pollution.
Traditionally, the polluter faced a potential claim for property damage or
bodily injury and, possibly, a fine. The increase in environmental liability
legislation during the past 10 or so years, however, means that a polluter is
now also likely to face the cost of remediating the pollution and, in some
cases, restoring damaged natural resources to their state immediately
before the damage.

Many companies remain unaware, however, that their public liability
and other general liability policies may not provide cover for a substantial
proportion of the costs arising from a pollution incident. Many companies
are also not aware that specialised policies exist which fill these gaps in
cover.

This chapter describes the extent of cover for environmental liabilities in
general liability insurance policies. It shows that the failure to recognise the
gap in this cover can have serious consequences for insureds. The chapter
then examines the range of environmental insurance policies and their
general features before describing the measures to be taken by an insured,
and its legal or other advisers, in purchasing environmental insurance
policies. To set this discussion in context, the chapter begins with an
overview of the format of general liability policies, application of the burden of proof and the rules of construction pertaining to them.

General Liability Insurance Policies

General liability policies provide some cover for environmental liabilities.   **22–002**
They do not, however, provide cover for all environmental liabilities; there
are invariably large gaps in cover.

Format

22–003   General liability insurance policies tend to have a similar format consisting of a schedule and a wording. The schedule sets out information about the specific policy including:

- the name of the insured;
- the names of any additional insureds;
- the limit of indemnity, including any sub-limits;
- the policy period, i.e. the time and date on which the policy begins and the time and date when it terminates;
- the amount of the deductible, also known as the excess, or in some cases, the self-insured retention, i.e. the amount to be paid by the insured before the insurer's obligation to pay the indemnity arises; and
- the premium paid by the insured for the policy.

The wording generally includes:

- an insuring clause (also known as a coverage clause) which specifies the liabilities for which the insurer will indemnify the insured;
- definitions of commonly used words in the policy;
- exclusions, i.e. liabilities which are not covered by the policy;
- the territory covered by the policy;
- clauses setting out the time and manner in which the insured should make a claim, any claims co-operation clauses, etc; and
- conditions including choice of law, jurisdiction and venue, the insurer's right to subrogate, the insured's right (or not) to assign the policy, the insured's and insurer's right to cancel the policy, severability of clauses, etc.

If a policy provides cover for various different types of liability, it may well contain general conditions and, perhaps, general definitions and exclusions. Each section of the policy may then have its own insuring clauses, definitions, exceptions, claims-related provisions and conditions.

A policy may include endorsements as well as the main wording. Endorsements serve various purposes. A typical purpose is to modify, add or delete a term or condition in the body of the policy. For example, an endorsement may modify or add an insuring clause, a definition or an exclusion. Another purpose is to indicate that the policy has been renewed for an additional period of time, perhaps with an increased limit of liability or additional cover. A further purpose is to add additional insureds.

Burden of proof

22–004   The insured bears the burden of proving that a claim falls within the insuring clause. If the insurer considers that the policy nevertheless excludes cover for the claim, the insurer bears the burden of proving that the relevant exclusion(s) apply. If an exclusion contains an exception that writes back cover that would otherwise be barred by the exclusion, English law appears to provide that the insured bears the burden of proving that the exception applies.[1] The applicable standard of proof in all cases is the balance of probabilities.

Rules of construction

A determination whether an insurance policy provides cover for environ- **22–005** mental liabilities, or any other liabilities, depends on the wording of the particular policy. There are no standard form wordings for insurance policies for United Kingdom risks.[2]

In making the determination, courts apply the rules of construction for contracts in order to ascertain

> "the meaning which the document would convey to a reasonable person having all the background knowledge which would reasonably have been available to the parties in the situation in which they were at the time of the contract".[3]

The interpretation is not limited to the four corners of the contract; extrinsic evidence may, if necessary, be considered. Thus, in determining the meaning of a word or phrase in an insurance policy or other contract, a court may examine "the background to the contract, the surrounding circumstances, the matrix, the genesis and aim".[4] This information is known as the matrix of facts. As explained by Lord Hoffmann, it

> "includes absolutely everything which would have affected the way in which the language of the document would have been understood by a reasonable man" with the exception of "the previous negotiations of the parties and their declaration of subjective intent".[5]

---

[1] *Rowett, Leakey and Company v Scottish Provident Institution* [1927] 1 Ch.55 (CA).
[2] The situation is different in the United States where there is a standardised policy form for the general liability policy, namely, the commercial general liability (CGL) policy drafted by the Insurance Services Office (ISO). As the CGL policy, which has been approved for use by individual states, is revised and standardised endorsements for it are introduced, the insurance regulatory agencies of the individual states decide whether to approve the particular revision or endorsement for use in that state. An insurer that wishes to use the CGL policy or any other ISO policy form must have a licence from the ISO authorising it to do so. The existence of a standardised policy does not mean that the terms and conditions of the CGL policy have the same meaning in all states. Insurance law is state law. Therefore, the meaning of a word or phrase in an insurance policy depends on the state's rules of construction and other principles of insurance law.
[3] *Investors Compensation Scheme v West Bromwich Building Society* [1998] 1 W.L.R. 896, [1998] 1 All E.R. 98 (HL).
[4] *Youell v Bland Welch & Company Ltd* [1992] 2 Lloyd's Rep. 127 (CA).
[5] ibid.

A word or phrase in a contract is construed in the context of the relevant clause and the entire policy. Thus, as Lord Hoffmann explained, the meaning which the contract

"would convey to a reasonable man is not the same thing as the meaning of its words. The meaning of words is a matter of dictionaries and grammars; the meaning of the document is what the parties using those words against the relevant background would reasonably have been understood to mean. The background may not merely enable the reasonable man to choose between the possible meanings of words which are ambiguous but even (as occasionally happens in ordinary life) to conclude that the parties must, for whatever reason, have used the wrong words or syntax".[6]

22–006   Unless the context requires otherwise, the meaning that a court gives to a word or phrase to be construed within a contract is its "primary meaning in ordinary speech".[7] This meaning is generally described as the word or phrase's natural and ordinary meaning, or its ordinary and plain meaning. As, again, Lord Hoffmann explained,

"[t]he 'rule' that words should be given their 'natural and ordinary meaning' reflects the common sense proposition that we do not easily accept that people have made linguistic mistakes, particularly in formal documents. On the other hand, if one would nevertheless conclude from the background that something must have gone wrong with the language, the law does not require judges to attribute to the parties an intention which they plainly could not have had".[8]

General Liability Policies

22–007   There are numerous and diverse types of insurance policies including life, casualty, marine, motor, medical, credit risk, political risk, disability, aviation and travel. The five main types of insurance policies which may provide cover for environmental liabilities are:

- public liability policies;
- property policies;
- professional indemnity policies;
- directors' and officers' liability policies; and
- employers' liability policies.

[6] ibid.
[7] *Charter Reinsurance Company Ltd v Fagan* [1997] A.C. 313, [1996] 2 W.L.R. 726, [1996] 3 All E.R. 46 (HL).
[8] *Investors Compensation Scheme v West Bromwich Building Society* [1998] 1 W.L.R. 896, [1998] 1 All E.R. 98 (HL).

Public liability policies

A public liability policy provides cover for third-party claims for bodily   **22–008**
injury and property damage against the insured. The policies provide cover
for common law liabilities and, in some cases, statutory liabilities.
Although policies are by no means standard in form, a typical public liability policy provides an indemnity from the insurer to the insured for:

"all sums which the insured shall become 'legally liable' to pay as
'damages' [or 'compensation' or 'claims'] for

(a) accidental bodily injury including death, or illness, and
(b) accidental loss or damage to property

occurring during the period of insurance in connection with the
business".

As the above insuring clause indicates, public liability policies are occur-
rence-based policies, providing cover for bodily injury and property
damage that occurs during the policy period. In many, if not most, cases,
the injury or damage occurs at the same time as, or shortly after, the
incident that caused it. As discussed further below, however, this is not
necessarily the case in environmental claims where injury or damage may
occur long after an individual or property has been exposed to pollutants
and even long after the policy period has terminated. This capacity for
public liability policies to be triggered long after their policy period has
terminated is often described as a "long tail" of liability. This long tail of
liability has meant that old policies have been, and will continue to be,
triggered by a claim against the insured for harm caused by exposure to
asbestos and other pollutants many years after the exposure occurred.
Mesothelioma, for example, does not develop until at least 10 years after an
individual is exposed to asbestos. The disease, which can be caused by
exposure to a single asbestos fibre, is invariably fatal.

The long tail of liability also means that old policies may be triggered by
proceedings brought by an enforcing authority under legislation that has a
retrospective as well as a prospective effect. This situation occurred in the
United States following enactment of the Comprehensive Environmental
Response, Compensation and Liability Act (CERCLA or Superfund) on
December 11, 1980,[9] under which "potentially responsible parties"
(PRPs) may be liable for remediating contamination from historic inci-
dents. It may also occur in the United Kingdom due to the enactment of
Part 2A of the Environmental Protection Act 1990 (EPA 1990),[10] under

---

[9] Pub. L. No. 96-510, 94 Stat. 2767 (1980), codified at 42 U.S.C. ss 9601 et seq.; see
generally V. Fogleman, *Environmental Liabilities and Insurance in England and the United
States* pp.457–632 (Witherbys, 2005).

[10] See Chapter 16 above; Part 2A came into force in England on April 1, 2000.

which "appropriate persons" may be liable for remediating contamination from historic incidents.

"Damages"

22–009   The first issue involving the application of a public liability policy to statutory liabilities is whether the words "damages" or "compensation" in the insuring clause provide cover for such liabilities. It is undisputed that the words "damages" and "compensation" provide cover for tort actions for bodily injury and property damage arising from a claimant's exposure to pollutants depending, of course, on other terms and conditions in the policy. It is unclear, however, whether such words also cover the costs of remediating contaminated land or polluted water or restoring damaged natural resources.

The issue of whether the word "damages" covers the cost of remedial measures was litigated in an English court for the first time as a result of a massive fire at a factory owned by Bartoline Ltd in East Yorkshire. The fire caused adhesives and hydrocarbons, including paraffin, turpentine and white spirits, which were stored at the factory, together with fire-fighting water, to enter and pollute two watercourses. The Environment Agency exercised its powers under the Water Resources Act 1991 (WRA 1991) and remediated the contamination by constructing dams and pumping out polluted water for treatment and disposal and by removing polluted silt and vegetation from the bed and banks of the water courses. The Agency subsequently invoiced Bartoline £622,681.78 for the works. Bartoline incurred additional costs of £147,988.14 for further works which it carried out to comply with a works notice issued by the Agency.

Bartoline submitted a claim for the remedial costs to Royal & Sun Alliance plc (RSA), its public liability insurer. The insuring clause of the policy provided that RSA agreed to indemnify Bartoline "against legal liability for damages in respect of . . . accidental loss or damage to Property . . . nuisance trespass to land or trespass to goods or interference with any easement right of air light water or way". RSA denied the claim on the basis that the word "damages" provides cover only for tort liabilities and not statutory liabilities such as those arising under the WRA 1991.

22–010   His Honour Judge Hegarty QC in the High Court concluded that the word "damages" in the RSA policy did not provide cover for statutory liabilities. In his lengthy judgment, he examined the distinction between common law and statutory liabilities. He also discussed cases in which courts had construed marine insurance policies to cover only common law liabilities. The judge concluded that the "established usage" of the word "damages" in a public liability policy is not to provide cover for statutory liabilities but only common law liabilities.[11] The case subsequently settled

---

[11] *Bartoline Ltd v Royal & Sun Allliance Insurance plc* [2007] 1 All E.R. (Comm) 1043 (Q.B. (Merc)).

for an undisclosed amount shortly before it was due to be heard by the Court of Appeal.

The High Court's construction of the word "damages" in the RSA policy to exclude cover for statutory liabilities does not mean that other public liability policies do not provide such cover. As noted above, a court construes a word or phrase in the context of an entire policy. If, for example, a policy excludes cover for pollution but includes a write back of cover for cleaning up contamination from a sudden and accidental pollution incident (see below), the policy may, depending on its other terms and conditions, provide cover for remedial costs.

In addition, some public liability insurers offer so-called "Bartoline endorsements" which are specifically designed to provide cover for some statutory environmental liabilities. The scope of these endorsements is not always clear. Some endorsements may offer only limited cover for environmental liabilities whilst others may offer broad cover.

"Compensation"

The word "compensation" in the insuring clause of a public liability policy   **22–011** may be broader than the word "damages". In a non-environmental case involving the issue of whether the word "compensation" included cover for exemplary as well as compensatory damages, Simon Brown L.J. (as he then was) accepted that "the natural and ordinary meaning of 'compensation' in the context of a legal liability to pay damages is one which excludes [such cover]". He considered, however, that the "meaning is not wholly clear and unambiguous", stating that such an interpretation "involves very much a literal, lawyers' understanding of the term and is one which would not command universal acceptance." He commented that "(m)any ... would regard 'compensation' to mean instead all damages (of whatsoever nature and however calculated) payable to the victim of a tort". He thus concluded that the word "compensation" in the policy at issue included exemplary as well as compensatory damages.[12]

Simon Brown L.J.'s judgment does not, of course, mean that the word "compensation" includes statutory as well as common law liabilities. Indeed, as noted above, his comments are limited to cover for damages for tort liabilities. The meaning of the word "compensation" in a particular policy also depends on the construction of the word in the context of the entire policy.

---

[12] *Lancashire County Council v Municipal Mutual Insurance Ltd* [1997] Q.B. 897 (CA).

"Legally liable"

22-012   The insuring clauses of public liability policies for United Kingdom risks, as indicated above, tend to use the term "legally liable" or, in some cases "legally obliged", in respect of the insurer's agreement to indemnify the insured. Under English law, "liability" to an injured person arises when the injury occurs. "Legal liability" does not arise, however, unless or until the parties agree to settle a claim arising from the injury or there is a judicial judgment or arbitration award regarding it.[13] The use of the term "legally liable" in the insuring clause of a policy means, therefore, that an insured is not under a duty to indemnify the insured until the insured's liability has been ascertained and quantified.[14]

It is comparatively easy to determine whether a policy provides cover for a judgment or an award because each provides conclusive proof of the insured's liability. It may, however, be difficult to determine whether a policy covers a particular settlement. If an issue regarding coverage arises, the insured may have to prove that the liability compromised by the settlement is insured by the policy and that the amount of the settlement is reasonable compared with the amount of damages if the matter had been adjudicated.[15]

Yorkshire Water Company was unable to meet this burden of proof in a claim arising from the collapse of its sewage sludge tip into the River Colne in Huddersfield, West Yorkshire. ICI, whose property next to the river flooded as a result of the collapse, had brought claims against the water company in nuisance, the rule in *Rylands v Fletcher*[16] and negligence. The claims had been settled by Yorkshire Water paying an agreed sum to ICI. The Official Referee's Court concluded that ICI's claims did not fall within any of the above causes of action, all of which were covered by the water company's public liability policy. In consequence the water company was not legally liable to ICI, and hence the payment to ICI under the insured's settlement of the claim was not covered by the policy.[17]

22-013   The use of the term "legally liable" does not mean that public liability policies for United Kingdom risks fail to provide cover for defence costs. An insurer generally provides such cover by obtaining the insured's consent to act and, subsequently, by acting on behalf of the insured in respect of a covered claim. The defence costs are generally included in rather than being additional to the indemnity provided by the policy. It is however rare

---

[13] *Post Office v Norwich Union Fire Insurance Society Ltd* [1967] 2 Q.B. 363, [1967] 2 W.L.R. 709, [1967] 1 All E.R. 577 (CA).

[14] *Bradley v Eagle Star Insurance Company Ltd* [1989] 1 A.C. 957, [1989] 2 W.L.R. 568, [1989] 1 All E.R. 961 (HL).

[15] *Lumbermens Mutual Casualty Company v Bovis Lend Lease Ltd* [2004] EWHC 1614 (QBD).

[16] (1868) LR 3 HL 330.

[17] *Yorkshire Water Services Ltd v Sun Alliance and London Insurance plc (No 2)* [1998] Env. L.R. 204 (QBD). For a discussion of other issues arising from the collapse of the sewage sludge tip, see text accompanying fn.21.

for a public liability policy for United Kingdom risks to include a duty by the insurer to defend the insured.[18]

The issue of whether an insured is legally liable may be relevant in claims for remediating contaminated land and polluted water. An enforcing authority cannot serve a remediation notice on an "appropriate person" under Part 2A of the EPA 1990 until the authority has notified that person of the contamination, a three-month minimum consultation period has expired and the authority has concluded that the appropriate person will not remediate the contamination in the absence of a remediation notice.[19] In respect of water pollution, the Environment Agency will not serve a works notice[20] under section 161A of the WRA 1991 on a person who caused or knowingly permitted the pollution until the Agency has provided that person with the opportunity to remediate the pollution voluntarily and the person has not carried out the requested remediation.

An insured may make a commercial decision to remediate the contamination or pollution in the absence of a remediation or works notice. Such a decision may result in the enforcing authority agreeing that the insured may carry out remediation at a lower cost than if the authority served a notice and, in the case of water pollution, that there will be no prosecution under section 85 of the WRA 1991. By taking such a course of action, however, the insured risks its insurers denying the claim (provided, of course, that it would otherwise be covered by the policy) because no legal liability on the part of the insured has arisen. Timely liaison by the insured with its insurers is therefore essential in such circumstances.

Claims

A somewhat similar issue to whether an insured is legally liable is whether a   **22–014** third party has made a claim against an insured and, thus, whether the policy has been triggered. If an insured carries out works to avoid a potential claim from arising, its public liability policy is unlikely to provide cover for the cost of the works in the absence of a clause which specifically provides such cover.

The issue arose in the episode concerning the collapse of Yorkshire Water's sewage sludge tip into the River Colne[21] considered above. Because the collapse caused flooding at properties owned by ICI, in an effort to avoid further flooding and claims, Yorkshire Water carried out

---

[18] In contrast, the standard CGL policy which is used in the United States contains a duty to defend and a duty to indemnify. Only the latter is subject to the limit of indemnity in the policy; the duty to defend does not typically have a limit.

[19] EPA 1990, ss.78B(3), 78C(1), (2), 78H(3), 78H(5)(b). An exception exists if the enforcing authority determines that an "imminent danger of serious harm, or serious pollution of controlled waters [is] being caused". Ibid. ss.78H(4), 78N(3)(a).

[20] See Anti-Pollution Works Regulations 1999, SI 1999/1006.

[21] See text accompanying fn.17.

remedial works on its own land at a cost of £4,601,061. Its insurers subsequently denied its claim for the costs of the works.

Yorkshire Water had a primary and an excess[22] public liability policy. The former provided that insurers agreed to indemnify Yorkshire Water "against legal liability for damages in respect of accidental ... loss of or damage to material property ... happening during any Period of Insurance in connection with the Business". The policy also provided that "The Insured at his own expense shall ... take reasonable precautions to prevent any circumstances or to cease any activity which may give rise to liability under this Policy".

22–015   The excess public liability policy provided that insurers agreed to

"indemnify the Insured against all sums which the Insured shall become legally liable to pay as damages or compensation in respect of ... loss of or damage to property ... happening in connection with the Business and occurring during the Period of Insurance".

The policy further provided that: "The insured at his own expense shall take reasonable precautions to prevent any Occurrence or to cease any activity which may give rise to liability under this Policy."

The Court of Appeal concluded that insurers were not liable for the water company's claim because:

- no "sums" had been paid or were payable to a third party;
- the cost of works carried out on the water company's own land was not a sum that the company was "legally liable" to pay to a third party claimant;
- the cost of the works was not "damages" because it was not a sum that was owed due to a breach of duty or obligation; and
- the cost of the works was not paid in respect of loss or damage to a third party's property.

The court also concluded that the policies obliged the water company to carry out measures to prevent further damage at its own expense, commenting that there was no implied term in them to provide cover for the reasonable cost of such measures.[23]

In contrast, in a case involving a complex public liability policy, the Court of Appeal concluded that costs incurred by an insured dredging company and an insured port authority in removing silt from third parties' land next to an estuary were covered. The dredging company, whose works

---

[22] An excess policy provides cover above a specified limit. For example, it may provide £1 million cover above the primary public liability policy's indemnity limit of £1 million. A further excess policy may provide, say, "£3 million excess £2 million", i.e. cover for the next £3 million above the first £2 million. Yet another excess policy may provide, say, £1 million excess £5 million, and so on.

[23] *Yorkshire Water Services Ltd v Sun Alliance and London Insurance plc (No. 1)* [1997] 2 Lloyd's Rep. 21 (CA).

in Southampton Water had resulted in silt being put into suspension and deposited on adjacent properties, faced claims for negligence and nuisance due to the presence of the silt. The claims included a demand for the cost of a study of the impact of the silt on a nature reserve. The court concluded that the cost of the study was covered by the public liability policy even though the study had concluded that the silt need not be removed because it would not cause any long-term damage.[24]

Timing of an occurrence

A public liability policy provides cover for bodily injury and property damage that occurs during the policy period. As indicated above, if the injury or damage results from an incident such as an explosion, it is relatively easy to determine when the injury or damage occurred because of the short length of time between the incident and the injury or damage. Environmental liabilities, however, often arise from injury or damage that occurs long after an individual or property has been exposed to pollutants. In many cases, the period between the incident and the discovery of the injury or damage includes a latency period during which the injury or damage is not capable of being diagnosed or otherwise discovered.

22–016

Courts have developed four theories to determine the time at which injury or damage takes place. The theories have been adopted by courts in the United States in cases involving claims for bodily injury and, to a much lesser extent property damage, resulting from exposure to asbestos. They have subsequently been applied to cases involving progressive environmental damage, in particular, soil and water pollution.[25] The four theories are:

- the exposure theory;
- the injury in fact theory;
- the manifestation theory; and
- the continuous trigger theory.

---

[24] *Jan de Nul (UK) Ltd v Axa Royale Belge S.A.* [2002] 1 All E.R. (Comm) 767 (CA).

[25] Progressive environmental damage arises when indivisible damage, which occurs during a lengthy period, has been caused, that is, when it is not possible to divide the harm between different persons. For example, assume that nine companies disposed of liquid hazardous waste in a pit, that the waste gradually polluted the groundwater, and that the plume of polluted groundwater migrated. Assume further that another company disposed of liquid hazardous waste at the same location but that its waste did not leak from the barrel that contained it. Assume still further that the regulatory authority subsequently required the 10 companies to clean up the pollution. In such a case, the nine companies are liable for an indivisible harm because it is almost always impossible to divide the harm caused by intermingled liquid chemicals in soil and groundwater. The remaining company, however, is liable only for removing its barrel of waste because the harm is distinct. The former situation is progressive environmental damage; the latter situation is not.

Application of the exposure theory means that policies on the risk when a property or individual is exposed to a pollutant are triggered. More than one policy may be triggered when the exposure occurs over more than one policy period. For example, the migration of a pollutant from a site, via groundwater, to third party properties may extend over a period of time. In addition, a worker may have been exposed to, and have ingested, a pollutant such as asbestos fibres over a period of many years.

22–017   Application of the injury-in-fact theory means that policies on the risk when actual injury or damage occurs are triggered. More than one policy may be triggered, particularly when contamination for which the insured is liable migrates to other properties and results in more than one claim for property damage against the insured or results in proceedings to clean up progressive environmental damage.

Application of the manifestation theory means that the policy on the risk when an injury is diagnosed or property damage manifests itself (that is, is discovered), are triggered. If a court applies the manifestation trigger, only one policy is triggered.

Application of the continuous trigger means that policies on the risk from the first exposure to a pollutant through to its manifestation, and in some cases beyond, are triggered. This theory was introduced in the United States in the notorious case of *Keene Corporation v Insurance Company of North America*[26] in which the District of Columbia Circuit Court of Appeals held that the exposure, injury-in-fact, and manifestation triggers all applied to claims for bodily injury arising from exposure to asbestos.

22–018   The issue of the appropriate trigger to apply under English law arose in a case for damages for harm caused by mesothelioma as a result of the negligent exposure of an individual to asbestos in the work place. Mr Green had been employed by a subcontractor to Bolton Metropolitan Borough Council between 1960 and 1963 and by another company between 1965 and 1970 and after 1973. During those periods, he had been negligently exposed to asbestos by both employers and, as a result, contracted mesothelioma. He died in November 1991, the same year in which he was diagnosed with the disease.

Bolton MBC was insured by a predecessor company to Commercial Union between 1960 and 1965. The public liability policies provided an indemnity to the insured for

"[a]ll sums which the Insured shall become legally liable to pay for compensation in respect of ... bodily injury to or illness of any person ... occurring ... during the Period of Indemnity as a result of an accident and happening".

---

[26] 667 F.2d 1034 (D.C. Cir. 1981), *cert. denied*, 455 U.S. 1007 (1982).

Between 1979 and 1991, Bolton MBC was insured by Municipal Mutual Insurance Ltd. The public liability policies provided an indemnity to the insured for

"all sums which the Insured shall become legally liable to pay as compensation arising out of ... accidental bodily injury or illness ... when such injury illness ... occurs during the currency of the Policy".

Bolton MBC first claimed against Municipal Mutual, which denied the claim on the basis that it was not liable for the insured having negligently exposed Mr Green to asbestos because the exposure occurred outside its policy periods. Bolton MBC then claimed against Commercial Union, which denied liability on the basis that it was not liable for injuries developed by Mr Green outside its policy periods. **22–019**

The Court of Appeal concluded that the policies on the risk when Mr Green was exposed to asbestos were not triggered because Mr Green had not suffered an actionable injury at that time. Longmore L.J., with whom Hallett and Auld L.JJ. agreed, concluded that the appropriate trigger is either the injury-in-fact or the manifestation trigger. The injury-in-fact occurred when the malignant tumour developed in about 1980. The manifestation of mesothelioma occurred when there were identifiable symptoms of the disease in 1990. The court did not have to determine whether the injury-in-fact or the manifestation trigger applied because Municipal Mutual was on the risk at both times.[27] Nor did the court have to determine whether more than one policy was triggered by the injury-in-fact trigger.

Longmore L.J. discussed the continuous trigger theory but rejected its application to public liability policies. He stated that:

"I am far from saying that what has been called this multiple trigger or, sometimes triple trigger theory ... might not be held, on some future occasion, to be appropriate for employers' liability policies in general, depending on the precise words used. ... It has been adopted in the United States avowedly for policy reasons in relation to the vastly greater numbers of asbestos-disease sufferers in that country. I see no reason to adopt it in this particular case where the same policy considerations are not present".

Allocation

If an occurrence, such as progressive environmental damage, takes place over more than one policy period, the issue may arise as to the proportion of the indemnity for which each insurer whose policy is triggered is liable. **22–020**

[27] *Bolton Metropolitan Borough Council v Municipal Mutual Insurance Ltd* [2006] 1 W.L.R. 1492, [2006] All E.R. (D) 66 (CA).

There are no English cases directly on point. There are, however, two cases that provide guidance as well as numerous United States cases on the allocation of liabilities between insurers in cases involving latent diseases and progressive environmental damage.[28]

The allocation issue arose in an English case in which an insured employer had negligently exposed an employee to asbestos between 1955 and October 1957 and between October 1959 and 1970. The employee was subsequently diagnosed with mesothelioma. The employer had purchased employers' liability policies from Syndicate 922 for the period of October 1959 to November 1968. Insurers claimed that they were liable for only 72.5 per cent of the £205,000 judgment against the employer for the employee's death from mesothelioma due to the amount of time during the exposure for which their policies were on risk.

Eady J. rejected insurers' arguments. He referred, among other things, to *Fairchild v Glenhaven Funeral Services Ltd*,[29] in which the House of Lords concluded that an employer is jointly and severally liable if it make a material contribution to an employee's risk of contracting mesothelioma by negligently exposing him to asbestos.[30] Eady J. concluded that an insurer that had issued an employers' liability policy to a company at any time during the period that the employer negligently exposed an employee to asbestos is fully liable for damages in a claim against the employer arising from the employee having developed mesothelioma.[31]

22–021   This line of thinking may perhaps be influenced by the desire to ensure the ready availability of compensation for industrial disease. If an English court were to follow the reasoning in a case involving liability for remediating progressive environmental damage, it may also conclude that each insurer whose policies were on risk during the progressive damage is liable for the entire loss if it made a material contribution to it (depending on the

---

[28] See generally V. Fogleman, *Environmental Liabilities and Insurance in England and the United States* (Witherbys, 2005) pp.52–537.

[29] [2003] 1 A.C. 32, [2002] 3 W.L.R. 89, [2002] 3 All E.R. 305 (HL).

[30] The House of Lords distinguished *Fairchild* in *Barker v Corus (UK) plc* [2006] UKHL 20 (HL), with the effect that an employer who negligently exposes an employee to asbestos is not necessarily jointly and severally liable for a claim by the employee for harm suffered due to the development of mesothelioma. Parliament subsequently enacted the Compensation Act 2006, section 3 of which imposes joint and several liability on a person who negligently exposes an individual to asbestos with the result that the individual develops mesothelioma. In effect, section 3 re-instates *Fairchild*.

[31] *Phillips v Syndicate 922* [2004] Lloyd's Rep I.R. 426 (QBD). Eady J. also concluded that insurers had failed to establish that a generally recognised custom or practice existed according to which each insurer whose policy was on the risk paid a proportion of a claim based on a time on the risk basis. He agreed that such a practice had existed between insurers (but not necessarily between insurers and their insureds) since the late 1980s but ruled that such a practice was not a custom or practice between insurers and their insureds during the 1950s and 1960s when the employee had been exposed to asbestos, or during the mid 1990s when the employee developed mesothelioma.

applicable remediation regime[32]). The insurer could then claim contribution from other insurers that were on the risk during the progressive damage.

The other English case in which the allocation issue arose concerned the pilfering and vandalism of machinery stored at the Port of Sunderland. The pilfering and vandalism occurred between March 1985 and September 1988. Different reinsurers had issued three facultative reinsurance contracts to Municipal Mutual Insurance, which insured the Port of Sunderland Authority, for three 12-month periods beginning in June 1986. The contracts provided that compensation was payable "in respect of or arising out of any one occurrence or in respect of or arising out of all occurrences of a series consequent on or attributable to one source or original cause".

Hobhouse L.J. concluded that the evidence showed that most of the pilfering and vandalism occurred between June 1987 and June 1988. He, therefore, held that, on the balance of probabilities, two-thirds of the losses occurred during the period of the second reinsurance contract. The losses that occurred during the first and third reinsurance contracts were not sufficiently high to exceed the excesses of those reinsurance contracts.[33]

If an English court were to follow the reasoning in the Sunderland case   **22–022** in respect of a claim for progressive environmental damage, it may well hold that the insured need not prove precisely the amount of damage that occurred during each policy period in order for insurers to be liable.

The decisions of the US courts can become relevant in reinsurance cases as demonstrated in *Wasa International Insurance Company Limited and AGF Insurance Company Limited v Lexington Insurance Company*.[34] Lexington had reached certain settlements under US law with the Aluminium Company of America (Alcoa). Lexington sought indemnification from Wasa and AGF, as reinsurers, which parties applied for a declaration from the High Court that they were not liable to follow the Lexington settlements and provide indemnity. The insurance at issue covered the risk of physical loss and damages relating to Alcoa's property on a worldwide basis. When Alcoa was required by the US Environmental Protection Agency to clean up the historic operational pollution on the sites, it turned to its insurers, one of whom was Lexington. In May 2000 the Washington Supreme Court held that for the three years from 1977 and 1980, under the insurance contract Lexington acquired joint and several liability for the

---

[32] Liability for remediating water pollution under the WRA 1991 is joint and several. Liability for remediating contaminated land under Part 2A of the EPA 1990 is modified joint and several liability. That is, after the exclusion tests have been applied, each remaining appropriate person in a liability group for a significant pollutant linkage is liable for remediating the contamination, including the share of contamination of excluded appropriate persons. If there is more than one person in a liability group, liability is proportionate between those persons.

[33] *Municipal Mutual Insurance Ltd v Sea Insurance Company Limited* [1998] Lloyd's Rep. I.R. 421 (CA).

[34] [2008] EWCA Civ 150.

remediation costs at the sites and this was so irrespective of whether the damage had been sustained before, during or after that three year period – a serious matter as the sites were operational between about 1942 and 1986.

In the English Courts, Lexington successfully argued, largely on the basis of *Vesta v Butcher*,[35] that the reinsurance contract was "back to back" with the insurance contract and on this basis any analysis of the time frame for liability had to match that of the Washington Supreme Court. The Court of Appeal held that if a US Court reached a decision in relation to liability under an insurance contract then prima facie that judgment would apply also to the reinsurance contract. This was so even if the judgment seemed surprising or unexpected because indemnification involved covering unexpected possibilities.

Pollution exclusions

22–023   Environmental claims that are covered by the insuring clauses of public liability policies may, nevertheless, be barred due to a pollution exclusion in the policy. Virtually all public liability policies for United Kingdom risks issued since 1990 have contained a pollution exclusion. In that year, the Association of British Insurers (ABI) recommended the inclusion of a model pollution exclusion in public liability policies to its members in order to bar cover for claims arising from gradual pollution. The ABI model exclusion and most, if not all, of the other pollution exclusions used in policies for United Kingdom risks are qualified. That is, the policies exclude liabilities arising out of pollution and then write back cover for liabilities arising from sudden and accidental pollution. They thus effectively bar cover for gradual pollution. In contrast, an absolute pollution exclusion excludes liabilities for both sudden and gradual pollution; it does not contain an exception.

Association of British Insurers Pollution Exclusion

22–024   The ABI model pollution exclusion provides that:

"A.   This policy excludes all liability in respect of Pollution or Contamination other than caused by a sudden identifiable unintended and unexpected incident which takes place in its entirety at a specific time and place during the Period of Insurance.

All Pollution or Contamination which arises out of one incident shall be deemed to have occurred at the time such incident takes place.

---

[35] [1989] AC 852.

B. The liability of the Company for all compensation payable in respect of all Pollution or Contamination which is deemed to have occurred during the Period of Insurance shall not exceed £. .. in the aggregate.

C. For the purpose of this Endorsement "Pollution or Contamination" shall be deemed to mean

   i.   all pollution or contamination of buildings or other structures or of water or land or the atmosphere; and

   ii.   all loss or damage or injury directly or indirectly caused by such pollution or contamination".

The purpose of the second sentence of paragraph A above is to avoid an insured claiming under more than one policy, and thus contending that more than one policy limit applies to a pollution incident. In effect, the clause deems all liability for pollution or contamination arising from a pollution incident into a single policy limit.

The ABI model exclusion is drafted robustly in respect of the abruptness of a pollution incident that is covered. A major reason for such drafting is the large number of decisions by courts in the United States which have concluded that the term "sudden and accidental" in the 1973 qualified exclusion to the CGL policy is ambiguous and that a reasonable meaning of the phrase is "unexpected and unintended". Such an interpretation does not bar cover for gradual pollution.[36]

The word "incident" in the ABI model exclusion has, however, created problems in determining the time at which a pollution event occurred. This is partly because the word "incident" is rarely, if ever, used in public liability policy wordings and, thus, does not have a legal or otherwise generally accepted meaning. For example, assume that oil leaks slowly from a tank and seeps to groundwater beneath the insured's property. Assume further that the plume of polluted groundwater migrates and abruptly bursts through the banks of a stream so that it pollutes the water in the stream. If the "incident" is the slow leakage or seepage, the pollution

---

[36] The highest courts of over 10 states have concluded that the word "sudden" in the phrase "sudden and accidental" in the 1973 CGL policy form is ambiguous and could reasonably mean "unexpected". See *Alabama Plating Company v United States Fidelity & Guaranty Company*, 690 So. 2d 331 (1996); *Hecla Mining Company v New Hampshire Insurance Company*, 811 P.2d 1083 (Colo. 1991); *Claussen v Aetna Casualty & Surety Company*, 259 Ga. 333, 380 S.E.2d 686 (1989); *Outboard Marine Corporation v Liberty Mutual Insurance Company*, 154 Ill. 2d 90, 180 Ill. Dec. 691, 607 N.E.2d 1204 (1992); *American States Insurance Company v Kiger*, 662 N.E.2d 945 (Ind. 1996); *Hudson v Farm Family Insurance Company*, 142 N.H. 144, 697 A.2d 501 (1997); *St Paul & Marine Insurance Company v McCormick & Baxter Creosoting Company*, 324 Or. 184, 923 P.2d 1200 (1996); *Textron, Inc v Aetna Casualty & Surety Company*, 754 A.2d 742 (R.I. 2000); *Greenville County v South Carolina Insurance Reserve Fund*, 313 S.C. 546, 443 S.E.2d 552 (1994); *Queen City Farms, Inc v Central National Insurance Company of Omaha*, 126 Wash. 2d 50, 882 P.2d 703 (1994); *Just v Land Reclamation Ltd*, 155 Wis. 2d 737, 456 N.W.2d 570 (1990).

exclusion would bar cover. If, however, the "incident" is the sudden rush of oil into the stream, the pollution exclusion would not bar cover.

Lloyd's Underwriters Non-Marine Association clause 1685

22–025 NMA 1685 provides, in pertinent part, that cover is barred for:

"(1) Personal Injury or loss of, or damage to, or loss of use of property directly or indirectly caused by seepage, pollution or contamination, provided always that this paragraph (1) shall not apply to liability for Personal Injury or Bodily Injury or loss of or physical damage to or destruction of tangible property, or loss of use of such property damaged or destroyed, where such seepage, pollution or contamination is caused by a sudden, unintended and unexpected happening during the period of this Insurance.

(2) The cost of removing, nullifying or cleaning up seeping, polluting or contaminating substances unless the seepage, pollution or contamination is caused by a sudden, unintended and unexpected happening during the period of this Insurance".

There are no reported cases construing the clause in the United Kingdom. The highest courts of Colorado, Rhode Island and Washington have concluded that NMA 1685 does not bar cover for gradual pollution.[37] This does not, of course, mean that an English court would necessarily reach the same conclusion as courts in the United States. Each jurisdiction has its own insurance law which it applies in construing insurance policies.

Other issues could, however, arise from the use of NMA 1685 in a public liability policy for United Kingdom risks. If a public liability policy contains the second clause of NMA 1685, an implication could be drawn that, by writing back cover for cleaning up "seepage, pollution or contamination" that is "sudden, unintended and unexpected", insurers intended the policy to provide cover for the cost of such remedial measures. That is, the insuring clause of an insurance policy grants coverage for liabilities under the policy; this is not a function of a write back to an exclusion. Therefore, a court could conclude that the words "damages" or "compensation" in the insuring clause included cover for statutory liabilities for remediating contamination.

---

[37] See *Public Service Company of Colorado v Wallis & Companies*, 986 P.2d 924 (Colo. 1999) (term "sudden, unintended and unexpected" is ambiguous; word "sudden" in term can be reasonably construed to have non-temporal as well as temporal meaning); *Textron, Inc. v Aetna Casualty & Surety Company*, 754 A.2d 742 (R.I. 2000); *Queen City Farms, Inc v Central National Insurance Company of Omaha*, 126 Wash. 2d 50, 882 P.2d 703 (1994). See generally V. Fogleman, *Environmental Liabilities and Insurance in England and the United States*, pp.537–558 (Witherby, 2005) (discussing interpretation of qualified pollution exclusions in CGL and excess general liability policies).

Other pollution exclusions

At the time of writing, there had been three reported decisions on the **22–026** application of pollution exclusions under English law,[38] only one of which involves non-marine pollution. The third party liability policy in the non-marine case excluded cover for nuisance resulting from "non-accidental pollution". The word "accident" was defined to mean "a sudden occurrence which is unintentional and unexpected for the policyholder". Moore-Bick J. concluded that the deposit of silt on a nature reserve during the dredging of the estuary next to it was not "accidental" because "it was not on any view the result of a sudden and unforeseen occurrence but of a particular method of working persisted in over a period of many weeks".[39]

The marine cases both involved the oil spill from the *Exxon Valdez* into Prince William Sound, Alaska, in 1989. The relevant policy term in the first case, which involved cover under reinsurance contracts, provided that "This contract excludes any loss arising from seepage, pollution or contamination on land unless such risks are insured on a sudden and accidental basis". The Commercial Court concluded that the exclusion applied only to seepage, pollution or contamination from a land-based source and did not apply to seepage, pollution or contamination from a vessel.[40]

The relevant policy term in the second case, which involved retrocession contracts,[41] provided that:

> "This contract excludes any loss arising from seepage, pollution or contamination on land unless such risks are insured solely on a sudden and accidental basis. This contract also excludes liability in respect of disposing or dumping of any waste materials or substances".

The contracts further provided that the exclusion was disapplied for "liability under ... Offshore Pollution Liability Agreement" and "[s]eepage, pollution or contamination covered by Protection and Indemnity policies". The Commercial Court concluded that by disapplying the exclusion to the Offshore Pollution Liability Agreement and the Protection and Indemnity policies, retrocessionaires intended the exclusion to apply to seepage,

---

[38] In contrast, many courts in the United States have construed the pollution exclusion in the CGL policy. The decisions have been inconsistent, however, some holding that it covers gradual pollution because the term "sudden and accidental" is ambiguous, and others that it does not because the term is not ambiguous. The inconsistency is due to insurance law in the US being state law. That is, the terms and conditions of insurance policies are construed according to the insurance law of the individual states.

[39] *Jan de Nul (UK) Ltd v N.V. Royale Belge* [2000] 2 Lloyd's Rep. 700, *aff'd* [2002] 1 All E.R. (Comm) 767 (CA).

[40] *Commercial Union Assurance Company plc v NRG Victory Reinsurance Ltd* [1998] 2 All E.R. 434, [1998] 2 Lloyd's Rep. 600 (CA).

[41] A retrocession contract is a contract between reinsurers. That is, a reinsurer may agree to reinsure losses under an insurance policy. In turn, the reinsurer may decide that it wishes to cede part of the risk to another reinsurer. There may be more than one retrocession agreement in place at any one time.

pollution or contamination that affects land regardless of whether it originated offshore or on land. Coleman J reasoned that liability under the Offshore Pollution Liability Agreement could only arise in respect of pollution or contamination that originated from a source that was not on land.[42]

Owned property exclusion

22–027 Public liability policies exclude liability for damage to an insured's own property. The reason for this is that cover for such property is provided by a property policy;[43] there is thus no need for overlapping cover. A typical owned property exclusion bars cover for damage to property owned or occupied by or in the care, custody or control of the insured or of any servant of the insured.

There is an argument that the owned property exclusion does not bar cover for damage to groundwater beneath an insured's site because, under English law, a landowner does not own groundwater in his land.[44] Some courts in the United States have ruled that the cost of remediating groundwater pollution is not excluded under similar owned property clauses.[45] The issue has not, however, been decided by an English court.

Property policies

22–028 Property policies provide cover for damage to, or destruction of, an insured's own property. The insured property to be covered by the policies is listed in a schedule and generally includes buildings and, in some cases, fences and other structures. Insured property does not typically include the land on which buildings and other insured property are located.

Property policies differ from public liability policies in many ways. For example, the damage for which a person is insured by a property policy is suffered directly by the insured rather than by a third party who may bring a claim against the insured. The limit of indemnity in a property policy is generally sufficient to cover the total loss of the insured property, whereas an insured under a public liability policy cannot know what the total

---

[42] *King v Brandywine Reinsurance Company (UK) Ltd* [2005] 2 All E.R. (Comm) 1 (CA).
[43] See, e.g. *Yorkshire Water Services Ltd v Sun Alliance & London Insurance plc (No 2)* [1998] Env. L.R. 204 (QBD)(public liability policy that excluded cover for "any loss of or damage to any property which ... is owned by ... or in the custody or control of [the water company]" did not cover losses on the company's own site).
[44] *Ballard v Tomlinson* (1885) L.R. 29 Ch D 115 (CA).
[45] See, e.g. *Alabama Plating Company v United States Fidelity & Guaranty Company*, 690 So. 2d 331 (Ala. 1996); *E.I. du Pont de Nemours & Company v Allstate Insurance Company*, 686 A.2d 152 (Del. 1996); *Olds-Olympic, Inc v Commercial Union Insurance Company*, 129 Wash. 2d 464, 918 P.2d 923 (1996). Groundwater is not owned by the landowner according to water law in Alabama, Delaware and Washington.

amount of potential third-party claims against it might be, and can only make an informed guess as to what limit of liability is reasonable. In addition, a property policy generally requires the damage to insured property to occur during the policy period whereas public liability policies may have a long tail of liability.

A property policy may cover environmental liabilities in respect of, say, buildings that are damaged due to a leak from a heating oil tank. Due to land not being insured property, however, the loss must occur to the building itself. For example, if oil that leaks from a heating oil tank damages the walls or foundations of a building, the policy may, depending on its wording, cover the damage. The value of the leaked oil may also be covered by the policy. If, however, the oil leaks into soil and groundwater next to the building, the policy does not generally provide cover for the costs of cleaning up the oil. Further, most property policies underwritten since the early 1990s contain qualified or absolute pollution exclusions.

Property policies include a debris removal clause which provides cover   22–029
for removing and disposing of the damaged remains of insured property, such as a building that has been destroyed by fire. This raises the question of the extent to which such a clause might cover the remediation of pollution. The debris removal clause does not typically cover the costs of remediating contamination such as oil that has leaked into the ground. This is because land is not generally insured property. In addition, the High Court has concluded that the plain and ordinary meaning of the word "debris" in a reinsurance contract did not include liquid but, rather, only damaged solids.[46] A court may well, therefore, apply this meaning to the word "debris" in a specific property policy depending, of course, on its entire wording.

In summary, therefore, a property policy is unlikely to provide cover for statutory environmental liabilities such as the costs of remediating contamination.

Professional indemnity policies

Professional indemnity policies provide cover for claims arising from pro-   22–030
fessional services. They are underwritten on a claims-made basis. That is, they provide cover for claims that arise during the policy period. They may have a retroactive date that bars cover for claims that arise from an act or omission that occurred before a specified date prior to the inception of the policy.

The professionals who are most at risk of receiving claims for environmental liabilities from, say, negligent advice are accountants, environmental consultants, solicitors and surveyors. The minimum terms and conditions for professional indemnity insurance for chartered accountants

---

[46] *King v Brandywine Reinsurance Company (UK) Ltd* [2004] 2 All E.R. (Comm) 443 (QBD).

are set out in requirements published by the Institute of Chartered Accountants and the Association of Chartered Certified Accountants. The minimum terms and conditions do not allow policies to include a pollution exclusion. The minimum terms and conditions for solicitors are set out in requirements published by the Law Society in similar terms to the accountants – without a pollution exclusion. The minimum terms and conditions for chartered surveyors are set out in requirements published by the Royal Institution for Chartered Surveyors. In contrast to the minimum terms and conditions of chartered accountants and solicitors, they specifically include a pollution exclusion.

There are no minimum levels and conditions for environmental consultants. Some environmental consultants purchase environmental insurance policies[47] that specifically provide cover for errors and omissions connected with pollution; others do not. One might question the value of professional indemnity cover for this type of professional service if it contains a pollution exclusion.

22–031 There has been one reported English case involving the issue of whether claims against a consultant were covered by a professional indemnity policy.[48] Claims were made against Encia Remediation Ltd, which had formerly been part of AIG Remediation Ltd before a management buy out. The claims arose out of civil engineering works for a proposed residential development on reclaimed land in West Hartlepool. Cracks had developed in some of the buildings as a result of the buildings having settled. The construction company claimed that Encia was liable due to an allegedly defective design and, in some cases, construction of piling. Encia's professional indemnity policy provided cover for negligence and negligent breach of contract in the professional conduct of Encia's business.

Insurers denied liability for the claim on the basis that the policy excluded cover for

"any liability arising out of any claim arising from the provision of advice, design or specification where the Insured contracts to manufacture, construct, erect, install or supply materials or equipment unless defined in the business stated in the schedule".

The schedule described Encia's business as "civil and environmental engineering and as more fully declared in the proposal forms and any accompanying information submitted with the proposal forms".

Creswell J. stated that the business of "civil and environmental engi-

---

[47] See para.22–042 (below).

[48] English courts have also decided underlying claims against environmental consultants. See, e.g. *Urban Regeneration Agency v Mott Macdonald Group Ltd* (2000) 12 Envtl. L. & Mgt. 24 (QBD) (environmental consultant liable for failing to carry out adequate site investigation and failing to exercise due care and skill during remediation after learning that there was more contaminated material than envisaged); *Lidl Properties v Clarke Bond Partnership* [1998] Env. L.R. 662 (QBD) (environmental consultant not liable due to retailer not relying on its estimate for cost of remedial works in purchasing site).

neering" covered many activities including the design and construction of piling as well as project management for the residential development. He concluded that the term "civil and environmental engineering" was sufficiently broad to cover the contract with the construction company.[49]

Directors' and officers' policies

Directors' and officers' liability policies provide cover for directors and officers of companies in the event of a claim against the director or officer personally rather than against their company. It is worth noting that in many environmental statutes, it is open to the regulator to prosecute a director or officer where the offence is committed with the consent or connivance of, or has been attributable to any neglect on their part.[50] The policies, which are underwritten on a claims-made basis, tend to provide cover, with a sub-limit of liability, for defence costs in prosecutions for environmental offences as well as cover for defence costs in civil environmental claims.

22–032

Employers' liability policies

Employers' liability policies provide cover to employers for the cost of compensating their employees for illness or injury during the course of their employment. The policies have been mandatory for most employers since 1972.[51] Industrial diseases may arise, among other things, from exposure to pollutants at the workplace. A particular problem arises in claims for harm from exposure to asbestos because of the long latency period.

22–033

The policies that respond to a claim from a disease such as mesothelioma were traditionally those that were on the risk at the time that the relevant employee is exposed to the pollutant. When this book went to print, it was not known whether this would continue to be the case because litigation known as the "employers' liability policy trigger litigation" was ongoing in order to determine which policies are liable for asbestos-related claims. The insuring clauses that are at issue in the test cases include the terms "injuries caused during the period of insurance" and injuries "contracted during the currency of the policy". Excess employers' liability policies at issue include the term "sustaining of personal injury by accident or disease arising out of and in the course of employment". A lengthy hearing in the litigation was held beginning in June 2008.

---

[49] *Encia Remediation Ltd v Canopius Managing Agents Ltd* [2007] EWHC 916 (Comm) (QBD).
[50] See for example section 157(1) of the EPA 1990 and section 217 WRA 1991.
[51] Employers Liability (Compulsory Insurance) Act of 1969.

Environmental Insurance Policies

22–034   Environmental insurance policies cover a wide range of environmental risks. The risks include: liability for remediating historic contamination; liability for bodily injury and property damage claims arising from incidents that occur during the policy period; and negligence by environmental consultants, laboratories and contractors. The policies have several features that distinguish them from general insurance policies.

First, environmental insurance policies are mostly underwritten on a claims-made-and-reported basis. As such, the policies provide cover for claims which arise against the insured during the policy period and which the insured must report to the insurer within the policy period or an extended reporting period.

Second, policies that provide cover in respect of land that is owned or occupied by the insured are written on a site-specific basis. That is, the site(s) that are covered by the policy are listed in a schedule to the policy. Sites may be added and deleted during the policy period as the insured acquires and disposes of them. Non-site-specific policies provide cover for the environmental risks of professionals, laboratories and contractors.

22–035   Third, the terms and conditions of most environmental insurance policies are negotiated between the insured's broker and, in some cases, the insured's solicitor, and insurers. This does not mean that the policies are bespoke; bespoke policies are negotiated only for some especially large and complex sites. Rather, each environmental insurer has a specimen policy to which it may add standardised and, in some cases bespoke, endorsements in order to tailor the policy to the insured's specific needs. The specimen policy is written in a menu-type style which sets out various insuring clauses to enable the insured to select the cover it requires. As with other insurance policies, an environmental insurance policy also contains a schedule that sets out the name of the insured, names of any additional insureds, the limit and sub-limits of indemnity, the limit of the deductible or self-insured retention, the policy period and so on.

Fourth, environmental underwriters generally review documentation about the environmental condition of, and polluting operations at, sites to be covered in deciding whether to offer cover. If cover is offered, the review will shape the limit of indemnity, the deductible and terms and conditions of the policy. Typical documentation includes any Phase I and Phase II environmental site assessments,[52] and details of any remediation including

---

[52] A Phase I assessment is a review of records and documentation pertaining to a site's past and current uses including a non-intrusive "walk over" of the site by the environmental consultant. A Phase II assessment includes intrusive investigations. See chapter 21.

verification reports.[53] This does not mean that insurers will not offer to underwrite a policy in the absence of such information. For example, there may be telephone calls in which underwriters gather information about sites from sources such as brokers, solicitors for the potential insured, and managers of the sites to be insured. If no information is available about the environmental condition of, or operations at, a site, insurers may still offer cover. In such a case, however, the premium is likely to be higher due to the lack of information. Insurers may also visit a site to gain information. For example, if insurers are considering whether to offer cover for operational risks at a large number of sites, they may visit selected sites in order to gain knowledge about the potential insured's environmental practices. If they are considering whether to offer cover for remediating any unknown contamination, they may visit the sites that are most likely to be contaminated.

Standardised operational risk policies are available for low-risk sites without the need for negotiating the terms and conditions. The policies provide cover on an annual, claims made basis and are renewable.

Types of policies

The following are the main types of environmental insurance policies: 22–036

- property transfer policies;
- third- and first- party policies for operational risks;
- stop loss remediation policies;
- lender liability policies;
- environmental consultant policies;
- environmental laboratories pollution liability policies;
- contractors' pollution liability policies; and
- homeowners' policies.

Property transfer policies

Property transfer policies are the most popular environmental insurance   22–037
policy sold in the United Kingdom. Their primary purpose is to provide cover for the cost of remediating historic contamination on an insured's site and any third-party claims for bodily injury and/or property damage arising from the contamination. The policies may also provide cover for other risks arising from the contamination, including diminution in the value of first- or third- party property, business interruption costs, costs arising from

---

[53] The principle of *uberrimae fides* – utmost good faith – applies to insurance contracts. The remedy for non-disclosure of material information is avoidance of the policy *ab initio*. It is, therefore, crucial for an insured to provide all relevant environmental information about a site to be insured.

delays in construction due to remedial works, relocation costs during remediation, personal liability of directors and officers, and defence costs

Policy periods are available up to 10 years. The policies are triggered by a claim against the insured or a notification or request by an enforcing authority, acting under its statutory powers, to the insured to remediate contamination. There is no need for an enforcing authority to issue a remediation notice under Part 2A of the EPA 1990[54] or a works notice under the WRA 1991[55] in order for the policy to be triggered.

The policies provide cover for claims and proceedings arising from historic contamination unknown to the insured at the inception of the policy or disclosed by that time to the insurers. The policies are, thus, generally available for known contaminated sites as well as sites that may be contaminated. In the case of contaminated sites, insurers decide whether to take the risk that an enforcing authority will require remediation during the policy period. Insurers may also carve out one or more contaminated areas of the site until they have been remediated. They may also exclude cover for remediation costs and other losses arising from a specified pollutant that is known to be present at the site.

22–038   Property transfer policies tend to be purchased mostly during transactions. In particular, they may be carefully worded to provide cover, subject to their terms and conditions, to back up an environmental indemnity in a sale and purchase agreement.

Third- and first- party policies for operational risks

22–039   The second most popular environmental insurance policy which is sold in the United Kingdom provides cover for the cost of remediating contamination and third- and first- party claims for bodily injury and property damage arising from accidental pollution that occurs during the policy period. The policies may also provide cover for liabilities under the Environmental Liability Directive,[56] relocation costs, business interruption costs, diminution in the value of third-party property, loss of rental income, directors and officers' personal liability, and defence costs.

Operational risk policies have become more popular since the *Bartoline* case, discussed above, raised awareness of the gaps in cover for environmental liabilities in public liability policies and due to the enactment of the Environmental Liability Directive. They also fill a gap in public liability policies by providing cover for the costs of remediating own-site con-

---

[54] See Chapter 16 above.
[55] See Chapter 11 above.
[56] Directive 2004/35/CE of the European Parliament and of the Council on environmental liability with regard to the prevention and remedying of damage, as amended. [2004] OJ L143/56.

tamination as well as contamination arising from gradual pollution incidents.

Stop loss remediation policies

A stop loss remediation policy, also known as a remediation cost cap policy, provides cover for costs that exceed the expected amount of the remedial works, as agreed between the insurer and insured, plus a buffer of between 10 and 25 per cent of that amount. The policy provides cover for unforeseen risks in remediating a contaminated site. Such risks can include more extensive contamination than anticipated, greater concentrations of contaminants, failure of the remedy, and changes in legislation requiring more remedial works than anticipated. Due to the extensive negotiations required to determine the expected cost of the remedial works, stop loss remediation policies are generally available only for projects that exceed £1 million.
    22–040

Lender liability policies

A lender liability policy provides cover to a bank or other lender in the event that a borrower who has provided collateral, in the form of land, defaults and an enforcing authority then requires the land to be remediated. The policy responds either by repaying the principal loan balance owed by the borrower or by covering the costs of remediating the contaminated land. The policies may also provide cover for third-party claims for bodily injury and property damage incurred by the lender as mortgagee in possession of the property.
    22–041

Environmental consultant policies

Environmental insurance policies for consultants provide cover for losses that result from their professional services. Such losses may include the consultant's client facing greater remedial costs due to the negligence of the consultant in identifying the nature or extent of pollutants when carrying out a survey. They may also include the cost of remediating contamination due to negligently carried out intrusive works.
    22–042

The policies typically provide cover up to the aggregate limit of indemnity for all projects carried out by the insured consultant during a period of one year or another specified time period. Policies are also available for specific projects. The purpose of such policies is to ensure that the limit of indemnity is not eroded by other claims against the consultant, as could be the case in the blanket policy. If a client wishes the environmental consultant to provide a policy for the client's project, the consultant will generally ask its client to pay the premium. The policies may also provide cover for completed operations and defence costs.

Environmental laboratories pollution liability policies

22–043   As locating pollution may depend on accurate analysis of samples obtained during intrusive investigation, laboratories may need professional liability cover, but this may be excluded in their professional liability policy. Laboratories that carry out environmental work may purchase policies to provide specific cover against claims arising out of their professional environmental services. The policies may also provide cover for completed operations and defence costs.

Contractors' pollution liability policies

22–044   Contractors that remediate contamination may purchase policies to provide cover against claims arising from their works. Due, among other things, to the use of sub-contractors, the policies are also available to other contractors, including construction, electrical, and general contractors. The policies are available on an occurrence basis, generally for an increased premium, as well as a claims-made basis. The policy may be site specific and can include cover for completed work.

Homeowners' policies

22–045   A policy is available to homeowners to provide cover for the costs of remedial works if the location of the home is determined to be "contaminated land" under Part 2A of the EPA 1990. The homeowner must not have known of the existence of the contamination when the policy was purchased. The policy also covers diminution in the value of the house due to the contamination provided that the house is sold during the policy period.

In addition, the National Home Building Council and Zurich Building Guarantees Insurance Company provide cover for the cost of remedial works as part of the guarantees that are offered for newly built or converted homes. The warranties have exclusions including the presence of any contamination that was not at the location of the home at the inception of the policy.

Finite Risk Programmes

Cover for environmental liabilities may be provided by a finite risk pro- **22–046**
gramme, which generally contains a funding element and an insurance
element. The funding element covers costs that are certain to be payable,
such as the cost of remediating contamination or meeting the closure
conditions for a waste disposal site. The insurance element covers potential
costs, such as the cost of indemnifying and defending claims for bodily
injury and property damage arising from exposure to the contamination or
waste.

Placing Policies

Environmental insurance policies are placed through brokers. The first **22–047**
step in placing a policy is for a potential insured or its solicitors to contact
the insured's broker. Most large, and some smaller, brokers have specialised environmental teams.

Before providing the broker with information regarding the environmental condition or polluting operations at the potential insured's sites, it
is advisable for the insured to enter into a confidentiality agreement with
the broker due to the sensitive and often confidential nature of the information. The broker will then prepare a market presentation of the risks that
are sought to be insured and provide that presentation to environmental
insurers. If an insurer is interested in offering cover, the broker will provide
the information regarding the potential insured's sites to that insurer.
Again, it is advisable for a potential insured to enter into confidentiality
agreements with any insurers to whom the information is provided. The
broker will request quotations for a range of policy limits, deductibles and
policy periods from each insurer to whom it provides information.

Insurers who wish to pursue an offer of cover will provide a quotation
that sets out the premiums for the various limits, deductibles and policy
periods it is willing to offer. The quotation is generally available for up to
30 days or another specified period but can almost always be renewed if
negotiations progress. The insurer will also provide its specimen policy and
identify any standard or bespoke endorsements that it wishes to attach to
that policy. The endorsements may include schedules for sites to be covered by the policy and known underground storage tanks (USTs).[57] The
quotation is contingent on the potential insured completing a proposal
form and providing other information, the review of which is satisfactory to

---

[57] The endorsement for USTs sets out information such as the age, capacity and contents of
each known UST on the sites to be insured. The purpose of the endorsement is to allow
insurers to assess the risk from each UST and to decide whether they are willing to provide
cover for claims arising from them. Cover is generally provided for USTs that are listed on
the schedule but not for other USTs, the existence of which is known to the insured.

insurers. The insurer may also visit one or more sites or ask for additional information before making a binding offer.

22–048   The broker will then provide the quotations to the potential insured together with an evaluation and comparison of them. If more than one insurer has submitted a quotation, the insured and its broker and solicitor can negotiate with the various insurers to obtain the appropriate cover. The negotiations may well include modifying clauses in the endorsements or adding endorsements. When the potential insured and an insurer have agreed the final version of the policy, the insurer binds the policy, the insured pays the premium and the insured's broker provides the final policy to the insured.

INDEX

Inquiries
adversarial procedure, 8–061
costs, 8–064
date for inquiries, 8–061
Habitats Directive, 10–036
judicial review, 8–062
participation, 8–062
planning permission, 8–059–8–062
representation, 8–061
third parties, 8–061, 8–062
witnesses, 8–061
Insects
statutory nuisance, prejudice to
health and, 17–011
Insolvency
contaminated land, 16–038
disclaimer of onerous property,
15–085
landfill, 15–085
remediation, 16–038
Inspection
air pollution, environmental
permitting regime and, 14–027
caveat emptor, 21–012
contaminated land, 16–009, 21–002
Drinking Water Directive, 11–026
infringement proceedings, 1–055
local authorities, 4–056
negligence, 4–056
noise, 17–020
nuisance, 17–019, 17–020
permits, 14–027
radioactive substances, 20–031
registers, 16–040
statutory nuisance, prejudice to
health and, 17–019, 17–020
warranties, 21–017
waste management regulation,
15–058, 15–063
Installations
see also **Nuclear installations**
air pollution, environmental
permitting regime and, 14–005–
14–016, 14–044
BAT (best available techniques),
14–017
capacities, 14–005
categories, 14–016
definition, 14–007–14–009
emergencies, 8–049
Environment Agency, 14–015
hazardous installations, 8–048–8–049
Integrated Pollution Prevention and

Control (IPPC) Directive,
14–005, 14–007–14–014,
14–044
Large Combustion Plant Directive,
14–048
local authorities, 14–015
offshore installations, 14–058
ozone depleting substances, 14–058
reform, 14–044
regulators, 14–015–14–016
scope, 14–005, 14–007–14–008
Solvent Emissions Directive, 14–046
small combustion plants, 14–048
terms, 14–007–14–008
Insurance
see also **Environmental insurance
policies**
brokers, 22–047
burden of proof, 22–004
confidentiality agreements with
brokers, 22–047
construction, rules of, 22–005–
22–006
contaminated land, caveat emptor
and, 21–015
criminal offences, 22–032
directors' and officers' policies,
22–032
employers' liability policies, 22–033
endorsements, 22–003, 22–047
Environmental Liability Directive,
5–006
extent of cover, 22–001
finite risk programmes, 22–046
format, 22–003
general liability insurance policies,
22–002–22–033
indemnities, 21–024
placing policies, 22–047–22–048
professional indemnity policies,
21–004, 22–030–22–031
property policies, 22–028–22–029
public liability policies, 22–009–
22–027
quotations, 22–047–22–048
reasonableness, 22–005
remediation, 22–005
Transfrontier Movements of Waste
Regulations, 15–143
Integration principle
environmental action programmes,
1–058
importance and logic, 1–059–1–060

Urban Waste Water Treatment
Directive, 11–074
variation of consents, 11–081
water pollution offences and
consents, 11–063
Transboundary pollution
air pollution, 14–052
Air Quality Framework Directives,
14–055
Environmental Liability Directive,
5–039
genetically modified organisms
(GMOs), 19–004, 19–027–
19–028
hazardous waste, 15–075
treaties and conventions, 1–005
**Transfrontier Movements of Waste
Regulations**
amber waste, 15–126, 15–128
Basel Convention, 15–126–15–127,
15–132, 15–135
categories, 15–126
common to all shipments, provisions,
15–128
consents to shipment, expiry of,
15–143
criminal offences, 15–144
definition of shipment, 15–131
disposal, 15–127, 15–129, 15–132,
15–134, 15–136–15–139,
15–141, 15–143–15–144
domestic rules, 15–144
energy recovery, 15–142
extraterritorial application of
standards, 15–137–15–140
fines, 15–144
green waste, 15–126, 15–128–
15–130
guarantees, 15–143
hazardous waste, 15–126, 15–132,
15–135
history, 15–125–15–127
imprisonment, 15–144
incineration, 15–142
information, supply of, 15–143
insurance, 15–143
Integrated Pollution Prevention and
Control (IPPC) Directive,
15–135
mixed wastes, 15–129–15–130
notifications, 15–143
objections concerning shipments
between Community, 15–133

objections to disposal shipments
within the Community, 15–134–
15–135
objections to recovery shipments
within the Community, 15–136
OECD, 15–126, 15–128
procedure, 15–143
prohibitions, 15–132
recovery, 15–127, 15–129, 15–132,
15–136–15–138, 15–140–
15–144
red waste, 15–126, 15–128
tracking, 15–130
Waste Framework Directive,
15–140
Transport
see also **Transfrontier Movements
of Waste Regulations**
air pollution, 14–059
car manufacturers, voluntary
agreements with, 7–042
COTIF (Convention on Carriage of
Goods by Rail), 18–054
dangerous goods, carriage of, 18–054
End–of–Life Motor Vehicles
Directive, 5–112–5–114
energy efficiency, 7–041
motor vehicles,
air pollution, 14–059
End–of–Life Motor Vehicles
Directive, 5–112–5–114
noxious substances in bulk, carriage
of, 1–009, 11–088
Office of the Renewable Fuels Agency
(RFA), 7–043
radioactive substances, 20–034,
20–036
Renewable Transport Fuel
Certificates (RTF certificates),
7–043
Renewable Transport Fuel
Obligation (RTFO), 7–043
road transport, 7–041–7–042
waste management regulation,
15–059–15–064
Traps
species protection, 10–067
Treaties and conventions
aircraft noise, 17–046
customary law, 1–004
EC states, participation of, 1–002
geographical coverage, 1–002
implementation, 1–003